BRITISH SHIPPING LAWS

General Editor

THE HON. SIR BUSHBY HEWSON
One of Her Majesty's Judges of the Probate, Divorce and Admiralty Division of the High Court of Justice

Editor

RAOUL P. COLINVAUX

of Gray's Inn, Barrister-at-Law

Volume 11

THE MERCHANT SHIPPING ACTS

AUSTRALIA
The Law Book Co. of Australasia Pty Ltd.
Sydney : Melbourne : Brisbane

CANADA AND U.S.A.
The Carswell Company Ltd.
Agincourt, Ontario

INDIA
N. M. Tripathi Private Ltd.
Bombay

ISRAEL
Steimatzky's Agency Ltd.
Jerusalem : Tel Aviv : Haifa

MALAYSIA : SINGAPORE : BRUNEI
Malayan Law Journal (Pte.) Ltd.
Singapore

NEW ZEALAND
Sweet & Maxwell (N.Z.) Ltd.
Wellington

PAKISTAN
Pakistan Law House
Karachi

Other Volumes in British Shipping Laws Series

Vol. 1.	Admiralty Practice
Vols. 2–3.	Carriage by Sea (*Carver*)
Vol. 4.	Collisions at Sea (*Marsden*)
Vol. 5.	C.I.F. and F.O.B. Contracts (*Sassoon*)
Vol. 6.	Forms and Precedents (*Colinvaux, Steel and Ricks*)
Vol. 7.	Law of General Average and York-Antwerp Rules (*Lowndes and Rudolf*)
Vol. 8.	International Conventions (*Singh*)
Vols. 9–10.	Marine Insurance (*Arnould*)
Vol. 12.	Civil Salvage (*Kennedy*)
Vol. 13.	Ship Owners (*Singh and Colinvaux*)

BRITISH SHIPPING LAWS

Volume 11

The Merchant Shipping Acts

Seventh Edition

BY

MICHAEL THOMAS, LL.B.
of the Middle Temple; one of Her Majesty's Counsel

and

DAVID STEEL, M.A.(OXON)
of the Inner Temple, Barrister

LONDON
STEVENS & SONS
1976

EDITIONS OF TEMPERLEY

First Edition	(1895)	*By R. Temperley*
Second Edition	(1907)	*By R. Temperley and H. S. Moore, assisted by A. Bucknill*
Third Edition	(1922)	*By R. Temperley and William Lennox McNair*
Fourth Edition	(1932)	
Fifth Edition	(1954)	*By The Hon. Sir William Lennox McNair and John Philippe Honour*
Sixth Edition	(1963)	*By Waldo Porges and Michael Thomas*
Seventh Edition	(1976)	*By Michael Thomas and David Steel*

Published in 1976 by
Stevens & Sons Limited of
11 New Fetter Lane London E.C.4
and printed in Great Britain
by The Eastern Press Limited
of London and Reading

SBN 420 43450 X

PREFACE

OVER the 12 years since the last edition of this work, there has been an enormous amount of national and international legislative activity in the field of merchant shipping.

Over a third of the sixth edition has been repealed and over a dozen new statutes concerned with merchant shipping have been enacted. These include the Merchant Shipping Act 1964, based on the 1960 Safety of Life at Sea Convention: the Merchant Shipping (Load Lines) Act 1967, based on the 1966 Load Lines Convention: the Merchant Shipping Act 1970, which evolved from the 1967 Pearson Report following the seamen's strike: and the Merchant Shipping (Oil Pollution) Act 1971, based on the 1969 Convention on Civil Liability for Oil Pollution Damage.

The reason that this book is not much larger than the previous edition is due to an increasing tendency to enact enabling legislation. The consequence is, that much substantive law is now contained in subordinate legislation. The appendices have accordingly been enlarged but there is a limit to the extent of material which can be published in a work of this kind.

We wish to thank Ian Lee who prepared the index and assisted with the checking of the proofs and Mrs. Susan Norbury who also assisted with the checking of proofs.

We also wish to record our thanks to our publishers for waiting so patiently for the birth of this new edition. Because of the lengthy progress of the book through the press (about 21 months), it has not been possible to be entirely consistent as to the style in which new legislation, repeals, etc., coming into effect while the book was in proof have been indicated: see particularly the Merchant Shipping Act 1974. But the effect of such changes has been noted in such a way as to draw the reader's attention to them at the appropriate place. The law is stated as at June 1975.

2 Essex Court,
Temple,
E.C.4.

MICHAEL THOMAS
DAVID STEEL

CONTENTS

PART 1

MERCHANT SHIPPING ACT 1894

Part I—Registry

Contents

MERCHANT SHIPPING ACT 1894

MERCHANT SHIPPING ACT 1894

Contents

MERCHANT SHIPPING ACT 1894

Contents

MERCHANT SHIPPING ACT 1894

MERCHANT SHIPPING ACT 1894

SECT. PARA.

2. PASSENGER STEAMERS

Survey of Passenger Steamers

General Equipment of Passenger Steamers

Keeping Order in Passenger Steamers

3. EMIGRANT SHIPS

Supplemental

MERCHANT SHIPPING ACT 1894

Contents

MERCHANT SHIPPING ACT 1894

MERCHANT SHIPPING ACT 1894

Contents

MERCHANT SHIPPING ACT 1894

MERCHANT SHIPPING ACT 1894

Contents

MERCHANT SHIPPING ACT 1894

Contents

MERCHANT SHIPPING ACT 1894

MERCHANT SHIPPING ACT 1894

PART TWO

MERCHANT SHIPPING ACT 1897

MERCHANT SHIPPING (MERCANTILE MARINE FUND) ACT 1898

MERCHANT SHIPPING (LIABILITY OF SHIPOWNERS AND OTHERS) ACT 1900

MERCHANT SHIPPING ACT 1906

Part I—Safety

MERCHANT SHIPPING ACT 1906

MERCHANT SHIPPING ACT 1906

MARITIME CONVENTIONS ACT 1911

PILOTAGE ACT 1913

PILOTAGE ACT 1913

MERCHANT SHIPPING (SAFETY AND LOAD LINE CONVENTIONS) ACT 1932

MERCHANT SHIPPING (SAFETY AND LOAD LINE CONVENTIONS) ACT 1932

PILOTAGE AUTHORITIES (LIMITATION OF LIABILITY) ACT 1936

SHIPS AND AIRCRAFT (TRANSFER RESTRICTION) ACT 1939

CROWN PROCEEDINGS ACT 1947

Part I—SUBSTANTIVE LAW

CROWN PROCEEDINGS ACT 1947

MERCHANT SHIPPING ACT 1948

Crew Accommodation and Food and Catering

Certification of Able Seamen

Certification of Ships' Cooks

Social Security

Supplemental

MERCHANT SHIPPING (SAFETY CONVENTION) ACT 1949

Construction and Equipment

MERCHANT SHIPPING (SAFETY CONVENTION) ACT 1949

MERCHANT SHIPPING (SAFETY CONVENTION) ACT 1949

MERCHANT SHIPPING ACT 1950

MERCHANT SHIPPING ACT 1952

CLEAN AIR ACT 1956

Dark Smoke

MERCHANT SHIPPING (LIABILITY OF SHIPOWNERS AND OTHERS) ACT 1958

MERCHANT SHIPPING (LIABILITY OF SHIPOWNERS AND OTHERS) ACT 1958

MERCHANT SHIPPING (MINICOY LIGHTHOUSE) ACT 1960

MERCHANT SHIPPING ACT 1964

Application of Act of 1949 *to new Convention*

New requirements for cargo ships

Damage Control and life-saving appliances

Radio installations and certificates

Miscellaneous

Contents

MERCHANT SHIPPING (LOAD LINES) ACT 1967

FISHING VESSELS (SAFETY PROVISIONS) ACT 1970

MERCHANT SHIPPING ACT 1970

Engagement and discharge of crews

Wages, etc.

Safety, health and welfare

Contents

MERCHANT SHIPPING ACT 1970

Contents

MERCHANT SHIPPING ACT 1970

MERCHANT SHIPPING ACT 1970

MERCHANT SHIPPING (OIL POLLUTION) ACT 1971

MERCHANT SHIPPING (OIL POLLUTION) ACT 1971

PREVENTION OF OIL POLLUTION ACT 1971

General provisions for preventing oil pollution

Shipping casualties

Enforcement

PREVENTION OF OIL POLLUTION ACT 1971

PROTECTION OF WRECKS ACT 1973

MERCHANT SHIPPING ACT 1974

Part I—THE INTERNATIONAL OIL POLLUTION COMPENSATION FUND

Contents

MERCHANT SHIPPING ACT 1974

APPENDICES

TABLE OF CASES

[*All references are to paragraph numbers*]

Table of Cases

PARA

TABLE OF STATUTES

Other than M.S. Acts and Acts printed in this edition

CITED INDIVIDUALLY

TABLE OF RULES AND ORDERS

[References in **bold** type denote where the text of the Statutory Instrument is printed.]

ABBREVIATIONS

All E.R.	All England Law Reports.
Asp.M.L.C.	Maritime Law Cases (New Series), by Aspinall.
B. & L.	Browning and Lushington's Admiralty Reports.
C.Rob.	C. Robinson's Admiralty Reports.
Com.Cas.	Commercial Cases.
Cox C.C.	E. W. Cox's Criminal Law Cases.
E.R.	English Reports.
F.	Fraser's Scottish Reports (Court of Session, 5th Series).
Ir.L.T.	Irish Law Times.
I.R. or Ir.R.	Irish Reports.
J.A.	Supreme Court of Judicature Act, 1873.
J.I.A.	Supreme Court of Judicature Act (Ireland), 1877.
L.G.R.	Local Government Reports.
Ll.L.R. or Lloyd's Rep. ...	Lloyd's List Law Reports.
L.T.	Law Times Reports (New Series)
L.T.(o.s.)	Law Times Reports (Old Series).
Lush.	Lushington's Admiralty Reports.
M.	Macpherson's Scottish Reports (Court of Session, 3rd Series).
M.L.C.(o.s.)	Maritime Law Cases (Old Series).
M.S.	Merchant Shipping.
M.S.A.	Merchant Shipping Act or Acts.
Moo.P.C.	Moore's Privy Council Cases.
N.I.	National Insurance.
R.	Rettie's Scottish Reports (Court of Session, 4th Series).
S.C....	Session Cases (Court of Session, from 1907).
S.L.R. or Sc.L.R.	Scottish Law Reporter.
S.I.	Statutory Instrument.
S.L.R. Act	Statute Law Revision Act.
Sc.L.T. or S.L.T.	Scots Law Times Reports.
(Sh.Ct.)	(Sheriff Court).
Sol.J. or S.J.	Solicitors' Journal.
S.R. & O.	Statutory Rules and Orders.
Swa.	Swabey's Admiralty Reports.
T.L.R.	Times Law Reports.
W.C. & Ins.Rep.	Workmen's Compensation and Insurance Reports.
W.L.R.	Weekly Law Reports.
W.R.	Weekly Reporter.
W.Rob.	W. Robinson's Admiralty Reports.

The headings to the sections reproduce the marginal notes to the sections, which appear in the Queen's Printers' copies of the Acts.

Part One

MERCHANT SHIPPING ACT 1894

[57 & 58 VICT. c. 60]

An Act to consolidate Enactments relating to Merchant Shipping.

[25th August, 1894]

BE it enacted, etc.:

PART I—REGISTRY

1 HISTORICAL NOTE.—The object of the Navigation Acts from 1660 onwards, by which the registration of British ships was made compulsory, appears to have been to confine the privileges of certain branches of British trade to ships not only owned exclusively by British subjects, but also built in the British Dominions, an exception being made in favour of ships taken as prize in time of war. Notwithstanding the breakdown of the economic policy of which the Navigation Acts were the expression, the registry, whilst still furnishing the criterion of the right to fly the British flag, has meantime gained a new importance as providing a proof of title to the property in the vessel. See generally for the history of registration of British shipping, Abbott's *Law of Merchant Ships, etc.*, Part I, Chap. 2. The policy of the modern Acts is explained by Wood V.-C. in *Liverpool Borough Bank* v. *Turner* (1860) 29 L.J.Ch. at p. 830: " There are two points of public policy which may be suggested in these Acts relating to shipping: the one a policy regarding the interests of the nation at large, relating to the question who shall be entitled to the privileges of the British flag . . . ; the other policy being similar to that which gave rise to the Acts for the registration of titles to land, the object being to determine what should be a proper evidence of title in those who deal with the property in question."

Qualification for owning British Ships

Qualification for owning British ship

2 **1.** A ship shall not be deemed to be a British ship [1] unless owned wholly by persons [2] of the following description (in this Act referred to as persons qualified to be owners of British ships); namely,

(*a*) *Natural-born* British subjects [3]:

(*b*) *Persons naturalized by or in pursuance of an Act of Parliament of the United Kingdom, or by or in pursuance of an Act or ordinance of the proper legislative authority in a British possession*;

(*c*) *Persons made denizens by letters of denization*; *and* [4]

(*d*) Bodies corporate [5] established under and subject to the laws of some part of Her Majesty's dominions, and having their principal place of business [5] in those dominions:

Provided that any person who either—

(*i*) *being a natural-born British subject has taken the oath of allegiance to a foreign sovereign or state or has otherwise become a citizen or subject of a foreign state; or*

(*ii*) *has been naturalized or made a denizen as aforesaid;*

shall not be qualified to be owner of a British ship unless, after taking the said oath, or becoming a citizen or subject of a foreign state, or on or after being naturalized or made denizen as aforesaid, he has taken the oath of allegiance to Her Majesty the Queen, and is during the time he is owner of the ship either resident in Her Majesty's dominions, or partner in a firm actually carrying on business in Her Majesty's Dominions.[4]

3 The words in italics were repealed by the British Nationality Act 1948, with effect from January 1, 1949. The result is to abolish the special provisions which previously applied, limiting the rights of naturalised British subjects, as compared with " natural-born " British subjects, in respect of the ownership of British ships.

[1] Though a certificate of registry is prima facie evidence (see ss. 64, 695) that a vessel is a British ship, proof that the owner is an alien will rebut this presumption: *R.* v. *Bjornsen* (1865) 34 L.J.M.C. 180; 10 Cox C.C. 74.

The term " British ship " is not defined in the Act. It would seem, however, that, unless she is employed by a government under letters of marque, the nationality of the owners is generally the criterion of the nationality of a vessel, at any rate so far as regards the duties and liabilities of her owners and persons belonging to her. Hence, a British-owned ship is a British ship for such purposes, even if she is not registered in this country, or if she is registered in, and carries the flag of, a foreign country: see *per* Brett L.J., *Chartered Mercantile Bank of India* v. *Netherlands India S.N. Co.* (1883) 10 Q.B.D. at pp. 534–536; and *per* Cockburn C.J., *Union Bank of London* v. *Lenanton, infra* (s. 2, note (1)).

The ule above stated seems to underlie in some degree the decisions on criminal jurisdiction (see note at head of s. 27 of M.S.A. 1970), and on concealment of national character (see s. 70), as well as those in cases of prize.

Where a vessel is registered as a British ship, she cannot divest herself of her national character and the liabilities attached to it, except by ceasing to be owned wholly by persons qualified to be owners of British ships and thereupon closing her British register: see ss. 70, 72, the provisions of Part I as to the register, and note (1) to s. 459; also M.S.A. 1906, s. 52. But if a vessel is not registered, when required by the Act to be registered, she will not be " recognised as a British ship " (s. 2 (2)) and thus " will not be entitled to the benefits . . . enjoyed by British ships " while still incurring certain of the liabilities of being a British ship. See s. 72. See, too, *Mortimer* v. *Wisker* [1914] 3 K.B. 699, where a vessel which, though required by the M.S.A. to be registered, was in fact not registered was held not to be " a ship registered in the United Kingdom " or " any other British ship " within the meaning of the Workmen's Compensation Act 1906, s. 7 (1). For, not being registered when registration was required, she could not be " recognised " as a British ship. For the purposes of the Sea Fish (Conservation) Act 1967 (c. 84), a " British-owned " fishing boat is defined by reference to qualification under this section; see *ibid.* s. 22 (1). See also reference to " British-ship " in s. 20 (3) of the Redundancy Payments Act 1965 (c. 62).

Certain government ships may be registered as British ships: see M.S.A. 1906, s. 80.

[2] This includes persons who own any interest arising under contract, or any equitable interest in the ship or any share therein, and the legal and equitable interest in a British ship can only be owned by the persons designated in s. 1. See ss. 9, 25, 57 and 71.

The test as to whether a person is " qualified to own a British ship " has been applied by the Sea Fisheries Act 1968 (c. 77), s. 19 (1).

[3] Before the amendment introduced by the British Nationality Act 1948 the words used were " natural-born British subjects." This term was previously defined by s. 1 of the British Nationality and Status of Aliens Act 1914 (as amended by Acts of 1918, 1922, 1933 and 1943); but these enactments have now, with immaterial exceptions, been repealed by the British Nationality Act 1948, which does not recognise the term " natural-born

British subjects." The term " British subject," which is now used in this section, includes those who have become British subjects by naturalisation. The present definition, if definition it can properly be called, of " British subject " will be found in s. 1 of the British Nationality Act 1948. The status of British subject (or, in the elegant alternative phrase offered by the Act, " Commonwealth citizen ") is dependent on citizenship either of the United Kingdom and Colonies (regarded for this purpose as a single unit) or of Canada, Australia, New Zealand, India, Southern Rhodesia, Ghana, Malaysia, the Republic of Cyprus, Nigeria, Sierra Leone, Jamaica, Trinidad and Tobago, Uganda, Kenya, Zanzibar, Malawi, Zambia, Malta, The Gambia, Guyana, Botswana, Lesotho, Singapore, Barbados, Mauritius, Swaziland, Tanzania, Tonga, Fiji, Sri Lanka, Bangladesh and Grenada. For Pakistan see the Pakistan Act 1973. The assumption is that each of these territories within the British Commonwealth will enact (if it has not already enacted) legislation defining its own " citizenship," and that anyone who is a local citizen *qua* any part of the British Commonwealth will be a British subject (or, if the title be preferred a " Commonwealth citizen ") *qua* the whole of the Commonwealth. For the conditions of qualification for citizenship of the United Kingdom and colonies, see ss. 4 to 18 of the Act, as amended by the Immigration Act 1971. There are special provisions in s. 2 of the Act to enable citizens of Eire (now Republic of Ireland) who desire to do so to continue their status as British subjects, provided they satisfy certain conditions. There are also provisions in the Act (see s. 3 (2)) and in the Ireland Act 1949 (see s. 3 (2) and s. 4), the general effect of which is to place citizens of the Republic of Ireland (formerly Eire) and Irish ships in the same position under the M.S. Acts as British subjects and British ships respectively.

[4] The deletion, by the British Nationality Act 1948, of sub-paragraphs (*b*) and (*c*) and the proviso to the section has the effect of removing the preferred position which a " natural-born " British subject previously enjoyed, as compared with a naturalised British subject. At the same time, the deletion of the proviso has swept away the discrimination which was previously suffered by a " natural-born " British subject who had undertaken allegiance to a foreign state.

[5] In deciding whether a British registered company is qualified to own a British ship, the nationality of the individual shareholders is for the purpose of this Act immaterial (*R.* v. *Arnaud* (1846) 9 Q.B. 806), though it may be material in a question of prize: *The St. Tudno* [1916] P. 291. The real criterion for the purpose of this Act is where " the principal place of business " is. This is in each case a question of fact which generally falls to be determined by an inquiry into the *locality of the control* of the business of the company. Thus in *The Polzeath* [1916] P. 241 (C.A.), where a ship was owned by a company which was registered in the United Kingdom, but was in fact controlled from Hamburg by the chairman of directors who held the majority of shares and resided there, the court held in proceedings for forfeiture under s. 76 that the principal place of business was not in His Majesty's dominions, and that therefore the ship was forfeit to the Crown. For a review of the authorities regarding a company's " place of business " see *The World Harmony* [1965] 1 Lloyd's Rep. 244 at p. 251 (Hewson J.). See also notes to R.S.C., Ord. 81, r. 3, in *Supreme Court Practice* 1973, and see notes, in the textbooks on company law, to s. 107 of the Companies Act 1948, which re-enacts s. 92 of the Companies Act 1929. If the control of the business of the company is exercised from within H.M. dominions, the individual shareholders may be aliens, but the control must be really effective and not a mere colourable cloak for the evasion of the provisions of the Act.

For the general position of companies registered in the United Kingdom but controlled by aliens, see *Daimler Co.* v. *Continental Tyre and Rubber Co.* [1916] 2 A.C. 307. For an example of an English company acquiring enemy character, see *Kuenigl* v. *Donnersmarck* [1955] 1 All E.R. 46.

Obligation to register British Ships

Obligation to register British ships

4 **2.**—(1) Every British [1] ship shall, unless exempted [2] from registry be registered under this Act.

(2) If a ship required by this Act to be registered is not registered under this Act she shall not be recognised as a British ship.[3]

(3) A ship required by this Act to be registered may be detained [4] until the master of the ship, if so required, produces the certificate of the registry of the ship.

5 As to the saving of registration before this Act, see s. 745 (1) (*e*).

As to the objects and policy of registration, see note at head of s. 1.

[1] If the Commissioners of Customs have doubt as to the title of a ship registered as a British ship to be so registered, they may call for proof of title: see M.S.A. 1906, s. 51.

A ship built in England to be delivered to a foreign purchaser at a foreign port, was held not to be a British ship so as to require to be registered, although being undelivered it was still the property of a British subject: *Union Bank of London* v. *Lenanton* (1878) 3 C.P.D. 243; and see notes to s. 1.

As this Act does not, except where specially provided, apply to ships belonging to Her Majesty (see s. 741), such ships are not required to be, and cannot be, registered as British ships, except in the case of certain " government ships," which may be registered as provided by M.S.A. 1906, s. 80.

For definition of " ship," see s. 742. See also M.S.A. 1921, s. 1 (3), by which the Secretary of State for Trade is empowered to declare that " lighters, barges or like vessels " registered under port regulations shall be deemed to be registered under the Merchant Shipping Acts.

[2] Exemptions from registry are dealt with in s. 3.

[3] It is not an offence under this Act to omit to register a ship required to be registered thereby. " The consequence of not registering is that the owner does not get the benefits of his British ownership ": *per* Bramwell L.J. in *Union Bank of London* v. *Lenanton* (1878) 3 C.P.D. 243 at p. 248. But apparently registration could be compelled by detention under subs. (3). Furthermore, failure to register a ship required to be registered deprives the ship of the benefit and advantages conferred by the M.S. Acts on British ships while leaving the ship exposed to the liabilities attached to British ships: see s. 72. However, since 1958, limitation of liability under Part VIII of this Act may be claimed in respect of any British ship, notwithstanding that it has not yet been registered: M.S. (Liability of Shipowners and Others) Act 1958, s. 4 (2).

But registration *ipso facto* does not give the courts of the country in which the register is any jurisdiction over the owners of the ship in respect of their share therein. Formerly, the Scottish courts had no jurisdiction over an English part-owner of a ship registered in Scotland, notwithstanding registration there: *Anderson* v. *Sillars* (1894) 22 Ct. of Sess.Cas. (4th Ser.) 105. But, in England, by virtue of the Supreme Court of Judicature (Consolidation) Act 1925, s. 22 (1) (*a*) (ii), re-enacting in effect the Admiralty Court Act 1861, s. 8, the High Court had Admiralty jurisdiction over disputes between co-owners of a ship " registered at any port in England." This section has now been repealed by the Administration of Justice Act 1956, s. 7 (2). The Admiralty jurisdiction of the High Court is no longer dependent upon registration. See Administration of Justice Act 1956, Part I (ss. 1–8), for the jurisdiction in England and Wales; *ibid.* Part V for the jurisdiction in Scotland; *ibid.* s. 55 for the provisions in respect of jurisdiction in Northern Ireland. As to claims falling to be determined in accordance with the provisions of the Rhine Navigation Convention see *ibid.* ss. 6, 49 and Sched. I, para. 6.

For the application of s. 2 to the question of determining a seaman's rights under the repealed Workmen's Compensation Acts, see *The Rigel* [1912] P. 99 (Irish light vessel), and *Mortimer* v. *Wisker* [1914] 3 K.B. 699 (C.A.) (ship's registry closed before sailing). These decisions are still apposite to the determination of the question whether a seaman is an " insured person " under the National Insurance (Industrial Injuries) Acts 1965–67.

No grant under the Industrial Development Act 1966, s. 5 (3), can be made in respect of a ship which is not registered; see also the Industrial Development (Ships) Act 1970.

[4] For provisions as to detention, see s. 692.

Exemptions from registry

6 **3.** The following ships are exempted from registry under this Act:—

(1) Ships not exceeding fifteen tons burden [1] employed solely in navigation on the rivers or coasts of the United Kingdom,[2] or on the rivers or coasts of some British possession [3] within which the managing owners of the ships are resident:

(2) Ships not exceeding thirty tons burden [1] and not having a whole or fixed deck, and employed solely in fishing or trading coastwise on the shores of Newfoundland or parts adjacent

thereto, or in the Gulf of St. Lawrence, or on such portions of the coasts of Canada as lie bordering on that gulf.

7 [1] " Tons burden " means the net register tonnage, ascertained in accordance with the regulations made under s. 1 of M.S.A. 1965 (§ 1258, *post*) which replaced the provisions that were contained in ss. 78 and 79 of this Act as later amended by M.S.A. 1907 and M.S.A. 1954. See *The Brunel* [1900] P. 24.

[2] " United Kingdom " here includes the Republic of Ireland. See note " Application to Northern Ireland and the Republic of Ireland " in notes to s. 742.

[3] " British possession " is defined by the Interpretation Act 1889, s. 18 (2) as " any part of Her Majesty's dominions exclusive of the United Kingdom."

As to powers of colonial legislatures to alter provisions of this Act and to regulate coasting trade and for special position of dominions, see ss. 735, 736 and notes thereto.

An exempted vessel which has in fact been registered may be transferred without a registered bill of sale: *Benyon* v. *Cresswell* (1848) 12 Q.B. 899. See note to s. 24, *infra*.

Her Majesty's ships are also exempt from registration (see s. 741) except for those government vessels registrable under M.S.A. 1906, s. 80.

As to the registration of fishing boats, see s. 373.

Procedure for Registration

As to procedure on re-registration or " registry anew," see ss. 44, 52.

Registrars of British ships

8 **4.**—(1) The following persons shall be registrars of British ships:—

(*a*) At any port in the United Kingdom, or Isle of Man, approved by the Commissioners of Customs [1] for the registry of ships, the chief officer of customs [2]:

(*b*) In Guernsey and Jersey, the chief officers of customs together with the governor:

(*c*) In Malta and Gibraltar, the governor:

(*d*) At Calcutta, Madras, and Bombay, the port officer:

(*e*) At any other port in any British possession approved by the governor of the possession for the registry of ships, the chief officer of customs, or, if there is no such officer there resident, the governor of the possession in which the port is situate, or any officer appointed for the purpose by the governor:

(*f*) At a port of registry established by Order in Council under this Act, persons of the description in that behalf declared by the Order.[3]

(2) Notwithstanding anything in this section Her Majesty may by Order in Council declare, with respect to any British possession named in the Order, not being the Channel Islands or the Isle of Man, the description of persons who are to be registrars of British ships in that possession.[4]

(3) A registrar shall not be liable to damages or otherwise for any loss accruing to any person by reason of any act done or default made by him in his character of registrar, unless the same has happened through his neglect or wilful act.

9 [1] The Commissioners of Customs are now the Commissioners of Customs and Excise; see the Customs and Excise Act 1952, s. 318 (1).

[2] The term "chief officer of customs" is used throughout the Act in place of various expressions in the repealed Acts, and is defined in s. 742.

[3] See s. 88 for establishment of such ports.

[4] The following officials have been constituted registrars. At Singapore, the officers for the time being acting as master attendant; Penang and Malacca, the harbour master, July 9, 1869; Gibraltar, the captain of the port, or persons discharging the duties of captain of the port, July 11, 1877; Tasmania, the collector of customs, the chief clerk of the customs, November 23, 1893 (see S.R. & O. & S.I.Rev. 1948, XIV, M.S. pp. 47–50); in British India at any port of registry, the Principal Officer, Mercantile Marine Department, or where there is no such officer, the port officer (S.R. & O. 1931 No. 672); this is now subject, however, to the provisions of the Indian Independence Act 1947 (see s. 18 thereof); Seychelles, the Port Officer, or, in his absence, the Collector of Customs (S.I. 1968 No. 1648).

An Order in Council was also made in respect of Burma, June, 1937 (S.R. & O. 1937 No. 534), but this has lapsed or is spent as a result of the Burma Independence Act 1947. As to Orders in Council generally, see s. 738, and as to saving of those made before January 1, 1895, s. 745.

Register book

10 **5.** Every registrar of British ships shall keep a book to be called the register book,[1] and entries in that book shall be made in accordance with the following provisions:—

(i) The property in a ship shall be divided into sixty-four shares [2]:

(ii) Subject to the provisions of this Act with respect to joint owners or owners by transmission,[3] not more than sixty-four individuals shall be entitled to be registered at the same time as owners of any one ship; but this rule shall not affect the beneficial title [4] of any number of persons or of any company represented by or claiming under or through any registered owner or joint owner:

(iii) A person shall not be entitled to be registered as owner of a fractional part of a share in a ship; but any number of persons not exceeding five may be registered as joint owners of a ship or of any share or shares therein:

(iv) Joint owners shall be considered as constituting one person only as regards the persons entitled to be registered, and shall not be entitled to dispose in severalty of any interest in a ship, or in any share therein in respect of which they are registered:

(v) A corporation may be registered as owner by its corporate name.

11 [1] As to inspection, and admissibility in evidence, of register book, see ss. 64, 695.

[2] Co-owners are of two classes: (1) Joint-owners, in whom is vested the property in a ship or share therein jointly with unity of title and no distinction of interest; and (2) part-owners, or co-owners properly so-called, in whom is vested in severalty distinct shares in the ship but with an undivided interest in the whole. The former are joint tenants of the property held; the latter are tenants in common with each other of their respective shares. Normally the relations of the co-owners *inter se* are regulated by express agreement, the management of the ship being relegated to a ship's manager or ship's husband who may or may not be a part-owner. Where, however, there is no agreement, their rights *inter se* are governed at any rate in English law by the broad principle that the will of the majority must prevail, provided that the interests of the dissentient minority can be properly protected. The power of sale will be exercised, though with reluctance, even on the application of a minority of part-owners: *The Nelly Schneider* (1878) 3 P.D. 152; *The Hereward*

[1895] P. 284. For the details of the working out of this principle, see Abbott, *Merchant Shipping*, 14th ed., Part I, Chap. 3; Maclachlan, *Merchant Shipping*, 7th ed., Chap. 3.

Formerly, the Admiralty jurisdiction of the High Court in respect of any question arising between the co-owners of a ship was dependent upon registration at an English port; see the Supreme Court of Judicature (Consolidation) Act 1925, s. 22 (1) (*a*) (ii). That section has now been repealed, and jurisdiction is no longer dependent upon registration; see the Administration of Justice Act 1956, s. 1 (1) (*c*). This jurisdiction is assigned to the Queen's Bench Division of the High Court and exercised by the Admiralty Court. County Courts do not have jurisdiction over questions of co-ownership.

For the jurisdiction in Scotland over disputes between co-owners, see the Adminstration of Justice Act 1956, s. 47 (2) (*q*) which was brought into force on January 1, 1957, by S.I. 1956 No. 2099.

[3] For transmission of the property in a ship, see s. 27, *infra*.

[4] See s. 57 for definition of " beneficial interest."

Survey and measurement of ship

12 6. Every British ship [1] shall before registry be surveyed by a surveyor of ships [2] and her tonnage ascertained in accordance with the tonnage regulations of this Act,[3] and the surveyor shall grant his certificate [4] specifying the ship's tonnage and build, and such other particulars descriptive of the identity of the ship as may for the time being be required by the [Department of Trade], and such certificate shall be delivered to the registrar before registry.

13 [1] See note (1) to s. 1, *supra*.

[2] See ss. 724 *et seq*., M.S.A. 1906, s. 75, and M.S.A. 1965, s. 1 (4), for appointment and powers of surveyors.

[3] For the rules for ascertaining register tonnage see M.S.A. 1965 (c. 47), s. 1 (§ 1258, *post*). As to pleasure yachts see Part 4 and the Schedule to the M.S. (Tonnage) (Amendment) Regulations 1975 (S.I. No. 594).

[4] As to form of certificate, see s. 65, and Part II of Sched. I.

Marking of ship

14 7.—(1) Every British ship [1] shall before registry be marked permanently and conspicuously to the satisfaction of the [Department of Trade] as follows:—

(*a*) Her name [2] shall be marked on each of her bows, and her name and the name of her port of registry [3] must be marked on her stern, on a dark ground in white or yellow letters, or on a light ground in black letters, such letters to be of a length not less than four inches, and of proportionate breadth;

(*b*) Her official number and the number denoting her registered tonnage shall be cut in on her main beam;

(*c*) A scale of feet denoting her draught of water shall be marked on each side of her stem and of her stern post in Roman capital letters or in figures, not less than six inches in length, the lower line of such letters or figures to coincide with the draught line denoted thereby, and those letters or figures must be marked by being cut in and painted white or yellow on a dark ground, or in such other way as the [Department of Trade] approve.

(2) The [Department of Trade] may exempt any class of ships from all or any of the requirements of this section, and a fishing boat entered in the fishing boat register, and lettered and numbered in pursuance of the Fourth Part of this Act, need not have her name and port of registry marked under this section.[4]

(3) If the scale of feet showing the ship's draught of water is in any respect inaccurate, so as to be likely to mislead, the owner of the ship shall be liable to a fine not exceeding one hundred pounds.

(4) The marks required by this section shall be permanently continued, and no alteration shall be made therein, except in the event of any of the particulars thereby denoted being altered in the manner provided by this Act.

(5) If an owner or master of a British ship [1] neglects to cause his ship to be marked as required by this section, or to keep her so marked, or if any person conceals, removes, alters, defaces, or obliterates, or suffers any person under his control to conceal, remove, alter, deface, or obliterate any of the said marks, except in the event aforesaid, or except for the purpose of escaping capture by an enemy, that owner, master, or person shall for each offence be liable to a fine not exceeding one hundred pounds, and on a certificate from a surveyor of ships,[5] or [Department of Trade] Inspector under this Act,[6] that a ship is insufficiently or inaccurately marked the ship may be detained [7] until the insufficiency or inaccuracy has been remedied.

15 [1] See note (1) to s. 1, *supra*.
[2] For provisions as to name of ship, alteration of name, etc., see s. 47, and M.S.A. 1906, s. 50.
[3] " Port of Registry " means the port at which a British ship is registered for the time being: see s. 13. Upon a change of registry, the name of the new port of registry must be substituted: see s. 53 (4).
[4] The exception as to fishing boats was new here, being rendered necessary by s. 373, *q.v.* Yachts belonging to certain yacht clubs are exempted by the Department of Trade. Small craft must be marked in accordance with the directions of the Commissioners of Customs and Excise: see Customs and Excise Act 1952, s. 68 (5).
[5] See ss. 724 *et seq.* for powers of surveyors.
[6] See ss. 728 *et seq.* for appointment of inspectors.
[7] See s. 692 for means of enforcing detention.

Application for registry

16 **8.** An application for registry of a ship shall be made in the case of individuals by the person requiring to be registered as owner, or by some one or more of the persons so requiring if more than one, or by his or their agent, and in the case of corporations by their agent, and the authority of the agent shall be testified by writing, if appointed by individuals, under the hands of the appointors, and, if appointed by a corporation, under the common seal of that corporation.

As to the power of the registrar to dispense with any evidence, see s. 60.

Declaration of ownership on registry

17 **9.** A person shall not be entitled to be registered as owner of a ship or of a share therein until he, or in the case of a corporation the person authorised by this Act [1] to make declarations on behalf of the corporation, has made and signed a declaration of ownership, referring to the ship as described in the certificate of the surveyor, and containing the following particulars:—

(i) A statement of his qualification to own a British ship, or in the case of a corporation, of such circumstances of the constitution and business thereof as prove it to be qualified to own a British ship [2]:

(ii) A statement of the time when and the place where the ship was built, or, if the ship is foreign built, and the time and place of building unknown, a statement that she is foreign built, and that the declarant does not know the time or place of her building; and, in addition thereto, in the case of a foreign ship, a statement of her foreign name, or, in the case of a ship condemned, a statement of the time, place, and court at and by which she was condemned:

(iii) A statement of the name of the master:

(iv) A statement of the number of shares in the ship of which he or the corporation, as the case may be, is entitled to be registered as owner:

(v) A declaration that, to the best of his knowledge and belief, no unqualified [2] person or body of persons is entitled as owner to any legal or beneficial interest [3] in the ship or any share therein.

18 As to retention of all declarations of ownership by the registrar, see s. 12; as to declarations by incapacitated persons, s. 55; as to the power of the registrar to dispense with declarations and other evidence, s. 60; as to the mode of making declarations, s. 61; and as to their admissibility in evidence, s. 64.

As to forms, see s. 65, and Part II of Sched. I.

[1] Declarations on behalf of a corporation may be made by the secretary or any other officer authorised by the corporation for the purpose. See s. 61 (2).

[2] As to the qualifications for owning a British ship, see s. 1 and notes thereto.

[3] As to the meaning of " beneficial interest," see s. 57 and notes thereto.

Evidence on first registry

19 **10.**—(1) On the first registry of a ship the following evidence shall [1] be produced in addition to the declaration of ownership [2]:—

(*a*) in the case of a British-built ship, a builder's certificate,[3] that is to say, a certificate signed by the builder of the ship, and containing a true account of the proper denomination and of the tonnage of the ship, as estimated by him, and of the time when and the place where she was built, and of the name of the person (if any) on whose account the ship was built, and if there has been any sale, the bill of sale under which the ship, or a share therein, has become vested in the applicant for registry:

(*b*) in the case of a foreign-built ship, the same evidence as in the case of a British-built ship, unless the declarant who makes the declaration of ownership declares that the time and place of her building are unknown to him, or that the builder's certificate cannot be procured, in which case there shall be required only the bill of sale under which the ship, or a share therein, became vested in the applicant for registry:

(*c*) in the case of a ship condemned by any competent court, an official copy of the condemnation.

(2) The builder shall grant the certificate required by this section, and such person as the Commissioners of Customs [4] recognise as carrying on the business of the builder of a ship, shall be included, for the purposes of this section, in the expression " builder of the ship."

(3) If the person granting a builder's certificate under this section wilfully makes a false statement in that certificate he shall for each offence be liable to a fine not exceeding one hundred pounds.[5]

20 [1] As to the power of the registrar to dispense with declarations and evidence, see s. 60.
[2] See s. 9.
[3] As to the effect of the builder's certificate in transferring the general property in the vessel to the purchaser, see *Goss* v. *Quinton* (1842) 4 Scott.N.R. 471 and *Woods* v. *Russell* (assignee in bankruptcy) (1822) 5 B. & Ald. 942; 106 E.R. 1436. The builder's certificate is one of the documents retained by the registrar on the registry of a ship, see s. 12.
[4] See note (1) to s. 4.
[5] For summary prosecution of offences, see s. 680.

Entry of particulars in register book

21 **11.** As soon as the requirements of this Act preliminary to registry have been complied with the registrar shall enter in the register book the following particulars respecting the ship [1]:—

(*a*) the name of the ship and the name of the port to which she belongs [2]:

(*b*) the details comprised in the surveyor's certificate [3]:

(*c*) the particulars respecting her origin stated in the declaration of ownership [3]: and

(*d*) the name and description of her registered owner or owners,[1] and if there are more owners than one, the proportions in which they are interested in her.[4]

22 [1] As to conclusiveness of the register as evidence of ownership, tonnage, nationality, etc. see ss. 64, 695, and cases cited in note (1) to s. 695.
[2] As to the effect of a difference between the name by which a ship was before registration described in a mortgage and the name in which both ship and mortgage were subsequently registered, see *Bell* v. *Bank of London* (1858) 3 H. & N. 730; 28 L.J.Ex. 116, cited in note to s. 31 on " Mistake or variation in name." See also s. 47 for rules as to changing ship's name; and M.S.A. 1906, s. 50 (1) and regulations made thereunder (S.R. & O. 1907

No. 740, as amended by S.R. & O. 1922 No. 729 and S.R. & O. 1936 No. 390) as to choice of name.

As to what is deemed to be the port to which a British ship belongs, see s. 13.

[3] See s. 6 as to surveyors' certificates, and s. 9 as to declarations of ownership.

[4] As to the rights of co-owners *inter se*, etc., see Abbott, *Merchant Ships, etc.*, 14th ed., Part 1, Chap. 3; Maclachlan, *Merchant Shipping*, 7th ed., Chap. 3; and note (2) to s. 5.

Documents to be retained by registrar

23 **12.** On the registry of a ship the registrar shall retain in his possession the following documents; namely, the surveyor's certificate, the builder's certificate, any bill of sale of the ship previously made, the copy of the condemnation (if any), and all declarations of ownership.

Port of registry

24 **13.** The port at which a British ship is registered for the time being shall be deemed her port of registry and the port to which she belongs.

For transfer of registry, see s. 53.

Certificate of Registry

Certificate of registry

25 **14.** On completion of the registry of a ship, the registrar shall grant a certificate of registry comprising the particulars respecting her entered in the register book, with the name of her master.

26 As to fees on registration, see M.S. (Mercantile Marine Fund) Act 1898, s. 3, and notes thereto, *post*. For the fees presently in force, see the M.S. (Fees) Regulations 1975 (No. 341).

As to form of certificate, see s. 65, and Part II of Sched. I.

As to admissibility in evidence of such certificates, see s. 64. The certificate of registry is prima facie evidence that the ship is British: *R.* v. *Bjornsen* (1865) 12 L.T. 473.

As to terminable certificates in colonies, see s. 90.

Custody of certificate

27 **15.**—(1) The certificate of registry shall be used only for the lawful navigation of the ship, and shall not be subject to detention by reason of any title, lien, charge, or interest whatever had or claimed by any owner, mortgagee, or other person to, on, or in the ship.

(2) If any person, whether interested in the ship or not, refuses on request to deliver up the certificate of registry when in his possession or under his control to the person entitled to the custody thereof for the purposes of the lawful navigation of the ship, or to any registrar, officer of customs, or other person entitled by law to require such delivery, any justice by warrant under his hand and seal, or any court capable of taking cognizance of the matter, may summon the person so refusing to appear before such justice or court, and to be examined touching such refusal, and unless it is proved to the satisfaction of such justice or court that there

was reasonable cause[1] for such refusal, the offender shall be liable to a fine not exceeding one hundred pounds,[2] but if it is shown to such justice or court that the certificate is lost, the person summoned shall be discharged, and the justice or court shall certify that the certificate of registry is lost.

(3) If the person so refusing is proved to have absconded so that the warrant of a justice or process of a court cannot be served on him, or if he persists in not delivering up the certificate, the justice or court shall certify the fact, and the same proceedings may then be taken as in the case of a certificate mislaid, lost, or destroyed, or as near thereto as circumstances permit.[3]

28 For definition of "Court," see s. 742.

The High Court has jurisdiction independently of this section, to order a certificate of registry to be delivered up to the owners of a ship: see *The Barbara,* 4 C.Rob. 2; *The Frances,* 2 Dods. 420. See also *The St. Olaf* (1876) 3 Asp.M.L.C. 268 where it was held that a master, whether co-owner or not, has no lien upon a certificate of registry or ship's papers in the case of wrongful dismissal by managing owners. A master who is wrongfully dismissed has no lien upon the certificate for wages or disbursements: *Gibson* v. *Ingo* (1847) 6 Hare 112.

In *The Celtic King* [1894] P. 175, the High Court ordered the certificate to be delivered up to the plaintiff, the purchaser from a mortgagee, by the defendants, to whom the ship was under contract, and who sought to restrain the plaintiff from dealing with the ship contrary to the terms of that contract. A pledge of a certificate of registry is, by virtue of this provision, illegal and void; and where the master, who was also sole owner, had pledged the certificate, he was held entitled to recover it by action from the pledgee for the purposes of navigation: *Wiley* v. *Crawford* (1861) 30 L.J.Q.B. 319; 1 B. & S. 253.

1 Where the master of a ship, at the port of discharge, and before the completion of the discharge, refused to deliver up the certificate to the managing owner, who demanded it without giving any reason and without dismissing the master, it was held that there was reasonable ground for the master's refusal: *Arkle* v. *Henzell* (1858) 27 L.J.M.C. 110; 8 E. & B. 828. See also *R.* v. *Walsh* (1834) 3 N. & M. 632; 1 A. & E. 481 (conviction under 3 & 4 Will. 4, c. 55, s. 27 (registry of vessels), for detaining certificate).

2 As to the recovery of fines, see ss. 680–682.

3 See s. 18.

Penalty for use of improper certificate

29 **16.** If the master or owner of a ship uses or attempts to use for her navigation a certificate of registry not legally granted in respect of the ship, he shall, in respect of each offence, be guilty of a misdemeanour, and the ship shall be subject to forfeiture under this Act.

For provisions as to forfeitures, see s. 76, and as to prosecution of offences, see ss. 680 *et seq.* By the Criminal Law Act 1967, s. 1, all distinctions between felony and misdemeanour were abolished.

Power to grant new certificate

30 **17.** The registrar of the port of registry of a ship may, with the approval of the Commissioners of Customs,[1] and on the delivery up to him of the certificate of registry of a ship, grant a new certificate in lieu thereof.

1 Now the Commissioners of Customs and Excise; see note (1) to s. 4.

Provision for loss of certificate

31 **18.**—(1) In the event of the certificate of registry of a ship being mislaid, lost, or destroyed, the registrar of her port of registry shall grant a new certificate of registry in lieu of her original certificate.

(2) If the port (having a British registrar or consular officer) at which the ship is at the time of the event, or first arrives after the event—

(*a*) is not in the United Kingdom, where the ship is registered in the United Kingdom; or,

(*b*) is not in the British possession in which the ship is registered; or,

(*c*) where the ship is registered at a port of registry established by Order in Council under this Act,[1] is not that port;

then the master of the ship, or some other person having knowledge of the facts of the case, shall make a declaration stating the facts of the case, and the names and descriptions of the registered owners of such ship to the best of the declarant's knowledge and belief, and the registrar or consular officer, as the case may be, shall thereupon grant a provisional certificate, containing a statement of the circumstances under which it is granted.

(3) The provisional certificate shall within ten days after the first subsequent arrival of the ship at her port of discharge in the United Kingdom, where she is registered in the United Kingdom, or in the British possession in which she is registered, or where she is registered at a port of registry established by Order in Council under this Act at that port, be delivered up to the registrar of her port of registry, and the registrar shall thereupon grant the new certificate of registry; and if the master without reasonable cause fails to deliver up the provisional certificate within the ten days aforesaid, he shall be liable to a fine not exceeding fifty pounds.[2]

32 [1] See s. 88, which provides for the establishment of foreign ports of registry by Order in Council.

[2] As to the recovery of fines, see ss. 680–682.

Endorsement of change of master on certificate

33 **19.** Where the master of a registered British ship is changed, *each of the following persons, that is to say*—

(*a*) *if the change is made in consequence of the sentence of a naval court, the presiding officer of that court; and*

(*b*) *if the change is made in consequence of the removal of the master by a court under Part VI of this Act, the proper officer of that court; and*

(*c*) *if the change occurs from any other cause,*[1] the registrar, or if there is none the British consular officer, at the port where the change occurs, shall endorse and sign on the certificate of registry a memorandum of the change,[2] and shall forthwith report the change to the Registrar-General of Shipping and Seamen[3]; and any officer of customs at any port in Her Majesty's dominions may refuse to admit any person to do any act there as master of a British ship unless his name is inserted in or endorsed on her certificate of registry as her last appointed master.[4]

34 [1] The words in italics will be repealed by M.S.A. 1970, s. 100 (3) (§ 1479, *post*), from a day to be appointed.
[2] As to fees for endorsing and signing this memorandum, see the Fees (Increase) Act 1923, s. 2 (1) (as amended by Merchant Shipping (Safety Convention Act) 1949, s. 37 (5) and Sched. III) and notes thereto. No fee has been fixed for this service.
[3] See M.S.A. 1970, s. 80, as to appointment of " Registrar-General of Shipping and Seamen."
[4] As to admissibility of endorsements on certificates in evidence, see s. 64.

Endorsement of change of ownership on certificate

35 **20.**—(1) Whenever a change occurs in the registered ownership of a ship, the change of ownership shall be endorsed[1] on her certificate of registry either by the registrar of the ship's port of registry, or by the registrar of any port at which the ship arrives who has been advised of the change by the registrar of the ship's port of registry.

(2) The master shall, for the purpose of such endorsement by the registrar of the ship's port of registry, deliver the certificate of registry to the registrar, forthwith after the change if the change occurs when the ship is at her port of registry, and if it occurs during her absence from that port and the endorsement under this section is not made before her return then upon her first return to that port.

(3) The registrar of any port, not being the ship's port of registry, who is required to make an endorsement under this section may for that purpose require the master of the ship to deliver to him the ship's certificate of registry, so that the ship be not thereby detained, and the master shall deliver the same accordingly.

(4) If the master fails to deliver to the registrar the certificate of registry as required by this section he shall, for each offence[2] be liable to a fine not exceeding one hundred pounds.

36 As to registry anew on change of ownership, see s. 51.
[1] As to admissibility of endorsements on certificates in evidence, see s. 64.
[2] As to prosecution of offences, see s. 680.

Delivery up of certificate of ship lost or ceasing to be British-owned

37 **21.**—(1) In the event of a registered ship being either actually or constructively lost,[1] taken by the enemy, burnt, or broken up, or ceasing by reason of a transfer to persons not qualified to be owners of British ships,[2] or otherwise, to be a British ship, every owner of the ship or any share in the ship shall, immediately on obtaining knowledge of the

event, if no notice thereof has already been given to the registrar, give notice thereof to the registrar at her port of registry, and that registrar shall make an entry thereof in the register book [3] [and the registry of the ship in that book shall be considered [4] as closed except so far as relates to any unsatisfied mortgages or existing certificates of mortgage entered therein.[5]]

(2) In any such case, except where the ship's certificate of registry is lost or destroyed, the master of the ship shall, if the event occurs in port immediately, but if it occurs elsewhere then within ten days after his arrival in port, deliver the certificate to the registrar, or, if there is none, to the British consular officer there, and the registrar, if he is not himself the registrar of her port of registry, or the British consular officer, shall forthwith forward the certificate delivered to him to the registrar of her port of registry.[3]

(3) If any such owner or master fails, without reasonable cause, to comply with this section, he shall for each offence be liable to a fine not exceeding one hundred pounds.[6]

38 [1] "The expression 'constructively lost' has no meaning as applied to a ship, except in connection with marine insurance, and a vessel which is a constructive total loss within the meaning of the term in marine insurance is 'constructively lost' within the meaning of [this section]": *per* Swinfen Eady L.J. in *Manchester Ship Canal Co.* v. *Horlock* [1914] 2 Ch. 199 at p. 208 (C.A.) (vessel abandoned and raised by canal company). For the meaning of the term in marine insurance, see Marine Insurance Act 1906, s. 60.

[2] As s. 24 only requires a bill of sale in the prescribed form on transfer to a person qualified to own a British ship, any form effective to transfer property will suffice when the transferee is not qualified. But the usual procedure in such cases is for the owner to execute a bill of sale in the prescribed form, and to give notice under this section to the registrar, who thereupon closes the registry (except as to unsatisfied mortgages) and, if required, gives a certificate to that effect to the purchaser. In the case of a transfer to an unqualified person executed *within* the country of the port of registry, the notice required by this section is sufficient authority to the registrar to close the register, even though no bill of sale or other instrument of transfer is produced to him. Where, however, the transfer takes place under a certificate of sale at some place *outside* the country of the port of registry, a bill of sale in the prescribed form, if the transfer is to a qualified person, or a bill of sale either in the prescribed form or in some other form effective to transfer property, if the transfer is to an unqualified person, must be produced to the registrar or British consular officer, together with the certificate of sale and certificate of registry. See s. 44 (5) (7) and (10) and notes thereto, *infra*. For qualification for ownership, see s. 1 and notes thereto.

[3] As to re-registration after survey as to seaworthiness, see s. 54.

[4] *Semble*, that the giving of notice to the registrar and his making an entry in the book are not conditions precedent to the registry being considered as closed, but that it is to be so considered on the happening of any one of the events whereby the ship may cease to be a British ship. See *Manchester Ship Canal Co.* v. *Horlock*, *supra*, and the terms of M.S.A. 1906, s. 52 (2).

[5] The words in square brackets are to be read into subs. (1) as if they were inserted there; see M.S.A. 1906, s. 52 (1). As to power of courts to enforce unsatisfied mortgages on ships sold to foreigners, see *ibid.*, s. 52 (2). As to unsatisfied mortgages on registry anew of a ship, see M.S.A. 1894, s. 52 (2).

[6] As to recovery of fines, see ss. 680–682.

Provisional certificate for ships becoming British-owned abroad

39 **22.**—(1) If at a port not within Her Majesty's dominions and not being a port of registry established by Order in Council under this Act,[1]

a ship becomes the property of persons qualified to own a British ship, the British consular officer there may grant to her master, on his application, a provisional certificate,[2] stating:—

(*a*) the name of the ship;

(*b*) the time and place of her purchase, and the names of her purchasers;

(*c*) the name of her master; and

(*d*) the best particulars respecting her tonnage, build, and description which he is able to obtain;

and shall forward a copy of the certificate at the first convenient opportunity to the Registrar-General of Shipping and Seamen.[3]

(2) Such a provisional certificate shall have the effect of a certificate of registry until the expiration of six months from its date, or until the ship's arrival at a port where there is a registrar (whichever first happens), and on either of those events happening shall cease to have effect.

40 [1] As to foreign ports of registry, see s. 88.
[2] As to form, see s. 65 and Part II of Sched. I.
[3] See note (3) to s. 19.

Temporary passes in lieu of certificates of registry

41 **23.** Where it appears to the Commissioners of Customs,[1] or to the governor of a British possession, that by reason of special circumstances it would be desirable that permission should be granted to any British ship to pass, without being previously registered, from any port in Her Majesty's dominions to any other port within Her Majesty's dominions, the Commissioners or the governor may grant a pass accordingly, and that pass shall, for the time and within the limits therein mentioned [2] have the same effect as a certificate of registry.

42 In practice such a pass is often granted to enable an unregistered vessel to proceed to a port for the purpose of registration survey.
[1] Now Commissioners of Customs and Excise; see note (1) to s. 4.
[2] Where the pass sufficiently fixes its duration by reference to the voyage to be undertaken, it will not be invalid by reason of no " time " being mentioned: *The Wills, No.* 66 (1914) 83 L.J.P. 162; 30 T.L.R. 676.

Transfers and Transmissions

43 JURISDICTION. The High Court in England has Admiralty jurisdiction to hear and determine (*inter alia*) . . . (a) any claim to the possession or ownership of a ship or to the ownership of any share therein; (b) any question arising between the co-owners of a ship as to possession, employment or earnings of that ship, together with power to settle outstanding accounts or to direct the sale of such ship or share therein; Administration of Justice Act 1956, s. 1 (1). (Formerly, jurisdiction over co-ownership was dependent upon registration in an English port; see Supreme Court of Judicature (Consolidation) Act 1925, s. 22 (1) (*a*) (ii) now repealed by Administration of Justice Act 1956, s. 7 (2).) The High Court in England has also by virtue of the Trustee Act 1925, s. 51 (6), jurisdiction to make vesting orders in respect of shares in British registered ships, vesting the right to transfer or call for a transfer of such shares or to receive the income thereof, in all cases where similar vesting orders as to stock might be made under the Trustee Act 1925, s. 51.

Restrictions on Transfer under Emergency Legislation. By s. 1 of the Ships and Aircraft (Transfer Restriction) Act 1939, it is unlawful except under the sanction of the Department of Trade and Industry to transfer any ship to which the Act applies or any share therein. See the Act and notes thereon, *post*, §§1054–1072. For general sanctions at present in force, see note to s. 1 of that Act.

Transfer of ships or shares

44 **24.**—(1) A registered ship [1] or a share therein (when disposed of to a person qualified to own a British ship [2]) shall be transferred by a bill of sale.[3]

(2) The bill of sale shall contain such description of the ship [4] as is contained in the surveyor's certificate, or some other description sufficient to identify the ship to the satisfaction of the registrar, *and shall be in the form marked A. in the first part of the First Schedule to this Act, or as near thereto as circumstances permit,*[5] and shall be executed by the transferor in the presence of, and be attested by, a witness or witnesses.[6]

45 For the definition of " ship " see s. 742; M.S.A. 1921, and *Gapp* v. *Bond, infra,* and cases there cited.

The sale or mortgage of a " ship " includes everything then on board necessary for the prosecution of the voyage, or subsequently brought on board in substitution therefor: *Coltman* v. *Chamberlain* (1890) 25 Q.B.D. 328; see also *Re Salmon, ex p. Gould* (1885) 2 Mor.Bky.Cas. 137; and *Langton* v. *Horton* (1842) 5 Beav. 9. A ship is " goods " within the definition in s. 62 of the Sale of Goods Act 1893, and (applying *ibid.* s. 52) specific performance of such a contract may be ordered in appropriate cases: *Behnke* v. *Bede Shipping Co.* [1927] 1 K.B. 649. See also *Lloyd del Pacifico* v. *Board of Trade* (1930) 35 Ll.L.R. 217.

The statutory control of restrictive trading agreements, the prohibition of such agreements as may be found to be contrary to the public interest, and the prohibition of collective enforcement of conditions regulating the resale price of goods, apply to ships; see the Restrictive Trade Practices Act 1956, s. 36 (1) where " ships " are included in the definition of " goods."

1 *Semble*, this section does not apply to a ship which, though required to be registered by s. 2, has in fact not been registered: *Union Bank of London* v. *Lenanton* (1878) 3 C.P.D. 243, *per* Bramwell L.J. cited in note (1) to s. 2. Nor to a vessel which, though exempted from registration under s. 3, has in fact been registered: *Benyon* v. *Cresswell* (1848) 12 Q.B. 899. Nor to a vessel which has been " constructively lost," and whose registry is considered as closed under s. 21 (*q.v.*): *Manchester Ship Canal Co.* v. *Horlock* [1914] 2 Ch. 199 (C.A.) (vessel abandoned and raised by canal company, and sold without bill of sale). In each of these cases transfer can take place without a registered bill of sale.

A transfer or assignment of any ship or vessel, or share thereof, is not a bill of sale within the Bills of Sale Acts 1878 and 1882. Hence, that which is a " ship or vessel " within this exception, and yet not a " registered ship " within the present section, can be validly transferred without registration of the instrument of transfer under either Act. See *The Union Bank of London* v. *Lenanton, supra,* where an assignment for value of a ship built in England for a foreign purchaser, to be delivered at a foreign port, and therefore unregistered, was held to be valid, although not registered either under the M.S.A. 1854, or the Bills of Sale Act 1854; *Gapp* v. *Bond* (1887) 19 Q.B.D. 200. A vessel used as a coal hulk and workshop may cease to be a ship, and the property in her may pass without a bill of sale: *European and Australian Royal Mail Co.* v. *Peninsular and Oriental S.N. Co.* (1864) 2 Mar.Law Cas. 351; 12 Jur.(N.S.) 909.

In the case of *Gapp* v. *Bond*, a dumb barge propelled by oars, which was not a " ship " within the M.S.A. 1854 or 1894, was held to be a " vessel " within the exceptions in the Bills of Sale Acts, and therefore transferable without registration. But see now M.S.A. 1921, s. 1 (1).

2 As to the qualifications for owning a British ship, see s. 1 and notes thereto. Upon a transfer to a person not qualified to own a British ship, no bill of sale is required unless the sale is effected under a certificate of sale at some place outside the country of the port of registry, in which case a bill of sale, though not necessarily in the prescribed form, must be produced to the registrar or British Consular Officer. See s. 44 (10). But even where the transfer is made to an unqualified person *within* the country of the port of registry, it is

usual for the owner to execute a bill of sale in the prescribed form and to give notice under s. 21 to the registrar, who thereupon closes the register (except as to unsatisfied mortgages) and if required, gives a certificate to that effect to the purchaser.

[3] Apart from the registration required by s. 26, the execution of the bill of sale transfers the property as between the parties thereto. See cases in note to s. 26. Moreover, the section applies only to the actual instrument of transfer, and not to an agreement to transfer, and therefore, such an agreement may be enforced, under s. 57, by a registered owner, though it is not a bill of sale and not registered; *Batthyany* v. *Bouch* (1881) 50 L.J.Q.B. 421; 4 Asp.M.L.C. 380; see also notes to s. 26.

As to the enforcement of equities generally, by or against the registered owner, see s. 57 and cases there cited.

[4] See note, " Mistake or variation in name," to s. 31 at § 63, *post*.

[5] The words in italics were repealed by M.S.A. 1965 s. 7 (2). As to the form of the prescribed bill of sale, see s. 65 (§ 125, *post*).

[6] As to proof without calling attesting witnesses, see s. 694.

Declaration of transfer

46 **25.** Where a registered ship or a share therein is transferred, the transferee shall not be entitled to be registered as owner thereof until he, or, in the case of a corporation, the person authorised by this Act [1] to make declarations on behalf of the corporation, has made and signed a declaration (in this Act called a declaration of transfer) referring to the ship, and containing—

(*a*) a statement of the qualification of the transferee to own a British ship, or if the transferee is a corporation, of such circumstances of the constitution and business thereof as prove it to be qualified to own a British ship; and

(*b*) a declaration that, to the best of his knowledge and belief, no unqualified person or body of persons is entitled as owner to any legal or beneficial interest [2] in the ship or any share therein.

47 As to the power of the registrar to dispense with declarations, see s. 60; as to declarations generally, ss. 61, 64; as to forms, s. 65, and Part II of Sched. I.

As to qualification for ownership, see s. 1 and notes thereto.

[1] Declarations on behalf of a corporation may be made by the secretary or other authorised officer. See s. 61 (2). [2] For definition of " beneficial interest," see s. 57.

Registry of transfer

48 **26.**—(1) Every bill of sale for the transfer of a registered ship or of a share therein, when duly executed, shall be produced to the registrar of her port of registry, with the declaration of transfer, and the registrar shall thereupon enter in the register book the name of the transferee as owner of the ship or share, and shall endorse on the bill of sale the fact of that entry having been made, with the day and hour thereof.

(2) Bills of sale of a ship or of a share therein shall be entered in the register book in the order of their production to the registrar.

49 As to the power of the registrar to dispense with declarations or other evidence, see s. 60. It is doubted whether the court has jurisdiction to order registration in the absence of a bill of sale. It is a matter for the registrar's discretion: but see *The Bineta* [1967] 1 W.L.R. 121.

The duty to register a transfer rests with the purchaser, and, apart from registration, the execution of the bill of sale (see s. 24) entirely divests the title of the vendor: *The Spirit of the Ocean* (1865) 34 L.J.Ad. 74; 12 L.T. 239. See also *Stapleton* v. *Haymen* (1864) 33 L.J.Ex. 170; 2 H. & C. 918, where the assignee in bankruptcy of the vendor was held not entitled to retake possession from the vendee, who, being an infant, had been refused registration as owner. See also *Watson* v. *Duncan* (1879) 6 Ct. of Sess.Cas. (4th Ser.) 1247. *Cf. The Two Ellens* (note to s. 37).

So that for repairs ordered by the vendee and completed before the registration of the bill of sale the vendor is not responsible although his name remains on the register: *Young* v. *Brander* (1806) 8 East 10; 103 E.R. 248. See also *M'Iver* v. *Humble* (1812) 16 East 169; 104 E.R. 1053.

Similarly a transfer by a bill of sale which is irregular by reason of non-registration is sufficient to entitle the transferee to maintain trover against a wrong-doer: *Sutton* v. *Buck* (1810) 2 Taunt. 302; 127 E.R. 1094.

Non-registration of a bill of sale by the first purchaser does not affect the title of a bona fide purchaser from him: *The Australia* (1859) 13 Moo.P.C. 132; 15 E.R. 50.

As to the enforcement of an agreement to transfer which is neither a bill of sale nor registered, see *Batthyany* v. *Bouch*, cited under s. 24.

As to the effect of registration under a "certificate of sale," where the bill of sale is apparently valid, but in fact *ultra vires* and void, see *Orr* v. *Dickinson*, *infra* (s. 44).

As to the enforcement of equities by or against the registered owner, see s. 57 and cases there cited.

As to fees on transfers, see M.S. (Mercantile Marine Fund) Act 1898, s. 3 and notes thereto, *post*; for the fees presently in force, see the M.S. (Fees) Regulations 1975 (S.I. No. 341).

As to fees payable on transfers of shares by different bills of sale, see *Harrowing Steamship Co.* v. *Toohey* [1900] 2 Q.B. 28; 9 Asp.M.L.C. 91.

Transmission of property in ship on death, bankruptcy, marriage, etc.

50 **27.**—(1) Where the property in a registered ship or share therein is transmitted to a person qualified to own a British ship [1] on the marriage,[2] death, or bankruptcy of any registered owner, or by any lawful means other than by a transfer under this Act [3]:—

(*a*) That person shall authenticate the transmission by making and signing a declaration (in this Act called a declaration of transmission) identifying the ship and containing the several statements hereinbefore required to be contained in a declaration of transfer, or as near thereto as circumstances admit, and also a statement of the manner in which and the person to whom the property has been transmitted.

(*b*) If the transmission takes place by virtue of marriage,[2] the declaration shall be accompanied by a copy of the register of the marriage or other legal evidence of the celebration thereof, and shall declare the identity of the female owner.

(*c*) If the transmission is consequent on bankruptcy, the declaration of transmission shall be accompanied by such evidence as is for the time being receivable in courts of justice as proof of the title of persons claiming under a bankruptcy.

(*d*) If the transmission is consequent on death, the declaration of transmission shall be accompanied by the instrument of representation, or an official extract therefrom.[4]

(2) The registrar, on receipt of the declaration of transmission so accompanied, shall enter in the register book the name of the person entitled under the transmission as owner of the ship or share the property in which has been transmitted, and, where there is more than one such

person, shall enter the names of all those persons, but those persons, however numerous, shall, for the purpose of the provision of this Act with respect to the number of persons entitled to be registered as owners, be considered as one person.

51 As to fees on transmission, see M.S. (Mercantile Marine Fund) Act 1898, s. 3 and notes thereto, *post*. For the fees presently in force, see the M.S. (Fees) Regulations 1975 (S.I. No. 341).

As to the power of the registrar to dispense with declarations, see s. 60; as to declarations generally, ss. 61, 64; as to forms, s. 65, Part II of Sched. I.

1 For persons qualified to own a British ship, see s. 1 and notes thereto.

2 Marriage *per se* can no longer cause transmission of the property in a ship. See Law Reform (Married Women and Tortfeasors) Act 1935, s. 2 and Halsbury, *Laws of England* (3rd ed.) title "Husband and Wife," Vol. 19, pp. 822–826.

3 These words comprehend only transmissions by operation of law unconnected with any direct act of the party to whom the property is transmitted. Hence, a transmission to a purchaser at a sale by licitation by order of a court is not such a transmission, and the registrar was held to be right in refusing to register such a purchaser in the absence of a conveyance by bill of sale: *Chasteauneuf* v. *Capeyron* (1882) 7 App.Cas. 127, 134. The difficulty arising in such a case appears, however, to be now met by the extension of the powers given by s. 29; see note (1) thereto.

4 For definition of "representation," see s. 742.

Order for sale on transmission to unqualified person

52 **28.**—(1) Where the property in a registered ship or share therein is transmitted on marriage,[1] death, bankruptcy, or otherwise [2] to a person not qualified to own a British ship,[3] then—

if the ship is registered in England or Ireland, the High Court [4]; or

if the ship is registered in Scotland, the Court of Session; or

if the ship is registered in any British possession, the court having the principal civil jurisdiction in that possession; or

if the ship is registered in a port of registry established by Order in Council under this Act,[5] the British court having the principal civil jurisdiction there;

may on application by or on behalf of the unqualified person, order a sale [6] of the property so transmitted, and direct that the proceeds of the sale, after deducting the expenses thereof, be paid to the person entitled under such transmission or otherwise as the court direct.

(2) The court may require any evidence in support of the application they think requisite, and may make the order on any terms and conditions they think just, or may refuse to make the order, and generally may act in the case as the justice of the case requires.

(3) Every such application for sale must be made within four weeks after the occurrence of the event on which the transmission has taken place, or within such further time (not exceeding in the whole one year from the date of the occurrence) as the court allow.

(4) If such an application is not made within the time aforesaid, or if the court refuse an order for sale, the ship or share transmitted shall thereupon be subject to forfeiture under this Act.[7]

53 [1] See note (2) to s. 27, *supra*.
[2] *Cf.* note (3) to s. 27.
[3] For persons qualified to own a British ship, see s. 1 and notes thereto.
[4] An application to the High Court under this section shall be assigned to the Queen's Bench Division and taken by the Admiralty Court: see R.S.C. Ord. 74, r. 1 (see App. 10, *post*). See also note (4) to s. 30. As to Ireland, see note "Application to Northern Ireland and the Republic of Ireland" after notes to s. 742, *post*.
[5] As to foreign ports of registry, see s. 88.
[6] The court may order either a sale generally or a particular sale: *Re The Santon* (1878) 26 W.R. 810.
[7] For an instance of forfeiture on failure of application in a case of transmission of a share to an alien, see *The Millicent* [1891] W.N. 162. As to time of forfeiture, *cf.* note (3) to s. 70.

Transfer of ship or sale by order of court

54 **29.** Where any court, whether under the preceding sections of this Act or otherwise,[1] order the sale of any ship or share therein, the order of the court shall contain a declaration vesting in some person named by the court the right to transfer that ship or share, and that person shall thereupon be entitled to transfer the ship or share in the manner and to the same extent as if he were the registered owner thereof; and every registrar shall obey the requisition of the person so named in respect of any such transfer to the same extent as if such person were the registered owner.

55 [1] A sale by order of the court in proceedings *in rem* gives to the purchaser a clean title against all the world. Those having claims against the ship before her sale must, thereafter, proceed against the fund in court. See *The Acrux* [1962] 1 Lloyd's Rep. 405 (applying dicta in *The Tremont* (1841) 1 Wm.Rob. 163, 164 and *Louis Castrique* v. *William Imrie and Another* (1869) L.R. 4 H.L. 414, 429, 448). But *cf. Chasteauneuf* v. *Capeyron and Delange* (1882) 7 App.Cas. 127.

As to the application of the Trustee Act 1925, to vesting orders of shares in British registered ships, see note at head of s. 24.

Power of court to prohibit transfer

56 **30.** Each of the following courts, namely:—

(*a*) in England or Ireland the High Court,[1]
(*b*) in Scotland the Court of Session,
(*c*) in any British possession the court having the principal civil jurisdiction in that possession [2]; and
(*d*) in the case of a port of registry established by Order in Council under this Act,[3] the British court having the principal civil jurisdiction there,

may, if the court think fit (without prejudice to the exercise of any other power of the court), on the application [1] of any interested person make an order prohibiting for a time specified any dealing [4] with a ship or any share therein, and the court may make the order on any terms or conditions they think just, or may refuse to make the order, or may discharge the order when made, with or without costs, and generally may act in the case as the justice of the case requires [5]; and every registrar, without being made a party to the proceeding, shall on being served with the order or an official copy thereof obey the same.

57 [1] An application to the High Court under this section shall be assigned to the Queen's Bench Division and taken by the Admiralty Court: See R.S.C. Ord. 74, r. 1 (App. 10, *post*). See also note 4 to s. 28.

[2] For a discussion of this subsection, see *Beneficial Finance Corporation Ltd.* v. *Price* [1965] 1 Lloyd's Rep. 556 (Sup.Ct. N.S.W.).

[3] See s. 88 for establishment of such ports.

[4] These sections, ss. 28, 29 and 30, confer on the High Court the jurisdiction previously enjoyed by the High Court of Admiralty under the 12th (repealed) section of the Admiralty Court Act 1861, which provided that the High Court of Admiralty should exercise the same powers over a British ship or share therein as had previously been conferred on the High Court of Chancery in England by M.S.A. 1854, ss. 63–65. M.S.A. 1854, s. 65 (now M.S.A. 1894, s. 30), has perhaps been treated as empowering the court to make the specified orders in all cases, and not merely in cases of transmissions to persons not qualified to own British ships referred to in its context, *i.e.* ss. 63, 64 (now M.S.A. 1894, ss. 27, 28). Thus in *The Ship Isis, ex p. Baker* (1868) 3 M.L.C.(o.s.) 52; [1868] W.N. 88, on an application being made in chambers by the purchaser of a barge who had agreed to pay in instalments but had fallen into arrears, an order was made restraining the vendor from transferring the barge to a third party on the purchaser giving security for the completion of the contract on his part. In *The Horlock* (1877) 2 P.D. 243 at p. 250, a similar order was made. But in neither case does it appear whether the order was made under this section or under the inherent jurisdiction of the Court of Chancery in the first case, or of the High Court in the second. The latter view would bring the decisions in these cases into harmony with the Scottish cases of *Roy* v. *Hamiltons* (1867) 5 Ct. of Sess.Cas. (3rd Ser.) 573; *McPhail* v. *Hamilton* (1878) 5 Ct. of Sess.Cas. (4th Ser.) 1017, in which it was held that M.S.A. 1854, s. 65, had not this extended application. The Admiralty jurisdiction of the High Court is now to be found in the Administration of Justice Act 1956, s. 1, which expressly preserves (*inter alia*) " jurisdiction which . . . was vested in the High Court of Admiralty immediately before the . . . 1st day of November 1875." See App. 8, § 3167, *post*.

In addition, jurisdiction was conferred on the High Court of Admiralty by the Admiralty Court Act 1861, s. 8, in suits between co-owners touching the ownership, possession, and employment and earnings of any ship registered in England or Wales. These powers were re-enacted in the Supreme Court of Judicature (Consolidation) Act 1925, s. 22 (1) (*a*) (ii), which has now been repealed and replaced by the Administration of Justice Act 1956, s. 1 (1) (*b*). Jurisdiction in such questions is no longer dependent upon registration in England.

[5] For instances of such orders, see *Nicholas* v. *Dracachis* (1875) 1 P.D. 72; *La Blanca and El Argentino* (1908) 77 L.J.P. 91 (on *ex parte* application by bank interested in mortgaged ships); and see note (4).

Mortgages

58 Scope of the Statutory Provisions. A mortgage of a ship is in general governed by the same principles, legal and equitable, as govern mortgages of other personal chattels, but the peculiar characteristics of ships as securities and the system of registration of ownership, bills of sale, and certificates of sale, have necessitated certain statutory provisions as to registration and transfers of mortgages and certificates of mortgages, which are contained in ss. 31 to 38. The scope of these sections is, however, limited, and for the general law relating to ships' mortgages, reference must be made to the general law relating to mortgages of personal chattels. In the notes to the following sections, only such cases have been selected for citation as contain statements of the law peculiar to ships' mortgages. These are for the most part collected in the notes to s. 34.

It should be borne in mind that the registration of a mortgage under these sections, while of the utmost importance in fixing priorities (see s. 33) and in limiting the effect of acts of bankruptcy by the mortgagor (see s. 36), is not essential to the validity of a mortgage, even on a British registered ship. See ss. 31 and 57, and notes thereto. But see the last note to s. 31 as to the necessity of registering certain mortgages under the Companies Act 1948.

Further, these provisions relate only to mortgages of British registered ships. Thus they do not affect mortgages of ships whilst building and before they are capable of being registered as ships; nor do they affect mortgages of unregistered British ships or foreign vessels, although the statutory forms provided by the Act are commonly used for mortgages of ships of the latter class. The nature of the rights conferred by such instruments will fall to be determined by the law of the flag. See *The Byzantion*, 38 T.L.R. 744; 127 L.T. 756; *The Colorado* [1923] P. 102.

The provisions may be adopted with respect to the mortgaging of aircraft; see Civil Aviation Act 1968, s. 16 (2) (*a*). For provisions relating to hovercraft, see § 1317, *post*.

59 HISTORY OF ADMIRALTY JURISDICTION. At common law the High Court of Admiralty had no jurisdiction over ships' mortgages. See *The Portsea* (1827) 2 Hagg.Adm. 84; *The Exmouth* (1828) 2 Hagg.Adm. 88n. (" The interest of the mortgagee is not a question for the Court of Admiralty.") By the Admiralty Court Act 1840, s. 3, a limited jurisdiction was given over claims of any mortgagee of a ship which was under arrest by process issuing from the court, or the proceeds of which after arrest had been paid into the registry of the court. Under this Act a claim of the mortgagee against the freight which had not been originally arrested was dismissed: *The Fortitude* (1843) 2 W.Rob. 217. However, by the Admiralty Court Act 1861, ss. 11 and 35, the jurisdiction was extended to include any claim in respect of any mortgage duly registered under the M.S.A. 1854 (now M.S.A. 1894) whether the ship or proceeds were under arrest or not, such jurisdiction being exercised by proceedings either *in rem* or *in personam*. Under the Supreme Court of Judicature (Consolidation) Act 1925, s. 22 (1) (*a*) (ix), the Admiralty jurisdiction of the High Court in England included jurisdiction to hear and determine " any claim in respect of a mortgage of any ship, being a mortgage duly registered in accordance with the provisions of the M.S. Acts 1894 to 1923, or in respect of any mortgage of a ship which is, or the proceeds whereof are, under the arrest of the court," and s. 3 of the Admiralty Court Act 1840, and ss. 11 and 35 of the Admiralty Court Act 1861, were repealed. See *ibid.* s. 226 (1). Now, by the Administration of Justice Act 1956, s. 1 (1) (*c*), the Admiralty jurisdiction of the High Court in England has been extended to include " any claim in respect of a mortgage of or charge on a ship or any share therein." (See App. 8, *post.*) The Supreme Court of Judicature (Consolidation) Act 1925, s. 22, has been repealed; *ibid.* s. 7 (2). " Ship " includes any description of vessel used in navigation; *ibid.* s. 8 (1). The effect of this recent change in the law is to provide jurisdiction in Admiralty over claims in respect of mortgages, registered or unregistered. Formerly, the holder of an unregistered mortgage had no right *in rem* against the vessel, unless she was already under the arrest of the court.

A sale of a ship by order of a competent court in proceedings *in rem* confers on the purchasers a valid title free of all charges and incumbrances. It is not open to mortgagees to proceed subsequently against such a ship in respect of any unsatisfied balance of moneys due to them under a pre-existing mortgage; see *The Acrux* [1962] 1 Lloyd's Rep. 405. But *cf. Chasteauneuf* v. *Capeyron* (1882) 7 App.Cas. 127.

60 RESTRICTIONS ON MORTGAGES UNDER EMERGENCY LEGISLATION. By s. 1 of the Ships and Aircraft (Transfer Restriction) Act 1939, it is unlawful except under the sanction of the Board of Trade (now Minister of Transport) to mortgage or transfer the mortgage of any ship to which the Act applies. See the text of that Act, and notes, *post*, §§ 1054–1072. For general sanctions at present in force, see note to s. 1 of that Act.

Mortgage of ship or share

61 **31.**—(1) A registered ship or a share therein may be made a security for a loan or other valuable consideration, and the instrument creating the security (in this Act called a mortgage) shall be in the form marked B in the first part of the First Schedule to this Act, or as near thereto as circumstances permit, and on the production of such instrument the registrar of the ship's port of registry shall record it in the register book.

(2) Mortgages shall be recorded by the registrar in the order in time in which they are produced to him for that purpose, and the registrar shall by memorandum under his hand notify on each mortgage that it has been recorded by him, stating the day and hour of that record.

62 " Ship." As to what vessels are included in this term, see s. 742 and M.S.A. 1921, s. 1 (1). As to what articles on board pass under the word " ship " in a mortgage, see note to s. 24. See also note (1) to s. 24.

Where the owner of an unfinished ship mortgaged it before registration, and then registered it in his own name as owner, and the mortgagee subsequently registered the mortgage, the property in the ship was held to be in the mortgagee; *Bell* v. *Bank of London* (1858) 3 H. & N. 730; 28 L.J.Ex. 116.

Stamp duty. See exemption in s. 721.

FEES. See M.S. (Mercantile Marine Fund) Act 1898, s. 3, and notes thereto, *post.* For the fees presently in force, see M.S. (Fees) Regulations 1975 (S.I. No. 341).

FORM. As to the power of the authorities to make alterations in the prescribed form, and of the registrar to reguse to register a mortgage in any other form, and other provisions as to forms, see s. 65.

COLLATERAL DEED OF COVENANTS. The detailed stipulations of the mortgage are often contained in a separate deed. See *The Benwell Tower* (1895) 8 Asp.M.C. 13; *The Cathcart* (1867) L.R. 1 A. & E. 314; 16 L.T. 211; *The Innisfallen* (1866) L.R. 1 A. & E. 72; *Brown* v. *Tanner* (1868) L.R. 3 Ch.App. 597. Such a collateral deed often contains covenants dealing with the following matters—interest, repayment of principal, insurances and renewals thereof, entry in " Protection and Indemnity," " Freight and Demurrage," etc. clubs, limitation on employment of ship, application of policy money, definition of default on which statutory or other powers to be exercised, etc.

Quaere whether reference in a statutory mortgage to the deed of covenants may be sufficient notice to bind third parties with knowledge of the contents of the collateral deed. *Brown* v. *Tanner* (1868) L.R. 3 Ch. 597.

For form of such deed of covenant, see *Encyclopaedia of Forms and Precedents.*

EQUITIES. As to the enforcement of equities by or against a registered mortgagee, see ss. 56, 57, and notes thereto.

UNREGISTERED MORTGAGE. Under M.S.A. 1854 it was held that a mortgage of a ship must be accompanied by the formalities required by that Act, and that a court of equity could give no effect to an unregistered contract to assign a ship as security for money: *Liverpool Borough Bank* v. *Turner* (1860) 29 L.J.Ch. 827; 1 Johns. & H. 159; affirmed 30 L.J.Ch. 379; 2 De G.F. & J. 502, cited in note (4) to s. 57.

But the effect of this decision was annulled by the enactment of M.S.A. 1862, s. 3 (1894, s. 57), as to the enforcement of equities. See s. 57, and cases there cited.

And it would seem that, even apart from s. 57, registration is not a condition of the validity of the mortgage, as between the parties to it or their representatives. See cases cited under s. 26: and *cf. The Two Ellens* (1871) L.R. 3 A. & E. 345, 355, cited in note to s. 37. But see as to the necessity of registering mortgages on ships belonging to any company registered in England or Wales, note " Registration of charges on ships under Companies Act 1948," *infra.*

As to the position of an unregistered mortgagee claiming freight as against the purchaser of the cargo, see *Keith* v. *Burrows* (1876) 1 C.P.D. at p. 734; 3 Asp.M.L.C. 280.

An equitable mortgage may be created by the deposit of the builder's certificate of an unfinished ship: *Ex p. Hodgkin, re Softley* (1875) L.R. 20 Eq. 746; *sub nom. Ex p. Winter, re Softley*, 44 L.J.Bky. 107; 33 L.T. 62; or of a registered mortgage of a ship: *Lacon* v. *Liffen* (1862) 32 L.J.Ch. 25; 7 L.T. 774.

In *Smith* v. *Owners of S.S. Zigurds* (*The Zigurds*) [1934] A.C. 209, it was held that ships' agents, who had taken an equitable assignment of freight and who had given notice thereof to the person from whom freight was due, took priority over a mortgagee of the ship, who had a prior equitable assignment of freight, but who had not given notice.

63 UNREGISTERED SHIP. It would seem that the mortgage of an unregistered ship being neither within the provisions of this Act nor the Bills of Sale Acts 1878, 1882, though valid as a security under the ordinary law of mortgage, need not be in the statutory form, and cannot be registered, so as to secure priority for the mortgagee by registration, under this Act.

MISTAKE OR VARIATION IN NAME. Where, before registration, a vessel was described in a mortgage as the " City of Bruxelles," and subsequently the owner registered the vessel and the mortgagee the mortgage, in the name " City of Brussels," this variation in name was held to be immaterial, and not to invalidate the mortgage, the identity of the vessel being established by the descriptions of her in the register and the original mortgage: *Bell* v. *Bank of London* (1858), *supra.*

The principle of this decision would seem not to be affected by s. 47.

POWER TO EXPUNGE. The court has inherent jurisdiction to expunge an invalid mortgage from the register: *Brond* v. *Broomhall* [1906] 1 K.B. 571; *Burgis* v. *Constantine* [1908] 2 K.B. 484; and to expunge an entry in a register after a mortgage has been redeemed: *The Yolanda Barbara* [1961] 2 Lloyd's Rep. 337.

Registration of charges on ships under Companies Act 1948. Any charge, including any mortgage, on a ship or any share of a ship belonging to any company registered in England created after November 1, 1929, is void against the liquidator or any creditor of the company unless particulars of the charge, together with the instrument creating the charge, are delivered to or received by the registrar of companies for registration within 21 days after the date of its creation, but without prejudice to any contract or obligation for repayment of the moneys thereby secured. When a charge becomes void under this provision, the money secured thereby becomes immediately repayable. Companies Act 1948, s. 95 (1) (2) (*h*) and (10). Registration *must* be effected by the company, but *may* be effected on the application of any person interested (s. 96). Where after November 1, 1929, any company registered in England acquires any property which is subject to a charge which would have required registration if created by the company after such acquisition, *e.g.* a ship subject to a mortgage, the company must similarly register the charge. *Ibid.* s. 97.

Relief against failure to register such charges properly and in due time may, in certain cases, be granted by the court. *Ibid.* s. 101. Copies of every instrument creating charges requiring registration, and a register of charges, must be kept at the registered office of the company, and must be open to inspection of any creditor or member of the company. *Ibid.* ss. 103, 104 and 105.

By virtue of s. 106 these provisions also apply to companies incorporated outside England, but having an established place of business in England, in respect of charges on " property in England," which presumably includes ships. It is not clear, however, under what circumstances a ship is " property in England." A ship would not be property in England merely because registered in England: *cf. The Natalie* [1973] 1 Lloyd's Rep. 216. Again, if not registered in England, it is unlikely that a ship would be held to be property in England merely by reason of the fact that she from time to time trades in English waters. See Dicey's *Conflict of Laws*, 8th ed., p. 516, as to the *situs* of ships, and compare the authorities there quoted as to the locality of shares or other securities.

Entry of discharge of mortgage

64 **32.** Where a registered mortgage is discharged, the registrar shall, on the production of the mortgage deed, with a receipt for the mortgage money endorsed thereon, duly signed and attested, make an entry in the register book to the effect that the mortgage has been discharged, and on that entry being made the estate (if any) which passed to the mortgagee shall vest in the person in whom (having regard to intervening acts and circumstances, if any) it would have vested if the mortgage had not been made.

65 The registrar has no Authority to erase an entry of a mortgage on its being discharged: *Chasteauneuf* v. *Capeyron* (1882) 7 App.Cas. 127. But the court has power to expunge the entry in a register after a mortgage has been redeemed; see *The Yolanda Barbara* [1961] 2 Lloyd's Rep. 337.

In *Bell* v. *Blyth* (1868) L.R. 4 Ch.App. 136, where the question was one of priorities, it was held that the entry of a discharge in the register discharged the mortgage, and that it could not be revived by a memorandum on the register that the discharge was given by mistake. But in *The Rose* (1873) L.R. 4 A. & E. 6, where there was also a mistaken entry of discharge, but apparently no question of priorities, the court pronounced that the purchaser from the mortgagee was entitled to be registered as owner. See also *Duthie* v. *Aiken* (1893) (Sc.) 20 Ct. of Sess.Cas. (4th Ser.) 214; 30 S.L.R. 229.

Priority of mortgages

66 **33.** If there are more mortgages than one registered in respect of the same ship or share, the mortgagees shall, notwithstanding any express, implied, or constructive notice, be entitled in priority, one over the other, according to the date at which each mortgage is recorded in the register book, and not according to the date of each mortgage itself.

67 A mortgagee by registering gets priority over a prior unregistered equitable mortgage of which he had notice: *Coombes* v. *Mansfield* (1855) 24 L.J.Ch. 513. And over unregistered debentures of prior date, of which he had notice: *Black* v. *Williams* [1895] 1 Ch. 408, cited in note to s. 57. See also as to tacking, priorities, etc. *Liverpool Marine Credit Co.* v. *Wilson* (1872) L.R. 7 Ch. 507. The section, however, relates only to such priorities as, apart from registration, would arise from the dates of the instruments and when the priorities depend, not upon the dates of the instruments, but upon a state of facts wholly independent of the dates of the instruments, this section does not apply: *The Benwell Tower* (1895) 8 Asp.M.L.C. 13. Thus the general principle that a first mortgage taken to cover future advances has not priority over a second mortgage as regards advances made after notice of the second mortgage (as to which see *Hopkinson* v. *Rolt* (1861) 9 H.L.Cas. 514), applies to mortgages of ships notwithstanding this section. *Ibid.*

Mortgagee not treated as owner

68 **34.** Except as far as may be necessary for making a mortgaged ship or share available as a security for the mortgage debt, the mortgagee shall not by reason of the mortgage be deemed the owner of the ship or share, nor shall the mortgagor be deemed to have ceased to be owner thereof.

69 The following notes contain a summary of the principal cases upon the rights and liabilities of mortgagor and mortgagee:

I. Introductory Notes

Apart from statutory provisions, a mortgage of a ship is in general governed by the same principles, legal and equitable, as govern mortgages of any other personal chattel. Williams and Bruce, *Admiralty Practice*, 3rd ed., Chap. 2. But the statutory provisions as to registration and transfers of mortgages and certificates of mortgage, which form a natural part of the system of registration of ownership, bills of sale and certificates of sale, introduce into the law applicable to mortgages of ships certain special features. Further, from the very nature of the subject-matter and the circumstances of its employment the interests of the mortgagee of a ship are exposed to many peculiar incidents and perils. " The mortgagee of a ship holds a security over a floating subject which in the very act of use as a ship may be withdrawn from the jurisdiction and control of the courts to which the mortgagee can have recourse, and in that use is exposed to the perils of the sea whereby the value of the security may be wholly or in great part destroyed." *Laming* v. *Seater* (1889) 16 Ct. of Sess.Cas. (4th Ser.) 828 at p. 832. Again, by the operation of maritime liens, either arising out of the old maritime law or created by statute, in the course of her trading, liabilities may be attached to the ship for damage done in collision, salvage awards, wages of crew and master's disbursements, etc., which may still further impair the security. Accordingly, the interests of the mortgagee of a ship have received the special consideration of the legislature and the courts in many respects.

70 II. Mortgagor in Possession—Mortgagee's Right to take Possession, etc.

The most valuable right that the mortgagee enjoys is the right to take possession and, if necessary, to sell the ship in order to realise his security. This right of taking possession he enjoys at common law independently of statute in the circumstances referred to below; moreover, in many cases provision is made in a deed of covenants collateral to the statutory mortgage whereby the mortgagee, although not in possession, is given greater control over the ship than he would enjoy at common law or under the statute and more advantageous rights of taking possession. See note " Collateral deed " to s. 31 and *Laming* v. *Seater*, *supra*.

Position of mortgagor. In general, till the mortgagee takes possession, the mortgagor is owner to all the world; he bears the expenses and he is to reap the profit: *Chinnery* v. *Blackburn* (1784) 1 Hy.Bl. 117n., *per* Lord Mansfield. Thus the mortgagee is not responsible for the wages of the master: *Annet* v. *Carstairs* (1813) 3 Camp. 354; nor for necessaries supplied to the ship on the credit of owner or master: *Jackson* v. *Vernon* (1789) 1 Hy.Bl. 114; *Twentyman* v. *Hart* (1816) 1 Stark. 366. See § 74, *post*.

The mortgagor remaining in possession retains all rights and powers of ownership, and his contracts with regard to the ship will be valid and effectual, provided they do not materially impair the security: *Collins* v. *Lamport* (1865) 34 L.J.Ch. 196; 11 L.T. 497; *The Heather Bell* [1901] P. 143, 272. He may insure: *Provincial Insurance Co. of Canada* v. *Leduc* (1874) L.R. 6 P.C. 224.

Where, therefore, a mortgagor in possession had entered into a beneficial charterparty, the mortgagee was restrained by injunction, at the suit of the charterer, from dealing with the ship so as to interfere with the execution of the charterparty; *The Heather Bell, supra.*

Where, before the mortgage is effected, the mortgagee has notice of a charterparty, then, whether the charterparty is beneficial or not, *semble*, he will be restrained from doing any act (*e.g.* exercising a power of sale) which would have the effect of preventing the performance of the charterparty: *De Mattos* v. *Gibson* (1859) 28 L.J.Ch. 498, *per* Lord Chelmsford at p. 502. But if the mortgagor is already unable to perform the charterparty (*e.g.* through lack of means), a mortgagee with such notice will not be restrained from exercising his power of sale: *Ibid.*; *The Lord Strathcona* [1925] P. 143. The wider proposition of Knight Bruce L.J. in *De Mattos* v. *Gibson*, 28 L.J.Ch. 165, that a purchaser of a personal chattel with notice of a restrictive covenant, *e.g.* the purchaser of a ship with notice of a charterparty (which *a fortiori* would apply to a mortgagee with notice of a charterparty) may be restrained from using the chattel in a manner inconsistent with the restrictive covenant, has been much criticised (*e.g. per* Buckley L.J. in *London County Council* v. *Allen* [1914] 3 K.B. 642 at p. 658, and *per* Scrutton L.J. in *Barker* v. *Stickney* [1919] 1 K.B. 121 at p. 132); but was approved by the Privy Council in its application to ships in *Lord Strathcona S.S. Co.* v. *Dominion Coal Co. Ltd.* [1926] A.C. 108; but see *Port Line Ltd.* v. *Ben Line Steamers Ltd.* [1958] 2 Q.B. 146.

And see "charterparties," *infra* under III.

If the mortgagee arrests the ship in an attempt to prevent her fulfilling a beneficial charterparty, he may be condemned in costs and damages even though he takes possession of his shares before she sails: *The Maxima* (1878) 4 Asp.M.L.C. 21; 39 L.T. 112.

The mortgagee, so long as he does not interfere and claim possession, will be taken to have allowed the mortgagor to enter into all engagements for the employment of the ship of the sort usually entered into by a person who has the apparent control and ownership of the ship, so long as they do not impair his security. Hence, where a ship was at the time of demand for possession by the mortgagee under engagement for a voyage, the mortgagee was held not entitled to damages for detention of the ship till the conclusion of the voyage: *Johnson* v. *Royal Mail S.P. Co.* (1867) L.R. 3 C.P. 38 as explained by Mathew L.J. in *Law Guarantee and Trust Soc.* v. *Russian Bank, etc.* [1905] 1 K.B. 815 at p. 826.

Where the mortgagee of a share in a ship has joined with the owners of the remainder of the shares in appointing the master, any act of the master which would be barratrous against the owners is equally barratrous against the mortgagee: *Small* v. *United Kingdom Mutual Insurance Co.* [1897] 2 Q.B. 42, as explained in *Samuel* v. *Dumas* [1924] A.C. 431.

RIGHTS OF MORTGAGEE. This section (s. 34) enacts in substance that the mortgagee shall be deemed owner for all the purposes necessary for making the ship available as a security for the mortgage debt: *per* Coleridge J., *Kitchen* v. *Irvine* (1858) 28 L.J.Q.B. 46. And to make the ship so available he may take possession of her, in the manner referred to below, and collect her freight: *per* Lord Campbell C.J., *Kitchen* v. *Irvine, sub nom. Dickinson* v. *Kitchen* (1858) 8 E. & B. 789.

IMPAIRMENT OF SECURITY. He may prevent her sailing uninsured if mortgagor agreed to insure: *Laming* v. *Seater* (1889) 16 Ct. of Sess.Cas. (4th Ser.) 828. But he cannot object to a charterparty being carried out simply on the ground that it would remove the ship out of the jurisdiction and render enforcement of the mortgage security more difficult: *The Fanchon* (1880) 50 L.J.Ad. 4; 5 P.D. 173. The onus is on him to show that his security would be prejudiced. *Ibid.* Nor can he arrest the ship until bail is given merely because the owner intends to send her on a foreign voyage: *The Highlander* (1843) 2 W.Rob. 109. As to the position when the mortgagee has notice of the charterparty before effecting the mortgage, see *De Mattos* v. *Gibson*, and *The Lord Strathcona, supra.*

Thus, where the mortgagee arrested the ship in an action for possession before the mortgage money became due and while she was under a charterparty not prejudicial to the security, the court, on the motion of the owners, ordered her release: *The Blanche* (1887) 6 Asp.M.L.C. 272.

Similarly, where the charterparty is not prejudicial to the security, a mortgagee of shares not in possession cannot maintain an action of restraint against co-owners who have let the ship without his consent: *The Innisfallen* (1866) L.R. 1 A. & E. 72.

A subsequent bottomry bond does not necessarily impair the mortgagee's security: *The Ripon City* [1897] P. 226 at p. 244; *The St. George* [1926] P. 217.

The judgment creditor of the mortgagor cannot take a ship in execution because that would impair the mortgagee's security: *Kitchen* v. *Irvine*, *Dickinson* v. *Kitchen* (1858) 8 E. & B. 789.

71 RIGHT TO TAKE POSSESSION. The mortgagee's right to take possession is generally regulated by the collateral deed of covenants which usually accompanies the mortgage deed. (See note, "Collateral deed," to s. 31.) But apart from such express agreement the mortgagee may take possession under the mortgage whenever the mortgagor is in default in the payment of interest or repayment of the principal, or where the mortgagor allows the ship to remain burdened with maritime liens which impair the security, even in the absence of such default; *The Manor* [1907] P. 339.

He may act on his own initiative and responsibility in the exercise of his rights at common law or under his special contract (if any), or may invoke the assistance of the court by arresting the ship in a mortgage action under the Administration of Justice Act 1956, s. 1 (1) (*c*).

Mode of taking possession. The taking of possession by the mortgagee may be actual or constructive. He may take actual possession by putting his own representative on board. He may dismiss the master, or with the concurrence of the master may reappoint him, in which case he will act henceforth as agent for the mortgagee. A mortgagee who cannot take actual possession by reason of the ship being in foreign seas may, by taking constructive possession, entitle himself to exercise all the rights of ownership. But in order to constitute constructive possession, acts must be done on his behalf which clearly indicate an intention to assume the right of ownership: *The Benwell Tower* (1895) 72 L.T. 664; 8 Asp.M.L.C. 13. Thus, where the mortgagee of shares joined with other co-owners in appointing a new ship's husband, the court held that he had effectually intervened: *Beynon* v. *Godden* (1878) L.R. 3 Ex.D. 263; 39 L.T. 82. Similarly, where actual possession is impossible, constructive possession may be obtained by giving notice to the mortgagor and the charterer and other persons interested, *e.g.* insurance brokers, underwriters and bill of lading holders: *Rusden* v. *Pope* (1868) L.R. 3 Ex. 269.

Chattels contained in vessel. In *The Humorous, The Mabel Vera* [1933] P. 109 (mortgage of two fishing vessels " and their appurtenances ") it was held that when the mortgagee took possession there passed to him fishing nets which had been appropriated to one of the vessels at the time of the mortgage, or those subsequently put on board in substitution, but that in the case of the other vessel, to which no nets had been appropriated at the time of the mortgage, nets on board when the mortgagee took possession did not pass to him.

Damages. Damages for wrongful arrest of a ship by the mortgagee were awarded to the mortgagor in *The Cathcart* (1867) L.R. 1 A. & E. 314; 16 L.T. 211; *The Egerateia* (1868) 38 L.J.Adm. 40.

Expenses of taking possession. As to mortgagee's right to have the expenses of taking possession, etc., allowed in taking the accounts, see *Wilkes* v. *Saunion* (1877) 7 Ch.D. 188.

Where, in order to obtain possession, the mortgagee is compelled to pay wages, disbursements, etc., he can recover the same from the mortgagor, or other owners if severally liable therefor: *The Orchis* (1889) 15 P.D. 38; *Johnson* v. *Royal Mail S. P. Co.* (1867) L.R. 3 C.P. 38.

See, too, " Power of sale " and " Right to foreclose," *infra*.

III. Mortgagee in Possession—Rights and Liabilities of

72 " When a mortgagee takes possession he becomes the master or owner of the ship, and his position is simply this: from that time everything which represents the earnings of the ship which had not been paid before, must be paid to the person who then is the owner, who is in possession ": *Keith* v. *Burrows* (1877) 2 App.Cas. 636 at p. 646. But see below, " Freight."

Charterparties. On taking possession, the mortgagee is entitled to the benefit of outstanding contracts made by the mortgagor: *Collins* v. *Lamport* (1865) 34 L.J.Ch. 196. And is in general bound by a charterparty entered into by the mortgagor: *Cory Bros.* v. *Stewart* (1885) 2 T.L.R. 508. Provided that it does not impair his security: *Collins* v. *Lamport* (1865) 34 L.J.Ch. 196; 11 L.T. 497; *The Heather Bell* [1901] P. 143, 272. Thus, where the mortgagors entered into a charterparty for the carriage of contraband of war to a port of one of two belligerents, and the ship was not insured against risk of capture, the court gave the mortgagees a declaration that the charter was not binding on them because it impaired their security: *Law Guarantee and Trust Society* v. *Russian Bank for Foreign Trade* [1905] 1 K.B. 815.

And where a ship, under an engagement of an unusual kind which would be prejudicial to its sale, was mortgaged to A without notice, and then to B with notice, A was held entitled (upon default of mortgagor) to sell her to B, and B to take free of the engagement: *The Celtic King* [1894] P. 175.

And see *De Mattos* v. *Gibson, The Lord Strathcona*, *supra*, under II, as to the effect of notice even where the charterparty impairs the security.

Freight. He becomes owner, and as such, and not ordinarily by virtue of any contract or antecedent right, is entitled to freight in the process of being earned: *Keith* v. *Burrows* (1877) 2 App.Cas. 636; *Gumm* v. *Tyrie* (1865) 6 B. & S. 298; 122 E.R. 1206; *Dean* v. *M'Ghie*

(1826) 4 Bing. 45; and to all freight which under the terms of the charterparty becomes due after he takes possession, although for services rendered in part previously. *Brown* v. *Tanner* (1868) L.R. 3 Ch. 597. But he is not entitled to freight still unpaid which became due on a voyage previous to his taking possession: *Shillito* v. *Biggart* [1903] 1 K.B. 683 (where the authorities are reviewed).

But in order to defeat the mortgagor's right to freight the mortgagee must take possession, actual or constructive, before the freight is paid: *Rusden* v. *Pope* (1868) L.R. 3 Ex. 269; *Beynon* v. *Godden* (1878) L.R. 3 Ex.D. 263.

Where actual possession was impossible owing to the ship being at sea, notice to mortgagor and charterer was held equivalent thereto: *Rusden* v. *Pope, supra.*

The mortgagee cannot recover freight which he has allowed the mortgagor to receive: *Wilson* v. *Wilson* (1872) L.R. 14 Eq. 32; *Willis* v. *Palmer* (1860) 29 L.J.C.P. 194; 7 C.B.(N.S.) 340; following *Gardner* v. *Casenove* (1856) 26 L.J.Ex. 17.

But where a charterparty provides for certain limited advances by the charterer on account of freight, the charterer cannot claim to set off against freight due to the mortgagee in possession further advances made to the captain in excess of the sum provided for in the charterparty: *Tanner* v. *Phillips* (1872) 42 L.J.Ch. 125.

The question whether the mortgagee is entitled to freight payable in advance or at some time before the mortgagee takes possession, which in fact has not been so paid, does not appear to have been decided; but it is submitted on principle that if, upon the true construction of the contract, the consideration for the payment of the advance freight has been fully executed (*e.g.* by receiving the goods on board) before possession is taken, the mortgagor and not the mortgagee will be entitled to payment. See *Oriental S.S. Co.* v. *Tyler* [1893] 2 Q.B. 518; *Byrne* v. *Schiller* (1871) L.R. 6 Ex. 20, 319; *Smith* v. *Pyman* [1891] 1 Q.B. 42, 742; B.S.L. Vol. 3, Carver, *Carriage by Sea*, 12th. ed., §§ 1144–1155.

As to appointment of receiver of freight at instance of mortgagee, see *Burn* v. *Herlofsen and anor.*; *The Faust* (1887) 6 Asp.M.C. 126; 56 L.T. 722 (C.A.); *Fairfield Shipping, etc., Co.* v. *London and East Coast Express Co.* [1895] W.N. 64.

See also further, as to freight, notes on " Mortgagee of shares " and " Mortgagee and third parties," *infra.*

MORTGAGEE OF SHARES. If the mortgagee of shares in a ship joins with other part-owners in appointing a receiver of freight before freight is due, they effectually intervene so as to entitle themselves to freight as against the owner of the mortgaged shares or his assigns: *Beynon* v. *Godden* (1878) L.R. 3 Ex.D. 263; 4 Asp.M.C. 10. The position of a mortgagee of shares when a ship is employed on a joint adventure by the co-owners may involve intricate questions of accounts, and the position is discussed in *Alexander* v. *Simms* (1854) 23 L.J.Ch. 721; *Green* v. *Briggs* (1848) 17 L.J.Ch. 323.

73 MORTGAGEE AND THIRD PARTIES. The right of the mortgagee to freight on taking possession cannot be defeated by an assignment of freight: *Brown* v. *Tanner* (1868) L.R. 3 Ch. 597; even if made prior to the registration of the mortgage, unless the mortgagee has notice thereof: *Wilson* v. *Wilson, etc.* (1872) 41 L.J.Ch. 423. A purchaser from the mortgagee stands in the same position: *Dobbyn* v. *Comerford* (1860) 10 Ir.Ch.Rep. 327.

For a case where a garnishee order, obtained by a creditor for owners' disbursements, upon the receivers of cargo attaching the freight due from them was discharged in favour of the mortgagee in possession, see *Japp* v. *Campbell* (1887) 57 L.J.Q.B. 79.

An unpaid vendor who supplied coal on the personal credit of the mortgagor has no claim on freight in the hands of the mortgagee, although the coal was used in earning the freight: *El Argentino* [1909] P. 236.

SECOND MORTGAGEE. For the position of a second mortgagee with respect to freight and taking possession, see *Liverpool Marine Credit Co.* v. *Wilson* (1872) L.R. 7 Ch.App. 507. " He has no legal right to take actual possession, and cannot therefore by his own act give himself that which is equivalent to possession. But as between himself and the mortgagor, the equitable right of the second mortgagee is the same as the legal right of the first mortgagee; just as in the case of land if the first mortgagee declines to take possession the second mortgagee may obtain a receiver and so have the possession and the benefits of the possessory right. . . . The legal owner's right is paramount to every equitable charge not affecting his own conscience; the equitable owner in the absence of special circumstances takes subject to all equities prior in date to his own estate or charge. The courts of equity, in appointing a receiver at the instance of an equitable incumbrancer take possession in fact on behalf of all, and so as not to disturb any legal right or interfere with equitable priorities." *Per* Sir W. M. James L.J., *ibid.* at p. 511.

MORTGAGEE'S PRIORITIES. The mortgagee is in no way affected by the personal debts of the owner of the ship except in so far as they attach to the ship. But the ship is in many cases the most tangible asset belonging to a defaulting owner within the jurisdiction of the court, and difficult questions frequently arise as between the rival claimants against the proceeds of the arrested ship. In practice the court, after allowing a reasonable time for creditors against the fund to come in, will order the proceeds to be paid out according to the following principles in satisfaction of the claims of those who have prosecuted their claims without laches to final judgment: see *The Markland* (1871) L.R. 3 A. & E. 340; *The Africano* [1894] P. 14.

74 MARITIME LIENS. The mortgagee, as regards his claim against the ship, is postponed to all maritime liens, *e.g.* for salvage, wages, disbursements, bottomry and damage, from the moment of their attachment.

Thus, he is postponed to liens for bottomry bonds even accruing after the date of the mortgage: *The Dowthorpe* (1843) 2 W.Rob. 73. And a bottomry bond retains its priority for a reasonable time after the voyage for which it was given: *The Royal Arch* (1857) Swab. 269; *The Duke of Bedford* (1829) 2 Hagg.Adm. 294; and its validity is not affected by non-disclosure to the mortgagee: *The Heligoland* (1859) Swab. 491; *The Staffordshire* (1872) L.R. 4 P.C. 194. But where practicable the lender on bottomry should see that the mortgagee has notice of the hypothecation before obtaining the bond: *The St. George* [1926] P. 217.

Similarly, the mortgagee is postponed to the master's claim for disbursements and wages in connection with the mortgaged ship: *The Mary Ann* (1865) L.R. 1 A. & E. 8; *The Feronia* (1868) L.R. 2 A. & E. 65; *The Julindur* (1853) 1 Spinks 71. In *The Leoborg* (*No.* 2) [1964] 1 Lloyd's Rep. 380, the question was raised (but not decided) as to whether or not a claim brought under the provisions of the Administration of Justice Act 1956, s. 3 (4), for wages earned on board a sister ship has priority over the mortgagee of the ship against which the claim is brought. For the position of the master in respect of claims for wages and disbursements at common law and under statute, see § 1374 and the cases there cited.

The mortgagee is postponed to a person claiming in respect of a damage claim arising subsequent to the mortgage: *The Aline* (1839) 1 W.Rob. 111. On principle it would seem that he would be postponed to a person claiming in respect of prior damage also, for the owner can only mortgage his ship subject to existing maritime liens.

The mortgagee has a right to defend an action against the ship for wages and disbursements, but can only rely on defences open to the owner: *The Chieftain* (1863) 32 L.J.Ad. 106; Br. & L. 104. As to his right to have the ship released on giving bail, see *The Ringdove* (1858) Swab. 310; *The Acacia* (1879) (Ir.) 4 Asp.M.C. 226; 41 L.T. 564.

REPAIRS, NECESSARIES, ETC. At common law there is no maritime lien for necessaries supplied to or repairs effected on a ship, although the civil law, which has been adopted in many foreign countries, does confer a maritime lien upon the ship in such cases. Foreign law cannot be adduced, in proceedings in an English court, to alter the English rule of ranking, under which the claims of " necessaries men " rank *pari passu*, and after those of a mortgagee. See *The Zigurds* [1932] P. 113, at p. 125. But a mortgagee under a French *hypothèque*, although he has not the same right of property as under an English mortgage, has the right to arrest the ship in the hands of a subsequent owner. Since this right resembles a maritime lien, the mortgagee is entitled under the *lex fori* to priority over necessaries men: *The Colorado* [1923] P. 102 (C.A.). Nor is any maritime lien to be implied from the statutes which, successively, provided the Admiralty Court and the Probate, Divorce and Admiralty Division of the High Court with jurisdiction over claims in respect of repairs and necessaries (see Admiralty Court Act 1861, s. 4 and Supreme Court of Judicature (Consolidation) Act 1925, s. 22 (1) (*a*) (x) and (vii), both of which are now repealed) and claims " in respect of goods or materials supplied to a ship for her operation or maintenance " which is currently the scope of the Admiralty jurisdiction of the High Court; see Administration of Justice Act 1956, s. 1 (1) (*m*): *The Pacific* (1862) 33 L.J.Ad. 120; Br. & L. 243 (overruling *The Skipwith* (1864) 10 L.T. 43); *The Troubadour* (1866) L.R. 1 A. & E. 302; 16 L.T. 156; *The Two Ellens* (1872) L.R. 4 P.C. 161; *The Heinrich Björn* (1886) 11 App.Cas. 270. The law in Scotland is the same: *The Arbonne* (1925) 23 Ll.L.R. 141. " The *res*, the ship, does not become chargeable with the debt for necessaries until the suit is actually instituted, and . . . all valid charges on the ship to which any person other than the owner of the ship who is liable for the necessaries is entitled must take precedence." *Per* Mellish L.J., *The Two Ellens* (*supra*) at p. 170. Therefore, the mortgagee takes priority over the claims of repairers and material men who have not issued proceedings before the date of the mortgage, from which date the mortgage becomes a valid charge upon the ship, even though the owner remains in possession. The right to sue *in rem* in Admiralty gives the plaintiff a charge upon the *res* from the date of the issue of the writ of summons: see *The Monica S.* [1967] 2 Lloyd's Rep. 113. Accordingly, a change of ownership occurring after the institution of proceedings but before service of process or arrest does not defeat a " statutory right of action *in rem* ": see *The Monica S.*, *supra*, but compare *The Banco*, *The Times*, December 10, 1970. Registration, it should be noticed, only affects the priorities as between mortgagees: see s. 33. A mortgagee whilst in possession is not liable for necessaries supplied to the order of the ship, unless the master in ordering them acted as agent of the mortgagee: *The Troubadour, supra*. The master has no implied authority to act as his agent in that respect. *Ibid.* But if duly authorised he will bind the mortgagee to the same extent as he would the owner of the ship: *Havilland* v. *Thompson* (1864) (Sc.) 3 Ct. of Sess.Cas. (3rd Ser.) 313. On equitable principles, a necessaries claimant might be preferred to a mortgagee if that mortgagee had stood by, knowing that the shipowners were insolvent, and that the claimant was carrying out work or supplying materials that were directly benefiting his interests. See *The Pickaninny* [1960] 1 Lloyd's Rep. 533. See *The Zigurds, supra*, generally for various attempts by repairers and " necessaries men " to obtain preference over an equitable mortgagee. Since a repairer has no maritime lien or similar charge upon the ship, he cannot proceed *in rem* if his contract was made with demise charterers and not the owners: see *Smith's Dock Co.* v. *The St. Merriel (Owners)* [1963] 2 W.L.R. 488.

75 Possessory liens, etc. If, however, the repairer, who has done work on the ship to the order of the owner, retains possession of the ship, the mortgagee seeking to take possession must first discharge the repairer's possessory lien: *Williams* v. *Allsupp* (1861) 30 L.J.C.P. 353; 10 C.B.(n.s.) 417; *The Turliani* (1875) 32 L.T. 841. And if the repairer is forced to give up his possessory lien by judicial process, *e.g.* by arrest of the ship at the suit of other necessaries men, the court will protect his rights and will give him priority over all claims except for maritime liens which have attached before the possessory lien: *The Gustaf* (1862) Lush. 506; 31 L.J.Ad. 207; *The Immacolata Concezione* (1883) 9 P.D. 37. *Quaere* if the repairer himself arrests the ship: *Jacobs* v. *Latour* (1828) 5 Bing. 130. The point was raised, but not decided in *The Andrea Ursula* [1971] 1 Lloyd's Rep. 145. But see, as to Ireland, *The Acacia* (1880) 4 Asp.M.C. 254. Although it is suggested in *The Aline* (1839) 1 W.Rob. 111, that the holder of a bottomry bond for the cost of repairs effected subsequent to the attachment of a maritime lien, *e.g.* for salvage, is entitled to priority over the maritime lien to the extent of the increased value of the ship due to the repairs, yet this suggestion, so far as it applies to a repairer's possessory lien unsupported by a bottomry bond, was disapproved of in *The Russland* [1924] P. 55, where Hill J. held that a ship-repairer's lien ranked after maritime liens, *e.g.* for salvage already accrued, and that, although the salvors had benefited, there was no principle on which the ship-repairer's claim could be preferred to that of the salvors.

For position when the possessory lien has been given up, see *The Lyons* (1887) 6 Asp.M.C. 199; 57 L.T. 818, where the mortgagee of a part was held entitled to his share of the proceeds of sale without contributing to the charges of material men who had no lien.

Use of the ship. If the mortgagee takes possession, he can only lawfully use the ship as a prudent man would use her, she being his own property. It is impossible to lay down the strict rule that he can never lawfully employ her to earn freight, or that after taking possession he must allow her to lie idle till he may prudently sell her. But he will be liable to the mortgagor for any loss sustained through his imprudent use and sale of the ship: *Marriott* v. *Anchor Reversionary Co.* (1861) 2 Giff. 457; affirmed 30 L.J.Ch. 571; 3 De G.F. & J. 177. Certain dicta of Wood V.-C. in *European and Australian R.M. Co.* v. *R.M.S.P. Co.* (1858) 4 Kay & J. 676, which imply that the mortgagee has an unlimited right to use the ship, were disapproved by Lord Campbell L.C. in the last-mentioned case.

The mortgagee cannot be compelled at the instance of other parties interested in the ship to join in a charterparty instead of selling her: *Samuel* v. *Jones* (1863) 7 L.T. 760.

76 Power of sale. A power of sale is conferred on every registered mortgagee by s. 35 (*q.v.*) even though no such power is given in the mortgage deed or covenants. Mortgagees, however, will generally find it advisable to obtain the concurrence of the owner in the sale, as the owner is in most cases able to effect a better sale than the mortgagee, in view of his knowledge of the particular characteristics of the ship. If the proceeds of sale after discharging the mortgage debt show a surplus in the hands of the mortgagee, he becomes a constructive trustee of such surplus for subsequent incumbrancers and the mortgagor; but not an express trustee, and hence the Statutes of Limitation are not barred: *Banner* v. *Berridge*, L.R. 18 Ch.D. 254. But now by the Limitation Act 1939, ss. 19 and 31, constructive trustees have the same right to plead limitation as express trustees.

But where the first mortgagee sold by arrangement with the second mortgagee, and a surplus resulted, then such arrangement and not the law of mortgage was held to create the trust: *Tanner* v. *Heard* (1857) 23 Beav. 555 (considered by Kay J. in the case last cited; 18 Ch.D. at pp. 261, 262).

Being a trustee, he cannot make any charge in connection with the sale: *Matthison* v. *Clarke* (1854) 3 Drew. 3; and no agreement between the parties as to commission can make such a charge valid: *The Benwell Tower* (1895) 72 L.T. 664.

For an instance of a wrongful sale by mortgagee, see *Broward* v. *Dumaresque* (1841) 3 Moo.P.C. 457. As to a sale decreed at the suit of mortgagee of shares, see *The Fairlie* (1868) 37 L.J.Ad. 66; and as to rights of mortgagee of minority of shares in distribution of proceeds of sale, see *The Ripon City* (*No.* 2) [1898] P. 78.

Where the second mortgagee arrests a ship and the first mortgagee procures her release by giving bail, the latter will be entitled to his costs and interest on money paid into court if the proceeds of sale are insufficient to satisfy the first mortgage: *The Western Ocean* (1870) L.R. 3 A. & E. 38.

RIGHT TO FORECLOSE. In principle there seems no reason why a mortgagee should not have a right to foreclose; for the right to foreclose is inherent in the very nature of a mortgage; *Re Bogg, Allison* v. *Paice* [1917] 2 Ch. 239, at p. 255. In practice, however, foreclosure actions by mortgagees of ships are rare, though not unknown. In *The Buttermere* (Fo. 211, July 24, 1883), reported in Williams & Bruce *Admiralty Practice*, 3rd ed. (1902) at p. 44, the mortgagee of two sixty-fourth shares in a ship claimed a decree of foreclosure, or in the alternative a sale of the mortgaged shares. The mortgagor appearing as defendant but making default in pleading, the court ordered that he should be precluded from all equity of redemption in the mortgaged shares, unless the amount due on the mortgage was paid within a month. The M.S. Acts do not appear to provide expressly any machinery by which the mortgagee, after obtaining an order for foreclosure, can perfect his title by becoming registered as owner. In the case of a sale by order of the court, the court may under s. 29 vest in some person named by the court—in practice the Admiralty Marshal—the right to transfer the ship in the same manner and to the same extent as if he were the registered owner, but there seems to be no corresponding power in the case of foreclosure. See as to the procedure on foreclosure in the case of registered land, Land Registration Act 1925, s. 34 (3).

Mortgagee to have power of sale

77 **35.** Every registered mortgagee shall have power absolutely to dispose of the ship or share in respect of which he is registered, and to give effectual receipts for the purchase money; but where there are more persons than one registered as mortgagees of the same ship or share, a subsequent mortgagee shall not, except under the order of a court of competent jurisdiction,[1] sell the ship or share, without the concurrence of every prior mortgagee.

For notes on this section, see note " Power of sale " under preceding section.

[1] For Admiralty jurisdiction of the High Court over claims in respect of mortgages, see Administration of Justice Act 1956, s. 1 (1) (*c*).

Mortgage not affected by bankruptcy

78 **36.** A registered mortgage of a ship or share shall not be affected by any act of bankruptcy [1] committed by the mortgagor after [2] the date of the record of the mortgage, notwithstanding that the mortgagor at the commencement of his bankruptcy had the ship or share in his possession, order, or disposition, or was reputed owner thereof, and the mortgage shall be preferred to any right, claim, or interest therein of the other creditors of the bankrupt or any trustee or assignee on their behalf.

79 [1] As to what are acts of bankruptcy, see Bankruptcy Act 1914, s. 1.

[2] Where a mortgage is granted by a mortgagor who has already committed an act of bankruptcy to a mortgagee without notice of the act of bankruptcy, the mortgagee is protected by s. 45 of the Bankruptcy Act 1914, re-enacting s. 49 of the Bankruptcy Act 1883: *The Ruby* (1900) 9 Asp.M.L.C. 146; 83 L.T. 438, following *Lyon* v. *Weld n* (1824) 2 Bing. 334.

Transfer of mortgages

80 **37.** A registered mortgage of a ship or share may be transferred to any person, and the instrument effecting the transfer shall be in the form marked C in the first part of the First Schedule to this Act, or as near thereto as circumstances permit, and on the production of such instrument the registrar shall record it by entering in the register book the name of the transferee as mortgagee of the ship or share, and shall by memorandum under his hand notify on the instrument of transfer that it has been recorded by him, stating the day and hour of the record.

81 The instrument of transfer is exempt from stamp duty; see s. 721.

As to fees on transfer of mortgages, see M.S. (Mercantile Marine Fund) Act 1898, s. 3, and notes thereto, *post*. For the fees presently in force, see M.S. (Fees) Regulations 1975 (S.I. No. 341).

For provisions as to forms, etc., and as to power of registrar to refuse to register transfer not in prescribed form, see s. 65.

As between the transferor and the transferee, the rights under the mortgage pass upon the execution of the instrument of transfer, and not upon registration thereof: *The Two Ellens* (1871) L.R. 3 A. & E. 345, 355, following *Stapleton* v. *Haymen*, cited in note to s. 26, *ante*.

Moreover, it seems that an agreement to transfer a mortgage can be enforced under s. 57, though it is not in the prescribed form, and is not registered. See note to s. 24, and *Batthyany* v. *Bouch*, there cited.

As to the power of the court to look behind the registered documents and enforce equities between the owner and the transferee of a mortgagee, see *The Cathcart* (1867) L.R. 1 A. & E. 314; 16 L.T. 211, cited in note to s. 57; and as to equities generally, see s. 57, and note (4) thereto.

The deposit of a mortgage as security by the registered mortgagee, who subsequently became bankrupt, was held to take the ship out of his " order and disposition ": *Lacon* v. *Liffen* (1862) 7 L.T. 774, cited in note to s. 31.

Restriction on transfer of mortgages under emergency legislation. See note at head of s. 31.

Transmission of interest in mortgage by death, bankruptcy, marriage, etc.

82 **38.**—(1) Where the interest of a mortgagee in a ship or share is transmitted on marriage,[1] death, or bankruptcy, or by any lawful means, other than by a transfer under this Act,[2] the transmission shall be authenticated by a declaration [3] of the person to whom the interest is transmitted, containing a statement of the manner in which and the person to whom the property has been transmitted, and shall be accompanied by the like evidence [3] as is by this Act required in case of a corresponding transmission of the ownership of a ship or share.[4]

(2) The registrar on the receipt of the declaration, and the production of the evidence aforesaid, shall enter the name of the person entitled under the transmission in the register book as mortgagee of the ship or share.

83 [1] Marriage *per se* can no longer cause a transmission of property. See note (2) to s. 27, *supra*.

[2] As to these words, see note (3) to s. 27.

[3] As to power of registrar to dispense with declarations and evidence, see s. 60; as to mode of making declarations, s. 61; and as to their admissibility in evidence, s. 64.

[4] See s. 27 for transmission of property in ship.

Certificates of Mortgage and Sale

Powers of mortgage and sale may be conferred by certificate

84 **39.** A registered owner, if desirous of disposing by way of mortgage or sale of the ship or share in respect of which he is registered at any place out of the country in which the port of registry [1] of the ship is situate, may apply to the registrar, and the registrar shall thereupon enable him to do so by granting a certificate of mortgage or a certificate of sale.

[1] For definition of ship's port of registry, see s. 13.

Requisites for certificates of mortgage and sale

85 **40.** Before a certificate of mortgage or sale is granted, the applicant shall state to the registrar, and the registrar shall enter in the register book, the following particulars: (that is to say,)

(i) the name of the person by whom the power mentioned in the certificate is to be exercised, and in the case of a mortgage the maximum amount of charge to be created, if it is intended to fix any such maximum, and in the case of a sale the minimum price at which a sale is to be made, if it is intended to fix any such minimum:

(ii) the place where the power is to be exercised, or if no place is specified, a declaration that it may be exercised anywhere, subject to the provisions of this Act:

(iii) the limit of time within which the power may be exercised.

Restrictions on certificates of mortgage and sale

86 **41.** A certificate of mortgage or sale shall not be granted so as to authorise any mortgage or sale to be made—

If the port of registry of the ship is situate in the United Kingdom, at any place within the United Kingdom; or

If the port of registry is situate within a British possession, at any place within the same British possession; or

If the port of registry is established by Order in Council under this Act,[1] at that port, or within such adjoining area as is specified in the order; or

By any person not named in the certificate.

[1] Foreign ports of registry may be established by Order in Council. See notes to s. 88 for a list of such Orders in Council.

Contents of certificates of mortgage and sale

87 **42.** A certificate of mortgage and a certificate of sale shall contain a statement [1] of the several particulars by this Act directed [2] to be entered in the register book on the application for the certificate, and in addition

thereto an enumeration of any registered mortgages [3] or certificates of mortgage or sale affecting the ship or share in respect of which the certificate is given.

[1] As to forms, see s. 65 and Part II of Sched. I.
[2] See s. 40 for the particulars directed to be entered.
[3] As to registration of mortgages, see s. 31.

Rules as to certificates of mortgage

88 **43.** The following rules shall be observed as to certificates of mortgage:—

(1) The power shall be exercised in conformity with the directions contained in the certificate:

(2) Every mortgage made thereunder shall be registered by the endorsement of a record thereof on the certificate by a registrar or British consular officer:

(3) A mortgage made in good faith thereunder shall not be impeached by reason of the person by whom the power was given dying before the making of the mortgage:

(4) Whenever the certificate contains a specification of the place at which, and a limit of time not exceeding twelve months within which, the power is to be exercised, a mortgage made in good faith to a mortgagee without notice shall not be impeached by reason of the bankruptcy of the person by whom the power was given:

(5) Every mortgage which is so registered as aforesaid on the certificate shall have priority over all mortgages of the same ship or share created subsequently to the date of the entry of the certificate in the register book; and, if there are more mortgages than one so registered, the respective mortgagees claiming thereunder shall, notwithstanding any express, implied, or constructive notice, be entitled one before the other according to the date at which each mortgage is registered on the certificate, and not according to the date of the mortgage [1]:

(6) Subject to the foregoing rules, every mortgagee whose mortgage is registered on the certificate shall have the same rights and powers and be subject to the same liabilities as he would have had and been subject to if his mortgage had been registered in the register book instead of on the certificate [2]:

(7) The discharge of any mortgage so registered on the certificate may be endorsed on the certificate by any registrar or British consular officer, on the production of such evidence as is by this Act [3] required to be produced to the registrar on the entry of the discharge of a mortgage in the register book; and on that endorsement being made, the interest, if any, which passed to the mortgagee shall vest

in the same person or persons in whom it would (having regard to intervening acts and circumstances, if any) have vested, if the mortgage had not been made:

(8) On the delivery of any certificate of mortgage to the registrar by whom it was granted he shall, after recording in the register book, in such manner as to preserve its priority, any unsatisfied mortgage registered thereon, cancel the certificate, and enter the fact of the cancellation in the register book; and every certificate so cancelled shall be void to all intents.

See note to the next section.
89 [1] *Cf.* s. 33 and note for priority of mortgages.
[2] See ss. 34–37 for powers of mortgagee.
[3] See s. 32 for entry of discharge of mortgage.

Rules as to certificates of sale

90 **44.** The following rules shall be observed as to certificates of sale:—

(1) A certificate of sale shall not be granted except for the sale of an entire ship:

(2) The power shall be exercised in conformity with the directions contained in the certificate [1]:

(3) A sale made in good faith thereunder to a purchaser for valuable consideration shall not be impeached by reason of the person by whom the power was given dying before the making of such sale:

(4) Whenever the certificate contains a specification of the place at which, and a limit of time not exceeding twelve months within which, the power is to be exercised, a sale made in good faith to a purchaser for valuable consideration without notice shall not be impeached by reason of the bankruptcy of the person by whom the power was given:

(5) A transfer made to a person qualified to be the owner of a British ship [2] shall be by a bill of sale in accordance with this Act [3]:

(6) If the ship is sold to a person qualified to be the owner of a British ship the ship shall be registered anew [4]; but notice of all mortgages enumerated on the certificate of sale shall be entered in the register book:

(7) Before registry anew there shall be produced to the registrar required to make the same the bill of sale by which the ship is transferred, the certificate of sale, and the certificate of registry of such ship [5]:

(8) The last-mentioned registrar shall retain the certificates of sale and registry, and after having endorsed on both of those instruments an entry of the fact of a sale having taken place,

shall forward them to the registrar of the port appearing thereon to be the former port of registry of the ship, and the last-mentioned registrar shall thereupon make a memorandum of the sale in his register book, and the registry of the ship in that book shall be considered as closed, except as far as relates to any unsatisfied mortgages [6] or existing certificates of mortgage entered therein:

(9) On such registry anew the description of the ship contained in her original certificate of registry may be transferred to the new register book, without her being re-surveyed, and the declaration to be made by the purchaser shall be the same as would be required to be made by an ordinary transferee [5]:

(10) If the ship is sold to a person not qualified to be the owner of a British ship, the bill of sale [7] by which the ship is transferred, the certificate of sale, and the certificate of registry shall be produced [5] to a registrar or British consular officer, and that registrar or officer shall retain the certificates of sale and registry, and, having endorsed thereon the fact of that ship having been sold to a person not qualified to be the owner of a British ship, shall forward the certificates to the registrar of the port appearing on the certificate of registry to be the port of registry of that ship; and that registrar shall thereupon make a memorandum of the sale in his register book, and the registry of the ship in that book shall be considered as closed except so far as relates to any unsatisfied mortgages [6] or existing certificates of mortgage entered therein:

(11) If, on a sale being made to a person not qualified to be the owner of a British ship, default is made in the production of such certificates as are mentioned in the last rule, that person shall be considered by British law as having acquired no title to or interest in the ship; and further, the person upon whose application the certificate of sale was granted, and the person exercising the power, shall each be liable to a fine not exceeding one hundred pounds [8]:

(12) If no sale is made in conformity with the certificate of sale, that certificate shall be delivered to the registrar by whom the same was granted; and he shall thereupon cancel it and enter the fact of the cancellation in the register book; and every certificate so cancelled shall be void for all intents and purposes.

91 Restrictions on transfer. See note at head of s. 31.

[1] Where a bill of sale, on the face of it made in conformity with the directions in the certificate, was registered, but the sale was in fact unauthorised, it was held that the bill of sale was void, and that therefore the transferee acquired no legal title by the registration, which must be treated as a nullity: *Orr* v. *Dickinson* (1859) 28 L.J.Ch. 516; 1 Johns. 1.

[2] As to qualification for ownership of a British ship, see s. 1 and notes thereto.
[3] See s. 24 for transfer by bill of sale.
[4] As to registry anew, *cf.* s. 52.
[5] As to the power of the registrar to dispense with evidence, see s. 60; as to declaration by ordinary transferee, s. 25; as to mode of making declarations, s. 61.
[6] As to the enforcement of such unsatisfied mortgages, see M.S.A. 1906, s. 52 (2).
[7] Where the sale is made to a qualified person whether within or without the country of the port of registry, a bill of sale in the prescribed form must be used. See ss. 24 and 44 (5). Where the sale is made to an unqualified person *within* the country of the port of registry no bill of sale is necessary, though a bill of sale in the prescribed form with or without modification is commonly used. See note (2) to s. 21. Where the sale is made to an unqualified person under a certificate of sale *without* the country of the port of registry, a bill of sale either in the prescribed form or in some other form effective to transfer property must be produced, together with the certificate of sale and certificate of registry.
[8] As to recovery of fines, see ss. 680 *et seq.*

Power of Commissioners of Customs in case of loss of certificate of mortgage or sale

92 **45.** On proof at any time to the satisfaction of the Commissioners of Customs [1] that a certificate of mortgage or sale is lost or destroyed, or so obliterated as to be useless, and that the powers thereby given have never been exercised, or if they have been exercised, then on proof of the several matters and things that have been done thereunder, the registrar may, with the sanction of the Commissioners, as circumstances require, either issue a new certificate, or direct such entries to be made in the register books, or such other things to be done, as might have been made or done if the loss, destruction, or obliteration has not taken place.

[1] Commissioners of Customs are now the Commissioners of Customs and Excise; see note (1) to s. 4.

Revocation of certificates of mortgage and sale

93 **46.**—(1) The registered owner of any ship or share therein in respect of which a certificate of mortgage or sale has been granted, specifying the places where the power thereby given is to be exercised, may, by an instrument under his hand, authorise the registrar by whom the certificate was granted to give notice to the registrar or British consular officer at every such place that the certificate is revoked.

(2) Notice shall thereupon be given accordingly and shall be recorded by the registrar or British consular officer receiving it, and after it is recorded the certificate shall be deemed to be revoked and of no effect so far as respects any mortgage or sale to be thereafter made at that place.

(3) The notice after it has been recorded shall be exhibited to every person applying for the purpose of effecting or obtaining a mortgage or transfer under the certificate.

(4) A registrar or British consular officer on recording any such notice shall state to the registrar by whom the certificate was granted whether any previous exercise of the power to which such certificate refers has taken place.

As to form of revocation, see s. 65 and Part II of Sched. I.

Name of Ship

Rules as to name of ship

94 **47.**—(1) A ship shall not be described by any name other than that by which she is for the time being registered.[1]

(2) A change shall not be made in the name of a ship without the previous written permission of the [Department of Trade].[2]

(3) Application for that permission shall be in writing, and if the [Department of Trade is] of opinion that the application is reasonable [it] may entertain it, and thereupon require notice [3] thereof to be published in such form and manner as [it thinks] fit.

(4) On permission being granted to change the name, the ship's name shall forthwith be altered in the register book, in the ship's certificate of registry, and on her bows and stern.[4]

(5) If it is shown to the satisfaction of the [Department of Trade] [2] that the name of any ship has been changed without [its] permission [it] shall direct that her name be altered into that which she bore before the change, and the name shall be altered in the register book, in the ship's certificate of registry, and on her bows and stern accordingly.

(6) Where a ship having once been registered has ceased to be so registered no person unless ignorant of the previous registry (proof whereof shall lie on him) shall apply to register, and no registrar shall knowingly register, the ship, except by the name by which she was previously registered, unless with the previous written permission of the [Department of Trade].[2]

(7) Where a foreign ship, not having at any previous time been registered as a British ship, becomes a British ship, no person shall apply to register, and no registrar shall knowingly register, the ship, except by the name which she bore as a foreign ship immediately before becoming a British ship, unless with the previous written permission of the [Department of Trade].[2]

(8) If any person acts, or suffers any person under his control to act, in contravention of this section, or omits to do, or suffers any person under his control to omit to do, anything required by this section, he shall for each offence be liable to a fine [5] not exceeding one hundred pounds, and (except in the case of an application being made under the section with respect to a foreign ship which not having at any previous time been registered as a British ship has become a British ship) the ship may be detained [6] until this section is complied with.

95 [1] As to effect of mistake or variation in description of vessel, see *Bell* v. *Bank of London* (1858) 28 L.J.Ex. 116, cited in note to s. 31.

[2] As to choice of ship's name, see M.S.A. 1906, s. 50, which gives the Department of Trade power to make regulations relating to ships' names. Regulations made under that section are contained in S.R. & O. No. 740 as amended by S.R. & O. 1922 No. 729 and S.R. & O. 1936 No. 390.

95

[3] In practice, notice of the proposed change of name is advertised in Lloyd's List, or other shipping papers, with a request that any objection may be notified to the Registrar-General of Shipping and Seamen, Cardiff.
[4] As to marking name upon ship see s. 7; and as to entry in register book, s. 11.
[5] As to recovery of fines, see ss. 680 *et seq.*
[6] For provisions as to detention of ships, see s. 692.

Registry of Alterations, Registry anew, and Transfer of Registry

Registry of alterations

96 **48.**—(1) When a registered ship is so altered as not to correspond with the particulars relating to her tonnage or description contained in the register book, then, if the alteration is made at any port having a registrar, that registrar, or, if it is made elsewhere, the registrar of the first port having a registrar at which the ship arrives after the alteration, shall, on application being made to him, and on receipt of a certificate from the proper surveyor stating the particulars of the alteration, either cause the alteration to be registered, or direct that the ship be registered anew.[1]

[(2) If default is made in registering anew a ship, or in registering an alteration of a ship so altered as aforesaid, the owner of the ship shall be liable on summary conviction [2] to a fine not exceeding one hundred pounds, and, in addition, to a fine not exceeding five pounds for every day during which the offence continues after conviction.]

97 The words in square brackets were substituted for subs. 2 by M.S.A. 1906, s. 53.
[1] As to registry anew, see ss. 50–52.
[2] As to summary procedure, see ss. 680–687.

Regulations for registry of alteration

98 **49.**—(1) For the purpose of the registry of an alteration in a ship, the ship's certificate of registry shall be produced to the registrar, and the registrar shall, in his discretion, either retain the certificate of registry and grant a new certificate of registry containing a description of the ship as altered, or endorse and sign on the existing certificate a memorandum of the alteration.

(2) The particulars of the alteration so made, and the fact of the new certificate having been granted, or endorsement having been made, shall be entered by the registrar of the ship's port of registry in his register book; and for that purpose the registrar to whom the application for the registry of the alteration has been made (if he is not the registrar of the ship's port of registry), shall forthwith report to the last-mentioned registrar the particulars and facts as aforesaid, accompanied, where a new certificate of registry has been granted, by the old certificate of registry.

Provisional certificate and endorsement where ship is to be registered anew

99 **50.**—(1) Where any registrar, not being the registrar of the ship's port of registry, on an application as to an alteration in a ship directs the ship

to be registered anew, he shall either grant a provisional certificate, describing the ship as altered, or provisionally endorse the particulars of the alteration on the existing certificate.

(2) Every such provisional certificate, or certificate provisionally endorsed, shall, within ten days after the first subsequent arrival of the ship at her port of discharge in the United Kingdom, if she is registered in the United Kingdom, or, if she is registered in a British possession, at her port of discharge in that British possession, or, if she is registered at a port of registry established by Order in Council under this Act,[1] at that port, be delivered up to the registrar thereof, and that registrar shall cause the ship to be registered anew.

(3) The registrar granting a provisional certificate under this section, or provisionally endorsing a certificate, shall add to the certificate or endorsement a statement that the same is made provisionally, and shall send a report of the particulars of the case to the registrar of the ship's port of registry, containing a similar statement as the certificate or endorsement.

[1] See notes to s. 88 for a list of foreign ports of registry.
As to form of certificate, see s. 65 and Part II of Sched. I.

Registry anew on change of ownership

100 **51.** Where the ownership of any ship is changed, the registrar of the port at which the ship is registered may, on the application of the owners of the ship, register the ship anew, although registration anew is not required under this Act.[1]

101 When the ship is registered anew under this section, a change of ownership must be endorsed in the ship's certificate of registry (see s. 20).

[1] Registry anew is required, where a ship is sold under a certificate of sale to a person qualified to be the owner of a British ship. See s. 44 (6).

Procedure for registry anew

102 **52.**—(1) Where a ship is to be registered anew, the registrar shall proceed as in the case of first registry,[1] and on the delivery up to him of the existing certificate of registry, and on the other requisites to registry, or in the case of a change of ownership such of them as he thinks material, being duly complied with, shall make such registry anew, and grant a certificate thereof.

(2) When a ship is registered anew, her former register shall be considered as closed, except so far as relates to any unsatisfied mortgage or existing certificates of sale or mortgage entered thereon, but the names of all persons appearing on the former register to be interested in the ship as owners or mortgagees shall be entered on the new register, and the registry anew shall not in any way affect the rights of any of those persons.

103 Part of this section is taken from M.S.A. 1854, s. 81, which applied only to registry anew upon a sale under a certificate of sale, as to which see now s. 44.

As to fees on registry anew, see M.S. (Mercantile Marine Fund) Act 1898, s. 3, and notes thereto, *post*. For the fees presently in force, see M.S. (Fees) Regulations 1975 (S.I. No. 341).
[1] See ss. 10–12 as to first registry.

Transfer of registry

104 **53.**—(1) The registry of any ship may be transferred from one port to another on the application to the registrar of the existing port of registry of the ship made by declaration in writing of all persons appearing on the register to be interested therein as owners or mortgagees, but that transfer shall not in any way affect the rights of those persons or any of them, and those rights shall in all respects continue in the same manner as if no such transfer had been effected.

(2) On any such application the registrar shall transmit notice thereof to the registrar of the intended port of registry with a copy of all particulars relating to the ship, and the names of all persons appearing on the register to be interested therein as owners or mortgagees.

(3) The ship's certificate of registry shall be delivered up to the registrar either of the existing or intended port of registry, and, if delivered up to the former, shall be transmitted to the registrar of the intended port of registry.

(4) On the receipt of the above documents the registrar of the intended port of registry shall enter in his register book all the particulars and names so transmitted as aforesaid, and grant a fresh certificate of registry, and thenceforth such ship shall be considered as registered at the new port of registry, and the name of the ship's new port of registry shall be substituted for the name of her former port of registry on the ship's stern.

105 As to fees on transfer of registry, see M.S. (Mercantile Marine Fund) Act 1898, s. 3, and notes thereto, *post*. For the fees presently in force, see M.S. (Fees) Regulations 1975, (S.I. No. 341).

Under s. 2 of the Ships and Aircraft (Transfer Restriction) Act 1939 an application to transfer under this section the registry of a ship to which that Act applies may not be granted without the approval of the Secretary of State for Trade. See text of the Act and notes thereon, *post*. For general sanctions at present in force, see note to s. 2 of that Act.

As to meaning of "port of registry," see s. 13.
As to "certificate of registry," see s. 14.

Restrictions on re-registration of abandoned ships

106 **54.** Where a ship has ceased to be registered as a British ship[1] by reason of having been wrecked or abandoned, or for any reason other than capture by the enemy or transfer to a person not qualified to own a British ship, the ship shall not be re-registered until she has, at the expense[2] of the applicant for registration, been surveyed by a surveyor of ships[3] and certified by him to be seaworthy.

107 [1] See s. 21 for delivery up of certificate. See also s. 17 for power to grant a new certificate with the permission of the Commissioners of Customs and Excise.
[2] As for the fees, see note to s. 53.
[3] See M.S.A. 1970, s. 76, for appointment of surveyors.

Incapacitated Persons

Provision for cases of infancy or other incapacity

108 **55.**—(1) Where by reason of infancy, lunacy, or any other cause any person interested in any ship, or any share therein, is incapable of making any declaration or doing anything required or permitted by this Act to be made or done in connection with the registry of the ship or share, the guardian or committee, if any, of that person, or, if there is none, any person appointed on application made on behalf of the incapable person, or of any other person interested, by any court or judge having jurisdiction in respect of the property of incapable persons, may make such declaration, or a declaration as nearly corresponding thereto as circumstances permit, and do such act or thing in the name and on behalf of the incapable person; and all acts done by the substitute shall be as effectual as if done by the person for whom he is substituted.

(2) The Trustee Act 1850, and the Acts amending the same, shall, so far as regards the court exercising jurisdiction in lunacy in Ireland, apply to shares in ships registered under this Act as if they were stock as defined by that Act.

109 Applications under this section are assigned to the Chancery Division: R.S.C., Ord., 74, r. 1 (App. 10, *post*).

Subs. (1) ceases to have effect in relation to persons within the jurisdiction of the judge under Part VIII of the Mental Health Act 1959; see *ibid*. s. 121 and Sched. V.

As to the power of the registrar to dispense with declarations, etc., see s. 60.

The guardian of an infant registered owner has no power, under subs. (1), to sell or mortgage a ship on behalf of the infant: *Michael* v. *Fripp* (1868) L.R. 7 Eq. 95.

"The words evidently go to minor unimportant acts, falling far short of an absolute disposition of the thing which is to be protected and taken care of." *Per* Malins V.-C., *ibid*. L.R. 7 Eq. at p. 100.

Subs. (2) represents so much of 18 & 19 Vict. c. 91, s. 10, as was left unrepealed by the Trustee Act 1893, s. 51. The remainder of s. 10 of 18 & 19 Vict. c. 91 is now represented by the Trustee Act 1925 (which repealed and replaced the Trustee Act 1893), s. 51 (6), by which the provisions of that Act as to vesting orders are applied to shares in registered ships as if they were stock.

Trusts and Equitable Rights

Notice of trusts not received

110 **56.** No notice of any trust, express, implied, or constructive, shall be entered in the register book or be receivable by the registrar,[1] and, subject to any rights and powers appearing by the register book to be vested in any other person,[2] the registered owner of a ship or of a share therein shall have power absolutely to dispose in manner in this Act provided [3] of the ship or share, and to give effectual receipts [4] for any money paid or advanced by way of consideration.

111 [1] As to equities generally, see the next section and notes thereto.

[2] *e.g.* under a mortgage (see s. 31), or under a certificate of sale or mortgage (see s. 40).

[3] Thus a registered owner who is a bare trustee cannot create a mortgage or an equity which is good against the beneficial owner, otherwise than by execution and registration under this Act: *Burgis* v. *Constantine* [1908] 2 K.B. 484.

[4] As the section enables a registered owner not only "absolutely to dispose" of shares, but also "to give effectual receipts" for the purchase-money, it enables him to enter into a valid contract as to the application of the purchase-money. Therefore the purchasers' right under such a contract to apply part of the purchase-money in discharge of the vendor's debt to the ship, a right in which the purchasers, being already part owners, were pecuniarily interested, took precedence over a prior unregistered mortgage: *Barclay* v. *Poole* [1907] 2 Ch. 284.

Equities not excluded by Act

112 **57.** The expression "beneficial interest," where used in this Part of this Act,[1] includes interests arising under contract and other equitable interests; and the intention of this Act is, that without prejudice to the provisions of this Act for preventing notice of trusts from being entered in the register book or received by the registrar, and without prejudice to the powers of disposition and of giving receipts conferred by this Act on registered owners and mortgagees,[2] and without prejudice to the provisions of this Act relating to the exclusion of unqualified persons from the ownership of British ships,[3] interests arising under contract or other equitable interests may be enforced by or against owners and mortgagees of ships in respect of their interest therein in the same manner as in respect of any other personal property.[4]

113 [1] The expression "beneficial interest" occurs in ss. 9, 71; "beneficially interested" in s. 58; and "beneficial title" in s. 5. For a discussion of the words "beneficial owner" within the meaning of s. 3 (4) of the Administration of Justice Act see *The Andrea Ursula* [1971] 1 Lloyd's Rep. 145.

[2] See ss. 35, 56, for powers of sale by mortgagee and owner.

[3] See s. 1 for qualification for ownership.

[4] Equities. Before M.S.A. 1862, s. 3 of which is re-enacted in the present section, it was held that a mortgage of a ship must be accompanied by the formalities required by the M.S.A. 1854, and that a court of equity could therefore give no effect to an unregistered contract for the assignment of a ship as security for money: *Liverpool Borough Bank* v. *Turner* (1860) 29 L.J.Ch. 827; 1 Johns. & H. 159; affirmed, 30 L.J.Ch. 379; 2 De G.F. & J. 502. Nor would it decree specific performance of an unregistered contract for the sale of a ship: *Hughes* v. *Morris* (1852) 21 L.J.Ch. 761. Contrast, *Batthyany* v. *Bouch*, *supra*.

A sale by licitation of a British ship without a conveyance by bill of sale did not create such an interest in the purchasers as rendered it compulsory on the registrar, under the M.S.A. 1854, to register them as owners: see *Chasteauneuf* v. *Capayron* (1882) 7 App.Cas. 127.

The Court of Chancery would, however, correct a mistake by which a person was registered as owner of a ship proved to be the property of another, and would direct the former to transfer to the latter, that being a case for which the Act (M.S.A. 1854) made no provision, and in which, therefore, the jurisdiction of the court was not taken away: *Holderness* v. *Lamport* (1861) 30 L.J.Ch. 489; 29 Beav. 129. And see, as to the effect of the registration of a bill of sale apparently, but not actually, valid, *Orr* v. *Dickinson* (1859) cited in note (1) to s. 44.

In consequence of the decision in *Liverpool Borough Bank* v. *Turner*, s. 3 of M.S.A. 1862 was enacted in order to provide for the enforcement of equities (see *per* Pollock C.B. in *Stapleton* v. *Haymen*, *infra*), and the following cases have been decided thereunder:

Cases under M.S.A. 1862 and this section. An owner who has executed a bill of sale absolute in terms may show that it was intended to operate as a security only, and the court will, for such purpose, look behind the register at the real character of the transactions: *Ward* v. *Beck* (1863) 32 L.J.C.P. 113; 13 C.B.(N.S.) 668; *The Innisfallen* (1866) L.R. 1 A. & E. 72. See also *The Jane* (1870) 23 L.T. 791.

Similarly, an owner may show that the transferee of a mortgage had by other arrangements, contemporaneous with and subsequent to the transfer, agreed to postpone repayment of the mortgage loan until a date subsequent to that named in the mortgage: *The Cathcart* (1867) L.R. 1 A. & E. 314; 16 L.T. 211.

But the court cannot look behind the register for the purpose of dispossessing a bona fide purchaser for value, whose name is on the register, but whose transferor had obtained title by fraud: *The Horlock* (1877) 2 P.D. 243.

The requirements as to the transfer of a ship contained in s. 55 of 1854 (1894, s. 24) apply only to the actual instrument of transfer, and not to an agreement to transfer, and therefore such an agreement may be enforced under this section by a registered owner though it is not a bill of sale and not registered: *Batthyany* v. *Bouch* (1881) *supra* (s. 24).

Indeed, independently of this section, the property in a ship passes, as between the vendor or his assigns and the purchaser, by a bill of sale, although not registered: *The Spirit of the Ocean* (1865), *supra* (s. 26); *The Two Ellens* (1871), *supra* (s. 37).

Hence the assignee in bankruptcy of the vendor could not retake possession from a purchaser who, being an infant, was refused registration as owner: *Stapleton* v. *Haymen* (1864) 33 L.J.Ex. 170; 2 H. & C. 918.

And the unregistered grantee of a bill of sale of shares in a ship, who has been in receipt of his proportion of the earnings, and therefore in possession of the shares, acquires a good title as against the trustee of the grantor's sequestered estates: *Watson* v. *Duncan* (1879) (Sc.) 16 S.L.R. 791.

The section does not entitle holders of unregistered debentures of a company owning ships to priority over subsequent registered mortgagees who had notice of the debentures: *Black* v. *Williams* [1895] 1 Ch. 408. See also *Barclay* v. *Poole* [1907] 2 Ch. 284, cited in note (4) to s. 56.

The court will now enforce a resultant trust in favour of a person who has advanced part of the purchase price, although under the old Registry Acts it could not: *The Venture* [1908] P. 218 (C.A.).

But such resultant trust will not take priority over a claim for necessaries supplied on the credit of the ship: *Foong Tai & Co.* v. *Buchheister & Co.* [1908] A.C. 458 (P.C.).

Liability of Beneficial Owner

Liability of owners

114 **58.** Where any person is beneficially interested,[1] otherwise than by way of mortgage,[2] in any ship or share in a ship registered in the name of some other person as owner, the person so interested shall, as well as the registered owner, be subject to all pecuniary penalties imposed by this or any other Act on the owners of ships or shares therein, so nevertheless that proceedings may be taken for the enforcement of any such penalties against both or either of the aforesaid parties, with or without joining the other of them.

[1] See s. 57 for meaning of "beneficial interest." See also *The Hopper* 66 [1908] A.C. 126.

[2] s. 34 provides that except as far as may be necessary for making a mortgaged ship or share available as a security for the mortgage debt, the mortgagee shall not by reason of the mortgage be deemed the owner of the ship or share. By entering into possession, the mortgagee may incur the liabilities of an owner. See notes to s. 34.

Managing Owner

Ship's managing owner or manager to be registered

115 **59.**—(1) The name and address of the managing owner for the time being of every ship registered at a port in the United Kingdom shall be registered at the custom house of that port.

(2) Where there is not a managing owner there shall be so registered the name of the ship's husband or other person to whom the management of the ship is entrusted by or on behalf of the owner; and any person whose name is so registered shall, for the purposes of this Act, be under

the same obligations, and subject to the same liabilities, as if he were the managing owner.

(3) If default is made in complying with this section the owner shall be liable, or if there are more owners than one each owner shall be liable in proportion to his interest in the ship, to a fine not exceeding in the whole one hundred pounds each time the ship leaves any port in the United Kingdom.

116 The term " managing owner " is not defined in the Act, the only other places in which it occurs being s. 426 (now repealed) (notice to the Department of Trade of loss of ship), and s. 696 (service of documents). As to the position and authority of the managing owner, and the effect of this section, and as to how far registration of the managing owner's name is evidence of his authority to bind his co-owners, see *Frazer* v. *Cuthbertson* (1880) 6 Q.B.D. 93 at p. 98.

" It (*i.e.* ' managing owner ') is a commercial and not a legal expression. . . . The section is part of the machinery designed to secure adequate protection for lives and property at sea; and provides, with that or a similar object, that a certain class of agents when they are appointed shall be registered, so that it may be known who in fact is managing the vessel. A managing owner registered under the Act is no more and no less than a managing owner before the Act. He binds those whose agent he is; he binds nobody besides." Whether the registered managing owner has authority to bind other owners " is in each case a question of fact. . . . There is no magic in the term managing owner which creates him a plenipotentiary for those owners whose agent he is not in fact." *Ibid. per* Bowen L.J., 6 Q.B.D. at p. 98.

As to his position and authority generally, see also *The Huntsman* [1894] P. 214; 70 L.T. 386; *Barker* v. *Highley* (1863) 15 C.B.(N.S.) 27; 1 M.L.C.(O.S.) 383; *Thomas* v. *Lewis* (*or Oxley*) (1878) 4 Ex.D. 18; *Doeg* v. *Trist* (1897) 2 Com.Cas. 153; *Pringle* v. *Dixon* (1896) 2 Com.Cas. 38; *Von Freeden* v. *Hull, Blythe & Co.* (1907) 96 L.T. 590. See also Abbott, *Merchant Ships, etc.*, 14th ed., pp. 55, 144; B.S.L. Vol. 2, Carver, *Carriage by Sea*, 12th ed., paras. 24–26; Halsbury, *Laws of England*, 3rd ed., Vol. 35, pp. 92–93.

As to his duty to procure charters, etc., and the principles of his remuneration, see *Williamson* v. *Hine* [1891] 1 Ch. 390.

For the duty of an owner or master to report any shipping casualty to the Secretary of State for Trade, see s. 73 of M.S.A. 1970; for service of documents on managing owner in lieu of master, see s. 696 of this Act.

s. 5 (4) of the Crown Proceedings Act 1947 contains, and defines for the purpose of that Act, the term " manager," and provides that the " manager " of one of H.M. ships (see s. 38 (2) of that Act) shall have the benefit of limitation of liability. See *post*, § 1075.

Declarations, Inspection of Register, and Fees

Power of registrar to dispense with declarations and other evidence

117 **60.** When under this Part of this Act any person is required to make a declaration on behalf of himself or of any corporation, or any evidence is required to be produced to the registrar, and it is shown to the satisfaction of the registrar that from any reasonable cause that person is unable to make the declaration, or that the evidence cannot be produced, the registrar may, with the approval of the Commissioners of Customs,[1] and on the production of such other evidence, and subject to such terms as they may think fit, dispense with the declaration or evidence.

As to declarations on behalf of incapacitated persons, see s. 55.

[1] Now Commissioners of Customs and Excise; see note (1) to s. 4.

Mode of making declarations

118 **61.**—(1) Declarations required by this Part of this Act shall be made before a registrar of British ships, or a justice of the peace, or a commissioner for oaths, or a British consular officer.

(2) Declarations required by this Part of this Act may be made on behalf of a corporation by the secretary or any other officer of the corporation authorised by them for the purpose.

119 This section summarises provisions contained in various sections of the Act of 1854. Subs. (1) omits certain restrictions as to the particular registrar, etc., before whom a declaration is to be made. Justices of the peace are empowered to take declarations by the Statutory Declarations Act 1835, s. 18. A commissioner for oaths is empowered by the Commissioners for Oaths Act 1889, as amended by the Commissioners for Oaths Act 1891, to take declarations at any place. See definition in s. 742. The provision as to corporations now made general in subs. (2) did not occur in all the sections of the Act of 1854.

As to who are " registrars of British ships " see s. 4.

As to meaning of " consular officer " see s. 742.

Application of fees

120 **62.** All fees authorised to be taken under this Part of this Act shall, except where otherwise in this Act provided, if taken in any part of the United Kingdom, be applied in payment of the general expenses of carrying into effect this Part of this Act, or otherwise as the Treasury may direct; if taken in a British possession be disposed of in such way as the Executive Government of the possession direct; and if taken at any port of registry established by Order in Council under this Act be disposed of as Her Majesty in Council directs.

121 For the fees at present in force under the M.S. Acts, see the M.S. (Fees) Regulations 1975 (S.I. No. 341).

Returns, Evidence, and Forms

Returns to be made by registrars

122 **63.**—(1) Every registrar in the United Kingdom shall at the expiration of every month, and every other registrar at such times as may be fixed by the Registrar-General of Shipping and Seamen, transmit to him a full return, in such form as the said Registrar-General may direct, of all registries, transfers, transmissions, mortgages, and other dealings with ships which have been registered by or communicated to him in his character of registrar, and of the names of the persons concerned in the same, and of such other particulars as may be directed by the said Registrar-General.

(2) Every registrar at a port in the United Kingdom shall on or before the first day of February and the first day of August in every year transmit to the Registrar-General of Shipping and Seamen a list of all ships registered at that port, and also of all ships whose registers have been transferred or cancelled at that port since the last preceding return.

Evidence of register book, certificate of registry, and other documents

123 **64.**—(1) A person, on payment of a fee [*not exceeding two shillings* [1]], to be fixed by the Commissioners of Customs,[2] may, on application to

the registrar at a reasonable time during the hours of his official attendance, inspect any register book.[3]

(2) The following documents shall be admissible in evidence in manner provided by this Act,[4] namely,

(*a*) Any register book under this Part of this Act on its production from the custody of the registrar or other person having the lawful custody thereof;

(*b*) A certificate of registry under this Act purporting to be signed by the registrar or other proper officer;

(*c*) An endorsement on a certificate of registry purporting to be signed by the registrar or other proper officer;

(*d*) Every declaration made in pursuance of this Part of this Act in respect of a British ship.

(3) A copy or transcript of the register of British ships kept by the Registrar-General of Shipping and Seamen under the direction of the [Secretary of State] shall be admissible in evidence in manner provided by this Act,[4] and have the same effect to all intents as the original register of which it is a copy or transcript.

124 [1] The words bracketed in italics, which had been substituted by the Fees Increase Act 1923, s. 1, Sched. I, were repealed as from November 19, 1952, by M.S. (Safety Convention) Act 1949, s. 37 (5), Sched. III.

For the fee currently in force, see M.S. (Fees) Regulations 1975 (S.I. No. 341) as made in pursuance of M.S. (Safety Convention) Act 1949, s. 33 (2), *post.*

[2] Now Commissioners of Customs and Excise; see note (1) to s. 4.

[3] This provision does not impose upon a shipwright, to whom the mortgagor has delivered a ship for repairs, the duty of inspecting the register (to see whether the ship is mortgaged or not), but merely gives him permission to do so: *Williams* v. *Allsup* (1861) 30 L.J.C.P. 353; 10 C.B.(N.S.) 417.

[4] See, as to admissibility of documents in evidence generally, ss. 694, 695, 719–721 and M.S.A. 1970, s. 75. M.S.A. 1854, s. 107, appears to be reproduced, with certain verbal modifications, by subs. (2) of this section and s. 695 combined; for cases, see note (3) to s. 695.

Forms of documents, and instructions as to registry

125 **65.**—(1) The several instruments and documents specified in the second part of the First Schedule to this Act [1] shall be in the form prescribed by the Commissioners of Customs,[2] with the consent of the [Secretary of State], or as near thereto as circumstances permit; and the Commissioners of Customs [2] may, with the consent of the [Secretary of State], make such alterations in the forms so prescribed, and also in the forms set out in the first part of the said Schedule, as they may deem requisite.

(2) A registrar shall not be required without the special direction of the Commissioners of Customs [2] to receive and enter in the register book any bill of sale, mortgage or other instrument for the disposal or transfer of any ship or share, or any interest therein which is made in any form other than that for the time being required under this Part of this Act, or

which contains any particulars other than those contained in such form; but the said Commissioners [2] shall, before altering the forms, give such public notice thereof as may be necessary in order to prevent inconvenience.

(3) The Commissioners of Customs [2] shall cause the said forms to be supplied to all registrars under this Act, for distribution to persons requiring to use the same, either free of charge, or at such moderate prices as they may direct.

(4) The Commissioners of Customs,[2] with the consent of the [Secretary of State], may also, for carrying into effect this Part of this Act, give such instructions to their officers as to the manner of making entries in the register book, as to the execution and attestation of powers of attorney, as to any evidence required for identifying any person, as to the referring to themselves of any question involving doubt or difficulty, and generally as to any act or thing to be done in pursuance of this Part of this Act, as they think fit.

126 [1] The forms of these instruments and documents were scheduled to the M.S.A. 1854, but to facilitate the alteration of them they are now left to be prescribed as here provided. For list of the forms prescribed on May 5, 1896, see S.R. & O. and S.I. Rev. 1948, XIV, *Merchant Shipping*, p. 87.

As to exemptions from stamp duty, see s. 721.

[2] Now Commissioners of Customs and Excise. See note (1) to s. 4.

Forgery and False Declarations

Forgery of documents

127 **66.** If any person forges, or fraudulently alters, or assists in forging or fraudulently altering, or procures to be forged or fraudulently altered, any of the following documents, namely, any register book, builder's certificate, surveyor's certificate, certificate of registry, declaration, bill of sale, instrument of mortgage, or certificate of mortgage or sale under this Part of this Act, or any entry or endorsement required by this Part of this Act to be made in or on any of those documents, that person shall in respect of each offence be guilty of felony[1] [and liable on conviction on indictment to imprisonment for not more than seven years].[2]

128 [1] By the Criminal Law Act 1967, s. 1, all distinctions between felony and misdemeanour were abolished.

[2] The words in brackets were added by the Criminal Law Act 1967 (c. 58), s. 10 (1), Sched. II, para. 22.

See also the provisions of the Forgery Act 1913, s. 3 (3) (*k*).

As to costs of prosecution for offences committed within the Admiralty jurisdiction, see the Costs in Criminal Cases Act 1973; as to prosecution of offences in Scotland see s. 702, and M.S.A. 1906, s. 82 (3).

False declarations

129 **67.**—(1) If any person in the case of any declaration made in the presence of or produced to a registrar under this Part of this Act, or in any document or other evidence produced to such registrar—

129

(i) wilfully makes, or assists in making, or procures to be made, any false statement concerning the title to or ownership of, or the interest existing in any ship, or any share in a ship; or

(ii) utters, produces, or makes use of any declaration, or document containing any such false statement, knowing the same to be false,

he shall, in respect of each offence, be guilty of a misdemeanour.

(2) If any person wilfully makes a false declaration touching the qualification of himself or of any other person, or of any corporation, to own a British ship or any share therein, he shall for each offence be guilty of a misdemeanour,[1] and that ship or share shall be subject to forfeiture under this Act,[2] to the extent of the interest therein of the declarant, and also, unless it is proved that the declaration was made without authority, of any person or corporation on behalf of whom the declaration is made.

[1] As to punishment of offences, see s. 680.
[2] See s. 76 for proceedings on forfeiture, and note (3) to s. 70.

National Character and Flag

National character of ship to be declared before clearance

130 **68.**—(1) An officer of customs shall not grant a clearance or transire for any ship until the master of such ship has declared to that officer the name of the nation to which he claims that she belongs, and that officer shall thereupon inscribe that name on the clearance or transire.

(2) If a ship attempts to proceed to sea without such clearance or transire, she may be detained until the declaration is made.

For provisions as to detention, see s. 692.
For procedure on clearance, see Customs and Excise Act 1952, s. 52.

Penalty for unduly assuming British character

131 **69.**—(1) If a person uses the British flag and assumes the British national character on board a ship owned in whole or in part by any persons not qualified to own a British ship,[1] for the purpose of making the ship appear to be a British ship, the ship shall be subject to forfeiture under this Act,[2] unless the assumption has been made for the purpose of escaping capture by an enemy or by a foreign ship of war in the exercise of some belligerent right.[3]

(2) In any proceeding for enforcing any such forfeiture the burden of proving a title to use the British flag and assume the British national character shall lie upon the person using and assuming the same.

132 [1] See s. 1 for qualification for ownership.
[2] See s. 76 for proceedings on forfeiture of ship, and note (3) to s. 70.
[3] As to the international aspects of the use of false flags, see Oppenheim, *International Law*, 7th ed., Vol. 2, p. 429, and W. E. Hall, *International Law*, 8th ed., p. 649.

Penalty for concealment of British or assumption of foreign character

133 **70.** If the master or owner of a British ship [1] does anything or permits anything to be done, or carries or permits to be carried any papers or documents, with intent to conceal the British character of the ship from any person entitled by British law to inquire into the same, or with intent to assume a foreign character,[2] or with intent to deceive any person so entitled as aforesaid, the ship shall be subject to forfeiture under this Act [3]; and the master, if he commits or is privy to the commission of the offence, shall in respect of each offence be guilty of a misdemeanour.[4]

134 [1] As to the meaning of "British ship," see ss. 1, 2, 72, and notes thereto.

[2] A ship was forfeited under this provision in *The Sceptre* (1876) 3 Asp.M.L.C. 269; 35 L.T. 429, where, in order to prevent her seizure as unseaworthy, the owner, by a representation to the collector of customs that he had sold her to foreigners, procured the closing of the register, and sailed her under a foreign register and flag, whilst he continued to own her and receive the profits of working her; and in *The Annandale* (1877) 3 Asp.M.L.C. 504; 37 L.T. 364, where she was nominally transferred to an Englishman resident abroad to enable her to sail under a foreign flag and evade the law as to inspection, etc., while her former owners preserved control over her.

[3] The corresponding words of M.S.A. 1854, s. 103 (2), were "shall be forfeited," and under these it was held that the property in the ship vested in the Crown immediately on the commission of the offence, and therefore a bona fide purchaser for value without notice, who purchased after the commission of the offence, but before seizure, had no title: *The Annandale* (1877) 2 P.D. 218; affirming 2 P.D. 179. It may be doubted whether the law remains the same under the different language of the present Act. The words "subject to forfeiture" occurred in the concluding part of M.S.A. 1854, s. 103, and were considered by Cotton L.J. in the case cited. *Cf. R.* v. *M'Cleverty* (*The Telegrafo or Restauracion*) (1871) L.R. 3 P.C. 673, a case of forfeiture for piracy.

The words "shall be forfeited" occur in s. 319.

As to procedure on forfeiture, see s. 76.

[4] As to the punishment of offences, see s. 680.

Penalty for acquiring ownership if unqualified

135 **71.** If an unqualified person [1] acquires as owner, otherwise than by such transmission as hereinbefore provided for,[2] any interest, either legal or beneficial,[3] in a ship using a British flag and assuming the British character, that interest shall be subject to forfeiture under this Act.[4]

136 [1] See s. 1 for qualification for ownership.

[2] See ss. 27, 28, for provisions regulating transmission.

[3] See s. 57 for meaning of "beneficial interest."

[4] See s. 76 for procedure on forfeiture, and note (3) to s. 70. The Commissioners of Customs and Excise can at any time call for proof of title: see M.S.A. 1906, s. 51, and the cases there cited.

Liabilities of ships not recognised as British

137 **72.** Where it is declared by this Act that a British ship shall not be recognised as a British ship,[1] that ship shall not be entitled to any benefits, privileges, advantages,[2] or protection usually enjoyed by British ships nor to use the British flag or assume the British national character, but so far as regards the payment of dues, the liability to fines and forfeiture, and the punishment of offences committed on board such ship, or by any persons belonging to her, such ship shall be dealt with in the same manner in all respects as if she were a recognised British ship.[3]

138 A similar provision as to fishing boats is contained in s. 373 (3).

[1] For the necessary qualifications for ownership of a British ship, see s. 1; for the obligation to register, s. 2 (in particular, as to effects of non-registration, note (3) to s. 2); and for exemption from registration, s. 3.

[2] As to the extension of the provisions relating to limitation of liability to ships from launching to registration, see M.S. (Liability of Shipowners and Others) Act 1958, s. 4.

[3] See M.S.A. 1970, s. 92.

National colours for ships, and penalty on carrying improper colours

139 **73.**—(1) The red ensign usually worn by merchant ships, without any defacement or modification whatsoever, is hereby declared to be the proper national colours for all ships and boats belonging to any British subject, except in the case of Her Majesty's ships or boats, or in the case of any other ship or boat for the time being allowed to wear any other national colours in pursuance of a warrant from Her Majesty or from the Admiralty.[1]

(2) If any distinctive national colours, except such red ensign or except the Union Jack with a white border,[2] or of any colours usually worn by Her Majesty's ships or resembling those of Her Majesty, or if the pendant usually carried by Her Majesty's ships or any pendant resembling that pendant, are or is hoisted on board any ship or boat belonging to any British subject without warrant from Her Majesty or from the Admiralty,[2] the master of the ship or boat, or the owner thereof, if on board the same, and every other person hoisting the colours or pendant, shall for each offence incur a fine not exceeding five hundred pounds.

(3) Any commissioned officer on full pay in the military or naval service of Her Majesty, or any officer of customs in Her Majesty's dominions, or any British consular officer, may board any ship or boat on which any colours or pendant are hoisted contrary to this Act, and seize and take away the colours or pendant, and the colours or pendant shall be forfeited to Her Majesty.[3]

(4) A fine under this section may be recovered with costs in the High Court [4] in England or Ireland, or in the Court of Session in Scotland, or in any Colonial Court of Admiralty or Vice-Admiralty Court within Her Majesty's dominions.

(5) Any offence mentioned in this section may also be prosecuted, and the fine for it recovered, summarily, provided that:—

(*a*) where any such offence is prosecuted summarily, the court imposing the fine shall not impose a higher fine than one hundred pounds; and

(*b*) nothing in this section shall authorise the imposition of more than one fine in respect of the same offence.

140 These provisions seem to embody the general maritime law: see *R.* v. *Ewen* (1856) 2 Jur.(N.S.) 454; and *The Minerva* (1800) 3 C.Rob. 34 and notes thereto. See also *R.* v. *Miller* (1823) 1 Hagg.Adm. 197 (where warrant for arrest for use of illegal colours was decreed), and *R.* v. *Benson*, 3 Hagg.Adm. 96.

s. 73 (1) and s. 74 (1) apply to ships of certain Indian States. S.R. & O. 1921 No. 1212; made under s. 734.

[1] In certain circumstances, British merchant ships and fishing vessels are allowed to wear the Blue Ensign by Admiralty warrant: (1) the officer commanding a ship other than a fishing vessel and at least one other officer in the ship's company must be officers on the Retired or Emergency Lists of the Royal Navy or a Commonwealth Navy, or officers on the Active or Retired Lists of any branch of the Reserves of such navies, (2) commodores on the Active or Retired Lists of the Royal Naval Reserve or Commonwealth Naval Reserves, may be allowed to fly the Blue Ensign in their own right without the requirement of an additional officer, (3) the skipper of a fishing vessel must be an officer on the Active or Retired Lists of the R.N.R. Patrol Service who holds or has held the substantive rank of Lieutenant or Skipper Lieutenant or above, and the crew must include a number of reservists as specified from time to time by the Admiralty. The vessel must hold a certificate issued by the Registrar of Royal Naval Reserves at the port where the articles are opened, showing particulars of reservists employed, and specifying the minimum number required to qualify. This certificate must be retained with the warrant and produced whenever required. See Queen's Regulations and Admiralty Instructions. Warrants are also granted to certain yacht clubs. See the *Navy List* and Lloyd's "*Register of yachts, ensigns and burgees for Yacht Clubs and distinguishing flags of yachtsmen,*" published each year in July.

[2] *i.e.* the "Pilot Jack." See Pilotage Act 1913, s. 45, *post,* and S.I. 1970, No. 1952, made thereunder, for pilot signals.

[3] See s. 70, note (3).

[4] See R.S.C. Ord. 74, r. 1.

Penalty on ship not showing colours

141 **74.**—(1) A ship belonging to a British subject shall hoist the proper national colours—

(*a*) on a signal being made to her by one of Her Majesty's ships (including any vessel under the command of an officer of Her Majesty's navy on full pay), and

(*b*) on entering or leaving any foreign port, and

(*c*) if of fifty tons gross tonnage or upwards, on entering or leaving any British port.

(2) If default is made on board any such ship in complying with this section, the master of the ship shall for each offence be liable to a fine not exceeding one hundred pounds.

(3) This section shall not apply to a fishing boat duly entered in the fishing boat register and lettered and numbered as required by the Fourth Part of this Act.

Saving for Admiralty

142 **75.** The provisions of this Act with respect to colours worn by merchant ships shall not affect any other power of the Admiralty in relation thereto.

The functions of the Admiralty under, *inter alia,* this section were transferred to the Secretary of State for Defence by the Defence (Transfer of Functions) Act 1964, s. 1 (2).
See generally Queen's Regulations and Admiralty Instructions.

Forfeiture of Ship

Proceedings on forfeiture of ship

143 **76.**—(1) Where any ship has either wholly or as to any share therein become subject to forfeiture [1] under this Part of this Act,

(*a*) any commissioned officer on full pay in the military or naval service of Her Majesty;

(*b*) any officer of Customs in Her Majesty's dominions; or

(*c*) any British consular officer,

may seize and detain [2] the ship, and bring her for adjudication before the High Court in England [3] or Ireland,[4] or before the Court of Session in Scotland, and elsewhere before any Colonial Court of Admiralty or Vice-Admiralty Court in Her Majesty's dominions,[5] and the court may thereupon adjudge the ship with her tackle, apparel, and furniture to be forfeited to Her Majesty, and make such order in the case as to the court seems just, and may award to the officer bringing in the ship for adjudication such portion of the proceeds of the sale of the ship, or any share therein, as the court think fit.

(2) Any such officer as in this section mentioned shall not be responsible either civilly or criminally to any person whomsoever in respect of any such seizure or detention as aforesaid, notwithstanding that the ship has not been brought in for adjudication, or if so brought in is declared not liable to forfeiture, if it is shown to the satisfaction of the court before whom any trial relating to such ship or such seizure or detention is held that there were reasonable grounds [6] for such seizure or detention; but if no such grounds are shown the court may award costs and damages to any party aggrieved, and make such other order in the premises as the court thinks just.[7]

144 [1] See s. 70, note (3). A ship or share therein may be subject to forfeiture (*inter alia*) under s. 16 (improper use of certificate); s. 28 (4) (transmission to unqualified person); s. 67 (2) (false declaration as to title); s. 69 (unduly assuming British character); under M.S.A. 1906, s. 51 (2) (on failure to prove title).

The machinery of this section has also been adopted under other statutes, *e.g.* under the Seal Fisheries (North Pacific) Act 1912, s. 3 (1), a vessel using any port in the United Kingdom for the purpose of equipping for hunting seals within prohibited areas in the North Pacific is subject to forfeiture under this section; under the Treaties of Washington Act 1922, s. 2 (4), any vessel built as a vessel of war or altered, armed or equipped so as to be adapted for use as a vessel of war within H.M. dominions, without licence from the Admiralty, is subject to forfeiture under this section; under the Ships and Aircraft (Transfer Restriction) Act 1939, which prohibits the transfer or mortgage of certain ships without the sanction of the Secretary of State for Trade (see the Act and notes thereon, *post*, §§ 1054 *et seq.*); and under the Sea Fish (Conservation) Act 1967, s. 156 (see, however, the Sea Fisheries Act 1968, s. 22 (1), Sched. 1, para. 38 (3), which will replace s. 15 (6) of the 1967 Act on coming into force).

[2] See, as to enforcement of detention, s. 692.

[3] Where the vessel in respect of which forfeiture is claimed is already detained by the court as prize, the High Court administering this section in its Admiralty jurisdiction as part of the municipal law has no jurisdiction to decree forfeiture: *The St. Tudno* (*No.* 2) [1918] P. 174.

[4] See note " Application to Northern Ireland and the Republic of Ireland " in notes to s. 742.

[5] Jurisdiction under this section was extended by M.S.A. 1911, *post*, to include " any British court in a foreign country being a court having Admiralty jurisdiction " (s. 1 (1), *ibid.*), and the expression " British court in a foreign country " means " any British court having jurisdiction out of His Majesty's dominions in pursuance of an Order in Council, whether made under any Act or otherwise " (s. 1 (3), *ibid.*). It had previously been held in *The Maori King* [1909] A.C. 562 (P.C.), that as s. 76 did not confer jurisdiction on any

court outside H.M. dominions, the Supreme Court of China and Corea at Shanghai had no jurisdiction to deal with a case of forfeiture.

[6] As to what are reasonable grounds, reference may be made to *The Evangelismos* (1858) Sw. 378; *Wilson* v. *The Queen* (1866) L.R. 1 P.C. 405; *Burns* v. *Nowell* (1880) 5 Q.B.D. 444.

[7] For an instance of proceedings under this section where the court refused relief under subs. (2) to British shareholders in a ship-owning limited company registered in but not having its " principal place of business " within the United Kingdom as required by s. 1, see *The Polzeath* [1916] P. 241 (C.A.), cited in note (5) to s. 1.

Measurement of Ship and Tonnage

145 **77–81.** [*Section* 77 (*rules for ascertaining register tonnage*), *section* 78 (*allowance for engine-room space on steamships*), *section* 79 (*deductions for ascertaining tonnage*), *section* 80 (*provisions as to deductions in case of certain steamships*) *and section* 81 (*measurement of ship with double bottoms for water ballast*), *were repealed by M.S.A.* 1965, *ss.* 5 (1), 7 (2), *Sched. II. Tonnage is now ascertained in accordance with regulations made under s.* 1 *of that Act* (§ 3054, *post*).]

Tonnage once ascertained to be the tonnage of ship

146 **82.** Whenever the tonnage of any ship has been ascertained and registered in accordance with the tonnage regulations of this Act, the same shall thenceforth be deemed to be the tonnage of the ship, and shall be repeated in every subsequent registry thereof, unless any alteration is made in the form or capacity of the ship, or unless it is discovered that the tonnage of the ship has been erroneously computed; and in either of those cases the ship shall be re-measured, and her tonnage determined and registered according to the tonnage regulations of this Act.

147 For provisions allowing the alteration of particulars relating to registered tonnage, see M.S.A., 1965, s. 1 (5) (§ 1258, *post*).

In an action of limitation of liability, evidence for the defendants, to prove that the registered tonnage of the plaintiff's ship was not the correct tonnage, was held admissible apparently under the section here re-enacted: *The Recepta* (1889) 14 P.D. 131.

See also *The Franconia*, cited in note to s. 84, and see note (16) to s. 503.

Fees for measurement

148 **83.** Such fees as the [Department of Trade] determines shall be paid in respect of the measurement of a ship's tonnage *not exceeding those specified in the Third Schedule*[1] *to this Act*, and those fees shall be paid into the Mercantile Marine Fund.[2]

149 [1] The words in italics were repealed by s. 37 (5) and Sched. III of M.S. (Safety Convention) Act 1949.

[2] The fees are now to be paid to the Exchequer: see M.S. (Mercantile Marine Fund) Act 1898, s. 1. This does not apply in those cases where measurement is undertaken by organisations appointed by the Board of Trade: see M.S.A. 1965, s. 1 (4). For the fee currently payable see M.S. (Fees) Regulations 1975 (S.I. No. 341).

Tonnage of ships of foreign countries adopting tonnage regulations

150 **84.**—(1) Whenever it appears to Her Majesty the Queen in Council that the tonnage regulations of this Act have been adopted by any foreign

country, and are in force there, Her Majesty in Council may order that the ships of that country shall, without being re-measured in Her Majesty's dominions, be deemed to be of the tonnage denoted in their certificates of registry or other national papers, in the same manner, to the same extent, and for the same purposes as the tonnage denoted in the certificate of registry of a British ship is deemed to be the tonnage of that ship [and any space shown by the certificate of registry of other national papers of any such ship as deducted from the tonnage shall, where a similar deduction in the case of a British ship depends on compliance with any conditions or on the compliance being evidenced in any manner, be deemed to comply with those conditions and to be so evidenced, unless a surveyor of ships certifies to the [Department of Trade] that the construction and the equipment of the ship as respects that space do not come up to the standard which would be required if the ship were a British ship registered in the United Kingdom].[1]

(2) Her Majesty in Council may limit the time during which the Order is to remain in operation, and make the Order subject to such conditions and qualifications (if any) as Her Majesty may deem expedient, and the operation of the Order shall be limited and modified accordingly.

(3) If it is made to appear to Her Majesty that the tonnage of any foreign ship, as measured by the rules of the country to which she belongs, materially differs from that which would be her tonnage if measured under this Act, Her Majesty in Council may order that, notwithstanding any Order in Council for the time being in force under this section, any of the ships of that country may, for all or any of the purposes of this Act, be re-measured in accordance with this Act.

151 [1] The words in brackets were added by M.S.A. 1965, s. 7, Sched. I.

The following is a list of the Orders in Council in force under the powers of this Act and those reproduced in subss. (1) (2). As to the saving of Orders made before January 1, 1895, see s. 745: Austria, Order in Council dated August 19, 1871, S.R. & O., Rev. 1948, Vol. XIV, p. 2; Belgium, Order in Council dated October 17, 1884, S.R. & O., Rev. 1948, Vol. XIV, p. 3; Denmark (S.R. & O. 1895 No. 571); Egypt, June 23, 1939 (S.R. & O. 1939 No. 709 as amended by S.R. & O. 1940 No. 1315); France (S.R. & O. 1904 No. 1433); Germany (S.R. & O. 1896 No. 56); Greece (S.R. & O. 1927 No. 63); Iceland (S.R. & O. 1925 No. 417); Italy (S.R. & O. 1906 No. 384); Japan (S.R. & O. 1923 No. 232); Netherlands (Order in Council dated May 3, 1888, S.R. & O., Rev. 1948, Vol. XIV, p. 15); Norway (S.R. & O. 1894 No. 161); Poland (S.R. & O. 1935 No. 309); Portugal (S.R. & O. 1926 No. 827); Russia (Order in Council dated November 20, 1880, S.R. & O., Rev. 1948, Vol. XIV, p. 20); Spain (S.R. & O. 1911 No. 544); Sweden (Order in Council dated August 18, 1882, S.R. & O., Rev. 1948, Vol. XIV, p. 22); United States of America (S.R. & O. 1895 No. 411); Finland (S.I. 1966 No. 390); Kuwait (S.I. 1971 No. 595); U.S.S.R. (S.I. 1972 No. 1817).

In *The Franconia* (1878) 3 P.D. 164, it was held that an Order in Council under M.S.A., 1862, s. 60 (subs. (1) of the present section), did not make the certificate of registry of a foreign ship conclusive evidence of the tonnage, but only such evidence as the register of a British ship would be, *i.e.* prima facie evidence; and that therefore the court was entitled to consider the legal effect of the measurements stated in such certificate, *i.e.* whether the crew space was to be deducted. *Cf.* s. 503 (2) (*b*), and M.S.A., 1906, s. 69, for measurement of foreign ships for limitation of liability, and s. 695 as to admissibility of documents.

For the ascertainment of the tonnage of a ship to which an order under this section applies, for the purposes of s. 4 of the M.S. (Oil Pollution) Act 1971, see *ibid.* s. 4 (2) (*a*) from a day to be appointed.

Space occupied by deck cargo to be liable to dues

152 **85.**—(1) If any ship, British or foreign, other than a home trade ship as defined by this Act,[1] carries as deck cargo, that is to say, in any uncovered space upon deck, or in any covered space not included in the cubical contents forming the ship's registered tonnage [and not exempted by regulations under the Merchant Shipping Act 1965,] [2] timber, stores, or other goods,[3] all dues payable on the ship's tonnage shall be payable as if there were added to the ship's registered tonnage the tonnage of the space occupied [4] by those goods at the time at which the dues become payable.

(2) The space so occupied shall be deemed to be the space limited by the area occupied by the goods and by straight lines inclosing a rectangular space sufficient to include the goods.

(3) The tonnage of the space shall be ascertained by an officer of the [Department of Trade] or of Customs [5] [in accordance with regulations made under the Merchant Shipping Act 1965,] [2] and when so ascertained shall be entered by him *in the ship's official log book, and also* [6] in a memorandum which he shall deliver to the master, and the master shall, when the said dues are demanded, produce that memorandum in like manner as if it were the certificate of registry, or, in the case of a foreign ship, the document equivalent to a certificate of registry, and in default shall be liable to the same penalty as if he had failed to produce the said certificate or document.[7]

(4) Nothing in this section shall apply to any ship employed exclusively in trading or going from place to place in any river or inland water of which the whole or part is in any British possession, or to deck cargo carried by a ship while engaged in the coasting trade of any British possession.

153 [1] "Home-trade ship" includes every ship employed in trading or going within the limits of the United Kingdom, the Channel Islands, and the Isle of Man, and the Continent of Europe between the River Elbe and Brest inclusive. See s. 742.

[2] The words in brackets were added by M.S.A. 1965, s. 7 (1), Sched. 1.

[3] "Stores or other goods" includes bunker coal carried in an uncovered space on deck for use on voyage: see *Cairn Line of S.S. Ltd.* v. *Corporation of Trinity House* [1907] 1 K.B. 604; affirmed [1908] 1 K.B. 528. "Other goods" includes horses and cattle: see *Richmond Hill S.S. Co.* v. *Corporation of Trinity House* [1896] 2 Q.B. 134.

[4] In the case of horses and cattle the space is the rectangular space which is reasonably necessary to hold the animal, allowing it due facility for movement. See *ibid.*

[5] An officer of Customs has no power to order measurement under Rule II: *Great Western Ry.* v. *Kassos Steam Navigation Co.* (1930) 38 Ll.L.R. 49; 144 L.T. 121.

[6] The words in italics were repealed by M.S.A. 1970, s. 100 (3), Sched. 5, as from January 1, 1973: S.I. 1972, No. 1972. See now *ibid.* s. 68.

[7] *i.e.* to a fine not exceeding one hundred pounds. See s. 15.

Surveyors and regulations for measurement of ships

154 **86.** All duties in relation to the survey and measurement of ships shall be performed by surveyors of ships under this Act [1] in accordance with regulations [2] made by the [Department of Trade].

155 [1] See ss. 724 *et seq.* as to surveyors and their powers, and, as to colonies, s. 727. This provision is now subject to M.S.A. 1965, s. 1 (4), and the M.S.A. 1974, s. 11 (4), Sched. 2, para. 1.

[2] The regulations under this section are contained in the "Instructions" to surveyors, issued by the Ministry of Transport from time to time.

Levy of tonnage rates under local Acts on the registered tonnage

156 **87.** Any persons having power to levy tonnage rates on ships may, if they think fit, with the consent of the [Department of Trade], levy those tonnage rates upon the registered tonnage of the ships as determined by the tonnage regulations of this Act,[1] notwithstanding that any local Act under which those rates are levied provides for levying the same upon some different system of tonnage measurement.

157 [1] See now the M.S.A. 1965, s. 1, and the regulations made thereunder.

Ports of Registry in Place under Foreign Jurisdiction Act

Foreign ports of registry

158 **88.** Where, in accordance with the Foreign Jurisdiction Act, 1890, Her Majesty exercises jurisdiction within any port, it shall be lawful for Her Majesty, by Order in Council, to declare that port a port of registry, and by the same or any subsequent Order in Council to declare the description of persons who are to be registrars of British ships at that port of registry, and to make regulations with respect to the registry of British ships thereat.

159 Orders in Council are in force under this section with respect to the following ports: Honiara (British Solomon Islands) (S.R. & O. 1912 No. 1862, as amended by S.I. 1948 No. 2063 and by S.I. 1969, No. 1061); Vila (New Hebrides) (S.R. & O. 1917 No. 1018, as amended by S.I. 1969 No. 1062).

Ships registered at ports specified in Orders in Council under this section are within the scope of the Ships and Aircraft (Transfer Restriction) Act 1939. See s. 4 (1) (*b*) (ii) of that Act, § 1548, *post*.

Registry in Colonies

Powers of Governors in colonies

160 **89.** In every British possession [1] the Governor of the possession shall occupy the place of the Commissioners of Customs [2] with regard to the performance of anything relating to the registry of a ship or of any interest in a ship registered in that possession, and shall have power to approve a port within the possession for the registry of ships.

161 Under the section of the Act of 1854 here reproduced a doubt arose whether certain powers, transferred since 1854 from the Commissioners of Customs and Excise to the Minister of Transport were still enjoyed by governors of colonies. Under the present section such powers are not conferred on governors. But as to the appointment of surveyors of ships, see s. 727.

[1] "British Possession" is defined in the Interpretation Act 1889, s. 18 (2); see § 1064, *post*.

[2] Now Commissioners of Customs and Excise, see note (1) to s. 4.

Terminable certificates of registry for small ships in colonies

162 **90.**—(1) The Governor of a British possession may, with the approval of a Secretary of State, make regulations providing that, on an application

for the registry under this Act in that possession of any ship which does not exceed sixty tons burden,[1] the registrar may grant, in lieu of a certificate of registry as required by this Act,[2] a certificate of registry to be terminable at the end of six months or any longer period from the granting thereof, and all certificates of registry granted under any such regulations shall be in such form and have effect subject to such conditions as the regulations provide.

(2) Any ship to which a certificate is granted under any such regulations shall, while that certificate is in force, and in relation to all things done or omitted during that period, be deemed to be a registered British ship.[3]

163 [1] " Tons burden " used with reference to registration means net registered tonnage and not gross tonnage: see *The Brunel* [1900] P. 24, and *ante*, s. 3, note (1).
[2] See s. 14.
[3] See s. 72 for liabilities of ships not recognised as British.

Application of Part I

Application of Part I

164 **91.** This Part of this Act shall apply to the whole of Her Majesty's dominions, and to all places where Her Majesty has jurisdiction.

As to power of colonial legislatures to alter provisions of the Act and to regulate coasting trade, see ss. 735, 736 and notes thereto.

PART II—MASTERS AND SEAMEN

165 [*Save as indicated, the whole of Part II of the Act, which dealt with the conditions of service, discipline and general welfare of merchant seamen, was repealed by M.S.A.* 1970, *s.* 100 (3), *Sched. V. The subject-matter of this Part is now dealt with in the latter Act. By virtue of the M.S.A.* 1970 (*Commencement No.* 1) *Order* 1972 (*S.I. No.* 1977) *various sections were repealed as from January* 1, 1973. *Only those sections which are repealed as from a date yet to be appointed have been included in this Part. They have been printed in italics in anticipation of their repeal in due course.*]

Certificates of Competency

166 As to the suspension and cancellation of certificates of competency by the Department of Trade, see ss. 469 *et seq.*

As to the qualifications of master and mariners generally, see Abbott, *Merchant Ships, etc.*, 14th ed., p. 149.

Certificates of competency to be held by officers of ships

167 **92.**—(1) *Every British* [1] *foreign-going ship* [2] *and every British home-trade passenger ship,*[2] *when going to sea* [3] *from any place in the United Kingdom, and every foreign steam ship* [4] *carrying passengers* [5] *between places in the United Kingdom, shall be provided with officers duly certificated under this Act according to the following scale:—*

(*a*) *In any case with a duly certificated master:*

[(*b*) *If the ship is of one hundred tons burden* [6] *or upwards, with at least one officer besides the master holding a certificate not lower than that of—*

(*i*) *Mate in the case of a home-trade passenger ship;*

(*ii*) *Second mate in the case of a foreign-going sailing ship of not more than two hundred tons burden; and*

(*iii*) *Only mate in the case of any other foreign-going ship.*[7]]

(*c*) *If the ship is a foreign-going ship, and carries more than one mate, with at least the first and second mate duly certificated* [8]*:*

(*d*) *If the ship is a foreign-going steam ship of one hundred nominal horse-power or upwards, with at least two engineers one of whom shall be a first-class and the other a first-class or second-class engineer duly certificated:*

(*e*) *If the ship is a foreign-going steam ship of less than one hundred nominal horse-power, or a sea-going home-trade passenger steam ship, with at least one engineer who is a first-class or second-class engineer duly certificated.*

(2) *If any person—*

(*a*) *having been engaged as one of the above-mentioned officers goes to sea as such officer without being duly certificated; or*

(*b*) *employs a person as an officer, in contravention of this section, without ascertaining that the person so serving is duly certificated,*

that person shall be liable for each offence to a fine not exceeding fifty pounds:

(3) *An officer shall not be deemed duly certificated, within the meaning of this section, unless he is the holder for the time being of a valid certificate of competency under this Act of a grade appropriate to his station in the ship, or of a higher grade.*[9]

168 For requirements on board fishing-boats, see s. 413, § 301, *post.*
For restrictions on the employment of aliens, see note §1342, *infra.*

[1] See, as to what are " British ships," s. 1; and as to the position of unrecognised British ships generally, s. 72.

[2] For definitions of " ship," " foreign-going ship," and " home-trade passenger ship," see s. 742.

[3] As to " sea-going ships " see note (1) to M.S.A. 1970, s. 96.

[4] By virtue of s. 743 these provisions as to steamships apply also to ships propelled by electricity and other mechanical power.

[5] As to who are " passengers," see notes to s. 267, and in particular *The Charles Livingston* (pilot boat) (1941) 69 Ll.L.R. 180, there cited (a decision under this section); see also notes to the Pilotage Act 1913, s. 11, and s. 26 of M.S. (Safety Convention) Act 1949.

[6] In *The Brunel* [1900] P. 24, the court held that " tons burden " in s. 3 meant net register tonnage, but intimated that the words might require a different interpretation in other parts of the Act. See note (1) to s. 3.

[7] The words in square brackets were substituted by M.S.A. 1906, s. 56, for the original subsection which was repealed by s. 85, *ibid.*

[8] As to the meaning of the word " mate," and generally on the requirements of this section, see the observations of Lord Merriman in *The Empire Jamaica* [1957] A.C. 386 at p. 396 *et seq.* See also note (9) to the Pilotage Act 1913, s. 11.

[9] Or of an appropriate certificate of service under s. 99.

Grades of certificates of competency

169 **93.**—(1) *Certificates of competency shall be granted, in accordance with this Act, for each of the following grades*[1]; *that is to say,*

Master of a foreign-going ship:
First mate of a foreign-going ship:
Second mate of a foreign-going ship:
Only mate of a foreign-going ship:
Master of a home-trade passenger ship:
Mate of a home-trade passenger ship:
First-class engineer:
Second-class engineer.

(2) *A certificate of competency for a foreign-going ship shall be deemed to be of a higher grade than the corresponding certificate for a home-trade passenger ship, and shall entitle the lawful holder thereof to go to sea in the corresponding grade in the last-mentioned ship*[2]; *but a certificate for a*

home-trade passenger ship shall not entitle the holder to go to sea as master or mate of a foreign-going ship.

170 Provisions governing examinations are to be found in ss. 96, 97 and M.S. (Certificates) Act 1914, s. 1, § 939, *post*. See also the other requirements in s. 98 (1).

[1] As to certificates of competency in cooking for "ship's cooks" to be carried by British foreign-going ships of 1,000 tons gross registered tonnage and upwards, see M.S.A. 1906, s. 27. See also M.S.A. 1948, s. 6, for further provisions relating to certificated cooks for foreign-going ships, and s. 5 of that Act for provisions relating to certificates of competency to be held by seamen rated as A.B.

[2] But the holder of a certificate of service, though entitled to act as master or mate of a foreign-going ship is not entitled to go to sea as a master or mate of a home-trade passenger ship. See s. 99 (4), *infra*.

171 **94–95.** [*These sections, which provided for the examination of master and mates by Local Marine Boards, were repealed by M.S.* (*Certificates*) *Act* 1914, *s.* 1 (3), *and replaced by section* 1 (1) *and* (2) *of that Act*, § 939, *post.*]

Engineers' certificates of competency

172 **96.**—(1) *For the purpose of granting certificates of competency as engineers to persons desirous of obtaining the same, examinations shall be held at such places as the* [*Department of Trade direct*].

(2) *The* [*Department of Trade*] *may appoint times for the examinations, and may appoint, remove, and re-appoint examiners to conduct the same, and determine the remuneration of those examiners, and may regulate the conduct of the examinations and the qualification of the applicants and may do all such acts and things as* [*it thinks*] *expedient for the purpose of the examinations.*

173 See notes on s. 1 of M.S. (Certificates) Act 1914, § 939, *post*, for rules relating to examinations.

Fees on examination

174 **97.** *An applicant for examination, whether as master, mate, or engineer, shall pay such fees,* [*not exceeding those specified in the Fourth Schedule to this Act*[1] *as the* [*Department of Trade direct*], *and the fees shall be paid to such persons as the* [*Department appoints*] *and carried to the Mercantile Marine Fund.*[2]

175 See s. 676 (2), as to time, etc., of payment of fees.

[1] The words in square brackets were repealed by M.S. (Safety Convention) Act 1949, s. 37 (5) and Sched. III.

[2] The fees are now to be paid to the Exchequer, see M.S. (Mercantile Marine Fund) Act 1898, s. 1. The fees now in force are contained in the M.S. (Fees) Regulations, 1975 (S.I. No. 341) made in pursuance of the M.S. (Safety Convention) Act 1949, s. 33 (2), *post*.

Grant of certificates on passing examination

176 **98.**—(1) *The* [*Department of Trade*] *shall, subject as hereinafter mentioned, deliver to every applicant who is duly reported by the*

examiners to have passed the examination satisfactorily, and to have given satisfactory evidence of his sobriety, experience, ability, and general good conduct on board ship, such a certificate of competency as the case requires.

(2) *The* [*Department of Trade*] *may in any case in which a report appears to* [*it*] *to have been unduly made, remit the case either to the examiners who made the report or to any other examiners, and may require a re-examination of the applicant, or a further inquiry into his testimonials and character, before granting him a certificate.*

For the rules relating to examinations, see notes to s. 1 of M.S. (Certificates) Act 1914, § 940, *post*.

Certificates of service for naval officers

177 **99.**—(1) *A person who has attained the rank of lieutenant, sub-lieutenant, navigating lieutenant, or navigating sub-lieutenant in Her Majesty's Navy, or of lieutenant in Her Majesty's Indian* [*Navy* [1]], *shall be entitled to a certificate of service* [2] *as master of a foreign-going ship without examination.*

(2) *A person who has attained the rank of engineer or assistant engineer in Her Majesty's Navy or Indian* [*Navy* [1]], *shall be entitled without examination, if an engineer, to a certificate of service* [2] *as first class engineer, and if an assistant engineer to a certificate of service as second class engineer.*

(3) *A certificate of service shall differ in form* [3] *from a certificate of competency, and shall contain the name and rank of the person to whom it is delivered, and the* [*Department of Trade*] *shall deliver a certificate of service to any person who proves himself to be entitled thereto.*

(4) *The provisions of this Act (including the penal provisions) shall apply in the case of a certificate of service as they apply in the case of a certificate of competency, except that the provisions* [4] *allowing a holder of a certificate of competency as master of a foreign-going ship to go to sea as master or mate of a home-trade passenger ship shall not apply.*

178 See also Q.R. and A.I., Art. 1045; and Appendix to the Navy List (1973), where these certificates of service are said to be granted by the Department of Trade at their discretion. Certificates of competency can only be granted after examination.

[1] The word " Navy " was substituted for " Marine Service " by the Government of India (Adaptation of Acts of Parliament) Order, 1937 (S.R. & O. 1937, No. 230), made under Government of India Act, 1935.

[2] As to fees for certificates of service, see Fees (Increase) Act, 1923, s. 2 (1) and note thereto *post*. The actual fees at present in force will be found in the M.S. (Fees) Regulations, 1975 (S.I. No. 341).

[3] As to power of the Department of Trade to prescribe forms, see s. 720.

[4] See s. 93 (2), as to certificates of competency.

Form and record of certificate

179 **100.**—(1) *All certificates of competency shall be made in duplicate, one part to be delivered to the person entitled to the certificate, and one to be preserved.*

(2) *Such last-mentioned part of the certificate shall be preserved, and a record of certificates of competency and the suspending, cancelling, or altering of the certificates and any other matter affecting them shall be kept, in such manner as the* [*Department of Trade directs*] *by the Registrar-General of Shipping and Seamen or by such other person as the* [*Secretary of State for Trade directs*].

(3) *Any such certificate and any record under this section shall be admissible in evidence in manner provided by this Act.*

180 As to power of the *Secretary of State* to prescribe forms, see s. 720, and as to admissibility in evidence, see s. 695, and notes thereto.

Loss of certificate

181 **101.** *If a master, mate, or engineer proves to the satisfaction of the* [*Department of Trade*] *that he has, without fault on his part, lost or been deprived of a certificate already granted to him, the* [*Department of Trade*] *shall, and in any other case may, upon payment of such fee* (*if any*) *as* [*the Department directs*], *cause a copy of the certificate to which, by the record kept in pursuance of this Act, he appears to be entitled, to be certified by the Registrar-General of Shipping and Seamen, or other persons directed to keep the record, and to be delivered to him; and a copy purporting to be so certified shall have all the effect of the original.*

182 In the case of a colonial certificate, this power is exercised by the authority granting such certificate; see the Orders in Council cited in note to s. 102.

Colonial certificates of competency

183 **102.** *Where the legislature of any British possession provides for the examination of, and grant of certificates of competency to, persons intending to act as masters, mates, or engineers on board ships, and the* [*Dept. of Trade*] *report to Her Majesty that* [*it is*] *satisfied that the examinations are so conducted as to be equally efficient with the examinations for the same purpose in the United Kingdom under this Act, and that the certificates are granted on such principles as to show the like qualifications and competency as those granted under this Act, and are liable to be forfeited for the like reasons and in like manner, Her Majesty may by Order in Council—*

(i) *declare that the said certificates shall be of the same force as if they had been granted under this Act: and*

(ii) *declare that all or any of the provisions of this Act, which relate to certificates of competency granted under this Act, shall apply to the certificates referred to in the Order: and*

(iii) *impose such conditions and make such regulations with respect to the certificates, and to the use, issue, delivery, cancellation, and suspension thereof, as Her Majesty may think fit, and impose fines not exceeding fifty pounds for the breach of those conditions and regulations.*

184 Orders in Council have been made in respect of the following places:

Canada (including Newfoundland), New Zealand, Hong Kong, Straits Settlements (now part of the Federation of Malaya) (Order in Council dated May 9, 1891 (S.R. & O., Rev. 1948, XIV, p. 99—as amended by S.R. & O. 1906 No. 810; S.R. & O. 1910 No. 823));

Australia (Merchant Shipping (Australian Certificates of Competency) Order (S.R. & O. 1923 No. 1288—as amended by S.R. & O. 1931 No. 692));

India (Merchant Shipping (Indian Certificates of Competency) Order 1931 (No. 1100));

Republic of Ireland (Merchant Shipping (Republic of Ireland) (Certificates of Competency) Order, 1954 (No. 640)).

South African Certificates of Competency are provided for in the South Africa Act 1962, s. 2 (2), Sched. III, para. 6; S.R. & O. 1931 No. 693 has now lapsed.

(*Note.*—The application of Order in Council dated May 9, 1891 (S.R. & O., Rev. 1948, XIV, p. 99) to Malta and Mauritius was revoked by Order in Council dated August 18, 1916 (No. 633).)

As to the saving of Orders in Council made before 1894, see s. 745.

Production of certificates of competency to superintendent

185 **103.**—(1) *The master of a foreign-going ship—*

(*a*) *on signing the agreement with the crew before a superintendent* [1] *shall produce to him the certificates of competency which the master, mates, and engineers of the ship are by this Act required to hold* [2]*: and*

(*b*) *in the case of a running agreement shall also, before the second and every subsequent voyage, produce to the superintendent the certificate of competency of any mate or engineer then first engaged by him who is required by this Act to hold a certificate.* [2]

(2) *The master or owner of every home-trade passenger ship of more than eighty tons burden* [3] *shall produce to some superintendent within twenty-one days after the thirtieth of June and the thirty-first of December in every year the certificates of competency which the master, mates, and engineers of the ship are by this Act required to hold.*

(3) *Upon the production of the certificates of competency, the superintendent shall, if the certificates are such as the master, mates, and engineers of the ship ought to hold, give to the master a certificate to the effect that the proper certificates of competency have been so produced.*

(4) *The master shall, before proceeding to sea, produce the superintendent's certificate to the chief officer of customs, and the ship may be detained* [4] *until the certificate is produced.*

186 [1] See M.S.A. 1970, ss. 1 and 2 (§§1346–1349, *post*), for provisions as to agreements with crew.

[2] See s. 92 as to certificates of competency.

[3] In *The Brunel* [1900] P. 24, the court held that " tons burden " in s. 3 meant net register tonnage, but intimated that the words might require a different interpretation in other parts of the Act. See note (1) to s. 3.

[4] As to enforcing detention, see s. 692.

Forgery, etc. of certificate of competency

187 **104.** *If any person—*

(*a*) *forges or fraudulently alters, or assists in forging or fraudulently altering, or procures to be forged or fraudulently altered, any certificate of competency, or an official copy of any such certificate; or*

(*b*) *makes, assists in making, or procures to be made, any false representation for the purpose of procuring either for himself or for any other person a certificate of competency; or*

(*c*) *fraudulently uses a certificate or copy of a certificate of competency which has been forged, altered, cancelled or suspended, or to which he is not entitled; or*

(*d*) *fraudulently lends his certificate of competency or allows it to be used by any other person,*

that person shall in respect of each offence be guilty of a misdemeanour.

188 The provisions of this section also apply in relation to certificates of competency granted under the M.S. (Certificates of Competency as A.B.) Regulations 1959 (No. 2148), made under M.S.A. 1948, s. 5 (see para. 11 of the Regulations), and also to certificates of competency granted in Commonwealth countries which are approved for the purposes of United Kingdom legislation by regulations made under M.S.A. 1948, s. 5 (4) (see the various regulations noted to that section at § 1102, *post*).

By s. 4 (4) of the Emergency Laws (Miscellaneous Provisions) Act 1953, this section (s. 104) has effect as if references to a certificate of competency included references to a British seaman's card.

As to punishment of offences see s. 680.

Apprenticeship to the Sea Service

189 **105.** [*This section which dealt with assistance given by superintendents was repealed with effect from January* 1, 1973: *see note at beginning of Part II to this Act*, § 165, *ante*.]

190 **106–107.** [*These two sections, which dealt with the apprenticeship of paupers in Great Britain and Ireland and the attestation of pauper apprenticeship, were repealed by the National Assistance Act* 1948, *as from July* 5, 1948. *See ss.* 62 (3) *and* 68 (2) *of and the* 7*th Schedule to that Act, and S.I.* 1948 *No.* 1218.]

191 **108–109.** [*These sections which dealt with special provisions as to apprenticeship to the sea service and production of indentures to superintendent before a voyage in a foreign-going ship were repealed with effect from January* 1, 1973: *see* § 165, *ante*.]

Licences to supply Seamen

Licence for supply of seamen

192 **110.** *The* [*Dept. of Trade*] *may grant to such persons as* [*it thinks*] *fit licences to engage or supply seamen* [1] *or apprentices for merchant ships in the United Kingdom, and any such licence shall continue for such period, and may be granted and revoked on such terms and conditions as* [*it thinks*] *proper.*

This section will be saved to the extent that any licence granted under this section shall have effect as if granted under s. 6 *of the M.S.A.* 1970: *see M.S.A.* 1970, *s.* 100 (2), *Sched. IV, para.* 5.

This section will be saved to the extent that any licence granted under this section shall have effect as if granted under s. 6 of the M.S.A. 1970: see M.S.A. 1970 s. 100 (2), Sched. IV, para. 5.

[1] " Seaman " is defined in s. 742, § 679, *post.*

Penalty for engaging seamen without licence

193 **111.**—(1) *A person shall not engage or supply a seaman or apprentice to be entered on board any ship* [1] *in the United Kingdom, unless that person either holds a licence* [2] *from the* [*Dept. of Trade*] *for the purpose, or is the owner* [3] *or master or mate of the ship, or is bona fide the servant and in the constant employment of the owner, or is a superintendent.*

(2) *A person shall not employ for the purpose of engaging or supplying a seaman or apprentice to be entered on board any ship in the United Kingdom any person, unless that person either holds a licence from the* [*Dept. of Trade*] *for the purpose, or is the owner or master or mate of the ship, or is bona fide the servant and in the constant employment of the owner, or is a superintendent.*

(3) *A person shall not receive or accept to be entered on board any ship any seaman or apprentice, if that person knows that the seaman or apprentice has been engaged or supplied in contravention of this section.*

(4) *If a person acts in contravention of this section he shall for each seaman or apprentice in respect of whom an offence is committed, be liable to a fine not exceeding twenty pounds,*[4] *and, if a licensed person, shall forfeit his licence.*

194 [1] " Any ship " here includes a foreign ship: *R.* v. *Stewart* [1899] 1 Q.B. 964; *Hart* v. *Alexander* (1898) 36 Sc.L.Rep. 64.

[2] The onus of proving the possession of a licence lies upon the defendant: *R.* v. *Johnston* (1886) 6 Asp.M.L.C. 14. See also *Nelson* v. *Richardson* (1884) 48 J.P. 457 for an instance of a conviction under similar previous provisions.

[3] A person having a contract enforceable in equity for the purchase of a share in a ship was held to be an " owner " within this exception, though the share had not been transferred to him by bill of sale, and he had not been registered as owner: *Hughes* v. *Sutherland* (1881) 7 Q.B.D. 160.

[4] The fine imposed by this section is a punishment for an offence, and not a civil debt: *R.* v. *Stewart, supra.*

Penalty for receiving remuneration from seamen for engagement

195 **112.**—(1) *A person shall not demand or receive directly or indirectly from a seaman or apprentice to the sea service, or from a person seeking employment as a seaman or apprentice to the sea service, or from a person on his behalf, any remuneration whatever for providing him with employment other than any fees authorised by this Act.*[1]

(2) *If a person acts in contravention of this section, he shall for each offence be liable to a fine not exceeding five pounds.*

[1] No fees are specifically authorised by the Act.

196 **113–125.** [*These sections dealt with Engagement of Seamen and Agreements with Lascars and have been repealed as from January* 1, 1973: *see* § 165, *ante.*]

Rating of Seamen

Rating of seamen

197 **126.**—(1) *A seaman shall not be entitled to the rating* [1] *of A.B., that is to say, of an able-bodied seaman, unless he has served at sea for* [*three years before the mast* [2]], *but the employment of fishermen in decked fishing vessels registered under the First Part of this Act shall only count as sea service up to the period of* [*two years of that employment* [2]]; *and the rating of A.B. shall only be granted after at least one year's sea service in a trading vessel in addition to* [*two or more years' sea service* [2]] *on board of decked fishing vessels so registered.*

(2) *The service may be proved by certificates of discharge, by a certificate of service from the Registrar-General of Shipping and Seamen* (*granted by the Registrar on payment of a fee* [*not exceeding one shilling*] [3]), *specifying in each case whether the service was rendered in whole or in part in steam ship or in sailing ship, or by other satisfactory proof.*[4]

198 As from May 1, 1953, this section ceased to have effect in relation to any seamen for the time being engaged in a British ship registered in the United Kingdom. See M.S.A. 1948, s. 5 (6), and M.S. (Certificate of Competency as A.B.) Regulations 1970 (S.I. No. 294) as amended by S.I. 1975 No. 341. The new provisions relating to the certification of such seamen as A.B.s are contained in the said section and regulations.

As to the saving for A.B.s rated before the enactment here reproduced, see s. 746 (3).

1 " Rating " means the station or position a person holds on the ship's articles.

2 The words in square brackets were substituted by M.S.A., 1906, s. 58 (1), for the words " four years before the mast "; " three years of that employment," and " three or more years' sea service," respectively.

3 The words bracketed in italics, which had been substituted by the Fees Increase Act 1923, s. 1, Sched. I, were repealed as from Nov. 19, 1952, by M.S. (Safety Convention) Act 1949, s. 37 (5) and Sched. III, *post.* The fee at present in force is contained in the M.S. (Fees) Regulations 1975 (S.I. No. 341) made in pursuance of s. 33 (2) of the 1949 Act.

4 The superintendent or other officer before whom a seaman is engaged must refuse to enter him as an A.B. unless the proof hereby required is given. See M.S.A. 1906, s. 58 (2). Any false statement or false representation as to rating is punishable by a fine not exceeding five pounds. *Ibid.*

199 **127–143.** [*These sections contained provisions with regard to Discharge of Seamen and Payment of Wages and were repealed, save as otherwise indicated, with effect from January* 1, 1973: *see* § 165, *ante.*]

200 **144.** [*This section, which provided for the time of payment of allotment notes, was repealed by M.S.A.* 1906, *s.* 85, *Sched. II.*]

201 **145–156.** [*These sections contained provisions with regard to seamen's money orders and savings banks and the rights of seamen in respect of wages and have been repealed, save as otherwise indicated, with effect from January* 1, 1973: *see* § 165, *ante.*]

Wages not to depend on freight

202 **157.**—(1) *The right to wages shall not depend on the earning of freight; and every seaman and apprentice who would be entitled to demand and recover any wages, if the ship in which he has served had earned freight, shall, subject to all other rules of law and conditions applicable to the case, be entitled to demand and recover the same, notwithstanding that freight has not been earned* [1]; *but in all cases of wreck or loss of the ship,*[2] *proof that the seaman has not exerted himself to the utmost to save the ship, cargo, and stores, shall bar his claim to wages.*

(2) *Where a seaman or apprentice who would, but for death, be entitled by virtue of this section to demand and recover any wages, dies before the wages are paid, they shall be paid and applied in manner provided by this Act with respect to the wages of a seaman who dies during a voyage.*[3]

203 [1] Subs. (1) was in substance a re-enactment of M.S.A. 1864, s. 183, whereby the rule of maritime law that " freight is the mother of wages," ceased to be the law of this country. The rule never applied to a master's wages: *Hawkins* v. *Twizell* (1856) 5 E. & B. 883.

[2] See notes (1) and (2) to s. 158, *post.*

[3] See M.S.A. 1970, s. 66, as to property of deceased seamen.

Wages on termination of service by wreck or illness

204 **158.** *Where the service of a seaman terminates before the date contemplated in the agreement, by reason of the wreck* [1] *or loss of the ship,*[2] *or of his being left on shore at any place abroad under a certificate granted as provided by this Act* [3] *of his unfitness or inability to proceed on the voyage,*[4] *he shall be entitled to wages up to the time of such termination, but not for any longer period.*[5]

205 The effect of this section is modified in important respects by s. 1 of the M.S. (International Labour Conventions) Act 1925 (*q.v.*), which in effect provides that a seaman shall be entitled to wages for each day up to two months during which he remains unemployed by reason of the wreck or loss of his ship, unless the owner shows that the unemployment was not due to the wreck or loss of the ship, or that the seaman was able to obtain suitable employment elsewhere; and this is so even though the seaman's engagement would have terminated before the expiration of the two months, had there been no wreck or loss of the ship. See notes to M.S. (International Labour Conventions) Act 1925, s. 1, § 974, *post.*

As to the question from what date the period of two months begins to run, see *The Terneuzen* [1938] P. 109.

[1] " Wreck." There must be " physical damage caused at sea by perils of the sea to the ship such that though repairable would make the ship unseaworthy for so long a time as to make the continuance of the voyage useless as a commercial venture ": *The Olympic* (Wages) [1913] P. 92 (C.A.). *Per* Vaughan Williams L.J., at p. 103. The meaning of " wreck," as thus laid down in *The Olympic*, was approved by the House of Lords (Lord Blanesburgh dissenting) in *Barras* v. *Aberdeen Steam Trawling and Fishing Co.* [1933] A.C. 402, on the basis that the legislature, in using the word " wreck " in s. 1 of the M.S. (International Labour Conventions) Act 1925, must be deemed to have intended that the word should have the meaning given to it by the Court of Appeal in *The Olympic*. In *Barras* v. *Aberdeen, etc.*, it was held, however, that there had not been a " wreck " of a steam trawler, for the purposes of an engineer's engagement to serve in her for 6 months, where the trawler was laid up for 14 days as the result of a collision.

The court will decide in each particular case whether there has in fact been a " wreck " or not, and abandonment to underwriters is immaterial: *Lloyd* v. *Sheen* (1905) 10 Asp. M.L.C. 75; 93 L.T. 174.

When a ship was scuttled in port in order to extinguish fire, and the crew were put on shore, the ship being subsequently raised and abandoned to underwriters as a constructive total loss, it was held that there was a " wreck " within the section: *The Woodhorn* (1891) 92 L.T. 113 (explained in *Sievewright* v. *Allen, infra*). Held, also, that the crew were not entitled to wages up to date of final settlement, as M.S.A. 1880, s. 4 (1894, s. 134 (*c*)) had no application to the case: *The Woodhorn, supra.*

[2] There is a " loss " within the meaning of this section where a ship is destroyed by explosion of a contraband cargo: *Collins* v. *Simpson S.S. Co.* (1907) 24 T.L.R. 178; or where the ship after capture is destroyed by a belligerent: *Sievewright* v. *Allen* [1906] 2 K.B. 81; but not it seems on mere capture and confiscation. *Per* Lord Alverstone C.J. and Ridley J. (Darling J. dissenting), at pp. 85, 87, *ibid.* Thus, where a ship was condemned for carrying contraband cargo and the owners had before capture broken their agreement with the crew by carrying such a cargo, it was held that the crew were entitled to their wages up to the date of their arrival in London and to damages for breach of their agreement: *Austin Friars Steam Navigation Co.* v. *Strack* [1905] 2 K.B. 315. See also *Burton* v. *Ponkorton* (1867) L.R. 2 Ex. 340: *The Justitia* (1887) 12 P.D. 145.

The detention of a vessel by a belligerent under the provisions of The Hague Convention, No. 6 of 1907, is not a " loss of the ship " within the meaning of this section: *Horlock* v. *Beal* [1916] 1 A.C. 486. The words " wreck or loss " refer to physical loss. " The Court of Appeal in *The Olympic, supra,* did not decide anything inconsistent with this view. They merely used the frustration of the voyage as a test by which to determine whether or not the physical injury inflicted amounted to a wreck." *Per* Earl Loreburn, at p. 493, *ibid.* See the discussion of *Horlock* v. *Beal* by the House of Lords in *Barras* v. *Aberdeen, etc.* (*supra*).

Apart altogether from this section, however, the seaman's contract of service may be dissolved and his right to wages terminated at common law by the doctrine of frustration if events happen, not amounting to " wreck or loss of the ship " (*e.g.* a long continued detention), which render the future performance of the contract of service impossible. *Ibid.*

206 [3] See now M.S.A. 1970, s. 4. Where seamen were left on shore to be called for on the return journey because they refused to continue a voyage with contraband of war on becoming aware that their destination was a port of a belligerent, it was held they were entitled to their wages until they reached the United Kingdom, on proof that they had not been discharged under their contract or under this Act, and that their ship had not been wrecked, though she had been stranded and abandoned to underwriters but subsequently refloated: *Lloyd* v. *Sheen* (1905) 10 Asp.M.L.C. 75; 93 L.T. 174.

[4] By the law maritime, a seaman disabled by an accident happening to him in the course of his duty was entitled to wages for the whole voyage, even though the accident prevented his performing the whole of it: *Chandler* v. *Greaves* (1792) 2 H.Bl. 606, n.; 6 T.R. 325, n. In *The Carolina* (1875) 34 L.T. 399; 3 Asp.M.L.C. 141 the entitlement of a seaman to wages was held to be determined, though he was still retained in the service of the ship by the master, by the commencement of a suit *in rem* for the recovery of wages. However in *The Fairport* (*No.* 2) [1966] 2 Lloyd's Rep. 7, it was held by Cairns J. that *The Carolina,* was wrongly decided and that the institution of a wages claim did not terminate the contract of service and that, therefore, wages continued to accrue after the proceedings were commenced. See also, as to cases of wreck, s. 157 (1).

[5] So long as a mariner is entitled to receive wages under this provision, he is not entitled to receive benefits under the National Insurance (Industrial Injuries) Acts 1965–1969 and the regulations made thereunder. For decisions as to wages claimed in cases of termination or suspension of services from other causes, than those above mentioned, see *Button* v. *Thompson* (dismissal at a foreign port for negligence and misconduct) (1869) L.R. 4 C.P. 330; *The Friends* (capture and imprisonment by enemy) (1801) 4 C.Rob. 143; *Beale* v. *Thompson* (embargo) (1804) 4 East 546; *Melville* v. *De Wolf* (1855) 24 L.J.Q.B. 200; 4 E. & B. 844; and *Cross* v. *Hyne* (1868) 3 M.L.C.(o.s.) 80 (sent home as a witness by consular officer). See *Horlock* v. *Beal* (*supra*), where many of the cases are reviewed. As to time of payment of wages the M.S.A. 1970, s. 7.

207 **159–164.** [*These sections contained further provisions with regard to the rights of seamen in respect of wages and provisions with regard to mode of recovering wages and were repealed with effect from January* 1, 1973: *see* § 165, *ante.*]

208 **165.** [*This section, which dealt with certain restrictions upon the right to sue for wages less than* £50, *was repealed by the Administration of Justice*

Act 1956, *as from October* 1, 1957. *See ibid. s.* 5 (1), *Sched. II, and the Administration of Justice Act* 1956 (*Commencement*) *Order*, 1957 (*No.* 1179).]

209 **166–184.** [*These sections contained provisions with regard to the mode of recovery of wages, powers of the court to rescind contracts, the property of deceased seamen, expenditure in connection with the maintenance and Assistance of seamen's families, destitute seamen, and were repealed save as otherwise indicated, with effect from January* 1, 1973: *see* § 165, *ante.*]

210 **185.** [*This section, which related to the relief of destitute lascars, and which had been amended by the Government of India* (*Adaptation of Acts of Parliament*) *Order* 1937 (*S.R. & O.* 1937 *No.* 230) *made under the Government of India Act* 1935, *and by the Burma Independence Act* 1947, *s.* 5, *Sched. IV, has been repealed, with effect from July* 5, 1948, *by the National Assistance Act* 1948. *See sections* 62 (3), 68 (2) *of and Sched. VII to that Act, and S.I.* 1948 *No.* 1218.]

211 **186–194.** [*Part of section* 193 *and the whole of section* 194 (*payments out of the Mercantile Marine Fund*) *were repealed by M.S.* (*Mercantile Marine Fund*) *Act* 1898, *s.* 8, *Sched. IV*; *sections* 186–193 *inclusive, which related to leaving seamen abroad and to distressed seamen, were repealed by M.S.A.* 1906, *s.* 85, *Sched. II, and those matters are now dealt with in Part IV of that Act* (*provisions as to relief and repatriation of distressed seamen, and seamen left behind abroad*), *sections* 28–49, *to which reference should be made, post.*]

212 **195–199.** [*These sections contained provisions with regard to volunteering into the navy and provisions, health and accommodation and were repealed with effect from January* 1, 1973: *see* § 165, *ante.*]

213 **200.** [*This section, which contained provisions for regulations respecting medicines, anti-scorbutics etc. has been repealed with effect from October 1,* 1974: *see* § 1384, *post.*]

214–215 **201–206.** [*These sections contained further provisions with regard to provisions, health and accommodation and were repealed as from January* 1, 1973; *see* § 165, *ante.*]

216 **207.** [*This section, which provided for the expenses of medical attendance in case of illness, was repealed by M.S.A.* 1906, *s.* 85, *Sched. II, itself now repealed*; *but see* § 1386, *post.*]

217 **208.** [*This section, which provided for the recovery of expenses from owner, was repealed by M.S.A.* 1906, *s.* 85, *Sched. II, itself now repealed*; *but see* § 1386, *post.*]

[The next page is p, 76]

Certain ships to carry medical practitioners

218 **209.**—(1) *Every foreign-going ship,*[1] *having one hundred persons or upwards on board, shall carry on board as part of her complement some duly qualified medical practitioner, and if she does not the owner shall for every voyage of the ship made without a duly qualified medical practitioner be liable to a fine not exceeding one hundred pounds.*

(2) *Nothing in this section shall apply to an emigrant ship within the meaning of the Third Part of this Act.*[2]

219 [1] For definition of "foreign-going ship" see s. 742.

[2] It would seem that a medical practitioner carried under s. 209 as part of a ship's complement is a "seaman" within the definition of s. 742 and must, therefore, under the M.S.A. 1970, ss. 1 and 2 sign the crew agreement.

Accommodation for seamen

220 **210.**—(1) *Every place in any British ship occupied by seamen or apprentices,*[1] *and appropriated to their use, shall have for each of those seamen or apprentices a space of not less than seventy-two cubic feet*[2] *and of not less than twelve superficial feet measured on the deck or floor of that place, and shall be subject to the regulations in the Sixth Schedule to this Act,*[3] *and those regulations shall have effect as part of this section, and if any of the foregoing requirements of this section is not complied with in the case of any ship, the owner of the ship shall for each offence be liable to a fine not exceeding twenty pounds.*

(2) *Every place so occupied and appropriated shall be kept free from goods and stores of any kind not being the personal property of the crew in use during the voyage, and if any such place is not so kept free, the master shall forfeit and pay to each seaman or apprentice lodged in that place the sum of one shilling for each day during which, after complaint*[4] *has been made to him by any two or more of the seamen so lodged, it is not so kept free.*

(3) *Such fees as the* [*Department of Trade fixes*] *shall be paid in respect of an inspection for the purposes of this section, not exceeding the fees specified in the Sixth Schedule to this Act.*[5]

221 This section does not apply to any ship to which regulations made under s. 1 of the M.S.A. 1948, or s. 1 of the M.S.A. 1950, apply. See s. 4 (3) of the Act of 1948, and para. 13 of Sched. I to the Act of 1950, *post*. The M.S. (Crew Accommodation) Regulations 1953 (No. 1036) (amended by S.I. 1954 No. 1660; 1961 No. 393; 1965 No. 1047; 1975 No. 341), have been made under M.S.A. 1948, s. 1, relating to crew accommodation in certain classes of ships. These regulations came into operation on January 1, 1954 (see S.I. 1953 No. 1036). See also *post* §§ 1095–1098. No regulations have so far been made under M.S.A. 1950, s. 1.

[1] Seamen and apprentices here includes lascars serving on a British ship trading between this country and India or Australia; and the Merchant Seamen (India) Act No. 13 of 1876, was held not to apply: *Peninsular and Oriental Steam Navigation Co.* v. *The King* [1901] 2 K.B. 686.

[2] This subsection is now amended (except as to lascars) by the M.S.A. 1906, s. 64 (*q.v.*), which provides that ships registered after the passing of the M.S.A. 1906, and not in course of construction on January 1, 1907, and not being fishing boats or ships of not more than 300 tons burden, must provide for seamen and apprentices (not being lascars) a space of not less than 120 cubic feet and of not less than 15 superficial feet measured on the deck or floor.

As to inclusion of mess and bath rooms and washing spaces, see *ibid.* subs. (2). From this exception of lascars and the decision in *P. & O. S.N. Co.* v. *The King, supra*, it appears that the accommodation for lascars in ships built after the passing of M.S.A. 1906, will be that specified in s. 210 without amendment.

[3] For regulations relating to tonnage, see M.S.A. 1965, s. 1.

[4] As to surveys consequent upon complaint as to deficiency of accommodation, see s. 463.

[5] The words in italics were repealed by M.S. (Safety Convention) Act 1949, s. 37 (5) and Sched. III. The fees at present in force for inspection of accommodation of seamen are contained in the M.S. (Fees) Regulations 1975 (S.I. No. 341) made in pursuance of s. 33 (2) of the 1949 Act.

222 *Sections* 211 *to* 266 *contained provisions with regard to facilities for making complaint, discipline, official logs, Local Marine Boards, Mercantile Marine Officers, registration of and returns respecting seamen, sites for Sailors Homes and the application of Part II of the Act and but for section* 256 *they were repealed as from January* 1, 1973, *save as otherwise indicated*: *see* § 165, *ante.*

222a **211–234.** [*These sections which contained provisions as to facilities for making complaint and as to discipline were repealed, save as otherwise indicated, with effect from January* 1, 1973: *see* § 165, *ante.*]

223 **235.** [*This section, which provided for the deduction from wages and payments to superintendents, etc., of fines, was repealed by M.S.A.* 1906, *s.* 85, *Sched. II, and the subject of the repealed section is now dealt with by section* 44 *of that Act, post.*]

224 **236–255.** [*These sections which contained further provisions as to discipline, provisions as to official logs, Local Marine Boards, Mercantile Marine Offices and registration of and returns respecting seamen and were repealed, save as otherwise indicated with effect from January* 1, 1973: *see* § 165, *ante.*]

Transmission of documents to registrar by superintendents and other officers

225 **256.**—(1) *All superintendents and all officers of customs shall take charge of all documents which are delivered or transmitted to or retained by them in pursuance of this Act, and shall keep them for such time (if any) as may be necessary for the purpose of settling any business arising at the place where the documents come into their hands, or for any other proper purpose, and shall, if required, produce them for any of those purposes, and shall then transmit them to the Registrar General of Shipping and Seamen, and he shall record and preserve them, and they shall be admissible in evidence in manner provided by this Act,*[1] *and they shall, on payment of a moderate fee fixed by the* [*Department of Trade*], *or without payment if the* [*Department so directs*], *be open to the inspection of any person.*

(2) *The documents aforesaid shall be public records and documents within the meaning of the Public Record Offices Acts* 1838 *and* 1877, *and*

those Acts shall, where applicable, apply to those documents in all respects as if specifically referred to therein.[2]

226 The provisions of this section are applied to radiotelegraph log books and radiotelephone log books by the M.S. (Radio) Rules, 1965 (S.I. No. 1107) as amended by S.I. 1969 No. 1315: made under M.S. (Safety Convention) Act 1949, s. 3, *post*.

Cf. ss. 714, 715, returns as to Merchant Shipping and production of log books.

[1] See ss. 694, 695, 719–721, admissibility and proof of documents. As to fees for the furnishing of copies see s. 695 (2) and notes thereto, *post*. The fees at present in force are contained in the M.S. (Fees) Regulations 1975 (S.I. No. 341).

[2] Subs. (2) has been repealed by the Public Records Act 1958, s. 13 (2).

227 **257–266.** [*These sections dealt with registration of and returns respecting seamen, sites for sailors' homes and the application of Part II of the Act and were repealed, save as otherwise indicated, with effect from January* 1, 1973: *see* § 165, *ante.*]

PART III—PASSENGER AND EMIGRANT SHIPS

228 This Part consolidated the Passengers Acts and certain sections of the Merchant Shipping Acts which related to steamers carrying passengers. Its provisions generally apply to passenger ships in addition to, and not in substitution for, those of other parts of the Act. It has been subsequently amended by Part II of M.S.A. 1906, by certain provisions of M.S. (Safety Convention) Act 1949 and by the M.S.A. 1970. These amendments include the alteration of the definition of " passenger steamer " (see 1906 Act, s. 13), and the application of certain provisions relating to surveys and passenger steamers' certificates to surveys for the purpose of issuing safety certificates, etc., and to such certificates (see 1949 Act, s. 13). The M.S.A. 1970, s. 100 (3) and Sched. 5, repealed all those provisions which related to emigrant ships as being obsolete.

As to legal proceedings under Part III, see section 356, and the general provisions of Part XIII, section 680 *et seq*.

As to the exemption of Italian ships from the provisions of the M.S.A. relating to passenger steamers and emigrant ships, see M.S. (Passenger Steamers and Emigrant Ships) Italian Ships Order 1929 (December 17, 1929, S.R. & O. No. 1154), made under M.S. (Equivalent Provisions) Act 1925, s. 1.

1. Definitions

For other definitions, see s. 742.

Definition of Passenger and Passenger Steamer

Definition of " passenger " and " passenger steamer "

229 **267.** For the purposes of this Part of this Act—

The expression " passenger " shall include any person carried in a ship other than the master and crew, and the owner, his family and servants [and persons on board the ship either in pursuance of the obligation laid upon the master to carry shipwrecked, distressed or other persons or by reason of any circumstance which neither the master nor the owner nor the charterer (if any) could have prevented or forestalled]; and [1]

The expression " passenger steamer," [2] shall mean every British steamship carrying passengers to, from, or between any places in the United Kingdom, except steam ferry boats working in chains (commonly called steam bridges) *and every foreign steamship carrying passengers between places in the United Kingdom.*[2]

230 [1] The words in italics (including the words in square brackets, which had been added by the M.S. (Safety and Load Line Conventions) Act s. 33) were repealed by M.S. (Safety Convention) Act 1949, s. 37 (5) and Sched. III, and the present definition of " passenger "

for the purposes of Part III of this Act is now contained in s. 26 of that Act which provides that " the expression ' passenger ' means any person carried in a ship, except—

(*a*) a person employed or engaged in any capacity on board the ship on the business of the ship,

(*b*) a person on board the ship either in pursuance of the obligation laid upon the master to carry shipwrecked, distressed or other persons, or by reason of any circumstance that neither the master nor the owner nor the charterer (if any) could have prevented or forestalled; and

(*c*) a child under one year of age."

231 [2] The definition of " passenger steamer " in this section was amended by M.S.A. 1906, s. 13 " so as to include every foreign steamship (whether originally proceeding from a port in the United Kingdom or from a port out of the United Kingdom) which carries passengers to or from any place, or between any places, in the United Kingdom," and the words in italics were repealed by s. 85, Sched. II, *ibid.* The definition also includes any ship " while on or about to proceed on a voyage or excursion in any case where a passenger steamer's certificate is required to be in force in respect of her ": see M.S.A. 1964, s. 17 (2). It is to be observed, however, that for the purposes of the M.S. (Safety and Load Line Conventions) Act 1932, and the M.S. (Safety Convention) Act 1949, " passenger steamer " is defined by s. 26 (2) of the 1949 Act, as " a steamer carrying more than twelve passengers."

" Passenger steamer." The mere presence on board of some person or persons " other than the master and crew, and the owner, his family and servants " is not in itself sufficient to constitute the ship a passenger steamer. It is in each case a question of fact. Is the ship one which is engaged in the business of carrying passengers? *Procurator-Fiscal, Greenock* v. *Kyle* (1929) 33 Ll.L.R. 114, followed and applied by Langton J. in *The Charles Livingston* (pilot boat) (1941) 69 Ll.L.R. 180. Thus, where the owner lent a steamer, without making any charge, to a party of more than twelve persons for an excursion on a river, and they gave the master a gratuity for himself and crew and coals, it was held that they were not " passengers," nor the ship a " passenger steamer," and that she was not " plying " (see s. 271) within the meaning of these provisions, and that therefore her owner could not be convicted for not having a certificate posted up as under M.S.A. 1854, s. 318 (1894, ss. 271, 281): *Hedges* v. *Hooker* (1889) 60 L.T. 822; 37 W.R. 491; disagreeing with *R.* v. *Divisional Justices of Dublin* (1884) 15 C.C.C. 379, *sub nom. Kiddle* v. *Kidston*, 14 L.R.Ir. 1. In *Duncan* v. *Graham and Others* [1951] 1 K.B 68, the Divisional Court in considering whether the owners of two fishing boats and the master of one of them had committed an offence against M.S.A. 1894, s. 271 (1), held that the expression " passenger steamer " meant a steamer " that is either used habitually, or at any rate substantially, for carrying passengers, or is constructed as a passenger steamer." (The head-note of this case in the Law Reports appears to be inaccurate.) See also *R.* v. *Fox* (1925) 21 Ll.L.R. 72 and *Weeks* v. *Ross*, *infra*. By way of illustration the following cases decided under the pilotage provisions of the M.S.A., now the Pilotage Act, s. 11, *post*, as to the meaning of " ship carrying passengers " should be referred to: *The Hanna* (guest of captain who worked his passage) (1866) L.R. 1 A. & E. 283; followed in *The Lion* (friend of captain not paying fare) (1869) L.R. 2 P.C. 525; *The Clymene* (distressed seamen) [1897] P. 295; *Hay* v. *Corporation of Trinity House* (distressed seamen) (1895) 65 L.J.Q.B. 90; 8 Asp.M.L.C. 77. The presence of even one passenger is sufficient to attract the provisions as to compulsory pilotage, but not to make the ship a passenger steamer.

" Home-trade passenger ship " and " ship " are defined for the purpose of the Act generally in s. 742.

" Steamship." The provisions of the Act as to steamers and steamships apply to ships propelled by electricity or other mechanical power with such modifications as the Secretary of State may prescribe. See s. 743.

In *The Mayor of Southport* v. *Morriss* [1893] 1 Q.B. 359, it was held that an electric launch used for carrying passengers on pleasure trips on a small artificial lake was not a " ship " within M.S.A. 1854, s. 2 (1894, s. 742), because, having regard to the size of the lake, she was not a vessel " used in navigation "; and that therefore she did not require a certificate under M.S.A. 1854, s. 318 (1894, s. 271). This case was distinguished by the Divisional Court in *Weeks* v. *Ross* [1913] 2 K.B. 229, where it was held that a small motor-boat carrying passengers on short trips up and down a river and canal used by sea-going ships was " used in navigation " and did require a certificate under s. 271.

" British ship." As to what constitutes a British ship, see ss. 1, and notes thereto, 2, 3; and as to the liabilities of British ships which are not recognised as British, and of persons belonging thereto, see s. 72.

"Foreign steamships." See M.S.A. 1906, s. 13. As to the exemption of Italian ships see M.S. (Passenger Steamers and Emigrant Ships) Italian Ships Order 1929 (S.R. & O. No. 1154), made under M.S. (Equivalent Provisions) Act 1925, s. 1.

Definition of Emigrant Ship, etc.

232 **268–270.** [*These sections which deal with the definition of an emigrant ship, etc., to which this Part applies, the scale for determining length of voyages and the definition of colonial voyage were repealed by M.S.A.* 1970, *s.* 100 (3), *Sched. V. as from January* 1, 1973: *see S.I.* 1972 *No.* 1977].

2. Passenger Steamers

For the application of the provisions relating to steamers to ships propelled by other mechanical power, see s. 743.

Survey of Passenger Steamers

Annual survey of passenger steamers

233 **271.**—(1) [Every passenger steamer [1] which carries [2] more than twelve passengers [1] shall be surveyed once at least in each year in the manner provided in this Part of this Act [3]; and no ship (other than a steam ferry boat working in chains) shall proceed to sea [4] or on any voyage or excursion with more than twelve passengers on board, unless there is in force in respect of the ship a certificate as to survey under this Part of this Act,[3] applicable to the voyage or excursion on which the ship is about to proceed, or that voyage or excursion is one in respect of which the [Department of Trade] has exempted the ship from the requirements of this subsection.] [5]

(2) A passenger steamer attempting to ply or go to sea may be detained [6] until such certificate as aforesaid is produced to the proper officer of Customs [6] [unless the voyage or excursion on which she is about to proceed is one in respect of which she has been exempted as aforesaid.] [7]

(3) *Provided that, while a steamer is an emigrant ship and the provisions of this Part of this Act as to the survey of the hull machinery and equipments of emigrant ships have been complied with, she shall not require a survey or certificate under this section.*[8]

234 As to "safety certificates," see M.S. (Safety Convention) Act 1949, ss. 7 *et seq.*; and to the relation of "safety certificates" to "passenger steamer certificates," see *ibid.* s. 13.

[1] As to the meaning of "passenger" and "passenger steamer" see note (2) to s. 267, citing *Hedges* v. *Hooker* and *Duncan* v. *Graham and Others*.

Foreign passenger steamers, having foreign certificates of survey, may in certain cases be exempted from further survey (see s. 363).

[2] "Which carries" means which in fact carries on a particular occasion, not which is fitted to carry: *Yeudall* v. *Sweeney*, 1922 S.C.(J.) 32.

[3] See s. 274. For the application of this provision to a motor boat, see *Weeks* v. *Ross* [1913] 2 K.B. 229, cited in note "ship" to s. 267; and *Young* v. *Ducherly* (1929) S.C.(J.) 57. Special passenger certificates are now issued for small motor vessels. See Board of Trade Circular No. 1704 (August 1935, reprinted in 1954).

4 Where the master of a vessel, which has not obtained the requisite certificate, carries passengers to sea without his owner's knowledge, he exceeds his authority, and the voyage is not rendered by this section illegal so as to vitiate a policy effected by the innocent owner: *Dudgeon* v. *Pembroke* (1874) L.R. 9 Q.B. 581; following *Cunard* v. *Hyde* (1858) 27 L.J.Q.B. 408; E.B. & E. 670; and *Wilson* v. *Rankin* (1865) L.R. 1 Q.B. 162. But it is otherwise if the owner is a party to the illegal act: *Cunard* v. *Hyde* (No. 2) (1859) 29 L.J.Q.B. 6; 2 E. & E. 1.

5 The words in brackets were substituted by M.S.A. 1964, s. 17 (1).

6 As to the power of detention, see s. 692. If the provisions requiring a passenger steamer to be surveyed and to have a passenger steamer's certificate are not obeyed, the master or owner of the steamer or of the tender by which the passengers are taken on board or landed is liable to a fine not exceeding ten pounds for every passenger carried. See M.S.A. 1906, s. 21.

As to fines for not posting certificate up on board, and for plying without having it posted up, see s. 281, and for carrying more passengers than it specifies, s. 283, extended by M.S.A. 1906, s. 22. As to exemption where certificate expires while steamer is abroad, see s. 278.

7 The words in brackets were added by M.S.A. 1964, s. 17 (1).

8 The words in italics were repealed by M.S.A. 1970, s. 100 (3), Sched. V. as from January 1, 1973: see S.I. 1972, No. 1977.

Mode of survey and declaration of survey

235 **272.**—(1) The owner of every passenger steamer [1] shall cause the same to be surveyed by a shipwright surveyor [2] of ships and an engineer surveyor of ships,[3] [and, in the case of a sea-going passenger steamer required to be provided with a radio installation, by a wireless telegraphy surveyor [4]] the shipwright surveyor being, in the case of an iron steamer, a person properly qualified in the opinion of the [Department of Trade] to survey an iron steamer.

(2) [5] The surveyors, if satisfied on the survey that they can with propriety do so, shall deliver to the owner declarations of survey in a form [6] approved by the [Department of Trade].

(3)–(5).[7]

236 1 Means apparently only a passenger steamer which carries more than twelve passengers. See s. 271. As to exemption of "Safety Convention passenger steamers," not registered in the United Kingdom, from the requirements of this section, see s. 15 of the M.S. (Safety Convention) Act 1949.

2 Now a "ship surveyor." See M.S.A. 1906, s. 75 (1). The surveys required to be made under this section may be made by the same person if he has been appointed both as a ship surveyor and an engineer surveyor. *Ibid.* s. 75 (3).

3 For provisions as to the appointment and control of surveyors of ships by the Secretary of State, their powers, etc., see ss. 724 *et seq.*, and M.S.A. 1906, s. 75. The Secretary may make regulations as to the performance of surveyors' duties, and the manner in which surveys are to be made (see s. 724 (3)). As to whether they have power to issue an instruction that declarations shall not be granted unless vessels satisfy certain requirements, *e.g.* as to the materials of which certain pipes are to be made, see *Denny* v. *Board of Trade*, *infra* (s. 275).

4 The words in square brackets were added by s. 9 (1) of the M.S. (Safety and Load Line Conventions) Act 1932, as amended by s. 35 (5) of the M.S. (Safety Convention) Act 1949, which substituted the words "radio installation" for "wireless telegraph installation." By s. 8 of the 1932 Act a person appointed to be a surveyor of ships under s. 724 may be appointed as a wireless telegraphy surveyor; persons appointed as wireless telegraphy surveyors are now known as "radio surveyors." M.S. (Safety Convention) Act 1949, s. 4.

"Passenger steamer" here clearly means a steamer carrying more than twelve passengers. See s. 26 (2) of M.S. (Safety Convention) Act 1949.

5 The provisions of this subsection are made applicable to surveys for the issue of safety certificates, etc., under the M.S. (Safety Convention) Act 1949. See s. 13 (2) of that Act.

[6] As to forms, see ss. 720 *et seq.* For the fees payable, see s. 277.
[7] Subss. (3)–(5) of this section, which related to the contents of the declarations of shipwright surveyors, engineer surveyors, and wireless telegraphy surveyors, ceased to have effect by virtue of s. 13 (1) of the M.S. (Safety Convention) Act 1949, and have been repealed by s. 37 (5) of and Sched. III to that Act.

Transmission of declaration

237 **273.**—(1) The owner of a steamer surveyed shall within fourteen days after the receipt by him of a declaration of survey transmit it to the [Department of Trade].

(2) If an owner fails without reasonable cause so to transmit a declaration of survey, he shall forfeit a sum not exceeding ten shillings for every day during which the transmission is delayed, and any sum so forfeited shall be payable on the granting of a certificate in addition to the fee, and shall be applied in the same manner as the fee.

The provisions of this section are made applicable to surveys for the issue of safety certificates, etc., under the M.S. (Safety Convention) Act 1949. See s. 13 (2) of that Act.

Ten shillings is now to be read as 50 new pence: see the Decimal Currency Act 1969, s. 10 (1).

Issue of passenger steamer's certificate

238 **274.** On the receipt of the declarations of survey, the [Department of Trade] shall, if satisfied that this Part of this Act has been complied with, issue in duplicate a passenger steamer's certificate, that is to say, a certificate stating such compliance and stating, according to the declarations—

(*a*) the limits (if any) beyond which the steamer is not fit to ply; and

(*b*) the number of passengers which the steamer is fit to carry, distinguishing, if necessary, the number to be carried in each part of the steamer, and any conditions and variations to which the number is subject.

As to form of certificate, see s. 720. For the issue of safety certificates, and passenger steamers' exemption certificates, see M.S. (Safety Convention) Act 1949, s. 7. For the power to cancel the survey certificate, see s. 279 and note thereto.

Appeal to court of survey

239 **275.**—(1) If the owner of a steamer feels aggrieved by the declaration of survey of a shipwright [1] or engineer surveyor [or wireless telegraphy surveyor [2]], or by the refusal of such a surveyor to give such a declaration, he may appeal to the court of survey [3] for the port or district where the steamer for the time being is, in manner directed by the rules of that court.

(2) On any such appeal the judge of the court of survey shall report to the [Department of Trade] on the question raised by the appeal and the [Department of Trade], when satisfied that the requirements of the report and of the foregoing provisions of this Part of this Act have been complied with, may grant a passenger steamer's certificate.

(3) Subject to any order made by the judge of the court of survey the costs of and incidental to the appeal shall follow the event.

(4) A shipwright or engineer surveyor [or wireless telegraphy surveyor [2]] in making a survey of a steamer for the purpose of a declaration of survey shall, if the owner of the steamer so requires, be accompanied on the survey by some person appointed by the owner, and in that case, if the surveyor and the person so appointed agree, there shall be no appeal under this section to the court of survey.

240 The provisions of this section are made applicable to surveys for the issue of safety certificates, etc., under the M.S. (Safety Convention) Act 1949. See s. 13 (2) of that Act. They are also applied by the Fishing Vessels (Safety Provisions) Act 1970, ss. 2 (2), 11 (4).

[1] Now a ship surveyor. See M.S.A. 1906, s. 75.

[2] The words in square brackets were introduced by s. 9 (3) of the M.S. (Safety and Load Line Conventions) Act 1932. Wireless telegraphy surveyors appointed under s. 724 of the M.S.A. 1894, as amended by s. 8 of M.S. (Safety and Load Line Conventions) Act 1932, are now known as " radio surveyors ": M.S. (Safety Convention) Act 1949, s. 4.

[3] As to courts of survey and procedure thereof, see ss. 487–489.

The provisions here re-enacted were held to exclude the right of appeal to the Court of Session: *Denny* v. *Board of Trade* (1880) 7 R. 1019; 17 Sc.L.R. 694.

Transmission of certificates

241 **276.**—(1) The [Department of Trade] shall transmit the passenger steamer's certificate in duplicate to a superintendent or some other public officer at the port mentioned by the owner of the steamer for the purpose, or at the port where the owner or his agent resides, or where the steamer has been surveyed or is for the time lying.

(2) The [Department of Trade] shall cause notice of the transmission to be given to the master or owner or his agent, and the officer to whom the certificate has been transmitted shall, on the owner, master, or agent applying and paying the proper fee and other sums (if any) mentioned in this Act as payable in that behalf, deliver to him both copies of the certificate.

(3) In proving the issue of a passenger steamer's certificate it shall be sufficient to show that the certificate was duly received by the said officer and that due notice of the transmission was given to the owner, master, or agent.

The provisions of this section are made applicable to safety, etc., certificates issued under the M.S. (Safety Convention) Act 1949. See s. 13 (8) of that Act.

Fees for certificates

242 **277.** The grantee of a passenger steamer's certificate shall pay such fees,[1] *not exceeding those specified in Part One of the Ninth Schedule to this Act*,[2] as the [Department of Trade fix].

[1] As to penalty for receiving improper fees, see s. 360 (3).

[2] The words in italics were repealed by M.S. (Safety Convention) Act 1949, s. 37 (5) and Sched. III, and by s. 33 of that Act the Secretary of State is given power to make

regulations prescribing the amount or maximum amount of the fees payable (*inter alia*) under this section of the principal Act. For the fees currently in force, see M.S. (Fees) Regulation 1975 (S.I. No. 341).

Duration of certificates

243 **278.**—(1) A passenger steamer's certificate shall not be in force for more than one year from the date of its issue, or any shorter time specified in the certificate, nor after notice is given by the [Department of Trade] to the owner, agent, or master of the steamer, that the Department have cancelled it.[1]

(2) If a passenger steamer is absent from the United Kingdom at the time when her certificate expires, a fine shall not be incurred for want of a certificate until she first begins to ply with passengers [2] after her next return to the United Kingdom.

[1] For powers of cancellation, see s. 279 and notes thereto.
[2] As to what amounts to "plying with passengers," see note to s. 267.

Cancellation of certificate

244 **279.**—(1) The [Department of Trade] may cancel a passenger steamer's certificate where they have reason to believe—

(*a*) that any declaration of survey on which the certificate was founded has been in any particular made fraudulently or erroneously; or,

(*b*) that the certificate has been issued upon false or erroneous information; or,

(*c*) that since the making of the declaration, the hull, equipment, or machinery have sustained any injury, or are otherwise insufficient.

(2) In every such case the [Department of Trade] may require the owner to have the hull, equipment or machinery of the steamer again surveyed, and to transmit further declarations of survey, before they re-issue the certificate or grant a fresh one in lieu thereof.

This section is applied by the M.S. (Safety Convention) Act 1949, to safety, etc., certificates issued thereunder. See s. 13 (8) of that Act. Also by the M.S.A. 1964, s. 3 (6) to certificates issued thereunder.

As to powers of cancellation in the event of subsequent alterations or damage, see *ibid.* s. 11 (4).

Delivery up of certificate

245 **280.**—(1) The [Department of Trade] may require a passenger steamer's certificate, which has expired or been cancelled, to be delivered up as [it directs].

(2) If any owner or master fails without reasonable cause to comply with such requirement, he shall for each offence be liable to a fine not exceeding ten pounds.

This section is applied by the M.S. (Safety Convention) Act 1949, s. 13 (8), the M.S.A. 1964, s. 3 (6), the M.S. (Load Lines) Act 1967, s. 27 (3) and the Fishing Vessels (Safety Provisions) Act 1970 to certificates issued under those Acts.

Posting up of certificate

246 **281.**—(1) The owner or master [1] of every passenger steamer required to have a passenger steamer's certificate shall forthwith on the receipt of the certificate by him or his agent cause one of the duplicates to be put up in some conspicuous place on board the steamer, so as to be legible to all persons on board, and to be kept so put up and legible while the certificate remains in force, and the steamer is in use.

(2) If the owner or master fails without reasonable cause to comply with this section [2] he shall for each offence be liable to a fine not exceeding ten pounds.[3]

(3) If a passenger steamer plies [4] or goes to sea with passengers on board, and this section is not complied with,[2] then for each offence the owner thereof shall be liable to a fine not exceeding one hundred pounds,[3] and the master shall also be liable to a further fine not exceeding twenty pounds.[3]

247 This section is applied by the M.S. (Safety Convention) Act 1949, s. 13 (8), the M.S.A. 1964, s. 3 (6) and the Fishing Vessels (Safety Provisions) Act 1970, s. 3 (4), to certificates issued under those Acts.

[1] The owner is the person responsible for default in the absence of agreement, see s. 359.

[2] As to the consequence of not having a certificate, see s. 271 and note (5) thereto. M.S.A. 1906, s. 21, does not appear to apply to this section.

[3] The penalties were increased by the M.S. (Load Lines) Act 1967, s. 25, Sched 1 as follows: Subs. (2) ten pounds was increased to twenty pounds; Subs. (3) one hundred pounds and twenty pounds increased to two hundred pounds and fifty pounds respectively.

[4] As to the meaning of " passenger " and " passenger steamer," see s. 267 and notes thereto, and see also s. 26 of M.S. (Safety Convention) Act 1949; and as to what amounts to " plying " within this section, see *Hedges* v. *Hooker*, there cited.

Penalty for forgery of certificate or declaration

248 **282.** If any person—

(*a*) knowingly and wilfully makes, or assists in making, or procures to be made, a false or fraudulent declaration of survey or passenger steamer's certificate; or

(*b*) forges, assists in forging, procures to be forged, fraudulently alters, assists in fraudulently altering, or procures to be fraudulently altered, any such declaration or certificate, or anything contained in, or any signature to any such declaration or certificate;

that person shall in respect of each offence be guilty of a misdemeanour.

This section is applied by the M.S. (Safety Convention) Act 1949, s. 13 (8), the M.S.A. 1964, s. 3 (6), the M.S. (Load Lines) Act 1967 s. 27 (3) and the Fishing Vessels (Safety Provisions) Act 1970, to certificates issued under those Acts.

As to the punishment of offences, see s. 680.

Penalty for carrying passengers in excess

249 **283.** The owner or master of any passenger steamer shall not receive on board thereof, or on or in any part thereof, any number of passengers

which, having regard to the time, occasion, and circumstances of the case, is greater than the number allowed by the passenger steamer's certificate, and if he does so, he shall for each offence be liable to a fine not exceeding twenty pounds,[1] *and also to an additional fine not exceeding five shillings for every passenger above the number so allowed, or if the fare of any passenger on board exceeds five shillings, not exceeding double the amount of the fares of all the passengers above the number so allowed, reckoned at the highest rate of fare payable by any passenger on board.*

By M.S.A. 1906, s. 22, it is an offence under this section to " have on board at any place " as well as to " receive on board " more passengers than the certificate permits.

See notes to s. 281.

No offence is committed where the Secretary has permitted more persons to be carried on board than are permitted by the M.S. Acts for the purpose of removing persons in consequence of a threat to their lives; see s. 27 of M.S. (Safety Convention) Act 1949.

[1] The penalty was increased to a fine not exceeding four hundred pounds on summary conviction, and a fine on conviction on indictment, irrespective of the number of passengers: see the M.S. (Load Lines) Act 1967, s. 25, Sched. 1. Accordingly, the words in italics are no longer applicable.

Colonial certificates for passenger steamers

250 **284.** Where the legislature of any British possession provides for the survey of, and grant of certificates for, passenger steamers, and the [Department of Trade] reports to Her Majesty the Queen that [it is] satisfied that the certificates are to the like effect, and are granted after a like survey, and in such manner as to be equally efficient with the certificates granted for the same purpose in the United Kingdom under this Act, Her Majesty in Council may—

(1) declare that the certificates granted in the said British possession shall be of the same force as if granted under this Act; and

(2) declare that all or any of the provisions of this Part of this Act which relate to passenger steamers' certificates shall, either without modification or with such modifications as to Her Majesty may seem necessary, apply to the certificates granted in the said British possession; and

(3) impose such conditions and make such regulations with respect to the certificates, and to the use, delivery, and cancellation thereof, as to Her Majesty may seem fit, and impose fines not exceeding fifty pounds for the breach of those conditions and regulations.

251 S. 21 (3) of the M.S. (Safety and Load Line Conventions) Act 1932, provided that this section, and any Orders in Council made thereunder should cease to apply to Safety Convention passenger steamers plying on international voyages. (For definitions of the relevant terms for the purposes of s. 21 (3), see ss. 38 and 73 (1) of that Act.) This repeal apparently remains effective by virtue of the Interpretation Act 1889, s. 38 (2), notwithstanding that s. 21 (3) of the 1932 Act has itself been repealed by M.S. (Safety Convention) Act 1949, s. 37 and Sched. III.

Orders in Council made under the repealed section remain in force under this Act by virtue of s. 745. The following Orders are now in force: Australia, April 16, 1924 (S.R. & O. No. 523); Hong Kong, March 22, 1928 (S.R. & O. No. 250); India, October 1, 1931

(S.R. & O. No. 848); Mauritius, February 27, 1905 (S.R. & O. No. 137); New Zealand, November 26, 1886 (S.R. & O. and S.I.Rev., 1948, XIV, p. 209); and Straits Settlements, July 5, 1929 (S.R. & O. No. 547).

General Equipment of Passenger Steamers

Equipment of passenger steamers with compasses, hose, deck shelters and safety appliances

252 **285.**—(1) A sea-going [1] passenger steamer shall have her compasses properly adjusted from time to time, to the satisfaction of the shipwright surveyor [2] and according to such regulations as may be issued by the [Department of Trade].

(2) [3]

(3) A home-trade passenger steamer shall be provided with such shelter for the protection of deck passengers (if any) as the [Department of Trade], having regard to the nature of the passage, the number of deck passengers to be carried, the season of the year, the safety of the ship, and the circumstances of the case, [require].

(4) A passenger steamer shall be provided with a safety valve on each boiler, so constructed as to be out of the control of the engineer when the steam is up, and, if the safety valve is in addition to the ordinary valve, so constructed as to have an area not less, and a pressure not greater, than the area of and pressure on the ordinary valve.[4]

(5) If a passenger steamer plies [5] or goes to sea from a port in the United Kingdom without being equipped as required by this section, then, for each matter in which default is made, the owner (if in fault) shall be liable to a fine not exceeding one hundred pounds, and the master (if in fault) shall be liable to a fine not exceeding fifty pounds.

253 See also s. 21 of M.S. (Safety Convention) Act 1949, as to provision for making distress signals.

Further provisions for the manning, construction and equipment of (*inter alia*) passenger steamers registered in the United Kingdom are contained in the M.S. (Safety Convention) Act 1949, ss. 1–6, 19 as prospectively amended by the M.S.A. 1970, s. 85 (1), (3) and Sched. 1.

[1] As to the meaning of "sea-going," see *The Salt Union* v. *Wood* [1893] 1 Q.B. 370, cited in note to s. 260. See also s. 432 for the general requirements for compasses.

[2] Now a "ship surveyor," see M.S.A. 1906, s. 75. As to such surveyors, see s. 724.

[3] This subsection, which dealt with fire extinguishing hoses, was repealed by ss. 5 (4), 39 (2) of and Part I of Sched. IV to the M.S. (Safety and Load Line Conventions) Act 1932. The subject-matter is now covered by the rule-making powers contained in section 427 (*q.v.*) and by the M.S. (Fire Appliances) Rules 1965 (S.I. No. 1106) made under that section.

[4] See also ss. 286, 433, as to limit of weight on safety valves.

[5] As to the meaning of "plies," see note (2) to s. 267, citing *Hedges* v. *Hooker* (1889) 60 L.T. 822; 37 W.R. 491, and other cases.

Prohibition of increasing weight on safety valve

254 **286.** A person shall not increase the weight on the safety valve of a passenger steamer beyond the limits fixed by the surveyor, and, if he does so, he shall, in addition to any other liability he may incur by so doing, be liable for each offence to a fine not exceeding one hundred pounds.

S. 433 prohibits the placing of an undue weight on the safety valve of any steamship.

Keeping Order in Passenger Steamers

Offences in connection with passenger steamers

255 **287.**—(1) If any of the following offences is committed in the case of a passenger steamer for which there is a passenger steamer's certificate [1] in force; (that is to say,)

(*a*) If any person being drunk or disorderly has been on that account refused admission thereto by the owner or any person in his employment, and, after having the amount of his fare (if he has paid it) returned or tendered to him, nevertheless persists in attempting to enter the steamer:

(*b*) If any person being drunk or disorderly on board the steamer is requested by the owner or any person in his employ to leave the steamer at any place in the United Kingdom, at which he can conveniently do so, and, after having the amount of his fare (if he has paid it) returned or tendered to him, does not comply with the request:

(*c*) If any person on board the steamer, after warning by the master or other officer thereof, molests or continues to molest any passenger:

(*d*) If any person, after having been refused admission to the steamer by the owner or any person in his employ on account of the steamer being full, and having had the amount of his fare (if he has paid it) returned or tendered to him, nevertheless persists in attempting to enter the steamer:

(*e*) If any person having gone on board the steamer at any place, and being requested, on account of the steamer being full, by the owner or any person in his employ to leave the steamer, before it has quitted that place, and having had the amount of his fare (if he has paid it) returned or tendered to him, does not comply with that request:

(*f*) If any person travels or attempts to travel in the steamer without first paying his fare, and with intent to avoid payment thereof:

(*g*) If any person, having paid his fare for a certain distance, knowingly and wilfully proceeds in the steamer beyond that distance without first paying the additional fare for the additional distance, and with intent to avoid payment thereof:

(*h*) If any person on arriving in the steamer at a point to which he has paid his fare knowingly and wilfully refuses or neglects to quit the steamer: and

(*i*) If any person on board the steamer fails, when requested by the master or other officer thereof, either to pay his fare or exhibit such ticket or other receipt, if any, showing the payment of his fare, as is usually given to persons travelling by and paying their fare for the steamer:

the person so offending shall for each offence be liable to a fine not exceeding forty shillings,[2] but that liability shall not prejudice the recovery of any fare payable by him.

256 (2) If any person on board any such steamer wilfully does or causes to be done anything in such a manner as to obstruct or injure any part of the machinery or tackle of the steamer, or to obstruct, impede, or molest the crew, or any of them, in the navigation or management of the steamer, or otherwise in the execution of their duty on or about the steamer, he shall for each offence be liable to a fine not exceeding twenty pounds.

(3) The master or other officer of any such steamer, and all persons called by him to his assistance, may, without any warrant, detain any person who commits any offence against this section and whose name and address are unknown to the master or officer, and convey the offender with all convenient despatch before some justice of the peace to be dealt with according to law, and that justice shall with all convenient despatch try the case in a summary manner.[2]

(4) If any person commits an offence against this section and on the application of the master of the steamer, or any other person in the employ of the owner thereof, refuses to give his name and address, or gives a false name or address, that person shall be liable to a fine not exceeding twenty pounds, *and the fine shall be paid to the owner of the steamer*.[3]

257 For power to exclude drunken passengers on home-trade passenger steamers, see s. 288.

As to the application of the Summary Jurisdiction Acts (now Magistrates' Courts Act 1952, as respects England and Wales), and the prosecution of offences generally, see ss. 680 *et seq.*; and see also, as to legal proceedings under this Part of the Act, ss. 356 *et seq.*

As to the master's authority over passengers apart from statute, see *Kay on Shipmasters and Seamen*, 2nd ed., Chap. 13; Maclachlan, 7th ed., p. 264; Halsbury's *Laws of England*, 3rd ed., Vol. 35, p. 547.

1 See s. 274, issue of passenger steamer's certificate.

2 The maximum fine in respect of offences under paras. (*a*) and (*b*) of subs. (1) has been increased to five pounds; see the Penalties for Drunkenness Act 1962, s. 1.

3 The words in italics were repealed by the Justices of the Peace Act 1949, s. 46, and Sched. VII, as from April 1, 1953 (see S.I. 1951 No. 1941).

Power to exclude drunken passengers on home-trade passenger steamers

258 **288.** The master of any home-trade passenger steamer may refuse to receive on board thereof any person who by reason of drunkenness or otherwise is in such a state, or misconducts himself in such a manner, as to cause annoyance or injury to passengers on board, and if any such person is on board, may put him on shore at any convenient place; and a person so refused admittance or put on shore shall not be entitled to the return of any fare he has paid.

For definition of "home-trade passenger steamer," see s. 742.

3. Emigrant Ships

259 **289–290.** [*These sections, which dealt with surveys of and equipment for emigrant ships, became obsolete and were repealed by the* M.S.A. 1970, s. 100 (3), Sched. V, *as from January* 1, 1973: *see* S.I. 1972 No. 1977.]

Number of, and Accommodation for, Passengers

260 **291.** [*This section, which dealt with regulations as to carrying of passengers generally, was repealed by M.S.A.* 1906, *s.* 85, *Sched. II, and replaced by section* 16 *of that Act.*]

261 **292–298.** [*These sections, which contained provisions relating to numbers and accommodation of passengers and to provisions, water and medical stores, became obsolete and were repealed by M.S.A.* 1970, *s.* 100 (3), *Sched. V, as from January* 1, 1973: *see S.I.* 1972 *No.* 1977.]

262 **299.** [*This section, which empowered the then Board of Trade to exempt emigrant ships from certain provisions of this Part of the Act if satisfied that the food, space, accommodation, etc., provided was superior to the standard required by this Part of the Act, was repealed by the M.S.A.* 1906, *s.* 85, *Sched. II, and a general dispensing power was given to the then Minister of Transport by section* 78 *of that Act.*]

263 **300–340.** [*These sections, which contained further provisions relating to emigrant ships, became obsolete and were repealed by M.S.A.* 1970, s. 100 (3), *Sched. V, as from January* 1, 1973: *see S.I.* 1972 No. 1977.]

264 **341–352.** [*These sections, which related to passage brokers and emigrant runners, were repealed as from December* 13, 1966, *by the Local Government Act*, 1966, *s.* 43 (2) (*a*), *Sched.* 3, *as regards England and Wales, and by the Local Government* (*Scotland*) *Act* 1966, *s.* 48 (2), *Sched.* 6, *as regards Scotland.*]

265 **353–355.** [*These sections, which related to frauds in procuring emigration and to emigration officers, became obsolete and were repealed by the M.S.A.* 1970, *s.* 100 (3), *Sched.* V, *as from January* 1, 1973: *see S.I.* 1972 *No.* 1977.]

Recovery of fines

266 **356.** All fines and forfeitures under the provisions of this Part of this Act (other than the provisions relating to passenger steamers only [1]) shall be sued for [2] by the following officers; that is to say,

(*a*) *any emigration officer* [3];
(*b*) any chief officer of customs [4]; and also

(*c*) in the British Islands,[5] any person authorised by the [Department of Trade] and any officer of customs authorised by the Commissioners of Customs [6]; and

(*d*) in a British possession [5] any person authorised by the Governor of that possession, or any officer of customs authorised by the Government department regulating the customs in that possession.

267 [1] See ss. 273, 280, 281, 283–287, and M.S.A. 1906, ss. 21–22, as to fines connected with passenger steamers. It seems that no special officers are appointed by the Act to take proceedings for offences under the provisions which relate to passenger steamers only.

[2] Although the words " sued for " hardly appear appropriate to cover proceedings taken under ss. 680–681, yet the provision made in those sections for legal proceedings generally appears to be intended to embrace proceedings under this Part of the Act. Where an offence may involve a liability to pay a fine exceeding £100, *e.g.* under s. 337, it cannot be dealt with summarily, s. 680 (*b*).

[3] The words in italics were repealed by M.S.A. 1970, s. 100, Sched. V, as from January 1, 1973: see S.I. 1972 No. 1977.

[4] See s. 742 for definition.

[5] See Interpretation Act 1889, s. 18 (1) (2), at § 687, *post*.

[6] Now Commissioners of Customs and Excise, see Customs and Excise Act 1952, s. 318 (1).

Recovery of passage and subsistence money, compensation, and damages

268 **357** and **358.** [*Section* 357 (*Recovery of passage and subsistance money, compensation, and damages*) *and section* 358 (*Protection of persons executing Act* 56 & 57 *Vict. c.* 61) *were repealed by M.S.A.* 1970, *s.* 100 (3) *Sched. V, as from January* 1, 1973; *see S.I.* 1972, *No.* 1977.]

Supplemental

Owner responsible for default in absence of agreement

269 **359.**—(1) In the absence of any agreement to the contrary, the owner of a ship shall be the person ultimately responsible as between himself and the other persons by this Part of this Act made liable in respect of any default in complying with any requirement thereof.

(2) [1]

As to whether the registered owner is responsible as owner in the case of a demised ship, *cf.* the cases cited in note (1) to s. 695.

[1] This subsection was repealed by M.S.A. 1970, s. 100 (3), Sched. V.

Forms and Fees

270 **360.**—(1) [1]

(2) [1]

(3) If any person employed under this Part of this Act demands or receives, directly or indirectly, otherwise than by the direction of the [Department of Trade], any fee, remuneration, or gratuity whatever in respect of any duty performed by him under this Part of this Act, he shall for each offence be liable to a fine not exceeding fifty pounds.

271 [1] Subsections 1 and 2 were repealed by M.S.A. 1970, s. 100 (3), Sched. V. as from January 1, 1973: see S.I. 1972 No. 1977.

Posting of abstracts of Part III in emigrant ships

272 **361–362.** [*Section* 361 (*Posting of abstracts of Part III on emigrant ships*) *and section* 362 (*By-laws by harbour authority*) *were repealed by M.S.A.* 1970, *s.* 100 (3), *Sched. V as from January* 1, 1973: *see S.I.* 1972 No. 1977.]

Exemption from survey of foreign passenger steamer in certain cases

273 **363.** Where a foreign ship is a passenger steamer *or emigrant ship* [1] within the meaning of this Part of this Act,[2] and the [Department of Trade is] satisfied, by the production of a foreign certificate of survey attested by a British consular officer at a port out of Her Majesty's dominions, that the ship has been officially surveyed at that port, and [is] satisfied that any requirements of this Act are proved by that survey to have been substantially complied with, the [Department] may, if [it thinks] fit, dispense with any further survey of the ship in respect of any requirement so complied with, and grant or direct one of [its] officers to grant a certificate, which shall have the same effect as if given upon survey under this Part of this Act [3]:

Provided that Her Majesty in Council may order that this section shall not apply in the case of an official survey at any port at which it appears to Her Majesty that corresponding advantages are not extended to British ships.[4]

274 [1] The words in italics were repealed by M.S.A. 1970, s.100 (3), Sched. V as from January 1, 1973: see S.I. 1972 No. 1977.

[2] See s. 267.

[3] See, as to passenger ships, ss. 271 *et seq.*

[4] The power contained in the proviso to this section appears never to have been exercised. But by M.S. (Passenger Steamers and Emigrant Ships) Italian Ships Order 1929 (S.R. & O. No. 1154, S.R. & O. Rev. XIV, p. 229) made under M.S. (Equivalent Provisions) Act 1925, s. 1, Italian ships, whilst in a port in the United Kingdom, are exempted from the provisions of the M.S. Acts relating to passenger steamers and emigrant ships on proof that they comply with the equivalent provisions of the law of Italy.

By s. 21 (3) of the M.S. (Safety and Load Line Conventions) Act 1932, this section ceased to apply to Safety Convention passenger steamers plying on international voyages as from January 1, 1934. (For definitions of the relevant terms for the purposes of s. 21 (3), see ss. 38 and 73 (1) of that Act.) This repeal apparently remains effective by virtue of the Interpretation Act 1889, s. 38 (2), notwithstanding that s. 21 (3) of the 1932 Act has itself been repealed by M.S. (Safety Convention) Act 1949, s. 37, and Sched. III.

Application of Part III as regards Emigrant Ships

Application to certain voyages

275 **364–365.** [*Section* 364 (*Application to certain voyages*) *and section* 365 (*Limited Application of Part III of Act to colonial voyages were repealed by M.S.A.* 1970, *s.* 100 (3), *Sched. V*, *as from January* 1, 1973; *see S.I.* 1972 *No.* 1977.]

Modification of provisions of Part III in their application to British possessions

276 **366.**—(1) The Governor of a British possession [1] may by proclamation—

(*a*) Determine what shall be deemed, for the purposes of this Part of this Act, to be the length of the voyage of any ship carrying steerage passengers from any port in that British possession to any other port; and

(*b*) Fix dietary scales for steerage passengers during the voyage; and

(*c*) Declare what medical stores shall be deemed necessary for the medical treatment of the steerage passengers during the voyage.

(2) Every such proclamation shall take effect from the issue thereof, and shall have effect without as well as within the possession, as if enacted in this Part of this Act.

(3) The governor of a British possession [1] may authorise such persons as he thinks fit to make a like survey of emigrant ships sailing from that possession as is by this Act required to be made by two or more competent surveyors in the case of emigrant ships sailing from the British Islands.[1]

(4) The governor of a British possession [1] may authorise any competent person to act as medical practitioner on board an emigrant ship proceeding on a colonial voyage.

[1] For definitions of "British Islands" and "British Possessions," see Interpretation Act 1889, s. 18 (1), (2), at § 687, *post*.

Powers of governors of colonies as to numbers of steerage passengers

277 **367.**—(1) The governor of each of the Australasian Colonies, that is to say, New South Wales, Victoria, South Australia, Western Australia, Queensland, Tasmania, New Zealand, and any colony hereafter established in Australia, may by proclamation make such rules as he thinks proper for determining the number of steerage passengers to be carried in any emigrant ship proceeding from one of such colonies to any other of those colonies, and for determining on what deck or decks, and subject to what reservations or conditions, steerage passengers may be carried in such ship.[1]

(2) The governor of any British possession may, if he thinks fit, declare by proclamation that ships intended to pass within the tropics from any port in such possession may convey steerage passengers, being natives of Asia or Africa, after the rate of one for every twelve superficial feet of the passenger deck instead of after the rate specified in the Tenth Schedule [2] to this Act.

(3) Every such proclamation shall take effect from the issue thereof, or such other day as may be named therein, and shall have effect without

as well as within the possession, as if it were enacted in this Part of this Act in substitution as respects the said ships for the Tenth Schedule [2] to this Act.

(4) The provisions of the Tenth Schedule [2] to this Act with respect to the number of superficial feet to be allowed to each steerage passenger shall not apply to any ship proceeding from any port in the Island of Ceylon to any port in British India [3] in the Gulf of Manar or Palk's Straits, and the legislature of Ceylon [4] may regulate by law the number of steerage passengers who may be carried on board such ships.

278 [1] Since the dates of the establishment of the Dominions of Australia and New Zealand the provisions of this subs. are of no operative effect.

[2] This schedule was repealed by the substitution of the regulations made by the Minister of Transport. The regulations were made on September 6, 1907 (No. 739) under the M.S.A. 1906, s. 17 (2), which in turn has been repealed by the M.S.A. 1970 s. 100 (3) Sched. 5.

[3] For meaning of references to "British India," see now s. 18 of Indian Independence Act 1947, and s. 1 of India (Consequential Provisions) Act 1949.

[4] As to legislative powers of Ceylon, see Ceylon Independence Act 1947, s. 1, Sched. I.

Power for legislature of India to apply Part III

279 **368.**—(1) The provisions of this Part of this Act (other than the provisions relating to passenger steamers only) shall not apply to British India, except as in this section provided.

(2) The [legislature of India [1]] may, by any Act passed for the purpose, declare that all or any provisions of this Part of this Act shall apply to the carriage of steerage passengers upon any voyage from any specified port in British India to any other specified port whatsoever; and may for the purposes of this Part of this Act—

(*a*) fix dietary scales for the voyage, and authorise the substitution of those scales for the scale enacted by this Act;

(*b*) determine what shall be deemed to be the length of any such voyage;

(*c*) determine the persons or officers who in British India shall take the place of emigration officers and officers of customs in the British Islands;

(*d*) declare the space necessary for steerage passengers, and the age at which two children shall be treated as one statute adult, in ships clearing out from any port in British India; and

(*e*) authorise the employment on board any ship of a medical practitioner duly qualified according to Indian law; and

(*f*) provide for the recovery and application in British India of fines and sums of money under this Part of this Act,

and the provisions of any such Act while in force shall have effect without as well as within British India as if enacted by this Act.

(3) Provided that any such Act shall be of no effect under this section,

unless it be reserved for the signification of Her Majesty's pleasure thereon or contain a suspending clause providing that the Act shall not come into operation until Her Majesty's pleasure thereon has been publicly signified in British India.

280 As to the meaning of references to "British India," see now s. 18 of the Indian Independence Act 1947.

There appears to be no provision, with reference to Acts passed under the power here reproduced, similar to that in s. 735 (2) (*q.v.*).

For provisions in this Part of the Act relating to passenger steamers only, see ss. 271–288.

[1] The words in square brackets were substituted for the words "Governor-General of India in Council" by the Government of India (Adaptation of Acts of Parliament) Order 1937 (S.R. & O. No. 230) made under the Government of India Act 1935, and a new section 368A inserted by that order was repealed by the Burma Independence Act 1947, s. 5, Sched. II; the order continues in force in relation to all Acts in so far as they operate otherwise than as part of the law of British India or India or Pakistan (see Indian Independence Act 1947, s. 18 (2), and India (Consequential Provisions) Act 1949, s. 1).

PART IV—FISHING BOATS

281 *The provisions of this Part are in large part replaced by the provisions of M.S.A.* 1970: *see s.* 95 *of that Act. By virtue of the M.S.A.* 1970 (*Commencement No.* 1) *Order* 1972 (*S.I. No.* 1972) *various sections were repealed as from January* 1, 1973. *Only those sections which are repealed as from a date yet to be appointed have been included in this Part. They have been printed in italics in anticipation of their repeal in due course.*

Part IV consolidated the M.S. (Fishing Boats) Acts 1883, 1887, certain sections of the Fisheries Acts 1868, 1883, and other enactments relating to fishing boats. Its provisions were then of general application to fishing boats (except in British possessions: see section 372), and were for the most part in lieu of the corresponding provisions of Part II (Masters and Seamen). Until August 16, 1920, the provisions did not embrace Scotland, but by the M.S. (Scottish Fishing Boats) Act 1920, *post*, their application was extended to include that country with certain necessary modifications of a purely formal character. For the limited application to Scotland prior to that date, see the note to § 948, *post*.

See also as to certain fishing vessels, section 744.

As to the restrictions on the employment of young persons and children on board British ships and British fishing boats registered in the fishing boat register, see Employment of Women, Young Persons and Children Act 1920, ss. 1 and 4, set out in notes at § 1344, *post*, and M.S. (International Labour Conventions) Act 1925, *post*. The general effect of these provisions is summarised in a note at §§ 1344 and 1345, *post*.

Application of Part IV, etc.

Application of Part IV

282 369.—(1) *This Part of this Act relates partly—*

(*a*) *to all fishing boats and to the whole fishing service; and partly*

(*b*) *to all fishing boats of twenty-five tons tonnage and upwards; and partly*

(*c*) *to fishing boats being trawlers of twenty-five tons tonnage and upwards, and where so expressly provided, to fishing boats being trawlers of whatever tonnage.*

(2) *The* [*Department of Trade*] *may, by order published in the London Gazette* [1]—

(*a*) *exempt from the date in the order mentioned, any class of such trawler or trawlers belonging to any port from the whole or any portion of this Part* [2] *of this Act, and* (*b*) *extend all or any of the provisions of this Part of this Act to any fishing boats referred to in the order,*

and may revoke or alter any such order by an order published in like manner, but such order shall not extend to any of the provisions relating to the fishing boat register, or to the boats and life-buoys to be carried on fishing boats.

(3) *The* [*Department of Trade*] *may, before making any order under this section, institute such inquiry, as in* [*its*] *opinion may be required for enabling* [*it*] *to make the order, by such person as the* [*Dept.*] *may appoint, and the person so appointed shall for the purpose of the inquiry have all the powers of a* [*Department of Trade*] *inspector under this Act.*[3]

(4) *The provisions of this Act with respect to fishing boats being trawlers*[4] *shall, save as otherwise expressly provided, apply to vessels employed as tenders or carriers to fishing boats or for the purpose of collecting and conveying to the land the catch of fishing boats.*[5]

283 This section is prospectively repealed by the M.S.A. 1970, s. 100 (3), Sched. V, from a day to be appointed.

[1] By order dated November 2, 1899, sea fishing boats registered at any port in the United Kingdom being (1) sailing trawlers under 50 tons registered tonnage, (2) paddle steamers employed as trawlers, are exempt from such portion of Part IV as was contained in ss. 399–408 relating to the engagement of seamen: S.R. & O. and S.I.Rev. 1948; *Merchant Shipping*, p. 276. See now M.S.A. 1970, s. 95 (§ 1474, *post*). The provisions of this Act relating to certificates of skippers and second hands (ss. 413–416), have been extended to embrace (1) all fishing boats engaged in seine net fishing of 50 tons gross tonnage and upwards propelled by steam or other mechanical power with the exception that s. 413 (4) and the general provisions in ss. 413–416 do not apply to such fishing boats as regards the skipper or second hand if such skipper or second hand is properly authorised by the Dept. of Trade to act as skipper or second hand respectively of fishing boats being liners or drifters of 50 tons gross tonnage and upwards, propelled by steam or other mechanical power (M.S. (Fishing Boats) Order 1923, S.R. & O. No. 949); and (2) all fishing boats, being liners or drifters or boats engaged in seine net or ring net fishing, of 25 tons gross tonnage or upwards propelled by steam or other mechanical power with the exception that s. 413 (1) does not apply in certain circumstances to such fishing boats not exceeding 50 tons gross tonnage (M.S. (Fishing Boats) Order 1948, S.I. No. 366). The 1948 Order also exempts from the provisions of s. 413 (1) in certain circumstances trawlers of 25 tons tonnage or upwards but not exceeding 50 tons. The circumstances in which this exemption applies are the same as those in which the exemptions referred to in (2) above, applies.

In the application of this section to Scotland, the *Edinburgh Gazette* is to be substituted for the *London Gazette*, and any order made thereunder, in so far as it affects Scotland is subject to the consent of the Secretary for Scotland. See M.S.A. 1906, s. 81, and M.S. (Scottish Fishing Boats) Act 1920, s. 1 (2) (*a*) and (*c*).

[2] This includes powers to exempt boats going to sea from ports in Scotland from the provisions of ss. 413–416. See M.S. Act 1906, s. 81 (2).

[3] See s. 729 for powers of an inspector of the Department of Trade.

[4] *i.e.* ss. 413–417.

[5] For powers of the Secretary of State to make regulations restricting conveyance of fish from trawlers to collecting and carrying vessels, see s. 417.

Definitions. " Fishing boat "—" Second hand "—" Voyage "

284 **370.** In this Part of this Act, unless the context otherwise requires—

The expression " fishing boat " means a vessel of whatever size, and in whatever way propelled, which is for the time being employed in sea fishing or in the sea-fishing service,[1] [. . .][2]

The expression " second hand " means, with respect to a fishing boat, the mate or person next to the skipper in authority or command on board the boat.[3]

The expression " voyage " shall mean a fishing trip commencing with a departure from a port for the purpose of fishing, and ending with the first return to a port thereafter upon the conclusion of the trip, but a return due to distress only shall not be deemed to be a return, if it is followed by a resumption of the trip.[3]

285 [1] The term " sea-fishing " is not defined in this Act, but see the Sea Fisheries Act 1868, s. 5: " The term ' sea fish ' does not include salmon, as defined by any Act relating to salmon, but, save as aforesaid, includes every description both of fish and of shell fish which is found in the seas to which this Act applies; and ' sea-fishing,' ' sea fishermen,' and other expressions referring to sea fish shall in this Act be construed to refer only to sea fish as before defined."

It seems that a " fishing boat " is generally a " ship " within the meaning of this Act as being a vessel which substantially goes to sea: see note (4) to s. 742, and *Ex p. Ferguson*, there cited, in which a fishing " coble " was held to be a ship. And if a fishing boat is a ship, she is required by s. 2 to be registered under Part I of the Act, unless she falls within the exemptions in s. 3.

As to fishing vessels engaged in the whale, seal or walrus fisheries, which are deemed to be " foreign-going ships " for the purposes of this Act, see s. 744, and M.S.A. 1906, s. 83.

[2] The words omitted which excluded from the definitions vessels used for catching fish otherwise than for profit were repealed by M.S.A. 1970, s. 100 (3) Sched. V.

[3] The words in italics are prospectively repealed by M.S.A. 1970, s. 100 (3), Sched. V.

Ascertainment of tonnage of fishing boat

286 **371.**—(1) *The tonnage of a fishing boat for the purpose of this Part of this Act shall be taken to be in the case of a steam trawler her gross tonnage, but in any other case her register tonnage.*

(2) *Where a fishing boat is registered under Part I of this Act,*[1] *her gross or register tonnage as ascertained for the purpose of that registry shall be her gross or register tonnage for the purpose of this Part of this Act.*[2]

(3) *Where a fishing boat is not so registered a certificate signed by a surveyor of ships under this Act*[3] *stating her gross or register tonnage, ascertained as in the case of a ship registered under Part I of this Act*[2] *shall be conclusive of that tonnage.*

This section is prospectively repealed by M.S.A. 1970, s. 100 (3) Sched. V from a day to be appointed.

[1] See note (1) to s. 370.

[2] As to measurement and tonnage of ships, see M.S.A. 1965, s. 1 (§ 1258, *post*).

[3] See ss. 724 *et seq.*

Extent of Part IV

287 **372.** This Part of this Act shall not, except where otherwise expressly provided, apply *to Scotland, or* to any British possession.

The words in italics were repealed by M.S. (Scottish Fishing Boats) Act 1920, s. 1 (3) and Sched. As to Scotland, see note at head of s. 369.

As to certain vessels engaged in the whale, seal or walrus fisheries, see s. 744 and M.S.A. 1906, s. 83.

As to the application of this Part to the Republic of Ireland, see note " Application to Northern Ireland and the Republic of Ireland " in notes to s. 742.

(I) PROVISIONS APPLYING TO ALL FISHING BOATS AND TO THE WHOLE FISHING SERVICE

288 The following sections shall apply to all fishing boats and the whole fishing service:

But see the power of exemption in s. 369 (2) and the notes thereto.

Fishing Boats Register

These provisions as to registration are in addition to the requirements as to registration under Part I which is obligatory on all fishing boats which are " ships " unless they come within the exemptions contained in s. 3.

Registry of British fishing boats

289 **373.**—(1) This section shall apply to the British Islands,[1] and to all British fishing boats, including those used otherwise than for profit, and the expression " fishing boat " in this section shall be construed accordingly.

(2) Subject to any exemptions made by the regulations under this section, every fishing boat shall be lettered and numbered and have official papers,[2] and shall for that purpose be entered in the fishing boat register.[3]

(3) If a fishing boat required to be so entered is not so entered, she shall not be entitled to any of the privileges or advantages of a British fishing boat,[4] but all obligations, liabilities, and penalties with reference to that boat, and the punishment of offences committed on board her, or by any persons belonging to her, and the jurisdiction of officers [5] and courts, shall be the same as if the boat were actually so entered.

(4) If a fishing boat required to be entered in the fishing boat register is not so entered, and is used as a fishing boat, the owner and skipper of such boat shall each be liable, for each offence, to a fine not exceeding twenty pounds, and the boat may be detained.

(5) Her Majesty, by Order in Council, may make regulations [6] for carrying into effect and enforcing the entry of fishing boats in the fishing boat register, and any convention with a foreign country relative to the registry, lettering, and numbering of fishing boats, which is for the time being in force by virtue of any statute, and may by such regulations—

(*a*) adopt any existing system of registry or lettering and numbering of boats, and provide for bringing any such system into conformity with the requirements of this Act and of any such convention, and the regulations; and (*b*) define the boats or classes of boats to which the regulations or any of them are to apply, and provide for the exemption [7] of any boats or classes of boats from the provisions of this section, and from the regulations or any of them; and

(*c*) apply to the entry of fishing boats in the fishing boat register, and to all matters incidental thereto, such (if any) of the enactments contained in this or any other Act relating to the registry of British ships, and with such modifications and alterations as may be found desirable; and

(*d*) impose fines not exceeding twenty pounds for the breach of any such regulations which cannot be punished by the application of any of those enactments.

(6) [Sections 8 and 9 of the Sea Fisheries Act 1968 (general powers of British sea-fishery officers, and powers of sea-fishery officers to enforce conventions) shall apply in relation to this section and any Order in Council thereunder, and to any convention mentioned in subsection (5) above, as they apply respectively in relation to any order mentioned in the said section 8 and any convention mentioned in the said section 9; and sections 10, 11, 12 and 14 of that Act (offences, and supplement provisions as to legal proceedings) shall apply accordingly.][8]

(7) *Section one hundred and seventy-six of the Customs Consolidation Act* 1876, *shall not apply to any fishing boat entered in the fishing boat register in pursuance of this Act.*[9]

290 [1] " British Islands " means the United Kingdom, Channel Islands, and the Isle of Man; see Interpretation Act 1889, s. 18 (1); § 687, *post*. As to the application to the Republic or Ireland, see note " Application to Northern Ireland and the Republic of Ireland " in notes to s. 742.

[2] The Sea Fisheries Act 1868, s. 26, as amended by the Sea Fisheries Act 1968, s. 22 (1), Sched. 1, para. 23, provides for the compulsory carrying of certificates of registry or official papers by sea fishing boats.

[3] The Contracts of Employment Act 1972, ss. 1–8, do not apply to a person employed as a skipper of or a seaman on a fishing boat required to be registered under this section; see *ibid.* s. 9 (2) (*c*).

[4] For restrictions on users of British-owned boats not registered under this Act, see the Sea Fish (Conservation) Act 1967, ss. 4 (1) and 5 (8). *Cf.* s. 72, *ante*, as to liabilities of ships not recognised as British.

[5] For powers of British sea-fishery officers in relation to such boats, see Sea Fish (Conservation) Act 1967, s. 15 (4) and the Sea Fisheries Act 1968, ss. 7–9.

[6] By the M.S. (Fishing Boats Registry) Order 1927 (S.R. & O. No. 642), all the earlier regulations as to the fishing boat registry were revoked and new regulations were made containing detailed provisions as to ports and places of registry, applications for registry, measurement of tonnage, change of ownership, marking and lettering, etc.

[7] A fishing boat which is not exempted from registration by regulations under this section is a " foreign fishing boat " for the purposes of the Fishery Limits Act 1964, see *ibid.* s. 3 (1). A fishing boat which is exempted from registration by regulations under this section is a " British fishing boat " by virtue of the Sea Fisheries Act 1968, s. 19 (1).

[8] The words in brackets were substituted by the Sea Fisheries Act 1968, s. 22 (1), Sched. 1, para. 32.

[9] Subs. (7) which is in italics was repealed by the Customs and Excise Act 1952, s. 320, Sched. XII, Part I, as from January 1, 1953. See now s. 68 (5) of that Act for provisions replacing s. 176 of the Customs Consolidation Act 1876.

Effect of registry of fishing boat

291 **374.** In all legal proceedings against the owner or skipper of, or any person belonging to, any boat entered in the fishing boat register, *either for an offence against the fishery regulations or regulations as to lights in the Sea Fisheries Act* 1868, *or* [1] for an offence [under the Sea Fisheries (Scotland) Amendment Act 1885, or under section 5, 6 or 10 of the Sea Fisheries Act 1968,][2] or for the recovery of damages for injury done by such boat, the register shall be conclusive evidence that the persons entered therein at any date as owners of the boat were at that date owners thereof, and that the boat is a British sea fishing-boat: Provided that—

(*a*) this enactment shall not prevent any proceedings being instituted against any person not so entered who is beneficially interested [3] in the boat; and

(*b*) this enactment shall not affect the rights of the owners among themselves, or the rights of any owner entered in the register against any person not so entered who is beneficially interested in the boat; and

(*c*) save as aforesaid, entry in the fishing boat register shall not confer, take away, or affect any title to or interest in any fishing boat.

[1] The words in italics were repealed by the Fishery Limits Act 1964, s. 3 (4), Sched. II.
[2] The words in brackets were substituted by the Sea Fisheries Act 1968, s. 22 (1), Sched. I, para. 33.
[3] See the definition of " beneficial interest," for the purposes of Part I of the Act, in s. 57.

292 **375.** [*This section, and Schedule XV, which related to life-saving appliances for fishing boats, were repealed by section* 2 *of the M.S. Act* 1937. *Fishing boats are now subject to the same rules regarding life-saving appliances as are other ships under section* 427.]

Discipline

293 **376–384.** [*These sections contained provisions relating to discipline and they were repealed as from January* 1, 1973: *see* § 281, *ante*.]

Provisions as to Deaths, Injuries, Ill-treatment, Punishments, and Casualties in Fishing Boats

Cf. the provisions as to keeping records of such events in official logs pursuant to M.S.A. 1970, s. 68 (§ 1439, *post*).

Record and report of death, injury, ill-treatment, punishment, casualties, etc.

294 **385.**—(1) *The skipper of a fishing boat shall keep a record of the following occurrences, namely—*

(i) *of every death, injury, ill-treatment, or punishment of any member of his boat's crew while at sea or of any person on board his boat, and*

(ii) *of every casualty to his fishing boat or any boat belonging to her.*

(2) *The skipper shall produce the record so kept to any superintendent when required by him, and shall also send the same to the superintendent at the port to which the boat belongs at such periods as the* [*Department of Trade requires*] *by any directions endorsed on the forms approved by* [*it*].

(3) *If any such occurrence has happened in the case of a fishing boat, the skipper of the boat shall make to the superintendent at the port where his boat's voyage ends, within twenty-four hours of the boat's arrival at that port, a report of the occurrence.*

(4) *The record and report under this section shall be in such form*[1] *and contain such particulars as the* [*Department of Trade requires*].

(5) *If a skipper fails without reasonable cause to comply with any requirement of this section, he shall for each offence be liable to a fine not exceeding twenty pounds.*

This section is prospectively repealed by the M.S.A. 1970, s. 100 (3) Sched. V from a day to be appointed.

[1] As to forms, see s. 720.

Inquiry as to death, injury, ill-treatment, punishment, etc.

295 **386.**—(1) *Where any such occurrence as in the last preceding section mentioned happens or is supposed to have happened, the superintendent at or nearest to the port at which the fishing boat arrives after the occurrence, or to which the boat belongs, may inquire into the cause and particulars of the occurrence, and, if a report as to the occurrence is made to him in pursuance of the said section, may make on the report an endorsement either that in his opinion the particulars in the report are true, or otherwise to such effect as in his opinion his information warrants.*

(2) *For the purpose of the inquiry, a superintendent shall have all the powers of a* [*Department of Trade*] *inspector under this Act.*[1]

(3) *If in the course of the inquiry it appears to the superintendent that any such occurrence as aforesaid has been caused or was accompanied by violence or the use of any improper means, he shall report the matter to the* [*Department of Trade*][2] *and shall also, if the emergency of the case in his opinion so requires, take immediate steps for bringing the offender to justice, and may for that purpose, if in his discretion he thinks it necessary, cause him to be arrested, and thereafter dealt with in due course of law.*

This section is prospectively repealed from a day to be appointed by the M.S.A. 1970, s. 100 (3) Sched. V.

[1] See s. 729 for powers of inspectors.

[2] If the fishing boat be a " ship " within the meaning of the Act (as to which see note to s. 370), and the casualty be within the definition in s. 464, the provisions of Part VI as to inquiries and formal investigations apply. Further, if there is any loss of life arising by reason of any casualty happening to, or on board, a boat belonging to a fishing vessel, the Secretary of State may if he thinks fit apply the provisions of Part VI and order an inquiry or formal investigation. See s. 468.

296 [*Sections* 387 *and* 388, *which contained provisions relating to Settlement of Disputes and Profits of Fishing Boats were repealed as from January* 1, 1973: *see* § 281, *ante*].

Agreements for Fishing Vessels in Scotland

297 **389.** [*This section, which provided for agreements for fishing vessels in Scotland to which Part IV did not as a whole apply, was repealed by the M.S.* (*Scottish Fishing Boats*) *Act* 1920, *s.* 1 (3) *and Schedule*].

Fees and Control of Superintendents

Fees payable on engagements and discharges

298 **390.**—(1) *The* [*Department of Trade*] *may fix the fees to be payable upon engagements or discharges of members of the crews of fishing boats when effected before a superintendent; and a superintendent may refuse to proceed with any such engagement or discharge unless the fee payable thereon has first been paid.*

(2) *All fees so paid shall be carried to the credit of the Mercantile Marine Fund.*[1]

This section is prospectively repealed by the M.S.A. 1970, s. 100 (3) Sched. V from a day to be appointed.

[1] Now the Exchequer. See M.S. (Mercantile Marine Fund) Act 1898, s. 1 (1) (*a*). There are no fees at present in force under this section.

299 **391–412.** [*These sections which contained further provisions relating to fees and control of superintendents and provisions relating to Apprenticeship and Agreement with Boys, Engagement of Seamen, Payment of Wages and Discharge of Seamen, were repealed as from January* 1, 1973: see § 281 *ante*].

Certificates of Skippers and Second Hands

Sections 413 *to* 417 *have been prospectively repealed by the M.S.A.* 1970, *s.* 100 (3) *Sched. V. from a day to be appointed and have been printed in italics.*

300 As to boats to which ss. 413–416 have been extended and as to exemption of certain boats from the provisions of s. 413 (1) in certain circumstances, see note (1) to s. 369.

As to the restrictions on employment of aliens as skippers or second hands of fishing boats registered in the United Kingdom, see the Aliens Restriction (Amendment) Act 1919, s. 5 (1), which is set out at § 1342, *post*, and also the Employment of Aliens in British Ships Order 1944, cited *ibid*.

Skippers and second hands to hold certificate of competency

301 **413.**—(1) *A fishing boat, being a trawler of twenty-five tons tonnage*[1] *or upwards, shall not go to sea from any port* [. . .][2] *unless provided with a duly certificated skipper and a duly certificated second hand.*[3]

(2) *If a boat goes to sea contrary to this section, the owner thereof shall for each offence be liable to a fine not exceeding twenty pounds.*

(3) *If any person, except in case of necessity—*

(*a*) *having been engaged to serve as skipper or second hand of a fishing boat, being a trawler of twenty-five tons tonnage and upwards, serves as skipper or second hand of that boat without being duly certificated; or*

(*b*) *employs any person as skipper or second hand of such a boat without ascertaining that he is duly certificated;*

that person shall for each offence be liable to a fine not exceeding twenty pounds.

(4) *A skipper or second hand shall not be deemed duly certificated for the purpose of this section unless he holds a certificate under this Part of this Act appropriate to his station in the boat or to a higher station.*

(5) *Where the skipper of such a boat is absent from his boat, a superintendent may, on the request of the owner of the boat, and on being satisfied that the absence is due to an unavoidable cause, authorise the second hand of the boat to act, for a period not exceeding one month, as the skipper of the boat during the skipper's absence, and the second hand when acting under that authority shall for the purposes of this section be deemed to be a duly certificated skipper.*

302 As to extension of these provisions, and restrictions upon the employment of aliens, see note at head of this section.

[1] As to ascertainment of tonnage, see s. 371.

[2] The words omitted were repealed by M.S.A. 1906, s. 85, Sched. II, and this section now applies to trawlers of 25 tons and upwards going to sea from any port in the United Kingdom; see M.S.A. 1906, s. 81. As to the application to the Republic of Ireland, see note "Application to Northern Ireland and the Republic of Ireland" in notes to s. 742.

[3] For boats exempted in certain circumstances from the provisions of this subsection, see note (1) to s. 369.

Granting of certificate of competency

303 **414.**[1]—(1) *Certificates of competency as skipper or as second hand of fishing boats, or any particular class of fishing boats, may be granted by the* [*Department of Trade*] *in the same manner as certificates of competency as master or mate under the Second Part of this Act,*[2] *and all the provisions of this Act with respect to or connected with the examination of applicants for certificates and the granting thereof, and the suspension and cancellation thereof, and inquiries and investigations into the conduct of the holders thereof,*[3] *and all other provisions of this Act relating to or connected with certificates of masters or mates, shall apply to the certificates as skipper or second hand of fishing boats, and the holders thereof, as if the certificates had been granted under Part II of this Act, and the holders thereof shall be entitled to such privileges, and subject to such liabilities as they would be if such certificates had been so granted.*

(2) *A certificate of competency as skipper of a fishing boat shall not be granted to any person unless he has previously held a certificate as second hand for at least twelve months.*

This section has been prospectively repealed by the M.S.A. 1970, s. 100 (3) from a day to be appointed.

As to extension of these provisions and restrictions upon the employment of aliens, see note at head of s. 413.

[1] This section applies to trawlers of 25 tons and upwards going to sea from any port in the United Kingdom. See M.S.A. 1906, s. 81.

[2] For the provisions of Part II as to such certificates, see ss. 92–104, and M.S.A.,1906, s. 56, and M.S. (Certificates) Act 1914.

Certificates granted under the repealed Act were saved by s. 745 (1) (*a*).

[3] See Part VI.

The " Regulations relating to the examination of skippers and second hands of fishing boats " (Exn. I, Fishing) 1959 (reprinted with amendments 1962) may be obtained from H.M. Stationery Office or through any bookseller.

Certificate of service

304 **415.**—(1) *If any person before the first day of September one thousand eight hundred and eighty-three* [1] *served as a skipper, or before the first day of July one thousand eight hundred and eighty-eight* [1] *served as a second hand in fishing boats, being trawlers of twenty-five tons tonnage* [2] *and upwards or such other fishing boats as the* [*Department of Trade considers*] *will have afforded that person sufficient experience, for a period amounting in all to not less than twelve months, that person shall be entitled to a certificate of service as skipper or second hand, as the case may be, of a fishing boat, limited, if he has been exclusively employed in a particular class of such fishing boats, to that particular class.*

(2) *If a person proves to the* [*Department of Trade*] *that he has served as required by this section and has been generally well conducted on board the boats in which he has served, the* [*Department of Trade*] *shall deliver a certificate of service to him.*

(3) *The certificate of service shall differ in form from a certificate of competency, and shall contain particulars of the name, place, and date of birth of the holder, and of the length and nature of his previous service.*

(4) *This act shall apply to a certificate of service so granted and to the holder thereof in like manner as it applies to a certificate of competency granted under this Part of this Act and to the holder thereof.*

This section has been prospectively repealed by the M.S.A. 1970, s. 100 (3) from a day to be appointed.

As to extension of these provisions and restrictions upon the employment of aliens, see note at head of s. 413.

[1] This section applies to trawlers of 25 tons and upwards going to sea from any port in the United Kingdom, but the date of the commencement of the M.S.A. 1906, *viz.*, June 1, 1907, is to be substituted for the dates mentioned in this section. See M.S.A. 1906, s. 81.

Certificates granted under the repealed Act were saved by s. 745 (1) (*a*).

[2] As to ascertainment of tonnage, see s. 371.

Registers of certificated skippers and second hands

305 **416.**[1]—(1) *The* [*Department of Trade*] *may cause a register*[2] *of certificated skippers and second hands to be kept in such form and by such person, and containing such particulars, as the* [*Department directs*].

(2) *Such register shall be admissible in evidence in manner provided by this Act,*[3] *and the absence of an entry in the register of any person or matter shall be evidence of the non-registration of such person or matter and if the question is whether the person has been certificated as a skipper or second hand, of his not being so certificated.*

This section has been prospectively repealed by the M.S.A. 1970, s. 100 (3) Sched. V, from a day to be appointed.

As to extension of these provisions, see note at head of s. 413.

1 This section applies to trawlers of 25 tons and upwards going to sea from any port in the United Kingdom See M.S.A. 1906, s. 81.

2 Such a register has been kept by the Registrar-General of Shipping and Seamen since December 1883.

3 As to admissibility in evidence, see ss. 695, 719, etc.

Conveyance of Fish from Trawlers

[Dept. of Trade] regulations as to conveyance of fish from trawlers

306 **417.**—(1) *The* [*Dept. of Trade*], *on the application of any owners of a fleet of fishing boats, or of any association of owners of fishing boats, or of any persons having the charge or command of a fleet of fishing boats, or without such application if the person or association entitled to make the application fails after request by the* [*Dept. of Trade*] *to do so, may make such regulations respecting the conveyance of fish from fishing boats catching fish as trawlers to vessels engaged in collecting and carrying fish to port, as may appear to the* [*Dept.*] *expedient for preventing loss of life, or danger to life or limb.*

(2) *All regulations so made*[1] *shall be laid for thirty days before both Houses of Parliament while in session, and shall not come into force till the expiration of those thirty days; and if either House within those thirty days resolves that the whole or any part of the regulations laid before them ought not to be in force, the same shall not have any force, without prejudice, nevertheless, to the making of any other regulation in its place.*

(3) *All regulations made under this section shall, whilst in force, have effect as if enacted in this Act.*

(4) *If any person to whom such a regulation applies fails without reasonable cause to comply therewith, he shall for each offence be liable to a fine not exceeding ten pounds.*

(5) *This section shall apply to fishing boats of whatever tonnage.*

This section has been prospectively repealed by the M.S.A. 1970, s. 100 (3) Sched V, from a day to be appointed.

The following is a list of such regulations now in force, with the dates thereof, and (in brackets) the date of the *London Gazette* in which they are published. As to the saving of such regulations under this Act, see s. 745: Great Northern Steamship Fishing Co. Ltd.,

May 17 (July 24), 1888. Great Grimsby Ice Co. Ltd., November 10 (December 28), 1888. Grimsby and North Sea Steam Trawling Co. Ltd., November 5 (December 28), 1888. Hull Steam Fishing and Ice Co. Ltd., May 17 (July 24), 1888. Short Blue Fleet (Messrs. Hewett's), March 28 (July 5), 1889. Hagerup, Doughty & Co., June 29, 1897, S.R. & O. 1897 No. 602. Kelsall Brothers & Beeching Ltd., May 8, 1897, S.R. & O. 1897 No. 427. Hull Steam Fishing Vessel Owners Association Ltd., February 6, 1905, S.R. & O. 1905 No. 411; October 7 1908, S.R. & O. 1908 No. 1177; August 1, 1911, S.R. & O. 1911 No. 908.

The regulations made since 1896 were not published in the *London Gazette*, and the last regulations have not been put on sale by the Queen's printers. See generally Annual Volume of S.I.'s published by H.M. Stationery Office, Class 10.

[1] The making of these regulations is now subject to the Statutory Instruments Act 1946.

PART V—SAFETY

307 By sections 23 (3) and 24 (1) (2) of M.S. (Safety Convention) Act 1949, certain ships in certain circumstances are deemed for the purposes of this Part of the Act to be unsafe by reason of improper loading, and by section 23 (4), *ibid.* goods declared by the rules made under that section to be dangerous in their nature are deemed to be dangerous goods for the purposes of this Part of the Act.

Prevention of Collisions

Collision regulations

308 **418.**—(1) Her Majesty may, on the joint recommendation of the Admiralty and the [Dept. of Trade], by Order in Council, make regulations [1] for the prevention of collisions at sea,[2] and may thereby regulate the lights to be carried and exhibited, the fog signals to be carried and used, and the steering and sailing rules to be observed, by ships,[3] and those regulations (in this Act referred to as the collision regulations) [4] shall have effect as if enacted in this Act.[5]

(2) The collision regulations, together with the provisions of this Part of [6] this Act relating thereto, or otherwise relating to collisions, shall be observed by all foreign ships within British jurisdiction,[7] and in any case arising in a British court [8] concerning matters arising within British jurisdiction foreign ships shall, so far as respects the collision regulations and the said provisions of this Act, be treated as if they were British ships.

309 REGULATIONS FOR PREVENTING COLLISIONS AT SEA.

HISTORICAL NOTE. The origin of the Collision Regulations as they exist today can be traced back to the body of customary rules of good seamanship which had been evolved by the seafaring communities of the world, without the assistance of the legislature, during the course of centuries. These rules from time to time were adjudicated upon by the Court of Admiralty, with the assistance of the Trinity Masters, whose chief function would appear to have been to advise the court upon these rules as recognised in practice, that is, upon what may be called the common law rules of seamanship. Some of these rules are of great antiquity, and their rudiments can be found in the ancient sea codes, such as the Ordinances of Oleron and Wisbury. Not until 1846 were any of these rules embodied in statutory enactments in this country, but in that year certain Trinity House Rules, which had been promulgated in 1840, were given statutory force by s. 7 of the Steam Navigation Act 1846 (9 & 10 Vict. c. 100). Since that date a number of statutes have extended the power of the executive to make rules for the regulation of traffic at sea, and have imposed varying penalties on disobedience. When examining judicial decisions on the Collision Regulations, great care must be exercised to ascertain what regulations were in force at the time of adjudication and the nature of the penalty for non-observance. The subject is exhaustively discussed and the matter set out in a convenient form under the heading of different periods in *British Shipping Laws* (Vol. 4), *Marsden on Collisions at Sea*, 11th ed., Chap. 23. See also Roscoe's *Admiralty Practice*.

PRESENT REGULATIONS. On September 1, 1965, new Collision Regulations (reproducing the regulations which had been approved by a number of countries, including the United Kingdom, at the International Conference on Safety of Life at Sea, which was held in London in 1960, Cmnd. 1949) came into force, revoking the previous (1954) regulations which in turn had revoked the 1910 regulations: see the Collision Regulations (Ships and Seaplanes on the Water) and Signals of Distress (Ships) Order, 1965, S.I. No. 1525. Additional regulations are contained in the Collision Regulations (Traffic Separation Schemes) Order 1972 (S.I. No. 809), as amended by S.I. 1972 No. 1267, 1974 No. 1890, which provided for regulating navigation in traffic separation schemes based on recommendations adopted by the Inter-Governmental Maritime Consultative Organisation. This Order came into force on September 1, 1972, save for the " off Kiel Lighthouse scheme " which came into force on December 1, 1972. The detailed interpretation of these regulations is beyond the scope of this note, but will be found fully discussed in *British Shipping Laws* (Vol. 4), *Marsden on Collisions at Sea*, 11th ed., Chap. 27A, and Halsbury's *Laws of England*, 3rd ed., Vol. 35, p. 592 *et seq.* The text of the regulations is set out in full in *Marsden* at §§ 990/2–990/35. As to application of the new Collision Regulations to foreign ships, see note (2) to s. 424.

APPLICATION OF REGULATIONS TO SEAPLANES. By s. 52 (1) of the Civil Aviation Act 1949, the provisions of ss. 418, 419, 421 and 424 of M.S.A. 1894, are applied, with certain modifications, to seaplanes on the surface of the water. The new power has been exercised and the Collision Regulations (see above) apply to seaplanes on the high seas as well as to vessels.

HOVERCRAFT. As to the position of hovercraft, see the Hovercraft Act 1968, s. 1.

310 [1] For extension of power to make regulations in connection with seaplanes see note, *supra*.

[2] There is no definition of this term " at sea " in this Act, and it has been doubted whether the extended application of the Collision Regulations imported by the Preliminary article thereto (" the high seas and in all waters connected therewith, navigable by sea-going vessels ") is not *ultra vires*. It should be noticed, however, that by s. 421 provision is made for rules as to the navigation of the waters of any harbour, river or other inland navigation. When such regulations are made by Order in Council, they are not the regulations for preventing collisions at sea, but they have the same force as if they formed part of such regulations: s. 421 (2). Compare *Salt Union* v. *Wood* [1893] 1 Q.B. 370, where it was held that a ship which only navigated the River Weaver and the tidal waters of the Mersey was not a " sea-going ship " within the provisions now embodied in s. 260 of this Act.

In *The Carlotta* [1899] P. 223, Gorell Barnes J. assumed, without deciding it, that the sea rules applied in the River Thames, an opinion which he endorsed in *The Hare* [1904] P. 331, in deciding that for other reasons they did not apply to the Manchester Ship Canal.

However, it was held in *The Anselm* [1907] P. 151, that the regulations applied to tidal waters connected with the sea navigable by sea-going vessels by reason of the directions in the Preliminary article to the regulations, and that it was too late to question in the Court of Appeal the validity of such directions. See also *The Concordia* (1866) L.R. 1 A. & E. 93; *The Velocity* (1869) L.R. 3 P.C. 44; *The Cologne* (1872) L.R. 4 P.C. 519; *The Khedive* (1880) 5 App.Cas. 876, in which the regulations were assumed to be applicable to rivers and narrow waters.

[3] " Ships." As to what vessels are included in this term, see s. 742 and note (4) thereto. The regulations state (Rule 1) that the rules are to be followed by " all vessels and seaplanes . . ." and " vessel " is defined as including " every description of water craft, other than a seaplane on the water, used or capable of being used as a means of transportation on water." See *Marsden*, 11th ed., Chap. 24, §§ 648–649. See also note (1) to s. 419 (Crown ships). For hovercraft, see note (above). As to enforcement of collision regulations as they apply to fishing boats by sea-fishery officers, see Sea Fisheries Act 1968, s. 8 (6). Also see the Fishing Vessels (Safety Provisions) Act 1970, s. 2.

[4] The meaning of " collision regulations " has been applied in the Fishing Vessels (Safety) Provisions Act 1970, s. 9 (1) as from a day to be appointed.

[5] Subject to the provisions of this Act, Orders in Council made under this section are to take effect as if they were enacted by Parliament. See s. 738 (3).

As to the interpretation of terms used in Orders in Council, see Interpretation Act 1889, s. 31, set out in notes to s. 742.

[6] The insertion of the words " this Part of " in this and the 424th section is in accordance with the construction put upon ss. 57, 58 of the M.S.A. 1862, in *The Amalia* (1863) 32 L.J.Ad. 191; 1 Moo.P.C.C.(N.S.) 471.

[7] As to the limits of British jurisdiction, see *The Saxonia* (1861) 31 L.J.Ad. 201; Lush. 410; *The Annapolis* (1861) 30 L.J.Ad. 201; Lush. 295; *R.* v. *Keyn, The Franconia* (1876) 46 L.J.M.C. 17; 3 Ex.D. 63, cited in note (2) to s. 686; and the Territorial Waters Jurisdiction Act 1878.

As to application to foreign ships beyond these limits, see s. 424, and S.I. 1965 No. 1525, applying the new regulations to the ships of those countries which have accepted the International Collision Regulations of 1960 (for list of those countries, see note (2) to s. 424).

[8] See the restrictions on the county court jurisdiction over actions *in personam* to enforce claims arising out of non-compliance with rules made under this section: County Courts Act 1959, s. 70.

Observance of collision regulations

311 **419.**—(1) All owners and masters of ships [1] shall obey the collision regulations, and shall not carry or exhibit any other lights, or use any other fog signals, than such as are required by those regulations.[2]

(2) If an infringement of the collision regulations is caused by the wilful default of the master or owner of the ship, that master or owner shall, in respect of each offence, be guilty of a misdemeanour.[3]

(3) If any damage to person or property arises from the non-observance by any ship of any of the collision regulations, the damage shall be deemed to have been occasioned by the wilful default [4] of the person in charge of the deck of the ship at the time, unless it is shown to the satisfaction of the court that the circumstances of the case made a departure from the regulation necessary.

(4) *Where in a case of collision it is proved to the court before whom the case is tried, that any of the collision regulations have been infringed, the ship by which the regulation has been infringed shall be deemed to be in fault, unless it is shown to the satisfaction of the court that the circumstances of the case made departure from the regulation necessary.*[5]

(5) The [Department of Trade] shall furnish a copy of the collision regulations to any master or owner of a ship who applies for it.

312 This section is applied (with certain modifications) to seaplanes on the surface of the water by the Civil Aviation Act 1949, s. 52 (1). See notes to s. 418. For hovercraft, see *ibid.*

[1] See note (3) to s. 418. As to foreign ships, see note to s. 424.

OWNERS. The extent of an owner's obligation to obey the collision regulations was considered in *The Lady Gwendolen* [1964] 2 Lloyd's Rep. 99; [1965] 1 Lloyd's Rep. 335 (C.A.).

HER MAJESTY'S SHIPS. By reason of s. 741 the Collision Regulations do not apply to "ships belonging to Her Majesty," whether ships of war or ships employed in the service of any government department: *Young* v. *S.S. Scotia* [1903] A.C. 501. *The Cybele* (1878) 3 P.D. 8, in which a Ramsgate Harbour vessel vested in the Board of Trade was held not to be a ship belonging to H.M., was doubted in the last-mentioned case in [1903] A.C. at p. 505. But as all H.M. ships are subject to precisely similar regulations for navigation (" the Queen's Regulations and Admiralty Instructions," made by Order in Council), the exemption in s. 741 is now of little practical importance in this connection. Further, where an uncompleted aircraft carrier belonging to the Crown, but not yet commissioned, was involved in a collision, the court held that, although neither the Collision Regulations (1910) nor Q.R. and A.I. applied to her, the Collision Regulations nevertheless contained a standard of care to which those in charge of her should have conformed: *The Albion* [1953] P. 117 at pp. 117, 128. See also *British Shipping Laws* (Vol. 4), *Marsden on Collisions at Sea,* 11th ed., Chap. 24, §§ 650–653. For the effect of s. 741 in the case of a collision between an H.M. ship and a merchant ship before the repeal of s. 419 (4), *infra*, see *H.M.S. Sanspareil* [1900] P. 267 (C.A.), with which compare *The Hero* [1911] P. 128; affirmed [1912] A.C. 300.

TUG AND TOW. It had long been doubted whether the identity of tug and tow was a rule of law or a mere question of fact to be decided on the circumstances of each case, and the cases, though conflicting, seemed to point to the conclusion that a ship and her tow must be considered in the application of the Collision Regulations as one ship, and therefore that the fault of the one must be considered the fault of the other. See *The Mary Hounsell* (1879) 4 P.D. 204; *The Quickstep* (1890) 15 P.D. 196. But in 1912 the House of Lords decided that the question of identity of the tow with the tug is one of fact, not of law, and must be decided upon the particular circumstances and facts of each case: *S.S. Devonshire* [1912] A.C. 634. The question is of importance in deciding the rights and liabilities of the owners of the tow and of cargo laden therein. See *The Umona*

[1914] P. 141; and Maritime Conventions Act 1911, s. 1, *infra*, where the subject is more fully discussed.

[2] This subsection means that, for the purposes covered by the regulations, the lights (and fog signals) as prescribed must be used and no others. It does not prohibit lights required for safety by reason of the general provisions of Article 29 of the regulations (now rule 29 of the new regulations): *Thomas Stone Shipping Ltd.* v. *Admiralty and Others, The Albion* [1953] P. 117, 118, 130.

[3] As to punishment of misdemeanours, see s. 680.

[4] These words do not relieve the owner from liability for damage caused by the act of his servant: *The Seine* (1859) Swa. 411.

The statute was not intended to alter the relation between shipowners and shippers, but to regulate the rights of shipowners *inter se*, and subs. (3) does not render a breach of the regulations barratry unless it was intentional: *Grill* v. *General Iron Screw Collier Co.* (1866) L.R. 1 C.P. 600, 611; affirmed L.R. 3 C.P. 476.

313 [5] The statutory presumptions of fault for breach of Collision Regulations (s. 419 (4)) and for failure to stand by (s. 422 (2)) were abolished by the repeal of these subsections by the Maritime Conventions Act 1911, s. 4 (1) (2), as regards all actions of damage by collisions in which proceedings had been commenced since December 16, 1911, even though the events out of which the actions arose had taken place before that date: *The Enterprise* [1912] P. 207; and s. 9 (2), *ibid.*

Since 1873, when the presumption, in what was in effect its final form, was first introduced by M.S.A. 1873, s. 17, on proof of infringement of any of the Collision Regulations applicable in the circumstances (*The Khedive* (1880) 5 App.Cas. 876 at p. 901, and *The Fanny M. Carvill* (1875) 32 L.T. 646 (P.C.)), a presumption of culpability was raised as against the ship guilty of such infringement, which could not be met by proof that the non-observance of the rule *did not in fact* contribute to the collision; but only by proof (1) that the infringement *could* not by any possibility have contributed to it; *The Fanny M. Carvill* (1875), *supra* (approved in *The Duke of Buccleugh* [1891] A.C. 310; 65 L.T. 422); see also *The Khedive, supra* (*per* Lord Blackburn, 5 App.Cas. at p. 894, and Lord Watson at p. 901); *The Hochung, The Lapwing* (1882) 7 App.Cas. 512; *The Hibernia* (1874) 31 L.T. 803; 24 W.R. 60; *The Magnet* (1875) L.R. 4 A. & E. 417; *The Englishman* (1877) 3 P.D. 18; *The Glamorganshire* (1888) 13 App.Cas. 454; 59 L.T. 572; *The Argo* (1900) 82 L.T. 602; 9 Asp.M.L.C. 74; *The Hermod* (1890) 62 L.T. 670; 6 Asp.M.L.C. 509; or (2) that the circumstances made the departure from the regulations necessary: *The Memnon* (1889) 59 L.T. 289; 6 Asp.M.L.C. 317 (C.A.) (see especially *per* Lord Herschell, 62 L.T. at p. 85); *The Hibernia, supra*; *The Lovebird* (1881) 6 P.D. 80; 44 L.T. 650; see also *The Arklow* (1883) 9 App.Cas. 136; *The Tirzah* (1878) 4 P.D. 33.

Under the present law the question for the court is: " Did this want of obeying the regulations in any way contribute to the collision? " not " Might it possibly have done so? " *Per* Bargrave Deane J. in *The Enterprise* [1912] P. 207 at p. 211 (the first case under the new rule). This imposes on the court the duty of examining more closely the steps leading up to the collision, and, it would seem, applying more strictly the maxim, " *Causa proxima non remota spectatur*." The onus is upon the party alleging breach of the regulations to prove the breach and that it contributed to the collision and the resulting damage: *Owners of S.S. Heranger* v. *Owners of S.S. Diamond* [1939] A.C. 94.

As to the revived authority of decisions prior to 1863, when a special liability for breach was first imposed, and as to the applicability of cases decided on the repealed presumption of fault, see *British Shipping Laws* (Vol. 4), *Marsden on Collisions at Sea*, 11th ed., Chap. 23.

DAMAGES. Under the old rule of Admiralty, where both vessels were to blame for a collision (even if one of them was at fault only by virtue of the repealed statutory presumption, *The Hochung, The Lapwing* (1882) 51 L.J.P.C. 92; 7 A.C. 512; *The Khedive, supra*), each vessel would be entitled to recover half the amount of her loss from the other, and in practice this involved only one liability, *viz.* that of the lesser sufferer, to pay the difference of these halves to the greater sufferer. This rule was fundamentally altered by the Maritime Conventions Act 1911, s. 1, *post*, which empowered the court to divide the loss in proportion to the degree in which each vessel was in fault, the rule of equal moieties being applied only where it is not possible to establish different degrees of fault.

Again, under the old rule of Admiralty, where two vessels were found to blame, the owners of the cargo on one vessel could only recover half their loss from the other vessel. *The Milan* (1861) 31 L.J.Adm. 105; Lush. 388, followed and approved as being a rule of Admiralty within the meaning of the Judicature Act 1873, s. 25 (9), in *The Drumlanrig* [1911] A.C. 16. Now where under the provisions of the Maritime Conventions Act 1911, s. 1, the damages have been assessed in proportion to the degree of fault, the owners of the cargo in one vessel can recover from the second vessel a proportion of her damages equal to the degree of fault of the second vessel: *The Umona* [1914] P. 141. See also Maritime Conventions Act 1911, s. 1, *infra*, where the question is more fully discussed.

Inspection as to lights and fog signals

314 **420.**—(1) A surveyor of ships may inspect any ship, British or foreign, for the purpose of seeing that the ship is properly provided with lights and the means of making fog signals, in conformity with the collision regulations, and if the surveyor finds that the ship is not so provided, he shall give to the master or owner notice in writing, pointing out the deficiency, and also what is, in his opinion, requisite in order to remedy the same.

(2) Every notice so given shall be communicated in the manner directed by the [Department of Trade] to the chief officer of customs [1] at any port at which the ship may seek to obtain a clearance or transire; and the ship shall be detained,[2] until a certificate under the hand of a surveyor of ships is produced to the effect that the ship is properly provided with lights and with the means of making fog signals, in conformity with the collision regulations.

(3) For the purpose of an inspection under this section a surveyor shall have all the powers of a [Department of Trade] inspector under this Act.[3]

(4) Where the certificate as to lights and fog signals is refused, an owner may appeal to the court of survey for the port or district where the ship for the time being is in manner directed by the rules of that court.[4]

(5) On any such appeal the judge of the court of survey shall report [4] to the [Department of Trade] on the question raised by the appeal, and the [Department of Trade], when satisfied that the requirements of the report and of this Act as to lights and fog signals have been complied with, may grant, or direct a surveyor of ships or other person appointed by [the Secretary of State] to grant, the certificate.

(6) Subject to any order made by the judge of court of survey the costs of and incidental to the appeal shall follow the event.

(7) A surveyor in making an inspection under this section shall, if the owner of the ship so require, be accompanied on the inspection by some person appointed by the owner, and, if in that case the surveyor and the person so appointed agree, there shall be no appeal under this section to the court of survey.

(8) Such fees as the [Department of Trade] may determine shall be paid in respect of an inspection of lights and fog signals under this section *not exceeding those specified in the Sixteenth Schedule to this Act.*[5]

315 Safety Convention ships (including passenger steamers) not registered in the U.K. are exempted from the provisions of this section where accepted Safety Convention certificates in respect of such ships are produced; see M.S. (Safety Convention) Act 1949, s. 16 (1) (2).

1 For definition of " Chief Officer of Customs," see s. 742.

2 As to enforcement of detention, see s. 692.

3 See ss. 729, 730, as to powers of inspector.

[4] As to courts of survey and rules thereof, see ss. 487–489; as to exclusion of rights of appeal to other courts, see *Denny* v. *Board of Trade* (1880) 7 R. 1019; 17 S.L.R. 694, cited in note to s. 275.

[5] The words in italics were repealed by M.S. (Safety Convention) Act 1949, s. 37 (5) and Sched. III. For the fee currently in force, see M.S. (Fees) Regulations 1975 (S.I. No. 341).

Saving for local rules of navigation in harbours, etc.

316 **421.**—(1) Any rules made before or after the passing of this Act under the authority of any local Act,[1] concerning lights and signals to be carried, or the steps for avoiding collision to be taken, by vessels navigating the waters of any harbour, river, or other inland navigation, shall, notwithstanding anything in this Act, have full effect.[2]

(2) Where any such rules are not and cannot be made, Her Majesty in Council on the application of any person having authority over such waters,[3] or, if there is no such person, any person interested in the navigation thereof, may make such rules,[1] and those rules shall, as regards vessels navigating the said waters, be of the same force as if they were part of the collision regulations.[4]

317 This section is applied with certain modifications to seaplanes on the surface of the water by the Civil Aviation Act 1949, s. 52 (1). See note to s. 418.

[1] The local rules made either under local Acts or by Order in Council under this section are numerous and are constantly changing. A list of the rules at present in force is contained in Halsbury's *Laws of England*, 3rd ed., Vol. 35, pp. 868–873, where the numerous judicial decisions on the rules are also noted. See also the list printed in *British Shipping Laws* (Vol. 4), *Marsden on Collisions at Sea*, 11th ed., Chap. 28, § 991. The more important of these local rules will also be found set out in full in Chaps. 29–39 of *Marsden.*

Under s. 52 of the Harbours, Docks and Piers Clauses Act 1847 a harbour master may give directions for regulating the manner in which vessels are to enter or go out of the harbour or dock. The Swansea Rules have been made under this provision.

Collision regulations for the dockyard ports are contained in Orders made under Dockyard Ports Regulation Act 1865 (28 & 29 Vict. c. 125), and such regulations as regards Her Majesty's and other vessels have the same effect as if they had been regulations made under the Merchant Shipping Acts. See s. 7, *ibid.* For a list of those in force, see *British Shipping Laws* (Vol. 4), *Marsden on Collisions at Sea*, 11th ed., Chap. 28, § 992.

As to the saving of Orders in Council under this Act, see s. 745.

[2] The distinction between rules made under a local Act, which by subs. (1) are to " have full effect," and those made by Order in Council, which under subs. (2) are to be " of the same force as if they were part of the Collision Regulations," would appear now to be of no practical importance since the termination of the statutory presumption of fault in case of breach of Collision Regulations. See note (5) to s. 419, and *cf. The Harton* (1884) 9 P.D. 44.

[3] Subs. (2) is extended to and includes power to make collision regulations for the sea channels or approaches to the River Mersey between the Rock Lighthouse and the furthest point seawards to which such sea channels or approaches respectively are for the time being buoyed on both sides. Mersey Channels Act 1897, s. 2.

[4] See, *e.g. The Ripon* (1885) 10 P.D. 65 (Humber Rules); *The Talbot* [1891] P. 184 (Mersey Rules).

Duty of vessel to assist the other in case of collision

318 **422.**—(1) In every case of collision between two vessels,[1] it shall be the duty of the master or person in charge[2] of each vessel, if and so far as he can do so without danger to his own vessel, crew, and passengers (if any)[3]—

(*a*) to render to the other vessel, her master, crew, and passengers (if any) such assistance as may be practicable, and may be necessary to save them from any danger caused by the collision, and to stay by the other vessel until he has ascertained that she has no need of further assistance,[4] and also

(*b*) to give to the master or person in charge of the other vessel the name of his own vessel and of the port to which she belongs, and also the names of the ports from which she comes and to which she is bound.

(2) *If the master or person in charge of a vessel fails to comply with this section, and no reasonable cause for such failure is shown, the collision shall, in the absence of proof to the contrary, be deemed to have been caused by his wrongful act, neglect, or default.*[5]

(3) If the master or person in charge fails without reasonable cause to comply with this section, he shall be guilty of a misdemeanour,[6] and, if he is a certificated officer, an inquiry into his conduct may be held, and his certificate cancelled or suspended.[6]

319 SALVAGE. The question whether the statutory obligation to stand by after collision debars salvage claims is discussed in Kennedy, *Civil Salvage*, 4th ed., pp. 30–31. The general rule would seem to be (1) that where the ship standing by is in no way to blame, she may rank as salvor if her services are really of the nature of salvage: *The Hannibal* and *The Queen* (1867) L.R. 2 A. & E. 53; approved in *Melanie* (*Owners*) v. *San Onofre* (*Owners*) [1925] A.C. 246; *The Beta* (1884) 5 Asp.M.L.C. 276; (2) where she has been wholly or in part to blame, no claim can be entertained for salvage services rendered: *Cargo ex Capella* (1867) L.R. 1 A. & E. 356; *The Glengaber* (1872) L.R. 3 A. & E. 534; *Duc d'Aumale* [1904] P. 60 (collision between tug and tow); *Beaverford* v. *The Kafiristan* [1938] A.C. 136.

[1] It should be noted that in s. 419 the term " ships " is used. As to what vessels are included in the term " ships," see definition of " ship " in s. 742 and note (4) thereto. *Ex p. Ferguson*, there cited, was decided under M.S.A. 1862, s. 33 (corresponding to 1894, s. 422), in which the term " ships " was used. The wider term " vessels " was substituted in 36 & 37 Vict. c. 85, s. 16, so as to apply s. 422 to collisions both in the sea and in harbours, rivers and other navigable waters. See ss. 418, 421. As to foreign ships, see s. 424 and notes thereto. As to H.M. ships, see s. 419, note (1).

[2] The words " master or " were first introduced in the Act of 1873; but the change does not appear to render the following decisions under the prior Act (1862, s. 33), inapplicable:

While the master is below, the duty to stand by is on the mate or other person in charge of the deck: *Ex p. Ferguson* (1871) L.R. 6 Q.B. 280.

But it seems that a compulsory pilot is not a " person in charge " within this section, and that the fact of his being on board does not of itself relieve the master or mate or other person in charge from the duty of rendering assistance: *The Queen* (1869) L.R. 2 A. & E. 354.

It seems that the statute makes it the duty of a tug to stand by and assist a vessel which has collided with the tug's tow: *The Hannibal* and *The Queen* (1867) L.R. 2 A. & E. 53. But this does not affect such tug's right, if any, to salvage reward or towage remuneration for services thus rendered: *Ibid.* and *The Harvest Home* [1904] P. 409 at p. 421.

[3] A vessel, unable actually to stay by the injured vessel, was held at fault for not lowering a boat, in *The Adriatic* (1875) 33 L.T. 102; 3 Asp.M.L.C. 16; and for not answering signals of distress, in *The Emmy Haase* (1884) 9 P.D. 81. See also (under the provisions of M.S.A. 1862), *The Queen of the Orwell* (1863) 7 L.T. 839; 11 W.R. 499. See also the duty to go to the assistance of a vessel in distress on receipt of a signal, M.S. (Safety Convention) Act 1949, s. 22.

[4] Failure to stand by has been excused where there was imminent risk of capture by the enemy: *The Thuringia* (1872) 1 Asp.M.L.C. 283; 41 L.J.P. 44. And where a steam trawler fouled her nets in attempting to avoid collision, *The Pitgavering* [1910] P. 215. See also

The Tryst [1909] P. 333, 342; *The Kirkwall* (1909) 100 L.T. 284 (C.A.); *The Effra* (1936) 55 Ll.L.R. 362.

[5] The words in italics were repealed by the Maritime Conventions Act 1911, s. 4 (2), *post*. The effect of the repeal of this statutory presumption of fault, together with that contained in s. 419 (4), is discussed above in note (5) to s. 419.

[6] As to the punishment of offences, see s. 680; and as to cancelling, etc., of certificates, see M.S.A. 1970, ss. 52 (1) (*c*) and 101 (4).

320 **423.** [*This section* (*Collisions to be entered in official log*) *was repealed by M.S.A.* 1970, *s.* 100 (3), *Sched. V as from January* 1, 1973: *see S.I.* 1972 *No.* 1977. *See now ibid. s.* 68 (§ 1439, *post*).]

Application of collision regulations to foreign ships

321 **424.** Whenever it is made to appear to Her Majesty in Council that the Government of any foreign country is willing that the collision regulations, or the provisions of this Part of this Act relating thereto or otherwise relating to collisions, or any of those regulations or provisions should apply to the ships of that country when beyond the limits of British jurisdiction,[1] Her Majesty may, by Order in Council, direct that those regulations and provisions shall, subject to any limitation of time, conditions and qualifications contained in the Order, apply to the ships of the said foreign country, whether within British jurisdiction or not, and that such ships shall for the purposes of such regulations and provisions be treated as if they were British ships.[2]

322 This section is applied (with certain modifications) to seaplanes on the surface of the water by the Civil Aviation Act 1949, s. 52 (1).

[1] When within British jurisdiction all foreign ships are subject to the collision regulations. See s. 418 (2).

[2] As from September 1, 1965, the new Collision Regulations (see note to s. 418) which came into force on that date, were applied to ships of the following foreign countries (*i.e.* being countries which have accepted the International Collision Regulations of 1960): Belgium, Burma, Cameroon, Denmark, Finland, France, Greece, Iceland, Israel, Kuwait, Japan, Liberia, Madagascar, Morocco, Netherlands, Norway, Paraguay, Peru, Philippines, Poland, Portugal, Roumania, Spain, Sweden, U.S.S.R., United Arab Republic, United States, Vietnam, Yugoslavia. (See Collision Regulations (Ships and Seaplanes on the Water) and Signals of Distress (Ships) Order, 1965 (S.I. No. 1525).)
The Collision Regulations of 1965, are printed in *British Shipping Laws* (Vol. 4), *Marsden on Collisions at Sea*, 11th ed. at § 990/2 *et seq*.

Report of Accidents and Loss of Ship

Report to [Secretary of State] of accidents to steamships

323 **425–426.** [*These sections* (*Reports to Dept. of Trade of accidents to steamships and Notices of Loss of British Ship to be given to the Dept. of Trade*) *were repealed by M.S.A.* 1970, *s.* 100 (3) *Sched. V*, *as from January* 1, 1973, *see S.I.* 1972 *No.* 1977.]

Life-saving Appliances

324 S. 427 as originally enacted was extended to apply to foreign ships in U.K. ports which they had entered for ordinary commercial purposes by M.S.A. 1906, ss. 4 and 6. Subsequently, by M.S. (Safety and Load Line Conventions) Act 1932, s. 5 (1), the scope of the

rule-making power in the section was widened to include additional matters with respect to which rules could be made, and finally by M.S. (Safety Conventions) Act 1949, s. 2, a new section 427 (which is here printed below in the text) was substituted, which consolidated the earlier amendments and made further modifications.

Rules as to life-saving appliances

325 [**427.**[1]—(1) The Department of Trade may, in relation to any ships to which this section applies, make rules [2] (in this Act called " rules for life-saving appliances ") with respect to all or any of the following matters, namely:

(*a*) the arranging of ships into classes, having regard to the services in which they are employed, to the nature and duration of the voyage, and to the number of persons carried;

(*b*) the number, description, and mode of construction of the boats, life rafts, line-throwing appliances, life-jackets, and lifebuoys to be carried by ships, according to the classes in which the ships are arranged;

(*c*) the equipment to be carried by any such boats and rafts and the methods to be provided to get the boats and other life-saving appliances into the water, including oil for use in stormy weather;

(*d*) the provision in ships of a proper supply of lights inextinguishable in water, and fitted for attachment to lifebuoys;

(*e*) the quantity, quality and description of buoyant apparatus to be carried on board ships *carrying passengers*,[3] either in addition to or in substitution for boats, life rafts, life-jackets and lifebuoys;

(*f*) the position and means of securing the boats, life rafts, life-jackets, lifebuoys and buoyant apparatus;

(*g*) the marking of the boats, life rafts, and buoyant apparatus so as to show their dimensions and the number of persons authorised to be carried on them;

(*h*) the manning of the lifeboats and the qualifications and certificates of lifeboat men;

(*j*) the provision to be made for mustering the persons on board, and for embarking them in the boats (including provision for the lighting of, and the means of ingress to and egress from, different parts of the ship);

(*k*) the provision of suitable means situated outside the engine-room whereby any discharge of water into the boats can be prevented;

(*l*) the assignment of specific duties to each member of the crew in the event of emergency;

(*m*) the methods to be adopted and the appliances to be carried in ships for the prevention, detection and extinction of fire;

(*mm*) the provision in ships of plans or other information relating to

325

the means of preventing, detecting, controlling and extinguishing outbreaks of fire[4];

(*n*) the practice in ships of boat-drills and fire-drills;

(*o*) the provision in ships of means of making effective distress-signals by day and by night;

(*p*) the provision, in ships engaged on voyages in which pilots are likely to be embarked, of suitable pilot-ladders, and of ropes, lights and other appliances designed to make the use of such ladders safe, and

(*q*) the examination [and maintenance] [4] at intervals to be prescribed by the rules of any appliances or equipment required by the rules to be carried.

326 (2) This section applies to—

(*a*) British ships,[5] except ships registered in a Dominion within the meaning of the Statute of Westminster 1931, or in India, Pakistan [Ceylon, Ghana, Malaysia, the Republic of Cyprus, Nigeria, Sierra Leone, Tanganyika, Jamaica, Trinidad and Tobago, Uganda, Kenya, Zanzibar, Malawi, Malta, The Gambia, Guyana, Barbados, Singapore, Mauritius, and Fiji] [6] or in any territory administered by Her Majesty's government in any such Dominion;

(*b*) other ships while they are within any port in the United Kingdom:

Provided that this section shall not apply to a ship by reason of her being within a port in the United Kingdom if she would not have been in any such port but for stress of weather or any other circumstance that neither the master nor the owner nor the charterer (if any) of the ship could have prevented or forestalled.]

327 [1] The text gives the new section substituted by s. 2 (1) of the M.S. (Safety Convention) Act 1949, *post*, involving modifications of and additions to the section as originally enacted. See note above.

[2] The rules at present in force are the M.S. (Fire Appliances) Rules 1965, S.I. No. 1106, as amended by S.I. 1974 No. 2185 and S.I. 1975 No. 330, the M.S. (Musters) Rules 1965, No. 1113 as amended by S.I. 1974 No. 2185 and S.I. 1975 No. 330, the M.S. (Pilots Orders) Rules 1965, S.I. No. 1046 as amended by S.I. 1972 No. 531, the M.S. (Life-Saving Appliances) Rules 1965, S.I. No. 1105, as amended by S.I. 1966 No. 744, S.I. 1969 No. 409 and S.I. 1975 No. 330, and the Fishing Vessels (Safety Provisions) Rules 1975 (S.I. No. 330). Because of their length, it is not practicable to print the text of these rules in an Appendix to this edition.

Safety Convention ships (including passenger steamers) not registered in the United Kingdom, are exempt from the rules for life-saving appliances, where accepted Safety Convention certificates in respect of such ships are produced; see M.S. (Safety Convention) Act 1949, s. 16 (1) (2).

[3] The words in italics were repealed by the M.S.A. 1964, s. 9 (*a*).

[4] The words in brackets were added by M.S.A. 1964, s. 9 (*b*).

[5] For meaning of "British ships," see s. 1 and note thereto.

[6] The words within square brackets represent the result of several amendments to this section. "Ceylon" was referred to in the original text of s. 2 (1) of M.S. (Safety Convention) Act 1949. References to the other countries have been added successively by

the Ghana Independence Act 1957, s. 4 (4), Sched. II, para. 7; the Federation of Malaya Independence Act 1957, s. 2 (1), Sched. I, para. 10 (*a*) as modified by the Malaysia Act 1963, s. 3 (2), Sched. II, para. 10 (1); the Cyprus Act 1960, s. 3 (2), Sched., para. 10 (1); the Nigeria Independence Act 1960, s. 3 (4), Sched. II, para. 7; the Sierra Leone Independence Act 1961, s. 3 (3), Sched. III, para. 8; the Tanganyika Independence Act 1961, s. 3 (4), Sched. II, para. 7; the Jamaica Independence Act 1962, s. 3 (5), Sched. II, para. 7; the Trinidad and Tobago Independence Act 1962, s. 3 (4), Sched. II, para. 7; the Uganda Independence Act 1962, s. 3 (4), Sched. III, para. 7; the Kenya Independence Act 1963, s. 4 (4), Sched. II, para. 7; the Zanzibar Act 1963, s. 1 (2), Sched. I, Part I, para. 8 (2); the Malawi Independence Act 1964, s. 4 (4), Sched. II, para. 7; the Malta Independence Act 1964, s. 4 (4), Sched. II, para. 7; the Gambia Independence Act 1964 s. 4 (4), Sched. II, para. 7; the Singapore Act 1966, s. 1 (2), Sched. para. 10; the Guyana Independence Act 1966, s. 5 (4), Sched. II, para. 7; the Barbados Independence Act 1966, s. 4 (5), Sched. II, para. 7; the Mauritius Independence Act 1968, s. 4 (3), Sched. II, para. 7; the Fiji Independence Act 1970, s. 4 (3), Sched. II, para. 6.

Duties of owners and masters as to carrying life-saving appliances

328 **428.** It shall be the duty of the owner and master of every British ship to see that his ship is provided, in accordance with the rules for life-saving appliances,[1] with such of those appliances as, having regard to the nature of the service on which the ship is employed, and the avoidance of undue encumbrance of the ship's deck, are best adapted for securing the safety of her crew and passengers.

[1] See s. 427 and notes thereto.

Appointment of consultative committee for framing rules

329 **429.**—(1) For the purpose of preparing and advising on the rules for life-saving appliances, the [Department of Trade] may appoint a committee, the members of which shall be nominated by the [Department] in accordance with the Seventeenth Schedule to this Act.

(2) A member of the committee shall hold office for two years from the date of his appointment, but shall be eligible for re-appointment.

(3) There shall be paid to the members of the committee, out of the Mercantile Marine Fund,[1] such travelling and other allowances as the [Department of Trade] may fix.

(4) Her Majesty may, by Order in Council, alter the Seventeenth Schedule to this Act.[2]

For rules as to life-saving appliances now in force, see notes to s. 427

[1] Now out of moneys provided by Parliament see M.S. (Mercantile Marine Fund) Act 1898, s. 1 (*b*).

[2] This power has not so far been exercised.

Penalty for breach of rules

330 **430.**[1]—(1) In the case of any ship—

(*a*) if the ship is required by the rules for life-saving appliances [1] to be provided with such appliances and proceeds on any voyage [2] or excursion without being so provided in accordance with the rules applicable to the ship; or

(*b*) if any of the appliances with which the ship is so provided are lost or rendered unfit for service in the course of the voyage or excursion through the wilful fault or negligence of the owner or master [3]; or

(*c*) if the master wilfully neglects to replace or repair on the first opportunity any such appliances lost or injured in the course of the voyage or excursion; or

(*d*) if such appliances are not kept so as to be at all times fit and ready for use;

[(*e*) if any provision of the rules for life-saving appliances applicable to the ship is contravened or not complied with [4];]

then the owner of the ship (if in fault) shall for each offence be liable to a fine not exceeding one hundred pounds, and the master of the ship (if in fault) shall for each offence be liable to a fine not exceeding fifty pounds.

(2) Nothing in the foregoing enactments with respect to life-saving appliances shall prevent any person from being liable under any other provision of this Act, or otherwise, to any other or higher fine or punishment than is provided by those enactments, provided that a person shall not be punished twice for the same offence.

(3) If the court before whom a person is charged with an offence punishable under those enactments thinks that proceedings ought to be taken against him for the offence under any other provision of this Act, or otherwise, the court may adjourn the case to enable such proceedings to be taken.

[1] For the rules at present in force, see notes to s. 427.
[2] In *Genochio* v. *Steward* (1909) 100 L.T. 525, the C.A. held that a vessel going from the River Ouse at King's Lynn to Lynn Roads to lighter a vessel was "proceeding on a voyage."
[3] As to duty to keep records of boat-drills, fire-drills and inspections of life-saving appliances, see M.S.A. 1970, s. 68 (2).
[4] The new sub-paragraph (*e*) was added by s. 5 (2) of the M.S. (Safety and Load Line Conventions) Act 1932.

Survey of ship with respect to life-saving appliances

331 [**431.**[1]—(1) A surveyor of ships [2] may inspect [3] any ship for the purpose of seeing that the rules for life-saving appliances [4] have been complied with in her case, and for the purpose of any such inspection shall have all the powers of a [Department of Trade] inspector under this Act.[5]

(2) If the surveyor finds that the rules for life-saving appliances [4] have not been complied with, he shall give written notice to the owner or master stating in what respect the said rules have not been complied with, and what, in his opinion, is required to rectify the matter.

(3) Every notice so given shall be communicated in manner directed by the [Department of Trade] to the Chief Officer of Customs [6] of any port at which the ship may seek to obtain a clearance or transire, and a clearance or transire shall not be granted to the ship and the ship shall be detained [7] until a certificate under the hand of a surveyor of ships is produced to the effect that the matter has been rectified.]

332 [1] The text gives the new section substituted by s. 5 (3) of the M.S. (Safety and Load Line Conventions) Act 1932, involving certain modifications of the section as originally enacted.

[2] See ss. 724 *et seq.*, and M.S.A. 1906, s. 75 as to appointment, powers, etc., of surveyors.

[3] As to fees for inspection of life-saving appliances, see the Fees (Increase) Act 1923, s. 2 (3), and notes thereto, *post*. For the fees presently in force, see M.S. (Fees) Regulations 1975 (S.I. No. 341).

[4] For the rules at present in force, see note at end of s. 427.

[5] See ss. 729, 730, as to powers of inspectors.

[6] For definition of " Chief Officer of Customs," see s. 742.

[7] See s. 692 as to detention of ship.

General Equipment

Adjustment of compasses and provision of hose

333 **432.**—(1) Every British sea-going [1] steamship,[2] if employed to carry passengers,[3] shall have her compasses properly adjusted from time to time; and every British sea-going steamship not used wholly as a tug shall be provided with a hose capable of being connected with the engines of the ship, and adapted for extinguishing fire in any part of the ship.

(2) If any such British sea-going steamship plies [1] or goes to sea from any port in the United Kingdom and any requirement of this section is not complied with, then for each matter in which default is made, the owner (if in fault) shall be liable to a fine not exceeding one hundred pounds, and the master (if in fault) shall be liable to a fine not exceeding fifty pounds.

[1] See, as to the meaning of " plies," note to s. 267.

[2] See s. 743 as to application to ships propelled by electricity, etc.

[3] See s. 285: vessels not carrying passengers are apparently not required to have their compasses adjusted.

Placing undue weight on safety valve

334 **433.** A person shall not place an undue weight on the safety valve of any steamship, and if he does so he shall, in addition to any other liability he may incur by so doing, be liable for each offence to a fine not exceeding one hundred pounds.

As to safety valves of passenger steamers, see ss. 272 (4) (*d*), 286.

Signals of Distress

335 **434.** [*This section, which dealt with signals of distress, was repealed, and re-enacted with modifications and extensions, by section* 25 *of the M.S.* (*Safety and Load Line Conventions*) *Act* 1932, *which latter section was repealed by M.S.* (*Safety Convention*) *Act* 1949, *and re-enacted with modifications by section* 21 *of that Act* (*see section* 21 *of the* 1949 *Act and the notes thereto*).]

336 **435.** [*This section, which dealt with the provision of signals of distress, inextinguishable lights, and lifebuoys, was repealed by M.S.* (*Safety Convention*) *Act* 1949. *The matter is now dealt with by paras.* (*d*) *and* (*o*) *of*

M.S.A. 1894, *s.* 427, *and by the rules made under that section. See* ante, §§ 325–326.]

Draught of Water and Load-Line

Ship's draught of water to be recorded

337 **436.**—(1) The [Dept. of Trade] may, in any case or class of cases in which [it thinks] it expedient to do so, direct any person appointed by [it] for the purpose, to record, in such manner and with such particulars as [it directs], the draught of water of any sea-going [1] ship, as shown on the scale of feet on her stem and stern post,[2] and the extent of her [freeboard [3]] in feet and inches, upon her leaving any dock, wharf, port, or harbour for the purpose of proceeding to sea, and the person so appointed shall thereupon keep that record, and shall forward a copy thereof to the [Department of Trade].

(2) That record or copy, if produced out of the custody of the [Department of Trade] shall be admissible in evidence in manner provided by this Act.[4]

(3) *The master of every British sea-going ship shall, upon her leaving any dock, wharf, port, or harbour for the purpose of proceeding to sea, record her draught of water and the extent of her* [*freeboard* [3]] *in the official log book (if any), and shall produce the record to any chief officer of customs whenever required by him, and if he fails without reasonable cause to produce the record shall for each offence be liable to a fine not exceeding twenty pounds.*[5]

(4) The master of a sea-going ship shall,[6] upon the request of any person appointed to record the ship's draught of water, permit that person to enter the ship and to make such inspections and take such measurements as may be requisite for the purpose of the record; and if any master fail to do so, or impedes, or suffers anyone under his control to impede, any person so appointed in the execution of his duty, he shall for each offence be liable to a fine not exceeding five pounds.

(5) [In this section the expression " freeboard " means, in the case of any ship which is marked with a deck-line, the height from the water to the upper edge of the deck-line, and, in the case of any other ship, the height amidships from the water to the upper edge of the deck from which the depth of hold as stated in the register is measured.[7]]

338 [1] For the meaning of " sea-going," see note (1) to M.S.A. 1970, s. 96.

[2] A ship's draught is marked on her stem and stern under s. 7 (1) (*c*).

[3] The word " freeboard " was substituted for " clear side " by s. 62 (1) of the M.S. (Safety and Load Line Conventions) Act 1932.

[4] See s. 695 as to admissibility.

[5] The words in italics were repealed by the M.S.A. 1970, s. 100 (3), Sched. V as from January 1, 1973: see S.I. 1972 No. 1977.

[6] As to declaration by master as to draught of ship on request of pilot, see Pilotage Act 1913, s. 31, *post*.

[7] The new subs. (5) was substituted by s. 62 (3) of the M.S. (Safety and Load Line Conventions) Act 1932.

339 **437–445.** [*These sections were repealed by the M.S.* (*Safety and Load Line Conventions*) *Act* 1932, *section* 67 (2) *and* 4*th Schedule, Part II. They related to the marking of deck-lines and load lines and regulations and penalties in connection therewith. These matters are now dealt with by Part II of the M.S.* (*Safety and Load Line Conventions*) *Act* 1932. *As to the Orders in Council made under the repealed sections* 444 *and* 445, *see section* 67 (2) *of that Act, and notes* (4) *and* (5) *thereto. These orders in Council are preserved in force with a limited effect.*]

Dangerous Goods

340 The operation of these sections, *viz.*: ss. 446–450 dealing with dangerous goods, is unaffected by the Carriage of Goods by Sea Act 1924, the schedule of which by Art. IV, Rule 6, contains certain provisions as to power of the master in dealing with dangerous goods. See *ibid.* s. 6 (2) and note to s. 448. That Act is prospectively repealed by the Carriage of Goods by Sea Act 1971, s. 6 (3), (5). The M.S. (Safety Convention) Act 1949, s. 23, contains further provisions relating to the carriage of dangerous goods on certain ships. See *post*, and see also note at head of s. 418.

Restrictions on carriage of dangerous goods

341 **446.**—(1) A person shall not send or attempt to send by any vessel, British or foreign, and a person not being the master or owner of the vessel, shall not carry or attempt to carry in any such vessel, any dangerous goods,[1] without distinctly marking their nature on the outside of the package [2] containing the same, and giving written notice of the nature of those goods and of the name and address of the sender or carrier thereof to the master or owner of the vessel at or before the time of sending the same to be shipped or taking the same on board the vessel.

(2) If any person fails without reasonable cause to comply with this section, he shall for each offence be liable to a fine not exceeding one hundred pounds; or if he shows that he was merely an agent in the shipment of any such goods as aforesaid, and was not aware and did not suspect and had no reason to suspect that the goods shipped by him were of a dangerous nature, then not exceeding ten pounds.

(3) For the purpose of this Part of this Act the expression " dangerous goods " means aquafortis, vitriol, naphtha, benzine, gun-powder, lucifer matches, nitro-glycerine, petroleum,[3] any explosives within the meaning of the Explosives Act 1875, and any other goods which are of a dangerous nature.[4]

342 [1] For definition of " dangerous goods," see subs. (3). For the purposes of Part V of the 1894 Act (which includes s. 446) " dangerous goods " also include any goods declared by rules made under s. 23 of the 1949 Act to be dangerous in their nature. See s. 23 (4) of the 1949 Act and the M.S. (Dangerous Goods) Rules 1965 S.I. No. 1067, as amended by S.I. 1968 No. 332 and S.I. 1972 No. 666. As to the common law liability of the shipper of dangerous goods towards the shipowner and the owners of other goods on board, see *British Shipping Laws* (Vol. 3), *Carver on Carriage by Sea* (12th ed.), Chap. 11, § 689, and *Scrutton on Charterparties and Bills of Lading* (18th ed.), Art. 50 at p. 100, *et seq.* See also *Brass* v. *Maitland* (1856) 6 E. & B. 470; 26 L.J.Q.B. 49; *Hutchinson* v. *Guion* (1858) 5 C.B.(N.S.) 149; 28 L.J.C.P. 63; *Farrant* v. *Barnes* (1862) 11 C.B.(N.S.) 553; 31

L.J.C.P. 137; *Bamfield* v. *Goole, etc. Transport Co.* [1910] 2 K.B. 94; *Mitchell, Cotts & Co.* v. *Steel Bros.* [1916] 2 K.B. 610 (goods dangerous as causing legal embargo). See, too, Carriage of Goods by Sea Act 1924, Sched., Art. IV, Rule 6, cited in note to s. 448.

[2] A motor car containing petrol in its tank has been held to be a "package containing" dangerous goods within this section: *L.N.W. Ry.* v. *Farey* (1920) 5 Ll.L.R. 90 (November 4, Ir.K.B.D.).

[3] The Petroleum (Consolidation) Act 1928, provides (ss. 7 and 9) for the making of by-laws as to the loading of ships with petroleum spirit and generally as to the precautions to be observed with respect to ships carrying petroleum spirit whilst in harbours and canals; (s. 8) for the notification by masters of ships carrying petroleum spirit and entering harbours within Great Britain of the nature of their cargo; and (s. 13) for the notification by masters of any accident causing loss of life or personal injury in connection with the carriage of petroleum spirit in any ship. "Petroleum" and "petroleum spirit" are defined by s. 23, *ibid.*

The Prevention of Oil Pollution Act 1971, also contains provisions restricting the discharge or escape of oil into navigable waters; see § 1531 *et seq.*, *post.*

[4] See note (1) above.

Penalty for misdescription of dangerous goods

343 **447.** A person shall not knowingly send or attempt to send by, or carry or attempt to carry in, any vessel, British or foreign, any dangerous goods under a false description, and shall not falsely describe the sender or carrier thereof, and if he act in contravention of this section he shall for each offence be liable to a fine not exceeding five hundred pounds.

Power to deal with goods suspected of being dangerous

344 **448.**—(1) The master or owner of any vessel, British or foreign, may refuse to take on board any package or parcel which he suspects to contain any dangerous goods, and may require it to be opened to ascertain the fact.

(2) Where any dangerous goods, or any goods, which, in the judgment of the master or owner of the vessel, are dangerous goods, have been sent or brought aboard any vessel, British or foreign, without being marked as aforesaid, or without such notice having been given as aforesaid, the master or owner of the vessel may cause those goods to be thrown overboard, together with any package or receptacle in which they are contained; and neither the master nor the owner of the vessel shall be subject to any liability, civil or criminal, in any court for so throwing the goods overboard.

345 In the case of goods carried under contracts which fall within the provisions of the Carriage of Goods by Sea Act 1924, the master has certain additional powers conferred on him by Art. IV, Rule 6, in the Schedule to the Act, which provides as follows: "Goods of an inflammable, explosive or dangerous nature to the shipment whereof the carrier, master or agent of the carrier, has not consented with knowledge of their nature and character, may at any time before discharge be landed at any place or destroyed or rendered innocuous by the carrier without compensation, and the shipper of such goods shall be liable for all damages and expenses directly or indirectly arising out of or resulting from such shipment.

"If any such goods shipped with such knowledge and consent shall become a danger to the ship and cargo they may in like manner be landed at any place or destroyed or rendered innocuous by the carrier without liability on the part of the carrier except to general average, if any."

Forfeiture of dangerous goods improperly sent or carried

346 **449.**—(1) Where any dangerous goods have been sent or carried, or attempted to be sent or carried, on board any vessel, British or foreign, without being marked as aforesaid, or without such notice having been given as aforesaid, or under a false description, or with a false description of the sender or carrier thereof, any court having Admiralty jurisdiction[1] may declare those goods, and any package or receptacle in which they are contained, to be, and they shall thereupon be, forfeited,[2] and when forfeited shall be disposed of as the court direct.

(2) The court shall have, and may exercise, the aforesaid powers of forfeiture and disposal notwithstanding that the owner of the goods has not committed any offence under the provisions of this Act relating to dangerous goods, and is not before the court, and has not notice of the proceedings, and notwithstanding that there is no evidence to show to whom the goods belong; nevertheless the court may, in their discretion, require such notice as they may direct to be given to the owner or shipper of the goods before they are forfeited.

[1] For the jurisdiction of the High Court, see Administration of Justice Act, 1956, s. 1 (1) (*s*). This matter is assigned to the Queen's Bench Division (Admiralty Court); see R.S.C. Ord. 74, r. 1. It is doubtful whether a claim for forfeiture under this section can be brought in a county court; see County Courts Act 1959, s. 56.

[2] *Cf.* s. 70, note (3), as to forfeiture.

Saving for other enactments relating to dangerous goods

347 **450.** The provisions of this Part of this Act relating to the carriage of dangerous goods shall be deemed to be in addition to and not in substitution for, or in restraint of, any other enactment for the like object, so nevertheless that nothing in the said provisions shall be deemed to authorise any person to be sued or prosecuted twice in the same matter.

See, *e.g.* the Explosives Act 1875, s. 33 *et seq.*; Explosive Substances Act 1883, s. 8. The operation of ss. 446–450 is expressly saved by the Carriage of Goods by Sea Act 1924, s. 6 (2).

Loading of Timber

348 **451.** [*This section, which contained provisions limiting the carriage of wood goods on deck during certain winter voyages, was repealed by the M.S.A.* 1906, *s.* 85, *Sched. II, and the subject-matter of the repealed section was then dealt with by section* 10 *of the M.S.A.* 1906. *That section was then repealed by M.S.* (*Safety and Load Line Conventions*) *Act* 1932, *Sched. IV, Part II, and the present provisions regarding loading of timber are contained in section* 61 *of that Act. See also note* (2) *to section* 61 *of that Act, for the Timber Cargo Regulations now in force.*]

Carriage of Grain

349 **452–456.** [*These sections which dealt with the carriage of grain were repealed by M.S.* (*Safety Convention*) *Act* 1949, *and their provisions were*

re-enacted with modifications by section 24 *of that Act. See section* 24 *of that Act, and notes thereto*, post.]

Unseaworthy Ships

As to unsafe lighters, barges, etc., see M.S.A. 1921, s. 2.

Sending unseaworthy ship to sea a misdemeanor

350 **457.**—(1) If any person sends or attempts to send, or is party to sending or attempting to send,[1] a British ship to sea in such an unseaworthy [2] state that the life of any person is likely to be thereby endangered, he shall in respect of each offence be guilty of a misdemeanor, unless he proves either that he used all reasonable means to insure her being sent to sea in a seaworthy state, or that her going to sea in such an unseaworthy state was, under the circumstances, reasonable and justifiable, and for the purpose of giving that proof he may give evidence [3] in the same manner as any other witness.

(2) If the master of a British ship knowingly takes the same to sea in such an unseaworthy state that the life of any person is likely to be thereby endangered, he shall in respect of each offence be guilty of a misdemeanor, unless he proves that her going to sea in such an unseaworthy state was, under the circumstances, reasonable and justifiable, and for the purpose of giving such proof he may give evidence [3] in the same manner as any other witness.

(3) A prosecution under this section shall not, except in Scotland, be instituted otherwise than by, or with the consent of, the [Department of Trade], or of the governor of the British possession in which the prosecution takes place.

(4) A misdemeanor under this section shall not be punishable upon summary conviction.[4]

(5) This section shall not apply to any ship employed exclusively in trading or going from place to place in any river or inland water of which the whole or part is in any British possession.

351 [1] Subs. (1). Under the similar enactment of 34 & 35 Vict. c. 110, s. 11, it was held that the offence was the " sending," and not the " knowingly sending," a ship to sea in an unseaworthy state, and that the indictment need not aver that the accused knew the ship to be in an unseaworthy state, nor contain averments negativing the use of reasonable means to make and keep the ship seaworthy: *R.* v. *Freeman* (1875) 9 I.R.C.L. 527.
[2] *Cf.* note to s. 458, " seaworthy," and note (2) to s. 459.
[3] *Cf.* Criminal Evidence Act 1898, which now allows defendants in criminal cases generally to give evidence. See *ibid.* s. 1.
[4] See s. 680 *et seq.* as to summary procedure.

Obligation of shipowner to crew with respect to use of reasonable efforts to secure seaworthiness

352 **458.**—(1) In every contract of service,[1] express or implied, between the owner of a ship and the master or any seaman thereof, *and in every*

8—S.M.T

instrument of apprenticeship whereby any person is bound to serve as an apprentice on board any ship,[2] there shall be implied, notwithstanding any agreement to the contrary, an obligation on the owner of the ship, that the owner of the ship, and the master, and every agent charged with the loading of the ship, or the preparing of the ship for sea, or the sending of the ship to sea, shall use all reasonable means to insure the seaworthiness [3] of the ship for the voyage at the time when the voyage commences and to keep her in a seaworthy condition for the voyage during the voyage.

(2) Nothing in this section—

(*a*) shall subject the owner of a ship to any liability by reason of the ship being sent to sea in an unseaworthy state where, owing to special circumstances, the sending of the ship to sea in such a state was reasonable and justifiable; or

(*b*) shall apply to any ship employed exclusively in trading or going from place to place in any river or inland water of which the whole or part is in any British possession.

353 [1] For agreements with the crew, see M.S.A. 1970, s. 1. See also *ibid.* ss. 6 and 51.

[2] The words in italics were repealed by M.S.A. 1970, s. 100 (3), Sched. V as from January 1, 1973, see S.I. 1972 No. 1972.

[3] At common law there is no implied warranty of seaworthiness by the owner *qua* the seaman's contract of service: *Couch* v. *Steele* (1853) 23 L.J.Q.B. 121; 3 E. & B. 402 cited in note (8) to s. 200. But the effect of this section, it is submitted, is to import into such contract the implied obligation defined in the section, a breach of which causing injury to the master or seaman would give rise to a claim for damages, such implied obligation taking the place of any other obligation which would be implied at common law arising from the relationship of master and servant.

In *Waddle* v. *Wallsend Shipping Co. Ltd.* [1952] 2 Lloyd's Rep. 105, Devlin J. at p. 129 held that this section being designed " to benefit the seaman and to enable him to escape some of the more drastic consequences of the doctrine of common employment " could since the abolition of that doctrine by the Law Reform (Personal Injuries) Act 1948, " now be treated as obsolete." He accordingly rejected the argument that the obligation as to seaworthiness implied by this section—namely, an obligation imposed only on the owner, the master and every agent charged with the loading of the ship or the preparing of the ship for sea or the sending of the ship to sea—supplanted the wider obligation which on the authority of *Wilsons and Clyde Coal Co. Ltd.* v. *English* [1938] A.C. 57, would be implied at common law, *viz.* an obligation imposed on the owners (the performance of which could not be delegated) to make the ship as safe as reasonable skill and care could make her. Had the necessary proof as to the cause of the loss been established he would have held the owners liable, for the failure of the ship repairers to ensure the ship's safety, such repairers not being within the section agents " charged with . . . preparing of the ship for sea." As Devlin J. was not satisfied as to the cause of the loss, these views were strictly *obiter* and it may be doubted whether they give full effect to the words " notwithstanding any agreement to the contrary." It is submitted that the preferable view is that the section is still an effective statutory provision which has the effect (1) of stating the extent of the owner's obligation as to seaworthiness, and (2) preventing the owner from contracting out of that obligation; but the section being a remedial section there is no justification for limiting the class of agents for which the owner would be vicariously liable to those specified in the section.

" Seaworthy " in this section means that the ship should be in a fit state, as to repairs, equipment and crew, and in all other respects, to encounter the ordinary perils of the voyage, and the negligence of the captain in not using with proper care the means of safety provided does not make the ship unseaworthy within the section: *Hedley* v. *Pinkney & Sons S.S. Co.* [1894] A.C. 222; affirming [1892] 1 Q.B. 58. And as the captain was a fellow-servant with a seaman, the owners (by reason of the doctrine of common employment which has now been abolished) were not liable for injury to the latter arising from such negligence: *Ibid.*; *Gillies* v. *Cairns* (1905) 8 Ct. of Sess.Cas. (5th Ser.), 174; 43 S.L.R

218 (where the court held that the shipowner was not responsible for latent defects or for patent defects which ought to have been remedied by the master or other fellow servant to whom the shipowner was entitled to leave the repair of such minor defect); unless, *semble*, his negligence had rendered the ship unseaworthy within the meaning of the section.

Neglect to stow a grain cargo so as to prevent it from shifting constituted a breach of the obligation created by this section: *Cunningham* v. *Frontier S.S. Co.* [1906] 2 Ir.K.B. 12.

For the purpose of marine insurance a " ship is deemed to be seaworthy when she is reasonably fit in all respects to encounter the ordinary perils of the seas of the adventure insured." Marine Insurance Act 1906, s. 39 (4). The effect and extent at common law of the implied or express warranty of seaworthiness contained in contracts of marine insurance and affreightment are beyond the scope of this note, but will be found exhaustively discussed in *British Shipping Laws* (Vol. 10), *Arnould on Marine Insurance*, 15th ed., § 694 *et seq.*; *British Shipping Laws* (Vol. 3); *Carver on Carriage by Sea* (12th ed.) Chap. 4 §102; and *Scrutton on Charterparties and Bills of Lading* (18th ed.), Art. 47 at p. 80 *et seq.*

As to the seaman's right to refuse to proceed to sea on the ground of unseaworthiness, see s. 463.

Power to detain unsafe ships, and procedure for detention

354 **459.**—(1) Where a British ship,[1] being in any port in the United Kingdom, is an unsafe ship,[2] that is to say, is by reason of the defective condition of her hull, equipments, or machinery, [or by reason of undermanning [3]], or by reason of overloading or improper loading, unfit to proceed to sea without serious danger to human life,[4] having regard to the nature of the service for which she is intended, such ship may be provisionally detained [5] for the purpose of being surveyed [or for ascertaining the sufficiency of her crew [3]], and either finally detained or released as follows:

(*a*) The [Department of Trade], if [it has] reason to believe, on complaint [4] or otherwise, that a British ship is unsafe, may order the ship to be provisionally detained as an unsafe ship for the purpose of being surveyed.

(*b*) When a ship has been provisionally detained there shall be forthwith served [6] on the master [7] of the ship a written statement of the grounds of her detention, and the [Department of Trade] may, if [it thinks] fit, appoint some competent person or persons to survey the ship and report [4] thereon to the [Department].

(*c*) The [Department of Trade] on receiving the report may either order the ship to be released or, if in [its] opinion the ship is unsafe, may order her to be finally detained, either absolutely, or until the performance of such conditions with respect to the execution of repairs or alterations, or the unloading or reloading of cargo [or the manning of the ship [3]], as the [Department thinks] necessary for the protection of human life, and the [Department] may vary or add to any such order.

(*d*) Before the order for final detention is made a copy of the report shall be served upon the master of the ship, and within seven days after that service the owner or master of the ship may appeal to the court of survey for the port or district where the ship is detained in manner directed by the rules of that court.[8]

(*e*) Where a ship has been provisionally detained, the owner or master of the ship, at any time before the person appointed under this section to survey the ship makes that survey, may require that he shall be accompanied by such person as the owner or master may select out of the list of assessors for the court of survey, and in that case if the surveyor and assessor agree, the [Department of Trade] shall cause the ship to be detained or released accordingly, but if they differ, the [Department of Trade] may act as if the requisition had not been made, and the owner and master shall have the like appeal touching the report of the surveyor as is before provided by this section.

(*f*) Where a ship has been provisionally detained, the [Department of Trade] may at any time, if [it thinks] it expedient, refer the matter to the court of survey for the port or district where the ship is detained.

(*g*) The [Department of Trade] may at any time, if satisfied that a ship detained under this section is not unsafe, order her to be released either upon or without any conditions.

(2) Any person appointed by the [Department of Trade] for the purpose (in this Act referred to as a detaining officer) shall have the same power as the [Department has] under this section of ordering the provisional detention of a ship for the purpose of being surveyed, and of appointing a person or persons to survey her; and if he thinks that a ship so detained by him is not unsafe may order her to be released.

(3) A detaining officer shall forthwith report to the [Department of Trade] any order made by him for the detention or release of a ship.

(4) An order for the detention of a ship, provisional or final, and an order varying the same, shall be served [6] as soon as may be on the master [7] of the ship.

(5) A ship detained under this section shall not be released by reason of her British register being subsequently closed.[1]

(6) The [Department of Trade] may with the consent of the Treasury appoint fit persons to act as detaining officers under this section, and may remove any such officer; and a detaining officer shall be paid such salary or remuneration (if any) out of money provided by Parliament as the Treasury direct, and shall for the purpose of his duties have all the powers of a [Department of Trade] inspector under this Act.[9]

(7) A detaining officer and a person authorised to survey a ship under this section shall for that purpose have the same power as a person appointed by a court of survey to survey a ship, and the provisions of this Act with respect to the person so appointed shall apply accordingly.[10]

355 By s. 3 (4) of the M.S. (Load Lines) Act 1967, a British load line ship registered in the U.K., which does not comply with the " conditions of assignment " of the Load Line Rules shall be deemed to be unsafe for the purpose of this section. See also s. 17 (4) (*a*) of the same Act as to British ships, not registered in the U.K., which have been subjected to material alterations so as to invalidate a Load Line Convention certificate. And see s. 13 (5) (*b*) of the same Act as to a foreign load line ship which neither produces a valid Load Line Convention certificate nor complies with the above-mentioned " conditions of assignment." See also ss. 23 (3) and 24 (1) (2) of M.S. (Safety Convention) Act 1949, as to circumstances in which certain ships are deemed to be unsafe for the purposes of Part V of M.S.A. 1894 (which includes s. 459), for non-compliance with rules relating to the carriage of dangerous goods or for not taking all necessary and reasonable precautions in connection with the carriage of grain.

1 As to the meaning of " British ship," see ss. 1, 2, 72, and notes thereto.

Where a vessel, registered as a British ship, was detained by the Department of Trade under M.S.A. 1873, s. 12, after a contract for her to transfer to a foreigner, but before completion of the transfer and before the closing of her British register, it was held that she was a British ship and therefore was not released by the subsequent completion of the transfer. *Granfelt* v. *Lord Advocate* (1874) (Sc.) 1 Ct. of Sess.Cas. (3rd Ser.) 782; 11 S.L.R. 337.

The detention does not prevent the transfer to a foreigner, and the closing of the British register. *Per* the Lord President, *ibid.*

Quaere, whether a vessel, registered as British, may be detained after transfer to a foreigner, but before the closing of the register. *Ibid.*

2 It should be noticed that the degree of danger in connection with the offence of sending a ship to sea in an " unseaworthy state " (s. 457) appears to be less than that required to make a vessel an " unsafe ship " within s. 459. It is not thought, however, that this has any practical importance except in so far as it lightens the burden of the prosecution under s. 457.

3 The words in square brackets were added by the M.S.A. 1897, s. 1. The powers given by this section now include power to muster the crew. *Ibid.*

When a British ship is detained under this section, the Department of Trade may inquire into the condition of her anchors and chains, and make such order as it thinks requisite. Anchors and Chain Cables Act, 1967, s. 1.

4 In *Lewis* v. *Gray* (1876) 45 L.J.C.P. 720; 1 C.P.D. 452, it was held, under M.S.A. Amendment Act 1873 (36 & 37 Vict. c. 85), s. 12, that neither the original information or complaint nor the report need state in terms that the vessel " cannot proceed to sea without serious danger to human life "; it is enough if the facts reported to the Secretary of State for Trade are such as ought reasonably to satisfy him that this is so.

See also *ibid.* as to when detention is justifiable—form of order for detention—appeal; and as to whether in the case of any excess of jurisdiction on the part of the Secretary of State for Trade the owner's common law remedy is taken away by this enactment.

As to the right of the Department of Trade to rely, in an action for illegal detention, upon a deficiency not mentioned in the notice of detention, subject to fair notice to the shipowner before the hearing, see *per* Brett L.J., *Thompson* v. *Farrer* (1882) 9 Q.B.D. 372 at p. 382. See also note (1) to s. 460.

5 As to the enforcement of detention, see s. 692.

6 Notice by registered letter is sufficient, see *Larsen* v. *Hart* (1900) 2 F. (Court of Justiciary Cases) 54; 37 S.L.R. 924; and see note (4) to s. 462.

7 As to service of documents on master, see s. 696.

8 As to courts of survey, see ss. 487–489.

9 As to the powers of a Department of Trade inspector, see ss. 723, 729, 730.

10 See s. 488 (4), as to powers of persons appointed by court of survey to survey a ship.

Liability for costs and damages

356 **460.**—(1) If it appears that there was not reasonable and probable cause, by reason of the condition of the ship [1] or the act or default of the owner, for the provisional detention of a ship under this Part of this Act as an unsafe ship, the [Department of Trade] shall be liable [2] to pay to the owner of the ship his costs of and incidental to the detention and survey of the ship, and also compensation for any loss or damage [3] sustained by him by reason of the detention or survey.

(2) If a ship is finally detained [4] under this Act, or if it appears that a ship provisionally detained was, at the time of that detention, an unsafe ship within the meaning of this Part of this Act,[5] the owner of the ship shall be liable to pay to the [Department of Trade] costs of and incidental to the detention and survey of the ship, and those costs shall, without prejudice to any other remedy, be recoverable as salvage is recoverable.[6]

(3) For the purpose of this section the costs of and incidental to any proceeding before a court of survey, and a reasonable amount in respect of the remuneration of the surveyor or officer of the [Department of Trade], shall be part of the costs of the detention and survey of the ship, and any dispute as to the amount of those costs may be referred to one of the officers following, namely, in England or Ireland [7] to one of the masters or registrars of the High Court,[8] and in Scotland to the auditor of the Court of Session, and the officer shall, on request by the [Department of Trade], ascertain and certify the proper amount of those costs.

(4) [9] . . .

357 [1] In an action for compensation for detention it was held (under M.S.A. 1846, ss. 6, 10) that the proper question to be left to the jury was whether the facts with regard to the ship as she lay, which would have been apparent to a person of ordinary skill on examining her and inquiring about her, would have given him reasonable and probable cause to suspect her safety, and to detain her for survey and inquiry. See also *Thompson* v. *Farrer* (1882) 9 Q.B.D. 372; *Lewis* v. *Gray* (1876) 45 L.J.C.P. 720; 1 C.P.D. 452, cited in note (4) to s. 459.

[2] An action under this section (formerly M.S.A. 1876, s. 10) is one in which the Crown has an interest so as to entitle the Attorney-General to demand, as of right, a trial at bar, and hence upon his waiving that right the court is bound (under the Crown Suits Act 1865, s. 46) to change the venue to any county wherein he elects to have the action tried. *Dixon* v. *Farrer* (1886) 18 Q.B.D. 43. See generally Halsbury's *Laws of England*, 3rd ed., Vol. 11, Crown Proceedings, pp. 19–20.

[3] General damages in respect of injury to the owners' reputation as shipowners, by reason of the detention of their ship, are not within the words "compensation for any loss or damage," and therefore are not recoverable: *Dixon* v. *Calcraft* [1892] 1 Q.B. 458.

[4] By s. 27 (2) of the M.S. (Load Lines) Act 1967, and s. 4 (4) of the Fishing Vessels (Safety Provisions) Act 1970, it is provided that in any of the numerous cases contemplated by the Acts in which a ship may be detained until a certain event occurs, this subsection shall apply as if the ship had been "finally detained." By s. 35 (2) of the M.S. (Safety Conventions) Act 1949, it is further provided that where a ship is detained under any provision of that Act which authorises the detention of a ship until the production of a certificate, this subsection shall also apply as if the ship had been "finally detained." The general effect of these extensions is to enable the Department of Trade under the above sections to recover its costs as herein provided.

[5] See s. 459 (1) as to the detention of unsafe ships.

[6] Presumably this refers to procedure only, for which see s. 547 *et seq.*, and does not confer the maritime lien enjoyed by salvors proper.

[7] *i.e.* Northern Ireland only; see the Irish Free State (Consequential Adaptation of Enactments) Order 1923 (S.R. & O. No. 405).

[8] The jurisdiction in England is assigned to the Queen's Bench Division (Admiralty Court); see R.S.C. Ord. 74, r. 1.

[9] Subs. (4), which prescribed the procedure for enforcing claims for costs or compensation against the Department of Trade, was repealed by the Crown Proceedings Act 1947, s. 39 (1), Sched. II; and such claims are now enforced in the same manner as other claims against the Department of Trade are enforced under that Act.

Power to require from complainant security for costs

358 **461.**—(1) Where a complaint is made to the [Department of Trade] or a detaining officer that a British ship [1] is unsafe, the [Department] or

officer may, if [they think] fit, require the complainant to give security to the satisfaction of the [Department] for the costs and compensation which he may become liable to pay as hereinafter mentioned.

(2) Provided that such security shall not be required where the complaint is made by one-fourth, being not less than three, of the seamen belonging to the ship,[2] and is not in the opinion of the [Department] or officer frivolous or vexatious, and the [Department] or officer shall, if the complaint is made in sufficient time before the sailing of the ship, take proper steps for ascertaining whether the ship ought to be detained.

(3) Where a ship is detained [3] in consequence of any complaint, and the circumstances are such that the [Department of Trade is] liable under this Act to pay to the owner of the ship any costs or compensation, the complainant shall be liable to pay to the [Department of Trade] all such costs and compensation as the [Department incur] or [is] liable to pay in respect of the detention and survey of the ship.

[1] As to the meaning of " British ship," see ss. 1, 2, 72 and notes thereto.
[2] See s. 463 (survey of ships alleged by seamen to be unseaworthy).
[3] See s. 459 as to power to detain unsafe ships and procedure for detention.

Application to foreign ships of provisions as to detention

359 **462.** Where a foreign ship *has taken on board all or any part of her cargo* [1] at a port in the United Kingdom, *and* [1] is *whilst at that port* [1] unsafe [by reason of the defective condition of her hull, equipments, or machinery, or [1]] by reason of overloading or improper loading, [or by reason of undermanning [1]], the provisions of this Part of this Act [2] with respect to the detention of ships shall apply to that foreign ship as if she were a British ship,[3] with the following modifications:

(i) a copy of the order for the provisional detention of the ship shall be forthwith served [4] on the consular officer [5] for the country to which the ship belongs at or nearest to the said port;

(ii) where a ship has been provisionally detained, the consular officer, on the request of the owner or master of the ship, may require that the person appointed by the [Department of Trade] to survey the ship shall be accompanied by such person as the consular officer may select, and in that case, if the surveyor and that person agree, the [Department of Trade] shall cause the ship to be detained or released accordingly, but if they differ, the [Department of Trade] may act as if the requisition had not been made, and the owner and master shall have the like appeal to a court of survey touching the report of the surveyor as is hereinbefore provided in the case of a British ship [6]; and

(iii) where the owner or master of the ship appeals to the court of survey, the consular officer, on his request, may appoint a competent person to be assessor [7] in the case in lieu of the assessor who, if the ship were a British ship, would be appointed otherwise than by the [Department of Trade].

360 By s. 17 (4) (*a*) of the M.S. (Load Lines) Act 1967, a British ship, not registered in the U.K., which has been subjected to material alterations so as to invalidate a Load Line Convention certificate shall be deemed to be unsafe for the purposes of this section. See also s. 13 (5) (*b*) of the same Act as to a foreign load line ship which neither produces a valid Load Line Convention certificate nor complies with the above-mentioned " conditions of assignment."

[1] The words in italics in this section were repealed by M.S.A. 1906, s. 85, Sched. II, and these two sets of words in square brackets were added by M.S.A. 1906, s. 2, and M.S.A. 1897, s. 1 (2), respectively. M.S.A. 1906, s. 2, enacts that s. 462 shall apply to the case of a ship which is unsafe by reason of the defective condition of her hull, equipments, or machinery, and shall apply with respect to any foreign ships being at any port in the United Kingdom, whether those ships take on board any cargo at that port or not. This provision as to foreign ships does not apply to ships not bound to a port in the United Kingdom, putting in under stress of weather; see M.S.A. 1906, s. 6.

[2] See s. 459 as to detention of unsafe ships.

[3] As to " British ship," see note (1) to s. 461. An Order in Council, under s. 734, is not needed in order to enforce the provisions of this section against a foreign ship: *Chalmers* v. *Scopenich* [1892] 1 Q.B. 735, cited in note (1) to s. 692; and see note (1) to s. 734.

The general provisions for enforcing detention are contained in s. 692. As to whether, in the absence of such an Order in Council, they also apply to a foreign ship which is subject to detention under s. 462, see *ibid.* and note to s. 692.

[4] Where a foreign ship was detained and the copy of the Order only referred to s. 459, and was sent by registered post to the consul, it was held that the notice was sufficient, and that the consul had been " forthwith served " within the meaning of this section: *Larsen* v. *Hart* (1900) 2 F. (Court of Justiciary Cases) 54; 37 S.L.R. 924.

[5] For definition of " Consular officer," see s. 742.

[6] See s. 459 (1) (*d*).

[7] See s. 487 (3) as to assessors in court of survey.

Survey of ships alleged by seamen to be unseaworthy

361 **463.**—(1) Whenever in any proceeding against any seaman *or apprentice* [1] belonging to any ship [2] for the offence of desertion, or absence without leave or for otherwise being absent from his ship without leave,[3] it is alleged by one-fourth, or if their number exceeds twenty by not less than five, of the seamen belonging to the ship, that the ship is by reason of unseaworthiness, overloading, improper loading, defective equipment, or for any other reason, not in a fit condition to proceed to sea, or that the accommodation in the ship is insufficient,[4] the court having cognizance of the case shall take such means as may be in their power to satisfy themselves concerning the truth or untruth of the allegation, and shall for that purpose receive the evidence of the persons making the same, and may summon any other witnesses whose evidence they may think it desirable to hear, and shall, if satisfied that the allegation is groundless, adjudicate in the case, but if not so satisfied shall before adjudication cause the ship to be surveyed.

(2) A seaman *or apprentice* charged with desertion, or with quitting his ship without leave, shall not have any right to apply for a survey under this section unless he has before quitting his ship complained to the master of the circumstances so alleged in justification.

(3) For the purposes of this section the court shall require any surveyor

of ships appointed under this Act,[5] or any person appointed for the purpose by the [Department of Trade], or, if such a surveyor or person cannot be obtained without unreasonable expense or delay, or is not, in the opinion of the court, competent to deal with the special circumstances of the case, then any other impartial surveyor appointed by the court, and having no interest in the ship, her freight, or cargo, to survey the ship, and to answer any question concerning her which the court think fit to put.

(4) Such surveyor or other person shall survey the ship, and make his written report to the court, including an answer to every question put to him by the court, and the court shall cause the report to be communicated to the parties, and, unless the opinions expressed in the report are proved to the satisfaction of the court to be erroneous, shall determine the questions before them in accordance with those opinions.

(5) Any person making a survey under this section shall for the purposes thereof have all the powers of a [Department of Trade] inspector under this Act.[6]

(6) The costs (if any) of the survey shall be determined by the [Department of Trade] according to a scale of fees [7] to be fixed by [it], and shall be paid in the first instance out of the Mercantile Marine Fund.[8]

(7) If it is proved that the ship is in a fit condition to proceed to sea, or that the accommodation is sufficient, as the case may be, the costs of the survey shall be paid by the person upon whose demand or in consequence of whose allegation the survey was made, and may be deducted by the master or owner out of the wages due or to become due to that person, and shall be paid over to the [Department of Trade].

(8) If it is proved that the ship is not in a fit condition to proceed to sea, or that the accommodation is insufficient, as the case may be, the master or owner of the ship shall pay the costs of the survey to the [Department of Trade], and shall be liable to pay to the seaman *or apprentice*, who has been detained in consequence of the said proceeding before the court under this section, such compensation for his detention as the court may award.

362 *Cf.* s. 483 (1) (*j*) as to survey by order of a naval court.

1 The words in italics were repealed by M.S.A. 1970, s. 100 (3), Sched. V as from January 1, 1973: see S.I. 1972 No. 1977.

2 Presumably the steps authorised by s. 89 of M.S.A. 1970 in the case of deserters from certain foreign ships amount to a " proceeding " within s. 463, so as to entitle the foreign seamen to the benefit of this section. For the application of s. 89, see note (2) thereto.

3 See M.S.A. 1970, s. 31, for provisions relating to absentees.

4 As to the accommodation to be provided for seamen in British ships, see s. 210, and notes thereto; see also M.S.A. 1948; and as to fishing boats, M.S.A. 1950. These provisions are prospectively repealed by the M.S.A. 1970, s. 100 (3) Sched. V on a day to be appointed. Thereafter they will be replaced by *ibid*, s. 20 and Sched. 2.

5 See s. 724 as to appointment of surveyors. *Cf.* M.S.A. 1906, s. 75, as to shipwright surveyors.

6 See ss. 729, 730 for powers of inspectors.

7 The fees at present in force for this service are contained in Part 7 of the Schedule to the M.S. (Fees) Order, 1924 (S.R. & O. 1924 No. 1056).

8 Now " out of moneys provided by Parliament." See M.S. (Mercantile Marine Fund) Act 1898, s. 1 (1) (*b*).

PART VI—SPECIAL SHIPPING INQUIRIES AND COURTS

363 §§ 364–403. Save for provisions relating to inquiries by colonial courts into shipping casualties and conduct of officers (s. 478), courts of survey (ss. 487–489) and scientific referees (s. 490), the whole of Part VI of the Act, which dealt with special shipping inquiries and courts, is prospectively repealed by M.S.A. 1970, s. 100 (3), Sched. V and is printed in italics. The subject-matter will thereafter be dealt with in the latter Act.

The following special shipping inquiries and courts are regulated by this Part of the Act: (i) Preliminary inquiries before inspecting officers of coastguards, or chief officers of customs, or the Secretary of State's nominee (section 465); (ii) formal investigations before courts of summary jurisdiction or wreck commissioners (section 466); (iii) inquiries into conduct of certificated officers before the Secretary of State's nominee, local marine board, or court of summary jurisdiction (section 471); (iv) rehearings and appeals (section 475); (v) inquiries and investigations before colonial courts (section 478); (vi) naval courts on the high seas and abroad (sections 480–486); (vii) courts of survey (sections 487–489); and (viii) references to scientific referees (section 490).

See also M.S.A. 1906: s. 66, shipping casualties appeals; s. 67, power to send a person sentenced to imprisonment home; and s. 68, naval appeals. Part VI of this Act, s. 66 of the M.S.A. 1906 and the Shipping Casualties and Appeals and Re-Hearing Rules 1923 apply to diving operations subject to certain modifications and substitutions: see the M.S. (Diving Operations) Regulations 1975 (S.I. No. 116), reg. 20 and Sched. 4.

Inquiries and Investigations as to Shipping Casualties

Shipping casualties

364 **464.** *For the purpose of inquiries and investigations under this Part of this Act a shipping casualty shall be deemed to occur:—*

(1) *when on or near the coasts of the United Kingdom* [1] *any ship* [2] *is lost, abandoned, or materially damaged;*

(2) *when on or near the coasts of the United Kingdom any ship has been stranded or damaged, and any witness is found in the United Kingdom* [3]*;*

(3) *when on or near the coasts of the United Kingdom* [1] *any ship causes loss or material damage to any other ship;*

(4) *when any loss of life ensues by reason of any casualty happening to or on board any ship on or near the coasts of the United Kingdom;*

(5) *when in any place any such loss, abandonment, material damage, or casualty as above mentioned occurs,* [4] *and any witness is found in the United Kingdom;*

(6) *when in any place any British ship* [5] *is stranded or damaged, and any witness is found in the United Kingdom* [3]*;*

(7) *when any British ship* [5] *is lost or is supposed to have been lost, and any evidence is obtainable in the United Kingdom as to the circumstances under which she proceeded to sea or was last heard of.* [3]

[1] " On or near the coasts of the United Kingdom"; *semble*, means within territorial waters. See *The Fulham* [1898] P. 206; and see note (2) to s. 546. As to colonies, see s. 478.

[2] " Ship"; as to the meaning of this term, see s. 742, and note (4) thereto.

In *Ex p. Ferguson* there cited, it was held that a fishing " coble " was a " ship " within the provisions of M.S.A. 1854, here re-enacted. Certain fishing boats are expressly exempted from the provisions as to naval courts: see s. 486. As to inquiries before superintendents regarding casualties to fishing boats and boats belonging thereto, see also ss. 385, 386, 468.

[3] The occurrences mentioned in paras. (2), (6), (7), were made subjects of inquiry by M.S.A. 1876, s. 32, as to the effect of which with regard to the jurisdiction to suspend certificates, see note (4) to s. 470. That Act did not apply to vessels trading in colonial rivers and inland waters; but if such exemption had any application to these provisions, it is now dropped: see subss. (5)–(7).

[4] Apparently the word " material " was inserted in para. (5) in consequence of the addition to the context of para. (2), which is not limited to cases of material damage; and the words " as above mentioned," in accordance with *Ex p. Story, infra* (s. 470), where it was held that " casualty " here means the casualty mentioned in the preceding subsection, *i.e.* one by which loss of life occurs.

[5] " British ship"; see ss. 1, 2, 72, and notes thereto.

Preliminary inquiry into shipping casualties

365 **465.**—(1) *Where a shipping casualty has occurred a preliminary inquiry may be held respecting the casualty by the following persons, namely:—*

(*a*) *where the shipping casualty occurs on or near the coasts of the United Kingdom,* [1] *by the inspecting officer of the coastguard or chief officer of customs* [2] *residing at or near the place at which the casualty occurs; or*

(*b*) *where the shipping casualty occurs elsewhere, by the inspecting officer of the coastguard or chief officer of customs residing at or near any place at which the witnesses with respect to the casualty arrive or are found or can be conveniently examined; or*

(*c*) *in any case by any person appointed for the purpose by the* [*Department of Trade*].

(2) *For the purpose of any such inquiry the person holding the same shall have the powers of a* [*Department of Trade*] *inspector under this Act.* [3]

[1] See s. 464, note (1).

[2] See definition of " chief officer of customs," s. 742. The result of this inquiry is entered in a Department of Trade form, and sworn to by the deponent. It is usually referred to as " the deposition " of the person examined. The form must be filled in and completed before being sworn, and no alteration should afterwards be made by the officers of customs. As to admissibility of depositions in evidence, see note (6) to s. 517.

[3] See ss. 729, 730, for powers of inspectors.

See as to examinations by receivers of wreck or other persons in cases of ships in distress, s. 517; as to inquiries by Department of Trade inspectors, ss. 728 *et seq.*; and as to inquiries in colonies, see s. 478.

Formal investigation of shipping casualties

366 **466.**—(1) *A person authorised as aforesaid to make a preliminary inquiry shall in any case where it appears to him requisite or expedient (whether upon a preliminary inquiry or without holding such an inquiry) that a formal investigation should be held, and in any case where the* [*Department of Trade*] *so directs, apply to a court of summary jurisdiction to hold a formal investigation, and that court shall thereupon hold the formal investigation.*[1]

(2) *A wreck commissioner appointed under this Act*[2] *shall at the request of the* [*Department of Trade*] *hold any formal investigation into a shipping casualty under this section, and any reference to the court holding an investigation under this section includes a wreck commissioner holding such an investigation.*

(3) *The court holding any such formal investigation shall hold the same with the assistance of one or more assessors of nautical, engineering, or other special skill or knowledge, to be appointed out of a list of persons for the time being approved for the purpose by a Secretary of State in such manner and according to such regulations as may be prescribed by rules made under this Part of this Act with regard thereto.*[3]

(4) *Where a formal investigation involves or appears likely to involve any question as to the cancelling or suspension of the certificate of a master, mate, or engineer,*[4] *the court shall hold the investigation with the assistance of not less than two assessors having experience in the merchant service.*

(5) *It shall be the duty of the person who has applied to a court to hold a formal investigation to superintend the management of the case, and to render such assistance to the court as is in his power.*

(6) *The court after hearing the case shall make a report to the* [*Department of Trade*] *containing a full statement of the case and of the opinion of the court thereon, accompanied by such report of, or extracts from, the evidence, and such observations as the court think fit.*[5]

(7) *Each assessor shall either sign the report or state in writing to the* [*Department of Trade*] *his dissent therefrom and the reasons for that dissent.*

367 (8) *The court may make such order as the court think fit respecting the costs of the investigation, or any part thereof,*[6] *and such order shall be enforced by the court as an order for costs under the Summary Jurisdiction Acts.*[7]

(9) *The* [*Department of Trade*] *may, if in any case* [*they think*] *fit so to do, pay the costs of any such formal investigation.*

(10) *For the purposes of this section the court holding a formal investigation shall have all the powers of a court of summary jurisdiction when acting as a court in exercise of their ordinary jurisdiction.*

(11) *Every formal investigation into a shipping casualty shall be conducted in such manner that if a charge is made against any person, that person shall have an opportunity of making a defence.*[8]

(12) *Formal investigations into shipping casualties under this section shall be held in some town hall, assize or county court, or public building, or in some other suitable place to be determined according to rules made under this Part of this Act with regard thereto, and, unless no other suitable place is in the opinion of the* [*Department of Trade*] *available, shall not be held in a court ordinarily used as a police court, and all enactments relating to the court shall for the purposes of the investigation have effect as if the place at which the court is held were a place appointed for the exercise of the ordinary jurisdiction of the court.*

(13) *Where an investigation is to be held in Scotland, the* [*Secretary of State for Trade*] *may remit the same to the Lord Advocate to be prosecuted in such manner as he may direct.*

368 [1] As to the conduct of the inquiry see Shipping Casualties Rules 1923, Nos. 10 to 17 set out *post*; §§ 3193–3194. See the provisions of s. 476, as to holding formal investigations before stipendiary magistrates who are members of local marine boards.

As to proceeding with an investigation, although the Secretary of State for Trade has no charge to make against the master or officers, see *Ex p. Minto* (1877) 35 L.T. 808; 25 W.R. 251.

[2] See M.S.A. 1970, s. 82: appointment of wreck commissioner.

[3] See s. 467, and the Shipping Casualties Rules 1923 (S.R. & O. No. 752), set out *post*, §§ 3192–3201. The Rules, as amended by S.I. 1975 No. 116, also apply to diving operations.

[4] For power to cancel or suspend certificates, see s. 470 (1) (*a*).

[5] For the form of the report, see Shipping Casualties Rules 1923, No. 17, *post*, §§ 3192–3201 and Appendix, Part I, Form No. 3 and note thereto, § 3021. It is improper for the commissioner to amend the report (other than to correct an accidental slip or omission) after it has been read out in open court: *The Corchester* [1957] P. 84, 86.

As to investigations in British possessions, see s. 478.

As to rehearings, see s. 475, and M.S.A. 1906, s. 66 (appeals).

[6] See Shipping Casualties Rules 1923, No. 16, *post*, § 3018. No provision is made for taxation and it is therefore necessary for the precise sum to be stated in the order. An order for costs to be paid may be made against the Secretary of State for Trade or any other party. It is sometimes used as a method of penalising parties.

[7] Now Magistrates' Courts Act 1952, as respects England and Wales.

[8] For illustrations of the application of this subsection, see *The Chelston* [1920] P. 400; *Nelson Steam Navigation Co. Ltd.* v. *Board of Trade* (1931) 40 Ll.L.R. 55; *The Princess Victoria* [1953] 2 Lloyd's Rep. 619; *The Seistan* [1959] 2 Lloyd's Rep. 607. In *The Princess Victoria*, it was held (at p. 635) that the requirements of the subsection were sufficiently complied with if the person concerned, although not a party and not named in any question put to the court, knew that his conduct was in issue and was aware of his rights. *Cf. The Seistan* where an assessor in a rider added to the findings of the court criticised the conduct of an engineer although no charge had been made against him and he had not given evidence at the inquiry.

List of assessors

369 **467.**—(1) *The list of persons approved as assessors*[1] *for the purpose of formal investigations into shipping casualties shall be in force for three years only, but persons whose names are on any such list may be approved for any subsequent list.*

(2) *The Secretary of State may at any time add or withdraw the name of any person to or from the list.*

(3) *The list of assessors in force at the passing of this Act shall, subject as aforesaid, continue in force till the end of the year one thousand eight hundred and ninety-five.*

[1] See Shipping Casualties Rules 1923, Nos. 22 to 26 and Appendix, Part II, *post*, §§ 3196, 3200.

Inquiry in case of loss of life from fishing vessel's boat

370 **468.** *When any loss of life arises by reason of any casualty happening to or on board any boat belonging to a fishing vessel, the* [*Secretary of State for Trade*] *may, if* [*he thinks*] *fit, cause an inquiry to be made or a formal investigation to be held as in the case of a shipping casualty, and the provisions of this Act relating thereto shall apply accordingly.*

See also ss. 385, 386, as to inquiries by superintendents into casualties connected with fishing vessels or fishing vessels' boats.

Power as to Certificates of Officers, etc.

Power of the [Secretary of State for Trade] as to certificate

371 **469.** *The* [*Secretary of State for Trade*] *may suspend or cancel the certificate of any master, mate, or engineer if it is shown that he has been convicted of any offence.*[1]

[1] It was held in a Scottish case that " any offence " in this section meant any " criminal " offence, *i.e.* an offence punishable by fine or deprivation of liberty, and did not include, *e.g.* drunkenness on board ship or incompetency for which a certificate could be cancelled by a court or tribunal inquiring into such a charge, and that the Board of Trade had no power to cancel or suspend certificates except when the holder had committed (and been convicted of) such a " criminal " offence: *Board of Trade* v. *Leith Local Marine Board*, 34 S.L.R. 139 at p. 141; (1896) 24 R. 177 at p. 182.

Power of court of investigation or inquiry as to certificates

372 **470.**—(1) *The certificate of a master, mate, or engineer may be cancelled or suspended—*

(*a*) *by a court holding a formal investigation into a shipping casualty under this Part of this Act,*[1] *or by a naval court constituted under this Act,*[2] *if the court find*[3] *that the loss or abandonment of, or serious damage to, any ship, or loss of life,*[4] *has been caused by*[5] *his wrongful act or default,*[6] *provided that, if the court holding a formal investigation is a court of summary jurisdiction, that court shall not cancel or suspend a certificate unless one at least of the assessors concurs in the finding of the court:*

(*b*) *by a court holding an inquiry under this Part of this Act*[7] *into the conduct of a master, mate, or engineer,*[8] *if they find that he is incompetent, or has been guilty of any gross act of misconduct, drunkenness, or tyranny, or that in a case of collision he has failed to render such assistance or give such information as is required under the Fifth Part of this Act*[9]*:*

(c) *by any naval or other court where under the powers given by this Part of this Act the holder of the certificate is superseded or removed by that court.*[10]

(2) *Where any case before any such court as aforesaid involves a question as to the cancelling or suspending of a certificate, that court shall, at the conclusion of the case or as soon afterwards as possible, state in open court the decision to which they have come with respect to the cancelling or suspending thereof.*[11]

(3) *The court shall in all cases send a full report on the case with the evidence to the [Secretary of State for Trade], and shall also, if they determine to cancel or suspend any certificate, send the certificate cancelled or suspended to the [Secretary of State for Trade] with their report.*[11]

(4) *A certificate shall not be cancelled or suspended by a court under this section, unless a copy of the report, or a statement of the case on which the investigation or inquiry has been ordered, has been furnished before the commencement of the investigation or inquiry to the holder of the certificate.*[12]

373 [1] As to these investigations, see ss. 466, 478. Where the investigation is instituted by the Secretary of State for Trade he must not act as a neutral party, but must advise the court whether or not he considers that the certificate in question should be cancelled or suspended: *The Carlisle* [1906] P. 301 at pp. 313 *et seq.* The Secretary of State may also ask the court to make recommendations in the general interests of safety. As to rehearings, see s. 475.

[2] As to naval courts, see ss. 480 *et seq.*

[3] There appears to be no decision indicating what burden of proof is required to be discharged for a finding under this section. The proceedings are always regarded as "quasi-criminal." It seems that the court is entitled to find that a fault of omission caused or contributed to the loss if proper action on the part of the officer concerned would "*in all probability*" have prevented the mistakes of another officer; see the judgment of the court in *The Corchester* [1957] P. 84 at p. 100.

[4] The occurrences mentioned in subss. (2), (6) and (7) of s. 464 were added to the subjects of preliminary inquiries and formal investigations by M.S.A. 1876, s. 32; but it was held in *Ex p. Story* (1878) 3 Q.B.D. 166, that the jurisdiction as to the suspension of certificates under 1854, s. 242 (1894, s. 470) was not thereby extended, and that there was no power to suspend the master's certificate where a ship had merely stranded without material damage to the ship or loss of life.

[5] See *The Arizona* (1880) 5 P.D. 123 in which the master's certificate was restored on appeal because there was no evidence to connect the casualty with his alleged default, though *semble* it would have been sufficient to show that the fault had contributed to the casualty. See also *The Corchester* [1957] P. 84 in which it was held that there must be specific findings (a) that the officer was guilty of a specific wrongful act or default and (b) that the casualty was caused or contributed to thereby.

[6] "Wrongful act or default"; these words were generally considered in *The Princess Victoria* [1953] 2 Lloyd's Rep. 619 at pp. 627–629 and were interpreted as "a breach of legal duty of any degree which causes or contributes to the casualty under investigation." They do not include an error of judgment at a moment of great difficulty and danger: *The Famenoth* (1882) 7 P.D. 207; 48 L.T. 28; *Watson* v. *Board of Trade* (1884) 22 S.L.R. 22. But they include conduct arising from a surrender of the judgment to the influence of unreasonable panic: *Brown* v. *Board of Trade* (1890) 18 R. 291; 28 S.L.R. 401. A master's certificate was suspended where the loss was due to his taking improper ballast. *The*

Golden Sea (1882) 7 P.D. 194. See, too, *Ewer* v. *Board of Trade* (1880) 7 R. 835 (master improperly leaving bridge).

374 [7] In *Board of Trade* v. *Leith Local Marine Board* (cited in note (1) to s. 469, *supra*), a local marine board holding an inquiry (by direction of the Board of Trade) into the conduct of an officer was held to be a " court " within the meaning of this paragraph.

[8] See ss. 471, 478, as to conduct of officers.

[9] See s. 422, as to " standing by " in case of collisions; and the M.S.A. 1970, s. 73 as to reporting casualties.

[10] See ss. 472, 483, as to removal, etc., of officers.

[11] See the Shipping Casualties Rules, 1923 (S.R. & O. 1923 No. 752), Nos. 15 and 17, *post*, § 3194, and note (5) to s. 466. In *The Kestrel* (1881) 6 P.D. 182; 45 L.T. 111, it was held that although the court holding the inquiry must, when it deals with a certificate, give its decision in open court, it need not then make any statement of the reasons for the decision (though it is usual to do so); hence the report to the Minister of Transport may state reasons for the decision which were not mentioned in open court when the decision was announced. The court has no power to recommend that a certificate be cancelled or suspended and there is no machinery for the Minister or any other authority to act on any such recommendation: *The Corchester* [1957] P. 84, 89. In addition to any recommendations the court wishes to make, it may also criticise any person whose wrongful conduct has caused or contributed to the casualty, even though he is not a party (*e.g.* see *The Princess Victoria* [1953] 2 Lloyd's Rep. 619 where the designated manager was criticised). As to the rights of such persons to appeal, see Merchant Shipping Act 1906, s. 66. An order to pay costs may be used as a method of penalising any party to the proceedings; see note (6) to s. 466, *supra*.

[12] In *The Chelston* [1920] P. 400, the Divisional Court held that, while the Shipping Casualty Rules 1907 governed the procedure in British wreck commissioner's courts wherever held, and the rights of British ship-masters in such courts must be ascertained by considering whether the local rules diminished the safeguards given to British ship-masters by the British rules, yet the Canada Shipping Act 1908, s. 36, which provided that " a certificate shall not be cancelled or suspended . . . unless the holder of the certificate has had an opportunity of making a defence," amply protected the rights of British ship-masters, and was not repugnant to M.S.A. 1894, s. 470 (4), or any other provision of the Act or the rules made thereunder. (The subject-matter of the Canada Shipping Act 1908, s. 36, is now dealt with by the Canada Shipping Act 1934, s. 561.)

Inquiry into conduct of certificated officer

375 **471.**—(1) *If the* [*Secretary of State for Trade*], *either on the report of a local marine board or otherwise,* [*has*] *reason to believe that any master, mate, or certificated engineer is from incompetency or misconduct unfit to discharge his duties, or that in a case of collision he has failed to render such assistance or give such information as is required under the Fifth Part of this Act,*[2] *the* [*Secretary of State*] *may cause an inquiry to be held.*

(2) *The* [*Secretary of State for Trade*] *may either* [*himself*] *appoint a person to hold the inquiry or direct the local marine board at or nearest the place at which it is convenient for the parties or witnesses to attend to hold the same, or where there is no local marine board before which the parties and witnesses can conveniently attend, or the local marine board is unwilling to hold the inquiry, may direct the inquiry to be held before a court of summary jurisdiction.*

(3) *Where the inquiry is held by a local marine board, or by a person appointed by the* [*Secretary of State for Trade*], *that board or person—*

(*a*) *shall hold the inquiry, with the assistance of a local stipendiary magistrate, or, if there is no such magistrate available, of a com-*

petent legal assistant appointed by the [Secretary of State for Trade]: and

(*b*) *shall have all the powers of a [Department of Trade] inspector under this Act*[3]; *and*

(*c*) *shall give any master, mate, or engineer against whom a charge is made an opportunity of making his defence either in person or otherwise,*[4] *and may summon him to appear; and*

(*d*) *may make such order with regard to the costs of the inquiry as they think just; and*

(*e*) *shall send a report upon the case to the [Secretary of State for Trade].*

(4) *Where the inquiry is held by a court of summary jurisdiction, the inquiry shall be conducted and the results reported in the same manner, and the court shall have the like powers, as in the case of a formal investigation into a shipping casualty under this Part of this Act,*[5] *provided that, if the [Secretary of State for Trade] so [directs], it shall be the duty of the person who has brought the charge against the master, mate, or engineer, to the notice of the [Secretary of State for Trade], to conduct the case, and that person shall in that case, for the purpose of this Act, be deemed to be the party having the conduct of the case.*

376 [2] See s. 422, as to " standing by " in cases of collision; and the M.S.A. 1970, s. 73 as to reporting casualties.

[3] See ss. 728–730 for powers of Department of Trade inspectors. These powers include a discretionary power to grant summonses for witnesses for the defence (see s. 729 (1) (*c*)). The expense of witnesses so summoned is to be borne by the public, and it is a proper course for the court before granting summonses to inquire who the witnesses are and what they are expected to prove, and to prevent a witness being vexatiously summoned: *R.* v. *Collingridge* (1864) 34 L.J.Q.B. 9, and *ibid. sub nom. R.* v. *Local Marine Board of London,* 12 W.R. 1109. False swearing at such an inquiry is indictable as perjury: *R.* v. *Tomlinson* (1866) L.R. 1 C.C.R. 49.

[4] " Proceedings of this kind, which are penal, if not criminal, should be as public as possible. Those who conduct such an inquiry should give the party charged every opportunity of having his attorney and counsel and witnesses present; " see *R.* v. *Collingridge, supra.* " Otherwise " seems to mean by his counsel or solicitor; *ibid.* The nature of the incompetency or misconduct alleged should be stated with reasonable particularity and a reasonable time before the hearing: *The Empire Antelope, The Radchurch* [1943] P. 79.

[5] See s. 466 as to formal investigations of shipping casualties; and as to the power to cancel or suspend certificates, see s. 470. A local marine board when holding an inquiry into the conduct of a certificated officer by order of the Secretary of State for Trade is a court within the meaning of s. 470 (1) (*b*), and has power to cancel a certificate of competency; see *Board of Trade* v. *Leith Local Marine Board,* 34 S.L.R. 139; (1896) 24 R. 177. A person appointed by the Secretary of State to hold the inquiry has the same power: *The Empire Antelope, The Radchurch* (*supra*). The tribunal should state their findings in such a way that both the officer concerned and the Secretary of State may know the reasons for the decision. Further, if the officer's previous record is good, a finding of incompetency should only be made if the circumstances are exceptional, and should not ordinarily be based on an isolated incident. (*Ibid.*)

As to similar inquiries in British possessions, see s. 478.

As to rehearings and appeals, see s. 475 and notes thereto; see, too, *The Carlisle* [1906] P. 301 there cited.

Removal of master by Admiralty Court

377 **472.**—(1) *Any of the following courts, namely:—*

In England and Ireland the High Court,[1]

In Scotland the Court of Session,

Elsewhere in Her Majesty's dominions any colonial Court of Admiralty or Vice-Admiralty Court,[2]

may remove the master of any ship within the jurisdiction of that court, if that removal is shown to the satisfaction of the court by evidence on oath to be necessary.[3]

(2) *The removal may be made upon the application of any owner of the ship or his agent, or of the consignee of the ship,*[4] *or of any certificated mate, or of one third or more of the crew of the ship.*

(3) *The court may appoint a new master instead of the one removed; but where the owner, agent, or consignee of the ship is within the jurisdiction of the court, such an appointment shall not be made without the consent of that owner, agent, or consignee.*

(4) *The court may also make such order and require such security in respect of the costs of the matter as the court thinks fit.*

378 [1] The jurisdiction is assigned in England to the Queen's Bench Division (Admiralty Court) by R.S.C., Ord. 74, r. 1; see *post*, Appendix 13, § 3039. As to Ireland see "Application to Northern Ireland and Republic of Ireland" in notes after s. 742.

[2] See ss. 2 and 9 of Colonial Courts of Admiraly Act 1890, for provisions relating to Colonial Courts of Admiralty and Vice-Admiralty Courts.

[3] As to what circumstances make a master's removal "necessary," see *The Royalist* (1863) B. & L. 46; 32 L.J.Adm. 105. As to endorsement of removal upon certificate of registry, etc., see s. 19. As to the power of the court to cancel or suspend the certificate of the master on removing him, see s. 470 (1) (*c*).

[4] The words of the repealed section were "upon application by the owner . . . or by the part-owner or consignee or . . . ," and thereunder the removal was ordered on the application of a part-owner in *The Royalist, supra.*

Delivery of certificate cancelled or suspended

379 **473.**—(1) *A master, mate, or engineer whose certificate is cancelled or suspended*[1] *by any court or by the* [*Secretary of State for Trade*] *shall deliver his certificate—*

(*a*) *if cancelled or suspended by a court to that court on demand:*

(*b*) *if not so demanded, or if it is cancelled or suspended by the* [*Secretary of State for Trade*], *to* [*the Secretary of State*], *or as* [*the Secretary of State directs*].

(2) *If a master, mate, or engineer fail to comply with this section, he shall, for each offence, be liable to a fine not exceeding fifty pounds.*

[1] For powers as to cancellation or suspension of certificates, see ss. 469, 470. A record of cancellations and suspensions is kept by the Secretary of State for Trade; see s. 100 (2)

Power of the Secretary of State for Trade to restore certificate

380 **474.** *The* [*Secretary of State for Trade*] *may, if* [*he thinks*] *that the justice of the case requires it, re-issue and return the certificate of a master, mate, or engineer which has been cancelled or suspended,*[1] *whether in the United Kingdom or in a British possession, or shorten the time for which it is suspended, or grant in place thereof a certificate of the same or any lower grade.*

[1] For powers as to cancellation or suspension of certificates, see ss. 469, 470. The granting of a certificate of a lower grade may be recommended by the court.

Rehearing of Investigations and Inquiries

Rehearing of inquiries and investigations

381 **475.**—(1) *The* [*Secretary of State for Trade*] *may, in any case where under this Part of this Act a formal investigation as aforesaid into a shipping casualty, or an inquiry into the conduct of a master, mate, or engineer has been held, order the case to be reheard either generally or as to any part thereof, and shall*[1] *do so*—

(*a*) *if new and important evidence which could not be produced at the investigation or inquiry has been discovered; or*

(*b*) *if for any other reason there has in* [*his*] *opinion been ground for suspecting that a miscarriage of justice has occurred.*

(2) *The* [*Secretary of State for Trade*] *may order the case to be reheard, either by the court or authority by whom the case was heard in the first instance, or by the wreck commissioner, or in England or Ireland by the High Court,*[2] *or in Scotland by the Senior Lord Ordinary, or any other judge in the Court of Session whom the Lord President of that court may appoint for the purpose, and the case shall be so reheard accordingly.*

(3) *Where on any such investigation or inquiry, a decision has been given with respect to the cancelling or suspension of the certificate of a master, mate, or engineer,*[3] *and an application for a rehearing under this section has not been made or has been refused, an appeal shall lie from the decision to the following courts; namely*—

(*a*) *If the decision is given in England or by a naval court, to the High Court*[4]*:*

(*b*) *If the decision is given in Scotland, to either division of the Court of Session:*

(*c*) *If the decision is given in Ireland, to the High Court in Ireland.*

(4) *Any rehearing or appeal under this section shall be subject to and conducted in accordance with such conditions and regulations as may be*

prescribed by rules made in relation thereto under the powers contained in this Part of this Act.[5]

82 [1] The words " and shall " in subs. (1) impose on the Secretary of State for Trade a duty, when new and important evidence which could not be produced at the investigation is discovered, to grant a rehearing, and he may be compelled by mandamus to grant it: *The Ida* (1886) 11 P.D. 37.

[2] For a recent example of a rehearing which was ordered by the High Court to be heard by a Divisional Court of the former Probate, Divorce and Admiralty Division assisted by assessors, see *The Seistan* [1959] 2 Lloyd's Rep. 607.

[3] It is uncertain whether under this section alone, a master who has been censured for negligence, but whose certificate has not been cancelled or suspended, would have a right of appeal. Probably he would, as the decision not to cancel or suspend his certificate is a " decision with respect to the cancelling or suspension of the certificate." He has, however, a clear right of appeal under M.S.A. 1906, s. 66, which provides that where an application for a rehearing has not been made or refused, the owner of the ship or any other person, who, having an interest in the investigation or inquiry, has appeared at the hearing and is affected by the decision of the court, may appeal from that decision in the same manner and subject to the same conditions in and subject to which a master may appeal against a decision with respect to the cancelling or suspension of his certificate; he is a person having an interest in the investigation: *The Royal Star* [1928] P. 48. Previous to the Act of 1906 an owner had no right of appeal, even where he had been condemned in costs, and thus, in effect, found guilty of a misdemeanour and subjected to a fine: *The Golden Sea* (1882) 7 P.D. 194.

[4] The appeal is to the Queen's Bench Division (Admiralty Court): see R.S.C., Ord. 74, r. 1 (§ 3190, *post*); and the Shipping Casualties Rules, 1923, No. 19, *post*, § 3195. The appeal is not a rehearing; see *The Princess Victoria* [1953] 2 Lloyd's Rep. 619, 624.

83 [5] See the Shipping Casualties Rules 1923, Nos. 19, 20 and 21, *post*, Appendix 5, § 3195, made under s. 479.

COSTS. See the Shipping Casualties Rules 1923, Nos. 20 and 21, *post*, § 3192. Before these rules the court laid down the rule (which, it seems, still applies) that an unsuccessful appellant would usually be condemned in costs, and that in the case of a successful appeal against a suspension of a certificate at the instance of the Department of Trade, the Department would be ordered to pay the appellant's costs unless he had been guilty of such misconduct as rendered an inquiry reasonable: *The Arizona* (1880) 5 P.D. 123. And in *The Carlisle* [1906] P. 301 (see at p. 308), the Board were ordered to pay the costs of a successful appellant against a suspension, because they had failed to advise the court below whether in their opinion on the evidence the certificate should be dealt with. Where the Department of Trade has acted with fairness and propriety throughout, even where appeal is successful, no costs will be allowed; see *The Throstlegarth* (1899) (unreported, but referred to in *The Carlisle* [1906] P. 312). Similarly, in the case of a successful appeal against the suspension of a certificate by a Court of Formal Investigation at Singapore, the inquiry being ordered not by the Board of Trade (now the Department of Trade) but by the Governor of the Straits Settlements, costs of the appeal were not awarded against the Board of Trade. *Secus*, the costs of the argument as to the appellant's right of appeal; see *The Royal Star* (*No.* 2) [1928] P. 144; following *The Grecian* (1920), reported [1928] P. 146n. See also *The Famenoth* (1882) 7 P.D. 207; *The Golden Sea* (*supra*); *The Kestrel* (1881) 6 P.D. 182; *Brown* v. *Board of Trade* (1890) 18 R. (Ct. of Sess.) 291. The court hearing the appeal has power to allow the successful appellant officers their costs, not only of the appeal, but also of the inquiries: *The Empire Antelope, The Radchurch* [1943] P. 79.

EVIDENCE. The court hearing the appeal will consider the evidence and, if it is insufficient to justify the suspension of the certificate, will reverse the decision: *The Arizona* (1880) 5 P.D. 123, cited in note to s. 470. See, too, *Turner* v. *Board of Trade* (1894) 22 R. 18, and *The Princess Victoria* [1953] 2 Lloyd's Rep. 619.

The court has power to receive fresh evidence on appeal or rehearing: see the Shipping Casualties Rules 1923, No. 20 (*h*), *post*, § 3195. Where it is desired to adduce fresh evidence on appeal, application for leave to do so should be made before the hearing of the appeal: *The Famenoth* (1882) 7 P.D. 207; 48 L.T. 28.

The court will not permit witnesses to be called on questions of nautical knowledge or skill—it is the duty of the nautical assessors to advise the court on such matters; *The Kestrel* (1881) 6 P.D. 182; 45 L.T. 111.

An appeal lies to the Court of Appeal from the Divisional Court if leave to appeal is obtained; see Supreme Court of Judicature (Consolidation) Act 1925, s. 31 (1) (*f*).

Supplemental Provisions as to Investigations and Inquiries

Investigations before stipendiary magistrate

384 **476.**—(1) *Where a stipendiary magistrate is in any place a member of the local marine board, a formal investigation at that place into a shipping casualty shall, whenever he happens to be present, be held before that stipendiary magistrate.*[1]

(2) *There shall be paid out of the Mercantile Marine Fund*[2] *to the stipendiary magistrate, if he is not remunerated out of money provided by Parliament under this Act, such remuneration by way of an annual increase of salary, or otherwise, as a Secretary of State, with the consent of the* [*Secretary of State for Trade*] *may direct.*

[1] *Cf.* s. 466 (1) (2), as to persons to hold formal investigations.
[2] Now " out of moneys provided by Parliament"; see M.S. (Mercantile Marine Fund) Act 1898, s. 1 (1) (*b*).

385 **477.** [*This section* (*Power to appoint Wreck Commissioners*) *was repealed by the M.S.A.* 1970, *s.* 100 (3), *Sched. V as from January* 1, 1973: *see S.I.* 1972 *No.* 1977. *See now ibid. s.* 82.]

Authority for colonial court to make inquiries into shipping casualties and conduct of officers

386 **478.**—(1) The legislature of any British possession may authorise any court or tribunal to make inquiries as to shipwrecks, or other casualties affecting ships, or as to charges of incompetency, or misconduct on the part of masters, mates, or engineers of ships, in the following cases; namely:—

(*a*) where a shipwreck or casualty occurs to a British ship on or near the coasts [1] of any British possession or to a British ship in the course of a voyage to a port within the British possession:

(*b*) where a shipwreck or casualty occurs in any part of the world to a British ship registered in the British possession:

(*c*) where some of the crew of a British ship which has been wrecked or to which a casualty has occurred, and who are competent witnesses to the facts, are found in the British possession:

(*d*) where the incompetency or misconduct has occurred on board a British ship on or near the coasts of the British possession, or on board a British ship in the course of a voyage to a port within the British possession:

(*e*) where the incompetency or misconduct has occurred on board a British ship registered in the British possession:

(*f*) when the master, mate, or engineer of a British ship who is charged with incompetency or misconduct on board that British ship is found in the British possession.

(2) A court or tribunal so authorised shall have the same jurisdiction over the matter in question as if it had occurred within their ordinary jurisdiction, but subject to all provisions, restrictions, and conditions which would have been applicable if it had so occurred.

(3) An inquiry shall not be held under this section into any matter which has once been the subject of an investigation or inquiry and has been reported on by a competent court or tribunal in any part of Her Majesty's dominions, or in respect of which the certificate of a master, mate, or engineer has been cancelled or suspended by naval court.

87 (4) Where an investigation or inquiry has been commenced in the United Kingdom with reference to any matter, an inquiry with reference to the same matter shall not be held, under this section, in a British possession.

(5) The court or tribunal holding an inquiry under this section shall have the same powers of cancelling and suspending certificates, and shall exercise those powers in the same manner as a court holding a similar investigation or inquiry in the United Kingdom.[2]

(6) The [Secretary of State for Trade] may order the rehearing of any inquiry under this section in like manner as he may order the rehearing of a similar investigation or inquiry in the United Kingdom,[3] but if an application for rehearing either is not made or is refused, an appeal [4] shall lie from any order or finding of the court or tribunal holding the inquiry to the High Court in England [5]: provided that an appeal shall not lie—

(*a*) from any order or finding on an inquiry into a casualty affecting a ship registered in a British possession, or

(*b*) from a decision affecting the certificate of a master, mate, or engineer, if that certificate has not been granted either in the United Kingdom or in a British possession, under the authority of this Act.

(7) The appeal shall be conducted in accordance with such conditions and regulations as may from time to time be prescribed by rules made in relation thereto under the powers contained in this Part of this Act.[6]

38 [1] *Quaere*, within territorial waters; see s. 464, note (1).

[2] See s. 470, as to certificates of officers.

[3] See s. 475, as to rehearing of inquiries, and as to the rights of the shipowner and other interested parties to appeal, see M.S.A. 1906, s. 66.

[4] A master who has been censured for negligence by a colonial court of inqury, but whose certificate has not been cancelled or suspended has, *semble*, a right of appeal under this section, and certainly has under M.S.A. 1906, s. 66, as being a person " interesed in the investigation or inquiry; " *The Royal Star*, *supra*, cited in note (3) to s. 475.

[5] The appeal is to a Divisional Court of the Queen's Bench Division (Admiralty Court). See R.S.C., Ord. 74 (App. 10, *post*, § 3190), and the Shipping Casualties Rules 1923, No. 19, *post*, § 3192.

[6] See s. 479.

Rules as to investigations and inquiries

389 **479.**—(1) *The Lord Chancellor may (with the consent of the Treasury so far as relates to fees) make general rules for carrying into effect the enactments relating to formal investigations, and to the rehearing of, or an appeal from, any investigation or inquiry held under this Part of this Act, and in particular with respect to the appointment and summoning of assessors, the procedure, the parties, the persons allowed to appear, the notice to those parties or persons or to persons affected, the amount and application of fees, and the place in which formal investigations are to be held.*

(2) *Any rule made under this section while in force shall have effect as if it were enacted in this Act.*

(3) *Any rule made under this section with regard to the rehearing of, or appeals from, any investigation or inquiries, as to the appointment of assessors, and as to the place in which formal investigations are to be held, shall be laid before both Houses of Parliament as soon as may be after it is made.*

The rules at present in force are the Shipping Casualties and Appeals and Rehearing Rules 1923, dated May 4, 1923 (S.R. & O. No. 752/L. 9), printed as Appendix 11, §§ 3192–3201.

The making of rules under this section is now subject to the Statutory Instruments Act 1946.

Naval Courts on the High Seas and Abroad

Cases in which naval courts may be summoned

390 **480.**[1] *A court (in this Act called a naval court) may be summoned by any officer in command of any of Her Majesty's ships on any foreign station,*[2] *or, in the absence of such an officer, by any consular officer, in the following cases; (that is to say,)*

(i) *Whenever a complaint which appears to that officer to require immediate investigation is made to him by the master of any British ship, or by a certificated mate, or by any one or more of the seamen belonging to any such ship;*

(ii) *Whenever the interest of the owner of any British ship or of the cargo thereof appears to that officer to require it; and*

(iii) *Whenever any British ship is wrecked, abandoned, or otherwise lost at or near the place where that officer may be, or whenever the crew or part of the crew of any British ship which has been wrecked, abandoned, or lost abroad arrive at that place.*

During the 1939–45 War, naval courts were given the function of trying British subjects, who were the masters or members of the crew of any ship other than a Dominion ship, in respect of offences committed in certain specified countries. See Regulation 47AAB of the Defence (General) Regulations 1939, which has now been revoked.

[1] " This fasciculus of clauses as to the holding of naval courts creates a special tribunal specially constituted of not less than three persons for the purpose of dealing with emergencies arising in foreign ports or on the high seas ": *per* Farwell L.J. in *Hutton* v. *Ras Steam Shipping Co. Ltd.* [1907] 1 K.B. 834 at p. 843. See also comments of Singleton

L.J. in *Canadian Pacific Ry.* v. *Gaud and Others* [1949] 2 K.B. 239, when considering s. 573 of the Canada Shipping Act, 1934, which is in almost identical terms.

[2] The words " on any foreign station " were specifically referred to and commented on by Singleton L.J. in *Canadian Pacific Ry.* v. *Gaud and Others, supra.*

Constitution of naval courts

91 **481.**—(1) *A naval court shall consist of not more than five and not less than three members, of whom, if possible, one shall be an officer in the naval service of Her Majesty not below the rank of lieutenant, one a consular officer, and one a master of a British merchant ship, and the rest shall be either officers in the naval service of Her Majesty, masters of British merchant ships, or British merchants, and the court may include the officer summoning the same, but shall not include the master or consignee of the ship to which the parties complaining or complained against belong.*[1]

(2) *The naval or consular officer in the court, if there is only one such officer, or, if there is more than one, the naval or consular officer who, according to any regulations for settling their respective ranks for the time being in force, is of the highest rank, shall be the president of the court.*

[1] As to the constitution of the court, see McMillan, *Shipping, Inquiries and Courts* (1929, Stevens & Sons Ltd.), pp. 62–64.

Functions of naval courts

92 **482.**—(1) *A naval court shall hear the complaint or other matter brought before them under this Act, or investigate the cause of the wreck, abandonment, or loss, and shall do so in such manner as to give every person against whom any complaint or charge is made an opportunity of making a defence.*[1]

(2) *A naval court may, for the purpose of the hearing and investigation, administer an oath, summon parties and witnesses, and compel their attendance and the production of documents.*

[1] *Cf.* s. 471 (3) (*c*), and note (4) thereto, as to publicity of inquiry.

Powers of naval courts

93 **483.**—(1) *Every naval court may, after hearing and investigating the case, exercise the following powers; (that is to say,)*

(*a*) *the court may, if unanimous that the safety of the ship or crew or the interest of the owner absolutely requires it, remove the master, and appoint another person to act in his stead; but no such appointment shall be made without the consent of the consignee of the ship if at the place where the case is heard:*

(*b*) *the court may, in cases in which they are authorised by this Act*[1] *and subject to the provisions of this Act, cancel or suspend the certificate of any master, mate, or engineer:*

(*c*) *the court may discharge a seaman from his ship:*

(*d*) *the court may order the wages of a seaman so discharged or any part of those wages to be forfeited, and may direct the same either to be retained by way of compensation to the owner, or to be paid into the Exchequer, in the same manner as fines under this Act:*

(*e*) *the court may decide any questions as to wages or fines or forfeitures arising between any of the parties to the proceedings:*

(*f*) *the court may direct that all or any of the costs incurred by the master or owner of any ship in procuring the imprisonment of any seaman or apprentice in a foreign port, or in his maintenance whilst so imprisoned, shall be paid out of and deducted from the wages of that seaman or apprentice, whether then or subsequently earned:*

(*g*) *the court may exercise the same powers with regard to persons charged before them with the commission of offences at sea or abroad as British consular officers can under the Thirteenth Part of this Act*[2]*:*

(*h*) *the court may punish any master of a ship or any of the crew of a ship respecting whose conduct a complaint is brought before them for any offence against this Act, which, when committed by the said master or member of the crew, is punishable on summary conviction, and shall for that purpose have the same powers as a court of summary jurisdiction would have if the case were tried in the United Kingdom*[3]*:*

Provided that—

(i) [. . .][4]

(ii) *copies of all sentences passed by any naval court summoned to hear any such complaint as aforesaid, shall be sent to the commander-in-chief or senior naval officer of the station:*

(*j*) *the court may, if it appears expedient, order a survey of any ship which is the subject of investigation to be made, and such survey shall accordingly be made, in the same way, and the surveyor who makes the same shall have the same powers as if such survey had been directed by a competent court in pursuance of the Fifth Part of this Act,*[5] *in the course of proceedings against a seaman or apprentice for the offence of desertion:*

(*k*) *The court may order the costs of the proceedings before them, or any part of those costs, to be paid by any of the parties thereto, and may order any person making a frivolous or vexatious complaint to pay compensation for any loss or delay caused thereby; and any costs or compensation so ordered to be paid shall be paid by that person accordingly, and may be recovered in the same manner in which the wages of seamen are recoverable,*[6] *or may, if the case admits, be deducted from the wages due to that person.*

(2) *All orders duly made by a naval court under the powers hereby*

given to it, shall in any subsequent legal proceedings be conclusive as to the rights of the parties.[7]

(3) *All orders made by any naval court shall, whenever practicable, be entered in the official log-book of the ship to which the parties to the proceedings before the court belong, and signed by the president of the court.*[8]

394 Certain punishments, etc. imposed by naval courts are now subject to review by the senior naval or consular officer present at the place where the court is held; see M.S.A. 1950, s. 3.

By M.S.A. 1906, s. 67, the naval court also has power to send a prisoner either to the United Kingdom or to any British possession to which that section has been applied, and for that purpose has the power given to consular officers by s. 689. The reviewing officer under M.S.A. 1950, s. 3, however, may revoke any direction by a naval court in exercise of their power (see subs. (4) of that section).

1 See s. 470 (1) (*a*) and (*c*), as to power of court as to certificates. No provision is made for assessors to assist a naval court, and the requirement for their concurrence in s. 470 (1) (*a*) does not, therefore, apply here.

2 See s. 689 as to conveyance of offenders.

3 See ss. 680 *et seq*., as to prosecution of offences.

4 The proviso omitted ceased to have effect by virtue of M.S.A. 1950, s. 3 (8), itself now repealed.

5 See s. 463 as to survey of unseaworthy ships.

6 See M.S.A. 1970, ss. 7 *et seq*. as to mode of recovering wages.

7 On questions of wages, fines, or forfeitures there is now an appeal to the High Court. Subs. (2) has no effect where the order of the naval court is quashed; but when the order is varied, the subsection applies as if the order, as so varied, were the order of the naval court. See M.S.A. 1906, s. 68 (2) and Merchant Shipping Rules 1908. This provision was in consequence of the defeat of a claim for wages: *Hutton* v. *Ras S.S. Co.* [1907] 1 K.B. 834, where a naval court had discharged and forfeited the wages of seamen who had lawfully refused to continue a voyage with a cargo of contraband.

8 As to official log books and entries therein, see M.S.A. 1970, s. 68.

Report of proceedings of naval courts

395 **484.**—(1) *Every naval court shall make a report to the [Secretary of State for Trade] containing the following particulars (that is to say):—*

(*a*) *a statement of the proceedings of the court, together with the order made by the court, and a report of the evidence;*

(*b*) *an account of the wages of any seaman or apprentice who is discharged from his ship by the court;*

(*c*) *if summoned to inquire into a case of wreck or abandonment, a statement of the opinion of the court as to the cause of that wreck or abandonment, with such remarks on the conduct of the master and crew as the circumstances require.*

(2) *Every such report shall be signed by the president of the court, and shall be admissible in evidence in manner provided by this Act.*[1]

1 See ss. 695 *et seq*., for admissibility of documents in evidence.

Penalty for preventing complaint or obstructing investigation

396 **485.** *If any person wilfully and without due cause prevents or obstructs the making of any complaint to an officer empowered to summon a naval court, or the conduct of any hearing or investigation by any naval court, he*

shall for each offence be liable to a fine not exceeding fifty pounds, or be liable to imprisonment, with or without hard labour,[1] *for any period not exceeding twelve weeks.*

[1] Imprisonment with hard labour has now been abolished: see Criminal Justice Act 1948, s. 1 (2).

Application of provisions as to naval courts

397 **486.**—(1) The provisions of this Part of this Act with regard to naval courts on the high seas and abroad shall apply to all sea-going ships registered in the United Kingdom (with the exception, *in their application elsewhere than in Scotland*, of fishing boats exclusively employed in fishing on the coasts [1] of the United Kingdom [2]) and to all ships registered in a British possession, when those ships are out of the jurisdiction of their respective governments, and where they apply to a ship, shall apply to the owners, master, and crew of that ship.

(2) For the purpose of the said provisions an unregistered British ship shall be deemed to have been registered in the United Kingdom.[3]

The words in italics are repealed by M.S. (Scottish Fishing Boats) Act 1920, s. 1 (3) and Schedule.

[1] See notes (1), (2) to s. 464, as to meaning of " ship on the coasts."

[2] " United Kingdom " here includes the Republic of Ireland. See note " Application to Northern Ireland and the Republic of Ireland," in notes to s. 742.

[3] *Cf.* s. 72 for similar applications of Act to unregistered British ships.

Courts of Survey

398 A right of appeal to a Court of Survey is granted by the M.S. Acts in the following cases: M.S.A. 1894, s. 275, from survey of passenger steamer; s. 420, from refusal of certificate as to lights and fog signals; s. 459, from order for detention of ship as unsafe; and M.S. (Safety Convention) Act 1949, s. 13 (2) (which (*inter alia*) extends the application of s. 275 of M.S.A. 1894) from refusal of safety certificate.

Where the appeal involves a question of construction or design, or of scientific difficulty, etc., the Secretary of State for Trade may refer the matter to a scientific referee. See s. 490.

As to power to detain unsafe ships, see s. 459; for liability for costs and damages, see s. 460 and Rules of the Court of Survey 1876 and 1877.

Constitution of court of survey

399 **487.**—(1) A court of survey for a port or district shall consist of a judge sitting with two assessors.

(2) The judge shall be such person as may be summoned for the case in accordance with the rules made under this Act [1] with respect to that court, out of a list approved for the port or district by a Secretary of State, of wreck commissioners appointed under this Act,[2] stipendiary or metropolitan police magistrates, judges of county courts, and other fit persons; but in any special case in which the [Secretary of State for Trade thinks] it expedient to appoint a wreck commissioner, the judge shall be such wreck commissioner.

(3) The assessors shall be persons of nautical, engineering, or other special skill and experience; subject to the provisions of the Fifth Part of this Act as regards foreign ships,[3] one of them shall be appointed by the [Secretary of State for Trade], either generally or in each case, and the other shall be summoned, in accordance with the rules made as aforesaid, by the registrar of the court, out of a list of persons periodically nominated for the purpose *by the local marine board of the port, or if there is no such board,*[4] by a body of local shipowners or merchants approved for the purpose by a Secretary of State, or, if there is no such list, shall be appointed by the judge. If a Secretary of State thinks fit at any time, on the recommendation of the government of any British possession or any foreign country, to add any persons to any such list, those persons shall, until otherwise directed by the Secretary of State, be added to the list, and if there is no such list shall form the list.

(4) The county court registrar or such other fit person as a Secretary of State may from time to time appoint shall be the registrar of the court, and shall, on receiving notice of an appeal or a reference from the [Secretary of State for Trade], immediately summon the court to meet forthwith in manner directed by the rules.

(5) The name of the registrar and his office, together with the rules made as aforesaid, relating to the court of survey, shall be published in the manner directed by the rules.

(6) In the application of this section to Scotland the expression " judge of a county court " means a sheriff, and the expression " county court registrar " means sheriff clerk.

(7) In the application of this section to Ireland [5] the expression " stipendiary magistrate " includes any of the justices of the peace in Dublin metropolis and any resident magistrate.

(8) In the application of this section to the Isle of Man the expression " judge of a county court " means the water bailiff, the expression " stipendiary magistrate " means the high bailiff, the expression " registrar of a county court " means a clerk to a deemster or a clerk to justices of the peace.

1 See s. 489, rules for procedure of Court of Survey.
2 See s. 82 of the M.S.A. 1970, power to appoint wreck commissioner.
3 See s. 462 (iii), appointment of assessors by foreign consular officers where the survey is on a foreign ship.
4 The words in italics were repealed by the M.S.A. 1970, s. 100 (3), Sched. V as from January 1, 1973: see S.I. 1972 No. 1977.
5 See note "Application to Northern Ireland and the Republic of Ireland " in notes following s. 742, § 689, *post*.

Power and procedure of court of survey

90 **488.**—(1) The court of survey shall hear every case in open court.
(2) The judge and each assessor of the court may survey the ship, and

shall have for the purposes of this Act all the powers of a [Department of Trade] inspector under this Act.[1]

(3) The judge of the court may appoint any competent person or persons to survey the ship and report thereon to the court.

(4) The judge of the court, any assessor of the court, and any person appointed by the judge of the court to survey a ship, may go on board the ship and inspect the same and every part thereof, and the machinery, equipment, and cargo, and may require the unloading or removal of any cargo, ballast, or tackle, and any person who wilfully impedes such judge, assessor, or person in the execution of the survey, or fails to comply with any requisition made by him, shall for each offence be liable to a fine not exceeding ten pounds.

(5) The judge of the court shall have the same power as the [Department of Trade has] to order the ship to be released or finally detained, but, unless one of the assessors concurs in an order for the detention of the ship, the ship shall be released.[2]

(6) The owner and master of the ship and any person appointed by the owner or master, and also any person appointed by the [Secretary of State for Trade], may attend at any inspection or survey made in pursuance of this section.

(7) The judge of the court shall send to the [Secretary of State for Trade] such report as may be directed by the rules, and each assessor shall either sign the report or report to the [Secretary of State for Trade] the reasons for his dissent.[3]

[1] See ss. 729 and 730, powers of Department of Trade inspectors.

[2] As to such powers of the Secretary of State for Trade see ss. 459 and 462. As to the enforcement of detention, see s. 692.

[3] See Appendix 6, *post*, § 3024, rule 31. Section 420 (appeals from refusal of certificate as to lights and fog-signals) also provides for reports by the courts to the Secretary of State for Trade.

Rules for procedure of court of survey, etc.

401 **489.** The Lord Chancellor may (with the consent of the Treasury so far as relates to fees) make general rules to carry into effect the provisions of this Act with respect to a court of survey, and in particular with respect to the summoning of, and procedure before, the court, the requiring on an appeal security for costs and damages, the amount and application of fees, and the publication of the rules, and those rules shall have effect as if enacted in this Act.

For the rules at present in force, *viz*. Rules of the Court of Survey 1876 and 1877, made under 39 & 40 Vict. c. 80, s. 9, and as to the saving thereof, see s. 745.

Scientific Referees

Reference in difficult cases to scientific persons

402 **490.**—(1) If the [Secretary of State for Trade is] of opinion that an appeal to a court of survey [1] involves a question of construction or design or of scientific difficulty or important principle, [he] may refer the matter to such one or more out of a list of scientific referees from time to time approved by a Secretary of State, as may appear to possess the special qualifications necessary for the particular case, and may be selected by agreement between the [Department of Trade] and the appellant, or in default of any such agreement by a Secretary of State, and thereupon the appeal shall be determined by the referee or referees, instead of by the court of survey.

(2) The [Secretary of State for Trade], if the appellant in any appeal so requires and gives security to the satisfaction of the [Secretary of State for Trade] to pay the costs of and incidental to the reference, shall refer that appeal to a referee or referees so selected as aforesaid.

(3) The referee or referees shall have the same powers as a judge of the court of survey.

[1] As to the cases in which an appeal lies to a Court of Survey, see note at head of s. 487.

403 **491.** [*This section* (*Payment to officers of court*) *was repealed by the M.S.A.* 1970, *s.* 100 (3), *Sched. V as from January* 1, 1973; *see S.I.* 1972 *No.* 1977.]

PART VII—DELIVERY OF GOODS

404 As to the respective rights and liabilities of the shipowner and the consignee or the holder of the bill of lading with regard to the exercise of the shipowner's lien on cargo at common law, under the Sufferance Wharfs Act (11 & 12 Vict. c. xviii), and under the sections of the M.S.A. 1862, here reproduced, see *per* Willes J. in *Meyerstein* v. *Barber* (1866) L.R. 2 C.P. 38 (affirmed by Ex.Ch. and H.L.; see *infra*, s. 494).

The general rights and obligations, as regards delivery of cargo, of shipowners, charterers, and consignees under charterparties and bills of lading, being for the most part regulated by common law and the particular terms of the special contract, are beyond the scope of these notes, but are exhaustively discussed in *British Shipping Laws* (Vols. 2 & 3), *Carver on Carriage by Sea* (13th ed.) and *Scrutton on Charterparties and Bills of Lading* (18th ed.).

Delivery of Goods and Lien for Freight

Definitions under Part VII

405 **492.** In this Part of this Act, unless the context otherwise requires—

The expression "goods" includes every description of wares and merchandise:

The expression "wharf" includes all wharves, quays, docks, and premises in or upon which any goods, when landed from ships, may be lawfully placed:

The expression "warehouse" includes all warehouses, buildings, and premises in which goods, when landed from ships, may be lawfully placed:

The expression "report" means the report required by the customs laws to be made by the master of an importing ship [1]:

The expression "entry" means the entry required by the customs laws to be made for the landing or discharge of goods from an importing ship [1]:

The expression "shipowner" includes the master of the ship and every other person authorised to act as agent for the owner or entitled to receive the freight, demurrage, or other charges payable in respect of the ship:

The expression "owner" used in relation to goods means every person who is for the time [2] entitled, either as owner or agent for the owner, to the possession of the goods,[3] subject in the case of a lien (if any), to that lien:

The expression "wharfinger"[4] means the occupier of a wharf as hereinbefore defined:

The expression "warehouseman"[4] means the occupier of a warehouse as hereinbefore defined.

[1] For the relevant provisions, see the Customs and Excise Act 1952, ss. 26 *et seq.*
[2] As to the position where the right to possession has passed from one party to another between the time of landing and the making of the deposit, see *A/s. Helsingörs, Sö, etc.* v. *Walton*, cited in note (3) to s. 496.
[3] As to the position of a consignee for sale taking delivery from the warehouseman, see *White & Co.* v. *Furness Withy & Co., infra* (s. 495).
[4] These expressions have been substituted for "wharf owner" and "warehouse owner" throughout these sections.

Power of shipowner to enter and land goods on default by owner of goods

406 **493.**—(1) Where the owner[1] of any goods imported in any ship from foreign parts into the United Kingdom[2] fails[3] to make entry thereof, or, having made entry thereof, to land the same or take delivery thereof, and to proceed therewith with all convenient speed, by the times severally hereinafter mentioned, the shipowner may[4] make entry of and land or unship the goods at the following times:—

(*a*) If a time for the delivery of the goods is expressed in the charter party, bill of lading, or agreement, then at any time after the time so expressed[5]:

(*b*) If no time for the delivery of the goods is expressed in the charter party, bill of lading, or agreement, then at any time after the expiration of seventy-two hours, exclusive of a Sunday or holiday, from the time of the report of the ship.

(2) Where a shipowner lands goods in pursuance of this section[6] he shall place them, or cause them to be placed—

(*a*) If any wharf or warehouse is named in the charter party, bill of lading, or agreement, as the wharf or warehouse where the goods are to be placed and if they can be conveniently there received, on that wharf or in that warehouse; and

(*b*) In any other case on some wharf or in some warehouse on or in which goods of a like nature are usually placed; the wharf or warehouse being, if the goods are dutiable, a wharf or warehouse duly approved by the Commissioners of Customs[7] for the landing of dutiable goods.

(3) If at any time before the goods are landed or unshipped[3] the owner of the goods is ready and offers to land or take delivery of the same, he shall be allowed to do so, and his entry shall in that case be preferred to any entry which may have been made by the shipowner.[8]

(4) If any goods are, for the purpose of convenience in assorting the same, landed at the wharf where the ship is discharged, and the owner

of the goods at the time of that landing has made entry and is ready and offers to take delivery thereof, and to convey the same to some other wharf or warehouse, the goods shall be assorted at landing, and shall, if demanded, be delivered to the owner thereof within twenty-four hours after assortment; and the expense of and consequent on that landing and assortment shall be borne by the ship owner.[9]

(5) If at any time before the goods are landed or unshipped [3] the owner thereof has made entry for the landing and warehousing thereof at any particular wharf or warehouse other than that at which the ship is discharging, and has offered and been ready to take delivery thereof,[10] and the shipowner has failed to make that delivery, and has also failed at the time of that offer to give the owner of the goods correct information of the time at which the goods can be delivered, then the shipowner shall, before landing or unshipping the goods, in pursuance of this section, give to the owner of the goods or of such wharf or warehouse as last aforesaid twenty-four hours' notice in writing of his readiness to deliver the goods, and shall, if he lands or unships the same without that notice, do so at his own risk and expense.[11]

407 [1] This includes an agent authorised to take delivery: *Euterpe S.S. Co.* v. *Bath & Sons* (1897) 2 Com.Cas. 196; *White & Co.* v. *Furness, Withy & Co.* [1895] A.C. 40, cited in note (3) to s. 495.

[2] " United Kingdom." See note " Republic of Ireland " in notes to s. 742.

[3] The section only applies where the owner of the goods has previously failed to take delivery as mentioned in subs. (1); hence, when not in default, he cannot take advantage of subs. (3): *Marzetti* v. *Smith* (1883) 49 L.T. 580; 5 Asp.M.C. 166 (C.A.), affirming 1 C. & E. 6. Nor of subs. (5). *Oliver* v. *Colven, infra.* See also *Glyn* v. *East and West India Dock Co.* (1882) 7 App.Cas. 591, 607 (H.L.), affirming 6 Q.B.D. 475. But the default need not be wilful. The shipowner is at liberty to land the goods under the section " whenever the delivery of them to the owner within the proper time has been prevented by the force of circumstances, whether the latter is or is not to blame ": *The Energie* (*Miedbrodt* v. *Fitzsimon*) (1875) L.R. 6 P.C. at p. 316; *The Clan Macdonald* (1883) 8 P.D. 178, 183.

[4] " The Act imposes no obligation. It is merely an empowering enactment of which the shipowner need not take advantage." *Per* Lord Herschell in *White & Co.* v. *Furness, Withy & Co., supra*; *Hick* v. *Rodocanachi* [1891] 2 Q.B. 626. He may have more advantageous rights under (1) special contract; *e.g.* by bill of lading containing the " London Clause," which empowers the shipowner to land the goods immediately on arrival: *Borrowman, Phillips* v. *Wilson* (1891) 7 T.L.R. 416. *Cf. Wilson* v. *London, Italian, etc., S.N. Co.* (1865) L.R. 1 C.P. 61, 66; *Oliver* v. *Colven* (1879) 27 W.R. 822; *Dennis* v. *Cork S.S. Co., infra*; or (2) by custom of the port. *Cf. Aste, Son and Kercheval* v. *Stumore Weston* (1884) C. & E. 319.

[5] See *Marzetti* v. *Smith, supra,* and other cases cited in note (3). The shipowner or master must exercise his discretion and act reasonably: *Smailes & Sons* v. *Hans Dessen* (1906) 11 Com.Cas. 74; 94 L.T. 492; (1907) 12 Com.Cas. 117; 95 L.T. 809 (C.A.). In the lower court Channell J. held that where the charterparty provides for discharge at a customary rate and gives the receiver days on demurrage over and above the lay days, a shipowner cannot land the goods subject to the lien given by s. 494, until it is evident that the goods cannot be discharged within the demurrage time allowed, but the Court of Appeal refused to decide this point.

408 [6] Where goods are stored with a warehouseman with directions that he is not to deliver to anyone without instructions, the goods are not landed in pursuance of this section, and therefore the owner of the goods is not entitled to delivery on depositing the freight under s. 495: *Dennis* v. *Cork S.S. Co.* [1913] 2 K.B. 393. A form of notice which, it is thought, satisfies s. 494 is printed as Appendix 8, § 3030, and referred to in the notes to that section.

[7] Now Commissioners of Customs and Excise; see Customs and Excise Act 1952, s. 318 (1), Sched. X. For provisions relating to approval see *ibid.* ss. 14, 80 *et seq.*

[8] It seems that where part of the goods has been landed before he is ready to take delivery, the goods-owner may still avail himself of the provision of subss. (3) and (5), provided that the shipowner can deliver the remainder without any further loss or injury than he would have incurred if the goods-owner had been ready before any of the goods were landed: *Wilson* v. *London-Italian, etc. S.N. Co., supra.*

The section does not entitle the goods-owner to demand delivery in a manner opposed to a custom of the port which is not inconsistent with the terms of the bill of lading: *Marzetti* v. *Smith, supra.*

[9] When goods are landed under subs. (4), subs. (5) does not apply, for the latter refers only to the discharging of cargo over side, and not to the landing of it for assortment on the wharf; and, therefore, the written notice referred to in subs. (5) is not required in cases under subs. (4): *The Clan Macdonald, supra.* But it is the duty of the goods-owner to take delivery of the goods within a reasonable time after he knows that he can have them, whether subs. (4) or subs. (5) applies. *Per* Sir J. Hannen, *ibid.* In the case cited, notice to the owner's lighterman that he could have the goods was considered sufficient notice to the owner under subs. (4).

[10] In order to entitle him to the benefit of subs. (5), the owner of the goods, when he makes an offer to take delivery of them, must be in a condition to receive the same if the offer be then accepted: *Beresford* v. *Montgomerie* (1864) 34 L.J.C.P. 41; 17 C.B.(N.S.) 379. And when such offer is made, the shipowner, if he then fails not only to make delivery of the goods, but also to give such owner information of the time at which they can be delivered, is bound to give twenty-four hours' notice before he lands the goods, although he was never asked to give such notice. *Ibid.*

[11] The concluding words of the section do not mean that where the goods are landed without such written notice they are to remain at shipowner's risk and expense for any time that the goods-owner thinks fit to leave them. The written notice is only required as a condition of the shipowner's right to land the goods at the goods-owner's risk and expense. The duty of the goods-owner remains, to take the goods within a reasonable time after he has notice, whether written or verbal, that he can receive them. *Per* Sir J. Hannen, *The Clan Macdonald, supra.*

The subsection was held inapplicable where the consignee's agent made a premature demand for the goods, and the shipowner, who was acting under the bill of lading and not under the Act, was unable to give delivery or correct information as to the time thereof owing to his bona fide ignorance of the position of the goods in the hold of the ship: *Oliver* v. *Colven, supra.*

Lien for freight on landing goods

409 **494.**[1] If at the time [2] when any goods are landed from any ship, and placed in the custody of any person as a wharfinger or warehouseman, the shipowner gives to the wharfinger or warehouseman notice in writing that the goods are to remain subject to a lien for freight or other charges [3] payable to the shipowner to an amount mentioned in the notice,[4] the goods so landed shall, in the hands of the wharfinger or warehouseman, continue subject to the same lien, if any, for such charges as they were subject to before the landing thereof [5]; and the wharfinger or warehouseman receiving those goods shall retain them until the lien is discharged as hereinafter mentioned, and shall, if he fails so to do, make good to the shipowner any loss thereby occasioned to him.[6]

410 [1] *Quaere* whether ss. 494–496 come into operation only when the shipowner has exercised his right of landing under s. 493: *Dennis* v. *Cork S.S. Co.* [1913] 2 K.B. 393, and Scrutton, *Charterparties*, 18th ed., p. 485. But in any event, s. 494 only applies to cases where the goods are stored with a notice that they "are to remain subject to a lien for freight or other charges" to the amount mentioned in the notice, and hence the operation of the sections may be excluded by a variation in the directions contained in the notice to the wharfinger or warehouseman. *Ibid.* The shipowner may, it seems, under the terms of his contract, have two courses open to him if the consignee does not take delivery. He may land the goods under s. 493 and give the requisite notice under s. 494, in which case the consignee

will be able to get possession on depositing the amount of freight, etc. mentioned in the notice, and the shipowner will in case of dispute only be able to obtain payment after taking legal proceedings (ss. 495–496). He may, on the other hand, if he has so provided in his contract of affreightment, land the goods under the terms of such special contract, which may empower him to insist on payment of freight before delivery, and in such a case the consignee will not be entitled to demand delivery from the warehouseman on mere deposit of freight with instructions to withhold payment to the shipowner, as he may when goods are landed in pursuance of s. 493.

A draft form of notice which it is thought satisfies the requirements of the statute is printed as Appendix 8, § 3030.

The common practice, which it is understood is prevalent among shipbrokers, of adding to the notice of lien for the captain's signature such words as " the cargo must not be delivered to anyone without my consent " would, it seems, be open to objection that such a notice takes the case out of the operation of the statute. See *Dennis* v. *Cork S.S. Co., supra.*

[2] There appears to be no decision as to whether the notice must be contemporaneous with the landing. The question is discussed in *Lawther* v. *Belfast Harbour Commissioners* (1864) 16 Ir.C.L.R. 182 at p. 191, but not decided. It should be noted that under the Bonded Warehouse Act 1845 (8 & 9 Vict. c. 91), s. 51 (now represented by this section), which provided a similar remedy in case of goods landed in a bonded warehouse, there was no limit as to the time within which the notice must be given, and it would seem that it might have been given at any time while the goods remained in the bonded store. It seems hardly probable that the legislature in repealing this enactment by M.S.A. 1862, s. 68, while extending its application to ordinary warehousemen and wharfingers, intended to restrict its operation by requiring notice contemporaneous with the landing.

[3] " Other charges " does not appear to be limited here to its ordinary meaning in shipping matters generally, *viz.* landing charges, dues on cargo, etc. In practice it is generally taken to include demurrage and dead freight where the shipowner has a lien for these. See *A/s. Helsingörs Sö, etc.* v. *Walton,* cited in note (3) to s. 496.

[4] If a master wilfully inserts in the stop order an amount which he knows to be in excess of that for which he has a lien, the delivery to the warehouseman is tantamount to a wrongful detention of the goods, and, as such, is an actionable breach of duty: *The Energie* (*Miedbrodt* v. *Fitzsimon*) (1875) L.R. 6 P.C. 306. But, as to whether he would be liable if the excess were slight and inserted bona fide, see *ibid.*, and *cf.* note (1) to s. 496.

[5] *i.e.* the shipowner's lien, which is not extended by the statute, that given to the warehouseman by s. 499 being another and a distinct lien: *The Energie, supra.*

[6] A warehouseman taking the custody of the goods under these provisions " is under an obligation cast upon him by the statute to deliver the goods to the same person to whom the shipowner was by his contract bound to deliver them, and is justified or excused by the same things as would justify or excuse the master." See *Glyn* v. *East and West India Dock Co., supra* (s. 493).

Whether the shipowner remains under any obligation to see that the goods are rightly delivered by the warehouseman appears doubtful. As to this, and generally as to the respective rights and duties of shipowner and warehouseman, see B.S.L., Vols. 2 and 3; Carver, *Carriage by Sea*, 12th ed., §§ 1037–1039; *Glyn* v. *East and West India Dock Co., supra*; *and Barber* v. *Meyerstein* (1870) L.R. 4 H.L. 317 at pp. 337, etc.; affirming L.R. 2 C.P. 38, 661.

Discharge of lien

411 **495.** The said lien for freight and other charges shall be discharged—

(1) Upon the production to the wharfinger or warehouseman of a receipt for the amount claimed as due, and delivery to the wharfinger or warehouseman of a copy thereof or of a release of freight from the shipowner,[1] and

(2) Upon the deposit by the owner of the goods [1] with the wharfinger or warehouseman of a sum of money equal in amount to the sum claimed [2] as aforesaid by the shipowner;

but in the latter case the lien shall be discharged without prejudice to any other remedy which the shipowner may have for the recovery of the freight.[3]

[1] See note (6) to s. 494; and as to meanings of " shipowner " and " owner of the goods," see s. 492.

[2] When the shipowner attempts to exercise his lien in respect of charges which he is not entitled to recover from the consignee, he may be ordered to pay to the latter interest on the extra sum deposited: *Red " R " S.S. Co.* v. *Allatini* (1908) 14 Com.Cas. 82, 93.

[3] Where the consignee for sale of goods under a bill of lading (being thus owner of the goods within these provisions but not within the Bills of Lading Act), made a deposit under the Act equivalent to the full amount of freight, accompanied by a notice to retain the deposit pending instructions, and accordingly had the goods delivered to him, it was held that the shipowner had no personal right of action against the consignee for the payment of the freight, as no promise to pay was to be implied from the receipt of the goods, and no liability for freight on his part was created by statute (*viz.*, s. 496): *White & Co.* v. *Furness, Withy & Co.* [1895] A.C. 40. The correct procedure in such a case is for the shipowner to claim a declaration as against the party making the deposit that he is entitled to the money deposited. See note (2) to s. 496 and *Montgomery* v. *Foy, Morgan & Co.*, there cited.

The cargo-owner cannot apparently by depositing the freight demand delivery from the warehouseman where the goods have been landed otherwise than in pursuance of s. 493, *e.g.* under a landing clause in his bill of lading: *Dennis* v. *Cork S.S. Co.* [1913] 2 K.B. 393. See note (1) to s. 494.

Provisions as to deposits by owners of goods

412 **496.**—(1) When a deposit as aforesaid is made with the wharfinger or warehouseman, the person making the same may, within fifteen days after making it, give to the wharfinger or warehouseman notice in writing to retain it, stating in the notice the sums, if any, which he admits to be payable to the shipowner, or, as the case may be, that he does not admit any sum to be so payable, but if no such notice is given, the wharfinger or warehouseman may, at the expiration of the fifteen days, pay the sum deposited over to the shipowner.

(2) If a notice is given as aforesaid the wharfinger or warehouseman shall immediately apprise the shipowner of it, and shall pay or tender to him out of the sum deposited the sum, if any, admitted by the notice to be payable, and shall retain the balance, or, if no sum is admitted to be payable, the whole of the sum deposited, for thirty days from the date of the notice.[1]

(3) At the expiration of those thirty days, unless legal proceedings [2] have in the meantime been instituted by the shipowner against the owner of the goods [3] to recover the said balance or sum, or otherwise for the settlement of any disputes which may have arisen between them concerning the freight or other charges as aforesaid, and notice in writing of those proceedings has been served on the wharfinger or warehouseman, the wharfinger or warehouseman shall pay the balance or sum to the owner of the goods.

(4) A wharfinger or warehouseman shall by any payment under this section be discharged from all liability in respect thereof.

413 [1] Where the amount inserted in the notice was manifestly and grossly in excess of that for which the master could bona fide claim a lien, the Privy Council held that the detention of the cargo thereunder was a wrongful act entitling the cargo-owner to damages, although the enactment assumed that in some cases the master might bona fide claim a lien for more than in fact was due to him, in which case he would incur no liability: *The Energie* (*Miedbrodt* v. *Fitzsimon*) (1875) 44 L.J.Ad. 25 at p. 32 (decided on the corresponding s. 72 of M.S.A. 1862). *Cf.* note (4) to s. 494.

[2] If the persons depositing the freight are consignees against whom the shipowner has no right of action for freight as not being parties to the contract of affreightment, the correct form of proceedings appears to be for the shipowner to apply as against the consignee for a declaration that he is entitled to be paid the freigh deposited with the warehouseman: *White & Co.* v. *Furness, Withy & Co., supra* (s. 495). And in such proceedings there is jurisdiction under Ord. 16, r. 11 (R.S.C.) to join the shippers of the cargo as defendants in order that they may counterclaim for short delivery and injury to the cargo: *Montgomery* v. *Foy, Morgan & Co.* [1895] 2 Q.B. 321.

By s. 29 (1) of the Arbitration Act 1950, the term " legal proceedings " in this section is deemed to include arbitration, thus altering the law as laid down in *Runciman* v. *Smyth* (1904) 20 T.L.R. 625. For the purposes of this section as so amended, an arbitration shall be deemed to be commenced when one party to the arbitration agreement serves on the other party or parties a notice requiring him or them to appoint or concur in appointing an arbitrator, or, where the arbitration agreement provides that the reference shall be to a person named or designated in the agreement, requiring him or them to submit the dispute to the person so named or designated (see subs. (2) of s. 29). Subs. (3) of s. 29 of that Act makes provision for the service of such notice as is mentioned in subs. (2).

[3] " Owner of the goods " here means the owner of the goods at the time when the deposit is made. Thus, where, after the goods had been landed subject to the shipowner's lien for demurrage, A purchased the goods from B, the shipper, and paid the deposit to release the goods, the claim for a declaration that the shipowner was entitled to be paid the deposit was properly made against A, not B: *A/s. Helsingörs Sö & Handelscompagni* v. *Walton* (1921) 9 Ll.L.R. 105.

Sale of goods by warehousemen

414 **497.**—(1) If the lien is not discharged, and no deposit is made as aforesaid, the wharfinger or warehouseman may, and, if required by the shipowner, shall, at the expiration of ninety days from the time when the goods were placed in his custody, or, if the goods are of a perishable nature, at such earlier period as in his discretion he thinks fit, sell by public auction, either for home use or for exportation, the goods or so much thereof as may be necessary to satisfy the charges hereinafter mentioned.

(2) Before making the sale the wharfinger or warehouseman shall give notice thereof by advertisement in two local newspapers circulating in the neighbourhood, or in one daily newspaper published in London, and in one local newspaper, and also, if the address of the owner of the goods has been stated on the manifest of the cargo, or on any of the documents which have come into the possession of the wharfinger or warehouseman, or is otherwise known to him, send notice of the sale to the owner of the goods by post.

(3) The title of a bona fide purchaser of the goods shall not be invalidated by reason of the omission to send the notice required by this section, nor shall any such purchaser be bound to inquire whether the notice has been sent.

It would seem that when once the power of sale has arisen, *i.e.* at the expiration of ninety days in the absence of a deposit, and the shipowner has requested the wharfinger to exercise such right, the goods-owner cannot then, as of right, tender a deposit and demand the goods before the sale has actually been effected.

Application of proceeds of sale

415 **498.** The proceeds of sale shall be applied by the wharfinger or warehouseman as follows, and in the following order:

(i) First, if the goods are sold for home use, in payment of any customs or excise duties owing in respect thereof; then

(ii) In payment of the expenses of the sale; then

(iii) In payment of the charges of the wharfinger or warehouseman and the shipowner according to such priority as may be determined by the terms of the agreement (if any) in that behalf between them; or, if there is no such agreement:—

(*a*) in payment of the rent, rates, and other charges due to the wharfinger or warehouseman in respect of the said goods; and then

(*b*) in payment of the amount claimed by the shipowner as due for freight or other charges in respect of the said goods;

and the surplus, if any, shall be paid to the owner of the goods.

Quaere, whether, if the proceeds of sale are insufficient to meet the claims of the warehouseman, he can claim the balance from the shipowner. It is submitted that he can on an undertaking by the shipowner, implied in the placing of the goods in his custody for the protection of the shipowner's interests, to indemnify him for all proper charges. But see Scrutton, *Charterparties*, 18th ed., p. 300, note (71). It seems doubtful whether he can recover in the alternative from the owner of the goods.

Warehouseman's rent and expenses

416 **499.** Whenever any goods are placed in the custody of a wharfinger or warehouseman, under the authority of this Part of this Act, the wharfinger or warehouseman shall be entitled to rent in respect of the same, and shall also have power, at the expense of the owner of the goods, to do all such reasonable acts as in the judgment of the wharfinger or warehouseman are necessary for the proper custody and preservation of the goods, and shall have a lien on the goods for the rent and expenses.[1]

[1] The lien created by this section is distinct from that of the shipowner for freight and other charges: *The Energie*, *supra* (s. 493), *per cur.* (1875) L.R. 6 P.C. at p. 316.

Warehousemen's protection

417 **500.** Nothing in this Part of this Act shall compel any wharfinger or warehouseman to take charge of any goods which he would not have been liable to take charge of if this Act had not been passed; nor shall he be bound to see to the validity of any lien claimed by any shipowner under this Part of this Act.

Saving for powers under local Acts

418 **501.** Nothing in this Part of this Act shall take away or abridge any powers given by any local Act to any harbour authority, body corporate, or persons, whereby they are enabled to expedite the discharge of ships or the landing or delivery of goods; nor shall anything in this Part of this Act take away or diminish any rights or remedies given to any shipowner or wharfinger or warehouseman by any local Act.

PART VIII—LIABILITY OF SHIPOWNERS

419 HISTORY OF LEGISLATION. The rule of maritime law, that the shipowner's liability in the case of collision is limited to the value of the ship and freight, which is vouched for by many writers of authority and is embodied in the laws of most foreign countries, finds no place in the English common law, and it may be doubted whether it is anywhere a rule of any great antiquity. The limitation of the shipowner's liability in English law is entirely the creature of statute, though on its introduction by 7 Geo. 2, c. 15 (amended by 26 Geo. 3, c. 86), in the cases specified in s. 502 of the present Act, the legislature adopting the rule of maritime law limited the owner's liability to the value of the ship and freight—which limit was also applied by 53 Geo. 3, c. 159, to damages by collision.

M.S.A. 1854, s. 504, extended the principle to cases of loss of life and personal injury, and provided that in such cases the value of the ship should be taken at not less than £15 per ton. This section was replaced by M.S.A. 1862, s. 54, which is reproduced in section 503 of the 1894 Act, under which the owner's liability was limited to £8 per ton, or £15 in case of loss of life, etc. By the Act of 1862, limitation of liability was extended to foreign ships in the cases under that section, but the application of M.S.A. 1854, s. 503 (section 502 of the 1894 Act), was not altered. See now section 502 of this Act and note (2) thereto. The principle was then further extended to the owners of British ships from the time of launching until registration, and to the owners of harbours, docks, piers, etc. See M.S. (Liability of Shipowners) Act 1898; M.S. (Liability of Shipowners and Others) Act 1900; and M.S.A. 1906, ss. 69, 70, 71.

As a consequence of the International Convention relating to the Limitation of the Liability of Owners of sea-going ships, signed at Brussels on October 10, 1957 (Cmnd. 353), the M.S. (Liability of Shipowners and Others) Act 1958, was passed. It came into force on August 1, 1958. Any claims arising out of occurrences before that date are governed by the law as it was set out in the 5th edition of this book: (see *ibid.* s. 9).

420 The effect of the 1958 Act is to increase substantially the scope of limitation of liability in respect of claims for loss of life or personal injury, claims for damage to property including harbour works, basins and waterways, and (from a date to be appointed) claims for wreck-raising charges. The right to limit no longer depends on negligence and it is no longer confined solely to acts or omissions in the navigation or management of the ship. Owners, charterers, persons interested in or in possession of the ship, managers, operators, masters and members of the crew may all be entitled to limit their liability, and the definition of " ship " has been extended. On the other hand, the financial limits have been raised so that

a greater fund will be available for distribution among claimants. The Act itself refers to gold francs but for the time being the declared sterling equivalents are £96·3911 per ton in the case of loss of life or personal injury (when 300 tons is the minimum multiple) and £31·0939 in the case of all other claims. See the detailed summary of the provisions of the 1958 Act at § 1208, *post.*

See further, for the history of the legislation on this subject, *British Shipping Laws* (Vol. 4); *Marsden on Collisions at Sea*, 11th ed., Chap. 6; *The Amalia* (1863) 32 L.J.Ad. 191; B. & L. 151; and an address by Mr. Dawson R. Miller published in the Annual Report of the Association of Average Adjusters for 1953.

For criticisms of the policy of this enactment, and as to its construction, see *The Northumbria* (1869) L.R. 3 A. & E. 6; *The Andalusian* (1878) 3 P.D. 182; *Chapman* v. *Royal Netherlands S.N. Co.* (1879) 4 P.D. 157 (C.A.); *The Ettrick* or *Prehn* v. *Bailey* (1881) 6 P.D. 127; 45 L.T. 399 (C.A.); *The Warkworth* (1884) 9 P.D. 20.

421 STATUTORY PROVISIONS AT PRESENT IN FORCE. M.S.A. 1894, Part VIII (Liability of Shipowners, ss. 502–509), contains the main statutory provisions as to limitation of liability. These have, however, been extended, adapted and modified by the following subsequent M.S. enactments:

(i) M.S. (Liability of Shipowners and Others) Act 1900, which extended the protection given to owners of ships by the principal Act to owners of docks and canals and to harbour or conservancy authorities in respect of loss or damage caused to any vessel or goods on board any vessel;

(ii) M.S.A. 1906, s. 69, which altered the method of calculating the tonnage of steamships for the purposes of limitation of liability;

(iii) M.S.A. 1921, which extended the protection given by the principal Act (except in respect of loss of life or personal injury to persons on board) to owners of lighters and barges used in navigation in Great Britain, however propelled, and provided for the registration of such vessels under Part I of the principal Act or under approved local systems of registration; and

(iv) M.S. (Liability of Shipowners and Others) Act 1958, which extended the protection of limitation substantially and increased the limitation funds. (See the note under " History of Legislation," *supra*, and the detailed summary of the Act at § 1208, *post.*)

In addition extensions or adaptations have been effected by the following enactments:

(v) Pilotage Authorities (Limitation of Liability) Act 1936, which conferred on pilotage authorities (otherwise than as owners of ships) a right to limit their liability in respect of a wide range of loss or damage.

(vi) The Crown Proceedings Act 1947, which applied the provisions of the M.S. Acts dealing with limitation of and exemption from liability to the liability of Her Majesty in respect of H.M. ships, the liability of demise or sub-demise charterers of ships from H.M. in United Kingdom right, and to the liability of managers of H.M. ships.

422 (vii) The Hovercraft Act 1968, which makes provision *inter alia* for the application of this Part of the 1894 Act to hovercraft: see now the Hovercraft (Civil Liability) Order, S.I. 1971 No. 720, art. 6 and Sched. 3, noted at § 1319, *post.* Part VIII of this Act as amended by ss. 1, 2 (1) and 8 (1) to (3) of the 1958 Act and as modified by the Hovercraft (Civil Liability) Order 1971, would read as follows:

502. The owner of a British hovercraft or any share therein, shall not be liable to make good to any extent whatever any loss or damage happening without his actual fault or privity in the following cases, namely:—

(i) where any goods, merchandise, or other things whatsoever taken in or put on board his hovercraft are lost or damaged by reason of fire on board the hovercraft; or

(ii) where any gold, silver, diamonds, watches, jewels, or precious stones taken in or put on board his hovercraft, the true nature and value of which have not at the time of shipment been declared by the owner or shipper thereof to the owner or captain of the hovercraft in the bills of lading or otherwise in writing, are lost or damaged by reason of any robbery, embezzlement, making away with, or secreting thereof.

503.—(1) Subject to the provisons of sub-section (2) below the owners of a hovercraft, British or foreign, shall not, where all or any of the following occurrences take place without their actual fault or privity; (that is to say,)

(*b*) Where any damage or loss is caused to any goods, merchandise or other things whatsoever on board the hovercraft;

(*c*) Where any loss of life or personal injury is caused to any person not carried in the hovercraft through the act or omission of any person (whether on board the hovercraft or not) in the navigation or management of the hovercraft or in the loading, carriage or discharge of its cargo or in the embarkation, carriage or disembarkation of its passengers, or through any other act or omission of any person on board the hovercraft;

(*d*) Where any loss or damage is caused to any property (other than any property mentioned in paragraph (*b*) of this sub-section) or any rights are infringed through the act or omission of any person (whether on board the hovercraft or not) in the navigation or management of the hovercraft, or in the loading, carriage or discharge of its cargo or in the embarkation, carriage or disembarkation of its passengers, or through any other act or omission of any person on board the hovercraft;

be liable to damages beyond the following amounts; (that is to say,)

(i) in respect of loss of life or personal injury, either alone or together with such loss, damage or infringement as is mentioned in paragraphs (*b*) and (*d*) of this sub-section an aggregate amount not exceeding £3·50 per kg. of the hovercraft's maximum authorised weight and

(ii) in respect of such loss, damage or infringement as is mentioned in paragraphs (*b*) and (*d*) of this sub-section, whether there be in addition loss of life or personal injury or not, an aggregate amount not exceeding £1 per kg. of the hovercraft's maximum authorised weight.

(2) The number by which the figure referred to in sub-section (1) (i) and (ii) above is to be multiplied shall be 8,000 in any case where the weight concerned is less than 8,000 kg.

(3) The limits set by this section to the liabilities mentioned therein shall apply to the aggregate of such liabilities which are incurred on any distinct occasion, and shall so apply in respect of each distinct occasion without regard to any liability incurred on another occasion.

504. Where any liability is alleged to have been incurred by the owner of a British or foreign hovercraft in respect of any occurrence in respect of which his liability is limited under section five hundred and three of this Act and several claims are made or apprehended in respect of that liability, then the owner may apply in England and Ireland to the High Court, or in Scotland to the Court of Session, or in a British possession to any competent court, and that court may determine the amount of the owner's liability and may distribute that amount rateably among the several claimants, and may stay (or in Scotland sist) any proceedings pending in any other court in relation to the same matter, and may proceed in such manner and subject to such regulations as to making persons interested parties to the proceedings, and as to the exclusion of any claimants who do not come in within a certain time, and as to requiring security from the owner, and as to payment of any costs, as the court thinks just.

505. All sums paid for or on account of any loss or damage in respect whereof the liability of owners is limited under the provisions of this Part of this Act and all costs and expenses incurred in relation thereto, may be brought into account among part owners of the same hovercraft in the same manner as money disbursed for the use thereof.

506. An insurance effected against the happening, without the owner's actual fault or privity, of any or all of the events in respect of which the liability of owners is limited under this Part of this Act shall not be invalid by reason of the nature of the risk.

423 The right to limit liability by these Acts is unaffected by the Maritime Conventions Act 1911 (see *ibid.* s. 1 (1) (*c*), and s. 2, *post*), or by the Carriage of Goods by Sea Act 1971, (see *ibid.* s. 6 (4)).

SUMMARY. The combined effect of the statutory provisions which are listed above may be summarised as follows, but reference should also be made to the relevant sections of the Acts and the notes thereto:

A. *Complete exemption.* In respect of certain claims (loss or damage to goods by fire, and loss or damage to undeclared valuables caused by criminal acts), owners of British ships may be able to escape liability altogether if the loss or damage occurred without their actual fault or privity (M.S.A. 1894, s. 502, as amended by M.S. (Liability of Shipowners and

Others) Act 1958, s. 8 (1)). For this purpose, " owners " is given a wide definition and includes any charterer, any person interested in or in possession of the ship and any manager or operator of the ship (M.S. (Liability of Shipowners and Others) Act 1958, ss. 3 (1), 8 (4)). Masters and members of the crew and their employers (if not otherwise protected) are also entitled to the same exemption from liability and in the case of masters and members of the crew, their liability is excluded notwithstanding actual fault or privity, except in the case of claims for loss or damage to undeclared valuables (*ibid.* s. 3 (2)). A " ship " in this context is also given a wide definition, and includes any structure, whether completed, commenced and intended for use in navigation as a ship or part of a ship (M.S. (Liability of Shipowners and Others) Act 1958, s. 4 (1)) and it includes unregistered British ships (*ibid.* s. 4 (2)). It also includes lighters, barges and like vessels used in navigation in Great Britain, however propelled, other than those used exclusively in non-tidal waters (M.S.A. 1921, s. 1 (1)). The provisions are also applicable to Crown ships and to the liability of Her Majesty, and demise or sub-demise charterers, and managers of Crown ships (Crown Proceedings Act 1947, s. 5).

B. *Limitation of Liability*. In respect of a much larger class of claims (loss of life, personal injury and loss or damage to property including damage to harbour works, basins and waterways and, from a date to be appointed, claims for wreck-raising expenses, whether arising from the navigation or management of the ship, or the loading, carriage or discharge of goods, or the embarkation, carriage or disembarkation of passengers, or from any act or omission of a person on board the ship) the owners of a ship, whether British or foreign, can limit their liability, if the loss or damage occurred without their actual fault or privity. Liability is limited to £96·3911 for each ton of the ship's registered tonnage (with the addition of engine room space) or £31·0939 (whichever is the greater) in the case of claims for loss of life and personal injury, and to £31·0939 for each ton in the case of other claims. These limitations cannot, however, be claimed if liability arises out of a contract of service governed by a foreign law which does not provide similar or lesser limits to liability (M.S.A. 1894, s. 503, as amended by M.S. (Liability of Shipowners and Others) Act 1958, ss. 1, 2).

For limitation purposes " owners " and " ship " are to be given the same extended definitions as in the previous paragraph A., but owners of certain lighters, barges and like vessels may not limit their liability for loss of life or personal injury caused to any person on board such craft (M.S.A. 1921, s. 3). In respect of claims arising out of acts or omissions in the course of their employment masters and members of the crew are entitled to the same limitation of their personal liability even where the loss or damage occurs by their actual fault or privity (M.S. (Liability of Shipowners and Others) Act 1958, ss. 3, 4).

The provisions are also applicable to Crown ships and to the liability of Her Majesty, and demise or sub-demise charterers, and managers of Crown ships (Crown Proceedings Act 1947, s. 5).

Owners of docks and canals and harbour or conservancy authorities can limit their liability in respect of loss or damage to any vessel or goods on board her to £31.0939 per ton of the tonnage on the largest British registered ship which is at the time of the casualty or has been within five years thereof within the area of their control (M.S.A. 1900, s. 2, as amended by M.S. (Liability of Shipowners and Others) Act 1958, s. 1). See also the Harbours Act 1964, s. 25 (1), which extends the provisions of the M.S. (Liability of Shipowners and Others) Act 1900, s. 2, to bodies administering schemes established by a control of movement order pursuant to the provisions of the Harbours Act 1964, ss. 20 *et seq.*

Lastly, pilotage authorities can similarly limit their liability in respect of loss or damage to any vessel or vessels or to any goods, merchandise or other things whatsoever on board any vessel or vessels or to any other kind of property whether on land or on water and whether fixed or moveable. The maximum amount of their liability is £100 multiplied by the number of licensed pilots for the pilotage district: Pilotage Authorities (Limitation of Liability) Act 1936, s. 1, *post*, § 1039.

Limitation of shipowner's liability in certain cases of loss of, or damage to, goods

424 **502.**[1] The owner [2] of a British *sea-going* [3] ship,[4] or any share therein, shall not be liable to make good to any extent whatever any loss or damage [5] happening without his actual fault or privity [6] in the following cases, namely:—

(i) where any goods, merchandise, or other things whatsoever taken in or put on board his ship are lost or damaged by reason of fire [7] on board the ship [8]; or

(ii) where any gold, silver, diamonds, watches, jewels, or precious stones taken in or put on board his ship, the true nature and value [9] of which have not at the time of shipment been declared by the owner or shipper thereof to the owner or master of the ship in the bills of lading or otherwise in writing, are lost or damaged by reason of any robbery, embezzlement, making away with, or secreting thereof.[10]

425 1 The operation of this section is unaffected by anything contained in the Carriage of Goods by Sea Act 1924: see *ibid.* s. 6 (2).

2 " Owners " was a term extended to include charterers by demise by M.S.A. 1906, s. 71. Limitation could also be claimed by owners, builders and other parties interested in a ship built in H.M. Dominions until registration; see M.S. (Liability of Shipowners) Act 1898, s. 1, and M.S.A. 1906, s. 70; and also certain hirers of lighters and barges, M.S.A. 1921, s. 1 (2). These enactments have all been repealed and it is now provided that " the persons whose liability in connection with a ship is excluded or limited by Part VIII of the Merchant Shipping Act 1894, shall include any charterer and any person interested in or in possession of the ship, and, in particular, any manager or operator of the ship" (M.S. (Liability of Shipowners and Others) Act 1958, ss. 3 (1), 8 (4)). The liability of a master or member of the crew for his own act or omission in that capacity or otherwise in the course of his employment, and the vicarious liability of his employer may also be excluded: *ibid.* s. 3 (2) (*a*), and the word " owner " must be construed to include such persons: *ibid.* s. 8 (4). But the personal liability of a master or member of a crew can only be excluded in respect of claims falling under paragraph (ii) of this section in the absence of his actual fault or privity (*ibid.* s. 3 (2) (*b*)), and in that context " owner " is not to be construed to include such persons: *ibid.* s. 8 (4). The decisions cited in note (1) to s. 503 appear also applicable to this section.

3 The word " sea-going " is now to be omitted: M.S. (Liability of Shipowners and Others) Act 1958, s. 8 (1).

4 " Ship." It is now provided that Part VIII of this Act shall apply to any structure, whether completed or in course of completion, launched and intended for use in navigation as a ship or part of a ship, and that the expression " ship " shall be construed accordingly (M.S. (Liability of Shipowners and Others) Act 1958, s. 4 (1)). Formerly, this section referred specifically to a " sea-going ship " (see note (3), *supra*) and further legislation (M.S. (Liability of Shipowners) Act 1898, s. 1 and M.S.A. 1906 s. 70, which has since been repealed by the 1958 Act), extended the application of Part VIII of this Act to certain ships which had been launched but not registered. Part VIII of this Act now applies to any British ship, whether or not it has yet been registered (M.S. (Liability of Shipowners and Others) Act 1958, s. 4 (2)). As to what vessels are included in the term " ship," see s. 742 and notes thereto. It should be noted that the words " intended for use " in M.S. (Liability of Shipowners and Others) Act 1958, s. 4 (1), extend the definition of " ship " in s. 742 where the word " used " is employed. By virtue of s. 1 (1) of M.S.A. 1921, the application of Part VIII, as amended or extended by any subsequent enactment, is extended to cover " lighters, barges, and other like vessels used in navigation in Great Britain, however propelled " (unless used exclusively in non-tidal waters, other than harbours). S. 1 (2) of that Act has, however, been repealed by M.S. (Liability of Shipowners and Others) Act 1958, s. 8 (6) and Schedule. The persons entitled to limit their liability in relation to such craft are now defined by *ibid.* s. 3 (1). See note (2), *supra*.

This section is also applied by s. 5 of the Crown Proceedings Act 1947, with any necessary modifications to the Crown in respect of H.M. ships and to the Crown, builders, owners and other persons interested in ships built by or for or to the order of Her Majesty in United Kingdom right from launching until completion as from February 13, 1947, and to managers, charterers or subcharterers by demise of H.M. ships retrospectively. In the context of that section, the expression " ship " now includes any structure to which Part VIII of this Act is applied by M.S. (Liability of Shipowners and Others) Act 1958, s. 4. See *ibid.* s. 8 (5).

5 The section does not exempt a shipowner from contribution to general average where goods are injured by water used in extinguishing fire any more than an exception of fire in a bill of lading would exempt him: *Schmidt* v. *Royal Mail S.S. Co.* (1876) 45 L.J.Q.B. 646; followed in *Greenshields, Cowie & Co.* v. *Stephens* [1908] A.C. 431. On the other hand, where the shipowner claims from cargo owners a general average contribution in respect of expenditure incurred by him as a result of fire, he may rely on this section (as he might have relied on an exception of fire in a bill of lading) in order to rebut the contention of

the cargo owners that he has been " in fault " so as to be debarred from claiming general average contribution on the principle of *The Carron Park*, 15 P.D. 203, and *Milburn* v. *Jamaica Fruit, etc., Co.* [1900] 2 Q.B. 540. See *Louis Dreyfus* v. *Tempus Shipping Co.* [1931] A.C. 726.

426 [6] See s. 503, note (4), " Fault or privity."

[7] Damage by smoke and water used in putting out a fire is damage by reason of fire within the meaning of this section: *The Diamond* [1906] P. 282.

" If the loss . . . happens without the owner's actual fault or privity, he is free from liability, even if his ship was unseaworthy. The benefit of the section extends to British sea-going vessels, and is not confined to *seaworthy* British sea-going vessels: *Virginia Carolina Chemical Co.* v. *Norfolk, etc., S.S. Co., infra*; *Ingram and Royle* v. *Services Maritimes du Tréport, infra*; *Louis Dreyfus* v. *Tempus Shipping Co., supra.* But if the unseaworthiness itself was not without the actual fault or privity of the owner, and if the fire was occasioned by the unseaworthiness, the owner is not relieved by the section from liability. The loss in that case has not happened without the owner's actual fault or privity, it has happened with his actual fault or privity, for the *causa causans* of the loss was the unseaworthiness which occasioned the fire which destroyed the goods " : *per* Buckley L.J. in *Lennard's Carrying Co.* v. *Asiatic Petroleum Co.* [1914] 1 K.B. 419 at pp. 431, 432 (C.A.); affirmed [1915] A.C. 705.

But the protection given by the statute may be excluded by the terms of the special contract. Thus, where a bill of lading contained a clause providing that the shipowner was not to be responsible for any loss of or damage to the goods received thereunder for carriage occasioned by (*inter alia*) fire or unseaworthiness, provided all reasonable means had been taken to provide against unseaworthiness, the Court of Appeal held that the effect of a bill of lading containing the above clause was to preclude the shipowner from setting up the section as an answer to a claim for the loss of goods shipped under the bill of lading, by reason of fire on board the ship caused by the unseaworthiness of the ship: *Virginia Carolina Chemical Co.* v. *Norfolk, etc. S.S. Co.* [1912] 1 K.B. 229 (C.A.). (The question of law was not adjudicated upon in the House of Lords. See *ibid.* [1913] A.C. 52.) *Cf. Ingram and Royle* v. *Services Maritimes du Tréport* [1914] 1 K.B. 541, where the C.A. held that the terms of the bill of lading employed in that case did not exclude the statute. The principle of the last-mentioned cases was approved in the House of Lords in *Louis Dreyfus* v. *Tempus Shipping Co., supra.* See also *The Kirknes* [1957] P. 51 where it was held (*obiter*) that the United Kingdom Standard Towage Conditions do not exclude the right to limit liability for damages.

[8] Where goods were destroyed by fire on board a lighter by which they were being conveyed to the ship, it was held, under similar words in 26 Geo. 3, c. 86, s. 2, that the owners were not entitled to limitation of liability: *Morewood* v. *Pollok* (1853) 1 E. & B. 743; see also note (6) to s. 503. But where goods heated by fire on board the ship were discharged into a lighter and then caught fire, the shipowner was held to be protected by this section: *Tempus Shipping Co.* v. *Louis Dreyfus* [1930] 1 K.B. 699. The words " on board " qualify " fire " not " lost or damaged." *Ibid.* at p. 709.

[9] A bill of lading describing the goods as " one box containing about 248 ounces of gold dust " was held not to be a sufficient declaration: *Williams* v. *African S.S. Co.* (1856) 1 H. & N. 300; 26 L.J.Ex. 69; 2 Jur.(N.S.) 693. *Semble*, the word " true " qualifies " nature " only, and not " value "; *ibid.* See also *Gibbs* v. *Potter* (1842) 10 M. & W. 70 (" 1338 hard dollars ").

[10] As to valuables brought on board by a passenger and remaining under his personal control, see *Smitton* v. *Orient S.N. Co.* (1907) 12 Com.Cas. 270; 23 T.L.R. 359. *Cf. Acton* v. *Castle Mail Packet Co.* (1895) 1 Com.Cas. 135; 8 Asp.M.C. 73.

Limitation of owner's liability in certain cases of loss of life, injury or damage

427 **503.**—(1) The owners [1] of a ship,[2] British or foreign,[3] shall not, where all or any of the following occurrences take place without their actual fault or privity [4]; (that is to say,)

(*a*) Where any loss of life or personal injury is caused to any person being carried in the ship [5];

(*b*) Where any damage or loss is caused to any goods, merchandise, or other things whatsoever on board the ship [6];

[(*c*) Where any loss of life or personal injury is caused to any person not carried in the ship [2] through the act or omission of any person (whether on board the ship or not) in the navigation or management [7] of the ship or in the loading, carriage or discharge of its cargo or in the embarkation, carriage or disembarkation of its passengers, or through any other act or omission of any person on board the ship;

(*d*) Where any loss or damage is caused to any property (other than any property mentioned in paragraph (*b*) of this subsection) or any rights are infringed through the act or omission of any person (whether on board the ship or not) in the navigation or management [7] of the ship, or in the loading, carriage or discharge of its cargo or in the embarkation, carriage or disembarkation of its passengers, or through any other act or omission of any person on board the ship [8];]

be liable to damages [9] beyond the following amounts [10]; (that is to say,)

(i) in respect of loss of life or personal injury, either alone or together with [such loss, damage or infringement as is mentioned in paragraphs (*b*) and (*d*) of this subsection [11]], an aggregate amount not exceeding [an amount equivalent to three thousand one hundred gold francs [12]] for each ton of their ship's tonnage [13]; and

(ii) in respect of [such loss, damage or infringement as is mentioned in paragraphs (*b*) and (*d*) of this subsection [11]], whether there be in addition loss of life or personal injury or not, an aggregate amount not exceeding [an amount equivalent to one thousand gold francs [12]] for each ton of their ship's tonnage.[13]

28 (2) For the purposes of this section—

(*a*) The tonnage of a steam ship [14] shall be her [registered tonnage with the addition of any engine-room space deducted for the purpose of ascertaining that tonnage [15]], and the tonnage of a sailing ship shall be her registered tonnage [16]:

Provided that there shall not be included in such tonnage any space occupied by seamen or apprentices and appropriated to their use which is certified under the regulations scheduled to this Act with regard thereto.[17]

(*b*) Where a foreign ship [18] has been or can be measured according to British law, her tonnage, as ascertained by that measurement, shall, for the purpose of this section, be deemed to be her tonnage.

(*c*) Where a foreign ship [18] has not been and cannot be measured according to British law, the surveyor general of ships in the United Kingdom, or the chief measuring officer of any British possession abroad, shall, on receiving from or by the direction of the court hearing the case, in which the tonnage of the ship is in question, such evidence concerning the dimensions of the ship as it may be practicable to furnish, give a certificate under his hand stating what would in his opinion have been the tonnage of the ship if she had been duly measured according to British law, and the tonnage so stated in that certificate shall, for the purposes of this section, be deemed to be the tonnage of the ship.

[(3) The limits set by this section to the liabilities mentioned therein shall apply to the aggregate of such liabilities which are incurred on any distinct occasion,[19] and shall so apply in respect of each distinct occasion without regard to any liability incurred on another occasion.[20]]

The operation of this section has been extended by the following enactments:

429 (i) M.S. (Liability of Shipowners and Others) Act 1900, s. 2, which enables the owners of docks and canals and harbour and conservancy authorities to limit liability for loss or damage to vessels and goods, etc., on board; see § 747, *post*.

(ii) M.S.A. 1921, s. 1, which extends the definition of " ship " to any lighter, barge and like vessel used in navigation in Great Britain, however propelled (unless used exclusively in non-tidal waters other than harbours) but limitation does not apply to claims for loss of life or personal injury caused to any person on board such craft (*ibid.* s. 3); see § 951, *post*.

(iii) Crown Proceedings Act 1947, s. 5, which applies the limitation provisions to Crown ships and to the liability of Her Majesty and demise or sub-demise charterers and managers of Crown ships; see § 1075, *post*.

(iv) M.S. (Liability of Shipowners and Others) Act 1958, which will, from a date to be appointed (s. 2 (5)), enable owners to limit their liability in respect of claims for wreck-raising expenses (s. 2 (2) (*a*)), and which already enables owners to limit in respect of claims for damage to harbour works, basins or navigable waterways (s. 2 (2) (*b*)). The same Act extends the right to limit to any charterer and any person interested in or in possession of the ship and, in particular, any manager or operator of the ship (ss. 3 (1), 8 (4)) and it enables masters, members of the crew and their employers (if not otherwise protected) to limit their liability, and in the case of masters and members of the crew, notwithstanding actual fault or privity if the claim arises from an act or omission in the course of their employment (s. 3 (2)). Further, the definition of " ship " is extended to include any structure, whether completed or in course of construction, launched and intended for use in navigation as a ship or part of a ship (s. 4 (1)) and any unregistered British ship (s. 4 (2)). See §§ 1212–1217, *post*.

(v) The Hovercraft Act 1968 extends the application of this section to hovercraft subject to certain modifications: *ibid.* s. 1 (1), § 1317, *post*. Owners of a hovercraft, among others, are enabled to limit their total liability in respect of any incident to a figure calculated in accordance with the weight of the hovercraft. This figure is £3·50 per kg. in respect of property and of injury or death caused to persons not on board the hovercraft. This limitation is restricted to hovercraft which are, at the time of the incident over navigable water or otherwise in a maritime environment. The text of Part VIII as modified is set out at § 1319, *post*. The text of the 1958 Act as modified is set out at § 1208, *post*.

The following enactments which previously extended the effect of s. 503 have been repealed by M.S. (Liability of Shipowners and Others) Act 1958, s. 8 (6) and Schedule:

(i) M.S. (Liability of Shipowners) Act 1898,
(ii) M.S. (Liability of Shipowners and Others) Act 1900, s. 1,
(iii) M.S.A. 1906, ss. 70 and 71,
(iv) M.S.A. 1921, s. 1 (2).

The operation of this section has been restricted by the following enactments:

(i) M.S.A. 1921, s. 3, which precludes the owners of a lighter, barge or like vessel from limiting their liability in respect of loss of life or personal injury; see § 954, *post*.

(ii) M.S. (Liability of Shipowners and Others) Act 1958, s. 2 (4), which provides that where liability for loss, injury or damage arises out of a contract of service which is governed by a foreign law, limitation cannot be claimed if that foreign law either sets no limit of liability, or sets a limit exceeding that in s. 503.

(iii) Nuclear Installations (Licensing and Insurance) Act 1959, s. 4 (5), which precludes a licensee of a nuclear site from limiting his liability for injury or damage caused by ionising radiations emitted from irradiated nuclear fuel in the course of carriage between places within the United Kingdom.

(iv) M.S. (Oil Pollution) Act 1971, s. 4 (1) (*a*) provides that s. 503 shall not apply to an owner's liability for oil pollution under s. 1 of the former Act: see § 1501, *post.*

(At some time in the future, legislative effect may be given to the International Convention on the Liability of Operators of Nuclear ships adopted at Brussels on May 25, 1962 which (*inter alia*) makes special provision for limitation of liability for " nuclear damage." S. 503 is expressly excluded by the Nuclear Installations Act 1965, s. 14 (1).)

The operation of these limitation provisions is expressly saved by the Maritime Conventions Act 1911, s. 1 (1) (*c*), and s. 2, *post*, and the Carriage of Goods by Sea Act 1924, s. 6 (2).

Similar protection is given to pilotage authorities (otherwise than as owners of ships) by the Pilotage Authorities (Limitation of Liability) Act 1936, s. 1 (§ 1039, *post*), the maximum liability being £100 multiplied by the number of licensed pilots in the pilotage district; but in their capacity as shipowners their right to limit liability is the same as that of other shipowners; *ibid.* s. 4, § 1043, *post.*

As to the rules of practice in limitation claims, see note (1) to s. 504.

430 [1] This term includes any charterer and any person interested in or in possession of the ship, and, in particular, any manager or operator of the ship. M.S. (Liability of Shipowners and Others) Act 1958, s. 3 (1), § 1214, *post.* It has also been held to include equitable or unregistered owners: *The Spirit of the Ocean* (1865) B. & L. 336; 34 L.J.Ad. 71.

The liability of a master or member of the crew for his own act or omission in that capacity, or otherwise in the course of his employment, together with the vicarious liability of his employer may also be limited. See M.S. (Liability of Shipowners and Others) Act 1958, s. 3 (2). In the case of masters and members of the crew, limitation applies notwithstanding their actual fault or privity. *Ibid.*

As to the extension to owners of docks and canals and to harbour and conservancy authorities, see M.S. (Liability of Shipowners and Others) Act 1900, s. 2, as amended by the M.S. (Liability of Shipowners and Others) Act 1958, s. 1 (1). See also s. 25 (1) of the Harbours Act 1964.

As to part owners, see note (4), *infra.*

As to the Crown and the liability of Her Majesty, managers, charterers or sub-charterers by demise of H.M. ships, see Crown Proceedings Act 1947, s. 5, as amended by M.S. (Liability of Shipowners and Others) Act 1958, s. 8 (5); §§ 1224–1225, *post.*

One who contracts to carry passengers and goods on a transit partly by land and partly by sea, and who fulfils the sea transit by one of his own ships, can limit his liability under this section in respect of loss or damage occurring at sea, notwithstanding that he is sued in his capacity as carrier and not as shipowner: *L. & S.W. Ry.* v. *James* (1872) L.R. 8 Ch. 241; *The Normandy* (1870) L.R. 3 A. & E. 152. But if the carriage by sea is not by the contractor's own ships but by ships owned by a third party, the contractor cannot limit his liability towards the passengers or the owners of the goods, though the shipowner can limit his liability towards the contractor: *Doolan* v. *Midland Ry.* (1877) 2 App.Cas. 792 at 805; 37 L.T. 317.

[2] By s. 742, the word " ship " is defined to include every description of vessel used in navigation not propelled by oars. It is provided by M.S. (Liability of Shipowners and Others) Act 1958, s. 4 (1), that Part VIII (the limitation provisions) of the 1894 Act shall apply to any structure, whether completed or in course of completion, launched and intended for use in navigation as a ship or part of a ship. By M.S.A. 1921, s. 1 (1) the word " ship " is to be construed as including every description of lighter, barge or like vessel used in navigation in Great Britain, however propelled, unless used exclusively in non-tidal waters, other than harbours. The limitation sections apply to any British ship, whether registered or not; M.S. (Liability of Shipowners and Others) Act 1958, s. 4 (2). In the case of any ship or structure that is unregistered or in the course of completion or construction, the tonnage is to be ascertained in accordance with the provisions of s. 503 (2) (*b*) and (*c*) which formerly applied only to foreign ships. See M.S. (Liability of Shipowners and Others) Act 1958, s. 4 (3). For the application of this section to H.M. ships, see Crown Proceedings Act 1947, s. 5, as amended by M.S. (Liability of Shipowners and Others) Act 1958, s. 8 (5). M.S. (Liability of Shipowners) Act 1898, s. 1, and M.S.A. 1906, s. 70, which previously extended the limitation provisions to ships built in H.M. dominions from the time of launching until the time of registration, have been repealed by M.S. (Liability of Shipowners and Others) Act 1958, s. 8 (6) and Schedule.

[3] It was at one time doubted whether the legislature had the right to limit the damages recoverable by a foreign ship in respect of a collision with a British vessel on the high seas. This doubt was, however, disposed of in *The Amalia* (1863) 1 Moo.P.C.C.(N.S.) 471; 32 L.J.Ad. 191, where it was held that the corresponding section in the repealed

Act placed British and foreign ships on the same footing and applied to a foreign ship whether she was the wrongdoer or the injured party, and whether the collision took place in British waters or not. Thus, where a collision took place on the high seas between a British and a Belgian vessel, and the latter was sunk, it was held that the owner of the British vessel was entitled to limit his liability. *Ibid.*

431 [4] " Fault or privity." The fact that the loss is occasioned by the fault of one of several part-owners, *e.g.* a master, did not deprive his co-owners of the right to have their liability limited, while the co-owner in fault remains liable in full: *The Spirit of the Ocean* (1865) 34 L.J.Ad. 74; B. & L. 336; *The Cricket* (1882) 48 L.T. 535, n.; 5 Asp.M.L.C. 53; *The Obey* (1866) L.R. 1 A. & E. 102; 12 Jur.(N.S.) 817; *Wilson* v. *Dickson* (1818) 2 B. & Ald. 2 (upon 53 Geo. 3, c. 159, s. 1).

Under s. 3 of the M.S. (Liability of Shipowners and Others) Act 1958, a master or member of the crew may, notwithstanding his actual fault or privity, limit his liability in relation to a claim arising from an act or omission in his capacity as master or member of the crew or (otherwise than in that capacity) in the course of his employment as a servant of the owners of the ship as defined in that section.

As to the circumstances which may or may not constitute " fault or privity," see *The Obey*, *supra*; *Kidston* v. *McArthur* (1878) 5 R. 936; *The Warkworth* (1884) 9 P.D. 20; on appeal, 9 P.D. 145, see note (7), *infra*; *The Satanita*, *infra*; *The Diamond* [1906] P. 282; *The Fanny* (1912) 28 T.L.R. 217, reversing on facts (1911) 27 T.L.R. 568 (appointment of incompetent master); *The Bristol City* [1921] P. 444 (C.A.) (damage due to sending unfinished vessel to sea without sufficient ground tackle); *Standard Oil Co. Ltd.* v. *Clan Line Steamers Ltd.* [1924] A.C. 100 (failure to communicate to master peculiar construction of tanks); *The Thames* [1940] P. 143 (failure by hirer of barge to inquire when it was last surveyed or to take steps to ascertain condition); *The Hans Hoth* [1952] 2 Lloyd's Rep. 341 (failure of master, a part-owner, to know local signals); *The Truculent* [1952] P. 1 (misleading light on a submarine); *The Hildina* [1957] 2 Lloyd's Rep. 247 (failure to fit a cut-out to a trawling winch); *The Empire Jamaica* [1957] A.C. 386 (H.L.) (appointment of an uncertificated officer); *Yuille* v. *B. & B. Fisheries* (*Leigh*) *Ltd., and Bates, the Radiant* [1958] 2 Lloyd's Rep. 596 (inadequate towropes, defective gearbox and lack of deck-lights); *The Norman* [1960] 1 Lloyd's Rep. 1 (H.L.) (failure to communicate the latest navigational information to a ship at sea); *The Anonity* [1961] 2 Lloyd's Rep. 117 (C.A.) (inadequate steps to prohibit use of galley stove at oil jetty); *The Lady Gwendolen* [1965] P. 294 (C.A.) (failure to ensure that ships were navigated safely in fog); *The Dayspring* [1968] 2 Lloyd's Rep. 204 (failure to heed sufficiently the warnings of a Court of Formal Investigation into a similar casualty); *The Hermes* [1969] 2 Lloyd's Rep. 347 (Can.) (failure of Department of Transport to set up system of control or of checking aids to navigation); *The Chugaway II* [1969] 2 Lloyd's Rep. 529 (Can.) (failure to instruct master not to tow under bridge at high water); *The Chickasaw* [1970] 1 Lloyd's Rep. 437 (U.S.) (failure to see that radio direction finder was in good order or to provide recent table of corrections); *The Alletta* [1972] 1 Lloyd's Rep. 375 (failure to instruct master to navigate with pilot and failure to provide copy of by-laws).

Proof that owners are in breach of a statutory duty or of an absolute common law duty does not of itself involve that they are guilty of fault or privity within the meaning of this section; *Admiralty* v. *Owners of Divina, The Truculent* [1952] P. 1 (defective lights); *Beauchamp* v. *Turrell* [1952] 2 Q.B. 207 (unsafe system of working); *Moore* v. *Metcalf Motor Coasters Ltd.* [1958] 2 Lloyd's Rep. 179 (unsafe gangway); *The Lady Gwendolen*, *supra*, (breach of the Collision Regulations); but see *Hook* v. *Consolidated Fisheries Ltd.* [1953] 2 Lloyd's Rep. 647 where it was conceded that a failure to provide a safe system of work would amount to actual fault or privity.

Difficult questions arise in this connection where the owners are a corporation. In *Smitton* v. *Orient S.N. Co.* (1907) 12 Com.Cas. 270 at p. 277, Channell J. held that in such a case " the statute referred to fault of the board of directors, the persons who have the general management of the affairs of the company." In *Lennard's Carrying Co.* v. *Asiatic Petroleum Co.* [1915] A.C. 705, Lord Dunedin, while considering that it was a question of fact to be decided upon the circumstances of each case, refused to assent to the proposition that the actual fault of the whole body of directors must be proved. Lord Haldane was of the opinion that the true construction required the fault or privity of somebody who is not merely a servant or agent for whom the company is liable upon the footing " *respondeat superior*," but somebody for whom the company is liable because his action is the very action of the company itself. *Cf.* Kennedy L.J., *ibid.* [1914] 1 K.B. at p. 437: " The person or persons with whom the chief management of the company's business resides." Lord Haldane's statement was accepted and applied by the Privy Council in *Paterson Steamships Ltd.* v. *Robin Hood Mills Ltd.* (1937) 58 Ll.L.R. 33. In *The Lady Gwendolen*, *supra*, Willmer L.J., considered that where a company has entrusted the management of its ships to a traffic department, the effective head of that department, although not a director, may be regarded as the *alter ego* of the company for the purposes of the shipping business.

See also *Paterson Steamships Ltd.* v. *Canadian Co-operative Wheat Producers Ltd.* [1934] A.C. 538, at p. 549, for a discussion of the words " actual fault or privity " in this section compared with the same words, used in a slightly different context, in a Canadian Act. See also *Tesco Supermarkets Ltd.* v. *Nattrass* [1972] A.C. 153, a decision under the Trade Descriptions Act 1968. In *Admiralty* v. *Owners of Divina, The Truculent* [1952] P. 1, the principles laid down by Lord Haldane in *Lennard's Carrying Co.* v. *Asiatic Petroleum Co., supra*, were applied in determining whether the Crown was entitled to limit its liability in respect of claims which arose out of a collision between *H.M.S. Truculent* and the *Divina*. The court held (*inter alia*) that there was a " fault " in relation to the lights exhibited by *H.M.S. Truculent* and that as that fault was one of which the Third Sea Lord, a responsible member of the Board of Admiralty, was or must be deemed to have been aware, the claim of the Crown to limit liability failed.

The *alter ego* of a defendant company may be personally liable to an injured plaintiff in damages. See *Yuille* v. *B. & B. Fisheries (Leigh) Ltd. and Bates, The Radiant* [1958] 2 Lloyd's Rep. 596.

Onus of proof. The onus of proving that the loss happened without their actual fault or privity lies upon the owners: *Lennard's Carrying Co.* v. *Asiatic Petroleum Co., supra*, followed in *Paterson Steamships Ltd.* v. *Robin Hood Mills Ltd.* (*loc. cit.*). In that case Lord Roche, delivering the judgment of the Privy Council, also said: " But another and very important principle is to be derived from a consideration of the section, namely, that the fault or privity of the owners must be fault or privity in respect of that which causes the loss or damage in question, a proposition which was acted upon and illustrated in *Lennard's Case*." Where a shipowner is at fault, it is for him to prove that the fault did not contribute to the loss: *The Norman* [1960] 1 Lloyd's Rep. 1. In *The Yarmouth* [1909] P. 293, the court held that a general manager of a company as representative of the shareholders was a proper person to give evidence of actual fault or privity of owners. In the same case the court held that the fault and privity of a paid agent of a company who was registered as managing owner, though in fact he held no shares either in the company or in the ship, was not such as to disentitle the owners from limiting their liability.

As to the case of loss or damage being caused by a breach of contract by the owners, see note (7).

432 5 A seaman who was a member of the crew on board a vessel is a " person being carried in the ship " within the meaning of s. 503: *Innes* v. *Ross*, 1957 S.L.T. 121 (Court of Session). So is a person who falls from the gangway while boarding a ship: *Moore* v. *Metcalf Motor Coasters Ltd.* [1958] 2 Lloyd's Rep. 179. Paragraph (a) does not apply in relation to hovercraft: see § 1320, *post*.

6 This includes passengers' luggage: *The Stella* [1900] P. 161. After a collision the cargo of a vessel in fault was transhipped by the master into other vessels, which were lost owing to the negligence of their masters and crews. The owners of the first vessel obtained a decree limiting their liability arising out of the collision. In an action against them for non-delivery of the cargo lost, it was held that the decree in the limitation action did not apply to the present claim, for the loss of the cargo did not occur on board the ship in respect of which the owners' liability was limited: *The Bernina* (1886) 12 P.D. 36. See also note (1).

7 If the injury arose from improper navigation or management, the original section 503 applied even though the act or omission complained of was also a breach of contract, but, if the act or omission complained of was a mere breach of contract, and did not amount to improper navigation or management, the section did not apply: *Wahlberg* v. *Young* (1876) 45 L.J.C.P. 783; 24 W.R. 847; *The Vigilant* [1921] P. 312. Thus, failure by a hired tug to tow at all, or to complete a towage, at a time when no act of towage is being performed at all, would be a mere breach of contract and would not amount to improper navigation or management. *Secus*, the faulty carrying out of an actual towage operation, which would be both a breach of contract and improper navigation or management. *Ibid.* It would seem that, *mutatis mutandis*, these principles still apply although the words " act or omission " have now been substituted for the word " improper " by M.S. (Liability of Shipowners and Others) Act 1958, s. 2 (1). (See note (8) below.)

In the present context " management of the ship " probably covers any mismanagement or mishandling of the ship's appliances: *The Athelvictor* [1946] P. 42, followed in *The Anonity* [1961] 1 Lloyd's Rep. 203; see also *The Teal* (1949) 82 Ll.L.R. 414, where Pilcher J., after holding that the acceptance by the plaintiff's servants, on board a barge, of leaky drums containing a dangerous cargo, constituted " improper management of ship," went on to say at p. 422 that " any negligent act of the shipowner's servants which is carried out in furtherance of the cargo-carrying adventure, and which endangers the safety of the ship herself, constitutes improper management of the ship, for the purposes of this limitation section, even though the negligent act be one which is carried out solely or primarily with reference to this cargo." In *The Tojo Maru* [1972] A.C. 242, it was held that the firing of a bolt gun under water by an employee of salvage contractors who had descended from the contractors' tug was not an act in the management of the tug.

The following cases in which the phrase " navigation or management of the ship," or similar phrases have been considered may be referred to by way of illustration, but (see *The Athelvictor, supra*) they are of no direct application to the construction of the phrase in these sections:

Carmichael v. *Liverpool Indemnity, etc. Association* (1887) 19 Q.B.D. 242 (C.A.) (improperly closed port); *Canada Shipping Co.* v. *British Shipowners', etc. Association* (1889) 23 Q.B.D. 342 (C.A.) (improperly cleaned holds); *Laurie* v. *Douglas*, 15 M. & W. 746 (getting adrift in dock); *Good* v. *London Mutual Association* (1871) L.R. 6 C.P. 563 (open sea-cock); *The Ferro* [1893] P. 38 (negligent stowage by stevedores); *The Glenochli* [1896] P. 10 (pumping through broken pipe); *The Rodney* [1900] P. 112 (clearing pipe with rod); *Rowson* v. *Atlantic Transport* [1903] 2 K.B. 666 and *Foreman & Ellams* v. *Federal S.N. Co.* [1928] 2 K.B. 424 (misuse of refrigerating machinery); *Gosse Millard* v. *Canadian Government Merchant Marine* [1929] A.C. 223 (negligence in securing hatches); *The Anonity* [1961] 2 Lloyd's Rep. 117 (improper use of galley stove at oil jetty).

TUG AND TOW. Where a tug and her tows are in the same ownership, and a collision with another vessel is caused by the negligent navigation of those on board the tug *and* the tows, their owners may limit on the combined tonnage of the tug and such of her tows as were in contact with the other vessel, or which, by their weight, contributed to the damage; *The Harlow* [1922] P. 175. In *The Freden* (1950) 83 Ll.L.R. 427 this principle was applied not only where the tug herself was not in collision but also where there was no negligence on board the tows. However in *The Sir Joseph Rawlinson* [1973] 1 Q.B. 285 it was held that where the collision between another ship and the tug and tow was due to the negligence of the tug's master, the owners could limit by reference to the tonnage of the tug alone. In *The Ran and The Graygarth* [1922] P. 80 the limit in such circumstances was held to be based on the tonnage of the tow but this decision was doubted in *The Bramley Moore* [1964] P. 200; *cf.* also the Canadian decisions in *Falconbridge Nickel Mines Ltd.* v. *Chimo Shipping Ltd.* [1969] 2 Lloyd's Rep. 277; vessel carrying barges for lightering and *The Kathy K* [1972] 2 Lloyd's Rep. 36. Where tug and tow are in different ownership, each owner is entitled to limit on the tonnage of his own vessel; see *The American and The Syria* (1874) L.R. 6 P.C. 127; *The Englishman* [1894] P. 239; *The Morgengry and The Blackcock* [1900] P. 1. In *The Bramley Moore, supra*, it was held that the provisions of the 1958 Act made it clear that, where those on board the tug were negligent and those on the tow were not, the owners of the tug could limit their liability to the tonnage of the tug alone.

433 [8] The passage in square brackets was substituted for the original text by M.S. (Liability of Shipowners and Others) Act 1958, s. 2 (1). Paragraph (2) has been extended by the M.S. (Oil Pollution) Act 1971, s. 15 (2) to cover liability for preventative measures to which s. 1 of that Act does not apply. The original paragraphs (*c*) and (*d*) were as follows:

" (*c*) Where any loss of life or personal injury is caused to any person carried in any other vessel by reason of the improper navigation of the ship;

(*d*) Where any loss or damage is caused to any other vessel, or to any goods, merchandise, or other things whatsoever on board any other vessel, by reason of the improper navigation of the ship."

By M.S. (Liability of Shipowners and Others) Act 1900, s. 1 (now repealed by the 1958 Act), the limitation set by the 1894 Act was extended to " all cases where . . . any loss or damage is caused to property or rights of any kind, whether on land or on water, or whether fixed or moveable, by reason of the improper navigation or management of the ship."

The effect of the 1958 Act is for the first time to extend the right to limit to (a) claims for loss of life or personal injury to *any* person not on board the " limiting " ship and (*b*) claims for loss or damage to *any* property (other than that on board the " limiting " ship) and for any rights infringed. Further, it is no longer necessary to prove that the loss of life or personal injury or damage to property or rights is due to the " improper navigation or management " or the ship. The benefit of limitation is conferred if the occurrence was caused through the act or omission of any person (whether on board the ship or not) in the navigation or management of the ship, or in loading, discharge or embarkation and disembarkation of passengers, or through any other act or omission of any person on board the ship.

Further, the right to limit is no longer excluded because the occurrence giving rise to the liability was not due to negligence. See M.S. (Liability of Shipowners and Others) Act 1958, s. 2 (1) and (3), § 1212, *post*. A shipowner liable for damage caused without negligence, by reason of the provisions of s. 74 of the Harbours, Docks, and Piers Clauses Act 1847, is now without doubt entitled to limit. That section (s. 74) provides: " The owner of every vessel or float of timber shall be answerable to the undertakers for any damage done by such vessel or float of timber, or by any person employed about the same, to the harbour, dock or pier, or the quays or works connected therewith, and the master or person having charge of such vessel or float of timber through whose wilful act or negligence any such damage is done shall also be liable to make good the same; . . ." In the 5th edition of this work, the view was expressed that a shipowner could not limit his liability in such cases, which accepted the curious result that an owner might actually be prejudiced by the fact that his servants had not been negligent. However, a Scottish court subsequently took a different view. See *G. & G. Hamilton* v. *British Transport Commission*, 1957 S.L.T. 198 (Court of Session).

See also note (7) above.

The words " through any other act or omission of any person on board the ship " require that the person concerned must be on board the ship when the act or omission which gives rise to the liability to damages occurs: see *The Tojo Maru* [1972] A.C. 242.

434 [9] " Damages." The statute limits the owner's liability in damages, and does not otherwise relieve him from the consequences of his wrongful act. Thus, where a ship, sunk by collision for which she was solely to blame, was raised by the Thames Conservators at the expense of the owner, who had paid into court the statutory amount of liability, he was held not entitled to any contribution by way of salvage or general average from the owner of salved cargo, since the necessity for the salvage or general average expenditure had been occasioned by the owner's default: *The Ettrick* (1881) 6 P.D. 127; 4 Asp.M.L.C. 465 (C.A.); affirming 50 L.J.Ad. 65. Neither under this section, nor under M.S. (Liability of Shipowners and Others) Act, 1900, is the owner of a ship which has sunk in the Manchester Ship Canal as a result of a collision for which she is solely to blame entitled to limit his liability as against the canal company which has statutory powers to raise the wreck and recover the expenses from the owner: *The Millie* [1940] P. 1; followed in *The Stonedale* (*No.* 1) [1956] A.C. 1. But where the claim for wreck-raising expenses by a government authority is in the nature of a claim for damages as opposed to a claim for a debt, the owner is entitled to seek to limit his liability: see *The Putbus* [1969] 1 Lloyd's Rep. 253. Similarly where the expenses of wreck-raising are part of the damages claimed by one vessel in respect of a collision for which another vessel is solely to blame, the shipowners are entitled to limit their liability for the whole of the damages, including these expenses: *The Arabert* [1961] 2 W.L.R. 215; 1 Lloyd's Rep. 363, not following *The Urka* [1953] 1 Lloyd's Rep. 478.

However, if and when the necessary statutory instrument is made, the liability to pay " damages " for the purpose of this section will include any obligation or liability in connection with the raising, removal or destruction of a ship or anything on board her; see M.S. (Liability of Shipowners etc.) Act 1958, s. 2 (2) (*a*) and s. 2 (5). A fund may be set up to compensate harbour authorities for any consequent loss when the provisions relating to wreck-raising expenses are brought into force. *Ibid.* s. 2 (6).

By the same Act, the liability to pay " damages " for the purpose of this section has been extended to include a claim in respect of damage (however caused) to harbour works, basins or navigable waterways; see *ibid.* s. 2 (2) (*b*).

It has been held that a shipowner cannot limit in respect of his liability to provide an indemnity under the United Kingdom Standard Towage Conditions for damage suffered by a tug because such liability arises out of a contractual obligation and is not within the meaning of the word " damages ": *The Kirknes* [1957] P. 52. The liability for loss of life of persons on board the tug, being a right of action in tort, can however be limited; *ibid.*

Section 1 of the Maritime Conventions Act 1911, which, as interpreted by the Court of Appeal in *The Cairnbahn* [1914] P. 25, enables vessels at fault to obtain contribution from one another in respect of their liability as joint-tortfeasors, expressly provides that nothing in that section ". . . shall be construed . . . as affecting the right of any person to limit his liability in the manner provided by law "; see Maritime Conventions Act 1911, s. 1 (1) and (*c*) at § 827, *post*. There is no case in which it has been decided whether or not a liability to make contribution under this section or under the Law Reform (Married Women and Tortfeasors) Act 1935, is a liability to " damages " within the terms of s. 503 of M.S.A. 1894, which may be limited accordingly. The right of contribution between vessels at fault in respect of claims for personal injuries or loss of life is expressly restricted to the amount directly recoverable as damages subject (*inter alia*) to statutory limitation of liability; see Maritime Conventions Act 1911, s. 3 (1) (proviso).

Where under yacht racing rules, infringement thereof entailed a liability on the owner of a yacht to " all damages " arising from improper navigation, this was held to mean that the owner had contracted out of his right to limitation of liability in respect of damage caused to a competing yacht: *The Satanita* [1897] A.C. 59.

435 Under the old Admiralty rule of equal division of loss where both ships were to blame, and the owners of the ship which sustained the lesser damage limited their liability and paid the amount into court, the owners of the other ship were entitled to a moiety of their damage, less a moiety of the damage sustained by the first ship, and to prove against the fund in court for the balance: *The Khedive* (*Stoomvaart Maatschappy Nederland* v. *Peninsular and Oriental S.N. Co.*) (*No.* 2) (1882) 7 App.Cas. 795; overruling *Chapman* v. *Royal Netherlands S.N. Co.* (1879) 4 P.D. 157. See also *per* Brett M.R., and Cotton L.J. in *The Hector* (*No.* 2) (1883) 8 P.D. 218 (C.A.).

This Admiralty rule as to the equal division of the loss in all cases of " both to blame " has been abrogated by the Maritime Conventions Act 1911, *post*, and the liability to make good the damage or loss is now to be in proportion to the degree in which each vessel was in fault, provided that if it is not possible to establish different degrees of fault, the liabilities shall be apportioned equally. But the principle of *The Khedive*, *supra*, appears still applicable in whatever degree the fault be apportioned.

The owner of cargo damaged on board the ship of the plaintiff in a limitation action is not precluded by the findings in the damage action to which he was not a party, and in which no one could be heard who was concerned to protect his interest, from showing the real value of the ship: *C. A. Van Eijck and Zoon* v. *Somerville* [1906] A.C. 489.

In all cases where the owner's liability is limited he is liable for interest upon the amount awarded from the date of the collision, whether the vessel injured was or was not earning freight; the amount limited by the statute takes the place of the amount which would be decreed as a *restitutio in integrum* apart from the statute, and therefore, like it, attaches to the *res* and bears interest from the moment the injury is inflicted. This rule, adopted by the Court of Admiralty, follows that which was observed by the Court of Chancery in limitation suits (where the ship was not earning freight), and differs from the rule at common law: *Nixon* v. *Roberts* (1861) 30 L.J.Ch. 844; *The Northumbria* (1869) L.R. 3 A. & E. 6; *The Amalia* (*No.* 2) (1864) 34 L.J.Ad. 21; 13 W.R. 111; *Straker* v. *Hartland* (1864) 34 L.J.Ch. 122; 2 H. & M. 570; *The Theems* [1938] P. 197; *Commonwealth of Australia* v. *Asiatic Steam Navigation Co., Ltd., and Others* [1955] 1 Lloyd's Rep. 503. As to the appropriate rate of interest, see *The Abadesa* [1968] P. 656, *The Mecca* [1968] P. 665, *Jefford and Jefford* v. *Gee* [1970] 2 Q.B. 130; *The Funabashi* [1972] 1 Lloyd's Rep. 371. The rule applies whether there are several claims or only one. *Smith* v. *Kirby* (1875) 1 Q.B.D. 131; 24 W.R. 207; *Owners of the S.S. Olga* v. *Owners of the S.S. Anglia* (1905) 7 F. 739. And equally in the case of life claims, although they are claims of a common law nature to which interest does not generally attach. *The Crathie* [1897] P. 178 at p. 184.

The statute does not relieve the owner from liability to pay costs; as to which, see s. 504, and note (10) thereto.

As to the release of a vessel arrested in a damage action, upon payment into court of the amount of statutory liability, and a sum to cover interest and costs, see *The Sisters* (1875) 32 L.T. 837; 2 Asp.M.L.C. 589. See, now, M.S. (Liability of Shipowners and Others) Act 1958, s. 5 (release of ship, property and security in certain circumstances) and s. 6 (restriction of enforcement of claims after security has been given).

As to payment into court, bail, stay of proceedings, etc., see *The Clutha* (1876) 45 L.J.Ad. 108; *The Alne Holme* (*No.* 2) (1882) 47 L.T. 302; 4 Asp.M.L.C. 593; *Milburn* v. *L. & S.W. Ry.* (1870) L.R. 6 Ex. 4; *The Expert* (1877) 36 L.T. 258; 3 Asp.M.L.C. 381 (reference as to distribution, etc.); *The Inventor* (1906) 10 Asp.M.L.C. 99; 93 L.T. 189; *The Charlotte* [1920] P. 78; 36 T.L.R. 204.

As to practice generally, see also s. 504, and notes thereto.

The statute does not affect the jurisdiction of the court to arrest freight in a damage action. " It may turn out that the conjoint value of the ship and freight may not amount to the statutory measure of liability ": *The Orpheus* (1871) L.R. 3 A. & E. 308, 312.

436 [10] The section does not prevent owners from contracting out of all liability for negligence, or from contracting to be liable for an amount exceeding their statutory liability: *The Stella* [1900] P. 161; *The Satanita* [1897] A.C. 59. But any exclusion by the terms of a contract must be clear: *The Kirknes* [1957] P. 51.

[11] The words in square brackets are substituted for " loss of or damage to vessels, goods, merchandise or other things " by the M.S. (Liability of Shipowners and Others) Act 1958, s. 2 (1). This follows the extended scope given to the right to limit by the 1958 Act. See note (8), *supra*.

12 The substitution of the sums referred to in square brackets for " fifteen pounds " in sub-para. (i) and " eight pounds " in sub-para. (ii) is the effect of the M.S. (Limitation of Liability of Shipowners and Others) Act 1958, s. 1 (1). For this purpose, a gold franc shall be taken to be a unit consisting of sixty-five and a half milligrams of gold of millesimal fineness nine hundred. *Ibid.* s. 1 (2). The sterling equivalents are £96·3911 and £31·0939 respectively. See the M.S. (Limitation of Liability) (Sterling Equivalents) Order 1973 (S.I. No. 1190), made under M.S. (Limitation of Liability of Shipowners and Others) Act 1958, s. 1 (3). As for hovercraft, see § 1320, *post.* For the effect upon a payment into court of a variation in the declared sterling equivalents, see *ibid.* s. 1 (4), § 1210, *post.* The sterling equivalents to be applied on any particular case are accordingly, those in force at the time the limitation decree is made or at the time the payment into court is made: see *The Abadesa* [1968] P. 656; *The Mecca* [1968] P. 665.

13 The number by which the sum specified in sub-para. (i) is to be multiplied shall be 300 in any case where the tonnage concerned is less than 300 tons. M.S. (Limitation of Liability of Shipowners and Others) Act 1958, s. 1 (1). As for hovercraft, see § 1320, *post.* As to marshalling the assets when there are both claims for loss of life or personal injury, and for loss of or damage to property, see s. 504, note (5).

14 As to the application of the Act to ships propelled by other mechanical power, see s. 743.

15 The words in square brackets are substituted for the words " gross tonnage without deduction on account of engine room " by the M.S.A. 1906, s. 69. See also the first part of note (13), *supra.*

437 16 For the provisions as to tonnage measurement, see the M.S. (Tonnage) Regulations 1967 (No. 172) as amended by S.I. 1967 No. 1093 and by S.I. 1972 No. 656 made under the M.S.A. 1965, s. 1, § 1259, *post.*

The tonnage to be taken as the basis of the owner's liability is that appearing on the ship's register in force at the time of the collision, and neither party is entitled to the benefit of any subsequent register: *The John McIntyre* or *The John Ormston* (1881) 6 P.D. 200; *The Dione* (1885) 52 L.T. 61; 5 Asp.M.L.C. 347. But the ship's register is not conclusive, and evidence may be given to show that the register was not made in accordance with the provisions of the Act. See *The Franconia* (1878) 3 P.D. 164 at p. 179; and *The Recepta* (1889) 14 P.D. 131, where evidence was admitted to show that the registered tonnage was not the correct tonnage at the time of collision. The copy of the register placed before the court must be a copy of the register at the time of the collision: *The Rosslyn* (1904) 10 Asp.M.L.C. 24; 92 L.T. 177. See also s. 82. For unregistered ships or structures in the course of completion or construction, see note (18), *infra.* M.S. (Liability of Shipowners) Act 1898, and M.S.A. 1906, s. 70, have now been repealed by M.S. (Liability of Shipowners and Others) Act 1958, s. 8 (6) and Sched. And as to foreign registers, see note (18).

The registered tonnage of a ship for the purpose of limiting liability for claims in respect of loss of life or personal injury shall be taken as 300 tons when the actual tonnage of the ship concerned is less than 300 tons. See M.S. (Liability of Shipowners and Others) Act 1958, s. 1 (1). As for hovercraft, see § 1320, *post.*

Under the M.S.A. 1889 (now repealed) in the case of a sailing ship, it was held that the master's and navigation spaces were to be deducted in calculating the register tonnage for the purpose of limiting liability: *The Pilgrim* [1895] P. 117. This section has placed steamships and sailing ships on an equal footing, in so far as both classes of ships now may deduct navigation and other spaces from their tonnage in arriving at the amount of their liability.

In cases where the limitation provisions are applied by the Crown Proceedings Act 1947, and the ship is not registered under the M.S. Acts, special provision is made for the calculation of the tonnage by s. 5 (5) of the Crown Proceedings Act 1947, *post.*

In the case of a British fishing vessel registered under Part IV but not Part I, a deduction may be made for crew space which has been certified by a Ministry of Transport surveyor for the purposes of registration under Part I of this Act: *Couper* v. *McKenzie* (1906) 43 S.L.R. 416. For provisions as to these crew spaces, see s. 210, and notes thereto.

17 The words in italics ceased to have effect by virtue of s. 4 (3) of M.S.A. 1948.

18 These provisions for ascertaining the tonnage of a foreign ship are now applied to any ship or structure which is unregistered or in the course of completion or construction but yet within the definition of " ship " for the purpose of the limitation provisions. See M.S. (Liability of Shipowners and Others) Act 1958, s. 4 (3). As to the tonnage of ships of a foreign country which has adopted the British tonnage regulations, see ss. 82, 84, and the notes thereto, and M.S.A. 1965, s. 1. For the appointment of the surveyor general of ships see s. 724 (2), § 652, *post.*

19 " On distinct occasions." Where a ship comes into collision with two vessels one after the other, and the two collisions take place substantially at the same time and as the result

of one act of improper navigation, the owner is entitled to limit his liability to one payment for the whole damage: *The Rajah* (1872) L.R. 3 A. & E. 539: *The Creadon* (1886) 54 L.T. 880; 5 Asp.M.L.C. 585. But where damage was caused to two vessels in succession by the improper starboarding of the ship in fault, it was held that as there was time between the two collisions to correct the mistake, the second collision took place on a " distinct occasion " from the first. The test is not the lapse of time but whether both collisions are the result of the same act of want of seamanship: *The Schwan* (*The Albano*) [1892] P. 419; 69 L.T. 34 (C.A.). The limitation of liability of owners of docks and canals and harbour and conservancy authorities in respect of loss or damage caused to vessels or cargo thereon is similarly restricted to losses or damages arising on " one distinct occasion." See M.S. (Liability of Shipowners and Others) Act 1900, s. 3. This limitation has now been made applicable also to the Crown; see Crown Proceedings Act 1947, s. 7. See also Pilotage Authorities (Limitation of Liability) Act 1936, s. 2, *post*, and the Harbours Act 1964, s. 25 (1).

20 The words in square brackets have been substituted by M.S. (Liability of Shipowners and Others) Act 1958, s. 8 (2), for the original text, which read as follows: " The owner of every sea-going ship or share therein shall be liable in respect of every such loss of life, personal injury, loss of or damage to vessels, goods, merchandise, or things as aforesaid arising on distinct occasions to the same extent as if no other loss, injury, or damage had arisen." This follows the greater scope given to the right to limit by the earlier paragraphs (*a*) to (*d*) as amended, and the wider meaning given to the word " damages " (see note (9), *supra*). For the meaning of " on distinct occasions " see note (19), above.

Power of courts to consolidate claims against owners, etc.

438 **504.** Where any liability is alleged [1] to have been incurred by the owner of a British or foreign ship [2] [in respect of any occurrence in respect of which his liability is limited under section five hundred and three of this Act [3]] and several claims are made or apprehended in respect of that liability, then the owner may apply in England and Ireland to the High Court,[4] or in Scotland to the Court of Session, or in a British possession to any competent court, and that court may determine the amount of the owner's liability and may distribute that amount rateably [5] among the several claimants,[6] and may stay any proceedings pending [7] in any other court in relation to the same matter, and may proceed in such manner and subject to such regulations as to making persons interested parties to the proceedings, and as to the exclusion of any claimants who do not come in within a certain time,[8] and as to requiring security [9] from the owner, and as to payment of any costs,[10] as the court thinks just.

439 This provision was extended by M.S.A. 1911, *post*, to include any British court in a foreign country having Admiralty jurisdiction. Similar provisions for consolidation of claims, where questions of limitation of total liability arise, are contained in the Pilotage Act 1913, s. 35 (3), and the Pilotage Authorities (Limitation of Liability) Act 1936, s. 3. For modifications of the section in its application to hovercraft, see § 1320, *post*.

1 Practice. Proceedings for relief under this section are now governed by R.S.C., Ord. 75, rr. 2 and 37 to 40. In limitation actions, the names of the plaintiffs must be stated in the writ and it is no longer sufficient to describe them as " Owners of S.S. —." See R.S.C., Ord. r. 37 (1). Further rules prescribe details of the procedure to be followed. A claim for limitation is heard by the Admiralty Registrar upon a summons supported by affidavits without pleadings. If the right to limit is not disputed, the registrar will order limitation, but if there is a dispute, he will order that the proceedings be heard by the judge and he will give appropriate directions and order pleadings to be delivered. As to the circumstances in which a court may, or must, order the release of a ship or other property from arrest, or release security that has been given, see M.S. (Liability of Shipowners and Others) Act 1958, s. 5, § 1218, *post*. R.S.C. Ord. 18, r. 22 preserves the right of any person to rely on the provisions of s. 503 of M.S.A. 1894, by way of defence. Accordingly, although in the Admiralty Court all questions of limitation are almost invariably

raised by separate action after the determination of liability and before assessment of damages in the damage action, it is competent, as usual in the Queen's Bench Division where liability and damages are usually determined in the same proceedings, to raise a plea under s. 503 by way of defence: *The Clutha* (1876) 45 L.J.Ad. 108; 35 L.T. 36; *London Rangoon Trading Co.* v. *Ellerman Lines Ltd.* (1923) 39 T.L.R. 284. In such a case, where a claim merits a higher sum of damages than the limit of liability, judgment will be given for the limit: *Wheeler* v. *London and Rochester Trading Co. Ltd.* [1957] 1 Lloyd's Rep. 69. In the Admiralty Court, it is not necessary that liability should be admitted before the plea is raised: *The Amalia* (1863) 32 L.J.Ad. 191; 1 Moo.P.C.C.(N.S.) 471; *The Sisters* (1875) 32 L.T. 837; 2 Asp.M.L.C. 589; and see *The Karo* (1887) 13 P.D. 24; but before a decree can be obtained in the limitation proceedings it seems that liability must be admitted or determined. See *Hill* v. *Audus* (1855) 24 L.J.Ch. 229; 1 K. & J. 263. However, a qualified admission of partial blame will be sufficient to entitle a shipowner to a limitation decree before a final apportionment of blame has been made. See *Commonwealth of Australia* v. *Asiatic Steam Navigation Co., Ltd. and Others* [1955] 1 Lloyd's Rep. 503 (High Ct. of Aus.). See further as to practice *British Shipping Laws* (Vol. 4); *Marsden on Collisions at Sea*, 11th ed., §§ 219, 409; Roscoe, *Admiralty Practice*, 5th ed., pp. 242, 243.

Where he admits liability, but not otherwise, the court will stay actions brought for the purpose of establishing liability. See *Miller* v. *Powell* (1875) 2 R. 976.

2 "Owner of a British or foreign ship" includes any charterers and any person interested in or in possession of the ship, and, in particular, any manager or operator of the ship (M.S. (Liability of Shipowners and Others) Act 1958, s. 3 (1)), and for the purposes of s. 2 of the M.S. (Liability of Shipowners and Others) Act 1900, a harbour or conservancy authority, and the owner of a canal or of a dock. See also note (1) to s. 503. As to the meaning of "ship," see note (2) to s. 503. For the modification of this section in its application to hovercraft, see § 1320, *post*.

440 3 The words in square brackets have been substituted by M.S. (Liability of Shipowners and Others) Act 1958, s. 8 (3), for the words "in respect of loss of life, personal injury or loss of or damage to vessels or goods." This follows the greater scope given to the right to limit by the earlier paragraphs (*a*) to (*d*) of s. 503 (1) as amended, and the wider meaning given to the word "damages" (see note (9) to s. 503, *supra*).

4 See R.S.C. Ord. 75, rr. 2 and 37 to 40.

5 The practice which has been established is in accordance with the terms of the International Convention relating to the Limitation of the Liability of Owners of Sea-going Ships, signed at Brussels on October 10, 1957, article 3 (1). Where the amount paid into court, at the higher rate, is insufficient to satisfy claims for loss of life and personal injuries, and for loss of goods, the court will marshal the assets; and the claimants in respect of loss of life, etc., are entitled to be paid first an amount equal to the difference between the higher rate and the lower rate, and then to rank *pari passu* with the claimants in respect of loss of goods against the balance of the fund: *The Victoria* (1888) 13 P.D. 125; and see *The Khedive* (*Stoomvaart, etc.*) v. *Peninsular and Oriental S.N. Co.* (*No.* 2) (1882) 7 App. Cas. 795. See also note (4) to s. 1 of the M.S. (Liability of Shipowners and Others) Act 1958, at § 1211, *post*, for the "minimum tonnage" of 300 introduced by that Act for claims for loss of life or personal injury. For similar provisions relating to hovercraft, see § 1319, *post*. But where no limitation proceedings have been instituted, the fund in court being merely the proceeds of the sale of a foreign ship, the life claimants have no priority over the claimants in respect of damage to property: *Canadian Pacific Ry.* v. *S.S. Storstad* [1920] A.C. 397.

For the mode of distributing the amount among several life claimants, see *Glaholm* v. *Barker* (1866) L.R. 2 Eq. 598.

For the mode of distributing the limitation fund where rival claimants seek to establish against the fund the same liability for payment of wreck-raising expenses, see *The Liverpool* (*No.* 2) [1960] 3 W.L.R. 597; [1960] 2 Lloyd's Rep. 66 (C.A.).

Where the owner has settled some of the claims out of court, he is entitled to have them taken into account in estimating the amount payable on the remaining claims: *Rankine* v. *Raschen* (1877) 4 R. 725. And this is so even though the payment is made under a judgment of a foreign court: *The Coaster* (1922) 91 L.J.P. 145; 38 T.L.R. 511. Formerly, if no payment had in fact been made, the owner could not put forward in his own right a contingent claim in respect of claims which might in the future be substantiated against him under a foreign judgment: *The Kronprinz Olav* [1921] P. 52 (C.A.). But see now M.S. (Liability of Shipowners and Others) Act 1958, s. 7 (1), by which a court may postpone distribution of part of a limitation fund if there are claims pending in a foreign court. And where all claims in respect of loss of life had been settled, an order was made, on payment into court of £8 per ton, restraining any action in respect of the collision: *The*

Foscolino (1885) 5 Asp.M.L.C. 420; 52 L.T. 866. When the ship has been sold in an action abroad, claimants in a limitation action in this country must give credit for any sums recovered by them out of the proceeds of the sale abroad: *The Crathie* [1897] P. 178.

A claimant gains no advantage over his fellow-claimants by his diligence in obtaining judgment in the Admiralty Court in respect of his claim: *Leycester* v. *Logan,* 3 K. & J. 446; *Jenkins* v. *Great Central Ry.* (*Shipping Gazette*, Jan. 13, 1912; Halsbury's *Laws of England*, 3rd ed., Vol. 35, Shipping, p. 779).

Formerly, effect was given to a possessory lien enjoyed by one claimant against a limitation fund even if the result was to deprive other claimants of all rights of recovery against the fund. See *Mersey Docks and Harbour Board* v. *Hay* (*The Countess*) [1923] A.C. 345. But it is now enacted by M.S. (Liability of Shipowners and Others) Act 1958, s. 7 (2), that " No lien or other right in respect of any ship or property shall affect the proportions in which under the said section five hundred and four any amount is distributed amongst several claimants."

441 [6] The section applies to claims under Lord Campbell's Act: *Glaholm* v. *Barker, supra*; *London & S.W. Ry.* v. *James, infra.* Although the Admiralty Division had formerly no jurisdiction *in rem* in cases under that Act (*per* Brett M.R., *The Vera Cruz* (1884) 9 P.D. 96), such jurisdiction was conferred by s. 5 of the Maritime Conventions Act 1911, *post*, which provided that " any enactment which confers on any court Admiralty jurisdiction in respect of damage shall have effect as though references to such damage included references to damages for loss of life or personal injury, and accordingly proceedings in respect of such damages may be brought *in rem* or *in personam* "; for present position see notes to that section.

As to claim by bottomry bondholder, see *The Empusa* (1879) 5 P.D. 6; and by the Crown, *The Zoe* (1886) 11 P.D. 72.

Where a vessel sank another belonging to the same owner and he limited his liability as owner of the former, underwriters, who had paid him insurance upon the latter, were held not entitled to claim upon the fund, as the owner himself could not have done so and they were no more than his assignees: *Simpson* v. *Thomson* (1877) 3 App.Cas. 279.

As to the right of plaintiffs in a limitation action to have credit for payments made by them, see note (5).

[7] " Proceedings pending, etc." Thus, under the Act of 1854, an injunction was granted by the Court of Chancery staying proceedings in the Admiralty Court, in *Leycester* v. *Logan* (1857) 3 K. & J. 446; 26 L.J.Ch. 36.

And actions which had been brought at common law, for breach of contract (except for loss by delay), and under Lord Campbell's Act, were restrained in *London & S.W. Ry.* v. *James* (1872) L.R. 8 Ch. 241; *The Normandy* (1870) L.R. 3 A. & E. 152.

But an action in the Queen's Bench Division under Lord Campbell's Act against the shipowners will not necessarily be transferred to the Admiralty Division on the owners obtaining a decree limiting their liability, when to transfer it will deprive the plaintiff of his right to have damages assessed by a jury: *Roche* v. *London & S.W. Ry.* [1899] 2 Q.B. 502; *The Nereid* (1889) 14 P.D. 78. See also M.S. (Liability of Shipowners and Others) Act 1958, s. 7 (1), by which a court may postpone the distribution of a limitation fund if there are claims pending in a foreign court. However, in *The Annie Hay* [1968] P. 341, it was doubted whether the court had power to order a stay of other proceedings arising out of the same event.

442 [8] The time may be extended. See *The Zoe, supra.* Where the usual advertisements have been issued, and all the known life claims have not been entered within the limit of time certified in the advertisements, the court will order any unappropriated balance of the fund available for the life claims to be paid back to the plaintiffs in the limitation action: *The Alma* [1903] P. 55.

[9] " Security." See now M.S. (Liability of Shipowners and Others) Act 1958, s. 6, for the restriction upon enforcement of claims founded upon a liability to which a limit is set by s. 503 when security has been given. On payment into court of £8 per ton actions for damage to ship and goods were stayed; but not actions for loss of life, though plaintiffs were ordered to give security for the difference between £8 and £15 per ton in respect of such claims: *The Nereid* (1889) 14 P.D. 78; and see *The Dione* (1885) 52 L.T. 61; 5 Asp. M.L.C. 347.

[10] Costs. The general practice before about 1930 was that the defendants in a limitation action should pay the costs other than those ordinarily incidental to obtaining a decree of limitation: *The Spirit of Ocean* (1865) 2 Asp. M.L.C. 192; *The Empusa* (1879) 5 P.D. 6; *The African S.S. Co.* v. *Swanzy and Kennedy* (1856) 25 L.J.Ch. 870; 2 K. & J. 660; *The Ponce* (1879) 4 Asp. M.L.C. 185n., *The Expert* (1877) 3 Asp. M.L.C. 381, 36 L.T. 258; *The Warkworth* (1884) 9 P.D. 145; *The Rijnstroon* (1899) 80 L.T. 422; *The Creadon*

(1886) 5 Asp. M.L.C. 585; *Carron* v. *Cayzer* (1885) 13 R. 114; *The Ant* (1924) 19 Ll.L.R. 211; *The Alde* [1926] P. 211; *The Ruapehu*, No. 2 [1929] P. 305. However there thereafter grew up a practice based on *Charlotte* v. *Theory and Others* (1921) 9 Ll.L.R. 341; *The Kathleen* (1925) 22 Ll.L.R. 80 that the plaintiff was ordered to pay all the costs of a limitation action unless the defendants had acted unreasonably in disputing the right to limit: see *The Teal* (1949) 82 Ll.L.R. 414; *The Hans Hoth* [1952] 2 Lloyd's Rep. 34; *The Empire Jamaica* [1955] P. 259; *The Hildina* [1957] 2 Lloyd's Rep. 247; *The Arabert* [1963] P. 102; *The Bramley Moore* [1964] P. 209. In the Court of Appeal the normal rule applied; see *The Empire Jamaica, supra*; affirmed [1957] A.C. 386; *The Bramley Moore, supra*. The more modern practice in the courts of first instance was doubted in *The Aunt May* [1968] 1 Lloyd's Rep. 141 at p. 154. The previous practice would now seem to have been reinstated: see *The Alletta* [1972] 1 Lloyd's Rep. 375.

Part owners to account in respect of damages

443 **505.** All sums paid for or on account of any loss or damage in respect whereof the liability of owners [1] is limited under the provisions of this Part of this Act, and all costs incurred in relation thereto, may be brought into account among part owners [2] of the same ship in the same manner as money disbursed for the use thereof.

For modifications of this section as it applies to hovercraft, see § , *post.*

[1] For the extended meaning of the word " owners " in relation to Part VIII of the Act, see M.S. (Liability of Shipowners and Others) Act 1958, s. 3 and s. 8 (4).

[2] The word " owner " in this context is *not* to be given the extended meaning referred to in note (1), *supra*. See M.S. (Liability of Shipowners and Others) Act 1958, s. 8 (4).

Insurances of certain risks not invalid

444 **506.** An insurance effected against the happening, without the owner's actual fault or privity, of any or all of the events in respect of which the liability of owners is limited under this Part of this Act shall not be invalid by reason of the nature of the risk.

This section corresponds to s. 55 of the Merchant Shipping Act Amendment Act 1862. Provision appears to have been made in the Act of 1862 *ex abundante cautela* to allay any apprehension there might be that such insurances could be impugned on the ground of want of interest or illegality. It seems, however, clear that they are valid apart from this section. See Hansard, *Parl. Deb.*, Vol. 166, p. 2227.

Cf. s. 335 as to similar provisions as to insurance of passage money.

S. 55 of the Act of 1862 only referred to cases of limitation of liability now covered by s. 503 of M.S.A. 1894; but s. 506 of M.S.A. 1894, in terms applies also to cases within s. 502 of this Act. By the Stamp Act 1891, s. 93 (1) (saved for this purpose by s. 30 (6) of the Finance Act 1959), contracts of insurance to which s. 55 of the Act of 1862 applied need not be made in a policy of sea insurance. *Quaere* whether, in these circumstances, s. 38 of the Interpretation Act 1889 (cited in notes to s. 742, *infra*), has extended the provisions of s. 93 (1) of the Stamp Act 1891, to cases of insurance of risks arising under s. 502 of M.S.A. 1894.

445 **507.** [*This section, which provided that the passenger lists under Part III of the Act were evidence that a person whose death was the subject of proceedings under this Part was a passenger at the time of death, was repealed by the M.S.A.* 1970, *s.* 100 (3) *and Sched.* 5 *as from January* 1, 1973: *see S.I.* 1972 *No.* 1977.]

446 **508.** [*This section, which preserved the liability of a master or seaman in that capacity when he was also an owner or part-owner of a ship, and*

also restricted limitation to British ships which were recognised as such throughout the Act, has been repealed by M.S. (*Liability of Shipowners and Others*) *Act* 1958, *s.* 8 (6) *and Schedule. See now ibid. ss.* 3 (2) *and* 4 (1), (2).]

Extent of Part VIII

447 **509.** This Part of this Act shall, unless the context otherwise requires, extend to the whole of Her Majesty's dominions.

448 This section does not apply to hovercraft, see § 1320, *post*.

The existing limitation enactments may, by Order in Council, be extended to the Isle of Man, any of the Channel Islands, or to any colony or any place outside Her Majesty's dominions where for the time being Her Majesty has jurisdiction. See M.S. (Liability of Shipowners and Others) Act 1958, s. 11. For the exercise of this power, see notes thereto.

The Crown Proceedings Act 1947 does not affect the law enforced in courts elsewhere than in England and Scotland or the procedure in any such courts. Accordingly the extended application of the provisions of Part VIII to the Crown and H.M. ships (as to which see notes to ss. 502 and 503, *supra*) would not be given effect to by other courts; *ibid.* s. 52. Power is given by s. 53 to extend the Act to Northern Ireland; this power was exercised by the Northern Ireland (Crown Proceedings) Order 1949 (S.I. 1949 No. 1836). The provisions of M.S. (Liability of Shipowners and Others) Act 1958 have been expressly extended to Northern Ireland; see *ibid.* s. 10 (1), and the reference in s. 8 of that Act to the Crown Proceedings Act, 1947, is a reference to that Act as it applies in Northern Ireland; M.S. (Liability of Shipowners and Others) Act 1958, s. 10 (2). As to the operation of Part VIII of the 1894 Act in Australia, see the *Commonwealth of Australia* v. *Asiatic Steam Navigation Co. Ltd., The River Loddon* [1955] 1 Lloyd's Rep. 503.

PART IX—WRECK AND SALVAGE

449 APPLICATION TO AIRCRAFT.—By the Civil Aviation Act 1949, s. 51, it is provided as follows:

" (1) Any services rendered in assisting, or in saving life from, or in saving the cargo or apparel of, an aircraft in, on or over the sea or any tidal water, or on or over the shores of the sea or any tidal water, shall be deemed to be salvage services in all cases in which they would have been salvage services if they had been rendered in relation to a vessel; and where salvage services are rendered by an aircraft to any property or person, the owner of the aircraft shall be entitled to the same reward for those services as he would have been entitled to if the aircraft had been a vessel.

The foregoing provisions of this subsection shall have effect notwithstanding that the aircraft concerned is a foreign aircraft, and notwithstanding that the services in question are rendered elsewhere than within the limits of the territorial waters adjacent to any part of His Majesty's dominions.

(2) His Majesty may by Order in Council direct that any provisions of any Act for the time being in force which relate to wreck, to salvage of life or property or to the duty of rendering assistance to vessels in distress shall, with such exceptions, adaptations and modifications, if any, as may be specified in the Order, apply in relation to aircraft as those provisions apply in relation to vessels.

(3) For the purposes of this section, any provisions of an Act which relate to vessels laid by or neglected as unfit for sea service shall be deemed to be provisions relating to wreck, and the expression " Act " shall be deemed to include any local or special Act and any provisions of the Harbours, Docks and Piers Clauses Act 1847, as incorporated with any local or special Act, whenever passed.

(4) Part VI of this Act applies to this section."

This section replaces the provisions of section 11 of the Air Navigation Act 1920, as substituted by section 28 of the Air Navigation Act 1936 (now repealed by the Civil Aviation Act 1949, s. 70 (1) and Twelfth Schedule). The Aircraft (Wreck and Salvage) Order in Council, 1938, (now partly revoked by S.I. 1964 No. 489) which was made under the Air Navigation Acts 1920 and 1936, and which applied with adaptations, the provisions of the M.S.A. as to wreck and salvage to aircraft, continues in force notwithstanding the repeal of the provisions under which it was made, and it has effect as if made under this section.

450 MOTOR VEHICLES.—A vehicle at a time when it is being driven on a journey, to or from any place, undertaken for salvage purposes pursuant to Part IX of the Merchant Shipping Act 1894, is exempted from the

requirements of compulsory third party insurance by the Road Traffic Act 1972, s. 144 (2) (*c*). There is also power to vary speed limits for motor vehicles used for salvage purposes pursuant to this part of the Act, Road Traffic Regulation Act 1967, s. 98.

Vessels in Distress

Definition of " wreck " and " salvage "

451 **510.** In this Part of this Act unless the context otherwise requires—

(1) The expression " wreck " [1] includes [2] jetsam, flotsam, lagan, and derelict found in or on the shores of the sea or any tidal water.[3]

(2) The expression " salvage " includes all expenses, properly incurred by the salvor in the performance of the salvage services.

452 [1] " Wreck."—As to rights of the Crown, see s. 523. This term was held not to include a barge which had parted from her moorings in the Thames and was drifting: *The Zeta* (1875) L.R. 4 A. & E. 460. Nor timber which had drifted from its moorings: *Palmer* v. *Rouse* (1858) 27 L.J.Ex. 437; 3 H. & N. 505; *Cargo ex Schiller* (1877) 2 P.D. 145 (C.A.); 36 L.T. 714; affirming 46 L.J.Ad. 9.

For the meaning of " wreck, jetsam, flotsam, lagan and derelict," see *Sir Henry Constable's Case* (1601) 3 Coke's Rep. Pt. 5, 106, a, b (or p. 214); *R.* v. *Forty Nine Casks of Brandy* (1836) 3 Hag.Adm. 257; *R.* v. *Two Casks of Tallow* (1837) 3 Hag.Adm. 294; *The Pauline* 2 Rob.Ad.R. 359, and *The Gas Float Whitton No.* 2 [1896] P. 42, and cases cited in preceding note. See also Kennedy: *Civil Salvage*, 4th ed., pp. 385–388.

See also on the meaning of " derelict " *Cossman* v. *West* (1887) 13 App.Cas. 160 at pp. 180, 181; *The Aquila* (1798) 1 C.Rob. 37; *The Coromandel* (1857) Swa. 205, at pp. 208, 209; *The Gertrude* (1861) 30 L.J.Ad. 130; *The Cosmopolitan* (1848) (Ir.) 6 Notes of Cas. Sup. xviii, xx–xxviii; *The Zeta, supra*; *The Genessee* (1848) 12 Jur. 401; and *The F.D. Lambert* [1917] P. 232, n.; and for the distinction between " wreck " and " derelict," see *The Sophie* (1841) 6 L.T. 370.

The definition has also been applied by the Milford Haven Conservancy Act 1958, s. 7 (a). For fishing boats and fishing gear deemed to be " wreck " within this definition, see the Sea Fisheries Act 1968, s. 17.

[2] As to the effect of the word " includes " in an interpretation clause see note (4) to s. 742.

[3] See note (2) to s. 546, and note (2) to s. 418. See definition of tidal water, s. 742, which expressly excludes a harbour.

Duty of receiver where vessel in distress

453 **511.**—(1) Where a British or foreign vessel [1] is wrecked, stranded, or in distress [2] at any place on or near the coasts [3] of the United Kingdom [4] or any tidal water [5] within the limits of the United Kingdom, the receiver of wreck [6] for the district in which that place is situate shall, upon being made acquainted with the circumstance, forthwith proceed there, and upon his arrival shall take the command of all persons present, and shall assign such duties and give such directions to each person as he thinks fit for the preservation of the vessel and of the lives of the persons belonging to the vessel (in this Part of this Act referred to as shipwrecked persons) and of the cargo and apparel of the vessel.

(2) If any person wilfully disobeys the directions of the receiver, he shall for each offence be liable to a fine not exceeding fifty pounds; but the

receiver shall not interfere between the master [7] and the crew of the vessel in reference to the management thereof, unless he is requested to do so by the master.

454 [1] See definition of " vessel " in s. 742.
[2] For the signals of distress and their use, see M.S. (Safety Convention) Act 1949, s. 21 and notes thereto.
[3] For the meaning of " on or near the coasts," see *The Fulham* [1898] P. at p. 213, and note (2) to s. 546.
[4] See note " Application to Northern Ireland and the Republic of Ireland " in notes to s. 742.
[5] See definition of " tidal water " in s. 742.
[6] See s. 566, as to appointment of receivers of wreck.
[7] See definition of " master " in s. 742.

Powers of the receiver in case of vessels in distress

455 **512.**—(1) The receiver may, with a view to such preservation as aforesaid of shipwrecked persons, or of the vessel,[1] cargo, or apparel—

(*a*) require such persons as he thinks necessary to assist him;

(*b*) require the master,[1] or other person having the charge, of any vessel near at hand to give such aid with his men or vessel, as may be in his power;

(*c*) demand the use of any waggon, cart, or horses that may be near at hand.

(2) If any person refuses without reasonable cause to comply with any such requisition or demand, that person shall, for each refusal, be liable to a fine not exceeding one hundred pounds [2]; *but a person shall not be liable to pay any duty in respect of any such waggon, cart, or horses, by reason only of the use of the same under this section.*

The words in italics were repealed as from January 1, 1945, by the Finance Act 1944, s. 49, Sched. V, consequent upon the repeal of the armorial bearings and carriage duties by s. 6 of that Act. For the exemption of motor vehicles from the requirements of third party insurance, and from speed limits, see the preliminary note " motor vehicles " at the beginning of Part IX.

[1] See definitions of " vessel " and " master " in s. 742.
[2] For summary prosecution of offences, see s. 680 (1).

Power to pass over adjoining lands

456 **513.**—(1) Whenever a vessel is wrecked, stranded, or in distress as aforesaid, all persons may, for the purpose of rendering assistance to the vessel, or of saving the lives of the shipwrecked persons, or of saving the cargo or apparel of the vessel, unless there is some public road [1] equally convenient, pass and repass, either with or without carriages or horses, over any adjoining lands without being subject to interruption by the owner or occupier, so that they do as little damage as possible, and may also, on the like condition, deposit on those lands any cargo or other article recovered from the vessel.

(2) Any damage sustained by an owner or occupier in consequence of the exercise of the rights given by this section shall be a charge on the

vessel, cargo, or articles in respect of or by which the damage is occasioned, and the amount payable in respect of the damage shall, in case of dispute, be determined and shall, in default of payment, be recoverable in the same manner as the amount of salvage is under this Part of this Act determined or recoverable.[2]

(3) If the owner or occupier of any land—

(*a*) impedes or hinders any person in the exercise of the rights given by this section by locking his gates, or refusing, upon request, to open the same, or otherwise; or

(*b*) impedes or hinders the deposit of any cargo or other article recovered from the vessel as aforesaid on the land; or

(*c*) prevents or endeavours to prevent any such cargo or other article from remaining deposited on the land for a reasonable time until it can be removed to a safe place of public deposit;

he shall for each offence be liable to a fine not exceeding one hundred pounds.[3]

[1] For definitions of public road, see Vehicles (Excise) Act 1971, s. 38 (1) and the Telegraph Act 1863, s. 3, as extended by the Telegraph Act 1892, s. 3.
[2] See ss. 547 *et seq.*, as to procedure in salvage cases.
[3] For summary prosecution of offences, see s. 680 (1).

Power of receiver to suppress plunder and disorder by force

457 **514.**—(1) Whenever a vessel is wrecked, stranded, or in distress as aforesaid, and any person plunders, creates disorder, or obstructs the preservation of the vessel or of the shipwrecked persons or of the cargo or apparel of the vessel, the receiver may cause that person to be apprehended.

(2) The receiver may use force for the suppression of any such plundering, disorder, or obstruction, and may command all Her Majesty's subjects to assist him in so using force.

(3) If any person is killed, maimed, or hurt by reason of his resisting the receiver or any person acting under the orders of the receiver in the execution of the duties of this Part of this Act committed to the receiver, neither the receiver nor the person acting under his orders shall be liable to any punishment, or to pay any damages by reason of the person being so killed, maimed, or hurt.

Liability for damage in case of a vessel plundered

458 **515.** Where a vessel is wrecked, stranded, or in distress as aforesaid, and the vessel or any part of the cargo and apparel thereof, is plundered, damaged, or destroyed by any persons riotously and tumultuously assembled together, whether on shore or afloat, compensation shall be made to the owner of the vessel, cargo, or apparel:

In England in the same manner, by the same authority, and out of the same rate, as if the plundering, damage, injury, or destruction, were an injury, stealing, or destruction in respect of which compensation is payable under the provisions of the Riot (Damages) Act 1886, and in the case of the vessel, cargo, or apparel not being in any police district,[1] as if the plundering, damage, injury, or destruction took place in the nearest police district;

In Scotland by the inhabitants of the county, city, or borough in or nearest to which such offence is committed, in manner provided by the Riot Act, with respect to prosecutions for repairing the damages of any churches and other buildings, or as near thereto as circumstances permit; and

[In Northern Ireland, in pursuance of an application in that behalf to the County Court] [2]

1 For the meaning of police district see the Police Act 1964, s. 62 (*a*).

2 This paragraph has been substituted for the original text by the Northern Ireland Act 1962, s. 23 (1). Compensation will not be made under this section in Northern Ireland unless the aggregate amount of the plunder, damage or destruction exceeds twenty pounds; *ibid.*

Exercise of powers of receiver in his absence

459 **516.**—(1) Where a receiver is not present, the following officers or persons in succession (each in the absence of the other, in the order in which they are named), namely, any chief officer of customs,[1] principal officer of the coast guard, officer of inland revenue, sheriff, justice of the peace, commissioned officer on full pay in the naval service of Her Majesty, or commissioned officer on full pay in the military service of Her Majesty, may do anything by this Part of this Act authorised to be done by the receiver.

(2) An officer acting under this section for a receiver shall, with respect to any goods or articles belonging to a vessel the delivery of which to the receiver is required by this Act,[2] be considered as the agent of the receiver, and shall place the same in the custody of the receiver; but he shall not be entitled to any fees payable to receivers, or be deprived by reason of his so acting of any right to salvage to which he would otherwise be entitled.[3]

1 For definition, see s. 742.

2 See s. 518 (*b*).

3 The effect of a corresponding provision in 9 & 10 Vict. c. 99, s. 15, was considered in *The Wear Packet* (1855) 2 Spinks Ecc. & Adm. Rep. 256.

Examination in respect of ships in distress

460 **517.**—(1) Where any ship,[1] British or foreign, is or has been in distress on [2] the coasts of the United Kingdom,[3] a receiver of wreck, or at the request of the [Secretary of State for Trade] a wreck commissioner [4] or

deputy approved by the [Dept.], or, in the absence of the persons aforesaid, a justice of the peace, shall, as soon as conveniently may be, examine on oath [5] (and they are hereby respectively empowered to administer the oath) any person belonging to the ship, or any other person who may be able to give any account thereof or of the cargo or stores thereof, as to the following matters; that is to say,—

(*a*) the name and description of the ship;
(*b*) the name of the master and of the owners;
(*c*) the names of the owners of the cargo;
(*d*) the ports from and to which the ship was bound;
(*e*) the occasion of the distress of the ship;
(*f*) the services rendered; and
(*g*) such other matters or circumstances relating to the ship, or to the cargo on board the same, as the person holding the examination thinks necessary.

(2) The person holding the examination shall take the same down in writing,[6] and shall send one copy thereof to the [Secretary of State for Trade], and another to the secretary of Lloyd's in London, and the secretary shall place it in some conspicuous situation for inspection.

(3) The person holding the examination shall, for the purposes thereof, have all the powers of a [Department of Trade] inspector under this Act.[7]

461 [1] See definition of " ship " in s. 742.
[2] Note this section does not apply to ships in distress near the coasts of the United Kingdom. *Cf.* ss. 511, 519. See also *The Fulham* [1898] P. 206; affirmed [1899] P. 251, cited in note (2) to s. 546 on the meaning of the words " on or near."
[3] See note " Application to Northern Ireland and the Republic of Ireland " in notes to s. 742.
[4] For appointment of wreck commissioners, see s. 82 of the M.S.A. 1970 (§ 1458, *post*).
[5] For the provisions for preliminary inquiries and formal investigations as to shipping casualties generally, see ss. 55 *et seq.* of the M.S.A. 1970 (§ 1423, *post*).
[6] A deposition made under M.S.A. 1854, s. 448, by a master was held inadmissible as evidence on behalf of his owners in an action brought against the ship for damages by collision, although the master had died before trial: *The Henry Coxon* (1878) 3 P.D. 156. But such a deposition, if now made, would clearly be admissible under the Civil Evidence Act 1968 (see *ibid.*, ss. 1, 2).
As to the admissibility of depositions taken on oath before a justice, see s. 691, and as to the admissibility of documents declared by the Act to be admissible in evidence, see s. 695.
[7] See ss. 728, 729, 730, for powers of inspectors.

Dealing with Wreck

Provision as to wreck found in the United Kingdom

462 **518.**[1] Where any person finds or takes possession of any wreck [2] within the limits of the United Kingdom [1] he shall,—

(*a*) If he is the owner thereof, give notice to the receiver of the district stating that he has found or taken possession of the same, and describing the marks by which the same may be recognised;

(*b*) If he is not the owner thereof, as soon as possible deliver the same to the receiver of the district:

and if any person fails,[3] without reasonable cause, to comply with this section, he shall, for each offence, be liable to a fine not exceeding one hundred pounds,[4] and shall in addition, if he is not the owner, forfeit any claim to salvage, and shall be liable to pay to the owner of the wreck if it is claimed, or, if it is unclaimed to the person entitled to the same, double the value thereof, to be recovered in the same way as a fine of a like amount under this Act.

463 [1] This section also applies to wreck found or taken possession of outside the limits of the United Kingdom and brought within such limits in the same way as it applies to wreck found within the limits of the United Kingdom. See M.S.A. 1906, s. 72. As for provisions relating to fishing boats and fishing gear, see s. 17 of the Sea Fisheries Act 1968. As to these limits, see Territorial Waters Jurisdiction Act 1878.

As to the meaning of " United Kingdom," see note " Application to Northern Ireland and the Republic of Ireland " in notes to s. 742.

[2] For definition of " wreck," see s. 510, and see *The Zeta*, cited in note (3), *infra*.

[3] The section is meant to prevent a criminal and improper detention, whereby it is sought to practise a fraud upon the Crown or the owner. Salvors who have restored the property to the owners do not forfeit their right to salvage because they have not complied with the requirements of this section: *The Zeta* (1875) L.R. 4 A. & E. 460. It does not apply to salvors who remain in possession for the safety of the vessel: *The Glynoeron* (1905) 21 T.L.R. 648. Nor to a person who takes possession of a stranded vessel under the *bona fide* belief that it is his property by purchase or otherwise: *The Liffey* (1887) 58 L.T. 351; 6 Asp.M.L.C. 255.

The right to prosecute under this section is not confined to officers of the Department of Trade; but may be exercised by a police officer without authorisation from that department: *Dowling* v. *Griffin* [1917] 2 Ir.R. 609.

[4] For summary prosecution of offences, see s. 680 (1).

Penalty for taking wreck at time of casualty

464 **519.**—(1) Where a vessel is wrecked, stranded, or in distress at any place on or near the coasts of the United Kingdom [1] or any tidal water [2] within the limits of the United Kingdom,[3] any cargo or other articles belonging to or separated from the vessel, which may be washed on shore or otherwise lost or taken from the vessel shall be delivered to the receiver.

(2) If any person, whether the owner or not, secretes or keeps possession of any such cargo or article, or refuses to deliver the same to the receiver or any person authorised by him to demand the same, that person shall for each offence be liable to a fine not exceeding one hundred pounds.[4]

(3) The receiver or any person authorised as aforesaid may take any such cargo or article by force from the person so refusing to deliver the same.

[1] See note " Application to Northern Ireland and the Republic of Ireland " in notes to s. 742.

[2] " Tidal water " is defined in s. 742.

[3] See note (2) to s. 546.

[4] For summary prosecution of offences, see s. 680 (1).

Notice of wreck to be given by receiver

465 **520.** Where a receiver takes possession of any wreck [1] he shall within forty-eight hours—

(*a*) cause to be posted in the custom house nearest to the place where the wreck was found or was seized by him a description thereof and of any marks by which it is distinguished; and

(*b*) if in his opinion the value of the wreck exceeds twenty pounds, also transmit a similar description to the secretary of Lloyd's in London, and the secretary shall post it in some conspicuous position for inspection.

[1] " Wreck " is defined in s. 510 (1), and see notes thereto.

Claims of owners to wreck

466 **521.**—(1) The owner of any wreck in the possession of the receiver, upon establishing his claim to the same to the satisfaction of the receiver within one year from the time at which the wreck came into the possession of the receiver, shall, upon paying the salvage, fees,[1] and expenses due, be entitled to have the wreck or the proceeds thereof delivered up to him.

(2) Where any articles belonging to or forming part of a foreign ship, which has been wrecked on or near [2] the coasts of the United Kingdom, or belonging to and forming part of the cargo, are found on or near those coasts, or are brought into any port in the United Kingdom, the consul-general of the country to which the ship, or in the case of cargo, to which the owners of the cargo may have belonged, or any consular officer of that country authorised in that behalf by any treaty or arrangement with that country, shall, in the absence of the owner and of the master or other agent of the owner, be deemed to be the agent of the owner, so far as relates to the custody and disposal of the articles.[3]

[1] See s. 567; fees of receivers of wreck.
[2] See note (2) to s. 546.
[3] S. 5 (2) of the Consular Conventions Act 1949 provides that the powers of a consul-general or other consular officer under this subsection of the M.S.A. shall extend to the custody and disposal of the wrecked ship itself as well as to the custody and disposal of articles as already provided.

Immediate sale of wreck by receiver in certain cases

467 **522.** A receiver may at any time sell any wreck in his custody, if in his opinion—

(*a*) it is under the value of five pounds, or

(*b*) it is so much damaged or of so perishable a nature that it cannot with advantage be kept, or

(*c*) it is not of sufficient value to pay for warehousing,

and the proceeds of the sale shall, after defraying the expenses thereof, be held by the receiver for the same purposes and subject to the same claims, rights, and liabilities as if the wreck had remained unsold.

Unclaimed Wreck

Right of Crown to unclaimed wreck

468 **523.** Her Majesty and Her Royal successors are entitled to all unclaimed wreck [1] found in any part of Her Majesty's dominions, except in places where Her Majesty or any of Her Royal predecessors has granted to any other person the right to that wreck.

See 17 Edw. 2, st. 2, c. 11; Prerog. Reg. Stat. temp. incert. c. 13 in rev. ed.

[1] See s. 510, and notes thereto, for definition of "wreck." Wreck found outside the limits of the United Kingdom, and brought within such limits, has to be delivered to the Receiver of Wreck, though the Crown may have no title to it. M.S.A. 1906, s. 72, extending s. 518 of this Act.

Notice of unclaimed wreck to be given to persons entitled

469 **524.**—(1) Where any admiral, vice-admiral, lord of the manor, heritable proprietor duly infeft, or other person is entitled for his own use to unclaimed wreck found on any place within the district of a receiver, he shall deliver to the receiver a statement containing the particulars of his title, and an address to which notices may be sent.

(2) When a statement has been so delivered and the title proved to the satisfaction of the receiver, the receiver shall, on taking possession of any wreck found at a place to which the statement refers, within forty-eight hours send to the address delivered a description of the wreck and of any marks by which it is distinguished.

Disposal of unclaimed wreck

470 **525.** Where no owner establishes a claim to any wreck, found in the United Kingdom [1] and in the possession of a receiver, within one year after it came into his possession, the wreck shall be dealt with as follows; that is to say,

(1) if the wreck is claimed by any admiral, vice-admiral, lord of a manor, heritable proprietor, or other person who has delivered such a statement to the receiver as hereinbefore provided, and has proved to the satisfaction of the receiver his title to receive unclaimed wreck found at the place where that wreck was found, the wreck, after payment of all expenses, costs, fees, and salvage due in respect thereof, shall be delivered to him;

(2) if the wreck is not claimed by any admiral, vice-admiral, lord of a manor, heritable proprietor, or other person as aforesaid, the receiver shall sell the same and shall pay the proceeds of the sale

(after deducting therefrom the expenses of the sale, and any other expenses incurred by him, and his fees,[2] and paying thereout to the salvors such amount of salvage as the [Secretary of State for Trade] may in each case, or by any general rule, determine) for the benefit of the Crown, as follows, that is to say:—

(*a*) if the wreck is claimed in right of Her Majesty's duchy of Lancaster, to the receiver-general of that duchy or his deputies as part of the revenues of that duchy;

(*b*) if the wreck is claimed in right of the duchy of Cornwall, to the receiver-general of that duchy or his deputies as part of the revenues of that duchy; and

(*c*) if the wreck is not so claimed, the receiver shall pay the proceeds of sale *to the Mercantile Marine Fund during the life of Her present Majesty, and* after the decease of Her present Majesty to her heirs and successors.[3]

[1] See note " Application to Northern Ireland and the Republic of Ireland " in notes to s. 742.
[2] See s. 567 as to receiver's fees.
[3] The words in italics have been repealed as spent by the Statute Law Revision Act 1908. The proceeds of unclaimed wreck have now to be paid to Her Majesty. See s. 676, note (3). It is understood, however, that in practice the proceeds of unclaimed wreck are paid into the Exchequer.

Disputed title to unclaimed wreck

471 **526.**—(1) Where any dispute arises between any such admiral, vice-admiral, lord of a manor, heritable proprietor, or other person as aforesaid and the receiver respecting title to wreck found at any place, or where more persons than one claim title to that wreck and a dispute arises between them as to that title, that dispute may be referred and determined in the same manner as if it were a dispute as to salvage to be determined summarily under this Part of this Act.[1]

(2) If any party to the dispute is unwilling to have the same so referred and determined, or is dissatisfied with the decision on that determination, he may within three months after the expiration of a year from the time when the wreck has come into the receiver's hands, or from the date of the decision, as the case may be, take proceedings in any court having jurisdiction in the matter for establishing his title.[2]

[1] See s. 548, summary disposal of salvage disputes.
[2] See s. 547 (2) and notes to that section for jurisdiction of the High Court and county courts.

Delivery of unclaimed wreck by receivers not to prejudice title

472 **527.** Upon delivery of wreck or payment of the proceeds of sale of wreck by a receiver, in pursuance of the provisions of this Part of this Act,[1] the receiver shall be discharged from all liability in respect thereof,

but the delivery thereof shall not prejudice or affect any question which may be raised by third parties concerning the right or title to the wreck, or concerning the title to the soil of the place on which the wreck was found.

[1] See s. 525 for disposal of unclaimed wreck.

Power to [Secretary of State for Trade] to purchase rights to wreck

473 **528.**—(1) The [Secretary of State for Trade] may, with the consent of the Treasury, out of the revenue arising under this Part of this Act, purchase for and on behalf of Her Majesty any rights to wreck possessed by any person other than Her Majesty.[1]

(2) For the purpose of a purchase under this section, the provisions of the Lands Clauses Acts relating to the purchase of lands by agreement shall be incorporated with this Part of this Act, and in the construction of those Acts for the purposes of this section this Part of this Act shall be deemed to be the special Act, and any such right to wreck as aforesaid shall be deemed to be an interest in land authorised to be taken by the special Act, and Her Majesty shall be deemed to be the promoter of the undertaking.

[1] See s. 523 for right of Crown, with certain exceptions, to unclaimed wreck.

Admiral not to interfere with wreck

474 **529.** No admiral, vice-admiral, or other person, under whatever denomination, exercising Admiralty jurisdiction, shall, as such, by himself or his agents, receive, take, or interfere with any wreck except as authorised by the Act.

Removal of Wrecks

475 Provisions giving power to remove wrecks etc. are also contained in the Harbours, Docks and Piers Clauses Act 1847 (as to s. 56 see *infra*, s. 530, note (8), and s. 534, note), in the Dockyard Ports Regulation Act 1865, and in various Acts referring to particular ports. The powers given by such Acts are, in some cases, more advantageous than those under this Act. See s. 534, and notes thereto.

By the Civil Aviation Act 1949, s. 10, which (*inter alia*) empowers the Secretary of State for Trade to make regulations for the investigation of any accident arising out of or in the course of air navigation, and occurring in or over the United Kingdom, or to British aircraft (registered in the United Kingdom) anywhere, it is provided that nothing in the section shall limit the powers of any authority under M.S.A. 1894, ss. 530–537, or any enactment amending those sections.

Removal of wreck by harbour or conservancy authority

476 **530.** Where any vessel [1] is sunk, stranded, or abandoned in any harbour [2] or tidal water [2] under the control of a harbour or conservancy authority,[2] or in or near any approach thereto, in such manner as in the opinion of the authority [3] to be, or be likely to become, an obstruction or

danger to navigation or to lifeboats engaged in lifeboat service in that harbour or water or in any approach thereto, that authority may [4]—

(*a*) take possession of,[5] and raise, remove, or destroy the whole or any part of the vessel; and

(*b*) light or buoy any such vessel or part until the raising, removal, or destruction thereof; and

(*c*) sell,[6] in such manner as they think fit, any vessel [7] or part so raised or removed, and also any other property recovered in the exercise of their powers under this section, and out of the proceeds of the sale reimburse themselves for the expenses incurred by them in relation thereto under this section,[8] and the authority shall hold the surplus, if any, of the proceeds in trust for the persons entitled thereto.

Provided as follows:

(1) A sale shall not (except in the case of property which is of a perishable nature, or which would deteriorate in value by delay) be made under this section until at least seven clear days' notice of the intended sale has been given by advertisement in some local newspaper circulating in or near the district over which the authority have control; and

(2) At any time before any property is sold under this section, the owner thereof shall be entitled to have the same delivered to him on payment to the authority of the fair market value thereof, to be ascertained by agreement between the authority and the owner, or failing agreement by some person to be named for the purpose by the [Secretary of State for Trade], and the sum paid to the authority as the value of any property under this provision shall, for the purposes of this section, be deemed to be the proceeds of sale of that property.

477 As to the common law duty of a canal company or conservancy, etc. authority in receipt of tolls to use reasonable care in making navigation secure, see *Parnaby* v. *Lancaster Canal Co.* (1839) 11 A. & E. 223; *Mersey Docks and Harbour Board Trustees* v. *Gibbs, infra*; *Queens of the River S.S. Co.* v. *Thames Conservators* (1906) 22 T.L.R. 419; *Workington Harbour and Dock Board* v. *Towerfield* (*Owners*) [1951] A.C. 112; *The Mars and Other Barges* (1948) 81 Ll.L.R. 452; *The Citos* (1925) 22 Ll.L.R. 275; *The Gregerso* [1971] 2 Lloyd's Rep. 220.

1 This does not include H.M. ships. See s. 741 and *Christie* v. *Trinity House* (1919) 35 T.L.R. 480, cited in note (4) to s. 531. See also definition of "vessel" in s. 742.

2 For definitions of these terms, see s. 742.

3 The opinion must be formed with a view to action within a reasonable time: *Christie* v. *Trinity House, supra*. See also note (4) to s. 531.

4 The question whether the permissive word "may" in the corresponding provision in the Wrecks Removal Act 1877, s. 4, imposed a duty on the harbour authority was considered in *The Douglas* (1882) 7 P.D. 151; and in *Dormont* v. *Furness Ry. Co.* (1883) 11 Q.B.D. 496. In the former case, Cotton L.J., *obiter*, seems to have considered that the power was obligatory. In the latter case, however, Kay J. declined to follow this expression of opinion; but (following *Mersey Docks and Trustees* v. *Gibbs* (1864–66) L.R. 1 H.L. 93; 11 H.L.Cas. 686, cited in note to s. 634), held the defendants, a harbour authority, liable for damage caused by a wreck which, after partially removing, they had negligently left unbuoyed, on the ground that, under their special Acts, they received certain funds to be

applied for such purposes, and accordingly they were under a duty to undertake the removal and to use reasonable care in so doing. *Semble*, there is no absolute warranty that the area within the jurisdiction of such an authority will be free from obstruction: *St. Just S.S. Co.* v. *Hartlepool Port and Commissioners* (1929) 34 Ll.L.R. 344. See also *Anchor Line* (*Henderson Brothers*) *Ltd.* v. *Dundee Harbour Trustees* (1922) 38 T.L.R. 299; *The Citos* (1925) 22 Ll.L.R. 275; *The Mars and Other Barges* (1948) 81 Ll.L.R. 452; *The Gregerso* [1971] 2 Lloyd's Rep. 220.

Where the management and control of the wreck, so far as relates to the protection of other vessels, has been legitimately transferred by the owners to the harbour authority, then, in the absence of negligence on the part of the owners, neither they nor the *res* are liable for a collision which occurs through insufficient lighting, buoying, or other protection: *The Utopia* [1893] A.C. 492, P.C.; *The Douglas* (1882) 7 P.D. 151; and see *Brown* v. *Mallett* (1848) 17 L.J.C.P. 227; 5 C.B. 599; *White* v. *Crisp* (1854) 23 L.J.Ex. 317; 10 Ex. 312. But where the owner, without abandonment or transfer of possession, employs a contractor on salvage operations, he is not relieved from his liabilities in regard to the protection of other vessels, and will be liable for damage caused by the negligent lighting of the wreck: *The Snark* [1900] P. 105.

5 Instead of acting under this section, the authority may agree with the owner or other salvor to allow him to attempt salvage on undertaking to indemnify the authority in respect of any liabilities incurred by the authority: *Trinity House* v. *Maritime Salvors Ltd.* (1923) 14 Ll.L.R. 91. In such event, if salvage is impossible, the authority has power to compromise its claim under the indemnity even though no liabilities or expenses have in fact been incurred: *Hocloch* v. *Isachsen* (1928) 32 Ll.L.R. 239 (C.A.).

478 6 This power carries with it, when exercised in relation to a registered ship, a power to transfer by statutory bill of sale, where necessary, free and discharged from encumbrances: *Manchester Ship Canal Co.* v. *Horlock* [1914] 1 Ch. 453; reversed on another point in C.A. [1914] 2 Ch. 199.

7 By virtue of s. 532, the term " vessel " here includes equipment, cargo, etc.

8 By virtue of this Act the authority have no personal remedy against the shipowner for the expenses of raising, etc. Nor have they any remedy at common law where the obstruction is caused through innocent misadventure, and not by negligent and improper acts for which the shipowner can be made liable. See *The Crystal* (*Arrow Shipping Co.* v. *Tyne Improvement Commrs.*) [1894] A.C. 508, *per* Lord Herschell L.C. at p. 516. Where, however, expenses are incurred in removing the wreck of A., sunk by the negligent navigation of B., the owners of B. will be liable in damages, either on the grounds of negligence or public nuisance from which the authority has suffered special damage in the expenditure of money in pursuance of their right or duty to abate it: *The Ella* [1915] P. 111; followed in *The Solway Prince* (1914) 31 T.L.R. 56; and approved, in so far as the decision was based on negligence, in *Dee Conservancy Board* v. *McConnell* [1928] 2 K.B. 159 (C.A.); and, the owners of a ship sunk by negligence for which they are responsible cannot escape liability by abandoning; *ibid.*

Such statutory remedy may, however, be given by their special Act, either expressly or by incorporation of s. 56 of the Harbours, Docks and Piers Clauses Act 1847, which provides: " The harbour master may remove any wreck or other obstruction to the harbour, dock or pier, or the approaches to the same, and also any floating timber which impedes the navigation thereof, and the expense of removing any such wreck, obstruction or floating timber shall be repaid by the owner of the same; and the harbour master may detain such wreck or floating timber for securing the expenses, and on non-payment of such expenses, on demand, may sell such wreck or floating timber, and out of the proceeds of such sale pay such expenses, rendering the overplus, if any, to the owner on demand." See note to s. 534. See for an example *Tyne Improvement Commissioners* v. *Armement Anversois S/A, The Brabo* [1949] A.C. 326 where an action for the expenses of removing a wreck against shipowners out of the jurisdiction was held to be not " properly brought " within R.S.C., Ord. 11, r. 1.

Thus under s. 77 of the Thames Conservancy Act 1894 (see now s. 120 of the Port of London Act 1968), the conservators (now the Port of London Authority) were held entitled to raise and sell a vessel sunk in the River Thames, and to recover any deficiency from the owners of the vessel, even after abandonment: *The Wallsend* [1907] P. 302. The owner may in turn recover these expenses in a damage action if the other party to the collision is found to be at fault. *Ibid.* For the expenses incurred under this section, the P.L.A. have a priority over the owners of a second vessel injured in collision by the fault of the sunk vessel, in as much as the *res* has been preserved by their action: *The Sea Spray* [1907] P. 133. See, too, *The Veritas* [1901] P. 304.

479 On the other hand, under s. 120 of the Medway Conservancy Act 1881, though a personal remedy for the recovery of expenses of removing the wreck is given, it is only

against the owner at the time the expenses were incurred. So, where before the expenses were incurred, the owner at the time of the casualty had abandoned, the authority could not recover against him under the Act: *Sheppey and Chemical Works* v. *Conservators of River Medway* (1926) 25 Ll.L.R. 32.

Similar powers are conferred by s. 56 of the Harbour, etc. Clauses Act 1847, but the particular form of words there used (" wreck," " owners of the same ") relieve the original owner of the vessel from liability for expenses incurred after abandonment of the vessel: *The Crystal, infra*; followed in *Barraclough* v. *Brown* [1897] A.C. 615 (Aire and Calder Navigation); *Boston Corporation* v. *Fenwick* (1923) 28 Com.Cas. 367; 129 L.T. 766.

Where expenses have been incurred both under this Act and under the Act last mentioned, the authority are not bound to apply the proceeds of the sale to such expenses *pro rata*, but may allocate them in the first place to the expenses under this Act and afterwards to those under the earlier Act, and then sue the owner for the balance of the latter expenses: *The Crystal* (*Arrow Shipping Co.* v. *Tyne Improvement Commissioners*) [1894] A.C. 508; 71 L.T. 346.

As to what may be properly taken into account in estimating such expenses, see *The Harrington* (1888) 13 P.D. 48; and see also *The Ousel* [1957] 1 Lloyd's Rep. 151 where salvors sought to allege that the expenses of a Board were unnecessarily high because the Board had dismissed the salvors' tugs too soon.

As to whether the ship and cargo, etc. are rateably liable for these expenses, see *The Ettrick* (1881) 6 P.D. 127; 45 L.T. 399; affirming 50 L.J.Ad. 65; 44 L.T. 817 and note to s. 534.

As to the right of the owner to recover such expenses from underwriters, see *Eglinton* v. *Norman* (1877) 46 L.J.Ex. 557; 36 L.T. 888; overruled on another point in *The Crystal, supra*.

A port authority which is required to exercise its statutory powers in order to remove a vessel can only recover the expenses of doing so. It cannot sue for salvage: see *The Citos* (1925) 22 Ll.L.R. 275 and *The Gregerso* [1971] 2 Lloyd's Rep. 220.

Power of lighthouse authority to remove wreck

480 **531.**—(1) Where any vessel [1] is sunk, stranded, or abandoned in any fairway, or on the seashore or on or near any rock, shoal, or bank, in the British Islands,[2] or any of the adjacent [3] seas or islands, and there is not any harbour or conservancy authority having power to raise, remove, or destroy the vessel, the general lighthouse authority [4] for the place in or near which the vessel is situate shall, if in their opinion [5] the vessel is, or is likely to become, an obstruction or danger to navigation or to lifeboats engaged in the lifeboat service, have the same powers in relation thereto as are by this Part of this Act conferred [6] upon a harbour or conservancy authority.

(2) All expenses incurred by the general lighthouse authority under this section, and not reimbursed in manner provided by this Part of this Act, shall be paid out of the Mercantile Marine Fund,[7] but shall be subject to the like estimate, account, and sanction as the expenses of a general lighthouse authority, other than establishment expenses.[8]

481 [1] This does not include H.M. ships. See s. 741 and *Christie* v. *Trinity House, infra*.

[2] This means the United Kingdom, the Channel Islands and the Isle of Man; see Interpretation Act 1889, s. 18 (1) and note " Application to Northern Ireland and the Republic of Ireland," both in notes to s. 742.

[3] The meaning of " adjacent " is not clear. It seems doubtful that it is restricted to seas or islands within the territorial sea. *Cf.* also *Wellington Corp.* v. *Lower Hutt Corporation* [1904] A.C. 773 and *Re Ecclesiastical Comrs. for England's Conveyance* [1936] Ch. 430.

[4] See definition of " General Lighthouse Authority " at s. 634. As to the rights of the servants of a general lighthouse authority to claim a salvage award in respect of services rendered by them outside their statutory duty, see *The Citos* (1925) 22 Ll.L.R. 275; *The Mars and Other Barges* (1948) 81 Ll.L.R. 452; *The Gregerso* [1971] 2 Lloyd's Rep. 220.

[5] In the case of Trinity House, the formation of this opinion can, *semble*, be delegated to an individual, so as to be the opinion of the corporation; but the opinion must be formed with a view to action within a reasonable time. Thus, where a trawler belonging to the Admiralty, after being wrecked in 1914, and being at that time, in the opinion of Trinity House, an obstruction and a danger to navigation, was sold to a private purchaser for a salvage speculation in 1918, and then without notice to him or the formation of any fresh opinion by the Trinity House was blown up by them, they having no knowledge of the sale, the owner was held entitled to damages: *Christie* v. *Trinity House* (1919) 35 T.L.R. 480.

[6] *i.e.*, s. 530.

[7] Now the General Lighthouse Fund. See M.S. (Mercantile Marine Fund) Act 1898 s. 1 (1) (*b*) (*c*).

[8] See ss. 660 *et seq.* as to expenses of lighthouse authorities.

Powers of removal to extend to tackle, cargo, etc.

482 **532.** The provisions of this Part of this Act relating to removal of wrecks shall apply to every article or thing or collection of things being or forming part of the tackle, equipments, cargo, stores, or ballast of a vessel in the same manner as if it were included in the term "vessel,"[1] and for the purposes of these provisions any proceeds of sale arising from a vessel and from the cargo thereof, or any other property recovered therefrom, shall be regarded as a common fund.

A defence is available to any person who, in the exercise of any power conferred by sections 530–532, discharges oil or a mixture containing oil into areas outside United Kingdom waters or into United Kingdom waters; see Prevention of Oil Pollution Act 1971, s. 7 (1).

[1] *Cf.* definition of "vessel" in s. 742.

Power for [Secretary of State for Trade] to determine certain questions between authorities

483 **533.** If any question arises between a harbour or conservancy authority on the one hand and a general lighthouse authority on the other hand as to their respective powers under this Part of this Act for the removal of wrecks,[1] in relation to any place being in or near an approach to a harbour or tidal water,[2] that question shall, on the application of either authority, be referred to the decision of the [Secretary of State for Trade], and the decision of that [Secretary] shall be final.

[1] See ss. 530, 531.

[2] For definitions of "harbour" and "tidal water," see s. 742.

Powers to be cumulative

484 **534.** The powers conferred by this Part of this Act on a harbour, conservancy, or lighthouse, authority, for the removal of wrecks shall be in addition to and not in derogation of any other powers for a like object.

485 See note preceding s. 530.

The authority will be taken to have acted under the statute most advantageous to it. Thus, when the Conservators of the Thames had raised a ship and cargo, it was held that they must be taken to have acted under the Thames Conservancy Act 1857, and not under the Removal of Wrecks Act 1877 (re-enacted in substance in the present Part IX), because the former gave a personal remedy against the shipowner: *The Ettrick*, *supra* (s. 530, note (8)).

A cargo-owner may take advantage of this principle as against a shipowner. Thus, in the case last cited, the shipowner being under the former Act primarily liable for the expenses, he was held not entitled to contribution from the cargo-owner.

Offences in respect of Wreck

486 See, also, as to assaults on officers, etc. saving wreck, Offences against the Person Act 1861 (24 & 25 Vict. c. 100), s. 37.

As to aircraft, see note at head of s. 530, *supra*.

Taking wreck to foreign port

487 **535.** If any person takes into any foreign port any vessel, stranded, derelict, or otherwise in distress, found on or near the coasts [1] of the United Kingdom [2] or any tidal water within the limits of the United Kingdom,[3] or any part of the cargo or apparel thereof, or anything belonging thereto, or any wreck found within those limits, and there sells the same, that person shall be guilty of felony,[4] and on conviction thereof shall be liable to be kept in penal servitude for a term not less than three years and not exceeding five years.[5]

1 *i.e. semble*, within the territorial limits. See *The Fulham* [1898] P. 206.
2 See note " Application to Northern Ireland and the Republic of Ireland " in notes to s. 742.
3 See note (2) to s. 546.
4 This should now be read as " shall be guilty of an offence." See the Criminal Law Act 1967, s. 12 (5) (*a*).
5 Penal servitude has now been abolished. Enactments conferring powers to pass sentences of penal servitude are to be construed as conferring power to sentence to imprisonment; Criminal Justice Act 1948, s. 1 (1).

Interfering with wrecked vessel or wreck

488 **536.**—(1) A person shall not without the leave of the master board or endeavour to board any vessel which is wrecked, stranded, or in distress, unless that person is, or acts by command of, the receiver or a person lawfully acting as such, and if any person acts in contravention of this enactment, he shall for each offence be liable to a fine not exceeding fifty pounds, and the master of the vessel may repel him by force.

(2) A person shall not—

(*a*) impede or hinder, or endeavour in any way to impede or hinder, the saving of any vessel stranded or in danger of being stranded, or otherwise in distress on or near any coast or tidal water, or of any part of the cargo or apparel thereof, or of any wreck;

(*b*) secrete any wreck, or deface or obliterate any marks thereon: or

(*c*) wrongfully carry away or remove any part of a vessel stranded or in danger of being stranded, or otherwise in distress, on or near any coast or tidal water, or any part of the cargo or apparel thereof, or any wreck,

and if any person acts in contravention of this enactment, he shall be liable for each offence to a fine not exceeding fifty pounds,[1] and that fine may be inflicted in addition to any punishment to which he may be liable by law under this Act or otherwise.

For definitions of " master," " vessel " and " tidal water," see s. 742 and for definition of " wreck," see s. 510 (1).

[1] For summary prosecution of offences, see s. 680 (1).

Summary procedure for concealment of wreck

489 **537.**—(1) Where a receiver suspects or receives information that any wreck [1] is secreted or in the possession of some person, who is not the owner thereof or that any wreck [1] is otherwise improperly dealt with he may apply to any justice of the peace for a search warrant, and that justice shall have power to grant such a warrant, and the receiver, by virtue thereof, may enter any house, or other place, wherever situate, and also any vessel, and search for, and seize, and detain any such wreck there found.[2]

(2) If any such seizure of wreck is made in consequence of information given by any person to the receiver, on a warrant being issued under this section, the informer shall be entitled, by way of salvage, to such sum not exceeding in any case five pounds as the receiver may allow.

[1] For definition of " wreck " see s. 510.

[2] The Scrap Metal Dealers Act 1964, s. 7 provides rights of entry onto, and inspection of, scrap metal stores.

Marine Store Dealers

490 **538–542.** [*These sections, which contained provisions relating to marine store dealers were repealed and replaced by the Scrap Metal Dealers Act* 1964. *The later Act does not however apply to Northern Ireland or to Scotland.*]

See also the Old Metal Dealers Act 1861, s. 5 of which provides that any dealer in old metals registered under that Act who is also a dealer in marine stores within the meaning of M.S.A. 1854, s. 480 (1894, s. 538), shall also conform to the regulations of the latter Act. See also the Prevention of Crimes Act 1871, s. 13; Public Stores Act 1875, s. 11; Public Health Acts Amendment Act 1907, s. 86; and Children and Young Persons Act 1933, s. 9.

Marking of Anchors

Marking of anchors

491 **543.**—(1) Every manufacturer of anchors shall mark on every anchor manufactured by him in legible characters and both on the crown and also

on the shank under the stock his name or initials, and shall in addition mark on the anchor a progressive number and the weight of the anchor.

(2) If a manufacturer of anchors fails without reasonable cause to comply with this section he shall be liable for each offence to a fine not exceeding five pounds.[1]

As to the testing of chain cables and anchors, see the Anchors and Chain Cables Act 1967, s. 1, and the Anchors and Chain Cables Rules 1967, S.I. No. 1453.

[1] For summary prosecution of offences, see s. 680 (1).

Salvage

492 The provisions of the Act relating to salvage are far from exhaustive, as the great bulk of the law of salvage has developed independently of statute. Accordingly, notes on the law of salvage are for the most part beyond the scope of this work. Reference should be made to Kennedy, *Civil Salvage*, 4th ed. (1958).

For the application of the law of salvage to aircraft in certain circumstances, see the Civil Aviation Act 1949, s. 51, which is set out in a note at head of s. 510, *supra.*

Salvage payable for saving life

493 **544.**—(1) Where services are rendered wholly or in part within British waters [1] in saving life from [2] any British or foreign vessel,[3] or elsewhere in saving life from any British vessel, there shall be payable to the salvor by the owner [4] of the vessel, cargo, or apparel saved, a reasonable amount of salvage,[5] to be determined in case of dispute in manner hereinafter mentioned.

(2) Salvage in respect of the preservation of life when payable by the owners of the vessel shall be payable in priority to all other claims for salvage.

(3) Where the vessel, cargo, and apparel are destroyed, or the value thereof is insufficient, after payment of the actual expenses incurred, to pay the amount of salvage payable in respect of the preservation of life, the [Secretary of State for Trade] may, in [his] discretion, award to the salvor, out of the Mercantile Marine Fund,[6] such sum as [he thinks] fit in whole or part satisfaction of any amount of salvage so left unpaid.[7]

494 The right to reward of salvors of life, who had not saved any property, was not recognised by the general maritime law or by the Court of Admiralty, there being no *res* to which the claim could attach; though, where both life and property had been saved by the same set of salvors, it was the practice of the court to give a larger amount of salvage than if the property only had been saved: *The Fusilier, infra*; *The Johannes* (1860) 30 L.J.Ad. 91; Lush. 182; 3 L.T. 757; *The Willem III, infra.* The earlier enactments on the subject were 1 & 2 Geo. 4, c. 75, ss. 8, 9, and 9 & 10 Vict. c. 99, s. 10, but the preservation of human life was first made a distinct ground of salvage award by the M.S.A. 1854. See *The Coromandel* (1857) Swa. 205; *The Bartley* (1857) Swa. 198; *The Eastern Monarch* (1860) Lush. 81.

That Act, moreover, put the life salvor in three respects in a superior position to the salvor or property—

(i) It gave him priority over all other claimants where the property was insufficient: *The Coromandel, supra*; *The Eastern Monarch, supra.*

(ii) It entitled him to reward out of any property that by any means escaped destruction. See note (4).

(iii) It empowered the Board of Trade (now the Secretary of State for Trade) to reward him out of the Mercantile Marine Fund. See *supra*, subs. (3).

As to policy of this legislation, see *The Fusilier, infra.*

The application of the provisions of M.S.A. 1854, was considerably extended by s. 9 of the Admiralty Court Act 1861; and the combined effect of those two statutes is reproduced in the present section with certain verbal modifications, apparently intended to give effect to the decisions in some of the cases cited in following notes.

The Maritime Conventions Act 1911, s. 6, imposes on the master the duty of rendering assistance to every person who is found at sea in danger of being lost; and the M.S. (Safety Conventions) Act 1949, s. 22, imposes a duty (subject to certain qualifications) on the master of a British ship registered in the U.K. when he receives a wireless distress call to proceed to the assistance of the persons in distress; but neither of these provisions affect any right to salvage.

495 [1] British waters include the open sea within three miles from the shore. See *The Leda* (1856) Swab. 40; 2 Jur.(N.S.) 119; *Gen. Iron Screw Collier Co.* v. *Schurmanns* (1860) 29 L.J.Ch. 877; 6 Jur.(N.S.) 883; *The Johannes* (1860) 30 L.J.Ad. 91; Lush. 182. See also s. 546, note (2), and Territorial Waters Jurisdiction Act 1878.

It is a question of fact in each case whether or not the services were rendered in part within British waters. Thus, where no part of the services rendered by the claimants was performed in British waters, the fact that other services were afterwards performed in British waters by other persons does not bring the claim within the statute: *The Willem III* (1871) L.R. 3 A. & E. 487; 25 L.T. 386 (decided upon Admiralty Court Act 1861, s. 9).

Again, where a British vessel rescued the crew of a foreign vessel 90 miles from the British coast, brought them in heavy weather to an English port, and the foreign vessel was afterwards brought within the jurisdiction by other salvors, Sir F. Jeune P. found as a fact that the life salvage services had been performed " in part within British waters," and therefore awarded life salvage: *The Pacific* [1898] P. 170. But the Scottish Court of Session in a similar case, but where the distance was 200 miles from British waters, refused life salvage on the ground that the salvage services were complete when the seamen were taken on board a seaworthy ship, and were therefore not rendered wholly or in part within British waters: *Jorgensen* v. *Neptune Steam Fishing Co. Ltd.* (1902) 4 F. (Ct. of Sess.Cas.) 992; 39 S.L.R. 765. *Cf.* the judgment in *The Pacific, supra.* [1898] P. at p. 175. See *Kennedy*, 4th ed., pp. 415–416.

[2] The corresponding words of the Act of 1854 were " the lives of the persons belonging to such ship or boat." These were held to include passengers as well as crew: see *The Fusilier* (1865) 34 L.J.Ad. 25; B. & L. 341; and were treated in 24 & 25 Vict. c. 10, s. 9, as equivalent to the words now used.

Where a steamship was in great danger and some of the crew left her in a boat in circumstances not amounting to desertion, smacksmen who subsequently saved them were held entitled to recover salvage against the steamship: *The Cairo* (1874) L.R. 4 A. & E. 184.

Where shipwrecked passengers and crew were taken off an island, which was uninhabited and without water, but on which they were not in any immediate danger, and brought to England, it was held that no life salvage services had been rendered: *The Cargo ex Woosung* (1875) 44 L.J.Ad. 45; 33 L.T. 394; 3 Asp.M.L.C. 50, 239 (C.A.).

[3] See definition of " vessel " at s. 742.

496 [4] The personal liability is not confined to the actual legal owner of the property saved, but extends to a person having an interest therein which has been saved by the property being brought into a position of security: *The Five Steel Barges* (1890) 15 P.D. 148; *Duncan* v. *Dundee Shipping Co.* (1878) 5 R. 742; *The Cargo ex Port Victor* [1901] P. 243; and *cf.* s. 547, note (3). As to what is a sufficient interest to create liability, see *The Five Steel Barges, supra.*

The action *in personam* lies, although the property has subsequently to the services been transferred to others (H.M. Govt.), and the lien lost. *Ibid.*

The owners of cargo which has escaped destruction are liable to contribute to life salvage, although the salvors may have rendered no direct benefit to the cargo; for benefit to the property is not the criterion of liability to pay life salvaged: *The Fusilier, supra.* See also *The Cargo ex Schiller* (1877) 1 P.D. 473; affirmed 2 P.D. 145; 36 L.T. 714; and other cases, *infra.*

As to the right of a life-salvor against cargo, which has been sold after action brought see *The Governor Maclean* (1865) 13 W.R. 728.

The liability for life salvage is, however, not a general personal liability, but is limited to the value of the property saved from destruction: *The Cargo ex Schiller, supra.* And where no *res* is saved to which the claim can attach, the action, whether upon an agreement or otherwise, will not lie: *The Renpor* (1883) 8 P.D. 115; *The Annie* (1886) 12 P.D. 50. Thus, where the ship was lost, but cargo and life were saved, the ship-owners were not, but the cargo-owner was, held liable for life salvage: *The Cargo ex Sarpedon* (1877) 3 P.D. 28; 37 L.T. 505; 26 W.R. 374; 3 Asp.M.L. 509.

But it is immaterial whether the property saved from destruction has been salved by "salvors," as the expression is ordinarily understood, or by other means. Thus, salvors of life alone were held entitled to salvage reward out of the proceeds of specie which the owners thereof had subsequently recovered from the wreck at their own expense: *The Cargo ex Schiller, supra*. See also *The Coromandel, supra*.

Where a harbour authority, acting under statutory powers, sold a sunken vessel which they had raised for less than the expenses, and recovered the difference from her owners, it was held that nothing was thereby saved to which a life salvage claim could attach: *The Annie, supra*. And if the owners of such vessel recover her value from the owners of a vessel through whose fault she was sunk, they are not liable for life salvage in respect of the sum so recovered. *Ibid.*

The wearing apparel of masters and seamen is not liable to contribute to salvage. See Kennedy, *Civil Salvage*, 4th ed., pp. 382–383. The wearing apparel of passengers and other effects carried by them for their daily personal use are also exempt: *The Willem III, supra*. As to the liability of passengers' luggage not in daily use, and of ship's provisions, see Kennedy, 4th ed., p. 383.

As to the apportionment of the salvors' costs between the owners of the ship and the cargo saved, see *The Peace* (1856) Swa. 115; *The Elton* [1891] P. 265.

Life salvage paid under this section of this Act is not recoverable under a Lloyd's policy in the usual form: *Nourse* v. *Liverpool Sailing Ship Owners, etc. Ass.* [1896] 2 Q.B. 16. But may be specially insured against. *Ibid.*

497 Salvage could not, until the Crown Proceedings Act 1947 took effect, be claimed for services to the property of the Crown: *The Scotia* [1903] A.C. 501; and see s. 546, note (1).

[5] As to the principle on which the court acts in awarding salvage for preservation of life alone, see *The Suevic* [1908] P. 154. "There must be actual danger to the persons whose lives are salved, or at least the apprehension of danger." *Ibid.* at p. 158, *per* Bucknill J.

Where passengers have been landed in safety from a stranded vessel, and the shipowners are by their contract under no obligation to carry them further, the master, if he arranges for a passing steamer to convey them to their destination, acts as agent for the passengers and not for the shipowner, and no claim by the second steamer for life salvage will attach: *The Mariposa* [1896] P. 273.

The court will set aside an inequitable agreement as to life salvage if the facts are such as to show compulsion or fraud: *The Medina* (1876) 35 L.T. 779; 2 P.D. 5 (C.A.).

[6] Now money provided by Parliament: see M.S. (Mercantile Marine Fund) Act 1898, s. 1 (1) (*b*).

[7] When no property is saved, this is the only reward a life salvor can obtain: *The Renpor, supra*.

Salvage of life from foreign vessels

498 **545.** When it is made to appear to Her Majesty that the government of any foreign country is willing that salvage should be awarded by British courts for services rendered in saving life from ships belonging to that country, when the ship is beyond the limits of British jurisdiction, Her Majesty may, by Order in Council, direct that the provisions of this Part of this Act with reference to salvage of life shall, subject to any conditions and qualifications contained in the Order, apply, and those provisions shall accordingly apply to those services as if they were rendered in saving life from ships within British jurisdiction.

No order has been made under this section.

Salvage of cargo or wreck

499 **546.** Where any vessel [1] is wrecked, stranded, or in distress at any place on or near [2] the coasts of the United Kingdom [3] or any tidal water within the limits of the United Kingdom, and services are rendered by

any person [4] in assisting that vessel or saving the cargo or apparel of that vessel or any part thereof, and where services are rendered by any person other than a receiver in saving any wreck,[5] there shall be payable to the salvor by the owner [6] of the vessel, cargo, apparel, or wreck, a reasonable amount of salvage to be determined in case of dispute in manner hereinafter mentioned.

500 The effect of this section, which reproduces s. 458 of the M.S.A. 1854, is to give the Admiralty Court jurisdiction over claims for services in the nature of salvage rendered otherwise than on the high seas. As regards services on the high seas, the Court of Admiralty had long exercised jurisdiction whatever the nationality of the salvors or the property salved, provided that the property had been brought within its jurisdiction. For the statutory steps by which the present position was reached, see Kennedy, *Civil Salvage*, 4th ed., Chapter 12.

501 [1] For definition of " vessel," see s. 742 and cases there cited in notes (3) and (4).

SALVAGE CLAIM AGAINST THE CROWN OR FOREIGN POWERS.

(*i*) *Apart from the Crown Proceedings Act* 1947:—

The Admiralty Court will not enforce claims *in rem* or *in personam* for salvage of ships or goods belonging to H.M. Government or to a foreign power. See *The Prins Frederick* (1820) 2 Dods. 451; *The Constitution* (1879) 4 P.D. 39; *The Parlement Belge* (1880) 5 P.D. 197; 42 L.T. 273 (C.A.) (collision); *Young* v. *S.S. Scotia* [1903] A.C. 501 (P.C.); even though the vessel is employed in ordinary commercial pursuits: *The Parlement Belge, supra*; *The Porto Alexandre* [1920] P. 30 (C.A.); unless the goods, though belonging to a sovereign power, are carried at a private charterer's risk; *Port Victor* (*Cargo ex*) [1901] P. 243. See, too, *The Jassy* [1906] P. 270. Hence, in *The Broadmayne* [1916] P. 64, where the ship was requisitioned by the government after a salvage claim had attached, an action instituted after the requisition was stayed for such time as the vessel remained under requisition in the service of the Crown, since, by reason of the requisition, the vessel, for the time being, belonged to the class of " things which are allowed to be, and from their nature must be exempt and free from all private rights and claims of individuals, inasmuch as if these claims were to be allowed against them, the arrest, the judicial possession and judicial sale incident to such proceedings would divert them from those public uses to which they are destined." *The Parlement Belge, supra* (1880) 5 P.D. at p. 210. The British Government usually, and foreign powers occasionally, submit to the jurisdiction of the court when claims are made against them. See Roscoe's *Admiralty Practice*, 5th ed. (1931), p. 256; *The Prins Frederick, supra* (foreign government); *The Marquis of Huntley* (1835) 3 Hagg.Adm. 246; *The Constitution, supra*.

(*ii*) *Claims against the Crown under the Crown Proceedings Act* 1947:—

By s. 8 of this Act the law relating to civil salvage whether of life or property (except ss. 551–554 of the M.S.A. 1894, or any corresponding provisions relating to aircraft) applies in relation to salvage services rendered after the commencement of the Act (*i.e.* January 1, 1948) in assisting any of H.M. ships or aircraft (as defined by s. 38 (2)) or in saving life therefrom, or in saving any cargo or apparel belonging to Her Majesty in United Kingdom right in the same manner as if the ship, aircraft, cargo or apparel belonged to a private person; but (i) no claim for salvage lies against the Crown in respect of anything done to, or suffered in relation to, any postal packets which then are being carried by sea and air (*ibid.*, s. 9 (6)) and (ii) proceedings *in rem* in respect of any claim against the Crown, the arrest, detention, or sale, of H.M. ships, aircraft, cargo or other property, and liens against such property are excluded in s. 29 (1) with power to the court, where proceedings *in rem* have been instituted against Crown property in the reasonable belief that it did not belong to the Crown, to order that the proceedings be treated as if they were *in personam* against the Crown: *ibid.*, s. 29 (2).

502 [2] Gorell Barnes J. held that a place 20 miles off the coast was not within these words, and thought (but without expressing a final opinion) that the limit to be placed upon them was the territorial limits of the Kingdom: *The Fulham* [1898] P. 206; affirmed [1899] P. 251. " Tidal water " is defined in s. 742.

[3] " United Kingdom " here includes the Republic of Ireland. See note " Application to Northern Ireland and the Republic of Ireland " in notes to s. 742.

[4] " Any person."—" What is a salvor? A person who without any particular relation to a ship in distress proffers useful service, and gives it as a volunteer adventurer without any pre-existing covenant that connected him with the duty of employing himself for the preservation of the ship "; *per* Lord Stowell in *The Neptune* (1824) 1 Hagg.Adm. 227, 236.

" A salvage service in the view of the Court of Admiralty may be described sufficiently for practical purposes as a service which saves or helps to save a recognised subject of salvage when in danger, if the rendering of such service is voluntary in the sense of being solely attributable neither to pre-existing contractual or official duty owed to the owner of the salved property nor to the interest of self-preservation." Kennedy, *Civil Salvage*, 4th ed., p. 5.

Under certain circumstances persons already in a " particular relation to the ship in distress " may be entitled to rank as salvors. For exampie:

503 Pilots.—A pilot may be entitled to salvage reward where the circumstances of the vessel when he takes charge are such as to make his services more than mere pilotage: *Akerblom* v. *Price* (1881) 7 Q.B.D. 129; followed in *The Santiago* (1900) 83 L.T. 439; 9 Asp. 147, where the pilot was on board the salving vessel. But he must show not merely that the ship was in distress, but that she was in danger of being lost, and that he was called upon to incur such unusual danger or responsibility, or to exercise such unusual skill or perform such an unusual kind of service, as to make it unjust that he should be paid otherwise than upon the terms of salvage reward: *Akerblom* v. *Price, supra*. And that which was originally a pilotage service may, by supervening casualties, become a service entitled to salvage reward: *Ibid*.; and *The Saratoga* (1861) Lush. 318. See also *The Frederick* (1838) 1 W.Rob. 16; *The Aglaia* (1886) 13 P.D. 160; *The Æolus* (1873) L.R. 4 A. & E. 29.

The burden of proof is on the pilot: *The Æolus, supra*. See, too, *The Bedeburn* [1914] P. 146. " It is not in the interests of the mercantile community to give any countenance to the idea that a pilot compulsorily in charge of a disabled vessel can easily convert himself into a salvor." *Ibid. per* Sir S. Evans P., at p. 151. For a recent example, see *The Driade* [1959] 2 Lloyd's Rep. 311.

For regulations as to salvage claims by local pilots and special local legislation in respect thereof, see Kennedy, *Civil Salvage*, 4th ed., pp. 44–45, notes (1)–(5).

504 Towage or salvage—". . . if in the performance of a contract of towage an unforeseen and extraordinary peril arises to the vessel towed, the [tug] is not at liberty to abandon the vessel, but is bound to render her the necessary assistance, and thereupon is entitled to salvage reward." *Per* Dr. Lushington in *The Saratoga* (1861) Lush. 318, at p. 321. In any case the court will examine a salvage claim by a tug under a towage contract " with the closest attention and not without some degree of jealousy." *The Minnehaha* (1861) Lush. 335, where the subject is discussed at length. The test is, whether supervening circumstances make the services wholly different from those contemplated by the parties when entering into the towage agreement: *The White Star* (1866) L.R. 1 A. & E. 68; *The Westbourne* (1889) 14 P.D. 132. See, too, *The Marechal Suchet* [1911] P. 1; *The Glenmorven*, 29 T.L.R. 412; [1913] P. 141; *The Leon Blum*, 31 T.L.R. 2, 582; [1915] P. 90, 290 (C.A.) (towage for fixed sum—" no cure, no pay, no salvage services "). But there can be no right to salvage when the danger to the tow was caused by the negligence of the tug: *The Duc d'Aumale* [1904] P. 60.

Miscellaneous salvors.—The servants of a general lighthouse authority engaged in performing their statutory duty of removing wrecks under s. 531 may be entitled to claim salvage if they render services outside their statutory duty: *The Citos* (1925) 22 Ll.L.R. 275. The same applies to servants of the Port of London Authority: *The Mars and other Barges* (1948) 81 Ll.L.R. 452. See also *The Gregerso* [1971] 2 Lloyd's Rep. 220.

For claims by ship's agents, passengers, tugboatmen, R.N. personnel, coastguards, lifeboat crews and other persons, see Kennedy, *Civil Salvage*, 4th ed., Chap. 3.

As to salvage by H.M. ships, see ss. 557 *et seq.*

[5] For the definition of " wreck," see s. 510.

[6] See s. 544, note (4), and s. 547, note (2).

Procedure in Salvage

Determination of salvage disputes

505 **547.**—(1) Disputes as to the amount of salvage [1] whether of life or property, and whether rendered within or without the United Kingdom arising between the salvor and the owners [2] of any vessel, cargo, apparel, or wreck, [3] shall, [4] if not settled by agreement, arbitration, or otherwise, be determined summarily in manner provided by this Act, in the following cases, namely:—

(*a*) In any case where the parties to the dispute consent:

(*b*) In any case where the value [5] of the property saved does not exceed one thousand pounds:

(*c*) In any case where the amount claimed [6] does not exceed in Great Britain three hundred pounds, and in Ireland two hundred pounds.

(2) Subject as aforesaid, disputes as to salvage shall be determined by the High Court in England or Ireland,[7] or in Scotland the Court of Session, but if the claimant does not recover in any such court in Great Britain more than three hundred pounds, and in any such court in Ireland more than two hundred pounds, he shall not be entitled to recover any costs, charges, or expenses incurred by him in the prosecution of his claim, unless the court before which the case is tried certify [8] that the case is a fit one to be tried otherwise than summarily in manner provided by this Act.[9]

06 (3) Disputes relating to salvage may be determined on the application either of the salvor or of the owner of the property saved, or of their respective agents.

(4) Where a dispute as to salvage is to be determined summarily under this section it shall be referred and determined as follows [10]:—

(*a*) In England it shall be referred to and determined by a county court having Admiralty jurisdiction by virtue of the County Courts Admiralty Jurisdiction Act, 1868, or any Act amending the same [11]:

(*b*) In Scotland it shall be referred to and determined by the sheriff's court:

(*c*) In Ireland it shall be referred to the arbitration of and determined by two justices of the peace, or a stipendiary magistrate, or the recorder of any borough having a recorder, or the chairman of quarter sessions in any county, and any such justices, stipendiary magistrate, recorder, or chairman are hereinafter included in the expression " arbitrators."

(5) Nothing in this Act relating to the procedure in salvage cases shall affect the jurisdiction or procedure in salvage cases of a county court having Admiralty jurisdiction by virtue of the County Courts Admiralty Jurisdiction Act, 1868,[12] or the Court of Admiralty (Ireland) Act, 1867, or any Act amending either of those Acts.

07 Jurisdiction of High Court in England and Wales—Subss. (2) and (3) of this section were repealed " so far as they relate to the High Court in England " by the Supreme Court of Judicature (Consolidation) Act 1925, s. 226, Sched. 6, and the jurisdiction of the High Court is now governed by the Administration of Justice Act 1956 (which replaces the Supreme Court of Judicature (Consolidation) Act 1925, ss. 22 and 33; see A.J.A. 1956, s. 7 (2)) and which provides:

" S. 1 (1) The Admiralty jurisdiction of the High Court shall be as follows, that is to say, jurisdiction to hear and determine any of the following questions or claims— . . .

(*j*) any claim in the nature of salvage (including any claim arising by virtue of the application, by or under section fifty-one of the Civil Aviation Act 1949, of the law relating to salvage to aircraft and their apparel and cargo); . . .

(3) The reference in paragraph (*j*) of subsection (1) of this section to claims in the nature of salvage includes a reference to such claims for services rendered in saving life from a ship or an aircraft or in preserving cargo, apparel or wreck, as under sections five hundred and forty-four to five hundred and forty-six of the Merchant Shipping Act 1894, or any Order in Council made under section fifty-one of the Civil Aviation Act 1949, are authorised to be made in connection with a ship or an aircraft.

(4) The preceding provisions of this section apply— . . .

(*b*) in relation to all claims, wheresoever arising (including, in the case of cargo or wreck salvage, claims in respect of cargo or wreck found on land); . . ."

For the jurisdiction for enforcing such claims, either *in rem* or *in personam*, see *ibid.* ss. 3 and 4.

This jurisdiction is assigned to the Queen's Bench Division and taken by the Admiralty Court by virtue of R.S.C., Ord. 74, r. 1, printed as Appendix 10, *post*, § 3190, the Supreme Court of Judicature (Consolidation) Act 1925, s. 56 (3) and the Administration of Justice Act 1970, ss. 1 and 2.

508 JURISDICTION OF COUNTY COURTS—This section and ss. 548 and 549 were repealed as respects the summary determination in a county court of disputes as to salvage by the County Courts (Amendment) Act 1934, ss. 13 (8), 34, Sched. V, Part I. The jurisdiction of County Courts in England and Wales is now governed by the County Courts Act 1959, which provides (in almost identical terms) that an Admiralty County Court (*i.e.*, a county court appointed to have Admiralty jurisdiction by order under *ibid.* s. 55; see *ibid.* s. 201) shall have similar jurisdiction subject to a limitation of amount (except where the parties otherwise agree) where the value of the property saved does not exceed £3,500. See *ibid.* s. 56 (1)–(3), (5).

As to saving for this section in Northern Ireland, see Administration of Justice Act 1956, s. 55 (1), Sched. I, Part I, paras. 1 (1) (*j*), 2 (1).

For the provisions relating to hovercraft, see the Hovercraft Act 1968, § 1317, *post*.

509 [1] The jurisdiction extends to a claim on an agreement for a fixed amount of salvage: *Beadnell* v. *Beeson* (1868) L.R. 3 Q.B. 439 (following *The William and John* (1863) 32 L.J.Ad. 102; B. & L. 49). And it includes the apportionment of the reward among the salvors: *Atkinson* v. *Woodall* (1862) 31 L.J.M.C. 174; 1 H. & C. 170; and *cf. The Glannibanta* (1876) 2 P.D. 45.

[2] " Owners " includes mortgagees and all interested in the property: *The Louisa* (1863) B. & L. 59; 9 Jur.(N.S.) 676; 11 W.R. 614. *Cf.* note (4) to s. 544.

[3] The jurisdiction extends only to the salvage of ship and cargo (and freight), or that which has formed part of one of them, and not to all property saved from peril at sea, and a floating beacon incapable of being navigated is not the subject of salvage: *The Gas Float Whitton* (*No. 2*) [1897] A.C. 337.

[4] These words were held to be imperative, and to oust the jurisdiction of the Court of Admiralty: *The William and John* (1863) 32 L.J.Ad. 102; B. & L. 49; *The Kate* (1864) 33 L.J.Ad. 122; B. & L. 218. But see now notes on jurisdiction of the High Court and County Courts, *supra*.

[5] *i.e.*, the value when first brought into safety: *The Stella* (1867) L.R. 1 A. & E. 340. *Cf. The Norma* (1859) Lush. 124. Under this section the Court of Session in Scotland held that it had no jurisdiction to entertain a salvage action where the value of the vessel had been conclusively determined during the proceedings as less than £1,000, the value of freight and cargo being nil: *The Craig-an-Eran* (1939) 63 Ll.L.R. 284.

[6] In *The William and John*, *supra*, it was held that this referred to the amount claimed antecedently to any legal proceedings. *Cf.* s. 549, note (4).

[7] See note " Application to Northern Ireland and the Republic of Ireland " in notes to s. 742. The jurisdiction of the Cinque Port Court is saved by s. 571.

[8] Where the question is merely one of *quantum*, time occupied, dangers incurred, etc. the court should not certify; but questions of disputed agreements made at sea or charges of misconduct or neglect are, because of their difficulty, grounds for certifying: *The Fenix* (1855) Swa. 13; *The John* (1860) Lush. 11; *The Comte Nesselrood* (1862) Lush. 454; 31 L.J.Ad. 77.

[9] As to repeal of subss. (2) and (3), so far as they relate to the High Court in England, see note " Jurisdiction of the High Court in England," *supra*.

[10] The salvage jurisdiction of justices and other persons as arbitrators under the repealed Acts is retained, with some modification, in Ireland, but is superseded in England and Scotland by the provisions of subs. (4) (*a*) (*b*). As to venue and as to assessors see s. 548.

[11] As to repeal of this section so far as relates to county courts in England, see note " Jurisdiction of County Courts," *supra*.

[12] See note *supra*, " Jurisdiction of County Courts."

Determination of disputes as to salvage summarily

510 **548.**—(1) Disputes as to salvage which are to be determined summarily in manner provided by this Act shall [1]—

(*a*) where the dispute relates to the salvage of wreck [2] be referred to a court or arbitrators having jurisdiction at or near the place where the wreck is found;

(*b*) where the dispute relates to salvage in the case of services rendered to any vessel or to the cargo or apparel thereof or in saving life therefrom be referred to a court or arbitrators having jurisdiction at or near the place where the vessel is lying,[3] or at or near the port in the United Kingdom into which the vessel is first brought after the occurrence by reason whereof the claim of salvage arises.

(2) Any court or arbitrators to whom a dispute as to salvage is referred for summary determination may, for the purpose of determining any such dispute, call in to their assistance any person conversant with maritime affairs as assessor, and there shall be paid as part of the costs of the proceedings to every such assessor in respect of his services such sum not exceeding five pounds as the [Secretary of State for Trade] may direct.

[1] See "Jurisdiction of County Courts," *supra*, and see note (10) to s. 547.
[2] For definition of "wreck," see s. 510.
[3] These words mean at or near the place where the ship is brought immediately after the accident, and do not include any place where she may afterwards be when a dispute arises: *Summers* v. *Buchan* (1891) 18 R. 879.

Appeal in case of salvage disputes

511 **549.**—(1) Where a dispute relating to salvage has been determined summarily in manner provided by this Act, any party aggrieved by the decision may appeal [1] therefrom—

(*a*) in Great Britain, in like manner as in the case of any other judgment in an Admiralty or maritime cause of the county court or sheriff's court, as the case may be [2]; and

(*b*) in Ireland,[3] to the High Court, but only if the sum in dispute [4] exceeds fifty pounds, and the appellant within ten days after the date of the award gives notice to the arbitrators of his intention to appeal and, within twenty days after the date of the award, takes such proceedings as, according to the practice of the High Court, are necessary for the institution of an appeal.

(2) In the case of an appeal from arbitrators in Ireland the arbitrators shall transmit to the proper officer of the court of appeal a copy on unstamped paper certified under their hands to be a true copy of the proceedings had before them or their umpire (if any) and of the award so made by them or him, accompanied with their or his certificate in writing of the gross value of the article respecting which salvage is claimed; and

such copy and certificate shall be admitted in the court of appeal as evidence in the case.

512 See note to s. 547, *supra*, " Jurisdiction of County Courts," and note (10) to s. 547.

[1] The court hearing the appeal will not disturb the award on a mere question of amount, unless plainly inadequate or exorbitant: *The Cuba* (1860) Lush. 14; 6 Jur.(N.S.) 152; *The Jeune Louise*, 37 L.J.Ad. 32; *The Harriett* (1857) Swa. 218; *The Clarissa* (1856) Swa. 129 (P.C.).

As to a similar rule in the Court of Appeal, see *The Lancaster* (1883) 9 P.D. 14; 49 L.T. 705 (C.A.); *The Star of Persia* (1887) 57 L.T. 839; 6 Asp.M.L.C. 220 (C.A.); *The Accomac* [1891] P. 349; 66 L.T. 335; 7 Asp.M.L.C. 153 (C.A.) (where a distinction is drawn between this rule and that with regard to setting aside the verdict of a jury on a question of fact); and *cf. The Thomas Allen* (1886) 12 App.Cas. 118; 56 L.T. 285.

" The amount of the award is so much a matter for judicial discretion that unless the judge has gone wrong on a matter of principle, so far as any principle can be laid down, in a salvage case, the court will decline to interfere." *Per* Buckley L.J. in *The Port Hunter*, 103 L.T. 550; [1910] P. 343 at p. 354. But see Roscoe's *Admiralty Practice*, 5th ed., p. 181. " The decisions of the Court of Appeal from 1891 to 1918 seem in fact to have reduced the rule to the simple formula that a Court of Appeal will vary a salvage award if it is greatly too large or too small."

As to the more stringent rule in the House of Lords, see *The Glengyle* [1898] A.C. 519; and in the Privy Council, see *The De Bay* (*Bird* v. *Gibb*) (1883) 8 App.Cas. 599.

As to admission of fresh evidence on appeal, see *The Generous, infra*.

As to costs on appeal, see Roscoe's *Admiralty Practice*, 5th ed., p. 369.

[2] This provision, so far as it relates to County Courts, has been repealed. See note " Jurisdiction of County Courts," *supra*. See also Sheriff Courts (Scotland) Act 1907; Sheriff Courts (Scotland) Act 1913; and *Spence* v. *Sinclair* (1883) 20 S.L.R. 726.

[3] See note " Northern Ireland and the Republic of Ireland " in notes to s. 742, and note (10) to s. 547.

[4] " Sum in dispute " does not mean the sum awarded by the justices and appealed against, but the sum claimed by the salvors: *The Andrew Wilson* (1863) 32 L.J.Ad. 104; B. & L. 56; *The Mary Ann* (1865) 34 L.J.Ad. 73; 12 L.T. 238; *The Generous* (1868) L.R. 2 A. & E. 57 (where the two preceding cases are explained); and *cf.* note (6) to s. 547.

When the sum in dispute exceeds £50, an appeal lies, even though the value of the property is under £1,000: *The Generous, supra*.

As to arbitrators in Ireland

513 **550.**—(1) The Lord Lieutenant in Ireland [1] may appoint, out of the justices for any borough or county, a rota of justices, by whom jurisdiction in salvage cases under this Part of this Act shall be exercised.

(2) Where no such rota is appointed the salvors may, by writing addressed to the justices' clerk, name one justice and the owner of the property saved may in like manner name another justice to be arbitrators; and if either party fails to name a justice within a reasonable time the case may be tried by two or more justices at petty sessions.

(3) Where a dispute as to salvage is referred to justices under this Act, they may, if a difference of opinion arises between them, or without such difference, if they think fit, appoint some person conversant with maritime affairs as umpire to decide the point in dispute.

(4) The arbitrators, within forty-eight hours after any such dispute has been referred to them, and the umpire (if any) within forty-eight hours after his appointment, shall make an award as to the amount of salvage payable, with power nevertheless for such arbitrators or umpire, by writing, duly signed, to extend the time for so making the award.

(5) There shall be paid to every umpire appointed as aforesaid, in respect of his services, such sum not exceeding five pounds as the [Secretary of State for Trade] may direct.

(6) All the costs of such arbitration, including any such payment to an umpire as aforesaid, shall be paid by the parties to the dispute, in such manner, and in such shares and proportions, as the arbitrators or umpire may direct by the award.

(7) The arbitrators or umpire may call for the production of any documents in the possession or power of either party which they or he may think necessary for determining the question in dispute, and may examine the parties and their witnesses on oath, and administer the oaths necessary for that purpose.

(8) A Secretary of State may determine the scale of costs to be awarded in salvage cases determined by arbitrators under this Part of this Act.

[1] See note " Application to Northern Ireland and Republic of Ireland " in notes to s. 742.

Valuation of property by receiver

514 **551.**—(1) Where any dispute as to salvage arises, the receiver of the district where the property is in respect of which the salvage claim is made, may, on the application of either party, appoint a valuer to value that property, and shall give copies of the valuation to both parties.

(2) Any copy of the valuation purporting to be signed by the valuer, and to be certified as a true copy by the receiver, shall be admissible as evidence in any subsequent proceeding.

(3) There shall be paid in respect of the valuation by the person applying for the same such fee [1] as the [Secretary of State for Trade] may direct.

Application to Crown.—Ss. 551–554 do not apply in relation to salvage services against the Crown. See Crown Proceedings Act 1947, s. 8.

[1] The fees at present in force for this service are contained in Part 20 of the Schedule to the Merchant Shipping (Fees) Order 1924 (S.R. & O. No. 1056).

Detention of property liable for salvage by a receiver

515 **552.**—(1) Where salvage is due to any person under this Act,[1] the receiver shall [2]—

(*a*) if the salvage is due in respect of services rendered in assisting any vessel, or in saving life therefrom, or in saving the cargo or apparel thereof, detain the vessel and cargo or apparel; and

(*b*) if the salvage is due in respect of the saving of any wreck,[3] and the wreck is not sold as unclaimed under the Act, detain the wreck.

(2) Subject as hereinafter mentioned, the receiver shall detain the vessel and the cargo and apparel, or the wreck (hereinafter referred to as

detained property) until payment is made for salvage, or process is issued for the arrest or detention thereof by some competent court.

(3) A receiver may release [4] any detained property if security is given to his satisfaction or, if the claim for salvage exceeds two hundred pounds and any question is raised as to the sufficiency of the security, to the satisfaction in England [5] or Ireland [6] of the High Court, and in Scotland of the Court of Session, including any division of that court, or the lord ordinary officiating on the bills during vacation.

(4) Any security given for salvage in pursuance of this section to an amount exceeding two hundred pounds may be enforced by such court as aforesaid in the same manner as if bail had been given in that court.

516 See note " Application to Crown " to s. 551.

[1] These words are not limited to the cases covered by ss. 544, 545 and 546, but embrace all salvage recoverable under this Act (see *inter alia*, s. 565), and therefore the receiver of wreck may detain a ship within his district for services rendered in salving her outside the limits prescribed by s. 546: *The Fulham* [1899] P. 251 (C.A.), affirming Gorell Barnes J. who held that the term " due under this Act " appeared to have been used as a general expression to cover any salvage which the Act contemplated being awarded by the courts mentioned in it, the jurisdiction of which was conferred or recognised by it. See *ibid.* [1898] P. 206 at p. 213. Nothing in the Administration of Justice Act 1956, or the County Courts Act 1959, which govern the jurisdiction of the High Court and county courts over salvage and the right to proceed *in rem*, affects the power of a receiver of wreck to detain a ship under this section; Administration of Justice Act 1956, s. 7 (1). County Courts Act 1959, s. 61 (2) (*b*). See notes to s. 547.

[2] *Semble*, the receiver has no discretion to refuse to detain if a claim for salvage is made; see judgment of Vaughan Williams L.J. in *The Fulham* [1899] P. at p. 264.

[3] See s. 510 for definition of " wreck."

[4] In *The Lady Katherine Barham* (1861) Lush. 404; 5 L.T. 693, it was held that, after such release by the receiver on security being given, salvors had no right to detain the property or arrest it by warrant of the Admiralty Court.

[5] See R.S.C. Ord. 74, r. 1. Appendix 10, *post*, § 3190.

[6] See " Application to Northern Ireland and the Republic of Ireland " in notes to s. 742.

Sale of detained property by receiver

517 **553.**—(1) The receiver may sell any detained property if the persons liable to pay the salvage in respect of which the property is detained are aware of the detention, in the following cases, namely—

(*a*) where the amount is not disputed, and payment of the amount due is not made within twenty days after the amount is due, or,

(*b*) where the amount is disputed, but no appeal lies from the first court to which the dispute is referred, and payment is not made within twenty days after the decision of the first court, or

(*c*) where the amount is disputed and an appeal lies from the decision of the first court to some other court, and within twenty days of the decision of the first court neither payment of the sum due is made nor proceedings are commenced for the purpose of appeal.

(2) The proceeds of sale of detained property shall, after payment of the expenses of the sale, be applied by the receiver in payment of the expenses, fees,[1] and salvage, and, so far as not required for that purpose,

shall be paid to the owners of the property, or any other persons entitled to receive the same.

See note " Application to Crown " to s. 551.
[1] See s. 567: receiver's fees.

Agreement as to salvage

8 **554.**—(1) Where services for which salvage is claimed are rendered either by the commander or crew or part of the crew of any of Her Majesty's ships or of any other ship, and the salvor [1] voluntarily agrees to abandon his lien upon the ship, cargo, and property alleged to be salved, then, upon the master entering into a written agreement attested by two witnesses to abide the decision of the High Court in England, or of a Vice-Admiralty Court or Colonial Court of Admiralty,[2] and thereby giving security in that behalf to an amount agreed on by the parties to the agreement, that agreement shall bind the ship, and the cargo, and freight respectively, and the respective owners of the ship, cargo, and freight, and their respective heirs, executors, and administrators, for the salvage which may be adjudged to be payable in respect of the ship, cargo, and freight respectively to the extent of the security given.

(2) Any agreement made under this section may be adjudicated on and enforced in the same manner as a bond executed under the provisions of this Part of this Act [3] relating to salvage by Her Majesty's ships, and on any such agreement being made the salvor and the master shall respectively make the statements required by this Part of this Act to be made in the case of the bond, but their statements need not be made on oath.

(3) The salvor shall transmit the statements made, as soon as practicable to the court in which the agreement is to be adjudicated upon.

See note " Application to Crown " to s. 551.
[1] In case of salvage by officers and crew of one of Her Majesty's ships, " salvor " means the person in command of such ship. See s. 742.
[2] See s. 742, and Colonial Courts of Admiralty Act 1890.
[3] See ss. 558 *et seq.*: salvage by Her Majesty's ships.

Apportionment of salvage under £200 by receiver

19 **555.**—(1) Where the aggregate amount of salvage payable in respect of salvage services rendered in the United Kingdom [1] has been finally determined, either summarily in manner provided by this Act [2] or by agreement [or by a county court in England [3]], and does not exceed two hundred pounds, but a dispute arises as to the apportionment thereof among several claimants, the person liable to pay the amount may apply to the receiver for liberty to pay the same to him; and the receiver shall, if he thinks fit, receive the same accordingly, and shall grant to the person paying the amount a certificate of the amount paid and of the services in respect of which it is paid, and that certificate shall be a full discharge

and indemnity to the person by whom the money is paid, and to his vessel, cargo, apparel, and effects against the claims of all persons whomsoever in respect of the services mentioned in the certificate.

(2) The receiver shall with all convenient speed distribute [4] any amount received by him under this section among the persons entitled to the same on such evidence, and in such shares and proportions, as he thinks fit, and may retain any money which appears to him to be payable to any person who is absent.

(3) A distribution made by a receiver in pursuance of this section shall be final and conclusive as against all persons claiming to be entitled to any portion of the amount distributed.

[1] " United Kingdom " here includes the Republic of Ireland. See note " Application to Northern Ireland and the Republic of Ireland " in notes to s. 742.
[2] See ss. 547 *et seq.*: determination of salvage disputes.
[3] The words in square brackets were inserted by the County Courts Act 1934, s. 56 (8), now repealed, but for this purpose replaced by County Courts Act 1959, s. 56 (8).
[4] As to the principles upon which the courts act in apportioning the amount due among different salvors, see Kennedy, *Civil Salvage*, 4th ed., Chap. 7.

Apportionment of salvage by Admiralty Courts

520 **556.** Whenever the aggregate amount of salvage payable in respect of salvage service rendered in the United Kingdom [1] has been finally ascertained, and exceeds two hundred pounds, and whenever the aggregate amount of salvage payable in respect of salvage services rendered elsewhere has been finally ascertained, whatever that amount may be, then, if any delay or dispute arises as to the apportionment thereof, any court having Admiralty jurisdiction may cause the same to be apportioned [2] amongst the persons entitled thereto in such manner as it thinks just, and may for that purpose, if it thinks fit, appoint any person to carry that apportionment into effect, and may compel any person in whose hands or under whose control the amount may be to distribute the same, or to bring the same into court to be there dealt with as the court may direct and may for the purposes aforesaid issue such processes as it thinks fit.

PRACTICE.—As to proceedings in the High Court under this section, see Administration of Justice Act 1956, s. 1 (1) and R.S.C. Ord. 75, r. 33. Such proceedings are by originating motion in Admiralty (see r. 33 (1), *ibid.*). In the county court, proceedings are commenced by originating application; see Ord. 46, r. 15, C.C.R.

[1] " United Kingdom " here includes the Republic of Ireland. See note " Application to Northern Ireland and the Republic of Ireland " in notes to s. 742.
[2] As to the principles upon which the court acts in apportioning the amount due among different salvors, see Kennedy, *Civil Salvage*, 4th ed., Chap. 7.

Salvage by Her Majesty's Ships

Salvage by Her Majesty's ships

521 **557.**—(1) *Where salvage services are rendered by any ship belonging to Her Majesty* [1] *or by the commander or crew thereof, no claim shall be*

allowed for any loss, damage, or risk caused to the ship or her stores, tackle, or furniture, or for the use of any stores or other articles belonging to Her Majesty, supplied in order to effect those services, or for any other expense or loss sustained by Her Majesty by reason of that service, and [1] no claim for salvage services by the commander or crew, or part of the crew of any of Her Majesty's ships shall be finally adjudicated upon, unless the consent of the Admiralty [2] to the prosecution of that claim is proved.

(2) Any document purporting to give the consent of the Admiralty for the purpose of this section, and to be signed by the Secretary to the Admiralty or on his behalf, shall be evidence of that consent.

(3) If a claim is prosecuted and the consent is not proved, the claim shall stand dismissed with costs.

22 The effect of subs. (1) as originally enacted was to prohibit claims for salvage services rendered by H.M. ships while permitting personal claims by commanders and crews subject to proof of consent by the Admiralty to the prosecution of their claims. By the M.S. (Salvage) Act 1916, s. 1, a limited right was given to the Admiralty to claim for services rendered by tugs and salvage vessels belonging to Her Majesty. By the M.S. (Salvage) Act 1940, a wider but still incomplete right to claim salvage for services rendered by or with the aid of Crown property was conferred on the Crown, and the M.S. (Salvage) Act 1916, and also the words now printed in italics in subs. (1) of this section were repealed. Now by s. 8 (2) of the Crown Proceedings Act 1947, the Crown's right to claim salvage in the courts of England and Scotland (and by order made under s. 53 (see note to s. 509) in N. Ireland) is fully equiparated to that of the private salvor by the provisions that " where after the commencement of this Act " (*i.e.* Jan. 1, 1948, *ibid.* s. 54) " salvage services are rendered by or on behalf of [Her] Majesty, whether in right of [Her] Government in the United Kingdom or otherwise, [Her] Majesty shall be entitled to claim salvage in respect of those services to the same extent as any other salvor, and shall have the same rights and remedies in respect of those services as any other salvor," and by s. 39, Sched. II, the M.S. (Salvage) Act 1940, was repealed.

23 [1] The following decisions under the repealed provision (see note above) though not now strictly relevant, may be noted:

A ship belonging to the Bombay Government, with a hired commander and crew, was held to be in the same position, with respect to these provisions (M.S.A. 1854, s. 484), as a Queen's ship: *The Cargo ex Woosung* (1876) 1 P.D. 260; 35 L.T. 8 (C.A.). *Cf. The Dalhousie* (1875) 1 P.D. 271, n.; 3 Asp.M.L.C. 240, n.

A ship owned by the Government, appearing in the Navy List, and exclusively employed in carrying coal for the navy under the dockyard authorities and the Admiralty, was held to be a ship belonging to His Majesty within the meaning of s. 741 of this Act, so that her master was exempt from liability to pay pilotage dues under this Act (see s. 591, now Pilotage Act 1913, s. 49, *post*), though neither master nor crew were in the navy: *Symons* v. *Baker* [1905] 2 K.B. 723.

The term " Her Majesty's ships " was held not to include every case in which any department of Her Majesty's service thinks proper to use a vessel for that service. Thus a tug and lifeboat owned and employed by the Board of Trade, as Trustees of Ramsgate Harbour, were held not to be ships belonging to Her Majesty within this provision: *The Cybele* (1878) 3 P.D. 8.

A transport, let to the Lords of the Admiralty under a charterparty which did not amount to a demise, and performing, by order of the officer of a Queen's ship, salvage services not within the terms of the charterparty, was held entitled to a share of the amount awarded as salvage: *The Nile* (1875) L.R. 4 A. & E. 449; *The Bertie* (1886) 55 L.T. 520; 6 Asp.M.L.C. 26. Similarly, the owners, master and crew of a tug requisitioned by the Admiralty under the Royal Proclamation of August 3, 1914, on terms subsequently arranged, which did not amount to a demise, were held not to be debarred from claiming salvage: *The Sarpen* [1916] P. 306 (C.A.). But when the terms of the charterparty amounted to a demise, the tug was held to be a ship " belonging to H.M." both within this section and M.S. (Salvage) Act 1916, s. 1 (now repealed) and therefore the Admiralty and not the original owners were held entitled to sue for salvage: *Admiralty Commissioners* v. *Page* [1919] 1 K.B. 299; affirmed under reversed names [1921] 1 A.C. 137.

See also *Master of Trinity House* v. *Clark* (1815) 4 M. & S. 288 (demise); *Weir* v. *Union S.S. Co.* [1900] A.C. 525, H.L.(E.). In the case of an enemy vessel detained at the outbreak of war under the " Chile " Order of 1914, and requisitioned by the Crown on terms which passed to the Crown the full dominion and control, the Admiralty were held not entitled to salvage as the vessel was " a ship belonging to H.M." within this section and, not being " a tug or a ship specially equipped with salvage plant," was not within M.S. (Salvage) Act 1916: *The Matti* [1918] P. 314. In *The Valverda* [1938] A.C. 173, it was held that subs. (1) could not be excluded by agreement.

As to " Government ships " registered as British ships, see M.S.A. 1906, s. 80.

524 [2] The object of this requirement appears to be to prevent claims being made where the service is not of real importance or hazardous or where it is within the scope of the salvor's public duty and therefore not entitled to reward. See Kennedy, *Civil Salvage*, 4th ed., pp. 76 *et seq.*

The consent of the Admiralty given in the usual form was held to cover a claim for salvage of life as well as of property: *The Alma* (1861) Lush. 378.

By virtue of the Defence (Transfer of Functions) Act 1964, the functions conferred by this section on the Admiralty are transferred to the Secretary of State charged with general responsibility for defence: see *ibid.*, ss. 1 (1) (*a*) and 2.

Where such consent is given, the officers and crew of Her Majesty's ships are entitled to salvage reward for services rendered to life, ship, and cargo, but their claim is limited to their personal services; and they cannot claim salvage reward for anything which fairly falls within the scope of their public duty to render protection to British ships and to the lives and cargoes on board of them. See *ibid.* and *The Cargo ex Ulysses* (1888) 13 P.D. 205; 37 W.R. 270; more fully reported in 58 L.J.P. 11; *The Rosalie*, 1 Spink. 188. And the fact that such salvors do not risk their own property is to be taken into consideration: *The Iodine* (1844) 3 Notes of Cases, 140; *The Earl of Eglington* (1855) Swa. 7.

Save for s. 558 (see note (5) thereto), the commander and crew of H.M. ships appear to have the same right to salvage remuneration for their personal services as the master and crew of a merchant ship: *The Cargo ex Woosung*, *infra* (s. 558), and *The Iodine*, *supra*.

In assessing the award, the court is entitled to take into consideration the fact that the commander of one of H.M. ships runs the risk of incurring official displeasure by endangering his ship: *The Domira* (1914) 30 T.L.R. 521 (C.A.).

For examples of the court's attitude towards claims by officers and crews of H.M. ships assisting merchantmen in time of war, see *The F. D. Lambert*, 119 L.T. 119; [1917] P. 232, n. (torpedo gunboat); *The Gorliz*, 119 L.T. 123; [1917] P. 233, n. (armed hopper and trawlers).

Where a neutral vessel carrying munitions for an allied government was rescued from war and marine perils by the officers and crew of two of H.M. ships, salvage award was granted on the ground that even if the salvage of the cargo fell within their public duty, they were under no duty to the neutral shipowners to salve the vessel: *The Carrie*, 33 T.L.R. 573; [1917] P. 224.

As to the right of the commander and crew of H.M. ships to detain the salved ship, etc., see ss. 558, 560, 562.

525 Prize salvage.—As a general rule, no salvage is granted to officers and crew of H.M. ships on the recapture of innocent neutral vessels from the enemy. This rule is, however, based on the presumption that, if innocent, they incur no peril by the capture; but when it is apparent that in defiance of international law the neutral ships would have been condemned in the captor's court, the rule does not apply and salvage is awarded. This practice was constantly followed by Lord Stowell: *The War Onskan* (1799) 2 C.Rob. 299; 1 Eng.P.C. 239; *The Eleanora Catharina* (1802) 4 C.Rob. 156; 1 Eng.P.C. 367; *The Sansom* (1807) 6 C.Rob. 410; and was during the war of 1914–18 adopted in *The Pontoporus* [1916] P. 100, and *The Svanfos, The Borgila* [1919] P. 189. By the Prize Salvage Act 1944, no proceeding to enforce a claim for services rendered in retaking a ship, aircraft or goods taken by an enemy may be instituted without the consent of the Secretary of State.

Salvage by Her Majesty's ships abroad

526 **558.**—(1) Where services are rendered at any place out of the limits of the United Kingdom [1] or the four seas adjoining thereto by the commander or any of the crew of any of Her Majesty's ships, in saving any vessel or cargo or property belonging to a vessel, the vessel, cargo, or property, alleged to be saved shall, if the salvor [2] is justified by the circum-

stances of the case in detaining it, be taken to some port where there is a consular officer or a colonial court of admiralty, or a vice-admiralty court.[3]

(2) The salvor [2] and the master, or other person in charge of the vessel, cargo, or property, saved shall within twenty-four hours after arriving at the port each deliver to the consular officer or judge of the colonial court of admiralty or vice-admiralty court, as the case may be, a statement on oath, specifying so far as possible, and so far as those particulars are applicable, the particulars set out in the first part of the Nineteenth Schedule to this Act, and also in the case of the master or other person his willingness to execute a bond [4] in the form, so far as circumstances will permit, set out in the second part of that Schedule.[5]

27 [1] " United Kingdom " here includes the Republic of Ireland. See note " Application to Northern Ireland and the Republic of Ireland " in notes to s. 742.

[2] *i.e.* the person in command of Her Majesty's ship; see definition, s. 742.

[3] See s. 742, and Colonial Courts of Admiralty Act 1890.

[4] See s. 559.

[5] This section and Schedule 19 appear to negative the power of an officer commanding a ship belonging to Her Majesty to enter into an agreement with the master of the salved ship as to the amount of remuneration. At any rate, if sent to render help to a wrecked ship, he cannot impose terms and refuse to give salvage services unless those terms are accepted. See *The Cargo ex Woosung* (1875) 44 L.J.Ad. 45; on appeal (1876) 1 P.D. 260, cited in note (2) to s. 557.

Provisions as to bond to be executed

528 **559.**—(1) The bond shall be in such sum as the consular officer [1] or judge thinks sufficient to answer the demand for salvage service, but the sum fixed shall not exceed one half of the amount which, in the opinion of the consular officer or judge, is the value of the property in respect of which salvage has been rendered.

(2) Where the vessel, cargo, or property in respect of which salvage services are rendered is not owned by persons domiciled in Her Majesty's dominions, the master [1] shall procure such security for the due performance of the bond [2] as the consular officer or judge thinks sufficient to be lodged with that officer or judge, or with that officer or judge and such other persons jointly as the salvor [1] may appoint.

(3) The consular officer or judge shall fix the amount of the bond within four days after the receipt of the statements required by this Part of this Act,[2] but if either of those statements is not delivered within the time required by this Part of this Act, he may proceed ex parte.

(4) A consular officer may for the purposes of this section take affidavits.

(5) Nothing in this section shall authorise the consular officer or judge to require the cargo of any ship to be unladen.

[1] For definitions of " consular officer," " master," " salvor," see s. 742.

[2] See s. 558.

Execution of bond

529 **560.**—(1) The consular officer or judge on fixing the sum to be inserted in the bond shall send notice thereof to the salvor and master, and on the execution of the bond by the master in the sum fixed in the presence of the consular officer or judge (who shall attest the same), and upon delivery thereof to the salvor, and in cases where security is to be lodged, on that security being duly lodged, the right of the salvor to detain the vessel, cargo, or property shall cease.

(2) The bond shall bind the respective owners of the vessel, cargo, and freight, and their heirs, executors, and administrators, for the salvage adjudged to be payable in respect of the vessel, cargo, and freight respectively.

Enforcement of bond

530 **561.**—(1) The bond shall be adjudicated on and enforced in the High Court in England, unless the salvor and master agree at the time of the execution of the bond that the bond may be adjudicated on and enforced in any specified colonial court of admiralty or vice-admiralty court, but that court shall in that case have the same power and authorities for the purpose as the High Court in England.

(2) The High Court in England shall have power to enforce any bond given in pursuance of this Part of this Act in any colonial court of admiralty or vice-admiralty court in any part of Her Majesty's dominions, and any court exercising admiralty jurisdiction in Scotland, Ireland,[1] the Isle of Man, or the Channel Islands shall assist that court in enforcing those bonds.

(3) Where security has been given for the performance of a bond, the persons with whom the security is lodged shall deal with the same as the court adjudicating upon the bond direct.

(4) The consular officer or judge shall at the earliest opportunity transmit the statements and documents delivered to him, and the notice of the sum fixed in the bond to the High Court in England or the colonial court of admiralty or vice-admiralty court in which the bond is to be enforced, as the case may be.

The jurisdiction of the High Court in England under the Act generally is assigned to the Queen's Bench Division and taken by the Admiralty Court: see R.S.C., Ord. 74, r. 1: see Appendix 10, *post*, § 3190. See, too, Supreme Court of Judicature (Consolidation) Act 1925, s. 56 (3), Administration of Justice Act 1956, s. 1 (1), and Administration of Justice Act 1970, ss. 1 and 2.

[1] See note "Application to Northern Ireland and the Republic of Ireland" in notes to s. 742.

Saving for other salvage rights

531 **562.**—(1) Nothing contained in this Part of this Act shall prejudice the right of the salvor,[1] where salvage services have been rendered by one

of Her Majesty's ships,[2] or by the commander or any of the crew thereof, to proceed for the enforcement of the salvage claim otherwise than in manner provided by this Act,[3] but the salvor shall have no right to detain the vessel, cargo, or property saved, unless he elects to proceed under this Part of this Act.

(2) Nothing contained in this Part of this Act shall affect the right of the salvor, where salvage services have been rendered by one of Her Majesty's ships or by the commander or any of the crew thereof, in any case which is not provided for therein.

[1] For definition, see s. 742.
[2] For provisions relating to salvage by H.M. ships, see ss. 557, 558.
[3] See ss. 547, 548 and notes thereto.

Exemption from stamp duty

2 **563.** Any bond, statement, agreement, or other document made or executed in pursuance of the provisions of this Part of this Act [1] relating to salvage by Her Majesty's ships shall, if made or executed out of the United Kingdom, be exempt from stamp duty.

[1] See ss. 557, 558 (2).

Punishment for forgery and false representations

3 **564.** If any person in any proceeding under the provisions of this Part of this Act relating to salvage by Her Majesty's ships [1]—

(*a*) forges, assists in forging, or procures to be forged, fraudulently alters, assists in fraudulently altering, or procures to be fraudulently altered, any document; or

(*b*) puts off or makes use of any forged or altered document, knowing the same to be so forged or altered; or

(*c*) gives or makes, or assists in giving or making, or procures to be given or made, any false evidence or representation, knowing the same to be false,

that person shall for each offence be liable to imprisonment, with or without hard labour,[2] for any period not exceeding two years, or, on summary conviction, to imprisonment, with or without hard labour, for any period not exceeding six months.

[1] For provisions relating to salvage by H.M. ships, see ss. 557, 558.
[2] Imprisonment with hard labour has now been abolished; see Criminal Justice Act 1948, s. 1 (2). Enactments conferring power to sentence to imprisonment with hard labour are to be construed as conferring power to sentence to imprisonment.

Jurisdiction of High Court in Salvage

Jurisdiction of High Court in salvage

4 **565.** *Subject to the provisions of this Act, the High Court, and in Scotland the Court of Session, shall have jurisdiction to decide upon all*

claims whatsoever relating to salvage, whether the services in respect of which salvage is claimed were performed on the high seas or within the body of any county, or partly on the high seas and partly within the body of any county, and whether the wreck in respect of which salvage is claimed is found on the sea or on the land, or partly on the sea and partly on the land.

This section was repealed by s. 226 of the Supreme Court of Judicature (Consolidation) Act 1925, so far as it relates to the High Court in England, and the subject-matter hereof is re-enacted in the Administration of Justice Act 1956, s. 1, which is set out in note " Jurisdiction of the High Court in England " in notes to s. 547. See also note " Jurisdiction of County Courts " which follows it.

This section has been repealed so far as it relates to Northern Ireland by the Administration of Justice Act 1956, s. 55 (1), Sched. I, Part III.

Accordingly the section only applies to Scotland.

Appointment of Receivers of Wreck

Appointment of receivers of wreck

535 **566.** The [Secretary of State for Trade] shall have the general superintendence throughout the United Kingdom [1] of all matters relating to wreck,[2] and may, with the consent of the Treasury, appoint any officer of customs or of the coastguard, or any officer of inland revenue, or, where it appears to [the Secretary of State] to be more convenient, any other person, to be a receiver of wreck (in this Part of this Act referred to as a receiver), in any district, and to perform the duties of receiver under this Part of this Act, and shall give due notice of the appointment.

[1] See note " Application to Northern Ireland and the Republic of Ireland " in notes to s. 742.

[2] See also the general provisions of ss. 713 *et seq.* as to the control of the Department of Trade.

Fees of Receivers of Wreck

Receivers' fees

536 **567.**—(1) There shall be paid to every receiver the expenses properly incurred by him in the performance of his duties, and also, in respect of the several matters specified in the Twentieth Schedule to this Act, such fees *not exceeding the amounts therein mentioned* [1] as may be directed by the [Secretary of State for Trade], but a receiver shall not be entitled to any remuneration other than those payments.

(2) The receiver shall, in addition to all other rights and remedies for the recovery of those expenses or fees, have the same rights and remedies in respect thereof as a salvor has in respect of salvage due to him.[2]

(3) Whenever any dispute arises in any part of the United Kingdom as to the amount payable to any receiver in respect of expenses or fees, that dispute shall be determined by the [Secretary of State for Trade], and the decision of [the Secretary of State] shall be final.

(4) All fees received by a receiver in respect of any services performed by him as receiver shall be carried to and form part of the Mercantile

Marine Fund,[3] but a separate account shall be kept of those fees, and the moneys arising from them shall be applied in defraying any expenses duly incurred in carrying into effect this Act in such manner as the [Secretary of State directs].

37 [1] The words printed in italics were repealed as from November 19, 1952, by M.S. (Safety Convention) Act 1949, s. 37 (5) and Schedule III, *post*. The fees of receivers of wreck are now contained in Part 20 of the Schedule to the M.S. (Fees) Regulations 1975 (S.I. No. 341) made in pursuance of s. 33 (2) of the 1949 Act.

[2] See s. 552, note (1).

[3] Now to the Exchequer. See M.S. (Mercantile Marine Fund) Act 1898, s. 1 (1) (*a*).

Where the receiver of wreck has incurred expense in burying carcases of frozen meat washed ashore from a vessel, he can recover his expenses from the local authority, who can in turn recover from the shipowner under s. 46 of the Diseases of Animals Act 1894 (now Diseases of Animals Act 1950, s. 75 (as amended by the Administration of Justice Act 1956, s. 7 (1)) save in relation to Northern Ireland where the earlier Act still substantially applies): *The Suevic* [1908] P. 292.

Remuneration for services by coastguard

38 **568.**—(1) Where services are rendered by any officers or men of the coastguard service in watching or protecting shipwrecked property, then, unless it can be shown that those services have been declined by the owner of the property or his agent at the time they were tendered, or that salvage has been claimed and awarded for those services, the owner of the property shall pay in respect of those services remuneration according to a scale to be fixed by the [Secretary of State for Trade]; and that remuneration shall be recoverable by the same means, and shall be paid to the same persons, and accounted for and applied in the same manner as fees received by receivers under the provisions of this Part of this Act.[1]

(2) The scale fixed by the [Secretary of State for Trade] shall not exceed the scale by which remuneration to officers and men of the coastguard for extra duties in the ordinary service of the Commissioners of Customs [2] is for the time being regulated.

[1] See s. 567.

[2] Now "Commissioners for Customs and Excise," see Customs and Excise Act 1952, s. 318 (1).

Duties on Wreck

Provisions as to duties, etc. on wrecked goods

39 **569.**—(1) *All wreck, being foreign goods brought or coming into the United Kingdom or Isle of Man, shall be subject to the same duties as if the same was imported into the United Kingdom or Isle of Man respectively, and if any question arises as to the origin of the goods, they shall be deemed to be the produce of such country as the Commissioners of Customs may on investigation determine.*[1]

(2) The Commissioners of Customs and Inland Revenue [2] shall permit all goods, wares, and merchandise saved from any ship stranded or

wrecked on her homeward voyage to be forwarded to the port of her original destination, and all goods, wares, and merchandise saved from any ship stranded or wrecked on her outward voyage to be returned to the port at which the same were shipped; but those Commissioners shall take security for the due protection of the revenue in respect of those goods.

[1] Subs. (1), which is in italics, was repealed by the Customs and Excise Act 1952, s. 320, Sched. XII, Part 1, as from January 1, 1953. For replacement provisions, see now s. 34 (3) of that Act, which provides as follows:

"Any goods brought or coming into the United Kingdom by sea otherwise than as cargo, stores or baggage carried in a ship shall be chargeable with the like duty, if any, as would be applicable to those goods if they had been imported as merchandise; and if any question arises as to the origin of the goods they shall be deemed to be the produce of such country as the Commissioners may on investigation determine."

[2] Now " Commissioners for Customs and Excise," see Customs and Excise Act 1952, s. 318 (1).

Supplemental

Powers of sheriff in Scotland

540 **570.** Any matter or thing which may be done under this Part of this Act by or to a justice of the peace, or a court of summary jurisdiction, may in Scotland be done by or to the sheriff of the county.

Saving for Cinque Ports

541 **571.** Nothing in this Part of this Act shall prejudice or affect any jurisdiction or powers of the Lord Warden or any officers of the Cinque Ports or of any court of those ports or of any court having concurrent jurisdiction within the boundaries of these ports,[1] and disputes as to salvage arising within those boundaries shall be determined in the manner in which they have been hitherto determined.

[1] See Cinque Ports Act 1821, for provisions relating to salvage disputes in the Cinque Ports.

PART X—PILOTAGE

542 The whole of this Part was repealed by the Pilotage Act 1913, which now regulates this subject and is set out *post*, §§ 850–938. Sections 572–632 are repealed by section 60 and Schedule, *ibid.* and section 633 (defence of compulsory pilotage in U.K. waters) as from January 1, 1918, by section 15 (3).

PART XI—LIGHTHOUSES

543 See also as to exemptions of lighthouses, etc. from rates, and of vessels belonging to lighthouse authorities from harbour dues, sections 731, 732; as to powers of lighthouse authorities to remove wreck, sections 531 *et seq.*

For definitions of " Lighthouse," " Buoys and beacons," see section 742.

As to Light Dues, see also the Merchant Shipping (Mercantile Marine Fund) Act 1898, *post.*

General Management

Management of lighthouses, buoys, and beacons

544 **634.**—(1) Subject to the provisions of this Part of this Act, and subject also to any powers or rights now lawfully enjoyed or exercised by any person or body of persons having by law or usage authority over local lighthouses, buoys, or beacons [1] (in this Act referred to as " local lighthouse authorities," [2]) the superintendence and management of all lighthouses, buoys, and beacons shall within the following areas be vested in the following bodies; namely,

(*a*) throughout England and Wales, and the Channel Islands,[3] and the adjacent [4] seas and islands, and at Gibraltar, in the Trinity House [5];

(*b*) throughout Scotland and the adjacent seas and islands, and the Isle of Man, in the Commissioners of Northern Lighthouses [6]; and

(*c*) throughout Ireland and the adjacent seas and islands, in the Commissioners of Irish Lights,[5]

and those bodies are in this Act referred to as the general lighthouse authorities [7] and those areas as lighthouse areas.

(2) Subject to the provisions of this Part of this Act, the general lighthouse authorities shall respectively continue to hold and maintain all property now vested in them in that behalf in the same manner and for the same purposes as they have hitherto held and maintained the same.

545 It seems that these authorities are not by these provisions constituted servants of the Crown so as to have been, before the passing of the Crown Proceedings Act 1947, exempt from liability to an action for negligence in the performance of their duties. See *Gilbert* v. *The Corporation of the Trinity House* (1886) 17 Q.B.D. 795; *Romney Marsh* v. *The Corporation of the Trinity House* (1870) L.R. 5 Ex. 204; affirmed (1872) L.R. 7 Ex. 247; *cf. Mersey Docks, etc. Trustees* v. *Gibbs* (1864–66) L.R. 1 H.L. 93; 11 H.L.Cas. 686; and see note (4) to s. 530.

[1] As to what are included in these terms, see s. 742.

[2] See ss. 652–657 as to local lighthouses.

[3] For the restrictions on the exercise by Trinity House of their powers in the Channel Islands, see s. 669.

[4] See note (3) to s. 531.

[5] See definitions in s. 742. Before the Act there mentioned the Port of Dublin Corporation had the control of lighthouses in Ireland. The functions of the Commissioners were, as regards the area which is now the Republic of Ireland, transferred to the Provisional Government by the Provisional Government Transfer of Functions Order 1922 (S.R. & O. No. 315) and the Commissioners retained their title until superseded by the body appointed by the Executive Council of the Irish Free State to exercise those functions.
[6] As to the constitution of this body, see s. 668.
[7] As to the expenses, etc., of general lighthouse authorities, see ss. 658–665.

Returns and information to [Secretary of State for Trade]

546 **635.** The general lighthouse authorities, and their respective officers, shall at all times give to the [Secretary of State for Trade] all such returns, explanations, or information, in relation to the lighthouses, buoys, or beacons within their respective areas, and the management thereof, as the [Secretary of State requires].

Power of [Secretary of State for Trade] to inspect on complaint made

547 **636.**—(1) The [Secretary of State for Trade] may, on complaint that any lighthouse, buoy, or beacon under the management of any of the general lighthouse authorities, or any work connected therewith, is inefficient or improperly managed or is unnecessary, authorise any person appointed by them to inspect the same.

(2) A person so authorised may inspect the same accordingly, and make any inquiries in respect thereof, and of the management thereof, which he thinks fit; and all officers and others having the care of any such lighthouses, buoys, or beacons, or concerned in the management thereof, shall furnish any information and explanations in relation thereto which the person inspecting requires.

Inspection by Trinity House

548 **637.** The Trinity House,[1] and any of their engineers, workmen, and servants, may at all times enter any lighthouse within any of the lighthouse areas [2] for the purpose of viewing their condition or otherwise for the purposes of this Act.

[1] For definition, see s. 742.
[2] See s. 634 (1).

Construction of Lighthouses, etc.

General powers of lighthouse authorities

549 **638.** A general lighthouse authority shall, within their area but subject, in the case of the Commissioners of Northern Lighthouses and the Commissioners of Irish Lights, to the restrictions enacted in this Part of this Act,[1] have the following powers (in this Act referred to as lighthouse powers), namely, powers—

(*a*) to erect or place any lighthouse, with all requisite works, roads, and appurtenances:

(*b*) to add to, alter, or remove any lighthouse:

(*c*) to erect [2] or place any buoy or beacon, or alter or remove any buoy or beacon:

(*d*) to vary the character of any lighthouse or the mode of exhibiting lights therein.

As to the liability of the authorities for negligence in the exercise of their powers, see note to s. 634.

[1] See s. 640.

[2] Development in the cause of exercising these powers is permitted by the Town and Country Planning General Development Order 1973 (S.I. No. 31, Art. 3, Sched. 1, Class XVIII G).

Powers as to land

550 **639.**—(1) A general lighthouse authority [1] may take and purchase any land which may be necessary for the exercise of their lighthouse powers,[2] or for the maintenance of their works or for the residence of the light keepers, and for that purpose the Lands Clauses Acts shall be incorporated with this Act and shall apply to all lighthouses to be constructed and all land to be purchased under the powers thereof.

(2) A general lighthouse authority may sell any land belonging to them.

[1] See s. 634.

[2] " Lighthouse powers " are defined in s. 638.

Restrictions on exercise of lighthouse powers by Commissioners

551 **640.**—(1) When the Commissioners of Northern Lighthouses or the Commissioners of Irish Lights propose to exercise any of their lighthouse powers,[1] they shall submit a scheme to the Trinity House [2] specifying the mode in which they propose to exercise the power, and their reasons for wishing to exercise the same, and they shall not exercise any such power until they have so submitted a scheme to the Trinity House and obtained the sanction of the [Secretary of State for Trade] in manner provided by this Act.

(2) The Trinity House shall take into consideration any scheme so submitted to them, and shall make a report, stating their approval or rejection of the scheme with or without modification, and shall send a copy of the report to the commissioners by whom the scheme is submitted.

(3) For the purpose of obtaining the sanction of the [Secretary of State for Trade] to any scheme so submitted to the Trinity House, the Trinity House shall send a copy of the scheme and of their report thereon, and of any communications which have passed with reference thereto between them and the commissioners by whom the scheme is submitted, to the [Secretary of State for Trade], and that [the Secretary of State] may give any directions [he thinks] fit with reference to the scheme, and may

grant or withhold [his] sanction either wholly or subject to any conditions or modifications [he thinks] fit.

(4) The commissioners by whom a scheme is submitted may, before a decision on the scheme is given by the [Secretary of State for Trade], forward either to that [Secretary of State] or to the Trinity House any suggestions or observations with respect to the scheme or the report of the Trinity House thereon, and the [Secretary of State for Trade] in giving any decision on the scheme shall consider those suggestions or observations.

(5) The decision of the [Secretary of State for Trade] with reference to any scheme shall be communicated by that [Secretary of State] to the Trinity House, and by the Trinity House to the commissioners by whom the scheme is submitted, and those commissioners shall act in conformity with the decision.

[1] " Lighthouse powers " are defined in s. 638. As to incorporation of Commissioners of Northern Lighthouses, see s. 668.
For meaning of " Commissioners of Irish Lights," see s. 742 and notes thereto.
[2] For definition, see s. 742.

Power of Trinity House to direct lighthouse works to be done

552 **641.**—(1) The Trinity House [1] may, with the sanction of the [Secretary of State for Trade], direct the Commissioners of Northern Lighthouses [2] or the Commissioners of Irish Lights [3]—

(*a*) to continue any lighthouse, buoy, or beacon [4]:
(*b*) to erect or place any lighthouse, buoy, or beacon, or add to, alter, or remove any existing lighthouse, buoy, or beacon:
(*c*) to vary the character of any lighthouse or the mode of exhibiting lights therein:

and the commissioners shall be bound within a reasonable time to obey any directions so given and sanctioned.

(2) For the purpose of obtaining the sanction of the [Secretary of State for Trade] to any direction under this section, the Trinity House shall make a written application to the [Secretary of State for Trade] showing fully the work which they propose to direct and their reasons for directing the same, and shall give notice in writing of the application to the commissioners to whom they propose to give the direction at their principal office in Edinburgh or Dublin, as the case may be.

(3) Before the [Secretary of State for Trade decides] on any such application an opportunity shall be given to the commissioners to whom it is proposed to give the direction for making any representation which they may think fit to make with regard to the application to the [Secretary of State for Trade] or the Trinity House.

[1] For meaning, see s. 742.
[2] As to incorporation, see s. 668.
[3] For meaning, see s. 742 and notes thereto.
[4] For meaning, see s. 742.

Additions to lighthouses

553 **642.** Where any improved light, or any siren or any description of fog signal has been added to an existing lighthouse, the light siren or signal may, for the purposes of this Part of this Act, be treated as if it were a separate lighthouse.

Cf. definition of " lighthouse," s. 742. *Cf.* provisions in Part V as to lights, fog signals, etc., in connection with the prevention of collisions. See ss. 418 *et seq.*

Light Dues

See also the Merchant Shipping (Mercantile Marine Fund) Act 1898, §§ 1112–1131, *post.*

Continuance of light dues

554 **643.** *Subject to any alterations to be made under the powers contained in this Part of this Act, a general lighthouse authority shall, in respect of any lighthouses, buoys, or beacons which at the commencement of this Act are under their management, continue to levy dues (in this Act called light dues), subject to the same limitations as to the amount thereof as are in force at the commencement of this Act; and those* light dues shall be payable in respect of all ships [1] whatever, except ships belonging to Her Majesty,[2] and ships exempted from payment thereof in pursuance of this Act.[3]

555 The words in italics were repealed by the Merchant Shipping (Mercantile Marine Fund) Act 1898, s. 8, Sched. IV.

[1] For meaning of " ships," see s. 742 and notes thereto.

[2] See the cases cited in note (1) to s. 557, as to the meaning of this term in that part of the Act. Reference may also be made to the following cases as to light dues before 1854: *Trinity House* (*Master*) v. *Clark* (1815) 4 M. & S. 288 (transport ship chartered to Crown, so as to transfer temporary ownership, held exempt); *Smithett* v. *Blythe* (1830) 1 B. & Ad. 509 (mail packets); *Hamilton* v. *Stow* (*Stone*) (1822) 1 D. & R. 274; 5 B. & Ad. 649. See also M.S.A. 1906, s. 80, as to " Government ships " registered under M.S. Acts.

[3] As to exemptions from light dues, see M.S. (Mercantile Marine Fund) Act 1898, s. 5, Sched. II, and note (1) thereto. *Cf.* s. 732, exemption of certain ships from harbour dues, etc. See also ss. 647–651 (publication, application and recovery of light dues) ss. 670–675 (colonial light dues) and ss. 655–657 (local light dues), and M.S. (Mercantile Marine Fund) Act 1898, s. 5 (scales of light dues).

556 **644–646.** [*Section* 644 (*dues for new lighthouses*), *section* 645 (*revision of light dues by Order in Council*), *and section* 646 (*regulation of light dues by lighthouse authorities*), *were repealed by M.S.* (*Mercantile Marine Fund*) *Act* 1898, *s.* 8, *Sched. IV*, *and the subject-matter of those sections is now dealt with by s.* 5 *of that Act, post.*]

Publication of light dues and regulations

557 **647.** Tables of all light dues, and a copy of the regulations for the time being in force in respect thereof, shall be posted up at all custom houses in the United Kingdom, and for that purpose each of the general lighthouse authorities [1] shall furnish copies of all such tables and regulations to the Commissioners of Customs [2] in London, and to the chief

officers of customs resident at all places where light dues are collected on account of that lighthouse authority; and those copies shall be posted up by the Commissioners of Customs [2] at the Custom House in London, and by the chief officers of customs [3] at the custom houses of the places at which they are respectively resident.

[1] See s. 634 as to these authorities.
[2] Now Commissioners of Customs and Excise; see Customs and Excise Act 1952, s. 318 (1).
[3] See definition, s. 742.

Application and collection of light dues

558 **648.**—(1) All light dues coming into the hands of any general lighthouse authority [1] under this Act shall be carried to the Mercantile Marine Fund.[2]

(2) Every person appointed to collect light dues by any of the general lighthouse authorities shall collect all light dues payable at the port at which he is so appointed, whether they are collected [3] on account of the authority by whom he was appointed or on account of one of the other general lighthouse authorities.

(3) Any person so appointed to collect light dues shall pay over to the general lighthouse authority by whom he was appointed, or as that authority directs, the whole amount of light dues received by him; and the authority receiving the dues shall keep accounts thereof, and shall cause the dues to be remitted to Her Majesty's Paymaster-General in such manner as the [Secretary of State for Trade directs].

As to ships liable to pay light dues, see s. 634. As to scale of light dues, see M.S. (Mercantile Marine Fund) Act 1898, s. 5, Sched. II, § 739, *post*.
[1] See s. 634 as to these authorities.
[2] Now the General Lighthouse Fund: see Merchant Shipping (Mercantile Marine Fund) Act 1898, s. 1 (1) (*c*), § 726, *post*.
[3] A receipt must be given, see s. 651.

Recovery of light dues

559 **649.**—(1) The following persons shall be liable to pay light dues for any ship in respect of which light dues are payable, namely,—

(*a*) the owner or master; or

(*b*) such consignees or agents thereof as have paid, or made themselves liable to pay, any other charge on account of the ship in the port of her arrival or discharge;

and those dues may be recovered in the same manner as fines of a like amount under this Act.[1]

(2) Any consignee or agent (not being the owner or master of the ship) who is hereby made liable for the payment of light dues in respect of any ship, may, out of any moneys received by him on account of that ship or belonging to the owner thereof, retain the amount of all light dues paid

by him together with any reasonable expenses he may have incurred by reason of the payment of the dues or his liability to pay the dues.[2]

560 As to ships liable to pay light dues, see s. 643. As to scale of light dues, see M.S. (Mercantile Marine Fund) Act 1898, s. 5, Sched. II.

[1] See ss. 680 *et seq.*, and note (2) to s. 681.

[2] As to competing claims of seamen for wages and of a person who has paid light dues, see *The Andalina* (1886) 12 P.D. 1; 56 L.T. 171.
Where the charterparty provides that the charterers shall pay " port charges," this includes all light dues which the ship may be required to pay at the particular port before she can obtain her clearance. *Newman & Dale* v. *Lamport & Holt* [1896] 1 Q.B. 20.

Distress on ship for light dues

561 **650.**—(1) If the owner or master of any ship fails, on demand of the authorised collector, to pay the light dues due in respect thereof, that collector may, in addition to any other remedy which he or the authority by whom he is appointed is entitled to use, enter upon the ship, and distrain the goods, guns, tackle, or anything belonging to, or on board, the ship, and detain that distress until the light dues are paid.

(2) If payment of the light dues is not made within the period of three days next ensuing the distress, the collector may, at any time during the continuance of the non-payment, cause the distress to be appraised by two sufficient persons or sworn appraisers, and thereupon sell the same, and apply the proceeds in payment of the light dues due, together with all reasonable expenses incurred by him under this section, paying the surplus (if any), on demand, to the owner or master of the ship.

As to ships liable to pay light dues, see s. 643. As to scale of light dues, see M.S. (Mercantile Marine Fund) Act 1898, s. 5, Sched. II.
The distress, or poinding and sale by direction of court or magistrate, under s. 693, extends to the ship herself.

Receipt for light dues

562 **651.** A receipt for light dues shall be given by the person appointed to collect the same to every person paying the same, and a ship may be detained [1] at any port where light dues are payable in respect of any ship, until the receipt for the light dues is produced to the proper officer of customs.

[1] For provisions as to detention, see s. 692.

Local Lighthouses

Inspection of local lighthouses

563 **652.**—(1) It shall be the duty of each of the general lighthouse authorities,[1] or of any persons authorised by that authority for the purpose, to inspect all lighthouses, buoys, and beacons situate within their area, but belonging to or under the management of any local lighthouse authority,[1]

and to make such inquiries in respect thereof and of the management thereof as they think fit.

(2) All officers and others having the care of any such local lighthouses, buoys, or beacons, or concerned in the management thereof, shall furnish all such information and explanations concerning the same as the general lighthouse authority require.

(3) All local lighthouse authorities and their officers shall at all times give to the general lighthouse authority all such returns, explanations, or information concerning the lighthouses, buoys, and beacons, under their management and the management thereof, as the general lighthouse authority require.

(4) The general lighthouse authority shall communicate to each local lighthouse authority the results of the inspection of their lighthouses, buoys, and beacons, and shall also make general reports of the results of their inspection of local lighthouses, buoys, and beacons to the [Secretary of State for Trade]; and those reports shall be laid before Parliament.[2]

[1] For definition, see s. 634.
[2] As to meaning of reference to laying of documents, etc., before Parliament, see now Laying of Documents before Parliament (Interpretation) Act 1948, s. 1.

Control of local lighthouse authorities by general lighthouse authorities

564 **653.**—(1) A general lighthouse authority [1] may, within their area, with the sanction of the [Secretary of State for Trade], and after giving due notice of their intention, direct a local lighthouse authority [1] to lay down buoys, or to remove or discontinue any lighthouse, buoy, or beacon,[1] or to make any variation in the character of any lighthouse, buoy, or beacon, or in the mode of exhibiting lights in any lighthouse, buoy, or beacon.

(2) A local lighthouse authority shall not erect or place any lighthouse, buoy, or beacon, or remove or discontinue any lighthouse, buoy, or beacon, or vary the character of any lighthouse, buoy, or beacon, or the mode of exhibiting lights in any lighthouse, buoy, or beacon, without the sanction of the general lighthouse authority.

(3) If a local lighthouse authority having power to erect, place, or maintain any lighthouse, buoy, or beacon, at any place within a lighthouse area,[1] fail to do so, or fail to comply with the direction of a general lighthouse authority under this section with respect to any lighthouse, buoy, or beacon, Her Majesty may, on the application of the general lighthouse authority, by Order in Council, transfer any powers of the local lighthouse authority with respect to that lighthouse, buoy, or beacon, including the power of levying dues, to the general lighthouse authority.

(4) On the making of any Order in Council under this section, the powers transferred shall be vested in the general lighthouse authority to whom they are transferred, and the lighthouse, buoy, or beacon in respect

of which the Order is made, and the dues leviable in respect thereof, shall respectively be subject to the same provisions as those to which a lighthouse, buoy, or beacon provided by that general lighthouse authority under this Part of this Act, and the light dues leviable under this Part of this Act are subject.

(5) Nothing in this section shall apply to local buoys and beacons placed or erected for temporary purposes.

1 For definitions, see ss. 634, 742.

Surrender of local lighthouses

565 **654.**—(1) A local lighthouse authority [1] may, if they think fit, surrender or sell any lighthouse, buoy, or beacon held by them to the general lighthouse authority [1] within whose area it is situated, and that general lighthouse authority may, with the consent of the [Secretary of State for Trade], accept or purchase the same.

(2) The purchase money for any lighthouse, buoy, or beacon so sold to a general lighthouse authority shall be paid out of the Mercantile Marine Fund.[2]

(3) On the surrender or sale of a lighthouse, buoy, or beacon under this section to a general lighthouse authority,—

(*a*) the lighthouse, buoy, or beacon surrendered or sold shall, together with its appurtenances, become vested in the general lighthouse authority, and shall be subject to the same provisions as if it had been provided by that authority under this Part of this Act [3]; and

(*b*) the general lighthouse authority shall be entitled to receive either the dues which were leviable in respect of the lighthouse, buoy, or beacon surrendered or sold at the time of the surrender or sale, or, if Her Majesty so directs by Order in Council, such dues as may be fixed by Order in Council, and those dues shall be subject to the same provisions and regulations as light dues for a lighthouse completed by a general lighthouse authority under this Act.[3]

1 For definitions, see ss. 634, 742.
2 Now the General Lighthouse Fund: see M.S. (Mercantile Marine Fund) Act 1898, s. 1 (1) (*c*).
3 See ss. 643–651.

Light dues for local lights

566 **655.**—(1) *If any lighthouse, buoy, or beacon is erected or placed, or reconstructed, repaired, or replaced by a local lighthouse authority, Her Majesty may, on the application of that authority, by Order in Council, fix such dues to be paid to that authority in respect of every ship which enters the port or harbour under the control of that authority or the estuary in which the*

lighthouse, buoy, or beacon is situate, and which passes the lighthouse, buoy, or beacon and derives benefit therefrom as Her Majesty may think reasonable.

(2) Any *dues fixed under this section* (*in this Act referred to as* local light dues [1]) shall be paid by the same persons and may be recovered in the same manner as light dues under this Part of this Act.[2]

(3) *Her Majesty may, by Order in Council, reduce, alter, or increase any local light dues, so that those dues, so far as possible, may be sufficient and not more than sufficient for the payment of the expenses incurred by the local lighthouse authority in respect of the lighthouse, buoys, or beacons for which the dues are levied.*

The words in italics were repealed by the Harbours Act 1964, s. 63 (3) Sched. 6.
[1] *i.e.* charges pursuant to the Harbours Act 1964, s. 29: see *ibid.* s. 29 (3).
[2] As to the recovery of light dues, see s. 649.

Application of local light dues

567 **656.**—(1) All local light dues [1] shall be applied by the authority by whom they are levied for the purpose of the construction, placing, maintenance, and improvement of the lighthouses, buoys, and beacons in respect of which the dues are levied, and for no other purpose.

(2) The local lighthouse authority to whom any local light dues [1] are paid shall keep a separate account of the receipt and expenditure of those dues, and shall, once in every year or at such other time as the [Secretary of State for Trade] may determine, send a copy of that account to the [Secretary of State for Trade], and shall send the same in such form and shall give such particulars in relation thereto as the [Secretary of State for Trade] requires.

[1] *i.e.* charges pursuant to the Harbours Act 1964, s. 29: see *ibid.* s. 29 (3).

Reduction of local light dues

568 [**657.** *This section which contained provision for the reduction of local light dues, was repealed by the Harbours Act* 1964, *s.* 63 (3), *Sched.* 6.]

Expenses of General Lighthouse Authorities

Payment of lighthouse expenses out of Mercantile Marine Fund

569 **658.** The expenses incurred by the general lighthouse authorities [1] in the works and services of lighthouses, buoys, and beacons [1] under this Part of this Act, or in the execution of any works necessary or expedient for the purpose of permanently reducing the expense of those works and services, shall be paid out of the Mercantile Marine Fund.[2]

A provision to the same effect is contained in s. 677 (*i*). *Cf.* ss. 648 (1), 654 (2).
[1] For definitions, see ss. 634, 742.
[2] Now the General Lighthouse Fund: see M.S. (Mercantile Marine Fund) Act 1898, s. 1 (1) (*b*), (*c*).

Establishments of general lighthouse authorities

570 **659.**—(1) Her majesty may by Order in Council fix [1] the establishments to be maintained by each of the general lighthouse authorities on account of the services of lighthouses, buoys, and beacons, or the annual or other sums to be paid out of the Mercantile Marine Fund [2] in respect of those establishments.[3]

(2) If it appears that any part of the establishments of the general lighthouse authorities is maintained for other purposes as well as for the purposes of their duties as general lighthouse authorities, Her Majesty may by Order in Council fix the portion of the expense of those establishments to be paid out of the Mercantile Marine Fund.

(3) An increase of any establishment or part of an establishment fixed under this section shall not be made without the consent of the [Secretary of State for Trade].

571 [1] This power has been extended by M.S.A. 1920, s. 1, " to fixing the annual or other sums to be paid out of " the General Lighthouse Fund " to members of the general lighthouse authority for England and Wales, and the sums so fixed shall have effect notwithstanding anything in any Act limiting the amount thereof."

[2] Now the General Lighthouse Fund: see M.S. (Mercantile Marine Fund) Act 1898, s. 1 (1) (*c*).

[3] This power has been exercised by Order in Council as follows:—

The office establishment of Trinity House was fixed by an Order in Council, February 16, 1903, and the engineering establishment by one of May 20, 1903. See also Trinity House (Establishment) Order 1951, dated January 21, 1951; and Trinity House (Remuneration of Members) Order 1968, November 28, 1968. As to Commissioners of Northern Lighthouses, the establishment was fixed by an Order in Council of May 31, 1951, as amended by an Order dated July 29, 1952; and as to Commissioners of Irish Lights, by an Order in Council dated March 20, 1905. These Orders in Council which in some cases have since been amended by subsequent Orders published in the *London Gazette*, are not set out in the Index to Statutory Rules and Orders and S.I.s in force.

As to the saving of Orders in Council, see s. 745.

Estimates or accounts of expenses sent to [Secretary of State for Trade]

572 **660.**—(1) An expense of a general lighthouse authority [1] in respect of the services of lighthouses, buoys, and beacons shall not be paid out of the Mercantile Marine Fund [2] or allowed in account, unless either it has been allowed as part of the establishment expenses under this Act, or an estimate or account thereof has been approved by the [Secretary of State for Trade].

(2) For the purpose of approval by the [Secretary of State for Trade] each of the general lighthouse authorities [1] shall submit to that [Secretary of State] an estimate of all expenses to be incurred by them in respect of lighthouses, buoys, or beacons, other than expenses allowed under this Act on account of their establishments, or, in case it is necessary in providing for any sudden emergency to incur any such expense without waiting for the sanction of an estimate, shall as soon as possible submit to the [Secretary of State for Trade] a full account of the expense incurred.

(3) The [Secretary of State for Trade] shall consider any estimates and

accounts so submitted to [him] and may approve them either with or without modification.

[1] For definitions, see ss. 634, 742.
[2] Now the General Lighthouse Fund: see M.S. (Mercantile Marine Fund) Act 1898, s. 1 (1) (*c*).

Advances by Treasury for lighthouse expenses

573 [**661.** *This section, which made provision for advances by the Treasury of lighthouse expenses, was repealed by the National Loans Act* 1968, *s.* 24 (2) *and Sched.* 6, *Part I.*]

Mortgage of Mercantile Marine Fund for lighthouse expenditure

574 **662.**[1]—(1) The [Secretary of State for Trade] may mortgage the Mercantile Marine Fund,[2] and any dues, rates, fees, or other payments payable thereto, or any part thereof, for the purpose of the construction and repair of lighthouses or other extraordinary expenses connected with the services of lighthouses, buoys, and beacons.

(2) Any mortgage under this section shall be made in such form and executed in such manner as the [Secretary of State for Trade] may direct.

(3) A person lending money on a mortgage under this section shall not be bound to inquire as to the purpose for which the money is raised or the manner in which it is applied.

[1] ss. 662 and 663 apply in the case of colonial lights: see M.S. (Mercantile Marine Fund) Act 1898, s. 2.
[2] Now the General Lighthouse Fund. See note (2) to s. 660.

Advances by Public Works Loan Commissioners

575 **663.**[1]—(1) The Public Works Loan Commissioners [2] may, for the purpose of the construction and repair of lighthouses or other extraordinary expenses connected with the service of lighthouses, buoys, and beacons, advance money upon mortgage of the Mercantile Marine Fund,[3] and the several dues, rates, fees, and payments to be carried thereto under this Act, or any of them, or any part thereof, without requiring any further security than that mortgage.

(2) Notwithstanding anything in this Act, every mortgage so made to the Public Works Loan Commissioners shall be made in accordance with the Acts regulating loans by the Public Works Loan Commissioners.

(3) An advance by the Public Works Loan Commissioners shall not prevent any lawful reduction of any dues, rates, fees, or other payments payable to the Mercantile Marine Fund [3] if that reduction is assented to by the Public Works Loan Commissioners.

[1] This section has been extended so that the Loans Commissioners may make loans to any authority in Great Britain: see the National Loans Act 1968, s. 3 (11) and Sched. 4 para. 2. See also note (1) to s. 662.

[2] See the Public Works Loans Acts 1875 to 1882.
[3] Now the General Lighthouse Fund: see M.S. (Mercantile Marine Fund) Act 1898, s. 1 (1) (*c*).

Accounts of general lighthouse authorities

576 **664.** Each of the general lighthouse authorities shall account to the [Secretary of State for Trade] foı their receipts from light dues and for their expenditure in respect of expenses paid out of the Mercantile Marine Fund,[1] in such form, and at such times, and with such details, explanations, and vouchers, as the [Secretary of State for Trade requires], and shall, when required by that [Secretary of State], permit all books of accounts kept by or under their respective direction to be inspected and examined by such persons as that [Secretary of State appoints] for that purpose.

[1] See note (3) to s. 663 above.

Power to grant pensions

577 [**665.** *This section, which contained a power to grant pensions, was repealed by the Superannuation Act* 1972, *ss.* 17 (2), 29 (2), (4), *Sched.* 7, *para.* 11, *Sched.* 8.]

Offences in connection with Lighthouses, etc.

Injury to lighthouses

578 **666.**—(1) A person shall not wilfully or negligently—

(*a*) injure any lighthouse or the lights exhibited therein, or any buoy or beacon;

(*b*) remove, alter, or destroy any light ship, buoy, or beacon; or

(*c*) ride by, make fast to, or run foul of any light ship or buoy.

(2) If any person acts in contravention of this section, he shall, in addition to the expenses of making good any damage so occasioned, be liable for each offence to a fine not exceeding fifty pounds.[1]

579 See also ss. 47, 48 of the Malicious Damage Act 1861, by which certain offences in connection with lights, buoys, etc., and the safety of ships generally, are made offences. The Criminal Damage Act 1971 did not repeal these sections.

[1] For summary prosecution of offences, see s. 680.

Prevention of false lights

580 **667.**—(1) Whenever any fire or light is burnt or exhibited at such place or in such manner as to be liable to be mistaken for a light proceeding from a lighthouse, the general lighthouse authority[1] within whose area the place is situate, may serve a notice upon the owner of the place where the fire or light is burnt or exhibited, or on the person having the charge of the fire or light, directing that owner or person, within a

reasonable time to be specified in the notice, to take effectual means for extinguishing or effectually screening the fire or light, and for preventing for the future any similar fire or light.

(2) The notice may be served either personally or by delivery of the same at the place of abode of the person to be served, or by affixing the same in some conspicuous spot near to the fire or light to which the notice relates.

(3) If any owner or person on whom a notice is served under this section fails, without reasonable cause, to comply with the directions contained in the notice, he shall be guilty of a common nuisance, and, in addition to any other penalties or liabilities he may incur, shall for each offence be liable to a fine not exceeding one hundred pounds.[2]

(4) If any owner or person on whom a notice under this section is served neglects for a period of seven days to extinguish or effectually screen the fire or light mentioned in the notice, the general lighthouse authority [1] may, by their servants or workmen, enter upon the place where the fire or light is, and forthwith extinguish the same, doing no unnecessary damage; and may recover the expenses incurred by them in so doing from the owner or person on whom the notice has been served in the same manner as fines may be recovered under this Act.[2]

See note to s. 666. As to exemption from liability for use of registered private signals, see s. 733.

[1] For definition, see s. 634.
[2] For summary prosecution of offences, see s. 680.

Commissioners of Northern Lighthouses

Incorporation of Commissioners of Northern Lights

581 **668.**—(1) The persons holding the following offices shall be a body corporate under the name of the Commissioners of Northern Lighthouses; that is to say,

(*a*) the Lord Advocate and the Solicitor-General for Scotland;

(*b*) the lords provosts of Edinburgh, Glasgow, and Aberdeen, and the provosts of Inverness and Campbeltown;

(*c*) the eldest bailies of Edinburgh and Glasgow;

(*d*) the sheriffs of the counties of the Lothians and Peebles, Lanark, Renfrew and Bute, Argyll, Inverness Elgin and Nairn, Ross Cromarty and Sutherland, Caithness Orkney and Shetland, Aberdeen Kincardine and Banff, Ayr, Fife and Kinross, Dumfries and Galloway; and

(*e*) any persons elected under this section.

(2) The Commissioners shall have a common seal; and any five of them shall constitute a quorum, and shall have power to do all such matters and things as might be done by the whole body.

(3) The Commissioners may elect the provost or chief magistrate of any royal or parliamentary burgh on or near any part of the coasts of Scotland and the sheriff of any county abutting on those coasts to be a member of their body.

As to subss. (1) (*dd*) (4) and (5) added by the M.S.A. 1974, s. 18, see § 1633, *post*.

Provision as to Channel Islands

Restriction on exercise of powers in Channel Islands

582 **669.**—(1) The powers of the Trinity House [1] under this Part of this Act with respect to lighthouses, buoys, or beacons already erected or placed, or hereafter to be erected or placed, in the islands of Guernsey or Jersey (other than their powers with respect to the surrender or purchase of local lighthouses, buoys, and beacons, and the prevention of false lights) shall not be exercised without the consent of Her Majesty in Council.

(2) Dues for any lighthouse, buoy, or beacon erected or placed in or near the islands of Guernsey, Jersey, Sark, or Alderney shall not be taken in the islands of Guernsey or Jersey without the consent of the States of those Islands respectively.

See s. 634 (1) (*a*), making Trinity House the authority for the Channel Islands.

[1] See s. 742 for definition of "Trinity House."

Lighthouses, etc., in Colonies

Dues for colonial lighthouses, etc.

583 **670.**—(1) Where any lighthouse, buoy, or beacon has, either before or after the passing of this Act, been erected or placed on or near the coasts of any British possession [1] by or with the consent of the legislature of that possession, Her Majesty may by Order in Council fix such dues (in this Act referred to as colonial light dues) to be paid in respect of that lighthouse, buoy, or beacon by the owner or master of every ship which passes the same and derives benefit therefrom, as Her Majesty may deem reasonable, and may by like order increase, diminish, or repeal such dues, and those dues shall from the time mentioned in the Order be leviable throughout Her Majesty's dominions.[2]

(2) Colonial light dues shall not be levied in any British possession unless the legislature of that possession has by address to the Crown, or by Act or Ordinance duly passed, signified its opinion that the dues ought to be levied.

584 [1] These lights, and certain others referred to in Schedule III to the M.S. (Mercantile Marine Fund) Act 1898, are "colonial lights"; *ibid.* s. 7. Amongst those mentioned is the Minicoy lighthouse which ceased to be a colonial light upon its transfer to the Government of India; see M.S. (Minicoy Lighthouse) Act 1960, s. 1.

[2] Since the Colonial Light Dues (Revocation) Order 1960 (S.I. No. 471), no order exercising this power is in force. The relevant orders were revoked by that S.I. as a consequence of United Kingdom adherence to the Convention on the Territorial Sea and Contiguous Zone.

Collection and recovery of colonial light dues

585 **671.**—(1) Colonial light dues [1] shall in the United Kingdom be collected and recovered so far as possible as light dues are collected and recovered under this Part of this Act.[2]

(2) Colonial light dues shall in each British possession be collected by such persons as the Governor of that possession may appoint for the purpose, and shall be collected by the same means, in the same manner, and subject to the same conditions so far as circumstances permit, as light dues under this Part of this Act,[2] or by such other means, in such other manner, and subject to such other conditions as the legislature of the possession direct.

[1] As to the transfer of colonial light dues to the General Lighthouse Fund, and the payment out of that fund of the expenses of colonial lights, etc., see M.S. (Mercantile Marine Fund) Act 1898, s. 2. But see note (2) to s. 670.
[2] As to the recovery of light dues, see s. 649.

Payment of colonial light dues to Paymaster-General

586 **672.** Colonial light dues levied under this Act shall be paid over to Her Majesty's Paymaster-General at such times and in such manner as the [Secretary of State for Trade directs], and shall be applied, paid, and dealt with by him for the purposes authorised by this Act, in such manner as [the Secretary of State directs].

Colonial light dues are now to be carried to the General Lighthouse Fund: see M.S. (Mercantile Marine Fund) Act 1898, s. 2. But see note (2) to s. 670.

587 [**673.** *This section which contained provision for the application of colonial light dues was repealed by the M.S.* (*Mercantile Marine Fund*) *Act* 1898, *s.* 8, *Sched. IV.*]

588 [**674.** *This section, which related to advances for construction and repair of colonial lighthouses, etc., was repealed by the National Loans Act* 1968, *s.* 24 (2) *and Sched.* 6, *Part I.*]

Accounts of colonial light dues

589 **675.**—(1) Accounts shall be kept of all colonial light dues received under this Act and of all sums expended in the construction, repair, or maintenance of the lighthouse, buoy, or beacon in respect of which those dues are received.

(2) These accounts shall be kept in such manner as the [Secretary of State for Trade directs], and shall be laid annually before Parliament [1] and audited in such manner as may be directed by Order in Council.[2]

[1] See note (2) to s. 652.
[2] These accounts must be audited by the Comptroller and Auditor-General; see Order in Council, May 13, 1875 (S.R. & O. Rev. 1904, Merchant Shipping, p. 302), and the saving in s. 745 (1) (*a*). But see note (2) to s. 670.

PART XII—MERCANTILE MARINE FUND

Sums payable to the Mercantile Marine Fund

590 **676.**—(1) The common fund called the Mercantile Marine Fund shall continue to exist under that name, and subject to the provisions of this Act there shall be accounted for and paid to that fund [1]—

(*a*) all fees, charges, and expenses payable in respect of the survey or measurement of ships under this Act [2]:

(*b*) all fees and other sums (other than fines and forfeitures [3]) received by the [Department of Trade] under the *Second and* Fifth Parts of this Act, *including all fees payable in respect of the medical inspection of seamen under the Second Part of this Act* [4]:

(*c*) the moneys arising from the unclaimed property of deceased seamen, except where the same are required to be paid as directed by the Accountant General of Her Majesty's Navy:

(*d*) *any sums recovered by the* [Department of Trade] *in respect of expenses incurred in relation to distressed seamen and apprentices under the Second Part of this Act* [5]:

(*e*) all fees and other sums payable in respect of any services performed by any person employed under the authority of the Third Part of this Act [6]:

(*f*) *all fees paid upon the engagement or discharge of members of the crews of fishing boats when effected before a superintendent* [7]:

(*g*) [8]

(*h*) any fees received by receivers of wreck under the Ninth Part of this Act [9]:

(*i*) all light dues or other sums received by or accruing to any of the General Lighthouse Authorities under the Eleventh Part of this Act [10]:

(*k*) all costs and expenses ordered by the court to be paid to the [Department of Trade] in pursuance of the Boiler Explosions Acts, 1882 and 1890:

(*l*) any sums which under this or any other Act are directed to be paid to the Mercantile Marine Fund.[11]

(2) All fees mentioned in this section shall be paid at such time and in such manner as the [Secretary of State for Trade directs].

591 [1] By the M.S. (Mercantile Marine Fund) Act 1898, s. 1 (1) (*a*), all these sums except those payable under s. 83, *ante* (see paragraphs (*a*) and (*b*) above) and those mentioned in paragraph (*i*), are now to be paid into the Exchequer. Payments in respect of paragraph (*i*) are to be made to the General Lighthouse Fund. *Ibid.* s. 1 (1) (*c*). As for payments under s. 83 *ante*, see the M.S.A. 1965, s. 1 (4), § 1258, *post*. See also note to s. 62 for general observations regarding fees chargeable under the M.S. Acts.

[2] See s. 724 (4), *post*, for fees of surveyors of ships.

3 Compare s. 716, of which subs. (1) partly covers the same ground.
4 See ss. 420 and 463 (6). The words in italics are prospectively repealed by the M.S.A. 1970, s. 100 (3), Sched. 5.
5 This paragraph is prospectively repealed by the M.S.A. 1970, s. 100 (3) and Sched. 5.
6 See s. 277.
7 This paragraph is prospectively repealed by the M.S.A. 1970, s. 100 (3), Sched. 5.
8 This subsection, which dealt with the proceeds from the sale of unclaimed wreck, has been repealed as spent by the Statute Law Revision Act 1908; the proceeds of unclaimed wreck have now to be paid to Her Majesty under s. 525 (2) (*c*), though it is understood that in practice they are paid into the Exchequer.
9 See s. 567.
10 See s. 648.
11 As to the application of fines coming into the hands of the Department of Trade, see s. 716 (2); and of fines generally, see s. 699.

Application of Mercantile Marine Fund

592 **677.** Subject to the provisions of this Act and to any prior charges that may be subsisting on the Mercantile Marine Fund under any Act of Parliament or otherwise there shall be charged on and payable out of that fund [1] the following expenses so far as they are not paid by any private person:—

(*a*) *the salaries and other expenses connected with Local Marine Boards and Mercantile Marine Offices, and with the examinations conducted under the Second and Fourth Parts of this Act* [2]:

(*b*) the salaries of all surveyors of ships [3] and officers appointed under this Act and all expenses incurred in connexion with the survey and measurement of ships under this Act,[4] *and the remuneration of medical inspectors of seamen under the Second Part of this Act* [5]:

(*c*) the salaries and expenses of persons employed under the Third Part of this Act [6]:

(*d*) the superannuation allowances, gratuities, pensions, and other allowances granted either before or after the passing of this Act to any of the said surveyors, officers, or persons:

(*e*) *the allowances and expenses paid for the relief of distressed British seamen and apprentices, including the expenses declared under this Act to be payable as such expenses, and any contributions to seamen's refuges and hospitals* [7]:

(*f*) any sums which the [Secretary of State for Trade], in [his] discretion, thinks fit to pay in respect of claims to moneys carried to the Mercantile Marine Fund [8] on account of the property of deceased seamen, or on account of the proceeds of wreck [9]:

(*g*) all expenses of obtaining depositions, reports, and returns respecting wrecks and casualties [10]:

(*h*) all expenses incurred in carrying into effect the provisions of this Act with regard to receivers of wrecks and the performance of their duties under this Act [11]:

(*i*) all expenses incurred by the general lighthouse authorities in the works and services of lighthouses, buoys and beacons, or in the execution of any works necessary or expedient for the purpose of permanently reducing the expense of those works and services [12]:

(*k*) any pensions or other sums payable in relation to the duties formerly performed by the Trinity House [13] in respect of lastage and ballastage in the River Thames:

(*l*) such expenses for establishing and maintaining on the coasts of the United Kingdom proper lifeboats with the necessary crews and equipments, and for affording assistance towards the preservation of life and property in cases of shipwreck and distress at sea, and for rewarding the preservation of life in such cases,[14] as the [Secretary of State for Trade directs]:

(*m*) such reasonable costs, as the [Secretary of State for Trade] may allow, of advertising or otherwise making known the establishment of, or alterations in, foreign lighthouses, buoys, and beacons to owners, and masters of, and other persons interested in, British ships:

(*n*) all costs and expenses incurred by the [Secretary of State for Trade] under the Boiler Explosions Acts 1882 and 1890 (so far as not otherwise provided for), including any remuneration paid in pursuance of section seven of the Boiler Explosions Act 1882, and any costs and expenses ordered by the court in pursuance of those Acts to be paid by the [Secretary of State for Trade]:

(*o*) any expenses which are charged on or payable out of the Mercantile Marine Fund under this or any other Act or Parliament.[15]

593 [1] The expenses enumerated in this section are now to be paid out of moneys provided by Parliament, except those mentioned in paragraph (*i*), which are to be paid out of the General Lighthouse Fund: see M.S. (Mercantile Marine Fund) Act 1898, s. 1 (1) (*b*) (*c*).

[2] This paragraph is prospectively repealed by the M.S.A. 1970, s. 100 (3) and Sched. 5.

[3] See s. 724.

[4] See s. 724 (4).

[5] The words in italics are prospectively repealed by the M.S.A. 1970, s. 100 (3) and Sched. 5.

[6] See s. 272.

[7] This paragraph is prospectively repealed by the M.S.A. 1970, s. 100 (3) and Sched. 5.

[8] These moneys are now paid into the Exchequer: see s. 676 (1) (*c*), and note to that section.

[9] See s. 522.

[10] See ss. 464 *et seq.* and s. 517.

[11] See s. 567.

[12] See the similar provision of s. 658.

[13] These were duties imposed by the Merchant Shipping Act 1854, s. 420 (now repealed). For definition of Trinity House, see s. 742.

[14] As to power of Secretary of State for Trade to award life salvage, see s. 544. The Sea Gallantry Medal—the only decoration for gallantry approved by the Crown which is not the subject of a Royal warrant—is awarded pursuant to this power.

[15] See, *e.g.* s. 429 (3).

Subsidy from Parliament to Mercantile Marine Fund

594 **678.** [*This section, which provided for a Treasury subsidy to the Mercantile Marine Fund, has been repealed by the M.S.* (*Mercantile Marine Fund*) *Act* 1898, *s.* 8 *and Sched. IV.*]

Accounts and audit

595 **679.**—(1) The accounts of the Mercantile Marine Fund [1] shall be deemed to be public accounts within the meaning of section thirty-three of the Exchequer and Audit Departments Act 1866,[2] and shall be examined and audited accordingly.

(2) The [Secretary of State for Trade] shall as soon as may be after the meeting of Parliament in every year cause the accounts of the Mercantile Marine Fund [1] for the preceding year to be laid before both Houses of Parliament.[3]

596 [1] Now the General Lighthouse Fund: see M.S. (Mercantile Marine Fund) Act 1898, s. 1 (1) (*c*).

[2] Repealed and replaced by the Exchequer and Audit Departments Act 1921, s. 10 (2) and Sched. II.

[3] By virtue of Treasury Minutes, dated December 3, 1889 and December 3, 1894 (S.R. & O. No. 726) made under the Parliamentary Returns Act 1869, s. 2, the accounts mentioned in subsection (2) are not to be laid before Parliament as a separate document since they are presented to Parliament with the Appropriation Accounts prepared under the Exchequer and Audit Departments Act 1866 (now repealed and replaced by the Exchequer and Audit Departments Act 1921). For the meaning of the expression "laid before Parliament," see the Laying of Documents before Parliament (Interpretation) Act 1948, s. 1 (1).

PART XIII—LEGAL PROCEEDINGS

597 As to the application of this Part, see section 712.

For certain special provisions as to legal proceedings under Part III (Passenger and Emigrant Ships), see section 356.

As to Special Shipping Inquiries and Courts, see Part VI at §§ 737 *et seq., post*.

For the meaning of " Summary Jurisdiction Acts," see Interpretation Act 1889, s. 13, set out in notes to section 742, *infra*.

Prosecution of Offences

Prosecution of offences

598 **680.**—(1) Subject to any special provisions of this Act [1] and to the provisions hereinafter contained with respect to Scotland,[2]—

(*a*) an offence under this Act declared to be a misdemeanour, shall be punishable by fine or by imprisonment not exceeding two years,[3] with or without hard labour,[4] but may, instead of being prosecuted as a misdemeanour, be prosecuted summarily in manner provided by the Summary Jurisdiction Acts, and if so prosecuted shall be punishable only with imprisonment for a term not exceeding six months, with or without hard labour, or with a fine not exceeding one hundred pounds:

(*b*) an offence under this Act made punishable with imprisonment for any term not exceeding six months, with or without hard labour, or by a fine [5] not exceeding one hundred pounds, shall be prosecuted summarily [6] in manner provided by the Summary Jurisdiction Acts.[7]

(2) Any offence committed or fine recoverable under a byelaw made in pursuance of this Act may be prosecuted or recovered in the same manner as an offence or fine under this Act.

599 [1] Misdemeanours under s. 457 are not punishable upon summary conviction: see s. 457 (4).

[2] See ss. 702 *et seq.* The provisions of s. 680 are, however, now applied to Scotland, and ss. 702, 703 amended accordingly. See M.S. Act 1906, s. 82 (2) (3) and (4).

[3] This was apparently new, the Act of 1854 having placed no limit upon imprisonment for a misdemeanour not prosecuted summarily.

[4] Imprisonment with hard labour has now been abolished: see Criminal Justice Act 1948, s. 1 (2). Enactments conferring power to sentence to imprisonment with hard labour are to be read as conferring power to sentence to imprisonment.

[5] If the fine is imposed as a punishment of an offence and is not in the nature of a civil debt, as, *e.g.* under s. 649, it can be recovered summarily under this section, and imprisonment can be awarded in default of payment or sufficient distress: *R.* v. *Stewart* [1899] 1 Q.B. 964.

[6] This provision does not exclude s. 25 of the Magistrates' Courts Act 1952 (formerly s. 17 of the Summary Jurisdiction Act 1879), under which a person charged with an offence in respect of which he is liable to imprisonment for a term exceeding three months is entitled to be tried by a jury: *Rex* v. *Goldberg* [1904] 2 K.B. 866.

[7] See note (1) to s. 681.

Application of Summary Jurisdiction Acts in certain cases

600 **681.**—(1) The Summary Jurisdiction Acts [1] shall, so far as applicable, apply—

(*a*) to any proceeding under this Act before a court of summary jurisdiction, whether connected with an offence punishable on summary conviction or not; and

(*b*) to the trial of any case before one justice of the peace, where, under this Act, such a justice may try the case.

(2) Where under this Act any sum may be recovered as a fine [2] under this Act, that sum, if recoverable before a court of summary jurisdiction, shall, in England, be recovered as a civil debt in manner provided by the Summary Jurisdiction Acts.

601 For special provisions as to summary procedure in salvage, see ss. 548 *et seq.*

[1] As to the meaning of this expression, see the Interpretation Act 1889, s. 13, set out in notes to s. 742. The Summary Jurisdiction Acts have now, as respects England and Wales, been substantially repealed and replaced by the Magistrates' Courts Act 1952.

[2] *e.g.* in s. 649 light dues, in s. 667 expenses incurred in extinguishing false lights, and in the Pilotage Act 1913, s. 49, pilotage dues are made recoverable "in the same manner as fines under this Act." These sums, being in the nature of civil debts and not fines imposed as a punishment for offences, can by this subsection be recovered as civil debts under the Summary Jurisdiction Acts (now Magistrates' Courts Act 1952). In such procedure the debtor is not liable to imprisonment in default of payment, unless proof of means has been given. Similarly, no warrant for arrest will be issued for apprehending any person for failing to answer the complaint. See Magistrates' Courts Act 1952, ss. 73, 47 (8) (formerly Summary Jurisdiction Act 1879, s. 35 (2)); and *R.* v. *Stewart* [1899] 1 Q.B. 964.

Appeal on summary conviction

602 **682.** [*This section, which made provision for appeal following summary conviction, was repealed by the Courts Act* 1971, *s.* 56 (4) *and Sched. II, Part IV. The appellate jurisdiction of quarter sessions was transferred to the Crown Court*: *ibid. s.* 8 *and Sched.* 1.]

Limitation of time for summary proceeding

603 **683.**—(1) Subject to any special provisions of this Act neither a conviction for an offence nor an order for payment of money shall be made under this Act in any summary proceeding instituted in the United Kingdom, unless that proceeding is commenced within six months after the commission of the offence or after the cause of complaint arises as the case may be; or, if both or either of the parties to the proceeding happen during that time to be out of the United Kingdom, unless the same is commenced, in the case of a summary conviction within two months, and in the case of a summary order within six months, after they both first happen to arrive, or to be at one time, within the United Kingdom.[1]

(2) Subject to any special provisions of this Act neither a conviction for an offence nor an order for payment of money shall be made under this Act in any summary proceeding instituted in any British possession,

unless that proceeding is commenced within six months after the commission of the offence or after the cause of complaint arises as the case may be; or, if both or either of the parties to the proceeding happen during that time not to be within the jurisdiction of any court capable of dealing with the case, unless the same is commenced in the case of a summary conviction within two months, and in the case of a summary order within six months, after they both first happen to arrive, or to be at one time, within that jurisdiction.[1]

(3) No law for the time being in force under any Act, ordinance, or otherwise, which limits the time within which summary proceedings may be instituted shall affect any summary proceeding under this Act.

(4) Nothing in this section shall affect any proceeding to which the Public Authorities Protection Act 1893, applies.[2]

604 [1] Where a seaman took proceedings against a person for attempting to persuade him to neglect to join his ship, it was held that " parties to the proceeding " meant the person committing the offence and the person against whom it was committed, and that if either of them left the kingdom during the six months after the commission of the offence an information might be laid within two months of his return: *Austin* v. *Olsen* (1868) L.R. 3 Q.B. 208.

[2] The Public Authorities Protection Act 1893 has been repealed by the Law Reform (Limitation of Actions, etc.) Act 1954.

Jurisdiction

605 Application under other enactments.—S. 684 is applied by s. 14 of the Sea Fish (Conservation) Act 1967, and s. 1 (4) of the Anchors and Chain Cables Act 1967.

By articles 25 and 26 of the Aliens Order 1953 (S.I. No. 1671), ss. 684, 685 and 686 are applied to jurisdiction under that Order and s. 693 is applied to fines, etc., paid by a master of a ship under that Order.

The Continental Shelf Act 1964, s. 3, as extended by the Mineral Working (Offshore Installations) Act 1971, s. 8, makes provision for the application of criminal and civil law to acts or omissions on areas of the sea bed designated in connection with the exploration and exploitation of the continental shelf. The areas have been defined by the Continental Shelf (Designation of Areas) Order 1964 (S.I. No. 697), and the Continental Shelf (Designation of Additional Areas) Orders, 1965 (S.I. No. 1531); 1968 (S.I. No. 891); 1971 (S.I. No. 594); made under section 1 of the Act and applied by the Prevention of Oil Pollution Act 1971, s. 3 (2) and the Mineral Workings (Offshore Installation) Act 1971, ss. 1 (2) (*a*) and 12 (1). Jurisdiction is conferred in respect of those areas by the Continental Shelf (Jurisdiction) Order 1968 (S.I. No. 892) as amended by S.I. 1971 No. 721 and S.I. 1974 No. 1490. Under section 2 of the Continental Shelf Act 1964, the Secretary of State can, by order, prohibit ships from entering designated areas without his consent: see the Continental Shelf (Protection of Installations) Orders, 1967 (S.I. No. 655), 1968 (S.I. No. 323), 1969 (S.I. No. 195).

Provision as to jurisdiction in case of offences

606 **684.** For the purpose of giving jurisdiction under this Act, every offence shall be deemed to have been committed and every cause of complaint to have arisen either in the place in which the same actually was committed or arose, or in any place in which the offender or person complained against may be.

See note at head of this section as to application.

In the limited immunity in respect of criminal liability given to British subjects or citizens of the Republic of Ireland who are not citizens of the United Kingdom by s. 3 (1) of the British Nationality Act 1948, contravention of any of the provisions of the Merchant Shipping Acts 1894–1948, is expressly excluded.

Jurisdiction over ships lying off the coasts

607 **685.**—(1) Where any district within which any court, justice of the peace, or other magistrate, has jurisdiction either under this Act or under any other Act or at common law for any purpose whatever is situate on the coast of any sea, or abutting on or projecting into any bay, channel, lake, river, or other navigable water, every such court, justice, or magistrate, shall have jurisdiction over any vessel being on, or lying or passing off, that coast, or being in or near that bay, channel, lake, river, or navigable water, and over all persons on board that vessel or for the time being belonging thereto, in the same manner as if the vessel or persons were within the limits of the original jurisdiction of the court, justice or magistrate.[1]

(2) The jurisdiction under this section shall be in addition to and not in derogation of any jurisdiction or power of a court under the Summary Jurisdiction Acts.[2]

See note at head of s. 684 as to application of these provisions under other enactments.

[1] See Archbold's *Criminal Pleading, etc.*, 38th ed., paras. 82 *et seq.* for notes on "Offences in the Admiralty Jurisdiction." Notwithstanding anything on the Colonial Laws Validity Act 1865, no colonial law within the meaning of that Act is by the Consular Relations Act 1968, s. 15, to be void or inoperative as being repugnant to this section or s. 686, *post,* by reason only of making provision corresponding to s. 5 of the 1968 Act.

[2] See now s. 3 of the Magistrates' Courts Act 1952 (formerly s. 46 of the Summary Jurisdiction Act 1879), which contains provisions somewhat similar to those of subs. (1).

Jurisdiction in case of offences on board ship

608 **686.**—(1) Where any person, being a British subject,[1] is charged with having committed any offence on board any British ship [2] on the high seas [3] or in any foreign port or harbour [3] or on board any foreign ship to which he does not belong,[4] or, not being a British subject, is charged with having committed any offence on board [5] any British ship on the high seas,[3] and that person is found within the jurisdiction [6] of any court in Her Majesty's dominions,[7] which would have had cognizance of the offence if it had been committed on board a British ship within the limits of its ordinary jurisdiction, that court shall have jurisdiction to try the offence as if it had been so committed.

(2) Nothing in this section shall affect the Admiralty Offences (Colonial) Act, 1849.[8]

609 See note at head of s. 684 as to application of these provisions under other enactments. By the M.S.A. 1970, ss. 77 (2) and 101 (4) nothing in this section is to be taken to limit the jurisdiction of any court in the United Kingdom to deal with an offence under s. 77 which has been committed in a country outside the United Kingdom by a person who is not a British subject.

The general law as to the criminal jurisdiction of British courts over offences within the Admiralty jurisdiction is beyond the scope of these notes and will be found exhaustively discussed in Archbold's *Criminal Pleading, etc.*, 38th ed., paras. 82 *et seq,* under "Offences in the Admiralty Jurisdiction." A warrant may be issued by a justice of the peace notwithstanding that the offence was committed outside England and Wales if an indictment for the offence may legally be preferred in England or Wales; see Magistrates' Courts Act 1952, s. 1 (4). See also note 1 to s. 685.

[1] As to who are "British subjects," see note (3) to s. 1, *ante.*

[2] As to offences on board a foreign ship within British territorial waters, see the Territorial Waters Jurisdiction Act, 1878. This statute, by providing that " an offence committed by any person, whether he is or is not a subject of Her Majesty, on the open sea within the territorial waters of Her Majesty's dominions is an offence within the jurisdiction of the Admiral," had the effect of reversing the decision in *R.* v. *Keyn, The Franconia* (1876) 46 L.J.M.C. 17; 2 Ex.D. 63. In that case the majority of the court had held that, inasmuch as Parliament by several statutes had only transferred to the Common Law Courts and the Central Criminal Court the jurisdiction formerly possessed by the Admiral, and as the Admiral had no jurisdiction to try offences by foreigners on board foreign ships, whether within or without the limit of three miles from the shore of England, the Central Criminal Court had no jurisdiction to try on the charge of manslaughter the master of a foreign ship by whose negligent navigation a British ship was sunk in collision with loss of life within three miles of the shore of England.

[3] Passengers have been held to be " persons belonging to " a ship within the meaning of certain other provisions: see note (2) to s. 544 and *The Fusilier* there cited. But *quaere* whether they would be held to be such within this section.

[4] Where a foreign ship ran into and sank a British ship and so caused the death by drowning of a passenger on board the latter, and the facts were such as to amount to manslaughter by the master of the former vessel, the offence was held not to have been committed on board a British ship: *R.* v. *Keyn, The Franconia, supra.* See the judgment of Bramwell J.A., 2 Ex.D. at p. 150.

610 It is immaterial, as to the liability of a foreigner to punishment or to the jurisdiction of the court to try him, that he was illegally and by force taken on board an English ship and there detained in custody at the time of the act alleged to be an offence, if such act was not committed for the purpose of releasing himself from the illegal duress: *R.* v. *Lopez, R.* v. *Sattler* (1858) 27 L.J.M.C. 48; Dears. & B.C.C. 525.

See also *Robey* v. *Vladinier* (1935) 53 Ll.L.R. 121 (stowaway arrested on arrival in U.K. port).

[5] The high seas means " where great ships can go " not just the waters outside territorial waters: see *R.* v. *Liverpool Justices, ex parte Molyneux* [1972] 1 Lloyd's Rep. 367. As to the jurisdiction in case of an offence on board a British ship lying at a foreign port in a river, but within the ebb and flow of the tide, see *R.* v. *Carr* (*No.* 2) (1882) 10 Q.B.D. 76.

[6] A person is " found within the jurisdiction " if he be brought within it, even against his will: *R.* v. *Lopez, R.* v. *Sattler, supra.*

[7] By the Foreign Jurisdiction Act 1890, Her Majesty has power by Order in Council to extend the provisions of the Merchant Shipping Acts to any foreign country in which for the time being Her Majesty has jurisdiction. (See also the general provisions of the Interpretation Act 1889, s. 38 (1), cited after notes to s. 742, *post*, as to references in any Act to provisions of any other Act which are repealed and re-enacted.) For the details of the individual orders and amending orders, see Guide to Government Orders title, Overseas Territories 4, Courts (1), or alternatively in the Chronological List of Instruments to Part I of the title Dominions and Dependencies in Vol. 6 of Halsbury's *Statutory Instruments*, and the Service to that work.

[8] That Act provides for trial in colonies of offences on the high seas.

Offences committed by British seamen at foreign ports to be within Admiralty jurisdiction

611 **687.** All offences against property or person committed in or at any place either ashore or afloat out of Her Majesty's dominions by any master, seaman, or apprentice who at the time when the offence is committed is, or within three months previously has been, employed in any British ship shall *be deemed to be offences of the same nature respectively, and* [1] be liable to the same punishments respectively, and be inquired of, heard, tried, determined, and adjudged in the same manner and by the same courts and in the same places as if those offences had been committed within the jurisdiction of the Admiralty of England; and the costs and expenses of the prosecution of any such offence may be directed to be

paid as in the case of costs and expenses of prosecutions for offences committed within the jurisdiction of the Admiralty of England.

The effect of this section appears to be that the offences therein indicated, when committed abroad, by the persons specified are to be treated as if committed within the Admiralty jurisdiction, and are to be tried in the same way as offences committed within that jurisdiction are triable. The statutes dealing with the trial of offences within the Admiralty jurisdiction are too numerous to be usefully dealt with in this note, but will be found set out in the yearly Index to the Statutes under the heading " Sea." See, too, Archbold's *Criminal Pleading, etc.*, 38th ed., paras. 82 *et seq*, " Offences in the Admiralty Jurisdiction."

[1] The words in italics were repealed by the Criminal Law Act 1967, ss. 10 (2), 11 (1), (2) and Sched. 3 Part III. As to Northern Ireland, see the Criminal Law Act (Northern Ireland) 1967, Sched. II.

Damage occasioned by Foreign Ship

Power to arrest foreign ship that has occasioned damage

612 **688.** [*This section, which gave power to United Kingdom courts to arrest a foreign ship found within the jurisdiction for damage caused by her to British property in any part of the world, has been repealed by the Administration of Justice Act* 1956, *ss.* 7 (1), 55 (1), 57 (2) *and Sched. I and replaced by ibid. s.* 3 (3) *and* (4) *which will be found set out in British Shipping Laws* (*Vol.* 4), *Marsden on Collisions at Sea*, 11*th ed.*, § 77.]

Provisions in case of Offences Abroad

Conveyance of offenders and witnesses to United Kingdom or British possession

613 **689.**—(1) Whenever any complaint is made to any British consular officer—

(*a*) that any offence against property or person has been committed at any place, either ashore or afloat, out of Her Majesty's dominions by any master, [or seaman],[1] who at the time when the offence was committed, or within three months before that time was employed in any British ship; or

(*b*) that any offence on the high seas has been committed by any master, [or seaman] [1] belonging to any British ship,

that consular officer may inquire into the case upon oath, and may, if the case so requires, take any steps in his power for the purpose of placing the offender under the necessary restraint and of sending him as soon as practicable in safe custody to the United Kingdom, or to any British possession in which there is a court capable of taking cognizance of the offence, in any ship belonging to Her Majesty or to any of Her subjects, to be there proceeded against according to law.

(2) The consular officer may order the master of any ship belonging to any subject of Her Majesty bound to the United Kingdom, or to such British possession as aforesaid to receive and afford a passage and subsistence during the voyage to any such offender as aforesaid, and to the

witnesses,[2] so that the master be not required to receive more than one offender for every one hundred tons of his ship's registered tonnage, or more than one witness for every fifty tons of that tonnage; and the consular officer shall endorse upon the agreement of the ship such particulars with respect to any offenders or witnesses sent in her as the [Secretary of State for Trade requires].

(3) Any master of a ship to whose charge an offender has been so committed shall, on his ship's arrival in the United Kingdom or in such British possession as aforesaid, give the offender into the custody of some police officer or constable, and that officer or constable shall take the offender before a justice of the peace or other magistrate by law empowered to deal with the matter, and the justice or magistrate shall deal with the matter as in cases of offences committed upon the high seas.

(4) If any master of a ship, when required by any British consular officer to receive and afford a passage and subsistence to any offender or witness, does not receive him and afford a passage and subsistence to him, or does not deliver any offender committed to his charge into the custody of some police officer or constable as hereinbefore directed, he shall for each offence be liable to a fine not exceeding fifty pounds.

(5) The expense of imprisoning any such offender and of conveying him and the witnesses to the United Kingdom or to such British possession as aforesaid in any manner other than in the ship to which they respectively belong, shall, where not paid as part of the costs of the prosecution, be paid out of moneys provided by Parliament.

See also the powers of a consular officer under s. 723.

[1] The words in brackets were substituted by the M.S.A. 1970, s. 100 (1) and Sched. 3, para. 2. As from January 1, 1973: see S.I. 1972 No. 1977.

[2] A seaman who is sent home as a witness is not entitled to any wages from the date of leaving the ship. *Melville* v. *de Wolf* (1855) 4 E. & B. 844.

Inquiry into cause of death on board ship

614 **690.** [*This section, which made provision for inquiry into the cause of any death on board a ship, was repealed by the M.S.A.* 1970, *s.* 100 (3) *and Sched.* 5. *As from January* 1, 1973: *see S.I.* 1972 *No.* 1977. *See now ibid., s.* 72.]

Depositions to be received in evidence when witness cannot be produced

615 **691.**—(1) Whenever in the course of any legal proceeding instituted in any part of Her Majesty's dominions before any judge or magistrate, or before any person authorised by law or by consent of parties to receive evidence, the testimony of any witness is required in relation to the subject-matter of that proceeding, then upon due proof, if the proceeding is instituted in the United Kingdom, that the witness cannot be found in that kingdom, or if in any British possession, that he cannot be found

in that possession, any deposition that the witness may have previously made on oath in relation to the same subject-matter before any justice or magistrate in Her Majesty's dominions, or any British consular officer elsewhere,[1] shall be admissible in evidence, provided that—

(*a*) if the deposition was made in the United Kingdom, it shall not be admissible in any proceeding instituted in the United Kingdom; and

(*b*) if the deposition was made in any British possession, it shall not be admissible in any proceeding instituted in that British possession; and

(*c*) if the proceeding is criminal it shall not be admissible, unless it was made in the presence of the person accused.

(2) A deposition so made shall be authenticated by the signature of the judge, magistrate, or consular officer before whom it is made; and the judge, magistrate, or consular officer shall certify, if the fact is so, that the accused was present at the taking thereof.

(3) It shall not be necessary in any case to prove the signature or official character of the person appearing to have signed any such deposition, and in any criminal proceeding a certificate under this section shall, unless the contrary is proved, be sufficient evidence of the accused having been present in manner thereby certified.

(4) Nothing herein contained shall affect any case in which depositions taken in any proceeding are rendered admissible in evidence by any Act of Parliament, or by any Act or ordinance of the legislature of any colony, so far as regards that colony, or interfere with the power of any colonial legislature to make those depositions admissible in evidence, or to interfere with the practice of any court in which depositions not authenticated as hereinbefore mentioned are admissible.

616 As to taking evidence for the purposes of claims by mariners for benefits under the National Insurance Act, 1965: see *ibid.* s. 100 (2) (*d*). For claims under the National Insurance (Industrial Injuries) Act 1965: see *ibid.* s. 75 (2) (*e*).

As to obtaining proofs of matters charged in an indictment for an offence committed outside the United Kingdom, see the Criminal Jurisdiction Act 1885, s. 2, and for the power to make provision for taking depositions, see the Evidence by Commission Act 1885, s. 3.

[1] See s. 737 for provision for foreign places where there is no British consular officer.

Detention of Ship and Distress on Ship

Enforcing detention of ship

617 **692.**—(1) Where under this Act a ship [1] is to be or may be detained, any commissioned officer on full pay in the naval or military service of Her Majesty, or any officer or the [Secretary of State], or any officer of Customs, or any British consular officer may detain the ship, and if the ship after detention or after service on the master of any notice of or order for detention proceeds to sea before it is released by competent authority

the master of the ship, and also the owner, and any person who sends the ship to sea, if that owner or person is party or privy to the offence, shall be liable for each offence to a fine not exceeding [two hundred pounds]. [2]

(2) Where a ship so proceeding to sea takes to sea when on board thereof in the execution of his duty any officer authorised to detain the ship, or any surveyor or officer of the [Dept. of Trade] or any officer of Customs, the owner and master of the ship shall each be liable to pay all expenses of and incidental to the officer or surveyor being so taken to sea, and also to a fine not exceeding one hundred pounds, or, if the offence is not prosecuted in a summary manner, not exceeding ten pounds for every day until the officer or surveyor returns, or until such time as would enable him after leaving the ship to return to the port from which he is taken, and the expenses ordered to be paid may be recovered in like manner as the fine.

(3) Where under this Act a ship is to be detained an officer of Customs shall, and where under this Act a ship may be detained an officer of Customs may, refuse to clear that ship outwards or to grant a transire to that ship.[3]

(4) Where any provision of this Act provides that a ship may be detained until any document is produced to the proper officer of Customs, the proper officer shall mean, unless the context otherwise requires, the officer able to grant a clearance or transire to such ship.

618 This section has been extended to apply to the detention of a ship under several statutes of which the following are now in force:

(i) Seal Fisheries North Pacific Act 1912, s. 3, prohibiting the use of a port in the United Kingdom for equipping vessels for the purpose of hunting seals in prohibited areas in the North Pacific; and

(ii) Diseases of Animals Act 1950; see s. 74 (3).

(iii) Agriculture (Miscellaneous Provisions) Act 1954: see s. 11 (1) and Sched. 2, para. 4.

The section is modified in relation to non-seagoing ships by s. 96 (2) of the M.S.A. 1970.

[1] Where a foreign ship had taken cargo on board at a port in the United Kingdom, and was whilst at that port unsafe by reason of overloading or improper loading, it was held that 39 & 40 Vict. c. 80, s. 34 (subss. (1) and (2) of the present section), applied to her by virtue of s. 13 of the same Act (1894, s. 462), although no Order in Council had been made under s. 37 of that Act (1894, s. 734) applying such provisions to the ships of the country to which she belonged. *Chalmers* v. *Scopenich* [1892] 1 Q.B. 735.

This decision rested partly on the fact that s. 13 of 39 & 40 Vict. c. 80 applied to foreign ships in such circumstances the provisions of that Act as to detention, including s. 34. It is to be observed that in the present Act s. 462 only expressly applies to such ships the provisions as to detention of Part V, which does not include s. 692. It is thought, however, that the authority of the decision is not affected by this change.

As to detention of foreign ships when unseaworthy, see s. 462, and M.S.A. 1906, s. 2.

[2] The words in brackets were substituted by the M.S.A. 1970, s. 88 for the previous maximum penalty of one hundred pounds.

[3] For further provisions relating to the power of Customs officers to refuse or cancel clearance of ships, see Customs and Excise Act 1952, s. 53.

Sums ordered to be paid leviable by distress on ship

619 **693.** Where any court, justice of the peace, or other magistrate, has power to make an order directing payment to be made of any seaman's wages, fines, or other sums of money, then, if the party so directed to pay the same is the master or owner of a ship, and the same is not paid at the

time and in manner prescribed in the order, the court, justice of the peace, or magistrate who made the order may, in addition to any other powers they may have for the purpose of compelling payment, direct the amount remaining unpaid to be levied by distress or poinding and sale of the ship, her tackle, furniture, and apparel.

See note at head of s. 685, as to application of these provisions under other enactments. Under the similar provision of 7 & 8 Vict. c. 112, s. 15, it was held that it was not competent for magistrates to levy distress at the suit of seamen for wages upon a vessel already under arrest of the Court of Admiralty. *The Westmoreland* (1845) 2 W.Rob. 394.

As to distress on tackle, etc., for light dues, independently of order of court, see s. 650.

Evidence, Service of Documents, and Declarations

Proof of attestation not required

620 **694.** Where any document is required by this Act to be executed in the presence of or to be attested by any witness or witnesses, that document may be proved by the evidence of any person who is able to bear witness to the requisite facts without calling the attesting witness or the attesting witnesses or any of them.[1]

[1] See also Evidence Act 1845, s. 1 (by which certain documents purporting to be sealed and signed may be received in evidence without proof of the seal and signature); see also Evidence Act 1938, s. 3 (proof of instruments requiring attestation).

Admissibility of documents in evidence

621 **695.**—(1) Where a document is by this Act declared to be admissible in evidence, such document shall, on its production from the proper custody,[1] be admissible in evidence in any court or before any person having by law or consent of parties authority to receive evidence, and, subject to all just exceptions, shall be evidence [and in Scotland sufficient evidence] [2] of the matters stated therein in pursuance of this Act or by any officer in pursuance of his duties as such officer.[3]

(2) A copy of any such document or extract therefrom shall also be so admissible [4] in evidence [and be evidence, and in Scotland sufficient evidence, of those matters] [2] if proved to be an examined copy or extract, or if it purports to be signed and certified as a true copy or extract by the officer to whose custody the original document was entrusted, and that officer shall furnish such certified copy or extract to any person applying at a reasonable time [5] for the same, upon payment of a reasonable sum for the same [*not exceeding one shilling* [6]], but a person shall be entitled to have—

(*a*) a certified copy of the particulars entered by the registrar in the register book on the registry of the ship, together with a certified statement showing the ownership of the ship at the time being; and (*b*) a certified copy of any declaration, or document, a copy of which is made evidence by this Act,

[on payment *of five shillings* [6]] for each copy.

(3) If any such officer wilfully certifies any document as being a true copy or extract knowing the same not to be a true copy or extract, he shall for each offence be guilty of a misdemeanour, and be liable on conviction to imprisonment for any term not exceeding eighteen months.

(4) If any person forges the seal, steamp, or signature of any document to which this section applies, or tenders in evidence any such document with a false or counterfeit seal, stamp, or signature thereto, knowing the same to be false or counterfeit, he shall for each offence be guilty of felony,[7] and be liable to penal servitude [8] for a term not exceeding seven years, or to imprisonment for a term not exceeding two years, with or without hard labour [8] and whenever any such document has been admitted in evidence, the court or the person who admitted the same may on request direct that the same shall be impounded, and be kept in the custody of some officer of the court or other proper person, for such period or subject to such conditions as the court or person thinks fit.

622 See also ss. 64, 256, 691, 719–722, as to admissibility in evidence of register book, certificate of registry, and other documents.

[1] As to the meaning of " proper custody," see *Hall* v. *Ball* (1841) 3 Man. & G. 242 at p. 247.

[2] The words in brackets were added by the M.S.A. 1970, s. 100 (1) and Sched. 3 para. 3.

[3] Since the names of the " registered owner " and of the " managing owner " are among the matters stated therein in pursuance of this Act (see ss. 11, 59), the register is evidence as to who are owners and managing owners, and it has been admitted as prima facie evidence that a ship-keeper was employed by the person registered as owner. *Hibbs* v. *Ross* (1866) L.R. 1 Q.B. 534.

But this section does not exclude evidence in explanation of the document. For instance, the registered owner is not necessarily the owner for all purposes. See *The Hopper 66* [1908] A.C. 126. Thus, where he had parted with the possession and control of his ship to charterers under a charterparty, under which the master was the servant of the charterer the owner, who was registered as such and as managing owner, was held not liable, either in contract or in tort, for loss of cargo carried under a bill of lading signed by the master. *Baumwoll, etc.* v. *Furness* (or *Scheibler* v. *Furness*) [1893] A.C. 8. *Cf. Steele* v. *Lester & Lilee* (1877) 47 L.J.C.P. 43; 3 C.P.D. 121, where the registered managing owner was held liable for the negligence of the master. In a case of a demised vessel the registered owner was held not liable upon an allotment note given by the master for wages earned on his ship. *Meiklerard* v. *West* (1876) 1 Q.B.D. 428; *Re The Great Eastern S.S. Co.* (1885) 5 Asp. M.C. 511.

But this section does not entitle the plaintiff in a salvage or collision action to tender, as evidence of the facts deposed to therein, the records of the examination of the ship's crew under s. 517. See *The Little Lizzie* (1870) L.R. 3 A. & E. 56; 23 L.T. 84; *Nothard* v. *Pepper* (1864) 10 L.T. 782; 17 C.B.(N.S.) 39. See, too, *McAllum* v. *Reid* (1870) L.R. 3 A. & E. 57, n. (attempt to use endorsement of master's certificate as evidence of negligence) and *The Kestrel* (1881) 6 P.D. 182 (reports of Courts of Formal Investigation).

As to the effect of registration as managing owner, see also note to s. 59.

As to the register as evidence of the national character of a ship, see *The Princess Charlotte* (1863) B. & L. 75; *The Laura* (1865) 3 Moo.P.C.C.(N.S.) 181; 13 L.T. 133; cases cited in notes to ss. 70, 72. As to evidence of tonnage, see s. 82, and cases there cited.

As to conclusiveness of documents, *cf. Lewis* v. *Jewhurst* (1866) 15 L.T. 275; and *Board of Trade* v. *Sailing Ship Glenpark* [1904] 1 K.B. 682.

[4] See also the Evidence Act 1851, as to the admissibility of examined or certified copies of public documents. As to copies of an entry on the official log book of a ship, see the M.S.A. 1970, s. 75 (1) (*b*), *post*.

[5] See *Small* v. *Bickley* (1875) 32 L.T. 726.

[6] The words printed within the square brackets, which had been inserted in substitution for the original text by the Fees Increase Act 1923, s. 1 (1), Sched. I, Part I, ceased to have effect by reason of the M.S. (Safety Convention) Act 1949, s. 37 (5) and Sched. III, which repealed the words in italics. Section 33 of that Act enables the Minister of Transport to fix fees for these services by regulations. Those in force are to be found in the M.S. (Fees) Regulations 1975 (S.I. No. 341).

[7] Now to be read as " shall be guilty of an offence ": see the Criminal Law Act 1967, s. 12 (5) (*a*).

[8] Penal servitude and imprisonment with hard labour have now been abolished: see the Criminal Justice Act 1948, s. 1 (2). Enactments conferring power on a court to pass such sentences are to be construed as conferring power to pass sentences of imprisonment subject to the same maximum period.

Service of documents

623 **696.**—(1) Where for the purposes of this Act any document is to be served on any person, that document may be served—

(*a*) in any case by delivering a copy thereof personally to the person to be served, or by leaving the same at his last place of abode; and,

(*b*) if the document is to be served on the master [1] of a ship, where there is one, or on a person belonging to a ship, by leaving the same for him on board that ship with the person being or appearing to be in command or charge of the ship; and,

(*c*) if the document is to be served on the master [1] of a ship, where there is no master, and the ship is in the United Kingdom, on the managing owner of the ship,[2] or if there is no managing owner, on some agent of the owner residing in the United Kingdom, or where no such agent is known or can be found, by affixing a copy thereof to the mast of the ship.

(2) If any person obstructed the service on the master [1] of a ship of any document under the provisions of this Act relating to the detention of ships as unseaworthy,[3] that person shall for each offence be liable to a fine not exceeding ten pounds, and if the owner or master of the ship is party or privy to the obstruction, he shall in respect of each offence be guilty of a misdemeanor.[4]

As to service of a demand in writing made by a Customs officer that the clearance be returned to him for the purpose of detaining a ship, see Customs and Excise Act 1952, s. 53.

[1] For definition of " master," see s. 742.
[2] See s. 59, as to registration of managing owner.
[3] See s. 459, as to detention of unsafe ships.
[4] As to prosecution of misdemeanours, see s. 680.

Proof, etc., of exemption

624 **697.** Any exception, exemption, proviso, excuse, or qualification, in relation to any offence under this Act, whether it does or does not accompany in the same section the description of the offence, may be proved by the defendant, but need not be specified or negatived in any information or complaint, and, if so specified or negatived, no proof in relation to the

matter so specified or negatived shall be required on the part of the informant or complainant.

Declarations

625 **698.** Any declaration required by this Act to be taken before a justice of the peace or any particular officer may be taken before a commissioner for oaths.

This section is founded on the Commissioners for Oaths Act 1891, s. 1.
For definition of Commissioner for Oaths, see s. 742.
As to declarations under Part I, see s. 61.

Application of Penalties and Costs of Prosecutions

Application of penalties

626 **699.**—(1) Where any court, justice of the peace, or other magistrate, imposes a fine under this Act for which no specific application is herein provided, that court, justice of the peace, or magistrate, may if they think fit direct the whole or any part of the fine to be applied in compensating any person for any wrong or damage which he may have sustained by the act or default in respect of which the fine is imposed, *or to be applied in or towards payment of the expenses of the proceedings.*[1]

(2) Subject to any directions under this section or to any specific application provided under this Act, all fines under this Act shall, notwithstanding anything in any other Act—

(*a*) if recovered in [Great Britain] [2] be paid into the Exchequer in such manner as the Treasury may direct, and be carried to and form part of the Consolidated Fund; and

(*b*) if recovered in any British possession, be paid over into the public treasury of that possession, and form part of the public revenue thereof.

As to the application of certain fees and fines coming into the hands of the Secretary of State for Trade, see s. 716 and s. 676 (1) (*b*).

[1] The words in italics were repealed by the Justices of the Peace Act 1949, s. 46 and Sched. VII, as from April 1, 1953 (see S.I. 1951 No. 1941).

[2] " Great Britain " was substituted for " United Kingdom " by the Northern Ireland Act 1962, s. 25 (1) (*a*) in order to secure that the proceeds of fines imposed upon the conviction of a person in Northern Ireland should not be paid thereafter into the Exchequer of the United Kingdom.

Expenses of prosecution of misdemeanor

627 **700.** Where an offence under this Act is prosecuted as a misdemeanor,[1] the court before whom the offence is prosecuted *may* in England *make the same allowances and order payment of the same costs and expenses as if the offence were a felony,*[2] and in any other part of Her Majesty's dominions may make such allowances and order payment of such costs and expenses

as are payable or allowable upon the trial of any misdemeanor or under any law for the time being in force therein.[3]

[1] See s. 680 (1) (*a*).
[2] The words in italics were repealed by the Criminal Law Act 1967, s. 10 (2) and Sched. 3, Part III. For Northern Ireland, see the Criminal Law Act (Northern Ireland) Act 1967, Sched. II.
[3] See generally the Costs in Criminal Cases Act 1973.

628 **701.** [*This section, which related to payment of costs of prosecution of offences committed in Admiralty jurisdiction was repealed by the Costs in Criminal Cases Act* 1908, *s.* 10 *and Schedule, and the subject-matter of the repealed section was contained in section* 4 (1) *of that Act. The relevant Act is now the Costs in Criminal Cases Act* 1973 *which consolidates previous legislation. See that Act.*]

See also s. 680 (prosecution of offences), which is now applied to Scotland by M.S.A. 1906, s. 82 (2).

As respects Scotland, the term " sheriff " includes sheriff's substitute, " felony " means a high crime and offence, and " misdemeanour " means an offence. See Interpretation Act 1889, s. 28.

Offences punishable as misdemeanors

629 **702.** In Scotland every offence which by this Act is described as a felony or misdemeanor may be prosecuted by indictment[1] or criminal letters at the instance of Her Majesty's Advocate before the High Court of Justiciary, or *by criminal libel at the instance of the procurator fiscal of the county before the sheriff*,[2] and shall be punishable with fine and with imprisonment with or without hard labour in default of payment, or with imprisonment with or without hard labour, or with both, as the court may think fit, or in the case of felony, with penal servitude where the court is competent thereto; and such court may also, if it think fit, order payment by the offender of the costs and expenses of the prosecution.

[1] From a conviction upon indictment an appeal lies to the High Court of Justiciary under the Criminal Appeal (Scotland) Act 1926.
[2] The words in italics were repealed by M.S.A. 1906, s. 82 (3), which also provides that every offence referred to in s. 702 may be prosecuted by indictment.

Summary proceedings

630 **703.** In Scotland, all prosecutions, complaints, actions, or proceedings under this Act, other than prosecutions for felonies *or misdemeanors*,[1] may be brought in a summary form before the sheriff of the county, or before any two justices of the peace of the county or burgh where the cause of such prosecution or action arises, or where the offender or defender may be for the time, and when of a criminal nature or for fines or penalties, at the instance of the procurator fiscal of court, or at the instance of any party aggrieved, with concurrence of the procurator fiscal of court;

and the court may, if it think fit, order payment by the offender or defender of the costs of the prosecution or action.

[1] The words in italics are repealed by the M.S.A. 1906, s. 82 (4), thus enabling offences which are not felonies to be prosecuted summarily.

Form of complaint

631 **704.** Where in any summary proceedings under this Act in Scotland any complaint or action is brought in whole or in part for the enforcement of a pecuniary debt or demand, the complaint may contain a prayer for warrant to arrest upon the dependence.

Warrants on summary proceedings

632 **705.** On any summary proceedings in Scotland the deliverance of the sheriff clerk or clerk of the peace shall contain warrant to arrest upon the dependence in common form, where that warrant has been prayed for in the complaint or other proceeding: Provided always, that where the apprehension of any party, with or without a warrant, is authorised by this Act, such party may be detained in custody until he can be brought at the earliest opportunity before any two justices or the sheriff who may have jurisdiction in the place, to be dealt with as this Act directs, and no citation or induciae shall in such case be necessary.

Backing arrestments

633 **706.** When it becomes necessary to execute such arrestment on the dependence against goods or effects of the defender within Scotland, but not locally situated within the jurisdiction of the sheriff or justices of the peace by whom the warrant to arrest has been granted, it shall be competent to carry the warrant into execution on its being endorsed by the sheriff clerk, or clerk of the peace of the county or burgh respectively within which such warrant comes to be executed.

Form of decree for payment of money

634 **707.** Where on any summary proceedings in Scotland there is a decree for payment of any sum of money against a defender, the decree shall contain warrant for arrestment, poinding, and imprisonment in default of payment.

Sentence and penalties in default of defender's appearance

635 **708.** In all summary complaints and proceedings for recovery of any penalty or sum of money in Scotland, if a defender who has been duly cited shall not appear at the time and place required by the citation, he shall be held as confessed, and sentence or decree shall be pronounced against him in terms of the complaint, with such costs and expenses as

to the court shall seem fit: Provided that he shall be entitled to obtain himself reponed against any such decree at any time before the same be fully implemented, by lodging with the clerk of court a reponing note, and consigning in his hands the sum decerned for, and the costs which had been awarded by the court, and on the same day delivering or transmitting through the post to the pursuer or his agent a copy of such reponing note; and a certificate by the clerk of court of such note having been lodged shall operate as a sist of diligence till the cause shall have been reheard and finally disposed of, which shall be on the next sitting of the court, or on any day to which the court shall then adjourn it.

Orders not to be quashed for want of form and to be final

636 **709.** No order, decree, or sentence pronounced by any sheriff or justice of the peace in Scotland under the authority of this Act shall be quashed or vacated for any misnomer, informality, or defect of form; and all orders, decrees, and sentences so pronounced shall be final and conclusive, and not subject to suspension, reduction, or to any form of review or stay of execution, except on the ground of corruption or malice on the part of the sheriff or justices, in which case the suspension, or reduction must be brought within fourteen days of the date of the order, decree, or sentence complained of: Provided that no stay of execution shall be competent to the effect of preventing immediate execution of such order, decree, or sentence.

See *Spence* v. *Sinclair* (1883) 20 S.L.R. 726.

General rules, so far as applicable, to extend to penalties and proceedings in Scotland

637 **710.** Nothing in this Act shall be held in any way to annul or restrict the common law of Scotland with regard to the prosecution or punishment of offences at the instance or by the direction of the Lord Advocate, or the rights of owners or creditors in regard to enforcing a judicial sale of any ship and tackle, or to give to the High Court in England any jurisdiction in respect of salvage in Scotland which it has not heretofore had or exercised.

See now Part V (ss. 45–50) of the Administration of Justice Act 1956 for the Admiralty jurisdiction and arrestment of ships in Scotland.

Prosecution of Offences in Colonies

Prosecution of offences in British possession

638 **711.** Any offence under this Act shall, in any British possession,[1] be punishable by any court or magistrate by whom an offence of a like character is ordinarily punishable, or in such other manner as may be

determined by any Act or ordinance having the force of law in that possession.

[1] This is defined as " any part of Her Majesty's dominions exclusive of the United Kingdom "; see Interpretation Act 1889, s. 18 (2), and notes to s. 742 at § 688, *post*.

Application of Part XIII

Application of Part XIII

639 **712.** This Part of this Act shall, except where otherwise provided, apply to the whole of Her Majesty's dominions.

As to the application of certain provisions of Part XIII by Order in Council to foreign countries where Her Majesty has jurisdiction, see note (7) to s. 686.

PART XIV—SUPPLEMENTAL

General Control of [Department of Trade]

Superintendence of merchant shipping by [Department of Trade]

640 **713.** The [Department of Trade] shall be the department to undertake the general superintendence of all matters relating to merchant shipping and seamen, and are authorised to carry into execution the provisions of this Act and of all Acts relating to merchant shipping and seamen for the time being in force, except where otherwise provided by those Acts, or except so far as those Acts relate to the revenue.

641 The powers of the Board of Trade with relation to merchant shipping were successively transferred to the Minister of Shipping (S.R. & O. 1939 No. 1470) and to the Minister of War Transport (S.R. & O. 1941 No. 654), and were then vested in the Minister of Transport (S.R. & O. 1946 No. 375), who was for a time styled the Minister of Transport and Civil Aviation (see S.I. 1953 No. 1204), but who was later restyled the Minister of Transport (see S.I. 1959 No. 1768). Thereafter the functions exercisable by the Minister of Transport in respect of merchant shipping, except those under the M.S. (Liability of Shipowners and Others) Act 1958 (c. 62), s. 2 (6) see (§ 1212, *post*), and except those exercisable under any order made pursuant to the M.S.A. 1906 (c. 48), s. 80 (§810, *post*), in relation to government ships in the service of the Minister of Transport, were transferred to the Board of Trade (see S.I. 1965 No. 145) as were also the Minister's functions under the Oil in Navigable Waters Acts 1955 and 1963. The functions of the Board of Trade relating to the construction, alteration and repair of ships were then transferred to the Minister of Technology (see S.I. 1966 No. 1410). By the Transfer of Functions (Sea Transport, etc.) Order 1968 (S.I. 1968 No. 2038) the function of the Minister of Transport in connection with the provision, acquisition, management and disposal of ships and shipping accommodation and functions exercisable by virtue of the M.S.A. 1906, s. 80 (§ 810, *post*), were transferred to the Board of Trade. With the dissolution of the Ministry of Transport (see S.I. 1970 No. 1681) and the restyling of the Ministry of Technology as the Department for Trade and Industry (see S.I. 1970 No. 1537), all functions under the Merchant Shipping Acts are now transferred to the Secretary of State. In 1974 the Department of Trade and Industry was divided into two: the Department of Trade, and the Department of Industry, and the functions of the D.T.I. with respect to merchant shipping were allocated to the former: S.I. 1974 No. 692. Any reference to the Board of Trade or their officers or Department in (*inter alia*) the Merchant Shipping Acts or in any Order in Council, order, rule, regulation or scheme made thereunder is now to be construed as a reference to the Secretary of State or his officers or Department.

The Secretary of State is also given the control and superintendence of particular matters by various sections throughout the Act. See, *e.g.* as to wreck, s. 566. He is also given dispensing powers (s. 78) and power to appoint advisory committees (s. 79) by the M.S.A. 1906.

Returns as to merchant shipping to [Department of Trade]

642 **714.** All consular officers and officers of customs abroad, and all *local marine boards and* [1] superintendents [2] shall make and send to the [Secretary of State for Trade] such returns or reports on any matter relating to British merchant shipping or seamen as the [Secretary of State] may require.

[1] The words in italics were repealed by the M.S.A. 1970, s. 100 (3) and Sched. 5, as from January 1, 1973: see S.I. 1972 No. 1977.

[2] For provisions as to superintendents, etc., see M.S.A. 1970, s. 81.

Production of log-books, etc., by superintendents

643 **715.** All superintendents shall, when required by the [Secretary of State for Trade], produce to that [Secretary of State] or to [his] officers all official log-books [1] and other documents which are delivered to them under this Act.

[1] For official log-books, now see M.S.A. 1970, s. 68.

Application of fees, fines, etc.

644 **716.**—(1) All fees and other sums (other than fines) received by the [Secretary of State for Trade] under the *Second, Fourth and* Fifth Parts of this Act shall be carried to the account of the Mercantile Marine Fund.[1]

(2) All fines coming into the hands of the [Secretary of State for Trade] under this Act shall be paid into the Exchequer as the Treasury may direct, and shall be carried to and form part of the Consolidated Fund.[2]

[1] By the M.S. (Mercantile Marine Fund) Act 1898, s. 1 (1) (*a*), these sums are now to be paid into the Exchequer, so that the distinction between them and fines has ceased. Compare subs. (1) with s. 676 (1) (*b*), which covers the same ground with respect to Parts II and V, but excepts forfeitures as well as fines.

As to the application of fines, forfeitures, fees, etc., generally, see ss. 62, 676, 699, etc.

[2] By s. 33 (4) of the M.S. (Safety Convention) Act 1949, *post*, the provisions of this subsection apply to fines under that Act as it applies to fines under this Act.

Legal proceedings

645 **717.** The [Secretary of State for Trade] may take any legal proceedings under this Act in the name of any of [his] officers.

Expenses of Commissioners of Customs

Expenses incurred by Commissioners of Customs

646 **718.** All expenses incurred by the Commissioners of Customs [1] in the conduct of suits or prosecutions, or otherwise in carrying into effect the provisions of this Act, shall be considered as expenses having reference to the Revenues of Customs, and shall be paid accordingly; but the [Secretary of State for Trade] may, with the consent of the Treasury, repay [out of moneys provided by Parliament] [2] all or any part of such of the expenses so paid as are under this Act chargeable on that fund.

[1] Now Commissioners of Customs and Excise: see Customs and Excise Act 1952, s. 318 (1).

[2] The amendment in square brackets is the effect of M.S. (Mercantile Marine Fund) Act 1898, s. 1 (1) (*b*).

Documents and Forms

Proof of documents

647 **719.** All documents purporting to be made, issued, or written by or under the direction of the [Secretary of State for Trade], and to be sealed

with the seal of the [Secretary of State], or to be signed by [his] secretary or one of [his] assistant secretaries, or, if a certificate, by one of the officers of the Marine Department, shall be admissible in evidence in manner provided by this Act.

See s. 695, etc. as to admissibility under the Act.

For an instance of the refusal of the court to admit as evidence a document purporting to issue from the Board of Trade which was not sealed or signed as provided by this section, see *The Yarmouth* [1909] P. 293, at p. 297.

Power of [Secretary of State for Trade] to prescribe forms

648 **720.**—(1) Subject to any special provisions of this Act [1] the [Secretary of State for Trade] may prepare and sanction forms for any book, instrument, or paper required under this Act, other than those required under the First Part of this Act,[2] and may make such alterations in these forms as [he thinks] fit.

(2) The [Secretary of State] shall cause every such form to be sealed with [his] seal or marked with some other distinguishing mark, and before finally issuing any form or making any alteration in a form shall cause public notice thereof to be given in such manner as the [Secretary of State thinks] requisite in order to prevent inconvenience.

(3) The [Secretary of State for Trade] shall cause all such forms to be supplied to all custom houses and mercantile marine offices in the United Kingdom, free of charge, or at such moderate prices as the [Secretary of State] may fix, or the [Secretary of State] may license any persons to print and sell the forms.

(4) Every such book, instrument, or paper, required under this Act shall be made in the form (if any) approved by the [Secretary of State for Trade], or as near thereto as circumstances permit, and unless so made shall not be admissible in evidence in any civil proceeding on the part of the owner or master of any ship.[3]

(5) Every such book, instrument, or paper, if made in a form purporting to be the proper form, and to be sealed or marked in accordance with this section, shall be deemed to be in the form required by this Act unless the contrary is proved.

1 *e.g.* the form of salvage bond under s. 558 is scheduled to the Act.
2 As to such forms, see s. 65 and Sched. I.
3 As to admissibility of documents generally, see ss. 694, 695.

Exemption from stamp duty

649 **721.** The following instruments shall be exempt from stamp duty:—

(*a*) any instruments used for carrying into effect the First Part of this Act [1]; and

(*b*) any instruments used by or under the direction of the [Secretary of State for Trade] in carrying into effect the *Second*,[2] Fifth, Eleventh, and Twelfth Parts of this Act; and (*c*) any instruments which are by those Parts of this Act required to be in a form approved by the [Secretary of State for Trade], if made in that form.

Exemptions from stamp duty are also contained in various sections dealing with particular instruments. See also general exemption (2) in Sched. I to Stamp Act 1891, relating to exemptions in respect of instruments for the sale, transfer or other disposition of ships; and see Finance Act 1944, s. 45, for exemption of certain assignments of wages in payment of contributions to certain approved bodies (see note (2) to s. 163). On the other hand, the exemption from stamp duty in respect of indentures of apprenticeship (s. 108 (1)) has been repealed by the Finance Act 1949, s. 52 (10), Sched. XI, Pt. V.

[1] See s. 65 and Sched. I.

[2] The word in italics is prospectively repealed by the M.S.A. 1970, s. 100 (3) and Sched. 5.

Offences as to use of forms

650 **722.**—(1) If any person—

(*a*) forges, assists in forging, or procures to be forged, the seal or any other distinguishing mark of the [Secretary of State for Trade] on any form issued by the [Secretary of State for Trade] under this Act; or

(*b*) fraudulently alters, or assists in fraudulently altering, or procures to be fraudulently altered, any such form,

that person shall in respect of each offence be guilty of a misdemeanor.[1]

(2) If any person—

(*a*) *when a form approved by the [Secretary of State] is, under the Second Part of this Act, required to be used, uses without reasonable cause a form not purporting to be a form so approved; or* [2]

(*b*) prints, sells, or uses any document purporting to be a form approved by the [Secretary of State for Trade], knowing the same not to be the form approved for the time being, or not to have been prepared or issued by the [Secretary of State for Trade],

that person shall, for each offence, be liable to a fine not exceeding ten pounds.[1]

[1] For the summary prosecution of misdemeanours, and the recovery of fines, see ss. 680 to 683.

[2] The words in italics are prospectively repealed by the M.S.A. 1970, s. 100 (3) and Sched. 5.

Powers for Enforcing Compliance with Act

Powers for seeing that Act is complied with

651 **723.**—(1) Where any of the following officers, namely:—

any officer of the [Department of Trade],

any commissioned officer of any of Her Majesty's ships on full pay,

any British consular officer,
the Registrar-General of Shipping and Seamen [1] or his assistant,
any chief officer of Customs [2] in any place in Her Majesty's dominions, or
any superintendent, [3]

has reason to suspect that the provisions of this Act, or any law for the time being in force relating to merchant seamen or navigation, is not complied with, that officer [4] may—

(*a*) require the owner, master, or any of the crew of any British ship to produce any official log books [5] or other documents relating to the crew or any member thereof in their respective possession or control;

(*b*) require any such master to produce a list of all persons on board his ship, and take copies of the official log books, or documents, or of any part thereof;

(*c*) muster the crew of any such ship [6]; and

(*d*) summon the master to appear and give any explanation concerning the ship or her crew or the official log books or documents produced or required to be produced.

(2) If any person, on being duly required by an officer authorised under this section, fails without reasonable cause to produce to that officer any such official log book or document as he is required to produce under this section, or refuses to allow the same to be inspected or copied, or impedes any muster of the crew required under this section, or refuses or neglects to give any explanation which he is required under this section to give, or knowingly misleads or deceives any officer authorised under this section to demand any such explanation, that person shall for each offence be liable to a fine not exceeding twenty pounds.

1 See s. 80 of the M.S.A. 1970.
2 As to who are included in this term, see s. 742.
3 See the M.S.A. 1970, s. 81.
4 The powers conferred by subs. (1) may be exercised by a British sea fishery officer: see the Sea Fisheries Act 1968, s. 8 (6).
5 See M.S.A. 1970, s. 68.
6 Power to muster the crew is also now exercisable under or for the purposes of s. 459 (unsafe ships), as amended by M.S.A. 1897, s. 1. For provisions as to mustering of persons on board ship (including the crew) in cases of emergency, see the M.S. (Musters) Rules 1965 (S.I. No. 1113), as amended by S.I. 1975 No. 330, made under s. 427, *ante*.

Surveyors of Ships

Appointment of surveyors

652 **724.**—(1) The [Secretary of State for Trade] may, at such ports as [he thinks] fit, appoint either generally or for special purposes, and on special occasion, any person [he thinks] fit to be a surveyor of ships for the purposes of this Act, and a person so appointed (in this Act referred to as a

surveyor of ships) may be appointed either as a [ship] [1] surveyor or as an engineer surveyor or as both.

(2) The [Secretary of State for Trade] may also appoint a surveyor-general of ships for the United Kingdom.[2]

(3) The [Secretary of State for Trade] may remove any surveyors of ships and fix and alter their remuneration, and may make regulations as to the performance of their duties, and in particular as to the manner in which surveys of [ships [3]] are to be made,[4] as to the notice to be given by them when surveys are required, and as to the amount and payment of any travelling or other expenses incurred by them in the execution of their duties, and may by such regulations determine the persons by whom and the conditions under which the payment of those expenses is to be made.

(4) If a surveyor of ships *demands or* [5] receives directly or indirectly any fee, remuneration, or gratuity whatever in respect of any duties performed by him under this Act otherwise than by the direction of the [Secretary of State for Trade], he shall for each offence be liable to a fine not exceeding fifty pounds.[6]

(5) The duties of a surveyor of ships shall be performed under the direction of the [Secretary of State for Trade], and in accordance with the regulations made by that [Secretary of State].[7]

653 As to saving of appointments made under the repealed Acts, see s. **745**.
For surveys of passenger ships, see ss. 271 *et seq*.

1 " Ship surveyor " was substituted for " shipwright surveyor " by M.S.A. 1906, s. 75.

2 Besides appointing a surveyor-general, the Secretary of State for Trade may appoint such other principal officers in connection with the survey of ships and other matters incidental thereto as he thinks fit. See M.S.A. 1906, s. 75 (4). By s. 8 of the M.S. (Safety and Load Line Conventions) Act 1932, a person appointed to be a surveyor of ships under this section may be appointed as a wireless telegraphy surveyor, and by s. 4 of M.S. (Safety Convention) Act 1949, such surveyors are to be known as " radio surveyors." A surveyor of ships may also inspect a fishing vessel to ensure that it complies with the provisions of the Fishing Vessels (Safety Provisions) Act, 1970, s. 1: see *ibid*. s. 1 (3). As regards the provisions of the Anchors and Chain Cables Act 1967, s. 1, see *ibid*. s. (1) 1 (*c*). The surveyor-general is the proper officer, when required, to certify the tonnage of a foreign ship, which has not been, and cannot be, measured according to British law. See s. 503 (2)(*c*).

3 The word " ships " was substituted for " passenger steamers " by s. 35 of the M.S. (Safety Convention) Act 1949, *post*.

4 Whether the Secretary of State for Trade has power to issue an instruction that declarations of survey shall not be made where vessels do not satisfy certain requirements, *e.g.* as to the material of which certain pipes are to be made, see *Denny* v. *Board of Trade* (1880) 7 R. 1019; 17 S.L.R. 694.

5 The words in italics were repealed by the Theft Act 1968, s. 33 (3) and Sched. 3, Part I.

6 For summary prosecution of offences, see s. 680 (1).

7 As to the general control of the Secretary of State for Trade see s. 713. The regulations under this section are contained in the " Instructions " to surveyors, issued by the Department of Trade from time to time.

Power of surveyor for purpose of survey of ships

654 **725.**—[*This section, which furnished various powers to surveyors for the purpose of survey of ships, was repealed by the M.S.A.* 1970, *s.* 10 (3) *and Sched.* 5 *as from January* 1, 1973: *see S.I.* 1972 *No.* 1977. *See now ibid. s.* 76.]

Returns by surveyors to [Secretary of State for Trade]

655 **726.**—(1) Surveyors of ships shall make such returns to the [Secretary of State for Trade] as that [Secretary of State] may require with respect to the build, dimensions, draught, burden, rate of sailing, room for fuel, and the nature and particulars of machinery and equipments of ships surveyed by them.

(2) The owner, master, and engineer of any ship so surveyed shall, on demand, give to the surveyors all such information and assistance within his power as they require for the purpose of those returns.

(3) If any owner, master, or engineer, on being applied to for that purpose, fails without reasonable cause to give any such information or assistance, he shall for each offence be liable to a fine not exceeding five pounds.[1]

[1] For summary prosecution of offences, see s. 680 (1).

Appointment of surveyors in colonies

656 **727.** The Governor of a British possession may appoint and remove surveyors of ships within the limits of the possession for any purposes of this Act to be carried into effect in that possession.

[*Department of Trade*] *Inspectors*

Appointment of inspectors to report on accidents, etc.

657 **728.** The [Secretary of State for Trade] may as and when [he thinks] fit appoint any person as an inspector to report to [him]—

(*a*) upon the nature and causes of any accident or damage which any ship has sustained or caused, or is alleged to have sustained or caused; or

(*b*) whether the provisions of this Act, or any regulations made under or by virtue of this Act, have been complied with; or

(*c*) whether the hull and machinery of any steamship [1] are sufficient and in good condition.[2]

[1] As to application to ships propelled by electricity, etc., see s. 743.
[2] As to surveys of alleged unsafe ships, see s. 459 (1) (*b*).

Powers of inspectors

658 **729.**—(1) An inspector so appointed (in this Act referred to as a [Department of Trade] inspector) and any person having the powers of a [Department of Trade] inspector [1]—

(*a*) may go on board any ship and inspect the same or any part thereof, or any of the machinery, boats, equipments, or articles on board thereof to which the provisions of this Act apply, not unnecessarily detaining or delaying her from proceeding on any voyage; and

(*b*) may enter and inspect any premises the entry or inspection of which appears to him to be requisite for the purpose of the report which he is directed to make; and

(*c*) may, by summons under his hand, require the attendance of all such persons as he thinks fit to call before him and examine for the purpose of his report, and may require answers or returns to any inquiries he thinks fit to make [2]; and

(*d*) may require and enforce the production of all books, papers, or documents which he considers important for the purpose of his report; and

(*e*) may administer oaths, or may, in lieu of requiring or administering an oath, require every person examined by him to make and subscribe a declaration of the truth of the statements made by him in his examination.[2]

(2) Every witness summoned under this section shall be allowed such expenses as would be allowed to a witness [3] attending on subpoena to give evidence before any court of record, or if in Scotland to a witness attending on citation the Court of Justiciary; and in case of any dispute as to the amount of those expenses, the same shall be referred in England or Ireland to one of the masters or registrars of the High Court,[4] and in Scotland to the Queen's and Lord Treasurer's Remembrancer, and the officer shall, on request made to him for that purpose under the hand of the inspector or person having the powers of an inspector, ascertain and certify the proper amount of those expenses.[2]

(3) If any person refuses to attend as a witness before a [Department of Trade] inspector, or before any person having the powers of a [Department of Trade] inspector, after having been required to do so in manner provided by this section and after having had a tender made to him of the expenses (if any) to which he is entitled under this section, or refuses or neglects to make any answer, or to give any return, or to produce any document in his possession, or to make or subscribe any declarations which an inspector or person having the powers of an inspector is hereby empowered to require, that person shall for each offence be liable to a fine not exceeding ten pounds.[5]

659 [1] Such powers are for special purposes conferred by various sections of the Act upon persons therein mentioned, *e.g.* ss. 420 (3), 431 (1), 459 (6), 463 (5), 488 (2) and 517 (3). See also the M.S.A. 1964, s. 7 (2), M.S. (Load Lines) Act 1967, ss. 11 (2), 17 (1) and 24 (6), the Fishing Vessels (Safety Provisions) Act 1970, s. 1 (3), the M.S.A. 1970, ss. 55 (2), 61 (2) and Sched. 2, Part I, para. 5 (2) and the Prevention of Oil Pollution Act 1971, s. 18 (3)–(5).

[2] See note (3) to s. 471, and cases there cited.

[3] See the Witnesses' Allowance Regulations 1971 (S.I. No. 107) as amended by S.I. 1971 No. 1259, made under the Costs in Criminal Cases Act 1952 (as substituted by the Criminal Appeal Act 1968, s. 52 (1) and Sched. 5, Pt I.) which *inter alia* increases the allowance in

respect of loss of wages payable to a seaman who is detained on shore to give evidence, and thereby misses his ship. See also R.S.C. Ord. 62 and the scales printed in the Appendices to R.S.C. in the *Supreme Court Practice*.

[4] See R.S.C. Ord. 74, r. 1, *post*, Appendix 13, § 3039. As to Ireland, see note, " Application to Northern Ireland and the Republic of Ireland " after notes to s. 742, § 689, *post*.

[5] For summary prosecution of offences, see s. 680 (1).

Penalty for obstructing inspectors in the execution of their duty

660 **730.** If any person wilfully impedes a [Department of Trade] inspector or any person having the powers of a [Department of Trade] inspector in the execution of his duty, whether on board a ship or elsewhere, that person shall for each offence be liable to a fine not exceeding ten pounds,[1] and may be seized and detained by the inspector or person having the powers of an inspector, or by any person or persons whom that inspector or person may call to his assistance, until he can be conveniently taken before some justice of the peace or other officer having proper jurisdiction.

[1] For summary prosecution of offences, see s. 680 (1).

Exemption from Rates and Harbour Dues

Exemption from rates

661 **731.** All lighthouses, buoys, beacons,[1] and all light dues, and other rates, fees, or payments accruing to or forming part of the mercantile marine fund,[2] and all premises or property belonging to or occupied by any of the general lighthouse authorities [3] or by the [Secretary of State for Trade], which are used or applied for the purposes of any of the services for which those dues, rates, fees, and payments are received, and all instruments or writings used by or under the direction of any of the general lighthouse authorities or of the [Secretary of State for Trade] in carrying on those services, shall be exempted from all public, parochial, and local taxes, duties, and rates of every kind.

This exemption does not apply to lighthouses, etc., under the control and management of local authorities. *Mersey Docks and Harbour Board* v. *Llaneilian* (1884) 14 Q.B.D. 770. *Cf. Mersey Docks Trustees* v. *Cameron* (1864) 35 L.J.M.C. 1; 11 H.L. 443. This section does not exempt from rates property belonging to or occupied by the Trinity House, except lighthouses, buoys, beacons, etc.; see the General Rate Act 1967, s. 41.

[1] For definitions of these terms, see s. 742.

[2] Now the General Lighthouse Fund. See M.S. (Mercantile Marine Fund) Act 1898, s. 1 (1) (*c*).

[3] See s. 634.

Exemption from harbour dues

662 **732.** All vessels belonging to or used by any of the general lighthouse authorities [1] or the [Secretary of State for Trade] shall be entitled to enter, resort to, and use any harbours, ports, docks, or piers in the United Kingdom [2] without payment of any tolls, dues, or rates of any kind.

[1] See s. 634.

[2] See note " Application to Northern Ireland and the Republic of Ireland " in notes to s. 742.

Private Signals

Registration of private code of signals

663 **733.**—(1) If a shipowner desires to use for the purpose of a private code any rockets, lights, or other similar signals, he may register those signals with the [Secretary of State for Trade], and that [Secretary of State] shall give public notice of the signals so registered in such manner as [he thinks] requisite for preventing those signals from being mistaken for signals of distress or signals for pilots.

(2) The [Secretary of State] may refuse to register any signals which in [his] opinion cannot easily be distinguished from signals of distress or signals for pilots.

(3) Where a signal has been registered under this section, the use or display thereof by any person acting under the authority of the shipowner in whose name it is registered shall not subject any person to any fine or liability under this Act for using or displaying signals improperly.[1]

[1] See s. 667, false lights; the Pilotage Act 1913, ss. 42 *et seq.*, pilot flags or signals; and the M.S. (Safety Convention) Act 1949, s. 21, signals of distress.

Application of Act to Foreign Ships by Order in Council

Application by Order in Council of provisions of Merchant Shipping Acts to foreign ships

664 **734.** Where it has been made to appear to Her Majesty that the Government of any foreign country is desirous that any of the provisions of this Act, or of any Act hereafter to be passed amending the same, which do not apply to the ships of that country,[1] should so apply and there are no special provisions in this Act for that application,[2] Her Majesty in Council may order [3] that such of those provisions as are in the Order specified shall (subject to the limitations, if any, contained therein) apply to the ships of that country, and to the owners, masters, seamen, and apprentices of those ships, when not locally within the jurisdiction of the government of that country, in the same manner in all respects as if those ships were British ships.

665 As to the application, under the Foreign Jurisdiction Acts, of certain provisions of this Act to foreign countries where Her Majesty has jurisdiction, see note (7) to s. 686.

As to power to exempt foreign ships from provisions of the Act applicable, see *e.g.* s. 363 (survey of passenger and emigrant ships).

As to general power to exempt foreign ships from provisions of the M.S. Acts when the foreign law contains equally effective provisions, see M.S. (Equivalent Provisions) Act 1925, s. 1.

[1] These words were apparently added in 1894 in consequence of the decision in *Chalmers* v. *Scopenich* [1892] 1 Q.B. 735, in which it was held that an Order in Council was not needed in order to enforce the provisions (as to detention of unsafe ships) now contained in ss. 462, 692 (see note thereto) against a foreign ship.

[2] These words were added to preserve the effect of such special provisions as are contained in s. 84 as to tonnage regulations, etc.; s. 424, as to collision regulations; s. 545, as to life salvage. As to the exercise of these special provisions, see notes to those sections.

[3] By the Collision Regulations (Ships and Seaplanes on the Water) and Signals of Distress (Ships) Order, 1965 (S.I. No. 1525) art. 3, made under ss. 418, 424, the collision regulations and distress signals are applied to all the major foreign countries as listed in the Second Schedule to the Order; see *British Shipping Laws* (Vol. 4), *Marsden on Collisions at Sea* (11th ed.) para. 642 and note to s. 424, *ante*.

Powers of Colonial Legislature

Power of Colonial Legislatures to alter provisions of Act

666 **735.**—(1) The Legislature of any British possession may by any Act or Ordinance, confirmed by Her Majesty in Council, repeal, wholly or in part, any provisions of this Act (other than those of the Third Part thereof which relate to emigrant ships),[1] relating to ships registered in that possession [2]; but any such Act or Ordinance shall not take effect until the approval of Her Majesty has been proclaimed in the possession, or until such time thereafter as may be fixed by the Act or Ordinance for the purpose.[3]

(2) Where any Act or Ordinance of the Legislature of a British possession has repealed in whole or in part as respects that possession any provision of the Acts repealed by this Act, that Act or Ordinance shall have the same effect in relation to the corresponding provisions of this Act as it had in relation to the provision repealed by this Act.[4]

667 The reference in this section and in s. 736 to the legislature of a British possession does not include reference to the Parliament of a Dominion: see Statute of Westminster 1931, s. 5; for meaning of " Dominion " see *ibid.* s. 1. It should be noted, however, that certain sections (including s. 5) of the Statute of Westminster did not apply to the Dominion of the Commonwealth of Australia, the Dominion of New Zealand, or Newfoundland, as part of the law of the Dominion unless the section had been adopted by the Dominion; see *ibid.* s. 10. These sections were not adopted by the Commonwealth of Australia until 1942 by the Statute of Westminster Adoption Act 1942, as from September 3, 1939, and by New Zealand until 1947, by the Statute of Westminster Adoption Act 1947, as from November 25, 1947. As from March 31, 1949, Newfoundland became part of the Dominion of Canada (see British North America Act, 1949) and accordingly no adoption by Newfoundland of the material sections is now required.

The effect of these provisions of the Statute of Westminster is that in the case of the Dominion of Canada, the Union of South Africa (no longer a member of the Commonwealth; see the South Africa Act 1962), the Irish Free State (now Republic of Ireland), and the Commonwealth of Australia and Dominion of New Zealand (from the respective dates of adoption of the material provisions), Acts of those Dominions altering the provisions of M.S.A. 1894, relating to ships registered in those countries no longer require confirmation under s. 735 and Acts of those Dominions regulating their own coasting trade are no longer subject to the limitations imposed by s. 736.

668 Sections 735 and 736 must also be construed as though reference therein to the legislation of a British possession does not include a reference to the Parliament of Ceylon (see Ceylon Independence Act 1947, s. 1, Sched. I, para. 3); or to the Parliament of Ghana (see Ghana Independence Act 1957, s. 1, Sched. I, para. 4); or to the legislature of the Federation of Malaya (see Federation of Malaya Independence Act 1957, s. 2 (1), Sched. I, para. 9); or to the legislature of the Republic of Cyprus (see Cyprus Act 1960, s. 1); or to any legislature established for Nigeria or any part thereof (see Nigeria Independence Act 1960, s. 1 (2) (*b*), Sched. I, para. 4); or to the legislature of Sierra Leone (see Sierra Leone Independence Act 1961, s. 1 (2), Sched. II, para. 4); or to the legislature of Tanganyika (see Tanganyika Independence Act 1961, s. 1 (2), Sched. I, para. 4); or to the legislature of Jamaica (see Jamaica Independence Act 1962, s. 1 (2), Sched. I, para. 4); or to the legislature of Trinidad and Tobago (see Trinidad and Tobago Independence Act 1962, s. 1 (2), Sched. I, para. 4); or to the legislature of Uganda (see Uganda Independence Act 1962, s. 1 (2), Sched. I, para. 4); or to the legislature of Kenya (see Kenya Independence Act 1963, s. 1 (2) Sched. I, para. 4);

or to the legislature of Malawi (see Malawi Independence Act 1964, s. 1 (2) Sched. I, para. 4 (*a*)); or to the legislature of Malta (see Malta Independence Act 1964, s. 1 (2) Sched. I, para. 4 (*a*)); or to the legislature of The Gambia (see The Gambia Independence Act 1964, s. 1 (2) Sched. I, para. 4 (*a*)); or to the legislature of Guyana (see Guyana Independence Act 1966, s. 1 (2) Sched. I, para. 4 (*a*)); or to the legislature of Barbados (see the Barbados Independence Act 1966, s. 1 (2) Sched. I, para. 4 (*a*)); or to the legislature of any associated state under the West Indies Act 1967 (see *ibid.* ss. 1 (3), 4 (4) Sched. I, para. 3 (*a*)); or to the legislature of Mauritius (see the Mauritius Independence Act 1968, s. 1 (2), Sched. I, para. 4 (a)); or to the legislature of Fiji (see the Fiji Independence Act 1970, s. 1 (2) Sched. I para. 4 (*a*)).

For the power of the legislatures of India and Pakistan to repeal or amend any Act in so far as it is part of the law of the Dominion, see the Indian Independence Act 1947, s. 6 (2).

" British possession " is defined by the Interpretation Act 1889, s. 18 (2) as " any part of Her Majesty's Dominions exclusive of the United Kingdom."

1 As to the application of such provisions to the colonies, see ss. 366 *et seq.*

2 As to the general power by Order in Council to exempt British ships registered in parts of H.M. Dominions outside Great Britain and Northern Ireland from the provisions of the M.S. Acts on proof that the local law contains equally effective provisions, see M.S. (Equivalent Provisions) Act 1925, s. 2.

3 It seems that, subject to the powers conferred by these sections, the Act, except where otherwise provided, applies to British possessions. See *The Rajah of Cochin* (1859) Swa. 473.

669 Dominion and Colonial legislation under this section has been confirmed by the following Orders in Council:—

(i) M.S. (Confirmation of Legislation) (Federation of Malaya) O. 1953 (No. 195), (but see the Federation of Malaya Independence Act 1957, s. 2, the Malaysia Act 1963, ss. 1 and 3 and the Singapore Act 1966, s. 1).
(ii) M.S. (C. of L.) (Cyprus) Order 1953 (S.I. No. 972) (see however the Cyprus Act 1960, ss. 1–3 and 6).
(iii) M.S. (C. of L.) (Sarawak) Order 1960 (S.I. No. 1963) (see however the Malaysia Act 1963, ss. 1 and 3).
(iv) M.S. (C. of L.) (North Borneo) Ord. 1960 (S.I. No. 2413) (see however the Malaysia Act 1963, ss. 1 and 3).
(v) M.S. (C. of L.) (Federation of Rhodesia and Nyasaland) Order 1961 (S.I. No. 1509) (the Federation was dissolved in 1964, see now the Zambia Independence Act 1964, s. 2, the Southern Rhodesia Act 1965 and the Southern Rhodesia Constitution Order 1965 (S.I. No. 1952)).
(vi) M.S. (C. of L.) (Hong Kong) Order 1965 (S.I. No. 1866).
(vii) M.S. (C. of L.) (Tasmania) Order 1967 (S.I. No. 250).
(viii) M.S. (C. of L.) (Queensland) Order 1972 (S.I. No. 446).
(ix) M.S. (C. of L.) (Bermuda) Order 1973 (S.I. No. 1317).

4 *Cf.* the similar provisions of s. 746 (2) as to local Acts.

Regulation of coasting trade by Colonial Legislature

670 **736.** The Legislature of a British possession may, by any Act or Ordinance, regulate the coasting trade of that British possession, subject in every case to the following conditions:

(*a*) the Act or Ordinance shall contain a suspending clause [1] providing that the Act or Ordinance shall not come into operation until Her Majesty's pleasure thereon has been publicly signified in the British possession in which it has been passed:

(*b*) the Act or Ordinance shall treat all British ships (including the ships of any other British possession) in exactly the same manner as ships of the British possession in which it is made:

(*c*) where by treaty made before the passing of the Merchant Shipping (Colonial) Act 1869 [2] (that is to say, before the thirteenth day of

May, eighteen hundred and sixty-nine), Her Majesty has agreed to grant to any ships of any foreign State any rights or privileges in respect of the coasting trade of any British possession, those rights and privileges shall be enjoyed by those ships for so long as Her Majesty has already agreed or may hereafter agree to grant the same, anything in the Act or Ordinance to the contrary notwithstanding.

See note to s. 735 as to construction of the reference in this section to the legislature of a British possession, and as to general effect on this section of the provisions of the Statute of Westminster 1931.

[1] See *Western Transport Pty. Ltd.* v. *Kropp, etc.* [1965] A.C. 914.
[2] Repealed by s. 745 and Sched. XXII to this Act.

Provision for Foreign Places where Her Majesty has Jurisdiction

Provision for foreign places where Her Majesty has jurisdiction

671 **737.** Where under this Act anything is authorised to be done by to or before a British consular officer, and in any place outside Her Majesty's dominions in which Her Majesty has jurisdiction there is no such officer, such thing may be done in that place by to or before such officer as Her Majesty in Council may direct.

The following Orders in Council made under this section with reference to the territories specified are at present in force:

672 (i) M.S. (Administration in the New Hebrides) Order 1955 (S.I. No. 707).
(ii) M.S. (Administration in the British Solomon Islands Protectorate) Order 1968 (S.I. No. 293).

Orders in Council

Provision as to Orders in Council

673 **738.**—(1) Where Her Majesty has power under this Act, or any Act hereafter to be passed amending the same, to make an Order in Council, Her Majesty may from time to time make that Order in Council, and by Order in Council revoke alter or add to any Order so made.

(2) Every such Order in Council shall be published in the London Gazette,[1] and shall be laid before both Houses of Parliament [2] within one month after it is made, if Parliament be then sitting, or if not, within one month after the then next meeting of Parliament.

(3) Subject to any special provisions of this Act, upon the publication of any such Order the Order shall, as from the date of the publication or any later date mentioned in the Order, take effect [3] as if it were enacted by Parliament.[4]

674 [1] See s. 740, as to publication in *London Gazette*.
[2] Such Orders in Council are now subject to the Statutory Instruments Act 1946. S. 4 (3) of that Act makes provision for copies of instruments to be laid before Parliament normally before they come into operation. See also the Laying of Documents before Parliament (Interpretation) Act 1948, s. 1.

[3] *Quaere*, does this provision prevent the court from inquiring whether the Order in Council is *ultra vires*? It is submitted, not. For it is only " such " an order as Her Majesty " has power to make under the Act " as is " to take effect as if it were enacted by Parliament." See *Minister of Health* v. *R., ex p. Yaffe* [1931] A.C. 494, and contrast *Institute of Patent Agents* v. *Lockwood* [1894] A.C. 347.

[4] As to interpretation of terms used in Orders in Council, see Interpretation Act 1889, s. 31, set out in notes to s. 742.

Transmission and Publication of Documents

Notices, etc., to be in writing and provision as to sending by post

75 **739.**—(1) Where by this Act any notice, authority, order, direction, or other communication is required or authorised to be given or made by the [Secretary of State for Trade], or the Commissioners of Customs,[1] or the Governor of a British possession,[2] to any person not being an officer of such [Secretary of State] or Commissioners, or Governor, the same shall be given or made in writing.

(2) Where any notice or document is by this Act required or authorised to be transmitted or sent, the same may be transmitted or sent by post.

[1] Now Commissioners of Customs and Excise, see Customs and Excise Act 1952, s. 318 (1).

[2] " British possession " is defined by the Interpretation Act 1889, s. 18 (2) as " any part of Her Majesty's dominions exclusive of the United Kingdom "; § 687, *post*.

Publication in London Gazette

76 **740.** Where a document is required by this Act to be published in the London Gazette, it shall be sufficient if notice thereof is published in accordance with the Rules Publication Act 1893.

The Rules Publication Act 1893 was repealed by the Statutory Instruments Act 1946, s. 12 (1). As to publication of statutory instruments in the *London Gazette*, see now s. 12 (2) of that Act. As to the Republic of Ireland, see note " Application to Northern Ireland and the Republic of Ireland " in notes to s. 742; § 689, *post*.

Exemption of Her Majesty's Ships

Exemption of Her Majesty's ships

77 **741.** This Act shall not, except where specially provided,[1] apply to ships belonging to Her Majesty.[2]

[1] See s. 73 (3) (seizing illegal colours); s. 516 (naval officer as receiver of wreck); ss. 557 *et seq.* (salvage); ss. 76, 692 (detention of ships by naval officers).

As to salvage by H.M. ships, see, too, Crown Proceedings Act 1947, s. 8, referred to in notes to s. 557, and set out *post*.

As to registration and application of the Merchant Shipping Acts to certain Government ships, see M.S.A. 1906, s. 80, and note to s. 419.

[2] As to what ships are included in this expression, see note (1) to s. 557 and *The Loredano* [1922] P. 201, cited in note (1) to Maritime Conventions Act 1911, s. 8, § 844, *post*. See also *Commonwealth of Australia* v. *Asiatic Steam Navigation Co. Ltd. and Others* (*the River Loddon*) [1955] 1 Lloyd's Rep. 503 (limitation of liability of an Australian Government ship). Also see the definition in the Crown Proceedings Act 1947, s. 38 (1), *post*.

Definitions and Provisions as to Application of Act

678 Many expressions, not included in s. 742, are defined in various sections throughout the Act. See INDEX under the words themselves. For the meanings of many expressions occurring but not defined in this Act, see also the Interpretation Act 1889, set out at end of notes to this section; § 687, *post*.

Definitions

679 **742.** In this Act,[1] unless the context otherwise requires, the following expressions have the meanings [2] hereby assigned to them, that is to say—

"Vessel" includes any ship or boat, or any other description of vessel used in navigation [3];

"Ship" includes every description of vessel used in navigation not propelled by oars [4];

"Foreign-going ship" [5] includes every ship employed in trading [5] or going between some place or places in the United Kingdom,[6] and some place or places situate beyond the following limits; that is to say, the coasts of the United Kingdom,[6] the Channel Islands, and Isle of Man, and the continent of Europe between the River Elbe and Brest inclusive;

"Home-trade ship" includes every ship employed in trading [5] or going within the following limits; that is to say, the United Kingdom,[6] the Channel Islands, and Isle of Man, and the continent of Europe between the River Elbe and Brest inclusive;

"Home-trade passenger ship" means every home-trade ship employed in carrying passengers [7];

"Master" includes every person (except a pilot) having command or charge of any ship [7a];

"Seaman" includes every person (except [masters and pilots]),[8] employed or engaged in any capacity on board any ship [9];

"Wages" includes emoluments [10];

"Effects" includes clothes and documents;

"Salvor" means, in the case of salvage services rendered by the officers or crew or part of the crew of any ship belonging to Her Majesty, the person in command of that ship;

"Pilot" means any person not belonging to a ship who has the conduct thereof;

680 "Court" in relation to any proceeding includes any magistrate or justice having jurisdiction in the matter to which the proceeding relates [11];

"Colonial Court of Admiralty" has the same meaning as in the Colonial Courts of Admiralty Act 1890;

"A Commissioner for Oaths" means a commissioner for oaths within the meaning of the Commissioners for Oaths Act 1889;

"Chief Officer of Customs" includes the collector, superintendent, principal coast officer, or other chief officer of customs at each port;

"Superintendent" shall, so far as respects a British Possession, include any shipping master or other officer discharging in that possession the duties of a superintendent [12];

"Consular Officer," when used in relation to a foreign country, means the officer recognised by Her Majesty as a consular officer of that foreign country [13];

"Bankruptcy" includes insolvency;

"Representation" means probate, administration, confirmation, or other instrument constituting a person the executor, administrator, or other representative of a deceased person;

"Legal personal representative" means the person so constituted executor, administrator, or other representative of a deceased person;

"Name" includes a surname;

"Port" includes place;

"Harbour" includes harbours properly so called, whether natural or artificial, estuaries, navigable rivers, piers, jetties, and other works in or at which ships can obtain shelter, or ship and unship goods or passengers [14];

"Tidal water" means any part of the sea and any part of a river within the ebb and flow of the tide at ordinary spring tides, and not being a harbour;

"Harbour authority" includes all persons or bodies of persons, corporate or unincorporate, being proprietors of, or instrusted with, the duty or invested with the power of constructing, improving, managing, regulating, maintaining, or lighting a harbour;

"Conservancy authority" includes all persons or bodies of persons, corporate or unincorporate, intrusted with the duty or invested with the power of conserving, maintaining or improving the navigation of a tidal water;

"Lighthouse" shall in addition to the ordinary meaning of the word include any floating and other light exhibited for the guidance of ships, and also any sirens and any other description of fog signals, and also any addition to a lighthouse of any improved light, or any siren, or any description of fog signal [14];

"Buoys and beacons" includes all other marks and signs of the sea;

"The Trinity House" shall mean the master wardens and assistants of the guild, fraternity, or brotherhood of the most glorious and undivided Trinity and of St. Clement in the parish of Deptford Strond in the county of Kent, commonly called the corporation of the Trinity House of Deptford Strond;

"The Commissioners of Irish Lights" means the body incorporated by that name under the local Act of the session held in the thirtieth and thirty-first years of the reign of Her present Majesty, chapter eighty-one intituled "An Act to alter the constitution of the Corporation for preserving and improving the Port of Dublin and for other purposes connected with that body and with the Port of Dublin Corporation," and any Act amending the same [15];

"Lifeboat service" means the saving, or attempted saving of vessels, or of life, or property on board vessels, wrecked or aground or sunk, or in danger of being wrecked or getting aground or sinking.

Any reference to failure to do any act or thing shall include a reference to refusal to do that act or thing.

681 1 The succeeding Merchant Shipping Acts provide that they "shall be construed as one" with earlier Merchant Shipping Acts. One of the consequences of this is that the definitions in this section may be used in the construction of the later Acts.

2 As to the construction of definitions or interpretation clauses in which the word "includes" is used, see note (4).

3 For the meaning of "vessel" in the provisions of Part IX as to removal of wreck, see s. 532. See also cases cited in note (4) under "ship."

In *Edwards* v. *Quickenden and Forester* [1939] P. 261 it was held that neither a skiff nor a rowing eight, which were in collision on the River Thames, was a "vessel" within the meaning of the Maritime Conventions Act 1911, and that therefore that Act did not apply, and that, as each was guilty of negligence, there could be no recovery by either against the other, under the then existing common law rule. Henn Collins J. said: "The definition 'ship' includes or embraces every description of vessel, which includes in turn, if one refers back to the definition 'vessel,' 'any ship or boat'; but by the definition of 'ship' any vessel of any description is only included if it is not propelled by oars. In other words, no vessel which is propelled by oars is within the definition 'vessel.'" It is suggested, however, that the skiff and the eight could properly be regarded as "boats" rather than "ships," and thus come within the definition of "vessels."

A vessel which has just been launched and is water-borne, though incapable of self-propulsion or self-direction, is a "vessel" within the definition: *The St. Machar* (1939) 65 Ll.L.R. 119.

682 4 "Ship"—The definition of ship given in this section has in its application to certain parts of the M.S. Acts been in effect extended by two later M.S. Acts as follows:—

(i) M.S. (Liability of Shipowners and Others) Act 1958, s. 4 (1), provides that Part VIII of the Merchant Shipping Act 1894, which deals with limitation of liability, "shall apply to any structure, whether completed or in course of completion, launched and intended for use in navigation as a ship or part of a ship," and that the expression "ship" in that Part VIII and in the 1958 Act shall be construed accordingly.

(ii) M.S.A. 1921, s. 1, which provides that, notwithstanding anything contained in s. 742, the 1894 Act shall have effect as though in the provisions of Part I (registry) and Part VIII (limitation of liability), as amended or extended by any subsequent enactment, "ship" included "every description of lighter, barge or like vessel used in navigation in Great Britain, however propelled: Provided that a lighter, barge, or like vessel used exclusively in non-tidal waters, other than harbours, shall not, for the purposes of this Act, be deemed to be used in navigation."

A further refinement of definition is introduced by the Crown Proceedings Act 1947, s. 5 (6) as amended by the M.S. (Liability of Shipowners and Others) Act 1958, s. 8 (5), which provides that for the purposes of the section (applying limitation of liability to Crown ships) the word "ship" shall have the meaning assigned to it by s. 742, M.S.A. 1894, but shall include also: (a) any structure to which Part VIII of the 1894 Act is applied by s. 4 of the M.S. (Liability of Shipowners and Others) Act 1958 (see under (i) above); and (b) every description of lighter, barge, etc., which comes within the definition in M.S.A. 1921, s. 1 (see under (ii) above).

In s. 30 (3) of the Crown Proceedings Act 1947 which deals with the limitation of actions, yet another definition is given for the purposes of that section: namely, "the expression 'ship' includes any boat or other description of vessel used in navigation."

The Anchors and Chain Cables Act 1967 also applies the definition of ship contained in this section: see *ibid.* s. 1 (7).

For provisions relating to hovercraft, see the Hovercraft Act 1968, § 1317, *post.*

The decisions cited in the following notes are for the most part decisions upon the original definition before these modifications, and accordingly care should be exercised in their application under present conditions.

The word " includes " in an interpretation clause is used by way of extension. Hence it would seem that the present clause does not exclude vessels which are at times propelled by oars, or vessels which are not used in navigation, in cases where, but for the clause, they would be within the term " ship." The purpose for which a vessel has been and is being used is material on the question of fact whether she is being used for navigation. See *St. John Pilot Commrs.* v. *Cumberland Ry. and Coal Co.* [1910] A.C. 208.

Accordingly a " coble," 24 feet long, partly decked, and having removable masts, etc. for sailing, and of a class which go 20 miles out to sea, was held to be a " ship " within the M.S.A. 1854, 1862, although she was fitted with oars with which she was propelled when in harbour. *Ex p. Ferguson and Hutchinson* (1871) L.R. 6 Q.B. 280.

And a hopper barge used for dredging, having a bow, stern and rudder, but not furnished with any means of propulsion, being of a class which is always towed, was held to be a ship within the M.S.A. 1854, ss. 2 and 458 (1894, ss. 544 and 742), Lord Coleridge C.J. observing that it was immaterial to consider whether she was " used in navigation." *The Mac* (1882) 7 P.D. 126; reversing 7 P.D. 38, etc.

83 In *The Mudlark* [1911] P. 116 Bargrave-Deane J., following *The Mac, supra,* granted a decree of limitation of liability to a hopper barge used for dredging purposes, with a rudder, but no means of propulsion, which was towed to her destination by a tug. So in *The Harlow* [1922] P. 175, dumb barges, not propelled by oars but fitted with rudders and used in tow of tugs for the carriage of goods in the River Thames were held to be " ships." As to dumb barges propelled by oars, see further below.

Where, however, the vessel was an electric launch of only about three tons burden, used for carrying passengers upon a small artificial lake, she was held not to be a ship, on the ground that, having regard to the size of the lake, she was not a vessel " used in navigation," it being apparently assumed that such a vessel would not be within the term " ship " unless brought within it by the extension in the interpretation clause. *Southport Corporation* v. *Morris* [1893] 1 Q.B. 359.

This case was distinguished in *Weeks* v. *Ross* [1913] 2 K.B. 229, where the court held to be a " vessel used in navigation " a small motor-boat carrying passengers on a river and canal connected by means of locks with a tidal estuary. In *Ex p. Ferguson, supra,* Blackburn J. said that every vessel which substantially goes to sea is a " ship," whether propelled by oars or not. And in *The C. S. Butler* (1874) L.R. 4 A. & E. 238; 31 L.T. 549, Sir R. Phillimore, professing to follow the last cited decision, held that a vessel was not a " ship " unless her real habitual business was to go to sea. See also *Oakes* v. *Monkland Iron Co., infra* (note 9).

It would appear, however, that the latter proposition is incorrect, and that a vessel, in order to be a ship, need not be sea-going: see *per* Cotton L.J. in *The Mac, supra,* and *Weeks* v. *Ross, supra.* As to " sea-going ship " see *The Salt Union* v. *Wood* [1893] 1Q.B. 370.

84 In *The Champion* [1934] P. 1 the question arose whether the Admiralty jurisdiction of county courts included jurisdiction to try a case of collision between two vessels, one of which was unquestionably a ship, and the other of which was a dumb barge, fitted with rowing chocks and a rudder, which at the time of the collision was in the tow of a tug. The court (Merriman P. and Bateson J.) held that even if the barge was not a ship, the county court, in its Admiralty jurisdiction, had jurisdiction to try a case of collision between two vessels one of which was a ship. This was decisive of the case, but the two learned judges further considered, and differed upon, the question whether the barge was properly to be considered a ship. Merriman P. took the view that the barge was not a ship since at many other times she was propelled by oars; the test was not, he held, whether she was in fact being propelled by oars at the material time. Bateson J., on the other hand, was of opinion that as the barge was at the material time being propelled by the steam of the tug she could not be regarded as " propelled by oars " within the meaning of those words in the definition of " ship." See now County Courts Act 1959, when " ships " is expressed to include any description of vessel used in navigation; *ibid.* s. 201.

A vessel which had been registered, but had for four years been used as a coal hulk, was held not to be a ship. *The European and Australian R.M. Co.* v. *Peninsular and Oriental S. Nav. Co.* (1864) 12 Jur.(N.S.) 909; 14 L.T. 704.

Nor, it seems, is a dumb barge propelled by oars a ship within the exception of " ship " in s. 4 of the Bills of Sale Act 1878, though it is a " vessel." See *Gapp* v. *Bond,* cited in note (1) to s. 24. See also *The Owen Wallis* (1874) L.R. 4 A. & E. 175; *Everard* v. *Kendall* (1870) L.R. 5 C.P. 428. But see now M.S.A. 1921 (lighters, barges, etc.), cited at head of this note.

But a dumb barge made fast to the side of a tug for towage has been held to be a " ship " for the purpose of the Collision Regulations. *The Lighter No.* 3 (1902) 18 T.L.R. 322. See, too, *The Mudlark*, *supra*, and *British Shipping Laws* (Vol. 4), *Marsden on Collisions at Sea* (11th ed.), paras. 149, 180, 428.

As to a vessel at the time of being launched, before receiving her engines and boilers, see *The Andalusian* (1878) 3 P.D. 182 (see note to s. 2); *The United States* (1865) 12 L.T. 33; 2 M.L.C.(o.s.) 166; and *cf. Re Softley, ex p. Winter* (or *ex p. Hodgkin*) (1875) L.R. 20 Eq. 746 (equitable mortgage of unfinished vessel before launch). See also *Gibson* v. *Small* (1853) 4 H.L.Cas. 353. But see M.S. (Liability of Shipowners and Others) Act 1958, referred to at head of this note.

In *The Craighall* [1910] P. 207 (C.A.), the C.A. held that a floating landing stage was not a " vessel " within R.S.C., Ord. 19, r. 28 (" preliminary acts "). See, too, *The Gas Float Whitton No.* 2 [1897] A.C. 337 (floating beacon not subject of salvage), cited in note (3) to s. 547; and *Marine Craft Constructors Ltd.* v. *Erland Blomquist Engineers Ltd.* [1953] 1 Lloyd's Rep. 514 (a pontoon stripped of its crane and used temporarily for carrying goods in tow of a tug); *Cook* v. *Dredging & Construction Co. Ltd.* [1958] 1 Lloyd's Rep. 334 (a blower boat was a " ship " for the purposes of the Docks Regulations 1934).

Where an insurance policy covered a vessel against loss by collision with " any other ship or vessel," it was held that a flying-boat, with which the insured vessel collided, was not a " ship or vessel." *Polpen Shipping Co. Ltd.* v. *Commercial Union Assurance Co. Ltd.* [1943] K.B. 161.

As to the meaning of the term " steamship " in a bill of lading, see *Fraser* v. *Telegraph Construction, etc. Co.* (1872) L.R. 7 Q.B. 566. In *Merchants' Marine Ins. Co.* v. *North of England P. & I. Ass.* (1926) 43 T.L.R. 107; 32 Com.Cas. 165, C.A., a pontoon carrying a crane but with no rudder or propelling machinery, capable of being moved but generally permanently moored was held not to be a " ship or vessel " within the rules of its insurance club. *Cf. The Titan* (1923) 14 Ll.L.R. 484; *Floating Elevator Hezekiah Baldwin* (1878) 8 Benedict 556 (American case).

As to whether a sunken wreck remains a vessel, see *Chandler* v. *Blogg* [1898] 1 Q.B. 32; *Pelton S.S. Co.* v. *North of England P. & I. Ass.* (1925) 22 Ll.L.R. 510.

It should be noticed that while the provisions of this Act with regard to transfer (s. 24) and mortgage (s. 31) apply only to " registered ships," the exception from the application of the Bills of Sale Acts 1878–1882, extends to transfers or assignments of any ship or vessel or any share therein. It would seem that the transfer or mortgage of a vessel " used in navigation " but " propelled by oars " is not governed by any of these Acts. See ss. 24 and 31 and notes thereto.

685 5 A " home trade ship " is exempt from the requirement of carrying a pilot in the River Thames by regulations under s. 11 (4) of the Pilotage Act 1913. A ship is not so exempted if it is calling first at a port within the limits referred to in s. 742 and then sailing to a port outside those limits; *Smith* v. *Van Der Veen* [1955] 1 Lloyd's Rep. 438. As to certain ships engaged in fishing being deemed to be foreign-going ships, see s. 744. As to meaning of " trading," see Pilotage Act 1913, *post*, s. 11, notes (19) and (20).

6 " United Kingdom " here includes the Republic of Ireland. See note " Application to Northern Ireland and the Republic of Ireland," *infra*.

7 As to who are " passengers," see s. 267 and notes thereto; Pilotage Act 1913, s. 11, note (5). A pilot cutter is not a " home-trade passenger ship." *The Charles Livingston* (1941) 69 Ll.L.R. 180.

7a The definition of master has been applied by the Administration of Justice Act 1956, Sched. 1, para. 8 (1), the County Courts Act 1959, s. 61 (1) and the Anchors and Chain Cables Act 1967, s. 1 (7).

8 The words in italics were substituted by the M.S.A. 1970, s. 100 (3) and Sched. 3, para. 4.

9 " Seamen."—In *R.* v. *Judge of City of London Court* (1890) 25 Q.B.D. 339, Lord Coleridge C.J. said that this definition would undoubtedly include such a person as a stevedore. And in *Re The Great Eastern S.S. Co.* (1885) 53 L.T. 594; 5 Asp.M.L.C. 511, following *Wells* v. *Osman* (1704) 2 Ld.Raym. 1044, persons were allowed to sue as seamen for wages in respect of services rendered to a vessel in port. That decision appears to have partly rested on the fact that they had been engaged for a voyage, though the vessel in fact never proceeded thereon. But in *Thomson* v. *Hart* (1890) (Sc.) 28 Sc.L.R. 28: 18 Ct. of Sess.Cas. (4th Ser.) Just. Cases 3, the definition was held to include a person engaged as store-keeper of a ship while in port, who had not yet been engaged for the voyage.

A steward in charge of a bar is " a seaman." *Thompson* v. *H. & W. Nelson* [1913] 2 K.B. 523.

The term appears to include medical practitioners, cooks etc. when part of the complement of the ship (see M.S.A. 1970, s. 43).

The term also includes lascars serving on a British ship. See *Peninsular and Oriental Steam Navigation Co.* v. *The King* [1901] 2 K.B. 686.

As to the position of a female acting as cook and steward, and partly as sailor, see *The Jane and the Matilda* (1823) 1 Hagg. 187.

In *Oakes* v. *Monkland Iron Co.* (1884) 21 S.L.R. 407 (Sc.), a fireman on a steam barge plying exclusively on an inland canal was held to be a " workman," and not a " seaman," within the Employers and Workmen Act 1875, ss. 10, 13.

As to the position of a person who messes with the master but helps in working the ship in return for his passage, see *The Hanna* (1866) L.R. 1 A. & E. 283.

Persons employed in the capacity of seamen are not excluded from the rights of seamen under the Act by the fact that the agreement with the master was oral, when required by former ss. 113, 114 to be in a certain form. *Re The Great Eastern S.S. Co.*, *supra*; (see now M.S.A. 1970, s. 1).

36 [10] A war bonus entered on the ship's articles has been held to be part of the crew's emoluments, and therefore part of their wages within M.S.A. 1906, s. 28. *Shelford* v. *Mosey* [1917] 1 K.B. 154.

A steward's commission on receipts from bar is part of his wages, and therefore is irrecoverable unless entered on the ship's articles (ss. 113, 114). *Thompson* v. *H. & W. Nelson* [1913] 2 K.B. 523. See too, *The Elmville* (*No.* 2) [1904] P. 422 (bonus).

" Wages " includes victualling allowance. *Kinley* v. *Sierra Nevada* (1924) 18 Ll.L.R. 294. " Wages " also includes the master's National Insurance contributions, where it has been agreed that these should be paid by the owner; *The Gee Whiz* [1951] 1 Lloyd's Rep. 145; and also claims for social benefit that have been incorporated in the contract of service; *The Arosa Kulm* (*No.* 2) [1960] 1 Lloyd's Rep. 97. See also *The Arosa Star* [1959] 2 Lloyd's Rep. 396. The master can include in a claim under s. 167 a claim for wages due after a wrongful determination of an ordinary mariner's contract of service, though not a special contract of service, *The British Trade* [1924] P. 104; the *Arosa Star* (*supra*). Wages also include deductions made by a master from crew's gross wages in respect of social service or trade union contributions which the crew or the master are liable to pay: see *The Fairport* [1965] 2 Lloyd's Rep. 183, *The Westport No.* 4 [1968] 2 Lloyd's Rep. 559. *In the Fairport* (No. 2) [1966] 2 Lloyd's Rep. 7, it was held that *The Carolina* (1875) 3 Asp. M.L.C. 141 was wrongly decided and accordingly that the institution of a wages claim did not terminate the contract of service and that wages continued to accrue after the proceedings were commenced. And see cases cited in note (3) to M.S.A. 1970, s. 7.

[11] This definition of " court " does not exclude every person not a " magistrate or justice," etc. See *Board of Trade* v. *Leith Local Marine Board* (1896) 24 R. 177.

[12] See s. 247 as to business of superintendents.

[13] " Consular officer " by the Interpretation Act 1889, s. 12 (20), includes consul-general, consul, vice-consul, consular agent, and any person for the time authorised to discharge the duties of consul-general, consul, or vice-consul.

[14] The definition of harbour has been applied by the Harbours Act 1964, s. 57 (1).

[15] Such an addition may be treated as a separate lighthouse: see s. 642. The definition has been applied by the Harbours Act 1964, s. 57 (1).

INTERPRETATION ACT 1889

37 NOTE.—The following definitions are contained in the Interpretation Act 1889, and unless the contrary intention appears, the several expressions there defined are to have the same meaning in the M.S. Acts; see Interpretation Act 1889, s. 12.

13.—(3) The expression " High Court," when used with reference to England or Ireland, shall mean Her Majesty's High Court of Justice in England or Ireland, as the case may be.

(6) The expression " the Summary Jurisdiction Act 1848," shall mean the Act of the session of the eleventh and twelfth years of the reign of Her present Majesty, chapter forty-three, intituled " An Act to facilitate the performance of the duties of justices of the peace out of sessions within England and Wales with respect to summary convictions and orders."

(7) The expression " the Summary Jurisdiction (England) Acts " and the expression " the Summary Jurisdiction (English) Acts " shall respectively mean the Summary Jurisdiction Act 1848, and the Summary Jurisdiction Act 1879, and any Act, past or future, amending those Acts or either of them.

(8) The expression " the Summary Jurisdiction (Scotland) Acts " shall mean

the Summary Jurisdiction (Scotland) Acts 1864 and 1881, and any Act, past or future, amending those Acts or either of them.

(9) [*Repealed by the Northern Ireland Act* 1962 *s.* 30, *Sched. IV.*]

(10) The expression "the Summary Jurisdiction Acts," when used in relation to England or Wales, shall mean the Summary Jurisdiction (England) Acts and when used in relation to Scotland, the Summary Jurisdiction (Scotland) Acts[1] . . .

(11) The expression "Court of Summary Jurisdiction" shall mean any justice or justices of the peace, or other magistrate, by whatever name called, to whom jurisdiction is given by, or who is authorised to act under, the Summary Jurisdiction Acts, whether in England, Wales, or Ireland, and whether acting under the Summary Jurisdiction Acts or any of them, or under any other Act, or by virtue of his commission, or under the common law.[2]

18.—(1) The expression "British Islands"[3] shall mean the United Kingdom, the Channel Islands,[4] and the Isle of Man.

(2) The expression "British possession" shall mean any part of Her Majesty's dominions[5] exclusive of the United Kingdom, and where parts of such dominions are under both a central and a local legislature, all parts under the central legislature shall, for the purposes of this definition, be deemed to be one British possession.

(3) The expression "Colony"[6] shall mean any part of Her Majesty's dominions[5] exclusive of the British Islands and of British India *and of British Burma*,[7] and where parts of such dominions are under both a central and a local legislature, all parts under the central legislature shall, for the purposes of this definition, be deemed to be one Colony.

(6) The expression "Governor" shall as respects Canada *and India*,[8] mean the Governor-General, and include any person who for the time being has the powers of the Governor-General, and as respects any other British possession [outside British India[8]], shall include the officer for the time being administering the government of that possession.

(7) The expression "Colonial legislature" and the expression "legislature," when used with reference to a British possession shall respectively mean the authority, other than the Imperial Parliament of Her Majesty the Queen in Council, competent to make laws for a British possession.

[18A.[8]—(1) In this Act and in every other Act, whether passed before or after the commencement of this Act,—

(i) the expression "British possession," when used in relation to British territories in India, shall, unless the contrary intention appears, mean British India as a whole, and references, in whatever words, to territories of the Crown abroad shall as respects India be construed accordingly;

(ii) the expression "Governor" shall, when used in relation to British India as a whole or to India as a whole, mean the Governor-General;

(iii) the expression "Governor-General" shall, when used in relation to British India or to India,—

(*a*) in relation to the period between the commencement of Part III of the Government of India Act, 1935, and the establishment of the Federation of India, mean the Governor-General in Council;

(*b*) in relation to any period after the commencement of the said Part III, be construed as including a reference to the Governor of a Province in India acting within the scope of any authority given to him under Part VI of the said Act;

(iv) the expression "Indian legislature" and, when used in relation to British India or to India, the expression "legislature" shall mean the authority, other than the Imperial Parliament competent to make laws for British India or for the relevant part of British India.

(2) . . .]

19. In this Act and in every Act passed after the commencement of this Act the expression "person" shall, unless the contrary intention appears, include any body of persons corporate or unincorporate.[9]

31. Where any Act, whether passed before or after the commencement of this Act, confers power to make, grant, or issue any instrument, that is to say, any Order in Council, order, warrant, scheme, letters patent, rules, regulations, or byelaws, expressions used in the instrument, if it is made after the commencement of this Act, shall, unless the contrary intention appears, have the same respective meanings as in the Act conferring the power.

38.—(1) Where this Act or any Act passed after the commencement of this Act repeals and re-enacts, with or without modification any provisions of a former Act, references in any other Act to the provisions so repealed, shall, unless the contrary intention appears, be construed as references to the provisions so re-enacted.

688 [1] The remainder of this paragraph has been repealed by the Northern Ireland Act 1962, s. 30, Sched. IV. The Summary Jurisdiction Acts have now, as respects England and Wales, been substantially repealed and replaced by the Magistrates' Courts Act 1952. For definition of "magistrates' court," see *ibid*. s. 124.

[2] As respects Northern Ireland, this paragraph has been repealed by the Northern Ireland Act 1962, s. 30, Sched. IV.

[3] But see note " Application to Northern Ireland and the Republic of Ireland," *infra.*

[4] The Channel Islands are not within the United Kingdom; see *Navigators and General Insurance Co., Ltd.* v. *Ringrose* [1962] 1 All E.R. 97, C.A.

[5] The Burma Independence Act 1947, s. 1 (1), the Ireland Act 1949, s. 1 (1), the Lesotho Independence Act 1966, the Aden etc. Act 1967, s. 1 (1) and the Uganda Act 1964 all recite that the territories concerned ceased to be part of Her Majesty's Dominions. Compare sovereignty and jurisdiction as it appears in the Federation of Malaya Independence Act 1957, s. 1 (2) (*b*), the Cyprus Act 1960, s. 1, and the Malaysia Act 1963, s. 1 (1).

[6] This definition of " colony " must now be read subject to s. 11 of the Statute of Westminster 1931, which provides that " notwithstanding anything contained in the Interpretation Act 1889, the expression ' colony ' shall not in any Act of the Parliament of the United Kingdom passed after the commencement of this Act include a Dominion or any Province or State forming part of a Dominion." Nor does the definition include Ceylon in any Acts of the Parliament of the United Kingdom passed on or after February 4, 1948, or in the Burma Independence Act 1947; see Ceylon Independence Act 1947, s. 4 (2). Nor does the definition include Ghana or any part thereof in any Act passed after March 16, 1957 (Ghana Independence Act 1957, s. 4 (1)), Nigeria or any part thereof in any Act passed after October 1, 1960 (Nigeria Independence Act 1960, s. 3 (1)), Sierra Leone or any part thereof in any Act passed after April 27, 1961 (Sierra Leone Independence Act 1961, s. 3 (1)), or Tanganyika in any Act passed after December 9, 1961, (Tanganyika Independence Act 1961, s. 3 (1)), or Jamaica in any Act passed after August 6, 1962 (Jamaica Independence Act 1962, s. 3 (1)), or Trinidad and Tobago in any Act passed after August 31, 1962 (Trinidad and Tobago Independence Act 1962, s. 3 (1)), or Uganda or any part thereof in any Act passed after October 9, 1962 (Uganda Independence Act 1962, s. 3 (1)), or Kenya in any Act passed after December 12, 1963 (Kenya Independence Act, s. 4 (1)), or Malawi in any Act passed on or after July 6, 1964 (Malawi Independence Act 1964, s. 4 (1)), or Malta in any Act passed on or after September 21, 1964 (Malta Independence Act 1964, s. 4 (1)), or The Gambia in any Act passed on or after February 18, 1965 (The Gambia Independence Act 1964), or Guyana in any Act passed on or after May 26, 1966 (Guyana Independence Act 1966, s. 5 (1)), or Barbados in any Act passed on or after November 30, 1966 (Barbados Independence Act 1966, s. 4 (1)), or Mauritius in any Act passed on or after March 12, 1968 (Mauritius Independence Act 1968, s. 4 (1)), or Fiji in any Act passed on or after October 10, 1970 (Fiji Independence Act 1970, s. 4 (1)). By virtue of the West Indies Act 1967, s. 3 (5) " colony " does not, in any Act passed after the appointed day, include an " associated state " within the meaning of *ibid.* s. 1 (3). The West Indies Act 1967 (Appointed Days) Order 1967 (S.I. No. 222) appointed February 27, 1967 for Antigua, St. Christopher, Nevis and Anguilla, March 1, 1967, for Dominica and St. Lucia and March 3, 1967, for Granada.

[7] The words in italics were added by the Government of India Act 1935, s. 311 (4) and repealed by the Burma Independence Act 1947, s. 5 (3), Sched. II, Part I.

[8] The words in italics were repealed and the words and new section in square brackets were added by the Government of India (Adaptation of Acts of Parliament) Order 1937 (S.R. & O. No. 230), art. 2, Sched., Part 1. This Order continues in force in relation to all Acts in so far as they operate otherwise than as part of the law of British India or India or Pakistan; see Indian Independence Act 1947, s. 18 (2), and India (Consequential Provisions) Act 1949, s. 1.
Wales.—The expression " England " in Acts of Parliament includes Wales. See 20 Geo. 2, c. 42, s. 3.

[9] The Crown is a corporation sole and therefore a person; *Boarland* (*Inspector of Taxes*) v. *Madras Electric Supply Corporation* (in liquidation) [1954] 1 All E.R. 52 at p. 57, C.A.

Application to Northern Ireland and the Republic of Ireland

39 Northern Ireland.—Such parts of the M.S. Acts as before the Government of Ireland Act 1920, applied to Northern Ireland continue to apply, subject to such modifications as have been or may be made by Irish Transfer Orders: Government of Ireland Act 1920, ss. 61, 69. The Supreme Court of Judicature of Northern Ireland, consisting of the High Court of Justice in Northern Ireland and the Court of Appeal in Northern Ireland, now exercises, so far as the M.S. Acts are concerned, the same jurisdiction in Northern Ireland as that previously exercised by the High Court of Justice in Ireland and the Court of Appeal in Ireland: *ibid.* ss. 38 and 40. The High Court of Appeal for Ireland, which was constituted with appellate jurisdiction throughout the whole of Ireland, by *ibid.* s. 38, was abolished by the

Irish Free State (Consequential Provisions) Act 1922, Sched. I, § 6. References to the Lord Lieutenant in any enactment in its application to Northern Ireland are to be construed as references to the Governor of Northern Ireland: *ibid.* Sched I, § 1, and references to the Lord Chancellor of Ireland are to be construed as references to the Lord Chief Justice of Northern Ireland. General Adaptation of Enactments (Northern Ireland), Order 1921, S.R. & O. No. 1804, Art. 5. See, too, the following note as to " Republic of Ireland."

Republic of Ireland.—The creation of the Irish Free State in 1922 (which became successively known as " Eire " by the Eire (Confirmation of Agreements) Act 1938, and is now known as the " Republic of Ireland " by the Republic of Ireland Act 1948 (No. 22 of 1948) (Eire)) necessitated certain changes in the interpretation of the phrases " the United Kingdom," " the United Kingdom of Great Britain," " Great Britain and Ireland," " Great Britain or Ireland," " the British Islands," or " Ireland," where appearing in Imperial Statutes passed before the establishment of the Irish Free State. Although by s. 1 of the Ireland Act 1949, that part of Ireland formerly known as Eire (and before that as the " Irish Free State ") and now known as the Republic of Ireland ceased as from April 18, 1949, to be part of H.M. dominions, it is deemed by virtue of ss. 3 and 4 of the Act to be still part of H.M. dominions for certain purposes (*e.g.* as respects any Act of Parliament or other enactment or instrument passed or made before the passing of the Ireland Act 1949 (or *semble* before the end of 1949), which contains a reference to H.M. dominions which would have extended to the Republic of Ireland had that part of Ireland remained part of H.M. dominions or any Act, enactment or instrument whenever passed or made which whether expressly or by implication is required to be construed in the same way as such an Act, enactment or instrument, it shall have effect as if that reference did so extend to include the Republic of Ireland). Consequently, save that the designation of Irish Free State has changed to Republic of Ireland, the changes in interpretation made necessary by the creation of the Irish Free State remain the same. The interpretation varies with the application of the statute to be interpreted.

690 (1) *In the application of the M.S. Acts to any part of Great Britain and Ireland other than the Republic of Ireland* references to " the United Kingdom " or " the United Kingdom of Great Britain and Ireland " or " Great Britain and Ireland " or " Great Britain or Ireland " or " the British Islands " or " Ireland " generally *exclude* the Republic of Ireland but *include* the Republic of Ireland in the following cases only: M.S.A. 1894, s. 3, s. 546, s. 555, s. 556 and s. 558, s. 742 so far as it defines " foreign-going ship " and " home-trade ship "; M.S. (Mercantile Marine Fund) Act 1898, Second Schedule, Rules 4 and 5; M.S.A. 1906, s. 77 (1), where the expression " United Kingdom " secondly occurs; the Pilotage Act 1913, s. 11 (5).

691 (2) *In the application of the M.S. Acts to parts of H.M. dominions outside the United Kingdom*, references to the " United Kingdom " or " the United Kingdom of Great Britain and Ireland " or " Great Britain and Ireland " or " Great Britain or Ireland " or " the British Islands " or " Ireland " must be construed as references both (a) to Great Britain and Ireland, or the British Islands, exclusive of the Republic of Ireland, or as the case may be, to Ireland exclusive of the Republic of Ireland, and (b) to the Republic of Ireland.

See Irish Free State (Consequential Adaptation of Enactments) Order 1923 (S.R. & O. No. 405), made under s. 6 of the Irish Free State (Consequential Provisions) Act 1922, which by virtue of s. 3 (1) (*b*) of the Ireland Act 1949, is one of those orders which are expressed to be not affected by the fact that the Republic of Ireland is no longer part of H.M. dominions, and which therefore remains in force and with the same effect as before but in relation to the newly designated Republic of Ireland instead of the old " Irish Free State."

Application of Act to ships propelled by electricity, etc.

692 **743.** Any provisions of this Act applying to steamers or steamships shall apply to ships propelled by electricity or other mechanical power with such modifications as the [Secretary of State for Trade] may prescribe for the purpose of adaptation.

Application of Act to certain fishing vessels

693 **744.** Ships engaged in the [whale, seal [1] or walrus fisheries [2]] shall be deemed to be foreign-going ships for the purpose of this Act, and not fishing boats,[3] with the exception *of ships engaged in the Newfoundland cod fisheries which belong to ports in Canada or Newfoundland, and* [4] [of ships

engaged in the whale fisheries off the coast of Scotland and registered at ports in Scotland [5]].

1 As to the restrictions on seal fishing, see the Conservation of Seals Act 1970.
2 The words in square brackets are substituted for the words " whale, seal, walrus, or Newfoundland cod fisheries " by s. 4 of M.S.A. 1950 (see notes to that section, *post*).
3 For provisions relating to fishing boats, see ss. 369 *et seq.*, *supra*, M.S.A. 1970, s. 95 and Sched. 2, and the Fishing Vessels (Safety Provisions) Act 1970.
4 The words in italics are omitted by virtue of s. 4 of M.S.A. 1950.
5 The words in square brackets were added by M.S.A. 1906, s. 83.

Repeal and Savings

Repeal

694 **745.**—(1) *The Acts mentioned in the Twenty-second Schedule to this Act are hereby repealed to the extent specified in the third column of that schedule.*

Provided that [1]—

(*a*) Any Order in Council, licence, certificate, byelaw, rule, or regulation made or granted under any enactment hereby repealed shall continue in force as if it had been made or granted under this Act [2];

(*b*) Any officer appointed, any body elected or constituted, and any *savings bank or* [3] office established, under any enactment hereby repealed shall continue and be deemed to have been appointed, elected, constituted, or established, as the case may be, under this Act;

(*c*) Any document [4] referring to any Act or enactment hereby repealed shall be construed to refer to this Act, or to the corresponding enactment of this Act;

(*d*) Any penalty may be recovered, and any offence may be prosecuted, under any provision of the Merchant Shipping Acts 1854 to 1892, which is not repealed by this Act,[5] in the same manner as fines may be recovered and offences prosecuted under this Act;

(*e*) Ships registered under the Merchant Shipping Act 1854, and the Acts amending the same, or duly registered before the passing of the Merchant Shipping Act 1854, shall be deemed to have been registered under this Act;

(*f*) Nothing in this Act shall affect the Behring Sea Award Act 1894,[6] and that Act shall have effect as if this Act had not passed.

(2) The mention of particular matters in this section shall not be held to prejudice or affect the general application of section thirty-eight of the Interpretation Act 1889, with regard to the effect of repeals.

(3) The tonnage of every ship not measured or remeasured in accordance with the Merchant Shipping Tonnage Act 1889,[7] shall be estimated

for all purposes as if any deduction prohibited by the Merchant Shipping (Tonnage) Act 1889,[7] had not been made, and the particulars relating to the ship's tonnage in the registry book and in her certificate of registry shall be corrected accordingly.

[1] The words in italics were repealed as spent by the Statute Law Revision Act 1908.
[2] Particulars of such Orders in Council, rules, etc., are given under the sections of the Act which respectively reproduce the provisions whereunder they were made. As to the interpretation of such orders, see *R.* v. *Abrahams* [1904] 2 K.B. 859.
[3] The words in italics were repealed by the M.S.A. 1970, s. 100 (3) and Sched. 5, as from January 1, 1973: see S.I. 1972 No. 1977.
[4] Such references in any other Act are similarly provided for by s. 38 (1) of the Interpretation Act 1889, set out at end of notes to s. 742.
[5] The unrepealed Acts within this collective title are the M.S. (Payment of Wages and Rating) Act 1880 and the M.S. (Expenses) Act 1880.
[6] That Act applies certain penal and other provisions of M.S.A. 1854 and 1876 to fur-seal fishing vessels in the North Pacific.
[7] That Act was repealed by this section and Sched. XXII to this Act.

Savings

695 **746.**—(1) Nothing in this Act shall affect the Chinese Passengers Act 1855.[1]

(2) Any local Act which repeals or affects any provisions of the Acts repealed by this Act shall have the same effect on the corresponding provisions of this Act as it had on the said provisions repealed by this Act.[2]

(3) *Nothing in this Act shall affect the rating of any seaman who was rated and served as A.B. before the second day of August one thousand eight hundred and eighty.*[3]

[1] The Act saved (now repealed in part) relates to ships conveying Asiatic emigrants from ports in China, or within 100 miles of the coast thereof.
[2] *Cf.* s. 735 (2) as to repeals in British possessions.
[3] This subsection was repealed as spent by the Statute Law Revision Act 1953, s. 1 and Sched. I.

Short Title and Commencement

Short title

696 **747.** This Act may be cited as the Merchant Shipping Act 1894.

Commencement

697 **748.** *This Act shall come into operation on the first day of January one thousand eight hundred and ninety-five.*

This section was repealed as spent by the Statute Law Revision Act 1908.

SCHEDULES

698 Editors' Notes.—With the exception of notes to repealed Schedules, all notes by the Editors upon the Schedules are printed as footnotes, and are preceded by the words "*Editors' Note*" or "*Editors' Notes*"; all other notes occur in the Schedules in the Queen's Printer's copy of the Act.

FIRST SCHEDULE

699 **Sections 24, 31, 37, 65**

PART I[1]

[*The forms in this Part of the Schedule are subject to alteration from time to time by the Commissioners of Customs, with the consent of the* [Department of Trade].]

Editors' Note:

[1] The forms in Part I of this Schedule substantially reproduce those issued by the Commissioners of Customs and Excise, with the consent of the Secretary of State for Trade in substitution for those contained in M.S.A. 1854.

700 FORM A—BILL OF SALE

[*This form was repealed by the M.S.A.* 1965, *ss.* 5 (1), 7 (2) *and Sched.* 2.]

701 FORM B—MORTGAGE[1]

[*Insert description of ship and particulars as in Bill of Sale*]

i. TO SECURE PRINCIPAL SUM AND INTEREST

(a) the undersigned in consideration of this day lent to (b) by do hereby for (c) and (d) heirs, covenant with the said firstly That (a) or (d) heirs, executors, or administrators, will pay to the said the said sum of together with interest thereon at the rate of per cent. per annum on the (f) day of next; and secondly, that if the said principal sum is not paid on the said day (a) or (d) heirs, executors, or administrators, will, during such time as the same or any part thereof remains unpaid, pay to the said interest on the whole or such part thereof as may for the time being remain unpaid, at the rate of per cent. per annum, by equal half-yearly payments on the day of and day of in every year; and for better securing to the said the repayment in manner aforesaid of the said principal sum and interest (a) hereby mortgage to the said shares, of which (e) the owner in the ship[1] above particularly described, and in her boats, guns, ammunition, small arms, and appurtenances.[2] Lastly (a) for (c) and (d) heirs, covenant with the said and assigns that (a) ha power to mortgage in manner aforesaid the above-mentioned shares, and that the same are free from incumbrances (g) .

In witness whereof (a) ha hereto subscribed (d) name and affixed (d) seal this day of One thousand eight hundred and .

Executed by the above-named
in the presence of .

(a) " I " or " we."
(b) " Me " or " us."
(c) " Myself " or " ourselves."
(d) " My " or " our."
(e) " I am " or " we are."
(f) Insert the day fixed for payment of principal as above.
(g) If any prior incumbrance add, " save as appears by the registry of the said ship."

NOTE.—The prompt registration of a mortgage deed at the port of registry of the ship is essential to the security of the mortgagee, as a mortgage takes its priority from the date of production for registry, not from the date of the instrument.

Editors' Notes:

1 The mortgage of a " ship " includes everything then on board necessary for the prosecution of the voyage or subsequently brought on board in substitution therefor. *Coltman* v. *Chamberlain* (1890) 25 Q.B.D. 328.

2 " Appurtenances " must be specified, and the term does not include nets and gear used on several mortgaged vessels, but not appropriated to any particular vessel. *Re Salmon, ex p. Gould* (1885) 2 Mor.Bky.Cas. 137.

See also notes to s. 34, *ante*.

ii. TO SECURE ACCOUNT CURRENT, ETC.

Whereas (a) .

Now (b) the undersigned in consideration of the premises for (c) and (d) heirs covenant with the said and (e) assigns, to pay to him or them the sums for the time being due on this security, whether by way of principal or interest, at the times and manner aforesaid. And for the purpose of better securing to the said the payment of such sums as last aforesaid (b) do hereby mortgage to the said shares, of which (f) the owner in the ship above particularly described, and in her boats, guns, ammunitions, small arms, and appurtenances.

Lastly, (b) for (c) and (d) heirs, covenant with the said and (e) assigns that (b) ha power to mortgage in manner aforesaid the above-mentioned shares, and that the same are free from incumbrances (g) .

In witness whereof (b) ha hereto subscribed (d) name and affixed (d) seal this day of One thousand eight hundred and .

Executed by the above-named
in the presence of . }

(a) Here state by way of recital that there is an account current between the mortgagor (describing him) and the mortgagee (describing him); and describe the nature of the transaction so as to show how the amount of principal and interest due at any given time is to be ascertained, and the manner and time of payment.
(b) " I " or " we."
(c) " Myself " or " ourselves."
(d) " My " or " our."
(e) " His " or " their."
(f) " I am " or " we are."
(g) If any prior incumbrance add, " save as appears by the registry of the said ship."

NOTE.—The prompt registration of a mortgage deed at the port of registry of the ship is essential to the security of the mortgagee, as a mortgage takes its priority from the date of production for registry, not from the date of the instrument.

Editors' Note: See also notes to s. 34, *ante*.

702 FORM C—TRANSFER OF MORTGAGE

[*To be indorsed on the original mortgage*]

([a]) the within-mentioned in consideration of this day paid to ([b]) by hereby transfer to ([c]) the benefit of the within written security. In witness whereof ([d]) ha hereunto subscribed ([e]) name and affixed ([e]) seal , this day of One thousand eight hundred and .

Executed by the above-named in the presence of . }

(a) " I " or " we."
(b) " Me " or " us."
(c) " Him " or " them."
(d) " I " or " we."
(e) " My " or " our."

PART II

Documents of which the forms are to be prescribed by the Commissioners of Customs [1] *and sanctioned by the* [*Board of Trade*].

Certificate of surveyor.
Declaration of ownership by individual owner.
Declaration of ownership on behalf of a corporation as owner.
Certificate of registry.
Provisional certificate.
Declaration of ownership by individual transferee.
Declaration of ownership on behalf of a corporation as transferee.
Declaration of owner taking by transmission.
Declaration by mortgagee taking by transmission.
Certificate of mortgage.
Certificate of sale.
Revocation of certificate of sale or mortgage.
[Bill of Sale] [2]

Editors' Note:

[1] Now " Commissioners of Customs and Excise "; see Customs and Excise Act 1952, s. 318 (1).

[2] The words in brackets were added by the M.S.A. 1965, ss. 5 (1), 7 (1) and Sched. 1.

SECOND SCHEDULE

703 [*This schedule which contained rules for the measurement of tonnage was repealed by the M.S.A.* 1965, *ss.* 5 (1), 7 (2) *and Sched.* 2. *See now ibid. s.* (1).]

THIRD–FOURTH SCHEDULES

704 [*These schedules, which prescribed maximum fees to be paid for the measurement of merchant ships and by applicants for examination, were repealed as from November* 19, 1952, *by M.S.* (*Safety Convention*) *Act* 1949, *s.* 37 (5) *and Third Schedule.*]

FIFTH SCHEDULE

[*This schedule is prospectively repealed by the M.S.A.* 1970, *s.* 100 (3), *Sched.* 5 *as from a day to be appointed.*]

Regulations to be observed with respect to Anti-Scorbutics

Furnishing of Anti-Scorbutics

Section 200

705 (1) *The anti-scorbutics to be furnished shall be lime or lemon juice, or such other anti-scorbutics* (*if any*) *of such quality, and composed of such materials, and packed and kept in such manner as Her Majesty by Order in Council may direct.*[1]

(2) *No lime or lemon juice shall be deemed fit and proper to be taken on board ship, for the use of the crew or passengers thereof, unless it has been obtained from a bonded warehouse for and to be shipped as stores.*

(3) *Lime or lemon juice shall not be so obtained or delivered from a warehouse as aforesaid, unless—*

(*a*) *it is shown, by a certificate under the hand of an inspector appointed by the* [*Secretary of State for Trade*], *to be proper for use on board ship, the certificate to be given upon inspection of a sample, after deposit of the lime or lemon juice in the warehouse; and*

(*b*) *it contains fifteen per cent. of proper and palatable proof spirit, to be approved by the inspector or by the proper officer of customs, and to be added before or immediately after the inspection thereof; and*

(*c*) *it is packed in such bottles at such time and in such manner and is labelled in such manner as the Commissioners of Customs*[2] *may direct.*

(4) *If the lime or lemon juice is deposited in a bonded warehouse, and has been approved as aforesaid by the inspector, the spirit, or the amount of spirit necessary to make up fifteen per cent., may be added in the warehouse, without payment of any duty thereon; and when any spirit has been added to any lime or lemon juice, and the lime or lemon juice has been labelled as aforesaid, it shall be deposited in the warehouse for delivery as ship's stores only, upon such terms and subject to such regulations of the Commissioners*

of Customs [2] *as are applicable to the delivery of ship's stores from the warehouse.*

(5) *The lime or lemon juice with which a ship is required by this Act to be provided shall be taken from the warehouse duly labelled as aforesaid, and the labels shall remain intact until twenty-four hours at least after the ship has left her port of departure on her foreign voyage.*

Serving out of Anti-Scorbutics

706 (6) *The lime or lemon juice shall be served out with sugar (the sugar to be in addition to any sugar required by the agreement with the crew).*

(7) *The anti-scorbutics shall be served out to the crew so soon as they have been at sea for ten days; and during the remainder of the voyage, except during such time as they are in harbour and are there supplied with fresh provisions.*

(8) *The lime or lemon juice and sugar shall be served out daily at the rate of an ounce each per day to each member of the crew, and shall be mixed with a due proportion of water before being served out.*

(9) *The other anti-scorbutics, if any, provided in pursuance of an Order in Council shall be served out at such times and in such quantities as the Order in Council directs.*

Editors' Notes:

1 " Instructions respecting Lime and Lemon Juice " were issued by the Board of Trade in June, 1913, and may be obtained in pamphlet form from the Government printers or through any bookseller, Circular 1534. By Order in Council dated April 22, 1927 (S.R. & O. No. 360), provision was made for the use of concentrated orange-juice as an anti-scorbutic.

2 Now Commissioners of Customs and Excise; see Customs and Excise Act 1952, s. 318 (1).

SIXTH SCHEDULE

[*This schedule is prospectively repealed by the M.S.A.* 1970, *s.* 100 (3) *as from a day to be appointed.*]

REGULATIONS TO BE OBSERVED WITH RESPECT TO ACCOMMODATION ON BOARD SHIPS

Sections 79, 210

707 (1) *Every place in a ship occupied by seamen or apprentices, and appropriated to their use, shall be such as to make the space which it is required by the Second Part of this Act to contain available for the proper accommodation of the men who are to occupy it, and shall be securely constructed, properly lighted and ventilated, properly protected from weather and sea, and as far as practicable properly shut off and protected from effluvium which may be caused by cargo or bilge water.*

(2) [. . .] [1]

(3) [. . .] [1]

(4) [. . .] [1]
(5) [. . .] [1]
(6) [. . .] [2]
(7) [. . .] [2]
(8) *When the accommodation is inspected at the same time with the measurement of the tonnage, no separate fee shall be charged for the inspection.*

708 *Editors' Notes:*

The Schedule does not apply to any ship to which regulations made under s. 1 of the M.S.A. 1948 or s. 1 of the M.S.A. 1950, apply. See s. 4 (3) of the Act of 1948, and para. 13 of the First Schedule to the Act of 1950, *post*.

[1] The words omitted were repealed by the M.S.A. 1965, ss. 5 (1), 7 (2) and Sched. 2. A foreign ship is entitled to deduct crew space upon limiting liability when such space is shown by its certificate of registry or other national papers as deducted as crew space from tonnage, unless a surveyor of ships certifies that the construction and equipment of the ship do not come up to the standard required by the Act for British ships. See M.S.A. 1906, s. 55.

[2] The words omitted were repealed by M.S. (Safety Convention) Act 1949, s. 37 (5), and Third Schedule. The fees at present in force for these services are contained in the M.S. (Fees) Regulations 1975 (S.I. No. 341), made in pursuance of s. 33 (2) of the 1949 Act.

SEVENTH AND EIGHTH SCHEDULES

709 [*These schedules which contained the constitution of Local Marine board (Seventh Schedule) and particulars to be registered by a master concerning birth or death at sea (Eighth Schedule) were repealed by the M.S.A.* 1970, *s.* 100 (3), *Sched. V as from January* 1, 1973: *see S.I.* 1972 *No.* 1977.]

NINTH SCHEDULE

710 [*This Schedule, which prescribed maximum fees to be paid for Passenger Steamers' Certificates and for Surveys of Emigrant Ships, was repealed as from November* 19, 1952, *by M.S.* (*Safety Convention*) *Act* 1949, *s.* 37 (5) *and Third Schedule. The fees at present in force for these services are contained in the M.S.* (*Fees*) *Regulations* 1975 (*S.I. No.* 341), *made in pursuance of s.* 33 (2) *of the* 1949 *Act.*]

TENTH–FOURTEENTH SCHEDULES

711 [*These Schedules, which contained regulations as to passenger and emigrant ships, were repealed by M.S.A.* 1906, *s.* 85, *Sched. II.*]

FIFTEENTH SCHEDULE

712 [*This Schedule, which contained regulations as to life-saving appliances for fishing boats, was repealed by M.S.A.* 1937, *s.* 2.]

SIXTEENTH SCHEDULE

713 [*This Schedule, which prescribed maximum fees to be paid for inspection of lights and fog signals, was repealed as from November* 19, 1952, *by M.S.* (*Safety Convention*) *Act* 1949, *s.* 37 (5) *and Third Schedule. The fees at present in force for these services are contained in the M.S.* (*Fees*) *Regulations* 1975 (*S.I. No.* 341), *made in pursuance of s.* 33 (2) *of the* 1949 *Act.*]

Section 429

SEVENTEENTH SCHEDULE

LIFE SAVING APPLIANCES

Constitution of the Committee

714 (1) Three shipowners selected by the Council of the Chamber of Shipping of the United Kingdom.

(2) One shipowner selected by the Shipowners Associations of Glasgow and one shipowner selected by the Liverpool Steamship Owners Association and the Liverpool Shipowners Association conjointly.

(3) Two shipbuilders selected by the Council of the Institution of Naval Architects.

(4) Three persons practically acquainted with the navigation of vessels selected by the shipmasters' societies recognised by the [Secretary of State for Trade] for this purpose.

(5) Three persons being or having been able-bodied seamen selected by seamen's societies recognised by the [Secretary of State for Trade] for this purpose.

(6) Two persons selected conjointly by the Committee of Lloyd's, the Committee of Lloyd's Register Society, and the Committee of the Institute of London Underwriters.

EIGHTEENTH SCHEDULE

715 [*This Schedule, which prescribed precautions to be taken in regard to the carriage of grain cargoes, was repealed as from November* 19, 1952, *by M.S.* (*Safety Convention*) *Act* 1949, *s.* 37 (5) *and Third Schedule. The provisions relating to the carriage of grain and the power of the* [*Secretary of State for Trade*] *to make rules prescribing particular precautions in relation thereto are now contained in s.* 24 *of that Act. See s.* 24 *of that Act and notes thereto, post.*]

Section 558

NINETEENTH SCHEDULE

PART I

STATEMENTS IN THE CASE OF SALVAGE BY HER MAJESTY'S SHIPS [1]

716 (1) Particulars to be stated both by the salvor and by the master or other person in charge of the vessel, cargo, or property saved:—

(*a*) the place, condition, and circumstances in which the vessel, cargo, or property was at the time when the services were rendered for which salvage is claimed:

(*b*) the nature and duration of the services rendered.

(2) Additional particulars to be stated by the salvor:—

(*a*) the proportion of the value of the vessel, cargo, and property, and of the freight which he claims for salvage, or the values at which he estimates the vessel, freight, cargo, and property respectively, and the several amounts that he claims [2] for salvage in respect of the same:

(*b*) any other circumstances which he thinks relevant to the said claim.

(3) Additional particulars [3] to be stated by the said master or other person in charge of the said vessel, cargo, or property:—

(*a*) a copy of the certificate of registry of the said vessel, and of the indorsements thereon, stating any change which (to his knowledge or belief) has occurred in the particulars contained in the certificate; and stating also to the best of his knowledge and belief, the state of the title to the vessel for the time being, and of the incumbrances and certificates of mortgage or sale, if any, affecting the same, and the names and places of business of the owners and incumbrancers:

(*b*) the name and place of business or residence of the freighter (if any) of the said vessel, and the freight to be paid for the voyage on which she then is:

(*c*) a general account of the quantity and nature of the cargo at the time the salvage services were rendered:

(*d*) the name and place of business or residence of the owner of the cargo and of the consignee thereof:

(*e*) the values at which the master or person making the statement estimates the vessel, cargo, and property, and the freight respectively, or if he thinks fit, in lieu of the estimated value of the cargo, a copy of the vessel's manifest:

(*f*) the amounts which the master thinks should be paid as salvage for the services rendered:

(*g*) an accurate list of the property saved in cases where the vessel is not saved:

(*h*) an account of the proceeds of the sale of the vessel, cargo, or property, in cases where the same or any of them are sold at the port where the statement is made:

(*i*) the number, capacities, and condition of the crew of the vessel at the time when the services were rendered: and

(*k*) any other circumstances he thinks relevant to the matters in question.

PART II

SALVAGE BOND

[*N.B.—Any of the particulars not known, or not required, by reason of the Claim being only against the Cargo, etc., may be omitted.*]

717 Whereas certain salvage services are alleged to have been rendered by the vessel [*insert names of vessel and of commander*], commander, to the merchant vessel [*insert names of vessel and master*], master, belonging to [*name and place of business or residence of owner of vessel*], freighted by [*the name of the freighter*], and to the cargo therein, consisting of [*state very shortly the descriptions and quantities of the goods, and the names and addresses of their owners and consignees*]:

And whereas the said vessel and cargo have been brought into the port of [*insert name and situation of port*], and a statement of the salvage claim has been sent to [*insert the name of the consular officer or judge of the colonial court of admiralty or vice-admiralty court and of the office he fills*], and he has fixed the amount to be inserted in this bond at the sum of [*state the sum*].

Now I, the said [*master's name*], do hereby, in pursuance of the Merchant Shipping Act 1894, bind the several owners for the time being of the said vessel and of the cargo therein and of the freight payable in respect of that cargo and their respective heirs, executors, and administrators, to pay among them such sum not exceeding the said sum of [*state the sum fixed*], in such proportions and to such persons as [*if the parties agree on any other court, substitute the name of it here*] the High Court in England shall adjudge to be payable as salvage for the services so alleged to have been rendered as aforesaid.

In the witness whereof I have hereunto set my hand and seal, this [*insert the date*] day of .

Signed, sealed, and delivered by the said [*master's name*].

(L.S.)

In the presence of [*name of consular officer or judge of the colonial court of admiralty or vice-admiralty court, and of the office he fills*].

Editors' Notes:

1 See s. 558 and note thereto.

2 See note (5) to s. 558, as to incapacity of officer commanding Her Majesty's ship to agree to amount of salvage.

[3] The master or other person in charge has also to add a statement of his willingness to execute a bond in form, so far as circumstances will permit, set out in Part II. See s. 558 (2).

Section 567

TWENTIETH SCHEDULE

MAXIMUM FEES AND REMUNERATION OF RECEIVERS

£ s. d.

718 For every examination on oath instituted by a receiver with respect to any vessel which may be or may have been in distress, a fee not exceeding 1 0 0

But so that in no case shall a larger fee than two pounds be charged for examinations taken in respect of the same vessel and the same occurrence, whatever may be the number of the deponents.

For every report required to be sent by the receiver to the secretary of Lloyd's in London, the sum of 0 10 0

For wreck taken by the receiver into his custody, a percentage of five per cent. upon the value thereof.

But so that in no case shall the whole amount of percentage so payable exceed twenty pounds.

In cases where any services are rendered by a receiver, in respect of any vessel in distress, not being wreck, or in respect of the cargo or other articles belonging thereto, the following fees instead of a percentage; (that is to say),

If that vessel with her cargo equals or exceeds in value six hundred pounds, the sum of two pounds for the first, and the sum of one pound for every subsequent day during which the receiver is employed on that service, but if that vessel with her cargo is less in value than six hundred pounds, one moiety of the above-mentioned sum.

Editors' Note:

The Twentieth Schedule, so far as it specifies the amount or the maximum amount of any fees, was repealed as from November 19, 1952, by M.S. (Safety Convention) Act 1949, s. 37, Sched. III, *post*.

For the fees at present in force see the M.S. (Fees) Regulations, 1975 (S.I. No. 341).

TWENTY-FIRST SCHEDULE

719 *Maximum Rates of Pilotage for the Thames and approaches thereto*

[*This Schedule has been repealed by the Pilotage Act* 1913, *s.* 60 *and Sched. II, post. But, see the saving in s.* 59, *ibid.*]

---

720 **Section 745** TWENTY-SECOND SCHEDULE [1]

REPEAL

Session and Chapter.	Short Title.	Extent of Repeal.
17 Edw. 2, stat. 2, c. 11. (Prerog. Reg. Stat. temp. incert. c. 13 in Rev. Edition.)	Prerogativa Regis	The words "wreck of the sea."
4 Geo. 4, c. 80.	An Act to consolidate and amend the several laws now in force with respect to trade within the limits of the charter of the East India Company, and to make further provision with respect to such trade.	Section twenty-seven, section twenty-eight, from "and for every omission" to "herein is required" and the word "omission" after "non-observance," and section thirty-four.
15 & 16 Vict. c. 26	The Foreign Deserters Act 1852.	The whole Act.
16 & 17 Vict. c. 84	An Act to amend the Passengers Act 1852, so far as relates to the passages of natives of Asia or Africa, and also passages between the Island of Ceylon and certain parts of the East Indies.	The whole Act.
17 & 18 Vict. c. 104	The Merchant Shipping Act 1854.	The whole Act.
17 & 18 Vict. c. 120.	The Merchant Shipping Repeal Act 1854.	Section sixteen.
18 & 19 Vict. c. 91.	The Merchant Shipping Act (Amendment) Act 1855.	The whole Act.
18 & 19 Vict. c. 119.	The Passengers Act 1855.	The whole Act.
19 & 20 Vict. c. 41.	The Seamen's Savings Bank Act 1856.	The whole Act.
24 & 25 Vict. c. 10.	The Admiralty Court Act 1861.	Sections nine, twelve, and twenty-four.
24 & 25 Vict. c. 52.	The Australian Passengers Act 1861.	The whole Act.
25 & 26 Vict. c. 63.	The Merchant Shipping Amendment Act 1862.	The whole Act.
26 & 27 Vict. c. 51.	The Passengers Act Amendment Act 1863.	The whole Act.
30 & 31 Vict. c. 114.	The Court of Admiralty (Ireland) Act 1867.	Sections thirty-five and forty-five.
30 & 31 Vict. c. 124.	The Merchant Shipping Act 1867.	The whole Act, except section one as far as "Act 1867," and section twelve.
31 & 32 Vict. c. 45.	The Sea Fisheries Act 1868.	Sections twenty-two to twenty-four.
31 & 32 Vict. c. 129.	The Colonial Shipping Act 1868.	The whole Act.
32 & 33 Vict. c. 11.	The Merchant Shipping (Colonial) Act 1869.	The whole Act.
33 & 34 Vict. c. 95.	The Passengers Act (Amendment) Act 1876.[2]	The whole Act.
34 & 35 Vict. c. 110.	The Merchant Shipping Act 1871.	The whole Act.
35 & 36 Vict. c. 73.	The Merchant Shipping Act 1872.	The whole Act, except sections one, ten, and seventeen.
36 & 37 Vict. c. 85.	The Merchant Shipping Act 1873.	The whole Act.

Session and Chapter.	Short Title.	Extent of Repeal.
37 & 38 Vict. c. 88.	The Births and Deaths Registration Act 1874.	Section thirty-seven, except sub-section (6), and except so far as the section relates to Her Majesty's ships.
38 & 39 Vict. c. 17.	The Explosives Act 1875.	Section forty-two.
39 & 40 Vict. c. 27.	The Local Light Dues Reduction Act 1876.	The whole Act.
39 & 40 Vict. c. 80.	The Merchant Shipping Act 1876.	The whole Act.
40 & 41 Vict. c. 16.	The Removal of Wreck Act 1877.	The whole Act.
42 & 43 Vict. c. 72.	The Shipping Casualties Investigation Act 1879.	The whole Act.
43 & 44 Vict. c. 16.	The Merchant Seamen Payment of Wages and Rating Act 1880.	The whole Act, except the first paragraph of section one and section eleven.
43 & 44 Vict. c. 18.	The Merchant Shipping Act (1854) Amendment Act 1880.	The whole Act.
43 & 44 Vict. c. 22.	The Merchant Shipping (Fees and Expenses) Act 1880.	Sections two, five, six and seven.
43 & 44 Vict. c. 43.	The Merchant Shipping (Carriage of Grain) Act 1880.	The whole Act.
45 & 46 Vict. c. 55.	The Merchant Shipping (Expenses) Act 1882.	The whole Act, except the first paragraph of section one and section eight.
45 & 46 Vict. c. 76.	The Merchant Shipping (Colonial Inquiries) Act 1882.	The whole Act.
46 & 47 Vict. c. 22.	The Sea Fisheries Act 1883.	Section eight.
46 & 47 Vict. c. 41.	The Merchant Shipping (Fishing Boats) Act 1883.	The whole Act.
49 & 50 Vict. c. 38.	The Riot (Damages) Act 1886.	In section six, paragraph (*a*), and the words "plundering, damage," before "injury"; and from "and as if" to the end of the section.
50 & 51 Vict. c. 4.	The Merchant Shipping (Fishing Boats) Act 1887.	The whole Act.
50 & 51 Vict. c. 62.	The Merchant Shipping (Miscellaneous) Act 1887.	The whole Act.
51 & 52 Vict. c. 24.	The Merchant Shipping (Life-saving Appliances) Act 1888.	The whole Act.
52 & 53 Vict. c. 5.	The Removal of Wrecks Act 1877, Amendment Act 1889.	The whole Act.
52 & 53 Vict. c. 29.	The Passenger Acts Amendment Act 1889.	The whole Act.
52 & 53 Vict. c. 43.	The Merchant Shipping Tonnage Act 1889.	The whole Act.
52 & 53 Vict. c. 46.	The Merchant Shipping Act 1889.	The whole Act.
52 & 53 Vict. c. 68.	The Merchant Shipping (Pilotage) Act 1889.	The whole Act.
52 & 53 Vict. c. 73.	The Merchant Shipping (Colours) Act 1889.	The whole Act.
53 & 54 Vict. c. 9.	The Merchant Shipping Act 1890.	The whole Act.
55 & 56 Vict. c. 37.	The Merchant Shipping Act 1892.	The whole Act.

721 *Editors' Notes*:

[1] The Twenty-Second Schedule was repealed as spent by the Statute Law Revision Act 1908.

[2] This date, which was no doubt intended for "1870," is printed "1876" in the Queen's Printer's copy of the Act.

Part Two

MERCHANT SHIPPING ACT 1897

(60 & 61 VICT. c. 59)

An Act to amend the Merchant Shipping Act 1894, with respect to the Power of Detention for Undermanning.

[6th August, 1897.]

BE it enacted, etc.

Extension of powers of detention for unsafety to undermanning

722 **1.**—(1) Section four hundred and fifty-nine of the Merchant Shipping Act 1894 (which gives power to detain unsafe ships), shall apply in the case of undermanning, and accordingly that section shall be construed as if the words " or by reason of undermanning " were inserted therein after the word " machinery," and as if the words " or for ascertaining the sufficiency of her crew," were inserted after the word " surveyed," and as if the words " or the manning of the ship " were inserted therein after the words " reloading of cargo," and the powers exercisable under or for the purposes of that section shall include power to muster the crew.[1]

(2) Section four hundred and sixty-two of the Merchant Shipping Act 1894 (which relates to foreign ships), shall also apply in the case of undermanning, and accordingly that section shall be construed as if the words " or by reason of undermanning " were inserted therein after the words " improper loading."

[1] It would seem that this power is to be exercised by the " detaining officer " appointed under s. 459 of M.S.A. 1894. A power to muster the crew of any ship in order to see that the provisions generally of the Act, etc., are complied with, is given to various officials by M.S.A. 1894, s. 723; see also note (6) to that section as to mustering of crew, etc., in cases of emergency.

Short title

723 **2.** This Act may be cited as the Merchant Shipping Act 1897.[1]

[1] This Act may now be cited with the rest of the Merchant Shipping legislation as the Merchant Shipping Acts 1894–1974: see note (1) to s. 21 of the M.S.A. 1971 (*post* § 1530) and s. 23 of the M.S.A. 1974 (*post* § 1639).

MERCHANT SHIPPING (EXEMPTION FROM PILOTAGE) ACT 1897

(60 & 61 Vict. c. 61)

724 [*This Act, which abolished certain exemptions from compulsory pilotage under* 6 *Geo.* 4, *c.* 125, *s.* 59, *was repealed by the Pilotage Act* 1913, *s.* 60, *and Sched. II.*]

MERCHANT SHIPPING (LIABILITY OF SHIPOWNERS) ACT 1898

(61 & 62 Vict. c. 14)

725 [*This Act, which extended Part VIII (the limitation of liability provisions) of M.S.A.* 1894, *to ships in the course of construction and to the owners, builders and other parties interested in such ships, was repealed by the Merchant Shipping (Liability of Shipowners and Others) Act* 1958, *s.* 8 (6) *and Schedule. See ibid. ss.* 3 (1) *and* 4 (1), (2) *for provisions now applicable.*]

MERCHANT SHIPPING (MERCANTILE MARINE FUND) ACT 1898

(61 & 62 Vict. c. 44)

An Act to amend the Law with regard to the Provision for the Payment of certain Expenses under the Merchant Shipping Act 1894, and with regard to the levying of Light Dues.

[12th August, 1898.]

Be it enacted, etc.

Abolition of Mercantile Marine Fund and constitution of General Lighthouse Fund

726 **1.**—(1) *As from the commencement of this Act*—

(*a*) All sums accounted for and paid to the Mercantile Marine Fund, except the light dues or other sums mentioned in paragraph (i) of section six hundred and seventy-six of the Merchant Shipping Act 1894, shall be paid into the exchequer[1]:

(*b*) All expenses charged on and payable out of the Mercantile Marine Fund, except the expenses relating to lighthouses, buoys, and beacons mentioned in paragraph (i) of section six hundred and seventy-seven of the same Act, and except also any expenses incurred by a general lighthouse authority under section five hundred and thirty-one of the same Act, shall, so far as they are not paid by any private person, be paid out of moneys provided by Parliament [2]:

(*c*) The said excepted sums shall be accounted for and paid to, and the said excepted expenses shall be charged on and payable out of, a fund which shall be called the General Lighthouse Fund, and references in Part XI and in sections five hundred and thirty-one and six hundred and seventy-nine of the Merchant Shipping Act 1894, to the Mercantile Marine Fund shall be construed as references to the General Lighthouse Fund.

(2) The General Lighthouse Fund shall be applied to the payment of the expenses by this Act charged thereon, and to no other purpose whatever.

(3) *The amount standing at the commencement of this Act to the credit of the Mercantile Marine Fund shall be carried to the credit of the General Lighthouse Fund and* [3] the liabilities of the Mercantile Marine Fund *existing at the commencement of this Act* [3] shall be discharged out of the General Lighthouse Fund.

[1] In so far as this section requires the payment of sums into the Exchequer, it does not apply to fees payable under the M.S.A. 1894, s. 83: See M.S.A. 1965, s. 1 (4).

[2] As to payments to the Government of India out of the General Lighthouse Fund in respect of the Minicoy Lighthouse, see the M.S. (Minicoy Lighthouse) Act 1960, s. 1 (3), *post*; see also note (2) to Sched. III to this Act.

[3] The words in italics were repealed as spent by the Statute Law Revision Act 1908.

[1A.[1] Pension rights of certain employees

(1) There shall be payable to or in respect of persons whose salaries are paid out of the General Lighthouse Fund such pensions, allowances or gratuities as may be determined in accordance with, in the case of such of those persons as are employed by the Secretary of State, arrangements made by him and, in the case of other such persons, arrangements made by a general lighthouse authority and approved by the Secretary of State, and those benefits shall be charged on and payable out of that Fund.

(2) *Section* 210 *of the Income and Corporation Taxes Act* 1970 (*contributions for widows' and certain other pensions not to qualify for tax relief*), *as amended by the Superannuation Act* 1972, *shall apply in relation to contributions made in pursuance of any such arrangements as are referred to in subsection* (1) *above by any person who is chargeable to income tax under the Income Tax Acts as it applies in relation to contributions made in accordance with a scheme under section* 1 *of the said Act of* 1972.[2]]

[1] This section was inserted by the Superannuation Act 1972, s. 17 (1). At the same time, s. 665 of the M.S.A. 1894 (power of general lighthouse authority to grant pensions) ceased to have effect.
[2] This subsection was repealed by the Finance Act 1972, s. 134 (7), Sched. 28, Part IV.

Transfer of certain light dues and charges to General Lighthouse Fund

727 **2.**—(1) All colonial light dues [1] shall, *after the commencement of this Act*,[2] be carried to the General Lighthouse Fund, subject to the prior payment thereout of any sums payable on account of money secured on those dues at the commencement of this Act in accordance with the conditions on which the money is secured.

(2) All sums which, at the commencement of this Act, are standing to the credit of the accounts kept by the [Secretary of State for Trade] with respect to colonial light dues (including any sum standing to the credit of the Basses Lights Fund [3]), shall be transferred and paid to the General Lighthouse Fund, but shall remain subject to any existing charges thereon.

(3) All expenses incurred in constructing or maintaining any colonial lights,[4] and the contributions made by Her Majesty's Government in respect of the lighthouse on Cape Spartel, Morocco, shall, *after the commencement of this Act*,[2] be paid out of the General Lighthouse Fund.

(4) Sections *six hundred and sixty-one*,[5] six hundred and sixty-two, and six hundred and sixty-three of the Merchant Shipping Act, 1894 (which relate to the advance and borrowing of money for the purpose of the construction and repair of lighthouses), shall apply in the case of colonial lights as they apply in the case of other lighthouses, buoys, or beacons.

(5) All expenses incurred *after the commencement of this Act* [2] by the [Secretary of State for Trade] or any of the general lighthouse authorities in making and maintaining communication between lighthouses and shore shall be paid out of the General Lighthouse Fund. Provided that such communications shall be available for private messages at reasonable charges, so far as may be compatible with the efficiency and safety of the lighthouse service, and all sums received in respect thereof shall be paid to the General Lighthouse Fund.

[1] See ss. 670–675 of the M.S.A. 1894, as to colonial light dues. Since the Colonial Light Dues (Revocation) Order 1960 (S.I. No. 471), they have ceased to be payable.
[2] The words in italics were repealed as spent by the Statute Law Revision Act 1908.
[3] See *post*, s. 7.
[4] See *post*, s. 7.
[5] The words in italics were repealed by the National Loans Act 1968, s. 24 (2) and Sched. 6, Part I.

Fees for registration, transfer, etc., of ships

728 **3.** Such fees shall be paid in respect of the registration, transfer (including [1] transmission), and mortgage of British ships [2] as the [Sec-

retary of State for Trade], with the consent of the Treasury, [determines], *not exceeding those specified in the First Schedule to this Act,*[3] and all such fees shall be paid into the Exchequer. Provided that fees shall not be payable under this section in respect of vessels [not exceeding ten tons gross register employed solely in fishing].[4]

29 [1] This inclusion is in terms not complete: Sched. I, Part 2 (now repealed) both as originally enacted and as amended by the Fees (Increase) Act 1923, s. 3 (now repealed), went further and embraced (as does Part X of Second Schedule to the M.S. (Fees) Regulations 1975 (S.I. No. 341) (see note (3) below), which now replaces Sched. I of the 1898 Act), also registry anew, transfer of registry, and transfer of mortgage.

But upon true principles of construction, this section and the schedule (now replaced by Part X of the Second Schedule to the 1975 Regulations) had to be read together, and as the word " transfer " had been extended in the schedule to include " transfer of mortgage," the same meaning had to be given to the word " transfer " in the section. Therefore, fees were held to be payable under this section to the registrar on the registration of the transfer of a mortgage of a British ship: *Re The New Zealand Shipping Co. Ltd.*, 87 L.J.K.B. 413; [1918] 1 K.B. 346. It is submitted that the position is the same when construing the material provisions of the 1975 Regulations with this section.

[2] This includes shares of ships: see Part X of the Second Schedule to the M.S. (Fees) Regulations 1975 (S.I. No. 341) (referred to in notes (1) and (3)), but not fees on the mortgage or transfer of mortgage of any ships for the purposes of the Cunard agreement: see Cunard Agreement (Money) Act 1904, s. 2 (repealed by the Statute Law Revision Act 1927).

[3] The words in italics were repealed as from November 19, 1952, by M.S. (Safety Convention) Act 1949, s. 37 (5) and Third Schedule, *post*. The fees at present in force are contained in Part X of the Second Schedule to the M.S. (Fees) Regulations 1975 (S.I. No. 341) made in pursuance of s. 33 (2) of the 1949 Act.

[4] The words " not exceeding . . . fishing " were substituted for the words " solely employed in fishing or sailing ships of under one hundred tons " by Fees (Increase) Act 1923, s. 1 (1), Sched. I, *post.*

30 **4.** [*This section, which dealt with the power to recover expenses incurred on account of distressed seamen, was repealed by M.S.A.* 1906, *s.* 85, *Sched. II, and this subject is now dealt with by section* 42 (4) *of that Act,* post.]

Scale of light dues

31 **5.**—(1) *On and after the commencement of this Act*[1] the general lighthouse authorities shall levy light dues with respect to the voyages made by ships or by way of periodical payment, and not with respect to the lights which a ship passes or from which it derives benefit, and the dues so levied shall take the place of the dues now levied by those authorities.

(2) The scale and rules set out in the Second Schedule to this Act shall have effect for the purpose of the levying of light dues in pursuance of this Act, but Her Majesty may, by Order in Council,[2] alter, either generally or with respect to particular classes of cases, the scale or rules and the exemptions therefrom.

(3) Before any Order in Council is made under this section, the draft thereof shall be laid before each House of Parliament for not less than thirty days on which that House is sitting, and if either House, before the

expiration of the thirty days during which the draft has been laid before it, presents an address to Her Majesty against the draft, or any part thereof, no further proceedings shall be taken thereon, but this shall be without prejudice to the making of any new draft Order.

732 [1] The words in italics were repealed as spent by the Statute Law Revision Act 1908.
[2] The Order in Council at present in force under this section modifying the rules and scales contained in Sched. II to the M.S. (Light Dues) Order 1972 (S.I. No. 456) as amended by S.I. 1973 No. 964, S.I. 1974 No. 868, and S.I. 1975 No. 432.

733 **6.** [*This section, which provided for a limited period a scale of allowance to be paid to the owners of British ships carrying boy sailors available for the Royal Naval Reserve, was repealed as spent by the Statute Law Revision Act* 1908.]

Definitions

734 **7.** In this Act, unless the context otherwise requires—

The expression " colonial lights "[1] means any lighthouses, buoys, or beacons on or near the coast of a British possession and maintained by the [Minister of Transport] out of moneys provided by Parliament or out of colonial light dues, and includes the lighthouses mentioned in the Third Schedule to this Act.

The expression " Basses Lights Fund " means the fund referred to in section five of the Public Works Loans Act 1887,[2] formed by the dues levied in respect of the Basses lights.

Other expressions have the same meaning as in the Merchant Shipping Act 1894.[3]

[1] As to the Minicoy lighthouse, see note (2) to Third Schedule.
[2] Section 5 of that Act was repealed; see Fourth Schedule.
[3] For definitions see M.S.A. 1894, s. 742 and notes thereon.

Repeal

735 **8.** *The enactments mentioned in the Fourth Schedule to this Act are hereby repealed to the extent specified in the third column of that schedule.*

This section was repealed as spent by the Statute Law Revision Act 1908.

Short title, construction, and commencement

736 **9.**—(1) This Act may be cited as the Merchant Shipping (Mercantile Marine Fund) Act 1898.

(2) This Act shall be construed as one [1] with the Merchant Shipping Act 1894, and that Act and the Merchant Shipping Act 1897, the Merchant Shipping (Exemption from Pilotage) Act 1897, and this Act may be cited together as the Merchant Shipping Acts 1894 to 1898.[2]

(3) *This Act shall come into operation on the first day of April, one thousand eight hundred and ninety-nine.*

37 [1] This means that every part of each of the Acts has to be construed "as if it had been contained in one Act, unless there is some manifest discrepancy, making it necessary to hold that the later Act has to some extent modified something found in the earlier Act"; *per* Earl of Selborne L.C. in *Canada Southern Ry. Co.* v. *International Bridge Co.* (1883) 8 App.Cas. 723 at p. 727; principle applied in *Hart* v. *Hudson Bros. Ltd.* [1928] 2 K.B. 629, at p. 634, and in *Phillips* v. *Parnaby* [1934] 2 K.B. 299, at pp. 302, 303. Thus definitions in any one of these Acts may be relevant to the construction of the provisions of another Act: *cf. Crowe* (*Valuation Officer*) v. *Lloyds British Testing Co. Ltd.* [1960] 1 Q.B. 592 with *Kirkness* v. *John Hudson & Co. Ltd.* [1955] A.C. 696.

[2] Now the Merchant Shipping Acts 1894 to 1974: see s. 23 of the M.S.A. 1974, *post.*

[3] Subs. (3) was repealed as spent by the Statute Law Revision Act 1908.

SCHEDULES

FIRST SCHEDULE

38 [*This Schedule, which prescribed maximum fees to be paid on the Registration, Transfer and Mortgage of Ships, was repealed as from November* 19, 1952, *by M.S.* (*Safety Convention*) *Act* 1949, *s.* 37 (5) *and Third Schedule, post. The scale of fees at present in force is contained in Part X of the Second Schedule to the M.S.* (*Fees*) *Regulations* 1975 (*S.I. No.* 341) *made under s.* 33 (2) *of the* 1949 *Act.*]

Editors' Note:

A fee is payable on each bill of sale. So where 166 bills of sale transferred 316 shares in six ships, it was held that the transferee was liable to pay a fee calculated on the tonnage in each bill of sale and not on the tonnage of each ship; *Harrowing Steamship Co.* v. *Toohey* [1900] 2 Q.B. 28.

SECOND SCHEDULE [1]

Light Dues

Scale of Payments [2]

39 1. Home-trade [3] sailing ships: 32p per 10 tons per voyage.

2. Foreign-going [3] sailing ships: 64p per 10 tons per voyage.

3. Home-trade [3] steamers:

Full rate: 64p per 10 tons per voyage.

Reduced rate (visiting cruise ships): 32p per 10 tons per voyage.

4. Foreign-going [3] steamers:

Full rate: £1·28 per 10 tons per voyage.

Reduced rate (visiting cruise ships): 64p per 10 tons per voyage.

5. In the place of payments per voyage, the following payments:—

(*a*) for pleasure yachts which the general lighthouse authority is satisfied are ordinarily kept or used outside any of the following countries and territories (including the territorial waters adjacent thereto), namely the United Kingdom, Isle of Man, Republic of Ireland, a payment in respect of any visit of 32p per 10 tons for every period of 30 days or less comprised in such visit;

(*b*) for tugs and pleasure yachts not included in sub-paragraph (*a*) of this paragraph an annual payment of £3·84 per 10 tons.

RULES

740 (1) A ship shall not in any year be required to make payments on account of light dues—

(*a*) if the ship is a home-trade ship, for more than 12 voyages; and

(*b*) if the ship is a foreign-going ship, for more than six voyages; and

(*c*) if the ship makes voyages during the year both as a home-trade and as a foreign-going ship, for more than 12 voyages, counting each voyage made as a foreign-going ship as two voyages.

Provided that in any year no steamer shall be required to pay more than £7·68 per 10 tons and no sailing vessel shall be required to pay more than £3·84 per 10 tons.

(2) A ship shall not pay dues both as a home-trade ship and as a foreign-going ship for the same voyage,[5] but a ship trading from a port outside home-trade limits, and discharging cargo or landing passengers [6] or mails at any port within home-trade limits, shall be deemed to be on one voyage as a foreign-going ship, until she has arrived at the last port of discharge of cargo or passengers brought from beyond home-trade limits; and a ship trading to a port outside home-trade limits, and loading cargo or receiving passengers or mails at any port within home-trade limits, shall be deemed to be on one voyage as a foreign-going ship from the time she starts from the first port of loading of cargo or passengers destined for a port beyond home-trade limits.

(3) The voyage of a home-trade ship shall be reckoned from port to port, but a home-trade ship shall not be required to pay dues for more than three voyages in one month.

(4) The voyage of a foreign-going ship trading outwards shall be reckoned from the first port of lading in the United Kingdom,[7] the Republic of Ireland or the Isle of Man of cargo destined for a port outside home-trade limits.

(5) The voyage of a foreign-going ship trading inwards shall be reckoned from her last port of lading outside home-trade limits to the last port in the United Kingdom, the Republic of Ireland or the Isle of Man at which any cargo laden outside those limits is discharged.

(6) Dues payable per voyage under this Act shall be payable and

collected only at ports where a ship loads or discharges cargo or passengers or mails.

(7) The annual payments shall be payable at the commencement of the year in respect of which they are made, provided that a new vessel shall pay only 32p per 10 tons for each month after the commencement of her first voyage till the first of April following.

(8) Every such payment as is referred to in paragraph 5 (*a*) of the scale shall be payable at the commencement of the period in respect of which it is made, provided that a vessel [8] shall not in any year be required to pay on account of light dues a sum greater than the sum which such vessel would be liable to pay under paragraph 5 (*b*) of the scale.

(9) For the purposes of this Schedule—

(*a*) A ship's tonnage shall be register tonnage reckoned in accordance with the Merchant Shipping Act 1965 with the addition required in section eighty-five of the Merchant Shipping Act 1894 as amended by the Merchant Shipping Act 1965 with respect to deck cargo, or in the case of an unregistered vessel, the tonnage reckoned in accordance with the Thames measurement adopted by Lloyd's Register.

(*b*) A year shall be reckoned from April 1.

(*c*) In calculating any payment of light dues where the vessel's tonnage is not a multiple of 10 tons, any excess not exceeding 5 tons shall be rounded down and any excess over 5 tons shall be rounded up to the nearest such multiple.

(*d*) A ship shall be treated as a visiting cruise ship if and only if it makes a call at one or more ports in the United Kingdom, Isle of Man or Republic of Ireland for the purpose of disembarking passengers for a visit ashore and for subsequent re-embarkation (whether or not at the same port) and at no time during that cruise does the ship—

(*a*) embark or disembark any other passengers; or

(*b*) load or discharge any cargo or mails—

at any such port.

(*e*) " Home-trade," in relation to any ship, means employed in trading or going within the following limits, that is to say the United Kingdom, the Channel Islands, the Isle of Man and the Republic of Ireland and the Continent of Europe between the north bank of the River Eider and Brest inclusive; and " home-trade limits " shall be construed accordingly.

(*f*) " Foreign-going," in relation to any ship means employed in trading or going between some place or places in the United Kingdom or the Republic of Ireland and some place or places situate beyond the following limits, that is to say the coasts of the United Kingdom, the Channel Islands, the Isle of Man and the Republic of Ireland and the Continent of Europe between the north bank of the River Eider and Brest inclusive.

EXEMPTIONS

741 There shall be exempted from dues under this Schedule:

Ships belonging to Her Majesty or to a foreign Government unless carrying cargo or passengers for freight or fares;

Sailing Ships (not being pleasure yachts) of less than one hundred tons, and all ships of less than twenty tons;

Vessels (other than tugs or pleasure yachts) when navigated wholly and bona fide in ballast, on which no freight is earned and without any passenger;

Ships putting in for bunkers, stores, or provisions for their own use on board;

Vessels for the time being employed in sea fishing or in sea fishing service, exclusive of vessels used for catching fish otherwise than for profit;

Ships putting in from stress of weather or for the purpose of repairing, or because of damage, provided they do not discharge or load cargo other than cargo discharged with a view to such repairs, and afterwards reshipped;

Dredgers and hoppers for the time being employed solely in dredging channels or deepening water for or on behalf of a harbour authority or a conservancy authority, within the area in which that authority has jurisdiction, or in disposing within or without such area, otherwise than by way of sale or exchange, of the spoil from such operations;

Sailing yachts of and above 100 tons, which are not registered in the United Kingdom, Isle of Man, Channel Islands or the Republic of Ireland, and which come into the territorial waters adjacent to the United Kingdom or the Republic of Ireland with the sole object of taking part in yacht racing, so long as such yachts are coming into, remaining in, or leaving such territorial waters solely in connection with such object, and hold a certificate in a form approved by the Secretary of State;

Ships making voyages entirely performed in waters in respect of which no lighthouse, buoy or beacon is maintained by a General Lighthouse Authority at the expense of the General Lighthouse Fund;

Yachts in respect of any year ending March 31 during the whole of which they are laid up.

Editors' Notes:

742 [1] This Schedule was substituted by the M.S. (Light Dues) Order 1972, S.I. No. 456 as amended by S.I. 1973 No. 964, and S.I. 1974 No. 868.

[2] As to the amendment of this Schedule by Orders in Council made under s. 5 and the Orders in Council at present in force, see note (2) to s. 5, *supra*.

[3] See, for the meanings of " home-trade ship," M.S.A. 1894, s. 742; " foreign-going ship," *ibid.* ss. 742, 744, and Order in Council dated July 24, 1901 (S.R. & O., and S.I. Rev., 1948, XIV, p. 676); and as to ships propelled by electricity, etc., M.S.A. 1894, s. 743.

[5] Where a ship in the course of loading cargo at two or more ports within home-trade limits destined for ports outside home-trade limits also carries local cargo between two such loading ports, she pays dues only as a foreign-going ship: *Corporation of Trinity House* v. *Owners of S.S. Cedar Branch* (1930) 46 T.L.R. 541. *Quaere*, whether home-trade dues would also be payable if the port of discharge of the local cargo is not also a port of loading for cargo destined for ports outside home-trade limits. Probably they would. For then the home-trade voyage and the foreign-going voyage would not be concurrent.

[6] See s. 267 of the M.S.A. 1894, and notes thereon, for explanation of term " passenger."

[7] " United Kingdom " here includes the Republic of Ireland. See note " Application to Northern Ireland and the Republic of Ireland " in notes to M.S.A. 1894, s. 742.

[8] " Vessel " does not refer to vessels propelled by oars, unless such vessels are also " ships," because light dues are only payable in respect of " ships." See s. 5 of this Act and M.S.A. 1894, s. 643, and definition of " ship " in s. 742 and notes (4) and (5) thereto.

THIRD SCHEDULE

743 I.—LIGHTHOUSES MAINTAINED BY THE [DEPARTMENT OF TRADE] OUT OF MONEY VOTED BY PARLIAMENT

Bahamas, 11 lighthouses as follows:— Gun Cay, Abaco, Cay Sal, Great Isaacs, Cay Lobos, Elbow Cay, Great Stirrup Cay, Castle Island, Inagua, Bird Rock, Watling Island.[1]

On *Sombrero*, one of the Leeward Islands.

Cape Pembroke, Falkland Islands.

744 II.—LIGHTHOUSES MAINTAINED BY THE [DEPARTMENT OF TRADE] OUT OF COLONIAL LIGHT DUES LEVIED UNDER THE MERCHANT SHIPPING ACT 1894

Great Basses,
Little Basses, } off the Coast of Ceylon.

Barberyn,
Dondra Head, } on the Coast of Ceylon.

Minicoy Island, between the Laccadive and Maldive Islands.[2]

[1] These words in italics are repealed by the Bahamas Independence Act 1973, s. 5 (2) (3) as from a day to be appointed.

[2] These words in italics were repealed by the M.S. (Minicoy Lighthouse) Act 1960, s. 1 (2), *post*. Under that Act the Secretary of State for Trade was empowered to transfer to the Government of India on an agreed date the Minicoy Lighthouse and sums in the General Lighthouse Fund in connection therewith, on which date the lighthouse ceased to be a colonial light within the meaning of this Act.

FOURTH SCHEDULE

745 ENACTMENTS REPEALED

Session and Chapter.	Short Title.	Extent of Repeal.
35 & 36 Vict. c. 55.	The Basses Lights Act 1872.	The whole Act.
44 & 45 Vict. c. 38.	The Public Works Loans Act 1881.	Section ten.
50 & 51 Vict. c. 37.	The Public Works Loans Act 1887.	Section five.
57 & 58 Vict. c. 60.	The Merchant Shipping Act 1894.	Section one hundred and ninety-three, the word " such " where it first occurs, and from " as follows; namely " to " citizen of a foreign country," inclusive. Section one hundred and ninety-four. Section six hundred and forty-three, to the words " and those," inclusive. Section six hundred and forty-four, six hundred and forty-five, six hundred and forty-six, six hundred and seventy-three, and six hundred and seventy-eight.

Editors' Note:
The Fourth Schedule was repealed as spent by the Statute Law Revision Act 1908.

MERCHANT SHIPPING (LIABILITY OF SHIPOWNERS AND OTHERS) ACT 1900

(63 & 64 VICT. c. 32)

An act to amend the Merchant Shipping Act 1894, with respect to the Liability of Shipowners and others.

[6th August, 1900.]

BE it enacted, etc.

746 **1.** [*This section, which extended the scope of the limitation of liability provided by section* 503 *of M.S.A.* 1894, *has been repealed by the M.S.* (*Liability of Shipowners and Others*) *Act* 1958, *s.* 8 (6) *and Schedule; see now ibid. s.* 2.]

Limitation of liability of harbour conservancy authority

747 **2.**—(1) The owners [1] of any dock [2] or canal, or a harbour authority or a conservancy authority, as defined [3] by the Merchant Shipping Act

1894, shall not, where without their actual fault or privity [4] any loss or damage [5] is caused to any vessel or vessels, or to any goods, merchandise, or other things whatsoever on board any vessel or vessels, be liable to damages beyond an aggregate amount [equivalent to one thousand gold francs [6]] for each ton of the tonnage of the largest registered British ship which, at the time of such loss or damage occurring, is, or within the period of five years previous thereto has been, within the area [7] over which such dock or canal owner, harbour authority, or conservancy authority, performs any duty or exercises any power. A ship shall not be deemed to have been within the area over which a harbour authority or a conservancy authority performs any duty, or exercises any powers, by reason only that it has been built or fitted out within such area, or that it has taken shelter within or passed through such area on a voyage between two places both situate outside that area, or that it has loaded or unloaded mails or passengers within that area.[8]

(2) For the purpose of this section the tonnage of ships shall be ascertained as provided by section five hundred and three, sub-section two,[9] of the Merchant Shipping Act 1894, and the register of any ship shall be sufficient evidence [10] that the gross tonnage and the deductions therefrom and the registered tonnage are as therein stated.

(3) Section five hundred and four [11] of the Merchant Shipping Act 1894, shall apply to this section as if the words " owner of a British or foreign ship " included a harbour authority, and a conservancy authority, and the owner of a canal or of a dock.

(4) For the purpose of this section the term " dock " shall include wet docks and basins, tidal docks and basins, locks, cuts, entrances, dry docks, graving docks, gridirons, slips, quays, wharves, piers, stages, landing-place, and jetties.[12]

(5) For the purposes of this section the term " owners of a dock or canal " shall include any person or authority having the control and management of any dock or canal, as the case may be.

(6) Nothing in this section shall impose any liability in respect of any such loss or damage on any such owners or authority in any case where no such liability would have existed if this Act had not passed.

748 This section, together with s. 503 of the M.S.A. 1894 (as amended) can, if not otherwise extended, by Order in Council be extended to the Isle of Man, the Channel Islands, or to any colony, or place where the Crown has jurisdiction; see M.S. (Liability of Shipowners and Others) Act 1958, s. 11 (1) (2). It has already been extended to the Isle of Man; see M.S. (Liability of Shipowners and Others) Act 1958 (Isle of Man) Order 1960 (S.I. No. 1379).

Application to Crown

By section 7 of the Crown Proceedings Act 1947 (§ 1079, *post*), it is declared that the provisions of the Merchant Shipping Acts 1894 to 1940, which limit the amount of the liability of the owners of docks and canals and of harbour and conservancy authorities apply for the purpose of limiting the liability of Her Majesty in Her capacity as the owner of any dock or canal or in Her capacity as a harbour or conservancy authority as defined for the purpose of this section (*i.e.* s. 2). The section also applies to any Government department and to any officer of the Crown in his capacity as such. See also M.S. (Liability of Shipowners and Others) Act 1958, s. 8 (5), *post*.

This section is also applied, with modifications, by the Harbours Act 1964, s. 25, for the purpose of limiting the liability of a body by whom a scheme established by a control of movement order is administered under the provisions of that Act.

749 [1] For meaning, see subs. (5).

[2] See subs. (4).

[3] For these definitions, see M.S.A. 1894, s. 742.

[4] See M.S.A. 1894, s. 503, note (4), § 431, *ante*.

[5] The right to limit liability depends not upon the quality of the act causing the damage but upon the locality within which the act was done. The damage must have been caused within the area over which the dock owner, etc., exercises some control, and, if so caused, it is immaterial in what capacity the dock owner incurred the liability. Thus, ship repairers, also owners of a dock at B, who were held liable for damage done to a ship whilst they were effecting repairs to the ship in a dock not owned by them at C, were not entitled to limit their liability in respect of such damage, their ownership of the dock at B being totally unconnected with their liability in respect of the repairs effected at C: *The City of Edinburgh* [1921] P. 274. But where ship repairers were held liable for damage caused to a vessel whilst within their own dock, they were not debarred from limiting their liability by reason of the fact that their liability was incurred not as dock owners but as ship repairers: *The Ruapehu* [1927] A.C. 523.

[6] The words in square brackets were substituted for " not exceeding eight pounds " by the M.S. (Liability of Shipowners and Others) Act 1958, s. 1 (1); see § 1210, *post*. The declared sterling equivalent of one thousand gold francs is £31·0939; see M.S. (Limitation of Liability) (Sterling Equivalents) Order 1973 (S.I. No. 1190) made under the M.S. (Liability of Shipowners and Others) Act 1958, s. 1 (3).

[7] The area must contain within its boundaries the particular spot within which the damage in respect of which limitation is claimed occurred. Thus ship repairers, owners of docks at A and at B, when seeking to limit their liability in respect of damage occurring within the area over which they exercised powers at A, were entitled to limit their liability on the tonnage of the largest vessel within the area at A and were not bound to take into account a larger vessel which had been within another area over which they exercised powers at B: *The Ruapehu* (*No.* 2) [1929] P. 305.

[8] It is to be observed that the latter part of this subsection does not apply to docks and canals belonging to persons who are not a harbour or conservancy authority, as defined by M.S.A. 1894, s. 742.

[9] s. 503 (2), as applied to this Act, is amended by the M.S.A. 1906, s. 69, *q.v.*

[10] *Quaere*, whether " sufficient," is to be read as meaning " conclusive." See *Board of Trade* v. *Sailing Ship Glenpark Ltd.*, 9 Asp.M.L.C. 550; [1904] 1 K.B. 682.

[11] Giving the courts power to consolidate claims against owners; see § 438, *ante*.

[12] The meaning of " dock " is discussed in *The Humorist* [1946] P. 438, where it was held that a warehouse built on the bed of a river, with an aperture in its walls for the delivery of goods into or from craft lying alongside is a " landing-place " and thus is a " dock " within this definition.

Limitation of liability where several claims arise on one occasion

750 **3.** The limitation of liability under this Act shall relate to the whole of any losses and damages which may arise upon any one distinct occasion,[1] although such losses and damages may be sustained by more than one person, and shall apply whether the liability arises at common law or under any general or private Act of Parliament,[2] and notwithstanding anything contained in such Act.

751 [1] See note (19) to M.S.A., 1894, s. 503, § 437, *ante*.

[2] Formerly, it had been held that this section did not deprive a dock authority of the advantages it enjoyed by way of a possessory lien over a vessel in respect of damage done by her. Thus, the rateable distribution provided for by M.S.A. 1894, s. 504 had regard to the rights of the claimants qualitatively as well as quantitatively: *Mersey Docks and Harbour Board* v. *Hay* (*The Countess*) [1923] A.C. 345. However, in this respect the law has been changed by the M.S. (Liability of Shipowners and Others) Act 1958, s. 7 (2)

which provides: " No lien or other right in respect of any ship or property shall affect the proportions in which under s. 504 any amount is distributed amongst several claimants."

Short title

52 **4.** This Act may be cited as the Merchant Shipping (Liability of Shipowners and Others) Act 1900.

Construction

53 **5.** This Act shall be construed as one [1] with the Merchant Shipping Act 1894, and that Act and the Merchant Shipping Act 1897, the Merchant Shipping (Exemption from Pilotage) Act 1897, the Merchant Shipping (Liability of Shipowners) Act 1898, the Merchant Shipping (Mercantile Marine Fund) Act 1898, and this Act, may be cited together as the Merchant Shipping Acts 1894 to 1900.[2]

[1] See note (1) to s. 9 of M.S. (Mercantile Marine Fund) Act 1898.
[2] Now the Merchant Shipping Acts 1894 to 1974: see § 1639, *post*.

SHIPOWNERS' NEGLIGENCE (REMEDIES) ACT 1905

(5 Edw. 7, c. 10)

54 [*This Act which, though not strictly one of the Merchant Shipping Acts, had been included in previous editions of this work, has been repealed by the Administration of Justice Act* 1956, *ss.* 7 (1), 55 (1), 57 (2), *Sched. I, Pt. I, para.* 7, *Pt. III*; *Sched. II*.]

MERCHANT SHIPPING ACT 1906

(6 Edw. 7, c. 48)

An Act to amend the Merchant Shipping Acts 1894 to 1900.

[21st December, 1906.]

Be it enacted, etc.

PART I—SAFETY

55 This Part of the Act marked an important stage in the progress made towards increasing safety at sea by legislative action. In particular, the new provisions had the effect (*inter alia*) of extending the application of certain provisions of M.S.A. 1894, relating to load-lines, detention, loading of grain cargoes, and life-saving appliances, to foreign ships while within any port in the United Kingdom, and of providing requirements for

the carriage of timber as deck cargo. Although most of the provisions of this Part of the Act, as well as the provisions of M.S.A. 1894, which had been extended have been repealed, they have been replaced by extensive provisions in the M.S. (Safety and Load Line Conventions) Act 1932, M.S. (Safety Convention) Act 1949, and M.S. (Load Lines) Act 1967, which are of far wider effect as they are based on International Conventions signed by a large number of seafaring nations. For notes to these Acts, see *post*.

For the law on this subject generally, see Part V (*i.e.* ss. 418–463) of M.S.A. 1894, Parts I and II of the M.S. (Safety and Load Line Conventions) Act 1932, the M.S. (Safety Convention) Act 1949, and the M.S. (Load Lines) Act 1967.

756 **1.** [*This section, which related to the application to foreign ships within any United Kingdom port of sections* 437–443 of *M.S.A.* 1894, *relative to load-lines, has been repealed by the M.S.* (*Safety and Load Line Conventions*) *Act* 1932, *s.* 67 (2) *and Fourth Schedule, Part II.*]

Detention of foreign ships when unsafe owing to defective equipment, etc.

757 **2.** Section four hundred and sixty-two of the principal Act (which relates to the detention of foreign ships)—

(1) shall apply in the case of a ship which is unsafe by reason of the defective condition of her hull, equipments, or machinery, and accordingly that section shall be construed as if the words " by reason of the defective condition of her hull, equipments, or machinery, or " were inserted before the words " by reason of overloading or improper loading "; and

(2) shall apply with respect to any foreign ships [1] being at any port in the United Kingdom,[2] whether those ships take on board any cargo at that port or not.

[1] For exceptions to the provisions of this section, see s. 6.
[2] See note " Application to Northern Ireland and the Republic of Ireland " in notes to M.S.A. 1894, s. 742.

758 **3.** [*This section, which related to the loading of grain cargoes on foreign ships in the United Kingdom, was repealed by M.S.* (*Safety Convention*) *Act* 1949, *s.* 37 (5) *and Third Schedule. As to carriage of grain generally, see section* 24 *of that Act, and notes thereto.*]

759 **4.** [*This section, which related to the application of the rules relating to life-saving appliances to foreign ships whilst in the United Kingdom, was repealed by M.S.* (*Safety Convention*) *Act* 1949, *s.* 37 (5) *and Third Schedule, post.*]

760 **5.** [*This section, which related to the appointed day, has been repealed as spent by the Statute Law Revision Act* 1927.]

Saving for ship coming in under stress of weather, etc.

61 **6.** Nothing in the foregoing provisions of this Part of this Act shall affect any foreign ship not bound to a port [1] of the United Kingdom [2] which comes into any port of the United Kingdom for any purpose other than the purpose of embarking or landing passengers,[3] or taking in or discharging cargo or taking in bunker coal.

[1] " Port " includes place. See M.S.A. 1894, s. 742 (definitions).
[2] See note " Application to Northern Ireland and the Republic of Ireland " in notes to M.S.A. 1894, s. 742.
[3] For meaning of " passengers," see notes to M.S.A. 1894, s. 267.

62 **7–8.** [*Sections* 7 *and* 8 *which amended sections* 437, 438 (*marking of deck-lines and load-lines*) *and extended section* 440 (*time of marking load-line*) *of M.S.A.* 1894, *were repealed by the M.S.* (*Safety and Load Line Conventions*) *Act* 1932, *s.* 67 (2) *and Fourth Schedule, Part II, their provisions being superseded by the provisions of Part II of that Act.*]

63 **9.**—[*This section which made provision for entry in the log-book of boat drills, etc. was repealed by the M.S.A.* 1970, *s.* 100 (3), *Sched.* 5 *as from January* 1, 1973: *see S.I.* 1972 *No.* 1977.]

64 **10.** [*This section was repealed by M.S.* (*Safety and Load Line Conventions*) *Act* 1932, *s.* 67 (2) *and Fourth Schedule, Part II. See section* 61 *of that Act for the present provisions regarding loading of timber, and note* (1) *thereto as to the Timber Cargo Regulations now in force.*]

65 **11.** [*This section, which related to summary prosecution for offences under the loading of grain provisions, was repealed by M.S.* (*Safety Convention*) *Act* 1949, *s.* 37 (5) *and Third Schedule. For general provisions relating to the carriage of grain, see now section* 24 *of that Act, post.*]

66 **12.** [*This section, which contained a prohibition as to the engagement of seamen, with insufficient knowledge of English, was repealed by the M.S.A.* 1970, *s.* 100 (3), *Sched.* 5 *as from January* 1, 1973: *see S.I.* 1972 *No.* 1977].

PART II—PASSENGER AND EMIGRANT SHIPS

The general provisions as to these ships are contained in M.S.A. 1894, Part III (ss. 267–368), although the provisions relating to emigrant ships were largely repealed by the M.S.A. 1970, s. 100 (3), Sched. 5. See also M.S. (Safety and Load Line Conventions) Act 1932, M.S. (Safety Convention) Act 1949, and the M.S. (Load Lines) Act 1967.

Inclusion of foreign steamships as passenger steamers

67 **13.** The definition of " passenger steamer " [1] in section two hundred and sixty-seven of the principal Act shall be amended so as to include every foreign steamship [2] (whether originally proceeding from a port in

the United Kingdom or from a port out of the United Kingdom) which carries passengers [1] to or from any place, or between any places, in the United Kingdom.[3]

[1] For explanation of these terms, see M.S.A. 1894, s. 267, and notes thereto; see also s. 26 of M.S. (Safety Convention) Act 1949 and s. 17 (2) of the M.S.A. 1964.

[2] As to the exemption of Italian ships, see M.S. (Passenger Steamers and Emigrant Ships) Italian Ships Order 1929 (December 17, 1929, S.R. & O. No. 1154), made under M.S. (Equivalent Provisions) Act 1925, s. 1.

[3] See note "Application to Northern Ireland and the Republic of Ireland" in notes to M.S.A. 1894, s. 742.

Definition of steerage passenger

768 **14.** [*This section, which substituted a new definition of steerage passenger for paragraph* (3) *of s.* 268 *of the M.S.A.* 1894, *has in common with the latter section been repealed by the M.S.A.* 1970, *s.* 100 (3), *Sched.* 5 *as from January* 1, 1973: *see S.I.* 1972 *No.* 1977.]

Passengers landed or embarked by means of tenders

769 **15.** Where a passenger steamer [1] takes on board passengers from a tender, or lands passengers by means of a tender, she shall be deemed to be taking the passengers on board from, or landing the passengers at, the port [2] from or to which the tender comes or goes, and passengers conveyed in a tender to or from a ship from or to a place in the United Kingdom [3] shall for the purposes of Part III of the principal Act,[4] and for the purposes of any returns [5] to be made under the Merchant Shipping Acts, be deemed to be passengers carried from or to a place in the United Kingdom.

[1] See note (1) to s. 13.

[2] "Port" includes place. See M.S.A. 1894, s. 742.

[3] See note "Application to Northern Ireland and the Republic of Ireland" in notes to M.S.A. 1894, s. 742.

[4] *i.e.* M.S.A. 1894. See s. 84 (1), *post*.

[5] As to such a return, see s. 76, *post*.

Restriction as to the decks on which passengers may be carried

770 **16.**[1]—(1) A ship shall not carry passengers,[2] *whether cabin or steerage passengers,*[3] on more than one deck below the water line.

(2) If this section is not complied with in the case of any ship the master of the ship shall for each offence be liable to a fine not exceeding five hundred pounds.[4]

771 [1] This section apparently takes the place of the repealed M.S.A. 1894, s. 291.

[2] For meaning, see notes to M.S.A. 1894, s. 267, and see also s. 26 of M.S. (Safety Convention) Act 1949.

[3] The words in italics were repealed by the M.S.A. 1970, s. 100 (3), Sched. 5 as from January 1, 1973: see S.I. 1972 No. 1977.

[4] The procedure for the recovery of this fine is apparently prosecution by indictment, M.S.A. 1894, s. 680 (prosecution of offences under the Act of 1894 generally), does not provide any summary remedy, as such procedure is limited to offences declared under this Act to be misdemeanours, and to offences under the Act made punishable with imprisonment for any term not exceeding six months, or by a fine not exceeding one hundred pounds.

Regulations substituted for Schedules 10, 11, 12, 13, and 14 of principal Act

72 **17–20.** [*These sections which contained provisions relating to emigrant vessels were repealed by the M.S.A.* 1970, *s.* 100 (3), *Sched.* 5 *as from January* 1, 1973: *see S.I.* 1972 *No.* 1977.]

Penalty on master or owner for non-compliance with provisions as to passenger steamers

73 **21.** If the provisions [1] of the Merchant Shipping Acts which require a passenger steamer to be surveyed and to have a passenger steamer's certificate are not complied with in the case of any such steamer, the master or owner of the steamer shall, without prejudice to any other remedy or penalty under the Merchant Shipping Acts,[2] be liable on summary conviction to a fine not exceeding ten pounds for every passenger [3] carried from or to any place in the United Kingdom,[4] and the master or owner of any tender by means of which passengers are taken on board or landed [5] from any such steamer shall be liable to a like penalty for every passenger so taken on board or landed.[3]

[1] For these provisions, see M.S.A. 1894, ss. 271, 272.
[2] As to such remedies and penalties, see M.S.A. 1894, ss. 271, 284.
[3] By virtue of the M.S. (Load Lines) Act s. 25 and Sched. 1, the penalty became irrespective of the number of passengers (a) on summary conviction, a fine not exceeding £400 and (b) on conviction on indictment, a fine. As to who must sue for such fines, see M.S.A. 1894, s. 356.
[4] See note " Application to Northern Ireland and the Republic of Ireland " in notes to M.S.A. 1894, s. 742.
[5] As to passengers landed or embarked by means of tenders, see s. 15.

Overcrowding of passenger steamers

74 **22.** If a passenger steamer [1] has on board at any place a number of passengers [1] which, having regard to the time, occasion, and circumstances of the case, is greater than the number allowed by the passenger steamer's certificate, the owner or master of the steamer shall, for the purposes of section two hundred and eighty-three of the principal Act, be deemed to have received those passengers on board at that place.[2]

[1] See note (1) to s. 13.
[2] This section makes it an offence " to have on board " as well as " to receive on board." Thus, it would seem, a conviction might be obtained for a breach of M.S.A. 1894, s. 283, at each port at which a passenger steamer calls, so long as she has an illegal number on board.

75 **23.** [*This section, which related to the sale of steerage passages, was repealed by the Local Government Act* 1966, *ss.* 35 (1), 43 (2), 44 (2); *Sched.* 3, *Pt.* 1 *and Sched.* 6, *Part* 1 *and also by the M.S.A.* 1970 (*see s.* 24 *below*).]

776 **24.** [*This section, relating to frauds in inducing persons to engage passages, which substituted a new section for section* 353 *of the M.S.A.* 1894, *was, together with s.* 23 *above, repealed by the M.S.A.* 1970, *s.* 100 (3), *Sched. V as from January* 1, 1973; *see S.I.* 1972 *No.* 1977.]

PART III—SEAMEN'S FOOD

777 **25–26.** [*These sections, which made provision for a Statutory Scale of Provisions for Crew* (*s.* 25) *and Inspection of Provisions and Water* (*s.* 26) *were repealed by the M.S.A.* 1970, *s.* 100 (3), *Sched. V, as from January* 1, 1973: *see S.I.* 1972 *No.* 1977.]

Certificated cooks for foreign-going ships

778 **27.**—(1) [. . . .] [1] *After the thirtieth day of June nineteen hundred and eight,*[1] *every British foreign-going ship* [2] *of a thousand tons and upwards gross tonnage,*[3] *going to sea from any place in the British Islands,*[4] *or on the continent of Europe between the River Elbe and Brest inclusive, shall be provided with and carry a duly certificated cook who is able to prove one month's service at sea in some capacity.*

(2) *A cook shall not be deemed to be duly certificated within the meaning of this section unless he is the holder of a certificate of competency in cooking granted by the* [*Secretary of State for Trade*] *or by some school of cookery or other institution approved for the purpose by that* [*Secretary*], *or, is the holder of certificates of discharge showing at least two years' service as cook previously to the said thirtieth day of June nineteen hundred and eight.*

(3) *The cook shall be rated in the ship's articles* [5] *as ship's cook or in the case of ships of not more than two thousand tons gross tonnage, or ships in which the crew, or the majority of the crew, provide their own provisions, either as ship's cook or as cook and steward.*

(4) *In the case of an emigrant ship, the ship's cook shall be in addition to the cook required by section three hundred and four of the principal Act.*[6]

(5) *If the requirements of this section are not complied with in the case of any ship, the master or owner of the ship shall, if there is no sufficient reason for the failure to comply with the requirements, for each offence be liable on summary conviction* [7] *to a fine not exceeding twenty-five pounds.*

779 This section is prospectively repealed by the M.S.A. 1970, s. 100 (3), Sched. 5, as from a day to be appointed.

M.S.A. 1948, s. 6, provides for the potential widening of the scope of this section in three ways: (i) by making provision for the recognition of certificates of competency as ship's cook granted under the law of any part of H.M. dominions outside the U.K.; (ii) by providing that by Order in Council the class of ships, mentioned in subs. (1), and the places of departure, also there mentioned, may be extended; (iii) by making it possible, by Order in Council, to extend the provisions of this section to the Isle of Man, the Channel Islands, or any colony, or any foreign country in which H.M. has jurisdiction. See *post*, § 1103.

[1] The words omitted were repealed as spent by Statute Law Revision Act 1927.
[2] Defined in M.S.A. 1894, s. 742.
[3] As to rules for ascertaining gross tonnage, see M.S.A. 1965, s. 1.

[4] See Interpretation Act 1889, s. 18, and note " Application to Northern Ireland and the Republic of Ireland," both of which are printed in the notes to M.S.A. 1894, s. 742.
[5] *i.e.* the agreement with the crew, as to which see M.S.A. 1970, s. 1.
[6] The provisions relating to emigrant ships were repealed by the M.S.A. 1970 (see note at head of § 767, *ante.*)
[7] As to summary procedure, see M.S.A. 1894, ss. 680 *et seq.*

PART IV—PROVISIONS AS TO RELIEF AND REPATRIATION OF DISTRESSED SEAMEN AND SEAMEN LEFT BEHIND ABROAD

These provisions were in substitution for M.S.A. 1894, ss. 186–193, which are repealed by this Act. This part was in turn repealed by the M.S.A. 1970, s. 100 (3), Sched. V, as from January 1, 1973, save as indicated: see S.I. 1972 No. 1977.

Deduction from wages and payment to superintendents, etc., of fines

780 **44.**[1]—(1) *Every fine imposed on a seaman for any act of misconduct for which his agreement* [2] *imposes a fine shall be deducted as follows (that is to say)*:—

(*a*) *if the offender is discharged in the United Kingdom,*[3] *and the offence, and the entry in the log book required by the Merchant Shipping Acts in respect thereof,*[4] *are proved to the satisfaction,* [. . . .] [5] *of the superintendent* [. . . .] [5] *the master or owner shall deduct the fine from the wages of the offender;*

(*b*) *if the offender enters His Majesty's naval service or is discharged abroad,*[6] *and the offence and the entry as aforesaid are proved to the satisfaction of the officer in command of the ship he so enters, or of the proper authority* [. . . .] [5] *as the case may be, the fine shall be deducted as aforesaid and an entry made in the official log book of the ship and signed by the officer or authority to whose satisfaction the offence is proved.*

(2) *Every fine so deducted shall be paid—*

(*a*) *if the offender is discharged in the United Kingdom,*[3] *to the superintendent;*

(*b*) *if the offender enters His Majesty's naval service, on the return of the ship to its port of destination, if that port is in the United Kingdom,*[3] *to the superintendent* [. . . .] [5] *and, if the port of destination is not in the United Kingdom,*[3] *to the proper authority as defined for the purpose of this Part of this Act;*

(*c*) *if the offender is discharged at any place out of the United Kingdom,*[3] *to the proper authority.*[7]

(3) *A proper authority shall remit any amounts received by them under this section at such times and in such manner, and render such accounts in respect thereof, as the* [*Secretary of State for Trade requires*].

(4) *If a master or owner fails without reasonable cause to pay any fine as required by this section, he shall for each offence be liable on summary*

conviction to a fine not exceeding six times the amount of the fine not so paid.

(5) *An act of misconduct for which any fine has been inflicted and paid by, or deducted from the wages of, the seaman, shall not be otherwise punished under the Merchant Shipping Acts.*[8]

781 The whole of this section is prospectively repealed by the M.S.A. 1970, s. 100 (3), Sched. 5 as from a day to be appointed.

[1] This section takes the place of s. 235 of M.S.A. 1894, which is repealed by M.S.A. 1906, s. 85, Sched. 2.
[2] See M.S.A. 1970, s. 34 *et seq.* as to disciplinary offences.
[3] See note " Application to Northern Ireland and the Republic of Ireland " in notes to M.S.A. 1894, s. 742.
[4] As to such entries in official log, see M.S.A. 1970, s. 68.
[5] The words omitted were repealed by the M.S.A. 1970, s. 100 (3), Sched. 5 as from January 1, 1973: see S.I. 1972 No. 1977.
[6] As to discharge, see M.S.A. 1970, s. 3.
[7] As to meaning of proper authority, see s. 49.
[8] This subsection only bars further punishments under the M.S. Acts. It has no application in cases of prosecutions under other enactments: see, *e.g. Lewis* v. *Morgan* [1943] 1 K.B. 376 (prosecution under Defence Regulations).

Definitions of " proper authority " and " seamen "

782 **49.** *For the purposes of this Part of this Act, unless the context otherwise requires—*

(1) *The expression " proper authority " means—*

(*a*) *as respects a place out of His Majesty's dominions, the British consular officer,*[1] *or if there is no such officer in the place, any two British merchants resident at or near the place, or if there is only one British merchant so resident, that British merchant; and*

(*b*) *as respects a place in a British possession*[2]*—*

(i) *in relation to the discharge or leaving behind of seamen, or the payment of fines, a superintendent,*[1] *or, in the absence of any such superintendent, the chief officer of customs*[1] *at or near the place; and*

(ii) *in relation to distressed seamen the governor of the possession, or any person acting under his authority; and*

(2) *The expression " seamen " includes not only seamen as defined by the principal Act,*[3] *but also apprentices to the sea service.*[4]

(3) *The provisions of this Part of this Act shall, for the purpose of sections two hundred and sixty to two hundred and sixty-six of the principal Act (which relate to the application of Part II of that Act), be construed as if they were contained in Part II of that Act.*

This section is prospectively repealed by the M.S.A. 1970, s. 100 (3), Sched. 5 as from a day to be appointed.

[1] Defined in M.S.A. 1894, s. 742, and see notes thereon.
[2] Defined by Interpretation Act 1889, ss. 18, 18A, set out after notes to M.S.A. 1894, s. 742.

[3] For such definition, see M.S.A. 1894, s. 742, and notes thereto.
[4] The provisions in the M.S.A. 1894 relating to apprenticeship to the sea service have been repealed by the M.S.A. 1970, s. 100 (3), Sched. 5 as from January 1, 1973: see S.I. 1972 No. 1977.

PART V—MISCELLANEOUS

Ships' names

783 **50.**—(1) The [Secretary of State for Trade] in conjunction with the Commissioners of Customs,[1] may make regulations [2] enabling the [Secretary of State for Trade] to refuse the registry of any ship by the name by which it is proposed to register [3] that ship if it is already the name of a registered British ship or a name so similar as to be calculated to deceive, and may by those regulations require notice to be given in such manner as may be directed by the regulations before the name of the ship is marked [2] on the ship, or before the name of the ship is entered in the register.

(2) If the registry of a ship by the name by which it is proposed to register that ship is refused by the [Secretary of State for Trade] or if any requirements of the regulations are not complied with in the case of any ship which it is proposed to register, that ship shall not be registered [4] under the name proposed, or until the regulations are complied with, as the case may be.

784 [1] Now Commissioners of Customs and Excise; see the Excise Transfer Order 1909 (S.R. & O. No. 197) made under the Finance Act 1908, s. 4.
[2] The regulations as to the registration of ships' names now in force are those of August 28, 1907 (S.R. & O. No. 740), as amended by M.S. (Ships' Names) Amendment Regulations 1922, dated June 23, 1922 (S.R. & O. No. 729), and by M.S. (Ships' Names) Amendment Regulations dated April 9, 1936 (S.R. & O. No. 390).
[3] As to entry of name in register, see M.S.A. 1894, s. 11; as to marking of name, see *ibid.* s. 7; for rules as to name of ship, *ibid.* s. 47.
[4] As to liabilities of British ships not registered, see M.S.A. 1894, s. 2 (2) and s. 72.

Power to inquire into the title of a registered ship to be registered

785 **51.**—(1) Where it appears to the Commissioners of Customs [1] that there is any doubt as to the title of any ship registered as a British ship to be so registered, they may direct the registrar of the port of registry of the ship to require evidence to be given to his satisfaction that the ship is entitled to be registered as a British ship.[2]

(2) If within such time, not less than thirty days, as the Commissioners fix, satisfactory evidence of the title of the ship to be registered is not so given, the ship shall be subject to forfeiture [3] under Part I of the principal Act.[4]

(3) In the application of this section to a port in a British possession, the Governor of the British possession, and, in the application of this section to foreign ports of registry,[5] the [Secretary of State for Trade], shall be substituted for the Commissioners of Customs.[1]

786 [1] See note (1) to s. 50.
[2] The main element in such title is that the ship shall be wholly owned by persons or corporations duly qualified as provided by M.S.A. 1894, s. 1 (see notes thereto). As to

sundry conditions precedent to registration, see *ibid.* s. 6 *et seq.* As the register gives no clue to the persons (if any) owning a beneficial interest in the ship or any share therein, s. 51 above enables the Commissioners of Customs to inquire as to such persons, and as to their capacity to own such property, and if an unqualified person has acquired as owner otherwise than by transmission any legal or beneficial interest in the ship, that interest is rendered subject to forfeiture by M.S.A. 1894, s. 71 (*q.v.*), and the whole ship by the present section.

[3] As to the meaning of these words, see note (3) to M.S.A. 1894, s. 70.

[4] See M.S.A. 1894, s. 76, as to procedure for effecting forfeiture.

Quaere, (1) whether upon the inquiry before the High Court under M.S.A. 1894, s. 76, the parties are confined as to evidence to the information supplied to the registrar or commissioners; and (2) what is the material date with reference to which it must be proved that the vessel was not entitled to be registered as a British ship. These points were left open in *The Polzeath* [1916] P. 241 at p. 255.

In *The St. Tudno* (*No.* 2) [1918] P. 174, the decree in a forfeiture action being a decree *in rem* and therefore not competent to issue against a *res* in the custody of the Prize Court, the court dismissed a forfeiture action at the suit of the Crown in respect of a vessel registered as a British ship which at the outbreak of war was seized as prize and ordered by the Prize Court to be detained by the Marshal and was subsequently requisitioned by the Admiralty.

[5] As to these, see M.S.A. 1894, s. 88.

Provisions with respect to mortgages of ships sold to foreigners

787 **52.**—(1) Subsection (1) of section twenty-one of the principal Act shall be read as if the following words were inserted at the end of that subsection, " and the registry of the ship in that book shall be considered as closed except so far as relates to any unsatisfied mortgages or existing certificates of mortgage entered therein."

(2) It is hereby declared that where the registry of a ship is considered as closed under subsection (1) of section twenty-one of the principal Act as amended by this section, or under subsection (10) of section forty-four of that Act, on account of a transfer to persons not qualified [1] to be owners of British ships, any unsatisfied registered mortgage (including mortgages made under a certificate of mortgage) may, if the ship comes within the jurisdiction of any court in His Majesty's dominions which has jurisdiction to enforce the mortgage, or would have had such jurisdiction if the transfer had not been made, be enforced by that court notwithstanding the transfer, without prejudice, in cases where the ship has been sold under a judgment of a court, to the effect of that judgment.

[1] For the necessary qualifications, see M.S.A. 1894, s. 1, and notes thereto.

Amendment of 57 and 58 Vict. c. 60, s. 48

788 **53.** The following subsection shall be substituted for subsection (2) of section forty-eight of the principal Act:—

(2) If default is made in registering anew a ship, or in registering an alteration of a ship so altered as aforesaid, the owner of the ship shall be liable on summary conviction [1] to a fine not exceeding one hundred pounds, and in addition to a fine not exceeding five pounds for every day during which the offence continues after conviction.[2]

[1] As to summary procedure, see M.S.A. 1894, s. 680 *et seq.*
[2] Before this amendment of M.S.A. 1894, s. 48, any unregistered alteration of a British ship which affected her tonnage caused her to be deemed not duly registered, and therefore not to be recognised as a British ship, thereby depriving her owners of (*inter alia*) the right (under s. 503, M.S.A. 1894) to limit their liability in case of collision. The effect of the new subsection is that the ship retains her rights as a recognised British ship, but the owner is subject to the named penalties.

789 **54–55.** [*These sections, which contained provisions relating to deduction of spaces used for water ballast in ascertaining tonnage (s.* 54) *and crew space in foreign ships (s.* 55) *were repealed by the M.S.A.* 1965, *s.* 7 (2), *Sched.* 2. *See now ibid. s.* 1.]

Second mate certificates allowed in small foreign-going sailing ships

790 **56.** *The following paragraph shall be substituted for paragraph* (*b*) *of subsection* (1) *of section ninety-two of the principal Act* (*which relates to the certificates of competency to be held by officers of ships*):—

" (*b*) *If the ship is of one hundred tons burden* [1] *or upwards with at least one officer besides the master holding a certificate not lower than that of*—

" (i) *mate in the case of a home-trade* [2] *passenger ship;*

" (ii) *second mate in the case of a foreign-going* [2] *sailing ship of not more than two hundred tons burden; and*

" (iii) *only mate in the case of any foreign-going* [2] *ship.*"

This section is prospectively repealed by the M.S.A. 1970, s. 100 (3), Sched. 5, as from a day to be appointed.

[1] In *The Brunel* [1900] P. 24, the court held that in M.S.A. 1894, s. 3, " tons burden " meant " net register tonnage," but intimated that in other parts of the Act another meaning might be required; see note (1) to s. 3, *ibid.*
[2] For definition, see M.S.A. 1894, s. 742.

791 **57.** [*This section which contained provisions relating to the powers of court in case of unreasonable delay in paying master's wages, was repealed by M.S.A.*, 1970, *s.* 100 (3), *Sched.* 5 *as from January* 1, 1973*: see S.I.* 1972, *No.* 1977.]

Title to be rated as A.B.

792 **58.**—(1) *For the purpose of reducing the period of service required as a qualification for the rating of A.B., the period of " three years before the mast " shall be substituted for the period of " four years before the mast," and " two years of that employment " shall be substituted for " three years of that employment," and " two or more years sea service " shall be substituted for " three or more years sea service," in section one hundred and twenty-six of the principal Act.*

(2) *Any superintendent or other officer before whom a seaman is engaged shall refuse to enter the seaman as A.B. on the agreement with the crew*

unless the seaman gives such satisfactory proof as is required by section one hundred and twenty-six of the principal Act of his title to be so rated; and if any seaman, for the purpose of obtaining a rating as A.B., makes any false statement or false representation, he shall be liable on summary conviction [1] *in respect of each offence to a fine not exceeding five pounds.*

This section is prospectively repealed by the M.S.A. 1970, s. 100 (3), Sched. 5, as from a day to be appointed.

As from May 1, 1953, this section ceased to have effect in relation to any seamen for the time being engaged in a British ship registered in the United Kingdom; see M.S.A. 1948, s. 5 (6), and M.S. (Certificates of Competency as A.B.) Regulations 1959 (S.I. No. 2148). The new provisions relating to the certification of such seamen as A.B.s are contained in the said section and regulations (as amended by S.I. 1962 No. 579 and S.I. 1975 No. 341).

[1] For summary procedure, see M.S.A. 1894, s. 680 *et seq.*

Notice of disrating of seaman

793 **59–63.** [*These sections which contained provisions relating to Notice of disrating of seaman* (*s.* 59), *Power to except claims from release on settlement of wages* (*s.* 60), *Obligation to offer allotment notes* (*s.* 61), *Time for payment of allotment note* (*s.* 62) *and Master to give facilities to seamen for remitting wages* (*s.* 63) *were repealed by the M.S.A.* 1970, *s.* 100 (3), *Sched.* 5 *as from January* 1, 1973: *see S.I.* 1972, *No.* 1977.]

Increase of crew space

794 **64.**—(1) *Subsection* (1) *of section two hundred and ten of the principal Act* (*which provides for the space required for each seaman or apprentice in any place in a British ship occupied by seamen or apprentices and appropriated to their use*) *shall be construed as if a space of not less than one hundred and twenty cubic feet and of not less than fifteen superficial feet measured on the deck or floor of that space were substituted for a space of not less than seventy-two cubic feet and of not less than twelve superficial feet measured on the deck or floor of that space.*

(2) *In estimating the space available for the proper accommodation of seamen and apprentices, there may be taken into account the space occupied by any mess rooms, bath rooms, or washing places appropriated exclusively to the use of those seamen and apprentices, so, however, that the space in any place appropriated to the use of seamen or apprentices in which they sleep is not less than seventy-two cubic feet and twelve superficial feet for each seaman or apprentice.*

(3) *Nothing in this section shall affect—*

(*a*) *any ship registered before the passing of this Act or which was in course of construction on the first day of January nineteen hundred and seven; or*

(*b*) *any ship of not more than three hundred tons burden* [1]; *or*

(*c*) *any fishing boat within the meaning of Part IV of the principal Act,*[2] *or require any additional space to be given in the case of places occupied solely by lascars and appropriated to their use.*

This section is prospectively repealed by the M.S.A. 1970, s. 100 (3), Sched. 5, as from a day to be appointed.

This section does not apply to any ship to which regulations made under s. 1 of the Merchant Shipping Act 1948, apply. See s. 4 (3) of the Act of 1948, § 1100, *post*.

[1] In *The Brunel* [1900] P. 24 the court held that " tons burden " in M.S.A. 1894, s. 3, means " net register tonnage," but intimated that a different meaning might be required in other parts of the Act.

[2] For application of Part IV to fishing boats, see M.S.A. 1894, s. 369; and for definition of " fishing boat," see *ibid.* s. 370.

Provisions as to failure to join ship and desertion

795 **65.**—[*This section which contained provisions as to failure to join ship and desertion was repealed by the M.S.A.* 1970, *s.* 100 (3), *Sched. 5 as from January* 1, 1973; *see S.I.* 1972, *No.* 1977.]

Appeal from decision on investigation as to shipping casualties

796 **66.**[1] *Where, on any investigation or inquiry under the provisions of Part VI of the principal Act, the court find that a shipping casualty* [2] *has been caused or contributed to by the wrongful act or default* [3] *of any person, and an application for rehearing has not been made under section four hundred and seventy-five or section four hundred and seventy-eight of the principal Act, or has been refused, the owner of the ship,*[2] *or any other person who, having an interest in the investigation or inquiry, has appeared at the hearing and is affected* [4] *by the decision of the court, may appeal from that decision in the same manner and subject to the same conditions in and subject to which a master may appeal under those sections against a decision with respect to the cancelling or suspension of his certificate.*

This section, together with ss. 67 and 68, were prospectively repealed by the M.S.A. 1970, s. 100 (3), Sched. 5 as from a day to be appointed. A substituted version of this section applies to diving operations: see the M.S. (Diving Operations) Regulations 1975 (S.I. No. 116), reg. 20 and Sched. 4.

[1] The effect of this section is to reverse the decisions in *The Golden Sea* (1882) 7 P.D. 194, and in *The Ida* (1886) 11 P.D. 37. As to costs of appeal, see *The Carlisle* [1906] P. 301, at p. 310.

[2] This section has effect as if the references to ships or activities connected with shipping included references to hovercraft or activities connected with hovercraft: see the Hovercraft (Application of Enactments) Order 1972 S.I. No. 971.

[3] As to the meaning of these words, see note (6) to s. 470, M.S.A. 1894.

[4] So a master who has been found guilty of negligence but whose certificate has not been suspended or cancelled has a right of appeal; *The Royal Star* [1928] P. 48.

Power of naval court to send a person sentenced to imprisonment home to undergo sentence

797 **67.**—(1) *The powers of a naval court under section four hundred and eighty-three of the principal Act (which deals with those powers) shall include a power to send an offender sentenced by the court to imprisonment either to the United Kingdom or to any British possession to which His Majesty by Order in Council has applied this section, as appears to them*

most convenient for the purpose of being imprisoned, and the court may take the same steps, and for that purpose shall have the same powers, as respects the orders which may be given to masters of ships as a consular officer has for the purpose of sending an offender for trial under section six hundred and eighty-nine of the principal Act, and subsections (2) (4) *and* (5) *of that section shall apply with the necessary modification.*[1]

(2) *Any master of a ship to whose charge an offender is committed under this section shall, on his ship's arrival in the United Kingdom or in a British possession, as the case may be, give the offender into the custody of some police officer or constable, and the offender shall be dealt with as if he had been convicted and sentenced to imprisonment by a court of competent jurisdiction in the United Kingdom or in the British possession, as the case may be.*

(3) *His Majesty may*[2] *by Order in Council apply this section to any British possession the Legislature of which consents to that application.*

[1] Any direction by a naval court under this section may be revoked by a reviewing officer under M.S.A. 1950; see s. 3 (4) of that Act.
[2] This power has not yet been exercised.

Appeal from naval courts

798 **68.**—(1) *Any person aggrieved by an order of a naval court ordering the forfeiture of wages, or by a decision of a naval court of a question as to wages, fines, or forfeitures, may appeal to the High Court*[1] *in such manner and subject to such conditions and provisions as may be provided by rules of court,*[2] *and on any such appeal the High Court may confirm, quash, or vary the order or decision appealed against as they think just.*[3]

(2) *Subsection* (2) *of section four hundred and eighty-three of the principle Act shall not have effect with respect to any order of a naval court which is quashed on an appeal under this section, and where an order of a naval court is varied on appeal, shall apply as if the order as so varied were the order originally made by the naval court.*

799 [1] See R.S.C. Ord. 74, r. 2 (§ 3190, *post*).

The appeal is to a Divisional Court of the Queen's Bench Division consisting, if possible, of judges of the Admiralty Court Division of the High Court. Notice must be given, within three months from the date on which the order or decision appealed from was pronounced, to all other parties to the proceedings whom the appellant may consider directly affected by the appeal, together with notice of the general grounds of the appeal. Further evidence on questions of fact may be given.

An appeal lies from the Divisional Court with leave to the Court of Appeal. Supreme Court of Judicature (Consolidation) Act 1925, s. 31 (1)(*f*).

[2] This subsection in its application to Northern Ireland has effect with the omission of the words " in such manner and subject to such conditions and provisions as may be provided by rules of court "; see the Northern Ireland Act 1962, s. 30 (2), Sched. I, Part I.

[3] This section was enacted to meet the case of *Hutton* v. *Ras S.S. Co.* [1907] 1 K.B. 834, in which case, a naval court having discharged and forfeited the wages of a crew who had lawfully refused to continue a voyage in a ship carrying contraband, an action by the crew for their wages was dismissed on the ground that the finding of the naval court was conclusive.

Calculation of tonnage of steamship for the purpose of limitation of liability

800 **69.** For the purpose of the limitation under the Merchant Shipping Acts of the liability of owners of ships, docks, or canals, and of harbour authorities and conservancy authorities,[1] the tonnage of a steamship shall be her registered tonnage,[2] with the addition of any engine-room space deducted for the purpose of ascertaining that tonnage, and the words " registered tonnage with the addition of any engine-room space deducted for the purpose of ascertaining that tonnage " shall accordingly be substituted in paragraph (*a*) of subsection (2) of section five hundred and three of the principal Act for " gross tonnage without deduction on account of engine-room."

The effect of this provision is that steamships can now deduct crew space for the purpose of arriving at their tonnage in limitation of liability actions.

[1] For the meaning of these terms, see M.S.A. 1894, s. 742, or Merchant Shipping (Liability of Shipowners and Others) Act 1900, s. 2.

[2] For the provisions as to tonnage measurement, see M.S.A. 1965, s. 1.

801 **70–71.** [*These sections which amended the provisions of Part VIII of the M.S.A.* 1894, *and s.* 1 *of the M.S.* (*Liability of Shipowners*) *Act* 1898 (*now repealed*) *have been repealed by the M.S.* (*Liability of Shipowners and Others*) *Act* 1958, *s.* 8 (6) *and Schedule. See now ibid. ss.* 3 (1) *and* 4.]

Delivery of wreck to receiver

802 **72.** Section five hundred and eighteen of the principal Act shall apply to wreck [1] found or taken possession of outside the limits of the United Kingdom, and brought within the limits of the United Kingdom,[2] as it applies to wreck found or taken possession of within the limits of the United Kingdom.

[1] As to the meaning of " wreck," see M.S.A. 1894, s. 510, and notes thereto. The section has effect as if references to activities connected with ships included activities connected with hovercraft: see the Hovercraft (Application of Enactments) Order 1972 (S.I. No. 971).

[2] As to these limits, see Territorial Waters Jurisdiction Act 1878. As to the meaning of " United Kingdom," see note " Application to Northern Ireland and the Republic of Ireland," in notes to M.S.A. 1894, s. 742.

803 **73.** [*This section, which dealt with alien pilotage certificates, was repealed by the Pilotage Act* 1913, *s.* 60, *and Schedule II, and the subject-matter thereof is dealt with in section* 24, *ibid.* (*q.v. post*), *and the Aliens Restriction Amendment Act* 1919, *s.* 4, *cited in notes to the last-mentioned section.*]

804 **74.** [*This section, which contained provisions as to superintendents, etc., was repealed by the M.S.A.* 1970, *s.* 100 (3), *Sched. V as from January* 1, 1973: *see S.I.* 1972 *No.* 1977.]

Substitution of ship surveyor for shipwright surveyor

805 **75.**—(1) Any person appointed to be a surveyor of ships [1] under section seven hundred and twenty-four of the principal Act may be appointed either as a ship surveyor or as an engineer surveyor, or as both, and any reference in that section or in any other section of the principal Act to a shipwright surveyor shall be construed as a reference to a ship surveyor.

(2) Any surveyor of ships who before the passing of this Act has been appointed as a shipwright surveyor, or both as a shipwright surveyor and an engineer surveyor, shall be deemed to have been appointed as a ship surveyor, or both as a ship surveyor and an engineer surveyor, as the case may be.

(3) The surveys required to be made under section two hundred and seventy-two of the principal Act by a ship surveyor and by an engineer surveyor may be made by the same person if that person has been appointed both as a ship surveyor and as an engineer surveyor, and that section shall be construed accordingly.

(4) The [Secretary of State for Trade] may, under subsection (2) of section seven hundred and twenty-four of the principal Act, in addition to appointing a surveyor-general of ships, appoint such other principal officers in connection with the survey of ships and other matters incidental thereto, as the [Secretary thinks] fit.

[1] As to powers of surveyors of ships, see M.S.A. 1970, s. 76.

Return to be furnished by masters of ships as to passengers

806 **76.**—(1) The master of every ship, whether a British or foreign ship, which carries any passenger [1] to a place in the United Kingdom [2] from any place out of the United Kingdom, or from any place in the United Kingdom to any place out of the United Kingdom, shall furnish to such person and in such manner as the [Secretary of State for Trade directs], a return giving the total number of any passengers so carried,[3] distinguishing, if so directed by the [Secretary], the total number of any class of passengers so carried, and giving, if the [Secretary of State for Trade] so [directs], such particulars with respect to passengers as may be for the time being required by the [Secretary].[4]

(2) Any passenger shall furnish the master of the ship with any information required by him for the purpose of the return.

(3) If the master of a ship fails to make a return as required by this section, or makes a false return, and if any passenger refuses to give any information required by the master of the ship for the purpose of the return required by this section, or gives any false information for the purpose, the master or passenger shall be liable for each offence on summary conviction [5] to a fine not exceeding twenty pounds.

[1] For meaning of "passenger," see M.S. (Safety Convention) Act 1949, s. 26, and notes to M.S.A. 1894, s. 267.

[2] See note "Application to Northern Ireland and the Republic of Ireland" in notes to M.S.A. 1894, s. 742.

[3] Including passengers conveyed to or from the ship in a tender. See s. 15.

[4] Rules and forms were prescribed by the Secretary of State for Trade under this section on August 16, 1960, and published as M.S. (Passenger Returns) Regulations 1960 (S.I. No. 1477) by which previous Orders were revoked and replaced.

[5] As to summary procedure, see M.S.A. 1894, ss. 680 *et seq.*

Return as to cattlemen brought to the United Kingdom

807 **77.**—(1) The master of every ship which carries any cattlemen to any port in the United Kingdom from any port out of the United Kingdom [1] shall furnish to such person and in such manner as the Secretary of State [2] directs, a return giving such particulars with respect to any cattlemen so carried as may be required for the time being by order of the Secretary of State, and every such cattleman shall furnish the master of the ship with any information required by him for the purpose of the return.

(2) If the master of a ship fails to make the return required by this section, or makes a false return, he shall be liable on summary conviction [3] to a fine not exceeding one hundred pounds, and if any cattleman refuses to give information required by the master for the purpose of the return under this section, or gives any false information for the purpose, he shall be liable on summary conviction to imprisonment with hard labour [4] for a term not exceeding three months.

(3) For the purpose of this section the expression "cattleman" means any person who is engaged or employed to attend during the voyage of the ship on any cattle carried therein as cargo.

[1] "United Kingdom" here includes the Republic of Ireland. See note "Application to Northern Ireland and the Republic of Ireland" in notes to M.S.A. 1894, s. 742.

[2] An order as to the Return of Cattlemen was made on July 23, 1923, and published as S.R. & O. 1923 No. 876.

[3] For summary procedure, see M.S.A. 1894, ss. 680 *et seq.*

[4] Imprisonment with hard labour has now been abolished; see Criminal Justice Act 1948, s. 1 (2). The section must now be construed as conferring power to sentence to imprisonment; *ibid.*

Dispensing powers of the [Secretary of State for Trade]

808 **78.**—(1) The [Secretary of State for Trade] may, if [he thinks] fit, and upon such conditions (if any) as [he thinks] fit to impose, exempt any ship from any specified requirement contained in, or prescribed in pursuance of, the Merchant Shipping Acts, or dispense with the observance of any such requirement in the case of any ship, if [he is] satisfied that that requirement has been substantially complied with in the case of that ship, or that compliance with the requirement is unnecessary in the circumstances of the case, and that the action taken or provision made as respects the subject-

matter of the requirement in the case of the ship is as effective as, or more effective than, actual compliance with the requirement.

(2) The [Secretary of State for Trade] shall annually lay before both Houses of Parliament a special report stating the cases in which [he has] exercised [his] powers under this section during the preceding year, and the grounds upon which [he has] acted in each case.

Under various sections of the M.S. Acts the Department of Trade or other branch of the Executive is also empowered to exempt ships, or classes of ships, from specific requirements of the Acts, *e.g.* M.S.A. 1894, s. 7 (2) (marking of ship), s. 363 (survey of foreign ships), s. 369 (application of Part IV to fishing boats); M.S. (Safety Convention) Act 1949, s. 28 (safety requirements); M.S. (Load Lines) Act 1967, ss. 18–22.

Power to appoint advisory committees

809 **79.**—(1) The [Secretary of State for Trade] may, if [he thinks] fit, appoint committees for the purpose of advising [him] when considering the making or alteration of any rules, regulations, or scales for the purpose of the Merchant Shipping Acts, consisting of such persons as [he] may appoint representing the interests principally affected, or having special knowledge of the subject-matter.

(2) There shall be paid to the members of any such committee, out of moneys provided by Parliament, such travelling and other allowances as the [Secretary of State for Trade fixes], with the consent of the Treasury.[1]

(3) Committees may be appointed under this section to advise the [Secretary of State for Trade] specially as regards any special rules, regulations, or scales, or generally as regards any class or classes of rules, regulations, or scales which the [Secretary of State] may assign to them.

[1] See the Minister for the Civil Service Order 1968 (S.I. No. 1656) as to the transfer of certain such functions of the Treasury to the Minister.

A standing Merchant Shipping Advisory Committee under this section is reappointed by the Secretary of State for Trade every two years, and includes representatives of the different interests involved.

Power to register Government ships under the Merchant Shipping Acts

810 **80.**—(1) His Majesty may by Order in Council[1] make regulations with respect to the manner in which Government ships may be registered as British ships for the purpose of the Merchant Shipping Acts, and those Acts, subject to any exceptions and modifications which may be made by Order in Council, either generally or as respects any special class of Government ships, shall apply to Government ships registered in accordance with those regulations as if they were registered in manner provided by those Acts.

(2) Nothing in this Act shall affect the powers of the Legislature of any British possession to regulate any Government ships under the control of the Government of that possession.

(3) In this section the expression " Government ships " means ships not forming part of His Majesty's Navy which belong to His Majesty, or

are held by any person on behalf of or for the benefit of the Crown, and for that reason cannot be registered under the principal Act.[2]

811 [1] For provisions as to Orders in Council, see M.S.A. 1894, s. 738.

[2] The Merchant Shipping Acts do not, except where specially provided, apply to ships " belonging to Her Majesty," M.S.A. 1894, s. 741. See note thereto, for various sections specially referring to such ships; as to what ships are included in the term, see note (1) to M.S.A. 1894, s. 557.

Regulations have been made under this section with respect to the registration as British ships of vessels in the service of Crown or Government Departments and as to the application of these Acts to such vessels by the following Orders in Council:— Admiralty, March 22, 1911 (S.R. & O. No. 338) as amended by S.I. 1964 No. 489; Ministry of Agriculture and Fisheries, February 9, 1920 (S.R. & O. No. 260); the Board of Trade (now Department of Trade), July 14, 1921 (S.R. & O. No. 1211) as amended by S.I. 1968 No. 2038; Government of Commonwealth of Australia, December 8, 1924 (S.R. & O. No. 1391); Government of Straits Settlements, August 10, 1926 (S.R. & O. No. 1036); Government of India, November 5, 1929 (S.R. & O. No. 986); Government of Union of South Africa, November 5, 1929 (S.R. & O. No. 987); Government of Northern Ireland, May 15, 1930 (S.R. & O. No. 336); New Zealand, July 10, 1946 (S.R. & O. No. 1086); Sierra Leone, 1951 (S.I. No. 143); Federation of Nigeria, 1957 (S.I. No. 861); Scottish Fishery Cruisers, Research Ships, etc., 1960 (S.I. No. 2217) as amended by S.I. 1973 No. 2001; Highland and Islands Shipping Services, *i.e.* vessels owned by the Secretary of State for Scotland, 1961 (S.I. No. 1514); British Antarctic Territory, 1963 (S.I. No. 1494); Colonial Governments, 1963 (S.I. No. 1631) as amended by S.I. 1965 No. 1867 and S.I. 1967 No. 1903; Western Australia, 1964 (S.I. No. 270); Ministry of Technology, 1966 (S.I. No. 269); Queensland, 1968 (S.I. No. 1092); South Australia, 1971 (S.I. No. 872).

For the effect of this section and of the Order in Council dated December 8, 1924 (Commonwealth of Australia vessels), see *Commonwealth of Australia* v. *Asiatic Steam Navigation Co. Ltd.* (*The River Loddon*) [1956] 1 Lloyd's Rep. 658.

In *The Matti* [1918] P. 314 (cited in note (1) to M.S.A. 1894, s. 557), the court held that this section (s. 80) did not empower the Crown to declare what class of ships was included in or excluded from the category of ships " belonging to Her Majesty " within the meaning of M.S.A. 1894, s. 557 (salvage by H.M. ships).

The meaning of " Government ships " has been applied by the Prevention of Oil Pollution Act 1971, ss. 16 (4) and 24 (3).

Application of certain sections of principal Act to Scotland

812 **81.**—(1) Sections four hundred and thirteen to four hundred and sixteen of the principal Act (which relate to certificates of skippers and second hands on trawlers) shall apply to fishing boats being trawlers of twenty-five tons tonnage and upwards, going to sea from any port of Scotland in like manner as they apply to such fishing boats going to sea from any port of England or Ireland, except that in section four hundred and fifteen the date of the commencement of this Act shall be substituted for the dates mentioned in that section, and Part IV of the principal Act shall be construed accordingly.

(2) The sections aforesaid as hereby applied to Scotland shall, notwithstanding anything contained in Part IV of the principal Act, be deemed to be portions or provisions of Part IV referred to in section three hundred and sixty-nine of the principal Act (conferring power on the [Secretary of State for Trade] to make exempting or extending orders), and that section (with the substitution of the Edinburgh Gazette for the London Gazette) and Part IV shall be construed accordingly: Provided that any

Order to be published in the Edinburgh Gazette under that section shall be subject to the consent of the Secretary for Scotland.

As to the general application of Part IV of the principal Act to Scotland, see M.S. (Scottish Fishing Boats) Act 1920.

Amendment of procedure in Scotland

813 **82.** The principal Act in its application to Scotland, is amended as follows:—

(1) *Subsection one of section two hundred and thirty-seven of the principal Act is hereby amended by the addition thereto of the following words: " And such person found on board without consent as aforesaid may be taken before any sheriff or justice of the peace without warrant, and such sheriff or justice may summarily hear the case, and on proof of the offence, convict such offender as aforesaid."* [1]

(2) The provisions of section six hundred and eighty of the principal Act shall apply to Scotland.

(3) *Section seven hundred and two of the principal Act shall be amended by the deletion of the words " by criminal libel at the instance of the procurator fiscal of the county before the sheriff," and* [2] every offence referred to in section seven hundred and two of the principal Act may be prosecuted by indictment.

(4) *The words " or misdemeanors " in section seven hundred and three of the principal Act are hereby repealed.* [2]

[1] The words in italics were repealed by the M.S.A. 1970, s. 100 (3), Sched. V, as from January 1, 1973: see S.I. 1972 No. 1977.

[2] The words in italics were repealed as spent by the Statute Law Revision Act 1927.

Amendment of section 744 of 57 & 58 Vict. c. 60, as respects Scottish whalers

814 **83.** Section seven hundred and forty-four of the principal Act (which relates to the application of that Act to certain fishing vessels) shall not apply to ships engaged in the whale fisheries off the coast of Scotland and registered at ports in Scotland, and accordingly there shall be added at the end of that section the words " and of ships engaged in the whale fisheries off the coast of Scotland registered at ports in Scotland."

PART VI—SUPPLEMENTAL

Construction of references to Merchant Shipping Acts

815 **84.**—(1) In this Act the expression " principal Act " means the Merchant Shipping Act 1894, and the expression " Merchant Shipping

Acts" means the Merchant Shipping Acts 1894 to 1900, and this Act.

(2) Any reference in this Act to any provision of the Merchant Shipping Acts 1894 to 1900, which has been amended by any subsequent Act or is amended by this Act, shall be construed as a reference to the provision as so amended.

Repeal

816 85. *The enactments mentioned in the Second Schedule to this Act are hereby repealed to the extent specified in the third column of that schedule.*[1]

[1] This section was repealed as spent by the Statute Law Revision Act 1927.

Short title and commencement

817 86.—(1) This Act may be cited as the Merchant Shipping Act 1906, and shall be construed as one [1] with the principal Act, and the Merchant Shipping Acts 1894 to 1900 and this Act may be cited together as the Merchant Shipping Acts 1894 to 1906.[2]

(2) *This Act shall, save as otherwise expressly provided, come into operation on the first day of June nineteen hundred and seven.*[3]

[1] "Construed as one."—See note (1) to s. 9 of M.S. (Mercantile Marine Fund) Act 1898.
[2] Now the Merchant Shipping Acts 1894 to 1974: see § 1639, *post*.
[3] This subsection was repealed as spent by the Statute Law Revision Act 1927.

SCHEDULES

818 [*The First Schedule was repealed by the M.S.A.* 1970, *s.* 100 (3), *Sched. V, as from January* 1, 1973: *see S.I.* 1972 *No.* 1977; *and the Second Schedule was repealed by the Statute Law Revision Act* 1927.]

MERCHANT SHIPPING ACT 1907

(7 EDW. 7, c. 52)

819 [*This Act, which amended s.* 78 *of the M.S.A.* 1894, *with respect to the deduction of space occupied by propelling power in ascertaining the tonnage of a ship, was repealed by the M.S.A.* 1965, *ss.* 5 (1), 7 (2) *and Sched. II. See now ibid. s.* 1.]

MERCHANT SHIPPING (SEAMEN'S ALLOTMENT) ACT 1911

(1 & 2 Geo. 5, c. 8)

820 [*This Act was repealed by the M.S.A.* 1970, *s.* 100 (3), *Sched.* 5, *as from January* 1, 1973: *see S.I.* 1972 *No.* 1977. *See now ibid. s.* 13.]

MERCHANT SHIPPING (STEVEDORES AND TRIMMERS) ACT 1911

(1 & 2 Geo. 5, c. 41)

821 [*This Act was repealed by the Administration of Justice Act* 1956, *ss.* 7 (1), 55 (1), 57 (2), *Sched. I, Pt.* 3, *para.* 7 (1), *Pt.* 3, *Sched. II.*]

MERCHANT SHIPPING ACT 1911

(1 & 2 Geo. 5, c. 42)

822 An Act to give jurisdiction under section seventy-six and Part VIII of the Merchant Shipping Act 1894, to certain British Courts in foreign countries. [16th December, 1911.]

Be it enacted, etc.

Introductory Note.—This statute was passed in consequence of the decision of the Privy Council in *The S.S. Maori King* [1909] A.C. 562 where it was held that a British Court in Shanghai had no jurisdiction to deal with a case of forfeiture. Although the importance of this Act has diminished since 1911, there are still British Courts in the Persian Gulf States (Bahrain, Qatar, Muscat and the Trucial States), and possibly in Tonga and the New Hebrides too, which derive their jurisdiction over forfeiture from this statute.

Extension of jurisdiction under section 76 and Part VIII of 57 & 58 Vict. c. 60 to certain British courts in foreign countries

823 **1.**—(1) Among the courts before which a ship may be brought for adjudication under section seventy-six of the Merchant Shipping Act 1894 (which relates to proceedings on forfeiture of a ship), there shall be included any British Court in a foreign country, being a court having Admiralty jurisdiction, as if such a court were included among the courts

specified in that section, and that section shall be construed and have effect accordingly.

(2) Any such British Court shall also have jurisdiction to entertain any proceedings under Part VIII of the Merchant Shipping Act 1894, and accordingly section five hundred and four of that Act (which relates to the power of courts to consolidate claims against owners) shall be construed and have effect as if such a court were included among the courts to which an application under that section may be made.

(3) In this Act the expression " British Court in a foreign country " means any British Court having jurisdiction out of His Majesty's Dominions in pursuance of an Order in Council whether made under any Act or otherwise.

Short title and construction

824 **2.** This Act may be cited as the Merchant Shipping Act 1911, and shall be construed as one [1] with the Merchant Shipping Act 1894, and the Merchant Shipping Acts 1894 to 1907, and this Act may be cited together as the Merchant Shipping Acts 1894 to 1911.[2]

[1] " Construed as one."—See note (1) to s. 9 of M.S. (Mercantile Marine Fund) Act 1898.
[2] Now the Merchant Shipping Acts 1894 to 1974: see § 1639, *post*.

MARITIME CONVENTIONS ACT 1911

(1 & 2 Geo. 5, c. 57)

An Act to amend the Law relating to Merchant Shipping with a view to enabling certain Conventions to be carried into effect.

[16th December, 1911.]

825 Introductory Note.—This Act marks a further stage of progress in the unification of international maritime law, and brings the English law as to the division of loss in collision actions and as to salvage into line with the practice of other maritime nations. Whilst the Collision Regulations had long enjoyed international recognition, the practice as to the proof of liability, the incidence of the loss caused by collisions at sea and the shipowners' rights in respect of limitation of liability varied widely in different countries. In England the statutory presumptions of fault which arose on proof of a breach of the Collision Regulations (M.S.A. 1894, s. 419 (4)), or of failure to stand by after collision (*ibid.* s. 422 (2)), were wholly arbitrary rules of law and sometimes led to harsh results. A further hardship was added by the old Admiralty rule of equal division of

loss on a finding of " both to blame " in cases where the colliding ships were in fault in different degrees.

At a conference held in Brussels in 1910, at which the principal maritime nations were represented, substantial agreement was reached on the rules as to division of loss and proof of liability and on the law of salvage, but the question of limitation of liability was reserved for further consideration. The result of these deliberations was embodied in two Conventions which were signed at Brussels on September 23, 1910, and duly ratified by the signatory Powers. Parliamentary Paper, Miscellaneous, No. 5 (1911), Cmd. 5558. For the text of the Collisions Convention, see *British Shipping Laws*, Vol. 4, *Marsden on Collisions at Sea*, 11th ed., § 1271 *et seq.*

The Maritime Conventions Act, 1911, provides the consequent alterations in the law of this country; while only minor amendments in the law of salvage were necessary in order to give effect to the Salvage Convention, the alterations in the law as to proof of liability and the division of loss are far-reaching and fundamental. An interesting account of the diverse practice of many foreign States will be found in the speech of Lord Gorell, delivered during the passage of the Bill through the House of Lords, see Hansard, *House of Lords Debates*, Vol. 10, col. 16. See, too, 12 *Law Quarterly Review*, 260. As to the omission from this Act of one of the resolutions of the Convention relating to salvage, see the speech of Lord Maugham in *The Beaverford* v. *The Kafiristan* [1938] A.C. 136 at p. 155.

Subsequently, the common law has been adapted to give the courts similar powers to apportion liability between joint tortfeasors, see the Law Reform (Contributory Negligence) Act 1945; and in *Davies* v. *Swan Motor Co.* (*Swansea*) *Ltd.* (*James, Third Party*) [1949] 2 K.B. 291, Evershed L.J. said (at p. 319): "I express the hope that there should be and will be no divergence of principle or of the application of principle between the Admiralty Courts and the Common Law Courts, in dealing with matters of contributory negligence under the Acts of 1911 and 1945 respectively. It seems to me that, broadly regarded, the intention of the two Acts was, in substance the same, so that similar principles should apply and be applied in the same way."

Whereas [1] *at the Conference held at Brussels in the year nineteen hundred and ten two conventions,*[2] *dealing respectively with collisions between vessels and with salvage, were signed on behalf of His Majesty, and it is desirable that such amendments should be made in the law relating to merchant shipping as will enable effect to be given to the conventions*:

826 [1] The preamble is repealed by the Statute Law Revision Act 1927, but such repeal is not to affect the operation or construction of the statute. Inasmuch, however, as in certain cases reference may be made to the Conventions mentioned in the preamble (as to which see next note), the preamble is here retained.

[2] For the Collisions Convention, see *British Shipping Laws*, Vol. 4, *Marsden on Collisions at Sea*, 11th ed., § 1271 *et seq.* Where the words of the statute are ambiguous, reference may be made to the Conventions in order to arrive at the true intention of the contracting parties; see *The Cairnbahn* [1914] P. 25. "If the words in the section which I have to construe (s. 1) were ambiguous I think I should be entitled to look at the conventions referred to in the preamble in order to see whether a reasonable construction could be given to the section which would carry out what was agreed by the high contracting parties to the conventions. It is not necessary to do this, because the words appear to be unambiguous and clear." *Per* Sir S. Evans P. [1914] P. at p. 29. See also *per* Lord Parker, *ibid.* at p. 30. See too, *Ellerman Lines* v. *Murray* (*The Croxteth Hall*); *White Star Line* v. *Comerford* (*The Celtic*) [1931] A.C. 126; *Salomon* v. *Commissioners of Customs and Excise* [1967] 2 Q.B. 116; *Post Office* v. *Estuary Radio Ltd.* [1968] 2 Q.B. 740; *The Annie Hay* [1968] P. 341; *Warwick Film Productions Ltd.* v. *Ersinger* [1969] 1 Ch. 508; *Corocraft Ltd.* v. *Pan American Airways, Inc.* [1969] 1 Q.B. 616.

BE it therefore enacted, etc.

By virtue of the Hovercraft (Civil Liability) Order 1971 (S.I. No. 720), ss. 1–3, 8 and 9 (4) of this Act apply as if references therein to vessels included references to hovercraft: *cf.* Hovercraft Act 1968, s. 1 (1), *post*, § 1317.

Provisions as to Collisions, etc.

Rule as to division of loss

827 **1.**—(1) Where, by the fault of two or more vessels,[1] damage or loss [2] is caused to one or more of those vessels,[3] to their cargoes or freight, or to any property on board,[4] the liability to make good [5] the damage or loss shall be in proportion [6] to the degree [7] in which each vessel was in fault: Provided that—

(*a*) if, having regard to all the circumstances of the case, it is not possible to establish different degrees of fault, the liability shall be apportioned equally [8]; and

(*b*) nothing in this section shall operate so as to render any vessel liable for any loss or damage to which her fault has not contributed; and

(*c*) nothing in this section shall affect the liability of any person under a contract of carriage or any contract,[9] or shall be construed as imposing any liability upon any person from which he is exempted by any contract or by any provision of law,[10] or as affecting the right of any person to limit his liability [11] in the manner provided by law.

(2) For the purposes of this Act, the expression "freight" includes passage money and hire, and references to damage or loss caused by the fault of a vessel shall be construed as including references to any salvage or other expenses, consequent upon that fault, recoverable at law by way of damages.

828 By s. 3 (1) of the Law Reform (Contributory Negligence) Act 1945, that Act does not apply to any claim to which this section applies and this Act (*i.e.* the M.C.A. 1911) has effect as if that Act had not been passed. The intention of the two Acts is the same, so that similar principles should be applied by the Common Law Courts and the Admiralty Courts in the same way. See *Davies* v. *Swan Motor Co.* (*Swansea*) (*Swansea Corporation and James* (*Third*

Parties)) [1949] 2 K.B. 291 *per* Evershed L.J. at p. 319. This section now applies in the case of vessels belonging to Her Majesty (as defined in s. 38 (2) of the Crown Proceedings Act 1947) as it applies in the case of other vessels; *ibid.* s. 6 (see notes to that section, *post*).

1 For definition of " vessel," see M.S.A. 1894, s. 742, and notes thereto. As to the position of hovercraft, see note at beginning of section and § 1317, *post*. In *Edwards* v. *Quickenden and Forester* [1939] P. 261, it was held that the Act did not apply to a collision between a skiff and a rowing eight on the River Thames.

" The Act personifies the vessel, treating it at one time as the actor, at another as suffering damage or loss, and at another as liable to make good such damage or loss. The truth is, of course, that for the purpose of ascertaining the legal effect, the word in one context connotes those responsible for the navigation of the vessel; in another those who are interested in her, her cargo or freight; and in another those who are in law answerable for the conduct of those in charge ": *per* Warrington J. in *The Cairnbahn* [1914] P. 25 at p. 34.

As to the proof of " fault," the rule is the same as in common law cases, namely, that the onus is on the party setting up a case of negligence to prove both the breach of duty and the consequent damage: *SS. Heranger* (*Owners*) v. *SS. Diamond* (*Owners*) [1939] A.C. 94. However, in *The Mimosa* (1944) 77 Ll.L.R. 217, Pilcher J. said: " The fact that one ship does not allege any fault against the other seems to me to be quite immaterial if the court after inquiring into all the facts find that such fault exists. I think, therefore, that this is a case in which liability should be apportioned." See, also, *The Shelbrit IV* (1945) 78 Ll.L.R. 50. The words are wide enough to include not only faults in navigation: see *The Norwhale* [1975] 2 W.L.R. 829.

It should be noted, however, that the negligence of an officer on board a ship is not always to be treated as " the fault of the vessel "; see *The Sobieski* [1949] P. 313, and *The Glaucus and the City of Florence* [1948] P. 95. In the former case a collision occurred between two vessels, the S and the E, as the result of the negligence of each of them and as the result, also, of the negligence of a senior escort officer, L, on board a naval vessel, the L A, which was escorting the S. L's negligence consisted of his failure to transmit information of the approach, detected by radar, of the E. It was held that L's negligence was not the negligence of his vessel, the L A. Therefore the Maritime Conventions Act had no application to the claim of the S against L, and that claim failed also at common law because of the contributory negligence of the S, the collision having occurred before the coming into force of the Law Reform (Contributory Negligence) Act 1945.

2 As to what may be recovered under the head of damages in a collision action, see Roscoe's *Measure of Damages in Maritime Collision*, 3rd ed., now incorporated in *British Shipping Laws*, Vol. 4, *Marsden on Collisions at Sea*, 11th ed., Part two.

" The word ' loss ' is wide enough to include that form of pecuniary prejudice which consists in compensating third parties for wrong done to them by the fault of persons for whose conduct the party prejudiced must answer ": *per* Lord Sumner in *The Cairnbahn* [1914] P. 25 at p. 33. See also *The Frankland* [1901] P. 161. But *cf. Drinkwater* v. *Kimber* [1952] 2 Q.B. 281 where the Court of Appeal placed a very different construction on the similar provisions contained in the Law Reform (Married Women and Tortfeasors) Act 1935 (reversed on unrelated grounds by the House of Lords).

The words do not cover claims for loss of life or personal injury, these being provided for by ss. 2 and 3; see *The Cedric* [1920] P. 193 at p. 197; *The Abadesa* [1966] 1 Lloyd's Rep. 118; and notes to s. 3.

The words " damage and loss " include the words " damages and losses " and accordingly the court can make different apportionments of liability for different heads of damage or loss resulting from the same event: *The Calliope* [1970] P. 172.

829 3 An innocent third vessel, not being one of " those vessels " who were " at fault," can, it seems, still recover the whole of her damage from either of the vessels by the fault of which damage to her has been caused, leaving the vessel which has paid to recover a proportionate share from the other vessel at fault: see *The Cairnbahn, supra*. In this case a collision occurred between a steamship and a barge in tow of and controlled by a tug. The tug-owners had no interest in the barge. The steamship and tug were found equally to blame for the collision. The owners of the innocent barge recovered the full amount of their damage from the steamship. In a subsequent action against the tug the steamship was held entitled to include in her claim for damages half the amount of damages which she had paid to the barge. To bring the case within the section it is not necessary that the two vessels on whom lies the liability to make good the damge should themselves have been in collision.

With this should be contrasted the decision in *The Umona* [1914] P. 141. There a collision occurred between a steamship and a dumb-barge in tow of and controlled by a tug whose owners also owned the barge. The fault was apportioned as to three-fourths to the steamship and one-fourth to the tug. The owners of cargo laden on the barge were held only entitled to recover from the steamship three-quarters of their damage in accordance with the doctrine enunciated in *The Milan* (1860) Lush. 388; 31 L.J.Ad. 105; followed in *The Drumlanrig* [1911] A.C. 16.

Only damage or loss to vessels is within the section; so that, in *Manchester Ship Canal Co.* (*Alpha*) v. *Helgoy* (1924) 18 Ll.L.R. 191 where a jetty belonging to the owners of vessel A was damaged in collision between vessels A and B, for which both A and B were equally to blame, though a moiety of the damage to A and B was recoverable from the owners of B and A respectively no part of the damage to the *jetty* was recoverable from the owners of B; for the claim in respect of the damage to the jetty is a common law claim and, as the collision causing the damage occurred before the coming into force of the Law Reform (Contributory Negligence) Act 1945, was defeated by the defence based on the contributory negligence of the servants of the owners of A. *Quaere*, however, whether this decision is consistent with certain passages in the judgment in *The Cairnbahn, supra*, which suggests that all forms of pecuniary loss suffered by owners of vessels involved in a collision are within the section. See, too, as to collision with wreck *The Manorbier Castle* (1922) 129 L.T. 31; 16 Asp.M.L.C. 151. For a different approach to similar provisions in the Law Reform (Married Women and Tortfeasors) Act 1935, see *Drinkwater* v. *Kimber* [1952] 2 Q.B. 281 (C.A.) (later reversed on unrelated grounds).

4 The innocent owner of cargo on board either of the colliding vessels could, prior to the Judicature Act 1873, recover in a common law action in tort the whole of his damages from either of the wrong-doing vessels unless defeated as regards the carrying vessel by the terms of the contract of carriage. In Admiralty, he could only recover half his damages against the other vessel if both were found to blame for the collision: *The Milan* (1860) Lush. 388; 31 L.J.Ad. 105. From 1873 until 1911, this Admiralty rule prevailed in all courts. Now, under this Act, he can recover from the other vessel a share of his damage proportionate to the degree in which such vessel was in fault; *The Umona, supra*. Nothing in this rule or the Act prevents the cargo owner from recovering his damages in full from the carrying vessel should the terms of the contract of carriage permit: *The Bushire* (1886) 5 Asp.M.C. 416; 52 L.T. 740.

5 These words are equivalent to " the burden of the damage or loss ": *per* Warrington J. in *The Cairnbahn, supra*, at p. 37. Further, as to liability, see note (6), *infra*.

6 At common law the doctrine of contributory negligence prior to the Law Reform (Contributory Negligence) Act 1945, prevented either party from recovering from the other damages for loss or injury for which both were to blame. In Admiralty, however, after considerable variation and uncertainty in practice, the rule of equal division of loss had long been applied where both vessels were held to blame. For the history of the rule in English law, see *British Shipping Laws*, Vol. 4, *Marsden on Collisions at Sea*, 11th ed., §§ 138–147. Although at one time it was intended that the common law rule should be extended to all courts, on the reorganisation of the judicial system in 1873 the Admiralty rule was finally adopted for application in all courts by the Judicature Act 1873, s. 25 (9).

This subsection provided that " in any cause or proceeding for damages arising out of a collision between two ships, if both ships shall be found to have been in fault the rules hitherto in force in the Court of Admiralty so far as they have been at variance with the rules in force in the courts of common law shall prevail." This subsection has now been repealed by the Maritime Conventions Act 1911, s. 9 (3), and the new rule of apportionment in accordance with the degree of fault enacted by s. 1 (1) is now of universal application, with the proviso, that if it is not possible to establish different degrees of fault the liability shall be apportioned equally.

7 In assessing degrees of fault, regard must be had both to the blameworthiness of the conduct alleged and to its causative potency: see *The British Aviator* [1965] 1 Lloyd's Rep. 271 at p. 277 (*per* Willmer L.J.).

8 The proviso means not that the liability shall be apportioned equally unless different degrees of fault are shown but that the court must apportion liability on proportion to the degree in which each vessel was at fault unless it is impossible so to do: *The Anneliese* [1970] 1 Lloyd's Rep. 355 at p. 362 (*per* Davies L.J). See also *The British Aviator, supra*; *The Lucile Bloomfield* [1967] 1 Lloyd's Rep. 541 at p. 351 (*per* Winn L.J.) as amended by *The Anneliese, supra*, at p. 363.

830 APPLICATION OF RULE WHEN LIABILITY IS LIMITED. In *Stoomvart Maatschappy Nederland* v. *Peninsular and Oriental S. N. Co.* (*The Voorwarts, The Khedive*) (1882) 7 App.Cas. 795 the House of Lords, following the rule laid down in *The Woodrop-Sims* (1816) 2 Dods.Ad. 83; *The Lord Melville* (1815) 5 Shaw's Sc.App.Cas. 395; *The Petersfield, Judith Randolph*, Marsd.Ad.Cas. 332, decided that upon a finding of both to blame only one liability arose, namely, a liability upon the part of the owners of the vessel that had done the greater damage to pay to the owners of the other vessel the difference between the moieties of the losses suffered by the two vessels, and that where the former limited their liability under the M.S.A. the latter were only entitled to prove against the fund in court for this difference. *Cf. The Tojo Maru* [1972] A.C. 242.

It is submitted that there is nothing in the present section to affect this rule as to unity of liability; but its application where both vessels are held to blame with unequal degrees of fault may give rise to anomalous results even more striking than those which occurred under the old rule. It may happen that the vessel which has been found to be at fault in the greater degree will, nevertheless, if she has also received the greater damage be entitled to some payment. Thus, for example, where the damage done to A amounts to £10,000, and to B £30,000, and the degree of fault in A is found to be one-third and in B two-thirds, A, though only one-third to blame, will have to pay B £3,333, *i.e.* the difference between £10,000 (one-third of B's damage) and £6,666 (two-thirds of A's damage). If A limits her liability, B can prove against the fund for £3,333.

THREE SHIPS INVOLVED.—It is possible that the effect of s. 1 is to extend the operation of the Admiralty rule of division of loss in certain cases. For it is not clear that the old rule ever applied to the case of two vessels being both in fault for a collision between one of them and a third vessel; the reference to the rule in the Judicature Act 1873, s. 25, *supra*, is confined to a collision between two ships both of which are to blame. This case of a collision with an innocent third ship is, however, covered by the words of the present section, as is also the case of fault of three vessels contributing to or causing a collision between two of them.

As to the method of apportioning liability for contribution to damage suffered by a third ship resulting from the collision of two others, see *The Miraflores and the Abadesa* [1967] 1 A.C. 826; [1967] 1 Lloyd's Rep. 191 (H.L.). In *The Boronkerk* [1973] 1 Lloyd's Rep. 63, the third vessel involved was not before the court. The point was left open as to how the section would operate should such third vessel be held in part to blame.

Where A, being towed by B, collides with C, and the court finds A and B one-half to blame and C one-half to blame, there is no obligation on the court to apportion the blame as between A and B. There is a joint and several liability in A and B to reimburse C in respect of a moiety of C's damage and a single liability in C to reimburse A and B in respect of a moiety of the damage, if any, sustained by them respectively: *The Socrates and the Champion* [1923] P. 76.

Where A collides with B while B is towing C, and the court finds that B and C are separately and distinctly at fault, the court will apportion blame as between B and C; see *The M.S.C. Panther and the Ericbank* [1957] P. 143 (distinguishing *The Socrates and the Champion* (*supra*)).

NO COLLISION.—The rule is not confined to cases where two vessels have actually been in collision. For example, where A, by her wash due to her excessive speed caused B, which was improperly moored, to break adrift and suffer damage, the loss was found to be due to the fault of both A and B, and was accordingly apportioned: *The Batavier III* (1925) 134 L.T. 155; 42 T.L.R. 8. See, too, *The Cairnbahn, supra.*

831 " FAULT."—No definition of " fault " is given in the Act or the Convention. The basis of liability in an action of damage by collision under the old Admiralty rule, and also, it seems, under the present section, is negligence causing or contributing to the *loss*. Under the old Admiralty rule for a finding of " both to blame " the vessels need not both have been guilty of acts of negligence contributing to the *collision*. See, for example, *The Margaret* (1881) 6 P.D. 76, where, in a collision between a schooner at anchor and a dumb barge, the schooner, whose only fault consisted in having an anchor improperly suspended in such a position that it holed and sank the barge, was held liable to pay for half the loss suffered by the barge whose sole negligence caused the collision. See, too, *The Monte Rosa* [1893] P. 23, 31. And presumably the same principle would be applied to cases under the present section. It is true that in *The Peter Benoit, infra*, the Court of Appeal and the House of Lords held that the fault for which the liability is to be apportioned under this section must be " fault causing or contributing to the collision." But this decision must be read *secundum subjectam materiam*. The court were considering the effect of a breach of a local by-law (which, in fact, contributed neither to the collision nor to the loss), and must not be taken to have questioned the proposition of law illustrated above by *The Margaret*, namely, that liability attaches to acts of negligence causing or contributing to the *loss*; see *The Kaiser Wilhelm II* (1916) 85 L.J.P. at p. 34; 31 T.L.R. 615.

CONTRIBUTORY NEGLIGENCE.—As to the principles to be applied when the acts of negligence of the two vessels are not simultaneous, see *British Shipping Laws*, Vol. 4, *Marsden on Collisions at Sea*, 11th ed., §§ 30–35, where the authorities are fully reviewed.

Costs.—Until the case of *The Modica* [1926] P. 72, the regular practice from the commencement of the Act in 1911 was that, where in a collision action it was found that each vessel had been to blame, although in different degrees, the court would apply in cases under this Act the old rule of making each vessel pay her own costs. This practice was based upon the rulings of Bargrave Deane J. in *The Rosalia* [1912] P. 109, and of Sir Samuel Evans P. in *The Bravo* (1912) 29 T.L.R. 122. In *The Modica, supra,* however, Hill J., after reviewing the authorities, laid down the principle that the court, being guided by the particular circumstances in each case, was at liberty in a proper case to give to the party least in fault such proportion of that party's costs as on the particular facts appeared just, and in modern practice an order apportioning the costs is frequently made. It is, however, in each case, both in the court of first instance and in the appellate tribunals, a matter of pure discretion and not of legal right, and, unless the judge can be shown to have taken into consideration matters which are immaterial to the issue, his decision as to costs is unappealable: *The Young Sid* [1929] P. 190. For a discussion of the methods of reflecting on an order for costs the fact that one party has done better than the other, see *The Osprey* [1967] 1 Lloyd's Rep. 76 at p. 94 (Brandon J.).

832 Appeal as to apportionment.—See *The Peter Benoit* (1915) 84 L.J.P. 87; 31 T.L.R. 227 (C.A.); 85 L.J.P. 12; 32 T.L.R. 124 (H.L.). " I do not think that this court ought lightly to interfere with the decision of the court below on the question of apportionment unless it sees quite clearly that there has been some mistake of fact or some mistake of law which has led the learned judge to the conclusion to which he came ": *per* Bankes L.J. (at p. 91). See too, *The Karamea* [1921] P. 76 (C.A.); [1922] 1 A.C. 68; *The Clara Camus* (1926) 134 L.T. 50 (C.A.); 136 L.T. 291 (H.L.). In *The Testbank* [1942] P. 75 the Court of Appeal indicated that they regarded the principles laid down in *The Karamea* as placing too strict a limitation on the discretion of the Court of Appeal. But in *The MacGregor* [1943] A.C. 197 the House of Lords expressly approved *The Karamea* and disapproved the statement of principle in *The Testbank*.

[9] See, for example, *Chartered Bank of India* v. *Netherlands India S.N. Co.* (1883) 10 Q.B.D. 521, where the owner of cargo damaged in collision between two vessels both belonging to the same shipowner and equally to blame was held only to be entitled to recover from the shipowner half the amount of the damage, *viz.* the half attaching to the non-carrying vessel, the claim for the other half being defeated by the negligence clause in the bill of lading under which the goods were carried. *Cf. The Cedric* [1920] P. 193 and note 1 under s. 3, *post.*

[10] *e.g.*, the defence of compulsory pilotage until its abolition (so far as U.K. waters are concerned) on January 1, 1918, by the Pilotage Act 1913, s. 15.

The rule in *Merryweather* v. *Nixan* (1799) 8 T.R. 186, which existed until the Law Reform (Married Women and Tortfeasors) Act 1935, that there was no right of contribution between joint tortfeasors was held not to be a provision of law exempting any person from any liability: *The Cairnbahn* [1914] P. 25 at p. 34.

[11] For notes on the provisions of the M.S.A. as to limitation of liability, see M.S.A. 1894, ss. 502–509, *supra*, and the M.S. (Liability of Shipowners and Others) Act 1958, *post*. There is no case in which it has been decided whether or not a liability to make contribution under this section (as interpreted in *The Cairnbahn, supra*) or under the Law Reform (Married Women and Joint Tortfeasors) Act 1935, is a liability to " damages " within the terms of s. 503 of M.S.A. 1894, which may be limited accordingly.

Damages for personal injuries

833 **2.** Where loss of life or personal injuries [1] are suffered by any person on board a vessel owing to the fault [2] of that vessel and of any other vessel or vessels, the liability of the owners [3] of the vessels shall be joint and several [4]:

Provided that nothing in this section shall be construed as depriving any person of any right of defence on which, independently of this section, he might have relied in an action brought against him by the person injured, or any person or persons entitled to sue in respect of such loss of life, or shall affect the right of any person to limit his liability [5] in cases to which this section relates in the manner provided by law.

834 This section now applies to vessels belonging to Her Majesty (as defined in s. 38 (2) of the Crown Proceedings Act 1947), as it applies in the case of other vessels; *ibid.* s. 6 (see notes to that section, *post*).

[1] Proceedings in respect of such damages may now be brought *in rem* or *in personam*: see s. 5 and notes thereto. As to the time within which claims may be brought under the Fatal Accidents Act 1846 for loss of life, and as to the limitation of time within which certain other claims can be brought, see s. 8 and notes thereto.

[2] As to the personification of the vessel, see s. 1, note (1). See also *ibid.* note (6).

[3] For meaning of this expression, see s. 9 (4) and note thereto.

[4] This would seem to confirm the practice before the Act. The doctrine of law whereby the owner of the innocent cargo laden on board a vessel partly to blame for a collision is able to recover from the other party to the collision only a proportion of his damages has no application to a claim for loss of life or personal injury. Thus a passenger or member of the crew who has not by his own negligence caused or contributed to the collision can recover damages in full from the other party to the collision: *The Bernina* (1888) 13 App. Cas. 1. But if the defendants in such an action can prove contributory negligence on the part of the plaintiffs themselves or on the part of any person standing in such a legal relation towards the plaintiffs as to cause the acts of that third person according to the ordinary principles of law to be regarded as their acts, this right of defence (*i.e.* contributory negligence) is preserved to them by the proviso but is now subject to the Law Reform (Contributory Negligence) Act 1945.

[5] For notes on the provisions of the M.S.A. as to limitation of liability, see M.S.A. 1894, ss. 502–509, *supra*, and M.S. (Liability of Shipowners and Others) Act 1958, *post*.

Right of contribution

835 **3.**—(1) [1] Where loss of life or personal injuries are suffered by any person on board a vessel owing to the fault [2] of that vessel and any other vessel or vessels, and a proportion of the damages [3] is recovered against the owners of one of the vessels which exceeds the proportion in which she was in fault,[4] they may recover by way of contribution [5] the amount of the excess from the owners of the other vessel or vessels to the extent to which those vessels were respectively in fault:

Provided that no amount shall be so recovered which could not, by reason of any statutory [6] or contractual limitation of, or exemption from, liability, or which could not for any other reason, have been recovered in the first instance as damages by the persons entitled to sue therefor.

(2) In addition to any other remedy provided by law, the persons entitled to any such contribution as aforesaid shall, for the purpose of recovering the same, have, subject to the provisions of this Act, the same rights and powers as the persons entitled to sue for damages in the first instance.[7]

836 This section now applies in the case of vessels belonging to Her Majesty (as defined in s. 386 of the Crown Proceedings Act 1947) as it applied in the case of other vessels; *ibid.* s. 6 (see notes to that section, *post*).

[1] Under subs. (1), if an innocent passenger on board ship A receives personal injuries in a collision between A and B, for which both ships are equally to blame, and recovers damages against A, A can recover a moiety from B subject to B's right to limit his liability in appropriate cases; for the passenger could have recovered against B in the first place. *Cf. The Abadesa* [1966] 1 Lloyd's Rep. 118.

An illustration of the working of the proviso is afforded by *The Cedric* [1920] P. 193. The representatives of the crew of a French sailing ship lost in collision with a British vessel, for which both were equally to blame, had recovered in full the amount of the claims from the British vessel. The owners of the latter were unable to recover a moiety of their damages in respect of these life claims in contribution from the French owners, on proof that by French law the representatives of the crew would have had no valid claim against the French ship. In *The Napier Star* [1939] P. 330 the two colliding ships were equally to blame. The personal representatives of members of the crew of ship A, killed in the collision, recovered damages from the owners of ship B. The latter were held not to be entitled to recover their proportion of these damages from the owners of ship A because the owners of ship A could have successfully set up the defence of common employment if they had been sued by the personal representatives. The owners of ship B were, however, held entitled to recover their proportion of the costs incurred in defending the actions against them. But it would appear that this decision would no longer be followed in view of the abolition of the defence of common employment by the Law Reform (Personal Injuries) Act 1948.

[2] As to the personification of the vessel, see s. 1, note (1). See also, *ibid.* note (6).

[3] Before this Act, a shipowner employer, who had paid compensation under the Workmen's Compensation Act 1906 (now repealed) to a seaman in respect of personal injury or to his dependants in respect of his death arising out of a collision for which both vessels were to blame, could not recover any part of the compensation so paid from the owners of the other vessel either as damages in Admiralty proceedings—for such a claim was not within the Admiralty rules or jurisdiction—or at common law—for the claim would have been defeated by the common law defence of contributory negligence. The present section, inasmuch as it only provides for contribution in respect of " damages," left the law in this respect unaltered: *The Molière* [1925] P. 27.

Costs incurred in unreasonably disputing liability cannot be made the subject of contribution: *The Cairnbahn* (*No.* 2) (1914) 30 T.L.R. 309, C.A.

[4] See note (6) to s. 1.

[5] It seems that this right of contribution can be enforced by the third party procedure provided for by R.S.C., Ord. 16.

Proceedings to enforce contribution must be commenced within one year of the date of payment: see s. 8.

[6] See M.S.A. 1894, ss. 503–509, *supra*, and M.S. (Liability of Shipowners and Others) Act 1958, *post*.

[7] *i.e.* a person claiming contribution can proceed *in rem* or *in personam*. See s. 5 and notes thereto.

Abolition of statutory presumptions of fault

837 **4.**—(1) *Sub-section* (4) *of section four hundred and nineteen of the Merchant Shipping Act* 1894 (*which provides that a ship shall be deemed in fault in a case of collision where any of the collision regulations have been infringed by that ship*), *is hereby repealed.*[1]

(2) The failure of the master or persons in charge of a vessel to comply with the provisions of section four hundred and twenty-two of the Merchant Shipping Act 1894 (which imposes a duty upon masters and persons in charge of vessels after a collision to stand by and assist the other vessel), shall not raise any presumption of law that the collision was caused by his wrongful act, neglect, or default, and accordingly sub-section (2) of that section shall be repealed.[2]

[1] As to the effect of the abolition of the statutory presumptions of fault formerly contained in the two subsections here repealed, see note (5) to M.S.A. 1894, s. 419, *supra*. This subsection is repealed as spent by the Statute Law Revision Act 1927.

[2] It should be noticed that, although this statutory presumption of fault no longer arises, failure to assist and stand by after a collision may still render the master or person in charge liable for a misdemeanour unless he can show reasonable cause; M.S.A. 1894, s. 422.

Jurisdiction in cases of loss of life or personal injury

838 **5.** Any enactment which confers on any court Admiralty jurisdiction in respect of damage shall have effect as though references to such damage included references to damages for loss of life or personal injury, and

accordingly proceedings in respect of such damages may be brought *in rem* or *in personam*.

839 Section 5 was repealed, so far as it relates to the High Court in England and Wales, by the Supreme Court of Judicature (Consolidation) Act 1925, s. 226 and was replaced by ss. 22 and 33 of that Act. These latter sections have now been repealed by the Administration of Justice Act 1956, s. 57 (2), Sched. 2 and replaced by ss. 1 and 3 of that Act. Section 1 (1) provides (*inter alia*):

" The Admiralty Jurisdiction of the High Court shall be as follows, that is to say, jurisdiction to hear and determine any of the following questions or claims:—

. . .

(*d*) any claim for damage done by a ship;
(*e*) any claim for damage received by a ship;
(*f*) any claim for loss of life or personal injury sustained in consequence of any defect in a ship or in her apparel or equipment, or of the wrongful act, neglect or default of the owners, charterers or persons in possession or control of a ship or of the master or crew thereof or of any other person for whose wrongful acts, neglects or defaults the owners, charterers, or persons in possession or control of a ship are responsible, being an act, neglect or default in the navigation or management of the ship, in the loading, carriage or discharge of goods on, in or from the ship or in the embarkation, carriage or disembarkation of persons on, in or from the ship; . . . ."

Sections 3 and 4 govern the mode of exercising that jurisdiction and make provision for actions *in personam* and actions *in rem*, either against the vessel concerned or against a sister-ship.

840 Section 5 of this present Act was also repealed, so far as it relates to county courts in England and Wales, by the County Courts Act 1934, s. 34 (1), Sched. V, Pt. 1, and was replaced by ss. 56 and 57 of that Act. These latter sections have now been repealed by the County Courts Act 1959, s. 204, Sched. III and replaced by s. 56 of that Act.

An Admiralty County Court (see the list contained in the County Courts (Admiralty Jurisdiction) Order 1949 (S.I. No. 2059) as amended by S.I. 1963 No. 2038) has for this purpose the same Admiralty jurisdiction as the High Court subject to a limitation of the amount of the claim to a sum not exceeding £1,000. Section 57 makes similar provision for actions *in personam* or *in rem*.

For the Admiralty jurisdiction and the arrest of ships in Scotland, see the Administration of Justice Act 1956 (Part V), ss. 45–50.

Further, section 5 of this present Act has also been repealed, so far as it relates to Northern Ireland, by the Administration of Justice Act 1956, s. 55 (1), Sched. I, Pt. 3 and provisions similar to those set out above are set out in Sched. I, Pt. 1 of that Act.

Provisions as to Salvage

General duty to render assistance to persons in danger at sea

841 **6.**—(1) The master or person in charge of a vessel shall, so far as he can do so without serious danger to his own vessel, her crew and passengers (if any), render assistance to every person, even if such person be a subject of a foreign State at war with His Majesty, who is found at sea in danger of being lost, and, if he fails to do so, he shall be guilty of a misdemeanour.[1]

(2) Compliance by the master or person in charge of a vessel with the provisions of this section shall not affect his right or the right of any other person to salvage.[2]

[1] A vessel which puts herself into unusual peril by reason of rendering assistance under this section is not to be regarded as negligent on that account. The principles of the common law as laid down in *Haynes* v. *Harwood* [1935] 1 K.B. 146, apply: *The Gusty and the Daniel M.* [1940] P. 159.

The section has effect as if the references to vessels or activities connected therewith included hovercraft and activities connected with hovercraft: *cf.* the Hovercraft (Application of Enactments) Order 1972, S.I. No. 971.

The duty of rendering assistance in answer to a distress signal is more particularly dealt with in s. 22 of the M.S. (Safety Convention) Act 1949, *post*.

All distinctions between a felony and a misdemeanour were abolished by the Criminal Law Act 1967, s. 1.

[2] *The Tower Bridge* [1936] P. 30 is a case in which salvage was awarded in such circumstances. For salvage provisions, see M.S.A. 1896, ss. 544 *et seq.*, and for the relevance to the right to salvage of the fact that assistance is rendered in compliance with a statutory obligation, see Kennedy's *Civil Salvage*, 4th ed., pp. 30–33.

Apportionment of salvage amongst owners, etc., of foreign ship

842 **7.** Where any dispute arises as to the apportionment of any amount of salvage among the owners, master, pilot, crew, and other persons in the service of any foreign vessel, the amount shall be apportioned by the court or person making the apportionment in accordance with the law of the country to which the vessel belongs.

See M.S.A. 1894, ss. 555 and 556 as to apportionment of salvage.

General Provisions

Limitation of actions

843 **8.** No action [1] shall be maintainable [2] to enforce any claim or lien against a vessel or her owners [3] in respect of any damage or loss to another vessel, her cargo or freight, or any property on board her, or damages for loss of life [4] or personal injuries suffered by any person on board her, caused by the fault [4a] of the former vessel, whether such vessel be wholly or partly in fault, or in respect of any salvage services,[5] unless proceedings therein are commenced [6] within two years from the date when the damage or loss or injury was caused or the salvage services were rendered, and an an action shall not be maintainable under this Act to enforce any contribution in respect of an overpaid proportion of any damages for loss of life or personal injuries unless proceedings therein are commenced within one year from the date of payment:

Provided that any court having jurisdiction to deal with an action to which this section relates may,[7] in accordance with the rules of court,[8] extend any such period, to such extent and on such conditions as it thinks fit, and shall,[9] if satisfied that there has not during such period been any reasonable opportunity [10] of arresting the defendant vessel within the jurisdiction of the court, or within the territorial waters of the country to which the plaintiff's ship belongs or in which the plaintiff resides or has his principal place of business, extend any such period to an extent sufficient to give such reasonable opportunity.

844 This section imposes an entirely new period of limitation in respect of the actions enumerated, subject to the proviso. It should be noted that the words of this section only apply to claims in respect of damage or loss to cargo or property or loss of life or personal injury which lie against the *other* vessel. Claims of this nature which lie against the vessel carrying the persons, cargo or property in question are not affected by this period of limitation: *cf. The Niceto de Larrinaga* [1966] P. 80; *The Alnwick* [1965] 1 Lloyd's Rep. 69 (reversed *ibid.* 320 on another point). Apart from actions which come within the terms of this section, it is not clear what period of limitation applies generally to claims within the Admiralty jurisdiction of the High Court which are enforceable *in rem.* The Limitation Act 1939, s. 2 (6) expressly excludes such actions in Admiralty from the provisions of that Act, except in regard to claims for

seaman's wages. It follows that the Law Reform (Limitation of Actions, etc.) Act 1954, s. 2 (1), which amends the 1939 Act by providing a three-year limitation period for actions for personal injuries, has no application to such actions in Admiralty. In regard to claims for loss or damage to cargo brought upon bills of lading which incorporate the Hague Rules, a one-year period of limitation may apply; see the Carriage of Goods by Sea Act 1924, Sched., Article III, r. 6. For claims under the Fatal Accidents Act 1846, see note (4) below.

The section has effect as if the references to vessels or activities connected therewith included hovercraft or activities connected with hovercraft: see the Hovercraft (Application of Enactments) Order 1972, S.I. No. 971.

The period of limitation under this section was suspended where any necessary party was an enemy or detained in enemy territory; see the Limitation (Enemies and War Prisoners) Act 1945; and the suspension may in certain cases still run: *The Atlantic Scout* [1950] P. 266.

[1] Prior to 1947 this section did not apply to actions brought by the Crown; see *The Loredano* [1922] P. 209. By the Crown Proceedings Act 1947, s. 30 (1), the provisions of this section were applied to certain of Her Majesty's ships, and by the Law Reform (Limitation of Actions, etc.) Act 1954, s. 5 (1) (2), the provisions of this section have been applied to all of Her Majesty's ships. The special limitation periods of six months under the Public Authorities' Protection Act 1893, and one year under the Limitation Act 1939, upon which public servants of the Crown were able to rely prior to 1947 (see, *e.g. The Danube II* [1921] P. 183) have been repealed by the Law Reform (Limitation of Actions, etc.) Act 1954, s. 1. Accordingly Her Majesty's ships are no longer in any different position from other ships for the purposes of this section.

[2] It should be observed that the effect of this section like that of most of the provisions of the Statutes of Limitation is not to extinguish the cause of action, but merely to bar the right to maintain the action. It does not therefore prevent the issue of a writ: *The P. L. M.* 8 [1920] P. 236; *The Dorie S.S. Co.* v. *Kamenetz Podolsk* (1923) 14 Ll.L.R. 512 (Sc.).

The defence (like " all matters which show the action or counterclaim not to be maintainable ") must be specially pleaded; see R.S.C. Ord. 18, r. 8. As to the effect of omitting to plead, see *Robinson's Settlement, Re, Gant* v. *Hobbs* [1912] 1 Ch. 717 at p. 728, *per* Buckley L.J. " If the defendant does not plead the defence, the court will deal with it in one of two ways. It may say that it is not open to him, that he has not raised it, and will not be allowed to rely upon it; or it may give him leave to amend by raising it, and protect the other party, if necessary, by letting the case stand over.... The rule leaves the party in mercy and the court will deal with him as is just."

An entry of unconditional appearance to a writ does not prevent the defendant from raising this defence: *The Llandovery Castle* [1920] P. 119.

If the defendant desires to raise any defence based on this section, he should raise it as a preliminary objection by way of summons or motion praying for an order that the action is not maintainable. On the hearing of such summons or motion the plaintiff may apply to the court for the exercise of its discretion in extending the time. (As to which see note (7).) If the objection is upheld the proper order is not that the writ should be set aside, but that the action is not maintainable; see *The P. L. M.* 8, *supra*.

[3] This presumably encompasses claims against " sister " vessels pursuant to s. 3 (4) of the Administration of Justice Act 1956: see *The Preveze* [1973] 1 Lloyd's Rep. 202. For the meaning of " owners " see s. 9 (4) and note thereto. As to the position of hovercraft, see the note above s. 1 and § 1317, *post*.

845 [4] It has been held that a claim against a vessel or her owners for damages for loss of life may be brought within two years from the date when the loss was caused, notwithstanding the provisions of the Fatal Accidents Act 1846, by which an action to recover damages for loss of life must be commenced within 12 months after the death of the deceased person: *The Caliph* [1912] P. 213. See also *The Alnwick* [1965] P. 357, where it was held that the two year period prevails over the 3 year period contained in s. 3 of the Law Reform (Limitation of Actions) Act 1954.

However, that limitation period of 12 months has now been extended to three years by the Law Reform (Limitation of Actions, etc.) Act 1954, s. 3. It has not been decided since that Act whether, in the case of a claim for loss of life which falls within the scope of section 8 of this Act, the three-year period or the two-year period applies. It was raised but not argued in *The Vadne* [1959] 2 Lloyd's Rep. 480 when Lord Merriman P. *obiter* (at p. 486) said that he thought that the two-year period applied.

[4a] These words are wide enough to include not only faults in navigation: *cf The Norwhale* [1975] 2 W.L.R. 829.

[5] This would appear to include claims for salvage against cargo-owners and it need not be limited to " claims against a vessel or her owners . . . in respect of any salvage services "; see *Burns, Philip & Co., Ltd.* v. *Nelson & Robertson Proprietary Ltd.* [1957] 1 Lloyd's Rep. 267 (a case in the High Court of Australia upon the similar provisions of an Australian

Statute in which the Brussels Convention of 1910 was referred to in order to reach a conclusion).

In *The Katcher I* [1969] P. 65, the plaintiff salvors were given leave to amend the writ to allege further services on the ground that the earlier and the later services constituted a composite or unitary service and did not raise a fresh cause of action which had become statute barred.

6 The period of limitation will cease to run if a writ *in rem* is issued: see *The World Harmony* [1967] P. 341; *The Monica S.* [1968] P. 741. The original writ remains in force for 12 months, but may be renewed.

For renewal of writ, see R.S.C. Ord. 6, r. 8. Even if application is not made within the prescribed time, the court can in its discretion enlarge the time for renewing the writ, despite the general rule of practice that the court will not by the renewal of writ revive a statute-barred debt: *Doyle* v. *Kaufman* (1878) 3 Q.B.D. 7, 340; *Hewett* v. *Barr* [1891] 1 Q.B. 98. See *The Espanoleto*, 36 T.L.R. 554; [1920] P. 223, where the facts were as follows: a collision having occurred in February, 1917, a writ *in rem* was issued in December, 1918, by which time the defendant vessel had left the jurisdiction. No application for renewal was made until March, 1920, when on an application *ex parte* the court granted a renewal, and the vessel, upon her first return to a port within the jurisdiction, was then arrested. Upon a motion to set aside the writ and the renewal and the warrant of arrest, and to discharge the undertaking to put in bail, Hill J. held that inasmuch as the period of limitation provided by this section was not absolute, the court should consider the application on its merits and inquire whether the circumstances were such that the court would have given leave to *issue* the writ notwithstanding that the time had expired, on the ground that the plaintiff had exercised due diligence in prosecuting his claim. If leave to issue the writ would have been given, *a fortiori* a renewal of a writ taken out within the prescribed time should be granted. In *The Owenbawn* [1973] 1 Lloyd's Rep. 56, Brandon J. envisaged three situations in which it was just to renew the writ: (a) where there is an express agreement deferring service (b) where there is an implied agreement to the same effect and (c) where there has been conduct by the defendant leading the plaintiff to suppose that it would be all right to defer service. See also *The World Harmony* [1965] 1 Lloyd's Rep. 244: [1967] P. 341; *Heaven* v. *Road and Rail Wagons Ltd.* [1965] 2 Q.B. 355; *Re Chittenden Decd.* [1970] 1 W.L.R. 1618; *The Preveze, supra.*

Where liability for damage has been proved or admitted, and the party liable has obtained a decree entitling him to limit his liability, claimants to the limitation fund may challenge the right of proof of other claimants who have not commenced proceedings within the periods prescribed by this section. For they are entitled to raise any defence which would have been open to the limiting person. But in such a case the court will generally consider the fact that limitation proceedings have been instituted as a sufficient ground for extending the time for commencing proceedings: *The Disperser* [1920] P. 228. *Secus*, if the non-issue of the writ resulted from the deliberate election of the claimant not to sue in this country; *The Nedenes* (1925) 23 Ll.L.R. 57.

846 7 In view of the decisions in *The World Harmony, supra* and *The Monica S., supra,* which held that an action *in rem* is brought or commences when the writ is issued, the lack of reasonable opportunity to *arrest* would not prevent a prospective plaintiff from ensuring that the time limit is complied with on the first instance. However, the same principles apply to the decision whether to extend time under this section or to renew the writ under R.S.C. Ord. 6, r. 8, see *The Owenbawn, supra.* The Court of Appeal will not interfere with the exercise of this discretion unless it is shown that a wrong principle has been applied: *The Kashmir* [1923] P. 85; *The James Westoll* [1923] P. 94n. *The Alnwick* (1965) 1 Lloyd's Rep. 69; [1965] P. 357 (C.A.). See also *The Heselmoor and The Sergeant* [1951] 1 Lloyd's Rep. 146 (where Willmer J. reviewed some of the earlier authorities), *The Sauria and The Trent* [1957] 1 Lloyd's Rep. 396, C.A. (where it was unsuccessfully contended that an admission of liability amounted to a contractual undertaking not to plead the defence of limitation). For further examples see *Bartlett* v. *Admiralty and anor., The Vadne* [1959] 2 Lloyd's Rep. 480 (discretion exercised) and *The Vadne* [1960] 1 Lloyd's Rep. 260 and *The Sunoak* [1960] 2 Lloyd's Rep. 213 (exercise of discretion refused). For a case in which the court exercised its discretion in favour of a counterclaiming defendant, see *The Fairplay XIV* [1939] P. 57.

There is no antithesis between the two limbs of the proviso. Thus, even in cases where there has been a reasonable opportunity of arresting, the court may extend the period if satisfied that there were reasonable grounds for not issuing the writ earlier. *The Arraiz* (1924) 19 Ll.L.R. 382; 132 L.T. 715.

The section applies whether the proceedings are *in rem* or *in personam. Ibid.*

8 Although no rules of court have yet been made under this section, the court may exercise its discretion as to extending time: *H.M.S. Archer* [1919] P. 1. For the application of this

reference to rules of the court in Northern Ireland, see the Northern Ireland Act 1962, s. 30 (2), Sched. 1 Part I.

[9] In the application of this section to Her Majesty's ships this section takes effect as if the words from "and shall, if satisfied" to the end of the section were omitted; see Crown Proceedings Act 1947, s. 30 as amended, § 1084, *post*.

[10] The proviso is considered effective with regard to any "sister" vessels named in the writ: *cf. The Preveze, supra, The Banco* [1971] P. 137; [1971] 1 Lloyd's Rep. 49. The fact that the vessel has been within the jurisdiction for a few days within the period does not necessarily disprove lack of reasonable opportunity to arrest: *The Largo Law* (1920) 123 L.T. 560; 15 Asp.M.L.C. 104.

Application of Act

847 **9.**—(1) This Act shall extend throughout His Majesty's dominions and to any territories under his protection, and to Cyprus:

Provided that it shall not extend to the Dominion of Canada, the Commonwealth of Australia, the Dominion of New Zealand, *the Union of South Africa, and Newfoundland.*[1]

(2) *This Act shall not apply in any case in which proceedings have been taken before the passing thereof and all such cases shall be determined as though this Act had not been passed.*[2]

(3) The provisions of this Act shall be applied in all cases heard and determined in any court having jurisdiction to deal with the case and in whatever waters the damage or loss in question was caused or the salvage services in question were rendered, and sub-section (9) of section twenty-five [3] of the Supreme Court of Judicature Act 1873, shall cease to have effect.

(4) This Act shall apply to any persons other than the owners [4] responsible for the fault of the vessel [5] as though the expression "owners" included such persons, and in any case where by virtue of any charter or demise, or for any other reason, the owners are not responsible for the navigation and management of the vessel, this Act shall be read as though for references to the owners there were substituted references to the charterers or other persons for the time being so responsible.

848 [1] The words "the Union of South Africa" were repealed by the South Africa Act 1962, s. 2 (3), Sched. 5; the words "and Newfoundland" were repealed by the Newfoundland (Consequential Provisions) Act 1950, s. 1, Sched., Part II.

[2] Subs. (2) was repealed as spent by the Statute Law Revision Act 1927.

[3] This subsection provided for the old Admiralty rule of division of loss prevailing over the common law rule of contributory negligence.

[4] This will include the commanding or navigating officer of a Queen's ship: *H.M.S. Archer* [1919] P. 1.

[5] See note (1) to s. 1 and cases there cited.

Short title and construction

849 **10.** This Act may be cited as the Maritime Conventions Act 1911, and shall be construed as one [1] with the Merchant Shipping Acts 1894 to 1907.

[1] See note (1) to s. 9 of M.S. (Mercantile Marine Fund) Act 1898.

PILOTAGE ACT 1913

(2 & 3 Geo. 5, c. 31)

An Act to consolidate and amend the Law relating to Pilotage.

[7th March, 1913.]

Be it enacted, etc.

850 Introductory Note.—The Pilotage Act 1913 embodies most of the recommendations of the Departmental Committee of the Board of Trade appointed in July, 1909, to inquire and report as to " the present state of the law and its administration with respect to pilotage in the United Kingdom and as to what changes, if any, are desirable." The report was forwarded to the President of the Board of Trade in March, 1911, and published as a Command Paper (1911 Cd. 5571). A very exhaustive inquiry had been made, and the recommendations of the Committee involved a codification of the law of pilotage, together with certain far-reaching changes.

The chief objects of this Act are (1) to provide the machinery for giving effect to such reorganisation or improvement of organisation as the [Secretary of State for Trade (replacing the Minister of Transport who in turn replaced the Board of Trade)] may recommend, (2) to render the law of pilotage accessible and so far as possible uniform, and (3) to make certain necessary changes in the law.

(1) *Organisation.*—The pilotage system of the United Kingdom, under the pressure of local or private interests, has developed with little assistance from the legislature until comparatively recent times. The earliest form of pilotage organisation apparently consisted of the establishment at important maritime centres of guilds of pilots, which in many cases were subsequently incorporated by Royal Charter under the style of the " Trinity House " of the port or district. The most important, the " Guild, Fraternity or Brotherhood of the Most Glorious and Undivided Trinity and of St. Clement in the parish of Deptford Strond," received its charter of incorporation from James I.

The powers given by these Royal Charters were for the most part afterwards confirmed and altered by private Acts of Parliament.

With the growth of municipal and private enterprise in the development of harbours and docks and rivers, new types of pilotage authorities were evolved, with the result that there are now four general classes of pilotage authorities: (1) Trinity Houses, (2) Harbours Authorities, (3) Municipal Corporations, and (4) Pilotage Boards, Trusts and Commissions. The Committee, while being unable to report that any particular class of pilotage authority was necessarily unfitted to possess pilotage powers, recommended that, in addition to a sufficient proportion of practical nautical men, each pilotage authority should include direct representation of shipowners and pilots. This recommendation is embodied in section 7 (1) (*f*).

The Committee also found that great uncertainty and controversy existed as to the limits of certain pilotage districts, which in many cases were defined in ancient charters by references to place-names which could no longer be traced or with relation to a set of local conditions which had ceased to exist. Section 7 (1) (*c*) now deals with this point.

851 (2) *Uniformity and accessibility of pilotage law.*—The report contains frequent references to the chaotic condition of the law of pilotage and the consequent uncertainty in administration. While the M.S. Acts of 1854 and of 1894 were in some degree consolidating statutes, the law of pilotage before the changes effected by the present Act was contained (i) in enactments of public general Acts, *e.g.* M.S.A. 1894, Part X; (ii) in provisional orders made by the Board of Trade under powers contained in M.S.A. 1894, ss. 575–576 and 578–580; (iii) in provisions of local Acts; (iv) in local customs, Royal Charters, provisions of repealed Acts kept alive by M.S.A. 1894, s. 574; and (v) in by-laws made by local pilotage authorities either under the powers given by M.S.A. 1894, s. 582, or wholly or partially under powers given by local Acts and, in the case of the London Trinity House as regards out-ports, by powers originally given by the repealed Act of 6 Geo. 4, c. 125, and believed to have been kept alive by M.S.A. 1854 and 1894. The control given to the Board of Trade over the by-laws made by pilotage authorities was found to be inadequate, no initiative being exercisable by the Board and considerable uncertainty existing as to the necessity for confirmation by the Board of by-laws of certain authorities.

The Pilotage Act 1913 now contains the general principles regulating pilotage in all districts, and makes provision for definition of the constitution and limits of jurisdiction of each pilotage authority by Pilotage Orders made by the Secretary of State for Trade, subject to confirmation by Parliament in certain cases. The Act, too, empowers the local pilotage authorities to make by-laws applying the general principles therein contained to local conditions, subject to the effective control of the Secretary of State for Trade, assisted by a Pilotage Advisory Committee.

852 (3) *Changes in laws of pilotage.*—The most far-reaching change effected by the Pilotage Act 1913 was the abolition (so far as U.K. waters are concerned) of the defence of " compulsory pilotage." (Section 15.) By this change the British law as to the civil liability of the owner of a vessel in the charge of a compulsory pilot for loss or damage caused by the vessel was brought into line with the law of the other principal maritime countries, and effect was given to Art. 5 of International Convention for the Unification of certain Rules of Law respecting Collisions, signed at

Brussels on September 23, 1910 (Cd. 5558), which is set out in *British Shipping Laws*, Vol. 4, *Marsden on Collisions at Sea*, 11th ed., § 1271 *et seq.*

One result of the abolition of this defence is to remove from the Superior Courts the intricate and costly litigation in connection with pilotage and to confine questions of pilotage law for the most part to courts of summary jurisdiction. Certain other changes are referred to in the notes following the sections below. The limitation of liability of pilotage authorities is dealt with by the Pilotage Authorities (Limitation of Liability) Act 1936, *post*.

PART I—REVISION OF PILOTAGE ORGANISATION

Improvement of pilotage organisation

853 **1.** The [Secretary of State for Trade] shall take steps to obtain information with respect to pilotage organisation at the various ports in the United Kingdom, and, by the exercise of [his] powers under this Act to make Pilotage Orders,[1] shall carry into effect any re-organisation or improvement of organisation which the [Secretary] may consider necessary or expedient at any port, and shall also at any port deal by Pilotage Order with any Act,[2] order, charter, custom, byelaw, regulation, or provision in force at the port with a view to rendering the law relating to pilotage at the various ports in the United Kingdom accessible and, so far as possible, uniform.

[1] As to the power of the [Secretary of State for Trade] to make Pilotage Orders, see s. 7.
[2] As to the saving of existing Acts, orders, etc., until superseded by Pilotage Order or by-law under this Act, see s. 59.

Recommendations with respect to pilotage byelaws

854 **2.**—(1) The [Secretary of State for Trade] shall also take steps to obtain information with respect to the byelaws as to pilotage in force at the various ports in the United Kingdom, and, after consulting with the pilotage authority at the port and considering any byelaws proposed by that authority, shall, when necessary or expedient and with a view to securing, so far as practicable, uniformity of administration and to carrying out any changes consequent on the passing of this Act, make recommendations for the substitution of new byelaws for those in force at the port, or in case there are no such byelaws in force, for the making of such byelaws as may be required at the port.

(2) If a pilotage authority fail to submit byelaws in accordance with the recommendations for confirmation by the [Secretary of State for Trade] under this Act, the [Secretary of State] may treat the byelaws recommended by the [Secretary of State] as if they were byelaws submitted to [him] by the pilotage authority for confirmation, and those byelaws, when con-

firmed by the [Secretary of State for Trade] in accordance with this Act, shall have the same effect as if they had been so submitted.

As to the general supervision over by-laws now directly exercised by the Minister of Transport, see s. 18 and notes thereto. For meaning of " pilotage authority," see s. 8, *post*.

855 **3–5.** [*These sections, which dealt with the appointment by the then Board of Trade of Commissioners for the purpose of Part I and for local inquiries and schemes for reorganisation and for the conduct of the local inquiries, were repealed as spent by the Statute Law Revision Act*, 1927.]

Consultation with pilots as to byelaws and schemes

856 **6.** The [Secretary of State for Trade], before making recommendations to a pilotage authority under this Act for the substitution of new byelaws for those in force in any port, and a pilotage authority, before submitting any scheme to the [Secretary of State] for the re-organisation or improvement of organisation of pilotage at their port shall, unless pilots are directly represented on the authority or on a pilotage committee of the authority, take steps to ascertain the opinion of the pilots at the port with respect to the matter in question.

PART II—GENERAL PILOTAGE LAW

Pilotage Orders

857 Under the repealed M.S.A. 1894, ss. 575–580, the Department of Trade was given power to deal with many of the matters referred to in this section by " provisional order."

Power of [Secretary of State for Trade] to make Pilotage Orders

858 **7.**—(1) The [Secretary of State for Trade] may, by Order made under this Act (in this Act referred to as a Pilotage Order)—

(*a*) make such rearrangement of pilotage districts and pilotage authorities as the [Secretary of State thinks] necessary or expedient; and

(*b*) establish new pilotage districts and new pilotage authorities and abolish existing pilotage districts and existing pilotage authorities in cases where it appears to the [Secretary of State] necessary or expedient; and

(*c*) define the limits of pilotage districts, distinguishing as respects any pilotage district in part of which pilotage is compulsory and in part of which pilotage is not compulsory, the part of the district in which pilotage is compulsory [1]; and

(*d*) provide for the incorporation of any pilotage authority, and make such alteration in the constitution of any pilotage authority with reference to their powers and duties as pilotage authority, and such provisions as to the appointment of committees (including, if it is thought fit, persons not members of the authority), and as to the relations between the authority and the committee, as the [Secretary of State for Trade thinks] necessary or expedient [2]; and

(*e*) empower a pilotage authority to delegate to a committee [3] thereof any of its powers and duties, and provide, if it seems necessary or desirable, that the decisions of the committee on questions so delegated shall not require confirmation by the pilotage authority; and

(*f*) make such provision for the direct representation of pilots and shipowners on any pilotage authority or committee of a pilotage authority as the [Secretary of State for Trade thinks] necessary or expedient [4]; and

(*g*) in cases where a pilotage authority have powers and duties as to other matters as well as pilotage, provide for their accounts as pilotage authority being kept separate from their accounts in relation to other matters [5]; and

(*h*) provide that pilotage shall be compulsory in any area where it has previously not been compulsory, or provide, in connection with any rearrangement of a pilotage district, that pilotage shall be non-compulsory in any area where it has been compulsory, subject to provision being also made for the payment of compensation to the pilots concerned for any loss or damage which may be incurred by them in consequence of such rearrangement [6]; and

(*i*) authorise, where it appears expedient, any pilotage authority to make byelaws providing for the grant of certificates (in this Act referred to as deep sea certificates) [7] certifying that persons are qualified to act as pilots of ships for any part of the sea or channels outside the district of any pilotage authority, so, however, that a pilot holding such a certificate shall not be entitled to supersede any other person as pilot of a ship; and

(*j*) provide that any Act (other than this Act), order, charter, custom, byelaw, regulation, or provision shall, so far as it relates to pilotage, cease to have effect within any pilotage district or as respects any pilotage authority, but may re-enact the whole or any part thereof so far as is not inconsistent with the provisions of this Act [8]; and

(*k*) provide for compensation being paid to any pilots for any loss or damage which may be incurred by them in consequence of any Order abolishing or rearranging any pilotage districts; and

(*l*) make any provisions which appear necessary or expedient for the purpose of giving full effect to the Order.

859 (2) Provision shall be made by Pilotage Order for the direct representation of pilots either on the pilotage authority or on the committee of the pilotage authority of any district where there are not less than six licensed pilots if a majority of the pilots licensed for the district signify in writing [9] to the [Secretary of State for Trade] that they desire such representation, and, where such provision is made,[10] provision shall also be made for the representation of shipowners on the authority or committee, as the case may be.

(3) A Pilotage Order establishing a pilotage authority for any pilotage district shall provide for the representation on the pilotage authority of any dock or harbour authority having jurisdiction within the district which was represented on the pilotage authority for the district at the time of the passing of this Act, and which desires to be so represented.

(4) A Pilotage Order shall not be made by the [Secretary of State for Trade] except—

(*a*) for any of the purposes of Part I of this Act; or

(*b*) on the application in writing of any person interested in the pilotage of any pilotage district or in the operation of the laws relating to pilotage in that district or the administration of those laws.

(5) A Pilotage Order shall require confirmation by Parliament—

(*a*) if it is an Order made for any of the purposes of Part I of this Act; and

(*b*) if, whatever the purpose for which it is made, a petition is presented to the [Secretary of State for Trade] against the Order by any person appearing to the [Secretary of State for Trade] to be interested in the administration of pilotage in the district within six weeks after the Order is published and the petition is not withdrawn.

(6) A Pilotage Order which does not require confirmation by Parliament shall have effect as if enacted in this Act.

(7) The provisions contained in the First Schedule to this Act shall have effect with respect to Pilotage Orders.[11]

860 [1] The Departmental Committee of the Board of Trade (1911) (Cd. 5571) reported many instances in which the limits of existing pilotage districts were ill-defined, and, in recommending that the limits of every pilotage authority should be clearly defined, suggested that, as a general rule, the limits should be where experience has shown that ships most usually begin to require the services of a pilot, and, where possible, should include those points where a pilot can most easily be taken on board under all conditions of weather. See Report, s. 86.

[2] Under the repealed M.S.A. 1894, s. 576, the Board of Trade could only incorporate new pilotage authorities on transfer of jurisdiction.

[3] Apart from this Act, certain pilotage authorities, *e.g.* harbour authorities, are empowered to delegate certain of their powers to a Pilotage Committee under their local Acts, *e.g.* Humber Conservancy Act 1907, s. 64 (1) and (2).

[4] By subs. (2), pilots and shipowners are given certain statutory rights to representation. See, too, the schemes of representation in the Appendix to the Pilotage Order (London) Confirmation Act 1913, and in the schedules to the Pilotage Orders Confirmation (No. 1) Act 1920 (Liverpool and Manchester).

[5] As to the receipts and expenses of pilotage authorities, see s. 21; and as to the saving for pilotage authorities of the power to apply money received in the name of pilotage for other purposes, see s. 58.

[6] It should be noticed that the Department of Trade may only provide for the abolition of compulsory pilotage in cases where a re-arrangement of the pilotage district is being made. See, too, s. 14, which provides against the extension of the defence of compulsory pilotage in areas in which pilotage is declared for the first time to be compulsory by Pilotage Order; but as to the abolition of the defence of compulsory pilotage, see s. 15 and notes thereto.

[7] See s. 17 (1) (*n*) for power of pilotage authority to provide by by-law for the grant of "deep sea certificates," and compare repealed M.S.A. 1894, s. 582 (10).

Prior to this Act, Hull, Leith and Newcastle Trinity Houses claimed to exercise the power of granting deep sea licences under private Acts or charters. As to Leith, see *Hossack* v. *Gray* (1865) 6 B. & S. 598, and *Randall* v. *Renton* (1902) 5 F. 16. In 1873, the London Trinity House and Tyne Pilotage Commissioners obtained an Order in Council authorising the grant of such licences under M.S.A. 1894, s. 582 (10).

For the power of the Trinity House (London Pilotage District) to make by-laws providing for the grant of deep sea certificates, see London Pilotage Order, s. 6, scheduled to Pilotage Order (London) Confirmation Act 1913; and for the like power of the Clyde Pilotage Authority, see the Clyde Pilotage Order, s. 14, scheduled to the Pilotage Orders Confirmation (No. 3) Act 1920.

[8] s. 40 provides that a Pilotage Order shall not diminish the powers of pilotage authorities as to pilot boats.

[9] Even without such request from a majority of the pilots, the Secretary of State for Trade may, under subs. (1) (*f*), provide for the direct representation of pilots and shipowners.

[10] *Quaere*, whether, where provision is made under subs. (1) (*f*) for representation of pilots, the shipowners are by virtue of these words also entitled to representation.

[11] *Cf.* the repealed M.S.A. (1894), s. 580 (making and confirming provisional orders).

The First Schedule of this Act gives power to the Secretary of State for Trade to make rules in relation to applications for Pilotage Orders. The Rules now in force are the Pilotage Authorities (Application) Rules 1964 (S.I. No. 1467).

861 Provisional orders have been made and confirmed by Parliament (in certain instances, for which see below, the orders so confirmed have been subsequently amended by Pilotage Orders not requiring confirmation) for the following districts:—

(1) London Pilotage District—confirmed by Act, c. clxv, of 1913;
(2) Pilotage districts of Liverpool and Manchester—confirmed by Pilotage Orders Confirmation (No. 1) Act 1920;
(3) Pilotage districts of Cork, Drogheda, Dundalk, Galway, Newry and Carlingford —confirmed by Pilotage Orders Confirmation (No. 2) Act 1920;
(4) Pilotage districts of the Clyde, Dundee, Fraserburgh and Peterhead—confirmed by Pilotage Orders Confirmation (No. 3) Act 1920;
(5) Output districts under jurisdiction of Corporation of Trinity House of Deptford Strond—confirmed by Pilotage Orders Confirmation (No. 1) Act 1921;
(6) Belfast, Coleraine, Londonderry, Portrush—confirmed by Pilotage Orders Confirmation (No. 2) Act 1921;
(7) Arbroath, Elgin, Lossiemouth, Eyemouth, Irvine, Thurso and Wick—confirmed by Pilotage Orders Confirmation (No. 3) Act 1921;
(8) Ballina, Limerick, Tralee, Fenit, Westport—confirmed by Pilotage Orders Confirmation (No. 4) Act 1921;
(9) Barry, Bristol, Cardiff, Gloucester, Llanelli, Newport, Port Talbot and Swansea —confirmed by Pilotage Orders Confirmation (No. 5) Act 1921;
(10) Arundel, Berwick and Lancaster—confirmed by Pilotage Orders Confirmation (No. 6) Act 1921;
(11) Aberdeen, Ardrossan, Ayr, Inverness, Montrose and Stonehaven—confirmed by Pilotage Orders Confirmation (No. 7) Act 1921;
(12) Humber, Boston, Spalding, King's Lynn and Wisbech—confirmed by Pilotage Orders Confirmation (No. 1) Act 1922;
(13) The Dee, Hartlepool, Sunderland, The Tees and The Tyne—confirmed by Pilotage Orders Confirmation (No. 2) Act 1922;
(14) Blyth, Buckie, Newcastle-upon-Tyne—confirmed by Pilotage Orders Confirmation (No. 3) Act 1922.
(15) The Forth (Trinity House of Leith), Borrowstounness, Burntisland, Charlestown, Grangemouth, Kirkcaldy, Leith and Methil—confirmed by Pilotage Orders Confirmation (No. 4) Act 1922.

862 Pilotage Orders not requiring confirmation by Parliament have been made for various districts and are printed as Statutory Rules and Orders or Statutory Instruments. Some of these Pilotage Orders have the effect of amending the Confirmation Act for the pilotage district covered by the Order. In each case, therefore, the Confirmation Acts above cited

should be considered with reference to the relevant Pilotage Orders for the same pilotage district. The Pilotage Orders not requiring confirmation are as follow:—

Aberdeen Pilotage Order 1924 (May 26, 1924; S.R. & O. No. 657/S.53);
Barry Pilotage (Amendment) Order 1939 (June 16, 1939; S.R. & O. No. 639);
Belfast Pilotage (Amendment) Order 1940 (August 7, 1940; S.R. & O. No. 1454);
Bridgwater Pilotage (Amendment) Order 1936 (December 21, 1936; S.R. & O. No. 1341);
Bristol—Pilotage Orders Confirmation (No. 5) Act 1921 (Amendment) Order 1935 (July 30, 1935; S.R. & O. No. 657), and the Bristol Pilotage (Amendment) Order 1946 (November 7, 1946; S.R. & O. No. 2016);
Burghead Pilotage Order 1935 (October 25, 1935; S.R. & O. No. 1041/S.46);
Clyde Pilotage (Amendment) Order (S.I.'s 1971 No. 887 & 1972 No. 288);
Dee Pilotage (Amendment) Order 1938 (September 21, 1938; S.R. & O. No. 1174);
Forth Pilotage Order 1947 (September 5, 1947; S.R. & O. No. 1938), repealing Pilotage Orders Confirmation (No. 4) Act 1922;
Humber Pilotage (Amendment) Order 1926 (September 20, 1926; S.R. & O. No. 1126), and Humber Pilotage (Amendment) Order 1939 (September 23, 1939; S.R. & O. No. 1196);
Ipswich Pilotage (Amendment) Order 1925 (July 23, 1925; S.R. & O. No. 723);
Irvine Pilotage (Amendment) Order 1954 (August 2, 1954; S.I. No. 950);
Isle of Wight Pilotage (Amendment) Order 1963 (S.I. 1964 No. 256);
Lerwick Pilotage Order 1928 (April 28, 1928; S.R. & O. No. 330);
Liverpool Pilotage (Amendment) Order 1942 (July 18, 1942; S.R. & O. No. 1378), Liverpool Pilotage (Amendment) Order 1947 (October 25, 1947; S.R. & O. No. 2292), Liverpool Pilotage (Amendment) Order 1950 (June 2, 1950; S.I. No. 1215), Liverpool Pilotage (Amendment) Order 1956 (February 27, 1956; S.I. No. 250), and Liverpool Pilotage (Amendment) Order 1960 (May 5, 1960; S.I. No. 379); Liverpool Pilotage (Amendment) Order 1963 (S.I. No. 1161); Liverpool Pilotage (Amendment) (No. 2) Order 1963 (S.I. 1964 No. 20) and Liverpool Pilotage (Amendment) Order 1969 (S.I. No. 41).
London Pilotage (Amendment) Order 1924 (December 29, 1924; S.R. & O. No. 1430); London Pilotage (Amendment) Order 1931 (December 10, 1931; S.R. & O. No. 1077); London Pilotage (Amendment) Order 1937 (December 10, 1937; S.R. & O. No. 1122); London Pilotage (Amendment) Order 1948 (April 5, 1948; S.I. No. 1154); London Pilotage (Amendment) Order 1953 (February 27, 1953; S.I. No. 695);
Manchester Pilotage (Amendment) Order 1949 (April 29, 1949; S.I. No. 1141); Manchester Pilotage (Amendment) Order 1953 (August 18, 1953; S.I. No. 1492);
Montrose Pilotage (Amendment) Order 1963 (S.I. 1964 No. 256);
Port Talbot Pilotage (Amendment) Order 1924 (July 22, 1924; S.R. & O. No. 808) and Port Talbot Pilotage (Amendment) Order 1958 (December 9, 1958; S.I. No. 2062);
Swansea Pilotage Order 1923 (June 20, 1923; S.R. & O. No. 714), and Swansea Pilotage (Amendment) Order 1958 (December 9, 1958; S.I. No. 2063);
Taw and Torridge Pilotage Order 1935 (December 17, 1935; S.R. & O. No. 1247);
Tees Pilotage (Amendment) Order 1955 (August 31, 1955; S.I. No. 1322);
Watchet Pilotage Order 1936 (December 21, 1936; S.R. & O. No. 1342);
Wisbech Pilotage Order 1949 (July 25, 1949; S.I. No. 1740);
Yarmouth and Southwold Pilotage (Amendment) Order (1963 No. 412).

Pilotage Districts and Authorities

Pilotage districts and pilotage authorities

863 **8.**—(1) For the purposes of this Act the districts established as pilotage districts under Pilotage Orders made under this Act shall be pilotage districts, and the pilotage authorities shall be the pilotage authorities as constituted by Pilotage Orders made under this Act.

(2) Until otherwise provided by Pilotage Order made under this Act, every pilotage district [1] which is, at the time of the passing of this Act, a pilotage district shall continue to be a pilotage district, and every pilotage authority which is a pilotage authority at the time of the passing of this Act [2] shall continue to be a pilotage authority.

[1] For the limits of pilotage districts existing at the time of the passing of the Act, see the report of the Departmental Committee on Pilotage (1911), Appendix B.

[2] See M.S.A. 1894, s. 573 (which was repealed by the Pilotage Act, 1913), which provided that " In this Act, pilotage authority includes all bodies and persons authorised to appoint or license pilots or to fix or alter rates of pilotage or to exercise any jurisdiction in respect of pilotage."

Advisory Committee

Power to appoint advisory committee

864 **9.**—(1) The [Secretary of State for Trade] may appoint an advisory committee for the purpose of advising [him] with reference to the exercise of [his] powers or the performance of [his] duties under this Act, consisting of such persons as [he] may appoint, being pilots, shipowners, representatives of pilotage authorities, representatives of dock and harbour authorities, or other persons representing the interests principally affected, or having special knowledge of the subject-matter.

(2) There shall be paid to the members of any such committee out of moneys provided by Parliament such allowances and expenses as the [Secretary of State for Trade] may fix with the consent of the Treasury.

Compulsory Pilotage

Continuation of existing compulsory districts and abolition of existing exemptions

865 **10.**—(1) Subject to the provisions of any Pilotage Order, pilotage shall continue to be compulsory [1] in every pilotage district in which it was compulsory at the time of the passing of this Act,[2] and shall continue not to be compulsory in every pilotage district in which it was not compulsory at the time of the passing of this Act, and subject to the provisions of this Act all exemptions from compulsory pilotage in force at the date of the passing of this Act shall cease to have effect.[3]

(2) Any reference in this Act to a pilotage district in which pilotage is compulsory shall, in the case of a district in which pilotage is compulsory only in part [4] of the district, be construed, if the context so requires, as a reference to that part of the district only.

866 [1] As to the abolition of compulsory pilotage " within any closed dock, lock, or other closed work," see s. 32 (2).

[2] The test as to whether pilotage was " compulsory at the time of the passing of this Act " is apparently twofold:—(1) Whether a charge for pilotage could be recovered whether a pilot was employed or not; and (2) Whether the employment of a qualified pilot could be enforced by a penalty: see *The Maria* (1839) 1 W.Rob. 95; *The SS. Beechgrove Co.* v. *Aktieselskabet Fjord of Kristiania* [1916] 1 A.C. 364 at p. 379; and Abbott, *Merchant Ships*, etc., 14th ed., p. 311.

In Continental codes the term compulsory pilotage is generally used in the former sense and imports no further obligation or exemption than the obligation to pay pilotage dues whether a pilot be in fact employed or not.

For the limits of districts existing at the time of the passing of this Act, reference should be made to the Report of the Departmental Committee on Pilotage (1911), Appendix B.

[3] Under the repealed M.S.A. 1894, s. 603 (1), all existing exemptions from compulsory pilotage were continued in force.
[4] As regards fees payable for pilotage by a vessel which has to cross both compulsory and optional pilotage limits, see *Arnold Malabre & Co.* v. *Kingston Pilotage Authority* [1972] 3 W.L.R. 587 (P.C.) (Jamaica).

Obligations where pilotage is compulsory

867 **11.**—(1) Every ship [1] (other than an excepted ship [2]) while navigating in a pilotage district [3] in which pilotage is compulsory for the purpose of entering, leaving, or making use [4] of any port [5] in the district, and every ship carrying passengers [6] (other than an excepted ship) while navigating for any such purpose as aforesaid in any pilotage district (whether pilotage is compulsory or not compulsory in that district) shall [7] be either—

(*a*) under the pilotage of a licensed pilot [8] of the district; or

(*b*) under the pilotage of a master or mate [9] possessing a pilotage certificate [10] for the district who is bona fide acting as master or mate of the ship.

(2) If any ship (other than an excepted ship) in circumstances in which pilotage is compulsory under this section, is not under pilotage as required by this section, after a licensed pilot of the district has offered to take charge [11] of the ship, the master of that ship shall be liable in respect of each offence to a fine [12] not exceeding double the amount of the pilotage dues [13] that could be demanded for the conduct of the ship.

(3) For the purposes of this Act the following ships are excepted ships [14]:—

(*a*) Ships belonging to His Majesty [15];

(*b*) Pleasure yachts;

(*c*) Fishing vessels [16];

(*d*) Ferry boats plying as such exclusively within the limits of a harbour authority;

(*e*) Ships of less than fifty tons gross tonnage [17];

(*f*) Ships exempted from compulsory pilotage by byelaw as hereinafter provided in this section.

(4) A pilotage authority may [18] by byelaw made under this Act exempt from compulsory pilotage in their district any of the following classes of ships, if not carrying passengers, up to such limit of gross tonnage in each case as may be fixed by the byelaw, that is to say:—

(i) Ships trading coastwise [19];

(ii) Home trade ships [20] trading otherwise than coastwise;

(iii) Ships whose ordinary course of navigation does not extend beyond the seaward limits of a harbour authority, whilst navigating within those limits or within such parts thereof as may be specified in the byelaw:

Provided that, if any such byelaw appears to the [Secretary of State for Trade] to exempt from compulsory pilotage ships of any class or description which were not at the date of the passing of this Act in practice exempted in the district to which the byelaw relates, the [Secretary of State] shall not confirm the byelaw, but may, if [he thinks] fit, submit to Parliament a Bill confirming the byelaw with or without modifications, and such Bill shall be treated as if it were a Bill confirming a Pilotage Order, and the provisions of this Act with respect to such Bills shall apply accordingly.

(5) For the purposes of this section, a ship which habitually trades to or from any port or ports outside the British islands [21] shall not be deemed to be trading coastwise, and a ship which habitually trades to or from any port outside the home trade limits shall not be deemed to be a home trade ship, by reason only that she is for the time being engaged on a voyage between ports in the British islands,[21] or within the home trade limits,[19] as the case may be.

868 [1] This section applies to all ships, British and foreign. See s. 61.

[2] " Excepted ships " are defined in subs. (3).

[3] The provisions for compulsory pilotage do not apply where the vessel is deemed not to be navigating within a pilotage district by virtue of a by-law made under s. 32: see *McMillan* v. *Crouch* [1972] 2 Lloyd's Rep. 325 (H.L.). See also s. 8.

[4] This was held to include the case of a ship stopping outside a port and receiving a letter of instructions from a motor-boat sent out from the port. " Making use of any port " means taking advantage of the facilities existing at the port: *Cannell, etc.* v. *Lawther, Latta & Co.* [1914] 3 K.B. 1135 (doubted in *Humber Conservancy Board* v. *Federated Coal and Shipping Co., infra*). But the words exclude the case of a ship merely passing through a compulsory pilotage district: *The Stranton* [1917] P. 177. *Semble*, it would exclude the case of a vessel passing through such a district and receiving a wireless message from the shore.

Vessels using the River Thames merely as a highway are not doing so " for the purpose of ... making use of " the Port of London, even if they make incidental use of such facilities as piers to embark and land passengers, and they are not therefore required to carry pilots; there is a custom that vessels in the charge of licensed watermen are not required to carry pilots within the watermen's district, and this custom is not excluded by the London Pilotage (Amendment) Order 1937; see *Thames Launches* v. *Trinity House Corporation* (*Deptford Strond*) (*No.* 2) [1962] Ch. 153 (where Wilberforce J. reviews historically the legislation affecting the Port of London in its dual capacity as a highway and as a port).

As to calling at a port to take on board or land a pilot belonging to some other district, see s. 13.

[5] Though by M.S.A. 1894, s. 742, " port " includes " place," a place to be a port within the meaning of this section must have some of the characteristics of a port. Thus Spurn Point, which has a trolley line, four houses, a signal station and a lighthouse, is not a port: *Humber Conservancy Board* v. *Federated Coal and Shipping Co.* [1928] 1 K.B. 492.

[6] *Cf. Clayton* v. *Albertsen* [1972] 1 W.L.R. 1443 (lorry drivers travelling on a " roll-on, roll-off " ship without payment are passengers); *The Alletta and England* [1965] 1 Lloyd's Rep. 479 (wife of master was not a passenger). It would seem that the following cases decided on the repealed statutes are applicable under this section (although it should be noted that they were decided at a time when shipowners commonly had the defence of compulsory pilotage).

A passenger ship, when not carrying passengers, is not within this provision: *The Lion* (1869) L.R. 2 P.C. 525; but any ship which *is* carrying passengers is within the provision. The carriage of even one passenger is sufficient to bring the ship within the section. See Interpretation Act 1889, s. 1 (1), and *The Hanna, infra*. Contrast the cases as to meaning of " passenger steamer " in M.S.A. 1894, Part III, in notes to s. 267, *supra*, in which the material question is not: " Was the steamer carrying passengers ? " but " Was the steamer a passenger steamer ? "

As to who are " passengers," see *The Lion, supra* (the wife and father-in-law of the captain not paying a fare not passengers); and *The Hanna* (1866) L.R. 1 A. & E. 283 (a friend of the captain who worked his passage not a passenger); and *The Clymene* [1897] P. 295 (distressed seamen are not passengers); *Hay* v. *Corporation of Trinity House* (1895) 65 L.J.Q.B. 90; 8 Asp.M.L.C. 77 (persons given passage on payment for food only and landed at bunkering port are not passengers).

The payment of a fare is necessary to constitute a " passenger " within the provisions as to pilotage: *The Lion, supra.*

869 [7] Navigation without a pilot in a compulsory area is not absolutely forbidden; but a ship in a compulsory area is under a continuing obligation to fly the pilot flag and to take a pilot on board if he offers. *Muller* v. *Trinity House* [1925] 1 K.B. 166. If no pilot offers, there is no obligation upon the owner to pay pilotage dues; *Ibid.* There is also a continuing obligation on the ship to keep a good lookout for the pilot signal, though she need not go out of her way to look for a pilot boat; *Rindby* v. *Brewis* (1926) 25 Ll.L.R. 26.

[8] The term " qualified pilot " was used throughout the repealed M.S.A. 1894, Part X (Pilotage). By *ibid.* s. 586 (1): " A pilot shall be deemed a qualified pilot . . . if duly licensed . . . to conduct ships to which he does not belong."

[9] This means any mate and not just the first mates: see note (2) to s. 23.

[10] As to pilotage certificates, see ss. 23–25.

[11] The Act does not define what constitutes an offer, but see s. 44: " makes a signal for the purpose of offering his services." The following cases deal with the offence of navigating in a compulsory pilotage district without employing a licensed pilot or certificated master or mate under the repealed statutes, but do not directly touch this point: *Usher* v. *Lyon* (1816) 2 Price 118; *Hammond* v. *Blake* (1830) 10 B. & C. 424; *Beilby* v. *Shepherd* (1848) 3 Ex. 40.

Under M.S.A. 1854, s. 343, the employment of an unqualified person on board an unexempted ship after the offer of a pilot licensed for exempted ships only was held not to be an offence: *Stafford* v. *Dyer* [1895] 1 Q.B. 566.

[12] It should be observed that no power is given by this section to the pilotage authority to charge double pilotage dues if the provisions as to compulsory pilotage are not observed. The proper course is for the authority to proceed by way of prosecution for the recovery of the fine under M.S.A. 1894, ss. 680–681, which are made applicable to offences under this Act by s. 62.

[13] As to the power of pilotage authority to fix by by-law the rate of payments to be made in respect of the services of a licensed pilot, see s. 17 (1) (*f*).

[14] As to the saving of exemptions from compulsory pilotage existing before the passing of this Act and affecting any district in particular until such time as provision has been made by pilotage order or by-law under this Act, see s. 59.

[15] See notes to M.S.A. 1894, s. 557 (salvage by H.M. ships), and cases there cited.

[16] *Cf.* definition of " fishing boat " in M.S.A. 1894, s. 370.

[17] As to method of ascertaining the gross tonnage of a ship, see M.S.A. 1965, s. 1.

[18] If no such by-law is made by the pilotage authority, interested parties may apply to the Secretary of State for Trade with a view to action by him; see s. 18.

[19] In *The Agricola* (1843) 2 W.R. 10 Dr. Lushington said (at p. 17) that the principle upon which vessels engaged in the coasting trade are exempt from compulsory pilotage is that the masters of such vessels, from their occupation and experience, are supposed to be so familiarly acquainted with the English coasts that it would be superfluous and oppressive upon the owners to impose upon them the necessity of employing a pilot; and a vessel which, after having made a voyage to Port Philip and Calcutta and thence back to London, was proceeding from London to Liverpool in ballast was held not to be engaged on a " coasting voyage " within the exemption. Similarly, a vessel ordinarily occupied in foreign trade, going from Liverpool to London, in order to sail thence for foreign parts, and not carrying passengers, but carrying a cargo shipped at Liverpool for London, is not within these words: *The Lloyds* or *Sea Queen* (1863) 32 L.J.Adm. 197; B. & L. 359; *Phillips* v. *Born* (1905) 93 L.T. 634; 10 Asp.M.C. 131; *The Winestead* [1895] P. 170 (a ship making regular voyages from London to Cardiff to complete loading, and then to the Mediterranean). Subs. (5) appears to adopt the principle of these decisions rather than that of the parallel line of cases under M.S.A. 1894, s. 625 (3), *e.g. The Rutland* [1897] A.C. 333; *Courtney* v. *Cole* (1887) 19 Q.B.D. 447.

Cf. the definition of " coasting ship " in the Customs and Excise Act 1952, s. 57.

[20] It is provided by M.S.A. 1894, s. 742, that " ' Home trade ship ' includes every ship employed in trading or going within the following limits; that is to say, the United Kingdom, the Channel Islands, the Isle of Man, and the Continent of Europe between the river Elbe and Brest inclusive." Where a ship which regularly trades within the home trade limits sets out on a voyage from a port in the U.K. to a port beyond the home trade limits, she ceases to be a home trade ship and is required to carry a pilot: *Smith* v. *Veen* [1955] 2 Q.B. 277.

[21] " British Islands " here includes the Republic of Ireland. See note " Application to Northern Ireland and the Republic of Ireland " following notes to M.S.A. 1894, s. 742.

Exemption from compulsory pilotage of ships belonging to certain public authorities

870 **12.** The provisions of this Act with respect to compulsory pilotage shall not apply to tugs, dredgers, sludge-vessels, barges, and other similar craft—

(*a*) belonging to or hired by a dock, harbour [1] or river authority whilst employed in the exercise of the statutory powers or duties of the authority and navigating within any pilotage district [2] which includes within its limits the whole or any part of the area of the authority; or

(*b*) belonging to a local authority whilst employed in the exercise of the statutory powers or duties of the authority and navigating within the pilotage district within which the port to which they belong is situate:

Provided that, where in any pilotage district any of the classes of vessels aforesaid were at the time of the passing of this Act in practice subject to compulsory pilotage, the pilotage authority [2] may by byelaw [3] provide that any of such classes of vessels shall continue to be so subject.

[1] For definition of " harbour authority," see M.S.A. 1894, s. 742.
[2] See s. 8.
[3] As to making and confirming by-laws, see s. 17.

Provision with respect to ships calling at a port for the purpose only of taking pilot

871 **13.** A ship calling at a port [1] in a pilotage district [2] for the purpose only of taking on board or landing a pilot [1] belonging to some other pilotage district shall not, for the purpose of the provisions of this Act relating to compulsory pilotage, be deemed to be navigating in the first-mentioned district for the purpose of entering, leaving, or making use of that port.

This section must be read in conjunction with s. 11, of which it is explanatory.
[1] For definitions of " port " and " pilot," see M.S.A. 1894, s. 742.
[2] See s. 8.

Provision against extension of defence of compulsory pilotage

872 **14.** Notwithstanding anything in any Pilotage Order made under this Act, any area in which pilotage was not compulsory at the date of the passing of this Act shall be deemed to be an area in which pilotage is not compulsory for the purpose of determining the liability of the owner or

master of a ship being navigated in the area for any loss or damage occasioned by or arising out of the navigation of such ship.

With the expiration of the suspensory period contained in s. 15 (2), this section would appear to be spent. It was apparently inserted to prevent the extension of the defence of compulsory pilotage during this period to areas in which pilotage might be made compulsory by Pilotage Order under s. 7 (1) (*h*). See *The Mickleham* [1918] P. 166 at p. 173.

Liability of owner or master in the case of a vessel under pilotage

873 **15.**—(1) Notwithstanding anything in any public or local Act,[1] the owner or master or a vessel navigating under circumstances in which pilotage is compulsory shall be answerable [2] for any loss or damage caused by the vessel or by any fault of the navigation of the vessel in the same manner as he would if pilotage were not compulsory.

(2) *This section shall not take effect until the first day of January, nineteen hundred and eighteen, or such earlier date* [3] *as His Majesty may fix by Order in Council, certifying that it is necessary to bring the section into operation in order to enable His Majesty to comply with an international convention.*

(3) *As from the date of the coming into operation of this section, section six hundred and thirty-three of the Merchant Shipping Act* 1894 *shall cease to have effect.*[4]

874 [1] These words were enacted *ex abundante cautela*, and do not have the effect of limiting the abolition of the defence of compulsory pilotage to cases only where it rested on a public or local Act: *The Chyebassa* [1919] P. 201, where compulsion arose from regulations made under the Defence of the Realm Consolidation Act 1914. See also *The Nord* [1916] P. 53; *The Penrith Castle* [1918] P. 142.

This section, which was designed to give effect to Article 5 of the " Convention for the Unification of certain Rules of Law respecting Collisions," signed at Brussels on September 23, 1910 (Cd. 5558) which is set out in *British Shipping Laws*, Vol. 4, *Marsden on Collisions at Sea*, 11th ed., § 1271 *et seq.*, effects a far-reaching alteration in the law as to the civil liability of the master or owner of a vessel navigating under the charge of a compulsory pilot for damage or loss caused by the vessel. For a historical review of the earlier English statute and case law on this subject, see the dissenting judgment of Bucknill L.J. given in the Court of Appeal in the case of *Workington Harbour and Dock Board* v. *Towerfield* (*Owners*) [1949] P. 10 (C.A.) at pp. 23–28, which was accepted by the House of Lords as accurate: [1951] A.C. 112.

M.S.A. 1894, s. 633, which was repealed by this section as from January 1, 1918, provided as follows:—" An owner or master of a ship shall not be answerable to any person whatever for any loss or damage occasioned by the fault or incapacity of any qualified pilot acting in charge of that ship within any district where the employment of a qualified pilot is compulsory by law." This section was probably merely declaratory of the common law, under which a compulsory pilot would, it appears, not be regarded as the servant or agent of the owner or master so as to make him liable for the pilot's negligence; see *per* Brett M.R., *The Hector* (1883) 8 P.D. 218, 224; *The Halley* (1868) L.R. 2 P.C. 193; *The Maria* (1839) 1 W.Rob. 95. The common law of America, at any rate so far as relates to the personal liability of the owner, is the same: *The City of Philadelphia* (1921) 9 Ll.L.R. 408.

A similar exemption from liability for damage done to a harbour, dock, quay, pier or work by a ship in charge of a compulsory pilot was contained in the Harbours, Docks and Piers Clauses Act 1847 (10 Vict. c. 27), s. 74, but was impliedly repealed by the present section: *The Mostyn* [1926] P. 46 (see *ibid.* on appeal on other points [1928] A.C. 57 (H.L.)).

It is doubtful, however, whether s. 15, in fact, gives full effect to Article 5, *supra*. By s. 61, the application of this Act is confined to the United Kingdom and the Isle of Man. If, then, damage is done by collision by a vessel while under the charge of a pilot compulsorily employed in the territorial waters of a country where the shipowner is not liable for the acts of such pilot, the defence of compulsory pilotage is still open to the shipowner in the English courts on the ground that he cannot be made liable in tort unless he is liable both by the law of this country and by the law of the place where the tort was committed: *The Arum* [1921] P. 12; followed in *The Waziristan, The Seirstad (Owners)* v. *Hindustan Shipping Co., Ltd.* [1953] 2 Lloyd's Rep. 361. Further it has been held that in the absence of evidence to the contrary the common law immunity of the shipowner from liability for the negligence of a person whom he is bound to receive on board, as laid down in *The Maria, supra,* and *The Halley, supra,* will be presumed to be recognised by the law of the foreign country: *The Arum, supra.* But *quaere,* whether the true presumption is not that the general law of England, whether derived from common law or statute, coincides with the law of the foreign country: *The Parchim* [1918] A.C. 157 at p. 161. It may be, however, that this presumption would not arise where the statute law (as here) is a direct reversal of the common law.

For another example of a successful defence of compulsory pilotage—in a case where the collision occurred in the territorial waters of an American state, where pilotage was compulsory and the common law defence of compulsory pilotage still subsisted, see *The City of Philadelphia, supra.*

As to the relationship between master and pilot compulsorily employed, see *The Tactician* [1907] P. 244; *The Elysia* [1912] P. 152; *The Ape* (1915) 84 L.J.P. 8; 31 T.L.R. 244; *The Alexander Shukoff* [1921] 1 A.C. 216; *The Cranley* (1920) 5 Ll.L.R. 302 (C.A.); *The Hans Hoth* [1952] 2 Lloyd's Rep. 341 (distinguishing *The Tactician* and *The Alexander Shukoff*); and *British Shipping Laws,* Vol. 4, *Marsden on Collisions at Sea,* 11th ed., § 289 *et seq.*

875 [2] Where damage to a ship under compulsory pilotage and to the works of a harbour authority whose private Act incorporates s. 74 of the Harbours, Docks and Piers Clauses Act 1847, was caused by the negligence of the compulsory pilot and the negligence of the authority, it was held in *Workington Harbour and Dock Board* v. *Towerfield (Owners)* [1951] A.C. 112 (H.L.) that the effect of s. 15 was (1) to debar the shipowner from making a claim whether based in tort or in contract, for the damage received by the ship and (2) to render him liable for a claim under s. 74 of the Act of 1847 for the damage done to the works of the harbour authority. "Answerable" is the equivalent of "responsible"; *ibid. per* Lord Porter at p. 133, Lord Normand at p. 145. It is to be noted that the events in question in this case occurred before the effective date of the Law Reform (Contributory Negligence) Act 1945.

[3] No earlier date was fixed.

[4] Subss. (2) and (3) were repealed as spent by the Statute Law Revision Act 1927.

Power of Pilotage Authorities to license Pilots and make Byelaws

Powers of pilotage authorities to license pilots for their district

876 **16.** Subject to the provisions of this Act, a pilotage authority [1] may license pilots [2] for their district, and do all such things as may be necessary or expedient for carrying into effect their powers and duties.

As to the power of Trinity House to license "exempt" pilots, see s. 54.

[1] See s. 8.

[2] "Pilot" is defined by M.S.A. 1894, s. 742.

Power of pilotage authorities to make byelaws

877 **17.**—(1) A pilotage authority may [1] by byelaws made under this Act—

(*a*) determine the qualification in respect of age, physical fitness, time of service, local knowledge, skill, character, and otherwise to be required from persons applying to be licensed by them as pilots, provide for the examination of such persons, and fix the term for which a licence is to be in force, and the conditions under which a licence may be renewed; and (*b*) fix the limit (if any) on the number of pilots to be licensed, and provide for the method in which and the conditions under which the list of pilots is to be filled up; and

(*c*) provide generally for the good government of pilots licensed by the authority, and of apprentices, and in particular for ensuring their good conduct and constant attendance to and effectual performance of their duties, whether at sea or on shore; and

(*d*) determine the system [2] to be adopted with respect to the supply and employment of pilots, and provide, so far as necessary, for the approval, licensing, and working of pilot boats in the district, and for the establishment and regulation of pilot boat companies; and

(*e*) provide for the punishment of any breach of any byelaws made by them for the good government of pilots or apprentices by the infliction of fines not exceeding twenty pounds (to be recoverable as fines are recoverable [3] under the Merchant Shipping Acts 1894 to 1907), without prejudice to their powers under this Act to revoke or suspend the licence in the case of any such breach of byelaw [4]; and

(*f*) fix for the district the rates of payments to be made in respect of the services [5] of a licensed pilot [6] (in this Act referred to as pilotage dues), and define the circumstances and conditions under which pilotage dues may be payable on different scales and provide for the collection and distribution of pilotage dues; and

(*g*) if and so far as it appears to the authority to be generally desired by the pilots concerned, provide for the pooling of pilotage dues earned by the licensed pilots or by any class of pilots in the district [7]; and

878 (*h*) provide for a deduction being made from any sums received by pilots of any sums required for meeting the administrative expenses of the authority, or any contributions required for any fund established for the payment of pensions or other benefits to pilots, their widows, or children (in this Act referred to as a pilots' benefit fund); and

(*i*) provide, if and so far as it appears to the authority to be generally desired by the pilots, for bonds [8] (the penalty of which shall not in any case exceed one hundred pounds) being given by pilots for the purpose of the provisions of this Act limiting pilots' liability; and

(*j*) establish, either alone or in conjunction with any other pilotage authority, pilots' benefit funds, and provide for the direct payment to any such fund of any contributions by pilots towards the fund, or of any part of the ordinary receipts of the pilotage authority, and also for the administration of any such fund and for the conditions of participation in any such fund; and (*k*) provide for the method of conducting the examination of masters and mates applying for pilotage certificates [9] so as to maintain a proper standard of efficiency; and

(*l*) prohibit the grant of pilotage certificates to masters or mates who do not hold at least *a mate's certificate of competency* [10] *recognised under Part II of the Merchant Shipping Act* 1894 [11]; and

(*m*) provide that a pilotage certificate shall not be renewed without re-examination unless the master or mate has made not less than a specified number of visits to the port as master or mate of any ship in respect of which the certificate is granted; and

(*n*) if the pilotage authority are an authority authorised to grant deep sea certificates by virtue of a Pilotage Order made with reference to that authority, provide for the grant of deep sea certificates [12]; and

(*o*) apply any byelaws made under this section for the good government of pilots and the punishment of any breach of any such byelaw, with any necessary modifications, to masters and mates holding pilotage certificates; and

(*p*) require the owners of ships, whose masters or mates hold pilotage certificates, to contribute towards the pilot fund or account of the pilotage district, and require the holders of such certificates to make a periodical return to them of the pilotage services rendered by them; provided that the contribution so required from an owner shall not exceed such proportion of the pilotage dues which would have been payable in respect of the ship if the master or mate had not held a pilotage certificate, as may be fixed by the [Secretary of State for Trade]; and

(*q*) provide for any matter for which provision is to be made or may be made under this Act by byelaw.

(2) A byelaw shall not take effect unless it has been submitted to the [Secretary of State for Trade] and confirmed by [him] with or without modifications.[13]

(3) Notice of any byelaw proposed to be submitted for confirmation under this section shall, before it is so submitted, be published in such manner as the [Secretary of State for Trade directs].

879 [1] Interested parties who object to the exercise of this power may make representations to the Department of Trade; see s. 18.

[2] An exhaustive examination of the systems employed by different pilotage authorities is contained in the Report of the Departmental Committee on Pilotage (1911), ss. 106–176. In many cases the system is based on mutual agreement between the pilotage authority and the pilots. Under this Act the system must be regulated by by-laws. Failure to maintain an adequate pilot service may render a pilotage authority liable to the owners of a ship which as a result suffers damage: *Anchor Line* (*Henderson Brothers*) *Ltd.* v. *Dundee Harbour Trustees* (1922) 38 T.L.R. 299 (H.L.).

As to the approval of pilot boats and the appointment or removal of their masters by the pilotage authority, see s. 38.

[3] *Cf.* repealed M.S.A. 1894, s. 582 (5), and see s. 680 (2), *ibid.* It seems that the fine being imposed as a punishment of an offence, and not being in the nature of a civil debt, can be recovered summarily under s. 680, and imprisonment can be awarded in default of payment or sufficient distress: *R.* v. *Stewart* [1899] 1 Q.B. 964. As to appeal, where the fine exceeds £2, see s. 28.
[4] As to revocation or suspension of a licence for breach of a by-law, see s. 26.
[5] *i.e.* services in fact rendered; see ss. 49, 55. A by-law professing to make dues payable although no services have been rendered is invalid: *Muller* v. *Trinity House* [1925] 1 K.B. 166.
[6] Before this Act, pilotage rates were fixed either (a) by by-law under M.S.A. 1894, s. 582 (6), or (b) by a local Act, or (c) by special agreement between the pilotage authority and the shipowner. This paragraph provides a uniform method.
[7] For an example of a by-law purporting to be made under this power but held *ultra vires*, see *McAlister* v. *Forth Pilotage Authority* (1943) 76 Ll.L.R. 32.
[8] Under M.S.A. 1894, s. 619 (ii), pilots' bonds were limited to pilots licensed by Trinity House. As to the limitation of the pilot's liability where a bond is given, see. s. 35.
[9] As to pilotage certificates, see ss. 23–25.
[10] As to certificates of competency, see M.S.A. 1894, s. 92 *et seq.* As to foreign certificates, see s. 25. As to the meaning of " a mate," see *The Empire Jamaica* [1957] A.C. 386.
[11] The M.S.A. 1970, s. 100 (1), Sched. 3, para. 5, prospectively substitutes for the words in italics the words " such certificate issued under the Merchant Shipping Act 1970, as may be specified in such bye-laws " as from a day to be appointed.
[12] As to the power of the Secretary of State for Trade by Pilotage Order to authorise a pilotage authority to make by-laws providing for the grant of " deep sea certificates," and as to such certificates generally, see s. 7 (1) (i) and note thereto.
[13] Under M.S.A. 1894, s. 583, a by-law required confirmation by Order in Council. Under the present section, power of approving or disapproving of a by-law is given directly to the Secretary of State for Trade, just as it was given to his predecessor in certain local Acts: *e.g.* Mersey Docks Consolidation Act 1858, and Clyde Navigation Act 1887. The change probably does little more than to make theory conform to practice.

There is no necessity for unanimous agreement by all affected parties before a by-law should be confirmed: *Forth* (*Trinity House of Leith*) *Pilotage Authority* v. *Lord Advocate and Others* (1949) 82 Ll.L.R. 1000.

880 Power of [Secretary of State for Trade] on representation to revoke or vary byelaws or require pilotage authority to make byelaws

18.—(1) If at any port [1] either—

(*a*) a majority of the licensed pilots [1] belonging to the port; or

(*b*) any number of persons, not less than six, being masters, owners, or insurers of vessels using the port; or

(*c*) a dock or harbour authority [1] not being the pilotage authority;

object to any byelaw in force at the port, or desire that any byelaw should be in force at the port which is not in force therein, they may make a representation to the [Secretary of State for Trade] to that effect, and the [Secretary of State for Trade] if the representation appears to [him] reasonable after giving the pilotage authority,[2] and, if [he thinks] fit, any other persons, an opportunity of making representations on the subject, may, by order, revoke, vary, or add to any byelaw to which objection is made, or require the pilotage authority to submit to [him] for confirmation a byelaw foı the purpose of giving effect to the representation.

(2) Any byelaw revoked by any such order shall cease to have effect, and any byelaw to which additions are made or which is varied or added to, shall have effect with the variations or additions made by the order.

(3) If a pilotage authority fail to submit to the [Secretary of State for

Trade] for confirmation a byelaw in accordance with an order made under this section, the [Secretary of State for Trade] may treat the byelaw which [he has] required the pilotage authority to submit to [him] as a byelaw submitted to [him] by the authority, and confirm it accordingly, and the byelaw so confirmed shall have effect as if it had been made and confirmed in accordance with this Act.

[1] For definitions of "harbour authority," "port" and "pilot," see M.S.A. 1894, s. 742. For power to license pilots, see s. 16.
[2] See s. 8.

Licensing of pilots by pilotage authority not to involve any liability

881 **19.** The grant or renewal of a licence to a pilot [1] by a pilotage authority [2] under the powers given to them by this Act does not impose any liability on the authority for any loss occasioned by any act or default of the pilot.

For provisions limiting the liability of pilotage authorities in case of loss or damage caused without their actual fault or privity, see Pilotage Authorities (Limitation of Liability) Act 1936.

This section is probably declaratory of the common law. See *Shaw, Savill and Albion* v. *Timaru Harbour Board* (1890) 15 App.Cas. 429; *Dudman and Browne* v. *Dublin Port and Docks Board* (1873) Ir.Rep. 7 C.L. 518; *Holman* v. *Irvine Harbour Trustees* (1877) 4 R. 406.

Quaere, whether in cases where the pilotage authority pay pilots fixed wages and treat them in other respects as their servants, the relationship of master and servant may not be established so as to fix the pilotage authority with responsibility for the pilot's negligence, *cf. The Bearn* [1906] P. 48. However, in *Fowles* v. *Eastern and Australian S.S. Co., Ltd.* [1916] 2 A.C. 556, the Privy Council held that the owners of a steamship damaged by the negligence of a compulsory pilot who was an "officer in the Government service" could not recover from the Queensland Government, on the ground that upon the interpretation of the relevant statutes the Government owed no duty to the owners to navigate the ship, and were not the "principals in the piloting of ships," their only duty being to provide a qualified man.

[1] For power to license pilots, see s. 16.
[2] See s. 8.

Form of pilot's licence, and production and return of pilot's licence to pilotage authority

882 **20.**—(1) A pilot's licence shall be in a form approved for the time being by the [Secretary of State for Trade].

(2) A licensed pilot shall, when required by the pilotage authority by whom the licence has been granted, produce his licence to the authority, and, in case his licence is revoked or suspended, shall deliver up [1] his licence to the authority.

(3) On the death of a licensed pilot, the person into whose hands his licence comes shall without delay transmit it to the pilotage authority [2] by whom it was granted.

(4) If any licensed pilot or other person fails to comply with the requirements of this section, he shall be liable in respect of each offence to a fine [3] not exceeding ten pounds.

For power to license pilots, see s. 16.

[1] Under the corresponding section in M.S.A. 1854, *viz.* s. 352, the pilotage authority had unrestricted power of ordering delivery up of the licence and was not as here limited to cases where the licence was revoked or suspended: *Henry* v. *Newcastle Trinity House* (1858) 8 E. & B. 723; 27 L.J.M.C. 57.
[2] See s. 8.
[3] As to the recovery of fines, see s. 62 and M.S.A. 1894, ss. 680–681.

Receipts and expenses of pilotage authority

883 **21.**—(1) All receipts of a pilotage authority in their capacity as such (other than any money received by them on behalf of and paid over to any pilot, or if the authority administer a pilots' benefit fund, any sums received by them as direct payments for that fund), shall be paid into a separate fund or account, to be called the pilot fund or account of the pilotage district.[1]

(2) All expenses incurred by a pilotage authority in the exercise of their powers or performance of their duties as such authority shall be paid out of their pilot fund or account, and, except so far as may be provided to the contrary by byelaw, subject to the payment of those expenses, the balance shall in each year be applied for the purposes of any pilots' benefit fund established in the district, and so far as not required for that purpose shall be applied for the benefit of pilots in such manner as may be determined by the pilotage authority with the approval of the [Secretary of State for Trade].

(3) A separate account shall be kept by any pilotage authority who administer a pilots' benefit fund of all moneys received by them as payments to that fund, or for the benefit of that fund, and money standing to the credit of that account shall not be applicable to any purpose other than the purposes of the fund.[2]

(4) Nothing in this section shall prevent a pilotage authority which owns or hires the pilot boats for the district from keeping a separate account in respect of such boats.

[1] As to the segregation of funds of an authority acting in a dual capacity, see ss. 6 and 7 of the Pilotage Authorities (Limitation of Liability) Act 1936. As to " pilotage authority " and " pilotage district," see s. 8. " Pilot " is defined in M.S.A. 1894, s. 744.
[2] Pilots' benefit funds, etc., are protected from being taken in execution or made available by any legal process in respect of any liability of the pilotage authority. See s. 5 of the Pilotage Authorities (Limitation of Liability) Act 1936.

Returns to be furnished and statements of accounts to be sent to [Secretary of State for Trade] by pilotage authorities

884 **22.**—(1) Every pilotage authority [1] shall deliver triennially, or, if the [Secretary of State for Trade] so [directs], at shorter intervals, to the [Secretary of State], in the form and at the time required by the [Secretary of State], returns [2] giving such particulars as the [Secretary of State] may by order prescribe with respect to pilotage in their district, and any returns so delivered shall, as soon as may be, be laid before both Houses of Parliament.

(2) Every pilotage authority shall in addition furnish annually to the [Secretary of State for Trade], at such time as the [Secretary of State directs], a statement of their accounts in the form prescribed by the [Secretary of State], duly audited, including a statement of the average gross and net earnings of pilots during the past year, and, where the authority administer a pilots' benefit fund, the separate accounts of that fund, including particulars of the investments, if any.

(3) Every pilotage authority shall allow the [Secretary of State for Trade], or any person appointed by the [Secretary of State] for the purpose, to inspect any books or documents in the possession of that authority relating to any matter in respect of which a return is required to be delivered or a statement is required to be furnished under this section.

(4) If a pilotage authority refuse or fail without reasonable cause to deliver any return or furnish any statement to the [Secretary of State for Trade] in accordance with this section, His Majesty may by order in Council suspend the pilotage authority for such time as His Majesty may direct, and thereupon the [Secretary of State for Trade] shall by order direct that, in the meantime, the powers of the authority shall be exercised, and the duties of the authority shall be performed, by such person as [he] may appoint for the purpose, and any such order shall take effect as if it were enacted in this Act.

[1] For meaning of "pilotage authority," see s. 8.
[2] The regulations as to pilotage returns at present in force are contained in the Pilotage Authorities (Returns) Order 1965 (S.I. No. 170).

Masters' and Mates' Certificates

Grant of masters' and mates' certificates by pilotage authorities

885 **23.**—(1) A pilotage authority may [1] grant a certificate (in this Act referred to as a pilotage certificate) to any person who is bona fide the master or mate [2] of any ship if that person applies for such a certificate, and if, after examination, they are satisfied that, having regard to his skill, experience, and local knowledge, he is capable of piloting the ship [3] of which he is master or mate within their district:

Provided that—

(*a*) A pilotage certificate shall not be granted to the master or mate of a ship unless he is a British subject,[4] except in the cases for which special provision is made by this Act [5]; and

(*b*) In any district where a byelaw [6] is in force prohibiting the grant of pilotage certificates to masters or mates who do not hold at least *a mate's certificate of competency recognised under Part II of the Merchant Shipping Act* 1894,[7] the pilotage authority shall not grant a certificate except to a master or mate holding *such a certificate of competency*.[6]

(2) A pilotage certificate shall be in a form approved for the time being by the [Secretary of State for Trade], and shall contain (in addition to any other particulars which may be prescribed) the name of the person to whom the certificate is granted, the name and draught of water of the ship [8] or ships in respect of which it is granted, the limits of the district in respect of which the certificate is granted, and the date on which it was granted.

(3) A pilotage certificate shall not be in force for more than a year from the date on which it is granted, but may be renewed annually by the pilotage authority, subject to the provisions of any byelaw made by that authority as to re-examination.[9]

(4) A pilotage certificate may [1] be granted so as to extend to more than one ship belonging to the same owner, while the master or mate is bona fide acting as master or mate of any such ship, provided that they are ships of substantially the same class.

(5) A pilotage authority may,[1] on the application of the master or mate of a ship, alter his pilotage certificate so as to relate to any other ship or ships of a not substantially greater draught of water or tonnage than that to which the certificate formerly related, to which the master or mate may be transferred, or so as to cover any ships of substantially the same class and belonging to the same owner as the ships to which the certificate already relates.

(6) A pilotage authority may,[1] for the purposes of this section, treat ships which are shown to their satisfaction to be bona fide under the management of the same person as manager, managing owner, demisee, or time charterer, as being ships owned by that person.[10]

886 1 As to appeals to the Department of Trade in case of complaint against pilotage authorities with respect to the exercise of their powers as to pilotage certificates, see s. 27.

2 This means any mate and not just the first mate or chief officer: see *The Empire Jamaica* [1957] A.C. 386 at p. 398. See also decision of Mr. Barry Sheen Q.C. dated January 5, 1970, pursuant to inquiry under s. 27.

3 When navigating in a pilotage district with a master or mate on board holding a pilotage certificate for that district, the ship must fly the pilot flag. See s. 41 (1).

4 As to who are now " British subjects," see British Nationality Act 1948, and note to M.S.A. 1894, s. 1.

5 As to aliens holding pilotage certificates, see s. 24 and notes thereto.

6 As to the power of pilotage authorities to make by-laws to this effect, see s. 17 (1) (*l*).

7 The M.S.A. 1970, s. 100 (1), Sched. 3, para. 6, prospectively substitutes for the words in italics the words " such certificate issued under the Merchant Shipping Act 1970 as is specified in the bye-law " and " a certificate so specified " as from a day to be appointed. As to certificates of competency, see M.S.A. 1894, s. 92 *et seq.* As to foreign certificates of competency, see s. 25.

8 Under the repealed M.S.A. 1894, s. 599, when a vessel changed owners, a fresh examination of the master was apparently necessary.

9 As to suspension or revocation of pilotage certificate by pilotage authority, see s. 26. As to fees, see s. 29.

10 This subsection is new. Under the repealed M.S.A. 1894, s. 599, the same owner must have had the whole of the shares in the ship in respect of which the certificate was originally granted as well as hold the whole of the shares in the ship to which the master or mate was transferred. A misstatement of the ownership of the first ship was held to invalidate a certificate to pilot ships belonging to the same owner: *The Bristol City* [1902] P. 10; *The Earl of Auckland* (1861) 30 L.J.Ad. 121; Lush. 164, 387.

Power to grant certificate to a master or mate, not being a British subject, under special circumstances

887 **24.**—(1) Notwithstanding anything in this Act, the provisions of this Act as to the renewal of a pilotage certificate shall apply, with respect to the renewal of a pilotage certificate granted before the first day of June nineteen hundred and six, to a master or mate who is not a British subject [1] in the same manner as they apply to a pilotage certificate granted to a master or mate who is a British subject.

(2) If any master or mate who is not a British subject shows to the satisfaction of the [Secretary of State for Trade] that he is the master or mate of a ship which is of substantially the same class, and is trading regularly between the same ports as a foreign ship which, on the first day of June nineteen hundred and six, was exempt from the obligation to carry a licensed pilot, or had habitually been piloted by a master or mate of the ship who held a pilotage certificate, the [Secretary of State for Trade] may authorise the master or mate to apply to the pilotage authority for a pilotage certificate under this Act, and the provisions of this Act as to the granting of a pilotage certificate shall, notwithstanding anything in this Act, extend to a master or mate so applying for a certificate, although he is not a British subject, as they extend to a master or mate who is a British subject:

Provided that if the Admiralty [2] at any time consider that, on the grounds of public safety, the provisions of this subsection should not be applicable with respect to any pilotage district or part of a pilotage district, they may make an order excluding that district or part of a district from the operation of those provisions and while any such order is in force with respect to any such district or part of a district, a certificate granted under those provisions shall not be of any effect within that district or part of a district.

888 [1] See note (4) to s. 23.

[2] By an Admiralty Order dated March 25, 1913 (published in the *London Gazette*, March 28, 1913), it was ordered that the provisions of s. 24 (2) should not be applicable with respect to the London Pilotage District, the Harwich Pilotage District and so much of the Humber Pilotage District as lies to the north of Grimsby.

The functions of the Admiralty were transferred to the Secretary of State by the Defence (Transfer of Functions) Act 1964, s. 1 (2).

The operation of this section is modified by the Aliens Restriction Act 1919, s. 4, which provides as follows: " No alien shall hold a pilotage certificate for any pilotage district in the United Kingdom; except that the provisions of section twenty-four of the Pilotage Act 1913, shall continue to apply to the renewal and issue of certificates entitling a master or mate of French nationality to navigate his ship into the ports of Newhaven or Grimsby."

Provision with respect to foreign certificates of competency

889 **25.** For the purposes of this Act, references [1] to *certificates of competency recognised under Part II of the Merchant Shipping Act*, 1894,[2]

shall be deemed to include references to any certificate of competency granted by the government of a foreign country, being a certificate of a class approved by the [Secretary of State for Trade], for the purpose.

[1] References occur in ss. 17 (1) (*l*) and 23 (1) (*b*).
[2] The M.S.A. 1970, s. 100 (1), Sched. 3, para. 7, prospectively substitutes for the words in italics, the words " certificates issued under the Merchant Shipping Act 1970," as from a day to be appointed.

Supplementary Provisions as to Licences and Certificates

Suspension or revocation of a pilot's licence or a pilotage certificate

890 **26.** A pilotage authority may suspend or revoke any pilot's licence or any pilotage certificate granted by them if it appears to them, after giving the holder thereof an opportunity of being heard,[1] that he has been guilty of any offence under this Act [2] or of any breach of any bye-law made by the authority, or of any other misconduct affecting his capability as a pilot, or that he has failed in or neglected his duty as a pilot, or that he has become incompetent to act as pilot; and a licence or certificate, if so revoked, shall cease to have effect, and, if so suspended, shall cease to have effect for the period for which it is suspended [3]:

Provided that in any case where pilots are directly represented on a committee of a pilotage authority, that committee may, until a Pilotage Order [4] is made regulating the relations between the authority and the committee, exercise the powers conferred on a pilotage authority by this section with respect to pilots' licenses as though they were the pilotage authority.

For definition of " pilot," see M.S.A. 1894, s. 742, and for definition of " Pilotage authority," see s. 8.
For power to license pilots, see s. 16.
[1] As to what constitutes a sufficient hearing, see *R.* v. *Trinity House* (1855) 26 L.T.(o.s.) 103; 4 W.R. 124; *Moore* v. *Clyde Pilotage Authority*, 1943 S.C. 457; *Soanes* v. *Trinity House Corpn.* (1950) 84 Ll.L.R. 432 and *Conway* v. *Clyde Pilotage Authority* (1951) S.L.T., Sh.Ct. 74.
[2] As to offences by pilots, see ss. 46–48.
[3] As to appeals by pilots, masters or mates, see ss. 27–28.
[4] See s. 7 (1) (*e*) as to powers of pilotage committee.

Appeal by pilot, master, or mate, against action of pilotage authority with respect to pilot's licence or pilotage certificate

891 **27.**—(1) If a complaint is made to the [Secretary of State for Trade] that a pilotage authority [1] have—

(*a*) without reasonable cause refused or failed to examine any candidate for a pilot's licence,[2] or a master or mate for a pilotage certificate, or to grant such a licence or certificate after examination; or

(*b*) conducted any examination for a pilot's licence or a pilotage certificate improperly or unfairly; or (*c*) imposed conditions on the granting of a pilot's licence or a pilotage certificate which they have no power to impose or which are unreasonable; or

(*d*) without reasonable cause refused or failed to renew a pilotage certificate, or, having obtained possession of any such certificate, refused or failed to return it [3]; or

(*e*) without reasonable cause suspended or revoked a pilotage certificate; or

(*f*) in any other manner failed properly to perform their duties under this Act with respect to the matters above-mentioned in this section, or improperly exercised any of their powers under this Act with respect to those matters;

the [Secretary of State for Trade] shall consider the complaint, and, if [he is] of opinion that the complaint is in any respect well founded, shall make such order as [he thinks] fit for the purpose of redressing the matter complained of, and the pilotage authority shall give effect to any order so made by the [Secretary of State for Trade].

(2) If a pilotage authority refuse or fail to give effect to any such order of the [Secretary of State for Trade], the [Secretary of State for Trade] may, for the purpose of giving effect to the order, exercise any powers of the pilotage authority, and anything done by the [Secretary of State for Trade] in the exercise of those powers shall have the same effect as if it had been done by the pilotage authority.

[1] For definition, see s. 8.
[2] For power to grant licences to pilots, see s. 16.
[3] A right of appeal is given to a *pilot* on suspension or refusal to renew his licence by s. 28.

Appeal by pilot against action of pilotage authority in suspending, etc., pilot's licence

92 **28.**—(1) If a pilot is aggrieved by the suspension or revocation by the pilotage authority of his licence, or by the refusal or failure of the pilotage authority to renew his licence, or by the refusal or failure of the pilotage authority who have obtained possession of his licence to return it to him, or by the imposition upon him by the pilotage authority of a fine exceeding two pounds, he may either appeal to a judge of county courts having jurisdiction within the port for which the pilot is licensed, or to a metropolitan police magistrate or stipendiary magistrate having jurisdiction within that port.

(2) For the purpose of hearing the appeal, the judge or magistrate shall sit with an assessor [1] of nautical and pilotage experience selected and summoned by the judge or magistrate.

(3) Objection may be taken to any person proposed to be summoned as an assessor, either personally or in respect of his qualification, and by either party to the appeal.

(4) The judge or magistrate may confirm or reverse the suspension or revocation of the licence, or make such order in the case as may seem just, and his decision shall be final, unless special leave to appeal from the same to the High Court on a question of law or a question of mixed law and fact is given by the judge or magistrate, or by the High Court, and in such case the decision of the High Court shall be final.

(5) The costs incurred by a pilotage authority under this section shall be payable out of any fund applicable to the general expenses of the pilotage authority.

(6) Rules with respect to the procedure under this section (including costs and the remuneration of assessors) may be made, as respects county court judges,[2] by the authority having power to make rules of practice under the County Courts Act 1888, and as respects metropolitan police and stipendiary magistrates [3] by a Secretary of State, but in either case with the concurrence of the Treasury as to fees.

(7) In Scotland the appeal under this section shall be to the sheriff having jurisdiction at the port where the decision is given, and may be heard by the sheriff sitting with an assessor as provided in this section, and rules [4] may be made by the Court of Session by Acts of Sederunt with respect to the procedure in case of those appeals in Scotland (including costs and the remuneration of assessors), subject to the concurrence of the Treasury as to fees. In the application of this section to Scotland, references to the Court of Session shall be substituted for references to the High Court.

(8) In the application of this section to Ireland [5]—

(*a*) The expression " judge of county courts " and " judge " shall respectively mean a county court judge and chairman of quarter sessions, and include recorder;

(*b*) The expressions " stipendiary magistrate " and " magistrate " shall respectively mean a magistrate appointed under the Constabulary (Ireland) Act 1836;

(*c*) [*This paragraph has been repealed by the County Courts Act* (*Northern Ireland*) 1959 (*N.I.*), *section* 154, *Sched. V.*]

893 [1] Under the repealed M.S.A. 1894, s. 610 (3), the assessor was selected from the Brethren of Trinity House, where the appellant was a pilot licensed by Trinity House for any district on the coast of England and Wales.

The judge or magistrate must sit with an assessor whatever the circumstances are; otherwise the court is not properly constituted: see *Soanes* v. *Corporation of Trinity House* (1950) 84 Ll.L.R. 432.

[2] The rules regulating appeals to county courts are contained in County Court Rules 1936, Ord. 46, r. 6, in force pursuant to the County Courts Act 1959, s. 102, see *The County Court Practice*, published annually.

[3] The rules regulating appeals to Stipendiary and Metropolitan Police magistrates were made on January 27, 1916, and are contained in S.R. & O. No. 62/L. 1, revoking the rules of March 14, 1890 and are printed in Appendix XIV, post.

[4] The rules regulating appeals to the sheriff in Scotland at present in force are contained in the codifying Act of Sederunt 1913, Book L, Chap. XI, dated June 4, 1913 (S.R. & O. No. 638/S. 44), as amended by Act of Sederunt of October 29, 1919 (S.R. & O. No.

1615/547). These rules, as so amended, though made with reference to M.S.A. 1894, s. 610, remained in force under this Act by virtue of s. 60 and are printed at Appendix XV, *post.*

[5] As to the application to Ireland, see note " Application to Northern Ireland and the Republic of Ireland " in notes to M.S.A. 1894, s. 742.

Fees in respect of pilots' licences and pilotage certificates

894 **29.** Such fees shall be payable on the examination for a pilot's licence, or for a pilotage certificate, and on the grant, renewal, or alteration of any such licence or certificate, as may be fixed by byelaw made under this Act.

Rights and Obligations of Licensed Pilots

A pilot in charge of a vessel is entitled to receive assistance from the crew; see *Alexander Shukoff* (*Owners*) v. *Gothland* (*Owners*) [1921] 1 A.C. 216.

Right of licensed pilot to supersede unlicensed persons

895 **30.**—(1) A pilot licensed [1] for a district may supersede any pilot not so licensed [2] who is employed to pilot a ship in the district.

(2) Where a licensed pilot supersedes an unlicensed pilot the master of the ship shall pay to the latter a proportionate sum for his services, and shall be entitled to deduct the sum so paid from the sum payable in respect of the services of the licensed pilot.

Any question as to the proportion payable to the licensed pilot and to the person whom the licensed pilot has superseded shall be referred to the pilotage authority [3] by whom the licensed pilot has been licensed, and their decision on the question shall be final.

(3) If in any pilotage district [3] a pilot not licensed [2] for the district pilots or attempts to pilot a ship after a pilot licensed for that district has offered [4] to pilot the ship, he shall be liable in respect of each offence to a fine not exceeding fifty pounds.

(4) If the master of a ship knowingly employs [5] or continues to employ a pilot not licensed for the district to pilot the ship within any pilotage district after a pilot licensed for that district has offered to pilot the ship,[6] or, in the case of an outward bound ship, without having taken reasonable steps (proof whereof shall lie on the master [7]) to obtain a licensed pilot, he shall be liable in respect of each offence to a fine not exceeding fifty pounds.

(5) If any person other than the master or a seaman being bona fide one of the crew of the ship is on the bridge of a ship, or in any other position (whether on board the ship or elsewhere) from which the ship is navigated,[8] that person shall, for the purposes of this section, be deemed to be piloting the ship unless the contrary is proved.

896 [1] " Pilot " is defined by M.S.A. 1894, s. 742. For power to license pilots, see s. 16.

[2] A deep sea pilot is not entitled to supersede any other person acting as pilot of a ship. See s. 7 (1) (*i*). *Semble* a pilot licensed to pilot ships of a deep draught would be entitled

to supersede a pilot not so licensed; but the latter pilot would receive a proper proportion of the fees: *The Carl XV* [1892] P. 324. The right of supersession does not apply where the vessel is deemed not to be navigating by virtue of a by-law made under s. 32, see *McMillan* v. *Crouch* [1972] 2 Lloyd's Rep. 325 (H.L.). See also *Babbs* v. *Press* [1971] 2 Lloyd's Rep. 383 and *Montague* v. *Babbs* [1972] 1 Lloyd's Rep. 65.

3 For definitions of " pilotage authority," " pilotage district"—see s. 8.

4 An offer must be made or communicated in relation to the particular movement of the vessel in question. A pilot flag displayed at a pilot station intended as an offer on behalf of licensed pilots available there is not sufficient: *Babbs* v. *Press* [1971] 2 Lloyd's Rep. 383 and *Montague* v. *Babbs* [1972] 1 Lloyd's Rep. 65. A pilot in charge of a vessel, licensed as a pilot for the first part of the voyage, does not commit an offence under this section by continuing in charge after the vessel has passed beyond the point covered by his licence, although a pilot qualified for the whole voyage has, at the port where the voyage commenced, offered to take charge for the whole voyage: *Blair* v. *Warden* (1898) 25 R.Ct. of Just. 93; 35 S.L.R. 932. Where a licensed pilot had offered his services to a master whose vessel was in the charge of an unlicensed pilot, and the master had refused the offer in the hearing of the unlicensed pilot who then completed his pilotage, it was held that the unlicensed pilot had committed an offence: *Smith* v. *Cocking* [1959] 1 Lloyd's Rep. 88. See further as to offers made outside the pilotage district, *Chandler* v. *Monroe* (1887) 3 T.L.R. 618.

5 The employment need not be for remuneration: *Lister* v. *Warne* (1935) 53 Ll.L.R. 96.

6 See note (11) to s. 11.

7 Under 6 Geo. 4, c. 125, s. 70, it was held that proof must be given that the master knew of the offer: *Chaney* v. *Payne* (1841) 1 Q.B. 712; 1 G. & D. 348. See, also, *Peek* v. *Carrington* (1821) 5 Moore 176; 2 B. & B. 399, under 52 Geo. 3, c. 39, s. 34, to the like effect.

As to the recovery of fines, see s. 62 and M.S.A. 1894, ss. 680–682.

8 The question whether a person on board a tug is " in a position from which " the tow is navigated is a question of fact. *Cf. Beilby* v. *Scott* (1840) 7 M. & W. 93 (under 6 Geo. 4, c. 125, s. 70).

Declaration as to draught of ship

897 **31.**—(1) A licensed pilot [1] may require the master of any ship which he is piloting to declare her draught of water, length and beam, and the master shall comply with any such request.

(2) If the master of a ship refuses to comply with any such request of a pilot, or makes or is privy to any other person making any false statement to the pilot in answer to the request, he shall be liable in respect of each offence to a fine not exceeding fifty pounds.[2]

1 For power to license pilots, see s. 16. " Pilot " is defined by M.S.A. 1894, s. 742.

2 As to the recovery of fines, see M.S.A. 1894, ss. 680–682.

Provision as to ships within harbour, dock, etc.

898 **32.**—(1) A ship while being moved within a harbour which forms part of a pilotage district [1] shall be deemed to be a ship navigating in a pilotage district,[2] except so far as may be provided by byelaw in the case of ships being so moved for the purpose of changing from one mooring to another mooring or of being taken into or out of any dock:

Provided that a byelaw shall in every case be made for the purpose aforesaid in any pilotage district where any class of persons other than licensed pilots [3] were in practice employed at the date of the passing of this Act for the purpose of changing the moorings of ships or of taking ships into or out of dock.

(2) A ship whilst being navigated within any closed dock, lock, or other closed work in a pilotage district shall notwithstanding anything in this Act [4] be deemed to be navigating in a district in which pilotage is not compulsory.

99 [1] See s. 8 as to "pilotage districts."
[2] See note 2 to section 30.
[3] For power to license pilots, see s. 16.
[4] This section would appear to exclude closed docks, etc., from the operation of s. 10, which provides that "pilotage shall continue to be compulsory in every pilotage district in which it was compulsory at the time of the passing of this Act." But, where the "compulsory pilotage" in such places depends, as it seems it invariably must, on some "enactment, order, etc, ... affecting any pilotage district in particular," the effect of s. 59 is to postpone the operation of s. 32 until provision is made by Pilotage Order under this Act: *The Port Hunter* (1915) 31 T.L.R. 181. Thus, under the Humber Pilotage Act 1832 (2 & 3 Will. 4, c. cv), pilotage in the docks at Hull remains compulsory until provision is made by Pilotage Order under the Pilotage Act 1913, while a vessel is coming in or going out, but not if she is being moved from one dock to another after she has come in: *ibid.*; *The Maria* (1867) L.R. 1 A. & E. 358; *The Rigsborg Minde* (1883) 8 P.D. 132.

See, too, the Mersey Docks Acts Consolidation Act 1858, s. 128, and the Mersey Docks (Pilotage, etc.) Act 1899, passed in consequence of the decision in *The Servia* [1898] P. 36.

Copies of pilotage provisions to be furnished to pilots

00 **33.**—(1) The pilotage authority [1] shall cause every pilot licensed [2] by them to be furnished with a copy of this Act as amended for the time being, and with a copy of any Pilotage Order for the time being in force in the district, and of any byelaws so in force.

(2) A licensed pilot shall produce any copy so furnished to him to the master of any ship or other person employing him when required to do so, and if he fails without reasonable cause to do so, he shall be liable in respect of each offence to a fine not exceeding five pounds.[3]

[1] See s. 8 as to "pilotage authority."
[2] For power to license pilots, see s. 16.
[3] As to recovery of fines, see M.S.A. 1894, ss. 680 *et seq.*

Allowance to licensed pilot taken out of his district

01 **34.**—(1) A master of a ship shall not, except under circumstances of unavoidable necessity, take a licensed pilot [1] without his consent beyond the district for which he is licensed, or beyond the point up to which he has been engaged to pilot the ship, and if a master of a ship acts in contravention of this section, he shall be liable in respect of each offence to a fine not exceeding twenty pounds.[2]

(2) Where a pilot [3] is taken beyond the district for which he is licensed, or beyond the point up to which he has been engaged to pilot the ship, either without his consent or under circumstances of unavoidable necessity, he shall be entitled, over and above his pilotage dues, to maintenance and to the sum of fifty-two and one half pence a day, recoverable in the same manner as pilotage dues.[4]

(3) The sum so to be paid shall be computed from and inclusive of the

day on which the ship passes beyond the district for which the pilot is licensed, or the point up to which the pilot was engaged to pilot her, and up to and inclusive of either the day of his being returned in the said ship to the place where he was taken on board, or, if he is discharged from the ship at a distance from that place, such day as will allow him sufficient time to return thereto; and in the last-mentioned case he shall be entitled to his reasonable travelling expenses.

[1] For power to license pilots, see s. 16.
[2] As to recovery of fines, see M.S.A. 1894, ss. 680 *et seq.*
[3] "Pilot" is defined by M.S.A. 1894, s. 742.
[4] As to the method of recovering pilotage dues, see s. 49. Under the repealed M.S.A. 1894, s. 594, the allowance to a pilot taken out of his district was not recoverable as "pilotage dues"; see *Morteo* v. *Julian* (1879) 4 C.P.D. 216.

Limitation of pilot's liability where bond is given

902 **35.**—(1) A licensed pilot,[1] who has given a bond in conformity with byelaws made for the purpose under this Act,[2] shall not be liable for neglect or want of skill beyond the penalty of the bond and the amount payable to him on account of pilotage in respect of the voyage in which he was engaged when he became so liable.

(2) *Any bond given by a pilot in conformity with byelaws made for the purpose under this Act shall not be liable to stamp duty, and* [3] a pilot shall not be called upon to pay any expense in relation to the bond other than the actual expense of preparing the same.

(3) Where any proceedings are taken against a pilot for any neglect or want of skill in respect of which his liability is limited as provided by this section, and other claims are made or apprehended in respect of the same neglect or want of skill, the court in which the proceedings are taken may determine the amount of the pilot's liability, and, upon payment by the pilot of that amount into court, may distribute that amount rateably among the several claimants, and may stay any proceedings pending in any other court in relation to the same matter, and may proceed in such manner and subject to such regulations as to making persons interested parties to the proceedings, and as to the exclusion of any claimants who do not come in within a certain time, and as to requiring security from the pilot, and as to payment of any costs as the court thinks just.[4]

903 As to the limitation of liability of the pilotage authorities themselves, see Pilotage Authorities (Limitation of Liability) Act 1936.

[1] For power to license pilots, see s. 16.
[2] As to the power of making by-laws for this purpose, see s. 17 (1) (*i*). Under M.S.A. 1894, only Trinity House pilots were entitled to limit their liability to the amount of their bond.
[3] The words in italics were repealed, with regard to England, Wales and Scotland, by the Finance Act 1971, s. 69, Sched. 14, Part VI, and with regard to Northern Ireland, by the Finance Act (Northern Ireland) s. 9, Sched. 3, Part 1.
[4] *Cf.* M.S.A. 1894, s. 504, which empowers the courts to consolidate claims against shipowners, etc. M.S.A. 1894 provided no such provision in the case of pilots. See *Deering* v. *Targetts & Sons* [1913] 1 K.B. 129, which illustrates the defect now remedied by this section.

As to the method by which this limitation may be claimed, see notes to M.S.A. 1894, s. 503.

Obligation on licensed pilot to produce his licence to employer

04 **36.**—(1) Every licensed pilot [1] when acting as such shall be provided with his licence, and shall, if requested, produce it to any person by whom he is employed, or to whom he offers his services as pilot.

(2) If a licensed pilot refuses to produce his licence in accordance with this section, he shall be liable, in respect of each offence, to a fine [2] not exceeding ten pounds.

[1] For power to license pilots, see s. 16.
[2] As to recovery of fines, see M.S.A. 1894, ss. 680 *et seq.*

Penalty on fraudulent use of licence

05 **37.** If any person not being a licensed pilot [1] for a district falsely represents himself to be a licensed pilot for that district, either by means of using a licence which he is not entitled to use or by any other means, he shall be liable in respect of each offence to a fine [2] not exceeding twenty pounds.

[1] For power to license pilots, see s. 16.
[2] As to recovery of fines, see M.S.A. 1894, ss. 680 *et seq.*

Pilot Boats and Pilot Signals

Approval of pilot boats

06 **38.** All vessels regularly employed in the pilotage service of any pilotage district [1] (in this Act referred to as " pilot boats ") shall be approved and licensed by the pilotage authority [1] of the district, and that authority may, at their discretion, appoint and remove the masters of those pilot boats.

[1] See s. 8 as to " pilotage district " and " pilotage authority."

Characteristics of pilot boats

07 **39.**—(1) Every pilot boat shall be distinguished by the following characteristics, namely:—

(*a*) On her stern the name of her owner and the port to which she belongs, painted in white letters at least one inch broad and three inches long, and on each bow the number of her licence:

(*b*) In all other parts a black colour, painted or tarred outside, or such other colour or colours as the pilotage authority of the district, with the consent of the [Secretary of State for Trade, direct]:

(*c*) When afloat a flag (in this Act called a pilot flag) of large dimensions compared with the size of the pilot boat, and of two colours, the upper horizontal half white, and the lower horizontal half red, to be placed at the mast head, or on a sprit or staff, or in some equally conspicuous situation.

(2) It shall be the duty of the master of the pilot boat to see that the pilot boat possesses all the above characteristics, and that the pilot flag is kept clean and distinct, so as to be easily discerned at a reasonable distance; and also that the names and numbers aforesaid are not at any time concealed; and if a master fails, without reasonable cause, to comply with the requirements of this section, he shall be liable in respect of each offence to a fine not exceeding twenty pounds.

As to the lights to be carried by pilot vessels when engaged on their station, see the Collision Regulations (Ships and Seaplanes on the Water) and Signals of Distress (Ships) Order, 1965 (S.I. 1965 No. 1525) Sched. 1, r. 8.

Pilotage order not to diminish powers of pilotage authorities as to pilot boats

908 **40.** A Pilotage Order in dealing with any Act, order, charter, custom, byelaw, regulation, or provision shall not provide for abolishing or diminishing any power of a pilotage authority to acquire, own, hire, build, renew, maintain, or work pilot boats.

Cf. s. 7 (1) (*j*) which provides that any Act, order, charter, custom, by-law, regulation or provision so far as it relates to pilotage ceases to have effect if a Pilotage Order is made for the district; as to power of pilotage authority to make by-laws providing for pilot boats and pilot boat companies, see s. 17 (1) (*d*); and as to keeping a separate account in respect of pilot boats, see s. 21 (4).

Display of pilot flag when pilot is on board ship

909 **41.** When a ship is navigating in a pilotage district, and has on board a pilot licensed [1] for that district, or a master or mate holding a pilotage certificate for that district, the master of the ship shall cause a pilot flag to be exhibited; and if he fails, without reasonable cause, to do so, he shall be liable in respect of each offence to a fine [2] not exceeding fifty pounds.

[1] For power to license pilots, see s. 16.
[2] As to recovery of fines, see M.S.A. 1894, ss. 680 *et seq.*

Penalty on ordinary boat displaying pilot flag

910 **42.** A pilot flag,[1] or a flag so nearly resembling a pilot flag as to be likely to deceive, shall not be displayed on any ship or boat not having a licensed pilot [2] or a master or mate holding a pilotage certificate on board, and, if any such flag is displayed on any such ship or boat, the master of that vessel shall, unless in the case of the display of a flag likely to deceive he proves that he had no intention to deceive, be liable for each offence to a fine not exceeding fifty pounds.[3]

[1] See s. 39.
[2] For power to license pilots, see s. 16.
[3] See note (2) to s. 41.

Obligation to display signal for pilot in certain circumstances

911 **43.**—(1) The master of a ship (other than an excepted ship [1]) shall when navigating in circumstances in which pilotage is compulsory under this Act, display a pilot signal,[2] and keep the signal displayed until a licensed pilot [3] comes on board.

(2) The master of a ship, whether navigating in circumstances in which pilotage is compulsory or not, which is being piloted in a pilotage district by a pilot not licensed [4] for the district, shall display a pilot signal and keep the signal displayed until a licensed pilot comes on board.

(3) If the master of any ship fails to comply with this section, he shall be liable in respect of each offence to a fine not exceeding twenty pounds.[5]

1 " Excepted ship " is defined in s. 11 (3).
2 As to the power of Her Majesty in Council to make rules as to pilot signals, see s. 45.
3 For power to license pilots, see s. 16.
4 As to the offence of continuing to employ a pilot not licensed for the district after a licensed pilot has offered, see s. 30 (4) and (5).
5 See note (2) to s. 41.

Facilities to be given for pilot getting on board ship

912 **44.**—(1) The master of a ship (other than an excepted ship [1]) which, in circumstances in which pilotage is compulsory under this Act, is not under pilotage as required in these circumstances, shall, if a licensed pilot [2] of the district makes a signal for the purpose of offering his services as pilot, by any practical means consistent with the safety of his ship, facilitate [3] the pilot getting on board the ship, and shall give the charge of piloting the ship to that pilot, or, if there are two or more licensed pilots offering at the same time, to such one of them as may, according to any byelaws for the time being in force in the district, be entitled or required to take charge of the ship.

(2) Where the master of a ship, whether in circumstances in which pilotage is compulsory or not, accepts the services of a licensed pilot, he shall, by any practical means consistent with the safety of his ship, facilitate the pilot getting on board the ship.

(3) If the master of any ship fails to comply with the provisions of this section, he shall be liable in respect of each offence to a fine [4] not exceeding double the amount of pilotage dues [5] that could be demanded for the conduct of the ship.

913 1 " Excepted ship " is defined in s. 11 (3).
2 For power to license pilots, see s. 16.
3 There is an implied obligation on the master to keep a good look-out for offers of pilotage, though he need not go out of his way to look for the pilot boat; *Rindby* v. *Brewis* (1926) 25 Ll.L.R. 26.
4 No power is given by this section to the pilotage authority to charge double pilotage dues. If the provisions of this section are not observed, the proper course is for the authority to proceed by way of prosecution for the recovery of the fine under M.S.A. 1894, ss. 680–681, which are made applicable to offences under the Act by s. 62.
5 As to power of pilotage authority to fix the amount of pilotage dues by by-law, see s. 17 (1) (*f*).

Signals to be displayed by ships requiring a pilot

914 **45.**—(1) His Majesty may by Order in Council make rules [1] as to the signals to be used or displayed where the services of a pilot [2] are required on any vessel, and those signals are in this Act referred to as pilot signals.

(2) If a vessel requires the services of a pilot, the master of that vessel shall use or display the pilot signals.

(3) If a master of a vessel uses or displays, or causes or permits any person under his authority to use or display, any of the pilot signals for any other purpose than that of summoning a pilot, or uses or causes or permits any person under his authority to use any other signal for a pilot, he shall be liable in respect of each offence to a fine not exceeding twenty pounds. [3]

915 [1] The rules at present in force are contained in the M.S. (Pilot Signals) Order 1970 (S.I. No. 1952). By day, the International Code Signals G. and P.T. each signifying " I require a pilot," and the Pilot Jack hoisted at the fore, when used or displayed together or separately are deemed to be signals for a pilot. By night, the same applies to the pyrotechnic light known as a blue light, every fifteen minutes, and a bright white light, flashed or shown at short or frequent intervals just above the bulwarks for about a minute at a time, and the International Code Signal P.T. by flashing.

[2] " Pilot " is defined by M.S.A. 1894, s. 742.

[3] See note (2) to s. 41.

Offences by Pilots

Penalty on pilot endangering ship, life, or limb

916 **46.** If any pilot, when piloting a ship, by wilful breach of duty or by neglect of duty, or by reason of drunkenness—

(*a*) does any act tending to the immediate loss, destruction, or serious damage of the ship, or tending immediately to endanger the life or limb of any person on board the ship; or

(*b*) refuses or omits to do any lawful act proper and requisite to be done by him for preserving the ship from loss, destruction, or serious damage, or for preserving any person belonging to or on board the ship from danger to life or limb;

that pilot shall in respect of each offence be guilty of a misdemeanour.

917 *Cf.* M.S.A. 1970, s. 27 (misconduct endangering ship or persons on board ship), and see notes thereto. *Cf. R.* v. *Gardner* (1859) 1 F. & F. 669, and *Deacon* v. *Evans* [1911] 1 K.B. 571. As to the question of the liability of the authority licensing the pilot, see s. 19 and notes thereto.

All distinctions between a felony and a misdemeanour were abolished by the Criminal Law Act 1967. As to punishment of offences of misdemeanours, see M.S.A. 1894, s. 680, which is made applicable to this Act by s. 62. In England there is now a general right of appeal to the Crown Court against summary conviction given by s. 83 of the Magistrates' Courts Act 1952, and the limitations in M.S.A. 1894, s. 682 (now repealed), of such appeals to cases where the fine inflicted exceeds £5 do not apply. From a conviction on indictment an appeal lies, in England, to the Criminal Division of the Court of Appeal under the Criminal Appeal Act 1968, and in Scotland to the High Court of Justiciary under the Criminal Appeal (Scotland) Act 1926. Before 1926 there was no right of appeal in Scotland. See M.S.A. 1894, ss. 702–710, as amended by M.S.A. 1906, s. 82 (3) and (4) and *Spence* v. *Sinclair* (1883) 20 S.L.R. 726.

Penalty on person obtaining charge of a ship by misrepresentation

918 **47.** If any person, by wilful misrepresentation of circumstances upon which the safety of a ship may depend, obtains, or endeavours to obtain, the charge of that ship, that person and every person procuring, abetting, or conniving at the commission of the offence shall, in addition to any liability for damages, be liable in respect of each offence to a fine not exceeding one hundred pounds.

As to recovery of fines, see M.S.A. 1894, ss. 680 *et seq.*

Offences by pilots

919 **48.**—(1) If a licensed pilot, either within or without the district for which he is licensed,—

(*a*) himself keeps, or is interested in keeping by any agent, servant, or other person, any premises licensed for the sale of intoxicating liquors, or sells or is interested in selling any intoxicating liquors, tobacco, or tea;

(*b*) is in any way directly or indirectly concerned in any corrupt practices relating to ships, their tackle, furniture, cargoes, crews, or passengers, or to persons in distress at sea or by shipwreck, or to their moneys, goods, or chattels;

(*c*) lends his licence;

(*d*) acts as pilot whilst suspended;

(*e*) acts as pilot when in a state of intoxication;

(*f*) employs, or causes to be employed, on board any ship which he is piloting any boat, anchor, cable, or other store, matter, or thing beyond what is necessary for the service of that ship, with intent to enhance the expenses of pilotage for his own gain or for the gain of any other person;

(*g*) refuses or wilfully delays, when not prevented by illness or other reasonable cause,[1] to pilot any ship within the district for which he is licensed, upon the signal [2] for a pilot being made by that ship, or upon being required to do so by the master, owner, agent, or consignee thereof, or by any officer of the pilotage authority by whom the pilot is licensed, or by any chief officer of Customs and Excise;

(*h*) unnecessarily cuts or slips, or causes to be cut or slipped, any cable belonging to any ship;

(*i*) refuses, otherwise than on reasonable ground of danger to the ship, when requested by the master, to conduct the ship which he is piloting into any port or place within the district for which he is licensed; or (*k*) quits the ship, which he is piloting, before the service for which he was engaged has been performed and without the consent of the master of the ship [3];

that pilot shall, in addition to any liability for damages, be liable in respect of each offence to a fine not exceeding one hundred pounds.

(2) If any person procures, aids, abets, or connives at the commission of any offence under this section, he shall, in addition to any liability for damages, be liable to a fine not exceeding one hundred pounds.

(3) The provisions of the law relating to Customs with respect to the recovery of penalties under that law,[4] and the application of such penalties,[4] shall apply in the case of any prosecution by any officer of Customs and Excise for the recovery of a fine in respect of any offence against this section.

920 For power to license pilots, see s. 16. As to recovery and application of penalties under Customs law, see Customs and Excise Act 1952, Part IX.

As to power of pilotage authority to suspend or revoke licences for offences under this Act, see s. 26.

1 A pilot is not bound to go on board a damaged ship for mere pilotage reward where the circumstances would entitle him to salvage; see *The Frederick* (1838) 1 W.Rob. 16.

2 See s. 45 and note thereto as to signals to be displayed by ships requiring a pilot.

3 It seems that a pilot is not entitled to quit a ship when emergencies arise which require extraordinary services from him such as would entitle him to salvage; see *The Saratoga* (1861) Lush. 318. It is his duty to stand by his ship although his services in doing so may entitle him to salvage remuneration; *The Santiago* (1900) 9 Asp.M.C. 147; 83 L.T. 439.

4 See Customs and Excise Act 1952, ss. 281–291.

Recovery, etc., of Pilotage Dues

Recovery of pilotage dues

921 **49.**—(1) The following persons shall be liable to pay pilotage dues for any ship for which the services of a licensed pilot are obtained, namely:—

(*a*) the owner or master;

(*b*) as to pilotage inwards, such consignees or agents as have paid or made themselves liable to pay any other charge on account of the ship in the port of her arrival or discharge;

(*c*) as to pilotage outwards, such consignees or agents as have paid or made themselves liable to pay any other charge on account of the ship in the port of her departure;

and those dues [1] may be recovered in the same manner as fines of like amount under the Merchant Shipping Act 1894,[2] but that recovery shall not take place until a previous demand has been made in writing.

(2) Any consignee or agent (not being the owner or master of the ship) who is hereby made liable for the payment of pilotage dues in respect of any ship may, out of any moneys received by him on account of that ship or belonging to the owner thereof, retain the amount of all dues paid by him, together with any reasonable expenses he may have incurred by reason of the payment of the dues or his liability to pay the dues.

922 [1] The allowances due to a pilot taken out of his district may be recovered in the same manner as pilotage dues; see s. 34 (2).

[2] By M.S.A. 1894, s. 681 (2), " where under this Act any sum may be recovered as a fine under this Act, that sum, if recoverable before a court of summary jurisdiction, shall, in England, be recovered as a civil debt, in the manner provided by the Summary Jurisdiction Acts "; see notes to that section and case there cited.

This remedy is not, however, exhaustive; pilotage dues may also be recovered in the Admiralty Court by proceedings *in rem* or *in personam*; *The Ambatielos and the Cephalonia* [1923] P. 68. But unless the vessel proceeded against is already under arrest or a foreign vessel, the pilot may be mulcted in costs if he neglects the cheaper summary method; *ibid.*

See, too, *Ross* v. *Walker* (1765) 2 Wilson 264; *The Nelson* (1805) 6 C.Rob. 227; *The Clan Grant* (1887) 6 Asp.M.C. 144; Coote's *Admiralty Practice*, 1st ed., p. 1; and Roscoe's *Admiralty Practice*, 5th ed., p. 222.

It is not certain whether or not a maritime lien exists for pilotage. The question was discussed but left open in *The Ambatielos and the Cephalonia, supra*.

For special provisions as to the collection of pilotage dues in the Port of London, see s. 55.

Receiving or offering improper rates of pilotage

923 **50.** A licensed pilot shall not demand or receive, and a master shall not offer or pay to any licensed pilot, dues in respect of pilotage services [1] at any other rates, whether greater or less, than the rates which may be demanded by law,[2] and, if a pilot or master acts in contravention of this enactment, he shall be liable in respect of each offence to a fine not exceeding ten pounds.

For power to license pilots, see s. 16.

[1] This applies only to pilotage services proper. Where the services rendered could not reasonably be considered to come within the scope of his contract as pilot, he may be entitled to salvage reward from the ship of which he is in charge or from a ship salved by her. See note to M.S.A. 1894, s. 546, and cases there cited. Certain local authorities restrict the right of pilots licensed by them to claim salvage reward; *e.g.* by the Liverpool Pilotage Order s. 25, scheduled to Pilotage Orders Confirmation (No. 1) Act 1920, no claim may be made by any pilot in respect of salvage services rendered to any vessel in the Liverpool Pilotage District without the written consent of the Pilotage Committee. Similarly, no claim may be made by the Liverpool Pilotage Committee as owners of any pilot boat in respect of any salvage services by any such boat: s. 26, *ibid*.

[2] Rates of payment for pilotage services may be fixed by by-law by the pilotage authority. See s. 17 (1)(*f*).

Pilotage rate for leading ships

924 **51.** If any boat or ship, having on board a licensed pilot, leads any ship which has not a licensed pilot on board when the last-mentioned ship cannot, from particular circumstances, be boarded, the pilot so leading the last-mentioned ship shall be entitled to the full pilotage rate for the distance run as if he had actually been on board and had charge of that ship.

As to the circumstances in which a pilot may be entitled to salvage reward from " the last-mentioned ship," *cf. The Santiago* (1900) 83 L.T. 439; 9 Asp.M.C. 147; and see s. 50, note (1) and M.S.A. 1894, s. 546, note (4).

For power to license pilots, see s. 16.

Special Provisions as to the Trinity House

Trinity House outport districts

925 **52.**—(1) For the purposes of this Act, any district [1] which at the time of the passing of this Act is under the authority of sub-commissioners appointed by the Trinity House [2] and any pilotage district which may be declared after the passing of this Act to be a Trinity House outport district, shall be deemed to be a Trinity House outport district.

(2) The powers and duties of the Trinity House under this Act as the pilotage authority of an outport district shall be exercised and performed through a committee appointed for the district in such manner and subject to such conditions as may be determined by a Pilotage Order, under the name of sub-commissioners or such other name as may be fixed by the Order, and any such Order may be made so as to apply to all or any one or more of the outport districts.

[1] For list of existing outport districts, see the Report of the Departmental Committee on Pilotage (1911), Appendix B.
[2] For definition of " Trinity House," see M.S.A. 1894, s. 742.

Trinity House Pilot Fund

926 **53.** Nothing in this Act shall oblige the Trinity House to maintain separate pilot funds for each of the pilotage districts of which they are the authority, and, if they maintain a single pilot fund for all those districts, the provisions of this Act as to pilot funds [1] shall apply as if all the districts of which they are the pilotage authority were a single pilotage district.

[1] For the provisions as to pilot funds, see s. 21.

Power of Trinity House to make provisions as to exempt pilots

927 **54.** Notwithstanding anything in this Act, the Trinity House may permit any person who, at the date of the passing of this Act, was licensed to pilot an exempted vessel in the Thames or Medway, to continue to pilot any vessel in those rivers belonging to a class which, at the date of the passing of this Act, were exempted vessels, and were, in the opinion of the Trinity House, in practice piloted by such persons, and any such person while so acting shall be deemed, for the purposes of this Act, to be a licensed pilot.

This class of " exempt " pilots was first authorised under a by-law dated February 5, 1873. They are licensed to pilot the numerous vessels which were exempted from compulsory pilotage by the operation of M.S.A. 1894, s. 625; *e.g.*, ships registered at the Port of London. Until special provision is made by by-law under s. 17 (1) (*f*), the present practice by which this class of pilots are free to make what bargains they please as to their remuneration will remain valid; see s. 59 and Report of the Departmental Committee on Pilotage (1911), § 154.

Collection of pilotage dues in Port of London by officers of Customs and Excise

928 **55.**—(1) The following pilotage dues [1] in respect of foreign ships, not being excepted ships,[2] trading to and from the port of London,[3] namely:—

(*a*) as to ships inwards, the full amount of pilotage dues for the distance piloted; and

(*b*) as to ships outwards, the full amount of dues for the distance required by law;

shall be paid to the chief officer of Customs and Excise in the port of London by the master, or by any consignees or agents of the ship who have paid, or made themselves liable to pay, any other charge for the ship in the port of London.

(2) The chief officer of Customs and Excise, on receiving any pilotage dues in respect of foreign ships, shall give to the person paying the dues a receipt in writing for the dues, and in the port of London the ship may be detained [4] until the receipt is produced to the proper officer of Customs and Excise of the port.

(3) The chief officer of Customs and Excise shall pay over to the Trinity House the pilotage dues received by him under this section, and the Trinity House shall apply the dues so received—

(*a*) in paying to any licensed pilot [5] who produces to them sufficient proof of his having piloted the ship such dues as would have been payable to him for pilotage services if the ship had been a British ship,[6] after making any deductions which they are authorised to make by byelaw under this Act; and

(*b*) in paying to any person not being a licensed pilot who produces to them sufficient proof of his having, in the absence of a licensed pilot, piloted the ship, such amount as the Trinity House think proper, not exceeding the amount which would, under similar circumstances, have been payable to a licensed pilot after making the said deductions; and

(*c*) in paying over to the Trinity House pilot fund [7] the residue, together with the amount of any deductions made as aforesaid.

(4) Nothing in this section shall affect the application of the provisions of this Act [8] as to the recovery of pilotage dues.

[1] See s. 17 (1)(*f*).
[2] See s. 11 (3) and (4) as to what ships are "excepted ships."
[3] For the port limits, see the Port of London Act 1968, s. 2 (1) and Sched. 1.
[4] For the procedure for enforcement of detention, see M.S.A. 1894, s. 692.
[5] For power to license pilots, see s. 16.
[6] As to "British ships," see M.S.A. 1894, s. 1, and notes thereto.
[7] See s. 53.
[8] As to the recovery of pilotage dues generally, see ss. 49–51.

Miscellaneous and General Provisions

Limit on expenditure

929 **56.** The expenditure under this Act out of money provided by Parliament shall not exceed six thousand pounds in any one year.

Application of 37 & 38 Vict. c. 40

930 **57.** The Board of Trade Arbitrations, etc., Act 1874, shall apply as if this Act were a special Act within the meaning of the first-mentioned Act.

The Board of Trade Arbitrations, etc., Act 1874, provides, by s. 2, that " where under the provisions of any special Act," as defined by s. 4, " the [Department of Trade] is required or authorised to sanction, approve, confirm or determine any appointment, matter or thing, or to make any order or to do any other act or thing for the purposes of such special Act the [Department of Trade] may make such inquiry as they think necessary " by any person authorised by order of the Department of Trade. S. 3 provides for the payment of the expenses of such inquiry by the parties who have applied for action by the Department of Trade.

Saving for pilotage authorities having power to apply money received in name of pilotage to other purposes

931 **58.** Notwithstanding anything in this Act, where a pilotage authority[1] is entitled by statute at the time of the passing of this Act to receive moneys in the name of pilotage and to apply part of such moneys to purposes other than those authorised under this Act, a Pilotage Order made under Part I of this Act in respect of that authority may provide for the apportionment of the moneys so received as between the pilot fund or account[2] and such other purposes.

[1] See s. 8 as to " Pilotage authority."
[2] See s. 21 (1) as to " Pilot fund or account."

Commencement of Act

932 **59.** *This Act shall (except as expressly provided) come into operation on the first day of April nineteen hundred and thirteen: Provided that*[1] Any enactment, order, charter, custom,[2] byelaw, regulation, or provision with reference to pilotage affecting any pilotage district in particular,[3] and in force at the time of the passing of this Act, including any exemptions from compulsory pilotage taking effect thereunder, shall remain in force notwithstanding anything in this Act or any repeal effected by this Act, until provision is made by Pilotage Order,[4] or in the case of a byelaw by byelaw, made under this Act superseding any such enactment, order, charter, custom,[2] byelaw, regulation, or provision.

933 [1] The words in italics were repealed as spent by the Statute Law Revision Act 1927.
[2] A custom, *semble*, may be superseded by the combined effect of a Pilotage Order and by-laws made under s. 17; *Buck* v. *Tyrrell* (1922) 10 Ll.L.R. 74. But for an example of a decision that a custom was compatible with and not superseded by a Pilotage Order, see *Thames Launches Ltd.* v. *Trinity House Corporation* (*Deptford Strond*) (*No.* 2) [1962] 1 Ch. 153 at pp. 190–191. The mere acquiescence of shipowners in the past in the enforcement by Trinity House of certain dues for which there is no longer any legal basis does not constitute such a custom as is preserved by this section: *Muller* v. *Trinity House* [1925] 1 K.B. 166 at p. 176.
[3] *e.g.* in *The Port Hunter* (1915) 31 T.L.R. 181, the court held that the Hull and Humber Pilotage Act 1832 remained in force until a Pilotage Order or new by-law was made, and that pilotage under the local Act was compulsory for a ship not moving about in a dock, but going out of the dock to sea.
[4] By s. 7 (1) (j), the Secretary of State for Trade may by Pilotage Order provide that any Act, order, etc., shall, so far as it relates to pilotage, cease to have effect.

Repeal

934 **60.**—(1) *The enactments mentioned in the Second Schedule to this Act are hereby repealed to the extent specified in the third column of that schedule.*

Provided that [1]—

(*a*) Any order in council, licence, certificate, byelaw, rule, or regulation made or granted under any enactment hereby repealed or in pursuance of any power which ceases in consequence of this Act, shall, subject to the provisions of this Act, continue in force as if it had been made or granted under this Act; and

(*b*) Any officer appointed, any body elected or constituted, and any officer established under any enactment hereby repealed shall continue and be deemed to have been appointed, elected, constituted, or established, as the case may be, under this Act;

(*c*) Any document referring to any Act or enactment hereby repealed shall be construed to refer to this Act or to the corresponding enactment of this Act.

(2) The mention of particular matters in this section shall not be held to prejudice or affect the general application of section thirty-eight of the Interpretation Act 1889,[2] as regards the effect of repeals.

[1] The words in italics were repealed as spent by the Statute Law Revision Act 1927.
[2] Part of this section is set out in the notes following M.S.A. 1894, s. 742 at § 687, *ante*.

Extent of Act

935 **61.** This Act extends to the United Kingdom and the Isle of Man, and applies to all ships, British and foreign.

As to the effect of this section in relation to the defence of compulsory pilotage, see note (1) to s. 15.

The repealed M.S.A. 1894, s. 572, contained a similar provision as to the application of Part X, *ibid.*; but it does not appear that in practice the provisions of that Act ever operated in the Isle of Man. The Isle of Man is nowhere mentioned in the periodical Pilotage Returns which were issued by the Board of Trade.

Short title

936 **62.** This Act may be cited as the Pilotage Act 1913, and shall be construed as one [1] with the Merchant Shipping Act 1894, and the Acts amending the same; and the Merchant Shipping Acts 1894 to 1907, and this Act may be cited together as the Merchant Shipping Acts 1894 to 1913.[2]

[1] See note (1) to s. 9 of M.S. (Mercantile Marine Fund) Act 1898.
[2] Now the Merchant Shipping Acts 1894 to 1974, see § 1639.

SCHEDULES

Section 7

FIRST SCHEDULE

Provisions as to Pilotage Orders

937 1. Subject to the provisions of this schedule, the [Secretary of State for Trade] may make rules [1] in relation to applications for Pilotage Orders, and to the payments to be made in respect thereof, and to the publication of notices and advertisements, and the manner in which and the time within which representations or objections with reference to any application are to be made, and as to the publication of Pilotage Orders.

2. Notice of an application for an Order shall be published once at least in each of two successive weeks in the month immediately succeeding the date of the application in such manner as may be prescribed by the rules made by the [Secretary of State for Trade].

3. The notice shall state the object which it is proposed to effect by the Order.

4. The [Secretary of State for Trade] on receiving any application for an Order shall refer the application to the pilotage authority of the district, if the authority are not themselves the applicants, and shall consider any objections which may be made to the proposed Order whether by the pilotage authority or by other persons appearing to the [Secretary of State for Trade] to be interested, and for that purpose shall allow at least six weeks to elapse between the date on which the application is referred to the authority and that on which the Order is made.

5. The [Secretary of State for Trade] may submit to Parliament for confirmation any Order which requires confirmation by Parliament.

6. If and when a Bill confirming any such Order is pending in either House of Parliament, a petition is presented against any Order comprised therein, the Bill, so far as it relates to that Order, may be referred to a Select Committee, or, if the two Houses of Parliament think fit so to order, to a Joint Committee of those Houses, and the petitioner shall be allowed to appear and oppose as in the case of private Bills.

7. Any Act confirming an Order under this Act may be repealed, altered, or amended by any subsequent Order made under this Act.

8. The [Secretary of State for Trade] may revoke, either wholly or partially, any Order made by [him] before the Order is confirmed by Parliament, but such revocation shall not be made whilst the Bill confirming the Order is pending in either House of Parliament.

9. The making of an Order shall be prima facie evidence that all the

requirements of this Act in respect of proceedings required to be taken previously to the making of the Order have been complied with.

Editors' Note.—

The rules at present in force under this Schedule are the Pilotage Orders (Application Rules 1964 (S.I. No. 1467).

[1] Compare repealed M.S.A. 1894, s. 580, as to making and confirming provisional orders.

---

938 Section 60

SECOND SCHEDULE [1]

ENACTMENTS REPEALED

Session and Chapter.	Short Title.	Extent of Repeal.
57 & 58 Vict. c. 60.	The Merchant Shipping Act 1894.	Sections five hundred and seventy-two to six hundred and thirty-two inclusive, and the twenty-first schedule.
60 & 61 Vict. c. 61.	The Merchant Shipping (Exemption from Pilotage) Act 1897.	The whole Act.
6 Edw. 7, c. 48.	The Merchant Shipping Act 1906.	Section seventy-three.

[1] *Editors' Note.*—This Schedule is repealed as spent by the Statute Law Revision Act 1927.

MERCHANT SHIPPING (CERTIFICATES) ACT 1914

(4 & 5 GEO. 5, c. 42)

An Act to amend the Law relating to Examinations for Certificates of Competency. [10th August, 1914.]

BE it enacted, etc.

This Act is prospectively repealed by the M.S.A. 1970, s. 100 (3), Sched. V as from a day to be appointed.

Examinations for certificates of competency as masters or mates

939 **1.**—(1) For the purpose of granting certificates of competency as masters or mates to persons desirous of obtaining such certificates, examinations shall be held at such places as the [Secretary of State for Trade directs].

(2) The [Secretary of State for Trade] may appoint times for the examinations, and may appoint, remove, and reappoint examiners to conduct the examinations, and determine the remuneration of those examiners, and may regulate the conduct of the examinations and the qualification of the applicants, and may do all such acts and things as [he thinks] expedient for the purpose of the examinations.

(3) *Sections ninety-four and ninety-five of the Merchant Shipping Act* 1894 *are hereby repealed.*[1]

940 The effect of this section is to remove the examinations for certificates of competency of masters and mates from the control of the local Marine Boards and to place them for all purposes under the direct control of the Department of Trade.

[1] Subs. (3) is repealed as spent by the Statute Law Revision Act 1927.

Short title and construction

941 **2.** This Act may be cited as the Merchant Shipping (Certificates) Act 1914, and the provisions of this Act shall be construed as if they were contained in Part II of the Merchant Shipping Act 1894; and the Merchant Shipping Acts 1894 to 1913, and this Act may be cited together as the Merchant Shipping Acts 1894 to 1914.[1]

[1] Now the Merchant Shipping Acts 1894 to 1974, see § 1639.

MERCHANT SHIPPING (CONVENTION) ACT 1914

(4 & 5 Geo. 5, c. 50)

942 [*This Act has been repealed by the M.S.* (*Safety and Load Line Conventions*) *Act* 1932, *s.* 74 (2), *Sched. IV, Part* 3. *The Convention to which this Act gave effect, was the result of an international conference held in London, shortly after the Titanic disaster, to consider what steps could be taken by the principal maritime States to render more effective their national laws as to the safety of life at sea. The Convention was signed on January* 20, 1914, *and a Bill introduced by the Board of Trade in May,* 1914, *was placed on the Statute Book in the form of this Act on August* 10, 1914. *Owing to the* 1914–18 *War, however, this Convention never became effective, and the operation of this Act was postponed from time to time by Orders in Council under section* 29.

In the Spring of 1929 *a further International Conference was held in London to consider what alterations were necessary to be made to the Convention agreed to in* 1914, *with the result that on May* 31, 1929, *a new Convention, entitled the International Convention for Safety of Life at Sea* 1929, *was signed by representatives of the principal maritime Powers. This latter Convention replaced and abrogated the earlier Convention, and the undertaking by the contracting Governments to give effect to its provisions necessitated fresh legislation repealing this Act and containing comprehensive provisions dealing with the construction of passenger vessels, life-saving appliances, radiotelegraphy, safety of navigation in general and safety certificates. The new provisions passed in this latter Convention were contained in Part I of the M.S.* (*Safety and Load Line Conventions*) *Act* 1932, *most of which, however, has now been repealed and replaced by the M.S.* (*Safety Convention*) *Act* 1949, *which is based on an International Convention for the Safety of Life at Sea signed on June* 10, 1948. *See further introductory notes to the* 1932 *and* 1949 *Acts, post.*]

BRITISH SHIPS (TRANSFER RESTRICTION) ACT 1915

(5 GEO. 5, c. 21)

BRITISH SHIPS (TRANSFER RESTRICTION) ACT 1916

(6 & 7 GEO. 5, c. 42)

943 *[These Acts, which had for their object the restriction of the transfer of ships, and the mortgage and transfer of mortgages of ships registered in the United Kingdom, to persons not qualified to own British ships, or to foreign-controlled companies, during the* 1914–18 *War and for a limited period thereafter, were repealed as spent by the Statute Law Revision Act* 1927.]

MERCHANT SHIPPING (SALVAGE) ACT 1916

(6 & 7 GEO. 5, c. 41)

944 *[This Act, which conferred on the Admiralty a limited right to claim salvage for services rendered by tugs and salvage vessels belonging to His Majesty, was repealed by the M.S. (Salvage) Act* 1940, *which conferred on the Crown considerably wider but still limited rights to claim salvage. The latter Act was itself repealed by the Crown Proceedings Act* 1947, *the relevant portions of which are printed at* §§ 1075–1092, *post.*]

MERCHANT SHIPPING (WIRELESS TELEGRAPHY) ACT 1919

(9 & 10 GEO. 5, c. 38)

945 *[This Act, which made further provisions with respect to wireless telegraphy on ships, was repealed as from November* 19, 1952, *by M.S. (Safety Convention) Act* 1949, *s.* 37 (5) *and Third Schedule, and its provisions were replaced by section* 3 *of that Act. See section* 3 *of that Act and notes thereto, post.*]

MERCHANT SHIPPING (AMENDMENT) ACT 1920

(10 & 11 GEO. 5, c. 2)

An Act to amend section six hundred and fifty-nine of the Merchant Shipping Act 1894. [26th March, 1920.]

BE it enacted, etc.

Amendment of section 659 of 57 & 58 Vict. c. 60

946 **1.** The power of His Majesty, under section six hundred and fifty-nine of the Merchant Shipping Act 1894, as amended by subsequent

enactments, by Order in Council to fix the annual or other sums to be paid out of the General Lighthouse Fund in respect of the establishment of the general lighthouse authorities, shall extend to fixing the annual or other sums to be paid out of that fund to members of the general lighthouse authority for England and Wales, and the sums so fixed shall have effect notwithstanding anything in any Act limiting the amount thereof.

Short title

947 **2.** This Act may be cited as the Merchant Shipping (Amendment) Act 1920, and shall be included amongst the Acts which may be cited together as the Merchant Shipping Acts 1894 to 1920.[1]

[1] Now the Merchant Shipping Acts 1894 to 1974, see § 1639.

MERCHANT SHIPPING (SCOTTISH FISHING BOATS) ACT 1920

(10 & 11 Geo. 5, c. 39)

An Act to provide for the extension to Scotland of Part IV of the Merchant Shipping Act 1894. [16th August, 1920.]

Be it enacted, etc.

Application to Scotland of Part IV of 57 & 58 Vict. c. 60

948 **1.**—(1) The provisions of Part IV of the Merchant Shipping Act 1894 (hereinafter referred to as the principal Act), in so far as those provisions do not at the passing of this Act apply to Scotland, shall, subject to the modifications contained in subsection (2) of this section, apply to Scotland, and accordingly references in those provisions to ports in England or Ireland shall be construed as references to ports in the United Kingdom.

(2) (*a*) In the application of the aforesaid provisions to Scotland the Edinburgh Gazette shall be substituted for the London Gazette, " burgh " shall be substituted for " borough," and " parish council " shall be substituted for " board of guardians."

(*b*) A decision by a superintendent under section three hundred and eighty-seven of the principal Act may be enforced in like manner as an order made on summary proceedings.

(*c*) An order under section three hundred and sixty-nine of the principal Act shall, in so far as it affects Scotland, be subject to the consent of the Secretary for Scotland.

(3) *The enactments mentioned in the Schedule to this Act are hereby repealed to the extent specified in the third column of that Schedule.*[1]

Before the passing of this Act, Scottish fishing boats were in general regulated by the provisions of M.S.A. 1894, Part II (Masters and Seamen), as applied by s. 263, *ibid.* and amended by M.S.A. 1906, s. 82, and only partially by M.S.A. 1894, Part IV (Fishing Boats). See ss. 372, 389, *ibid.* and M.S.A. 1906, s. 81. By virtue of the present Act, the provisions of Part IV are now of general application.

[1] Subs. (3) was repealed as spent by the Statute Law Revision Act 1927.

Short title and commencement

949 **2.**—(1) This Act may be cited as the Merchant Shipping (Scottish Fishing Boats) Act 1920; and this Act and the Merchant Shipping Acts 1894 to 1914, may be cited together as the Merchant Shipping Acts 1894 to 1920.[1]

(2) *This Act shall come into operation on the first day of October nineteen hundred and twenty.*[2]

[1] Now the Merchant Shipping Acts 1894 to 1974, see § 1639.
[2] Subs. (2) was repealed as spent by the Statute Lnw Revision Act 1927.

950 **Section 1** SCHEDULE[1]

ENACTMENTS REPEALED

Session and Chapter.	Short Title.	Extent of Repeal.
57 & 58 Vict. c. 60.	The Merchant Shipping Act 1894.	In sub-section (1) of section two hundred and sixty-three, the words "with respect to Scotland or." In sub-section (2) of section two hundred and sixty-three, the words "subject as in this section mentioned with respect to Scotland." Sub-section (3) of section two hundred and sixty-three. In section three hundred and seventy-two the words "to Scotland or." Section three hundred and eighty-nine. In section four hundred and eighty-six, the words "in their application elsewhere than in Scotland." In sub-section (3) of section six hundred and ninety the words "except in Scotland."

Editors' Note.—
[1] This Schedule was repealed as spent by the Statute Law Revision Act 1927.

MERCHANT SHIPPING ACT 1921

(11 & 12 Geo. 5, c. 28)

An Act to amend the Merchant Shipping Acts 1894 to 1920.

[28th July, 1921.]

Be it enacted, etc.

Application of Parts I and VIII of the Merchant Shipping Act 1894, to lighters, etc.

951 **1.**—(1) Notwithstanding anything in section seven hundred and forty-two of the Merchant Shipping Act 1894 (hereinafter referred to as " the principal Act "), the principal Act shall have effect as though in the provisions of Parts I and VIII thereof (which relate respectively to the registry of ships and to the limitation of the liability of the owners of ships), as amended or extended by any subsequent enactment, the expression " ship " included every description of lighter, barge, or like vessel used in navigation in Great Britain,[1] however propelled [2]:

Provided that a lighter, barge, or like vessel used exclusively in non-tidal waters, other than harbours, shall not, for the purposes of this Act, be deemed to be used in navigation.[3]

(2) [*This subsection, which for the purpose of Part VIII of the M.S.A.* 1894, *extended the meaning of* " *owner* " *to include certain hirers, has been repealed by M.S.* (*Liability of Shipowners and Others*) *Act* 1958, *section* 8 (6) *and Sched. and replaced by ibid. section* 3 (1).]

(3) Where the [Secretary of State for Trade is] satisfied that there are in force in any port, under any Act or order, regulations for the measurement or registration of lighters, barges, or like vessels, which provide for the measurement of their tonnage in substantial agreement with the provisions of the Merchant Shipping Acts 1894 to 1920, and for an adequate system of identification of the vessels and their owners, [he] may by order declare that vessels measured or registered in accordance with such regulations shall, for the purposes of this Act, be deemed to be measured or registered under Part I of the principal Act.[4]

952 [1] This expression does not include any part of Ireland. *Cf.* use of the expression " United Kingdom " in various parts of the M.S. Acts.

[2] " Ship " is defined by s. 742 of M.S.A. 1894, as including " every description of vessel used in navigation not propelled by oars." For the purposes of registration, the effect of this present section is to extend the definition in the 1894 Act to this additional class of vessels (lighters, barges, etc.) so that such vessels must, unless exempted under s. 3 of the 1894 Act, be registered either under *ibid.* s. 2, or under an approved local system of registration under subs. (3) of this section. For the purposes of limitation of liability, it is no longer material whether or not the ship has been registered; M.S. (Liability of Shipowners and Others) Act 1958, s. 4 (2). Prima facie, limitation can be claimed in respect of a ship which falls within any one of three relevant definitions; that is to say, the M.S.A. 1894, s. 742 (*supra*); M.S.A. 1921, s. 1 (1) (Lighters, barges, etc.) (this section) and M.S. (Liability of Shipowners and Others) Act 1958, s. 4 (1) which provides that the expression " ship "

in Part VIII (the limitation provisions) of the principal Act shall apply to " any structure, whether completed or in course of completion, launched and intended for use in navigation as a ship or part of a ship." But see s. 3 of this Act which appears to prevent the owners of any lighter, barge, etc. from limiting their liability for loss of life or personal injury caused to any person carried therein.

[3] This extended meaning of " ship," with its proviso, is incorporated in the Crown Proceedings Act 1947, s. 5 (6) as amended by the M.S. (Liability of Shipowners and Others) Act 1958, s. 8 (5), which defines " ship " for the purposes of that section, relating to the limitation of liability in respect of Crown ships.

[4] Orders have been made under the subsection adopting, in lieu of measurement and registration under Part I of the principal Act, measurement and registration under local regulations in force at the following ports:—London (December 21, 1921, S.R. & O. 1921 No. 2030), and Rochester (November 9, 1922, S.R. & O. 1922 No. 1262) printed in S.R. & O. Rev. (1948) XIV, pp. 26 and 27.

Use of unsafe lighters, etc.

953 2.—(1) If any person uses or causes or permits to be used in navigation any lighter, barge, or like vessel when, through the defective condition of its hull or equipment or by reason of overloading or improper loading or through undermanning, it is so unsafe that human life is likely to be thereby endangered, he shall be liable on summary conviction to a fine not exceeding one hundred pounds or to imprisonment for a term not exceeding six months.

(2) A prosecution under this section shall not, except in Scotland, be instituted otherwise than by, or with the consent of, the [Secretary of State for Trade].

Cf. M.S.A. 1894, ss. 457–463 (unseaworthy ships).

Saving for workmen

954 3. This Act shall not affect the liability of the owners of any lighter, barge, or like vessel in respect of loss of life or personal injury caused to any person carried therein.

This section appears to curtail the application of s. 503 of M.S.A. 1894, to owners of lighters and barges, etc., by excluding their right to limit their liability in the cases referred to in s. 503 (1) (*a*).

Short title, construction and commencement

955 4.—(1) This Act may be cited as the Merchant Shipping Act 1921, and shall be construed as one [1] with the Merchant Shipping Acts 1894 to 1920, and those Acts and this Act may be cited together as the Merchant Shipping Acts 1894 to 1921.[2]

(2) *This Act shall come into operation on the first day of January, one thousand nine hundred and twenty-two.*[3]

[1] See note (1) to s. 9 of M.S. (Mercantile Marine Fund) Act 1898.
[2] Now the Merchant Shipping Acts 1894 to 1974; see § 1639.
[3] The words in italics were repealed as spent by the Statute Law Revision Act 1950.

OIL IN NAVIGABLE WATERS ACT 1922

(12 & 13 Geo. 5, c. 40)

956 [*This Act, which made some provision against the discharge or escape of oil into navigable waters, was repealed by the Oil in Navigable Waters Act* 1955, *s.* 24 (1) *and replaced by the provisions of that Act. The Oil in Navigable Waters Acts* 1955 *to* 1971 *are now consolidated in the Prevention of Oil Pollution Act* 1971: *see* § 1531, *post.*

FEES (INCREASE) ACT 1923

(13 & 14 Geo. 5, c. 4)

An Act to provide for the increase of certain fees and the imposition of certain new fees in respect of various services, and for purposes connected therewith. [26th April, 1923.]

Be it enacted, etc.

Increase of certain fees under Merchant Shipping Acts

957 **1.**—(1) The provisions of *the Merchant Shipping Act* 1894, *and of* the Merchant Shipping (Mercantile Marine Fund) Act 1898, specified in the first column of Part I of the First Schedule to this Act so far as they *limit the amount of fees chargeable under those Acts or* grant exemptions from any *such* fees, shall have effect subject to the amendments mentioned in the third column of that Part of the Schedule:

Provided that no fees shall be payable under section three of the Merchant Shipping (Mercantile Marine Fund) Act 1898, in respect of vessels not exceeding ten tons gross register employed solely in fishing.

(2) *For the Schedules of the said Acts mentioned in Part II of the First Schedule to this Act there shall be substituted the Schedules by that Part directed to be substituted therefor.*

The words in italics were repealed as from November 19, 1952, by M.S. (Safety Convention) Act 1949, s. 37 (5), and Third Schedule, *post*.

Charge of new fees for certain services under the Merchant Shipping Acts

958 **2.**—(1) Where—

(*a*) under section nineteen of the Merchant Shipping Act 1894, a Registrar of Shipping endorses and signs on the certificate of registry of a ship a memorandum of the change of the master; *or*

(*b*) *a certificate of service is granted in pursuance of section ninety-nine of the Merchant Shipping Act* 1894 [1]; *or*

(*c*) *an indenture of apprenticeship to the sea service is recorded by a Superintendent or by the Registrar-General of Shipping and Seamen* [2];

there shall be payable such fees as the [Secretary of State for Trade] may determine [. . .] [3]

(2) *There shall be payable upon all engagements and discharges of seamen effected in the presence of a superintendent under section one hundred and fifteen, subsection* (2) *of section one hundred and sixteen, and section one hundred and twenty-seven of the Merchant Shipping Act* 1894, *such fees as may be fixed by the* [*Secretary of State for Trade*] [. . .] [3] *and the superintendent may refuse to proceed with any engagement or discharge unless the fees payable have been first paid by the master or owner of the ship.*[1]

(3) On the inspection of a ship—

(*a*) under section four hundred and thirty-one of the Merchant Shipping Act 1894, either during the construction of the ship or otherwise, for the purpose of seeing that the ship is properly provided, in accordance with the provisions of the Merchant Shipping Acts 1894 to 1921, or any rules made thereunder, with life-saving appliances;

(*b*) [. . .] [3]

there shall be paid in respect of the inspection such fees as the [Secretary of State for Trade] may determine, [. . .] [3]

(4) *Where under section two hundred and six of the Merchant Shipping Act* 1894, *or section twenty-six of the Merchant Shipping Act* 1906, *any provisions are inspected either before shipment or on board a ship, there shall be payable in respect of such inspection such fees as the* [*Secretary of State for Trade*] *may determine* [. . .] [3] *but it shall not be obligatory that such an inspection should be made, and accordingly in subsection* (1) *of the first mentioned section for the words "shall be inspected" there shall be substituted the words "may be inspected," and for the words "shall certify" there shall be substituted the words "may certify"; and subsection* (3) *of the same section shall be repealed:*

Provided that, where provisions which have been inspected and sealed by an inspecting officer are found on board any ship within such time as may be prescribed by the [*Secretary of State for Trade*] *as the time for which the seals are to hold good, no fee shall be charged for the verification of the seals.*[1]

59 The fees at present in force for (*inter alia*) these services are now contained in the M.S. (Fees) Regulations 1975 (S.I. No. 341), made in pursuance of M.S. (Safety Convention) Act 1949, s. 33. For fees for divers other services, see the Schedule to the M.S. (Fees) Order 1924 (S.R. & O. No. 1056).

[1] The words in italics are prospectively repealed by the M.S.A. 1970, s. 100 (3), Sched. V as from a day to be appointed.

[2] The words in italics are repealed by the M.S.A. 1970, s. 100 (3), Sched. V as from January 1, 1973: see S.I. 1972 No. 1977.

[3] The words omitted were repealed as from November 19, 1952, by M.S. (Safety Convention) Act 1949, s. 37 (5) and Third Schedule.

Limitation on fees to be fixed under Merchant Shipping Acts

960 **3.** *The amount of the fees to be charged under the Merchant Shipping Acts,* 1894 *to* 1921, *as amended by this Act shall be so fixed that the amount estimated by the* [*Department of Trade*] *to be produced thereby in any year shall not exceed one-half of the amount certified by the* [*Department of Trade*] *to be the aggregate estimated cost in that year of the administration of the services in respect of which the fees are payable.*[1]

[1] s. 3 was repealed by the Economy (Miscellaneous Provisions) Act 1926, s. 19 (2), Sched. IV and the subject-matter thereof was then dealt with by *ibid.* s. 18. That section (*i.e.* s. 18) however, was subsequently repealed by the British Shipping (Assistance) Act 1935, s. 7.

961 **4–9.** [*These sections of the Fees* (*Increase*) *Act* 1923, *are omitted, as they do not relate to the Merchant Shipping Acts.*]

Repeals

962 **10.** *The enactments mentioned in the Third Schedule to this Act are hereby repealed to the extent mentioned in the third column of that Schedule.*

This section was repealed as spent by the Statute Law Revision Act 1950.

Short title, construction and extent

963 **11.**—(1) This Act may be cited as the Fees (Increase) Act 1923.

(2) This Act, so far as it amends the Merchant Shipping Acts 1894 to 1921, shall be construed as one [1] with those Acts, and those Acts and this Act so far as it amends those Acts may be cited together as the Merchant Shipping Acts 1894 to 1923.[2]

(3) This Act, so far as it relates to matters with respect to which the Parliament of Northern Ireland has not power to make laws, shall extend to Northern Ireland.

[1] See note (1) to s. 9 of M.S. (Mercantile Marine Fund) Act 1898.
[2] Now the Merchant Shipping Acts 1894 to 1974; see § 1639.

SCHEDULES

Section 1

FIRST SCHEDULE

PART I

64 AMENDMENTS OF PROVISIONS OF MERCHANT SHIPPING ACTS RELATING TO FEES

Enactment amended.	Services in respect of which Fees chargeable.	Amendments.
Merchant Shipping (Mercantile Marine Fund) Act 1898 (61 & 62 Vict. c. 44):— S. 3.	Registration transfer and mortgage of ships.	For the words " solely employed in fishing or sailing ships of under one hundred tons " there shall be substituted the words " not exceeding ten tons gross register employed solely in fishing."

Editors' Note.—

Part I of this Schedule, in so far as it amended the M.S.A. 1894, was repealed as from November 19, 1952, by the M.S. (Safety Convention) Act 1949, s. 37 (5) and Third Schedule, and those amendments have therefore been omitted from the text of this Schedule.

Part II, which substituted new Schedules for those which prescribed fees under M.S.A. 1894, and M.S. (Mercantile Marine Fund) Act 1898, was repealed *in toto* as from November 19, 1952, by M.S. (Safety Convention) Act 1949, s. 37 (5) and Third Schedule.

SECOND SCHEDULE

65 [*This Schedule, which prescribed maximum fees to be paid for Certificates and Records, Engagement and Discharge of Seamen, and Inspection of Life-Saving Appliances and Wireless Telegraphy Equipment, was repealed as from November* 19, 1952, *by M.S.* (*Safety Convention*) *Act* 1949, *s.* 37 (5) *and Sched. III. The fees at present in force are contained in the M.S.* (*Fees*) *Regulations* 1975 (*S.I. No.* 341), *made in pursuance of s.* 33 *of the M.S.* (*Safety Convention*) *Act* 1949, *post. As to fees under M.S.* (*Load Lines*) *Act* 1967, *see note* (1) *to s.* 26 *of that Act.*

966 **Section 10**

THIRD SCHEDULE

ENACTMENTS REPEALED

Session and Chapter.	Short Title.	Extent of Repeal.
41 & 42 Vict. c. 49.	The Weights and Measures Act 1878.	In section thirty-seven the words " nor shall any fee be payable on the verification or re-verification of any local standard."
52 & 53 Vict. c. 21.	The Weights and Measures Act 1889.	In section eight the words " not being standards for the use of a local authority or their officers and."
57 & 58 Vict. c. 60.	The Merchant Shipping Act 1894.	Subsection (3) of section two hundred and six. The Third Schedule. The Ninth Schedule.
61 & 62 Vict. c. 44	The Merchant Shipping (Mercantile Marine Fund) Act 1898.	The First Schedule.

Editors' Note.—This Schedule was repealed as spent by the Statute Law Revision Act 1950.

MERCHANT SHIPPING ACTS (AMENDMENT) ACT 1923

(13 & 14 GEO. 5, c. 40)

967 [*This Act, which contained a provision relating to the expenses of the medical attendance of masters and seamen suffering from venereal disease was repealed by the Merchant Shipping Act* 1970 *as from January* 1, 1973: *see S.I.* 1972 *No.* 1977.]

MERCHANT SHIPPING (EQUIVALENT PROVISIONS) ACT 1925

(15 & 16 GEO. 5, c. 37)

An Act to provide for the exemption, in certain circumstances, of Foreign ships and British ships registered outside the United Kingdom from certain provisions of the Merchant Shipping Acts.

[30th June, 1925.]

BE it enacted, etc.

Power to exempt foreign ships from certain provisions of Merchant Shipping Acts

968 **1.** Where His Majesty is satisfied that—

(*a*) ships of a foreign country are required by the law of that country to comply with any provisions which are substantially the same as or equally effective with any provisions of the Merchant Shipping Acts which apply to foreign ships while they are within a port of the United Kingdom; and

(*b*) that country has made or has undertaken to make provision for the exemption of British ships, while they are within a port of that country, from the corresponding requirement of the law of that country;

His Majesty may,[1] by Order in Council, direct that any such provisions of the Merchant Shipping Acts as aforesaid shall not apply to any ship of that country within a port of the United Kingdom if it is proved that the ship complies with the corresponding provision of the law of that country applicable to that ship.[2]

69 [1] By M.S. (Wireless Telegraphy) French Ships Order 1926 (February 25, 1926, S.R. & O. No. 218) made under this section, French ships, whilst in a port in the United Kingdom, are exempted from the provisions of the M.S. Acts relating to wireless telegraphy, on proof that they comply with the corresponding provisions of the law of France applicable to such ships.

By M.S. (Passenger Steamers and Emigrant Ships) Italian Ships Order 1929 (December 17, 1929, S.R. & O. No. 1154), made under this section, Italian ships, whilst in a port in the United Kingdom, are exempted from certain provisions of the M.S. Acts relating to passenger steamers and emigrant ships, on proof that they comply with the corresponding provision of the law of Italy applicable to such ships.

These Orders in Council must now, however, be read subject to what is stated in note (2) below.

[2] s. 21 (2) of the M.S. (Safety and Load Line Conventions) Act 1932 provided that this Act and any Orders in Council made thereunder (see note (1) above) should cease to apply to—

(i) Safety Convention ships, being passenger steamers plying on international voyages, in respect of the exemption of such ships from any provision of the M.S. Acts relating to the survey and certification of passenger steamers, to life-saving appliances or to wireless telegraphy; and

(ii) other Safety Convention ships so plying, in respect of the exemption of such ships from any provision of the M.S. Acts relating to wireless telegraphy.

This apparently remains effective by virtue of the Interpretation Act 1889, s. 38 (2), notwithstanding that s. 21 (2) of the 1932 Act has itself been repealed by M.S. (Safety Convention) Act 1949, s. 37 and Third Schedule.

For definitions, for the purposes of that section, of " Safety Convention ships," " passenger steamers " and " international voyages " under the 1932 Act, see ss. 38 and 73 (1) of that Act. For the countries (including France and Italy) which acceded to the Safety Convention, see note to s. 37 of the 1932 Act in earlier editions.

Further, by s. 55 of the 1932 Act, this Act and Orders in Council made thereunder cease to apply to Load Line Convention ships plying on international voyages in respect of the exemption of such ships from any of the provisions of Part II of the 1932 Act.

For definition of " Load Line Convention ships," see s. 41 (2) of that Act; for definition of " international voyage," see s. 66. For the countries which have acceded to the Load Line Convention, see note (2) to s. 65 of that Act in the 6th edition.

Power to exempt British ships registered out of the United Kingdom from certain provisions of Merchant Shipping Acts

70 **2.** Where His Majesty is satisfied that British ships registered in a part of His Majesty's dominions outside the United Kingdom, or ships registered in a port of a territory over which His Majesty exercises jurisdiction, are required by the law of that part of His Majesty's dominions or the law

in force in that territory to comply with any provisions which are substantially the same as, or equally effective with, any of the provisions of the Merchant Shipping Acts which apply to such ships if, but only if, they are within a port of the United Kingdom, His Majesty may, by Order in Council, direct that any such provisions of the Merchant Shipping Acts as aforesaid shall not apply to any ship registered in that part of His Majesty's dominions, or in that territory, whilst within a port in the United Kingdom, if it is proved that the ship complies with the corresponding provision of the law of the part of His Majesty's dominions or territory in which the ship is registered.[1]

[1] See note (1) to s. 1.

Short title, construction, etc.

971 **3.**—(1) This Act may be cited as the Merchant Shipping (Equivalent Provisions) Act 1925, and shall be construed as one [1] with the Merchant Shipping Acts 1894 to 1923, and those Acts and this Act may be cited together as the Merchant Shipping Acts 1894 to 1925.[2]

(2) In this Act the expression " the Merchant Shipping Acts " means the Merchant Shipping Acts 1894 to 1923, and includes any Orders in Council, rules and regulations made thereunder, and the expression " United Kingdom " means Great Britain and Northern Ireland.

[1] See note (1) to s. 9 of M.S. (Mercantile Marine Fund) Act 1898.
[2] Now the Merchant Shipping Acts, 1894 to 1974; see § 1639.

MERCHANT SHIPPING (INTERNATIONAL LABOUR CONVENTIONS) ACT 1925

(15 & 16 Geo. 5, c. 42)

[*The whole of this Act is prospectively repealed by the Merchant Shipping Act* 1970, *s.* 100 (3), *Sched. V as from a day to be appointed and as printed in italics.*]

An Act to give effect to certain Draft Conventions adopted by the International Labour Conference relating respectively to an unemployment indemnity for seamen in the case of loss or foundering of their ship, the minimum age for the admission of young persons to employment as trimmers and stokers, and the compulsory medical examination of children and young persons employed at sea. [31st July, 1925.]

972 Whereas *at Genoa the General Conference of the International Labour Organisation of the League of Nations on the ninth day of July, nineteen*

hundred and twenty, adopted a draft convention [1] *concerning unemployment indemnity for seamen in case of loss or foundering of their ship, and at Geneva on the eleventh day of November, nineteen hundred and twenty-one, adopted two other draft conventions,* [1] *namely, a draft convention fixing the minimum age for the admission of young persons to employment as trimmers and stokers, and a draft convention* [1] *concerning the compulsory medical examination of children and young persons employed at sea*:

And whereas the said conventions [1] *contain (together with other provisions) the provisions set out in Parts I, II and III respectively of the First Schedule to this Act*:

And whereas it is expedient that for the purpose of giving effect to the said draft conventions [1] *such provision should be made as is contained in this Act*:

BE *it enacted, etc.*:

Amendment of section 158 of Merchant Shipping Act 1894

73 **1.**—(1) *Where by reason of the wreck or loss* [2] *of a ship on which a seaman is employed his service terminates before the date contemplated in the agreement, he shall, notwithstanding anything in section one hundred and fifty-eight of the Merchant Shipping Act* 1894, *but subject to the provisions of this section, be entitled, in respect of each day on which he is in fact unemployed during a period of two months from the date of the termination of the service,* [3] *to receive wages,* [4] *at the rate to which he was entitled at that date.*

(2) *A seaman shall not be entitled to receive wages under this section if the owner shows* [3] *that the unemployment was not due to the wreck or loss of the ship and shall not be entitled to receive wages under this section in respect of any day if the owner shows that the seaman was able to obtain suitable employment on that day.*

(3) *In this section the expression* " *seaman* " *includes every person employed or engaged in any capacity on board any ship, but, in the case of a ship which is a fishing-boat, does not include any person who is entitled to be remunerated only by a share in the profits or the gross earnings of the working of the boat.*

74 [1] If the words of the operative part of the statute are ambiguous, reference may be made to the Conventions in order to explain the ambiguity, see the notes to the preamble of the Maritime Conventions Act 1911, § 826, *supra*.

[2] As to what constitutes " wreck or loss," see notes to M.S.A. 1894, s. 158, and particularly *Barras* v. *Aberdeen Steam Trawling and Fishing Co.* [1933] A.C. 402, cited in that note. The injury to the ship alleged to have terminated the services must be such as to make the continuance of the voyage useless as a commercial venture; *The Terneuzen* [1938] P. 109. And as to relative advantages to the seaman of proving termination of his services " by wreck or loss," or by " discharge otherwise than in accordance with the terms " of his agreement, see notes (1) and (2) to M.S.A. 1894, s. 158.

[3] The section gives the seaman not an indemnity, but a conditional safeguard. Thus, the seaman cannot claim more than two months' wages even though his contemplated services would normally have continued beyond the two months. But he may be able to claim for the whole two months even though his services would normally have terminated within the

two months. If the seaman proves that he was in fact unemployed for two months, the employer may defeat the claim, either in whole or in part, by proving under subs. (2) either (a) that the unemployment was not due to the wreck or loss of the ship, or (b) that, in respect of any particular day, the seaman was able to obtain suitable employment. But proof by the employer that according to the terms of his engagement the seaman's services would have terminated within the two months does not constitute proof that the unemployment was not due to the wreck or the loss of the ship: *Ellerman Lines* v. *Murray* (*The Croxteth Hall*); *White Star Line* v. *Comerford* (*The Celtic*) [1931] A.C. 126.

The determination of the " date of the termination of the service " may be of importance, since it is from that date that the period of two months begins to run. In *The Terneuzen* (*supra*) it was held that the relevant date was the date of the final abandonment of the venture, which was, in that case, more than three months after the stranding, and some weeks after salvage efforts were abandoned.

4 No claim for subsistence allowance arising out of a special agreement outside the " ship's articles " is maintainable under this section; *The Croxteth Hall and The Celtic, supra*; *ibid.* [1930] P. 197. The seaman's right under this section is a right to receive wages, and not an " unemployment indemnity "; hence a superintendent has jurisdiction, under M.S.A. 1899, s. 387, to determine a dispute as to the seaman's right under this section: *Bruce* v. *Neish* (1934) 50 Ll.L.R. 127 (Ct. of Session).

Employment of young persons as trimmers or stokers

975 **2.**—(1) *Subject to the provisions of this section, no young person* [1] *shall be employed or work as a trimmer or stoker in any ship:*

Provided that—

(*a*) *The foregoing provision shall not apply—*

(i) *to the employment of a young person* [1] *on such work as aforesaid in a school-ship or training-ship if the work is of a kind approved by the* [*Secretary of State for Trade*] *and is carried on subject to supervision by officers of the* [*Secretary of State*]; *or*

(ii) *to the employment of a young person* [1] *on such work as aforesaid in a ship which is mainly propelled otherwise than by means of steam*; *or*

(iii) *to the employment of a young person* [1] *subject to and in accordance with the provisions contained in paragraph* (*c*) *of Article* 3 *of the draft convention set out in Part II of the First Schedule to this Act*; *and*

(*b*) *Where in any port a trimmer or stoker is required for any ship and no person over the age of eighteen years is available to fill the place, a young person over the age of sixteen years may be employed as a trimmer or stoker, but in any such case two young persons over the age of sixteen years shall be employed to do the work which would otherwise have been performed by one person over the age of eighteen years.*

(2) *There shall be included in every agreement* [2] *with the crew a list of the young persons* [1] *who are members of the crew, together with particulars of the dates of their birth, and, in the case of a ship* [1] *in which there is no such agreement, the master of the ship shall, if young persons are employed therein, keep a register of those persons with particulars of the dates of*

their birth and of the dates on which they become or cease to be members of the crew.

(3) *There shall be included in every agreement with the crew* [2] *a short summary of the provisions of this section.*

[1] For definitions of "young person" and "ship," see s. 5, *post.*
[2] For the general provisions for the engagement of seamen and agreements with the crew, see M.S.A. 1970, ss. 1 and 2.

Medical examination of young persons

76 **3.**—(1) *Subject to the provisions of this section, no young person* [1] *shall be employed in any capacity in any ship,*[1] *unless there has been delivered to the master of the ship a certificate granted by a duly qualified medical practitioner certifying that the young person is fit to be employed in that capacity:*

Provided that—

- (*a*) *the foregoing provisions shall not apply to the employment of a young person in a ship in which only members of the same family are employed; and*
- (*b*) *a superintendent or consular officer may on the ground of urgency authorise a young person to be employed in a ship notwithstanding that no such certificate as aforesaid has been delivered to the master of the ship, but a young person in whose case any such authorisation is given shall not be employed beyond the first port at which the ship calls after the young person has embarked thereon, except subject to and in accordance with the foregoing provisions of this section.*

(2) *A certificate under this section shall remain in force for a period of twelve months from the date on which it is granted and no longer:*

Provided that, if the said period of twelve months expires at some time during the course of the voyage of the ship in which the young person is employed, the certificate shall remain in force until the end of the voyage.

[1] For definitions of "young person" and "ship," see s. 5, *post.*

Penalties

77 **4.**—(1) *If any young person* [1] *is employed in any ship* [1] *in contravention of the provisions of this Act, the master of the ship shall be liable to a fine not exceeding forty shillings, or, in the case of a second or subsequent offence, not exceeding five pounds, and where a young person is taken into employment in any ship in contravention of the provisions of this Act on the production by, or with the privity of, the parent of a false or forged certificate or on a false representation by the parent that the young person is of an age at which such employment is not in contravention of the said provisions, that*

parent shall be liable on summary conviction to a fine not exceeding forty shillings.[3]

(2) *If the master of a ship*[1] *fails to keep such a register as is required to be kept by him under this Act, or, on being so required by an officer of the* [*Secretary of State for Trade*] *or any other person having power to enforce compliance with the provisions of the Merchant Shipping Acts,* 1894 *to* 1923,[2] *refuses or neglects to produce for inspection by that officer or person any such register as aforesaid or any certificate delivered to him under this Act, he shall be liable to a fine not exceeding twenty pounds.*[3]

[1] For definitions of "young person" and "ship," see s. 5, *post*.
[2] For powers of enforcing compliance with the M.S.A. 1894, see *ibid.* s. 723.
[3] For summary prosecution for fines, see M.S.A. 1894, s. 680 (1).

Interpretation

978 **5.** *In this Act—*

The expression "young person" means a person who is under the age of eighteen years:

The expression "ship" means any sea-going ship or boat of any description which is registered in the United Kingdom as a British ship, and includes any British fishing-boat entered in the fishing-boat register, but does not include any tug, dredger, sludge vessel, barge, or other craft whose ordinary course of navigation does not extend beyond the seaward limits of the jurisdiction of the harbour authority of the port at which such vessel is regularly employed, if and so long as such vessel is engaged in her ordinary occupation.

A new subsection (2) to the effect that India includes Burma was inserted by the Government of India (Adaptation of Acts of Parliament) Order 1937 (S.R. & O. No. 230), made under the Government of India Act 1935, but was repealed as from January 4, 1948, by the Burma Independence Act 1948, s. 5, Sched. II.

Power to apply Act to British possessions

979 **6.**—(1) *His Majesty may by Order in Council direct*[1] *that the provisions of this Act shall, subject to such modifications and adaptations, to be specified in the Order, as appear to His Majesty necessary or expedient in the circumstances of the case, apply to ships registered in any British possession*[2] *outside the United Kingdom, other than the Dominions mentioned in the Second Schedule to this Act, as they apply to ships registered in the United Kingdom.*

(2) *The reference in this section to British possessions*[2] *shall include a reference to territories which are under His Majesty's protection and territories in respect of which a mandate*[3] *has been accepted by His Majesty, other than any such territories in respect of which the mandate is being exercised by the Government of any of the Dominions mentioned in the said Second Schedule.*

(3) *An Order in Council made under this section may be varied or revoked by a subsequent Order.*

80 [1] This power has been exercised by the following Orders:—Isle of Man, March 22, 1927 (S.R. & O. No. 266); Guernsey, March 22, 1927 (S.R. & O. No. 267); Jersey, March 22, 1927 (S.R. & O. No. 268); Bermuda, Cyprus, Fiji, Jamaica, Mauritius, Seychelles, Straits Settlements and Trinidad, July 25, 1927 (S.R. & O. No. 715) amended by S.R. & O. 1941 No. 372; Hong Kong, March 3 and December 18, 1936 (S.R. & O.s Nos. 194 and 1381); Ceylon 1937 (S.R. & O. No. 235); the Gambia and British Solomon Islands Protectorate, May 5, 1939 (S.R. & O. No. 540) (which Order also substitutes the word " territories " for " Colonies " in S.R. & O. 1927, No. 715); Gibraltar, Granada, St. Lucia, St. Vincent, Nigeria, March 7, 1940 (S.R. & O. No. 369); Aden, Falkland Islands, Sierra Leone, March 14, 1941 (S.R. & O. No. 372); Dominica, Leeward Islands, February 9, 1942 (S.R. & O. No. 267); British Guiana, August 6, 1942 (S.R. & O. No. 1578); Barbados, November 14, 1951 (S.I. No. 1950). Ceylon, Fiji, Jamaica, Mauritius, Trinidad, The Gambia, Guyana, Cyprus, Nigeria and Sierra Leone are now self-governing countries within the Commonwealth and as such may abrogate United Kingdom law.

[2] " British possession " is defined by the Interpretation Act 1889, s. 18 (2), which is set out in the notes to M.S.A. 1894, s. 742.

[3] As to application of provisions relating to mandated territories to " trust territories " under the United Nations, see Mandated and Trust Territories Act 1947, and generally see Halsbury's *Laws of England*, 3rd ed., Vol. 5, Commonwealth and Dependencies 435.

Short title and construction

81 7. *This Act may be cited as the Merchant Shipping (International Labour Conventions) Act* 1925, *and shall be construed as one* [1] *with the Merchant Shipping Acts* 1894 *to* 1923, *and those Acts and this Act may be cited together as the Merchant Shipping Acts* 1894 *to* 1925.[2]

[1] See note (1) to s. 9 of M.S. (Mercantile Marine Fund) Act 1898.

[2] Now the Merchant Shipping Acts 1894 to 1974; see § 1639.

SCHEDULES

FIRST SCHEDULE

Preamble
Section 2

PART I

82 DRAFT CONVENTION CONCERNING UNEMPLOYMENT INDEMNITY IN CASE OF LOSS OR FOUNDERING OF THE SHIP

ARTICLE 1

For the purpose of this Convention, the term " seamen " includes all persons employed on any vessel engaged in maritime navigation.

For the purpose of this Convention, the term " vessel " includes all ships and boats, of any nature whatsoever, engaged in maritime navigation, whether publicly or privately owned; it excludes ships of war.

ARTICLE 2

In every case of loss or foundering of any vessel the owner or person with whom the seaman has contracted for service on board the vessel shall pay to

each seaman employed thereon an indemnity against unemployment resulting from such loss or foundering.

This indemnity shall be paid for the days during which the seaman remains in fact unemployed at the same rate as the wages payable under the contract, but the total indemnity payable under this Convention to any one seaman may be limited to two months' wages.

ARTICLE 3

Seamen shall have the same remedy for recovering such indemnities as they have for recovering arrears of wages earned during the service.

ARTICLE 4

Each member of the International Labour Organisation which ratifies this Convention engages to apply it to its colonies, protectorates and possessions which are not fully self-governing:

(*a*) *Except where owing to the local conditions its provisions are inapplicable; or*

(*b*) *Subject to such modifications as may be necessary to adapt its provisions to local conditions.*

Each member shall notify to the International Labour Office the action taken in respect of each of its colonies, protectorates and possessions which are not fully self-governing.

PART II

983 DRAFT CONVENTION FIXING THE MINIMUM AGE FOR THE ADMISSION OF YOUNG PERSONS TO EMPLOYMENT AS TRIMMERS OR STOKERS

ARTICLE 1

For the purpose of this Convention, the term " vessel " includes all ships and boats, of any nature whatsoever, engaged in maritime navigation, whether publicly or privately owned; it excludes ships of war.

ARTICLE 2

Young persons under the age of eighteen years shall not be employed or work on vessels as trimmers or stokers.

ARTICLE 3

The provisions of Article 2 shall not apply:

(*a*) *To work done by young persons on school-ships or training-ships, provided that such work is approved and supervised by public authority;*

(*b*) *To the employment of young persons on vessels mainly propelled by other means than steam;*

(*c*) *To young persons of not less than sixteen years of age, who, if found physically fit after medical examination, may be employed as trimmers or stokers on vessels exclusively engaged in the coastal trade of India and of Japan, subject to regulations made after consultation with the most representative organisations of employers and workers in those countries.*

ARTICLE 4

When a trimmer or stoker is required in a port where young persons of less than eighteen years of age only are available, such young persons may be employed and in that case it shall be necessary to engage two young persons in place of the trimmer or stoker required. Such young persons shall be at least sixteen years of age.

ARTICLE 5

In order to facilitate the enforcement of the provisions of this Convention every shipmaster shall be required to keep a register of all persons under the age of eighteen years employed on board his vessel, or a list of them in the articles of agreement, and of the dates of their births.

ARTICLE 6

Articles of agreement shall contain a brief summary of the provisions of this Convention.

ARTICLE 11

Each member of the International Labour Organisation which ratifies this Convention engages to apply it to its colonies, possessions and protectorates, in accordance with the provisions of Article 421 *of the Treaty of Versailles and of the corresponding Articles of the other Treaties of Peace.*

PART III

84 DRAFT CONVENTION CONCERNING THE COMPULSORY MEDICAL EXAMINATION OF CHILDREN AND YOUNG PERSONS EMPLOYED AT SEA

ARTICLE 1

For the purpose of this Convention, the term " vessel " includes all ships and boats, of any nature whatsoever, engaged in maritime navigation, whether publicly or privately owned; it excludes ships of war.

ARTICLE 2

The employment of any child or young person under eighteen years of age on any vessel, other than vessels upon which only members of the same family are employed, shall be conditional on the production of a medical certificate attesting fitness for such work, signed by a doctor who shall be approved by the competent authority.

ARTICLE 3

The continued employment at sea of any such child or young person shall be subject to the repetition of such medical examination at intervals of not more than one year, and the production, after each such examination, of a further medical certificate attesting fitness for such work. Should a medical certificate expire in the course of a voyage, it shall remain in force until the end of the said voyage.

ARTICLE 4

In urgent cases, the competent authority may allow a young person below the age of eighteen years to embark without having undergone the examination provided for in Articles 2 *and* 3 *of this Convention, always provided that such an examination shall be undergone at the first port at which the vessel calls.*

ARTICLE 9

Each member of the International Labour Organisation which ratifies this Convention engages to apply it to its colonies, possessions and protectorates, in accordance with the provisions of Article 421 *of the Treaty of Versailles and of the corresponding Articles of the other Treaties of Peace.*

Section 6 SECOND SCHEDULE

985 DOMINIONS TO WHICH ACT MAY NOT BE APPLIED BY ORDER IN COUNCIL

British India.

The Dominion of Canada.

The Commonwealth of Australia (including Papua and Norfolk Island).

The Dominion of New Zealand.

The Union of South Africa.

The Irish Free State.

Newfoundland.

Editors' Notes:

The words " the Union of South Africa " were repealed by the South Africa Act 1962, s. 2 (3), Sched. V. The Union of South Africa is now a republic outside the Commonwealth.

The word " Newfoundland " was repealed by the Newfoundland (Consequential Provisions) Act 1950, s. 1 (2), Sched., Part II. Newfoundland is now part of Canada (see British North America Act 1949).

As to meaning of references to " British India," see now s. 18 of the Indian Independence Act 1947.

For the reference to " Irish Free State," see note " Republic of Ireland " following notes to M.S.A. 1894, s. 742. The Republic of Ireland is no longer within the Commonwealth.

MERCHANT SHIPPING (LINE-THROWING APPLIANCE) ACT 1928

(18 & 19 GEO. 5, c. 40)

986 [*This Act, which made provisions for line-throwing appliances on certain ships, was repealed as from November* 19, 1952, *by M.S.* (*Safety Convention*) *Act* 1949, *s.* 37 (5) *and Third Schedule. Such provision is now made in section* 427 *of M.S.A.* 1894, *as substituted by section* 2 *of the* 1949 *Act.*]

MERCHANT SHIPPING (SAFETY AND LOAD LINE CONVENTIONS) ACT 1932

(22 GEO. 5, c. 9)

An Act to give effect to an International Convention for the Safety of Life at Sea, signed in London on the thirty-first day of May, nineteen hundred and twenty-nine, to give effect to an International Load Line Convention signed in London on the fifth day of July, nineteen hundred and thirty, and to amend the provisions of the Merchant Shipping Acts 1894 to 1928 relating to passenger steamers, life-saving appliances, wireless telegraphy, load lines, timber cargoes and other matters affected by the said Conventions. [17th March, 1932.]

987 INTRODUCTORY NOTE.—This Act was passed to give effect to two International Conventions, the International Convention for the Safety of Life at Sea (referred to as " the Safety Convention "), which was signed on May 31, 1929, and the International Load Line Convention, which was signed on July 5, 1930. The object of the Safety Convention was to establish in common agreement uniform principles and rules directed to promoting safety of life at sea; the object of the Load Line Convention was similarly to establish uniform principles and rules with regard to the limits to which ships on " international voyages " might be loaded. This Safety Convention, however, was superseded by a later International Convention for the safety of life at sea which was signed on June 10, 1948, and Part I of the Act (sections 1–39), which dealt with construction and

surveys, life-saving appliances, wireless telegraphy in ships, safety certificates (including the exemption from certain liabilities of ships holding valid Safety Convention certificates), and various miscellaneous provisions for furthering safety of life at sea (including provisions as to distress signals, carriage of dangerous goods on passenger steamers, helm orders, watertight doors, etc., has for the most part been repealed and replaced by the M.S. (Safety Convention) Act 1949, which is based on the 1948 Convention (see notes to that Act, *post*). The 1948 Convention was itself superseded by the International Convention for the Safety of Life at Sea 1960, upon which is based the M.S.A. 1964, *post*. The Load Line Convention was superseded by a later International Convention on Load Lines signed on April 5, 1966, and Part II of the Act which provided as to the marking and submersion of load lines, as to load line certificates and the effect thereof, as to what ships were exempt, and as to the loading of timber, was for the most part repealed and replaced by the M.S. (Load Lines) Act 1967, which is based on the 1966 Convention (§ 1272, *post*).

This Act came into operation on January 1, 1933. It repealed certain sections of the M.S.A. 1894, and of the M.S.A. 1906, relating to matters dealt with by this Act. It also repealed the M.S. (Convention) Act 1914 *in toto*. That Act, which was printed in the fourth edition of this work, never came into operation. It was founded on an International Convention signed on January 20, 1914, but its operation was postponed owing to the 1914–18 War. After that war, the Act, though it remained on the Statute Book, was kept in suspense by Orders in Council postponing its operation from year to year. The 1929 Safety Convention, to which effect was given by this (*i.e.* the 1932) Act, rendered the 1914 Act obsolete.

The countries which had (prior to the coming into force of the M.S. (Safety Convention) Act 1949) ratified or acceded to the Safety Convention (and had thus become " countries to which the Safety Convention applies " for the purposes of the Act) are listed in the note at § 1163, *post*. The countries which had (prior to the coming into force of the M.S. (Load Lines) Act 1967) ratified or acceded to the Load Line Convention (and had thus become " countries to which the Load Line Convention applies " for the purposes of the Act) are listed in note (2) to section 65 of this Act.

988 WHEREAS a Convention (in this Act referred to as " the Safety Convention ") which is set out in the First Schedule to this Act, was signed on behalf of the Government of the United Kingdom in London on the thirty-first day of May, nineteen hundred and twenty-nine, for promoting safety of life at sea by establishing in common agreement uniform principles and rules directed thereto:

And whereas a Convention (in this Act referred to as " the Load Line Convention ") which is set out in the Second Schedule to this Act, was signed on behalf of the Government of the United Kingdom in London on the fifth day of July, nineteen hundred and thirty, for promoting safety of life and property at sea, by establishing in common agreement uniform principles and rules with regard to the limits to which ships on international voyages may be loaded:

And whereas it is expedient to give effect to the said Conventions and to amend the provisions of the Merchant Shipping Acts 1894 to 1928, relating to passenger steamers, life-saving appliances, wireless telegraphy, load lines, timber cargoes and other matters affected by the said Conventions:

Be it therefore enacted, etc.

See note (1) to section 1 of M.S. (International Labour Conventions) Act 1925, as to making reference to Conventions when the words of the operative part of the statute are ambiguous.

PART I

SAFETY OF LIFE AT SEA

Construction and Surveys

989 **1.** [*This section, which related to construction and survey regulations, was repealed by M.S.* (*Safety Convention*) *Act* 1949, *s.* 37 (5) *and Third Schedule. See section* 1 *of that Act for the present provisions relating to construction rules, and the notes to that section for the rules now in force.*]

990 **2.** [*This section, which made amendments as to declarations of survey, was repealed by M.S.* (*Safety Convention*) *Act* 1949, *s.* 37 (5) *and Third Schedule.*]

991 **3.** [*This section, which related to the alteration of ships and additional surveys, was repealed by M.S.* (*Safety Convention*) *Act* 1949, *s.* 37 (5) *and Third Schedule. See section* 11 *of that Act for the present provisions relating to notice of alterations of ships and additional surveys.*]

Life-Saving Appliances

992 **4.** [*This section, which dealt with life-saving appliances rules, was repealed by M.S.* (*Safety Convention*) *Act* 1949, *s.* 37 (5) *and Third Schedule. See section* 2 *of that Act and section* 427 *of M.S.A.* 1894, *for the present provisions relating to rules for life-saving appliances, and the notes to those sections for the rules now in force.*]

Amendments of Merchant Shipping Acts as to life-saving appliances

993 5.—(1).[1]

(2) Subsection (1) of section four hundred and thirty of the principal Act (which imposes penalties for failure to comply with the rules for life-

saving appliances) shall be amended by inserting after paragraph (*d*) thereof the following paragraph:—

" (*e*) if any provision of the rules for life-saving appliances applicable to the ship is contravened or not complied with."

(3) The following section shall be substituted for section four hundred and thirty-one of the principal Act:—

[*The new section will be found printed as section* 431 *of the M.S.A.* 1894.]

(4).[1]

(5).[1]

[1] These subsections were repealed by M.S. (Safety Convention) Act 1949, s. 37 (5), and Third Schedule. See s. 2 of that Act, and s. 427 of M.S.A. 1894, for the present provisions relating to rules for life-saving appliances, and notes to those sections for the rules now in force.

Wireless Telegraphy

994 **6** and **7.** [*These sections, which related to wireless telegraphy, were repealed by M.S.* (*Safety Convention*) *Act* 1949, *s.* 37 (5) *and Third Schedule. See section* 3 *of that Act for the present provisions relating to radio* (*formerly wireless telegraphy*) *rules and section* 5 *as to rules for direction-finders.*]

Appointment of wireless telegraphy surveyors

995 **8.** A person appointed to be a surveyor of ships under section seven hundred and twenty-four of the principal Act may be appointed as a wireless telegraphy surveyor [1]:

Provided that the functions of the [*Secretary of State for Trade*] *under the said section with respect to surveyors of ships shall not be exercised with respect to wireless telegraphy surveyors* [1] *except with the approval of the Postmaster-General.*[2]

[1] Now known as " radio surveyors "; see s. 4 of M.S. (Safety Convention) Act 1949.
[2] The words in italics were repealed by the Post Office Act 1969, s. 137 (1) and Sched. 8 Part II.

Survey of passenger steamers by wireless telegraphy surveyors

996 **9.**—(1) The surveys of a passenger steamer [1] required by the principal Act shall, in the case of every survey made after the commencement of this Part of this Act [2] in respect of a sea-going steamer which is not [exempt from the obligations imposed by the radio rules [3]], include a survey by a wireless telegraphy surveyor, and accordingly subsection (1) of section two hundred and seventy-two of that Act shall be amended by inserting after the words " engineer surveyor of ships " the words " and, in the case of a sea-going passenger steamer [1] required to be provided with a [radio installation],[4] by a wireless telegraphy surveyor." [5]

(2).[6]

(3) Section two hundred and seventy-five of the principal Act (which provides for appeals to a court of survey by persons aggrieved by the declaration of survey of a ship or engineer surveyor) shall be amended by inserting the words " or wireless telegraphy surveyor " after the words " engineer surveyor " in both places where they occur.

997 [1] " Passenger steamer " is defined as a steamer carrying more than 12 passengers; see M.S. (Safety Convention) Act 1949, s. 26 (2). For the definition of " passenger," see s. 26 (1) of that Act.

[2] January 1, 1933 (S.R. & O. 1932 No. 917).

[3] The reference to an exemption from the obligations imposed by the " radio rules " was substituted by s. 35 (6) of M.S. (Safety Convention) Act 1949, for the previous reference to an exemption " under the M.S. (Wireless Telegraphy) Act 1919, from the obligations imposed by that Act." The 1919 Act was repealed by s. 37 of and Third Schedule to the 1949 Act. As to power of exemption by Department of Trade, see s. 28 of the 1949 Act, *post*.

[4] The reference to " radio installation " was substituted for " wireless telegraph installation " by s. 35 (5) of M.S. (Safety Convention) Act 1949.

[5] By s. 4 of M.S. (Safety Convention) Act 1949, " wireless telegraphy surveyors " are to be known as " radio surveyors."

[6] This subsection was repealed by M.S. (Safety Convention) Act 1949, s. 37 (5), and Third Schedule.

998 **10.** [*This section, which related to surveys of ships other than passenger steamers by wireless telegraphy surveyors, was repealed by M.S.* (*Safety Convention*) *Act* 1949, *s.* 37 (5) *and Third Schedule.*]

Certificates

999 **11.** [*This section, which dealt with the issue of safety certificates and passenger steamers' exemption certificates, was repealed by M.S.* (*Safety Convention*) *Act* 1949, *s.* 37 (5) *and Third Schedule. See section* 7 *of that Act for the present provisions relating to the issue for passenger steamers of safety certificates and exemption certificates, and section* 32 *and First Schedule, para.* 2, *for transitional provisions relating to certificates in force at the commencement of that Act.*]

Modification of safety certificates as respects life-saving appliances

1000 **12.**—(1) If, on any international voyage,[1] a British passenger steamer [1] registered in the United Kingdom in respect of which a safety certificate [2] is in force has on board a total number of persons less than the number stated in that certificate to be the number for which the life-saving appliances on the steamer provide, the [Secretary of State] or any person authorised by [him] for the purpose, may, at the request of the master of the steamer, issue a memorandum stating the total number of persons carried on the steamer on that voyage, and the consequent modifications which may be made for the purpose of that voyage in the particulars with respect to life-saving appliances [3] stated in the certificate, and that memorandum shall be annexed to the certificate.

(2) Every such memorandum shall be returned to the [Secretary of State for Trade] at the end of the voyage to which it relates, and, if it is not so returned, the master of the steamer shall be liable to a fine not exceeding twenty pounds.[4]

[1] For definitions of "international voyage" and "passenger steamer," see now M.S. (Safety Convention) Act 1949, ss. 26, 36.
[2] As to issue of safety certificates, see now M.S. (Safety Convention) Act 1949, ss. 7 *et seq.*
[3] See M.S.A. 1894, s. 427, and notes thereto, as to rules for life-saving appliances.
[4] As to recovery of fines, see M.S.A. 1894, ss. 680 *et seq.*

1001 **13.** [*This section, which dealt with wireless telegraphy certificates, etc., was repealed by M.S. (Safety Convention) Act* 1949, *s.* 37 (5) *and Third Schedule. See section* 9 *of that Act for the present provisions relating to the issue for cargo ships of radio (formerly wireless telegraphy) certificates and exemption certificates and section* 32 *and First Schedule, para.* 2, *for transitional provisions relating to certificates in force at the commencement of that Act.*]

1002 **14.** [*This section, which related to prohibition on proceeding to sea without certificate, was repealed by M.S. (Safety Convention) Act* 1949, *s.* 37 (5) *and Third Schedule. See section* 12 *of that Act for the present provisions relating to prohibition on proceeding to sea without appropriate certificates.*]

1003 **15.** [*This section, which contained miscellaneous provisions as to certificates, was repealed by M.S. (Safety Convention) Act* 1949, *s.* 37 (5) *and Third Schedule. Miscellaneous provisions as to certificates (and surveys) are now contained in section* 13 *of that Act.*]

Provisions as to Safety Convention Ships not registered in the United Kingdom

1004 **16.** [*This section, which related to certificates of Convention ships not registered in the United Kingdom, was repealed by M.S. (Safety Convention) Act* 1949, *s.* 37 (5) *and Third Schedule. See section* 14 *of that Act for the present provisions relating to certificates of Convention ships not registered in United Kingdom.*]

1005 **17.** [*This section, which related to modifications as to survey of passenger steamers holding Convention certificates, was repealed by M.S. (Safety Convention) Act* 1949, *s.* 37 (5) *and Third Schedule. See section* 15 *of that Act for the present provisions relating to modified surveys of passenger steamers holding Convention certificates.*]

1006 **18** and **19.** [*These sections, which dealt with miscellaneous privileges of passenger steamers holding Convention certificates and with wireless* *telegraphy applicable to ships holding Convention certificates, were repealed by M.S. (Safety Convention) Act* 1949, *s.* 37 (5) *and Third Schedule. See section* 16 *of that Act for the present provisions relating to miscellaneous privileges of ships holding Convention certificates.*]

007 **20.** [*This section, which related to the duty to produce Convention certificates, was repealed by M.S. (Safety Convention) Act* 1949, *s.* 37 (5) *and Third Schedule. See section* 17 *of that Act for the present provisions relating to the duty to produce Convention certificates.*]

008 **21.** [*This section, which related to modification of existing provisions for exemption of ships not registered in United Kingdom, was repealed by M.S. (Safety Convention) Act* 1949, *s.* 37 (5) *and Third Schedule.*]

Miscellaneous Provisions for furthering Safety of Life at Sea

009 **22.** [*This section, which dealt with duties as to watertight doors and other contrivances, was repealed by M.S. (Safety Convention) Act* 1949, *s.* 37 (5) *and Third Schedule. See section* 19 *of that Act for the present provisions relating to openings in passenger steamers' hulls and watertight bulkheads.*]

010 **23.** [*This section, which prohibited the submersion of subdivision load lines, was repealed by the M.S. (Load Lines) Act* 1966, *s.* 33 (1) *and Sched.* 2. *See section* 23 *of that Act for the present provisions relating to subdivision load lines.*]

Report of dangers to navigation

011 **24.**—(1) The master of any British ship registered in the United Kingdom, on meeting with dangerous ice, a dangerous derelict, a tropical storm or any other direct danger to navigation,[1] shall send information accordingly, by all means of communication at his disposal and in accordance with rules to be made for the purposes of this section,[2] to ships in the vicinity and to such authorities on shore as may be prescribed by those rules.

(2) Rules for the purposes of this section [2] shall be made by the [Secretary of State for Trade] *and shall make such provision as appears to the* [*Secretary of State*] *to be necessary for the purpose of giving effect to the provisions of Article forty-four (so far as it relates to safety signals) and of Regulation XLVI of the Safety Convention.*[3]

(3) If the master of a ship fails to comply with the provisions of this section, he shall for each offence be liable to a fine not exceeding fifty pounds.[4]

(4) Every person in charge of a wireless telegraph station which is under the control of the Postmaster General,[5] or which is established or installed under licence of the Postmaster General,[5] shall, on receiving the signal prescribed by the said rules for indicating that a message is about to be sent under this section, refrain from sending messages for a time sufficient to allow other stations to receive the message, and, if so required by the [Department of Trade], shall transmit the message in such manner as may be required by the [Dept.], and compliance with this subsection shall be deemed to be a condition of every licence granted by the Postmaster General [5] under the Wireless Telegraphy Act 1904 [6]:

Provided that nothing in this subsection shall interfere with the transmission by wireless telegraphy of any signal of distress or urgency prescribed under the next following section of this Act.[3]

(5) For the purposes of this section, the expression " tropical storm " means a hurricane, typhoon, cyclone, or other storm of a similar nature, and the master of a ship shall be deemed to have met with a tropical storm if he has reason to believe that there is such a storm in his vicinity.

(6) *The Derelict Vessels (Report) Act* 1896, *shall cease to have effect.*[7]

1012 This section, and the rules made under it, have effect as if references to ships or activities connected therewith included hovercraft or activities connected with hovercraft: see the Hovercraft (Application of Enactments) Order 1972, S.I. No. 971.

1 The matters of which information is to be sent include:

(*a*) Air temperature below freezing point associated with gale force winds causing severe ice accretion on the superstructure of ships; and

(*b*) Winds of force 10 or above on the Beaufort Scale for which no storm warning has been received;

see the M.S.A. 1964, s. 16 (§ 1253, *post*).

2 The rules made under this section at present in force are the M.S. (Navigational Warnings) Rules 1965 (S.I. No. 1051).

3 For power to apply provisions to British ships registered outside the U.K., see s. 36 (3). The words in italics were repealed by M.S. (Safety Convention) Act 1949, s. 37 (5) and Third Schedule. See note (4) below, as to proviso in M.S. (Safety Convention) Act 1949, similar to the proviso previously contained in subs. (6) of this section.

4 As to the recovery of fines, see M.S.A. 1894, ss. 680–682. See further, as to summary prosecution of offences, s. 72, *post*.

5 The first reference to the Postmaster General is to be construed as referring to the Minister of Posts and Telecommunications and the second and third references are to be construed as including references to that Minister: see the Post Office Act 1969, s. 3 (1) (i). As from April 1974, responsibility for the Post Office Corporation (including wireless telegraphy) was transferred to the Secretary of State for Industry.

6 The Wireless Telegraphy Act 1904 expired on June 1, 1954, by virtue of the Wireless Telegraphy Act 1949, s. 18, and S.I. 1954 No. 437, and has been replaced by that Act.

By s. 21 (4) of M.S. (Safety Convention) Act 1949 nothing in this subsection, *i.e.* 24 (4), shall interfere with the transmission of signals prescribed under that section (*i.e.* s. 21) of that Act.

7 This subsection was repealed as spent by the Statute Law Revision Act 1950.

1013 **25–26.** [*These sections, which related to signals of distress and the obligation to render assistance on receiving wireless distress call, were repealed by M.S. (Safety Convention) Act* 1949, *s.* 37 (5) *and Third Schedule. See sections* 21 *and* 22 *of that Act for the present provisions relating to signals of distress and the obligation to assist vessels, etc., in distress.*]

Signalling lamps

14 **27.** No British ship registered in the United Kingdom, being a ship of over one hundred and fifty tons gross tonnage, shall proceed to sea on an international voyage,[1] unless the ship is provided with a signalling lamp of a type approved by the [Secretary of State for Trade], and if any ship proceeds or attempts to proceed to sea in contravention [2] of this section, the owner or master thereof shall for each offence be liable to a fine not exceeding twenty pounds.[3]

[1] For definition, see M.S. (Safety Convention) Act 1949, s. 36.
[2] For definition, see s. 73 (1).
[3] As to the recovery of fines, see M.S.A. 1894, ss. 680–682.

15 **28.** [*This section, which related to the carriage of dangerous goods, was repealed by M.S.* (*Safety Convention*) *Act* 1949, *s.* 37 (5) *and Third Schedule. See section* 23 *of that Act for present provisions relating to the carriage of dangerous goods.*]

Method of giving helm orders

16 **29.**—(1) No person on any British ship registered in the United Kingdom [1] shall when the ship is going ahead give a helm or steering order containing the word " starboard " or " right " or any equivalent of " starboard " or " right," unless he intends that the head of the ship shall move to the right, or give a helm or steering order containing the word " port " or " left " or any equivalent of " port " or " left," unless he intends that the head of the ship shall move to the left.

(2) Any person who contravenes [2] the provisions of this section shall for each offence be liable to a fine not exceeding fifty pounds.[3]

[1] By virtue of the power given by s. 36, the provisions of this section have been made applicable to the Isle of Man, the Channel Islands, colonies, and foreign countries in which Her Majesty exercises jurisdiction, and to British ships registered in any such territories: M.S. (Helm Orders) Order in Council (August 13, 1935, S.R. & O. 1935 No. 837).
[2] As to meaning of " contravenes," see s. 73 (1).
[3] As to recovery of fines, see M.S.A. 1894, ss. 680–682. See further, as to summary prosecution of offences, s. 72, *post*.

Careful navigation near ice

017 **30.**—(1) The master of a British ship registered in the United Kingdom, when ice is reported on or near his course, shall at night either proceed at a moderate speed or change his course so as to keep amply clear of the ice reported and of the area of danger.

(2) If the master of any such ship fails to comply with this section, he shall for each offence be liable to a fine not exceeding one hundred pounds.[1]

For power to apply provisions to British ships registered outside the U.K., see s. 36 (3).
[1] As to recovery of fines, see M.S.A. 1894, ss. 680–682.

Notice of Atlantic routes

1018 **31.**—(1) The owner of any line of passenger steamers [1] crossing the North Atlantic from or to any port in the United Kingdom by regular routes shall give public notice, in such manner as may be directed [2] by the [Secretary of State for Trade], of the routes which it is proposed that the ships belonging to the line should follow, and of any changes which may be made in those routes.

(2) If the owner of any such line of passenger steamers [1] fails to comply with this section, he shall for each offence be liable to a fine not exceeding twenty pounds. [3]

[1] " Passenger steamer," for the purposes of this Act, is defined by s. 26 (2) of M.S. (Safety Convention) Act 1949, as " a steamer carrying more than twelve passengers."
[2] The M.S. (North Atlantic Routes) Directions, 1932 (S.R. & O. 1932 No. 1045), have been made under this section.
[3] As to recovery of fines, see M.S.A. 1894, ss. 680–682. See further, as to summary prosecution of offences, s. 72, *post*.

1019 **32.** [*This section, which related to contribution towards a service for watching ice and derelicts in the North Atlantic, was repealed by M.S.* (*Safety Convention*) *Act* 1949, *s.* 37 (5) *and Third Schedule. See section* 25 *of that Act for the present provisions relating to contribution towards a North Atlantic ice service.*]

Supplemental

1020 **33.** [*This section was repealed by M.S.* (*Safety Convention*) *Act* 1949, *s.* 37 (5) *and Third Schedule. See section* 26 (1) *of that Act for present definition of " passenger " for the purposes of Part III of M.S.A.* 1894, *and of this Act of* 1932.]

1021 **34.** [*This section, which gave power to the Board of Trade to amend rules and regulations to correspond with amendments of Safety Convention, was repealed by M.S.* (*Safety Convention*) *Act* 1949, *s.* 37 (5) *and Third Schedule.*]

1022 **35.** [*This section, which required certain rules and regulations to be laid before Parliament, was repealed by M.S.* (*Safety Convention*) *Act* 1949, *s.* 37 (5) *and Third Schedule. See section* 34 *of that Act for the present provisions relating to the exercise of the power to make rules and regulations under that Act.*]

Application of Part I to British possessions, protectorates and mandated territories

1023 **36.**—(1) His Majesty may by Order in Council direct that the provisions of this Part of this Act and (so far as may appear to His Majesty to be expedient for the purpose of giving effect to the provisions of this Part of this Act) the provisions of any other Act relating to Merchant Shipping, including any enactments for the time being in force amending or substituted for the provisions of this Part of this Act or any other such Act, shall extend, with such exceptions, adaptations or modifications (if any) as may be specified in the Order, to the Isle of Man, any of the Channel Islands and any colony.[1]

(2) The Foreign Jurisdiction Act 1890, shall have effect as if the provisions of this Part of this Act were included among the enactments which, by virtue of section five of that Act, may be extended by Order in Council to foreign countries in which for the time being His Majesty has jurisdiction.[2]

(3) His Majesty may by Order in Council direct—

(*a*) that any provision of this Part of this Act, which is expressed to apply only to British ships [3] or passenger steamers registered in the United Kingdom, shall apply to British ships or passenger steamers [4] as the case may be, registered in any country or part of His Majesty's dominions to which the provisions of this Part of this Act can be extended by virtue of the foregoing provisions of this section;

(*b*) that any reference in this Part of this Act to a port in the United Kingdom shall be construed as including a reference to a port in any such country or part of His Majesty's dominions as aforesaid.[5]

024 References in this section to Part I of this Act include references to M.S. (Safety Convention) Act 1949, the M.S.A. 1964 and the Post Office Act 1969, s. 3 (1)–(5). See s. 30 of that Act, as amended by s. 1 of the M.S.A. 1964 and s. 3 (6) of the Post Office Act 1969.

[1] Orders in Council have been made under this subsection as follows:
(i) M.S. Safety Convention (Isle of Man) Order 1934 (S.R. & O. No. 1414);
(ii) M.S. Safety Convention (Jersey) No. 1 Order 1935 (S.R. & O. No. 560);
(iii) M.S. Safety Convention (Guernsey) No. 1 Order 1935 (S.R. & O. No. 562);
(iv) M.S. Safety Convention (Hong Kong) No. 1 Order 1935 (S.R. & O. No. 692) as amended by S.I. 1953 No. 592 and modified by S.I. 1970 No. 285;
(v) M.S. Safety Convention (Straits Settlement) No. 1 Order 1935 (S.R. & O. No. 715);
(vi) M.S. (Helm Orders) Order 1935 (S.R. & O. No. 837)—(see note (1) to s. 29);
(vii) M.S. Safety Convention (Hong Kong) No. 1 Order 1953 (S.I. No. 592) as amended by S.I. 1965 No. 2011 and modified by S.I. 1970 No. 285;
(viii) M.S. (Safety Convention) (Hong Kong) Order 1965 (S.I. No. 201) as modified by S.I. 1970 No. 285;
(ix) The Wireless Telegraphy (Channel Islands) Orders S.I. 1969 No. 1369 and S.I. 1969 No. 1371;
(x) M.S. (Safety Convention) (Burmuda) Order 1973 (S.I. No. 1315) as amended by S.I. 1975 No. 413.

[2] See the M.S. (Helm Orders) Order 1935 (S.R. & O. No. 837) as amended by S.R. & O. 1943 No. 388.

[3] See M.S.A. 1894, s. 1, and notes thereto.

[4] For meaning of " passenger steamer," see M.S. (Safety Convention) Act 1949, s. 26 (2).

[5] Orders in Council have been made under this subsection as follows:
(i) M.S. Safety Convention (Isle of Man) Order 1934 (S.R. & O. No. 1414);
(ii) M.S. Safety Convention (Jersey) No. 2 Order 1935 (S.R. & O. No. 561);
(iii) M.S. Safety Convention (Guernsey) No. 2 Order 1935 (S.R. & O. No. 563);
(iv) M.S. Safety Convention (Hong Kong) No. 2 Order 1935 (S.R. & O. No. 693);

(v) M.S. Safety Convention (Straits Settlement) No. 2 Order 1935 (S.R. & O. No. 716);
(vi) M.S. (Helm Orders) Order 1935 (S.R. & O. No. 837)—(see note (1) to s. 29);
(vii) M.S. Safety Convention (Hong Kong) No. 2 Order 1953 (S.I. No. 593);
(viii) M.S. (Safety Convention) (Bermuda) (No. 2) Order 1973 (S.I. No. 1316).

1025 **37.** [*This section, which provided for Orders in Council declaring the countries to which the Safety Convention applied, has been repealed by the M.S.* (*Safety Convention*) *Act* 1949, *s.* 37 (5), *Sched. III. The comparable provision in that Act is s.* 31, *post.*]

1026 **38.** [*This section, which related to interpretation of Part I, was repealed by M.S.* (*Safety Convention*) *Act* 1949, *s.* 37 (5) *and Third Schedule. See section* 36 *of that Act for interpretation of terms thereunder.*]

Commencement of Part I and repeal

1027 **39.**—(1) *This Part of this Act shall come into operation on such date as His Majesty in Council may appoint.*[1]

(2) *The enactments set out in Part I of the Fourth Schedule to this Act shall be repealed, to the extent specified in the third column of that Part of that Schedule, as from the commencement of this Part of this Act.*

This section was repealed as spent by the Statute Law Revision Act 1950.

[1] The appointed day was January 1, 1933 (S.R. & O. 1932 No. 917).

PART II

LOAD LINE AND LOADING

1028 [*The whole of this part, save for parts of s.* 62, *was repealed and replaced by the provisions of M.S.* (*Load Lines*) *Act* 1967: *see* § 1272, *post.*]

Supplemental

Amendment of sections 436 and 454 of the principal Act

1029 **62.**—(1) In subsections (1) and (3) of section four hundred and thirty-six *and in subsection* (1) *of section four hundred and fifty-four* [1] of the principal Act the expression " freeboard " shall be substituted for the expression " clear side."

(2) *Subsection* (3) *of the said section four hundred and thirty-six shall cease to have effect with respect to load line ships.*[2]

(3) The following subsection shall be substituted for subsection (5) of the said section four hundred and thirty-six, namely—

" (5) In this section the expression ' freeboard ' means, in the case of any ship which is marked with a deck-line, the height from the water to the upper edge of the deck-line, and, in the case of any other ship, the height amidships from the water to the upper edge of the deck from which the depth of the hold as stated in the register is measured."

[1] The words in italics were repealed by M.S. (Safety Convention) Act 1949, s. 37 (5) and Sched. III, *post*.
[2] This subsection was repealed by the M.S. (Load Lines) Act 1967, Sched. II.

PART III

GENERAL

030 **68.** [*This section, which contained provisions as to rules and regulations, was repealed by the M.S.* (*Load Lines*) *Act* 1967, *Sched. II.*]

Notice to be given to Consular officer where proceedings taken in respect of foreign ships

031 **69.** Where any foreign ship is detained [1] under this Act,[2] and where any proceedings are taken under this Act [2] against the master or owner of any such ship, notice shall forthwith be served on the Consular officer for the country to which the ship belongs at or nearest to the port where the ship is for the time being, and such notice shall specify the grounds on which the ship has been detained or the proceedings have been taken.

Section 4 of the Consular Relations Act 1968, makes provision for Orders in Council excluding or limiting the jurisdiction of any court in the U.K. with respect to proceedings relating to the remuneration or any contract of service of the Master or crew of a ship belonging to a state specified in such an Order unless notice is given to a consular officer and no objection is made.

[1] See, *e.g.* ss. 23 (4), 53 (3) (4) (5), 54, 56, 57.
[2] This includes a reference to the M.S. (Safety Convention) Act 1949 (see *ibid.* s. 35 (4)) the M.S.A. 1964 (see *ibid.* s. 1) and M.S. (Load Lines) Act 1967 (see *ibid.* s. 27 (1)).

Cost of detaining ships

032 [*This section, which contained provision as to the costs of detaining ships, together with section* 71, *which contained provisions as to the forgery of certificates and s.* 72, *which contained provisions relating to summary prosecution of offences, were repealed by the M.S.* (*Load Lines*) *Act* 1967, *Sched. II.*]

Interpretation and construction

033 **73.**—(1) In this Act the following expressions have the meanings hereby respectively assigned to them, that is to say:—

"Contravention" includes, in relation to any provision, failure to comply with that provision, and the expression "contravenes" shall be construed accordingly;

"The Merchant Shipping Acts" means the Merchant Shipping Acts 1894 to 1928, and this Act;

" Passenger " has the same meaning as it has for the purpose of Part III of the principal Act;

" Passenger steamer " means a steamer carrying more than twelve passengers [1];

" The principal Act " means the Merchant Shipping Act 1894.

(2) In this Act [2] references to a ship constructed before or after any date shall be construed as references to a ship the keel of which has been laid before or after that date, as the case may be.

(3) For the purpose of any provision of this Act relating to Safety Convention ships,[3] Safety Convention passenger steamers or Load Line Convention ships [3] not registered in the United Kingdom, a passenger steamer or other ship registered in any of the Channel Islands or in the Isle of Man shall be deemed to be registered in the United Kingdom.

(4) Any references in this Act to any provision of the Merchant Shipping Acts 1894 to 1928, which has been amended by any subsequent Act, including this Act, shall be construed as a reference to that provision as so amended.

[1] The words in italics were repealed by M.S. (Safety Convention) Act 1949, s. 37 (5), and Sched. III. See s. 26 of that Act for present definitions of " passenger " and " passenger steamer " in this Act.
[2] This includes a reference to the M.S. (Safety Convention) Act 1949 (see *ibid.* s. 35 (4)) and the M.S.A. 1964 (see *ibid.* s. 1).
[3] For " Safety Convention ships," see the M.S. (Safety Convention) Act 1949, ss. 14 to 17: for " Load Line Convention Ships," see the M.S. (Load Lines) Act 1967.

Short title, citation and repeal

1034 **74.**—(1) This Act may be cited as the Merchant Shipping (Safety and Load Line Conventions) Act 1932, and shall be construed as one [1] with the Merchant Shipping Acts, 1894 to 1928, and those Acts and this Act may be cited together as the Merchant Shipping Acts 1894 to 1932.[2]

(2) *The enactments set out in Part III of the Fourth Schedule to this Act shall be repealed, to the extent specified in the third column of that Part of that Schedule, as from the passing of this Act.*[3]

[1] See note (1) to s. 9 of M.S. (Mercantile Marine Fund) Act 1898.
[2] Now the Merchant Shipping Acts 1894 to 1974: see § 1639, *post*.
[3] Subs. (2) was repealed as spent by the Statute Law Revision Act 1950.

1035

FIRST SCHEDULE

[*This Schedule contained the* 1929 *Convention and was superseded by the* 1948 *Convention, which in turn was superseded by the* 1960 *Convention.*]

. . . . . .

1036

SECOND SCHEDULE

[*This Schedule was repealed by the M.S. (Load Lines) Act* 1967, *Sched. II.*]

. . . . .

THIRD SCHEDULE

037 [*This Schedule which prescribed rules with respect to Watertight Doors and other Contrivances, was repealed by M.S.* (*Safety Convention*) *Act* 1949, *s.* 37 (5) *and Third Schedule. See s.* 19 *of that Act for the present provisions relating to the power of the Secretary of State to make such rules. See notes to that section for the rules at present in force.*]

FOURTH SCHEDULE

038 [*This Schedule, which contained the enactments repealed, was itself repealed as spent by the Statute Law Revision Act* 1950.]

PILOTAGE AUTHORITIES (LIMITATION OF LIABILITY) ACT 1936

(26 Geo. 5 & 1 Edw. 8, c. 36)

An Act to make provision with respect to the liability of pilotage authorities and others. [16th July, 1936.]

Be it enacted, etc.

Introductory Note.—The broad effect of this Act is to extend to Pilotage Authorities (other than as shipowners) similar privileges for limiting their liability as has been granted to dock, canal, harbour, and conservancy authorities by the M.S. (Liabilities of Shipowners and Others) Act 1900, s. 2 (as amended by the M.S. (Liability of Shipowners and Others) Act 1958).

Limitation of liability of pilotage authorities

039 **1.**—(1) A pilotage authority (as defined in this Act) [1] shall not, where without their actual fault or privity [2] any loss or damage is caused to any vessel or vessels [3] or to any goods, merchandise or other things whatsoever on board any vessel or vessels or to any other property or rights of any kind, whether on land or on water or whether fixed or moveable, be liable to damages [4] beyond the amount of one hundred pounds multiplied by the number of pilots holding licences from the pilotage authority [5] under section sixteen of the Pilotage Act 1913, for the pilotage district [6] of the pilotage authority at the date when the loss or damage occurs.

(2) Nothing in this section shall impose any liability in respect of any

such loss or damage as aforesaid on any pilotage authority in any case where no such liability would have existed if this Act had not been passed.

1040 [1] The definition is in s. 8 (1).
[2] As to meaning of the phrase " without their actual fault or privity," see note (4) to s. 503 of M.S.A. 1894.
[3] " Vessel " is defined in M.S.A. 1894, s. 742.
[4] See note (9) to s. 503 of M.S.A. 1894.
[5] Where the pilotage authority covers more than one pilotage district, s. 8 (2) in effect provides that the number of licensed pilots which is the relevant factor for the calculation is the number in the particular pilotage district, not the total number holding licences in all the districts covered by the pilotage authority. The question might conceivably arise—which pilotage district? It may then be the district in which the fault giving rise to the liability to damage occurs, or the district in which the loss or damage takes place. But both the fault and the loss or damage might take place outside any pilotage district!
[6] As to pilotage districts, see Pilotage Act 1913, s. 8.

Limitation of liability where several claims on one occasion

1041 **2.** The limitation of liability under section one of this Act shall relate to the whole of any losses and damages which may arise upon any one distinct occasion [1] although such losses and damages may be sustained by more than one person, and shall apply whether the liability arises at common law or under any public general or local Act of Parliament and notwithstanding anything contained in such Act.

[1] As to position where a pilotage authority are the owners of a ship, see s. 4. See a similar provision in s. 3 of M.S. (Liability of Shipowners) Act 1900. As to the meaning of " on distinct occasions," see note (19) to s. 503, M.S.A. 1894.

Power of courts to consolidate claims

1042 **3.** Where any liability is alleged to have been incurred by a pilotage authority [1] in respect of any loss or damage to which section one of this Act applies and several claims are made or apprehended in respect of that liability, then the pilotage authority may apply [2] in England to the High Court, or in Scotland to the Court of Session, or in Northern Ireland to the High Court of Justice in Northern Ireland, or in the Isle of Man to the High Court of Justice of the Isle of Man, and that court may determine the amount of liability of the pilotage authority and may distribute that amount rateably [3] among the several claimants,[4] and may stay any proceedings pending [5] in any other court in relation to the same matter, and may proceed in such manner and subject to such regulations as to making persons interested parties to the proceedings, and as to the exclusion of any claimants who do not come in within a certain time,[6] and as to requiring security from the pilotage authority, and as to payment of any costs,[7] as the court thinks just.

[1] See s. 8 for definition of " pilotage authority."
[2] The same right to apply for the consolidation of claims, where a question of limitation of liability arises, is contained in s. 504 of M.S.A. 1894, and also in s. 35 (3) of Pilotage Act 1913.
[3] See note (5) to s. 504 of M.S.A. 1894.
[4] See note (6) to s. 504 of M.S.A. 1894.

[5] See note (7) to s. 504 of M.S.A. 1894.
[6] See note (8) to s. 504 of M.S.A. 1894.
[7] See note (10) to s. 504 of M.S.A. 1894.

Act not to apply to pilotage authority as owners of ships

043 **4.** Where any pilotage authority [1] are the owners of any ship, nothing in this Act shall affect any limitation of liability conferred on them or other rights to which they are entitled as such owners by or under Part VIII of the Merchant Shipping Act 1894, and the Merchant Shipping (Liability of Shipowners and others) Act 1900, as respectively amended by subsequent Acts,[2] and accordingly the foregoing provisions of this Act shall not apply to any loss or damage the liability for which can be limited under the said enactments.

[1] For definition of "pilotage authority," see s. 8.
[2] See, in particular, the M.S. (Liability of Shipowners and Others) Act 1958, *post*.

Saving for funds for benefit of pilots, etc.

044 **5.** No pilots' benefit fund,[1] pilotage annuity fund or other fund formed or maintained by a pilotage authority for the benefit of pilots, their widows or children, shall be capable of being charged or attached or taken in execution or made available by any legal process or otherwise for meeting any liability of or any claim against the pilotage authority.

[1] As to pilots' benefit funds, see ss. 17 (1) (*j*), 21 of Pilotage Act 1913.

As to funds of authorities acting in dual capacity

045 **6.** If any body of persons corporate or unincorporate are the owners of any dock [1] or canal (including any body of persons having the control or management of any dock or canal) or are a harbour authority [2] or a conservancy authority [2] and that body or a committee of that body are also a pilotage authority,[3] then—

(i) No funds, revenues, moneys or other property whatsoever belonging to such body in any capacity other than as pilotage authority [4] shall be capable of being charged or attached or taken in execution or made available by any legal process or otherwise for meeting any liability of, or any claim against, such body or any committee of such body in their capacity as pilotage authority; and

(ii) No funds, revenues, moneys or other property whatsoever belonging to such body or a committee of such body in their capacity as pilotage authority [4] shall be capable of being charged or attached or taken in execution or made available by any legal process or otherwise for meeting any liability of, or any claim against, such body in any capacity other than as pilotage authority.[3]

[1] There is a definition of "dock" in s. 3 of M.S. (Liability of Shipowners) Act 1900. Presumably that definition, which is in very wide terms, would apply here.

2 " Harbour authority " and " Conservancy authority " are defined in s. 742, M.S.A. 1894; these definitions apply by virtue of s. 9, *post*.
3 For definition of " pilotage authority," see s. 8.
4 S. 21 (1) of the Pilotage Act 1913 provides for the payment of all receipts of a pilotage authority in their capacity as such into a separate fund, called the " pilot fund."

As to funds of certain Trinity Houses

1046 **7.**—(1) No funds, revenues, moneys or other property whatsoever belonging to the Trinity House [1] or the Trinity House of Newcastle-upon-Tyne,[2] in any capacity other than as pilotage authority,[3] shall be capable of being charged or attached or taken in execution or made available by any legal process or otherwise for meeting any liability of, or any claim against, either such body in their capacity as pilotage authority.

(2) No funds, revenues, moneys or other property whatsoever belonging to the Trinity House [1] or any committee or sub-commissioners of the Trinity House or the Trinity House of Newcastle-upon-Tyne,[2] in their capacity as pilotage authority,[3] shall be capable of being charged or attached or taken in execution or made available by any legal process or otherwise for meeting any liability of, or any claim against, any such body in any capacity other than as pilotage authority.

1 For definition of " the Trinity House," see M.S.A. 1894, s. 742.
2 For definition of " the Trinity House of Newcastle-upon-Tyne," see s. 9.
3 See note (4) to s. 6.

Meaning of pilotage authority

1047 **8.**—(1) In this Act " pilotage authority " means a body of persons or authority incorporated, constituted or established as a pilotage authority by a Pilotage Order made under the Pilotage Act 1913,[1] and where any existing body of persons or authority constituted or established for other purposes and with other duties or any committee of any such existing body of persons or authority are constituted or established a pilotage authority by any such Order includes that body of persons, authority or committee.

(2) Where any body of persons or authority are incorporated, constituted or established by any such Order or Orders as the pilotage authority for more than one pilotage district, this Act shall have effect as though such body of persons or authority were a separate pilotage authority for each separate pilotage district.[2]

1 For a list of such orders, see note (11) to s. 7, Pilotage Act 1913.
2 For the effect of this subsection and a possible difficulty of construction, see note (5) to s. 1.

Definitions

1048 **9.** In this Act unless the context otherwise requires—

words and expressions to which meanings are assigned by the Merchant Shipping Act 1894, as amended by subsequent Acts, shall have the same respective meanings; and the expression "the Trinity House of Newcastle-upon-Tyne" means the Corporation of the Master Pilots and Seamen of the Trinity House of Newcastle-upon-Tyne.

Extent of Act

49 **10.** This Act extends to Great Britain, Northern Ireland and the Isle of Man.

Short title and construction

50 **11.**—(1) This Act may be cited as the Pilotage Authorities (Limitation of Liability) Act 1936, and shall be construed as one [1] with the Pilotage Act 1913, and the Acts amending that Act.

(2) The Pilotage Act 1913, and this Act may be cited together as the Pilotage Acts 1913 and 1936.

[1] See note (1) to s. 9 of M.S. (Mercantile Marine Fund) Act 1898.

MERCHANT SHIPPING ACT 1937

(1 Edw. 8 & 1 Geo. 6, c. 23)

51 [*This Act, in so far as it contained provisions relating to the submergence of load lines, was repealed and replaced by the provisions of the M.S. (Load Lines) Act* 1967, *Sched. II. Section* 2, *which contained provisions as to life-saving appliances of fishing boats, had already been repealed by the Statute Law Revision Act* 1950.]

MERCHANT SHIPPING (SUPERANNUATION CONTRIBUTIONS) ACT 1937

(1 Geo. 6, c. 4)

52 [*This Act, which contained an amendment to s.* 163 *of the M.S.A.* 1894 *as respects contributions out of wages to certain funds established for the provision of superannuation and other benefits, was repealed by the M.S.A.* 1970, *s.* 100 (3), *Sched. V as from January* 1, 1973, *see S.I.* 1972 *No.* 1977.]

SEA FISH INDUSTRY ACT 1938

(1 & 2 Geo. 6, c. 30)

53 [*Part IV of this Act, which was expressly made a part of the Merchant Shipping Acts and which amended and added to the provisions of the M.S.A.* 1894 *relating to the crews of fishing boats, was repealed by the M.S.A.* 1970, *s.* 100 (3), *Sched. V as from January* 1, 1973; *see S.I.* 1972 *No.* 1977.]

SHIPS AND AIRCRAFT (TRANSFER RESTRICTION) ACT 1939

(2 & 3 Geo. 6, c. 70)

An Act to impose restrictions on certain transactions in respect of ships *and aircraft and parts of aircraft*; and for purposes connected with the matter aforesaid. [1st September, 1939.]

Be it enacted, etc.

The words in italics were repealed by the Statute Law (Repeals) Act 1971.

1054 Introductory Note.—In the 1914–18 War, the British Ships (Transfer Restriction) Acts 1915 and 1916 were passed, restricting the transfer or mortgage or transfer of mortgage of British registered ships to unqualified persons or to " foreign-controlled companies." These Acts, which were of a temporary character, expired, and were repealed as spent by the Statute Law Revision Act 1927. The present Act was passed immediately before the outbreak of the 1939–45 War. Its object was to ensure that the executive had the fullest powers to prevent British or British-registered ships passing to or coming into the control of persons of either enemy or neutral status and thereby being in danger of being lost to the British economy and war effort. The Act excluded from its operation British ships registered in a Dominion (other than Newfoundland) or India or Burma; but parallel legislation in these countries achieved the same result. The Act was to remain in force until " the emergency that was the occasion of the passing of this Act " was declared by Order in Council to have come to an end; see s. 13 (2). However, it was provided by the Emergency Laws (Repeal) Act 1959, s. 4 (1) that the Act should expire at the expiration of the 31st day of December 1964, " except as respects things previously done or omitted to be done." But by virtue of the Emergency Laws (Re-enactments and Repeals) Act 1964, s. 16, the Act continued in force until the end of 1969. It was further provided that the Act could continue in force by Order in Council, and by virtue of the Defence Powers (Continuance) Order 1969 (S.I. No. 1836); this Act remained in force until the end of 1974.

Restriction on transfer and mortgage of ships

1055 **1.**—(1) It shall be unlawful, except under the sanction [1] of the [Secretary of State for Trade]—

(*a*) to transfer any ship to which this Act applies [2] or any share in such a ship, or (*b*) to mortgage any such ship or any share therein, or to transfer a mortgage of any such ship or share;

and if any person purports to effect any transfer or mortgage which is unlawful by virtue of this subsection, then, in addition to the transfer or mortgage being void, he shall be guilty of an offence.[3]

(2) Any ship or share in a ship which has been the subject of any transaction unlawful by virtue of this section shall be subject to forfeiture; and accordingly section seventy-six of the Merchant Shipping Act 1894, as amended by any subsequent enactment (which section prescribes the procedure for the forfeiture of ships) shall apply in relation to ships which have become subject to forfeiture under this section, as it applies in relation to ships which have become subject to forfeiture under Part I of that Act.

56 [1] Sanctions can be given either generally or in relation to a particular case, and upon such terms and conditions as the Secretary of State for Trade may determine; see s. 7. See also the Emergency Laws (Repeal) Act 1959, s. 4 (2)–(4) which provides:

"4. (2) After the passing of this Act, the [Secretary of State for Trade] shall not withhold—

(*a*) his sanction under section one of the said Act of 1939 to any transfer or mortgage, or

(*b*) his approval under section two of that Act of the transfer of the registry of any ship.

except where it appears to him expedient so to do in the interests of national defence, having regard in particular to any agreement or arrangement concluded in respect of defence matters, or any consultations held in respect or such matters, between Her Majesty's Government in the United Kingdom and the government of any country outside the United Kingdom.

(3) The said [Secretary of State] may give his sanction under the said section one to any transfer or mortgage notwithstanding that the transfer or mortgage has already been effected, and thereupon that transfer or mortgage shall be deemed for the purposes of the said section one to have been effected under the sanction of that Minister:

Provided that the giving under this subsection of sanction to any mortgage or transfer shall not affect any penalty or forfeiture by virtue of the said Act of 1939 imposed in connection with that transfer or mortgage before the giving of that sanction.

(4) Any sanction or approval under the said Act of 1939 may be expressed to be, and if so expressed shall be, irrevocable, either unconditionally or subject to compliance with any terms or conditions attached thereto, for a specified period."

The restrictions on the transfer or mortgage or transfer of mortgage of ships, imposed by this Act for strategic reasons, have been progressively relaxed since the war by successive general sanctions dated October 11, 1945, January 17, 1947, July 21, 1950, September 8, 1958, and June 3, 1959. These have all been superseded by the most recent general sanction dated June 3, 1959, which permitted the free transfer of any ship to which the Act applies, the mortgage or transfer of any such ship to all countries abroad, with two exceptions: (i) the sale of former naval craft abroad and (ii) the sale of ships of high speed or fitted with specified equipment to countries of the Sino-Soviet bloc. The sanction does not imply exemption from the requirements of the Exchange Control Act 1947. A Press Notice No. 184 issued by the [Department of Trade] on June 3, 1959, explains the terms of the sanction. Reference should be made to the Department of Trade to ascertain its precise terms, and to ascertain whether any other sanctions have subsequently come into force.

[2] See s. 4 for the ships to which this Act applies. "Ship" has the same meaning as in M.S.A. 1894, s. 742.

[3] For the penalties, see s. 1 (2) (forfeiture) and s. 6.

Restriction on transfer of registry of ships

1057 **2.** Notwithstanding anything in section fifty-three of the Merchant Shipping Act 1894, an application made (whether before or after the commencement of this Act) for the transfer of the registry of a ship to which this Act applies [1] from any port at which the ship is registered for the time being, shall not be granted except with the approval [2] of the [Secretary of State for Trade].

[1] See s. 4.
[2] As to the power of giving approval, and the restrictions thereon, see note (1) to s. 1. A general sanction dated September 9, 1939, which is still in force, allows transfers of registry of ships (a) from ports of countries and territories referred to in s. 11 (1) of the Act to ports in the same country or territory and (b) from ports of the countries or territories (other than the U.K.) referred to in the said s. 11 (1) to ports in the U.K. Reference should however, be made to the Ministry to ascertain the sanctions in force at any given time.

1058 **3.** [*Section* 3, *which related to aircraft, was repealed by the Emergency Laws (Miscellaneous Provisions) Act* 1947, *s.* 11.]

Ships and aircraft to which this Act applies

1059 **4.**—(1) The ships to which this Act applies are—

(*a*) all British ships,[1] except ships registered

(i) in a Dominion,[2] or

(ii) in any territory administered by His Majesty's Government in a Dominion, or

(iii) in India *or Burma* [3]; and

(*b*) all other ships being ships

(i) which are registered in, or licensed under the law of, any colony [4] or British protectorate *or any territory in respect of which a mandate on behalf of the League of Nations has been accepted by His Majesty and is being exercised by His Majesty's Government in the United Kingdom*,[5] or

(ii) which, in pursuance of an Order in Council under section eighty-eight of the Merchant Shipping Act 1894,[6] are registered at any port within which His Majesty exercises jurisdiction in accordance with the Foreign Jurisdiction Act 1890.

1060 [1] See s. 1 of the M.S.A. 1894, and notes thereto.
[2] " Dominion " means any Dominion within the meaning of the Statute of Westminster, 1931; see s. 12 (as amended). This Act does not apply to any ship by reason only of its being registered in, or licensed under the law of Ceylon, Ghana, Malaysia, Nigeria, Sierra Leone, Tanzania, Jamaica, Trinidad and Tobago, Uganda, Kenya, Malawi, Malta, The Gambia, Guyana, Barbados, Mauritius, and Fiji, and the penal provisions of the Act do not apply to persons in these territories (but without prejudice to the operation with respect to any ship to which the Act does apply of the provisions thereof relating to forfeiture of ships); see the Ceylon Independence Act 1947, s. 4, Sched. II, para. 7; the Ghana Independence Act 1957, s. 4 (4), Sched. II, para. 10; the Federation of Malaya Independence Act 1957, s. 2 (1), Sched. I, para. 12; the Malaysia Act 1963, s. 3 (2) and Sched. 2, para. 1; the Nigeria Independence Act 1960, s. 3 (4), Sched. II, para. 10; the

Sierra Leone Independence Act 1961, s. 3 (3), Sched. III, para. 11; the Tanganyika Independence Act 1961, s. 3 (4), Sched. II, para. 10; Zanzibar Act 1963, s. 1 (2) and Sched. 1, para. 10; the Tanzania Act 1969, s. 3 (1); the Jamaica Independence Act 1962, s. 3 (5), Sched. II, para. 10; the Trinidad and Tobago Independence Act 1962, s. 3 (4), Sched. II, para. 10; the Uganda Independence Act 1962, s. 3 (4), Sched. III, para. 10. Kenya Independence Act 1962, s. 4 (4) and Sched. 2, para. 10; Malawi Independence Act 1964, s. 4 (4) and Sched. 2, para. 10; Malta Independence Act 1964, s. 4 (4) and Sched. 2, para. 10; The Gambia Independence Act 1964, s. 4 (4), Sched. 2, para. 9; Guyana Independence Act 1966, s. 5 (4) and Sched. 2, para. 9; Barbados Independence Act 1966, s. 4 (5) and Sched. 2, para. 9; Mauritius Independence Act 1968, s. 4 (5), Sched. 2, para. 9; and Fiji Independence Act 1970, s. 4 (3) and Sched. 2, para. 7. See also note (7) to s. 10 for the effect of these provisions upon the forfeiture of a ship.

[3] The words in italics were repealed by the Burma Independence Act 1947, s. 5, Sched. II, Part I.

[4] For definition, see Interpretation Act 1889, s. 18, and note thereto, cited following notes to M.S.A. 1894, s. 742.

[5] The words in italics were repealed by the Statute Law (Repeals) Act 1971.

[6] For a list of these orders now in force, see note to M.S.A. 1894, s. 88.

[7] Subsection (2) related to aircraft and, as a result of the repeal of s. 3, it has ceased to have effect. It was repealed by the Statute Law Repeals Act 1971.

Offences by corporations

961 5. [Where an offence under this Act committed by a body corporate is proved to have been committed with the consent or connivance of, or to be attributable to any neglect on the part of, any director, manager, secretary or other similar officer of the body corporate or any person who was purporting to act in any such capacity, he, as well as the body corporate, shall be guilty of that offence and shall be liable to be proceeded against and punished accordingly.

In this section, the expression " director," in relation to a body corporate established by or under any enactment for the purpose of carrying on under national ownership any industry or part of an industry or undertaking, being a body corporate whose affairs are managed by its members, means a member of that body corporate.]

This section was substituted for the original s. 5 by the Emergency Laws (Repeal) Act 1959, s. 4 (5). The principal consequence is to shift the burden of implicating a director in the offence of a body corporate from the accused person to the prosecution. Also, the former s. 5 did not include this extended definition of " director."

Penalties and legal proceedings

62 6.—(1) [1] Any person guilty of an offence under this Act shall be liable—

(*a*) on conviction on indictment, to imprisonment for a term not exceeding two years or a fine or to both such imprisonment and a fine, or

(*b*) on summary conviction, to imprisonment for a term not exceeding six months or to a fine not exceeding one hundred pounds or to both such imprisonment and such fine.

(2) Proceedings against any person for the purposes of this Act may be taken before the court having jurisdiction in the place where that person is for the time being.

(3) [1] Any summary proceedings which may be taken against a person for an offence under this Act committed by him outside the countries and territories to which this Act extends may, notwithstanding any limitation imposed by law on the time for taking proceedings, be commenced in any competent court within six months from the date on which he first sets foot within the jurisdiction of that court after the commission of the offence.

(4) In any proceedings a document purporting to state that a sanction or approval has been given under this Act, and to be signed on behalf of [*the Minister of Civil Aviation or*] the [Secretary of State for Trade], as the case may be, or by a person who is empowered by this Act to do anything which may be done thereunder by the [Secretary of State], shall be evidence of the facts stated in the document.

1063 *Omission of references to Minister of Civil Aviation.*—By s. 2 (1) of the Ministry of Civil Aviation Act 1945 (now repealed), for references to the " Secretary of State " in the Ships and Aircraft (Transfer Restriction) Act 1939, there were substituted references to the " Minister of Civil Aviation." Now, however, by s. 11 (2) of the Emergency Laws (Miscellaneous Provisions) Act 1947, any reference in this Act to the " Minister of Civil Aviation" shall be omitted. Accordingly the words in italics have ceased to have effect.

[1] In the application of this Act to the Channel Islands, subsections (1) and (3) of this section are modified by the Ships and Aircraft (Transfer Restriction) (Channel Islands) Order in Council 1939 (S.R. & O. 1939 No. 1192), as follows:—For subsection (1) there are substituted the words " Any person guilty of an offence under this Act shall be liable on conviction before the Royal Court to imprisonment for a term not exceeding two years with or without hard labour, or to a fine or to both such imprisonment and a fine." In subsection (3) the word " summary " is omitted.

Incidental provisions as to sanctions and approvals

1064 **7.** For the avoidance of doubt it is hereby declared that any sanction or approval under this Act may be given either generally or in relation to a particular case; and any such sanction or approval may be given on such terms, and subject to such conditions, as may be determined by [*the Minister of Civil Aviation or*] the [Secretary of State for Trade].

As to omission of the words in italics, see note to s. 6.

Power to impose charges

1065 **8.**—(1) The Treasury may by order [1] authorise the making of such charges as may be specified in the order in respect of the giving of any sanction under section one [2] of this Act; and any such order may be varied or revoked by a subsequent order of the Treasury.

(2) Any such order as aforesaid shall be laid before the Commons House of Parliament [1] as soon as may be after it is made, but, notwithstanding anything in subsection (4) of section one of the Rules Publication Act, 1893,[3] shall be deemed not to be a statutory rule to which that section applies.

(3) Any such order as aforesaid imposing or increasing a charge shall cease to have effect on the expiration of the period of twenty-eight days beginning with the day on which the order is made, unless at some time

before the expiration of that period it has been approved by a resolution of the Commons House of Parliament, without prejudice, however, to the validity of anything previously done under the order or to the making of a new order.

In reckoning any period of twenty-eight days for the purposes of this subsection, no account shall be taken of any time during which Parliament is dissolved or prorogued, or during which the Commons House is adjourned for more than four days.

(4) Without prejudice to the preceding provisions of this section, there may be charged in respect of the giving of any sanction under this Act, or in respect of the approving under this Act of any transfer of the registry of a ship, such fee, not exceeding five pounds, as [*the Minister of Civil Aviation or*] [4] the [Secretary of State for Trade] may with the approval of the Treasury determine.

(5) All sums received by virtue of this section or of an order made thereunder shall be paid into the Exchequer of the United Kingdom.

[1] These orders are now subject to the provisions of the Statutory Instruments Act 1946. As to meaning of references to laying before Parliament, see the Laying of Documents before Parliament (Interpretation) Act 1948, s. 1. No orders have so far been made under this section.
[2] The words in italics were repealed by the Statute Law (Repeals) Act 1971.
[3] That Act was repealed by the Statutory Instruments Act 1946, s. 12 (1).
[4] See note to s. 6.

Exercise of powers of [Secretary of State for Trade]

066 **9.**—(1) [*The Minister of Civil Aviation and*] [1] the [Secretary of State for Trade] may respectively make arrangements whereby any sanction or approval which may be given under this Act by [*the Minister of Civil Aviation or*] [1] the [Secretary of State] is given on [his] behalf outside the United Kingdom by such persons, and at such places, as [*the Minister of Civil Aviation or*] [1] the [Secretary of State] may determine; and any sanction or approval given in pursuance of such arrangements shall be deemed for the purposes of this Act to be a sanction or approval given by [*the Minister of Civil Aviation or*] [1] the [Secretary of State], *as the case may be*.[2]

(2) *Anything required or authorised under this Act to be done by, to or before the* [*Secretary of State for Trade*] *may* (*without prejudice to any arrangements in force under the preceding subsection*) *be done by, to or before the* [*Secretary of State*], *any secretary, under-secretary or assistant-secretary of the* [*Secretary of State*] *or any person authorised in that behalf by the* [*Secretary of State*].[3]

[1] See note to s. 6.
[2] The words in italics were repealed by the Statute Law (Repeals) Act 1971.
[3] This subsection was repealed by the Transfer of Functions (Shipping and Construction of Ships) Order 1965 (S.I. No. 145).

Extra-territorial operation of penal provisions of Act

1067 **10.** The penal provisions of this Act shall apply to all persons in any country or territory to which this Act extends [1] or on board any ship *or aircraft* [2] to which this Act applies,[3] and to all other persons being British subjects [4] or British protected persons,[4] except persons in any of the following countries and territories, that is to say,—

(*a*) any Dominion,[5]

(*b*) any territory administered by His Majesty's Government in a Dominion,

(*c*) India, *Burma* [6] and Southern Rhodesia, and

(*d*) any other country or territory being a country or territory under His Majesty's protection or suzerainty, and not being a country or territory to which this Act extends;

but nothing in this section shall be taken to restrict the operation of the provisions of this Act relating to the forfeiture of ships.[7]

1068 [1] See s. 11.

[2] The words in italics were repealed by the Statute Law Repeals Act 1971.

[3] See s. 4.

[4] See note (3) to M.S.A. 1894, s. 1. For definition of "British protected persons," see British Nationality Act 1948, s. 32; and see British Protectorates, Protected States and Protected Persons Order 1969 (S.I. No. 1832).

[5] See s. 12 for meaning of "Dominion." For the position of various commonwealth independent states, see note (2) to s. 4.

[6] The word in italics was repealed by the Burma Independence Act 1947, s. 5 (3), Sched. II, Part I.

[7] As to forfeiture, see s. 1 (2). This provision apparently means that if, for example, a transfer takes place in a Dominion, without the sanction of the Secretary of State for Trade of a ship registered in the U.K. or a colony, that ship is subject to forfeiture under s. 1 (2) on its arrival in the U.K. or a colony.

Extent of Act

1069 **11.**—(1) This Act extends to the following countries and territories, that is to say,—

(*a*) the United Kingdom,

(*b*) the Channel Islands [1] and the Isle of Man,[1]

(*c*) *Newfoundland, and* [2] any colony [3] except Southern Rhodesia or a colony administered by His Majesty's Government in a Dominion,

(*d*) any British protectorate, and

(*e*) *any territory in respect of which a mandate on behalf of the League of Nations has been accepted by His Majesty and is being exercised by His Majesty's Government in the United Kingdom* [4];

and also extends (in so far as His Majesty has jurisdiction therein) to any other country or territory being a foreign country or territory in which for the time being His Majesty has jurisdiction, and not being a country or territory administered by His Majesty's Government in a Dominion.

(2) This Act shall, in its application to any country or territory outside the United Kingdom, have effect subject to such adaptations and modifications, if any, as may be prescribed by or under an Order of His Majesty in Council [5]; and any such Order may be varied or revoked by a subsequent Order of His Majesty in Council.

70 [1] As to the Channel Islands, see note (5).
[2] The words in italics were repealed by the Newfoundland (Consequential Provisions) Act 1950, s. 1 (1), Schedule. Newfoundland is now part of the Dominion of Canada (see British North America Act 1949).
[3] See note (4) to s. 4.
[4] The words in italics were repealed by the Statute Law (Repeals) Act 1971.
[5] The only Order in Council made under this subsection is the Ships and Aircraft (Transfer Restriction) (Channel Islands) Order in Council 1939 (S.R. & O. No. 1192), which makes minor modifications to s. 6 (1) and (3) in the application of those subsections to the Channel Islands. These modifications are set out in note (1) to s. 6.

Interpretation

71 **12.** In this Act the following expressions have the meanings hereby respectively assigned to them, that is to say:—

" *aircraft* " *means any flying machine, glider or airship or any balloon (whether fixed or free)* [1];

" Dominion " means any Dominion within the meaning of the Statute of Westminster 1931, *except Newfoundland* [2]; and

" ship " has the same meaning as in the Merchant Shipping Act 1894.[3]

[1] The words in italics were repealed by the Statute Law (Repeals) Act 1971.
[2] The words in italics were repealed by the Newfoundland (Consequential Provisions) Act 1950, s. 1 (2), Schedule. Newfoundland is now part of the Dominion of Canada (see British North America Act 1949). See also note (2) to s. 4.
[3] See s. 742 of M.S.A. 1894, and note (4) thereto.

Short title and duration of Act

72 **13.**—(1) This Act may be cited as the Ships and Aircraft (Transfer Restriction) Act 1939.

(2) *This Act shall continue in force until such date as His Majesty may by Order in Council declare to be the date on which the emergency that was the occasion of the passing of this Act came to an end, and shall then expire except as respects things previously done or omitted to be done.*[1]

[1] This subsection was repealed by the Emergency Laws (Repeal) Act 1959, s. 4 (1), s. 10 (3), Sched. IV, Part 2. As to the duration of this Act, see the Introductory Note, § 1054, *ante*.

MERCHANT SHIPPING (SALVAGE) ACT 1940

(3 & 4 Geo. 6, c. 43)

73 [*This Act was repealed by the Crown Proceedings Act* 1947.]

CROWN PROCEEDINGS ACT 1947

(10 & 11 Geo. 6, c. 44)

An Act to amend the Law relating to the civil liabilities and rights of the Crown and to civil proceedings by and against the Crown, to amend the Law relating to civil liabilities of persons other than the Crown in certain cases involving the affairs or property of the Crown, and for purposes connected with the matters aforesaid. [31st July, 1947.]

Be it enacted, etc.

1074 Introductory Note.—The general purpose of this Act is to put the Crown in the same position as the private individual as regards legal liability for the acts of its servants and as regards the procedure for the enforcement of such liability. The portions of the Act printed below are those which relate directly and particularly to the rights and liabilities which are the concern of the Merchant Shipping Acts. For this purpose, the main provisions are these: (1) The Crown is given the benefit of the provisions relating to limitation of liability in respect of H.M. ships and in respect of Crown docks and harbours, and the benefit of the provisions of the Maritime Conventions Act 1911 relating to apportionment of liability; (2) The Crown is made liable to salvage claims and is put in the same position as a private salvor as regards claims for salvage. It should be noted that the Act applies only to proceedings against or by the Crown in respect of liabilities and rights of H.M. Government in the United Kingdom. It does not extend to proceedings against or by the Crown in respect of liabilities or rights of a Dominion Government.

Part I

Substantive Law

. . . .

Liability in respect of Crown ships, etc.

1075 **5.**—(1) The provisions of the Merchant Shipping Acts 1894 to 1940, which limit the amount of the liability of the owners of ships [1] shall, with any necessary modifications, apply for the purpose of limiting the liability of His Majesty in respect of His Majesty's ships [2]; and any provision of the said Acts which relates to or is ancillary to or consequential on the provisions so applied shall have effect accordingly.

(2) Without prejudice to the provisions of the preceding subsection, where a ship is built at any port or place within His Majesty's dominions, and His Majesty is interested in her by reason of the fact that she is built by or on behalf of or to the order of His Majesty in right of His Government

in the United Kingdom, the provisions of the Merchant Shipping Acts 1894 to 1940,[3] which limit the amount of the liability of the owners of ships shall, with any necessary modifications, apply for the purpose of limiting the liabilities in respect of that ship of His Majesty, her builders, her owners, and any other persons interested in her; and any provision of the said Acts which relates to or is ancillary to or consequential on the provisions so applied shall have effect accordingly.

This subsection shall have effect only in respect of the period from and including the launching of the ship until the time of her completion,[4] and shall not in any event have effect in respect of any period during which His Majesty is not so interested in the ship as aforesaid. In relation to a ship built to the order of His Majesty in right of His Government in the United Kingdom, the time of her completion shall be taken for the purposes of this subsection to be the time when His Majesty, acting in His said right, finally takes delivery of her under the building contract.[5]

(3) Where any ship has been demised or sub-demised by His Majesty acting in right of His Government in the United Kingdom, then, whether or not the ship is registered for the purposes of the Merchant Shipping Acts 1894 to 1940, the provisions of those Acts [1] which limit the amount of the liability of the owners of ships shall, in respect of the period for which the demise or sub-demise continues, apply, with any necessary modifications, for the purpose of limiting the liabilities in respect of the ship of any person entitled to her by demise or sub-demise; and any provision of the said Acts which relates to or is ancillary to or consequential on the provisions so applied shall have effect accordingly.

This subsection shall be deemed always to have had effect.

(4) Where by virtue of any arrangement between His Majesty and some other person (not being a servant of His Majesty) that other person (hereinafter referred to as " the manager " [6]) is entrusted with the management of any of His Majesty's ships, the provisions of the Merchant Shipping Acts 1894 to 1940,[1] which limit the amount of the liability of the owners of ships shall apply for the purpose of limiting the manager's liability in respect of the ship while so entrusted; and any provision of the said Acts which relates to or is ancillary to or consequential on the provisions so applied shall have effect accordingly.

This subsection shall be deemed always to have had effect.

(5) Where for the purposes of any enactment as applied by this section it is necessary to ascertain the tonnage of any ship, and that ship is not registered for the purposes of the Merchant Shipping Acts 1894 to 1940,[7] the tonnage of the ship shall be taken for the purposes of that enactment to be the tonnage arrived at by:—

(*a*) ascertaining her tonnage in accordance with [regulations made under the Merchant Shipping Act 1965] [8] and deducting from her tonnage as so ascertained ten per cent. thereof; or (*b*) where it is impossible to ascertain her tonnage as provided by paragraph (*a*) of this subsection, taking her estimated tonnage as certified for the purposes of this paragraph, and deducting from her estimated tonnage as so certified ten per cent. thereof.[9]

1076 Where it is necessary to ascertain the tonnage of a ship in the manner provided by paragraph (*b*) of this subsection, the Chief Ships Surveyor of the Ministry of Transport, or the officer for the time being discharging the functions of the said surveyor, shall, upon the direction of the court concerned, and after considering such evidence of the dimensions of the ship as it may be practicable to obtain, estimate what her tonnage would have been found to be if she could have been duly measured for the purpose, and issue a certificate stating her tonnage as so estimated by him.

(6) For the purposes of this section the expression " ship " [9] has the meaning assigned to it by section seven hundred and forty-two of the Merchant Shipping Act 1894, but includes also:—

(*a*) [any structure to which Part VIII of that Act is applied by section four of the Merchant Shipping (Liability of Shipowners and Others) Act 1958; and] [10]

(*b*) every description of lighter, barge or like vessel used in navigation in Great Britain, however propelled, so, however, that a vessel used exclusively in non-tidal waters, other than harbours, shall not for the purposes of this paragraph be deemed to be used in navigation.

(7) Any reference in this section to the provisions of the Merchant Shipping Acts 1894 to 1940, which limit the amount of the liability of the owners of ships shall be construed as including a reference to any provision of those Acts which negatives the liability of the owner of a ship,[1] and accordingly any reference in this section to limiting the liability of any person shall be construed as including a reference to negativing his liability.

(8) Relief shall not be available by virtue of [sections three and four of the Merchant Shipping (Liability of Shipowners and Others) Act 1958] [11] in any case in which it is available by virtue of this section.

1077 [1] Reference to the relevant provisions, including the M.S. (Liability of Shipowners and Others) Act 1958, both for limitation of liability and for complete exemption (see subs. (7) of this section), will be found in the note " Statutory Provisions at Present in Force " at the beginning of Part VIII of M.S.A. 1894. The effect of the present section is summarised in that note and in the notes to ss. 502–508. For the definition of " ship " for the purposes of this section, see subs. (6) and note (9).

[2] For the definition of " His Majesty's ships," see s. 38 (2). The effect of this provision in relation to the Crown was considered in *Admiralty* v. *The Divina* (*Owners*); *The Truculent* [1952] P. 1. The expression " His Majesty " is not used in any personal sense, but in a corporate sense. In that case, the Board of Admiralty were held to be in the position of owners of His Majesty's ship in question.

[3] For the relevant provisions, see now the M.S. (Liability of Shipowners and Others) Act 1958, ss. 4, 8 (5).

[4] *Cf. ibid.* s. 4 (1).

5 The occasion of "final delivery" is normally, if not invariably, fixed by the building contract.

6 See M.S.A. 1894, s. 59, and note thereto as to the meaning of the term "managing owner."

7 As to the ascertainment of tonnage of a registered ship, see M.S.A. 1894, s. 503 (2), and note (16) to that section.

8 The words within square brackets were substituted by the M.S.A. 1965, s. 7 (1) and Sched. 1.

9 As to the different definitions of "ship" for different parts of the M.S.A. see note (4) to s. 742, M.S.A. 1894; notes (2) and (3) to M.S.A. 1921, s. 1, and M.S. (Liability of Shipowners and Others) Act 1958, s. 4 (1). Note also the different definition in s. 30 (3) of this Act for the purposes of that section. See also the Hovercraft Act 1968 and the Hovercraft (Civil Liability) Order 1971 (S.I. No. 720), art. 8 (1).

10 This paragraph within square brackets was substituted for a reference to the definition of "ship" contained in the M.S. (Liability of Shipowners) Act 1898 (now repealed), by the M.S. (Liability of Shipowners and Others) Act 1958, s. 8 (5). For the application of this substitution to Northern Ireland, see *ibid.* s. 10 (2).

11 This reference within square brackets was substituted for a reference to the M.S. (Liability of Shipowners) Act 1898 (now repealed), by the M.S. (Liability of Shipowners and Others) Act 1958, s. 8 (5). For the application of this substitution to Northern Ireland, see *ibid.* s. 10 (2).

Application to Crown ships of rules as to division of loss, etc.

78 **6.** The provisions of sections one, two and three of the Maritime Conventions Act 1911 (which relate to the apportionment of damage or loss caused by vessels) shall apply in the case of vessels belonging to His Majesty as they apply in the case of other vessels.

This section is applied to hovercraft by the Hovercraft (Civil Liability) Order 1971 (S.I. No. 720), art. 8 (2).

Liability in respect of Crown docks, harbours, etc.

79 **7.**—(1) It is hereby declared that the provisions of the Merchant Shipping Acts 1894 to 1940, which limit the amount of the liability of the owners of docks and canals, and of harbour and conservancy authorities,[1] apply for the purpose of limiting the liability of His Majesty in His capacity as the owner of any dock or canal, or in His capacity as a harbour or conservancy authority, and that all the relevant provisions of the said Acts have effect in relation to His Majesty accordingly.

(2) In this section the expressions "dock", "harbour", "owner", "harbour authority" and "conservancy authority" have respectively the same meanings as they have for the purposes of section two of the Merchant Shipping (Liability of Shipowners and Others) Act 1900.[2]

(3) In this section references to His Majesty include references to any Government department and to any officer of the Crown in his capacity as such.

1 For these provisions, see the M.S. (Liability of Shipowners and Others) Act 1900, s. 2 (as amended by the M.S. (Liability of Shipowners and Others) Act 1958, s. 1 (1)).

2 The definitions of "harbour authority" and "conservancy authority" will be found in M.S.A. 1894, s. 742, to which M.S. (Liability of Shipowners and Others) Act 1900, refers. "Dock" and "owners of a dock or canal" are defined in subss. (4) and (5) respectively of s. 2 of M.S. (Liability of Shipowners and Others) Act 1900. "Canal" remains undefined for the purpose of this Act or the M.S. Acts. There is a definition of

the word in the Telegraph Act 1863, for the purposes of that Act, but it can scarcely be applicable in this context, since the word is there defined to include " navigation " and " any dock."

Salvage claims against the Crown and Crown rights to salvage

1080 **8.**—(1) Subject to the provisions of this Act, the law relating to civil salvage, whether of life or property,[1] except sections five hundred and fifty-one to five hundred and fifty-four of the Merchant Shipping Act 1894, or any corresponding provisions relating to aircraft, shall apply in relation to salvage services rendered after the commencement of this Act in assisting any of His Majesty's ships [2] or aircraft, or in saving life therefrom, or in saving any cargo or apparel belonging to His Majesty in right of His Government in the United Kingdom, in the same manner as if the ship, aircraft, cargo or apparel belonged to a private person.[3]

(2) Where after the commencement of this Act [4] salvage services are rendered by or on behalf of His Majesty, whether in right of His Government in the United Kingdom or otherwise, His Majesty shall be entitled to claim salvage in respect of those services to the same extent as any other salvor, and shall have the same rights and remedies in respect of those services as any other salvor.[5]

[1] See note at head of s. 544, M.S.A. 1894. The provisions of the M.S. Acts as to salvage are contained in the M.S.A. 1894, ss. 544 to 571, s. 710 (Scotland) and s. 742 (definition of " salvor "), and in the Maritime Conventions Act 1911, ss. 6 and 7. As to aircraft, see the Aircraft (Wreck and Salvage) Order 1938 (S.R. & O. No. 136).
[2] The definition is in s. 38 (2).
[3] As to proceedings *in rem*, see s. 29.
[4] The commencement date was January 1, 1948 (S.R. & O. 1947 No. 2527).
[5] As to the effect of this subsection, see note immediately following text of s. 557, M.S.A. 1894.

Liability in connection with postal packets

1081 **9.** [*This section, which included provisions relating to liability for salvage in connection with postal packets was repealed by the Post Office Act* 1969, *s.* 141 *and Sched. II, Part II.*]

Transitional provisions

1082 **12.**—(1) When this Act comes into operation,[1] the preceding provisions of this Part of this Act (except subsections (3) and (4) of section five thereof and any provision which is expressly related to the commencement of this Act [2]) shall be deemed to have had effect as from the beginning of the thirteenth day of February, nineteen hundred and forty-seven:

Provided that where by virtue of this subsection proceedings are brought against the Crown in respect of a tort alleged to have been committed on or after the said thirteenth day of February and before the commencement of this Act, the Crown may rely upon the appropriate provisions of the law relating to the limitation of time for bringing proceedings as if this Act had at all material times been in force.

(2) Where any civil proceedings brought before the commencement of this Act have not been finally determined, and the court for the time being seized of those proceedings is of opinion that having regard to the provisions of this section the Crown ought to be made a party to the proceedings for the purpose of disposing completely and effectually of the questions involved in the cause or matter before the court, the court may order that the Crown be made a party thereto upon such terms, if any, as the court thinks just, and may make such consequential orders as the court thinks expedient.

[1] January 1, 1948. See note (1) to s. 54, *post*.
[2] *e.g.* s. 8 (2).

. . . . . .

PART IV

MISCELLANEOUS AND SUPPLEMENTAL

. . . .

Exclusion of proceedings in rem against the Crown

1083 **29.**—(1) Nothing in this Act shall authorise proceedings in rem in respect of any claim against the Crown, or the arrest, detention or sale of any of His Majesty's ships [1] or aircraft, or of any cargo or other property belonging to the Crown, or give to any person any lien on any such ship, aircraft, cargo or other property.[2]

(2) Where proceedings in rem have been instituted in the High Court or in a county court against any such ship, aircraft, cargo or other property, the court may, if satisfied, either on an application by the plaintiff for an order under this subsection or an application by the Crown to set aside the proceedings, that the proceedings were so instituted by the plaintiff in the reasonable belief that the ship, aircraft, cargo or other property did not belong to the Crown, order that the proceedings shall be treated as if they were in personam duly instituted against the Crown in accordance with the provisions of this Act, or duly instituted against any other person whom the court regards as the proper person to be sued in the circumstances, and that the proceedings shall continue accordingly.

Any such order may be made upon such terms, if any, as the court thinks just; and where the court makes any such order it may make such consequential orders as the court thinks expedient.

[1] See definition in s. 38 (2).
[2] The provisions of this subsection are also covered by the Administration of Justice Act 1956, s. 7 (3) and the County Courts Act 1959, s. 61 (2).

Limitation of actions

1084 **30.**—(1) Section eight of the Maritime Conventions Act 1911 (which relates to the limitation of actions in respect of damage or loss caused to or by vessels and the limitation of actions in respect of salvage services), shall *except in the case of proceedings in respect of any alleged fault of a ship of war or a ship for the time being appropriated to the service of the armed forces of the Crown or to the service of the Post Office* [1] apply in the case of His Majesty's ships as it applies in the case of other vessels:

Provided that the said section eight, as applied by this section, shall have effect as if the words from " and shall, if satisfied " to the end of the said section eight were omitted therefrom.[2]

(2) [3]

(3) In this section the expression " ship " includes any boat or other description of vessel used in navigation, and the expression "His Majesty's ships " shall be construed accordingly.[4]

1085 [1] The words in italics were repealed by the Law Reform (Limitation of Actions, etc.) Act 1954, ss. 5 (2), 8 (3) and Sched. For the application of this repeal to Northern Ireland, see *ibid.* s. 5 (4).

[2] As to the effect of this section, see note (1) to s. 8 of the Maritime Conventions Act 1911.

[3] This subsection, which entitled the Crown to rely upon the special limitation periods for proceedings against public authorities, has been repealed by the Law Reform (Limitation of Actions, etc.) Act 1954, s. 8 (3) and Sched., in consequence of the repeal, by s. 1 of that Act, of the Public Authorities Protection Act 1893, the Limitation Act 1939, s. 21, and similar enactments.

[4] See also the Hovercraft (Civil Liability) Order 1971 (S.I. No. 720) Art. 8 (2).

Interpretation

1086 **38.**—(1) Any reference in this Act to the provisions of this Act shall, unless the context otherwise requires, include a reference to rules of court or county court rules made for the purposes of this Act.

(2) In this Act, except in so far as the context otherwise requires or it is otherwise expressly provided, the following expressions have the meanings hereby respectively assigned to them, that is to say:—

" Agent," when used in relation to the Crown, includes an independent contractor employed by the Crown;

" Civil proceedings " includes proceedings in the High Court or the county court for the recovery of fines or penalties, but does not include proceedings on the Crown side of the King's Bench Division;

" His Majesty's aircraft " does not include aircraft belonging to His Majesty otherwise than in right of His Government in the United Kingdom;

" His Majesty's ships " means ships of which the beneficial interest is vested in His Majesty or which are registered as Government ships for the purposes of the Merchant Shipping Acts 1894 to 1940, or which are for the time being demised or subdemised to or in the exclusive possession of the Crown, except that the said expression does not include any ship in which His Majesty is interested otherwise than in right of His Government in the United Kingdom unless that ship is for the time being demised or subdemised to His Majesty in right of His said Government or in the exclusive possession of His Majesty in that right[1];

" Officer," in relation to the Crown, includes any servant of His Majesty, and accordingly (but without prejudice to the generality of the foregoing provision) includes a Minister of the Crown;

" Order " includes a judgment, decree, rule, award or declaration;

" Prescribed " means prescribed by rules of court or county court rules, as the case may be;

" Proceedings against the Crown " includes a claim by way of set-off or counterclaim raised in proceedings by the Crown;

" Ship " has the meaning assigned to it by section seven hundred and forty-two of the Merchant Shipping Act 1894[2];

" Statutory duty " means any duty imposed by or under any Act of Parliament.

087 (3) Any reference in this Act to His Majesty in His private capacity shall be construed as including a reference to His Majesty in right of His Duchy of Lancaster and the Duke of Cornwall.[3]

(4) Any reference in Parts III or IV of this Act to civil proceedings by or against the Crown, or to civil proceedings to which the Crown is a party, shall be construed as including a reference to civil proceedings to which the Attorney General, or any Government department, or any officer of the Crown as such is a party:

Provided that the Crown shall not for the purposes of Part III and IV of this Act be deemed to be a party to any proceedings by reason only that they are brought by the Attorney General upon the relation of some other person.

(5) Any reference in this Act to the armed forces of the Crown shall be construed as including a reference to the following forces:—

(*a*) the Women's Royal Naval Service;

(*b*) the Queen Alexandra's Royal Naval Nursing Service; and

(*c*) any other organisation established under the control of the Admiralty, the Army Council or the Air Council.

(6) References in this Act to any enactment shall be construed as references to that enactment as amended by or under any other enactment, including this Act.

[1] Note, however, the special definition of " His Majesty's ships " in s. 30 (3) for the purposes of that section.

[2] Note, however, the special definitions of " ship " in s. 5 (6) and in s. 30 (3) for the purposes of those sections, respectively.

[3] See also the Mineral Workings (Offshore Installations) Act 1971, s. 11 (6).

Savings

1088 **40.**—(1) Nothing in this Act shall apply to proceedings by or against, or authorise proceedings in tort to be brought against, His Majesty in His private capacity.

(2) Except as therein otherwise expressly provided, nothing in this Act shall:—

(*a*) affect the law relating to prize salvage, or apply to proceedings in causes or matters within the jurisdiction of the High Court as a prize court or to any criminal proceedings; or

(*b*) authorise proceedings to be taken against the Crown under or in accordance with this Act in respect of any alleged liability of the Crown arising otherwise than in respect of His Majesty's Government in the United Kingdom, or affect proceedings against the Crown in respect of any such alleged liability as aforesaid; or

(*c*) affect any proceedings by the Crown otherwise than in right of His Majesty's Government in the United Kingdom; or

(*d*) subject the Crown to any greater liabilities in respect of the acts or omissions of any independent contractor employed by the Crown than those to which the Crown would be subject in respect of such acts or omissions if it were a private person; or

(*e*) *subject the Crown, in its capacity as a highway authority, to any greater liability than that to which a local authority is subject in that capacity; or*[1]

(*f*) affect any rules of evidence or any presumption relating to the extent to which the Crown is bound by any Act of Parliament; or

(*g*) affect any right of the Crown to demand a trial at bar or to control or otherwise intervene in proceedings affecting its rights, property or profits; or

(*h*) affect any liability imposed on the public trustee or on the Consolidated Fund of the United Kingdom by the Public Trustee Act 1906;

and, without prejudice to the general effect of the foregoing provisions, Part III of this Act shall not apply to the Crown except in right of His Majesty's Government in the United Kingdom.

(3) A certificate of a Secretary of State:—

(*a*) to the effect that any alleged liability of the Crown arises otherwise than in respect of His Majesty's Government in the United Kingdom;

(*b*) to the effect that any proceedings by the Crown are proceedings otherwise than in right of His Majesty's Government in the United Kingdom;

shall, for the purposes of this Act, be conclusive as to the matter so certified.

[1] Subsection 2 (*e*) has been repealed, as from August 3, 1964, by the Highways (Miscellaneous Provisions) Act 1961, s. 1 (6), (8).

PART VI

EXTENT, COMMENCEMENT, SHORT TITLE, ETC.

Extent of Act

089 **52.** Subject to the provisions hereinafter contained with respect to Northern Ireland, this Act shall not affect the law enforced in court elsewhere than in England and Scotland, or the procedure in any such courts.

Provisions as to Northern Ireland

090 **53.**—(1) His Majesty may by Order in Council provide for extending this Act to Northern Ireland with such additions, exceptions and modifications as appear to His Majesty to be expedient.

(2) An Order in Council under this section may provide for amending the law both in its application to the Crown in right of His Majesty's Government in the United Kingdom and in its application to the Crown in right of His Majesty's Government in Northern Ireland.

(3) An Order in Council under this section may provide for amending the law:—

(*a*) with respect to the right of the Crown to sue in a county court in Northern Ireland; and

(*b*) with respect to the award of costs to or against the Crown in Northern Ireland.

(4) An Order in Council under this section may be varied or revoked by a further Order in Council made thereunder.

(5) An Order in Council under this section may include such provisions as appear to His Majesty to be incidental to or consequential on any provision contained in such an Order by virtue of the preceding provisions of this section.

(6) *So far as any provision contained in an Order in Council under this section deals with a matter with respect to which the Parliament of Northern Ireland has power to make laws, it shall, for the purposes of section six of the Government of Ireland Act 1920 (which relates to the power of the Parliament of Northern Ireland), be deemed to be a provision of an Act passed before the appointed day.*[1]

(7) An Order in Council under this section shall be laid before Parliament as soon as may be after it is made, and, if either House of Parliament,

within the next twenty-eight days on which that House has sat after such an Order is laid before it, resolves that the Order be annulled, the Order shall thereupon cease to have effect except as respects things previously done or omitted to be done, without prejudice, however, to the making of a new Order.

Notwithstanding anything in subsection (4) *of section one of the Rules Publication Act* 1893, *such an Order shall be deemed not to be a statutory rule to which that section applies.*[2]

1091 As to making these Orders in Council, see now the Statutory Instruments Act 1946.

The Northern Ireland (Crown Proceedings) Order 1949 (S.I. No. 1836) made under this section as amended by the Northern Ireland Act 1962, s. 7 (9), Sched. 1, Part II and by S.I. 1971 (No. 212), extends the Act (other than Parts V and VI thereof) to Northern Ireland with certain additions, exceptions and modifications.

For the application to Northern Ireland of the amendments made to this Act by the M.S. (Liability of Shipowners and Others) Act 1958, see *ibid.* s. 10 (2). For the application to Northern Ireland of the amendment made to this Act by the Law Reform (Limitation of Actions, etc.) Act 1954, see *ibid.* s. 5 (4).

[1] Words in italics repealed by Northern Ireland Constitution Act 1973, s. 41, Sched. 6.

[2] Words in italics repealed by S.L.R. Act 1953.

Short title and commencement

1092 **54.**—(1) This Act may be cited as the Crown Proceedings Act 1947.

(2) *This Act shall come into operation on such day, not later than the first day of January, nineteen hundred and forty-eight, as His Majesty may by Order in Council appoint.*[1]

[1] Subs. (2) was repealed as spent by the Statute Law Revision Act 1950. The appointed day was January 1, 1948; see the Crown Proceedings Act 1947 (Commencement) Order 1947 (S.R. & O. No. 2527).

MERCHANT SHIPPING ACT 1948

(11 & 12 Geo. 6, c. 44)

An Act to amend the provisions of the Merchant Shipping Acts relating to matters affected by certain International Conventions adopted at Seattle in the year nineteen hundred and forty-six.

[13th July, 1948.]

1093 Introductory Note.—This Act, parts of which came into force at different times (see note (2) to section 10, *post*), was passed to give effect to various International Conventions adopted at the 28th (Maritime) Session of the International Labour Conference held at Seattle in 1946. The objects of the Act are:

(1) To regulate the standards of crew accommodation in British ships (other than fishing boats). This matter is dealt with in sections 1–4 of the Act, which (*inter alia*) empower the Secretary of State for

Trade to make regulations, after consultation with representative organisations of owners of British ships and of seamen employed therein, with respect to new accommodation in British ships registered in the United Kingdom or ships being constructed to the order of persons qualified to be owners of British ships and which have not been registered in the United Kingdom or elsewhere. Provision is also made by section 3 for inspections of crew accommodation in certain circumstances by surveyors of ships, and by section 4, amendments are made in those provisions of the M.S. Acts 1894 and 1906 which relate to crew accommodation, being consequential on the provisions of section 1 of the Act. These provisions (*i.e.* sections 1–4) are applied, with certain modifications, to British fishing boats, by the M.S.A. 1950 (see *post*), which latter Act, unlike this Act, came into force for all purposes on December 10, 1950. The general effect of the provisions (which, together with regulations made under section 1, came into force on January 1, 1954) is to improve considerably the standard of crew accommodation in ships to which the provisions apply and in the case of such ships to replace the existing provisions of the M.S. Acts relating to this subject. (See M.S.A. 1894, s. 210, Sched. VI; M.S.A. 1906, s. 64.)

(2) To provide for the certification as A.B.s of seamen engaged in British ships registered in the United Kingdom. These provisions are contained in section 5 of the Act which came into operation on April 7, 1952, and in relation to such seamen the provisions as from a prescribed date (see notes to section 5, *post*) replace those contained in the M.S.A. 1894, s. 126 and M.S.A. 1906, s. 58, relating to this subject.

(3) To make further provisions relating to the certification of ships' cooks. Provision is made in section 6 of the Act for the extension of the provision of section 27 of the M.S.A. 1906, and for the recognition in certain circumstances of certificates granted in any part of H.M. dominions outside the United Kingdom.

(4) To provide for social security of seafarers. Section 7 of the Act deals with this subject and extends section 34 of the M.S.A. 1906, by making the owner generally liable for the expense of maintaining a member of the crew during any period of unemployment after being cured of any injury or illness until his conveyance and return to a proper return port.

The whole Act is prospectively repealed by the M.S.A. 1970, *s.* 100 (3). *Sched. V as from a day to be appointed. Accordingly, it is printed in italics save for section* 7 *which was repealed on January* 1, 1973, *see S.I.* 1972 *No.* 1977.

1094 WHEREAS at a session of the International Labour Conference held at Seattle in the year nineteen hundred and forty-six certain Conventions were adopted, dealing respectively with crew accommodation on board ship, the certification of able seamen, food and catering for crews on board ship, the certification of ships' cooks, and social security for seafarers:

And whereas it is expedient to make such amendments in the law relating to merchant shipping as will enable effect to be given to those Conventions or certain parts thereof, and otherwise to amend the Merchant Shipping Acts with respect to matters dealt with by those Conventions:

BE it therefore enacted, etc.

See note (1) to section 1 of the M.S. (International Labour Conventions) Act 1925, as to making reference to Conventions when words of the operative part of the statute are ambiguous.

Crew Accommodation and Food and Catering

Accommodation for seamen

1095 **1.**—(1) *The [Secretary of State]* [1] *may, after consultation* [2] *with such organisation or organisations as appear to him* [3] *to be representative both of owners of British ships* [4] *and of seamen employed therein, make regulations* [5] *with respect to the crew accommodation to be provided in ships of any class specified in the regulations, being ships in respect of which such regulations are authorised to be made by the next following section.*

(2) *Without prejudice to the generality of the foregoing subsection, regulations made thereunder* [5] *may, in particular—*

(*a*) *prescribe the minimum space per man which must be provided in any ship to which the regulations apply by way of sleeping accommodation for seamen* [6] *and apprentices, and the maximum number of persons by whom any specified part of such sleeping accommodation may be used;*

(*b*) *regulate the position in any such ship in which the crew accommodation or any part thereof may be located, and the standards to be observed in the construction, equipment and furnishing of any such accommodation;*

(*c*) *require the submission to a surveyor of ships* [7] *of plans and specifications of any works proposed to be carried out for the purpose of the provision or alteration of any such accommodation, and authorise the surveyor to inspect any such works;*

(*d*) *provide for the maintenance and repair of any such accommodation, and prohibit or restrict the use of any such accommodation for purposes other than those for which it is designed;*

and may make different provision in respect of different classes of ships and in respect of crew accommodation provided for different classes of persons.

[(2A) *The* [*Secretary of State*] *may exempt any ships or classes of ships from any requirements of regulations made under this section, either absolutely or subject to such conditions as he thinks fit.*[8]]

(3) *In this Act the expression " crew accommodation " includes sleeping rooms, mess rooms, sanitary accommodation, hospital accommodation, recreation accommodation, store rooms and catering accommodation provided for the use of seamen* [6] *and apprentices, not being accommodation which is also used by or provided for the use of passengers* [9]*:*

Provided that regulations made under this section may provide that any store rooms comprised in the crew accommodation of a ship shall, to such extent as may be prescribed by the regulations, be disregarded in estimating the space to be deducted from the tonnage of the ship under section seventy-nine of the principal Act in respect of crew accommodation.[10]

(4) *If the provisions of any regulations made under this section are contravened in the case of a ship, the owner or master of the ship shall be liable to a fine not exceeding one hundred pounds.*[11]

96 [1] *i.e.* The Secretary of State for Trade. See s. 12 (1) and note thereto.

[2] As to the effect of similar words appearing in s. 1 (1) of the New Towns Act 1946, see *Rollo* v. *Minister of Town and Country Planning* (1948) 64 T.L.R. 25, though having regard to the difference in subject-matter the principles stated in that case may well not apply under this section.

[3] Under these words the Secretary of State has the sole right to decide whether or not a particular organisation is representative of the interests concerned; see *Robinson* v. *Sunderland Corporation* [1899] 1 Q.B. 751, where similar words in s. 36 of the Public Health Act 1875 (now repealed and replaced by the Public Health Act 1936) were considered and judicially construed.

[4] See M.S.A. 1894 s. 1, note (1).

[5] The regulations generally in force are contained in the M.S. (Crew Accommodation) Regulations 1953 (S.I. No. 1036) as amended by S.I. 1954 No. 1660, S.I. 1961 No. 393, S.I. 1965 No. 1047 and S.I. 1975 No. 341. These regulations, upon repeal of this section, shall have effect as if made under s. 20 of the M.S.A. 1970: see *ibid.* Sched. 4, para. 6.

[6] See definitions in M.S.A. 1894, s. 742.

[7] See M.S.A. 1894, s. 724.

[8] Subs. (2A) was added by s. 1 (1) of the M.S.A. 1952.

[9] The term is presumably intended to be used in the sense of the definition in M.S. (Safety Convention) Act 1949, s. 26.

[10] The words omitted were repealed by the M.S.A. 1965, s. 7 (2) and Sched. 2.

[11] For summary prosecution of offence, see M.S.A. 1894, s. 680.

Application of section one

97 **2.**—(1) *Subject to the provisions of this section, regulations made under section one of this Act may apply—*

(*a*) *to any British ship* [1] *for the time being registered in the United Kingdom, whether so registered before or after the date on which the regulations come into force* [2]*; and*

(*b*) *to any ship which, at any time after that date, is being constructed to the order of a person qualified under the principal Act to be the owner of a British ship* [3] *and has not been registered in the United Kingdom or elsewhere, not being a fishing boat*[4] *or a ship being constructed for use as a fishing boat:*

Provided that, subject to the provisions of any Order in Council made under section nine of this Act, such regulations shall not apply to any ship under construction which is being constructed at any place in His Majesty's dominions outside the United Kingdom or in any foreign country or territory in which His Majesty has for the time being jurisdiction, or is intended on her first registration to be registered at any such place.

(2) *Where any ship to which regulations made under section one of this Act apply was a British ship*[1] *registered in the United Kingdom immediately before the date on which those regulations came into force,*[2] *then, unless and until, after that date, the ship is re-registered*[5] *in the United Kingdom or undergoes substantial structural alterations or repairs (not being repairs carried out in consequence of damage or in an emergency)—*

(*a*) *any requirements of the regulations (including any subsequent regulations amending or substituted for those regulations) relating to matters specified in paragraph (a) or paragraph (b) of subsection* (2) *of section one of this Act (in this section referred to as "the construction requirements") shall be deemed to be complied with in the case of the ship if the corresponding requirements of the law in force immediately before that date*[6] *are so complied with; and*

(*b*) *any requirements of any such regulations relating to matters specified in paragraph (c) of the said subsection* (2) *(in this section referred to as "the survey requirements") shall not apply to any works other than works proposed to be carried out for the purpose of any such alterations or repairs as aforesaid.*[7]

(3) *Where regulations made under section one of this Act become applicable—*

(*a*) *to a ship under construction of which the keel was laid before the date on which those regulations came into force*[2]*;*

(*b*) *to a ship registered as a British ship*[1] *in the United Kingdom after that date, not being a ship to which such regulations applied while she was under construction,*

or where any such ship as is mentioned in the last foregoing subsection is re-registered,[5] *altered or repaired as mentioned in that subsection, then, if, upon application made to him by the owner of the ship, the [Secretary of State]*[8] *is satisfied, after consultation*[9] *with the owner of the ship or an organisation which appears to him to be representative of owners of British ships, and with an organisation which appears to him to be representative of seamen employed in British ships, that such steps if any as are reasonable and practicable have been taken for securing compliance with the construction requirements* [10] *of the regulations in the case of the ship, he shall certify accordingly.*

(4) *In determining for the purposes of the last foregoing subsection what steps for securing compliance with the construction requirements* [10] *of any regulations are reasonable and practicable, the* [*Secretary of State*] [8] *shall have regard to the age of the ship, to the purpose for which she is or is intended to be used and to the nature of any alterations or repairs which are carried out, or* [11] *to the extent to which the construction of the ship had been completed before the date on which the regulations came into force,*[2] *as the case may be.*

(5) *Where any such certificate is issued by the* [*Secretary of State*] [8] *as aforesaid, then, subject to compliance with such conditions, if any, as may be specified in the certificate—*

(*a*) *the construction requirements* [10] *of the regulations (including any subsequent regulations amending or substituted for those regulations) shall be deemed to be complied with in the case of the ship, and*

(*b*) *the survey requirements* [12] *of any such regulations shall not apply to any works other than works proposed to be carried out for the purpose of any such alterations or repairs as are mentioned in subsection* (2) *of this section*:

Provided that on the occurrence of any such event as is mentioned in the said subsection (2), *the provisions of this subsection shall cease to have effect in relation to the ship, but without prejudice to the issue of a further certificate under subsection* (3) *of this section.*

098 Subsections (2) to (5) of this section are applied with modifications in relation to fishing boats for the purposes of s. 1 of M.S.A. 1950, by s. 1 (5) of that Act and Sched. I, paras. 1–4, thereto.

1 See M.S.A. 1894, s. 1, note (1).
2 The regulations came into force on January 1, 1954. See note (5) to s. 1.
3 See M.S.A. 1894, s. 1, and notes thereto.
4 Presumably the definition in M.S.A. 1894, s. 370, applies.
5 See M.S.A. 1894, ss. 48–54. It would seem that " re-registered " is intended to have the same meaning as the words " registered anew " in M.S.A. 1894, s. 48 (1), in contradistinction to a " registry of alterations," but the wording is obscure.
6 See M.S.A. 1894, s. 210, and M.S.A. 1906, s. 64.
7 That is, " substantial alterations or repairs (not being carried out in consequence of damage or in an emergency)."
8 *i.e.* the Secretary of State for Trade; see s. 12 (1) and note thereto.
9 See notes (2) and (3) to s. 1.
10 See subs. (2) (*a*).
11 The words following " or " are applicable only to the ships covered by subs. (3) (*a*).
12 See subs. (2) (*b*).

Inspections of crew accommodation

099 3.—(1) *Whenever a ship to which regulations made under section one of this Act apply* [1] *is registered or re-registered* [2] *in the United Kingdom, whenever a complaint in respect of the crew accommodation in any such ship* *is duly made in accordance with the regulations, and on such other occasions as may be prescribed by the regulations, a surveyor of ships* [3] *shall inspect the crew accommodation.*[4]

(2) *If, upon any such inspection, the surveyor is satisfied that the crew accommodation* [4] *complies with the regulations, he shall (except where the inspection is made in consequence of a complaint) give to the registrar of British ships* [5] *a certificate specifying as space deductible under section seventy-nine of the principal Act* [6] *the whole of the space comprised in that accommodation, except any part thereof required by the regulations to be disregarded in estimating the space so to be deducted.*

(3) *If, upon any such inspection, it appears to the surveyor that the accommodation* [4] *does not comply in all respects with the regulations, he may give to the registrar a certificate specifying as space deductible as aforesaid such part of the space comprised in the accommodation as he considers appropriate having regard to the extent to which it complies with the regulations, but if he does not give such a certificate he shall report to the registrar that no space is deductible as aforesaid:*

Provided that the surveyor shall not be required to make such a report as aforesaid—

(*a*) *if the inspection is made on the occasion of the registration or re-registration* [2] *of the ship; or*

(*b*) *if it appears to him that the failure to comply with the regulations is not substantial and will be remedied within a reasonable time.*

(4) *Where any certificate is given or report made under the foregoing provisions of this section in respect of a ship already registered, any certificate previously given thereunder in respect of that ship shall cease to have effect, and the registered tonnage of the ship shall be altered accordingly.*

(5) *In respect of any inspection of a ship carried out by a surveyor for the purposes of this section, there shall be paid such fees as may be prescribed by regulations made under section one of this Act.*[7]

(6) *Regulations made under section one of this Act may require the master of any ship to which the regulations apply, or any officer authorised by him for the purpose, to carry out such inspections of the crew accommodation* [4] *as may be prescribed by the regulations, and to record in the official log such particulars of any such inspection as may be so prescribed.*[8]

This section is applied with modifications in relation to fishing boats for the purposes of M.S.A. 1950, s. 1, by s. 1 (5) of that Act and Sched. I, paras. 5–10, thereto.

1 See s. 2 and note (5) to s. 1.
2 See note (5) to s. 2.
3 See M.S.A. 1894, s. 724, for definition.
4 See definition in s. 1 (3).
5 See M.S.A. 1894, s. 4, as to registrars of British ships.
6 Section 79 of the M.S.A. 1894 was repealed by the M.S.A. 1965, ss. 5 (1), 7 (1), and Sched. 2. See now *ibid.* s. 1.
7 Fees for such inspections are prescribed by reg. 36 of the M.S. (Crew Accommodation) Regulations 1953 (S.I. 1953 No. 1036) as amended by M.S. (Fees) Regulations 1975 (S.I. No. 341).

[8] As to entries in the official log, see M.S.A., 1970, s. 68. The powers given by this subsection are exercised in reg. 34 of the M.S. (Crew Accommodation) Regulations 1953 (S.I. 1953 No. 1036) as amended by M.S. Fees (Regulations) 1975 (S.I. No. 341).

Amendments consequential on section 1

100 **4.**—(1) [1]

(2) [1]

(3) *Section two hundred and ten of the principal Act* [2] *and the Sixth Schedule to that Act, and section sixty-four of the Merchant Shipping Act* 1906, *shall not apply to any ship to which regulations made under section one of this Act apply (but without prejudice to the provisions of subsection* (2) *of section two of this Act); and the proviso to paragraph (a) of subsection* (2) *of section five hundred and three of the principal Act* [2] *shall cease to have effect:*

Provided that any certificate given in relation to any such ship as aforesaid, under paragraph (3) *of the said Sixth Schedule before the date on which the regulations apply thereto shall have effect for the purposes of this Act and of the principal Act* [2] *as if it had been given under the last foregoing section.*

The section is applied with modifications in relation to fishing boats for the purposes of s. 1 of M.S.A. 1950, by s. 1 (5) of that Act, and Sched. I, paras. 11–13, thereto.

[1] The subsections omitted were repealed by the M.S.A. 1965, s. 7 (2), and Sched. 2.
[2] *i.e.* M.S.A. 1894; see s. 12 (1), *post*.

Certification of Able Seamen

Rating of seamen

101 **5.**—(1) *After such date as may be prescribed by regulations* [1] *made under the following provisions of this section, a seaman* [2] *engaged in any British ship* [3] *registered in the United Kingdom shall not be rated as A.B. unless he is the holder of a certificate of competency granted in pursuance of those regulations.*

(2) *The* [*Secretary of State*] [4] *may make regulations* [1] *providing for the grant of certificates of competency as A.B. for the purposes of this section; and such regulations shall in particular direct that no such certificate shall be granted to any person unless—*

(*a*) *he has reached such minimum age as may be prescribed by the regulations; and*

(*b*) *he has performed such qualifying service at sea as may be so prescribed; and*

(*c*) *he has passed such examination as may be so prescribed;*

Provided that the regulations may authorise the grant of a certificate thereunder to any person, notwithstanding that he has not complied with the conditions aforesaid, if he shows, in such manner as may be prescribed by the regulations, that he was serving as A.B., or in an equivalent or superior deck rating, on the date on which the regulations came into force, or had so served at any time before that date.[5]

(3) *Regulations made under this section may make such consequential provisions as appear to the [Secretary of State] to be necessary or expedient, including provision—*

(*a*) *for the payment of such fees as may be prescribed by the regulations in respect of any application for the grant or replacement of a certificate thereunder;*

(*b*) *for applying to certificates granted under the regulations, subject to such adaptations and modifications as may be so prescribed, the provisions of section one hundred and four of the principal Act (which relates to forgery and other offences relating to certificates of competency of ships' officers granted under that Act).*

(4) *Where provision is made by the law of any part of His Majesty's dominions outside the United Kingdom for the grant of certificates of competency as A.B., and the [Secretary of State] reports to His Majesty that he is satisfied that the conditions under which such a certificate is granted require standards of competency not lower than those required for the grant of a certificate in pursuance of regulations made under this section, His Majesty may by Order in Council direct that certificates granted in that part of His Majesty's dominions shall have the same effect for the purposes of this section as if they had been granted in pursuance of such regulations as aforesaid; and any such Order may apply to any such certificate any of the provisions of the regulations relating to certificates granted thereunder.*[6]

(5) *Any superintendent* [7] *or other officer before whom, at any time after such date as may be prescribed by regulations* [1] *made under this section, a seaman is engaged in any British ship* [3] *registered in the United Kingdom, shall refuse to enter the seaman as A.B. on the agreement with the crew* [8] *unless the seaman produces a certificate of competency granted in pursuance of the regulations or such other proof that he is the holder of such a certificate as may appear to the superintendent or other officer to be satisfactory.*

(6) *As from such date as may be prescribed by regulations* [1] *made under this section, section one hundred and twenty-six of the principal Act and section fifty-eight of the Merchant Shipping Act* 1906, *shall cease to have effect in relation to any seamen for the time being engaged in a British ship registered in the United Kingdom.*

1102 [1] The regulations now in force are the M.S. (Certificates of Competency as A.B.) Regulations 1970 (S.I. No. 294) as amended by M.S. (Fees) Regulations 1975 (S.I. No. 341).

[2] "Seaman" is defined in M.S.A. 1894, s. 742.

[3] See M.S.A. 1894, s. 1, note (1).

[4] *i.e.* the Secretary of State for Trade.

[5] See M.S.A., 1894, s. 126, and M.S.A., 1906, s. 58.

[6] The following Orders in Council have been made under this subsection:—

(i) the M.S. (Certificate of Competency as A.B.) (New Zealand) Order 1956 (S.I. No. 1895);

(ii) the M.S. (Certificates of Competency as A.B.) (Barbados) Order 1957 (S.I. No. 1371);
(iii) the M.S. (Certificates of Competency as A.B.) (Republic of Ireland) Order 1958 (S.I. No. 1048);
(iv) the M.S. (Certificates of Competency as A.B.) (Canada) Order 1959 (S.I. No. 2213);
(v) the M.S. (Certificates of Competency as A.B.) (Mauritius) Order 1960 (S.I. No. 1662);
(vi) the M.S. (Certificates of Competency as A.B.) (Trinidad and Tobago) Order 1960 (S.I. No. 1663);
(vii) the M.S. (Certificates of Competency as A.B.) (Ghana) Order 1963 (S.I. No. 1316);
(viii) the M.S. (Certificates of Competency as A.B.) (Nigeria) Order 1964 (S.I. No. 700);
(ix) the M.S. (Certificates of Competency as A.B.) (Gilbert and Ellice Islands Colony) Order 1972 (S.I. No. 1105).

[7] See M.S.A. 1970, s. 81.
[8] See M.S.A. 1970 ss. 1 and 2.

Certification of Ships' Cooks

Certificated cooks for foreign-going ships

103 **6.**—(1) *Where provision is made by the law of any part of His Majesty's dominions outside the United Kingdom for the issue of certificates of competency as ship's cook, and the Minister reports to His Majesty that he is satisfied that the conditions under which such certificates are granted require standards of competency not lower than those required for the grant of certificates of competency in cooking for the purposes of section twenty-seven of the Merchant Shipping Act* 1906, *His Majesty may by Order in Council direct that the holders of such certificates granted in that part of His Majesty's dominions shall be deemed to be duly certificated within the meaning of the said section twenty-seven.*[1]

(2) *If the Minister* [2] *reports to His Majesty that he is satisfied that it is the wish of such organisation or organisations as appear to him* [3] *to be representative both of owners of British ships* [4] *and of seamen employed therein that the provisions of the said section twenty-seven should, with such exceptions, adaptations and modifications, if any, as may be specified in such report, apply—*

(*a*) *to such classes of British ships, other than the class mentioned in the said section,*[5] *as may be specified in the report, or*

(*b*) *to British ships going to sea from such places, other than places mentioned in the said section,*[5] *as may be so specified,*

and that it is expedient that the provisions of the said section should so apply, His Majesty may by Order in Council direct that the said provisions shall, with such exceptions, adaptations and modifications as aforesaid, apply to that class of ships or to ships going to sea from those places:

Provided that nothing in this subsection shall authorise the said provisions to be applied to ships registered in any Dominion within the meaning of the Statute of Westminster 1931 [. . .] [6] *or in India, Pakistan,* [*Ceylon, Ghana, Malaysia, the Republic of Cyprus, Nigeria, Sierra Leone, Tanganyika,*

Jamaica, Trinidad and Tobago, Uganda, Kenya, Zanzibar, Malawi, Malta, The Gambia, Guyana, Singapore, Barbados, or Mauritius].[7]

(3) *His Majesty may by Order in Council direct that the provisions of the said section twenty-seven shall extend, with such exceptions, adaptations and modifications, if any, as may be specified in the Order, to any country or territory to which, under the following provisions of this Act,*[8] *any of the provisions of this Act can be extended.*

1104 This section has not yet come into operation; see s. 10 as to commencement of the Act.

[1] Despite the fact that the section has yet to come into force, two Orders in Council have purported to have been made pursuant to it; see:—
 (i) the M.S. (Certificates of Competency as Ship's Cook) (Canada) Order 1963 (S.I. No. 374);
 (ii) the M.S. (Certificates of Competency as Ship's Cook) (Republic of Ireland) Order 1964 (S.I. No. 701).

[2] *i.e.* the Secretary of State for Trade. See s. 12 (1) and note thereto.

[3] See note (3) to s. 1.

[4] As to " British ship " see M.S.A. 1894, s. 1, and notes thereto.

[5] The " class mentioned " is foreign-going ships of 1,000 tons and upwards gross tonnage, going to sea from any place in the British Islands, or on the continent of Europe between the River Elbe and Brest inclusive.

[6] The words omitted were repealed by the Newfoundland (Consequential Provisions) Act 1950, s. 1 (4) and Part II of Schedule thereto. Newfoundland is now part of the Dominion of Canada (see British North America Act 1949).

[7] The passage printed in square brackets is the effect of a number of amendments to this subsection made successively by the Ghana Independence Act 1957, s. 4 (4), Sched. II, para. 8; the Federation of Malaya Independence Act 1957, s. 2 (1), Sched. I, para. 10 (*b*) (as construed in accordance with the Malaysia Act 1963, s. 3 (2) and Sched. 2, para. 1); the Cyprus Act 1960, s. 3 (2), Sched., para. 10 (2); the Nigeria Independence Act 1960, s. 3 (4), Sched. II, para. 8; the Sierra Leone Independence Act 1961, s. 3 (3), Sched. III, para. 9; the Tanganyika Independence Act 1961, s. 3 (4), Sched. II, para. 8; the Jamaica Independence Act 1962, s. 3 (5), Sched. II, para. 8; the Trinidad and Tobago Independence Act 1962, s. 3 (4), Sched. II, para. 8; the Uganda Independence Act 1962, s. 3 (4), Sched. III, para. 8; the Kenya Independence Act 1963, s. 4 (4) and Sched. 2, para. 8; the Zanzibar Act 1963, s. 1 (2) and Sched. 1, para. 8 (2); the Malawi Independence Act 1964, s. 4 (4) and Sched. 2, para. 8; the Malta Independence Act 1964, s. 4 (4) and Sched. 2, para. 8; The Gambia Independence Act 1964, s. 4 (4) and Sched. 2, para. 8; the Guyana Independence Act 1966, s. 4 (4) and Sched. 2, para. 8; the Singapore Act 1966, s. 1 and Sched., para. 11; the Barbados Independence Act 1966, s. 4 (5) and Sched. 2, para. 8; the Mauritius Independence Act 1968, s. 4 (3) and Sched. 2, para. 8.

[8] See s. 9, below.

1105 **7.** [*This section, which related to expenses of maintenance in case of injury or illness, was repealed by the M.S.A.* 1970, *s.* 100 (3), *Sched.* 5, *as from January* 1, 1973; *see S.I.* 1972 *No.* 1977.]

Supplemental

Payment of fees into the Exchequer

1106 **8.** *Any fees received by the* [*Secretary of State*] [1] *under this Act or regulations made thereunder shall be paid into the Exchequer.*

[1] *i.e.* the Secretary of State for Trade. See s. 12 (1) and note thereto.

Application to British possessions, etc.

1107 **9.**—(1) *His Majesty may by Order in Council direct* [1] *that any of the provisions of this Act (including any enactments for the time being in force* *amending or substituted for the said provisions) shall extend, with such exceptions, adaptations and modifications, if any, as may be specified in the Order, to the Isle of Man, any of the Channel Islands,* [. . .] [2] *or any colony.*

(2) *The Foreign Jurisdiction Act* 1890, *shall have effect as if the provisions of this Act were included among the enactments which, by virtue of section five of that Act, may be extended by Order in Council to foreign countries in which for the time being His Majesty has jurisdiction.*

(3) *His Majesty may by Order in Council direct that any provision of this Act shall apply, subject to such exceptions, adaptations and modifications, if any, as may be specified in the Order, to ships registered in any country or territory to which the provisions of this Act can be extended by virtue of subsection* (1) *or subsection* (2) *of this section, or under construction in any such country or territory, or to be registered on first registration in any such country or territory, as it applies to ships registered, under construction or to be registered on first registration, as the case may be, in the United Kingdom.*[3]

108 This section is applied with modifications in relation to fishing boats for the purposes of s. 1 of M.S.A. 1950 by s. 1 (5) of that Act and Sched. I, paras. 14–17, thereto.

[1] The following Orders have been made under this subsection:
 (i) M.S.A. 1948 (Cayman Islands) Order 1960 (S.I. No. 1371), as amended by S.I. 1966 No. 84;
 (ii) the M.S.A. 1948 (Isle of Man Ships) Order 1960 (S.I. No. 1377);
 (iii) M.S.A. 1948 (Isle of Man) Order 1960 (S.I. No. 1378).

[2] The word omitted was repealed by the Newfoundland (Consequential Provisions) Act 1950, s. 1 (1) and Part I of Schedule thereto. Newfoundland is now part of the Dominion of Canada (see British North America Act 1949).

[3] No orders appear to have been made under this subsection.

Commencement

109 **10.**—(1) *This Act shall come into operation on such date as the* [*Secretary of State*] [1] *may by order appoint, and different dates may be appointed for the purposes of different provisions of this Act.*[2]

(2) *The date or dates to be appointed for the purposes of the coming into operation of the provisions of this Act hereinafter mentioned shall be the date or dates on which the relevant Conventions come into force for the United Kingdom, that is to say—*

(*a*) *in respect of sections one to four of this Act, the Conventions dealing with crew accommodation on board ship and with food and catering for crews on board ship;*

(*b*) *in respect of section five, the Convention dealing with the certification of able seamen;*

(*c*) *in respect of section six, the Convention dealing with the certification of ships' cooks; and*

(*d*) *in respect of section seven, the Convention dealing with social security for seafarers:*

Provided that if the [*Secretary of State*] *is satisfied that it is the wish of such organisation or organisations as appear to him to be representative both of owners of British ships and of seamen employed therein, that any such provision of this Act as aforesaid should come into operation on a date earlier than the date aforesaid, and that it is expedient that it should come into operation on that date, he may appoint that date as the date on which that provision is to come into operation.*[2]

1110 For text of the various Conventions, see Cmd. 7109.
[1] *i.e.* the Secretary of State for Trade. See s. 12 (1) and note thereto.
[2] By M.S.A. 1948 (Commencement No. 1) Order 1952 (S.I. 1952 No. 739), the whole of s. 5, and ss. 8–12 in so far as they relate to the rating of seamen and were not in operation in relation thereto, came into operation on April 7, 1952, notwithstanding that the convention dealing with the certification of able seamen had not come into force for the U.K. By M.S.A. 1948 (Commencement No. 2) Order 1953 (S.I. 1953 No. 1035), the whole of ss. 1–4 inclusive, and ss. 8–12 in so far as they relate to crew accommodation on board ship and to food and catering for crews on board ship and are not in operation in relation thereto, came into operation on January 1, 1954, notwithstanding that the conventions dealing with crew accommodation on board ship and with food and catering for crews on board ship had not come into force for the U.K. Accordingly, s. 6 has not yet come into operation and s. 7 never came into operation.

Regulations and orders

1111 **11.**—(1) *Any power of the Secretary of State to make regulations or orders under the foregoing provisions of this Act shall be exercisable by statutory instrument.*

(2) *Any Order in Council made under the foregoing provisions of this Act and any instrument containing regulations made under section one of this Act shall be subject to annulment in pursuance of a resolution of either House of Parliament.*

Subs. (2) of this section is applied with modifications in relation to fishing boats for the purposes of s. 1 of M.S.A. 1950, by s. 1 (5) of that Act and Sched. I, paras. 14–17, thereto.

Interpretation, construction and citation

1112 **12.**—(1) *In this Act the following expressions have the meanings hereby respectively assigned to them, that is to say—*

" crew accommodation " has the meaning assigned to it by section one of this Act;

" Minister " means the Minister of Transport [1];

" owner," in relation to a ship under construction, means the person to whose order she is constructed;

" principal Act " means the Merchant Shipping Act 1894.

(2) *Except so far as the context otherwise requires, any reference in this Act to any other enactment shall be construed as a reference to that enactment as amended, extended or applied by or under any other enactment, including this Act.*

(3) *This Act shall be construed as one* [2] *with the Merchant Shipping Acts* 1894 *to* 1938, *and without prejudice to the generality of this provision, references in those Acts to the Merchant Shipping Acts shall be construed as including references to this Act.*

(4) *This Act may be cited as the Merchant Shipping Act* 1948, *and the Merchant Shipping Acts* 1894 *to* 1938, *and this Act may be cited together as the Merchant Shipping Acts* 1894 *to* 1948.[3]

[1] Now the Secretary of State for Trade.
[2] See note (1) to s. 9 of M.S. (Mercantile Marine Fund) Act 1898.
[3] Now the Merchant Shipping Acts 1894 to 1974: see § 1639.

MERCHANT SHIPPING (SAFETY CONVENTION) ACT 1949

(12 & 13 Geo. 6, c. 43)

An Act to enable effect to be given to an International Convention for the Safety of Life at Sea, signed in London on the tenth day of June, nineteen hundred and forty-eight; to amend the provisions of the Merchant Shipping Acts 1894 to 1948, relating to the construction of passenger steamers, to life-saving appliances, wireless and radio navigational aids and to other matters affected by the said Convention, and to amend the provisions of those Acts relating to fees.

[14th July, 1949.]

1113 Introductory Note.—The provisions of this Act came into force on November 19, 1952 (see S.I. No. 1418, made under section 37). The earlier history of the development of the progress towards international uniformity in relation to safety of life at sea will be found in the introductory note to M.S. (Safety and Load Line Conventions) Act 1932, *ante*. The main object of the present Act was to give effect to the International Convention for the Safety of Life at Sea, which was signed on behalf of H.M. Government on June 10, 1948. This Convention, the text of which is published in Cmd. 7492, as between the contracting Governments replaced and abrogated the International Convention for Safety of Life at Sea of 1929.

The Act made changes in the law relating to construction and equipment of ships, life-saving appliances, wireless telegraphy in ships, safety certificates, fees, and other miscellaneous matters including distress signals, carriage of dangerous goods and grain. The Act also made provision for contribution towards a North Atlantic ice service (see section 25). Almost the whole of Part I of the M.S. (Safety and Load Line Conventions) Act 1932 was replaced or substituted by sections in the Act. The 1948 Convention was replaced by the International Convention for the Safety of Life at Sea, signed in London on June 17, 1960 (Cmnd. 2812). This Act, therefore, has effect as if (a) for reference therein, except in the preamble, to the Safety Convention there were substituted references to the 1960 Convention; and (b) reference therein to this Act, except in s. 37 (1) and (4), included references to the M.S.A. 1964 (see *ibid.* s. 1).

1114 Whereas a Convention (in this Act referred to as " the Safety Convention ") was signed on behalf of the government of the United Kingdom in London on the tenth day of June, nineteen hundred and forty-eight, for promoting safety of life at sea by establishing in common agreement uniform principles and rules directed thereto:

And whereas it is intended that the Safety Convention shall replace the International Convention for the Safety of Life at Sea 1929, which is set out in the First Schedule to the Merchant Shipping (Safety and Load Line Conventions) Act 1932:

And whereas it is expedient to enable effect to be given to the Safety Convention, and to amend the provisions of the Merchant Shipping Acts 1894 to 1948, relating to the construction of passenger steamers, to life-saving appliances, wireless and radio navigational aids and to other matters affected by the Safety Convention, and to amend the provisions of those Acts relating to fees:

BE it therefore enacted, etc.

See note (1) to section 1 of M.S. (International Conventions) Act 1925, as to making reference to conventions when words of the operative part of the statute are ambiguous.

Construction and Equipment

Construction rules

1115 **1.**—(1) The [Secretary of State] [1] may make rules [2] (in this Act called " construction rules ") prescribing the requirements that the hull, equipments and machinery of British passenger steamers [3] registered in the United Kingdom shall comply with; and the rules shall include such requirements as appear to the [Secretary of State] [1] to implement the provisions of the Safety Convention [4] prescribing the requirements that the hull, equipments and machinery of passenger steamers shall comply with, except so far as those provisions are implemented by the rules for life-saving appliances,[5] the radio rules,[6] the rules for direction-finders [7] or the collision regulations.[8]

(2) The powers conferred on the [Secretary of State] [1] by this section shall be in addition to the powers conferred by any other enactment enabling him to prescribe the requirements that passenger steamers shall comply with.

1116 [1] *i.e.* the Secretary of State for Trade; see s. 36.

[2] The rules at present in force under this section are the M.S. (Construction) Rules 1965 (S.I. No. 1103). This power has been extended to include rules requiring the provision of damage control plans and stability information for passenger steamers: see M.S.A. 1964, s. 8. As to cargo ships, see *ibid.* s. 2. For power of the Secretary of State to exempt from rules, see s. 28.

[3] For definition, see s. 26. As to what ships are " British," see M.S.A. 1894, s. 1 and notes thereto.

[4] See Introductory Note, § 1113, *ante*.

[5] See s. 2.

[6] See s. 3.

[7] See s. 5.

[8] These are defined by s. 36 as meaning regulations made under s. 418 of M.S.A. 1894. Those currently in force will be found in *British Shipping Laws*, Vol. 4, *Marsden on Collisions at Sea*, 11th ed. and the Supplement thereto.

Rules for life-saving appliances

1117 **2.**—(1) For section four hundred and twenty-seven of the Merchant Shipping Act 1894 (in this Act referred to as " the principal Act "), there shall be substituted the following section:—

[*The new section as amended subsequently will be found printed in the text as section* 427 *of the M.S.A.* 1894.]

(2) The rules for life-saving appliances [1] shall include such requirements as appear to the Secretary of State [2] to implement the provisions of the Safety Convention [3] relating to the matters mentioned in the said section four hundred and twenty-seven.

(3) [4]

[1] See s. 427 of M.S.A. 1894.
[2] *i.e.* the Secretary of State for Trade.
[3] See note (4) to s. 1.
[4] The subsection omitted, which substituted a subsection for s. 9 (1) of the M.S.A. 1906, was repealed by the M.S.A. 1970 as from January 1, 1973; see S.I. 1972 No. 1977.

[The next page is 466]

Radio rules

1118 **3.**[1] (1) The [Secretary of State for Trade] may make rules [2] (in this Act called " radio rules ") requiring ships to which this section applies to be provided with radio equipment of such a nature (but not including a radio navigational aid [3]) as may be prescribed by the rules and to maintain such a radio service and to carry such number of radio officers or operators, of such grades and possessing such qualifications, as may be so prescribed; and the rules may contain provisions for preventing so far as practicable electrical interference by other apparatus on board with the equipment provided under the rules.

(2) This section applies to—

(*a*) sea-going ships [4] registered in the United Kingdom;

(*b*) other sea-going ships while they are in the United Kingdom or the territorial waters thereof.

(3) Radio rules shall include such requirements as appear to the [Secretary of State for Trade] to implement the provisions of the Convention [5] for the Safety of Life at Sea signed in London on 17th June 1960 as from time to time amended, so far as those provisions relate to radio telegraphy and radio telephony.

(4) Without prejudice to the generality of the preceding provisions of this section, radio rules may—

(*a*) prescribe the duties of radio officers and operators, including the duty of keeping a radio log-book;

(*b*) apply to any radio log-book required to be kept under the rules any of the provisions of any regulations with respect to official log-books made under section 68 of the Merchant Shipping Act 1970.

(5) If any radio officer or operator contravenes any rules made in pursuance of subsection (4) (*a*) of this section, he shall be liable to a fine not exceeding £10, and if radio rules are contravened in any other respect in relation to any ship, the owner or master of the ship shall be liable on conviction on indictment to a fine not exceeding £500, or on summary conviction to a fine not exceeding £100.

(6) If a ship to which this section applies is not provided with radio equipment or radio officers or operators in conformity with radio rules the ship, if in the United Kingdom, may be detained.[6]

1119 [1] This section was substituted by s. 85 of the M.S.A. 1970: § 1461, *post*.

For further provisions relating to the regulation of wireless telegraphy on ships, see the Wireless Telegraphy Act 1949 (s. 6 of which applies certain provisions of that Act to British sea-going ships and also deals with foreign sea-going ships while within the United Kingdom).

[2] The rules at present in force under this section are the M.S. (Radio) Rules 1965 (S.I. No. 1107) as amended by S.I. 1969 No. 1315 and the M.S. (Radio) (Fishing Vessels) Rules 1974 (S.I. No. 1919). The rules made under this section may prescribe requirement for

such portable radio apparatus as boats or life raft may be required to carry by the rules for life-saving appliances made under the M.S.A. 1894, s. 427: see M.S.A. 1964, s. 10.

[3] For definition of " radio navigational aid," see s. 36.

[4] *Cf. The Salt Union* v. *Wood* [1893] 1 Q.B. 370, where the court held that a sea-going ship is one that in fact goes to sea, and not merely could go to sea; and that a steamer of 142 tons gross register, exclusively used to carry salt on the River Weaver and the tidal waters of the River Mersey, but not beyond the port of Liverpool, was not a " sea-going " ship within M.S.A. 1854, s. 109; see M.S.A. 1894, s. 260.

As to " British ships," see M.S.A. 1894, s. 1 and notes thereto. As to the issue of certificates in respect of fishing vessels that comply with the radio rules; see the Fishing Vessels (Safety Provisions) Act 1970, ss. 3, 4 and 9 (1).

[5] See § 1113, *ante*.

[6] As to the procedure for detention, see M.S.A. 1894, s. 692. See also as to notice of detention of foreign ships, s. 35 (4), *post*.

Radio surveyors

120 **4.** Wireless-telegraphy surveyors appointed under section seven hundred and twenty-four of the principal Act [1] as amended by section eight of the Merchant Shipping (Safety and Load Line Conventions) Act 1932, shall be known as radio surveyors.

[1] " Principal Act " is defined by s. 36 of the M.S.A. 1894.

[The next page is 468]

Rules for direction-finders

1121 5.[1]—(1) The [Secretary of State] [2] may make rules [3] (in this Act called " rules for direction-finders ") requiring ships to which this section applies to be provided with a direction-finder of such a nature as may be prescribed by the rules.

(2) This section applies to—

(*a*) British ships [4] registered in the United Kingdom;

(*b*) other ships while they are within any port in the United Kingdom,

being ships of sixteen hundred tons gross tonnage [5] *or upwards.*[6]

(3) The said rules shall include such requirements as appear to the [Secretary of State] [2] to implement the provisions of the Safety Convention [7] relating to direction-finders.

(4) Without prejudice to the generality of the preceding provisions of this section, rules under this section may provide for the position of the direction-finder in the ship, for the communication between the direction-finder and the bridge, for testing the direction-finder at intervals and as occasion may require and for recording the result of the tests.

(5) If any of the said rules is not complied with in relation to any ship, the owner or master of the ship shall be liable to a fine not exceeding one hundred pounds.[8]

1122 [1] This section replaces, with modifications and additions, s. 6 (2) of the M.S. (Safety and Load Line Conventions) Act 1932, which is repealed by s. 37 (5) and the Third Schedule, *post*.

[2] *i.e.* the Secretary of State for Trade. For power to exempt from rules, see s. 28.

[3] The rules at present in force under this section are the M.S. (Direction-Finders) Rules 1965 (S.I. No. 1112). For power of Secretary of State to exempt from rules, see s. 28.

[4] As to " British ships," see M.S.A. 1894, s. 1 and notes thereto. As to the issue of certificates in respect of fishing vessels that comply with the rules for direction-finders, see the Fishing Vessels (Safety Provisions) Act 1970, ss. 3, 4 and 9 (1).

[5] See note (8) to s. 3.

[6] The words in italics were repealed by the M.S.A. 1970, ss. 85 (2), 100 (3) and Sched. 5 as from the 1st November, 1974.

[7] See note (4) to s. 1.

[8] As to the recovery of fines, see M.S.A. 1894, ss. 680–682.

Further provisions as to radio navigational aids

1123 6.[1]—(1) The [Secretary of State for Trade] may make rules [2]—

(*a*) requiring ships to which this section applies to be provided with such radio navigational aids,[3] other than direction-finders, as may be specified in the rules and prescribing requirements which such radio navigational aids are to comply with;

(*b*) prescribing requirements which radio navigational aids, other than direction-finders and other than such as are provided in pursuance of rules made under the preceding paragraph, are to comply with when carried in ships to which this section applies;

(*c*) prescribing requirements which apparatus designed for the purpose of transmitting or reflecting signals to or from radio navigational aids is to comply with if it is apparatus in the United Kingdom or apparatus off the shores of the United Kingdom but maintained from the United Kingdom;

and the requirements prescribed under paragraph (*a*) or (*b*) of this subsection may include requirements relating to the position and method of fitting of the radio navigational aids.

(2) This section applies to—

(*a*) ships [4] registered in the United Kingdom;

(*b*) other ships while they are within any port in the United Kingdom.

(3) If a ship to which this section applies proceeds, or attempts to proceed, to sea without carrying such navigational aids as it is required to carry by rules made under subsection (1) of this section or carrying radio navigational aids not complying with rules made under that subsection, the owner or master of the ship shall be liable on summary conviction to a fine [5] not exceeding £100.

(4) If any person establishes or operates any such apparatus as is mentioned in subsection (1) (*c*) of this section and the apparatus does not comply with rules made thereunder, he shall be liable on summary conviction to a fine not exceeding £100.

[1] This section was substituted by the M.S.A. 1970 s. 85: see § 1461, *post*.
[2] No rules have so far been made under the section. The power to make rules is exercisable by statutory instrument (see s. 34 (1)). For power to exempt from rules, see s. 28.
[3] For definition, see s. 36. See also the Fishing Vessels (Safety Provisions) Act 1970, s. 9 (1).
[4] As to the issue of certificates in respect of fishing vessels that comply with the rules for radio navigational aids, see the Fishing Vessels (Safety Provisions) Act 1970, ss. 3 and 4.
[5] As to the recovery of fines, see M.S.A. 1894, ss. 680–682.

Certificates

Issue for passenger steamers of safety certificates and exemption certificates

1124 7.[1]—(1) If the [Secretary of State],[2] on receipt of declarations of survey [3] in respect of a British passenger steamer [4] registered in the United Kingdom, is satisfied that the steamer complies with the construction rules,[5] rules for life-saving appliances,[6] radio rules [7] and rules for direction-finders [8] applicable to the steamer and to such international voyages [3] as she is to be engaged on, and that she is properly provided with the lights, shapes and means of making fog-signals required by the collision regulations,[3] he shall, on the application of the owner, issue in respect of the steamer a certificate showing that the steamer complies with the requirements of the Safety Convention [9] applicable as aforesaid; and any certificate issued under this subsection is hereafter in this Act referred to as a " general safety certificate " [10]:

Provided that if the voyages on which the steamer is to be engaged are short international voyages [3] and she complies only with such of those rules as are applicable to those voyages, the certificate shall show that the steamer complies with the requirements of the Safety Convention applicable to her as a steamer plying on short international voyages; and any such certificate is hereafter in this Act referred to as a " short-voyage safety certificate ".[10]

(2) If the [Secretary of State],[2] on receipt of declarations of survey [3] in respect of any such passenger steamer [4] as aforesaid is satisfied that the steamer is exempt, by virtue of any exercise by him of a power in that behalf conferred on him by this Act [11] or conferred on him by the rules in question, from any of the requirements of the construction rules,[5] rules for life-saving appliances,[6] radio rules [7] or rules for direction-finders [8] applicable to the steamer and to such international voyages [4] as she is to be engaged on, whether short voyages or otherwise, that she complies with the rest of those requirements and that she is properly provided with the lights, shapes and means of making fog-signals required by the collision regulations,[3] he shall, on the application of the owner, issue in respect of the steamer—

(*a*) an exemption certificate stating which of the requirements of the Safety Convention [8] applicable as aforesaid the steamer is exempt from and that the exemption is conditional on the steamer's plying only on the voyages and being engaged only in the trades and complying with the other conditions (if any) specified in the certificate, and

(*b*) a certificate showing that the steamer complies with the rest of those requirements;

and any certificate issued under paragraph (*b*) of this subsection is hereafter in this Act referred to as a " qualified safety certificate " or a " qualified short-voyage safety certificate," as the case may be.[10]

1125 [1] This section replaces, with modifications, the provisions of s. 11 of the M.S. (Safety and Load Line Conventions) Act 1932, which section is repealed by s. 37 (5) and the Third Schedule, *post*.

[2] *i.e.* the Secretary of State for Trade.

[3] For definitions of " declaration of survey," " international voyage," " short international voyage," and " collision regulations," see s. 36.

[4] For definition, see. s. 26.

[5] See s. 1.

[6] See s. 2.

[7] See s. 3.

[8] See s. 5.

[9] See note (4) to s. 1.

10 For further provisions as to safety certificates, see ss. 10 and 13, which (*inter alia*) confer on the Secretary of State the power to issue certificates on partial compliance with rules and lay down the periods of duration of certificates. As to fishing vessels, see the Fishing Vessels (Safety Provisions) Act 1970, ss. 3, 4 and 9 (1).

No express power to prescribe forms of safety certificates, etc., is given in this Act corresponding with the power given in the M.S. (Safety and Load Line Conventions) Act 1932, s. 15 (3), now repealed. There is, however, a general power to prescribe forms given in M.S.A. 1894, s. 720, and it is to be supposed that if and when it is decided to prescribe forms for safety certificates, etc., under the 1949 Act, the Secretary of State will act under this general power. For prescribed forms of " accepted Safety Convention Certificates," which relate only to Safety Convention ships not registered in the United Kingdom, see the M.S. (Accepted Safety Convention Certificates) Regulations 1952 (S.I. 1952 No. 1954), and the M.S. (Accepted Safety Convention Certificates) Regulation 1965 (S.I. No. 1145), made under s. 14, *post*.

As to fees, see s. 33 (1) and notes thereto. The fees at present in force for safety certificates are contained in the M.S. (Fees) Regulations 1975 (S.I. No. 341).

11 For power conferred by the Act to exempt ships from rules or regulations made under the Act, see s. 28. *Cf.* the absolute exemption from certain provisions of the Act, given by s. 29 to certain classes of ships.

Issue for cargo ships of safety-equipment certificates and exemption certificates

26 **8.**—(1) If the [Secretary of State],[1] on receipt of declarations of survey [2] in respect of a British ship [3] registered in the United Kingdom, not being a passenger steamer,[4] is satisfied that the ship complies with the rules for life-saving appliances [5] applicable to the ship and to such international voyages [2] as she is to be engaged on, and that she is properly provided with the lights, shapes and means of making fog-signals required by the collision regulations,[2] he shall, on the application of the owner, issue in respect of the ship a certificate showing that the ship complies with such of the requirements of the Safety Convention relating to those matters [6] as are applicable as aforesaid; and any certificate issued under this subsection is hereafter in this Act referred to as a " safety-equipment certificate ".[7]

(2) If the [Secretary of State],[1] on the receipt of declarations of survey [2] in respect of any such ship as aforesaid, is satisfied that the ship is exempt, by virtue of any exercise by him of a power in that behalf conferred on him by this Act [8] or conferred on him by the rules for life-saving appliances, from any of the requirements of those rules applicable to the ship and to such international voyages [2] as she is to be engaged on, and that she complies with the rest of those requirements and is properly provided with the lights, shapes and means of making fog-signals required by the collision regulations,[2] he shall, on the application of the owner, issue in respect of the ship—

(*a*) an exemption certificate [7] stating which of the requirements of the Safety Convention, being requirements the subject of the rules for life-saving appliances and applicable as aforesaid,[6] the ship is exempt from and that the exemption is conditional on the ship's plying only on the voyages and complying with the other conditions (if any) specified in the certificate, and (*b*) a certificate showing that the ship complies with the rest of those requirements;

and any certificate issued under paragraph (*b*) of this subsection is hereafter in this Act referred to as a " qualified safety-equipment certificate ".[7]

[1] *i.e.* the Secretary of State for Trade.

[2] For definitions of " declaration of survey," " international voyage " and " collision regulations," see s. 36.

[3] As to " British ships " see M.S.A. 1894, s. 1, and notes thereto.

[4] For definition of " passenger steamer," see s. 26.

[5] See s. 2.

[6] See note (4) to s. 1.

[7] No rules have so far been prescribed relating to the forms of certificates to be used. See also note (10) to s. 7 as to " forms."

As to fees, see s. 33 (1) and notes thereto. The fees at present in force for safety-equipment certificates are contained in the M.S. (Fees) Regulations 1975 (S.I. No. 341). See also for further provisions relating to safety-equipment certificates, ss. 10 and 13.

[8] For power conferred by the Act to exempt ships from rules or regulations made under the Act, see s. 28. *Cf.* the absolute exemption from certain provisions of the Act, given by s. 29 to certain classes of ships.

Issue for cargo ships of radio certificates and exemption certificates

1127 **9.**[1]—(1) If the [Secretary of State],[2] on receipt of declarations of survey [3] in respect of a British ship [4] registered in the United Kingdom not being a passenger steamer,[5] is satisfied that the ship complies with the radio rules [6] and rules for direction-finders [7] applicable to the ship and to such international voyages [3] as she is to be engaged on, he shall, on the application of the owner, issue in respect of the ship a certificate showing that the ship complies with such of the requirements of the Safety Convention relating to radiotelegraphy, radiotelephony and direction-finders as are applicable as aforesaid [8]; and any certificate issued under this subsection is hereafter in this Act referred to as a " radio certificate ".[9]

(2) If the [Secretary of State],[2] on receipt of declarations of survey [3] in respect of any such ship as aforesaid, is satisfied that the ship is exempt, by virtue of any exercise by him of a power in that behalf conferred on him by this Act [10] or conferred on him by the rules in question, from any of the requirements of the radio rules [6] or rules for direction-finders [7] applicable to the ship and to such international voyages [3] as she is to be engaged on, and that she complies with the rest of the requirements of the radio rules and rules for direction-finders, he shall, on the application of the owner, issue in respect of the ship—

(*a*) an exemption certificate [9] stating which of the requirements of the Safety Convention relating to radiotelegraphy, radiotelephony and direction-finders, being requirements applicable as aforesaid,[8] the ship is exempt from and that the exemption is conditional on the ship's plying only on the voyages and complying with the other conditions (if any) specified in the certificate, and (*b*) a certificate showing that the ship complies with the rest of those requirements;

and any certificate issued under paragraph (*b*) of this subsection is hereafter in this Act referred to as a " qualified radio certificate." [9]

(3) Where any British ship [4] registered in the United Kingdom is wholly exempt from the requirements of the radio rules [6] and the rules for direction-finders,[7] the [Secretary of State] [2] shall on the application of the owner issue an exemption certificate [9] stating that the ship is wholly exempt from the requirements of the Safety Convention relating to radiotelegraphy, radiotelephony and direction-finders [8] and specifying the voyages on which, and conditions (if any) on which, the ship is so exempt.

[1] This section replaces, with modifications, the provisions of s. 13 of the M.S. (Safety and Load Line Conventions) Act 1932, which section is repealed by s. 37 (5) and the Third Schedule, *post*.
[2] *i.e.* the Secretary of State for Trade.
[3] For definitions of " declaration of survey " and " international voyage," see s. 36.
[4] For meaning of " British ship," see M.S.A. 1894, s. 1.
[5] For definition of " passenger steamer," see s. 26. As to fishing vessels, see the Fishing Vessels (Safety Provisions) Act 1970, ss. 3, 4 and 9 (1).
[6] See s. 3.
[7] See s. 5.
[8] As to " Safety Convention," see note (4) to s. 1.
[9] No rules have yet been prescribed under this Act for the forms of certificates to be used. See also note (10) to s. 7 as to " forms."
As to fees, see s. 33 (1) and notes thereto. The fees at present in force for radio certificates and radio exemption certificates are contained in Part 2 of the Second Schedule to the M.S. (Fees) Regulations 1975 (S.I. No. 341). For further provisions relating to radio certificates, see ss. 10 and 13.
[10] See s. 28 as to power to exempt from safety requirements.

Issue of general safety certificates, etc., on partial compliance with rules

28 **10.** Where a ship complies with all the requirements of the construction rules,[1] rules for life-saving appliances,[2] radio rules [3] or rules for direction-finders [4] applicable to the ship and to the voyages on which she is to be engaged so far as those requirements are requirements of the Safety Convention applicable as aforesaid,[5] the [Secretary of State] [6] may issue in respect of the ship a general safety certificate,[7] short-voyage safety certificate,[7] safety-equipment certificate [8] or radio certificate,[9] as the case may be, notwithstanding that she is exempt from, or for some other reason does not comply with, any requirements of those rules that are not applicable requirements of the Safety Convention.

[1] See s. 1.
[2] See s. 2.
[3] See s. 3.
[4] See s. 5.
[5] As to " Safety Convention," see note (4) to s. 1.
[6] *i.e.* the Secretary of State for Trade; see s. 36 and note (3) thereto.
[7] For definition, see s. 7 (1).
[8] For definition, see s. 8 (1).
[9] For definition, see s. 9 (1).

Notice of alterations and additional surveys

1129 **11.**[1]—(1) The owner or master of a passenger steamer [2] in respect of which any passenger steamer's certificate issued under the principal Act,[3] or any certificate issued under this Act,[4] is in force shall, as soon as possible after any alteration is made in the steamer's hull, equipments or machinery affecting the efficiency thereof or the seaworthiness of the steamer, give written notice to the [Secretary of State] [5] containing full particulars of the alteration.

(2) The owner or master of a ship in respect of which any certificate issued under this Act [4] is in force, other than a passenger steamer,[2] shall, as soon as possible after any alteration is made in the appliances or equipments required by the rules for life-saving appliances,[6] the radio rules,[7] the rules for direction-finders [8] or the collision regulations [9] to be carried by the ship, being an alteration affecting the efficiency or completeness of those appliances or equipments, give written notice to the [Secretary of State] [5] containing full particulars of the alteration.[10]

(3) If notice of any alteration is not given as required by this section, the owner or master of the ship shall be liable to a fine not exceeding fifty pounds.[11]

(4) If the [Secretary of State] [5] has reason to believe that since the making of the last declaration of survey [9] in respect of any such ship as aforesaid—

(*a*) any such alteration has been made as is mentioned in subsection (1) or, as the case may be, in subsection (2) of this section; or

(*b*) the hull, equipments or machinery of the ship (being a passenger steamer [2]) have sustained any injury or are otherwise insufficient; or

(*c*) the appliances or equipments of the ship (not being a passenger steamer) mentioned in subsection (2) of this section have sustained any injury or are otherwise insufficient;

the [Secretary of State] may, without prejudice to his powers under section two hundred and seventy-nine of the principal Act [3] (which relates to the cancellation of certificates and additional surveys), require the ship to be again surveyed to such extent as he thinks fit, and, if such requirement is not complied with, may cancel any passenger steamer's certificate issued in respect of the ship under the principal Act [3] or any certificate issued in respect of the ship under this Act.[4]

(5) For the purpose of this section the expression " alteration " in relation to anything includes the renewal of any part of it.

1130 [1] This section replaces, with modifications, the provisions of s. 3 of the M.S. (Safety and Load Line Conventions) Act 1932, which section is repealed by s. 37 (5) and the Third Schedule, *post*.

[2] For definition, see s. 26.

[3] " Principal Act " means M.S.A. 1894. See s. 36, *post*. As to issue of passenger steamers' certificates under M.S.A. 1894, see s. 274 of that Act.
[4] This subsection is applied with modifications by the M.S.A. 1964, s. 4 (2), see *ibid.* § 1240 *post*. As to issue of certificates to passenger steamers, under this Act, see s. 7. As to issue of certificates to ships other than passenger steamers, see ss. 8 and 9.
[5] *i.e.* the Secretary of State for Trade.
[6] See s. 2.
[7] See s. 3.
[8] See s. 5.
[9] For definitions of " collision regulations " and " declaration of survey," see s. 36.
[10] This subsection is extended by the M.S.A. 1964, s. 4 (1): see *ibid.* § 1240, *post*.
[11] As to the recovery of fines, see M.S.A. 1894, s. 680 *et seq.*

Prohibition on proceeding to sea without appropriate certificates

31 **12.**[1]—(1) No British ship [2] registered in the United Kingdom shall proceed to sea on an international voyage [3] from a port in the United Kingdom unless there is in force in respect of the ship—

(*a*) if she is a passenger steamer,[4] a general safety certificate, a short-voyage safety certificate, a qualified safety certificate or a qualified short-voyage safety certificate [5] which (subject to the provisions of this section relating to short-voyage safety certificates) is applicable to the voyage on which the ship is about to proceed and to the trade in which she is for the time being engaged;

(*b*) if she is not a passenger steamer, both—

(i) a safety-equipment certificate or a qualified safety-equipment certificate,[6] and

(ii) a radio certificate or a qualified radio certificate, or an exemption certificate [7] stating that she is wholly exempt from the requirements of the Safety Convention relating to radiotelegraphy, radiotelephony and direction-finders [8]:

Provided that this subsection shall not prohibit a ship, not being a passenger steamer, from proceeding to sea as aforesaid if there is in force in respect of the ship such certificate or certificates as would be required if she were a passenger steamer.

(2) For the purposes of this section, a qualified certificate shall not be deemed to be in force in respect of a ship unless there is also in force in respect of the ship the corresponding exemption certificate; and an exemption certificate shall be of no effect unless it is by its terms applicable to the voyage on which the ship is about to proceed.

(3) If any ship proceeds, or attempts to proceed, to sea in contravention of this section—

(*a*) in the case of a passenger steamer,[4] the owner or master of the steamer shall, without prejudice to any other remedy or penalty [9] under the Merchant Shipping Acts,[10] be liable on summary conviction to a fine not exceeding ten pounds [11] for every passenger carried on board the steamer,[11] and the owner or master of any tender by means of which passengers have been taken on board the steamer shall be liable on summary conviction to a like fine [11] for every passenger so taken on board [12]; and

(*b*) in the case of a ship not being a passenger steamer, the owner or master of the ship shall be liable to a fine not exceeding one hundred pounds.[11]

(4) The master of every British ship [2] registered in the United Kingdom shall produce to the officer of customs from whom a clearance for the ship is demanded for an international voyage [3] the certificate or certificates required by the foregoing provisions of this section to be in force when the ship proceeds to sea; and a clearance shall not be granted, and the ship may be detained,[13] until the said certificate or certificates are so produced.

(5) Where the [Secretary of State] [14] permits any passenger steamer [4] in respect of which there is in force a short-voyage safety certificate, whether qualified or not,[5] to proceed to sea on an international voyage [3] from a port in the United Kingdom not exceeding twelve hundred nautical miles in length between the last port of call in the United Kingdom and the final port of destination, the certificate shall for the purposes of this section be deemed to be applicable to the voyage on which the steamer is about to proceed notwithstanding that the voyage exceeds six hundred nautical miles between the said ports.

(6) Where an exemption certificate [15] issued in respect of any British ship [2] registered in the United Kingdom specifies any conditions on which the certificate is issued and any of those conditions is not complied with, the owner or master of the ship shall be liable to a fine not exceeding one hundred pounds.[12]

1132 [1] This section replaces with modifications, the provisions of s. 14 of the M.S. (Safety and Load Line Conventions) Act 1932, which section is repealed by s. 37 (5) and the Third Schedule, *post*.

The section imposes a prohibition on proceeding to sea without appropriate certificates, but certain classes of ships by virtue of the provisions of s. 29 are exempted from this prohibition. See also as to exemption of H.M. ships, s. 741 of M.S.A. 1894.

[2] As to "British ships," see M.S.A. 1894, s. 1, and notes thereto.

As to ships exempted from the prohibition, see s. 29, *post*.

[3] For definition of "international voyage," see s. 36.

[4] For definition of "passenger steamer," see s. 26.

[5] As to issue of general safety certificates and short-voyage safety certificates, see s. 7 (1) and s. 10.

As to issue of qualified safety certificates and qualified short-voyage safety certificates, see s. 7 (2).

[6] As to issue of safety equipment certificates and qualified safety equipment certificates, see s. 8 and s. 10.

[7] As to issue of radio certificates, qualified radio certificates and exemption certificates relating to exemption from the requirements of the Safety Convention relating to radiotelegraphy, radiotelephony and direction-finders, see s. 9.

[8] As to "Safety Convention" and the requirements thereof relating to radiotelegraphy, radiotelephony and direction-finders, see note (4) to s. 1.

[9] For example, the owner would in addition be liable to the penalty prescribed by s. 430 of M.S.A. 1894, if the ship not only had no certificate, but was also deficient in the prescribed life-saving appliances.

10 " The Merchant Shipping Acts " means the Merchant Shipping Acts 1894 to 1948, and this Act; see s. 36.
11 This penalty has been increased to a fine, on summary conviction, not exceeding £400 irrespective of the number of passengers and, on conviction on indictment, a fine, see the M.S. (Load Lines) Act 1967, s. 25, Sched. 1.
12 As to the recovery of fines, see M.S.A. 1894, ss. 680–682.
13 As to detention, see s. 35 (2) of this Act; s. 9 of the M.S. (Load Lines) Act 1967; ss. 459 *et seq.* and s. 692 of M.S.A. 1894. For provisions as to clearance of ships and further provisions relating to the power of Customs officers to refuse or cancel such clearance, see Customs and Excise Act 1952, ss. 52 and 53.
14 *i.e.* the Secretary of State for Trade; see s. 36 and note (3) thereto.
15 As to exemption certificates generally, see ss. 7 (2), 8 (2), 9 (2) and 9 (3).

Miscellaneous provisions as to surveys and certificates

33 **13.**[1]—(1) *Subsections (3) to (5) of section two hundred and seventy-two of the principal Act (which prescribe the contents of declarations of survey) shall cease to have effect.*[2]

(2) Subsection (2) of section two hundred and seventy-two of the principal Act (which requires a surveyor to deliver declarations of survey to the owner of a ship), section two hundred and seventy-three of that Act (which requires the owner to deliver the declaration to the [Secretary of State] [3]) and section two hundred and seventy-five of that Act (which relates to appeals to the court of survey) shall apply to surveys for the purpose of the issue of any certificate in respect of a ship under this Act [4] as they apply to surveys for the purpose of the issue of passenger steamers' certificates.[5]

(3) A safety certificate [6] or radio certificate [7] or an exemption certificate stating that a ship is wholly exempt from the provisions of the Safety Convention relating to radiotelegraphy, radiotelephony and direction-finders,[8] shall be in force for one year, and a safety-equipment certificate [9] shall be in force for twenty-four months, from the date of its issue, or for such shorter period as may be specified in the certificate:

Provided that no such certificate shall remain in force after notice is given by the [Secretary of State] [3] to the owner or master of the ship in respect of which it has been issued that the [Secretary of State] [3] has cancelled the certificate.[10]

(4) An exemption certificate, other than a certificate stating that a ship is wholly exempt from the provisions of the Safety Convention relating to radiotelegraphy, radiotelephony and direction-finders, shall be in force for the same period as the corresponding qualified certificate.[11]

(5) The [Secretary of State] [3] or any person authorised by him for the purpose may grant an extension of any certificate issued under this Act [4] in respect of a British ship [12] registered in the United Kingdom for a period not exceeding one month from the date when the certificate would, but for the extension, have expired, or, if the ship is absent from the United Kingdom on that date, for a period not exceeding five months from that date.[13]

(6) Any general safety certificate or short-voyage safety certificate,[7]

whether qualified or not, may be combined in one document with a passenger steamer's certificate.[5]

(7) Any certificate issued by the [Secretary of State] [3] under this Act,[4] and any passenger steamer's certificate,[5] whether or not combined in one document with a safety certificate under the last preceding subsection, shall be admissible in evidence.

(8) The following provisions of the principal Act shall apply to and in relation to certificates issued by the [Secretary of State] [3] and ships certified, under this Act [4] in the same manner as they apply to and in relation to passenger steamers' certificates [5] and passenger steamers,[14] namely, section two hundred and seventy-six (which relates to the transmission of a certificate to the owner of the steamer), section two hundred and seventy-nine (which relates to the cancellation of certificates), section two hundred and eighty (which relates to the surrender of certificates no longer in force), section two hundred and eighty-one (which relates to the posting up of a certificate on board) and section two hundred and eighty-two (which relates to the forging and falsification of certificates).[15]

(9) The [Secretary of State] [3] may request the government of a country to which the Safety Convention applies [16] to issue in respect of a British ship [12] registered in the United Kingdom any certificate the issue of which is authorised under this Act [17]; and a certificate issued in pursuance of such a request and containing a statement that it has been so issued shall have effect for the purposes of this Act as if it had been issued [4] by the [Secretary of State] [3] and not by the government of that country.

1134 [1] This section replaces with modifications the provisions of s. 15 of the M.S. (Safety and Load Line Conventions) Act 1932, which section is repealed by s. 37 (5) and the Third Schedule, *post*. The section also makes further amendments to M.S.A. 1894.

[2] This subsection was repealed as spent by the Statute Law Revision Act 1953, s. 1, Sched. I.

[3] *i.e.* the Secretary of State for Trade.

[4] As to issue of safety certificates, see s. 7; safety equipment certificates, see s. 8; radio certificates and whole exemption certificates, see s. 9. See also s. 10 as to issue of certificates on partial compliance with rules.

[5] The provisions applied by this subsection are also applied by s. 2 (4) of the M.S.A. 1964. As to issue of passenger steamer's certificates, see s. 274, M.S.A. 1894.

[6] See s. 7.

[7] See s. 9.

[8] As to issue of exemption certificate stating that a ship is wholly exempt from the requirements of the Safety Convention relating to radiotelegraphy, radiotelephony and direction-finders, see s. 9 (3).

As to " Safety Convention " and the requirements thereof relating to radiotelegraphy, radiotelephony and direction-finders, see note (4) to s. 1.

[9] See s. 8.

[10] This subsection is excluded by the M.S.A. 1964, s. 12. The certificate may be cancelled under s. 279 of M.S.A. 1894, which is made applicable by subs. (8) of this section.

[11] As to issue of exemption certificates and qualified certificates, see s. 7 (2), 8 (2) and 9 (2).

[12] As to " British ship," see M.S.A. 1894, s. 1, and notes thereto.

[13] This subsection is not prejudiced by the M.S.A. 1964, s. 3 (5).

[14] For definition of " passenger steamer," see s. 26.

[15] The provisions applied by this subsection, save the M.S.A. 1894, s. 276, are also applied by s. 3 (6) of the M.S.A. 1964.

[16] As to the countries to which the Safety Convention applies, see ss. 31 and 36.

[17] As to the issue of exemption certificates following such a request, see the M.S.A. 1964, s. 13.

Safety Convention Ships not registered in the United Kingdom

Certificates of Convention ships not registered in United Kingdom

135 **14.**[1]—(1) The [Secretary of State] [2] may, at the request of the government of a country to which the Safety Convention applies,[3] issue in respect of a ship registered in that country any certificate the issue of which in respect of British ships registered in the United Kingdom is authorised under *the preceding provisions of* [4] this Act [5] if he is satisfied that it is proper for him to do so; and a certificate issued in pursuance of such a request and containing a statement that it has been so issued shall have effect for the purposes of this Act as if it had been issued by the said government and not by the [Secretary of State].[2]

(2) The [Secretary of State] [2] shall make such regulations [6] as appear to him to be necessary for the purpose of securing that certificates issued in accordance with the Safety Convention [7] by the government of any country other than the United Kingdom in respect of Safety Convention ships [8] not registered in the United Kingdom,[9] or having effect under the preceding subsection as if so issued, shall be accepted as having the same force as corresponding certificates issued by the [Secretary of State] [2] under this Act [10]; and any certificate required by those regulations to be so treated is in this Act referred to as an " accepted Safety Convention certificate."

(3) A surveyor of ships,[11] for the purpose of verifying—

(*a*) that there is in force in respect of a Safety Convention ship [8] not registered in the United Kingdom [9] an accepted Safety Convention certificate, or

(*b*) that the condition of the hull, equipments and machinery of any such Safety Convention ship corresponds substantially with the particulars shown in such a certificate; or,

(*c*) except where such a certificate states that the ship is wholly exempt from the provisions of the Safety Convention relating to radiotelegraphy and radiotelephony,[12] that the number, grades and qualifications of radio officers or operators on board correspond with those shown in the certificate; or

(*d*) that any conditions on which such a certificate, being the equivalent of an exemption certificate, [13] is issued are complied with,

shall have all the powers of a [Department of Trade] inspector [14] under the Merchant Shipping Acts.

(4) Where there is attached to an accepted Safety Convention certificate in respect of a Safety Convention passenger steamer [8] not registered in the United Kingdom [9] a memorandum which

(*a*) has been issued by or under the authority of the government of the country in which the steamer is registered; and (*b*) modifies for the purpose of any particular voyage, in view of the number of persons carried on that voyage, the particulars stated in the certificate with respect to life-saving appliances,

the certificate shall have effect for the purpose of that voyage as if it were modified in accordance with the memorandum.[15]

1136 [1] This section replaces with modifications, the provisions of s. 16 of the M.S. (Safety and Load Line Conventions) Act 1932, which section is repealed by s. 37 (5) and the Third Schedule, *post*.

[2] *i.e.* the Secretary of State for Trade.

[3] As to meaning of " Country to which the Safety Convention applies," see s. 36 and notes thereto.

[4] The words in italics were repealed by the M.S.A. 1964, s. 18 (4).

[5] As to issue of, and rules relating to, certificates under the Act in the case of British ships registered in the United Kingdom, see ss. 7–13.

As to fees for certificates issued under this Act, including certificates issued under subs. (1) of this section, see s. 33 (1) and notes thereto.

[6] The regulations at present in force under this subsection are the M.S. (Accepted Safety Convention Certificates) Regulations 1952 (S.I. 1952 No. 1954) and the M.S. (Accepted Safety Convention Certificates) Regulations 1965 (S.I. No. 1145).

For power to exempt from regulations, see s. 28.

[7] See note (4) to s. 1.

[8] As to meaning of " Safety Convention ships," see s. 36.

As to meaning of " Safety Convention passenger steamer," see ss. 26 and 36.

[9] For the purpose of any provision in this Act or in M.S. (Safety and Load Line Conventions) Act 1932, relating to Safety Convention ships or Safety Convention passenger steamers not registered in the United Kingdom, a passenger steamer or other ship registered in any of the Channel Islands or in the Isle of Man shall be deemed to be registered in the United Kingdom; see s. 73 (3) of M.S. (Safety and Load Line Conventions) Act 1932, as amended by s. 35 (4), *post*.

[10] This refers to the certificates issued under the Act to British ships registered in the United Kingdom; see note (5) above.

[11] As to appointment of surveyors, see M.S.A. 1894, s. 724.

[12] See note (8) to s. 13.

[13] As to issue of exemption certificates by the Minister (*i.e.* in the case of British ships and passenger steamers registered in the U.K.), see ss. 7 (2), 8 (2), 9 (2), (3).

[14] As to the powers of a Department of Trade inspector, see M.S.A. 1894, s. 729, and notes thereto.

[15] This subsection provides parallel relaxation of the regulations to that which may be granted to British passenger steamers registered in the United Kingdom under s. 12 (1) of the M.S. (Safety and Load Line Conventions) Act 1932.

Modified survey of passenger steamers holding Convention certificates

1137 **15.**[1]—(1) Where an accepted Safety Convention certificate [2] is produced in respect of a Safety Convention passenger steamer [3] not registered in the United Kingdom [4]—

(*a*) the steamer shall not be required to be surveyed under the Merchant Shipping Acts by a surveyor of ships [5] except for the purpose of determining the number of passengers that she is fit to carry;

(*b*) on receipt of any declaration of survey [6] for the purpose aforesaid, the [Secretary of State] [7] shall issue a certificate under section two hundred and seventy-four of the principal Act [8] containing only a statement of the particulars set out in paragraph (*b*) of that section (which relates to the said number of passengers); and a certificate so issued shall have effect as a passenger steamer's certificate.[9]

(2) Where there is produced in respect of any such passenger steamer as aforesaid an accepted Safety Convention certificate,[2] and also a certificate issued by or under the authority of the government of the country in which the steamer is registered showing the number of passengers that the steamer is fit to carry, and the [Secretary of State] [7] is satisfied that that number has been determined substantially in the same manner as in the case of a British passenger steamer registered in the United Kingdom, he may if he thinks fit dispense with any survey of the steamer for the purpose of determining the number of passengers that she is fit to carry and direct that the last-mentioned certificate shall have effect as a passenger steamer's certificate.

1138 [1] This section replaces, with modifications, the provisions of s. 17 of the M.S. (Safety and Load Line Conventions) Act 1932, which section is repealed by s. 37 (5) and the Third Schedule, *post*.
[2] " Accepted Safety Convention certificate " has the meaning assigned to it by s. 14. See s. 36.
[3] See note (8) to s. 14.
[4] See note (9) to s. 14. The same applies to this section.
[5] As to appointment of surveyors, see M.S.A. 1894, s. 724.
[6] " Declaration of Survey " means a declaration made under s. 272 of M.S.A. 1894; see s. 36, *post*.
[7] *i.e.* the Secretary of State for Trade.
[8] " Principal Act " means M.S.A. 1894. See s. 36.
[9] As to issue of passenger steamers' certificates under M.S.A. 1894, see s. 274 of that Act.

Miscellaneous privileges of ships holding Convention certificates

1139 **16.**[1]—(1) Where an accepted Safety Convention certificate [2] is produced in respect of a Safety Convention passenger steamer [3] not registered in the United Kingdom,[4] the steamer shall be exempt from paragraphs (*d*) and (*f*) or subsection (1) of section two hundred and ninety of the principal Act [5] (which relate to the equipments of emigrant ships) and section four hundred and twenty of that Act (which relates to lights and fog-signals) and from the rules for life-saving appliances.[6]

(2) Where an accepted Safety Convention certificate,[2] being the equivalent of a safety-equipment certificate, is produced in respect of a Safety Convention ship [3] (other than a passenger steamer) not registered in the United Kingdom,[4] the ship shall be exempt from section four hundred and twenty of the principal Act [5] (which relates to lights and fog-signals) and from the rules for life-saving appliances.[6]

(3) Where an accepted Safety Convention certificate [2] is produced in respect of a Safety Convention ship [3] not registered in the United Kingdom,[4] and the certificate shows that the ship complies with the requirements of the Safety Convention relating to radiotelegraphy, radiotelephony and direction-finders,[7] or that she is exempt from some of those requirements and complies with the rest, or that she is wholly exempt from those

requirements, the ship shall be exempt from the provisions of the radio rules [8] and the rules for direction-finders.[9]

[1] This section replaces, with modifications, the provisions of ss. 18 and 19 of the M.S. (Safety and Load Line Conventions) Act 1932, which sections are repealed by s. 37 (5) and the Third Schedule, *post*.
[2] " Accepted Safety Convention certificate " has the meaning assigned to it by s. 14. See s. 36.
[3] See note (8) to s. 14.
[4] See note (9) to s. 14 as to ships registered in the Channel Islands or Isle of Man.
[5] " Principal Act " means M.S.A. 1894. See s. 36. S. 290 of the 1894 Act was repealed by the M.S.A. 1970, s. 100 (3), Sched. 5 as from January 1, 1973; see S.I. 1972 No. 1977.
[6] As to rules for life-saving appliances, see s. 2.
[7] See note (4) to s. 1 as to " Safety Convention."
[8] As to radio rules, see s. 3.
[9] As to rules for direction-finders, see s. 5.

Further provisions as to the production of Convention certificates

1140 **17.**[1]—(1) The master of every Safety Convention ship [2] not registered in the United Kingdom [3] shall produce to the officer of customs from whom a clearance for the ship is demanded in respect of an international voyage [2] from a port in the United Kingdom accepted Safety Convention certificates [4] that are the equivalent of the certificates issued by the [Secretary of State] [5] under this Act that would be required to be in force in respect of the ship if she were a British ship so registered [6]; and a clearance shall not be granted, and the ship may be detained,[7] until such certificates are so produced.

(2) The production of an accepted Safety Convention certificate [4] being the equivalent of—

(*a*) a qualified certificate, or

(*b*) an exemption certificate,[8] other than a certificate stating that a ship is wholly exempt from the provisions of the Safety Convention relating to radiotelegraphy, radiotelephony and direction-finders,[9]

shall not avail for the purposes of either of the last two preceding sections unless there is also produced the corresponding exemption certificate or qualified certificate as the case may be.

1141 [1] This section replaces, with modifications, the provisions of s. 20 of the M.S. (Safety and Load Line Conventions) Act 1932, which section is repealed by s. 37 (5) and the Third Schedule, *post*.
[2] As to meaning of " Safety Convention ship " and " international voyage," see s. 36.
[3] See note (9) to s. 14 as to ships registered in the Channel Islands or Isle of Man.
[4] " Accepted Safety Convention certificate " has the meaning assigned to it by s. 14; see s. 36.
[5] *i.e.* the Secretary of State for Trade.
[6] As to the issue of certificates under this Act to British ships registered in the United Kingdom and the certificates required to be in force, in respect of such ships, see ss. 7–13.
[7] As to detention, see s. 35 (2) of this Act; s. 9 of the M.S. (Load Lines) Certificate 1967, ss. 459 *et seq.* and 692 of M.S.A. 1894. As to clearance, see note (13) to s. 12.
[8] As to qualified and exemption certificates generally, see ss. 7 (2), 8 (2), 9 (2) and (3).
[9] As to exemption certificate stating that a ship is wholly exempt from the provisions of the Safety Convention relating to radiotelegraphy, radiotelephony and direction-finders, see s. 9 (3) and notes thereto.

Miscellaneous Provisions for furthering Safety of Life at Sea

142 **18.** [*This section, which contained provisions relating to information about ships' stability, was repealed by the M.S.* (*Load Lines*) *Act* 1967, *s.* 33 (1) *and Sched. II. Subsection* 5 *was also repealed by the M.S.A.* 1970, *s.* 100 (3), *Sched. V as from January* 1, 1973; *see S.I.* 1972 *No.* 1977.]

Openings in passenger steamers' hulls and watertight bulkheads

143 **19.**[1]—(1) The [Secretary of State] [2] may in relation to British passenger steamers [3] registered in the United Kingdom make rules [4] for any of the following matters—

(*a*) for closing and keeping closed the openings in steamers' hulls and in watertight bulkheads;

(*b*) for securing, keeping in place and inspecting contrivances for closing any such openings as aforesaid;

(*c*) for operating the mechanisms of contrivances for closing any such openings as aforesaid and for drills in connection with the operation thereof;

(*d*) *for requiring entry to be made in the official log-book or other record to be kept of any of the matters aforesaid.*[5]

(2) If any of the said rules is not complied with in relation to any such steamer as aforesaid, the master of the steamer shall be liable to a fine not exceeding one hundred pounds.[6]

144 [1] This section replaces, with modifications, s. 22 of the M.S. (Safety and Load Line Conventions) Act 1932, which section is repealed by s. 37 (5) and the Third Schedule, *post.*

By s. 29 of the Act, certain classes of ships (*e.g.* troop-ships) are exempt from any provision imposing a penalty for the contravention of any rules relating to openings in ships' hulls and watertight bulkheads. Subs. (2) of this section, therefore, which provides for such a penalty, does not apply to such classes of ships as are specifically exempted by s. 29.

[2] *i.e.* Secretary of State for Trade.

[3] As to "British ships," see M.S.A. 1894, s. 1. As to meaning of "passenger steamer," see s. 26, *post.*

[4] The rules at present in force under this section are the M.S. (Closing of Openings in Hulls and in Watertight Bulkheads) Rules 1965 (S.I. No. 1114). For power to exempt from rules, see s. 28.

[5] The words in italics were repealed by the M.S.A. 1970, s. 100 (3), Sched. V as from January 1, 1973; see S.I. 1972 No. 1977.

[6] As to recovery of fines, see M.S.A. 1894, s. 680 *et seq.* As to application of fines, see s. 33 (4), *post.*

145 **20.** [*This section, which contained an amendment to s.* 23 *of the M.S.* (*Safety and Load Line Conventions*) *Act* 1932, *relating to the loading of passenger steamers, by the M.S.* (*Load Lines*) *Act* 1967 *s.* 33 (1) *and Sched.* 2.]

Signals of distress

1146 **21.**[1]—(1) His Majesty in Council may prescribe what signals shall be used by ships as signals of distress.[2]

(2) Rules may be made [3] by the [Secretary of State] [4] prescribing the circumstances in which, and the purposes for which, any signal prescribed by Order in Council under the last preceding subsection is to be used and the circumstances in which it is to be revoked.

(3) If the master of a ship uses or displays or causes or permits any person under his authority to use or display—

(*a*) any signal prescribed by Order in Council under this section except in the circumstances and for the purposes prescribed by the rules made [3] under this section; or

(*b*) any private signal, whether registered or not,[5] that is liable to be mistaken for any signal so prescribed by Order in Council,

he shall be liable to a fine not exceeding fifty pounds [6] and shall further be liable to pay compensation for any labour undertaken, risk incurred or loss sustained in consequence of the signal's having been supposed to be a signal of distress; and that compensation may, without prejudice to any other remedy, be recovered in the same manner as salvage.[7]

(4) Nothing in subsection (4) of section twenty-four of the Merchant Shipping (Safety and Load Line Conventions) Act 1932 (which requires persons in charge of wireless stations to give facilities for the reception of reports relating to dangers to navigation), shall interfere with the transmission of signals prescribed under this section.

1147 In this section and ss. 22 and 23, references to vessel or activities connected therewith include references to hovercraft and activities connected therewith: see the Hovercraft (Application of Enactments) Order 1972 (S.I. No. 971).

1 This section replaces, with modifications, s. 25 of the M.S. (Safety and Load Line Conventions) Act 1932, which section is repealed by s. 37 (5) and the Third Schedule, *post*.

2 Signals of distress have been prescribed by the Collision Regulations (Ships and Seaplanes on the Water) and Signals of Distress (Ships) Order 1965 (S.I. No. 1525), made under this section, which came into force on September 1, 1965. See r. 31 of the Collision Regulations, printed in the Supplement to *British Shipping Laws*, Vol. 4, *Marsden on Collisions at Sea*, 11th ed.

3 The rules in force under this subsection are the M.S. (Signals of Distress) Rules 1965 (S.I. No. 1550). For power to exempt from rules, see s. 28.

4 *i.e.* Secretary of State for Trade.

5 As to registration of private signals, see s. 733 of M.S.A. 1894.

6 As to recovery of fines, see M.S.A. 1894, s. 680 *et seq.* As to application of fines, see s. 23 (4), *post*.

7 See s. 547 *et seq.* of M.S.A. 1894, for "Procedure in Salvage." The provision as to compensation for misuse of distress signals is substantially the same as was contained in s. 434 (2) of the M.S.A. 1894, which section was repealed, and re-enacted with modifications, by s. 25 of the M.S. (Safety and Load Line Conventions) Act 1932. This latter section has now been repealed, and re-enacted with further modifications, by the present section. It has been held that that subsection of the M.S.A. 1894, did not by implication give any right to compensation for labour undertaken, risk incurred or loss sustained in going out in response to signals properly displayed, although, on arrival, the proffered services were not required: *The Elswick Park* [1904] P. 76. This decision is equally applicable to the present section.

Obligation to assist vessels, etc., in distress

1148 **22.**[1]—(1) The master of a British ship [2] registered in the United Kingdom, on receiving at sea a signal of distress or information from any source that a vessel or aircraft is in distress, shall proceed with all speed to the assistance of the persons in distress (informing them if possible that he is doing so) unless he is unable, or in the special circumstances of the case considers it unreasonable or unnecessary, to do so, or unless he is released under the provisions of subsection (3) or subsection (4) of this section.

(2) Where the master of any ship in distress has requisitioned any British ship [2] registered in the United Kingdom that has answered his call, it shall be the duty of the master of the requisitioned ship to comply with the requisition by continuing to proceed with all speed to the assistance of the persons in distress.

(3) A master shall be released from the obligation imposed by subsection (1) of this section as soon as he is informed of the requisition of one or more ships other than his own and that the requisition is being complied with by the ship or ships requisitioned.

(4) A master shall be released from the obligation imposed by subsection (1) of this section, and, if his ship has been requisitioned, from the obligation imposed by subsection (2) of this section, if he is informed by the persons in distress, or by the master of any ship that has reached the persons in distress, that assistance is no longer required.

(5) If a master fails to comply with the preceding provisions of this section, he shall be guilty of a misdemeanour.[3]

(6) *If the master of a British ship registered in the United Kingdom, on receiving at sea a signal of distress or information from any source that a vessel or aircraft is in distress, is unable, or in the special circumstances of the case considers it unreasonable or unnecessary, to go to the assistance of the persons in distress, he shall forthwith cause a statement to be entered in the official log-book, or if there is no official log-book cause other record to be kept, of his reasons for not going to the assistance of those persons, and if he fails to do so he shall be liable to a fine not exceeding one hundred pounds.*[4]

(7) *The master of every British ship registered in the United Kingdom for which an official log is required shall enter or cause to be entered in the official log-book every signal of distress or message that a vessel, aircraft or person is in distress at sea.*[4]

(8) Nothing in this section shall affect the provisions of section six of the Maritime Conventions Act 1911 [5]; and compliance by the master of a ship with the provisions of this section shall not affect his right, or the right of any other person, to salvage.[6]

As for hovercraft, see s. 21.

1 This section replaces with very slight modifications, the provisions of s. 22 of the M.S. (Safety and Load Line Conventions) Act 1932, which section is repealed by s. 37 (5) and the Third Schedule, *post*.
2 As to " British ship," see M.S.A. 1894, s. 1, and notes thereto.
3 As to prosecution of offences and recovery of fines, see M.S.A. 1894, s. 680 *et seq.*
4 The words in italics were repealed by the M.S.A. 1970, s. 180 (3), Sched. V, as from January 1, 1973; see S.I. 1972 No. 1977.
5 That section deals with the general duty of masters and persons in charge of vessels to render assistance to persons in danger at sea; see § 841, *ante*.
6 As to the relevance to the right to salvage of the fact that assistance is rendered in compliance with a statutory obligation, see Kennedy's *Civil Salvage*, 4th ed., pp. 30–33.

Carriage of dangerous goods

1149 **23.**[1]—(1) The [Secretary of State] [2] may make rules [3] for regulating in the interests of safety the carriage of dangerous goods [4] in ships to which this section applies.

(2) This section applies to—

(*a*) British ships [5] registered in the United Kingdom;

(*b*) other ships while they are within any port in the United Kingdom, or are embarking or disembarking passengers within the territorial waters [6] of the United Kingdom, or are loading or discharging cargo or fuel within those waters.

(3) If any of the rules made in pursuance of this section is not complied with in relation to any ship,[7] the owner or master of the ship shall be liable on conviction on indictment to a fine not exceeding three hundred pounds, or on summary conviction to a fine not exceeding one hundred pounds,[8] and the ship shall be deemed for the purposes of Part V of the principal Act to be unsafe by reason of improper loading.[9]

(4) Any goods declared by the rules made under this section to be dangerous in their nature shall be deemed to be dangerous goods for the purposes of Part V of the principal Act.[10]

1150 As for hovercraft, see s. 21.

1 This section replaces with modifications, the provisions of s. 28 of the M.S. (Safety and Load Line Conventions) Act 1932, which section is repealed by s. 37 (5) and the Third Schedule, *post*.
2 *i.e.* the Secretary of State for Trade.
3 The rules at present in force under this section are the M.S. (Dangerous Goods) Rules 1965 (S.I. No. 1067) as amended by S.I. 1968 No. 332 and S.I. 1972 No. 666. For power of Minister to exempt from rules, see s. 28.
4 See also M.S.A. 1894, ss. 446–450. For other enactments relating to dangerous goods, see the Explosives Acts 1875, s. 33 *et seq.*; 1883, s. 8, etc.; Petroleum (Consolidation) Act 1928, ss. 7, 8; Port of London Act 1968, ss. 149 to 151. As to carriage of grain, see s. 24, *post*. As to loading of timber, see s. 61 of the M.S. (Safety and Load Line Conventions) Act 1932.
5 As to " British ship," see M.S.A. 1894, s. 1, and notes thereto.
6 As to what are territorial waters of the United Kingdom, see Territorial Waters Jurisdiction Act 1878, and note (2) to s. 686 of M.S.A. 1894.
7 *i.e.* any ship to which the section applies.
8 As to recovery of fines, see M.S.A. 1894, ss. 680–682.
9 As to detention of ships unsafe *inter alia* by reason of improper loading under Part V of M.S.A. 1894 (the " principal Act ") see s. 459 *et seq.* and s. 592 of that Act. See also, as to detention, s. 9 of the M.S. (Load Lines) Act 1967.
10 See ss. 446–450 of M.S.A. 1894.

Carriage of grain

1151 **24.**[1]—(1) Where grain is loaded on board any British ship [2] registered in the United Kingdom, or is loaded within any port in the United Kingdom on board any ship, all necessary and reasonable precautions shall be taken to prevent the grain from shifting [3]; and if such precautions as aforesaid are not taken, the owner or the master of the ship, or any agent of the owner who was charged with the loading or with sending the ship to sea laden with the grain, shall be guilty of an offence under this subsection,[4] and the ship shall be deemed for the purposes of Part V of the principal Act to be unsafe by reason of improper loading.[5]

(2) Where any ship, having been loaded with grain outside the United Kingdom without the taking of all necessary and reasonable precautions to prevent the grain from shifting,[3] enters any port in the United Kingdom so laden, the owner or master of the ship shall be guilty of an offence under this subsection,[4] and the ship shall be deemed for the purposes of Part V of the principal Act to be unsafe by reason of improper loading [5]:

Provided that this subsection shall not have effect if the ship would not have entered any such port but for stress of weather or any other circumstance that neither the master nor the owner nor the charterer (if any) could have prevented or forestalled.

(3) Without prejudice to the generality of the two preceding subsections, any particular precaution prescribed by rules [6] made by the [Secretary of State] [7] under this subsection, in relation to the loading of ships generally or of ships of any class, as being a precaution to be treated for the purposes of those subsections as a necessary or reasonable precaution to prevent grain from shifting, shall be so treated in the case of ships generally, or of ships of that class, as the case may be:

Provided that this subsection shall not apply where a ship is loaded in accordance in all respects with any provisions approved by the [Secretary of State] [7] as respects the loading in question other than rules made under this subsection.

(4) If any person commits an offence under subsection (1) or subsection (2) of this section he shall be liable on conviction on indictment to a fine not exceeding three hundred pounds, or on summary conviction to a fine not exceeding one hundred pounds.[8]

1152 (5) On the arrival at a port in the United Kingdom from a port outside the United Kingdom of any ship carrying a cargo of grain, the master shall cause to be delivered to the proper officer of Customs in the United Kingdom, together with the report required by the Customs Consolidation Act 1876,[9] a notice stating—

(*a*) the draught of water and freeboard, as defined by Part V of the principal Act,[10] of the said ship after the loading of her cargo was completed at the final port of loading; and (*b*) the following particulars of the grain carried, namely,

(i) the kind of grain and the quantity thereof, stated in cubic feet, quarters, bushels, or tons weight;

(ii) the mode in which the grain is stowed, and

(iii) the precautions taken to prevent the grain from shifting;

and if the master fails to deliver any notice required by this subsection, or if in any such notice he makes any statement that he knows to be false in a material particular or recklessly makes any statement that is false in a material particular, he shall be liable to a fine not exceeding one hundred pounds.[8]

(6) Any person having a general or special authority in that behalf from the [Secretary of State] [7] may, for securing the observance of the provisions of this section, inspect any grain, and the mode in which it is stowed, and for that purpose shall have all the powers of a Ministry of Transport inspector under the principal Act.[11]

(7) In this section the expression " grain " includes wheat, maize, oats, rye, barley, rice, pulses and seeds, and the expression " ship carrying a cargo of grain " means a ship carrying a quantity of grain exceeding one-third of the ship's registered tonnage, reckoning one hundred cubic feet, or two tons weight, of grain as equivalent to one ton of registered tonnage.

1153 [1] This section replaces with modifications the amended provisions of ss. 452–456 of M.S.A. 1894, which sections are repealed by s. 37 (5) and the Third Schedule, *post*.

[2] As to " British ship," see M.S.A. 1894, s. 1, and notes thereto.

[3] Whether all necessary and reasonable precautions have been taken is a question of fact: see *Paterson Steamships, Ltd.* v. *Canadian Co-operative Wheat Producers, Ltd.* [1934] A.C. 538 at p. 543, where s. 452 (1) which is replaced by the present section, was considered. See also *The Standale* (1938) 61 Ll.L.R. 223, where Langton J. regarded the regulations laid down in Schedule 18 to M.S.A. 1894 (now repealed), as showing the standard which " reasonable people have considered to be the proper precautions," even though the Schedule was not strictly applicable to the ship in question.

[4] As to maximum fines for such an offence, see subs. (4).

[5] See note (9) to s. 23.

[6] The rules at present in force under this subsection are the M.S. (Grain) Rules 1965 (S.I. No. 1062). As to power to exempt from rules under this Act, see s. 28, *post*.

[7] *i.e.* Secretary of State for Trade.

[8] As to prosecution of offences and the recovery of fines, see M.S.A. 1894, ss. 680–682.

[9] See now s. 26 of the Customs and Excise Act 1952, which relates to the report to be made on importation of goods.

[10] " Principal Act " means M.S.A. 1894; see s. 36. As to draught of water and freeboard, see M.S.A. 1894, s. 436.

[11] As to the powers of a Department of Trade inspector under the principal Act, see M.S.A. 1894, s. 729, and notes thereto.

Contribution towards a North Atlantic ice service

1154 **25.**[1] Any sums required for the contribution from the United Kingdom towards maintaining, in accordance with the Safety Convention,[2] a service in the North Atlantic for the study and observation of ice, and for ice patrol, shall be paid by the [Secretary of State] [3] out of moneys provided by Parliament.

[1] This section replaces with slight modification, the provisions of s. 32 of the M.S. (Safety and Load Line Conventions) Act 1932, which section is repealed by s. 37 (5) and the Third Schedule, *post*.
[2] As to " Safety Convention," see note (4) to s. 1.
[3] *i.e.* the Secretary of State for Trade.

Supplemental

Definition of " passenger " and " passenger steamer "

155 **26.**[1]—(1) In Part III of the principal Act,[2] in the Merchant Shipping (Safety and Load Line Conventions) Act 1932, and in this Act the expression " passenger " means any person carried in a ship, except—

(*a*) a person employed or engaged in any capacity on board the ship on the business of the ship,

(*b*) a person on board the ship either in pursuance of the obligation laid upon the master to carry shipwrecked, distressed or other persons, or by reason of any circumstance that neither the master nor the owner nor the charterer (if any) could have prevented or forestalled, and

(*c*) a child under one year of age.

(2) In the Merchant Shipping (Safety and Load Line Conventions) Act 1932, and in this Act, the expression " passenger steamer " means a steamer carrying more than twelve passengers.[3]

156 [1] This section, besides defining " passenger " and " passenger steamer " for the purposes of this Act, extends the definition of these words to M.S.A. 1894, Part III, in the case of " passenger " and to the M.S. (Safety and Load Line Conventions) Act 1932, in the case of " passenger " and " passenger steamer." It does not affect the definition of " passenger steamer " in M.S.A. 1894, Part III, as amended by M.S.A. 1906.

As a result of the above substitution of definitions, that part of s. 267 of M.S.A. 1894, which defined " passenger," s. 33 of the M.S. (Safety and Load Line Conventions) Act 1932, which amended that definition, and the definitions of " passenger " and " passenger steamer " in s. 73 (1) of the M.S. (Safety and Load Line Conventions) Act 1932, were repealed by s. 37 (5) and the Third Schedule, *post*. The new definition of " passenger " slightly modifies the previous one but no change has been made by the new definition of " passenger steamer."

[2] " Principal Act " means M.S.A. 1894. See s. 36.
[3] This definition is applied by the M.S. (Load Lines) Act 1967, s. 23 (3). Contrast this definition with the definition in s. 267 of M.S.A. 1894, in which the carrying of "passengers," even though less in number than 12, brings the steamer within the definition. See note (2) to that section. See also the M.S.A. 1964, s. 17 (2) where it is provided that references in the " M.S. Acts " to a passenger steamer are to be construed as including any ship while on or about to proceed on a voyage or excursion in any case where a passenger steamer's certificate is required to be in force in respect of her.

Removing persons in case of danger

157 **27.** Where the [Secretary of State] [1] for the purpose of enabling persons to be moved from any place in consequence of a threat to their lives has permitted more persons to be carried on board a ship than are permitted

under the Merchant Shipping Acts [2] apart from this section,[3] the carriage of that excess of persons shall not be an offence under those Acts.

[1] *i.e.* the Secretary of State for Trade.
[2] See definition in s. 36 (1).
[3] By M.S.A. 1894, s. 283, the owner or master of any passenger steamer is not permitted to receive on board (and by M.S.A. 1906, s. 22, to have on board) a greater number of passengers than the number allowed by the passenger steamer's certificate.

Power of [Secretary of State] [1] to exempt from safety requirements

1158 **28.**—(1) The [Secretary of State] [1] may exempt any ships or classes of ships from any requirements of the rules for life-saving appliances [2] or any rules or regulations made under this Act, either absolutely or subject to such conditions as he thinks fit.

(2) Without prejudice to the preceding provisions of this section where a ship not normally engaged on international voyages [3] is required to undertake a single international voyage, the [Secretary of State] [1] may, if he is of opinion that the ship complies with safety requirements that are adequate for that voyage, exempt the ship from any of the safety requirements imposed by or under the Merchant Shipping Acts.[4]

[1] *i.e.* the Secretary of State for Trade.
[2] See s. 2.
[3] For definition of "international voyage," see s. 36.
[4] See the M.S.A. 1894, ss. 418 *et seq.* and the M.S.A., s. 19 for safety requirements generally. As to issue of exemption certificates and qualified cargo ship safety construction certificates in respect of certain ships exempted from safety requirements by virtue of this section, see the M.S.A. 1964, s. 3 (2).

Exemption of certain ships from certain provisions of this Act

1159 **29.**—(1) Nothing in this Act—

(*a*) prohibiting or preventing a ship from proceeding to sea unless there are in force in relation to the ship, or are produced, the appropriate certificates issued by the [Secretary of State] [1] under this Act or the appropriate accepted Safety Convention certificates [2];

(*b*) conferring powers on a surveyor of ships for the purpose of verifying the existence, validity or correctness of any Safety Convention certificate or that the conditions on which any such certificate was issued are complied with [3];

(*c*) *requiring information about a ship's stability to be carried on board* [4];

(*d*) imposing a penalty for the contravention of any rules relating to openings in ships' hulls and watertight bulkheads,[5]

shall, *unless in the case of information about a ship's stability the* [*Secretary of State*] *otherwise orders*,[4] apply to any troopship,[6] pleasure yacht [7] or fising vessel,[8] or to any ship of less than five hundred tons gross tonnage other than a passenger steamer [9] or to any ship not propelled by mechanical means.[10]

(2) Nothing in the preceding subsection shall affect the exemption conferred by section seven hundred and forty-one of the principal Act [11] on ships belonging to His Majesty.

(3) Notwithstanding that any provision of this Act is expressed to apply to ships not registered in the United Kingdom while they are within any port in the United Kingdom, that provision [12] shall not apply to a ship that would not be within any such port but for stress of weather or any other circumstance that neither the master nor the owner nor the charterer (if any) of the ship could have prevented or forestalled.

1160 1 *i.e.* the Secretary of State for Trade.

2 As to prohibition on proceeding to sea without appropriate certificates, see ss. 12, 17. As to issue of certificates to British ships registered in the United Kingdom, see ss. 7 to 10. As to " accepted Safety Convention certificates," see ss. 14 to 17.

3 The provisions here referred to conferring such powers on a surveyor of ships are contained in s. 14 (3).

4 The words in italics were repealed by the M.S. (Load Lines) Act 1967, s. 33 (1) and Sched. 2.

5 As to " openings in passenger steamers' hulls and watertight bulkheads," and the penalty for contravening any rules made in relation thereto, see s. 19.

6 In no previous Act relating to Merchant Shipping have " troopships " been specifically exempted from certain safety provisions as they are under this section. The term " troopships " is not defined and, *semble,* means ships solely employed in the carriage of troops.

7 For other exemptions of pleasure yachts, see M.S. (Load Lines) Act 1967, s. 1 (*c*).

8 Presumably the definition of " fishing boat " in M.S.A. 1894, s. 370 applies. For general provisions as to fishing boats, see M.S.A. 1894, Part IV and M.S.A. 1970, s. 95 and Sched. 2.

9 For definition of " passenger steamer," see s. 26.

10 This subsection is modified by the M.S.A. 1964, s. 15 in relation to certificates issued under s. 9, *ante.*

11 " Principal Act " means M.S.A. 1894; see s. 36.

12 *e.g.* s. 24 which relates to the carriage of dangerous goods on, *inter alia,* such ships.

Application to colonies, etc.

1161 **30.** Section thirty-six of the Merchant Shipping (Safety and Load Line Conventions) Act 1932 (which enables Orders in Council to be made applying Part I of that Act to territories outside the United Kingdom), shall have effect as if references therein to Part I of that Act included references to this Act.

For Orders in Council made under the M.S. (Safety and Load Line Conventions) Act 1932, s. 36, see notes (1) and (5) to that section at § 1024, *ante.*

Countries to which Safety Convention applies

1162 **31.** His Majesty, if satisfied—

(*a*) that the government of any country has accepted, or denounced, the Safety Convention; or

(*b*) that the Safety Convention extends, or has ceased to extend, to any territory,

may by Order in Council make a declaration to that effect.

This section should be read as if for the reference to the Safety Convention there is substituted a reference to the 1960 Convention: see Introductory Note § 1235, M.S.A 1964, s. 1.

1163 The following Orders in Council were made under this section prior to its amendment:

1. The M.S. (Safety Convention Countries) (Various) Order 1952 (S.I. No. 2034) which declared that the U.K., Belgium, Canada, Denmark, France, Iceland, Israel, Italy, Japan, Netherlands, New Zealand, Norway, Pakistan, Philippines, Portugal, Sweden, South Africa, U.S.A. and Yugoslavia had accepted the Convention, and that the Convention extended to Guernsey, Jersey and the Isle of Man.
2. The M.S. (Safety Convention Countries) (Various) Order 1953 (S.I. No. 733) which declared that India, Spain and Liberia had accepted the Convention, and that the Convention extended to Alaska, Hawaii, Puerto Rico, Spanish Morocco, Spanish West Africa, and Spanish Guinea.
3. The M.S. (Safety Convention Countries) (Various) (No. 2) Order 1953 (S.I. No. 1559) which declared that Chile had accepted the Convention, and that the Convention extended to Hong Kong, Singapore and Italian Somaliland.
4. The M.S. (Safety Convention Countries) (Various) Order 1954 (S.I. No. 143) which declared that Finland, Ireland and Vietnam had accepted the Convention, and that the Convention extended to the Federation of Malaya.
5. The M.S. (Safety Convention Countries) (Various) (No. 2) Order 1954 (S.I. No. 639) which declared that Greece and Panama had accepted the Convention.
6. The M.S. (Safety Convention Countries) (Various) (No. 3) Order 1954 (S.I. No. 1462) which declared that Cambodia, Nicaragua, U.S.S.R., Switzerland, Haiti, Egypt and Poland had accepted the Convention.
7. The M.S. (Safety Convention Countries) (Various) Order 1955 (S.I. No. 427) which declared that Roumania and Netherlands Antilles had accepted the Convention.
8. The M.S. (Safety Convention Countries) (Various) (No. 2) Order 1955 (S.I. No. 1803) which declared that the German Federal Republic, Cuba, Monaco, and Dominica had accepted the Convention.
9. The M.S. (Safety Convention Countries) (Various) (No. 1) Order 1956 (S.I. No. 234) which declared that the Convention extended to the Comoro Islands, French Equatorial Africa, French Somaliland, French West Africa, Madagascar, French Morocco, New Caledonia, the French possessions in Oceania, Saint Pierre and Miquelon, the Trust Territories of Togoland and Cameroons under French administration and Tunisia.
10. The M.S. (Safety Convention Countries) (Various) (No. 2) Order 1956 (S.I. No. 1213) which declared that Brazil and Venezuela had accepted the Convention.
11. The M.S. (Safety Convention Countries) (Various) (No. 3) Order 1956 (S.I. No. 2040) which declared that Argentina and Bulgaria had accepted the Convention.
12. The M.S. (Safety Convention Countries) (Various) (No. 1) Order 1957 (S.I. No. 1372) which declared that Hungary, Turkey and Czechoslovakia had accepted the Convention.
13. The M.S. (Safety Convention Countries) (Various) (No. 2) Order 1957 (S.I. No. 1877) which declared that the Cape Verde Islands, Portugese Guinea, St. Tomé and Principe Islands, Angola, Mozambique, Portuguese India, Macao and Portuguese Timor had accepted the Convention.
14. The M.S. (Safety Convention) (Ghana) Order 1958 (S.I. No. 1960) which declared that Ghana had accepted the Convention.
15. The M.S. (Safety Convention) (Kuwait) Order 1959 (S.I. No. 1042) which declared that Kuwait had accepted the Convention.
16. The M.S. (Safety Convention) (Australia) Order 1960 (S.I. No. 472) which declared that Australia had accepted the Convention.
17. The M.S. (Safety Convention) (Republic of Korea) Order 1960 (S.I. No. 1384) which declared that Korea had accepted the Convention.
18. The M.S. (Safety Convention) (Uruguay) Order 1961 (S.I. No. 1003) which declared that Uruguay had accepted the Convention.
19. The M.S. (Safety Convention) (Mexico) Order 1962 (S.I. No. 1091) which declared that Mexico had accepted the Convention.
20. The M.S. (Safety Convention Countries) (Various) Order 1964 (S.I. No. 702) which declared that Cyprus and Nigeria had accepted the Convention and that it had ceased to extend to Togo and Upper Volta.

21. The M.S. (Safety Convention Countries) (Various) (No. 2) Order 1964 (S.I. No. 1575) which declared that Algeria, Cameroon, Central Africa, Congo (Brazzaville), Dahomey, Guinea, Ivory Coast, Malagasy, Mauritania, Morocco, Niger, Senegal, Somalia and Tunisia had accepted the Convention.

See also note (2) to para. 3 of the First Schedule, *post*, as to treatment, for a limited period, of countries to which the 1929 Safety Convention apply as if they were countries to which the 1948 Convention applied.

For orders made under this section as amended by the M.S.A. 1964, s. 1, relating to the 1960 Convention, see *ibid.* § 1236, *post.*

Transitional provisions

164 **32.** Without prejudice to the effect of section thirty-eight of the Interpretation Act 1899,[1] the provisions of the First Schedule to this Act [2] shall have effect for the purpose of the transition from the law in force before the commencement of this Act [3] to the provisions of this Act.

[1] s. 38 of the Interpretation Act 1889 deals generally with the effect of repeals in Acts passed after the commencement of that Act and of repeals in that Act itself.

[2] See § 1172, *post.*

[3] The date of commencement of this Act was November 19, 1952; see s. 37 and notes thereto.

Provision as to certain fees and fines under the Merchant Shipping Acts

165 **33.**[1]—(1) There shall be paid in respect of any certificate issued by the [Secretary of State] [2] under this Act,[3] including a certificate issued by him under subsection (1) of section fourteen of this Act, and in respect of any inspection of a ship under this Act for the purpose of seeing that she is properly provided with a radio installation and radio officers or operators in conformity with the radio rules,[4] such fees as may be prescribed by regulations made by the [Secretary of State] [2] with the approval of the Treasury.[5]

(2) The [Secretary of State] [2] with the approval of the Treasury may make regulations [6] prescribing the amount or the maximum amount of the fees payable under the enactments specified in the Second Schedule to this Act [7]; and so much of those enactments as fixes the amount or the maximum amount of any such fees shall cease to have effect.

(2) Any fees payable under subsection (1) of this section shall be paid into the Exchequer.

(4) Subsection (2) of section seven hundred and sixteen of the principal Act [8] (which provides for the application of fines) shall apply to fines under this Act as it applies to fines under that Act.[9]

166 [1] This section, besides empowering the Secretary of State to prescribe by regulations with the approval of the Treasury, the fees to be paid in respect of certificates issued by him under this Act, also empowers him (see subs. (2)) to make regulations relating to fees payable under certain sections of previous enactments specified in the Second Schedule to this Act, namely the M.S.A. 1894, the M.S. (Mercantile Marine Fund) Act 1898 and the Fees (Increase) Act 1923. Those parts of sections in these previous enactments which prescribe the amount or maximum amount of any such fees are repealed by s. 37 (5) and the Third Schedule, *post*, and by subs. (2) of this section cease to have effect. Regulations have now been made under this section, which introduce new scales of fees; see notes (5) and (6) below.

[2] *i.e.* the Secretary of State for Trade.
[3] As to certificates issued under this Act, see ss. 7–13.
[4] See s. 3 (7).
[5] The prescribed fees are contained in Parts 1 to 4 of the regulations referred to in note (6) below.
[6] The regulations at present in force under this section are the M.S. (Fees) Regulations 1975 (S.I. No. 341).
[7] See § 1174, *post*.
[8] " Principal Act " means M.S.A. 1894; see s. 36.
[9] This subsection no longer applies to fines upon the conviction of a person in Northern Ireland; see the Northern Ireland Act 1962, s. 25 (1) (*c*).

Rules and regulations

1167 **34.**—(1) The power to make rules and regulations under *the preceding provisions of this Act or the First Schedule to*[1] this Act,[2] or to make rules for life-saving appliances,[3] shall be exercisable by statutory instrument.[4]

(2) Any statutory instrument by which any such power as aforesaid is exercised shall be subject to annulment in pursuance of a resolution of either House of Parliament.[4]

[1] The words in italics were repealed by the M.S.A. 1964, s. 18 (4).
[2] As to power to make rules or regulations under the Act, see ss. 1, 3, 5, 6, 14 (2), 19, 21, 23, 24.
For general power to prescribe forms, see M.S.A. 1894, s. 720.
[3] See s. 2 as to rules for life-saving appliances.
[4] For definition, see the Statutory Instruments Act 1946. As to statutory instruments which are subject to annulment by resolution of either House of Parliament, see s. 5 (1) of that Act.

Consequential amendments of Merchant Shipping Acts

1168 **35.**—(1) In subsection (3) of section seven hundred and twenty-four of the principal Act,[1] for the words " passenger steamers " there shall be substituted the word " ships."

(2) Where a ship is detained under any provision of this Act authorising the detention of a ship until the production of a certificate,[2] subsection (2) of section four hundred and sixty of the principal Act (which makes the owner of a ship liable to pay to the [Secretary of State] [3] his costs in connection with her detention and survey) shall apply as if she had been finally detained under that Act.

(3) *So far as Part I of the Merchant Shipping (Safety and Load Line Conventions) Act* 1932 *requires that any rules or regulations shall implement the International Convention for the Safety of Life at Sea* 1929 *it shall cease to have effect.*[4]

(4) Section sixty-nine of the said Act of 1932 (which requires notice to be given to a consular officer of the detention of a foreign ship, or of proceedings against her master or owner, under that Act), and subsection (3) of section seventy-three of that Act (which requires ships registered in the Channel Islands or the Isle of Man to be treated for the purpose of

any provisions of that Act relating to Safety Convention ships not registered in the United Kingdom as if they were registered in the United Kingdom), shall have effect as if any reference therein to that Act included a reference to this Act.

(5) In subsection (1) of section two hundred and seventy-two of the principal Act and in subsection (1) of section nine of the said Act of 1932, for any reference to a wireless telegraph installation there shall be substituted a reference to a radio installation.[5]

(6) In subsection (1) of section nine of the said Act of 1932 (which relates to the survey of passenger steamers by radio surveyors), for any reference to an exemption under the Merchant Shipping (Wireless Telegraphy) Act 1919,[6] from the obligations imposed by that Act, there shall be substituted a reference to an exemption from the obligations imposed by the radio rules.[5]

[1] " Principal Act " means M.S.A. 1894; see s. 36.
[2] For provisions relating to detention of ships under this Act until the production of a certificate, see ss. 3 (8), 12 (4), 17 (1).
[3] *i.e.* the Secretary of State for Trade.
[4] The words in italics were repealed as spent by the Statute Law Revision Act 1953, s. 1, Sched. I.
[5] As to rules relating to radio installations, referred to as " radio rules," see s. 3 and notes thereto.
[6] The M.S. (Wireless Telegraphy) Act 1919, is repealed by s. 37 (5) and the Third Schedule of this Act.

Interpretation

169 **36.**—(1) In this Act the following expressions have the meanings hereby respectively assigned to them, that is to say:—

" Accepted Safety Convention certificate " has the meaning assigned to it by section fourteen of this Act;

" Collision regulations " means regulations made under section four hundred and eighteen of the principal Act;

" Construction rules " means rules made under section one of this Act;

" Country to which the Safety Convention applies " means—

(*a*) a country the government of which has been declared under section thirty-one of this Act to have accepted the Safety Convention, and has not been so declared to have denounced that Convention[1];

(*b*) a territory to which it has been so declared that the Safety Convention extends, not being a territory to which it has been so declared that that Convention has ceased to extend[1];

" Declaration of survey " means a declaration made under section two hundred and seventy-two of the principal Act;

" International voyage " means a voyage from a port in one country to a port in another country, either of those countries being a country to which the Safety Convention applies,[1] and " short international voyage " means an international voyage—

1170 (*a*) in the course of which a ship is not more than two hundred nautical miles from a port or place in which the passengers and crew could be placed in safety and

(*b*) which does not exceed six hundred nautical miles in length between the last port of call in the country in which the voyage begins and the final port of destination;

so however that for the purpose of the definitions contained in this paragraph—

(i) no account shall be taken of any deviation by a ship from her intended voyage due solely to stress of weather or any other circumstance that neither the master nor the owner nor the charterer (if any) of the ship could have prevented or forestalled; and

(ii) every colony, overseas territory, protectorate or other territory for whose international relations a government that has accepted the Safety Convention is responsible, or for which the United Nations are the administering authority, shall be deemed to be a separate country;

" *The Merchant Shipping Acts " means the Merchant Shipping Acts 1894 to 1948, and this Act*[2]*;*

" The Minister " means the Minister of Transport [3];

" The principal Act " means the Merchant Shipping Act 1894;

" Radio navigational aid " means radio apparatus on board a ship being apparatus designed for the purpose of determining the position or direction of ships or other objects;

" Radio rules " means rules made under section three of this Act;

" Rules for direction-finders " means rules made under section five of this Act;

" Rules for life-saving appliances " means rules made under section four hundred and twenty-seven of the principal Act as amended by section two of this Act;

" Safety Convention ship " means a ship registered in a country to which the Safety Convention applies [4]; and the expression " Safety Convention passenger steamer " [5] shall be construed accordingly.

(2) If any amendment of the Safety Convention comes into force, references in this Act to the Safety Convention shall, unless the context otherwise requires, be construed as references to the Safety Convention as amended.

[1] See note to s. 31.
[2] The words in italics were repealed by the M.S.A. 1964, s. 18 (4): see now *ibid.* s. 19 (2).
[3] Now the Secretary of State for Trade.
[4] See note (1) above.
[5] For definition of " passenger steamer," see s. 26.

Commencement, construction, citation and repeal

71 37.—(1) This Act shall come into force on such day as His Majesty may by Order in Council appoint.[1]

(2) Except so far as the context otherwise requires, any reference in this Act to any other enactment shall be construed as a reference to that enactment as amended, extended or applied by or under any other enactment including this Act.

(3) Except so far as the context otherwise requires, this Act shall be construed as one [2] with the Merchant Shipping Acts 1894 to 1948, and, without prejudice to the generality of this provision, references in those Acts to the Merchant Shipping Acts shall be construed as including references to this Act.

(4) This Act may be cited as the Merchant Shipping (Safety Convention) Act 1949, and the Merchant Shipping Acts 1894 to 1948 and this Act may be cited together as the Merchant Shipping Acts 1894 to 1949.[3]

(5) *The enactments mentioned in the Third Schedule to this Act are hereby repealed to the extent specified in the third column of that Schedule.*[4]

[1] The Act came into force on November 19, 1952; see M.S. (Safety Convention) Act 1949 (Commencement) Order 1952 (S.I. 1952 No. 1418) made under this subsection.
[2] See note (1) to s. 9 of M.S. (Mercantile Marine Fund) Act 1898.
[3] See § 1639.
[4] This subsection was repealed as spent by the Statute Law Revision Act 1953, s. 1, Sched. I.

SCHEDULES

2 Section 32

FIRST SCHEDULE

Transitional Provisions

1. Any rules or regulations made, or having effect as if made, under any enactment repealed by this Act shall, until revoked, have effect as if they had been made under the corresponding provision of this Act.

2.—(1) *Any general safety certificate, short-voyage safety certificate, qualified safety certificate, passenger steamer's exemption certificate, wireless telegraphy certificate or wireless telegraphy exemption certificate in force in respect of any ship at the commencement of this Act shall continue in force until the date shown on the certificate, subject however to any cancellation of the certificate under the principal Act or this Act; and section twelve of this Act shall have effect accordingly.*

(2) *Section eleven of this Act shall have effect as if any such certificate as aforesaid had been issued under this Act.*

(3) *Where in respect of a ship there is in force at the commencement of this Act a wireless telegraphy certificate or a wireless telegraphy exemption*

certificate, that certificate shall be treated for the purposes of paragraph (*b*) *of subsection* (1) *of section twelve of this Act as a radio certificate or as an exemption certificate stating that she is wholly exempt from the requirements of the Safety Convention relating to radiotelegraphy, radiotelephony and direction-finders, as the case may require.*

(4) *Nothing in the said paragraph* (*b*) *shall prohibit a ship from proceeding to sea without a safety-equipment certificate (whether or not qualified) until after the expiration of twenty-four months from the date of the commencement of this Act, nor a ship of less than sixteen hundred tons gross tonnage from proceeding to sea without a radio certificate (whether or not qualified), or a certificate stating that she is wholly exempt from the provisions of the Safety Convention relating to radiotelegraphy, radiotelephony and direction-finders, until after the expiration of one year from that date.*

(5) *Subsection* (5) *of section thirteen of this Act shall apply to any certificate as is mentioned in sub-paragraph* (1) *of this paragraph as it applies to certificates issued under this Act.*

3.—(1) *The [Secretary of State]* [1] *may by regulations provide—*

(*a*) *that any country to which the International Convention for the Safety of Life at Sea* 1929 *applies shall, for such purposes, for such a period and subject to such conditions as may be specified by or under the regulations, be treated for the purposes of this Act as if it were a country to which the Safety Convention applies; and*

(*b*) *that any certificate purporting to have been issued in accordance with the said Convention of* 1929 *and complying with such of the regulations made under subsection* (2) *of section sixteen of the Merchant Shipping (Safety and Load Line Conventions) Act* 1932 *as are applicable in the circumstances may, for such purposes, for such a period and subject to such conditions as may be specified by or under the regulations, be treated as if it were an accepted Safety Convention certificate within the meaning of this Act.*

(2) *Without prejudice to any general provisions of this Schedule regarding the validity of regulations made under any Act repealed by this Act, regulations made under subsection* (2) *of section sixteen of the said Act of* 1932 *shall continue in force so far as they are required for the purposes of this paragraph.*

4. *Nothing in section seventeen of this Act shall require the master of a ship of less than sixteen hundred tons gross tonnage other than a passenger steamer to produce an accepted Safety Convention certificate being the equivalent of a radio certificate (whether or not qualified), or a certificate stating that she is wholly or partly exempt from the provisions of the Safety Convention relating to radiotelegraphy, radiotelephony and direction-*

finders, before the expiration of twelve months after the date of the commencement of this Act; nor the master of any ship to produce an accepted Safety Convention certificate being the equivalent of a safety-equipment certificate (whether or not qualified) before the expiration of twenty-four months after that date; and the provisions of that section relating to clearance and detention of ships shall have effect accordingly.

Editors' Notes:—

The words in italics were repealed by the M.S.A. 1964, s. 18 (4).

73 [1] *i.e.* The Secretary of State for Trade.

74 **Section 33** SECOND SCHEDULE

ENACTMENTS FIXING THE AMOUNT OF FEES

The Merchant Shipping Act 1894, sections 64 (1), 77 (2),[1] 83, 97, 125 (3), 126 (2), 210 (3), 277, 306 (2), 360 (2), 420 (8), 567 (1), 695 (2).

The Merchant Shipping (Mercantile Marine Fund) Act 1898, section 3.

The Fees (Increase) Act 1923, section 2 (1) to (4).

[1] s. 77 (2) was repealed by the M.S.A. 1965, ss. 1, 7 (2) and Sched. 2.

75 **Section 37** THIRD SCHEDULE [1]

[1] This schedule was repealed as spent by the Statute Law Revision Act 1953, s. 1, Sched. I.

MERCHANT SHIPPING ACT 1950

(14 GEO. 6, c. 9)

An Act to provide for regulating crew accommodation in fishing boats and for amending the Merchant Shipping Acts 1894 to 1949, with respect to the engagement and discharge of crews, the review of punishments imposed by naval courts, fishing boats engaged in the Newfoundland cod fisheries, and proceedings in summary courts in Northern Ireland; and for purposes connected with the matters aforesaid. [12th July, 1950.]

BE it enacted, etc.

76 INTRODUCTORY NOTE.—This Act, which came into force for all purposes on December 10, 1950 (see note to section 8, *post*), has now been largely repealed by the M.S.A. 1970, s. 100 (3), Sched. V, as from a date to be appointed. As enacted, however, it had as its objects:

(1) The regulation of standards of crew accommodation in British fishing boats. This matter is dealt with in section 1 of the Act and the First Schedule thereto, and these provisions substantially correspond with those provisions of the M.S.A. 1948, which relate to crew accommodation in other British ships and which are applied with modification for the purposes of section 1 of the 1950 Act (see paragraphs 1–13 of the First Schedule). The provisions (*inter alia*) empower the Secretary of State for Trade, after consultation with representative organisations of owners of British fishing boats and of seamen employed therein, to make regulations with respect to crew accommodation in British fishing boats registered in the United Kingdom or fishing boats being constructed to the order of persons qualified to be owners of British ships and which have not been registered in the United Kingdom or elsewhere. Provision is also made for inspections of crew accommodation in such fishing boats by surveyors of ships in certain circumstances (see paragraphs 5–10 of First Schedule, applying, with modifications, the provisions of section 3 of the M.S.A. 1948), and consequential amendments are made in those provisions of the M.S. Acts 1894 and 1906 which relate to crew accommodation (see paragraphs 11–13 of First Schedule, applying, with modifications, the provisions of section 4 of the M.S.A. 1948). The general effect of the provisions would have been to improve considerably the standard of crew accommodation in fishing boats to which the new provisions apply and in the case of such boats to replace the existing provisions of the M.S. Acts (applying to such boats) relating to this subject (see M.S.A. 1894, s. 210, Sched. VI). However no regulations have been made under the section.

(2) The amendment of a miscellaneous body of provisions of the M.S. Acts relating to the engagement and discharge of crews, the review of punishments imposed by naval courts, fishing boats engaged in the Newfoundland cod fisheries, and proceedings in summary courts in Northern Ireland. Section 2 of the Act and the Second Schedule (now repealed as from January 1, 1973: see S.I. 1972 No. 1977) enacted in permanent form the provisions of Defence (General) Regulation 45AA and of the Fourth Schedule to the Defence (General) Regulations 1939, by amending certain provisions of Part II of the M.S.A. 1894, and those amendments had the effect of extending to certain home trade ships certain provisions relating to the engagement and discharge of crews of foreign-going ships and of modifying those provisions. Section 3 enacts in permanent form the provisions of Defence (General) Regulation 48B by providing for the review of punishments

imposed by naval courts by the senior naval or consular officer present at the place where the court is held. Section 4 amends section 744 of the M.S.A. 1894, and section 5 removes any doubt as to the meaning of the expression "Summary Jurisdiction Acts" in the M.S. Acts in relation to Northern Ireland.

Regulations with respect to crew accommodation in fishing boats

7 **1.**[1]—(1) *The [Secretary of State]* [2] *may, after consultation* [3] *with such organisation or organisations as appear to him* [4] *to be representative of owners of British fishing boats* [5] *and with such organisation or organisations as appear to him to be representative of seamen employed in British fishing boats, make regulations,*[6] *with respect to the crew accommodation* [7] *to be provided in fishing boats of any class specified in the regulations, being—*

(*a*) *British fishing boats registered in the United Kingdom,*[8] *whether under Part I or Part IV of the principal Act* [9] *and whether so registered before or after the date on which the regulations come into force; or*

(*b*) *boats which at any time after the said date are being constructed for use as fishing boats and are being so constructed to the order of any person qualified under the principal Act to be the owner of a British ship,*[10] *and have not been registered in the United Kingdom or elsewhere:*

Provided that, subject to the provisions of any Order in Council made under the First Schedule to this Act, such regulations shall not apply to any fishing boat under construction which is being constructed at any place in His Majesty's dominions outside the United Kingdom, in India, in the Republic of Ireland or in any protectorate, protected state, trust territory or mandated territory within the meaning of the British Nationality Act 1948,[11] *or is intended on her first registration to be registered at any such place.*

(2) *Without prejudice to the generality of the preceding subsection, regulations made thereunder may, in particular—*

(*a*) *prescribe the minimum space per man which must be provided in any fishing boat to which the regulations apply by way of sleeping accommodation for seamen* [12] *and apprentices, and the maximum number of persons by whom any specified part of such accommodation may be used;*

(*b*) *regulate the position in any such fishing boat in which the crew accommodation* [7] *or any part thereof may be located, and the standards to be observed in the construction, equipment and furnishing of any such accommodation;*

(*c*) *require the submission to a surveyor of ships* [13] *of plans and specifications of any works proposed to be carried out for the purpose of the provision or alteration of any such accommodation, and authorise the surveyor to inspect any such works;*

(*d*) *provide for the maintenance and repair of any such accommodation, and prohibit or restrict the use of any such accommodation for purposes other than those for which it is designed;*

and may make different provision in respect of different classes of fishing boats and in respect of crew accommodation provided for different classes of persons.

[(2A) *The* [*Secretary of State*] [2] *may exempt any fishing boats or classes of fishing boats from any requirements of regulations made under this section, either absolutely or subject to such conditions as he thinks fit.*] [14]

(3) *If the provisions of any regulations made under this section are contravened in the case of any fishing boat, the owner* [15] *or skipper of the fishing boat shall be liable to a fine not exceeding one hundred pounds.*[16]

(4) [. . . . . . .] [17].

(5) *The provisions of the First Schedule* [18] *to this Act* (*being provisions contained in sections two, three, four, nine and eleven of the Merchant Shipping Act* 1948, *set out with modifications*) *shall have effect in relation to fishing boats to which regulations made under this section apply.*

(6) *The power of the* [*Secretary of State*] [2] *to make regulations under this section shall be exercisable by statutory instrument, and any such statutory instrument shall be subject to annulment in pursuance of a resolution of either House of Parliament.*[19]

1178 [1] This section is prospectively repealed by the M.S.A. 1970, s. 100 (3), Sched. V as from a day to be appointed.

[2] *i.e.* the Secretary of State for Trade.

[3] See note (2) to s. 1 of M.S.A. 1948.

[4] See note (3) to s. 1 of M.S.A. 1948.

[5] For definition, see s. 7 (1).

[6] No regulations have so far been made under this section.

[7] The subsection omitted was repealed by the M.S.A. 1965, s. 7 (2), Sched. 2.

[8] As to registration generally, see M.S.A. 1894, Part I, which applies to all boats which are " ships " unless they come within the exemptions contained in s. 3 of that Act; see also M.S.A. 1894, ss. 373, 374, for additional requirements of registration in the case of fishing boats.

[9] " Principal Act " means M.S.A. 1894; see s. 7 (1).

[10] As to the qualifications for owning a British ship and for meaning of the expression " British ship," see M.S.A. 1894, s. 1, and notes thereto.

[11] See *ibid.* ss. 30 and 32.

[12] See definition in M.S.A. 1894, s. 742.

[13] As to appointment and powers of surveyors, see M.S.A. 1894, ss. 724–727. As to inspection of crew accommodation of fishing boats by a surveyor of ships under this Act, see paras. 5–9 of the First Schedule, *post*.

[14] Subsection (2A) is added to this section by M.S.A. 1952, s. 1 (2).

[15] The expression " owner " in relation to a fishing boat under construction, means the person to whose order she is being constructed; see s. 7 (1).

[16] As to the recovery of fines, see M.S.A. 1894, ss. 680–682.

[17] The subsection omitted was repealed by the M.S.A. 1965, s. 7 (2), Sched. 2.

[18] See §§ 1187–1192, *post*.

[19] As to such statutory instruments subject to annulment by resolution of either House of Parliament, see s. 5 (1) of the Statutory Instruments Act 1946.

9 **2.** [*This section, which contained provisions relating to the engagement and discharge of crew, was repealed by the M.S.A.* 1970, *s.* 100 (3), *Sched. V, as from January* 1, 1973; *see S.I.* 1972 *No.* 1977. *For the present provisions, see ibid. ss.* 1 *to* 3.]

Review of punishments imposed by naval courts

80 **3.**[1]—(1) *Where a naval court summoned under Part VI of the principal Act*[2] *imposes*[3] *on any person any one or more of the following punishments, that is to say:—*

(*a*) *sentences him to imprisonment;*

(*b*) *imposes on him any fine or forfeiture of wages;*

(*c*) *removes or discharges him from his ship; or*

(*d*) *in the case of a certificated officer, cancels or suspends his certificate;*

the order of the court, so far as it imposes any such punishment, shall be subject to review by the senior naval or consular officer[4] *(hereafter in this section referred to as " the reviewing officer ") present at the place where the court is held:*

Provided that, if the senior naval or consular officer present at the said place is a member of the naval court, the functions of the reviewing officer under this section shall be exercised in relation to that court by the naval commander-in-chief or the naval officer within whose command the said place is situated.

(2) *The reviewing officer may, in reviewing any such order, confirm or refuse to confirm the order so far as it imposes on any person any such punishment, or vary the order, as respects any such punishment imposed thereby, as follows:—*

(*a*) *in the case of imprisonment, reduce the term thereof or substitute a fine, forfeiture of wages or removal or discharge from his ship;*

(*b*) *in the case of a fine or forfeiture of wages, reduce the amount thereof or substitute removal or discharge from his ship;*

(*c*) *in the case of any other punishment, being a punishment imposed on a certificated officer, substitute any punishment which is lower in the following scale:—*

cancellation of certificate,
suspension of certificate,
removal or discharge from his ship; or

(*d*) *in the case of suspension of certificate, reduce the period thereof:*

Provided that the reviewing officer shall not substitute under this subsection any punishment which the naval court could not have imposed.[3]

(3) *Where any such order imposes two or more such punishments as are referred to in subsection* (1) *of this section, whether of the same kind or*

different kinds, the reviewing officer may, in exercising his powers under the last foregoing subsection, deal separately with each such punishment.

(4) *Where any such naval court imposes a sentence of imprisonment and directs the offender to be sent to the United Kingdom or any other place under section sixty-seven of the Merchant Shipping Act* 1906,[5] *the reviewing officer may revoke that direction.*

(5) *The place of imprisonment, whether on land or on board ship, of any person sentenced by any such naval court shall, unless he is sent to the United Kingdom or any other place under the said section sixty-seven, be a place approved in writing by the reviewing officer as a proper place for the purpose.*

(6) *Where any order reviewed under this section requires the offender to pay the costs of the proceedings or any part thereof, the reviewing officer may also revoke that requirement or may vary it, but not so as to increase the amount payable by the offender in respect of those costs.*

(7) *The reviewing officer shall, on reviewing an order under this section, record his decision in writing, and if he refuses to confirm the order (so far as it imposes any such punishment as aforesaid), the order shall to that extent cease to have effect and if he varies the order, it shall thereafter have effect as if it had been made by the court as so varied.*

(8) [. . .] [6]

1181 [1] This section is prospectively repealed by the M.S.A. 1970, s. 100 (3), Sched. V as from a day to be appointed.

[2] " Principal Act " means M.S.A. 1894; see s. 7 (1). As to the summoning of Naval Courts, see M.S.A. 1894, s. 480.

[3] As to powers of Naval Courts, see *ibid.* s. 483.

[4] For definition, see M.S.A. 1894, s. 742, and note (13) thereto.

[5] Under that section the court has power to send a prisoner either to the United Kingdom or to any British possessions to which that section has been applied, and for that purpose has the power given to Consular officers by s. 689 of M.S.A. 1894.

[6] The subsection omitted was repealed as spent by the Statute Law Revision Act 1953, s. 1, Sched. I.

Amendment of s. 744 of the Merchant Shipping Act 1894

1182 **4.** A ship shall not be deemed to be a foreign-going ship [1] for the purposes of the principal Act [2] by reason only that she is engaged in the Newfoundland cod fisheries, and accordingly section seven hundred and forty-four of that Act [3] shall have effect with the substitution for the words " whale, seal, walrus or Newfoundland cod fisheries " of the words " whale, seal or walrus fisheries " and with the omission of the words " of ships engaged in the Newfoundland cod fisheries which belong to ports in Canada or Newfoundland and ".

[1] For definition, see M.S.A. 1894, s. 742.

[2] " Principal Act " means M.S.A. 1894; see s. 7 (1).

[3] Under s. 744 of M.S.A. 1894, as it existed before the amendment provided in this section, ships engaged *inter alia* in the Newfoundland cod fisheries were deemed to be foreign-going ships and therefore subject to *e.g.* the provisions in ss. 92 and 93 of that Act relating to certificates of competency.

Removal of doubts as to meaning of Summary Jurisdiction Acts in relation to Northern Ireland

83 5. [*This section which removed doubts as to the meaning of Summary Jurisdiction Acts in relation to Northern Ireland was repealed by the Northern Ireland Act* 1962, *s.* 30 (2), *Sched.* 4, *Pt. IV*: *see now ibid. s.* 27.]

Payment of fees into the Exchequer

84 **6.** *Any fees* [1] *received by the* [*Secretary of State*] [2] *under or by virtue of this Act or regulations made thereunder shall be paid into the Exchequer.*

This section is prospectively repealed by the M.S.A. 1970, s. 100 (3), Sched. V as from a day to be appointed.

1 As to fees payable under or by virtue of this Act, see First Schedule, para. 9.

2 *i.e.* the Secretary of State for Trade.

Interpretation

85 7.—(1) In this Act, the following expressions have the meanings hereby respectively assigned to them, that is to say:

" crew accommodation " includes sleeping rooms, mess rooms, sanitary accommodation, hospital accommodation, recreation accommodation, store rooms and catering accommodation provided for the use of seamen and apprentices;

" fishing boat " has the same meaning as in Part IV of the principal Act,[1] except that it includes a vessel which is being constructed for the purpose of being employed in sea fishing or in the sea-fishing service;

" local authority " means the Common Council of the City of London,[2] the council of a metropolitan borough,[3] the council of any county, county borough or county district in England and Wales or Northern Ireland, and, in Scotland, any county, town or district council;

" the Minister " means the Minister of Transport [4];

" owner," in relation to a fishing boat under construction, means the person to whose order she is being constructed;

" pilotage authority " has the same meaning as in the Pilotage Act 1913 [5];

" the principal Act " means the Merchant Shipping Act 1894;

and any reference in this Act to the re-registration of a fishing boat [6] shall not include a reference to a re-registration which is only required in consequence of a change in the ownership of the boat.

(2) Except so far as the context otherwise requires, any reference in this Act to any other enactment shall be construed as a reference to that enactment as amended, extended, or applied by or under any other enactment, including this Act.

[1] See M.S.A. 1894, s. 370.
[2] See the City of London (Various Powers) Act 1958, s. 5.
[3] See the London Government Act 1963, ss. 1, 4 (2) (*a*) and Sched. 1.
[4] Now the Secretary of State for Trade.
[5] See Pilotage Act 1913, ss. 7 and 8.
[6] For references to re-registration of fishing boats, see paras. 1, 2, 5 and 7 of First Schedule.

Short title, construction, citation and commencement

1186 **8.**—(1) This Act may be cited as the Merchant Shipping Act 1950.

(2) This Act shall be construed as one [1] with the Merchant Shipping Acts 1894 to 1949, and, without prejudice to the generality of this provision, references in those Acts to the Merchant Shipping Acts shall be construed as including references to this Act; and the said Acts and this Act may be cited together as the Merchant Shipping Acts 1894 to 1950.[2]

(3) This Act shall come into operation on such date as the [Secretary of State] [3] may by order appoint,[4] and different dates may be appointed for the purpose of different provisions of this Act, and the power of the Secretary of State to make orders under this subsection shall be exercisable by statutory instrument.

[1] See note to s. 9 of M.S. (Mercantile Marine Fund) Act 1898.
[2] See now § 1639.
[3] *i.e.* Secretary of State for Trade.
[4] By the M.S.A. 1950 (Commencement) Order 1950 (S.I. No. 1845 (*c*)), made under this subsection, the Act came into force on December 10, 1950.

SCHEDULES

Section 1 FIRST SCHEDULE

PROVISIONS OF MERCHANT SHIPPING ACT 1948, APPLIED WITH MODIFICATIONS FOR THE PURPOSES OF SECTION ONE OF THIS ACT

This schedule is prospectively repealed by the M.S.A. 1970, s. 100 (3), Sched. V, as from a day to be appointed.

1187 *Application of regulations to fishing boats already registered, under construction, etc.* (*Section* 2 (2) *to* (5) *of* 1948 *Act*)

1. *Where any fishing boat to which regulations made under section one of this Act apply was registered in the United Kingdom under Part I or Part IV of the principal Act* [1] *immediately before the date on which those regulations came into force, then, unless and until, after that date, the fishing boat is re-registered* [2] *in the United Kingdom or undergoes substantial structural alterations or repairs* (*not being repairs carried out in consequence of damage* [3] *or in an emergency*)—

(*a*) *any requirements of the regulations* (*including any subsequent regulations amending or substituted for those regulations*) *relating to matters specified in paragraph (a) or paragraph (b) of subsection (2) of section one of this Act (in this Schedule referred to as " the construction requirements ") shall—*

(i) *in the case of a fishing boat to which corresponding requirements under the law in force immediately before that date* [4] *were applicable, be deemed to be complied with if those requirements are complied with;*

(ii) *in any other case, not apply; and*

(*b*) *any requirements of any such regulations relating to matters specified in paragraph (c) of the said subsection (2) (in this Schedule referred to as " the survey requirements ") shall not apply to any works other than works proposed to be carried out for the purpose of any such alterations or repairs as aforesaid.*[5]

2. *Where regulations made under section one of this Act become applicable—*

(*a*) *to a fishing boat under construction of which the keel was laid before the date on which those regulations came into force;*

(*b*) *to a fishing boat registered in the United Kingdom under Part I or Part IV of the principal Act* [1] *after that date, not being a fishing boat to which such regulations applied while she was under construction,*

or where any such fishing boat as is mentioned in the preceding paragraph is re-registered,[2] *altered or repaired as mentioned in that paragraph, then, if, upon application made to him by the owner of the fishing boat, the [Secretary of State]* [6] *is satisfied, after consultation* [7] *with the owner of the fishing boat or an organisation or organisations appearing to* [8] *the [Secretary of State]* [6] *to be representative of owners of British fishing boats,*[9] *and with an organisation or organisations appearing to the [Secretary of State]* [6] *to be representative of seamen employed in British fishing boats, that such steps, if any, as are reasonable and practicable have been taken for securing compliance with the construction requirements* [10] *of the regulations in the case of the fishing boat, he shall certify accordingly.*

3. *In determining for the purposes of the last preceding paragraph what steps for securing compliance with the construction requirements* [10] *of any regulations are reasonable and practicable, the [Secretary of State]* [6] *shall have regard to the age of the fishing boat, to the purpose for which she is or is intended to be used and to the nature of any alterations or repairs which are carried out, or* [11] *to the extent to which the construction of the fishing boat had been completed before the date on which the regulations came into force, as the case may be.*

4. *Where any such certificate is issued by the Minister as aforesaid, then, subject to compliance with such conditions, if any, as may be specified in the certificate—*

1187

(*a*) *the construction requirements* [10] *of the regulations (including any subsequent regulations amending or substituted for those regulations) shall be deemed to be complied with in the case of the fishing boat; and*

(*b*) *the survey requirements* [12] *of any such regulations shall not apply to any works other than works proposed to be carried out for the purpose of any such alterations or repairs as are mentioned in paragraph* 1 *of this Schedule:*

Provided that on the occurrence of any such event as is mentioned in the said paragraph 1, *the provisions of this paragraph shall cease to have effect in relation to the fishing boat, but without prejudice to the issue of a further certificate under paragraph* 2 *of this Schedule.*

Editors' Notes:—

1188 For meaning of " fishing boat " see s. 7 (1).

[1] *i.e.* M.S.A. 1894; see s. 7 (1).
[2] See note (5) to s. 2 of M.S.A. 1948.
[3] See note (7) to s. 2 of M.S.A. 1948.
[4] See M.S.A. 1894, s. 210 and M.S.A. 1906, s. 64. Certain fishing boats were excluded from those provisions; see M.S.A. 1894, s. 263 (1).
[5] See note (7) to s. 2 of M.S.A. 1948.
[6] *i.e.* the Secretary of State for Trade.
[7] See note (2) to s. 1 of M.S.A. 1948.
[8] See note (3) to s. 1 of M.S.A. 1948.
[9] As to qualifications for owning a British ship, see M.S.A. 1894, s. 1.
[10] See para. 1 (*a*).
[11] The words following " or " are applicable only to the fishing boats covered by para. 2 (*a*).
[12] See para. 1 (*b*).

Inspection of crew accommodation (*Section* 3 *of* 1948 *Act*)

1189 5. *Whenever a fishing boat to which regulations made under section one of this Act apply is registered or re-registered* [1] *in the United Kingdom under Part I or Part IV of the principal Act* [2] *and whenever a complaint in respect of crew accommodation* [3] *in any such fishing boat is duly made in accordance with the regulations, and on such other occasions as may be prescribed by the regulations, a surveyor of ships* [4] *shall inspect the crew accommodation.*

6. *If, upon any such inspection, the surveyor is satisfied that the crew accommodation* [3] *complies with the regulations, he shall (except where the inspection is made in consequence of a complaint) give to the registrar of British ships* [5] *a certificate specifying as space deductible under section seventy-nine of the principal Act* [2] *the whole of the space comprised in that accommodation, except any part thereof required by the regulations to be disregarded in estimating the space so to be deducted.*

7. *If, upon any such inspection, it appears to the surveyor that the accommodation* [3] *does not comply in all respects with the regulations, he may give to the registrar a certificate specifying as space deductible as aforesaid such part of the space comprised in the accommodation as he considers appropriate having regard to the extent to which it complies with*

the regulations, but if he does not give such a certificate he shall report to the registrar that no space is deductible as aforesaid:

Provided that the surveyor shall not be required to make such a report as aforesaid—

(*a*) *if the inspection is made on the occasion of the registration or re-registration*[1] *of the fishing boat; or*

(*b*) *if it appears to him that the failure to comply with the regulations is not substantial and will be remedied within a reasonable time.*

8. *Where any certificate is given or report made under either of the two last preceding paragraphs in respect of a fishing boat already registered, any certificate previously given thereunder in respect of that fishing boat shall cease to have effect, and the register tonnage of the fishing boat shall be altered accordingly.*

9. *In respect of any inspection of a fishing boat carried out by a surveyor for the purposes of this Schedule, there shall be paid such fees as may be prescribed by regulations made under section one of this Act.*

10. *Regulations made under section one of this Act may require the skipper of any fishing boat to which the regulations apply, or any officer authorised by him for the purpose, to carry out such inspections of the crew accommodation*[3] *as may be prescribed by the regulations, and to record, in such manner as may be so prescribed, such particulars of any such inspection as may be so prescribed.*

Editors' Notes:—

For meaning of " fishing boat " see s. 7.

1 See note (5) to s. 2 of M.S.A. 1948.
2 *i.e.* M.S.A. 1894. See s. 7.
3 For definition, see s. 7 (1).
4 See M.S.A. 1894, s. 724.
5 See M.S.A. 1894, s. 4.

Consequential amendments of principal Act (*Section* 4 *of* 1948 *Act*)

190 11. *In relation to fishing boats to which regulations made under section one of this Act apply, section seventy-nine of the principal Act*[1] *(which authorises certain deductions in ascertaining the register tonnage of ships) shall have effect as if in sub-paragraph* (*a*) (i) *of subsection* (1) *for the words " any space occupied by seamen or apprentices and appropriated to their use, which is certified under the regulations scheduled to this Act with regard thereto " there were substituted the words " any space provided by way of crew accommodation which is certified under the Merchant Shipping Act* 1950, *to be space deductible under this section."*

12. [. . .][2]

13. *Section two hundred and ten of the principal Act and the Sixth Schedule to that Act shall not apply to any fishing boat to which regulations made under section one of this Act apply (but without prejudice to the provisions of paragraph* 1 *of this Schedule):*

Provided that any certificate given in relation to any such fishing boat as aforesaid, under paragraph (3) *of the said Sixth Schedule before the date on which the regulations apply thereto shall have effect for the purposes of this Act and of the principal Act as if it had been given under paragraph* 6 *of this Schedule.*

Editors' Notes:

For meaning of " fishing boat " see s. 7 (1).

[1] *i.e.* M.S.A. 1894; see s. 7 (1). S. 79 was repealed by the M.S.A. 1965, s. 7 (2), Sched. 2. See now *ibid.* s. 1.

[2] The paragraph omitted was repealed by the M.S.A. 1965, s. 7 (2), Sched. 2.

Application to certain countries and territories (*Sections* 9 *and* 11 (2) *of* 1948 *Act*)

1191 14. *His Majesty may by Order in Council*[1] *direct that any of the provisions of section one of this Act or of this Schedule (including any enactments for the time being in force amending or substituted for the said provisions) shall extend, with such exceptions, adaptations and modifications, if any, as may be specified in the Order, to the Isle of Man, any of the Channel Islands or any colony.*

15. *The Foreign Jurisdiction Act* 1890 *shall have effect as if the provisions of section one of this Act and of this Schedule were included among the enactments which, by virtue of section five of that Act, may be extended by Order in Council to countries in which for the time being His Majesty has jurisdiction.*[2]

16. *His Majesty may by Order in Council*[1] *direct that any of the provisions of section one of this Act or of this Schedule shall apply, subject to such exceptions, adaptations and modifications, if any, as may be specified in the Order, to fishing boats*[3] *registered in any country or territory to which the said provisions can be extended by virtue of either of the two last preceding paragraphs, or under construction in any such country or territory, or to be registered on first registration in any such country or territory, as it applies to fishing boats registered in the United Kingdom under Part I or Part IV of the principal Act, under construction in the United Kingdom or to be so registered on first registration, as the case may be.*

17. *Any Order in Council made under the preceding provisions of this Schedule shall be subject to annulment in pursuance of a resolution of either House of Parliament.*[4]

Editors' Notes:

1192 [1] No orders under these paragraphs of the Schedule have so far been made.

[2] No orders have so far been made under the Foreign Jurisdiction Act 1890, extending s. 1 of and this Schedule to the 1950 Act to any countries in which H.M. has jurisdiction.

[3] For meaning of " fishing boat," see s. 7.

[4] The making of these Orders in Council is now subject to the Statutory Instruments Act 1946, and the Orders are known as " statutory instruments." See s. 5 (1) as to such statutory instruments subject to annulment by resolution of either House of Parliament.

SECOND SCHEDULE

[*This schedule, which contained amendments to the M.S.A.* 1894, *relating to the engagement and discharge of crews, was repealed by the M.S.A.* 1970, *s.* 100 (3), *Sched. V as from January* 1, 1973: *see S.I.* 1972 *No.* 1977.]

MERCHANT SHIPPING ACT 1952

(15 & 16 GEO. 6 & 1 ELIZ. 2, c. 14)

An Act to enable the [Secretary of State for Trade] to grant exemptions from requirements as to crew accommodation imposed under the Merchant Shipping Act 1948, and the Merchant Shipping Act 1950.

[13th March, 1952.]

BE it enacted, etc.

This Act is prospectively repealed by the M.S.A. 1970 as from a day to be appointed.

Power of [Secretary of State] to exempt from requirements as to crew accommodation

1193 [*This section amended section* 1 *of the Merchant Shipping Act* 1948 *by adding a new subsection* (2A) *and section* 1 *of the Merchant Shipping Act* 1950 *by adding a new subsection* (2A). *See those Acts, ante.*]

Short title and citation

1194 **2.** *This Act may be cited as the Merchant Shipping Act* 1952, *and this Act and the Merchant Shipping Acts* 1894 *to* 1950 *may be cited together as the Merchant Shipping Acts* 1894 *to* 1952.[1]

[1] See now § 1639.

MERCHANT SHIPPING ACT 1954

(2 & 3 ELIZ. 2, c. 18)

1195 [*This Act, which contained provisions regulating the computation of the deduction formerly permitted under the M.S.A.* 1894, *s.* 78, *in respect of the space occupied by propelling power for the purposes of ascertaining the registered tonnage of a ship, was repealed by the M.S.A.* 1965, *s.* 7 (2), *Sched.* 2: *see now ibid. s.* 1.]

CLEAN AIR ACT 1956

(4 & 5 Eliz. 2, c. 52)

An Act to make provision for abating the pollution of the air.

[5th July, 1956]

Be it enacted, etc.:

Introductory Note. This Act is expressed to make provision for abating the pollution of the air, but it only deals with those forms of air pollution which can be attributed to the discharge of smoke, dust and grit from chimneys. It is intended to give effect to recommendations made in the Report of the Committee on Air Pollution (Cmd. 9322). It has a limited application to "vessels" (see s. 20) and only those sections relevant to merchant shipping are included in this book. Subject to certain special defences being established, the Act makes it an offence for vessels to emit dark smoke for longer than certain permitted periods if they are within prescribed waters (ss. 1, 20). Notification of an offence must be given to the owner or master of the vessel soon after the incident (s. 30). Vessels of the Royal Navy and Government ships employed on naval business are exempt from these provisions, although both a local authority and the Secretary of State have certain obligations if such vessels cause a nuisance by emitting dark smoke (s. 22). Penalties for the offence are laid down (s. 27) and the necessary powers of entry upon vessels are conferred upon local authorities (Sched. III). The sections which create the offence dealt with in this note, came into force on June 1, 1958, and to that extent the Act applies to Scotland without modification, but not to Northern Ireland (s. 36).

Dark Smoke

Prohibition of dark smoke from chimneys

1196 **1.**[1]—(1) Subject to the provisions of this Act, dark smoke [2] shall not be emitted from a chimney [3] of any building,[1] and if, on any day,[3] dark smoke [2] is so emitted, the occupier of the building [1] shall be guilty of an offence.[4]

(2) Emissions of smoke from any chimney [3] lasting for not longer than such periods as may be specified by the [Secretary of State] [5] by regulations [6] shall, in such classes of case and subject to such limitations as may be so specified, be left out of account for the purposes of this section.

(3) In any proceedings for an offence under this section, it shall be a defence to prove [7] either—

(*a*) that the contravention complained of was solely due to the lighting up of a furnace [1] which was cold and that all practicable [8] steps had been taken to prevent or minimise the emission of dark smoke; or

(*b*) that the contravention complained of was solely due to some failure of a furnace [1] or of apparatus used in connection with a furnace,[1] that that failure could not reasonably have been foreseen, or, if foreseen, could not reasonably have been provided against, and that the contravention could not reasonably have been prevented by action taken after the failure occurred; or

(*c*) that the contravention complained of was solely due to the use of unsuitable fuel, that suitable fuel was unobtainable, that the least unsuitable fuel which was available was used and that all practicable [8] steps had been taken to prevent or minimise the emission of dark smoke as the result of the use thereof; or

(*d*) that the contravention complained of was due to the combination of two or more of the causes specified in paragraphs (*a*) to (*c*) of this subsection and that the other conditions specified in those paragraphs are satisfied in relation to those causes respectively.

(4) This section shall apply in relation to a chimney [3] serving the furnace [1] of any boiler or industrial plant [8] (being a boiler or plant attached to a building or for the time being fixed to or installed on any land) as it applies in relation to a chimney of a building:

Provided that in relation to any such chimney as aforesaid which is not a chimney of a building, the reference in this section to the occupier of the building shall be construed as a reference to the person having possession of the boiler or plant.

1197 [1] This section applies to vessels within certain prescribed waters as it applies to buildings; for references to " occupier of the building " must be substituted references to " the owner of and the master or other officer or person in charge of the vessel "; and references to a " furnace " include references to " an engine of the vessel "; see generally s. 20, *post*.

[2] For definition of " dark smoke " and means of proof, see s. 34 (2), *post*.

[3] For definition of " chimney " and " day," see s. 34 (1), *post*.

[4] The section appears to impose an absolute criminal liability without proof of intention. An owner and a master will therefore be liable if a member of the crew causes the emission of dark smoke, provided he is acting within the scope of his authority even though contrary to instructions; see generally *Stone's Justices' Manual* (published annually), Vol. 1, Part III—" Criminal responsibility—guilty animus " and cases there cited. See, however, the special defences available under subss. (2) and (3) of this section, and ss. 2 and 30, *post*. For penalties, see s. 27, *post*.

[5] *i.e.* the Secretary of State for the Environment; in Scotland, the Secretary of State for Scotland; see s. 34 (1), *post*.

[6] The following regulations, made by statutory instrument in accordance with s. 33 of this Act, are at present in force:
(i) the Dark Smoke (Permitted Periods) Regulations 1958 (No. 498), and
(ii) the Dark Smoke (Permitted Periods) (Vessels) Regulations 1958 (No. 878).
For present purposes, only the latter are relevant. These permit dark smoke to be emitted from a chimney of a vessel for the following periods:
(1) from a forced draught oil-fired boiler furnace, or an oil engine—a total of ten minutes in any two hours;
(2) from a natural draught oil-fired boiler furnace (except for those cases referred to in (4) below)—a total of ten minutes in any one hour;
provided that in either case, continuous emissions of dark smoke caused otherwise than by the soot blowing of a water-tube boiler shall not exceed four minutes;

(3) from a coal-fired boiler furnace—
(a) when the vessel is at anchor or made fast to the shore or bottom—a total of ten minutes in any one hour;
(b) when the vessel is under way or aground—a total of twenty minutes in any one hour;
(4) from a natural draught oil-fired furnace or a coal-fired boiler furnace in the case of (a) a vessel with funnels shortened for the purpose of navigating the Manchester Ship Canal, or (b) a tug at anchor or made fast to the shore or bottom, but preparing to get under way or supplying power to other vessels or to shore installations, or (c) a vessel at anchor or made fast to the shore or bottom but using main power for dredging, lifting, pumping or performing some other special operation for which she is designed—a total of five minutes in any one hour (provided that in the case of natural draught oil-fired boiler furnaces, a continuous emission of dark smoke caused otherwise than by the soot blowing of a water-tube boiler shall not exceed ten minutes);
(5) from any other source—a total of five minutes in any one hour.

The regulations also limit the emission of " black smoke " (defined as smoke which is as dark or darker than shade 4 on the Ringelmann Chart) which in the case of any vessel, must not be emitted for more than a total of three minutes in any period of thirty minutes. As to " Ringelmann Chart," see note (1) to s. 34, *post.*

[7] The burden of proof resting upon a defendant is to satisfy the court of the probability of the matters which he is required to prove: see *R.* v. *Carr-Briant* [1943] K.B. 607.

[8] For the meaning of " practicable " and " industrial plant," see s. 34 (1), *post.*

. . . . .

Vessels

1198 **20.**—(1) Sections one *and two* [1] of this Act shall apply in relation to vessels [2] in waters to which this section applies as they apply in relation to buildings, but as if for the references to the occupier of the building there were substituted references to the owner of, and to the master or other officer or person in charge of, the vessel [2] and as if references to a furnace included references to an engine of the vessel.[2]

(2) For the purposes of this Act a vessel [2] in any waters to which this section applies which are not within the district of any local authority [3] shall be deemed to be within the district of the local authority [3] whose district includes that point on land which is nearest to the spot where the vessel [2] is.

(3) The waters to which this section applies are—

(*a*) all waters not navigable by sea-going ships; and

(*b*) all waters navigable by sea-going ships which are within the seaward limits of the territorial waters of the United Kingdom [4] and are contained within any port, harbour, river, estuary, haven, dock, canal or other place so long as a person or body of persons is empowered by or under any Act to make charges in respect of vessels [2] entering it or using facilities therein.

In this subsection " charges " means any charges with the exception of light dues, local light dues and any other charges payable in respect of lighthouses, buoys or beacons and of charges in respect of pilotage.

(4) Save as provided in this section, nothing in this Act [5] applies to smoke, grit or dust from any vessel.[1]

[1] The words in italics were repealed by the Clean Air Act 1968, s. 14 (2) and Sched. 2.
[2] " Vessel " is not defined in this Act but, in respect of England and Wales (except London) by virtue of s. 31 (1) of this Act and the Public Health Act 1936, s. 343 (1), see the M.S.A. 1894, s. 742. Within the County of London and the Port of London, " vessel " includes a boat and every description of vessel used in navigation; see (by virtue of ss. 31 (1) and 32 (1), (2) of this Act) the Public Health (London) Act 1936, s. 304 (1).
[3] See note (5) to s. 2 in 6th ed.
[4] The territorial waters of the United Kingdom extend for three miles from low-water mark; see the Territorial Waters Jurisdiction Act 1878, s. 7. *R.* v. *Kent Justices, ex p. Lye* [1967] 2 Q.B. 153; *Post Office* v. *Estuary Radio Ltd.* [1967] 3 All E.R. 663. In any particular dispute over the limits of territorial waters, the court will treat as conclusive evidence the statement of an appropriate officer of the Crown; *The Fagernes* [1927] P. 311. The reference to " this Act " includes a reference to the Clean Air Act 1968; see *ibid.* s. 14 (1), Sched. 1, para. 1.

. . . . . .

Crown premises, etc.

1199 **22.**—(1) It shall be part of the functions of the local authority,[1] in cases where it seems to them proper so to do, to report to the responsible [Secretary of State] any cases of—

. . . . . .

(*d*) emissions of dark smoke [2] from any vessel [3] of Her Majesty's navy, or any Government ship [4] in the service of the [Secretary of State] [5] while employed for the purposes of Her Majesty's navy, which appear to them to constitute such a nuisance as aforesaid,[6]

and on receiving any such report the said [Secretary of State] shall inquire into the circumstances and, if his inquiry reveals that there is cause for complaint, shall employ all practicable means [7] for preventing or minimising the emission of the smoke, grit or dust or for abating the nuisance and preventing a recurrence thereof, as the case may be. . . .

(3) Section twenty of this Act shall, with the omission of the reference in subsection (1) thereof to the owner, apply to vessels [1] owned by the Crown, except that it shall not apply to vessels of Her Majesty's navy or to Government ships in the service of the [Secretary of State] [5] while employed for the purposes of Her Majesty's navy. . . .

(5) In this section " Government ship " has the same meaning as in section eighty of the Merchant Shipping Act 1906.[8]

[1] See note (5) to s. 2, *ante.*
[2] For definition of " dark smoke " see s. 34 (2), *post.*
[3] See note (1) to s. 20 in 6th ed.
[4] See subs. (5) to this section, and the M.S.A. 1906, s. 80, § 810, *ante.*
[5] The words in brackets were substituted by the Defence (Transfer of Functions) (No. 1) Order 1964, S.I. No. 488 Art. 2, Sched. 1, Pt. 1.
[6] This appears to refer back to paragraph (*c*) of this subsection, which deals with Crown premises and relates to " emissions of smoke, whether dark smoke or not, from any such premises which appear to them to constitute a nuisance to the inhabitants of the neighbourhood."
[7] For meaning of " practicable " and " practicable means," see s. 34 (1), *post.*
[8] See § 810, *ante.*

. . . . . .

Penalties

1200 **27.**—(1) A person [1] guilty of an offence under section one of this Act shall be liable on summary conviction,[2] in the case of dark smoke from a chimney of a private dwelling, to a fine not exceeding ten pounds,[3] and, in the case of dark smoke from any other chimney, to a fine not exceeding one hundred pounds. . . .

(5) Any offence under any provision of this Act for which the maximum penalty which may be imposed does not exceed ten pounds [4] may in Scotland be prosecuted in any court of summary jurisdiction within the meaning of the Summary Jurisdiction (Scotland) Act 1954, having jurisdiction in the place where the offence was committed.

1 This may be the owner of or the master or other officer or person in charge of a vessel; see s. 20, *ante*.

2 For summary jurisdiction and procedure, see the Magistrates' Courts Act 1952. By s. 104 of that Act, an information must be laid within six months of the time when the alleged offence was committed. See also the special defence provided by s. 30, *post*, if a proper notification of the offence has not been given in due time.

3 The maximum fine has been increased to £20 by the Criminal Justice Act 1967, s. 92 (1) and Sched. 3, Pt. 1.

4 The limit has been raised to £50 by the Clean Air Act 1968, s. 14 (1), Sched. 1, para. 7.

. . . . . .

Enforcement

1201 **29.**—(1) It shall be the duty of the local authority [1] to enforce the provisions of this Act [2]:

Provided that nothing in this section shall be construed as extending to the enforcement of—

(*a*) any of the provisions of the Alkali, &c. Works Regulation Act 1906; or

(*b*) any building [regulations].[3]

(2) A local authority [1] in England and Wales may institute proceedings for an offence under section one of this Act in the case of any smoke [4] which affects any part of their district notwithstanding that the smoke is emitted from a chimney outside their district [and may institute proceedings for an offence under Section 1 of the Clean Air Act 1968, in the case of any smoke which affects any part of their district notwithstanding that the smoke is emitted from premises outside their district.] [5]

(3) Nothing in this section shall be construed as authorising a local authority in Scotland to institute proceedings for an offence against this Act.[2]

1 For the powers of entry conferred upon local authorities, see Sched. III, *post*. The local authorities are district councils or London borough councils.

2 The reference to this Act includes a reference to the Clean Air Act 1968; see *ibid.* s. 14 (1), Sched. I, para. 1.

3 The word in brackets was substituted by the Public Health Act 1961, ss. 5 (1), 11 (2) and Sched. 1, Pt. III.

4 See s. 34 (1), *post*, for the meaning of " smoke."

5 The words in brackets were added by the Clean Air Act 1968, s. 14 (1), Sched. I, para. 8.

Duty to notify occupiers of offences

1202 **30.**—(1) If, in the opinion of an authorised officer [1] of the local authority,[2] an offence is being or has been committed under section one or section eleven of this Act or a nuisance to which section sixteen of this Act applies exists or has existed, he shall, unless he has reason to believe that notice thereof has already been given by or on behalf of the local authority,[2] as soon as may be notify the occupier of the premises, the person having possession of the boiler or plant, the owner of the railway locomotive engine or the owner or master or other officer or person in charge of the vessel, as the case may be, and, if his notification is not in writing, shall, within forty-eight hours after he became aware of the offence, confirm the notification in writing.

(2) In any proceedings for an offence under section one or section eleven of this Act it shall be a defence to prove [3] that the provisions of subsection (1) of this section have not been complied with in the case of the offence, and if no such notification as is required by that subsection has been given before the end of the two days next following the day of the offence, the said subsection (1) shall be deemed not to have been complied with unless the contrary is proved.

[1] This term has, by virtue of s. 31 (1) of this Act (not printed in this book) the meaning given to it by the Public Health Act 1936, s. 343 (1); " an officer of the council authorised by them in writing, either generally or specially, to act in matters of any specified kind, or in any specified matter; provided that the medical officer of health, surveyor and sanitary inspector of a council shall, by virtue of their appointments, be deemed to be authorised officers for the purposes of matters within their respective provinces." Sanitary inspectors are now known as public health inspectors; see the Sanitary Inspectors (Change of Designation) Act 1956. As to Scotland, see s. 34 (1), *post.*

[2] See note 1 to s. 29, *ante.*

[3] See note (7) to s. 1 as to burden of proof.

. . . . .

Interpretation

1203 **34.**—(1) In this Act, except so far as the context otherwise requires,—

" appointed day " means such day as the [Secretary of State] may by order appoint and different days may be appointed for different purposes, different areas and different provisions of this Act; . . .

" authorised officer " means, as respects Scotland, any officer of a local authority authorised by them in writing, either generally or specially, to act in matters of any specified kind or in any specified matter; . . .

" chimney " includes structures and openings of any kind from or through which [smoke, grit, dust or fumes may be emitted and, in particular, includes flues] [1] and references to a chimney of a building include references to a chimney which serves the whole or a part of a building but is structurally separate therefrom;

" day " (except in the expression " the appointed day ") means a period of twenty-four hours beginning at midnight; . . .

[" fumes " means any airborne solid matter smaller than dust] [2] . . .

" industrial plant " includes any still, melting pot or other plant used for any industrial or trade purposes, and also any incinerator used for or in connection with any such purposes;

" local authority," as respects Scotland, means a county or town council;

[" The Secretary of State "] means, as respects England and Wales, [3] the Secretary of State for Environment and, as respects Scotland, the Secretary of State for Scotland; . . .

" owner," as respects Scotland, has the like meaning as in the Public Health (Scotland) Act 1897;

" port health authority " means, as respects Scotland, a port local authority constituted under Part X of the Public Health (Scotland) Act 1897;

" practicable " means reasonably practicable having regard, amongst other things, to local conditions and circumstances, to the financial implications and to the current state of technical knowledge, and " practicable means " includes the provision and maintenance of plant and the proper use thereof;

" smoke " includes soot, ash, grit and gritty particles emitted in smoke.

(2) In this Act " daik smoke " means smoke which, if compared in the appropriate manner with a chart of the type known at the date of the passing of this Act as the Ringelmann Chart, [4] would appear to be as dark as or darker than shade 2 on the chart.

For the avoidance of doubt it is hereby declared that, in proceedings brought under or by virtue of section one [5] or section sixteen of this Act, the court may be satisfied that smoke is or is not dark smoke as hereinbefore defined notwithstanding that there has been no actual comparison thereof with a chart of the said type; and, in particular, and without prejudice to the generality of the preceding provisions of this subsection, if the [Secretary of State] [6] by regulations [7] prescribes any method of ascertaining whether smoke is dark smoke as so defined, proof in any such proceedings that that method was properly applied, and that the smoke was thereby ascertained to be or not to be dark smoke as so defined, shall be accepted as sufficient. . . .

(8) Any reference in this Act to any enactment shall, except so far as the context otherwise requires, be construed as a reference to that enactment as amended by or under any subsequent enactment (including this Act).

[1] The words in brackets were substituted by the Clean Air Act 1968, s. 14 (1), Sched. 1, para. 10.
[2] The words in brackets were added by the Clean Air Act 1968, s. 14 (1), Sched. 1, para. 10.
[3] Now includes the Secretary of State for Wales as regards Wales and Monmouth (see S.I. 1965 No. 319). Formerly the Minister of Housing and Local Government.
[4] The chart, which is described in Appendix V of the Report of the Committee on Air Pollution (Cmd. 9322) is named after its designer, Professor Ringelmann of France.
[5] The reference to s. 1 of this Act, includes a reference to the Clean Air Act 1968, s. 1: see *ibid.* s. 14, Sched. 1, para. 11.
[6] *i.e.* the Secretary of State for the Environment.
[7] This power has not yet been exercised.

. . . . .

Provisions as to Northern Ireland

1204 **36.** The provisions of this Act other than this section, shall not extend to Northern Ireland, but, notwithstanding anything in the Government of Ireland Act 1920, the Parliament of Northern Ireland shall have power to make laws for any purposes similar to any of the purposes of this Act.

Short title and commencement

1205 **37.**—(1) This Act may be cited as the Clean Air Act 1956.

(2) This Act shall come into operation on the appointed day.[1]

[1] For meaning of " appointed day," see s. 34 (1) (*supra*). The Act came into force in two stages. The Clean Air Act 1956 (Appointed Day) Order 1956 (No. 2022), brought the whole Act, except for ss. 1, 2, 5–9, 16, 19, 20, 22 (1) (*a*) (*c*) (*d*) (3) and 35 (1) (2) and Sched. IV, into operation on December 31, 1956. The remainder of the Act, which includes all the provisions relevant to vessels, came into operation on June 1, 1958; see the Clean Air Act 1956 (Appointed Day) Order 1958 (No. 167).

. . . . .

Sections 31, 32

THIRD SCHEDULE

Modifications of, and Provisions Supplementary to, Public Health Acts, &c.

Part I

Public Health Act 1936

1206 1. Section two hundred and eighty-seven (which confers a power of entry on premises)—

(*a*) shall not, except in relation to work under subsection (2) of section twelve of this Act, apply in relation to any premises being a private dwelling; but

(*b*) shall apply in relation to any vessel [1] as it applies in relation to premises.

2. Section two hundred and ninety-seven shall have effect as if the reference to a daily penalty in respect of a continuing offence included a reference to a daily penalty in respect of a repetition of an offence.

3. Sections three hundred and seventeen, three hundred and nineteen, three hundred and forty-one and three hundred and forty-two [2] (which relate respectively to repeals and alterations of local Acts, to regulations made by the Minister, to the application of the Act to Crown property and to the application of portions of the Act to London) shall not apply.

PART II

Public Health (London) Act 1936 [3]

PART III

Scottish Enactments

Public Health (Scotland) Act 1897

1207 Section eighteen (which confers a power of entry on premises) shall have effect subject to the following modification and to any other necessary modifications consequential thereon, that is to say, that the purposes for which the power of entry may be exercised shall include the purposes of enforcing the provisions of this Act enforceable by the local authority, of exercising any of the powers of the authority under this Act and of ascertaining whether there is or has been on, or in connection with, the premises any contravention of those provisions or whether any of the powers of the authority under this Act ought to be exercised:

Provided that—

(*a*) the said section eighteen shall not, except in relation to work under subsection (2) of section twelve of this Act, apply in relation to any premises being a private dwelling; and

(*b*) except in the case of a factory within the meaning of the Factories Act 1937, or of any other premises in which persons are employed otherwise than in domestic service, admission to any premises shall not be demanded as of right unless twenty-four hours' notice of the intended entry has been given to the occupier.

This paragraph shall apply in relation to vessels [1] as it applies in relation to premises.

Housing (Scotland) Act 1950

Section twenty-two shall have effect as if the reference to section five or section eight of that Act included a reference to section twelve of this Act.

Section one hundred and sixty-one (which imposes a penalty for obstructing the execution of works) shall have effect as if, in subsection (1), the words " Part II of " and paragraph (*b*) were omitted.

Editors' note:
[1] For meaning of " vessels," see note (2) to s. 20, *ante*.
[2] s. 342 of the Public Health Act 1936 was repealed by the London Government Act 1965, s. 93 (1), Sched. 18, Part II.
[3] This part was repealed by the London Government Act 1963, s. 93 (1), Sched. 18, Part II.

MERCHANT SHIPPING (LIABILITY OF SHIPOWNERS AND OTHERS) ACT 1958

(6 & 7 ELIZ. 2, c. 62)

An Act to amend Part VIII of the Merchant Shipping Act 1894, and section two of the Merchant Shipping (Liability of Shipowners and others) Act 1900; and for purposes connected therewith.

[1st August, 1958]

BE it enacted, etc.:

1208 INTRODUCTORY NOTE. The provisions of this Act came into force on August 1, 1958 (see s. 9). The main object of this Act is to give effect to the International Convention relating to the Limitation of the Liability of Owners of Sea-going Ships, signed at Brussels on October 10, 1957. The text of this Convention is published in Cmnd. 353, and is set out in *British Shipping Laws*, Vol. 4, Marsden's *Collisions at Sea* (11th ed.), § 1286–91. The statute law relating to Limitation of Liability has already been summarised at the beginning of Part VIII of the M.S.A. 1894, § 410, *ante*. The principal alterations in the law made by this present Act may be summarised as follows:

(i) The limits set to liability by s. 503 of M.S.A. 1894, and s. 2 of M.S.A. 1900, are increased from £15 to an amount equivalent to 3,100 gold francs, and from £8 to an amount equivalent to 1,000 gold francs. The Secretary of State for Trade is empowered to declare the sterling equivalents of these amounts. Where there are claims against the larger fund, the amount specified must be multiplied by 300 wherever the tonnage of the ship concerned is less than 300 tons (s. 1).

(ii) The right to limit liability for loss of life or personal injury has been extended to claims of persons not on board the limiting ship, and the right to limit liability for loss or damage to property or rights has been extended to claims in respect of any property or rights wherever situated (s. 2 (1)).

(iii) It is no longer necessary that loss of life or personal injury, or damage to property or rights in respect of which limitation is claimed, should have been caused by reason of the improper navigation or management of the ship. Nor is the right to limit excluded by reason only that the occurrence giving rise to the liability was not due to negligence. It is sufficient if the occurrence was caused through the act or omission of any person (whether on board the ship or not) in the navigation or management of the ship or in loading, discharging or embarkation and disembarkation of passengers or through any other act or omission of any person on board the ship (s. 2 (1) and (3)).

(iv) The liability to " damages " (to which limitation was confined by s. 503 of M.S.A., 1894) now includes any liability otherwise than in damages arising in respect of any damage caused to harbour works, basins or navigable waterways and, when the necessary statutory instrument is made, will include any liability, otherwise than in damages, arising in connection with the raising, removal or destruction of any ship which is sunk, stranded or abandoned, or of anything on board such a ship. There is power to set up a fund to compensate harbour authorities for loss consequent upon bringing into force limitation of liability for wreck-raising charges (s. 2 (2) (5) (6) (7)).

(v) The benefit of the right to limit has been extended to any charterer and to any person interested in or in possession of the ship, and to any manager or operator of the ship, and to any employer of a person who by s. 3 (2) is entitled, to limit his personal liability (s. 3 (1) (2)). Further, the master and members of the crew have been given the right to limit their personal liability. This right is irrespective of their actual fault or privity, except in respect of the loss of or damage to undeclared valuables in circumstances of dishonesty (s. 3 (2)).

(vi) For the purposes of limitation, the definition of " ship " has been extended to include any structure, whether completed or in the course of construction, launched and intended for use in navigation as a ship or part of a ship, and the limitation provisions apply to a British ship whether or not it has been registered (s. 4 (1) (2)).

(vii) Restrictions are imposed upon the enforcement of judgments in respect of liabilities for which limitation may be claimed, after adequate security has been given (s. 6).

(viii) Contingent claims before a foreign court may now be taken into consideration in the distribution of a limitation fund, and liens no longer affect the proportions in which distribution is to be made (s. 7).

(ix) In certain cases, ships or property that have been arrested in connection with a claim founded upon a liability which may be limited, may be entitled to be released after adequate security has been given. In certain circumstances, the court will be obliged to order release, but these provisions are subject to the Brussels Convention coming into force by sufficient ratification (s. 5).

1209 By virtue of the Hovercraft (Civil Liability) Order 1971 S.I. No. 270, Art. 6 and Sched. 3, made under the Hovercraft Act 1968, s. 1 (1) this Act applies with modifications to various claims arising out of the operation of hovercraft: see § 1319, *post*.

This Act (other than ss. 1, 2 (1) and 8 (1) to (3)) as modified by the Hovercraft (Civil Liability) Order 1971, would read as follows:

2.—(2) For the purposes of subsection (1) of section 503 of the Merchant Shipping Act 1894 as applied by the Hovercraft (Civil Liability) Order 1971, where any obligation or liability arises in respect of any damage (however caused) to harbour works, basins or navigable waterways, the occurrence giving rise to the obligation or liability shall be treated as one of the occurrences mentioned in paragraphs (*b*) and (*d*) of that subsection, and the obligation or liability as a liability to damages.

(3) The application of the said section five hundred and three of the Merchant Shipping Act 1894 as applied by the Hovercraft (Civil Liability) Order 1971 to any liability shall not be excluded by reason only that the occurrence giving rise to the liability was not due to the negligence of any person.

3.—(1) The persons whose liability in connection with a hovercraft is excluded or limited by Part VIII of the Merchant Shipping Act 1894 as applied by the Hovercraft (Civil Liability) Order 1971 shall include any charterer and any person interested in or in possession of the hovercraft and, in particular, any manager or operator of the hovercraft.

(2) In relation to a claim arising from the act or omission of any person in his capacity as captain or member of the crew or (otherwise than in that capacity) in the course of his employment as a servant of the owners or of any such person as is mentioned in subsection (1) of this section,—

(*a*) the persons whose liability is excluded or limited as aforesaid shall also include the captain, member of the crew or servant, and, in a case where the captain, or member of the crew is the servant of a person whose liability would not be limited apart from this paragraph, the person whose servant he is; and

(*b*) the liability of the captain, member of the crew or servant himself shall be excluded or limited as aforesaid notwithstanding his actual fault or privity in that capacity, except in the case mentioned in paragraph (ii) of section five hundred and two of the said Act of 1894 as applied by the Hovercraft (Civil Liability) Order 1971.

5.—(1) Where a hovercraft or other property is arrested in connection with a claim which appears to the court to be founded on a liability to which a limit is set by section five hundred and three of the Merchant Shipping Act 1894 as applied by the Hovercraft (Civil Liability) Order 1971 or security is given to prevent or obtain release from such an arrest, the court may order the release of the hovercraft, property or security, if the conditions specified in subsection (2) of this section are satisfied; but where the release is ordered the person on whose application it is ordered shall be deemed to have submitted to the jurisdiction of the court to adjudicate on the claim (or, in Scotland, to have prorogated that jurisdiction).

(2) The said conditions are—

(*a*) that security which in the opinion of the court is satisfactory (in this section referred to as " guarantee ") has previously been given, whether in the United Kingdom or elsewhere, in respect of the said liability or any other liability incurred on the same occasion and the court is satisfied that, if the claim is established, the amount for which the guarantee was given or such part thereof as corresponds to the claim will be actually available to the claimant; and

(*b*) that either the guarantee is for an amount not less than the said limit or further security is given which, together with the guarantee, is for an amount not less than the limit.

(4) For the purposes of this section—

(*a*) a guarantee given by the giving of security in more than one country shall be deemed to have been given in the country in which security was last given;

(*b*) any question whether the amount of any security is (either by itself or together with any other amount) not less than any limit set by section five hundred and three of the Merchant Shipping Act 1894 as applied by the Hovercraft (Civil

Liability) Order 1971, shall be decided as at the time at which the security is given;

(*c*) where part only of the amount for which a guarantee was given will be available to a claimant that part shall not be taken to correspond to his claim if any other part may be available to a claimant in respect of a liability to which no limit is set as mentioned in sub-section (1) of this section.

(7) In the application of this section to Scotland the references to arrest shall be construed as referring to arrestment on the dependence of an action or in rem and for the references to release from arrest or to the ordering of such a release there shall be substituted references to the recall of an arrestment.

6.—(1) No judgment or decree for a claim founded on a liability to which a limit is set by section five hundred and three of the Merchant Shipping Act 1894 as applied by the Hovercraft (Civil Liability) Order 1971 shall be enforced, except so far as it is for costs (or, in Scotland, expenses), if security for an amount not less than the said limit has been given, whether in the United Kingdom or elsewhere, in respect of the liability or any other liability incurred on the same occasion and the court is of opinion that the security is satisfactory and is satisfied that the amount for which it was given or such part thereof as corresponds to the claim will be actually available to the person in whose favour the judgment or decree was given or made.

(2) For the purposes of this section—

(*a*) any question whether the amount of any security is not less than any limit set by section five hundred and three of the Merchant Shipping Act 1894 as applied by the Hovercraft (Civil Liability) Order 1971 shall be decided as at the time at which the security is given;

(*b*) where part only of the amount for which security has been given will be available to the person in whose favour the judgment or decree was given or made that part shall not be taken to correspond to his claim if any other part may be available to a claimant in respect of a liability to which no limit is set as mentioned in subsection (1) of this section.

7.—(1) In making any distribution in accordance with section five hundred and four of the Merchant Shipping Act 1894 as applied by the Hovercraft (Civil Liability) Order 1971, the court may, if it thinks fit, postpone the distribution of such part of the amount to be distributed as it deems appropriate having regard to any claims that may later be established before a court of any country outside the United Kingdom.

(2) No lien or other right in respect of any hovercraft or property shall affect the proportions in which under the said section five hundred and four as so applied any amount is distributed amongst several claimants.

8.—(4) In Part VIII of the Merchant Shipping Act 1894, as applied by the Hovercraft (Civil Liability) Order 1971, the expression " owner " shall be construed as including, where it occurs in section five hundred and two, every person whose liability is excluded by section three of this Act, and elsewhere, except in the second place where it occurs in section five hundred and five, every person whose liability is limited by that section.

As to limitation of liability for oil pollution see the M.S. (Oil Pollution) Act 1971, and in particular ss. 5 (4) (*b*) and 7 (*b*).

Increase in liability of shipowners and others

1210 1.—(1) In ascertaining the limits set to the liability of any persons by section five hundred and three of the Merchant Shipping Act 1894,[1] or section two of the Merchant Shipping (Liability of Shipowners and others) Act 1900,[2] there shall be substituted—

(*a*) for the amount of fifteen pounds mentioned in the said section five hundred and three, an amount equivalent to three thousand one hundred gold francs [3];

(*b*) for each of the amounts of eight pounds mentioned in the said sections, an amount equivalent to one thousand gold francs [3];

and the number by which the amount substituted by paragraph (*a*) of this subsection is to be multiplied shall be three hundred in any case where the tonnage concerned is less than three hundred tons.[4]

(2) For the purposes of this section a gold franc shall be taken to be a unit consisting of sixty-five and a half milligrams of gold of millesimal fineness nine hundred.

(3) The [Secretary of State for Trade] may from time to time by order made by statutory instrument [5] specify the amounts which for the purposes of this section are to be taken as equivalent to three thousand one hundred and one thousand gold francs respectively.[3]

(4) Where money has been paid into court (or, in Scotland, consigned in court) in respect of any liability to which a limit is set as aforesaid, the ascertainment of that limit shall not be affected by a subsequent variation of the amounts specified under subsection (3) of this section unless the amount paid or consigned was less than that limit as ascertained in accordance with the order then in force under that subsection.[6]

211 [1] See § 427, *ante*. S. 503 of the 1894 Act has been amended by ss. 1 and 2 of this Act, and is the principal provision which defines the class of claims for which liability may be limited.

[2] See § 747, *ante*. S. 2 of the M.S. (Liability of Shipowners and Others) Act 1900, enabled dock and canal owners, and harbour and conservancy authorities, to limit their liability for loss or damage to vessels or goods on board them to £8 for each ton of the tonnage of the largest registered British ship which was at the time of the occurrence, or which had been during the previous five years, within the area of the dock or canal owners or the harbour or conservancy authority. The limit has been raised by this section to an amount equivalent to one thousand gold francs.

[3] In exercise of the powers given by subs. (3) of this section, the Secretary of State for Trade has declared sterling equivalents of the amounts here specified as follows: £108·1677 for 3,100 gold francs and £34·8928 for 1,000 gold francs: see the M.S. (Limitation of Liability) (Sterling Equivalents) Order 1974 (S.I. No. 536).

[4] It is to be noted that the "minimum tonnage multiple" of 300 applies only to cases previously covered by the limit of £15, *i.e.* where loss of life or personal injury has occurred, either alone or together with loss of or damage to property. In this respect the Act departs from the Convention, Article 3 of which applied the "minimum tonnage" of 300 to all claims. Although it may be possible to read s. 503 as predicating two separate limitation funds, one out of which loss of life or personal injury claimants may be satisfied *pro tanto*, and one out of which other claimants may be satisfied *pro tanto*, the established practice is that referred to in note (5) to s. 504 at § 440, *ante*, and set out in Article 3 of the Convention. It is therefore probable that where claims for both kinds of liability result from an occurrence involving a ship of less than three hundred tons, the limitation provisions will be applied as follows:

(i) claims for loss of life or personal injury will be satisfied as far as possible out of a fund consisting of the difference between 300 × £108·1677 and the result of multiplying the actual tonnage of the ship by £34·8928. (To this extent, the smaller the actual tonnage of the ship, the greater the fund initially available to claimants for loss of life or personal injury whenever there are other claimants.)

(ii) the unsatisfied portion (if any) of claims for loss of life or personal injury will thereafter rank equally with other claimants against the fund obtained by multiplying the actual tonnage of the ship by £34·8928.

For ascertaining the tonnage of a ship, see s. 503 (2) at § 428, *ante*.

[5] See Statutory Instruments Act 1946.

[6] See also *The Abadesa* [1968] P. 656; *The Mecca* [1968] P. 665.

Amendments as to nature of liability limited by M.S.A. 1894, s. 503

212 **2.**—(1) In subsection (1) of section five hundred and three of the Merchant Shipping Act 1894, the following paragraphs shall be substituted for paragraphs (*c*) and (*d*)—

"(*c*) where any loss of life or personal injury is caused to any person not carried in the ship through the act or omission of any person (whether on board the ship or not) in the navigation or management of the ship or in the loading, carriage or discharge of its cargo or in the embarkation, carriage or disembarkation of its passengers, or through any other act or omission of any person on board the ship;

(*d*) where any loss or damage is caused to any property (other than any property mentioned in paragraph (*b*) of this subsection) or any rights are infringed through the act or omission of any person (whether on board the ship or not) in the navigation or management of the ship, or in the loading, carriage or discharge of its cargo or in the embarkation, carriage or disembarkation of its passengers, or through any other act or omission of any person on board the ship" [1];

and for the words "loss of or damage to vessels, goods, merchandise or other things," both where they occur in paragraph (i) and where they occur in paragraph (ii), there shall be substituted the words "such loss, damage or infringement as is mentioned in paragraphs (*b*) and (*d*) of this subsection." [2]

(2) For the purposes of the said subsection (1), where any obligation or liability arises—

(*a*) in connection with the raising, removal or destruction of any ship which is sunk, stranded or abandoned or of anything on board such a ship,[3] or

(*b*) in respect of any damage (however caused) to harbour works, basins or navigable waterways,[4]

the occurrence giving rise to the obligation or liability shall be treated as one of the occurrences mentioned in paragraphs (*b*) and (*d*) of that subsection, and the obligation or liability as a liability to damages.

(3) The application of the said section five hundred and three to any liability shall not be excluded by reason only that the occurrence giving rise to the liability was not due to the negligence of any person.[5]

(4) Nothing in the said section five hundred and three shall apply to any liability in respect of loss of life or personal injury caused to, or loss of or damage to any property or infringement of any right of, a person who is on board or employed in connection with the ship under a contract of service with all or any of the persons whose liabilities are limited by that section, if that contract is governed by the law of any country outside the United Kingdom [6] and that law either does not set any limit to that liability or sets a limit exceeding that set to it by that section.

(5) Paragraph (*a*) of subsection (2) of this section shall not come into force until such day as the [Secretary of State for Trade] may by order made by statutory instrument [7] appoint.[3]

(6) The [Secretary of State for Trade] may by order make provision for the setting up and management of a fund, to be used for the making to harbour or conservancy authorities of payments needed to compensate them for the reduction, in accordance with paragraph (*a*) of subsection (2) of this section, of amounts recoverable by them in respect of the obligations and liabilities mentioned in that paragraph, and to be maintained by contributions from such authorities raised and collected by them in respect of vessels in like manner as other sums so raised by them,[8] and any such order may contain such incidental and supplementary provisions as appear to the [Secretary of State] to be necessary or expedient.[9]

(7) The power to make an order under subsection (6) of this section shall include power to vary or revoke any such order by a subsequent order and any such power shall be exercisable by statutory instrument,[7] which shall be subject to annulment in pursuance of a resolution of either House of Parliament.

213 [1] Paragraphs (*c*) and (*d*) of s. 503 (1) of M.S.A. 1894, formerly read as follows:

" (*c*) When any loss of life or personal injury is caused to any person carried in any other vessel by reason of the improper navigation of the ship;

(*d*) When any loss or damage is caused to any other vessel, or to any goods, merchandise, or other things whatsoever on board any other vessel, by reason of the improper navigation of the ship; "

The effect of those paragraphs was extended to " all cases where .... any loss or damage is caused to property or rights of any kind, whether on land or on water, or whether fixed or movable, by reason of the improper navigation or management of the ship " by M.S. (Liability of Shipowners and Others) Act 1900, s. 1 (now repealed by this present Act, s. 8 (6) and Schedule).

For the definition of " ship " see section 4 (1) of this present Act, and note (2) to s. 503.

[2] See § 427 where s. 503 (1) is set out as amended by this Act, and see the notes thereto.

[3] This provision is not effective until such day as the Secretary of State may appoint. See subs. (5) of this section. No order has yet been made. When this paragraph is brought into force, it will override decisions to the contrary in *The Millie* [1940] P. 1 and *The Stonedale No.* 1 [1956] A.C. 1. However, it only applies to liability for wreck raising expenses incurred through the exercise of statutory powers thereby giving rise to a claim in debt and not for damages: see *The Putbus* [1969] 1 Lloyd's Rep. 253.

[4] See note (5), *infra.*

[5] The use of the word " improper " in s. 503 (1), M.S.A. 1894, and s. 1, M.S. (Liability of Shipowners and Others) Act 1900, led to the view expressed by the editors in the 5th edition of this work that the sections required some act of negligence as a condition precedent to limitation. As an example, they considered that a claim arising under s. 74 of the Harbours, Docks and Piers Clauses Act 1847 (which does not depend upon proof of negligence: *The Mostyn* [1928] A.C. 57) would not be fit for limitation.

This led to the curious result that a shipowner might be prejudiced by the fact that his servants had not been negligent. Subsequently, a Scottish court took a different view (*G. & G. Hamilton* v. *British Transport Commission*, 1957 S.L.T. 198 (Ct. of Sess.). However, the word " improper " no longer appears in s. 503 (1) as amended, and this subs. (3) removes all doubt. Further, a liability for damage to harbours, works, basins or navigable waterways, which is probably co-terminous with a liability under s. 74 of the Harbours, Docks and Piers Clauses Act 1847, is expressly brought within the limitation provisions as a " liability to damages " (see subs. (2) (*b*), *supra*). The right to limit seems not, however, to be generally extended to liabilities other than those " to damages," such as a contractual liability to indemnify irrespective of negligence or breach of contract: see *The Kirknes* [1957] P. 52.

[6] This means Great Britain and Northern Ireland; see the Royal and Parliamentary Titles Act 1927, s. 2 (2). It does not include the Channel Islands or the Isle of Man, but see s. 11 of this present Act.

[7] See Statutory Instruments Act 1946.

[8] As to the collection of rates by harbour authorities, see the Harbours, Docks and Piers Clauses Act 1847, ss. 25 *et seq.*

[9] This power has not yet been exercised. Presumably it will not be exercised before an order is made under subs. (5) of this section. This was the effect of a statement made in the House of Lords by the Minister without Portfolio on July 1, 1958 (see 210 H. of L. Official Report 423).

For definitions of " harbour authority " and " conservancy authority," see M.S.A. 1894, s. 742.

Extension to other persons of provisions applying to shipowners

1214 **3.**—(1) The persons whose liability in connection with a ship is excluded [1] or limited by Part VIII of the Merchant Shipping Act 1894, shall include any charterer and any person interested in or in possession of the ship, and, in particular, any manager or operator of the ship.[2]

(2) In relation to a claim arising from the act or omission of any person in his capacity as master [3] or member of the crew or (otherwise than in that capacity) in the course of his employment as a servant of the owners or of any such person as is mentioned in subsection (1) of this section,—

(*a*) the persons whose liability is excluded or limited as aforesaid shall also include the master, member of the crew or servant, and, in a case where the master or member of the crew is the servant of a person whose liability would not be excluded or limited apart from this paragraph, the person whose servant he is; and

(*b*) the liability of the master,[3] member of the crew or servant himself shall be excluded or limited as aforesaid notwithstanding his actual fault or privity in that capacity, except in the case mentioned in paragraph (ii) of section five hundred and two of the said Act of 1894.

1215 [1] See § 424, *ante*. This is a reference to s. 502 by which liability may be excluded altogether. These are cases where undeclared valuables are lost or damaged in circumstances of dishonesty.

[2] This extends the class of persons entitled to exclude or limit their liability under Part VIII of the M.S.A. 1894, in accordance with Article 6 (2) of the Convention. See also note (2) to s. 502. For the definition of " ship," see s. 4 (1) of this present Act, and note (4) to s. 502 and note (2) to s. 503 of M.S.A. 1894.

[3] For the definition of " master," see s. 742 of M.S.A. 1894. In *The Annie May* [1968] 1 Lloyd's Rep. 141, it was held that the words " any person in his capacity as master " includes an *owner* acting in the capacity of master. This conclusion was in line with Article 6 (3) of the Convention which provides: " If, however, the master or member of the crew is at the same time the owner, co-owner, charterer, manager or operator of the ship, the provisions of this paragraph shall only apply when the act, neglect or default in question is an act, neglect or default committed by the person in question in his capacity as master or as member of the crew of the ship." On the other hand, as noted in the previous edition of this work, the words " in that capacity " were clearly intended to prevent a master-owner from limiting his liability *qua* owner when the loss or damage occurs owing to his fault or privity in respect of some matter for which owners are normally responsible (*e.g.* unseaworthiness or faulty equipment). It should be noted that s. 508 of M.S.A. 1894, which expressly left unaffected the liability of a master or seaman, who was also an owner or part-owner of the ship to which he belonged has been repealed; see s. 8 (6) and Schedule to this present Act.

Unregistered ships and ships in course of completion or construction

16 **4.**—(1) Part VIII of the Merchant Shipping Act 1894, shall apply to any structure, whether completed or in course of completion, launched and intended for use in navigation as a ship or part of a ship, and the expression " ship " in the said Part VIII and in this Act shall be construed accordingly.[1]

(2) The said Part VIII shall apply to any British ship[2] notwithstanding that it has not yet been registered.[3]

(3) The tonnage of any ship or structure to which the said Part VIII applies by virtue of this section shall, for the purposes of that Part, be ascertained as provided by subsection (2) of section five hundred and three of the said Act of 1894 with regard to foreign ships.[4]

17 [1] Formerly, the combined effect of M.S. (Liability of Shipowners) Act 1898, s. 1, and M.S.A. 1906, ss. 70, 85 and Sched. II, was to entitle owners, builders and other parties interested in any British ship, built in H.M. Dominions, to limit their liability from the time of its launch until registration so long as it remained capable of registration and had not become a foreign ship; see *The Harlow* [1922] P. 175. The relevant sections of those Acts have now been repealed; see s. 8 (6) and Schedule to this present Act. See also s. 742 of M.S.A. 1894, for the definition of " ship " and s. 1 of M.S.A. 1921, by which the application of Part VIII of M.S.A. 1894, is extended to cover " lighters, barges, and other like vessels used in navigation in Great Britain, however propelled " unless used exclusively in non-tidal waters, other than harbours.

[2] As to " British ship," see note (1) to s. 1 of M.S.A. 1894.

[3] Formerly, exclusion or limitation of liability could only be claimed in respect of a British ship which was recognised as a British ship within the meaning of the M.S.A. 1894; *ibid.* s. 508 (now repealed by s. 8 (6) and Schedule to this present Act). This entailed registration, under Part I of the 1894 Act or special exemption from registration under *ibid.* s. 23 or, in the case of fishing boats, registration under Part IV of the 1894 Act.

[4] See § 428, *ante.* This subsection replaces M.S. (Liability of Shipowners) Act 1898, s. 3 (now repealed by s. 8 (6) and Schedule to this present Act).

Release of ship, etc.

18 **5.**—(1) Where a ship[1] or other property is arrested[2] in connection with a claim which appears to the court to be founded on a liability to which a limit is set[3] by section five hundred and three of the Merchant Shipping Act 1894,[4] or security is given to prevent or obtain release from such an arrest, the court[2] may, and in the circumstances mentioned in subsection (3) of this section shall,[3] order the release of the ship, property or security, if the conditions specified in subsection (2) of this section are satisfied[4]; but where the release is ordered the person on whose application it is ordered shall be deemed to have submitted to the jurisdiction of the court to adjudicate on the claim (or, in Scotland, to have prorogated that jurisdiction).

(2) The said conditions are—

(*a*) that security which in the opinion of the court is satisfactory (in this section referred to as " guarantee ") has previously been given, whether in the United Kingdom or elsewhere, in respect of the said liability or any other liability incurred on the same occasion and the court is satisfied that, if the claim is established, the amount for which the guarantee was given or such part thereof as corresponds to the claim will be actually available to the claimant; and

(*b*) that either the guarantee is for an amount not less than the said limit or further security is given which, together with the guarantee, is for an amount not less than that limit.

(3) The circumstances mentioned in subsection (1) of this section are that the guarantee was given in a port which, in relation to the claim, is the relevant port (or, as the case may be, a relevant port) and that that port is in a Convention country.[5]

(4) For the purposes of this section—

(*a*) a guarantee given by the giving of security in more than one country shall be deemed to have been given in the country in which security was last given;

(*b*) any question whether the amount of any security is (either by itself or together with any other amount) not less than any limit set by section five hundred and three of the Merchant Shipping Act 1894, shall be decided as at the time at which the security is given;

(*c*) where part only of the amount for which a guarantee was given will be available to a claimant that part shall not be taken to correspond to his claim if any other part may be available to a claimant in respect of a liability to which no limit is set as mentioned in subsection (1) of this section.

1219 (5) In this section—

"Convention country" means any country in respect of which the Convention is in force (including any country to which the Convention extends by virtue of Article 14 thereof)[5];

"relevant port"—

(*a*) in relation to any claim, means the port where the event giving rise to the claim occurred or, if that event did not occur in a port, the first port of call after the event occurred; and

(*b*) in relation to a claim for loss of life or personal injury or for damage to cargo, includes the port of disembarkation or discharge.

"the Convention" means the International Convention relating to the Limitation of the Liability of Owners of Seagoing Ships signed in Brussels on the tenth day of October, nineteen hundred and fifty-seven.[5]

(6) If Her Majesty by Order in Council declares that any country specified in the Order is a Convention country within the meaning of this section, the Order shall, while in force, be conclusive evidence that

the country is a Convention country; but any Order in Council under this section may be varied or revoked by a subsequent Order in Council.[6]

(7) In the application of this section to Scotland the references to arrest shall be construed as referring to arrestment on the dependence of an action or in rem and for the references to release from arrest or to the ordering of such a release there shall be substituted references to the recall of an arrestment.

20 1 For the meaning of "ship," see s. 4, *ante*, and note (1) thereto.

2 For the Admiralty jurisdiction of the High Court over actions *in rem*, see the Administration of Justice Act 1956, ss. 1 and 3. For the comparable jurisdiction of the county courts, see County Courts Act 1959, ss. 56 and 57.

3 It is not clear how this section would operate if the right to limit is not admitted.

4 For a full discussion of the meaning and operation of this section, see *The Putbus* [1969] 1 Lloyd's Rep. 253 where it was held that if the conditions specified in subsection (2) are satisfied, the court should exercise its discretion in favour of the release, unless there are exceptional circumstances. However it is not clear to what extent the court must be satisfied that the claim is one " founded on a liability to which a limit is set " if, for example, it is alleged that the owner of the vessel was actually at fault.

5 By Article 11 (1) of the Convention, it is provided that the Convention shall come into force " six months after the date of deposit of at least ten instruments of ratification, of which at least five are by states that have each a tonnage equal or superior to one million gross tons of tonnage. The Convention came into force on May 31, 1968. By March, 1972, the Convention had been ratified by the United Kingdom, France, Spain, Denmark, Finland, Israel, Netherlands, Norway, Portugal, Sweden, and Switzerland. The Convention has also been acceded to by Ghana, Algeria, the United Arab Republic, Singapore, Iran, the Congo, New Hebrides, Guiana, Iran, Malagache Republic and Iceland and extended to the Isle of Man, Jersey, Guernsey and many other British possessions: see Singh, *International Conventions of Merchant Shipping* (B.S.L. Vol. 8, 2nd ed.). Accordingly, the obligatory provision of this section is not yet effective. " Port " in this section includes " place "; s. 742 of M.S.A. 1894.

6 No Order in Council has yet been made for the reasons set out in note (3) (*supra*). The power to make Orders in Council is exercisable by statutory instrument; see Statutory Instruments Act 1946, s. 1 (1).

Restriction on enforcement after giving of security

1 **6.**—(1) No judgment or decree for a claim founded on a liability to which a limit is set by section five hundred and three of the Merchant Shipping Act 1894,[1] shall be enforced, except so far as it is for costs (or, in Scotland, expenses), if security for an amount not less than the said limit has been given, whether in the United Kingdom or elsewhere, in respect of the liability or any other liability incurred on the same occasion and the court is of opinion that the security is satisfactory and is satisfied that the amount for which it was given or such part thereof as corresponds to the claim will be actually available to the person in whose favour the judgment or decree was given or made.[2]

(2) For the purposes of this section—

(*a*) any question whether the amount of any security is not less than any limit set by section five hundred and three of the Merchant Shipping Act 1894,[1] shall be decided as at the time at which the security is given;

(*b*) where part only of the amount for which security has been given will be available to the person in whose favour the judgment or decree was given or made that part shall not be taken to correspond to his claim if any other part may be available to a claimant in respect of a liability to which no limit is set as mentioned in subsection (1) of this section.

[1] See § 427, *ante*, where s. 503 of M.S.A. 1894, is set out as amended by ss. 1, 2 and 8 (2) of this present Act.

[2] It appears that this section gives effect to Article 2 (4) of the Convention, which provides: " After the fund has been constituted, no claimant against the fund shall be entitled to exercise any right against any other assets of the ship-owner in respect of his claim against the fund, if the limitation fund is actually available for the benefit of the claimant."

Distribution of limitation fund

1222 7.—(1) In making any distribution in accordance with section five hundred and four of the Merchant Shipping Act 1894, the court [1] may, if it thinks fit, postpone the distribution of such part of the amount to be distributed as it deems appropriate having regard to any claims that may later be established before a court [2] of any country outside the United Kingdom.[3]

(2) No lien or other right in respect of any ship or property shall affect the proportions in which under the said section five hundred and four any amount is distributed amongst several claimants.[4]

1223 [1] *i.e.* the High Court in England, Wales and Ireland, the Court of Session in Scotland, or any competent court in a British possession; *cf.* s. 504 at § 438, *ante*.

[2] *Quaere* whether this includes arbitration proceedings abroad.

[3] *Cf. The Kronprinz Olav* [1921] P. 52, in which it was decided by the Court of Appeal that if no payment has in fact been made in respect of a foreign judgment, the owner could not put forward in his own right a contingent claim in respect of claims which might in the future be substantiated against him under a foreign judgment; but that the court had a discretion if application were made in good time to delay the distribution pending the final ascertainment of the claims in a foreign court. The present Act would appear to give a wider discretion than hitherto.

[4] This subsection overrides the decision in *Mersey Docks and Harbour Board* v. *Hay* (*The Countess*) [1923] A.C. 345, where it was held by the House of Lords that if one claimant had a possessory lien over the ship, effect must be given to his superior right even to the extent of depriving other claimants of all right of recovery against the fund. *Cf.* Article 3 (2) of the Convention.

Minor and consequential amendments and repeals

1224 8.—(1) *In section five hundred and two of the Merchant Shipping Act* 1894, *the word " sea-going " shall be omitted.*[1]

(2) For subsection (3) of section five hundred and three of the Merchant Shipping Act 1894, there shall be substituted the following subsection—

" (3) The limits set by this section to the liabilities mentioned therein shall apply to the aggregate of such liabilities which are incurred on any distinct occasion,[2] and shall so apply in respect of each distinct occasion without regard to any liability incurred on another occasion." [3]

(3) In section five hundred and four of the Merchant Shipping Act 1894, for the words " in respect of loss of life, personal injury or loss of or

damage to vessels or goods " there shall be substituted the words " in respect of any occurrence in respect of which his liability is limited under section five hundred and three of this Act." [4]

(4) In Part VIII of the Merchant Shipping Act 1894, the expression " owner " [5] shall be construed as including, where it occurs in section five hundred and two, every person whose liability is excluded by section three of this Act, and elsewhere, except in the second place where it occurs in section five hundred and five,[6] every person whose liability is limited by that section.

(5) In section five of the Crown Proceedings Act 1947, the following shall be substituted for paragraph (*a*) of subsection (6)—

> " (*a*) any structure to which Part VIII of that Act is applied by section four of the Merchant Shipping (Liability of Shipowners and Others) Act 1958; and "

and in subsection (8) for the reference to the Merchant Shipping (Liability of Shipowners) Act 1898,[7] there shall be substituted a reference to sections three and four of this Act.[8]

(6) *The enactments mentioned in the Schedule to this Act are hereby repealed to the extent specified in the third column of that Schedule.*[1]

5 [1] These subsections were repealed by the Statute Law (Reform) Act 1974.

[2] For discussion of " distinct occasions," see note (19) to s. 503 of M.S.A. 1894.

[3] See § 427, *ante*, where s. 503 of M.S.A. 1894, is set out as amended by this Act. This passage has been substituted for " (3) The owner of every sea-going ship or share therein shall be liable in respect of every such loss of life, personal injury, loss or damage to vessels, goods, merchandise, or things as aforesaid arising on distinct occasions to the same extent as if no other loss, injury or damage had arisen." *Cf.* Article 2 (1) of the Convention. See also note (20) to s. 503 of M.S.A. 1894.

[4] See § 438, *ante*, where s. 504 of M.S.A. 1894, is set out as amended by this Act. This amendment gives effect to the wider class of claims in respect of which limitation may now be claimed.

[5] See generally, note (2) to s. 502 and note (1) to s. 503 of M.S.A. 1894.

[6] This is the section which governs the rights of part owners *inter se*; see § 443, *ante*.

[7] The M.S. (Liability of Shipowners) Act 1898, s. 4 of which extended the definition of " ship " for limitation purposes, has been repealed by s. 8 (6) and the Schedule to this present Act.

[8] See § 1075, *ante*, where s. 5 of the Crown Proceedings Act 1947, is set out as amended by this section.

Saving for occurrences taking place before commencement

6 **9.** Nothing in this Act applies in relation to any liability arising from an occurrence which took place before the commencement of this Act.[1]

[1] The Act came into force upon receiving the Royal Assent on August 1, 1958. It should also be noted that s. 2 (2) (*a*) is as yet only partly effective because no order has been made under s. 2 (5), and that s. 5 is not yet fully effective for the reasons given in note (3) thereto.

Provisions as to Northern Ireland

7 **10.**—(1) This Act extends to Northern Ireland.[1]

(2) In the application of this Act to Northern Ireland the reference in

section eight to the Crown Proceedings Act 1947, is a reference to that Act as it applies in Northern Ireland.[2]

(3) For the purposes of section six of the Government of Ireland Act 1920 (which relates to the powers of the Parliament of Northern Ireland to make laws), this Act shall be deemed to have been passed before the day appointed for the purposes of that section.

[1] See also the note " Application to Northern Ireland and the Republic of Ireland " to s. 742 of M.S.A. 1894, at § 689, *ante*.

[2] For the application of the Crown Proceedings Act 1947, to Northern Ireland, see *ibid.* s. 53, and the Northern Ireland (Crown Proceedings) Order 1949 (No. 1836).

Application to British possessions, etc.

1228 **11.**—(1) Her Majesty may by Order in Council[1] direct that the provisions of this Act, and (so far as they do not so extend apart from the Order) the existing limitation enactments, shall extend, with such exceptions, adaptations and modifications as may be specified in the Order, to—

(*a*) the Isle of Man;[2]

(*b*) any of the Channel Islands;

(*c*) any colony, or any country or place outside Her Majesty's dominions in which for the time being Her Majesty has jurisdiction, or any territory consisting partly of one or more colonies and partly of one or more such countries or places.

(2) In this section " the existing limitation enactments " means Part VIII of the Merchant Shipping Act 1894, section two of the Merchant Shipping (Liability of Shipowners and others) Act 1900, and any incidental or supplementary provisions of any enactment applying the said Part or section.[3]

1229 [1] The power to make Orders in Council is exercisable by Statutory Instrument; see Statutory Instruments Act 1946, s. 1 (1).

[2] This power has been exercised by M.S. (Liability of Shipowners' and Others) Act 1958 (Isle of Man) Order 1960 (No. 1379). The Shipowners' Liability (Colonial Territories) Order 1963 S.I. No. 1379, as amended by S.I. 1964 No. 1658; the M.S. (Liability of Shipowners and Others) Act 1958 (Jersey) Order, 1964, S.I. No. 928; the M.S. (Liability of Shipowners and Others) Act 1958 (Guernsey) Order 1964 S.I. No. 929; the Shipowners' Liability (New Hebrides) Order 1965, S.I. No. 1307; the Shipowners' Liability (British Guiana) Order 1965, S.I. No. 1868 (see the Guyana Independence Act 1966, s. 1, Sched. 1), the Shipowners' Liability (St. Helena) Order 1966, S.I. No. 1406.

[3] See, *e.g.* Merchant Shipping Act 1911, s. 1 (2); Merchant Shipping Act 1921, s. 1 (1) and Crown Proceedings Act 1947, ss. 5, 7.

Construction, short title and citation

1230 **12.**—(1) Any reference in this Act to any other enactment is a reference thereto as amended, and includes references thereto as applied, by or under any subsequent enactment, including, except where the context otherwise requires, this Act.

(2) This Act shall be construed as one with the Merchant Shipping Acts 1894 to 1954.[1]

(3) This Act may be cited as the Merchant Shipping (Liability of Shipowners and Others) Act 1958, and this Act and the Merchant Shipping Acts 1894 to 1954 may be cited together as the Merchant Shipping Acts 1894 to 1958.

[1] Accordingly, definitions in earlier Acts (*e.g.* in s. 742 of M.S.A. 1894) may be relevant to the construction of the provisions of this Act. See generally on the effect of this subsection, *Phillips* v. *Parnaby* [1934] 2 K.B. 299 at p. 302, and *Kirkness* (*Inspector of Taxes*) v. *John Hudson & Co. Ltd.* [1955] A.C. 696.

---

31 **Section 8 (6)**

SCHEDULE

Enactments Repealed

[This schedule was repealed by the Statute Law (Reform) Act 1974].

1231 *M.S.* (*Liability of Shipowners and Others*) *Act 1958*

Table of Statutes referred to in this Act

Short Title	Session and Chapter
Merchant Shipping Act 1894	57 & 58 Vict. c. 60.
Merchant Shipping (Liability of Shipowners) Act 1898	61 & 62 Vict. c. 14.
Merchant Shipping (Liability of Shipowners and others) Act 1900	63 & 64 Vict. c. 32.
Government of Ireland Act 1920	10 & 11 Geo. 5. c. 67.
Crown Proceedings Act 1947	10 & 11 Geo. 6. c. 44.

MERCHANT SHIPPING (MINICOY LIGHTHOUSE) ACT 1960

(8 & 9 Eliz. 2, c. 42)

An Act to enable the lighthouse on Minicoy Island and sums held in the General Lighthouse Fund in connection therewith to be transferred to the Government of India, and for purposes connected with the matter aforesaid. [2nd June, 1960]

Whereas the lighthouse on Minicoy Island (in this Act referred to as " the lighthouse ") between the Laccadive and Maldive Islands, is a colonial light within the meaning of the Merchant Shipping (Mercantile Marine Fund) Act 1898, but has, since the second day of April, nineteen hundred and fifty-six, been administered by the Government of India:

And whereas it is expedient that the lighthouse and the sums held in the General Lighthouse Fund in connection therewith should be transferred to the Government of India;

1232 Introductory Note: This Act enabled the Minister of Transport (who then exercised the powers in relation to merchant shipping now exercised by the Secretary of State for Trade) to transfer the Minicoy Lighthouse to the Government of India, and to conclude a financial settlement in respect of the lighthouse dues collected since April 2, 1956. Minicoy Island, which lies off the south-west coast of India, became part of the territory of the Republic of India after the Indian Independence Act 1947, but the lighthouse remained the property of the United Kingdom Government. However, by agreement between the respective governments, the management of the lighthouse was taken over by the Indian

Government on April 2, 1956, although the lighthouse dues continued to be paid to the General Lighthouse Fund in this country; see *Hansard*, H.C. Vol. 623, col. 1137. The Act, which came into force on June 2, 1960, may be cited with the earlier Merchant Shipping legislation as the Merchant Shipping Acts 1894 to 1960; see s. 2 (2).

Be it therefore enacted, etc.:

Power to transfer to India Minicoy Lighthouse and assets attributable thereto

3 **1.**—(1) The [Secretary of State for Trade] (in this Act referred to as " the [Secretary of State "] shall have power to transfer to the Government of India on such date as may be agreed between him and that Government all the interest held by him in the lighthouse and in the appurtenances thereto.[1]

(2) On the date referred to in the foregoing subsection the lighthouse shall cease to be a colonial light [2] within the meaning of the Act of 1898,[3] and accordingly section six hundred and seventy of the Merchant Shipping Act 1894 (which empowers Her Majesty to fix colonial light dues) shall cease to have effect in relation to the lighthouse, and in the Third Schedule to the Act of 1898, the words " Minicoy Island, between the Laccadive and Maldive Islands " shall be repealed.

(3) There shall be paid to the Government of India out of the General Lighthouse Fund [4] (in this section referred to as " the Fund ") the following sums, that is to say—

(*a*) such sum as the [Secretary of State], with the consent of the Treasury, may determine to be equivalent to the excess of the proportion of the Fund attributable to light dues in respect of the lighthouse for the period ending with the second day of April, nineteen hundred and fifty-six,[4] over the aggregate of the expenses in connection with the lighthouse relating to that period and falling to be paid out of the Fund;

(*b*) a sum equal to interest at the rate of four per cent. per annum on the sum payable by virtue of the foregoing paragraph for the period beginning with the third day of April, nineteen hundred and fifty-six,[5] and ending with the day on which the last mentioned sum is paid;

(*c*) all the sums carried to the Fund and attributable to light dues due in respect of the lighthouse after the second day of April, nineteen hundred and fifty-six [5];

(*d*) in respect of each of the sums referred to in the last foregoing paragraph, a sum equal to interest at the rate of four per cent. per annum thereon for the period beginning with the relevant day and ending with the day on which the sum so referred to is paid.

(4) In the last foregoing subsection,—

(*a*) in paragraph (*a*), the reference to expenses falling to be paid out of the Fund includes a reference to expenses which fell to be paid out of the Basses Lights Fund [2] (the balance of which was transferred to the Fund by the Act of 1898), and

(*b*) in paragraph (*d*), " relevant day " means, in relation to a sum referred to in paragraph (*c*) of that subsection, the thirtieth day of September falling in the year in which that sum was carried to the Fund, and for the purposes of this paragraph a year shall be treated as a period of twelve months ending with the thirty-first day of March.

[1] The Secretary of State's power has not yet been exercised.
[2] See definitions in the M.S. (Mercantile Marine Fund) Act 1898, s. 7.
[3] *i.e.* the M.S. (Mercantile Marine Fund) Act 1898; see s. 2 (1), *post*.
[4] See M.S. (Mercantile Marine Fund) Act 1898, ss. 1, 2.
[5] *i.e.* the date upon which the Government of India by agreement took over the administration of the Minicoy lighthouse; see Introductory Note to this Act.

Interpretation and citation

1234 2.—(1) In this Act—

" the Act of 1898 " means the Merchant Shipping (Mercantile Marine Fund) Act 1898, and

" the General Lighthouse Fund " means the fund of that name established under the Act of 1898.[1]

(2) This Act may be cited as the Merchant Shipping (Minicoy Lighthouse) Act 1960, and this Act and the Merchant Shipping Acts 1894 to 1958, may be cited together as the Merchant Shipping Acts 1894 to 1960.

[1] See the M.S. (Mercantile Marine Fund) Act 1898, ss. 1, 2.

MERCHANT SHIPPING ACT 1964

[1964, c. 47]

An Act to enable effect to be given to an International Convention for the Safety of Life at Sea signed in London on 17th June, 1960; to amend section 271 of the Merchant Shipping Act 1894; and for purposes connected therewith. [10th June, 1964]

1235 Introductory Note. The Act provides for additions to and modifications of the Merchant Shipping (Safety Convention) Act 1949, to enable the United Kingdom to give effect to the International Convention for the Safety of Life at Sea, signed in London on June 17, 1960. This Convention came into force (in accordance with the provisions of Article XI of the

Convention) on May 26, 1965, replacing the International Convention for the Safety of Life at Sea signed in London on June 10, 1948.

S. 1 applies the Merchant Shipping (Safety Convention) Act 1949, to the new Convention. Ss. 2 to 7 give effect to the requirements of the Convention for the construction and survey of the hull, machinery and equipment of cargo ships. Ss. 3 to 7 provide for certification and the enforcement of the new requirements. Ss. 8 to 15 modify existing safety requirements in respect of damage control in passenger ships, life-saving appliances and radio installations to bring them into line with the standards of the new Convention. There are also provisions for inclining tests to establish ships' stability, and minor amendments of the 1949 Act. S. 16 requires masters of ships at sea to report additional weather hazards. S. 17 amends section 271 of the Merchant Shipping Act 1894, to ensure that no ship can sail with more than twelve passengers aboard unless it carries a passenger certificate issued on annual survey.

The Act applies to Scotland and to Northern Ireland.

The provisions of this Act, subject to certain modifications and exceptions, have been extended to Hong Kong; see the M.S. (Safety Convention) (Hong Kong) Order S.I. 1965 No. 2011.

Application of Act of 1949 *to new Convention*

Application of Act of 1949 to Convention of 1960

6 **1.** For the purpose of enabling effect to be given to the International Convention for the Safety of Life at Sea signed in London on 17th June 1960 (in this Act referred to as " the Convention ") which replaces the International Convention for the Safety of Life at Sea signed in London on 10th June 1948 (in this Act referred to as " the Safety Convention ") the Merchant Shipping (Safety Convention) Act 1949 (in this Act referred to as " the Act of 1949 "), shall have effect as if—

(*a*) for references therein, except in the preamble, to the Safety Convention there were substituted references to the Convention [1]; and

(*b*) references therein to that Act, except in subsections (1) and (4) of section 37 (commencement and citation), included references to this Act.

[1] The following countries have been declared to have accepted the 1960 Convention by Orders in Council made under section 31 of the 1949 Act as amended by this section; (i) United Kingdom, Algeria, Cuba, Denmark, France, Ghana, Greece, Haiti, Iceland, Japan, Liberia, Malagasy, Morocco, Netherlands, Norway, Paraguay, Peru, Spain, Tunisia, United States, Vietnam, Yugoslavia: see S.I. 1965 No. 1121; (ii) Canada, Finland, Germany, Korea, Kuwait, Saudi Arabia, Netherlands Antilles: see S.I. 1965 No. 1526; (iii) Burma, Cyprus, United Arab Republic, Russia, Philippines, Malaysia, Hong Kong: see S.I. 1965 No. 2012; (iv) Israel, Panama, Ivory Coast, Nigeria, Sweden, Guam, Puerto Rico, Virgin Islands (U.S.A.): see S.I. 1966 No. 396; (v) Switzerland, Belgium, New Zealand, Pakistan, India: see S.I. 1966 No. 946; (vi) Argentina, Iran, Italy, Lebanon, Poland, Portugal, Turkey, Mexico: see S.I. 1966 No. 1412; (vii) Chile, Gambia, Indonesia, Roumania, Trinidad and Tobago: S.I. 1967 No. 476; (viii) Somalia, Brazil, Ireland:

see S.I. 1967 No. 1552; (ix) Australia, Bulgaria, Czechoslovakia, Mauritania, Nicaragua, South Africa: see S.I. 1968 No. 467; (x) Congo, Guinea, Jamaica, Maldive Islands, Uruguay: see S.I. 1969 No. 152; (xi) Honduras, Singapore, Southern Yemen, Syria, Venezuela: see S.I. 1970 No. 159; (xii) Hungary, Monaco, Nauru, Senegal, Zambia: see S.I. 1971 No. 217; (xiii) Bermuda: see S.I. 1973 No. 1315 as amended by 1975 S.I. No. 413.

New requirements for cargo ships

Cargo ship construction and survey rules

1237 2.—(1) The [Secretary of State for Trade] may make rules [1] (in this Act referred to as " cargo ship construction and survey rules ") prescribing requirements for the hull, equipment and machinery of ships to which this section applies and requiring any such ships which are registered [2] in the United Kingdom to be surveyed to such extent, in such manner and at such intervals as may be prescribed by the rules.

(2) The said rules shall include such requirements as appear to the [Secretary of State for Trade] to implement the provisions of the Convention relating to the hull, equipment and machinery of such ships, except so far as those provisions are implemented by any other [3] rules or regulations made under the Merchant Shipping Acts.

(3) This section applies to—

(*a*) sea-going [4] ships of not less than five hundred tons gross tonnage [5]; and

(*b*) sea-going [4] ships of not less than such lower tonnage and of such description as the [Secretary of State] may by order made by statutory instrument specify [6];

other than passenger steamers,[7] troopships, pleasure yachts, fishing vessels and ships not propelled by mechanical means; except that it applies to ships not registered in the United Kingdom only while they are within a port in the United Kingdom and are not exempted [8] from the cargo ship construction and survey rules under the following provisions of this Act.

(4) The matters with regard to which fees may be prescribed by regulations under section 33 of the Act of 1949 [9] shall include surveys required by the cargo ship construction and survey rules, and the provisions applied by section 13 (2) of that Act (which relate to the delivery of declarations of survey and appeals to the court of survey) shall apply to such surveys whether or not they are made for the purpose of the issue of any certificate.

(5) In relation to surveys required by the cargo ship construction and survey rules which are carried out otherwise than by a surveyor of ships appointed under the Merchant Shipping Acts [10]—

(*a*) so much of the said section 33 as requires fees to be paid into the Exchequer shall not apply; and (*b*) the provisions applied by the said section 13 (2) shall apply with such modifications as may be prescribed by the cargo ship construction and survey rules; and

(*c*) the definition of " declaration of survey " in section 36 (1) of the Act of 1949 shall not apply.

(6) An order under subsection (3) (*b*) of this section may be varied or revoked by a subsequent order.

1 See the M.S. (Cargo Ship Construction and Survey) Rules 1965 (S.I. No. 1104) and the M.S. (Cargo Ship Construction and Survey) (Tankers and Combination Carriers) Rules 1975 S.I. No. 750.
2 For registration of ships in the United Kingdom, see Merchant Shipping Act 1894, s. 2.
3 See the M.S. (Safety Convention) Act 1949, ss. 2 (life saving), 3 (radio) and 5 (direction-finders); and the M.S.A. 1894, ss. 427 (life-saving) and 418 (collisions).
4 " Sea-going ship " is one that in fact goes to sea, not one which merely could go to sea; see *The Salt Union* v. *Wood* [1893] 1 Q.B. 370.
5 For ascertainment of tonnage see the M.S.A. 1965, s. 1.
6 No order had been made up to the date of writing this text.
7 See s. 26 (2) of the M.S. (Safety Convention) Act 1949.
8 See ss. 15, 16, *post*.
9 See M.S. (Fees) Regulations 1975 (S.I. No. 341).
10 See ss. 724–727 of the M.S.A. 1894 and s. 76 of the M.S.A. 1970.

Cargo ship safety construction certificates and exemption certificates

238 3.—(1) If the [Secretary of State for Trade] or such person as he may authorise for the purpose is satisfied, on receipt of declarations of survey [1] in respect of a ship to which section 2 of this Act applies and which is registered in the United Kingdom, that the ship complies with the cargo ship construction and survey rules applicable to the ship and such voyages as she is to be engaged on he shall, on the application of the owner, issue in respect of the ship—

(*a*) if the ship is of not less than five hundred tons gross tonnage and is to be engaged on international voyages,[2] a certificate in the form prescribed by the Convention;

(*b*) in any other case, a certificate showing that she complies with the said rules;

and any such certificate is in this Act referred to as a cargo ship safety construction certificate.

(2) If the [Secretary of State], on receipt of declarations of survey in respect of such a ship, is satisfied that the ship is exempt, by virtue of any exercise by him of a power conferred on him by section 28 of the Act of 1949 or the cargo ship construction and survey rules, from any of the requirements of those rules applicable to the ship and to such voyages as she is to be engaged on, and that she complies with the rest of those requirements, he shall, on the application of the owner, issue in respect of the ship—

(*a*) if she is of not less than five hundred tons gross tonnage and is to be engaged on international voyages—

(i) an exemption certificate stating which of the requirements of the Convention, being requirements implemented by the rules and applicable as aforesaid, the ship is exempt from and that the exemption is conditional on the ship's plying on the voyages and complying with the other conditions (if any) specified in the certificate; and

(ii) a certificate showing that the ship complies with the rest of those requirements;

(*b*) in any other case, a certificate showing that the ship complies with such of the requirements of the cargo ship construction and survey rules applicable to the ship and to the voyages she is to be engaged on as she is not exempt from;

and any certificate issued under paragraph (*a*) (ii) or paragraph (*b*) of this subsection is in this Act referred to as a qualified cargo ship safety construction certificate.

(3) A certificate issued under this section, other than an exemption certificate, shall remain in force for five years or such shorter period as may be specified in it, but without prejudice to the [Secretary of State's] power to cancel it; and an exemption certificate issued under this section shall remain in force for the same period as the corresponding qualified certificate.

(4) The [Secretary of State] may by order [3] made by statutory instrument extend the period for which a certificate under this section may be issued to a period not exceeding six years.

(5) Without prejudice to the power of extension conferred by section 13 (5) of the Act of 1949, where a certificate under this section is in force in respect of a ship and the certificate was issued for a shorter period than is allowed under the foregoing provisions of this section, the Minister or any person authorised by him for the purpose may, if satisfied on receipt of declarations of survey in respect of the ship that it is proper to do so, grant an extension of the certificate for a period not exceeding one year, and not exceeding, together with the period for which it was issued and any period by which it has been previously extended under this subsection, the longest period for which it could have been issued under this section.

(6) In relation to a certificate issued or extended under this section by a person authorised by the [Secretary of State]—

(*a*) the provisions applied by section 13 (8) of the Act of 1949 (which relate to the transmission, cancellation, surrender, posting-up and falsification of certificates issued by the [Secretary of State]) except section 276 of the principal Act (transmission of certificates); and

(*b*) section 33 of the Act of 1949 (fees);

shall apply as they apply in relation to certificates issued by the [Secretary of State], except that so much of the said section 33 as requires fees to be paid into the Exchequer shall not apply.

(7) An order under subsection (4) [4] of this section may be varied or revoked by a subsequent order.

39 [1] " Declaration of survey ": see Merchant Shipping Act 1894, s. 272 and Merchant Shipping (Safety Convention) Act 1949, s. 36 (1).

[2] " International voyage ": see Merchant Shipping (Safety Convention) Act 1949, s. 36 (1).

[3] No order under this subsection had been made at the date of writing this text.

[4] *Ibid.*

Notice of alterations and additional surveys

40 **4.**—(1) The duty of the owner or master [1] of a ship [1] under subsection (2) of section 11 of the Act of 1949 to notify alterations and renewals shall extend, in relation to any ship in respect of which a certificate under section 3 of this Act is in force, to the hull, machinery and any equipment other than that mentioned in that subsection, but may, if the certificate was issued by a person authorised under the said section 3, be discharged by notifying him instead of the [Secretary of State].

(2) Subsection (4) of the said section 11 (additional survey and cancellation of certificates) shall have effect, in relation to any such ship, as if—

(*a*) paragraph (*a*) thereof extended to any alteration or renewal which is notifiable by virtue of this section; and

(*b*) paragraph (*b*) and not paragraph (*c*) thereof were applicable, notwithstanding that the ship is not a passenger steamer [2];

and the power of the [Secretary of State] under that subsection to cancel such a certificate shall be exercisable also where the ship has not been submitted for survey as required by the cargo ship construction and survey rules.[3]

[1] For definition, see s. 742 of the M.S.A. 1894.

[2] For definition, see s. 26 of the M.S. (Safety Convention) Act 1949.

[3] See s. 2 (1), *ante*.

Prohibition on proceeding to sea without appropriate certificates

41 **5.**—(1) No ship to which section 2 of this Act applies and which is registered in the United Kingdom shall proceed to sea unless there is in force in respect of the ship either—

(*a*) a cargo ship safety construction certificate [1]; or

(*b*) a qualified cargo ship safety construction certificate [2] and, if the ship is about to proceed on an international voyage,[3] a corresponding exemption certificate; or

(*c*) such certificate or certificates as would be required if she were a passenger steamer,[4]

applicable to the ship and to the voyage on which she is about to proceed.

(2) If any ship proceeds, or attempts to proceed, to sea in contravention of this section the owner or master of the ship shall be liable to a fine not exceeding one hundred pounds.

(3) The master of every ship to which section 2 of this Act applies and which is registered in the United Kingdom shall produce to the officer of customs from whom a clearance [5] for the ship is demanded the certificate or certificates required by the foregoing provisions of this section; and the clearance shall not be granted, and the ship may be detained, until the said certificate or certificates are so produced.

1 See s. 3, *ante*.
2 *Ibid.*
3 See s. 36 (1) of the M.S. (Safety Convention) Act 1949.
4 See s. 26 (2) of the M.S. (Safety Convention) Act 1949.
5 See s. 52 of the Customs and Excise Act 1952.

Exemption of ships holding appropriate certificates

1242 **6.** Where there is produced in respect of a ship not registered in the United Kingdom—

(*a*) an accepted Safety Convention certificate [1] equivalent to a cargo ship safety construction certificate [2]; or

(*b*) accepted Safety Convention certificates equivalent respectively to a qualified cargo ship safety construction certificate [3] and to a corresponding exemption certificate [4];

the ship shall be exempt from the cargo ship construction and survey rules.[5]

1 See the M.S. (Safety Convention) Act 1949, ss. 14 and 36 (1).
2 See s. 3, *ante*.
3 *Ibid.*
4 See s. 13, *post*.
5 See s. 2 (1), *ante*.

Penalty for non-compliance with rules and power to detain

1243 **7.**—(1) If the cargo ship construction and survey rules [1] are contravened in any respect in relation to a ship, the owner or master of the ship shall be liable on conviction on indictment to a fine not exceeding five hundred pounds, or on summary conviction to a fine not exceeding one hundred pounds.

(2) A surveyor of ships [2] may inspect any ship for the purpose of seeing that she complies with the provisions of the cargo ship construction and survey rules (other than those relating to survey) and for that purpose shall have all the powers of a [Department of Trade] inspector [3] under the Merchant Shipping Acts; and if he finds that the ship fails to comply with those provisions he shall give to the owner or master notice in writing stating in what respect she fails to comply with them and what in his opinion is requisite to remedy the failure.

(3) Every notice under subsection (2) of this section shall be communicated in manner directed by the [Secretary of State] to the chief officer of customs of any port at which the ship may seek to obtain a clearance or transire; and the ship shall be detained until a certificate under the hand of a surveyor of ships is produced to the effect that the failure has been remedied.

[1] See s. 2 (1) *ante*.
[2] For appointment of surveyor of ships, see M.S.A. 1894, s. 724.
[3] For the powers of an inspector, see M.S.A. 1894, s. 729.

Damage control and life-saving appliances

Damage control plans and stability information for passenger steamers

244 **8.** Construction rules [1] (that is to say, rules made under section 1 of the Act of 1949 relating to the hull, equipment and machinery of British passenger steamers [2] registered in the United Kingdom) may require the provision in such ships,—

(*a*) of plans exhibited as provided by or under the rules, and of other information, relating to the boundaries of watertight compartments, the openings therein, the means of closing such openings and the arrangements for correcting any list due to flooding; and

(*b*) of information necessary for the guidance of the master in maintaining sufficient stability to enable the ship to withstand damage.

[1] See the M.S. (Passenger Ship Construction) Rules 1965 (S.I. No. 1104).
[2] See s. 17 (2) of this Act, *post*.

Extension of power to make rules for life-saving appliances

245 **9.** Subsection (1) of section 427 of the principal Act [1] (which empowers the [Secretary of State for Trade] to make rules for life-saving appliances) shall be amended as follows:—

(*a*) in paragraph (*e*) (buoyant apparatus required to be carried on board ships carrying passengers) the words " carrying passengers " shall be omitted;

(*b*) after paragraph (*m*) there shall be inserted the following paragraph:—

" (*mm*) the provision in ships of plans or other information relating to the means of preventing, detecting, controlling and extinguishing outbreaks of fire ";

(*c*) in paragraph (*q*) (examination of appliances and equipment required by the rules to be carried) after the word " examination " there shall be inserted the words " and maintenance ".

[1] *i.e.* the M.S.A. 1894.

Radio installations and certificates

Requirements for portable radio apparatus carried in survival craft

1246 **10.**—(1) Radio rules[1] may prescribe requirements for such portable radio apparatus as boats or life rafts may be required to carry by the rules for life-saving appliances.[2]

(2) Subsection (6) of section 3 of the Act of 1949 (detention of ships not conforming with radio rules) shall apply in relation to portable radio apparatus so required to be carried by the boats or life rafts on any ship as it applies in relation to the radio equipment of the ship.[3]

1247 [1] See the M.S. (Radio) Rules 1965 (S.I. No. 1107) as amended by S.I. 1969 No. 1315 and the M.S. (Radio) (Fishing Vessels) Rules 1974 (S.I. No. 1919) made under the M.S. (Safety Convention) Act 1949, s. 3.

[2] See the M.S.A. 1894, s. 427.

[3] Substituted by the M.S.A. 1970, s. 100 (1), Sched. 3, para. 10, as from November 1, 1974.

Radio installations

1248 **11.**[1] *For subsection* (4) *of section* 3 *of the Act of* 1949 (*which specifies the radio installations to be required under the radio rules*) *there shall be substituted the following subsection*:—

" (4) *The radio installation required under the said rules to be provided*—

(*a*) *for a passenger steamer of whatever tonnage, or for any ship of sixteen hundred tons gross tonnage or upwards which is neither a passenger steamer nor a fishing vessel, shall be a radiotelegraph installation*; *and*

(*b*) *for any other ship shall be either a radiotelephone installation or a radiotelegraph installation, at the option of the owner*."

[1] This section is prospectively repealed by the M.S.A. 1970, s. 100 (3) and Sched. 5 as from a day to be appointed.

Renewal of radio certificates for small cargo ships

1249 **12.** Where a radio certificate[1] or qualified radio certificate[1] is in force in respect of a ship of less than five hundred tons gross tonnage, other than a passenger steamer,[2] and the ship is surveyed by a radio surveyor[3] at a time not earlier than two months before the end of the period for which the certificate is in force, then, if on receipt of the declaration of survey[4] a new certificate is issued before the end of that period,—

(*a*) the current certificate may be cancelled; and

(*b*) the new certificate may, notwithstanding anything in section

13 (3) of the Act of 1949, be issued for a period ending not later than twelve months after the end of the first-mentioned period.

[1] See the M.S. (Safety Convention) Act 1949, s. 9.
[2] See *ibid.*, s. 26 (2).
[3] See *ibid.*, s. 4.
[4] See *ibid.*, s. 36 (1).

Miscellaneous

Issue of exemption certificates where Convention country issues corresponding qualified certificates

50 **13.** Where the [Secretary of State], under section 13 (9) of the Act of 1949, requests the government of a country to which the Convention applies to issue in respect of a ship such certificates as he is authorised to issue under subsection (2) of section 7, 8 or 9 of that Act or under paragraph (*a*) of section 3 (2) of this Act, and that government is willing to issue, in pursuance of that request, a qualified certificate thereunder but is not willing to issue the corresponding exemption certificate, the [Secretary of State] may issue that exemption certificate in respect of the ship.

251 **14.**—[*This section, which contained provision relating to information about ship's stability, was repealed by the M.S.* (*Load Lines*) *Act* 1967, *s.* 33 *and Sched.* 2. *See now, s.* 2.]

Modification of s. 29 of Act of 1949

252 **15.** Subsection (1) of section 29 of the Act of 1949 (which exempts certain ships from certain provisions) shall not prevent the application—

(*a*) to any ship of three hundred tons gross tonnage [1] or upwards, of so much of the provisions mentioned in paragraphs (*a*) and (*b*) of that subsection as relates to certificates issued under section 9 of that Act or equivalent accepted Safety Convention certificates [2];

(*b*) to any ship to which section 2 of this Act applies and which is registered in the United Kingdom, of so much of the provisions mentioned in paragraph (*a*) of that subsection as relates to certificates issued under section 3 of this Act;

by reason only that she is of less than five hundred tons gross tonnage.

[1] For ascertainment of gross tonnage, see the M.S.A. 1965, s. 2.
[2] See M.S. (Safety Convention) Act 1949, s. 14.

Extension of duty to report dangers to navigation

253 **16.** The matters of which information is to be sent by the master of a ship in accordance with rules under section 24 of the Merchant Shipping (Safety and Load Line Conventions) Act 1932, shall include—

(*a*) air temperatures below freezing point associated with gale force winds causing severe ice accretion on the superstructure of ships; and

(*b*) winds of force 10 or above on the Beaufort Scale for which no storm warning has been received.

Ships carrying passengers

Amendment of Merchant Shipping Act 1894, s. 271

1254 **17.**—(1) For subsection (1) of section 271 of the principal Act (which prohibits passenger steamers [1] carrying more than twelve passengers [2] from sailing without a certificate of survey) there shall be substituted the following subsection:—

"(1) Every passenger steamer which carries more than twelve passengers shall be surveyed once at least in each year in the manner provided in this Part of this Act; and no ship (other than a steam ferry boat working in chains) shall proceed to sea or on any voyage or excursion with more than twelve passengers on board, unless there is in force in respect of the ship a certificate as to survey under this Part of this Act, applicable to the voyage or excursion on which the ship is about to proceed, or that voyage or excursion is one in respect of which the [Secretary of State for Trade] has exempted the ship from the requirements of this subsection."

and at the end of subsection (2) of that section (which enables a passenger ship to be detained until such a certificate is produced) there shall be inserted the words "unless the voyage or excursion on which she is about to proceed is one in respect of which she has been exempted as aforesaid".

(2) References in the Merchant Shipping Acts to a passenger steamer shall be construed as including any ship while on or about to proceed on a voyage or excursion in any case where a passenger steamer's certificate is required to be in force in respect of her.

[1] See M.S.A. 1894 s. 267 and M.S. (Safety Convention) Act 1949, s. 26 (2); see also *Duncan* v. *Graham* [1951] 1 K.B. 68.
[2] See M.S. (Safety Convention) Act 1949, s. 26 (1).

Supplementary

Transitional provisions and repeals

1255 **18.**—[This section which contained transitional provisions and repeals was repealed by the Statute Law (Reform) Act 1974.]

Commencement, construction, citation and extent

1256 **19.**—(1) This Act shall come into force on such day as Her Majesty may by Order in Council appoint.[1]

(2) In the Act of 1949 " the Merchant Shipping Acts " shall mean the Merchant Shipping Acts 1894 to 1958, and this Act; and this Act shall be construed as one with those Acts.

(3) This Act may be cited as the Merchant Shipping Act 1964, and the Merchant Shipping Acts 1894 to 1958, and this Act may be cited together as the Merchant Shipping Acts 1894 to 1964.

(4) This Act extends to Northern Ireland.

[1] **See the M.S.A. 1964 (Commencement) Order, 1965 (S.I. No. 317) appointing May 26, 1965.**

MERCHANT SHIPPING ACT 1965

[1965 c. 47]

An Act to amend the law relating to the measurement of the tonnage of merchant ships and the marking of load lines.

[5th August, 1965]

1257 INTRODUCTORY NOTE. The Act repealed the former provisions for ascertaining the registered tonnage of ships. In particular sections 77 to 81 and Schedule 2 of the M.S.A. 1894, section 54 and 55 of the M.S.A. 1906 and the whole of the M.S.A.'s 1907 and 1954 were all repealed: see Schedule 2. Such tonnage is now ascertained in accordance with regulations of the Department of Trade. Such regulations also enabled the recommendation of the Inter-Government Maritime Consultative Organisation (I.M.C.O.) as to exemption from measurement of 'tweendeck space on certain ships to be implemented: see section 1 (3).

The Act came into operation on March 1, 1967, see the Merchant Shipping Act 1965 (Commencement) Order 1967 (S.I. 1965 No. 157). The Act extends to Northern Ireland, and may be extended to the Isle of Man, the Channel Islands and any colony: see sections 5 and 6.

Tonnage regulations

1258 **1.**—(1) The tonnage of any ship to be registered under the principal Act (whether under Part I or Part IV thereof) [1] shall be ascertained in accordance with regulations [2] made by the [Department of Trade] by statutory instrument; and those regulations shall, as respects anything done after the commencement of this Act, be taken to be the provisions referred to in the principal Act as the tonnage regulations of that Act.

(2) Regulations under this section—

(*a*) may make different provision for different descriptions [3] of ships or for the same description of ships in different circumstances;

(*b*) may make any provision thereof dependent on compliance with such conditions, to be evidenced in such manner, as may be specified in the regulations;

(*c*) may provide for the ascertainment of any space to be taken into account for the purposes of section 85 of the principal Act (payment of dues where goods carried in spaces not forming part of registered tonnage) and may exempt any space from being taken into account for those purposes; and

(*d*) may prohibit or restrict the carriage of goods or stores [4] in spaces not included in the registered tonnage of a ship and may provide for making the master and the owner each liable to a fine not exceeding one hundred pounds where such a prohibition or restriction is contravened.[5]

(3) Regulations under this section may make provision for assigning to a ship, either instead of or as an alternative to the tonnage ascertained in accordance with the other provisions of the regulations a lower tonnage applicable where the ship is not loaded to the full depth to which it can be safely loaded,[6] and for indicating on the ship by such mark as may be specified in the regulations, that such a lower tonnage has been assigned to it and, where it has been assigned to it as an alternative, the depth to which the ship may be loaded for the lower tonnage to be applicable.

(4) Regulations under this section may provide for the measurement and survey of ships to be undertaken, in such circumstances as may be specified in the regulations and notwithstanding sections 6 and 86 of the principal Act, by persons appointed by such organisations as may be authorised in that behalf by the [Department of Trade]; and so much of section 83 of the principal Act and section 1 of the Merchant Shipping (Mercantile Marine Fund) Act 1898, as requires the payment of fees into the Exchequer shall not apply to fees payable under the said section 83 to persons appointed in pursuance of this subsection.

(5) *Regulations under this section may make provision for the alteration (notwithstanding section* 82 *of the principal Act) of the particulars relating to the registered tonnage of any ship registered before the coming into operation of the regulations.*[7]

(6) *Regulations under this section may provide for the issue of documents certifying the registered tonnage of any ship or the tonnage which is to be taken for any purpose specified in the regulations as the tonnage of a ship not registered in the United Kingdom.*[8]

(7) Any statutory instrument made under this section shall be subject to annulment in pursuance of a resolution of either House of Parliament.

1259 [1] *i.e.* under the M.S.A. 1894. Part I relates to British ships, see s. 2, and Part IV to British fishing boats, see s. 373.

[2] See the Merchant Shipping (Tonnage) Regulations 1967 (S.I. No. 172) as amended by S.I. 1967 No. 1093, 1972 No. 656, 1975 No. 594. These regulations have also been applied by s. 12 (2) of the Industry Act 1972. Where tonnage dues were paid to a dock company on an erroneous computation of tonnage (see *The City of Dublin Steam Packet Co.* v. *Thompson* (1866) 34 L.J.C.P. 316; affm. 85 L.J.C.P. 198), the court held that the ship-owners could not recover the dues already paid, see *Moss* v. *Mersey Docks and Harbour Board* (1872) 26 L.T. 425.

[3] For the ascertainment of the tonnage of a ship of a description with respect to which no provision is made by regulations under this section for the purposes of s. 4 of the M.S. (Oil Pollution) Act 1971, see s. 4 (2).

[4] " Stores " include bunker coal: see *Cairn Line of Steamships, Ltd.* v. *Trinity House Corporation* [1908] 1 K.B. 528.

[5] Any reference in regulations made under this section to regulations made under the M.S.A. 1948, s. 1 (Accommodation of Seamen) is to be construed as including a reference to regulations made under the M.S.A. 1970, s. 20: see ss. 100, 101 (4) and Sched. 4, para. 7.

[6] See s. 2 of the M.S. (Load Lines) Act 1967.

[7] By the M.S.A. 1970, s. 91, there is substituted for subsections (5) and (6) the following subsections as from a day to be appointed:— " (5) Regulations under this section may make provision for the alteration (notwithstanding section 82 of the principal Act) of the particulars relating to the registered tonnage of a ship. (6) Regulations under this section may provide for the issue by the [Department of Trade] or by persons appointed by such organisations as may be authorised in that behalf by the [Department of Trade] of cer-

tificates of the registered tonnage of any ship or of the tonnage which is to be taken for any purpose specified in the regulations as the tonnage of a ship not registered in the United Kingdom, and for the cancellation and delivery up of such certificates in such circumstances as may be prescribed by the regulations. (6A) Regulations under this section requiring the delivery up of any certificate may make a failure to comply with the requirement an offence punishable on summary conviction with a fine not exceeding £100."

[8] *Ibid.*

1260 **2.** [*This section, which contained provisions relating to load lines indicating greater than minimum freeboard, was repealed by the M.S.* (*Load Lines*) *Act* 1967, *s.* 33, *Sched. II.*]

Transitional provision

1261 **3.** The provisions made with respect to the ascertainment of tonnage by the Merchant Shipping (Fishing Boats Registry) Order 1927,[1] shall have effect as if contained in, and accordingly may be amended or revoked by, regulations under this Act.[2]

[1] S.R. & O. 1927 (No. 642)

[2] See note 2 to s. 1, *ante*.

1262 **4.** [*This section, which contained provisions relating to the exercise of powers of the* [*Department of Trade*], *was repealed by the Industrial Expansion Act* 1968, *ss.* 17, 18 (2) *and Sched.* 4. *See now s.* 14.]

Provisions as to Northern Ireland

1263 **5.**—(1) This Act extends to Northern Ireland.

(2) In the application of this Act to Northern Ireland the amendment [1] made by this Act in the Crown Proceedings Act 1947, is an amendment to that Act as it applies in Northern Ireland.

[1] See Sched. 1, *post*.

Application to British possessions, etc.

1264 **6.** Her Majesty may by Order in Council direct that the provisions of this Act shall extend, with such exceptions, adaptations and modifications as may be specified in the Order,[1] to—

(*a*) the Isle of Man;

(*b*) any of the Channel Islands;

(*c*) any colony, or any country or place outside Her Majesty's dominions in which for the time being Her Majesty has jurisdiction, or any territory consisting partly of one or more colonies and partly of one or more such countries or places.

[1] Orders under this section are: (a) the M.S. (Tonnage) (Hong Kong) Order 1967 (S.I. No. 1764); (b) the M.S.A. 1965 (Guernsey) Order 1969 (S.I. No. 147); (c) the M.S.A. 1965 (Isle of Man) Order 1969 (S.I. No. 740); (d) the M.S.A. 1965 (Jersey) Order 1969 (S.I. No. 741); (e) the M.S. (Tonnage) (Overseas Territories) Order 1971 (S.I. No. 383) as amended by S.I. 1972 No. 447.

Amendments and repeals

1265 **7.**—(1) The enactments mentioned in Schedule 1 to this Act shall have effect subject to the amendments specified in relation thereto in the second column of that Schedule, being minor amendments and amendments consequential on the foregoing provisions of this Act.

(2) *The enactments mentioned in Schedule 2 to this Act are hereby repealed to the extent specified in the third column of that Schedule.*[1]

[1] This subsection was repealed by the Statute Law (Reform) Act 1974.

Interpretation, construction, citation and commencement

66 **8.**—(1) In this Act " the principal Act " means the Merchant Shipping Act 1894.

(2) This Act shall be construed as one with the Merchant Shipping Acts 1894 to 1964.

(3) This Act may be cited as the Merchant Shipping Act 1965, and the Merchant Shipping Acts 1894 to 1964, and this Act may be cited together as the Merchant Shipping Acts 1894 to 1965.

(4) This Act shall come into operation on such day as Her Majesty may by Order in Council appoint.[1]

[1] See the M.S.A. 1965 (Commencement) Order 1967 (S.I. No. 157) which appointed March 1, 1967.

267

SCHEDULES

Section 7 (1)

SCHEDULE 1

MINOR AND CONSEQUENTIAL AMENDMENTS

Enactment amended	Amendment
The Merchant Shipping Act 1894 57 & 58 Vict. c. 60.	In section 84, there shall be added at the end of subsection (1) the words " and any space shown by the certificate of registry of other national papers of any such ship as deducted from the tonnage shall, where a similar deduction in the case of a British ship depends on compliance with any conditions or on the compliance being evidenced in any manner, be deemed to comply with those conditions and to be so evidenced, unless a surveyor of ships certifies to the Board of Trade that the construction and the equipment of the ship as respects that space do not come up to the standard which would be required if the ship were a British ship registered in the United Kingdom." In section 85, in subsection (1) after the words " forming the ship's registered tonnage " there shall be inserted the words " and not exempted by regulations under the Merchant Shipping Act 1965," and in subsection (3) for the words from " in manner directed " to " this Act " there shall be substituted the words " in accordance with regulations made under the Merchant Shipping Act 1965." In section 371, in subsection (1), the words from " in the case " to " any other case " shall be omitted. At the end of Part II of Schedule 1 there shall be added the words " Bill of sale."
The Merchant Shipping (Safety and Load Line Conventions) Act 1932 22 & 23 Geo. 5. c. 9.	In section 43 (1) (*c*) for the words " can be safely loaded " there shall be substituted the words " may be loaded."
The Crown Proceedings Act 1947 10 & 11 Geo. 6. c. 44.	In section 5 (5) (*a*) for the words from " section seventy-seven " in the first place where they occur to " section seventy-seven " in the second place where they occur there shall be substituted the words " regulations made under the Merchant Shipping Act 1965."

1268 **Section 7 (2)** SCHEDULE 2

ENACTMENTS REPEALED

Chapter	Short Title	Extent of Repeal
57 & 58 Vict. c. 60.	The Merchant Shipping Act 1894.	In section 24 (2) the words from " and shall be in " to " permit." Sections 77 to 81. In section 84 (1) the words from " and any space " to the end of the subsection. In section 371, in subsection (1) the words from " in the case " to " any other case " and subsections (2) and (3). In Schedule 1, in Part I, Form A—Bill of Sale. Schedule 2. In Schedule 6, paragraphs (2) to (5).
6 Edw. 7. c. 48	The Merchant Shipping Act 1906.	Sections 54 and 55.
7 Edw. 7. c. 52	The Merchant Shipping Act 1907.	The whole Act.
11 & 12 Geo. 6. c. 44.	The Merchant Shipping Act 1948.	In section 1, the proviso to subsection (3). In section 4, subsections (1) and (2).
14 Geo. 6. c. 9	The Merchant Shipping Act 1950.	Section 1 (4). In Schedule 1, paragraph 12.
2 & 3 Eliz. 2. c. 18.	The Merchant Shipping Act 1954.	The whole Act.

MERCHANT SHIPPING ACT 1967

[1967 c. 26]

An Act to amend section 92 of the Merchant Shipping Act 1894.

[10th May 1967]

1269 INTRODUCTORY NOTE. Section 92 of the Merchant Shipping Act 1894 required British foreign-going ships and home trade passenger ships to carry certain officers holding statutory certificates of competency only when the ships have gone to sea from the United Kingdom. This Act requires British ships registered in the United Kingdom to carry these certificated officers when going to sea from any place outside the United Kingdom. It also provides that such a ship may in certain circumstances sail for a limited time short of one of the required certificated officers and alters the penalties for non-compliance with the requirements.

The Act has been prospectively repealed by the M.S.A. 1970, s. 100 (3), Sched. V as from a day to be appointed.

1270 **Extension of, and new penal provision for, section 92 of Merchant Shipping Act 1894**

1.—(1) *Section* 92 *of the Merchant Shipping Act* 1894 *shall be amended in accordance with the following provisions of this section.*

(2) *In subsection* (1) (*which requires every British foreign-going ship and every British home trade passenger ship, when going to sea from any place in the United Kingdom, and, in certain circumstances, other ships, to be provided with officers duly certificated under that Act according to the scale set out in that subsection) after the words " from any place in the United Kingdom " there shall be inserted the words " every ship registered in the United Kingdom, being a foreign-going ship or a home trade passenger ship, when going to sea from a place outside the United Kingdom."*

(3) *After subsection* (1), *there shall be inserted the following subsection*:

" (1A) *If, on an occasion on which a ship of a particular description registered in the United Kingdom, being a foreign-going ship or a home trade passenger ship, goes to sea from a place outside the United Kingdom, one, but only one, of the duly certificated officers with which a ship of that description is required to be provided by the foregoing provisions of this section is not provided, but all reasonable steps were taken to secure the provision on that occasion of a duly certificated person as that officer, so much of the foregoing subsection as requires a ship of that description to be provided with that officer when going to sea from a place outside the United Kingdom shall not apply to the ship during whichever is the shorter of the following periods beginning with the day on which the ship goes to sea from that place on that occasion, that is to say—*

(*a*) *the period of twenty-eight days*; *and*

(*b*) *the period ending with the day on which the ship is provided with a duly certificated person as that officer.*"

(4) *For subsection* (2) (*which penalises a person engaged as such an officer as is mentioned in the said subsection* (1) *who goes to sea without being duly certificated and any person who employs another as an officer in contravention of the said subsection* (1) *without ascertaining that that other is duly certificated*) *there shall be substituted the following subsection*:—

" (2) *If the requirements of subsection* (1) *of this section are not complied with in a case in which they apply to a ship, the master or owner of the ship shall be liable to a fine not exceeding one hundred pounds* ".

Interpretation and construction

271 **2.**—(1) *This Act may be cited as the Merchant Shipping Act* 1967, *and this Act and the Merchant Shipping Acts* 1894 *to* 1965 *may be cited together as the Merchant Shipping Acts* 1894 *to* 1967.[1]

(2) *Any reference in an Act passed before the passing* [1] *of this Act to section* 92 *of the Merchant Shipping Act* 1894 *shall, unless the contrary intention appears, be construed as referring to that section as amended by this Act.*

[1] This Act received the Royal Assent on May 10, 1967.

MERCHANT SHIPPING (LOAD LINES) ACT 1967

[1967 c. 27]

An Act to make further provision as to load lines and related matters; to increase penalties under certain provisions of the Merchant Shipping Acts 1894 to 1965 relating to passenger steamers; and for purposes connected with the matters aforesaid.

[10th May 1967]

1272 INTRODUCTORY NOTE. This Act gives effect to the International Convention on Load Lines 1966 (Cmnd. 3070) which replaced the International Convention respecting Load Lines 1930. The Act replaces the former provisions relating to load lines contained in Part II of the Merchant Shipping (Safety and Load Line Conventions) Act 1932 and the Merchant Shipping Act 1937.

The Act also enables a number of matters in the Act of 1932 to be dealt with by statutory instrument, extends the powers of exemption of the Department of Trade, and increases the amounts of maximum fines. There are also special provisions relating to load lines on passenger steamers and the carriage of deck cargo.

The Act came into force on July 21, 1968; see the Merchant Shipping (Load Lines) Act 1967 (Commencement) Order 1968 (S.I. No. 1108). The 1966 Convention came into force on the same day. Section 25 and Schedule 1 of the Act came into force on the passing of the Act, May 10, 1967.

General provisions

Ships to which Act applies

1273 **1.** This Act applies to all ships [1] except—

(*a*) ships of war;

(*b*) ships solely engaged in fishing; and

(*c*) pleasure yachts.

[1] For meaning of " ship " see s. 742 of the M.S.A. 1894.

Load line rules

1274 **2.**—(1) The [Department of Trade] shall make rules [1] in accordance with the following provisions of this Act (in this Act referred to as " the load line rules "); and in making those rules the [Department] shall have regard in particular to the Convention of 1966.

(2) The load line rules shall make provision—

(*a*) for the surveying and periodical inspection of ships to which this Act applies [2];

(*b*) for determining freeboards to be assigned from time to time to such ships;

(*c*) for determining, in relation to any such ship, the deck which is to be taken to be the freeboard deck of the ship, and for requiring the position of that deck to be indicated on each side of the ship by a mark of a description prescribed by the rules; and

(*d*) for determining, by reference to that mark and the freeboards for the time being assigned to any such ship, the positions in which each side of the ship is to be marked with lines of a description prescribed by the rules, indicating the various maximum depths to which the ship may be loaded in circumstances prescribed by the rules.

(3) The load line rules shall include the following provisions, that is to say—

(*a*) provisions specifying such requirements in respect of the hulls, superstructures, fittings and appliances of ships to which this Act applies as appear to the [Department of Trade] to be relevant to the assignment of freeboards to such ships;

(*b*) provisions whereby, at the time when freeboards are assigned to a ship in accordance with the load line rules, such particulars relating to those requirements as may be determined in accordance with the rules are to be recorded in such manner as may be so determined; and

(*c*) provisions for determining by reference to those requirements and that record whether, at any time after freeboards have been so assigned to a ship and while they continue to be so assigned, the ship is for the purposes of this Act to be taken to comply, or not to comply, with the conditions of assignment;

and those provisions shall be set out separately in the load line rules under the title of " rules as to conditions of assignment ".

(4) The load line rules shall also include provisions requiring such information relating to the stability of any ship to which freeboards are assigned thereunder, and such information relating to the loading and ballasting of any such ship, as may be determined in accordance with the rules to be provided for the guidance of the master of the ship in such manner as may be so determined.

(5) In relation to any matter authorised or required by this Act to be prescribed by the load line rules, those rules may make different provision by reference to (or to any combination of) any of the following, that is to say, different descriptions of ships, different areas, different seasons of the year and any other different circumstances.

(6) Except in so far as the context otherwise requires, in this Act " deck-line " means such a mark as is referred to in paragraph (*c*) of subsection (2) of this section and " load lines " means such lines as are referred to in paragraph (*d*) of that subsection.

[1] See the Merchant Shipping (Load Line) Rules 1968 (S.I. No. 1053) as amended by S.I. 1970 No. 1003 and S.I. 1975 No. 595.
[2] See s. 1, *ante*. As to exemptions, see ss. 18 to 22, *post*.

Ships registered in United Kingdom

Compliance with load line rules

1275 **3.**—(1) Subject to any exemption [1] conferred by or under this Act, no ship to which this Act applies, being a ship registered [2] in the United Kingdom, shall proceed or attempt to proceed to sea unless—

(*a*) the ship has been surveyed in accordance with the load line rules;
(*b*) the ship is marked with a deck-line [3] and with load lines [3] in accordance with those rules;
(*c*) the ship complies with the conditions of assignment; and
(*d*) the information required by those rules to be provided as mentioned in section 2 (4) of this Act is provided for the guidance of the master of the ship in the manner determined in accordance with the rules.

(2) If any ship proceeds or attempts to proceed to sea in contravention of the preceding subsection, the owner or master of the ship shall be guilty of an offence and liable on summary conviction to a fine not exceeding £200.

(3) Any ship which in contravention of subsection (1) of this section attempts to proceed to sea without being surveyed and marked as mentioned in paragraphs (*a*) and (*b*) of that subsection may be detained [4] until she has been so surveyed and marked.

(4) Any such ship as is mentioned in subsection (1) of this section which does not comply with the conditions of assignment shall be deemed to be unsafe for the purposes of section 459 of the Merchant Shipping Act 1894 (power to detain unsafe ships, and procedure for detention).

[1] See ss. 18 *et seq., post.*
[2] See s. 2 of the M.S.A. 1894.
[3] See s. 2 (6), *ante.*
[4] For enforcement of detention see s. 692 of the M.S.A. 1894, and as to costs of detention see s. 460 (2).

Submersion of load lines

1276 **4.**—(1) Where a ship to which this Act applies, being a ship registered in the United Kingdom, is marked with load lines, the ship shall not be so loaded [1] that—

(*a*) if the ship is in salt water and has no list, the appropriate load line on each side of the ship is submerged, or (*b*) in any other case, the appropriate load line on each side of the ship would be submerged if the ship were in salt water and had no list.

(2) If any ship is loaded in contravention [2] of the preceding subsection, the owner or master [3] of the ship shall [4] (subject to subsection (5) of this section) be guilty of an offence and liable on summary conviction—

(*a*) to a fine not exceeding £400, and

(*b*) to such additional fine,[5] not exceeding an amount calculated in accordance with the next following subsection, as the court thinks fit to impose, having regard to the extent to which the earning capacity of the ship was increased by reason of the contravention.

(3) Any additional fine imposed under subsection (2) (*b*) of this section shall not exceed £400 for every complete inch, and for any fraction of an inch over and above one or more complete inches, by which—

(*a*) in a case falling within paragraph (*a*) of subsection (1) of this section, the appropriate load line on each side of the ship was submerged, or

(*b*) in a case falling within paragraph (*b*) of that subsection, the appropriate load line on each side of the ship would have been submerged as therein mentioned;

and, if the amount by which that load line was or would have been submerged was less than a complete inch, any such additional fine shall not exceed £400.

(4) If the master of a ship takes the ship to sea when she is loaded in contravention of subsection (1) of this section, or if any other person, having reason to believe that the ship is so loaded, sends or is party to sending her to sea when she is loaded in contravention of that subsection, then (without prejudice to any fine to which he may be liable in respect of an offence under subsection (2) of this section) he shall be guilty of an offence under this subsection and liable—

(*a*) on conviction on indictment, to a fine;

(*b*) on summary conviction, to a fine not exceeding £400.

(5) Where a person is charged with an offence under subsection (2) of this section, it shall be a defence to prove that the contravention was due solely to deviation or delay and that the deviation or delay was caused solely by stress of weather or other circumstances which neither the master nor the owner nor the charterer (if any) could have prevented or forestalled.

(6) Without prejudice to any proceedings under the preceding provisions of this section, any ship which is loaded in contravention of subsection (1) of this section may be detained until she ceases to be so loaded.

(7) For the purposes of the application of this section to a ship in any circumstances prescribed by the load line rules in accordance with section 2 (2) (*d*) of this Act, " the appropriate load line " means the load line which, in accordance with those rules, indicates the maximum depth to which the ship may be loaded in salt water in those circumstances.

1277 [1] *Quaere* whether this refers to the condition of the ship on loading or to the condition of the ship at any point of her voyage. It is thought to be the latter, even though the condition does not result from any default by the owner or master; *cf. Radcliffe* v. *Buckwell* [1927] 2 K.B. 273; [1927] All E.R. 386.

[2] The fact that a ship was overloaded in the course of performing a contract of carriage, and that the master was subsequently prosecuted for an offence under this section, is not a defence to a claim by the shipowners for the balance of freight due upon the contract; *St. John Shipping Corporation* v. *Joseph Rank* [1957] 1 Q.B. 267.

[3] *Quaere* whether the owner of a ship, which without his knowledge or consent is overloaded, is responsible for the act of the master so as to be liable for the penalty; *cf. Massey* v. *Morris* [1894] 2 Q.B. 412.

[4] The absolute liability of the owner or master under subs. (2) of this section (subject only to the defence provided by subs. (4)) should be contrasted with the former provisions of the repealed s. 442 (1) of M.S.A. 1894, which provided that an offence was committed if without reasonable cause the owner or master failed in his duties as to marking or allowed the ship to be overloaded. For decisions on the old section, see *Massey* v. *Morris*, 63 L.J.M.C. 185; *Crabtree* v. *Fern Spinning Co.* (1901) 66 J.P. 181; *Radcliffe* v. *Buckwell* [1927] 2 K.B. 273.

[5] There must be some evidence of increased earning capacity; *Rutberg* v. *Williams* [1961] 2 All E.R. 649.

Miscellaneous offences in relation to marks

1278 **5.** Where a ship to which this Act applies, being a ship registered in the United Kingdom, is marked in accordance with any requirements as to marking imposed by or under this Act, then if—

(*a*) the owner or master of the ship fails without reasonable cause to keep the ship so marked, or

(*b*) any person conceals, removes, alters, defaces or obliterates, or causes or permits any person under his control to conceal, remove, alter, deface or obliterate, any mark with which the ship is so marked, except where he does so under the authority of a person empowered under the load line rules [1] to authorise him in that behalf,

he shall be guilty of an offence and liable on summary conviction to a fine not exceeding £200.

[1] See note 1 to s. 2.

Issue of load line certificates

1279 **6.**—(1) Where a ship to which this Act applies, being a ship registered in the United Kingdom, has been surveyed and marked in accordance with the load line rules,[1] the appropriate certificate shall be issued to the owner of the ship on his application.

(2) For the purposes of this section the appropriate certificate—

(*a*) in the case of an existing ship [2] of not less than 150 tons gross tonnage, and in the case of a new ship,[2] of not less than 24 metres in length,[3] is a certificate to be called an " International Load Line Certificate (1966)," and

(*b*) in the case of any other ship, is a certificate to be called a " United Kingdom load line certificate."

(3) Subject to the next following subsection, any certificate required by subsection (1) of this section to be issued—

(*a*) shall be issued by the [Department of Trade] or by a person authorised in that behalf by the [Department],[4] and

(*b*) shall be in such form, and shall be issued in such manner, as may be prescribed by the load line rules.[1]

(4) The [Department of Trade] may request a Contracting Government, other than Her Majesty's Government in the United Kingdom, to issue an International Load Line Certificate (1966) in respect of any ship to which this Act applies which is a ship registered in the United Kingdom and falling within subsection (2) (*a*) of this section; and the following provisions of this Act shall have effect in relation to such a certificate so issued, which contains a statement that it has been issued at the request of Her Majesty's Government in the United Kingdom, as they have effect in relation to an International Load Line Certificate (1966) issued by the [Department of Trade].

[1] See note 1 to s. 2.
[2] See s. 32 (4).
[3] See s. 32 (6).
[4] *e.g.* an authorised Classification Society.

Effect of load line certificate

280 7. Where a certificate, issued in pursuance of the last preceding section and for the time being in force, is produced in respect of the ship to which the certificate relates,—

(*a*) the ship shall be deemed to have been surveyed in accordance with the load line rules, and

(*b*) if lines are marked on the ship corresponding in number and description to the deck-line [1] and load lines [1] as required by the load line rules, and the positions of those lines so marked correspond to the positions of the deck-line and load lines as specified in the certificate, the ship shall be deemed to be marked as required by those rules.

[1] See s. 2 (6), *ante*.

Duration, endorsement and cancellation of load line certificates

1281 **8.**—(1) The load line rules [1] shall make provision for determining the period during which any certificate issued under section 6 of this Act is to remain in force, including—

(*a*) provision enabling the period for which any such certificate is originally issued to be extended within such limits and in such circumstances as may be prescribed by the rules, and

(*b*) provision for cancelling any such certificate in such circumstances as may be so prescribed.

(2) While any such certificate is in force in respect of a ship, there shall be endorsed on the certificate such information relating to—

(*a*) periodical inspections of the ship in accordance with the load line rules, and

(*b*) any extension of the period for which the certificate was issued,

as may be prescribed by the rules.

[1] See note 1 to s. 2.

Ships not to proceed to sea without load line certificate

1282 **9.**—(1) Subject to any exemption [1] conferred by or under this Act, no ship to which this Act applies, being a ship registered in the United Kingdom, shall proceed or attempt to proceed to sea unless the appropriate certificate is in force in respect of the ship.

(2) Before any such ship proceeds to sea, the master of the ship shall produce the appropriate certificate to the officer of customs from whom a clearance [2] for the ship is demanded; and a clearance shall not be granted, and the ship may be detained, until the appropriate certificate is so produced.

(3) If any ship proceeds or attempts to proceed to sea in contravention of this section, the master of the ship shall be guilty of an offence and liable on summary conviction to a fine not exceeding £200.

(4) In this section " the appropriate certificate " means the certificate which is the appropriate certificate for the purposes of section 6 of this Act.

[1] See ss. 18 *et seq.*, *post.*
[2] See s. 52 of the Customs and Excise Act 1952.

Publication of load line certificate and entry of particulars in official log-book

1283 **10.**—(1) Where a certificate is issued in respect of a ship under section 6 of this Act—

(*a*) the owner of the ship shall forthwith [1] on receipt of the certificate cause it to be framed and posted up in some conspicuous place on board the ship, and shall cause it to be kept so framed and posted up and legible so long as the certificate remains in force [2] and the ship is in use, and

(*b*) *the master of the ship, before making any other entry in any official log-book relating to the ship, shall enter in it the particulars as to the positions of the deck-line and the load lines which are specified in the certificate.*[3]

(2) Before any ship to which this Act applies, being a ship registered in the United Kingdom, leaves any dock, wharf, harbour or other place for the purpose of proceeding to sea, the master of the ship—

(*a*) *shall enter in the official log-book such particulars relating to the depth to which the ship is for the time being loaded as may be prescribed by regulations made by the* [*Department of Trade under this Act, and* [3]

(*b*) subject to the next following subsection, shall cause a notice [to be posted up in some conspicuous place on board the ship, which shall be in such form and containing such particulars relating to the depth to which the ship is for the time being loaded as may be specified in regulations [4] made by the [Department of Trade] under this Act;] [5]

and, where such a notice has been posted up, the master of the ship shall cause it to be kept so posted up and legible until the ship arrives at some other dock, wharf, harbour or place.

(3) The regulations may exempt home trade [6] ships, or any class of home trade ships specified in the regulations, from the requirements as to notices contained in the last preceding subsection.

(4) If the owner or master of a ship fails to comply with any requirement imposed on him by the preceding provisions of this section, he shall be guilty of an offence and liable on summary conviction to a fine not exceeding £50.

1284 [1] On meaning of forthwith, see *Re Southam, ex p. Lamb* (1881) 19 Ch.D. 169, 173; *Re Muscovitch, ex p. Muscovitch* [1939] Ch. 694, 697; *Sameen* v. *Abeyewickrema* [1963] A.C. 597; *Hillingdon London B.C.* v. *Cutler* [1968] 1 Q.B. 124.

[2] See s. 8 (1), *ante*.

[3] The words in italics were repealed by the M.S.A. 1970, s. 100 and Sched. 3, para. 12, and Sched. 5 as from January 1, 1973. See S.I. 1972 No. 1977.

[4] See the M.S. (Load Lines) (Particulars of Depth of Loading) Regs. 1972 (S.I. No. 1841).

[5] The words in square brackets were substituted by the M.S.A. 1970, s. 100 and Sched. 3, para. 12 as from January 1, 1973; see S.I. 1972 No. 1977.

[6] There is no special definition in this Act. But see the definition in s. 742 of M.S.A. 1894: " Every ship employed in trading or going within the following limits; that is to say, the United Kingdom, the Channel Islands and the Isle of Man, and the continent of Europe between the River Elbe and Brest inclusive."

Inspection of ships

285 **11.**—(1) A ship surveyor or engineer surveyor [1] may inspect any ship to which this Act applies, being a ship registered in the United Kingdom, for the purpose of seeing that the provisions of this Act have been complied with in respect of the ship.

(2) For the purposes of any such inspection any such surveyor shall have all the powers of a [Department of Trade] inspector under the Merchant Shipping Act 1894.[2]

[1] For appointment, see s. 724 of the M.S.A. 1894.
[2] See s. 729 of the M.S.A. 1894.

Ships not registered in United Kingdom

Valid convention certificates

1286 **12.**—(1) This section applies to any ship which, being a ship to which this Act applies and not being registered in the United Kingdom,—

(*a*) is registered in a Convention country [1] or, not being registered in any such country or elsewhere, flies the flag of a Convention country, and

(*b*) is either an existing ship [2] of not less than 150 tons gross tonnage or a new ship [2] of not less than 24 metres in length.

(2) The [Department of Trade] may, at the request of the Government of the parent country [1] of a ship to which this section applies, issue in respect of the ship a certificate in such form as may be prescribed by the load line rules, if the [Department is] satisfied that they could properly issue a certificate in respect of the ship under section 6 (1) of this Act if the ship were registered in the United Kingdom.

(3) The load line rules [3] shall make such provision as appears to the [Department of Trade] to be appropriate for securing that certificates which are issued as International Load Line Certificates (1966) in respect of ships to which this section applies, and are so issued by Governments other than Her Majesty's Government in the United Kingdom, shall be recognised for the purposes of this Act in such circumstances as may be prescribed by the rules.

(4) Certificates issued as mentioned in subsection (2) or subsection (3) of this section shall be included among the certificates to be called " International Load Line Certificates (1966)."

(5) In this Act " valid Convention certificate ", means a certificate which either—

(*a*) has been issued under subsection (2) of this section and is for the time being in force, or

(*b*) having been issued as mentioned in subsection (3) of this section, is produced in circumstances in which it is required by the load line rules to be recognised for the purposes of this Act.

[1] See s. 32 (1).
[2] See s. 32 (4).
[3] See note 1 to s. 2.

Compliance with load line rules

287 **13.**—(1) Subject to the next following subsection, and to any exemption [1] conferred by or under this Act, no ship to which this Act applies, not being a ship registered in the United Kingdom, shall proceed or attempt to proceed to sea from any port in the United Kingdom unless—

(*a*) the ship has been surveyed in accordance with the load line rules;

(*b*) the ship is marked with a deck-line and with load lines in accordance with those rules;

(*c*) the ship complies with the conditions of assignment; and

(*d*) the information required by those rules to be provided as mentioned in section 2 (4) of this Act is provided for the guidance of the master of the ship in the manner determined in accordance with the rules.

(2) The preceding subsection does not apply to a ship in respect of which a valid Convention certificate is produced.

(3) If any ship proceeds or attempts to proceed to sea in contravention of the preceding provisions of this section, the owner or master of the ship shall be guilty of an offence and liable on summary conviction to a fine not exceeding £200.

(4) Any ship which in contravention of this section attempts to proceed to sea without being surveyed and marked as mentioned in paragraphs (*a*) and (*b*) of subsection (1) of this section may be detained until she has been so surveyed and marked.

(5) If any such ship as is mentioned in subsection (1) of this section, not being a ship in respect of which a valid Convention certificate is produced, does not comply with the conditions of assignment, then—

(*a*) if the ship is a British ship, she shall be deemed to be unsafe for the purposes of section 459 of the Merchant Shipping Act 1894, or

(*b*) if the ship is a foreign ship, section 462 [2] of that Act shall have effect in relation to the ship as if she were unsafe by reason of one of the matters specified in that section.

[1] See s. 18.

[2] Where a foreign ship is detained or proceedings are taken against the master or owner of such a ship, notice must be given to the appropriate consular officer in accordance with the M.S. (Safety and Load Line Conventions) Act 1932, s. 69 and s. 27 (1) of this Act.

Submersion of load lines

288 **14.**—(1) Where a ship to which this Act applies, not being a ship registered in the United Kingdom, is within any port in the United Kingdom, and is marked with load lines, the ship shall not be so loaded that—

(*a*) if the ship is in salt water and has no list, the appropriate load line on each side of the ship is submerged, or (*b*) in any other case, the appropriate load line on each side of the ship would be submerged if the ship were in salt water and had no list.

(2) Subsections (2), (3), (5) and (6) of section 4 of this Act shall have effect for the purposes of this section as if any reference in those subsections to subsection (1) of that section, or to paragraph (*a*) or paragraph (*b*) of the said subsection (1), were a reference to subsection (1), or (as the case may be) to the corresponding paragraph of subsection (1), of this section:

Provided that, in the case of a ship to which section 12 of this Act applies, the ship shall not be detained, and no proceedings shall be brought by virtue of this subsection, unless the ship has been inspected by a ship surveyor or engineer surveyor in pursuance of section 17 of this Act.

(3) In relation to a ship in respect of which a valid Convention certificate is produced, " load line " in subsection (1) of this section means a line marked on the ship in the position of a load line specified in that certificate; and for the purposes of the application of the relevant provisions to such a ship in any circumstances for which a particular load line is specified in the certificate, the " appropriate load line " means the load line which, in accordance with the certificate, indicates the maximum depth to which the ship may be loaded in salt water in those circumstances.

(4) Where a valid Convention certificate is not produced in respect of a ship, then, for the purposes of the application of the relevant provisions to that ship in any circumstances prescribed by the load line rules in accordance with section 2 (2) (*d*) of this Act, " the appropriate load line " means the load line which, in accordance with those rules, indicates the maximum depth to which the ship may be loaded in salt water in those circumstances.

(5) In subsections (3) and (4) of this section " the relevant provisions " means the provisions of subsection (1) of this section and any provisions of section 4 of this Act as applied by subsection (2) of this section.

United Kingdom load line certificates

1289 **15.**—(1) Where a ship to which this Act applies, not being a ship registered in the United Kingdom, has been surveyed and marked in accordance with the load line rules, then on the application of the owner of the ship a United Kingdom load line certificate shall be issued to him by the [Department of Trade] or by a person authorised[1] in that behalf by the [Department].

(2) Subject to the next following subsection, the provisions of sections 7 and 8 of this Act shall have effect in relation to a certificate issued under the preceding subsection as they have effect in relation to a certificate issued under section 6 of this Act.

(3) Any certificate issued under subsection (1) of this section in respect of a ship to which section 12 of this Act applies shall be valid only so long

as the ship is not plying on international voyages,[2] and shall be cancelled by the [Department of Trade] if they have reason to believe that the ship is plying on international voyages.

[1] *e.g.* an authorised Classification Society.
[2] See s. 32 (2), (3).

Production of certificate to customs officer

290 **16.**—(1) Subject to any exemption conferred by or under this Act, before a ship to which this Act applies, not being a ship registered in the United Kingdom, proceeds to sea from any port in the United Kingdom, the master of the ship shall produce the appropriate certificate to the officer of customs from whom a clearance [1] for the ship is demanded; and a clearance shall not be granted, and the ship may be detained, until the appropriate certificate is so produced.

(2) For the purposes of this section the appropriate certificate—

(*a*) in the case of a ship to which section 12 of this Act applies, where a clearance for the ship is demanded in respect of an international voyage,[2] is a valid Convention certificate [3];

(*b*) in the case of any such ship, where a clearance for the ship is demanded in respect of any other voyage, is either a valid Convention certificate or a United Kingdom load line certificate for the time being in force in respect of the ship; and

(*c*) in any other case, is a United Kingdom load line certificate for the time being in force in respect of the ship.

[1] See s. 32 (1) and the Customs and Excise Act 1952, s. 52.
[2] See s. 32 (2), (3).
[3] See s. 12 (5).

Provisions as to inspection

291 **17.**—(1) Subject to the following provisions of this section, a ship surveyor or engineer surveyor [1] may inspect any ship to which this Act applies, not being a ship registered in the United Kingdom, while the ship is within any port in the United Kingdom; and for the purposes of any such inspection any such surveyor shall have all the powers of a [Department of Trade] inspector under the Merchant Shipping Act 1894.[2]

(2) Any such surveyor may go on board any ship to which section 12 of this Act applies, while the ship is within any port in the United Kingdom, for the purpose of demanding production of any International Load Line Certificate (1966) or United Kingdom load line certificate for the time being in force in respect of the ship.

(3) If on any such demand a valid Convention certificate is produced to the surveyor in respect of the ship, the powers of the surveyor under subsection (1) of this section shall be limited to seeing—

1291

(*a*) that the ship is not loaded beyond the limits allowed by the certificate;

(*b*) that lines are marked on the ship in the positions of the load lines specified in the certificate;

(*c*) that no material alterations have taken place in the hull or superstructures of the ship which affect the position in which any of those lines ought to be marked; and

(*d*) that the fittings and appliances for the protection of openings, the guard rails, the freeing ports and the means of access to the crew's quarters have been maintained on the ship in as effective a condition as they were in when the certificate was issued.

(4) If on an inspection of a ship under this section the ship is found to have been so materially altered in respect of the matters referred to in paragraph (*c*) or paragraph (*d*) of the last preceding subsection that the ship is manifestly unfit to proceed to sea without danger to human life, then—

(*a*) if the ship is a British ship, she shall be deemed to be unsafe for the purposes of section 459 of the Merchant Shipping Act 1894, or

(*b*) if the ship is a foreign ship, section 462 [3] of that Act shall have effect in relation to the ship as if she were unsafe by reason of one of the matters specified in that section.

(5) Where a ship is detained under the provisions of that Act as applied by the last preceding subsection, the [Department of Trade] shall order the ship to be released as soon as they are satisfied that the ship is fit to proceed to sea without danger to human life.

1292 [1] For appointment, see s. 724 of the M.S.A. 1894.
[2] See s. 729 of the M.S.A. 1894.
[3] See note 2 to s. 13.

Exemptions

Power to make exemption orders

1293 **18.**—(1) If in the opinion of the [Department of Trade] the sheltered nature and conditions of international voyages [1]—

(*a*) between near neighbouring ports in the United Kingdom and in another Convention country, or

(*b*) between near neighbouring ports in any two or more countries or territories outside the United Kingdom,

make it unreasonable or impracticable to apply the provisions of this Act to ships plying on such voyages, and the [Department] are satisfied that the Government of the other country or territory (or, as the case may be, of each of the other countries or territories) concurs in that opinion, the [Department] may by order specifying those ports direct that ships plying on international voyages between those ports, or any class of such ships specified in the order, shall be exempt from the provisions of this Act.

(2) The [Department of Trade] may by order direct that ships under 80 tons register engaged solely in the coasting trade,[2] or any class of such ships specified in the order, shall be exempt from the provisions of this Act while not carrying cargo, or (if the order so provides) shall be exempt from the provisions of this Act whether carrying cargo or not.[3]

(3) Any order under this section may be made subject to such conditions as the [Department of Trade] think fit; and, where any such order is made subject to conditions, the exemption conferred by the order shall not have effect in relation to a ship unless the ship complies with those conditions.

294 [1] See s. 32 (2), (3).

[2] There is no definition in the Act of the words " coasting trade." As to its meaning see note 19 to s. 11 of the Pilotage Act 1913. *Cf.* definition of " coasting ships " in s. 57 of the Customs and Excise Act 1952. Reference may be made to *Anglo-American Oil Co.* v. *Lewis* (1923) 17 Ll.L.R. 61, where it was held that a barge, normally used to carry oil fuel to vessels in the port of Liverpool, was " employed in the coasting trade " within the meaning of s. 441 of the M.S.A. 1894, while she was being towed in to Southampton for use in that port. But it must be realised that in that case the barge was over 80 tons, and thus did not fall within the exemption of s. 438 (1) of the M.S.A. 1894; and that the words of the relevant section (s. 441 of M.S.A. 1894, now repealed) were " employed in the coasting trade," and not " engaged solely in the coasting trade."

[3] See the Merchant Shipping (Load Lines) (Exemption) Order 1968 (S.I. No. 1116).

Further powers to exempt ships

295 **19.**—(1) In this section any reference to exempting a ship is a reference to exempting the ship either—

(*a*) from all the provisions of this Act and of the load line rules,[1] or

(*b*) from such of those provisions as are specified in the instrument conferring the exemption.

(2) On the application of the owner of a ship to which this Act applies, which is registered in the United Kingdom and is either an existing ship [2] of not less than 150 tons gross tonnage or a new ship [2] of not less than 24 metres in length, the [Department of Trade] may exempt the ship if in their opinion the ship embodies features of a novel kind such that, if the ship had to comply with all the requirements of this Act and of the load line rules, the development of those features and their incorporation in ships engaged on international voyages [3] might be seriously impeded.

(3) On the application of the owner of a ship to which this Act applies, which is registered in the United Kingdom and is either—

(*a*) an existing ship [2] of less than 150 tons gross tonnage or a new ship [2] of less than 24 meteres in length, or

(*b*) a ship (not falling within the preceding paragraph) which does not ply on international voyages,[3]

the [Department of Trade] may exempt the ship.

(4) Without prejudice to the last preceding subsection, where a ship to which this Act applies, which is registered in the United Kingdom and is either an existing ship [2] of not less than 150 tons gross tonnage or a new ship [2] of not less than 24 metres in length, does not normally ply on international voyages [3] but is, in exceptional circumstances, required to undertake a single international voyage, the [Department of Trade], on the application of the owner of the ship, specifying the international voyage in question, may exempt the ship while engaged on that voyage.

(5) Any exemption conferred under this section may be conferred subject to such conditions as the [Department of Trade] think fit; and, where any such exemption is conferred subject to conditions, the exemption shall not have effect unless those conditions are complied with.

[1] See note 1 to s. 2.
[2] See s. 32 (4).
[3] See s. 32 (2), (3).

Issue of exemption certificates

1296 **20.**—(1) Where the [Department of Trade] exempt a ship under the last preceding section, the [Department] shall issue the appropriate certificate to the owner of the ship.

(2) For the purposes of this section the appropriate certificate—

(*a*) where the exemption is conferred under subsection (2) or subsection (4) of the last preceding section, is a certificate to be called an " International Load Line Exemption Certificate," and

(*b*) where the certificate is conferred under subsection (3) of that section, is a certificate to be called a " United Kingdom load line exemption certificate."

(3) Any certificate issued under this section shall be in such form, and shall be issued in such manner, as may be prescribed by the load line rules.[1]

[1] See note 1 to s. 2.

Duration and termination of exemptions, and duration, endorsement and cancellation of exemption certificates

1297 **21.**—(1) The load line rules [1] shall make provision for determining the period during which any exemption conferred under section 19 of this Act, or any certificate issued under section 20 of this Act, is to remain in force, including—

(*a*) provision enabling the period for which any such exemption or certificate is originally conferred or issued to be extended within such limits and in such circumstances as may be prescribed by the rules, and (*b*) provision for terminating any such exemption, and for cancelling any such certificate, in such circumstances as may be so prescribed.

(2) While any such certificate is in force in respect of a ship, there shall be endorsed on the certificate such information relating to—

(*a*) periodical inspections of the ship in accordance with the load line rules, and

(*b*) any extension of the period for which the certificate was issued, as may be prescribed by the rules.

[1] See note 1 to s. 2.

International Load Line Exemption Certificates

298 **22.**—(1) The load line rules [1] shall make such provision as appears to the [Department of Trade] to be appropriate for securing that exemption certificates which, in accordance with the Convention of 1966, are issued in respect of ships to which section 12 of this Act applies, and are so issued by Governments other than Her Majesty's Government in the United Kingdom, shall in such circumstances as may be prescribed by the rules have the like effect for the purposes of this Act as if they were valid Convention certificates.

(2) Certificates issued as mentioned in the preceding subsection shall be included among the certificates to be called " International Load Line Exemption Certificates."

[1] See note 1 to s. 2.

Subdivision load lines and deck cargo

Subdivision load lines

299 **23.**—(1) Where in pursuance of any rules [1] for the time being in force under section 1 of the Merchant Shipping (Safety Convention) Act 1949 a passenger steamer to which this Act applies, being a ship registered in the United Kingdom, is marked with subdivision load lines, and the lowest of those lines is lower than the line which, apart from this subsection, would be the appropriate load line for the purposes of section 4 of this Act, the said section 4 shall have effect as if that subdivision load line were the appropriate load line for the purposes of that section.

(2) Where in pursuance of any such rules, or in pursuance of the Convention referred to in that Act as the Safety Convention or any law of any country made for the purpose of giving effect to that Convention, a passenger steamer to which this Act applies, not being a ship registered in the United Kingdom, is marked with subdivision load lines, and the lowest of those load lines is lower than the line which, apart from this subsection, would be the appropriate load line for the purposes of section 14 of this Act, that section shall have effect as if that subdivision load line were the appropriate load line for the purposes of that section.

(3) In this section " passenger steamer " has the meaning assigned to it by section 26 of the Merchant Shipping (Safety Convention) Act 1949.

[1] See the Merchant Shipping (Passenger Ship Construction) Rules 1965 (S.I. No. 1103) rule 21.

Deck cargo

1300 **24.**—(1) The [Department of Trade] shall make regulations [1] (in this section referred to as " the deck cargo regulations ") prescribing requirements to be complied with where cargo is carried in any uncovered space on the deck [2] of a ship to which this Act applies; and different requirements may be so prescribed in relation to different descriptions of ships, different descriptions of cargo, different voyages or classes of voyages, different seasons of the year or any other different circumstances.

(2) If the load line rules provide (either generally or in particular cases or classes of cases) for assigning special freeboards to ships which are to have effect only where a cargo of timber is so carried, then (without prejudice to the generality of the preceding subsection) the deck cargo regulations may prescribe special requirements to be complied with in circumstances where any such special freeboard has effect.

(3) In prescribing any such special requirements as are mentioned in the last preceding subsection, the [Department of Trade] shall have regard in particular to the provisions of Chapter IV of the Convention of 1966.

(4) If any provisions of the deck cargo regulations are contravened [3]—

(*a*) in the case of a ship registered in the United Kingdom, or

(*b*) in the case of any other ship while the ship is within any port in the United Kingdom,

the master of the ship shall (subject to the next following subsection) be guilty of an offence [3] and liable on summary conviction to a fine not exceeding £1,000.

(5) Where a person is charged with an offence under the last preceding subsection, it shall be a defence to prove that the contravention was due solely to deviation or delay and that the deviation or delay was caused solely by stress of weather or other circumstances which neither the master nor the owner nor the charterer (if any) could have prevented or forestalled.

(6) For the purpose of securing compliance with the deck cargo regulations, any person authorised in that behalf by the [Department of Trade] may inspect any ship to which this Act applies which is carrying cargo in any uncovered space on her deck; and for the purposes of any such inspection any such person shall have all the powers of a [Department of Trade] inspector under the Merchant Shipping Act 1894.

01 [1] See the Merchant Shipping (Load Lines) (Deck Cargo) Regulations 1968 (S.I. No. 1089).
[2] The corresponding provision of the M.S. (Safety and Load Line Conventions) Act 1932, s. 61, related only to timber deck cargo.
[3] It was held under the corresponding provision (see note 2 above) that where part of the deck cargo was stowed on one deck and part on another, the maximum height being exceeded in both places, there was only one offence; see *R.* v. *Campbell, ex p. Nomikos* [1956] 1 W.L.R. 622.
[4] See §§ 1034–1037, *ante*.

Miscellaneous and supplementary provisions

Increase of penalties for offences in connection with passenger steamers

02 **25.**—(1) A person who after the passing [1] of this Act commits an offence under any of the enactments specified in column 1 of Schedule 1 to this Act shall (instead of being liable on summary conviction to the penalty specified in column 2 of that Schedule) be liable, on conviction as mentioned in column 3 of that Schedule, to the penalty specified in the said column 3.

(2) Section 1 of this Act shall not have effect for the purposes of this section.

[1] May 10, 1967.

Provisions as to fees

03 **26.**—(1) In respect of any survey or inspection carried out in pursuance of the load line rules, and in respect of any certificate issued under this Act, there shall be paid such fee as may be prescribed by regulations [1] made by the [Department of Trade] with the approval of the Treasury.

(2) Subject to the next following subsection, any fees payable under the preceding subsection shall be paid into the Exchequer.

(3) The last preceding subsection shall not apply to any fee paid in respect of—

(*a*) a survey or inspection which is carried out otherwise than by a surveyor of ships appointed under the Merchant Shipping Act 1894, or

(*b*) a certificate issued otherwise than by the [Department of Trade].[2]

[1] See the M.S. (Fees) Regulations 1975 (S.I. No. 341), which revokes the Merchant Shipping (Load Lines) (Fees) Regulation 1968 (S.I. No. 1117) as amended by S.I. 1971 No. 644 and by S.I. 1971 No. 1352.
[2] *e.g.* an authorised Classification society.

Miscellaneous supplementary provisions

04 **27.**—(1) Without prejudice to the operation of section 34 (2) of this Act, section 69 of the Merchant Shipping (Safety and Load Line Conventions) Act 1932 (notice to be given to consular officer where proceedings taken in respect of foreign ships) shall have effect as if any reference therein to that Act included a reference to this Act.

(2) Where a ship is detained under any provision of this Act which provides for the detention of a ship until an event specified in that provision occurs, section 460 (2) of the Merchant Shipping Act 1894 (which relates to the costs of detention) shall apply as if the ship had been finally detained under that Act.

(3) The provisions of section 280 of that Act (delivery up of certificate) and of section 282 of that Act (penalty for forgery of certificate or declaration) shall have effect in relation to any certificate which can be issued under this Act as they have effect in relation to a passenger steamer's certificate.

(4) Section 436 (3) of that Act (which provides for recording the draught of water and the freeboard of ships) shall not have effect in relation to ships to which this Act applies, except any such ship which, by virtue of any order made or exemption conferred under this Act, is exempt from all the provisions of this Act.

(5) Any certificate issued under this Act shall be admissible in evidence.

Application of Act in relation to certain territories outside United Kingdom

1305 **28.**—(1) Her Majesty may by Order in Council [1] direct that the provisions of this Act shall extend, with such exceptions, adaptations or modifications as may be specified in the Order, to—

(*a*) the Isle of Man;

(*b*) any of the Channel Islands;

(*c*) any colony;

(*d*) any territory outside Her Majesty's dominions in which for the time being Her Majesty has jurisdiction.

(2) In respect of any territory falling within any of paragraphs (*a*) to (*d*) of the preceding subsection, Her Majesty may by Order in Council specifying that territory, give either or both of the following directions, that is to say—

(*a*) that, with such exceptions, adaptations or modifications as may be specified in the Order, the provisions of this Act shall have effect as if references in this Act to a ship registered in the United Kingdom included references to a ship registered in that territory;

(*b*) that, with such exceptions, adaptations or modifications as may be so specified, the provisions of this Act shall have effect as if references in this Act to a port in the United Kingdom included references to a port in that territory.

(3) If, in the case of any country or territory outside the United Kingdom, it appears to Her Majesty in Council—

(*a*) that the provisions which, as part of the law of that country or territory, have effect for marking ships with load lines, and for the issue of certificates in respect of ships so marked, are based on the same principles as the corresponding provisions of this Act and are equally effective, and

(*b*) that provision has been, or in pursuance of any agreement will be, made by the law of that country or territory for recognising United Kingdom load line certificates as having the like effect in ports of that country or territory as certificates issued under the provisions referred to in the preceding paragraph,

Her Majesty may by Order in Council [2] direct (subject to the next following subsection) that certificates issued under those provisions shall have the like effect for the purposes of this Act as if they were United Kingdom load line certificates.

(4) An Order in Council under subsection (3) of this section shall not have effect in relation to any ship which—

(*a*) plies on international voyages, and

(*b*) is a ship of a Convention country, and

(*c*) is either an existing ship of not less than 150 tons gross tonnage or a new ship of not less than 24 metres in length.

(5) In this section any reference to the provisions of this Act shall be construed as including a reference to the provisions of any rules or regulations made under this Act.

[1] See the M.S. (Load Lines) (Hong Kong) Order 1970 (S.I. No. 285) and the M.S. (Load Lines (Bermuda) Order 1975 S.I. No. 412.

[2] See the Merchant Shipping (Load Lines Certificates) (Various Countries) Order 1968 (S.I. No. 1110) which exercised the power under subs. (3) with respect to the countries of Denmark, France, India, Netherlands, Surinam and Netherlands Antilles, Norway and Sweden.

Application of Act to certain unregistered British ships

306 **29.**—(1) This section applies to ships which—

(*a*) are British ships to which this Act applies, but

(*b*) are not registered, whether in the United Kingdom or elsewhere.

(2) The [Department of Trade] may by order [1] specify a class of ships to which this section applies and direct that, in such circumstances as may be specified in the order, the provisions of this Act relating to ships registered in the United Kingdom shall have effect in relation to ships of that class as if they were registered in the United Kingdom.

[1] No order has yet been made under this section.

Provisions as to orders, rules and regulations, and as to functions of [Department of Trade]

307 **30.**—(1) Any Order in Council, order, rules or regulations made under this Act may contain such transitional or other incidental and supple-

mentary provisions as may appear to Her Majesty in Council, or (as the case may be) to the [Department of Trade] to be appropriate.

(2) Any power of the [Department of Trade] to make an order under this Act shall include power to revoke or vary the order by a subsequent order.

(3) Any power to make orders under section 18 or section 29 of this Act, and any power to make rules or regulations under any provision of this Act, shall be exercisable by statutory instrument; and any statutory instrument containing any such order, rules or regulations shall be subject to annulment in pursuance of a resolution of either House of Parliament.

(4) *Without prejudice to the operation of section* 34 (2) *of this Act, section* 4 *of the Merchant Shipping Act* 1965 (*exercise of powers of* [*Department of Trade*]) *shall have effect for the purposes of this Act as it has effect for the purposes of that Act.*[1]

[1] This subsection was repealed by the Industrial Expansion Act 1968, s. 18 (2) and Sched. 4.

1308 **Convention countries**

31.—(1) Her Majesty, if satisfied—

(*a*) that the Government of a country has accepted or acceded to, or has denounced, the Convention of 1966, or

(*b*) that the Convention of 1966 extends, or has ceased to extend, to a particular territory,

may by Order in Council [1] make a declaration to that effect.

(2) In this Act " Convention country " means a country or territory which is either—

(*a*) a country the Government of which has been declared under this section to have accepted or acceded to the Convention of 1966, and has not been so declared to have denounced that Convention, or

(*b*) a territory to which it has been so declared that the Convention of 1966 extends, not being a territory to which it has been so declared that that Convention has ceased to extend,

and " Contracting Government " means any such Government as is referred to in paragraph (*a*) of this subsection.

[1] It has been declared that the following countries have acceded to or accepted the 1966 Convention:

(*a*) United Kingdom, Denmark, France, India, Israel, Italy, Liberia, Malagasy, Maldive Islands, Mauritania, Morocco, Netherlands, Surinam and Netherlands Antilles, Norway, Panama, Republic of Peru, Somalia, South Africa, Sweden, Switzerland, Trinidad and Tobago, Tunisia, United States, U.S.S.R.: see M.S. (Load Lines Convention) (Various Countries) Order 1968 (S.I. No. 1109);

(*b*) Congo, Finland, Greece, Japan, Spain, Vietnam; see M.S. (Load Lines Convention) (Various Countries) (No. 2) Order 1968 (S.I. No. 1646);

(*c*) Australia, Ghana, Ireland, Kuwait and Turkey; see M.S. (Load Lines Convention) (Various Countries) Order 1969 (S.I. No. 151);

(*d*) United Arab Republic, Belgium, Bulgaria, Cuba, West Germany, Nigeria, Pakistan, Philippines, Yugoslavia; see M.S. (Load Lines Convention) (Various Countries) (No. 2) Order 1969 (S.I. No. 1084);

(*e*) Brazil, Cyprus, Czechoslovakia, Korea, Poland, Southern Yemen; see M.S. (Load Lines Convention) (Various Countries) Order 1970 (S.I. No. 158);

(*f*) Canada, Iceland, Lebanon, Mexico, Monaco, New Zealand, Portugal, Zambia; see the M.S. (Load Lines Convention) (Various Countries) Order 1971 (S.I. No. 216).

Interpretation

09 **32.**—(1) In this Act, except in so far as the context otherwise requires, the following expressions have the meanings hereby assigned to them respectively, that is to say:—

" alteration " includes deterioration;

" clearance " includes a transire;

" Convention country " and " Contracting Government " have the meanings assigned to them by section 31 (2) of this Act;

" parent country ", in relation to a ship, means the country or territory in which the ship is registered, or, if the ship is not registered anywhere, means the country or territory whose flag the ship flies;

" valid Convention certificate " has the meaning assigned to it by section 12 (5) of this Act.

(2) In this Act, subject to the next following subsection, " international voyage " means a voyage between—

(*a*) a port in the United Kingdom and a port outside the United Kingdom, or

(*b*) a port in a Convention country (other than the United Kingdom) and a port in any other country or territory (whether a Convention country or not) which is outside the United Kingdom.

(3) In determining, for the purposes of the last preceding subsection, what are the ports between which a voyage is made, no account shall be taken of any deviation by a ship from her intended voyage which is due solely to stress of weather or any other circumstance which neither the master nor the owner nor the charterer (if any) of the ship could have prevented or forestalled; and for the purposes of that subsection any colony, protectorate or other dependency, any territory for whose international relations a Government is separately responsible, and any territory for which the United Nations are the administering authority, shall be taken to be a separate territory.

(4) In this Act " new ship " means a ship whose keel is laid, or which is at a similar stage of construction, on or after the material date, and " existing ship " means a ship which is not a new ship; and for the purposes of this subsection the material date—

1309

(*a*) in relation to a ship whose parent country is a Convention country other than the United Kingdom, is the date as from which it is declared under section 31 of this Act either that the Government of that country has accepted or acceded to the Convention of 1966 or that it is a territory to which that Convention extends, and

(*b*) in relation to any other ship, is the date of the commencement of this Act.[1]

(5) Any reference in this Act to the gross tonnage of a ship shall be construed as a reference to the tonnage of the ship as ascertained in accordance with the tonnage regulations of the Merchant Shipping Act 1894 [2]; and, where in accordance with those regulations alternative tonnages are assigned to a ship, the gross tonnage of the ship shall, for the purposes of this Act, be taken to be the larger of those tonnages.

(6) For the purposes of this Act the length of a ship shall be ascertained in accordance with regulations [3] made by the [Department of Trade] under this Act.

(7) Any reference in this Act to any provision of the Convention of 1966 shall, in relation to any time after that provision has been amended in pursuance of Article 29 of that Convention, be construed as a reference to that provision as so amended.

(8) Except in so far as the context otherwise requires, any reference in this Act to an enactment shall be construed as a reference to that enactment as amended or extended by or under any other enactment.

1310 [1] July 21, 1968.

[2] See now the M.S. (Tonnage) Regulations 1967 (S.I. No. 172 as amended by S.I. 1967 No. 1093, S.I. 1972 No. 656 and S.I. 1975 No. 594) of the M.S.A. 1965 which replace the tonnage provisions of the M.S.A. 1894.

[3] See the M.S. (Load Lines) (Length of Ship) Regulations 1968 (S.I. No. 1072).

Repeals and transitional provisions

1311 **33.**—(1) Subject to the following provisions of this section, the enactments specified in Schedule 2 to this Act are hereby repealed to the extent specified in the third column of that Schedule.

(2) The repeal effected by the preceding subsection shall not affect the operation of any enactment as part of the law of any territory outside the United Kingdom, and accordingly shall not affect any Order in Council made under subsection (1) of section 64 of the Merchant Shipping (Safety and Load Line Conventions) Act 1932, or made by virtue of the Foreign Jurisdiction Act 1890 as modified by subsection (2) of that section, or any power to revoke or vary any such Order in Council.

(3) Without prejudice to the last preceding subsection and to the operation of section 38 of the Interpretation Act 1889 (which relates to the effect of repeals), for the purposes of the transition from the law in

force immediately before the commencement of this Act to the provisions of this Act the [Department of Trade] may by regulations [1] provide that those provisions shall have effect subject to such transitional provisions as may be contained in the regulations.

[1] See the M.S. (Load Lines) (Transitional Provisions) Regulations 1968 (S.I. No. 1052).

Short title, construction, citation, commencement and extent

12 **34.**—(1) This Act may be cited as the Merchant Shipping (Load Lines) Act 1967.

(2) This Act shall be construed as one with the Merchant Shipping Acts 1894 to 1965, and, without prejudice to the generality of this provision, references in those Acts to the Merchant Shipping Acts shall be construed as including references to this Act; and this Act shall be included among the Acts which may be cited together as the Merchant Shipping Acts 1894 to 1967.

(3) Section 25 of, and Schedule 1 to, this Act shall come into operation on the passing [1] of this Act; and all the other provisions of this Act shall come into operation on such day as Her Majesty may by Order in Council appoint.[2]

(4) For the purposes of the operation in relation to this Act of sections 36 and 37 of the Interpretation Act 1889 (which relate respectively to the meaning of " commencement " with reference to an Act and to the exercise of statutory powers between the passing and the commencement of an Act) the day appointed under the last preceding subsection shall be taken to be the date on which this Act comes into operation; and references in this Act to the commencement of this Act shall be construed accordingly.

(5) This Act extends to Northern Ireland.

[1] May 10, 1967.
[2] July 21, 1968: see introductory note § 1272, *ante*.

SCHEDULES

1313 **Section 25**

SCHEDULE 1

INCREASE OF PENALTIES

Enactment	Old penalty	New penalty
Merchant Shipping Act 1894.		
Section 281 (2) (Failure to post up passenger certificate).	A fine not exceeding £10.	On summary conviction, a fine not exceeding £20.
Section 281 (3) (Going to sea without posting up passenger certificate).	In the case of the owner, a fine not exceeding £100, and in the case of the master, a fine not exceeding £20.	On summary conviction, in the case of the owner, a fine not exceeding £200, and in the case of the master a fine not exceeding £50.
Section 283 (Carrying passengers in excess).	A fine not exceeding £20 and an additional fine not exceeding five shillings for every passenger above the number allowed by the passenger steamer's certificate, or if the fare of any passenger aboard exceeds five shillings, not exceeding double the amount of the fares of all the passengers above the amount so allowed, reckoned at the highest rate of fare payable by any passenger aboard.	Irrespective of the number of passengers, on summary conviction, a fine not exceeding £400; and, on conviction on indictment, a fine.
Merchant Shipping Act 1906.		
Section 21 (Non-compliance with provisions as to passenger steamers).	A fine not exceeding £10 for each passenger carried.	Irrespective of the number of passengers, on summary conviction, a fine not exceeding £400; and, on conviction on indictment, a fine.
Merchant Shipping (Safety Convention) Act 1949.		
Section 12 (3) (*a*) (Going to sea without appropriate certificates).	A fine not exceeding £10 for each passenger carried.	Irrespective of the number of passengers, on summary conviction, a fine not exceeding £400; and, on conviction on indictment, a fine.

14 **Section 33**

SCHEDULE 2

ENACTMENTS REPEALED

Chapter	Short Title	Extent of Repeal
22 & 23 Geo. 5. c. 9.	The Merchant Shipping (Safety and Load Line Conventions) Act 1932.	Section 23. Sections 40 to 61. Section 62 (2). Sections 63 to 68. Sections 70 to 72. Schedule 2.
1 Edw. 8 & 1 Geo. 6. c. 23.	The Merchant Shipping Act 1937.	The whole Act.
12, 13 & 14 Geo. 6. c. 43.	The Merchant Shipping (Safety Convention) Act 1949.	Sections 18 and 20. In subsection (1) of section 29, paragraph (*c*) and the words from " unless in the case of " to " Minister otherwise orders."
1964 c. 47.	The Merchant Shipping Act 1964.	Section 14.
1965 c. 47.	The Merchant Shipping Act 1965.	Section 2, and, in Schedule 1, the entry relating to the Merchant Shipping (Safety and Load Line Conventions) Act 1932.

ANCHORS AND CHAIN CABLES ACT 1967

[1967 c. 64]

An Act to make new provision in substitution for the Anchors and Chain Cables Act 1899. [27th July 1967]

Be it enacted etc.:

Rules for testing anchors and chain cables

315 **1.**—(1) The [Department of Trade] shall make rules [1] with respect to the testing of anchors and chain cables for use in ships registered in the United Kingdom, and such rules may in particular—

(*a*) prescribe the manner in which tests of anchors and cables are to be carried out, the tensile strains and breaking strains to be employed in such tests and the requirements to be fulfilled by equipment used for the purposes of such tests;

(*b*) provide for the marking of anchors and cables which have passed such tests and for the issue of certificates in respect of such anchors and cables;

(*c*) provide for the supervision of such tests and marking, and for the inspection of such equipment, by surveyors of ships [2] appointed under the Merchant Shipping Act 1894 or by such other persons as the [Department of Trade] may authorise for the purpose;

(*d*) provide for the payment of fees in respect of such supervision and inspection and in respect of the issue of certificates under the rules; and

(*e*) provide that the rules shall not apply to anchors or cables of such classes or descriptions as may be specified in the rules or which are exempted therefrom by the [Department of Trade] in accordance with any provision in that behalf contained in the rules.

(2) No ship registered in the United Kingdom shall have on board as part of her equipment an anchor or chain cable, being an anchor or cable which was first taken on board after the commencement of this Act, unless—

(*a*) the anchor or cable has been marked, and a certificate in respect of it has been issued, in accordance with rules under this section; or

(*b*) the anchor or cable is one to which those rules do not apply by virtue of any provision therein made under paragraph (*e*) of subsection (1) of this section;

and if this subsection is contravened in respect of any ship the owner or master of the ship shall be liable on summary conviction to a fine not exceeding four hundred pounds.

(3) If any person applies to any anchor or cable which has not passed the tests prescribed by rules under this section any mark prescribed by those rules for denoting that it has passed those tests, or any other mark calculated to suggest that it has passed those tests, he shall be liable on summary conviction to a fine not exceeding four hundred pounds.

(4) Section 684 of the Merchant Shipping Act 1894 (jurisdiction) shall apply for the purposes of this section as it applies for the purposes of that Act.

(5) Any fees payable by virtue of this section in respect of any functions of a surveyor of ships appointed under the said Act of 1894 shall be paid into the Exchequer.

(6) The power to make rules under this section shall be exercisable by statutory instrument, and any such statutory instrument shall be subject to annulment in pursuance of a resolution of either House of Parliament.

(7) In this section " anchor " and " chain cable " include any shackle attached to or intended to be used in connection with the anchor or cable, and " ship " and " master " have the same meanings respectively as in the said Act of 1894.

(8) The powers of the [Department of Trade] under this section or any rules made thereunder may be exercised by the [Secretary of State for Trade] . . . [Department], any secretary, under-secretary or assistant

secretary of the [Department] or any person authorised in that behalf by the [Secretary of State].

[1] See the Anchor and Chain Cables Rules 1970 (S.I. No. 1453).
[2] See the M.S.A. 1894, s. 724.

Short title, repeal, saving, commencement and extent

316 **2.**—(1) This Act may be cited as the Anchors and Chain Cables Act 1967.

(2) The Anchors and Chain Cables Act 1899 is hereby repealed.

(3) Any anchor or cable tested or marked, and any certificate issued, before the commencement of this Act under the said Act of 1899 shall be deemed to have been tested or marked, or, as the case may be, issued, in accordance with rules under section 1 of this Act.

(4) This Act shall come into force [1] on such day as Her Majesty may by Order in Council appoint.

(5) This Act extends to Northern Ireland.

[1] This Act came into force on October 19, 1970; see S.I. 1970 No. 1443.

HOVERCRAFT ACT 1968

[1968 c. 59]

An Act to make further provision with respect to hovercraft.

[26th July 1968]

Be it enacted etc.:

Power to make Orders in Council with respect to hovercraft

317 **1.**—(1) Her Majesty may by Order in Council [1, 2] make such provision as She considers expedient—

(*a*) [2] with respect to the registration of hovercraft [3];

(*b*) [2] for securing the safety of hovercraft and persons and property in hovercraft and at hoverports,[3] and for preventing hovercraft from endangering other persons and property;

(*c*) [2] for prohibiting or restricting the use of hovercraft unless the prescribed [3] certificates as to fitness are in force and the prescribed conditions as to maintenance and repair are satisfied with respect to them;

(*d*) for prohibiting persons from taking charge or otherwise acting as members of the crew of a hovercraft or from engaging in or being employed in connection with the maintenance or repair of hovercraft, in such capacities as may be prescribed, unless the prescribed conditions as to qualifications and other matters are satisfied with respect to those persons;

(*e*)[2] with respect to the investigation of accidents involving hovercraft;

(*f*) for regulating the noise and vibration which may be caused by hovercraft;

(*g*) for providing that no action shall lie, and no proceedings in pursuance of [Part III of the Control of Pollution Act 1974][3a] shall be brought, in respect of nuisance by reason only of noise and vibration caused by hovercraft in respect of which the requirements imposed in pursuance of paragraph (*f*) above are complied with;

(*h*)[1] for applying in relation to hovercraft or to persons, things or places connected with hovercraft—

(i) any enactment[3] or instrument relating to ships,[4] aircraft, motor vehicles or other means of transport or to persons, things or places connected therewith (other than an enactment or an instrument made under an enactment mentioned in paragraph (*i*) below or section 2 (1) of this Act),

(ii) any rules of law relating to ships or to persons, things or places connected with ships (other than rules relating to maritime liens),

and, without prejudice to the generality of the foregoing provisions of this paragraph, for providing that any enactment (other than an enactment mentioned as aforesaid) shall have effect as if references in it, in whatever terms, to ships, aircraft or motor vehicles or activities connected therewith included references to hovercraft or activities connected with hovercraft;

(*i*)[1] for applying the following enactments, and any instrument made under them, in relation to the following matters respectively, that is to say—

(i) in relation to the carriage of persons and their baggage by hovercraft, the Carriage by Air Act 1961 and the Carriage by Air (Supplementary Provisions) Act 1962,

(ii) in relation to the carriage of property by hovercraft (except baggage in relation to which provisions of the Acts aforesaid are applied), the Carriage of Goods by Sea Act 1924 and Part VIII of the Merchant Shipping Act 1894 so far as that Part relates to property on board a ship,

(iii) in relation to loss of life or personal injury connected with a hovercraft which is caused to persons not carried by the hovercraft, in relation to loss or damage connected with a hovercraft which is caused to property not carried by the hovercraft and in relation to infringements of rights through acts or omissions connected with a hovercraft, the said Part VIII;

(*j*)[1] for substituting references to hovercraft for references in any enactment or instrument to vehicles designed to be supported on a cushion of air;

(*k*) for repealing the provisions of any enactment or instrument (including provisions of the Schedule to this Act) in so far as it appears to Her Majesty that those provisions are not required having regard to any provision made or proposed to be made by virtue of this section;

(*l*)[2] with respect to the application of the Order to the Crown and the extra-territorial operation of any provision made by or under the Order;

(*m*) for the extension of any provisions of the Order, with or without modifications, to Northern Ireland, any of the Channel Islands, the Isle of Man, any colony and any country or place outside Her Majesty's dominions in which for the time being Her Majesty has jurisdiction;

(*n*)[2] for imposing penalties in respect of any contravention[3] of a provision made by or under the Order, not exceeding, in respect of any one contravention, a fine of £400 on summary conviction and imprisonment for twelve months and a fine on conviction on indictment;

(*o*)[2] for detaining any hovercraft in order to secure compliance with any provision made by or under the Order or any hovercraft in respect of which such a contravention as aforesaid is suspected to have occurred; and

(*p*)[2] for requiring the payment of fees in respect of any matter relating to hovercraft which is specified in the Order and for determining with the approval of the Treasury the amount of any such fee or the manner in which that amount is to be determined.

1318 (2) Nothing in any of the paragraphs of the foregoing subsection shall be construed as prejudicing the generality of any other of those paragraphs, and in particular paragraph (*n*) shall not prejudice paragraph (*h*).

(3) An Order under this section may—

(*a*) make different provision for different circumstances or for hovercraft of different descriptions;

(*b*) provide for exemptions from any of the provisions of the Order;

(*c*) provide for the delegation of functions exercisable by virtue of the Order;

(*d*) include such incidental, supplemental and consequential provisions as appear to Her Majesty to be expedient for the purposes of the Order;

(*e*) authorise the making of regulations and other instruments for any of the purposes of this section (except the purposes of paragraphs (*g*) to (*k*) of subsection (1)) and apply the Statutory Instruments Act 1946 to instruments made under the Order;

(*f*) provide that any enactment, instrument or rule of law applied by the Order shall have effect as so applied subject to such modifications [1] as may be specified in the Order; and

(*g*) be revoked or varied by a subsequent Order under this section.

(4) No recommendation shall be made to Her Majesty in Council to make an Order under this section containing provisions authorised by paragraphs (*f*) to (*k*) of subsection (1) unless a draft of the Order has been approved by a resolution of each House of Parliament; and any other Order in Council under this section, except an Order extending only to territory (other than Northern Ireland) which is mentioned in paragraph (*m*) of subsection (1), shall be subject to annulment in pursuance of a resolution of either House of Parliament.

1319 [1] See the Hovercraft (Application of Enactments) Order 1972 (S.I. No. 971) and App. 6, *post*. See also the Hovercraft (Civil Liability) Order 1971 (S.I. No. 720) made under s. 1 (1) (*h*) and (*i*). The provisions of this Order which relate to the Merchant Shipping Acts are as follows:

Interpretation

2.—(1) In this Order, unless the context otherwise requires, "navigable water" means any water which is in fact navigable by ships or vessels, whether or not the tide ebbs and flows there, and whether or not there is a public right of navigation in that water.

(2) The Interpretation Act 1889 shall apply to the interpretation of this Order as it applies to the interpretation of an Act of Parliament.

Overall Limitation of Liability

6. Part VIII of the Merchant Shipping Act 1894 and the Merchant Shipping (Liability of Shipowners and Others) Act 1958 shall apply, subject to the modifications set out in Schedule 3 to this Order, in relation to—

(*a*) personal injury (including loss of life);

(*b*) loss of or damage to property,

caused to a person or to property (except passengers or baggage carried by the hovercraft) by an act or omission of any person (whether on board the hovercraft or not) in the navigation or management of a hovercraft, in the loading, carriage or discharge of its cargo or in the embarkation, carriage or disembarkation of its passengers, or through any other act or omission of any person on board the hovercraft, as they apply in relation to injury, loss, damage and infringement of rights caused in the navigation or management of a ship:

Provided that the aforesaid provisions shall not apply unless at the time of the incident causing the damage the hovercraft was on or over navigable water, or on or over the foreshore, or place where the tide normally ebbs and flows, or was proceeding between navigable water and a hoverport, or was on or over a hoverport either preparing for or after such transit.

Application of the Maritime Conventions Act 1911

7.—Sections 1, 2, 3, 8 and 9 (4) of the Maritime Conventions Act 1911 shall apply as if references therein to vessels included references to hovercraft.

Application of the Crown Proceedings Act 1947

8.—(1) Section 5 (1) of the Crown Proceedings Act 1947 shall apply in relation to hovercraft in the circumstances described in Article 6 of this Order subject to the following modifications:—

(i) for "ships" wherever it appears, there shall be substituted "hovercraft";

(ii) For "1940" there shall be substituted "1970";

(iii) After the word "Acts" where it secondly appears there shall be inserted the words "as applied to hovercraft".

(2) Sections 6 and 30 of the said Act of 1947 shall apply in the case of hovercraft as they apply in the case of vessels.

(3) The said sections 5 (1), 6 and 30 as extended to Northern Ireland by virtue of the Northern Ireland (Crown Proceedings) Order 1949 shall also apply in relation to hovercraft in the circumstances described, and subject to the same modifications as in paragraphs (1) and (2) above.

320 SCHEDULE 3

Article 6

OVERALL LIMITATION OF LIABILITY

MODIFICATIONS OF PART VIII OF THE MERCHANT SHIPPING ACT 1894 AS AMENDED BY THE MERCHANT SHIPPING (LIABILITY OF SHIPOWNERS AND OTHERS) ACT 1958

The following are the modifications of Part VIII of the Merchant Shipping Act 1894 as amended by the Merchant Shipping (Liability of Shipowners and Others) Act 1958, referred to in Article 6 of this Order:—

A. *Part VIII as amended by sections* 1, 2 (1) *and* 8 (1) *to* (3) *of the* 1958 *Act*

(1) For " ship ", wherever it appears, there shall be substituted " hovercraft ".

(2) The words " Subject to the provisions of sub-section (2) below " shall be inserted at the beginning of sub-section (1) of section 503.

(3) In section 503 (1), paragraph (*a*) shall not apply.

(4) In section 503 (1) (i) for " an amount equivalent to three thousand one hundred gold francs for each ton of their ship's tonnage " there shall be substituted " £3·50 per kg. of the hovercraft's maximum authorised weight ".

(5) In section 503 (1) (ii) for " an amount equivalent to one thousand gold francs for each ton of their ship's tonnage " there shall be substituted " £1 per kg. of the hovercraft's maximum authorised weight ".

(6) The following shall be substituted for section 503 (2):

" The number by which the figure referred to in sub-section (1) (i) and (ii) above is to be multiplied shall be 8,000 in any case where the weight concerned is less than 8,000 kg."

(7) In section 504 there shall be added " (or in Scotland sist) " after " stay ", and " (or in Scotland expenses) " after " costs ".

(8) In section 505 there shall be added " and expenses " after " costs ".

(9) Sections 507 and 509 shall not apply.

B. *The* 1958 *Act, other than sections* 1, 2 (1) *and* 8 (1) *to* (3)

(1) For " ship ", wherever it appears, there shall be substituted " hovercraft ".

(2) For " master ", wherever it appears, there shall be substituted " captain ".

(3) To " the said section five hundred and three " and " the Merchant Shipping Act 1894 " wherever it appears, there shall be added " as applied by the Hovercraft (Civil Liability) Order 1971 ".

(4) For section 2 (2) there shall be substituted:

" For the purposes of sub-section (1) of section 503 of the Merchant Shipping Act 1894 as applied by the Hovercraft (Civil Liability) Order 1971, where any obligation or liability arises in respect of any damage (however caused) to harbour works, basins or navigable waterways, the occurrence giving rise to the obligation or liability shall be treated as one of the occurrences mentioned in paragraphs (*b*) and (*d*) of that sub-section, and the obligation or liability as a liability to damages."

(5) Section 2 (4)–(7) shall not apply.

(6) Section 4 shall not apply.

(7) In section 5 (1) " and in the circumstances mentioned in sub-section (3) of this section shall " shall be omitted.

(8) Section 5 (3), (5) and (6) shall not apply.

(9) In section 7 (2), after " four " there shall be added " as so applied ".

(10) Section 8 (5) and (6) shall not apply.

(11) Sections 9–12 shall not apply.

321 [2] See the Hovercraft (General) Order 1972 (S.I. No. 674) as amended by S.I. 1972 No. 1741, and App. 6, *post*. The Hovercraft (Fees) Regulations 1972 (S.I. 1972 No. 852) have been made under Art. 35 of S.I. 1972 No. 674.

[3] For meaning of " hovercraft ": " hoverport ": " prescribed ": " enactment ": " contravention ": and " modifications ": see s. 4 (1).

[3a] The words in square brackets were substituted by the Control of Pollution Act 1974, s. 18, Sched. 3.

4 Additional enactments and instruments with respect to which provision may be made include:
(i) M.S.A. 1970: see s. 100 and Sched. 3, para. 13.
(ii) M.S. (Oil Pollution) Act 1971; see s. 17.
(iii) Prevention of Oil Pollution Act 1971; see s. 31.
(iv) Civil Aviation Act 1971; see s. 69 (1), Sched. 10, para. 25.
(v) Diseases of Animals Act 1950, as amended, see Agriculture (Miscellaneous Provisions) Act 1972, s. 2 (2).

Admiralty jurisdiction etc.

1322 **2.**—(1) Subject to subsection (3) of this section, the following enactments, that is to say, Parts I and V of the Administration of Justice Act 1956, Part I of Schedule 1 to that Act and sections 56, 57, 60, 61 and 70 (6) of the County Courts Act 1959 (which among other things relate to Admiralty jurisdiction) shall have effect as if references to ships (except references to Her Majesty's ships and the reference in section 4 (1) and the first reference in section 8 (1) of the said Act of 1956 and the corresponding references in the said Schedule 1) included references to hovercraft [1] and as if references to Her Majesty's ships included references to hovercraft belonging to the Crown in right of the Government of the United Kingdom or the Government of Northern Ireland; and section 4 of the Sheriff Courts (Scotland) Act 1907 (which relates to the jurisdiction of the sheriffs) shall apply in relation to hovercraft as it applies in relation to ships.

(2) Subject to subsection (3) of this section, the law relating to maritime liens [2] shall apply in relation to hovercraft and property connected with hovercraft as it applies in relation to ships and property connected with ships, and shall so apply notwithstanding that the hovercraft is on land at any relevant time.

(3) Her Majesty may by Order in Council [3] provide that the enactments mentioned in subsection (1) and the law mentioned in subsection (2) of this section as extended by those subsections shall not apply in relation to hovercraft in such circumstances as may be specified in the Order or shall have effect, in all circumstances involving hovercraft or such circumstances involving hovercraft as may be specified in the Order, subject to such modifications as may be so specified; and subsection (3) of section 1 of this Act shall apply to an Order under this subsection as it applies to an Order under that section but as if paragraphs (*c*), (*e*) and (*f*) were omitted.

(4) No recommendation shall be made to Her Majesty in Council to make an Order under this section unless a draft of the Order has been approved by a resolution of each House of Parliament.

(5) Nothing in subsection (1) of this section affects any Order in Council made before the passing of this Act under section 56 of the said Act of 1956 (which among other things provides for the application of Part I of that Act to the Channel Islands, the Isle of Man, the colonies and certain other territories) but nothing in this subsection shall be construed

as prejudicing the powers to make Orders in Council under that section with respect to the said Part I or any of its provisions as extended by subsection (1) of this section; and the references in subsections (1) and (3) of that section to the said Part I shall include references to subsection (2) of this section.

(6) Subsection (1) of this section shall apply for the purposes of any proceedings begun on or after the date of the coming into operation of this section, whenever the cause of action arose, but shall not affect any proceedings begun before that date.

323 [1] For definition of " hovercraft," see s. 4 (1).

[2] A maritime lien has been defined as a privileged claim upon property in respect of service done to it or injury caused by it, and is carried into effect by the special legal process of arrest: see *The Bold Buccleugh* (1852) 7 Moo.P.C.C. 267, 284; *The Tervaete* [1922] P. 259, 270. See generally Vol. 35 *Halsbury's Laws of England*, p. 781 ff. The maritime liens recognised by English law are those in respect of bottomry and respondentia bonds (now obsolete), salvage, seamen's wages, and damage.

[3] No Order has yet been made.

Application of certain enactments to hovercraft

324 3. The enactments mentioned in the Schedule to this Act shall have effect subject to the modifications there specified (which provide for the application of those enactments in relation to hovercraft).

Interpretation etc.

325 **4.**—(1) In this Act—

" contravention " includes failure to comply;

" enactment " includes an enactment of the Parliament of Northern Ireland, an enactment contained in a local Act and an enactment contained in any Act passed after and in the same Session as this Act;

" hovercraft " [1] means a vehicle which is designed to be supported when in motion wholly or partly by air expelled from the vehicle to form a cushion of which the boundaries include the ground, water or other surface beneath the vehicle;

" hoverport " means any area, whether on land or elsewhere, which is designed, equipped, set apart or commonly used for affording facilities for the arrival and departure of hovercraft;

" modifications " includes additions, omissions and amendments; and

" prescribed " means prescribed by an Order in Council under section 1 of this Act or by an instrument made under such an Order.

(2) Subject to section 2 (5) of this Act, any reference in this Act to any enactment or instrument is a reference to it as amended, and includes a reference to it as applied, by or under any other enactment.

(3) Except as otherwise provided by or under this Act or an enactment passed before the date of the passing of this Act, a hovercraft shall not be treated as being a ship, aircraft or motor vehicle for the purposes of any such enactment or any instrument having effect by virtue of any such enactment.[2]

[1] This definition of hovercraft is applied by the Transport Act 1968, s. 159 (1) and by the Post Office Act 1969, s. 86 (1). A hovercraft within the meaning of this Act is not an aircraft for the purposes of the Civil Aviation Act 1971 (see s. 64 (2)) nor the Aerodromes Act (N.I.) 1971 (see s. 19 (2)). As to the meaning of hovercraft for the purposes of the Road Traffic Act 1972, see s. 192.

[2] This subsection came into operation on June 29, 1972, see the Hovercraft Act 1968 (Commencement) Order 1972, No. 979.

Northern Ireland

1326 **5.**—(1) Nothing in this Act restricts the power of the Parliament of Northern Ireland to make laws, and any laws made by that Parliament in the exercise of that power shall have effect notwithstanding anything in this Act.

(2) No recommendation shall be made to Her Majesty in Council to make an Order under this Act containing provisions which extend to Northern Ireland and relate to matters in respect of which the Parliament of Northern Ireland has power to make laws unless a draft of those provisions has been approved by a resolution of each House of that Parliament.

(3) The reference to the Treasury in paragraph (*p*) of section 1 (1) of this Act shall be construed as a reference to the Ministry of Finance for Northern Ireland in relation to the fees to be specified in any provision to be made by virtue of that paragraph so far as the provision is to extend to Northern Ireland and relate to matters in respect of which the Parliament of Northern Ireland has power to make laws.

Financial provisions

1327 **6.**—(1) Any expenses incurred or sums received under this Act by any Minister of the Crown or government department (*except the Postmaster General*)[1] shall be defrayed out of moneys provided by Parliament or paid into the Consolidated Fund, as the case may be.

(2) Any increase attributable to this Act in the sums which, under any other enactment, are payable out of or into the Consolidated Fund or the National Loans Fund or out of moneys provided by Parliament shall be paid out of or into that Fund or out of moneys so provided, as the case may be.

[1] The words in italics were repealed by the Post Office Act 1969, s. 141 and Sched. 11, Part II.

Short title and commencement

7.—(1) This Act may be cited as the Hovercraft Act 1968.

(2) This Act, except section 4 (3),[1] shall come into operation on the expiration of the period of one month beginning with the date on which it is passed,[2] and section 4 (3) of this Act shall come into operation on such date as the [Department of Trade] may appoint by order made by statutory instrument.

[1] See note (2) to s. 4.

[2] The Act received the Royal Assent on July 26, 1968, and accordingly came into force on August 26, 1968.

SCHEDULE

Section 3

MODIFICATIONS OF ENACTMENTS

328 1. In the following enactments, that is to say—

(*a*) the definition of "vessel" in section 2 of the Dockyard Port Regulation Act 1865;

(*b*) the Petroleum (Consolidation) Act 1928;

(*c*) the Petroleum (Consolidation) Act (Northern Ireland) 1929;

(*d*) section 32 (5) of the British Nationality Act 1948;

(*e*) section 2 (1) of the Docking and Nicking of Horses Act 1949; and

(*f*) the Commonwealth Immigrants Act 1962,

any reference to a ship shall include a reference to a hovercraft, and any reference to the master of a ship in the said Acts of 1928, 1929 *and* 1962 *and section* 5 *of the Commonwealth Immigrants Act* 1968[1] shall be construed accordingly; and in section 10 of the said Acts of 1928 and 1929 the references to aircraft shall include references to hovercraft.

2. In the Explosives Act 1875, any reference to a ship shall include a reference to a hovercraft used at sea and any reference to a boat shall include a reference to any other hovercraft used in a harbour or on inland water within the meaning of that Act, so however that in the definition of "magazine" in section 108 the reference to any ship shall include a reference to any hovercraft.

3. In section 23 (1) of the Prevention of Damage by Pests Act 1949 and section 6 of the Pests Act 1954, any reference to a vessel shall include a reference to a hovercraft.

4. In the following enactments, that is to say—

(*a*) *section* 19 (1) *of the Road Traffic Act* 1962[2];

(*b*) section 29 (1) of the Road Traffic Act (Northern Ireland) 1964;

(*c*) section 10 (9) of the Finance Act 1966;

(*d*) section 101 (1) of the Road Traffic Regulation Act 1967; and

(*e*) section 13 (4) of the Sea Fisheries (Shellfish) Act 1967,

for the words "vehicle designed to be supported on a cushion of air" there shall be substituted the words "hovercraft within the meaning of the Hovercraft Act 1968".

5. In section 57 (1) of the Harbours Act 1964, in the definition of "ship", for the words from "hover vehicles" onwards there shall be substituted the words "hovercraft within the meaning of the Hovercraft Act 1968".

6. *In section* 1 (3) *of the Drugs* (*Prevention of Misuse*) *Act* 1964, *the references to a medical store-carrying ship shall include references to a hovercraft used in such circumstances as the Secretary of State may specify by order made by statutory instrument, and the reference to the master of such a ship shall be construed accordingly.*[3]

7. In section 13 (1) of the Industrial Development Act 1966 and section 14 (1) of the Industrial Investment (General Assistance) Act (Northern Ireland) 1966, in the definition of "hover vehicle", for the words from "a vehicle" onwards there shall be substituted the words "a hovercraft within the meaning of the Hovercraft Act 1968 and includes part of such a hovercraft".

[1] The words in italics were repealed by the Immigration Act 1971, ss. 34 (1), 35 (1) and Sched. 6.

[2] The words in italics were repealed by the Road Traffic Act 1972, s. 205 (1), Sched. 9.

[3] This subsection was repealed by the Misuse of Drugs Act 1971, s. 39 (2) and Sched. 6.

FISHING VESSELS (SAFETY PROVISIONS) ACT 1970

[1970 c. 27]

An Act to make further provision for the safety of fishing vessels.

[29th May 1970]

Be it enacted, etc.:

Introduction

Fishing vessel construction rules

1329 **1.**—(1) The [Department of Trade] may make rules [1] (in this Act referred to as " fishing vessel construction rules ") prescribing requirements for the hull, equipment and machinery of fishing vessels [2] of any description registered in the United Kingdom (including any description framed by reference to the areas in which the vessels operate or the dates on which they were first registered in the United Kingdom or on which their construction was begun).

(2) The [Department of Trade] may exempt any fishing vessel or description of fishing vessel from any requirement of the fishing vessel construction rules, either generally or for a specified time or with respect to a specified voyage or to voyages in a specified area, and may do so subject to any specified conditions.

(3) A surveyor of ships [3] may inspect any fishing vessel for the purpose of seeing that it complies with the fishing vessel construction rules, and for that purpose shall have all the powers of a [Department of Trade] inspector [4] under the Merchant Shipping Act 1894.

(4) If—

(*a*) the fishing vessel construction rules are contravened with respect to any vessel; or

(*b*) a vessel is, under subsection (2) of this section, exempted from any requirement subject to a condition and the condition is not complied with;

the owner or master of the vessel shall be liable on summary conviction to a fine not exceeding £400.

1330 [1] See the Fishing Vessels (Safety Provisions) Rules 1975 (S.I. No. 330) as amended by S.I. 1975 No. 471.
[2] For definitions, see s. 9 (1).
[3] See the M.S.A. 1894, s. 724.
[4] See the M.S.A. 1894, s. 729.

Fishing vessel survey rules

1331 **2.**—(1) The [Department of Trade] may make rules [1] (in this Act referred to as " fishing vessel survey rules ") for the surveying and periodical inspection of fishing vessels registered in the United Kingdom, or any description of such fishing vessels, for the purpose of ensuring their compliance with the requirements of the fishing vessel construction rules, the rules for life-saving appliances,[2] the radio rules,[3] the rules for direction-finders [4] and the rules for radio navigational aids [5] applicable to them.

(2) Section 275 of the Merchant Shipping Act 1894 (appeals to the court of survey) shall apply to surveys carried out under the fishing vessel survey rules with such modifications as may be prescribed by the rules.

1332 [1] See the Fishing Vessels (Safety Provisions) Rules 1975 (S.I. No. 330), as amended by S.I. 1975 No. 471.

[2] *i.e.* the M.S. (Pilots Ladders) Rules 1965 (S.I. No. 1046) as amended by S.I. 1972 No. 531; M.S. (Life Saving Appliances) Rules 1965 (S.I. No. 1105) as amended by S.I. 1966 No. 744, S.I. 1969 No. 409 and S.I. 1975 No. 330; The M.S. (Fire Appliances) Rules 1965 (S.I. No. 1106 as amended by S.I. 1975 No. 330); the M.S. (Musters) Rules 1965 (S.I. No. 113 as amended by S.I. 1975 No. 330).

[3] *i.e.* the M.S. (Radio) (Fishing Boats) Rules 1965 (S.I. No. 1108) as amended by S.I. 1969 No. 1316.

[4] *i.e.* the M.S. (Direction-Finders) Rules 1965 (S.I. 1965 No. 1112).

[5] There are no such rules as yet.

Fishing vessel certificates

1333 **3.**—(1) If the [Department of Trade] or any person authorised by them for the purpose are satisfied, on receipt of a declaration of survey in respect of a fishing vessel surveyed under the fishing vessel survey rules, that the vessel complies with such of the requirements of—

(*a*) the fishing vessel construction rules;

(*b*) the rules for life-saving appliances [1]; or

(*c*) the radio rules, the rules for direction-finders and the rules for radio navigational aids [2];

as are or will be applicable to the vessel, then, subject to subsection (2) of this section, the [Department] or person shall, on the application of the owner, issue a certificate showing that the vessel complies with those requirements; and for this purpose any requirement from which the vessel has been exempted under section 1 (2) of this Act or any other provision of the Merchant Shipping Acts shall be deemed not to be applicable to it.

(2) Fishing vessel survey rules may require, in the case of such certificate to be issued under this section as may be specified in the rules, that the [Department of Trade] or person authorised to issue it shall not issue the certificate unless satisfied that the vessel in respect of which it is to be issued is provided with the lights, shapes and means of making fog signals required by the collision regulations.[3]

(3) A certificate issued under this section shall be in such form as may be prescribed by the fishing vessel survey rules; and those rules may make provision for the duration, extension or cancellation of any such certificate and for the endorsement on it of information relating to the inspection, in accordance with the rules, of the vessel to which it relates and of any extension of the period for which the certificate was issued.

(4) Sections 280 to 282 of the Merchant Shipping Act 1894 (delivery up and posting up of certificates and penalty for forgery) shall apply in relation to any certificate provided for by this section as they apply in relation to a passenger steamer's certificate.

(5) Any certificate issued under this section shall be admissible in evidence.

[1] See note (2) to s. 2.
[2] See notes (3), (4) and (5) to s. 2.
[3] See the Collision Regulations (Ships and Seaplanes on the Water) and Signals of Distress (Ships) Order 1965 (S.I. No. 1525).

Prohibition on going to sea without appropriate certificates

1334 **4.**—(1) No fishing vessel required to be surveyed under the fishing vessel survey rules shall go to sea unless there are in force certificates issued under section 3 of this Act showing that the vessel complies with such of the requirements of the fishing vessel construction rules, the rules for life-saving appliances,[1] the radio rules,[2] the rules for direction-finders [3] and the rules for radio navigational aids [4] as are applicable to the vessel.

(2) If any fishing vessel goes to sea or attempts to go to sea in contravention of this section, the owner or master of the vessel shall be liable on summary conviction to a fine not exceeding £200.

(3) The master of any fishing vessel registered in the United Kingdom shall on demand produce to any officer of customs or of the [Department of Trade] any certificate required by this Act; and the fishing vessel may be detained until the certificate is so produced.

(4) Where a fishing vessel is detained under this section, section 460 (2) of the Merchant Shipping Act 1894 (which relates to the costs of detention) shall apply as if the vessel had been finally detained under that Act.

[1] See note (2) to s. 2.
[2] See note (3) to s. 2.
[3] See note (4) to s. 2.
[4] See note (5) to s. 2.

Notice of alterations

1335 **5.**—(1) Where a certificate issued under section 3 of this Act is in force in respect of a fishing vessel and—

(*a*) the certificate shows compliance with requirements of the fishing vessel construction rules and an alteration is made in the vessel's hull, equipment or machinery which affects the efficiency thereof or the seaworthiness of the vessel; or

(*b*) the certificate shows compliance with requirements of the rules for life-saving appliances [1] and an alteration is made affecting the efficiency or completeness of the appliances or equipment which the vessel is required to carry by those rules; or (*c*) the certificate shows compliance with requirements of the rules mentioned in section 3 (1) (*c*) of this Act and an alteration is made affecting the efficiency or completeness of the equipment which the vessel is required to carry by those rules;

the owner or master shall, as soon as possible after the alteration is made, give written notice containing full particulars of it to the [Department of Trade] or, if the certificate was issued by another person, to that person; and if the notice is not given as required by this section the owner or master shall be liable on summary conviction to a fine not exceeding £50.

(2) In this section " alteration " in relation to anything includes the renewal of any part of it.

[1] See note (2) to s. 2.

Fees

336 **6.** The [Department of Trade] may with the consent of the Treasury make regulations [1] prescribing fees to be paid in respect of the doing of any thing in pursuance of this Act, and any such fee shall be paid into the Consolidated Fund except—

(*a*) a fee paid in respect of a survey or inspection carried out otherwise than by a surveyor of ships [2] appointed under the Merchant Shipping Act 1894; and

(*b*) a fee paid in respect of a certificate issued otherwise than by the [Department of Trade].

[1] No regulations have yet been made.
[2] See the M.S.A. 1894, s. 724.

Regulations and rules

337 **7.**—(1) Any regulations or rules made under this Act shall be made by statutory instrument which shall be subject to annulment in pursuance of a resolution of either House of Parliament.

(2) Before making any rules under this Act the [Department of Trade] shall consult [1] with organisations in the United Kingdom appearing to them representative of persons who will be affected by the rules.

[1] For meaning of consult, see *Rollo* v. *Minister of Town and Country Planning* [1948] L.J.R. 817 and *Re Union of Whippingham and East Cowes Benefices etc.* [1954] A.C. 245.

Power to extend Act to certain territories outside the United Kingdom, and to fishing vessels registered therein

338 **8.** Her Majesty may by Order in Council [1] give with respect to any of the following territories, that is to say—

(*a*) the Isle of Man;

(*b*) any of the Channel Islands;

(*c*) any colony;

(*d*) any territory outside Her Majesty's dominions in which for the time being Her Majesty has jurisdiction;

either or both of the following directions—

(i) that the provisions of this Act and of regulations and rules made thereunder shall apply to fishing vessels registered in that territory, with such exceptions, adaptations or modifications as may be specified in the Order, as they apply to fishing vessels registered in the United Kingdom;

(ii) that the provisions of this Act and of any regulations and rules made thereunder shall extend to that territory, with such exceptions, adaptations or modifications as may be specified in the Order, as part of the law of that territory.

[1] No order has yet been made.

Interpretation

1339 **9.**—(1) In this Act—

" collision regulations " means regulations made under section 418 of the Merchant Shipping Act 1894;

" fishing vessel " means a vessel which is for the time being used for or in connection with sea fishing but does not include a vessel used for fishing otherwise than for profit;

" fishing vessel construction rules " has the meaning assigned to it by section 1 of this Act;

" fishing vessel survey rules " has the meaning assigned to it by section 2 of this Act;

" radio rules " means rules made under section 3 of the Merchant Shipping (Safety Convention) Act 1949;

" rules for direction-finders " means rules made under section 5 of the Merchant Shipping (Safety Convention) Act 1949;

" rules for life-saving appliances " means rules made under section 427 of the Merchant Shipping Act 1894;

" rules for radio navigational aids " means rules made under section 6 of the Merchant Shipping (Safety Convention) Act 1949; and

" the Merchant Shipping Acts " means the Merchant Shipping Acts 1894 to 1967, the Merchant Shipping Act 1970 and this Act.

(2) References in this Act to any enactment are references thereto as amended by any other enactment.

Expenses

340 **10.** Any expenses incurred by the [Department of Trade] under this Act shall be defrayed out of moneys provided by Parliament.

Citation, construction, commencement and extent

11.—(1) This Act may be cited as the Fishing Vessels (Safety Provisions) Act 1970.

(2) This Act, the Merchant Shipping Acts 1894 to 1967 and the Merchant Shipping Act 1970 may be cited together as the Merchant Shipping Acts 1894 to 1970.

(3) This Act shall be construed as one with the Merchant Shipping Acts 1894 to 1967 and the Merchant Shipping Act 1970.

(4) This Act shall come into force on such day as the [Department of Trade] may by order made by statutory instrument appoint, and different days may be so appointed for different provisions and for different descriptions of fishing vessel.[1]

(5) This Act extends to Northern Ireland.

[1] This Act came into force on April 30, 1975: see the Fishing Vessels (Safety Provisions) Act 1970 (Commencement) Order 1975 (S.I. No. 337).

MERCHANT SHIPPING ACT 1970

[1970 c. 36]

1341 An Act to make fresh provision in place of certain enactments relating to merchant ships and seamen and to repeal some of those enactments without replacement; to make further provision relating to merchant ships and seamen; and for purposes connected therewith.

[29th May 1970]

Introduction

On May 26, 1966, the then Minister of Labour appointed a Court of Inquiry under the provisions of the Industrial Courts Act 1919 to inquire into various matters concerning the shipping industry. At the time the court was appointed, there was an industrial dispute between shipowners and the National Union of Seamen. Included in the terms of reference of the court, which was under the chairmanship of Lord Pearson, were the provisions of law, particularly the Merchant Shipping Acts, which were relevant to the terms and conditions of service of seamen, taking into account the national interest, technological change and the need for an efficient and competitive shipping industry, and to the relations between shipowners, officers and seamen.

This Act was in large part prompted by the recommendations contained in Part II of the Final Report of the Court of Inquiry (the " Pearson Report ") which was presented in February 1967 (Cmnd. 3211). The

Act marked an important stage in the progress towards revising the provisions of the Merchant Shipping Acts so that they were more in accord with modern conditions. To this end, the provisions of the Merchant Shipping Acts 1894 to 1967 relating to the conditions of service, discipline and general welfare of merchant seamen were replaced. The Act also replaced the corresponding provisions of those Acts relating to skippers and crews of fishing vessels (although these were outside the scope of the inquiry), the provisions relating to shipping inquiries and investigations, and repeals other provisions which were obsolete.

In accordance with the recommendations contained in the Pearson Report, this Act is to a large extent an enabling one. There are some twenty-five provisions empowering the Department of Trade to make regulations.

The Act received the Royal Assent on May 29, 1970. Most provisions were brought into force on January 1, 1973: see the M.S.A. 1970 (Commencement No. 1) Order 1972 (S.I. 1972 No. 1977). Those sections which are not yet in force are printed in italics. They include in particular those provisions relating to manning and certification and to inquiries. [N.B.: ss. 85 and 86, and Sched. 1 came into force November 1974: see M.S.A. 1970 (Commencement No. 3) Order 1974 (S.I. No. 1908).]

The position of seamen under the National Insurance Acts, 1965–69 is beyond the scope of these notes, and reference should be made to those Acts and the textbooks thereon.

For statutory provisions relating to the mercantile marine uniform, see British Mercantile Marine Uniform Act 1919, and see also Mercantile Marine (Uniform) Order 1921, published in *London Gazette*, December 16, 1921, at pp. 10248–10251.

Restriction on Employment of Aliens

1342 By the Aliens Restriction (Amendment) Act 1919, certain restrictions are imposed on the employment of aliens in the mercantile marine. The important provisions are as follows:

Section 5.—(1) No alien shall act as master, chief officer, or chief engineer of a British merchant ship registered in the United Kingdom, or as skipper or second hand of a fishing boat registered in the United Kingdom, except in the case of a ship or boat employed habitually in voyages between ports outside the United Kingdom:

Provided that this prohibition shall not apply to any alien who has acted as master, chief officer, or chief engineer of a British ship, or as skipper or second hand of a British fishing boat, at any time during the war, and is certified by the Admiralty to have performed good and faithful service in that capacity.

(2) No alien shall be employed in any capacity on board a British ship registered in the United Kingdom at a rate of pay less than the standard rate of pay for the time being current on British ships for his rating:

Provided that, where the [Secretary of State for Trade] is satisfied that aliens of any particular race (*other than former alien enemies*),[1] are habitually employed afloat in any capacity, or in any climate, for which they are specially fitted, nothing in this section shall prejudice the right of aliens of such race to be employed upon British ships at rates of pay which are not below those for the time being fixed as standard rates for British subjects of that race.

(3) No alien shall be employed in any capacity on board a British ship registered in the United Kingdom unless he has produced to the officer before whom he is engaged satisfactory proof of his nationality.

(4) Any person who engages an alien for employment on a British ship in contravention of the provisions of this section shall be guilty of an offence under this Act.

Section 13.—(4) A person who is guilty of an offence against this Act shall be liable on summary conviction to a fine not exceeding one hundred pounds or to imprisonment, with or without hard labour, for a term not exceeding six months, or in a second or subsequent conviction, 12 months, or, in either case, to both such fine and imprisonment.

1343 [1] The words in italics in s. 5 and the whole of s. 12, which prohibited the employment of " former enemy aliens " on board British ships registered in the United Kingdom, were repealed by the Former Enemy Aliens (Disabilities Removal) Act 1925, s. 1.

The master of a ship which comes to any port in the United Kingdom must make a return in a prescribed form giving particulars in respect of any officers or members of the crew who are aliens or who were engaged outside the United Kingdom; see Aliens Order, 1953 (No. 1671), article 10, and Aliens (Landing and Embarkation) (Forms) Order, 1954 (No. 392), made thereunder.

As to the holding of pilotage certificates by aliens, see the Aliens Restriction (Amendment) Act 1919, s. 4, cited in note (2) to Pilotage Act 1913, s. 24, § 888, *ante*.

It is interesting to note that these provisions represent a return to the policy of the Navigation Acts, which required, under certain conditions, that the master and a varying proportion of the crew should be British subjects: see Abbott, *Merchant Ships, etc.*, 14th ed., p. 150.

Restriction on Employment of Young Persons and Children

344 By the Employment of Women, Young Persons and Children Act 1920, which gives effect to certain Conventions adopted at the general Conference of the International Labour Organisation of the League of Nations, held at Genoa in July 1920, certain restrictions are imposed on the employment of children and young persons on board ship. The most important provisions are as follows:

Section 1.—(2) No child shall be employed in any ship except to the extent to which and in the circumstances in which such employment is permitted under the Convention set out in Part IV of the Schedule to this Act.

(5) There shall be included in every agreement with the crew entered into under the Merchant Shipping Act 1894, a list of the young persons under the age of sixteen years who are members of the crew, together with particulars of the dates of their birth, and in the case of a ship in which there is no such agreement, the master of the ship shall, if young persons under the age of sixteen years are employed therein, keep a register of those persons with particulars of the dates of their birth and of the dates on which they become or cease to be members of the crew, and the register so kept shall at all times be open to inspection.

(6) . . . This section, so far as it relates to employment in a ship, shall have effect as if it formed part of the Merchant Shipping Acts 1894 to 1920.

In the case of employment . . . in any ship

(*b*) If any child is employed in any ship in contravention of this Act, the master of the ship shall be liable for each offence to a fine not exceeding forty shillings, or, in the case of a second or subsequent offence, not exceeding five pounds, and where a child is taken into employment in any ship in contravention of the Act on the production, by or with the privity of the parent, of a false or forged certificate or on the false representation of his parent that the child is of an age at which such employment is not in contravention of this Act, that parent shall be liable on summary conviction to a fine not exceeding forty shillings; and

(*d*) If the master of a ship fails to keep such a register so required to be kept by him as aforesaid, or refuses or neglects when required to produce it for inspection by an officer of the [Department of Trade], or any other person having power to enforce compliance with the provisions of the Merchant Shipping Acts 1894 to 1920, he shall be liable to a fine not exceeding twenty pounds; . . .

Section 4. In this Act—

The expression " child " means a person under the age of fourteen years [1];

The expression " young person " means a person who has ceased to be a child and who is under the age of eighteen years; . . .

The expression " ship " means any sea-going ship or boat of any description which is registered in the United Kingdom as a British ship and includes any British fishing boat entered in the fishing boat register.

SCHEDULE

Part IV

345 Convention fixing the Minimum Age for Admission of Children to Employment at Sea

Article 1

For the purpose of this Convention, the term " vessel " includes all ships and boats, of any nature whatsoever, engaged in maritime navigation whether publicly or privately owned; it excludes vessels of war.

Article 2

Children under the age of fourteen years shall not be employed or work on vessels other than vessels upon which only members of the same family are employed.

ARTICLE 3

The provisions of Article 2 shall not apply to work done by children on school ships or training ships, provided that such work is approved and supervised by public authority.

ARTICLE 4

In order to facilitate the enforcement of the provision of this Convention, every shipmaster shall be required to keep a register of all persons under the age of sixteen years employed on board his vessel or a list of them in the articles of agreement, and of the dates of their birth.

[1] These words in italics, which defined the expression " child," were repealed by s. 121 of and Sched. IX, Part I, to the Education Act 1944. A " child " is now defined as being any person who is not for the purposes of the Education Act 1944, over compulsory school age (see *ibid.* s. 58). The upper limit of compulsory school age is now (1975) 16 years.

As to the restrictions on the employment of " young persons " as trimmers or stokers, see M.S. (International Labour Conventions) Act 1925, s. 2, *ante*; and as to the medical examination of young persons employed on board ship, see *ibid.* s. 3, *ante*.

Be it enacted etc.:

Engagement and discharge of crews

Crew agreements

1346 **1.**—(1) Except as provided under subsection (5) of this section an agreement in writing shall be made between each person employed as a seaman in a ship registered in the United Kingdom and the persons employing [1] him and shall be signed both by him and by or on behalf of them.

(2) The agreements made under this section with the several persons employed in a ship shall be contained in one document (in this Act referred to as a crew agreement) except that in such cases as the [Secretary of State for Trade] may approve—

(*a*) the agreements to be made under this section with the persons employed in a ship may be contained in more than one crew agreement; and

(*b*) one crew agreement may relate to more than one ship.

(3) The provisions and form of a crew agreement [2] must be of a kind approved by the [Secretary of State for Trade] [3] and different provisions and forms may be so approved for different circumstances.[4]

(4) Subject to the following provisions of this section, a crew agreement shall be carried in the ship to which it relates whenever the ship goes to sea.[5]

(5) The [Secretary of State for Trade] may make regulations [6] providing for exemptions from the requirements of this section—

(*a*) with respect to such descriptions of ship as may be specified in the regulations or with respect to voyages in such areas or such description of voyages as may be so specified; or

(*b*) with respect to such descriptions of seamen as may be specified in the regulations;

and the [Secretary of State for Trade] may grant other exemptions from those requirements (whether with respect to particular seamen or with respect to seamen employed by a specified person or in a specified ship or in the ships of a specified person) in cases where the [Secretary of State is] satisfied that the seamen to be employed otherwise than under a crew agreement will be adequately protected.

(6) Where, but for an exemption granted by the [Secretary of State for Trade], a crew agreement would be required to be carried in a ship or a crew agreement carried in a ship would be required to contain an agreement with a person employed in the ship, the ship shall carry such document evidencing the exemption as the [Secretary of State for Trade] may direct.

(7) Regulations [6] under this section may enable ships required under this section to carry a crew agreement to comply with the requirement by carrying a copy thereof, certified in such manner as may be provided by the regulations.

(8) If a ship goes to sea or attempts to go to sea in contravention of the requirements of this section the master or the person employing [7] the crew shall be liable on summary conviction to a fine not exceeding £100 and the ship, if in the United Kingdom, may be detained.

347 [1] In all cases, the agreement is made with the seaman's employer and not with the Master as formerly required by s. 113 of the M.S.A. 1894. Certain provisions of the Race Relations Act 1968 do not apply to employment on a ship if the person employed was engaged outside Great Britain: see *ibid.*, s. 8 (8) (9); or if the employment takes place mainly outside Great Britain: *ibid.* s. 8 (7).

[2] The provisions of the Contracts of Employment Act 1972 do not apply to a master of or seamen on a sea-going British ship of 80 tons gross or more, nor to certain persons employed to do a seaman's work in part, nor to a skipper or seamen on a registered fishing boat; see the Contracts of Employment Act 1972, s. 9 (2).

[3] For a full note on the approval of crew agreements, see Appendix 1, *post.*

[4] This provision adopts the recommendation of the Pearson Report that there be more flexibility on the forms of agreement.

[5] See s. 97 (2), *post.* Also compare s. 96 and note (1) thereto.

[6] See the M.S. (Crew Agreements, Lists of Crew and Discharge of Seamen) Regulations 1972 (S.I. No. 918) and the M.S. (Crew Agreements, Lists of Crew and Discharge of Seamen) (Fishing Vessels) Regulations 1972 (S.I. No. 919) set out in Appendix 1, *post.*

[7] This may not be the owner. By virtue of s. 113 of the 1894 Act (which is replaced by this section) the owner was liable and only then when it was a home-trade ship. In the case of a foreign-going ship only the master was liable.

Regulations relating to crew agreements

348 **2.**—(1) The [Secretary of State for Trade] may make regulations [1]—

(*a*) requiring such notice [2] as may be specified in the regulations to be given to a superintendent [3] or proper officer,[4] except in such circumstances as may be so specified, before a crew agreement is made or an agreement with any person is added to those contained in a crew agreement;

(*b*) providing for the delivery to a superintendent or proper officer or the Registrar General of Shipping and Seamen [5] of crew agreements and agreements added to those contained in a crew agreement and of copies of crew agreements and of agreements so added;

(*c*) requiring the posting in ships of copies of or extracts from crew agreements;

(*d*) requiring copies of or extracts from crew agreements to be supplied to members of the crew demanding them and requiring copies of or extracts from documents referred to in crew agreements to be made available, in such circumstances as may be specified in the regulations, for inspection by members of the crew; and

(*e*) requiring any document carried in a ship in pursuance of section 1 of this Act to be produced on demand to an officer of customs and excise.

(2) Regulations under this section may make a contravention of any provision thereof an offence punishable on summary conviction with a fine not exceeding £50 or such less amount as may be specified in the regulations.

1349 [1] See the M.S. (Crew Agreements, Lists of Crew, and Discharge of Seamen) Regulations 1972 (S.I. No. 918) and the M.S. (Crew Agreements, Lists of Crew and Discharge of Seamen) (Fishing Vessels) Regulations 1972 (S.I. No. 919), set out in Appendix 1, *post*. For further provisions relating to fishing vessels, see s. 95 (1) and Sched. 2, Pt. I, *post*.

[2] Superintendents (and proper officers) no longer attend as a matter of course at and witness the engagement and discharge of seamen on U.K. registered ships nor do masters need to obtain a clearance certificate from a superintendent before sailing in addition to clearance by an officer of Customs and Excise.

[3] See s. 742 of the M.S.A. 1894.

[4] See s. 97 (1), *post*.

[5] See s. 80, *post*.

Discharge of seamen

1350 **3.**—(1) The [Secretary of State for Trade] may make regulations [1] prescribing the procedure to be followed [2] in connection with the discharge of seamen from ships registered in the United Kingdom.[3]

(2) Without prejudice to the generality of subsection (1) of this section, regulations under this section may make provision—

(*a*) requiring notice [4] of such a discharge to be given at such time as may be specified in the regulations to the superintendent [5] or proper officer [6] at a place specified in or determined under the regulations;

(*b*) requiring such a discharge to be recorded, whether by entries in the crew agreement [5] and discharge book [7] or otherwise, and requiring copies of any such entry to be given to a superintendent or proper officer or the Registrar General of Shipping and Seamen.[8]

(3) Regulations under this section may provide that in such cases as may be specified in the regulations, or except in such cases as may be specified in or determined under the regulations, a seaman shall not be discharged outside the United Kingdom from a ship registered in the United Kingdom without the consent of the proper officer.

(4) Regulations under this section may make a contravention of any provision thereof an offence punishable on summary conviction with a fine not exceeding £100 or such less amount as may be specified in the regulations.

351 [1] See the M.S. (Crew Agreements, Lists of Crew, and Discharge of Seamen) Regulations 1972 (S.I. No. 918), and the M.S. (Crew Agreements, Lists of Crew, and Discharge of Seamen) (Fishing Vessels) Regulations 1972 (S.I. No. 919), set out in Appendix 1, *post*.

[2] It is wrong for the court to inquire into the circumstances of the discharge. If the procedure has not been followed, the dismissal is illegal and the agreement continues to run: *Hassan* v. *Trader Navigation Co.* [1965] 2 Lloyd's Rep. 378.

[3] As to the discharge of seamen when a ship ceases to be registered in the U.K., see s. 5, *post*.

[4] See note (2) to s. 2, *ante*.

[5] See s. 742 of the M.S.A. 1894.

[6] See s. 97 (1), *post*.

[7] See s. 71, *post*.

[8] See s. 80, *post*.

Seamen left behind abroad otherwise than on discharge

352 **4.** Regulations [1] made under section 3 of this Act may apply any provision thereof, with such modifications as appear to the [Secretary of State for Trade] to be appropriate, to cases where a seaman employed in a ship registered in the United Kingdom is left behind outside the United Kingdom otherwise than on being discharged from the ship.

[1] The regulations are set out in Appendix 1, *post*. They do not as yet apply any of the provisions of s. 3 to the situation envisaged.

Discharge of seamen when ship ceases to be registered in U.K.

353 **5.** Where a ship registered in the United Kingdom ceases to be so registered, any seaman employed in the ship shall be discharged from the ship unless he consents in writing to continue his employment in the ship; and sections 7 to 10 of this Act shall apply in relation to his wages as if the ship had remained registered in the United Kingdom.

Restrictions on making arrangements for employment of seamen

354 **6.**[1]—(1) *A person shall not for reward make arrangements for finding seamen for persons seeking to employ seamen or for finding employment for seamen, unless—*

(*a*) *he is the holder of a licence* [2] *under this section* [3] *authorising him to do so or is in the regular employment of the holder of such a licence; or* (*b*) *he is in the regular employment of the persons seeking to employ the seamen or makes the arrangements in the course of acting as ship's agent for those persons or is the master of the ship in which the seamen are to serve or an officer acting under his authority; or*

(*c*) *the employment is such as is exempted from the provisions of this subsection by regulations made by the* [*Secretary of State for Trade*].

(2) *A person shall not demand or directly or indirectly receive from any person any remuneration for providing him with employment as a seaman.*

(3) *The* [*Secretary of State for Trade*] *may grant licences for the purposes of this section for such periods, on such terms and subject to such conditions, including conditions providing for revocation, as they think fit.*

(4) *If a person acts in contravention of subsection* (1) *of this section he shall be liable on summary conviction to a fine not exceeding* £50 *and if a person acts in contravention of subsection* (2) *of this section he shall be liable on summary conviction to a fine not exceeding* £20.

This section is not yet in force.

1355 [1] This section does not apply to fishing vessels: see s. 95 (1), *post*.

[2] The onus of proving that he holds a licence rests with the defendant; see *R.* v. *Johnston* (1886) 55 L.T. 265; *Nelson* v. *Richardson* (1884) 48 J.P. 457.

[3] Licences granted under s. 110 of the M.S.A. 1894, are saved by virtue of s. 100 and Sched. 4, para. 5, *post*.

Wages, etc.

Payment of seamen's wages

1356 **7.**—[1] (1) Except as provided by or under this Act or any other enactment,[2] the wages [3] due to a seaman under a crew agreement [2] relating to a ship shall be paid to him in full at the time when he leaves the ship on being discharged therefrom (in this section and section 8 of this Act referred to as the time of discharge).

(2) If the amount shown in the account delivered to a seaman under section 8 (1) of this Act as being the amount payable to him under subsection (1) of this section is replaced by an increased amount shown in a further account delivered to him under section 8 (3) of this Act, the balance shall be paid to him within seven days [4] of the time of discharge; and if the amount so shown in the account delivered to him under section 8 (1) of this Act exceeds £50 and it is not practicable to pay the whole of it at the time of discharge, not less than £50 nor less than one-quarter of the amount so shown shall be paid to him at that time and the balance within seven days of that time.

(3) If any amount which, under the preceding provisions of this section, is payable to a seaman is not paid at the time at which it is so payable the seaman shall be entitled to wages at the rate last payable under the crew agreement for every day on which it remains unpaid

during the period of fifty-six days following the time of discharge; and if any such amount or any amount payable by virtue of this subsection remains unpaid after the end of that period it shall carry interest at the rate of 20 per cent. per annum.

(4) Subsection (3) of this section does not apply if the failure to pay was due to a mistake, to a reasonable dispute as to liability or to the act or default of the seaman or to any other cause, not being the wrongful act or default of the persons liable to pay his wages or of their servants or agents; and so much of that subsection as relates to interest on the amount due shall not apply if a court in proceedings for its recovery so directs.

(5) Where a seaman is employed under a crew agreement relating to more than one ship the preceding provisions of this section shall have effect, in relation to wages due to him under the agreement, as if for any reference to the time of discharge there were substituted a reference to the termination of his employment under the crew agreement.

(6) Where a seaman, in pursuance of section 5 of this Act,[5] is discharged from a ship outside the United Kingdom but returns to the United Kingdom under arrangements made by the persons who employed him, the preceding provisions of this section shall have effect, in relation to the wages due to him under a crew agreement relating to the ship, as if for the references in subsections (1) to (3) to the time of discharge there were substituted references to the time of his return to the United Kingdom, and subsection (5) were omitted.

357 [1] As regards fishing vessels, this section applies as set out in Sched. 2, Part II: see s. 95 (1), *post*.
[2] See s. 97 (1), *post*.
[3] See note (3) to s. 18: § 1376, *post*.
[4] See *Goldsmiths' Co.* v. *West Metropolitan Ry.* [1904] 1 K.B. 1: *Stewart* v. *Chapman* [1951] 2 K.B. 792; and *Cartwright* v. *MacCormack etc.* [1963] 1 W.L.R. 18.
[5] *i.e.*, when a ship ceases to be registered in the U.K.

Account of seaman's wages

358 **8.**[1]—(1) Subject to subsection (4) of this section and to regulations made under section 9 or 62 of this Act, the master of every ship registered in the United Kingdom shall deliver to every seaman employed in the ship under a crew agreement [2] an account of the wages due to him under that crew agreement and of the deductions subject to which the wages are payable.

(2) The account shall indicate that the amounts stated therein are subject to any later adjustment [3] that may be found necessary and shall be delivered not later than twenty-four hours before the time of discharge [4] or, if the seaman is discharged without notice or at less than twenty-four hours' notice, at the time of discharge.

(3) If the amounts stated in the account require adjustment the persons who employed the seaman shall deliver to him a further account stating

the adjusted amounts; and that account shall be delivered not later than the time at which the balance of his wages is payable to the seaman.

(4) Where a seaman is employed under a crew agreement relating to more than one ship any account which under the preceding provisions of this section would be required to be delivered to him by the master shall instead be delivered to him by the persons employing him and shall be so delivered on or before the termination of his employment under the crew agreement.

(5) If a person fails without reasonable cause to comply with the preceding provisions of this section he shall be liable on summary conviction to a fine not exceeding £20.

1359 [1] As regards fishing vessels, this section applies as set out in Sched. 2, Part II: see s. 95 (1), *post*.
[2] See s. 97 (1), *post*.
[3] The section recognises the possible need for adjustment. The Pearson Report expressed the view that a master should not be required to produce an exact account at a time when he may well be required to navigate his ship.
[4] See s. 7 (1), *ante*.

Regulations relating to wages and accounts

1360 **9.** The [Secretary of State for Trade] may make regulations [1]—

(*a*) authorising deductions to be made from the wages [2] due to a seaman under a crew agreement [3] (in addition to any authorised by any provision of this Act or of any other enactment [3] for the time being in force) in cases where a breach of his obligations under the agreement is alleged against him and such conditions, if any, as may be specified in the regulations are complied with, or in such other cases as may be specified in the regulations;

(*b*) regulating the manner in which any amounts deducted under the regulations are to be dealt with;

(*c*) prescribing the manner in which wages due to a seaman under a crew agreement are to be or may be paid;

(*d*) regulating the manner in which such wages are to be dealt with and accounted for in circumstances where a seaman leaves his ship in the United Kingdom otherwise than on being discharged therefrom;

(*e*) prescribing the form and manner in which any account required to be delivered by section 8 of this Act is to be prepared and the particulars to be contained therein (which may include estimated amounts).

1361 [1] See the M.S. (Seamen's Wages and Accounts) Regulations 1972 (S.I. No. 1700) and the M.S. (Seamen's Wages and Accounts) (Fishing Vessels) Regulations 1972 (S.I. No. 1701).
[2] See note (2) to s. 7.
[3] See s. 97 (1).

Power of superintendent or proper officer to decide disputes about wages

362 **10.**—(1) Any dispute relating to the amount payable to a seaman employed under a crew agreement [1] may be submitted by the parties to a superintendent or proper officer [1] for decision; but the superintendent or proper officer shall not be bound to accept the submission or, if he has accepted it, to decide the dispute, if he is of opinion that the dispute, whether by reason of the amount involved or for any other reason, ought not to be decided by him.

(2) The decision of a superintendent or proper officer on a dispute submitted to him under this section shall be final.

[1] See s. 97 (1).

Restriction on assignment of and charge upon wages

363 **11.**—(1) Subject to subsections (2) and (3) of this section, the following provisions shall have effect with respect to the wages due or accruing to a seaman employed in a ship registered in the United Kingdom, that is to say,—

(*a*) the wages shall not be subject to attachment or arrestment;

(*b*) an assignment thereof before they have accrued shall not bind the seaman and the payment of the wages to the seaman shall be valid notwithstanding any previous assignment or charge; and

(*c*) a power of attorney or authority for the receipt of the wages shall not be irrevocable.

(2) Nothing in this section shall affect the provisions of this Act with respect to allotment notes.

(3) Nothing in this section applies to any disposition relating to the application of wages—

(*a*) in the payment of contributions to a fund declared by regulations [1] made by the [Secretary of State for Trade] to be a fund to which this section applies; or

(*b*) in the payment of contributions in respect of the membership of a body declared by regulations [1] made by the [Secretary of State for Trade] to be a body to which this section applies;

or to anything done or to be done for giving effect to such a disposition.

[1] See the M.S. (Seaman's Wages) (Contributions) Regulations 1972 (S.I. No. 1699).

Power of court to award interest on wages due otherwise than under crew agreement

364 **12.** In any proceedings by the master of a ship or a person employed in a ship otherwise than under a crew agreement [1] for the recovery of any sum due to him as wages the court, unless it appears to it that the delay in

paying the sum was due to a mistake, to a reasonable dispute as to liability or to the act or default of the person claiming the amount or to any other cause, not being the wrongful act or default of the persons liable to make the payment or their servants or agents, may order them to pay, in addition to the sum due, interest on it at the rate of twenty per cent. per annum or such lower rate as the court may specify, for the period beginning seven days after the sum became due and ending when the sum is paid.

[1] See s. 91 (1).

Allotment notes

1365 **13.**—(1) Subject to the following provisions of this section, a seaman may, by means of an allotment note issued in accordance with regulations [1] made by the [Secretary of State for Trade], allot to any person or persons part of the wages to which he will become entitled in the course of his employment in a ship or ships registered in the United Kingdom.

(2) A seaman's right to make an allotment under this section shall be subject to such limitations as may, by virtue of the following provisions of this section, be imposed by regulations made by the [Secretary of State for Trade].

(3) Regulations [1] made by the [Secretary of State for Trade] for the purposes of this section may prescribe the form of allotment notes and—

(*a*) may limit the circumstances in which allotments may be made;

(*b*) may limit (whether by reference to an amount or by reference to a proportion) the part of the wages that may be allotted and the number of persons to whom it may be allotted and may prescribe the method by which that part is to be calculated;

(*c*) may limit the persons to whom allotments may be made by a seaman to persons of such descriptions or persons standing to him in such relationships as may be prescribed by the regulations;

(*d*) may prescribe the times and the intervals at which payments under allotment notes are to be made.

(4) Regulations [1] under this section may make different provision in relation to different descriptions of seamen and different circumstances.

[1] See the M.S. (Seamen's Allotments) Regulations 1972 (S.I. No. 1972).

Right of person named in allotment note to sue in own name

1366 **14.**—(1) A person to whom any part of a seaman's wages has been allotted by an allotment note issued in accordance with regulations made under section 13 of this Act shall have the right to recover that part in his own name and for that purpose shall have the same remedies as the seaman has for the recovery of his wages.

(2) In any proceedings brought by a person named in such an allotment note as the person to whom any part of a seaman's wages has been allotted it shall be presumed, unless the contrary is shown, that the seaman is entitled to the wages specified in the note and that the allotment has not been varied or cancelled.

Right, or loss of right, to wages in certain circumstances

367 **15.**—(1) *Where a ship registered in the United Kingdom is wrecked*[1] *or lost*[1] *a seaman whose employment in the ship is thereby terminated before the date contemplated in the agreement*[2] *under which he is so employed shall, subject to the following provisions of this section, be entitled to wages at the rate payable under the agreement at the date of the wreck or loss for every day on which he is unemployed in the two months following that date unless it is proved that he did not make reasonable efforts to save the ship and persons and property carried in it.*

(2) *Where a ship registered in the United Kingdom is sold while outside the United Kingdom or ceases to be so registered and a seaman's employment in the ship is thereby terminated before the date contemplated in the agreement*[2] *under which he is so employed, then, unless it is otherwise provided in the agreement, he shall, subject to the following provisions of this section, be entitled to wages at the rate payable under the agreement at the date on which his employment is terminated for every day on which he is unemployed in the two months following that date.*

(3) *A seaman shall not be entitled to wages by virtue of subsection* (1) *or subsection* (2) *of this section for a day on which he was unemployed, if it is shown—*

(*a*) *that the unemployment was not due to the wreck or loss of the ship or, as the case may be, the termination of his employment on the sale of the ship or its ceasing to be registered in the United Kingdom; or*

(*b*) *that the seaman was able to obtain suitable employment for that day but unreasonably refused or failed to take it.*

This section is not yet in force.

[1] See notes to the M.S.A. 1894, s. 158 and note (2) to the M.S. (International Labour Conventions) Act 1925.

[2] See s. 97 (1).

Protection of certain rights and remedies

368 **16.**—(1) A seaman's[1] lien,[2] his remedies for the recovery of his wages, his right to wages in case of the wreck or loss of his ship, and any right he may have or obtain in the nature of salvage[3] shall not be capable of being renounced by any agreement.[4]

(2) Subsection (1) of this section does not affect such of the terms of any agreement made with the seamen belonging to a ship which, in

accordance with the agreement, is to be employed on salvage service,[5] as provide for the remuneration to be paid to them for salvage services rendered by that ship.[6]

1369 [1] It seems that this section applies only to seamen, and not to masters: *The Wilhelm Tell* [1892] P. 337. As to who are included in the term " seamen," see the M.S.A. 1894, s. 742.

[2] This lien extends to ship and freight, even though the freight be due from sub-charterers, *The Andalina* (1886) 12 P.D. 1; 56 L.T. 171. As the seamen's lien is independent of statute, the subject generally is beyond the scope of these notes. See, however, cases relating thereto cited in notes on the master's similar (though statutory) lien for wages and disbursements, s. 18; and see Abbott, *Merchant Ships, etc.*, 14th ed., and Maclachlan, *Merchant Shipping*, 7th ed., and *The British Trade* [1924] P. 104, where the authorities are reviewed.

A volunteer who pays off a seaman's lien for wages (or a master's, *semble*, for disbursements) without leave of the court acquires no lien on the ship. See *The Petone* [1917] P. 198, where the authorities are reviewed by Hill J. and the question of transferability of maritime liens discussed. *Secus*, where payment is made with leave of court: *The Kammerhevie Rosenkranz* (1822) 1 Hagg.Adm. 62; *The Fair Haven* (1866) L.R. 1 A. & E. 67; *The Bridgewater* (1877) 3 Asp.M.C. 506; *The Leoborg* (*No.* 2) [1964] 1 Lloyd's Rep. 380. See, too, Abbott, *Merchant Ships, etc.* 14th ed., p. 1043. But in Scotland apparently, so long as payment is made on the credit of the ship, a volunteer even without leave will obtain a maritime lien without any formal assignment: *Clark* v. *Bowring*, 1908 S.C. 1168.

[3] For salvage generally, see Kennedy, *Civil Salvage*, 4th ed. This section extends to an assignment of a right to salvage for valuable consideration, whether such assignment be made before or after the salvage service has been rendered: *The Rosario* (1876) 2 P.D. 41.

But this section does not render void an agreement as to the *apportionment* of salvage whether made before or after services rendered: *The Afrika* (1880) 5 P.D. 192; *The Wilhelm Tell, supra*. And such an agreement will be upheld by the court only in so far as it is really equitable: *The Enchantress* (1860) 30 L.J.Adm. 15; Lush. 93; *The Afrika, supra*; *The Wilhelm Tell, supra*. See also note (5), *infra*. For the court has jurisdiction in this respect apart from statute, and thus, before the Act of 1854, would overrule an inequitable agreement between the owners and crew, and make a fresh apportionment of the salvage. See *The Beulah* (1842) 2 N. of Cas. 61; *The Louisa* (1843) 2 Wm.Rob. 22; *The Pride of Canada* (1863) 9 L.T. 546. *Cf.* s. 168.

But an agreement for an apportionment of the amount awarded after making certain deductions is inoperative by virtue of this section: *The Saltburn* (1894) 6 R. 702; 7 Asp. M.L.C. 474.

For provisions as to jurisdiction with regard to apportionment, see the M.S.A. 1894, s. 556.

[4] A towage agreement between tug-owners and shipowners on the terms " no salvage charges " will not bar the claim of the master and crew when salvage services have in fact been rendered: *The Leo Blum* [1915] P. 290. *Cf.*, too, *The Margery* [1902] P. 157; *The Pensacola* (1864) Br. & L. 306 (agreement between tug-owner and dock company—no bar to claim by master and crew for live-salvage). See also *Att.-Gen.* v. *Fargrove Steam Navigation Co.* (1908) 24 T.L.R. 430 (C.A.).

[5] By the agreement with the crew of a trawler, under which she was to be employed in fishing in the North Sea, it was provided that the crew and apprentices should participate in any salvage earnings in the proportion set forth in the agreement. *Held*, that she was not a " ship which according to the agreement was to be employed on salvage service," within the meaning of M.S.A. 1862, s. 18 (1894, s. 156 (2)); *The Wilhelm Tell, supra*. This agreement was, however, upheld as being an equitable agreement for apportionment, and therefore not within 1854, s. 182 (1894, s. 156 (1)). See note (3), *supra*.

[6] The section does not fetter the discretion of the court as to the agreements mentioned in subs. (2), but simply renders them not illegal, and places them on the same footing on which they stood before any legislation on the subject: *The Ganges* (1869) L.R. 2 A. & E. 370. The court, therefore, will uphold such an agreement only if it be equitable. See *ibid.*; *The Pride of Canada, supra*; and cases cited in note (3), *supra*.

Neither the agreement for the vessel to be employed in salvage services, nor the stipulation that the seaman shall waive his claim for salvage, need be in writing, but both must be clearly proved by those who dispute his right; *The Pride of Canada* (1863) B. & L. 208.

Claims against seaman's wages for maintenance, etc. of dependants

370 **17.**—(1) Where, during a seaman's employment in a ship, expenses are incurred by a responsible authority [1] for the benefit of any dependant of his and the expenses are of a kind specified in regulations [2] under this section and such further conditions, if any, as may be so specified are satisfied, the authority may by notice in writing complying with the regulations [2] require the persons employing the seaman—

(*a*) to retain for a period specified in the notice such proportion of his net wages as may be so specified; and

(*b*) to give to the responsible authority as soon as may be notice in writing of the seaman's discharge from the ship;

and the persons employing the seaman shall comply with the notice (subject to subsection (3) of this section) and give notice in writing of its contents to the seaman.

(2) For the purposes of this section—

(*a*) the following persons, and no others, shall be taken to be a seaman's dependants, that is to say, his spouse and any person under the age of sixteen whom he is liable, for the purposes of any enactment [3] in force in any part of the United Kingdom, to maintain or in respect of whom he is liable under any such enactment to make contributions to a local authority; and

(*b*) expenses incurred for the benefit of any person include (in addition to any payments made to him or on his behalf) expenses incurred for providing him with accommodation or care or for exercising supervision over him;

but no expenses shall be specified in regulations under this section unless they are such that a magistrates' court has power under any enactment in force in any part of the United Kingdom to order the making of payments in respect thereof.

(3) Not more than the following proportion of a seaman's net wages shall be retained under subsection (1) of this section (whether in pursuance of one or more notices) that is to say,—

(*a*) one-half if the notice or notices relate to one dependant only;

(*b*) two-thirds if the notice or notices relate to two or more dependants.

371 (4) Where a responsible authority [1] have served a notice under this section on the persons employing a seaman a magistrates' court may, on the application of the authority, make an order for the payment to the authority of such sum, not exceeding the proportion of the seaman's wages which those persons were required by virtue of this section to retain, as the court, having regard to the expenses incurred by the authority and the seaman's means, thinks fit.

(5) Any sums paid out of a seaman's wages in pursuance of an order under this section shall be deemed to be paid to him in respect of his wages; and the service, on the persons who employed the seaman, of such an order or of an order dismissing an application for such an order shall terminate the period for which they were required to retain the wages.

(6) An application for an order under this section for the payment of any sum by the persons who employed a seaman shall be deemed, for the purposes of any proceedings, to be an application for an order against the seaman; but the order, when served on those persons, shall have effect as an order against them and may be enforced accordingly.

(7) Parts I and III of the Maintenance Orders Act 1950 shall have effect as if an order under this section were included among those referred to in subsections (1) and (2) of section 4, subsections (1) and (2) of section 9 and subsections (1) and (2) of section 12 of that Act; and any sum payable by any persons under an order made under this section in any part of the United Kingdom may, in any other part of the United Kingdom, be recovered from them as a debt due to the authority on whose application the order was made.

(8) Any notice or order under this section may be served by registered post [4] or recorded delivery service.[4]

(9) The [Secretary of State for Trade] may make regulations specifying—

(*a*) the expenses in respect of which a notice may be served by a responsible authority under subsection (1) of this section;

(*b*) any conditions that must be satisfied if such a notice is to be served;

(*c*) the period that may be specified in such a notice (being a period beginning with the service of the notice and ending a specified number of days after the seaman's discharge from his ship);

(*d*) the form of such a notice and the information to be contained therein; and

(*e*) the amounts to be deducted from a seaman's wages in computing his net wages for the purposes of this section;

and the amounts specified under paragraph (*e*) of this subsection may include amounts allotted by allotment notes issued under section 13 of this Act.

(10) In this section " responsible authority " means the Secretary of State [for Health and Social Security], the Ministry of Health and Social Services for Northern Ireland, or any local authority; but any application to be made or notice to be given under this section by or to a responsible authority may, if the authority is the Secretary of State [for Health and Social Security] or the Ministry of Health and Social Services for Northern

Ireland, be made or given on behalf of the Secretary of State or Ministry by or to the Supplementary Benefits Commission or, as the case may be, the Supplementary Benefits Commission for Northern Ireland.

(11) In this section " local authority " includes a welfare authority constituted under the Public Health and Local Government (Administrative Provisions) Act (Northern Ireland) 1946 and "magistrates' court"—

(*a*) in relation to Scotland, means the sheriff, and

(*b*) in relation to Northern Ireland, means a court of summary jurisdiction.

1372 [1] See subs. (10).

[2] See the M.S. (Maintenance of Seamen's Dependants) Regs. 1972 (S.I. No. 1635) as amended by S.I. 1972 No. 1875.

[3] See s. 97 (1).

[4] See Inland Post Regulations 1968 (S.I. No. 1253).

Remedies of master for remuneration, disbursements, etc.

1373 **18.** The master of a ship [1] shall have the same lien [2] for his remuneration,[3] and all disbursements [4] or liabilities properly made or incurred by him on account of the ship, as a seaman [5] has for his wages.

1374 By the law maritime, though a seaman has a lien for wages, a master has no lien for either wages or disbursements. See *Bristow* v. *Whitmore* (1861) 9 H.L.Cas. 391; *Smith* v. *Plummer* (1818) 1 B. & Ald. 575. A lien was given to a master in 1844 for wages by 7 & 8 Vict. c. 112, and by M.S.A. 1854, s. 191; and for disbursements by M.S.A. 1889, s. 1. These provisions are now re-enacted in this section.

For the history of the jurisdiction over a master's disbursements, see the judgment of Lord Herschell L.C. in *Morgan* v. *Castlegate S.S. Co., The Castlegate* [1893] A.C. 38, 46, 47.

As to the nature of the master's lien, see *The Bold Buccleugh* (1851) 7 Moo.P.C. 267, 284; *The Feronia, infra* (note (2)). See also *The Edwin, infra* (note (4)).

In the case of the master the old rule that " freight is the mother of wages " never had any application: *Hawkins* v. *Twizell* (1856) 5 E. & B. 883.

[1] Foreign Ship. In *The Milford* (1858) Swa. 362; 4 Jur.(N.S.) 417, and *The Jonathan Goodhue* (1859) Swa. 524, it was held that M.S.A. 1854, s. 191 (1894, s. 167 (1)), extended notwithstanding s. 109 (1894, ss. 260 *et seq.*), to claims by masters of foreign ships. It is the *lex fori* which applies, and not the *lex loci contractus*, because we are " construing an English statute with regard to property which is within the English jurisdiction ": *per* Phillimore J. in *The Tagus* [1903] P. 44. But the jurisdiction as to such claims and as to wages generally in the case of foreign ships is discretionary only: notice must be given to the consul of the state to which the ship belongs and the suit has frequently been dismissed on his protest. See the first two cases cited in this note, and *The Golubchick* (1840) 1 W.Rob. 143; *The Herzogin Marie* (1861) Lush. 292; 5 L.T. 88; *The Octavie* (1863) B. & L. 215; 9 L.T. 695 (under Admiralty Court Act 1861, s. 10, now repealed); *The Timor* (1863) 9 L.T. 397; 12 W.R. 219; *The Nina* (1867) L.R. 2 A. & E. 44; on appeal, L.R. 2 P.C. 38; *The Leon XIII* (1883) 8 P.D. 121 (C.A.). See also R.S.C., Ord. 5, r. 16 (*c*), which requires that in an action for wages against a foreign vessel, notice of the commencement of the action be given to the consul of the state to which the vessel belongs, if there be one resident in London. See also s. 4 of the Consular Relations Act 1968.

As to reimbursement to foreign consul out of proceeds of compulsory sale of foreign ship in respect of payments made by him to master and crew for wages and " viaticum," see *The Julina* (1876) 35 L.T. 410.

For proceedings against vessel belonging to an alien enemy coming to this country under a British licence, see *The Vrow Mina* (1813) 1 Dods. 234.

1375 [2] Seaman's lien: see s. 16. By the law maritime, a seaman has a lien on the freight as well as upon the ship for wages, and this lien extends to freight due from sub-charterers: *The Andalina* (1886) 12 P.D. 1, 56 L.T. 171.

MASTER'S LIEN—COMPETING CLAIMS—PRIORITIES. The master's lien takes precedence of all others except those for subsequent salvage, collision, seamen's wages, and bottomry bonds by which the master has bound himself personally or which are given on a subsequent voyage, and the possessory lien of shipwrights and material-men in respect of work done, etc., before wages earned. See the cases following:

(i) Salvage. The master is in the same position as the seamen, and therefore his claim is deferred to that of a subsequent salvor; *The Panthea* (1871) 1 Asp.M.L.C. 133; *The Selina* (1842) 2 Notes of Cases, 18.

The priority also of the salvage lien over the lien for wages subsequently earned appears to be established by *The Gustaf* (1862) Lush. 506; 31 L.J.Ad. 207; and to have been admitted in *The Elin* (1883) 8 P.D. 39.

(ii) Damage. It would seem that similarly his claim is deferred to a damage claim, whether subsequent or not. See *ibid.* and *The Elin* (1883) 52 L.J.P. 55; 8 P.D. 39, 129, following *The Linda Flor* (1857) Swa. 309.

(iii) Seamen. Since the master is no longer by law liable to pay the seamen their wages, their claim against the *res* for wages is presumably no longer preferred to his for wages or disbursements. *Cf. The Salacia* (1862) 32 L.J.Ad. 41; Lush. 545, followed in *The Mons* [1932] P. 109.

(iv) Bottomry bondholder and cargo owner. A master having given a bottomry bond binding himself, ship and freight, cannot claim wages in priority to the bondholder: *The William* (1858) Swa. 346 (master being sole owner); *The Jonathan Goodhue* (1859) Swa. 524. But this rule is only for the protection of the bondholder, and will not be acted upon where he would not be prejudiced by the master's being paid before him; and a cargo owner has no equity to enforce the rule even when the master is a part-owner: *The Edward Oliver* (1867) L.R. 1 A. & E. 379; *The Daring* (1868) L.R. 2 A. & E. 260; *The Eugenie* (1873) L.R. 4 A. & E. 123. If, however, the master has not bound himself personally to pay the bond, then the general rule as to maritime liens in the nature of awards for services rendered applies. Hence his claim in respect of the voyage during which the bond was given or a subsequent voyage takes precedence of the bond, while his claim in respect of a prior voyage is deferred to it: *The Salacia, supra*; *The Hope* (1873) 1 Asp. M.L.C. 563.

Whether seamen's wages earned on a prior voyage are deferred to the claim of the bondholder is uncertain. In *The Union* (1860) 30 L.J.Ad. 17; Lush. 128, the court laid down the rule that seamen's wages have precedence over a bottomry bond, whether they were earned before or after the date of the bond. As the wages seem to have been earned on the voyage on which the bond was granted, this statement may in part be considered only a dictum, and the decision in *The Hope, supra*, raised a doubt whether it is not too wide. See Abbott, *Merchant Ships, etc.*, 14th ed., pp. 213, 294; Maclachlan, *Law of Merchant Shipping*, 7th ed., p. 187. Since this section, unlike the equivalent section of the M.S.A. 1894 (s. 167) which it replaces, does not contain the proviso that the seaman's lien shall apply " so far as the case permits," the matter seems to be resolved in favour of the decision in *The Hope, supra*.

The master and crew of a foreign ship arrested in this country are entitled to priority over a bottomry bondholder in respect of their " viaticum " home: *The Constancia* (1866) 15 W.R. 183.

(v) Mortgagee. The master's lien takes precedence of a claim of a mortgagee of ship or shares: *The Mary Ann, supra* (p. 110); *The Feronia* (1868) L.R. 2 A. & E. 65; *The Hope, supra*; *The Arosa Star* [1959] 2 Lloyd's Rep. 396. And such precedence is not affected by the master being also a part-owner; *The Feronia* (1868) L.R. 2 A. & E. 65; *The Joseph Dexter* (1869) 20 L.T. 820; provided he is not a mortgagor; *The Jenny Lind* (1872) L.R. 3 A. & E. 529; and provided he has not guaranteed the mortgage debt. *The Bangor Castle* (1896) 76 L.T. 768.

As to the position of a master who is also a mortgagee, see *The Repulse* (1845) 2 W.Rob. 398.

As to the effect of delay in enforcing lien during which a mortagee becomes interested without notice, see *The Chieftain* (1863) B. & L. 212.

(vi) Purchaser. The master can enforce his lien although the ship is in the hands of purchasers: *The Bengal* (1859) Swa. 468; *The Fairport* (1882) 8 P.D. 48; but he may lose it by laches; *The Bold Buccleugh* (1850) 7 Moore P.C. 267; *The Europa* (1863) 2 Moore P.C.(N.S.) 1; Br. & L. 89.

(vii) Shipwright, Material-man, etc. The possessory lien of a shipwright or material-man takes precedence of the master's lien for wages earned after the shipwright's work was done or the materials supplied, but not generally over that for wages previously earned. See *The Panthea, supra*; *The Gustaf* (1862) 31 L.J.Ad. 207; Lush. 506; *The Immacolata Concezione* (1883) 9 P.D. 37. As to a foreign master's right to " viaticum " home as against shipwright, see case last cited, followed in *The Tagus* [1903] P. 44; *The Tergeste* [1903] P. 26.

Where the master, being also part-owner, ordered necessaries, he was held liable for the price, both as the master giving the order and as owner, and his claim for wages was deferred to that of the material-men; *The Jenny Lind, supra,* and *The Eva* [1921] P. 454. But where he was not a part-owner, his claim appears to have been preferred in *The Lepanto* [1892] P. 122.

As to priority of a claim for costs by solicitors employed by the master, see *The Heinrich* (1872) L.R. 3 A. & E. 505. *Cf. The Livietta* (1883) 8 P.D. 209, where the cost of sending the crew of a foreign ship home was given priority over the claim of the salvor's solicitors for his costs.

(viii) Trustee in Bankruptcy. See *Re T. C.* (1877) Ir.Rep. 11 Eq. 151.

The master's lien is lost by his electing to take a bill on the owners for his wages instead of cash; *The William Money* (1827) 2 Hagg. 136. But not by his taking a mortgage for balance due; *The Albion* (1872) 27 L.T. 723; 1 Asp.M.L.C. 481 (in Vice-Adm. Court); *The Tagus, supra.*

As to the effect of his allowing wages to remain at interest in the managing owner's hands, see *The Rainbow* (1885) 53 L.T. 91; 5 Asp.M.L.C. 479.

A release of his personal claim against the owner does not release the ship from his lien; *The Chieftain, supra.*

1376 [3] There is no definition of remuneration. It is presumed to be the equivalent of seamen's wages. The fact that a claim for salary, wages, victualling and expenses arises under a special contract does not prevent a master from suing *in rem.* See *Pearson* v. " *Seapro* " (*Owners*) (1931) 40 Ll.L.R. 337.

" Wages " includes " emoluments ": see s. 742 of the M.S.A. 1894 and includes a bonus agreed to be paid on special conditions in addition to the agreed wages; *The Elmville* (*No.* 2) [1904] P. 422; *Shelford* v. *Mosey* [1917] 1 K.B. 154. It also includes the master's National Insurance contributions, where it has been agreed that these should be paid by the owner; *The Gee Whiz* [1951] 1 Lloyd's Rep. 145; and also claims for social benefits that have been incorporated in the contract of service; *The Arosa Kulm* (*No.* 2) [1960] 1 Lloyd's Rep. 97. See also *The Arosa Star* [1959] 2 Lloyd's Rep. 396. Deductions made by the master from the crew's gross wages in respect of social service or trade union contributions are within the section; *The Fairport* [1965] 2 Lloyd's Rep. 183, *The Westport No.* 4 [1968] 2 Lloyd's Rep. 559. However, a social service fund cannot proceed *in rem* to recover unpaid contributions; *The Acrux* [1965] 1 Lloyd's Rep. 565. A master's claim for damages for wrongful dismissal is a claim for wages within the meaning of the County Courts Act 1959, s. 56 (1) (*l*); see *The Blessing* (1877) 3 P.D. 35, a decision on the County Courts Admiralty Jurisdiction Act 1868, s. 3 (2) (now repealed), and he can proceed *in rem* in the High Court under the Administration of Justice Act 1956, s. 1 (1) (*o*). The master can include a claim for wages due after a wrongful determination of an ordinary mariner's contract of service; *The British Trade* [1924] P. 104; *The Arosa Star, supra.* However, when suing on a special contract as distinct from a mariners' contract, he has no lien for such damages; *The British Trade* [1924] P. 104. *Aliter*, a seaman suing on a mariner's contract; *The Great Eastern* (1867) L.R. 1 A. & E. 384.

Damages for wrongful dismissal. He is entitled to reasonable notice before dismissal in the absence of express agreement; *Creen* v. *Wright* (1876) 1 C.P.D. 591. Similarly the law will presume that the terms of his engagement for one voyage extend to a succeeding voyage performed without a new agreement express or clearly implied; *The Gananoque* (1862) Lush. 448. Where a master was engaged for a voyage out and home and was wrongfully discharged abroad he was held entitled to wages until he could obtain other suitable employment and possibly until the termination of the entire voyage; *The Camilla* (1858) Swab. 312. The Redundancy Payments Act 1965 does not apply to merchant seamen: see Redundancy Payments (Merchant Seamen Exclusion) Order 1973 (S.I. No. 1281).

377 [4] The master has no lien for disbursements for which he had no authority to pledge the shipowner's credit *e.g.* for coals where the charterer is bound to the knowledge of the master to provide them; *The Castlegate* [1893] A.C. 38. See also, *The Ripon City* [1897] P. 266; *The Beeswing* (1885) 53 L.T. 554; *The Turgot* (1886) 11 P.D. 21; *The Durham City* (1889) 14 P.D. 85; *The Marco Polo* (1871) 24 L.T. 804; for a general discussion of the extent of a master's authority see Halsbury's *Laws of England*, 3rd ed., Vol. 35, pp. 131–137.

Moreover, the lien exists in respect of those disbursements only, in the case of which it was supposed to have been created by the Admiralty Court Act 1861, that is, those made in the ordinary course of his employment as master, for which he could have pledged the owner's credit without express authority; *The Orienta* [1895] P. 49. And he can only so pledge his owner's credit if he is in a position where it is necessary for the purposes of his duty that the goods should be supplied and he cannot have recourse to his owners before ordering them. *Per* Lord Esher, *ibid.* Hence no lien to the prejudice of mortgagees is created in respect of a master's liability on a bill drawn by him upon his owners for coal ordered by them at a home port. *Ibid.*

The master can recover the expenses of defending himself against a false charge of murder, maliciously brought against him by some of the crew, where the charge originated in the performance of his duty in censuring them for misconduct; *The James Seddon* (1866) L.R. 1 A. & E. 62. But not the amount of a bond given for damages caused by his own default; *The Limerick* (1876) 1 P.D. 292, 411.

He can recover the costs incurred by him in unsuccessfully defending an action on a dishonoured bill of exchange drawn by him on his owners for coals supplied to the ship, if such defence was reasonably necessary in the interests of the ship: *The Elmville* (*No.* 2) [1904] P. 422; see also *The Ripon City, supra*; and *Ceylon Co.* v. *Goodrich* [1904] P. 319.

He can also recover disbursements made to privileged claimants, and is in such case entitled to stand in their shoes and have the benefit of any right they might have against the *res*; so if he has paid the wages of the crew he has a lien for the amount paid with the same priority as they would have had: *The Tagus* [1903] P. 44.

The position of a volunteer who pays off privileged claimants is different. If he does so by leave of the court, he is entitled to have the benefit of any right that they may have had against the *res*. Such leave is often given in the case of a mortgagee or bondholder. See *The Fair Haven* (1866) L.R. 1 A. & E. 67. If, however, he pays off such claims without leave of the court, he does not obtain any right *in rem* which the claimants may have enjoyed. See *The Petone* [1917] P. 198, where the authorities are exhaustively reviewed by Hill J. and the question of the transferability of maritime liens discussed. *The Petone* was approved and followed in *The Leoborg* (*No.* 2) [1964] 1 Lloyd's Rep. 380.

The master's lien is not affected by the fact that he was engaged by a person fraudulently in possession of the ship, provided he was not privy to the fraud. See *The Edwin* (1864) 33 L.J.Adm. 197; B. & L. 281.

Where a master has bound himself and the ship for the supply of necessaries to the ship, and subsequently his successor as master similarly binds himself for further supplies of necessaries, the claims of the two masters rank *pari passu*. See *The Mons* [1932] P. 109.

The master in a wages action is not bound to account for gratuities lawfully given to him; *The Parkdale* [1897] P. 53. See also the Prevention of Corruption Act 1906.

[5] This provision does not entitle a master to the rights accorded to seamen under s. 7 for delay in payment of wages. *Cf. The Arina* (1886) 12 P.D. 118 (overruling *The Princess Helena* (1861) Lush. 190; 30 L.J.Adm. 137).

A master cannot as a rule sue for wages until he is discharged or the service is terminated; *The Hemisphere Borealis*, 5 Ir.Jur.(N.S.) 180. But if compelled by ill-health to leave the ship abroad he may sue at once; *The Rajah of Cochin* (1859) Swa. 473.

Presumably this subsection enables the master to bring an action for wages at any time within a period of six years from the date on which the cause of action accrued. See the Limitation Act 1939, s. 2 (1) (*b*).

As to the master's right to wages during period of unemployment due to wreck or loss of his ship, see M.S. (International Labour Conventions) Act 1925, s. 1, *post*.

Safety, health and welfare

Safety Regulations

1378 **19.**—(1) *The [Secretary of State for Trade] may make regulations for securing, as far as practicable, safe working conditions and safe means of access for masters and seamen employed in ships registered in the United Kingdom and for requiring the reporting of injuries sustained by them.*

(2) *Without prejudice to the generality of the preceding subsection, regulations under this section may—*

(*a*) *require the maintenance, inspection and testing of any equipment and impose conditions on its use*;

(*b*) *require, prohibit, or regulate the use of any material or process*;

(*c*) *require the provision and use of any protective clothing or equipment*;

(*d*) *limit the hours of employment of seamen in any specified operation or in any specified circumstances;*

(*e*) *make provision for the discharge, by persons appointed from among the persons employed in a ship, of functions in connection with the arrangements to be made under the regulations.*

(3) *Regulations under this section may make different provisions for different descriptions of ship and for ships of the same description in different circumstances.*

(4) *The [Secretary of State for Trade] may grant exemptions from any requirement of regulations under this section in respect of any ship or description of ship.*

(5) *Regulations under this section may make a contravention of any provision thereof an offence punishable on summary conviction with a fine not exceeding, if the offence is committed by the master or owner, £200, and, if it is committed by any other person, £20.*

This section is not yet in force. For its application to non sea-going ships, see s. 96 (1).

Crew accommodation

1379 **20.**—(1) *The [Secretary of State for Trade] may make regulations*[1] *with respect to the crew accommodation*[2] *to be provided in ships*[3] *registered in the United Kingdom.*

(2) *Without prejudice to the generality of the preceding subsection, regulations made under this section may, in particular—*

(*a*) *prescribe the minimum space per man which must be provided by way of sleeping accommodation for seamen and the maximum number of persons by whom a specified part of such sleeping acccommodation may be used;*

(*b*) *regulate the position in the ship in which the crew accommodation or any part thereof may be located and the standards to be observed in the construction, equipment and furnishing of any such accommodation;*

(*c*) *require the submission to a surveyor of ships of plans and specifications of any works proposed to be carried out for the purpose of the provision or alteration of any such accommodation and authorise the surveyor to inspect any such works; and*

(*d*) *provide for the maintenance and repair of any such accommodation and prohibit or restrict the use of any such accommodation for purposes other than those for which it is designed.*

(3) *Regulations under this section may make different provision with respect to different descriptions of ships or with respect to ships which were registered in the United Kingdom at different dates or the construction of which was begun at different dates and with respect to crew accommodation provided for seamen of different descriptions.*

(4) *Regulations under this section may exempt ships of any description from any requirements of the regulations and the* [*Secretary of State for Trade*] *may grant other exemptions from any such requirement with respect to any ship.*

(5) *Regulations made under this section may require the master of a ship or any officer authorised by him for the purpose to carry out such inspections of the crew accommodation as may be prescribed by the regulations.*

(6) *If the provisions of any regulations made under this section are contravened in the case of a ship the owner or master shall be liable on summary conviction to a fine not exceeding* £200, *and the ship, if in the United Kingdom, may be detained.*

(7) *In this section " crew accommodation " includes sleeping rooms, mess rooms, sanitary accommodation, hospital accommodation, recreation accommodation, store rooms and catering accommodation provided for the use of seamen but does not include any accommodation which is also used by or provided for the use of passengers.*

This section is not yet in force.

1380 [1] By virtue of s. 100 (2) and Sched. 4, para. 6, the following regulations made under s. 1 of the M.S.A. 1948 will have effect as if made under this section:

(i) The M.S. (Crew Accommodation) Regs. 1953 (S.I. No. 1036) as amended by S.I. 1954 No. 1660, S.I. 1961 No. 393, S.I. 1965 No. 1047, S.I. 1975 No. 341, and as affected by the repeal of the proviso to subs. (3) of that section by the M.S.A. 1965, s. 7 (2) and Sched. 2.

(ii) The M.S. (Crew Accommodation) (Isle of Man) Regs. 1960 (S.I. No. 1967).

[2] Space for crew accommodation is deducted from the space included in the measurement of the tonnage in arriving at the register tonnage of a ship, see s. 1 of the M.S.A. 1965 and Sched. 4, para. 7, *post*.

[3] This included non sea-going ships, see s. 96 (1), *post*.

Provisions and water

1381 **21.**—(1) The [Secretary of State for Trade] may make regulations [1] requiring such provisions and water to be provided for seamen employed in ships registered in the United Kingdom or any description of such ships as may be specified in the regulations; and regulations under this section may make different provision for different circumstances and different descriptions of seamen.

(2) Regulations under this section may require a ship to carry such weighing and measuring equipment as may be necessary to ensure that the quantities of provisions and water supplied to seamen employed in the ship are in accordance with the regulations.

(3) The [Secretary of State for Trade] may exempt any ship from any requirement of regulations made under this section, either generally or in respect of a particular voyage.

(4) If the provisions of any regulations made under this section are not complied [2] with in the case of a ship the master or owner shall be liable on summary conviction to a fine not exceeding £100 unless he proves that the failure to comply was not due to his neglect or default.

(5) If a person empowered under this Act to inspect the provisions and water to be supplied to the seamen employed in a ship is not satisfied that they are in accordance with regulations made under this section the ship, if in the United Kingdom, may be detained.

[1] See the M.S. (Provisions and Water) Regs. 1972 (S.I. No. 1871) and the M.S. (Provisions and Water) (Fishing Vessels) Regs. 1972 (S.I. No. 1872), both amended by S.I. 1975 No. 733.

[2] For complaints, see s. 22.

Complaints about provisions or water

382 **22.**—(1) If three or more seamen employed in a ship registered in the United Kingdom consider that the provisions or water provided for the seamen employed in that ship are not in accordance with regulations made under section 21 of this Act (whether because of bad quality, unfitness for use or deficiency in quantity) they may complain to the master, who shall investigate the complaint.

(2) If the seamen are dissatisfied with the action taken by the master as a result of his investigation or by his failure to take any action they may state their dissatisfaction to him and may claim to complain to a superintendent or proper officer [1]; and thereupon the master shall make adequate arrangements to enable the seamen to do so as soon as the service of the ship permits.

(3) The superintendent or proper officer to whom a complaint has been made under this section shall investigate the complaint and may examine the provisions or water or cause them to be examined.

(4) If the master fails without reasonable cause to comply with the provisions of subsection (2) of this section he shall be liable on summary conviction to a fine not exceeding £20, and if he has been notified in writing by the person making an examination under subsection (3) of this section that any provisions or water are found to be unfit for use or not of the quality required by the regulations, then,—

(*a*) if they are not replaced within a reasonable time the master or owner shall be liable on summary conviction to a fine not exceeding £100 unless he proves that the failure to replace them was not due to his neglect or default; and

(*b*) if the master, without reasonable cause, permits them to be used he shall be liable on summary conviction to a fine not exceeding £100.

[1] See s. 97 (1).

Other complaints

383 **23.**—(1) If a seaman employed in a ship registered in the United Kingdom considers that he has cause to complain about the master or any

other seaman employed in the ship or about the conditions on board the ship he may complain to the master.

(2) If the seaman is dissatisfied with the action taken by the master on the complaint or by his failure to take any action he may state his dissatisfaction to him and, if the ship is outside the United Kingdom, claim to complain to a proper officer [1]; and thereupon the master shall make adequate arrangements to enable the seaman to do so as soon as the service of the ship permits.

(3) If the master of a ship fails without reasonable cause to comply with the provisions of this section he shall be liable on summary conviction to a fine not exceeding £20.

[1] See s. 97 (1).

Medical stores

1384 **24.**—(1) The [Department of Trade] may make regulations [1] requiring ships registered in the United Kingdom, or such descriptions of ships registered in the United Kingdom as may be specified in the regulations, to carry such medicines and other medical stores (including books containing instructions and advice) as may be specified in the regulations; and the regulations may make different provision for different circumstances.

(2) If a ship goes to sea [2] or attempts to go to sea without carrying the medical stores which it is required to carry by regulations under this section the master or owner shall be liable on summary conviction to a fine not exceeding £100 unless he proves that the failure to carry the stores was not due to his neglect or default.[3]

(3) If a person empowered under this Act to inspect the medical stores carried in a ship is not satisfied that the ship carries the stores which it is required to carry by regulations under this section, the ship, if in the United Kingdom, may be detained.

This section was brought into force by the Merchant Shipping Act 1970 (Commencement No. 2) Order 1974 (S.I. 1974 No. 1194).

[1] See the M.S. (Medical Scales) (Fishing Vessels) Regs. 1974 (S.I. No. 1192) and the M.S. (Medical Scales) Regs. 1974 (S.I. No. 1193).

[2] See s. 97 (2).

[3] It is submitted that, notwithstanding these penalties and s. 699 (application of penalties), a seaman has a right of action in respect of injury caused to him by non-compliance with the requirements of this section, since the obligation was primarily intended to be for the benefit of a class. In *Couch* v. *Steel* (1853) 23 L.J.Q.B. 121; 3 E. & B. 402 (under 7 & 8 Vict. c. 112, s. 18 now M.S.A. 1894, s. 200) the court held that the fact that a penalty was recoverable for breach of the statutory duty to provide medicines did not interfere with the right of the seaman at common law to maintain an action in respect of the special damage resulting to him fron the breach of this duty. The general principle laid down in this case, that where there is a statutory duty any person suffering from a breach thereof may bring an action for damages under the statute, was questioned by the Court of Appeal in *Atkinson* v. *Newcastle Waerworks Co.* (1877) 2 Ex.D. 441 and cannot now be regarded as sound since *Groves* v. *Wimborne* [1898] 2 Q.B. 402 (C.A.). See *Solomons* v. *R. Gertzenstein Ltd.* [1954] 2 Q.B. 243 (C.A.). Yet the decision in its particular application to this section appears to be correct; see *ibid., per* Romer L.J. at pp. 265–266. See also, for the duty of care: *McRobbie* v. *George Robb & Sons Ltd.* [1953] 1 Lloyd's Rep. 615 (Sc.).

Medical treatment on board ship

385 **25.** Where a ship registered in the United Kingdom does not carry a doctor among the seamen employed in it the master shall make arrangements for securing that any medical attention on board the ship is given either by him or under his supervision by a person appointed by him for the purpose.

Expenses of medical treatment, etc. during voyage

386 **26.** If a person, while employed [1] in a ship registered in the United Kingdom, receives outside the United Kingdom [2] any surgical or medical treatment or such dental or optical treatment (including the repair or replacement of any appliance) as cannot be postponed without impairing efficiency, the reasonable [3] expenses thereof shall be borne by the persons employing him; and if he dies while so employed and is buried or cremated outside the United Kingdom, the expenses of his burial or cremation shall also be borne by those persons.

387 [1] The employer would not be liable after the date of desertion; *Anchor Line* (*Henderson Brothers*) *Ltd.* v. *Mohad* [1922] 1 A.C. 146.

[2] The employer would not be liable for charges incurred after the seaman has been brought back to a port in the U.K.; *Anderson* v. *Rayner* [1903] 1 K.B. 589.

[3] If the seaman is incurable and incapable of being removed to a U.K. port, the employer is presumably not bound to bear the cost of treatment for the rest of the seaman's life.

Offences by seamen, etc.

Quite apart from his statutory powers, a master has authority over his crew to enforce obedience to his lawful commands for the navigation of the ship and the preservation of good order: *Lamb* v. *Burnett* (1831) 1 G. & J. 291; *The Lima* (1837) 3 Hagg.Adm. 346. He is justified in arresting and confining in a reasonable manner and for a reasonable time any person on board his ship if (1) he has reasonable cause to believe that such arrest or confinement is necessary for the preservation of good order and discipline or for the safety of the vessel or the persons or property on board and (2) in fact he believes that the arrest or the confinement is so necessary: *Hook* v. *Cunard S.S. Co.* [1953] 1 W.L.R. 682; [1953] 1 All E.R. 1021.

For the jurisdiction of the English Courts over crimes committed on board ships see ss. 686, 687 and notes thereto.

For an interesting article on the history of the master's disciplinary powers, see 34 L.Q.R. 347.

Misconduct endangering ship or persons on board ship

388 **27.**—(1) If the master or any member of the crew [1] of a ship registered in the United Kingdom—

(*a*) does any act which causes [2] or is likely to cause the loss or destruction of or serious damage to the ship or the death of or serious injury to a person on board the ship; or

(*b*) omits to do anything required to preserve [3] the ship from loss, destruction or serious damage or to preserve any person on board the ship from death or serious injury;

and the act or omission is deliberate, or amounts to a breach or neglect of duty,[4] or he is under the influence of drink or a drug at the time of the act or omission, he shall be liable, on conviction on indictment, to imprisonment for a term not exceeding two years or to a fine, and, on summary conviction, to a fine not exceeding [£400].[5]

(2) In this section " breach or neglect of duty ", except in relation to a master, includes any disobedience to a lawful command.

1389 [1] As to the application of this section to other persons, see s. 32.
[2] It need not be proved that any actual loss, etc., followed from the act: *B.* v. *Gardner* (1859) 1 F. & F. 669.
[3] As to barring of claim to wages by proof of misconduct in cases of wreck, see s. 15.
[4] Neglect of duty does not mean mere want of proper care in the performance of duty; so that neither the act of the master in placing a look-out man in a bad position, nor the failure by the look-out man to keep a good watch is a criminal offence within this section: *Deacon* v. *Evans* [1911] 1 K.B. 571.
[5] Substituted by the M.S.A. 1974, s. 19, § 1634, *post.*

Drunkenness, etc. on duty

1390 **28.** If a seaman employed in a ship registered in the United Kingdom is, while on duty, under the influence[1] of drink or a drug[2] to such an extent that his capacity to carry out his duties is impaired, he shall be liable on summary conviction to a fine not exceeding £50.

[1] This is a new offence based on a recommendation in para. 311 of the Pearson Report.
[2] As to a defence in proceedings for such an offence where drugs were taken for medicinal purposes, see s. 33.

Wilful disobedience to certain lawful commands

1391 **29.** [*This section has been repealed by the M.S.A.* 1974, *s.* 19, § 1634, *post.*]

Continued or concerted disobedience, neglect of duty, etc.

1392 **30.** If a seaman[1] employed in a ship[2] registered in the United Kingdom—

(*a*) persistently and wilfully neglects his duty; or

(*b*) persistently and wilfully disobeys lawful commands[3]; or

[(*c*) combines with other seamen employed in that ship—

(i) to disobey lawful commands which are required to be obeyed at a time while the ship is at sea;

(ii) to neglect any duty which is required to be discharged at such a time; or

(iii) to impede, at such a time, the progress of a voyage or the navigation of the ship,[4]

he shall be liable on summary conviction to a fine not exceeding £100.

For the purposes of this section a ship shall be treated as being at sea at any time when it is not securely moored in a safe berth.] [5]

[1] As to the application of sub-paras. (*b*) and (*c*) to other persons, see s. 32.
[2] This section is excluded in relation to fishing vessels; see s. 95 (1).
[3] See note (3) above. See also *Page* v. *Williams* [1965] 1 W.L.R. 10 where it was held that continued disobedience to a single command constituted an offence under the M.S.A. 1894, s. 376 (*f*) (an equivalent section to s. 225 but applicable only to fishing boats).
[4] During a civil war in Spain the crew of a vessel combined to refuse to proceed to a port for the purpose of loading a cargo of nitrate, which could be used for the manufacture of munitions, for carriage to Spain. It was held, following *Palace Shipping Co. Ltd.* v. *Caine* [1907] A.C. 386, that they were not guilty of an offence under this paragraph. The proposed voyage was "something outside the scope of the bargain into which they had entered": *Robson* v. *Sykes* (1938) 61 Ll.L.R. 16. See also *Pugh* v. *Henville and others* (*supra*).
[5] The subsection in brackets was substituted by the M.S.A. 1974, s. 19, § 1634, *post*.

Absence without leave at time of sailing

393 **31.** [*This section has been repealed by the M.S.A.* 1974, *s.* 19, § 1634, *post.*]

Offences committed by certain other persons

394 **32.** Where a person goes to sea [1] in a ship [2] without the consent of the master or of any other person authorised to give it or is conveyed in a ship in pursuance of section 62 (5) (*b*) of this Act, sections 27, *29*, 30 (*b*) and 30 (*c*) of this Act shall apply as if he were a seaman employed in the ship.

[1] See s. 97 (2).
[2] This section is excluded in relation to fishing vessels, see s. 95 (1).

Defence of drug taken for medical purposes

395 **33.** In proceedings for an offence under section 27 or section 28 of this Act it shall be a defence to prove that at the time of the act or omission alleged against the defendant he was under the influence of a drug taken by him for medical purposes and either that he took it on medical advice and complied with any directions given as part of that advice or that he had no reason to believe that the drug might have the influence it had.

Disciplinary offences

Disciplinary offences

396 **34.**—(1) For the purpose of maintaining discipline on board ships [1] registered in the United Kingdom the [Secretary of State for Trade] may make regulations [2] specifying any misconduct on board as a disciplinary offence and enabling the master, or such officer as may under the regulations be required or authorised to exercise the powers of the master, to impose fines on seamen committing disciplinary offences.

(2) The fine that may be so imposed on a seaman for a disciplinary offence shall be such as may be provided in the regulations either by

reference to his pay for such period as may be specified in the regulations, calculated in such manner as may be so specified, or by reference to an amount so specified; but the period so specified shall not exceed five days and the amount so specified shall not exceed [£20].[3]

(3) Regulations under this section shall prescribe the procedure to be followed in dealing with disciplinary offences.

(4) Regulations under this section shall enable the master to remit, in such circumstances as may be specified in the regulations, the whole or part of any fine imposed thereunder.

(5) Regulations under this section may make different provision for different descriptions of ship and for seamen employed in different capacities.

1397 [1] The section is excluded in relation to fishing vessels by s. 95 (1) (*a*).
[2] See the M.S. (Disciplinary Offences) Regs. 1972 (S.I. No. 1294) as amended by S.I. 1974 No. 2047.
[3] Substituted by the M.S.A. 1974, s. 19, § 1634, *post*.

Appeal against fine for disciplinary offences

1398 **35.**[1]—(1) A seaman on whom a fine has been imposed for a disciplinary offence may, in accordance with regulations [2] made by the [Secretary of State for Trade], appeal against the decision to a superintendent or proper officer [3] and on such an appeal the superintendent or proper officer may confirm or quash the decision and may remit the whole or part of the fine.

(2) Regulations under this section shall provide for the procedure to be followed on any such appeal, including the time within which notice of an intended appeal is to be given by the appellant to the master and by the master to the superintendent or proper officer and the place at which the appeal is to be heard.

[1] This section is excluded in relation to fishing vessels by s. 95 (1) (*a*).
[2] See the M.S. (Disciplinary Offences) Regs. 1972 (S.I. No. 1294) as amended by S.I. 1974 No. 2047.
[3] See s. 97 (1).

Power to provide for ship's disciplinary committees

1399 **36.**—(1) *The* [*Secretary of State for Trade*] *may make regulations providing for the setting up in ships* [1] *to which the regulations apply of committees of persons employed in the ships, to be known as ship's disciplinary committees and for the exercise by members of those committees of all or any of the powers of the master in dealing with disciplinary offences.*

(2) *Regulations under this section may contain such provisions excluding, modifying or adding to the provisions of regulations under section* 34 *of this Act as appear to the* [*Secretary of State for Trade*] *necessary or expedient for the proper and effective discharge by members of a ship's disciplinary committee of functions otherwise exercisable by the master.*

(3) *Regulations under this section may be so made as to apply to ships generally or to any description of ship specified in the regulations and either*

in all circumstances or in such circumstances as may be so specified, or to apply to such ships or to ships of such descriptions as may for the time being be specified in a direction of the [*Secretary of State for Trade*].

(4) *No regulations shall be made under this section unless a draft thereof has been laid before Parliament and approved by resolution of each House of Parliament.*[2]

00 This section, which contains the most radical change in the law relating to discipline recommended by the Pearson Report, is not yet in force.

[1] This section is excluded in relation to fishing vessels by s. 95 (1) (*a*).

[2] *Cf.* s. 99.

Prohibition of double prosecutions

01 **37.** Where any conduct is both a disciplinary offence and an offence against any provision of the Merchant Shipping Acts, then if it has been dealt with as a disciplinary offence it shall not be dealt with as an offence against that provision.

This section is excluded in relation to fishing vessels by s. 95 (1) (*a*).

It only bars further punishments under the M.S. Acts. It has no application in cases of prosecutions under other enactments: see, *e.g. Lewis* v. *Morgan* [1943] 1 K.B. 376 (prosecution under Defence Regulations).

Payment of fines for disciplinary offences

02 **38.**—(1) Subject to subsection (3) of this section, the amount of a fine imposed on a seaman [1] for a disciplinary offence, so far as not remitted by the master or on appeal, may be deducted from his wages or otherwise recovered by the persons employing him and shall be paid by them (whether or not it has been so deducted or otherwise recovered) to a superintendent or proper officer.[2]

(2) Subject to subsection (3) of this section—

(*a*) if the wages or part of the wages are paid by the master on behalf of the persons employing the seaman, or the master is the person employing the seaman, the said amount shall be paid at the time when the seaman leaves the ship at the end of the voyage or, if earlier, when his employment in the ship is terminated;

(*b*) in any other case the master shall at that time notify the amount to those persons and they shall pay it when the next payment in respect of the seaman's wages falls to be made by them.

(3) Where an appeal against such a fine is pending at the time mentioned in subsection (2) of this section no amount shall by reason of the fine be deducted, recovered, paid or notified under the preceding provisions of this section until the appeal has been disposed of; but regulations [3] under section 35 of this Act may provide for the amount of the fine to be provisionally deducted from the seaman's wages pending the appeal.

(4) Any amount paid under this section to a superintendent or proper officer shall be transmitted by him to the [Secretary of State for Trade] and any amount required to be so paid but remaining unpaid shall be recoverable by the [Secretary of State for Trade].

(5) The [Secretary of State for Trade] shall pay any sums received by them in pursuance of this section into the Consolidated Fund.

1403 [1] The section is excluded in relation to fishing vessels by s. 95 (1) (*a*).
[2] See s. 97 (1).
[3] See the M.S. (Disciplinary Offences) Regs. 1972 (S.I. No. 1294) as amended by S.I. 1974 No. 2047.

Civil liability for absence without leave, smuggling and fines imposed under immigration laws

Civil liability for absence without leave

1404 **39.**—(1) The following provisions of this section shall apply with respect to the liability of a seaman employed in a ship registered in the United Kingdom to damages for being absent from his ship at a time when he is required under his contract of employment to be on board.

(2) If he proves that his absence was due to an accident or mistake or some other cause beyond his control and that he took all reasonable precautions to avoid being absent his absence shall not be treated as a breach of contract.

(3) Where subsection (2) of this section does not apply, then—

(*a*) if no special damages are claimed his liability shall be £10;
(*b*) if special damages are claimed his liability shall not be more than £100.

(4) In the application of this section to Scotland for the references to special damages there shall be substituted references to damages in respect of specific expense incurred or loss sustained.

Civil liability for smuggling

1405 **40.** If a seaman employed in a ship registered in the United Kingdom is found in civil proceedings before a court in the United Kingdom to have committed an act of smuggling,[1] whether within or outside the United Kingdom, he shall be liable to make good any loss or expense that the act has caused to any other person.

[1] For smuggling offences, see Archbold's *Criminal Pleading, Evidence and Practice* (38th ed.) and see also Customs and Excise Act 1952.

Civil liability for fines imposed under immigration laws

1406 **41.**—(1) The following provisions of this section shall apply where, at a time when a ship registered in the United Kingdom is in the national or territorial waters of any country outside the United Kingdom, a seaman employed in the ship is absent without leave and present in that country in contravention of that country's laws.

(2) If, by reason of the contravention, a penalty is incurred under those laws by the persons employing the seaman the penalty shall be treated as being attributable to his absence without leave and may, subject to the provisions of section 39 of this Act, be recovered from him as special damages for breach of contract (or, in Scotland, as damages in respect of specific expense incurred or loss sustained).

(3) If, by reason of the contravention, a penalty is incurred under those laws by any other person the amount thereof, or, if that amount exceeds £100, £100, may be recovered by him from the seaman.

Trade disputes

Trade disputes involving seamen

407 **42.**—(1) The Conspiracy and Protection of Property Act 1875,[1] except section 5, shall apply to seamen as it applies to other persons.

(2) Notwithstanding anything in any agreement, a seaman employed in a ship registered in the United Kingdom may terminate his employment in that ship by leaving the ship in contemplation or furtherance [2] of a trade dispute [3] after giving to the master not less than forty-eight hours' notice of his intention to do so, and shall not be compelled (unless the notice is withdrawn) to go to sea [4] in the forty-eight hours following the giving of such a notice; but such a notice shall be of no effect unless at the time it is given the ship is in the United Kingdom and securely moored in a safe berth.

(3) *In this section " trade dispute " has the same meaning as in section* 5 (3) *of the Trade Disputes Act* 1906.[5]

408 [1] s. 16 of this Act formerly provided that the Act did not apply to seamen.
[2] See *Conway* v. *Wade* [1909] A.C. 506, 512 *per* Lord Loreburn L.C. See also *Bent's Brewery Co. Ltd.* v. *Hogan* [1945] 2 All E.R. 570 and *R.* v. *Tearse* [1945] 1 K.B. 1.
[3] See subsection (3).
[4] See s. 97 (1).
[5] This section was repealed by the Trade Union and Labour Relations Act 1974, s. 25, Sched. 8. See now s. 29 (1) of that Act. Prior to the 1974 Act subs. (3) of s. 42 of the M.S.A. 1970 was amended by the Industrial Relations Act 1971 as follows: " (3) In this section 'industrial dispute' has the same meaning as in the Industrial Relations Act 1971."

Manning and certification

Manning

409 **43.**—(1) *Subject to subsection* (2) *of this section, the* [*Secretary of State for Trade*] *may make regulations—*

(*a*) *requiring ships to which this section applies* [1] *to carry such number of qualified officers of any description, qualified doctors and qualified cooks and such number of other seamen or qualified seamen of any description as may be specified in the regulations; and* (*b*) *prescribing or enabling the* [*Secretary of State for Trade*] *to specify standards of competence to be attained and other conditions to be satisfied (subject to any exceptions allowed by or under the regulations) by officers and other seamen of any description in order to be qualified*[2] *for the purposes of this section.*

(2) *The* [*Secretary of State for Trade*] *shall not exercise his power to make regulations requiring ships to carry seamen other than doctors and cooks except to the extent that it appears to him necessary or expedient in the interests of safety.*

(3) *Regulations under this section may make different provision for different descriptions of ships or for ships of the same description in different circumstances.*

(4) *Without prejudice to the generality of paragraph* (*b*) *of subsection* (1) *of this section, the conditions prescribed or specified under that paragraph may include conditions as to nationality, and regulations made for the purposes of that paragraph may make provision, or enable the* [*Secretary of State for Trade*] *to make provision, for—*

(*a*) *the manner in which the attainment of any standard or the satisfaction of any other condition is to be evidenced;*

(*b*) *the conduct of any examinations, the conditions for admission to them and the appointment and remuneration of examiners; and*

(*c*) *the issue, form and recording of certificates and other documents;*

and different provisions may be so made or enabled to be made for different circumstances.

(5) *If a person makes a statement which he knows to be false or recklessly makes a statement which is false in a material particular for the purpose of obtaining for himself or another person a certificate or other document which may be issued under this section he shall be liable on summary conviction to a fine not exceeding* £100.

This section is not yet in force.

1410 The Pearson Report considered that the system of certificates of competency, as derived from the M.S.A. 1894, was sound in principle but felt that existing statutory provisions were too rigid and detailed, particularly in view of the development of new functions for officers and seamen.

The special provisions relating to apprenticeship to the sea service have been repealed and not replaced.

[1] See s. 49. As to exemptions, see s. 44.

[2] As to special certificates of competency, see s. 50.

Power to exempt from manning requirements

1411 **44.**—(1) *The* [*Secretary of State for Trade*] *may exempt any ship or description of ship from any requirements of regulations made under section* 43 *of this Act.*

(2) *An exemption given under this section may be confined to a particular period or to one or more particular voyages.*

This section is not yet in force.

Prohibition of going to sea undermanned

412 **45.** *Subject to section* 44 *of this Act, if a ship* [1] *to which this section applies goes to sea* [2] *or attempts to go to sea* [3] *without carrying such officers and other seamen as it is required to carry under section* 43 *of this Act the owner or master shall be liable on summary conviction to a fine not exceeding* £200 *and the ship, if in the United Kingdom,*[3] *may be detained.*[4]

This section is not yet in force.

413 The present position as regards crew manning is contained in Notice M. No. 489.

[1] See s. 49.

[2] See s. 97 (1).

[3] See s. 96 (2) which provides that in relation to non-sea-going ships, this section shall have effect as if for the words " goes to sea or attempts to go to sea " there were substituted the words " plies or attempts to ply " and the words " if in the United Kingdom " were omitted.

[4] In relation to non-sea-going ships, the M.S.A. 1894, s. 629 is amended: see s. 96 (2).

Unqualified persons going to sea as qualified officers or seamen

414 **46.**—(1) *If a person goes to sea* [1] *as a qualified officer or seaman of any description without being such a qualified officer or seaman he shall be liable on summary conviction to a fine not exceeding* £100.

(2) *In this section* " *qualified* " *means qualified for the purposes of section* 43 *of this Act.*

This section is not yet in force.

[1] See s. 97 (1).

Production of certificates and other documents of qualification

415 **47.** *Any person serving or engaged to serve in any ship* [1] *to which this section applies and holding any certificate or other document which is evidence that he is qualified for the purposes of section* 43 *of this Act shall on demand produce it to any superintendent, surveyor or proper officer* [2] *and (if he is not himself the master) to the master of the ship; and if he fails to do so without reasonable cause he shall be liable on summary conviction to a fine not exceeding* £20.

This section is not yet in force.

[1] See s. 49.

[2] See s. 97 (1).

Crew's knowledge of English

416 **48.**—(1) Where in the opinion of a superintendent or proper officer [1] the crew of a ship [2] to which this section applies consists of or includes persons who may not understand orders given to them in the course of their duty because of their insufficient knowledge of English and the absence of adequate arrangements for transmitting the orders in a language of which they have sufficient knowledge, then—

(*a*) if the superintendent or proper officer has informed the master of that opinion the ship shall not go to sea [1]; and

(*b*) if the ship is in the United Kingdom it may be detained.

(2) If a ship goes to sea or attempts to go to sea in contravention of this section the owner or master shall be liable on summary conviction to a fine not exceeding £200.

[1] See s. 97 (1).
[2] See s. 49.

Application of sections 43, 45, 47 and 48

1417 **49.** *Sections* 43, 45, 47 *and* 48 *of this Act apply to every ship registered* [1] *in the United Kingdom and also to any ship registered elsewhere which carries passengers—*

(*a*) *between places in the United Kingdom or between the United Kingdom and the Isle of Man or any of the Channel Islands; or*

(*b*) *on a voyage which begins and ends at the same place in the United Kingdom and on which the ship calls at no place outside the United Kingdom.*

This section is not yet in force.
[1] See ss. 92–94 as to unregistered ships and ships registered outside the U.K.

Special certificates of competency

1418 **50.**—(1) *The* [*Secretary of State for Trade*] *may issue and record documents certifying the attainment of any standard of competence relating to ships or their operation, notwithstanding that the standard is not among those prescribed or specified under section* 43 (1) (*b*) *of this Act; and may, in relation thereto, make regulations for purposes corresponding to those mentioned in section* 43 (4) *of this Act.*

(2) *If a person makes a statement which he knows to be false or recklessly makes a statement which is false in a material particular for the purpose of obtaining for himself or another person a document which may be issued under this section he shall be liable on summary conviction to a fine not exceeding* £100.

This section is not yet in force.

Restriction on employment of persons under eighteen on board ship

1419 **51.**—(1) *A person under school-leaving age shall not be employed in any ship registered in the United Kingdom except as permitted by regulations under this section.*

(2) *The* [*Secretary of State for Trade*] *may make regulations—*

(*a*) *prescribing circumstances in which and conditions subject to which persons under school-leaving age who have attained such age as may be specified in the regulations may be employed in a ship in such capacities as may be so specified;*

(*b*) *prescribing circumstances and capacities in which persons over school-leaving age but under the age of eighteen or under such lower age as may be specified in the regulations must not be employed in a ship registered in the United Kingdom or may be so employed only subject to such conditions as may be specified in the regulations.*

(3) *Regulations made for the purposes of this section may make different provision for different employments and different descriptions of ship and any other different circumstances.*

(4) *If any person is employed in a ship in contravention of this section or if any condition subject to which a person may be employed under regulations made for the purposes of this section is not complied with, the owner or master shall be liable on summary conviction to a fine not exceeding* £100.

(5) *For the purposes of this section a person employed in a ship shall be deemed to be over school-leaving age if he has, and under school-leaving age if he has not, attained the age which is the upper limit of the compulsory school age (in Scotland school age) under the enactments* [1] *relating to education in the part of the United Kingdom in which he entered into the agreement under which he is so employed or, if he entered into that agreement outside the United Kingdom or is employed otherwise than under an agreement, under the enactments relating to education in England and Wales; and if he is treated for the purposes of those enactments as not having attained that age he shall be so treated also for the purposes of this section.*

This section is not yet in force.

[1] See s. 97 (1).

Disqualification of seamen, inquiries and investigations

Inquiry into fitness or conduct of officer

420 **52.**—(1) *If it appears to the* [*Secretary of State for Trade*] *that an officer—*

(*a*) *is unfit to discharge his duties, whether by reason of incompetence or misconduct or for any other reason; or*

(*b*) *has been seriously negligent in the discharge of his duties; or*

(*c*) *has failed to comply with the provisions of section* 422 *of the Merchant Shipping Act* 1894 (*duty to give assistance and information after collision*);

the [*Secretary of State for Trade*] *may cause an inquiry to be held by one or more persons appointed by them and, if they do so, may, if they think fit, suspend, pending* [1] *the outcome of the inquiry, any certificate issued to the officer in pursuance of section* 43 *of this Act and require the officer to deliver it to them.*

(2) *Where a certificate issued to an officer has been suspended under subsection* (1) *of this section the suspension may, on the application of the officer, be terminated by the High Court or, if the inquiry is held in Scotland, by the Court of Session, and the decision of the court on such an application shall be final.*

(3) *An inquiry under this section shall be conducted in accordance with rules made under section* 58 (1) *of this Act and those rules shall require the persons holding the inquiry to hold it with the assistance of one or more assessors.*

(4) *The persons holding an inquiry under this section into the fitness or conduct of an officer—*

(*a*) *may, if satisfied of any of the matters mentioned in paragraphs* (*a*) *to* (*c*) *of subsection* (1) *of this section, cancel or suspend any certificate issued to him under section* 43 *of this Act or censure him;*
(*b*) *may make such order with regard to the costs of the inquiry as they think just; and*
(*c*) *shall make a report on the case to the* [*Secretary of State for Trade*];

and if the certificate is cancelled or suspended the officer (*unless he has delivered it to the* [*Secretary of State for Trade*] *in pursuance of subsection* (1) *of this section*) *shall deliver it forthwith to the persons holding the inquiry or to the* [*Secretary of State for Trade*].

(5) *Any costs which a person is ordered to pay under subsection* (4) (*b*) *of this section may be recovered from him by the* [*Secretary of State for Trade*].

This section is not yet in force.
[1] This power to suspend pending the outcome of the inquiry is new.

Disqualification of holder of certificate other than officer's

1421 **53.**—(1) *Where it appears to the* [*Secretary of State for Trade*] *that a person who is the holder of a certificate to which this section applies is unfit to be the holder of such a certificate, whether by reason of incompetence or misconduct or for any other reason,* [*he*] *may give him notice in writing that* [*he is*] *considering the suspension or cancellation of the certificate.*

(2) *The notice must state the reasons why it appears to the* [*Secretary of State for Trade*] *that that person is unfit to be the holder of such a certificate and must state that within a period specified in the notice, or such longer period as the* [*Secretary of State for Trade*] *may allow, he may make written representations to the* [*Secretary of State*] *or claim to make oral representations to the* [*Secretary of State*].

(3) *After considering any representations made in pursuance of the*

preceding subsection the [*Secretary of State*] *shall decide whether or not to suspend or cancel the certificate and shall give the holder of it written notice of* [*his*] *decision.*

(4) *Where the decision is to suspend or cancel the certificate the notice shall state the date from which the cancellation is to take effect, or the date from which and the period for which the suspension is to take effect, and shall require the holder to deliver the certificate to the* [*Secretary of State*] *not later than the date so specified unless before that date he has required the case to be dealt with by an inquiry under section* 54 *of this Act.*

(5) *Where, before the date specified in the notice, he requires the case to be dealt with by such an inquiry, then, unless he withdraws the requirement, the suspension or cancellation shall not take effect except as ordered in pursuance of the inquiry.*

(6) *The* [*Secretary of State for Trade*] *may make regulations prescribing the procedure to be followed with respect to the making and consideration of representations in pursuance of this section, the form of any notice to be given under this section and the period to be specified in any such notice as the period within which any steps are to be taken.*

(7) *This section applies to every certificate issued under section* 50 *of this Act and to any certificate issued under section* 43 *of this Act other than one certifying that a person is qualified as an officer.*

This section is not yet in force.

Inquiry into fitness or conduct of seaman other than officer

422 **54.**—(1) *Where a person has, before the date mentioned in section* 53 (4) *of this Act, required his case to be dealt with by an inquiry under this section the* [*Secretary of State for Trade*] *shall cause an inquiry to be held by one or more persons appointed by* [*him*].

(2) *An inquiry under this section shall be conducted in accordance with rules made under section* 58 (1) *of this Act and those rules shall require the persons holding the inquiry to hold it with the assistance of one or more assessors.*

(3) *The persons holding an inquiry under this section—*

(*a*) *may confirm the decision of the* [*Secretary of State for Trade*] *and cancel or suspend the certificate accordingly;*

(*b*) *may, where the decision was to cancel the certificate, suspend it instead;*

(*c*) *may, where the decision was to suspend the certificate, suspend it for a different period;*

(*d*) *may, instead of confirming the decision of the* [*Secretary of State for Trade*], *censure the holder of the certificate or take no further action;*

(*e*) *may make such order with regard to the costs of the inquiry as [he thinks] just; and*

(*f*) *shall make a report on the case to the [Secretary of State for Trade];*

and if the certificate is cancelled or suspended it shall be delivered forthwith to the persons holding the inquiry or to the [Secretary of State for Trade].

(4) *Any costs which a person is ordered to pay under subsection* (3) (*e*) *of this section may be recovered from him by the [Secretary of State for Trade].*

This section is not yet in force.

Inquiries and investigations into shipping casualties

1423 **55.**—(1) *Where any of the following casualties has occurred, that is to say,—*

(*a*) *the loss or presumed loss, stranding, grounding, abandonment of or damage to a ship; or*

(*b*) *a loss of life caused by fire on board or by any accident to a ship or ship's boat, or by any accident occurring on board a ship or ship's boat; or*

(*c*) *any damage caused by a ship;*

and, at the time it occurred, the ship was registered in the United Kingdom or the ship or boat was in the United Kingdom or the territorial waters thereof, the [Secretary of State for Trade]—

(i) *may cause a preliminary inquiry into the casualty to be held by a person appointed for the purpose by the [Secretary of State]; and*

(ii) *may (whether or not a preliminary inquiry into the casualty has been held) cause a formal investigation into the casualty to be held, if in England, Wales or Northern Ireland, by a wreck commissioner and, if in Scotland, by the sheriff.*

(2) *A person appointed under this section to hold a preliminary inquiry shall for the purpose of the inquiry have the powers conferred on an inspector by section* 729 *of the Merchant Shipping Act* 1894.

This section is not yet in force.

Formal investigation into shipping casualty

1424 **56.**—(1) *A wreck commissioner or sheriff holding a formal investigation into a casualty under section* 55 *of this Act shall conduct it in accordance with rules under section* 58 (1) *of this Act, and those rules shall require the assistance of one or more assessors and, if any question as to the cancellation or suspension of an officer's certificate is likely to arise, the assistance of not less than two assessors.*

(2) *Subsections* (1), (3) *and* (4) *of section* 77 *of the Magistrates' Courts Act* 1952 (*which provide for the attendance of witnesses and the production of evidence*) *shall apply in relation to a formal investigation held by a wreck commissioner as if the wreck commissioner were a magistrates' court and the investigation a complaint; and the wreck commissioner shall have power to administer oaths for the purposes of the investigation.*

(3) *Where a formal investigation is held in Scotland the sheriff shall, subject to any rules made under section* 58 (1) *of this Act, dispose of it as a summary application, and, subject to section* 57 *of this Act, his decision on the investigation shall be final.*

(4) *If as a result of the investigation the wreck commissioner or sheriff is satisfied, with respect to any officer, of any of the matters mentioned in paragraphs* (*a*) *to* (*c*) *of section* 52 (1) *of this Act and, if it is a matter mentioned in paragraph* (*a*) *or* (*b*) *of that section, is further satisfied that it caused or contributed to the casualty, he may cancel or suspend any certificate issued to the officer under section* 43 *of this Act or censure him; and if he cancels or suspends the certificate the officer shall deliver it forthwith to him or to the* [*Secretary of State for Trade*].

(5) *The wreck commissioner or sheriff may make such order with regard to the costs of the investigation as he thinks just and shall make a report on the case to the* [*Secretary of State for Trade*].

(6) *Any costs which a person is ordered to pay under the preceding subsection may be recovered from him by the* [*Secretary of State for Trade*].

(7) *In its application to Northern Ireland this section shall have effect as if in subsection* (2) *for the references to subsections* (1), (3) *and* (4) *of section* 77 *of the Magistrates' Courts Act* 1952 *there were substituted references to subsections* (1) *and* (3) *of section* 120 *and subsection* (1) *of section* 122 *of the Magistrates' Courts Act* (*Northern Ireland*) 1964.

This section is not yet in force.

Re-hearing of an appeal from inquiries and investigations

25 **57.**—(1) *Where an inquiry or formal investigation has been held under the preceding provisions of this Act the* [*Secretary of State for Trade*] *may order the whole or part of the case to be re-heard, and shall do so*—

(*a*) *if new and important evidence which could not be produced at the inquiry or investigation has been discovered; or*

(*b*) *if there appear to the* [*Secretary of State*] *to be other grounds for suspecting that a miscarriage of justice may have occurred.*

(2) *An order under subsection* (1) *of this section may provide for the re-hearing to be as follows,*—

(*a*) *if the inquiry or investigation was held in England, Wales or Northern Ireland, by the persons who held it, by a wreck commissioner or by the High Court;*

(*b*) *if it was held in Scotland, by the persons who held it, by the sheriff or by the Court of Session.*

(3) *Any re-hearing under this section which is not held by the High Court or the Court of Session shall be conducted in accordance with rules made under section* 58 (1) *of this Act; and section* 56 *of this Act shall apply in relation to a re-hearing of an investigation by a wreck commissioner or sheriff as it applies in relation to the holding of an investigation.*

(4) *Where the persons holding the inquiry or investigation have decided to cancel or suspend the certificate of any person or have found any person at fault, then, if no application for an order under subsection* (1) *of this section has been made or such an application has been refused, that person or any other person who, having an interest in the inquiry or investigation, has appeared at the hearing and is affected by the decision or finding, may appeal to the High Court or the Court of Session, according as the inquiry or investigation was held in England, Wales or Northern Ireland or in Scotland.*

This section is not yet in force.

Rules as to inquiries, investigations and appeals

1426 **58.**—(1) *The* [*Secretary of State for Trade*] *may make rules for the conduct of inquiries under sections* 52 *and* 54 *of this Act and of formal investigations under section* 55 *of this Act and for the conduct of any re-hearing under section* 57 *of this Act which is not held by the High Court or the Court of Session.*

(2) *Without prejudice to the generality of the preceding subsection, rules under this section may provide for the appointment and summoning of assessors, the manner in which any facts may be proved, the persons allowed to appear, and the notices to be given to persons affected.*

(3) *Rules of court made for the purpose of rehearings under section* 57 *of this Act which are held by the High Court, or of appeals to the High Court, may require the court, subject to such exceptions, if any, as may be allowed by the rules, to hold such a rehearing or hear such an appeal with the assistance of one or more assessors.*

This section is not yet in force.

Failure to deliver cancelled or suspended certificate

1427 **59.** *If a person fails to deliver a certificate as required under section* 52 *or* 56 *of this Act he shall be liable on summary conviction to a fine not exceeding* £50; *and if a person fails to deliver a certificate as required under section* 53 *or* 54 *of this Act he shall be liable on summary conviction to a fine not exceeding* £10.

This section is not yet in force.

Power to restore certificate

428 **60.** *Where a certificate has been cancelled or suspended under this Act or under section* 478 *of the Merchant Shipping Act* 1894, *the* [*Secretary of State for Trade*], *if of opinion that the justice of the case requires it, may re-issue the certificate or, as the case may be, reduce the period of suspension and return the certificate, or may grant a new certificate of the same or a lower grade in place of the cancelled or suspended certificate.*

This section is not yet in force.

Inquiries into deaths of crew members and others

429 **61.**—(1) Subject to subsection (4) of this section, where—

(*a*) any person dies in a ship registered in the United Kingdom; or

(*b*) the master of or a seaman employed in such a ship dies in a country outside the United Kingdom;

an inquiry into the cause of the death shall be held by a superintendent or proper officer [1] at the next port where the ship calls after the death and where there is a superintendent or proper officer, or at such other place as the [Secretary of State for Trade] may direct.

(2) The superintendent or proper officer holding the inquiry shall for the purpose of the inquiry have the powers conferred on an inspector by section 729 of the Merchant Shipping Act 1894.

(3) The person holding the inquiry shall make a report of his findings to the [Secretary of State for Trade] and the [Secretary of State] shall make a copy of the report available—

(*a*) if the deceased person was employed in the ship and a person was named as his next of kin in the crew agreement [1] or list of the crew in which the deceased person's name last appeared, to the person so named;

(*b*) in any case, to any person requesting it who appears to the [Secretary of State for Trade] to be interested.

(4) No inquiry shall be held under this section in a case where, in England, Wales or Northern Ireland, a coroner's inquest is to be held or, in Scotland, an inquiry is to be held under the Fatal Accidents Inquiry (Scotland) Act 1895 or the Fatal Accidents and Sudden Deaths Inquiry (Scotland) Act 1906.

[1] See s. 97 (1).

Relief and repatriation of seamen left behind

Relief and return of seamen left behind, etc.

430 **62.**—(1) Where—

(*a*) a person employed as a seaman [1] in a ship registered in the United Kingdom is left behind [2] in any country outside the

United Kingdom or is taken to such a country on being shipwrecked; or

(*b*) a person who became so employed under an agreement entered into outside the United Kingdom is left behind in the United Kingdom or is taken to the United Kingdom on being shipwrecked;

the persons who last employed him as a seaman shall make such provision for his return and for his relief and maintenance [3] until his return and such other provisions as may be required by regulations [4] made by the [Secretary of State for Trade].

(2) The provisions to be so made may include the repayment of expenses incurred in bringing a shipwrecked seaman ashore and maintaining him until he is brought ashore and the payment of the expenses of the burial or cremation of a seaman who dies before he can be returned.

(3) The [Secretary of State for Trade] may also make regulations providing for the manner in which any wages due to any person left behind or taken to any country as mentioned in subsection (1) of this section, and any property of his left on board ship, are to be dealt with.

(4) The [Secretary of State for Trade] may make regulations requiring a superintendent or proper officer [3]—

(*a*) to make such provision as may be prescribed by the regulations with respect to any matter for which provision may be required to be made by regulations under the preceding provisions of this section; and

(*b*) to make the like provision with respect to citizens [5] of the United Kingdom and Colonies found in distress in any country outside the United Kingdom after being employed in ships registered in, or belonging to the government of, such a country.

(5) Without prejudice to the generality of the preceding provisions, regulations made under this section may make provision—

(*a*) for determining the place to which a person is to be returned;

(*b*) for requiring the master of any ship registered in the United Kingdom to convey a person [6] to a place determined in accordance with the regulations and for enabling a superintendent or proper officer to give the master directions for that purpose;

(*c*) for the making of payments in respect of the conveyance of a person in accordance with the regulations; and

(*d*) for the keeping of records and the rendering of accounts.

(6) Regulations under this section may make a contravention of any provision thereof an offence punishable on summary conviction with a fine not exceeding £100 or such less amount as may be specified in the regulations.

(7) This section applies to a person left behind on being discharged in pursuance of section 5 of this Act, whether or not at the time he is left behind the ship is still registered in the United Kingdom.

1431 [1] This includes a master: see s. 67.
[2] See s. 97 (4). See also s. 63 as to the limit of an employer's liability for such persons.
[3] See s. 97 (1).
[4] See the M.S. (Repatriation) Regs. 1972 (S.I. No. 1805).
[5] See the British Nationality Act 1948, and see note (3) to M.S.A. 1894, s. 1.
[6] Such a person is treated as a seaman for the purposes of ss. 27, 29, 30 (*b*) and (*c*) of this Act. Such persons are not passengers for the purposes of Part III of M.S.A. 1894. See the definition of " passengers " in s. 26 of M.S. (Safety Conventions) Act 1949, replacing the definition formerly contained in s. 267 of M.S.A. 1894, as amended by s. 33 of M.S. (Safety and Load Line Conventions) Act 1932. Moreover, a ship carrying such persons is not, on that account, liable to compulsory pilotage as carrying passengers; *The Clymene* [1897] P. 295, followed in *The Charles Livingston* (1941) 69 Ll.L.R. 180.

Limit of employer's liability under s. 62

1432 **63.** Where a person left behind in or taken to any country as mentioned in section 62 (1) of this Act remains there after the end of a period of three months the persons who last employed him as a seaman [1] shall not be liable under that section to make provision for his return or for any matter arising after the end of that period, unless they have before the end of that period been under an obligation imposed on them by regulations under that section to make provision with respect to him.

[1] This includes a master: see s. 67.

Recovery of expenses incurred for relief and return, etc.

1433 **64.**—(1) Where any expenses are incurred in respect of any matter for which the employers of a seaman [1] are required to make provision under section 62 of this Act, then—

(*a*) if the expenses are incurred by the [Secretary of State for Trade], or are incurred by the government of any country outside the United Kingdom and repaid to them on behalf of the Crown, the [Secretary of State for Trade] may recover them from the employers;

(*b*) if the expenses are incurred by the seaman he may recover them from the employers unless they prove either that under the terms of his employment they were to be borne by him or that he would not have been left behind but for his own wrongful act or neglect.

(2) Where, in the case of any seaman, expenses are incurred by the [Secretary of State for Trade] or are incurred by the government of any country outside the United Kingdom and repaid to them on behalf of the Crown—

(*a*) in respect of any matter for which, but for section 63 of this Act, the seamen's last employers would have been required to make provision under section 62 of this Act; or (*b*) in respect of any matter for which provision is required to be made under section 62 (4) (*b*) of this Act;

the [Secretary of State for Trade] may recover them from the seamen (or, if he has died, from his personal representatives).

[1] This includes a master: see s. 67.

Property of deceased seamen

Custody, etc. of property of deceased seamen

1434 **65.**—(1) The [Secretary of State for Trade] may make regulations [1] providing for the custody of and dealing with—

(*a*) any property [2] left on board a ship registered in the United Kingdom by a seaman [3] dying [4] while or after being employed in the ship;

(*b*) any property left in a country outside the United Kingdom by a seaman dying while or within six months after being employed in such a ship; and

(*c*) any property left in a country outside the United Kingdom by a citizen [5] of the United Kingdom and colonies dying while or within six months after being employed as a seaman in a ship registered outside the United Kingdom;

until it is disposed of by or under the directions of the [Secretary of State for Trade]; and for the recovery by the [Secretary of State for Trade] of any wages [6] which, at the time of a seaman's death, were due to him in respect of his employment in a ship registered in the United Kingdom.

(2) Regulations under this section may require the recording of particulars and the rendering of accounts and may enable the [Secretary of State for Trade] or any person having custody of any such property to sell it by auction or otherwise and account for the proceeds.

(3) Regulations under this section may make a contravention of any provision thereof an offence punishable on summary conviction with a fire not exceeding £100.

1435 [1] See the M.S. (Property of Deceased Seamen) Regs. 1972 (S.I. No. 1697).
[2] As for the disposal of property of deceased seamen where the assets do not exceed £500, see s. 66.
[3] This includes a master: see s. 67.
[4] See s. 97 (5).
[5] See the British Nationality Act 1948, and note (3) to the M.S.A. 1894, s. 1.
[6] See the notes to s. 7.

Disposal of property of deceased seamen

1436 **66.**—(1) Where, on the death of a seaman,[1] any assets come into the hands of the [Secretary of State for Trade] by virtue of section 65 of this Act the Board may satisfy out of them any expenses incurred by the Board in respect of the seaman or his property.

(2) If the value of the residue of the assets does not exceed £500, the [Secretary of State for Trade] may at any time pay or deliver it to any of the persons mentioned in subsection (3) of this section or distribute it among them, unless a grant of representation, or in Scotland confirmation, has then been made and the [Secretary of State for Trade] know of it; and the Board shall thereby be discharged from any further liability in respect of the residue.

(3) The persons referred to in subsection (2) of this section are—

(*a*) any person appearing to the [Secretary of State for Trade] to be a person named as the seaman's next of kin in the crew agreement [2] or list of the crew in which the seaman's name last appeared;

(*b*) any person appearing to the [Secretary of State for Trade] to be his widow or a child [3] of his;

(*c*) any person appearing to the [Secretary of State for Trade] to be beneficially entitled, under a will [4] or on intestacy,[5] to the seaman's estate or any part of it;

(*d*) any person appearing to the [Secretary of State for Trade] to be a creditor of the seaman.

(4) If it appears to the [Secretary of State for Trade] that any of the persons to whom any assets may be paid or delivered under this section is resident in a foreign state the [Secretary of State for Trade] may pay or deliver them to him by paying or delivering them to a consular officer of that state for transmission to him.

(5) In this section " child " includes an adopted child and an illegitimate child.

437 [1] This includes a master; see s. 67.

[2] See s. 97 (1).

[3] See subs. 5.

[4] The will of a seaman made at sea, so far as concerns the disposal of personal estate, is regulated by the common law, being exempted by s. 11 of the Wills Act 1837, from the formalities required by that Act. It need not, therefore, be in writing or attested. Although to come within the exemption the will must have been made by the seaman while *at* sea, the seaman need not actually be *on* the sea. He may be *at* sea although temporarily ashore during a voyage (*In the Goods of Lay* (1840) 2 Curteis 375), or on board a ship in harbour in his own country so long as he is " subject to the restraint of the service " of the sea; *In the Goods of McMurdo* (1867) L.R. 1 P. & D. 540. See also *In the Estate of Thomas* (1918) 34 T.L.R. 626, and the cases there cited. Where a seaman made a will ashore, being at the time in contemplation of sailing on a fresh or specific voyage within a very few days, he was held to have been " at sea " when the will was made: *In the Goods of Newland* [1952] P. 71; *In the Goods of Wilson, Wilson* v. *Coleclough* [1952] P. 92, applying *In the Goods of Hale* [1915] 2 I.R. 362. Oral evidence may be given of the contents of a seaman's will, if it cannot be found, to rebut the presumption that it has been destroyed *animo revocandi*: *In the Estate of Wilson, Walker* v. *Treasury Solicitor* (1961) 105 S.J. 531. But words spoken in the course of a casual conversation about family matters would not be sufficient: *In the Estate of Knibbs* [1962] 1 W.L.R. 852. It may be made by a seaman under the age of 18. See the Wills (Soldiers and Sailors) Act 1918, s. 1. Certain restrictions on the power of a seaman to dispose by will of money or property in the charge of the Admiralty have been abolished as from August 14, 1953, except where the death has occurred or the will has been made before that date: Navy and Marine (Wills) Act 1953

(repealing the Navy and Marines (Wills) Acts of 1865, 1930 and 1939). As to the disposal of real estate by a sailor even under 18, see the Wills (Soldiers and Sailors) Act 1918, s. 3.

As to informal written wills of seamen generally, see also *In the Goods of Parker* (1859) 28 L.J.P. 91 (part only of letter testamentary); *In the Goods of D. Saunders* (1865) L.R. 1 P. & D. 16 (naval surgeon returning as passenger).

[5] This means " without leaving a will "; see *Re Skeats, Thain* v. *Gibbs* [1936] Ch. 683. See also the Administration of Estates Act 1925, s. 55 (vi).

Application of sections 62 to 66 to masters

Application of sections 62 to 66 to masters

1438 **67.** In sections 62 to 66 of this Act " seaman " (notwithstanding the definition in section 742 of the Merchant Shipping Act 1894) includes the master of a ship.

Documentation, reports and returns

Official log books

1439 **68.**—(1) Except as provided by regulations [1] under this section an official log book in a form approved by the [Secretary of State for Trade] shall be kept in every ship registered in the United Kingdom.

(2) The [Secretary of State for Trade] may make regulations [2] prescribing the particulars to be entered [3] in official log books, the persons by whom such entries are to be made, signed or witnessed, and the procedure to be followed in the making of such entries and in their amendment or cancellation.[4]

(3) The regulations may require the production or delivery of official log books to such persons, in such circumstances and within such times as may be specified therein.

(4) Regulations under this section may exempt [5] ships of any description from any requirements thereof, either generally or in such circumstances as may be specified in the regulations.

(5) Regulations under this section may make a contravention of any provision thereof an offence punishable on summary conviction with a fine not exceeding £20.

(6) If a person wilfully destroys or mutilates or renders illegible any entry in an official log book he shall be liable on summary conviction to a fine not exceeding £100.

1440 [1] See the M.S. (Official Log Books) Regs. 1972 (S.I. No. 1874) and the M.S. (Official Log Books) (Fishing Vessels) Regs. 1972 (S.I. No. 1873), as amended by S.I. 1975 No. 330.

[2] See note (1). Also see the M.S. (Crew Agreements, Lists of Crew and Discharge of Seamen) Regs. 1972 (S.I. No. 918); the M.S. (Crew Agreements, Lists of Crew and Discharge of Seamen) (Fishing Vessels) Regs. 1972 (S.I. No. 919); the M.S. (Disciplinary Offences) Regs. 1972 (S.I. No. 1294), as amended by S.I. 1974 No. 2047; the M.S. (Repatriation) Regs. 1972 (S.I. No. 1805).

[3] The entry of an offence in the log, though defamatory, is made on a privileged occasion and an action for libel cannot be sustained without proof of malice: see *Moore* v. *Canadian Pacific S.S. Co.* [1945] 1 All E.R. 128; 78 Ll.L.R. 120.

[4] As to the admissibility in evidence and the inspection of official log books, see s. 75 (1) (*b*). Failure to comply with the regulations under subs. (2) does not render the entry inadmissible: see *Robinson* v. *Robson* [1943] 1 K.B. 401.

[5] See s. 97 (6).

Lists of crew

441 **69.**—(1) Except as provided by regulations [1] made under this section the master of every ship registered in the United Kingdom shall make and maintain a list of the crew [2] containing such particulars as may be required by the regulations.

(2) The [Secretary of State for Trade] may make regulations—

(*a*) specifying the particulars to be entered in a list of the crew;

(*b*) limiting the time for which a list of the crew may remain in force;

(*c*) providing for the maintenance by such persons and either in such place as may be specified in the regulations or, if it is so specified, in the ship, of a copy or copies of each list of a crew, and for the notification to such persons of any changes therein;

(*d*) for the production of a list of the crew to such persons, in such circumstances and within such time as may be specified in the regulations; and

(*e*) for the delivery to a superintendent or proper officer [3] or the Registrar General of Shipping and Seamen,[4] in such circumstances as may be specified in the regulations, of a list of the crew or a copy thereof maintained under the regulations and for the notification to him of any changes in such a list.

(3) Regulations under this section may enable a list of the crew to be contained in the same document as a crew agreement [3] and may treat any particulars entered in the crew agreement as forming part of the particulars entered in the list.

(4) Regulations under this section may exempt [5] from the requirements thereof such descriptions of ship as may be specified in the regulations and may make different provision for different circumstances.

(5) Regulations under this section may make a contravention of any provision thereof an offence punishable on summary conviction with a fine not exceeding £20.

442 [1] See the M.S. (Crew Agreements, Lists of Crew and Discharge of Seamen) Regs. 1972 (S.I. No. 918) and the M.S. (Crew Agreements, Lists of Crew and Discharge of Seamen) (Fishing Vessels) Regs. 1972 (S.I. No. 919).

[2] As to the admissibility in evidence and availability for inspection of lists of crew see s. 75 (1).

[3] See s. 97 (1).

[4] See s. 80.

[5] See s. 97 (6).

British seamen's cards

1443 **70.**—(1) The [Secretary of State] may make regulations [1] providing

(*a*) for the issue to British seamen of cards (in this section referred to as " British seamen's cards ") in such form and containing such particulars with respect to the holders thereof and such other particulars (if any) as may be prescribed by the regulations, and for requiring British seamen to apply for such cards;

(*b*) for requiring the holders of British seamen's cards to produce them to such persons and in such circumstances as may be prescribed by the regulations;

(*c*) for the surrender of British seamen's cards in such circumstances as may be prescribed by the regulations;

(*d*) for any incidental or supplementary matters for which the [Secretary of State thinks] it expedient for the purposes of the regulations to provide;

and any provision of the regulations having effect by virtue of paragraph (*a*) of this subsection may be so framed as to apply to all British seamen or any description of them and as to have effect subject to any exemptions [2] for which provision may be made by the regulations.

(2) Regulations under this section may make a contravention of any provision thereof an offence punishable on summary conviction with a fine not exceeding £10.

(3) In this section " British seamen " means persons who are not aliens [3] within the meaning of the British Nationality Act 1948 and are employed, or ordinarily employed, as masters or seamen.

(4) If a person makes a statement which he knows to be false or recklessly makes a statement which is false in a material particular for the purpose of obtaining for himself or another person a British seaman's card he shall be liable on summary conviction to a fine not exceeding £100.

1444 [1] See the M.S. (Seamen's Documents) Regs. 1972 (S.I. No. 1295) as amended by S.I. 1974 No. 1734.

[2] See s. 97 (6).

[3] See the British Nationality Act 1948, s. 32.

Discharge books

1445 **71.**—(1) The [Secretary of State for Trade] may make regulations [1] providing—

(*a*) for the issue to persons who are or have been employed in ships registered in the United Kingdom of discharge books in such form and containing such particulars with respect to the holders thereof and such other particulars (if any) as may be prescribed by the regulations and for requiring such persons to apply for such discharge books;

(*b*) for requiring the holders of discharge books to produce them to such persons and in such circumstances as may be prescribed by the regulations;

(*c*) for the surrender of discharge books in such circumstances as may be prescribed by the regulations;

(*d*) for any incidental or supplementary matters for which the [Secretary of State thinks] it expedient for the purposes of the regulations to provide;

and any provision of the regulations having effect by virtue of paragraph (*a*) of this subsection may be so framed as to apply to all such persons as are mentioned in that paragraph or any description of such persons and as to have effect subject to any exemptions [2] for which provision may be made by the regulations.

(2) Regulations under this section may make a contravention of any provision thereof an offence punishable on summary conviction with a fine not exceeding £10.

[1] See the M.S. (Seamen's Documents) Regs. 1972 (S.I. No. 1295) as amended by S.I. 1974 No. 1734.
[2] See s. 97 (6).

Returns of births and deaths in ships, etc.

1446 **72.**—(1) The [Secretary of State for Trade] may make regulations [1]—

(*a*) requiring the master of any ship registered in the United Kingdom to make a return [2] to a superintendent or proper officer [3] for transmission to the Registrar General of Shipping and Seamen [4] of any birth or death [5] occurring in the ship and of the death, wherever occurring outside the United Kingdom, of any person employed in the ship, and to notify any such death to such person (if any) as the deceased may have named to him as his next of kin; and

(*b*) requiring the master of any ship not registered in the United Kingdom which calls at a port in the United Kingdom in the course of or at the end of a voyage to make a return to a superintendent for transmission to the Registrar General of Shipping and Seamen of any birth or death of a citizen of the United Kingdom and Colonies which has occurred in the ship during the voyage.

(2) Regulations under this section may require the Registrar General of Shipping and Seamen to send a certified copy of any return made thereunder to the Registrar General for England and Wales, the Registrar General of Births, Deaths and Marriages for Scotland or the Registrar General for Northern Ireland, as the case may require.

(3) The Registrar General to whom any such certified copies are sent shall record the information contained therein in a register kept by him for the purpose and to be called the marine register, and may also record in that register such additional information as appears to him desirable for the purpose of ensuring the completeness and correctness of the register; and the enactments relating to the registration of births and deaths in England, Scotland and Northern Ireland shall have effect as if the marine register were a register of births (other than still-births) or deaths or certified copies of entries in such a register and had been transmitted to the Registrar General in accordance with those enactments.[3]

(4) Regulations under the preceding provisions of this section may make a contravention of any provision thereof an offence punishable on summary conviction with a fine not exceeding £20.

(5) Regulations under this section may contain provisions for authorising the registration of the following births and deaths occurring outside the United Kingdom in circumstances where no return is required to be made under the preceding provisions of this section—

(*a*) any birth or death of a citizen of the United Kingdom and Colonies which occurs in a ship not registered in the United Kingdom;

(*b*) any death of a citizen of the United Kingdom and Colonies who has been employed in such a ship which occurs elsewhere than in the ship; and

(*c*) any death of a person who has been employed in a ship registered in the United Kingdom which occurs elsewhere than in the ship.

1447 [1] See the M.S. (Returns of Births and Deaths) Regs. 1972 (S.I. No. 1523).
[2] Such returns are admissible in evidence and, in some circumstances, open to public inspection; see s. 75 (1) (*d*).
[3] See s. 97 (1).
[4] See s. 80.
[5] See s. 97 (5).

Reports of shipping casualties

1448 **73.**[1]—(1) Where any such casualty as is mentioned in section 55 (1) of this Act has occurred in the case of a ship or ship's boat [2] and, at the time it occurred, the ship was registered in the United Kingdom, the owner or master of the ship shall, as soon as practicable, and in any case not later than twenty-four hours after the ship's arrival at the next port, report [3] the casualty to the [Secretary of State for Trade], giving a brief description of it and stating the time and place where it occurred, the name and official number of the ship, its position at the time of the report and the next port of call.

(2) If the owner or master of a ship fails without reasonable cause to comply with the preceding provisions of this section he shall be liable on summary conviction to a fine not exceeding £100.

449 [1] For the duty of the master of a British ship registered in the U.K. to send information about dangers to navigation encountered on the voyage, see M.S. (Safety and Load Line Conventions) Act 1932, s. 24.
[2] See s. 97 (1).
[3] Provided a report is sent under this section, in the case of a boiler explosion, no further notice is required under the Boiler Explosions Act 1882: see the Boiler Explosions Act 1890, s. 2.

Handing over of documents on change of master

450 **74.** If a person ceases to be the master of a ship registered in the United Kingdom during a voyage of the ship he shall deliver to his successor the documents relating to the ship or its crew which are in his custody; and if he fails without reasonable cause to do so he shall be liable on summary conviction to a fine not exceeding £100.

Admissibility in evidence and inspection of certain documents

75.—(1) The following documents shall be admissible in evidence and, when in the custody of the Registrar General of Shipping and Seamen,[1] shall be open to public inspection, that is to say,—

(*a*) crew agreements,[2] lists of crews made under section 69 of this Act and notices given under this Act of additions to or changes in crew agreements and lists of crews;

(*b*) the official log book of any ship kept under section 68 of this Act and, without prejudice to section 695 (2) of the Merchant Shipping Act 1894, any document purporting to be a copy of an entry therein and to be certified as a true copy by the master of the ship;

(*c*) documents purporting to be submissions to or decisions by superintendents or proper officers [2] under section 10 of this Act;

(*d*) returns or reports under section 72 of this Act or under regulations made under section 19 of this Act.

(2) A certificate issued under section 43 of this Act shall be admissible in evidence.

[1] See s. 80.
[2] See s. 97.

Inspections

Inspections

451 **76.**—(1) For the purpose of seeing that the provisions of the Merchant Shipping Acts [1] and regulations and rules made thereunder are duly complied with any of the following persons, that is to say,—

(*a*) a surveyor of ships;

(*b*) a superintendent;

(*c*) any person appointed by the [Secretary of State for Trade], either generally or in a particular case, to exercise powers under this section;

may at all reasonable times [2] go on board a ship and inspect the ship and its equipment or any part thereof, any articles on board, and any document carried in the ship in pursuance of the Merchant Shipping Acts or regulations or rules made thereunder; and if the ship is registered in the United Kingdom the powers conferred by this subsection may also be exercised outside the United Kingdom and may be so exercised by a proper officer [3] as well as by the persons mentioned in paragraphs (*a*) to (*c*) of this subsection.

(2) A person exercising powers under this section shall not unnecessarily detain or delay a ship but may, if he considers it necessary in consequence of an accident or for any other reason, require a ship to be taken into dock for a survey of its hull or machinery.

(3) Where any such person as is mentioned in paragraphs (*a*) to (*c*) of subsection (1) of this section has reasonable grounds for believing [4] that there are on any premises provisions or water intended for supply to a ship registered in the United Kingdom which, if provided on the ship, would not be in accordance with regulations under section 21 of this Act, he may enter the premises and inspect the provisions or water for the purpose of ascertaining whether they would be in accordance with those regulations.

(4) If any person obstructs a person in the exercise of his powers under this section, or fails to comply with a requirement made under subsection (2) thereof, he shall be liable on summary conviction to a fine not exceeding £100.

1452 [1] See § 1639.
[2] See, for instance, *Small* v. *Bickley* (1875) 32 L.T. 726.
[3] See s. 97 (1).
[4] The person must both have reasonable grounds for believing and actually believe; see *R.* v. *Banks* [1916] 2 K.B. 621; *R.* v. *Harrison* [1938] 3 All E.R. 134.

Stowaways, unauthorised presence on board ship and master's power of arrest

Stowaways

1453 77.—(1) If a person, without the consent of the master or of any other person authorised to give it, goes to sea [1] or attempts to go to sea in a ship registered in the United Kingdom he shall be liable on summary conviction to a fine not exceeding £100 or to imprisonment for a period not exceeding three months.[2]

(2) Nothing in section 686 of the Merchant Shipping Act 1894 shall be taken to limit the jurisdiction of any court in the United Kingdom to deal with an offence under this section which has been committed in a country outside the United Kingdom by a person who is not a British subject.[3]

[1] See s. 97 (2).
[2] Accordingly there is no right to claim trial by jury: see the Magistrates' Courts Act 1952, s. 25.

[3] The offence is a continuing one and hence it can be regarded as committed on board a ship on the high seas, thus giving jurisdiction under s. 686 (1) in respect of a person who is not a British subject: *Robey* v. *Vladinier* (1935) 53 Ll.L.R. 121.

Unauthorised presence on board ship

1454 **78.** Where a ship registered in the United Kingdom or any other country is in a port in the United Kingdom and a person who is neither in Her Majesty's service nor authorised [1] by law to do so—

(*a*) goes on board the ship without the consent of the master or of any other person authorised to give it; or

(*b*) remains on board the ship after being requested to leave by the master, a constable,[2] or an officer of the [Secretary of State for Trade] or of customs and excise;

he shall be liable on summary conviction to a fine not exceeding £20.

[1] Some instances of persons being authorised to go on board ships for specified purposes are to be found in Harbours, Docks, and Piers Clauses Act 1847, s. 44; Public Health Act 1936, s. 267; Explosives Act 1875, s. 75; the Petroleum (Consolidation) Act 1928, s. 18; Diseases of Animals Act 1950, s. 73; Foreign Enlistment Act 1870, s. 23; Customs and Excise Act 1952, s. 19; M.S.A. 1894, ss. 536, 684, 685, 692, 696; Prevention of Damage by Pests Act 1949, s. 23. As to proof of authorisation, see s. 697.

[2] This means the office not the rank of constable; see Halsbury's *Laws*, Vol. 30, p. 97 and the Police Act 1964, s. 18.

Master's power of arrest

1455 **79.** The master of any ship registered in the United Kingdom may cause any person on board the ship to be put under restraint if and for so long as it appears to him necessary or expedient in the interest of safety or for the preservation of good order or discipline on board the ship.

Quite apart from these statutory powers, a master has authority over his crew to enforce obedience to his lawful commands for the navigation of the ship and preservation of good order; *Lamb* v. *Burnett* (1831) 1 Cr. & J. 291, *The Lima* (1837) 3 Hagg.Adm. 346. He is justified in arresting and confining in a reasonable manner and for a reasonable time any person on board his ship if (1) he has reasonable cause to believe that such arrest or confinement is necessary for the preservation of order and discipline or for the safety of the vessel or the persons or property on board and (2) he in fact believes that the arrest or confinement is so necessary; *Hook* v. *Cunard Steamship Co.* [1953] 1 W.L.R. 682; [1953] 1 All E.R. 1021.

For the jurisdiction of the English courts over crimes committed on board ships, see ss. 686, 687 and notes thereto, and the full treatment of this topic in Archbold, *Criminal Pleading, etc.*, 38th ed., paras. 81–87.

For an interesting article on the history of the master's disciplinary powers, see 34 L.Q.R. 347.

Administrative provisions

Registrar General of Shipping and Seamen

1456 **80.**—(1) The [Secretary of State for Trade] shall appoint, and may remove, an officer to be styled the Registrar General of Shipping and Seamen, who shall exercise such functions as are conferred on him by the Merchant Shipping Acts and keep such records and perform such other duties as the [Secretary of State for Trade] may direct.

(2) The [Secretary of State for Trade] may appoint and remove persons to perform on behalf of the Registrar General of Shipping and Seamen such of his functions as the Board or the Registrar General of Shipping and Seamen may direct.

Appointment of Superintendents

1457 **81.** The [Secretary of State for Trade] shall appoint, and may remove, officers to be styled mercantile marine superintendents, who shall exercise the functions conferred on superintendents by the Merchant Shipping Acts.[1]

[1] See § 1639.

Appointment of wreck commissioners

1458 **82.**—(1) The Lord Chancellor may appoint such number of persons as he thinks fit to be wreck commissioners and may remove any wreck commissioners appointed by him.

(2) Before appointing a person to act as wreck commissioner in Northern Ireland the Lord Chancellor shall consult the Lord Chief Justice of Northern Ireland.

Remuneration of wreck commissioners and assessors

1459 **83.** There shall be paid to any wreck commissioner or assessor appointed under this Act such remuneration, out of moneys provided by Parliament, as the Lord Chancellor may with the consent of the Treasury determine.

Fees

1460 **84.** The [Secretary of State for Trade] may with the consent of the Treasury make regulations [1] prescribing fees to be paid in respect of the issue or recording of any certificate, licence or other document or the doing of any other thing in pursuance of this Act.

[1] See the M.S. (Fees for Seamen's Documents) Regs. 1972 (S.I. No. 1930) as amended by S.I. 1974 No. 1777. See also s. 99.

Miscellaneous

Amendment of Merchant Shipping (Safety Convention) Act 1949

1461 **85.**—(1) *For sections* 3 *and* 6 *of the Merchant Shipping (Safety Convention) Act* 1949 *there shall be substituted the sections set out in Schedule* 1 *to this Act.*

(2) *In section* 5 (2) *of that Act (rules for direction finders) the words "being ships of sixteen hundred tons gross tonnage or upwards" shall be omitted.*

(3) *Before making rules* [1] *under any of those sections the [Secretary of State for Trade] shall consult with organisations in the United Kingdom appearing to them representative of persons who will be affected by the rules.*

[1] See the M.S. (Radio) (Fishing Vessels) Rules 1974 (S.I. No. 1919).

Nautical publications

1462 **86.**—(1) *The [Secretary of State for Trade] may make rules* [1] *specifying such charts, directions or information as appear to the [Secretary of State] necessary or expedient for the safe operation of ships and those rules may require ships registered in the United Kingdom, or such descriptions of ships registered in the United Kingdom as may be specified in the rules, to carry, either at all times or on such voyages as may be specified in the rules, copies of the charts, directions or information so specified.*

(2) *If a ship goes to sea* [1] *or attempts to go to sea without carrying copies of the charts, directions or information which it is required to carry by rules under this section the master or owner shall be liable on summary conviction to a fine not exceeding* £100.

This section and the preceding section came into force in November 1974, by virtue of the M.S.A. 1970 (Commencement No. 3) Order, 1974 S.I. No. 1908.

[1] See the M.S. (Carriage of Nautical Publications) Rules 1975 S.I. No. 700.

[2] See s. 97 (1).

The merchant navy uniform

1463 **87.**—(1) *The [Secretary of State for Trade] may make regulations prescribing a uniform, to be known as the merchant navy uniform,*[1] *for the use of persons serving in ships registered in the United Kingdom, and distinguishing marks to be worn, as part of the uniform, by persons so serving in different positions or in different circumstances.*

(2) *Regulations under this section may prescribe the persons by whom and the circumstances in which the merchant navy uniform or any part of it may be worn.*

(3) *If a person wears the merchant navy uniform or any part of it, or wears anything bearing the appearance of the uniform or any part of it, when he is not authorised by regulations under this section to wear the uniform or that part he shall be liable on summary conviction to a fine not exceeding* £50.

(4) *Where any design,*[2] *within the meaning of the Registered Designs Act* 1949, *which forms part of the merchant navy uniform has been registered under that Act* [3] *and the [Secretary of State for Trade is] the registered proprietor thereof [his] copyright in the design shall, notwithstanding section* 8 *of that Act, continue so long as the design remains so registered.*

(5) *Nothing in this section shall prohibit or restrict the use of the merchant navy uniform or any part of it for the purposes of any stage, film or television performance, unless the use is such as to bring the uniform into disrepute.*

This section is not yet in force.

1464 [1] This section in its application to fishing vessels has effect as if the words " fishing fleet uniform " were substituted for the words " merchant navy uniform ": see s. 95 (3).
[2] See the Registered Designs Act 1949, s. 8.
[3] The registration of any design under Part II of the Patents and Designs Act 1907 is to be deemed to be a registration under the 1949 Act: see s. 100 (2) and Sched. 4, para. 10.

Increase of penalty for sailing while ship under detention

1465 **88.** In section 692 (1) of the Merchant Shipping Act 1894 (enforcing detention of ship) for the words " one hundred pounds " there shall be substituted the words " two hundred pounds ".

This section applies to non-sea-going ships: see s. 96 (1).

Dealing with deserters under reciprocal arrangements

1466 **89.**[1]—(1) Subject to subsection (5) of this section, this section applies to any country to which, immediately before the coming into operation of the repeal by this Act of section 238 of the Merchant Shipping Act 1894, that section applied by virtue of an Order in Council [2] made under it or having effect as if made under it.

(2) Where a seaman deserts in the United Kingdom from a ship registered in a country to which this section applies, a justice of the peace may, on the application of a consular officer of that country and on information on oath, issue a warrant for the arrest of the seaman.

(3) Where a seaman has been arrested on a warrant issued under this section a magistrates' court may, on proof of the desertion, order him to be conveyed on board his ship.

(4) Where a seaman is liable to be arrested under this section, any person who, knowing or believing that he has deserted, does without lawful authority or reasonable excuse any act with intent to impede his arrest shall be liable on summary conviction to a fine not exceeding £20.

(5) Her Majesty may by Order in Council direct that this section shall cease to apply to any country specified in the Order.

(6) In its application to Scotland this section shall have effect as if for the reference to a justice of the peace there were substituted a reference to a sheriff, magistrate or justice of the peace, for the reference to a magistrates' court a reference to a court of summary jurisdiction within the meaning of the Summary Jurisdiction (Scotland) Act 1954, and for the reference to information on oath a reference to evidence on oath.

(7) In its application to Northern Ireland this section shall have effect as if in subsection (3) for the reference to a magistrates' court there were substituted a reference to a court of summary jurisdiction.

[1] This section is excluded in relation to fishing vessels by s. 95 (1).
[2] Orders in Council now in force under this section are as follows:
Brazil, Nov. 28, 1888; Colombia, Dec. 28, 1866; Denmark (M.S. (Foreign Deserters) (Kingdom of Denmark) Order 1963 (No. 375)); Estonia and Finland, Aug. 14, 1934 (S.R. & O. 1934 No. 893); Federal Republic of Germany (M.S. (Foreign Deserters) (Federal Republic of Germany) Order 1958 (No. 142)); Greece (M.S. (Foreign Deserters)

(Kingdom of Greece) Order 1954 (No. 144)); Italian Republic (M.S. (Foreign Deserters) (Italian Republic) Order 1958 (No. 143)); Japan, Oct. 3, 1911 (S.R. & O. 1911 No. 961); Latvia, Aug. 14, 1934 (S.R. & O. 1934 No. 893); United States of Mexico (M.S. (Foreign Deserters) (United States of Mexico) Order 1955 (No. 426)); Netherlands, March 9, 1854; Nicaragua, March 1, 1907 (S.R. & O. 1907 No. 162); Norway (M.S. (Foreign Deserters) (Kingdom of Norway) Order 1951 (No. 1942)); Peru, Aug. 18, 1852; Portugal, Aug. 14, 1934 (S.R. & O. 1934 No. 893); Roumania, Feb. 29, 1908 (S.R. & O. 1908 Nos. 204, 205); Spain (M.S. (Foreign Deserters) (Spanish State) Order 1963 (No. 617)); Turkey, May 18, 1865; Yugoslavia, Aug. 14, 1934 (S.R. & O. 1934 No. 893); Belgium, 1964 S.I. No. 1403.

Adaptation to metric units

467 **90.**[1] The [Secretary of State for Trade] may by regulations [2] provide for such adaptations of any enactments contained in the Merchant Shipping Acts [3] as appear to them appropriate for the purpose of replacing references therein to units other than metric units by references to metric units which are either equivalent thereto or such approximations thereto as appear to the [Secretary of State] desirable for the purpose of securing that the enactments as adapted are expressed in convenient terms.

1 This section applies to non-sea-going ships; see s. 96 (1).
2 See the M.S. (Metrication) Regulations 1973 (S.I. No. 1979).
3 See § 1639.

Tonnage measurement and certificates

468 **91.**[1] *For subsections* (5) *and* (6) *of section 1 of the Merchant Shipping Act* 1965 (*tonnage regulations*) *there shall be substituted the following subsections—*

" (5) *Regulations under this section may make provision for the alteration* (*notwithstanding section* 82 *of the principal Act*) *of the particulars relating to the registered tonnage* [2] *of a ship.*

(6) *Regulations under this section may provide for the issue by the* [*Secretary of State for Trade*] *or by persons appointed by such organisations as may be authorised in that behalf by the* [*Secretary of State for Trade*] *of certificates of the registered tonnage of any ship or of the tonnage which is to be taken for any purpose specified in the regulations as the tonnage of a ship not registered in the United Kingdom, and for the cancellation and delivery up of such certificates in such circumstances as may be prescribed by the regulations.*

(6A) *Regulations under this section requiring the delivery up of any certificate may make a failure to comply with the requirement an offence punishable on summary conviction with a fine not exceeding* £100."

This section is not yet in force.

469 1 This section applies to non-sea-going ships; see s. 96 (1).
2 In a limitation action, evidence that the registered tonnage is not the correct tonnage is admissible; see *The Recepla* (1889) 14 P.D. 131.

Unregistered ships and ships registered outside the United Kingdom

Unregistered British ships

1470 **92.** The [Secretary of State for Trade] may make regulations [1] specifying any description of British ships which are not registered in the United Kingdom or elsewhere and directing that such of the provisions of this Act and of regulations and rules made thereunder as may be specified in the regulations shall extend to ships of that description and to masters and seamen employed in them, with such exceptions, adaptations or modifications as may be so specified.

[1] See the M.S. (Unregistered Ships) Regs. 1972 (S.I. No. 1876) and the M.S. (Unregistered Fishing Vessels) Regs. 1972 (S.I. No. 1877).

Ships registered in independent Commonwealth countries

1471 **93.**[1]—(1) Her Majesty may by Order in Council direct that such of the provisions of this Act and of regulations and rules made thereunder as may be specified in the Order shall extend, with such exceptions, adaptations or modifications as may be so specified, to ships registered in any independent Commonwealth country so specified and to masters and seamen employed in them.

(2) The modifications that may be made by an Order in Council under this section with respect to the ships registered in any country and the masters and seamen employed in them include the substitution, for any provision of this Act or of regulations or rules made thereunder, of a corresponding provision of the law of that country, with such exceptions, adaptations or modifications as appear to Her Majesty expedient.

(3) In this section " independent Commonwealth country " means any country for the time being specified in section 1 (3) of the British Nationality Act 1948.[2]

1472 [1] This section is excluded in relation to fishing vessels by s. 95 (1).
[2] See also note (3) to the M.S.A. 1894, s. 1.

Power to extend Act to certain territories outside the United Kingdom, and to ships registered therein

1473 **94.** Her Majesty may by Order in Council give with respect to any of the following territories, that is to say—

(*a*) the Isle of Man;

(*b*) any of the Channel Islands;

(*c*) any colony;

(*d*) any territory outside Her Majesty's dominions in which for the time being Her Majesty has jurisdiction;

either or both of the following directions—

(i) that such of the provisions of this Act and of regulations and rules made thereunder as may be specified in the Order shall apply to ships registered in that territory and to masters and seamen employed in them, with such exceptions, adaptations or modifications as may be specified in the Order, as they apply to ships registered in the United Kingdom and to masters and seamen employed in them;

(ii) that such of the provisions of this Act and of any regulations and rules made thereunder as may be specified in the Order shall extend to that territory, with such exceptions, adaptations or modifications as may be specified in the Order, as part of the law of that territory.

Fishing vessels and non-sea-going ships

Fishing vessels

74 **95.**—(1) In the application of this Act to fishing vessels [1] and persons serving in them—

(*a*) sections 6, [30 and] 32, 34 to 38, 89 and 93 do not apply and the provisions contained in Part I of Schedule 2 to this Act apply in addition to the other provisions of this Act; and

(*b*) sections 7 and 8 apply as set out in Part II of that Schedule;

and nothing in Schedule 2 to this Act applies to fishing vessels not registered in the United Kingdom or to persons serving in them.

(2) *Section* 15 *of this Act does not apply to so much of the wages* [2] *of a seaman employed in a fishing vessel as is in any manner related to the catch.* [3]

(3) *In its application to persons serving in fishing vessels section* 87 *of this Act shall have effect as if for the words* " *merchant navy uniform* ", *wherever they occur, there were substituted the words* " *fishing fleet uniform* ". [3]

(4) Nothing in section 11 of this Act shall affect the operation of Part II of the Administration of Justice Act 1970 in relation to wages due to a person employed in a fishing vessel; and the provisions of the Magistrates' Courts Act (Northern Ireland) 1964 and the Judgments (Enforcement) Act (Northern Ireland) 1969 relating to the attachment of wages shall apply in relation to such wages as they apply in relation to other wages.

(5) The [Secretary of State for Trade] may grant exemptions from any requirements of this Act or of any regulations made under this Act—

(*a*) with respect to any fishing vessel or to a fishing vessel of any description; or (*b*) with respect to any person or a person of any description serving in a fishing vessel or in a fishing vessel of any description;

and nothing in any other provision of this Act conferring a power to provide for or grant exemptions shall be taken to restrict the power conferred by this subsection.

(6) In this Act " fishing vessel " means a vessel which is for the time being employed in sea fishing, but does not include a vessel used otherwise than for profit.[4]

[1] See subs. (6).
[2] See notes to s. 7.
[3] This subsection is not yet in force.
[4] *Cf.* the definition of fishing vessel in the M.S.A. 1894, s. 370 (as amended by s. 100 (3), Sched. 5 of this Act) which no longer distinguishes between those vessels which catch fish for a profit and those which do not.

Non-sea-going ships

1475 **96.**—(1) The preceding provisions of this Act other than sections 19, 20, 43 to 60, 88, 90 and 91 do not apply to ships which are not sea-going ships[1] or to masters or seamen employed in ships which are not sea-going ships.

(2) In relation to ships which are not sea-going ships section 45 of this Act shall have effect as if for the words " goes to sea or attempts to go to sea " there were substituted the words " plies or attempts to ply " and the words " if in the United Kingdom " were omitted; and where such a ship may be detained in pursuance of that section, section 692 of the Merchant Shipping Act 1894 shall have effect, in relation to it, as if subsections (2) to (4) were omitted and in subsection (1) for the words " proceeds to sea " there were substituted the word " plies ", for the words " sends the ship to sea " there were substituted the words " causes the ship to ply " and the words " any British consular officer " were omitted.

[1] See s. 97 (2). A " sea-going " ship is one that in fact goes to sea, and not merely could go to sea; hence a steamer of 142 tons gross register, exclusively used to carry salt on the River Weaver and the tidal water of the River Mersey, but not beyond the port of Liverpool, was held not a " sea-going " ship within the M.S.A. 1854, s. 109; see *The Salt Union* v. *Wood* [1893] 1 Q.B. 370.

Supplementary

Interpretation

1476 **97.**—(1) In this Act—

" crew agreement " has the meaning assigned to it by section 1 (2) of this Act;

" enactment " includes an enactment of the Parliament of Northern Ireland;

" proper officer " means a consular officer appointed by Her Majesty's Government in the United Kingdom and, in relation to a port in a country outside the United Kingdom which is not a foreign country, also any officer exercising in that port functions similar to those of a superintendent;

" relief and maintenance " includes the provision of surgical or medical treatment and such dental and optical treatment (including the repair or replacement of any appliance) as cannot be postponed without impairing efficiency;

" ship's boat " includes a life-raft; and

" the Merchant Shipping Acts " means the Merchant Shipping Acts 1894 to 1967, the Fishing Vessels (Safety Provisions) Act 1970 and this Act.

(2) References in this Act to going to sea include references to going to sea from any country outside the United Kingdom.

(3) For the purposes of this Act a seaman is discharged from a ship when his employment in that ship is terminated.

(4) For the purposes of this Act a seaman discharged from a ship in any country and left there shall be deemed to be left behind in that country notwithstanding that the ship also remains there.

(5) References in this Act to dying in a ship include references to dying in a ship's boat and to being lost from a ship or ship's boat.

(6) Any power conferred by this Act to provide for or grant an exemption includes power to provide for or grant the exemption subject to conditions.

(7) If the Parliament of Northern Ireland passes provisions amending or replacing any enactment of that Parliament referred to in this Act the reference shall be construed as a reference to the enactment as so amended or, as the case may be, as a reference to those provisions.

Expenses and receipts

1477 **98.**—(1) Any expenses incurred by the [Secretary of State for Trade] under this Act shall be defrayed out of moneys provided by Parliament.

(2) Any fees received by the [Secretary of State for Trade] under this Act shall be paid into the Consolidated Fund.

Regulations and rules

1478 **99.**—(1) Any regulations or rules made under this Act shall be made by statutory instrument, which, except in the case of regulations made under section 36 of this Act or paragraph 2 of Schedule 2 to this Act, shall be subject to annulment in pursuance of a resolution of either House of Parliament.

(2) Before making regulations under any provision of this Act other than sections 84 and 90 the [Secretary of State for Trade] shall consult with organisations in the United Kingdom appearing to them repre-

sentative of masters and seamen who will be affected by the regulations and of persons employing such masters and seamen.

Amendments, savings, transitional provisions and repeals

1479 **100.**—(1) The enactments mentioned in Schedule 3 to this Act shall have effect subject to the minor and consequential amendments specified therein.

(2) This Act shall have effect subject to the savings and transitional provisions contained in Schedule 4 to this Act.

(3) The enactments specified in Schedule 5 to this Act (which include some which are obsolete and some not affected by the preceding provisions of this Act) are hereby repealed to the extent specified in the third column of that Schedule.

Citation, construction and commencement

1480 **101.**—(1) This Act may be cited as the Merchant Shipping Act 1970.

(2) This Act, the Merchant Shipping Acts 1894 to 1967 and the Fishing Vessels (Safety Provisions) Act 1970 may be cited together as the Merchant Shipping Acts 1894 to 1970.

(3) This Act shall be construed as one [1] with the Merchant Shipping Acts 1894 to 1967 and the Fishing Vessels (Safety Provisions) Act 1970.

(4) This Act shall come into force on such date as the [Secretary of State for Trade] may by order made by statutory instrument appoint, and different days may be so appointed for different provisions of this Act.[2]

[1] See §§ 1530 and 1639.

[2] See the M.S.A. 1970 (Commencement No. 1) Order 1972 (S.I. No. 1977), the M.S.A. 1970 (Commencement No. 2) Order 1974 (S.I. No. 1194) and the M.S.A. 1970 (Commencement No. 3) Order 1974 (S.I. No. 1908).

SCHEDULES

Section 85 *SCHEDULE* 1

Sections substituted for sections 3 *and* 6 *of Merchant Shipping* (*Safety Convention*) *Act* 1949

Radio rules

1481 3.—(1) *The* [*Secretary of State for Trade*] *may make rules* (*in this Act called* " *radio rules* ") *requiring ships to which this section applies to be provided with radio equipment of such a nature* (*but not including a radio navigational aid*) *as may be prescribed by the rules and to maintain such a radio service and to carry such number of radio officers or operators, of such grades and possessing such qualifications, as may be so prescribed*; *and the rules may contain provisions for preventing so far as practicable electrical interference by other apparatus on board with the equipment provided under the rules.*

(2) *This section applies to—*

- (*a*) *sea-going ships registered in the United Kingdom*;
- (*b*) *other sea-going ships while they are in the United Kingdom or the territorial waters thereof.*

(3) *Radio rules shall include such requirements as appear to the* [*Secretary of State for Trade*] *to implement the provisions of the Convention for the Safety of Life at Sea signed in London on* 17*th June* 1960 *as from time to time amended, so far as those provisions relate to radio telegraphy and radio telephony.*

(4) *Without prejudice to the generality of the preceding provisions of this section, radio rules may—*

- (*a*) *prescribe the duties of radio officers and operators, including the duty of keeping a radio log-book*;
- (*b*) *apply to any radio log-book required to be kept under the rules any of the provisions of any regulations with respect to official log-books made under section* 68 *of the Merchant Shipping Act* 1970.

(5) *If any radio officer or operator contravenes any rules made in pursuance of subsection* (4) (*a*) *of this section, he shall be liable to a fine not exceeding* £10; *and if radio rules are contravened in any other respect in relation to any ship, the owner or master of the ship shall be liable on conviction on indictment to a fine not exceeding* £500, *or on summary conviction to a fine not exceeding* £100.

(6) *If a ship to which this section applies is not provided with radio equipment or radio officers or operators in conformity with radio rules the ship if in the United Kingdom may be detained.*

Radio navigational aids

482 6.—(1) *The* [*Secretary of State for Trade*] *may make rules—*

- (*a*) *requiring ships to which this section applies to be provided with such radio navigational aids,*[1] *other than direction-finders, as may be specified in the rules and prescribing requirements which such radio navigational aids are to comply with*;
- (*b*) *prescribing requirements which radio navigational aids, other than direction-finders and other than such as are provided in pursuance of rules made under the preceding paragraph, are to comply with when carried in ships to which this section applies*;
- (*c*) *prescribing requirements which apparatus designed for the purpose of transmitting or reflecting signals to or from radio navigational aids is to comply with if it is apparatus in the*

United Kingdom or apparatus off the shores of the United Kingdom but maintained from the United Kingdom;

and the requirements prescribed under paragraph (a) or (b) of this subsection may include requirements relating to the position and method of fitting of the radio navigational aids.

(2) *This section applies to—*

(*a*) *ships registered in the United Kingdom;*

(*b*) *other ships while they are within any port in the United Kingdom.*

(3) *If a ship to which this section applies proceeds, or attempts to proceed, to sea without carrying such navigational aids as it is required to carry by rules made under subsection* (1) *of this section or carrying radio navigational aids not complying with rules made under that subsection, the owner or master of the ship shall be liable on summary conviction to a fine not exceeding* £100.

(4) *If any person establishes or operates any such apparatus as is mentioned in subsection* (1) (*c*) *of this section and the apparatus does not comply with rules made thereunder, he shall be liable on summary conviction to a fine not exceeding* £100.

This Schedule came into force in November 1974 by virtue of the M.S.A. 1970 (Commencement No. 3) Order 1974 (S.I. No. 1908).

[1] For the meaning, see the M.S. (Safety Convention) Act 1949, s. 36 (1).

SCHEDULE 2

FISHING VESSELS

PART I

ADDITIONAL PROVISIONS

Regulations relating to crew agreements

1483 1.—(1) The [Secretary of State for Trade] may make regulations [1] prescribing the procedure to be followed in connection with the making of crew agreements between persons employed in fishing vessels [2] and persons employing them and prescribing the places where such crew agreements are to be made or where an agreement with any person may be added to those contained in such a crew agreement.

(2) Regulations under this paragraph may make a contravention of any provision thereof an offence punishable on summary conviction with a fine not exceeding £50 or such less amount as may be specified in the regulations.

Offences

2.[3]—(1) *For the purpose of maintaining discipline on board fishing vessels and ensuring the safe and efficient operation of such vessels the*

[*Secretary of State for Trade*] *may by regulations specify any misconduct on board of or in relation to a fishing vessel which, but for section* 95 (1) (*a*) *of this Act, would be an offence under section* 29, 30 *or* 31 *thereof, and provide for its being an offence punishable on summary conviction with a fine not exceeding* £100 *or such less amount as may be specified in the regulations.*

(2) *Regulations under this paragraph may apply section* 32 *of this Act with such modifications as may be required to substitute in it for the reference to section* 29, 30 (*b*) *and* 30 (*c*) *of this Act a reference to the corresponding provisions of the regulations.*

(3) *Regulations under this paragraph may make different provision for different descriptions of fishing vessel or fishing vessels of the same description in different circumstances.*

(4) *No regulations shall be made under this paragraph unless a draft thereof has been laid before Parliament and approved by resolution of each House of Parliament.*

Production of certificates and other documents of qualification

484 3. *Any person serving or engaged to serve in a fishing vessel and holding any certificate or other document which is evidence that he is qualified for the purposes of section* 43 *of this Act shall on demand produce it to any person who is a British sea-fishery officer for the purposes of the Sea Fisheries Acts* (*within the meaning of the Sea Fisheries Act* 1968); *and if he fails to do so without reasonable cause he shall be liable on summary conviction to a fine not exceeding* £20.

Hours of work

485 4.—(1) *The* [*Secretary of State for Trade*] *may make regulations prescribing maximum periods of duty and minimum periods of rest for seamen employed in fishing vessels, and such regulations may make different provision for different descriptions of fishing vessels or seamen employed in them or for fishing vessels and seamen of the same description in different circumstances.*

(2) *If any provision of regulations made under this paragraph is contravened in the case of any seaman employed in a fishing vessel the persons employing him and the master shall each be liable on summary conviction to a fine not exceeding* £100.

Reports of and inquiries into injuries

486 5.—(1) *Where the master or a member of the crew of a fishing vessel is injured during a voyage, an inquiry into the cause and nature of the injury may be held by a superintendent or proper officer.*

(2) *The superintendent or proper officer holding an inquiry under this section shall for the purposes of the inquiry have the powers conferred on an*

inspector by section 729 of the Merchant Shipping Act 1894 *and shall make a report of his findings to the* [*Secretary of State for Trade*].

[1] See the M.S. (Crew Agreements, Lists of Crew and Discharge of Seamen)(Fishing Vessels) Regs. 1972 (S.I. No. 919).

[2] See s. 95 (6).

[3] Paras. 2–5 of Sched. 2, Pt. I are not yet in force.

PART II

SECTIONS 7 AND 8 SET OUT AS THEY APPLY TO FISHING VESSELS AND PERSONS EMPLOYED IN THEM

Payment of seamen's wages

1487 7. Except as provided by or under this Act or any other enactment, the wages due to a seaman under a crew agreement relating to a fishing vessel [1] shall be paid to him in full.

Accounts of wages and catch

1488 8.—(1) Subject to regulations made under section 9 or 62 of this Act, the persons employing any seaman under a crew agreement relating to a fishing vessel shall deliver to him at a time prescribed by regulations under this section an account of the wages due to him under that crew agreement and of the deductions subject to which the wages are payable.

(2) Where the wages of any person employed in a fishing vessel are in any manner related to the catch the persons employing him shall at a time prescribed by regulations under this section deliver to the master an account (or, if the master is the person employing him, make out an account) showing how those wages (or any part thereof related to the catch) are arrived at and shall make the account available to the crew in such manner as may be prescribed by the regulations.

(3) Where there is a partnership between the master and any members of the crew of a fishing vessel the owner of the vessel shall at a time prescribed by regulations under this section make out an account showing the sums due to each partner in respect of his share and shall make the account available to the partners.

(4) The [Secretary of State for Trade] may make regulations prescribing the time at which any account required by this section is to be delivered or made out and the manner in which the account required by subsection (2) or (3) of this section is to be made available.

(5) If a person fails without reasonable cause to comply with the preceding provisions of this section he shall be liable on summary conviction to a fine not exceeding £20.

[1] See s. 95 (6).

SCHEDULE 3

Section 100

MINOR AND CONSEQUENTIAL AMENDMENTS

The Conspiracy and Protection of Property Act 1875

489 1. For section 16 of the Conspiracy and Protection of Property Act 1875 there shall be substituted the following section:—

" 16. Section 5 of this Act does not apply to seamen."

The Merchant Shipping Act 1894

2. In subsection (1) of section 689 of the Merchant Shipping Act 1894 for the words " seamen or apprentice ", in both places, there shall be substituted the words " or seaman ".

3. In subsection (1) of section 695 of that Act, after the words " shall be evidence " there shall be inserted the words " and in Scotland sufficient evidence "; and in subsection (2) of that section, after the words " admissible in evidence " there shall be inserted the words " and be evidence, and in Scotland sufficient evidence, of those matters ".

4. In section 742 of that Act, in the definition of " seaman ", for the words " masters, pilots and apprentices duly indentured and registered " there shall be substituted the words " masters and pilots ".

The Pilotage Act 1913

5. *In section* 17 (1) (*l*) *of the Pilotage Act* 1913 *for the words from " a mate's certificate " to "* 1894 *" there shall be substituted the words " such certificate issued under the Merchant Shipping Act* 1970 *as may be specified in the byelaws ".*

6. *In paragraph* (*b*) *of the proviso to section* 23 (1) *of that Act for the words from " a mate's certificate " to "* 1894 *" there shall be substituted the words " such certificate issued under the Merchant Shipping Act* 1970 *as is specified in the byelaw " and for the words " such a certificate of competency " there shall be substituted the words " a certificate so specified ".*

7. *In section* 25 *of that Act for the words " certificates of competency recognised under Part II of the Merchant Shipping Act* 1894 *" there shall be substituted the words " certificates issued under the Merchant Shipping Act* 1970 *".*

The Illegal Trawling (*Scotland*) *Act* 1934

8. In section 1 (6) of the Illegal Trawling (Scotland) Act 1934 for the words " at each mercantile marine office " there shall be substituted the words " at the office of each mercantile marine superintendent ".

The Pensions (Navy, Army, Air Force and Mercantile Marine) Act 1939

1490 9. In section 6 (3) of the Pensions (Navy, Army, Air Force and Mercantile Marine) Act 1939, for the words from " section one hundred and seventy-six " to " deceased seamen " there shall be substituted the words " section 66 of the Merchant Shipping Act 1970 (disposal of property of deceased seamen) ".

The Merchant Shipping Act 1964

10. *For subsection* (2) *of section* 10 *of the Merchant Shipping Act* 1964 *there shall be substituted the following subsection—*

" (2) *Subsection* (6) *of section* 3 *of the Act of* 1949 (*detention of ships not conforming with radio rules*) *shall apply in relation to the portable radio apparatus so required to be carried by the boats or life rafts on any ship as it applies in relation to the radio equipment of the ship.*"

The Administration of Estates (Small Payments) Act 1965

11. In section 6 of the Administration of Estates (Small Payments) Act 1965 there shall be added at the end of subsection (1) (*b*) the words " and

(*c*) section 66 (2) of the Merchant Shipping Act 1970 ".

The Merchant Shipping (Load Lines) Act 1967

12. In section 10 (2) of the Merchant Shipping (Load Lines) Act 1967, paragraph (*a*) shall be omitted, and in paragraph (*b*) for the words from " in such form " to the end of the paragraph there shall be substituted the words " to be posted up in some conspicuous place on board the ship, which shall be in such form and containing such particulars relating to the depth to which the ship is for the time being loaded as may be specified in regulations made by the [Secretary of State for Trade] under this Act; ".

The Hovercraft Act 1968

13. The enactments and instruments with respect to which provision may be made by an Order in Council under section 1 (1) (*h*) of the Hovercraft Act 1968 shall include this Act and any instrument made under it.

The Income and Corporation Taxes Act 1970

14. In section 414 (1) of the Income and Corporation Taxes Act 1970 the word " or " shall be added at the end of paragraph (*a*), and paragraph (*c*) and the word " or " preceding it shall be omitted.

Paragraphs 5, 6, and 7 of Schedule 3 are not yet in force.

SCHEDULE 4

Section 100

SAVINGS AND TRANSITIONAL PROVISIONS

491 1. The repeals made by this Act shall not be taken to extend to any country outside the United Kingdom and shall not affect any Order in Council providing for the extension of any enactments to any country outside the United Kingdom or any power to vary or revoke such an Order in Council.

2. The repeal by this Act of sections 145 and 146 of the Merchant Shipping Act 1894 shall not affect the operation, in relation to a seaman's money order issued before the coming into force of the repeal, of regulations under section 145 (2) or of section 146.

3. The repeal by this Act of sections 148 to 153 of the Merchant Shipping Act 1894 shall not affect the operation of those sections in relation to any deposit received under section 148 before the coming into force of the repeal; but the [1] [Secretary of State for Trade] may by regulations make provision for the repayment of such deposits within such period as may be specified by or under the regulations and for the transfer to the National Savings Bank of any deposit not repaid before the end of that period.

4. The repeal by this Act of section 254 of the Merchant Shipping Act 1894 shall not affect the operation of that section in relation to any return made under it and any marine register book kept under that section shall be treated as part of a marine register kept under section 72 of this Act.

5. *Any licence granted under section* 110 *of the Merchant Shipping Act* 1894 *shall have effect as if granted under section* 6 *of this Act.*

6.[2] *Any regulations made under section* 1 *of the Merchant Shipping Act* 1948 *shall have effect as if made under section* 20 *of this Act.*

7. *Any reference in regulations made under section* 1 *of the Merchant Shipping Act* 1965 *to regulations made under section* 1 *of the Merchant Shipping Act* 1948 *shall be construed as including a reference to regulations made under section* 20 *of this Act.*

8. *The references in section* 57 *of this Act to an inquiry or formal investigation held under this Act shall be construed as including references to an inquiry or formal investigation held under section* 466, 468 *or* 471 *of the Merchant Shipping Act* 1894.

9. *The references in section* 60 *of this Act to a certificate which has been cancelled or suspended under this Act shall be construed as including references to a certificate which has been cancelled or suspended under the provisions repealed by this Act.*

1491 *Merchant Shipping Act 1970*

10. *For the purposes of section* 87 *of this Act the registration of any design under Part II of the Patents and Designs Act* 1907 *shall be deemed to be a registration under the Registered Designs Act* 1949.

[1] See the Seamen's Savings Bank Regs. 1972 (S.I. No. 1304).
[2] Paragraphs 5 to 10 of Schedule 4 are not yet in force.

SCHEDULE 5

Section 100

Enactments Repealed

1492

Chapter	Short Title	Extent of Repeal
57 & 58 Vict. c. 60.	The Merchant Shipping Act 1894.	*In section* 19, *the words from* " *each* " *to* " *cause* ".[1] In section 85 (3), the words " in the ship's official log book, and also ". Part II.[2] Sections 268 to 270. Section 271 (3). Sections 289 to 355. In section 356, paragraph (*a*). Sections 357 and 358. Section 359 (2). In section 360, subsections (1) and (2). Sections 361 and 362. In section 363 the words " or emigrant ship ". Sections 364 and 365. *Section* 369.[1] In section 370, in the definition of " fishing boat ", the words from " but " to " profit " and *the definitions of* " *second hand* " *and* " *voyage* ".[1] *Section* 371.[1] Sections 376 to 417.[3] Section 423. Sections 425 and 426. Section 436 (3). In section 458 (1), the words from " and in every " to " on board any ship ". In section 463, the words " or apprentice " wherever they occur. Part VI except section 478 and sections 487 to 490.[4] In section 487 (3), the words from " by the local marine board " to " board ". Section 507. *In section* 676, *in subsection* (1), *in paragraph* (*b*), *the words* " *Second and* " *and the words from* " *including* " *to the end of the paragraph, and paragraphs* (*d*) *and* (*f*).[1]

Chapter	Short Title	Extent of Repeal
57 & 58 Vict. c. 60 —*cont.*	The Merchant Shipping Act 1894—*cont.*	*In section 677, paragraph (a), in paragraph (b) the words from " and the remuneration " to the end of the paragraph, and paragraph (e).*[1] Section 690. In section 714, the words " local marine boards and ". *In section 716, the words " Second, Fourth and ".*[1] *In section 721, the word " Second ".*[1] *In section 722, subsection (2) (a).*[1] Section 725. In section 745 (1) (b), the words " savings bank or ". Schedules 5 to 8.[5]
6 Edw. 7, c. 48.	The Merchant Shipping Act 1906.	Sections 9 and 12. Section 14. In section 16 (1), the words " whether cabin or steerage passengers ". Sections 17 to 20. Sections 23 and 24. Parts III and IV.[6] Sections 56 to 68.[7] Section 74. *Section 81.*[1] Section 82 (1). Schedule 1.
1 & 2 Geo. 5. c. 8.	The Merchant Shipping (Seamen's Allotment) Act 1911.	The whole Act.
4 & 5 Geo. 5. c. 42.	The Merchant Shipping (Certificates) Act 1914.	*The whole Act.*[1]
9 & 10 Geo. 5. c. 62.	The British Mercantile Marine Uniform Act 1919.	*The whole Act.*[1]
9 & 10 Geo. 5. c. 92.	The Aliens Restriction (Amendment) Act 1919.	*Section 5.*[1]
10 & 11 Geo. 5. c. 65.	The Employment of Women, Young Persons and Children Act 1920.	*In section 1, subsections (2) and (5), and in subsection (6) the sub-paragraph beginning " This section, so far as it relates to employment in a ship " and, in the sub-paragraph following it, the words " or in any ship " and paragraphs (b) and (d).*[1] *Schedule, Part IV.*
13 & 14 Geo. 5. c. 4.	The Fees (Increase) Act 1923.	In section 2, subsection (1) (*b*) and (*c*), the word " or " preceding subsection (1) (*b*) and subsections (2) and (4).
13 & 14 Geo. 5. c. 40.	The Merchant Shipping Acts (Amendment) Act 1923.	The whole Act.

1494

Chapter	Short Title	Extent of Repeal
15 & 16 Geo. 5. c. 42.	The Merchant Shipping (International Labour Conventions) Act 1925.	*The whole Act.*[1]
24 & 25 Geo. 5. c. 18.	The Illegal Trawling (Scotland) Act 1934.	In section 6 the words " mercantile marine office ".
1 & 2 Geo. 6. c. 4.	The Merchant Shipping (Superannuation Contributions) Act 1937.	The whole Act.
1 & 2 Geo. 6. c. 30.	The Sea Fish Industry Act 1938.	Part IV.
9 & 10 Geo. 6. c. 26.	The Emergency Laws (Transitional Provisions) Act 1946.	In Schedule 2, the entry relating to the Merchant Shipping Act 1894.
11 & 12 Geo. 6. c. 10.	The Emergency Laws (Miscellaneous Provisions) Act 1947.	Section 2 (2).
11 & 12 Geo. 6. c. 44.	The Merchant Shipping Act 1948.	The whole Act.[8]
12 & 13 Geo. 6. c. 29.	The Consular Conventions Act 1949.	Section 5 (1).
12 & 13 Geo. 6. c. 43.	The Merchant Shipping (Safety Convention) Act 1949.	Section 2 (3). In section 5 (2) the words " being ships of sixteen hundred tons gross tonnage or upwards ". Section 18 (5). Section 19 (1) (*d*). In section 22, subsections (6) and (7).
14 Geo. 6. c. 9.	The Merchant Shipping Act 1950.	Sections 1 to 3.[9] *Section* 6.[1] Schedules 1 and 2.[10]
15 & 16 Geo. 6. and 1 Eliz. 2. c. 14.	The Merchant Shipping Act 1952.	*The whole Act.*[1]
1 & 2 Eliz. 2. c. 20.	The Births and Deaths Registration Act 1953.	Section 13 (3).
1 & 2 Eliz. 2. c. 47.	The Emergency Laws (Miscellaneous Provisions) Act 1953.	Section 4.
1963 c. 49.	The Contracts of Employment Act 1963.	Section 6 (2) (*b*).
1964 c. 47.	The Merchant Shipping Act 1964.	*Section* 11.[1]
1965 c. 19 (N.I.).	The Contracts of Employment and Redundancy Payments Act (Northern Ireland) 1965.	Section 6 (1) (*b*).
1965 c. 32.	The Administration of Estates (Small Payments) Act 1965.	In Part I of Schedule 1, the entry relating to the Merchant Shipping Act 1894.

1495

Chapter	Short Title	Extent of Repeal
1966 c. 20.	The Ministry of Social Security Act 1966.	Section 37. In section 38, paragraph (*c*) and the word " and " preceding that paragraph. Schedule 5. In Schedule 6, paragraphs 1 and 2.
1966 c. 28 (N.I.).	The Supplementary Benefits &c. Act (Northern Ireland) 1966.	Section 41. Schedule 4.
1967 c. 25 (N.I.).	The Births and Deaths Registration Act (Northern Ireland) 1967.	Section 28 (5).
1967 c. 26.	The Merchant Shipping Act 1967.	*The whole Act.*[1]
1967 c. 27.	The Merchant Shipping (Load Lines) Act 1967.	In section 10, in subsection (1), paragraph (*b*) and the word " and " immediately preceding that paragraph, and in subsection (2), paragraph (*a*).
1968 c. 34 (N.I.).	The Children and Young Persons Act (Northern Ireland) 1968.	In Schedule 7, paragraphs 1 and 2.
1496 1969 c. 48.	The Post Office Act 1969.	In Part III of Schedule 6 the entry relating to section 141 of the Merchant Shipping Act 1894.
1970 c. 10.	The Income and Corporation Taxes Act 1970.	In section 414, in subsection (1), paragraph (*c*) and the word " or " preceding that paragraph, and in subsection (7) the definition of " seamen's savings bank ".

[1] These repeals are not yet effective.
[2] The repeal of ss. 92 to 104, 110 to 112, 126, 157 to 158, 207 to 210 and 256 are not yet effective. The repeal of s. 200 was made effective by the Merchant Shipping Act (Commencement No. 2) Order 1974 (S.I. 1974 No. 1194).
[3] The repeal of ss. 385 and 386, 389 and 390, and 413 to 417 are not effective.
[4] Only the repeal ss. 477 and 491 are yet effective.
[5] Only the repeals of Schedules 7 and 8 are yet effective.
[6] The repeal of ss. 27 and 49 are not yet effective nor the complete repeal of s. 44.
[7] The repeals of ss. 56, 58, 64, 66, 67 and 68 are not effective.
[8] Only the repeal of s. 7 is as yet effective.
[9] The repeal of ss. 1 and 3 are not yet effective.
[10] The repeal of Sched. 1 is not yet effective.

MERCHANT SHIPPING (OIL POLLUTION) ACT 1971

[1971 c. 59]

An Act to make provision with respect to civil liability for oil pollution by merchant ships; and for connected purposes. [27th July 1971]

BE it enacted etc.:

This Act is primarily aimed at giving effect to the International Convention on Civil Liability for Oil Pollution Damage agreed at Brussels in November 1969 (Cmnd. 4403). Prompted by increasing public disquiet at incidents involving large crude oil tankers. It imposes strict liability on a shipowner for oil pollution damage in the U.K. (subject to various exceptions).

The Act received the Royal Assent on July 27, 1971. It partly came into force on September 9, 1971: see the M.S. (Oil Pollution) Act 1971 (Commencement) Order 1971 (S.I. No. 1423). The rest of the Act came into force on June 19, 1975: see the M.S. (Oil Pollution) Act 1971 (Commencement No. 2) Order 1975 (S.I. No. 867). They deal with limitation of liability and compulsory insurance.

Liability for oil pollution

1497 **1.**—(1) Where, as a result of any occurrence taking place while a ship [1] is carrying a cargo of persistent oil [2] in bulk, any persistent oil carried by the ship (whether as part of the cargo or otherwise) is discharged or escapes from the ship, the owner [3] of the ship shall be liable,[4] except as otherwise provided by this Act,—

(*a*) for any damage [5] caused in the area of the United Kingdom by contamination resulting from the discharge or escape; and

(*b*) for the cost of any measures reasonably taken after the discharge or escape for the purpose of preventing or reducing any such damage in the area of the United Kingdom; and

(*c*) for any damage [4] caused in the area of the United Kingdom by any measures so taken.

(2) *Where a person incurs a liability under subsection* (1) *of this section he shall also be liable for any damage or cost for which he would be liable under that subsection if the references therein to the area of the United Kingdom included the area of any other Convention country.*[6]

(3) Where persistent oil is discharged or escapes from two or more ships and—

(*a*) a liability is incurred under this section by the owner of each of them; but

(*b*) the damage or cost for which each of the owners would be liable cannot reasonably be separated from that for which the other or others would be liable;

each of the owners shall be liable, jointly with the other or others, for the whole of the damage or cost for which the owners together would be liable under this section.

(4) For the purposes of this Act, where more than one discharge or escape results from the same occurrence or from a series of occurrences having the same origin,[7] they shall be treated as one; but any measures taken after the first of them shall be deemed to have been taken after the discharge or escape.

(5) The Law Reform (Contributory Negligence) Act 1945 and, in Northern Ireland, the Law Reform (Miscellaneous Provisions) Act (Northern Ireland) 1948 shall apply in relation to any damage or cost for which a person is liable under this section, but which is not due to his fault, as if it were due to his fault.

1498 [1] As for hovercraft, see s. 17.
[2] This expression is not defined in the Act. The convention contains a definition of " oil " as being " any persistent oil such as crude oil, fuel oil, heavy diesel oil, lubricating oil and whale oil ": see Art. 1 (5). " Persistent oil " is defined in the Oil Pollution (Compulsory Insurance) Regulations 1975 (S.I. No. 869) for the purposes of s. 10 (1) of this Act.
[3] See s. 20 (1) (2).
[4] Service of notice of writ in a claim under this section can be served out of the jurisdiction with the leave of the court: see R.S.C., Ord. r. 1 (i) (ii).
[5] See s. 20 (1).
[6] For Convention country, see s. 19 (1).
[7] Compare the phrase " distinct occasion " in the M.S.A. 1894, s. 503, as amended by the M.S. (Liability of Shipowners and Others) Act 1962, s. 8 (2).

Exceptions from liability under s. 1

1499 2. The owner [1] of a ship [2] from which persistent oil [3] has been discharged or has escaped shall not incur any liability under section 1 of this Act if he proves that the discharge or escape—

(*a*) resulted from an act of war, hostilities, civil war, insurrection or an exceptional, inevitable and irresistible natural phenomenon; or
(*b*) was due wholly to anything done or left undone by another person, not being a servant or agent of the owner, with intent to do damage [4]; or
(*c*) was due wholly to the negligence or wrongful act of a government or other authority in exercising its function of maintaining lights or other navigational aids for the maintenance of which it was responsible.

[1] See s. 20 (1) (2).
[2] As for hovercraft, see s. 17.
[3] See note (2) to s. 1.
[4] See s. 20 (1).

Restriction of liability for oil pollution

1500 3. Where, as a result of any occurrence taking place while a ship [1] is carrying a cargo of persistent oil [2] in bulk, any persistent oil carried by the ship is discharged or escapes then, whether or not the owner incurs a liability under section 1 of this Act,—

(*a*) he shall not be liable otherwise than under that section for any such damage [3] or cost as is mentioned therein; and

(*b*) no servant or agent of the owner nor any person performing salvage operations with the agreement of the owner shall be liable for any such damage [3] or cost.

[1] As for hovercraft, see s. 17.
[2] See note (2) to s. 1.
[3] See s. 20 (1).

Limitation of liability under s. 1

1501 4.—(1) *Where the owner* [1] *of a ship* [2] *incurs a liability under section* 1 *of this Act by reason of a discharge or escape which occurred without his actual fault or privity* [3]—

(*a*) *section* 503 *of the Merchant Shipping Act* 1894 (*limitation of liability*) *shall not apply in relation to that liability*; *but*

(*b*) *he may limit that liability in accordance with the provisions of this Act, and if he does so his liability* (*that is to say, the aggregate of his liabilities under section* 1 *resulting from the discharge or escape*) *shall not exceed* 2,000 *gold francs for each ton of the ship's tonnage nor* (*where that tonnage would result in a greater amount*) 210 *million gold francs*.

(2) *For the purposes of this section the tonnage of a ship shall be ascertained as follows*:—

(*a*) *if the ship is a British ship* [4] (*whether registered in the United Kingdom or elsewhere*) *or a ship to which an Order under section* 84 *of the Merchant Shipping Act* 1894 *applies, its tonnage shall be taken to be its registered tonnage increased, where a deduction has been made for engine room space in arriving at that tonnage, by the amount of that deduction*;

(*b*) *if the ship is not such a ship as is mentioned in the preceding paragraph and it is possible to ascertain what would be its registered tonnage if it were registered in the United Kingdom, that paragraph shall apply* (*with the necessary modifications*) *as if the ship were so registered*;

(*c*) *if the ship is not such a ship as is mentioned in paragraph* (*a*) *of this subsection and is of a description with respect to which no provision is for the time being made by regulations under section* 1 *of the Merchant Shipping Act* 1965 (*tonnage regulations*) [5] *its tonnage shall be taken to be* 40 *per cent. of the weight* (*expressed in tons of* 2,240 *lbs.*) *of oil which the ship is capable of carrying*;

(*d*) *if the tonnage of the ship cannot be ascertained in accordance with the preceding paragraphs the Chief Ship Surveyor of the* [*Department of Trade*] *shall, if so directed by the court, certify what, on the evidence specified in the direction, would in his opinion be the tonnage of the ship if ascertained in accordance with those paragraphs, and the tonnage stated in his certificate shall be taken to be the tonnage of the ship.*

(3) *For the purposes of this section a gold franc shall be taken to be a unit of sixty-five and a half milligrams of gold of millesimal fineness nine hundred.*

(4) *The Secretary of State may from time to time by order made by statutory instrument specify the amounts which for the purposes of this section are to be taken as equivalent to* 2,000 *gold francs and* 210 *million gold francs respectively.*[6]

(5) *Where the amounts specified by an order under the preceding subsection are varied by a subsequent order the variation shall not affect the limit of any liability under section* 1 *of this Act if, before the variation comes into force,*[7] *an amount not less than that limit (ascertained in accordance with the order then in force) has been paid into court*[8] *(or, in Scotland, consigned in court) in proceedings for the limitation of that liability in accordance with this Act.*

502 [1] See s. 20 (1) (2).
[2] As for hovercraft, see s. 17.
[3] See note (4) to s. 503 of the M.S.A. 1894.
[4] See note (1) to s. 1 of the M.S.A. 1894.
[5] See the M.S. (Tonnage) Regulations 1967 (S.I. No. 172) as amended by S.I. 1967 No. 1093, S.I. 1972 No. 656, and S.I. 1975 No. 594.
[6] £69·7856 and £7,327,488 respectively: see the M.S. (Limitation of Liability for Oil Pollution) (Sterling Equivalents) Order 1975 (S.I. No. 868).
[7] *Cf.* the M.S. (Liability of Shipowner and Others) Act 1958, s. 1 (4).
[8] See s. 20 (1).

Limitation actions

503 **5.**—(1) *Where the owner of a ship*[1] *has or is alleged to have incurred a liability under section* 1 *of this Act he may apply to the court*[2] *for the limitation of that liability to an amount determined in accordance with section* 4 *of this Act.*

(2) *If on such an application the court finds that the applicant has incurred such a liability and is entitled to limit it, the court shall, after determining the limit of the liability and directing payment into court of the amount of that limit,—*

(*a*) *determine the amounts that would, apart from the limit, be due in respect of the liability to the several persons making claims in the proceedings; and*

(*b*) *direct the distribution of the amount paid into court (or, as the case may be, so much of it as does not exceed the liability) among those persons in proportion to their claims, subject to the following provisions of this section.*

(3) *No claim shall be admitted in proceedings under this section unless it is made within such time as the court may direct or such further time as the court may allow.*

(4) *Where any sum has been paid in or towards satisfaction of any claim in respect of the damage* [2] *or cost to which the liability extends,—*

(*a*) *by the owner or the person referred to in section* 12 *of this Act as* "*the insurer*"; *or*

(*b*) *by a person who has or is alleged to have incurred a liability, otherwise than under section* 1 *of this Act, for the damage or cost and who is entitled to limit his liability in connection with the ship by virtue of the Merchant Shipping* (*Liability of Shipowners and Others*) *Act* 1958 [3];

the person who paid the sum shall, to the extent of that sum, be in the same position with respect to any distribution made in proceedings under this section as the person to whom it was paid would have been.

(5) *Where the person who incurred the liability has voluntarily made any reasonable sacrifice or taken any other reasonable measures to prevent or reduce damage to which the liability extends or might have extended he shall be in the same position with respect to any distribution made in proceedings under this section as if he had a claim in respect of the liability equal to the cost of the sacrifice or other measures.*

(6) *The court may, if it thinks fit, postpone the distribution of such part of the amount to be distributed as it deems appropriate having regard to any claims that may later be established before a court of any country outside the United Kingdom.*

1504 [1] As for hovercraft, see s. 17.
[2] See s. 20 (1).
[3] *i.e.* "any charterer and any person interested in or in possession of the ship, and, in particular, any manager or operator of the ship"; see *ibid.* s. 3.

Restriction on enforcement of claims after establishment of limitation fund

1505 6.—(1) *Where the court has found that a person who has incurred a liability under section* 1 *of this Act* [1] *is entitled to limit that liability to any amount and he has paid into court a sum not less than that amount—*

(*a*) *the court* [2] *shall order the release of any ship or other property arrested in connection with a claim in respect of that liability or any security given to prevent or obtain release from such an arrest*; *and*

(*b*) *no judgment or decree for any such claim shall be enforced, except so far as it is for costs* (*or, in Scotland, expenses*);

if the sum paid into court, or such part thereof as corresponds to the claim, will be actually available to the claimant or would have been available to him if the proper steps in the proceedings under section 5 *of this Act had been taken.*

(2) *In the application of this section to Scotland, any reference (however expressed) to release from arrest shall be construed as a reference to the recall of an arrestment.*

506 [1] For the position where the person has incurred a corresponding liability in another Convention country, see s. 8.

[2] See s. 20 (1).

Concurrent liabilities of owners and others

507 **7.** *Where, as a result of any discharge or escape of persistent oil* [1] *from a ship,*[2] *the owner* [3] *of the ship incurs a liability under section* 1 [4] *of this Act and any other person incurs a liability, otherwise than under that section, for any such damage or cost as is mentioned in subsection* (1) *of that section, then, if—*

(*a*) *the owner has been found, in proceedings under section* 5 [4] *of this Act, to be entitled to limit his liability to any amount and has paid into court a sum not less than that amount; and*

(*b*) *the other person is entitled to limit his liability in connection with the ship by virtue of the Merchant Shipping (Liability of Shipowners and Others) Act* 1958;

no proceedings shall be taken against the other person in respect of his liability, and if any such proceedings were commenced before the owner paid the sum into court, no further steps shall be taken in the proceedings except in relation to costs.

508 [1] See note (2) to s. 1.

[2] As for hovercraft, see s. 17.

[3] See s. 20 (1) (2).

[4] For the position where the owner or other person has incurred a corresponding liability in another Convention country; see s. 8.

Establishment of limitation fund outside United Kingdom

509 **8.** *Where the events resulting in the liability of any person under section* 1 *of this Act also resulted in a corresponding liability under the law of another Convention country* [1] *sections* 6 *and* 7 *of this Act shall apply as if the references to sections* 1 *and* 5 *of this Act included references to the corresponding provisions of that law and the references to sums paid into court included references to any sums secured under those provisions in respect of the liability.*

[1] See s. 19 (1).

Extinguishment of claims

1510 **9.** No action to enforce a claim in respect of a liability incurred under section 1 of this Act shall be entertained by any court in the United Kingdom unless the action is commenced not later than three years after the claim arose nor later than six years after the occurrence or first of the occurrences resulting in the discharge or escape by reason of which the liability was incurred.

Compulsory insurance against liability for pollution

1511 **10.**—(1) *Subject to the provisions of this Act relating to Government ships,*[1] *subsection* (2) *of this section shall apply to any ship carrying in bulk a cargo of more than* 2,000 *tons of persistent oil of a description specified in regulations made by the Secretary of State.*[1a]

(2) *The ship shall not enter or leave a port in the United Kingdom or arrive at or leave a terminal in the territorial sea*[2] *of the United Kingdom nor, if the ship is registered in the United Kingdom, a port in any other country or a terminal in the territorial sea of any other country, unless there is in force a certificate complying with the provisions of subsection* (3) *of this section and showing that there is in force in respect of the ship a contract of insurance or other security satisfying the requirements of Article VII of the Convention (cover for owner's liability).*

(3) *The certificate must be—*

- (*a*) *if the ship is registered in the United Kingdom, a certificate issued by the Secretary of State;*
- (*b*) *if the ship is registered in a Convention country*[3] *other than the United Kingdom, a certificate issued by or under the authority of the government of the other Convention country; and*
- (*c*) *if the ship is registered in a country which is not a Convention country, a certificate issued by the Secretary of State or a certificate recognised for the purposes of this paragraph by regulations made under this section.*[3a]

(4) *The Secretary of State may by regulations provide that certificates in respect of ships registered in any, or any specified, country which is not a Convention country shall, in such circumstances as may be specified in the regulations, be recognised for the purposes of subsection* (3) (*c*) *of this section if issued by or under the authority of the government of the country designated in the regulations in that behalf; and the country that may be so designated may be either or both of the following, that is to say—*

- (*a*) *the country in which the ship is registered; and*
- (*b*) *any country specified in the regulations for the purposes of this paragraph.*[3a]

(5) *Any certificate required by this section to be in force in respect of a ship shall be carried in the ship and shall, on demand, be produced by the*

master to any officer of customs or of the [*Department of Trade*] *and, if the ship is registered in the United Kingdom, to any proper officer within the meaning of section* 97 (1) *of the Merchant Shipping Act* 1970.

(6) *If a ship enters or leaves, or attempts to enter or leave, a port or arrives at or leaves, or attempts to arrive at or leave, a terminal in contravention of subsection* (2) *of this section, the master or owner* [4] *shall be liable on conviction on indictment to a fine, or on summary conviction to a fine not exceeding* £35,000.

(7) *If a ship fails to carry, or the master of a ship fails to produce, a certificate as required by subsection* (5) *of this section the master shall be liable on summary conviction to a fine not exceeding* £400.

(8) *If a ship attempts to leave a port in the United Kingdom in contravention of this section the ship may be detained.*[5]

(9) *Regulations under this section shall be made by statutory instrument,*[6] *which shall be subject to annulment in pursuance of a resolution of either House of Parliament.*

1512 [1] See s. 14.
[1a] See Oil Pollution (Compulsory Insurance) Regulations 1975 (S.I. No. 869).
[2] The territorial waters of the United Kingdom extend for three miles from low-water mark; see the Territorial Waters Jurisdiction Act 1878, s. 7. In any particular dispute over the limits of territorial waters, the court will treat as conclusive evidence the statement of an appropriate officer of the Crown: *The Fagerives* [1927] P. 311.
[3] See s. 19 (1).
[3a] See note (2) above.
[4] Both the owners and master may be prosecuted and convicted of an offence under this section arising out of the same facts: *cf. R.* v. *Federal Steam Navigation Co.*; *R.* v. *Moran, The Times*, July 11, 1973, C.A.
[5] See M.S.A. 1894, s. 692.
[6] See note (2) above.

Issue of certificate by Secretary of State

1513 **11.**—(1) *Subject to subsection* (2) *of this section, if the Secretary of State is satisfied, on an application for such a certificate as is mentioned in section* 10 *of this Act in respect of a ship* [1] *registered in the United Kingdom or any country which is not a Convention country,*[2] *that there will be in force in respect of the ship, throughout the period for which the certificate is to be issued, a contract of insurance or other security satisfying the requirements of Article VII of the Convention,*[2] *the Secretary of State shall issue such a certificate to the owner.*

(2) *If the Secretary of State is of opinion that there is a doubt whether the person providing the insurance or other security will be able to meet his obligations thereunder, or whether the insurance or other security will cover the owner's liability under section* 1 *of this Act in all circumstances, he may refuse the certificate.*

(3) *The Secretary of State may make regulations* [2a]—

(*a*) *prescribing the fee to be paid on an application for a certificate to be issued by him under this section; and* (*b*) *providing for the cancellation and delivery up of such a certificate in such circumstances as may be prescribed by the regulations.*

(4) *If a person required by regulations under subsection* (3) (*b*) *of this section to deliver up a certificate fails to do so he shall be liable on summary conviction to a fine not exceeding* £200.

(5) *The Secretary of State shall send a copy of any certificate issued by him under this section in respect of a ship registered in the United Kingdom to the Registrar General of Shipping and Seamen,*[3] *and the Registrar shall make the copy available for public inspection.*

(6) *Regulations under this section shall be made by statutory instrument,*[4] *which shall be subject to annulment in pursuance of a resolution of either House of Parliament.*

1514 [1] As for hovercraft, see s. 17.
[2] See s. 19 (1).
[2a] See Oil Pollution (Compulsory Insurance) Regulations 1975 (S.I. No. 869).
[3] See the M.S.A. 1970, s. 80.
[4] See note (3) above.

Rights of third parties against insurers

1515 **12.**—(1) *Where it is alleged that the owner* [1] *of a ship* [2] *has incurred a liability under section* 1 *of this Act as a result of any discharge or escape of oil occurring while there was in force a contract of insurance or other security to which such a certificate as is mentioned in section* 10 *of this Act related, proceedings to enforce a claim in respect of the liability may be brought against the person who provided the insurance or other security* (*in the following provisions of this section referred to as* " *the insurer* ").

(2) *In any proceedings brought against the insurer by virtue of this section it shall be a defence* (*in addition to any defence affecting the owner's liability*) *to prove that the discharge or escape was due to the wilful misconduct of the owner himself.*

(3) *The insurer may limit his liability in respect of claims made against him by virtue of this section in like manner and to the same extent as the owner may limit his liability but the insurer may do so whether or not the discharge or escape occurred without the owner's actual fault or privity.*

(4) *Where the owner and the insurer each apply to the court* [3] *for the limitation of his liability any sum paid into court in pursuance of either application shall be treated as paid also in pursuance of the other.*

(5) *The Third Parties* (*Rights against Insurers*) *Act* 1930 *and the Third Parties* (*Rights against Insurers*) *Act* (*Northern Ireland*) 1930 *shall not apply in relation to any contract of insurance to which such a certificate as is mentioned in section* 10 *of this Act relates.*

1516 [1] See s. 20 (1) (2).
[2] As for hovercraft, see s. 17.
[3] See s. 20 (1).

Jurisdiction of United Kingdom courts and registration of foreign judgments

1517 **13.**—(1) Paragraph (*d*) of section 1 (1) of the Administration of Justice Act 1956 and paragraph 1 (1) (*d*) of Schedule 1 to that Act (Admiralty jurisdiction in claims for damage done by ships) shall be construed as extending to any claim in respect of a liability incurred under this Act, and the Admiralty jurisdiction of the Court of Session shall extend to any case arising out of any such claim.

(2) *Where any persistent oil*[1] *is discharged or escapes from a ship but does not result in any damage caused by contamination in the area of the United Kingdom and no measures are reasonably taken to prevent or reduce such damage in that area, no court in the United Kingdom shall entertain an action (whether in rem or in personam) to enforce a claim arising from—*

(*a*) *any damage*[2] *caused in the area of another Convention country*[3] *by contamination resulting from the discharge or escape;*

(*b*) *any cost incurred in taking measures to prevent or reduce such damage in the area of another Convention country*[3]*; or*

(*c*) *any damage caused by any measures so taken.*

(3) *Part I of the Foreign Judgments (Reciprocal Enforcement) Act* 1933 *shall apply, whether or not it would so apply apart from this section, to any judgment given by a court in a Convention country to enforce a claim in respect of a liability incurred under any provision corresponding to section* 1 *of this Act; and in its application to such a judgment that Part shall have effect with the omission of subsections* (2) *and* (3) *of section* 4 *of that Act.*

518 [1] See note (2) to s. 1.
[2] See s. 20 (1).
[3] See s. 19 (1).

Government ships

519 **14.**—(1) Nothing in the preceding provisions of this Act applies in relation to any warship or any ship[1] for the time being used by the government of any State for other than commercial purposes.

(2) *In relation to a ship owned by a State and for the time being used for commercial purposes it shall be a sufficient compliance with subsection* (2) *of section* 10 *of this Act if there is in force a certificate issued by the government of that State and showing that the ship is owned by that State and that any liability for pollution damage as defined in Article I of the Convention*[2] *will be met up to the limit prescribed by Article V thereof.*

(3) *Every Convention State*[2] *shall, for the purposes of any proceedings brought in a court in the United Kingdom to enforce a claim in respect of a liability incurred under section* 1 *of this Act, be deemed to have submitted to*

the jurisdiction of that court, and accordingly rules of court may provide for the manner in which such proceedings are to be commenced and carried on; but nothing in this subsection shall authorise the issue of execution, or in Scotland the execution of diligence, against the property of any State.

1520 [1] As for hovercraft, see s. 17.
[2] See s. 19 (1).

Liability for cost of preventive measures where s. 1 does not apply

1521 **15.**—(1) Where,—

(*a*) after an escape or discharge of persistent oil [1] from a ship,[2] measures are reasonably taken for the purpose of preventing or reducing damage in the area of the United Kingdom which may be caused by contamination resulting from the discharge or escape; and

(*b*) any person incurs, or might but for the measures have incurred, a liability, otherwise than under section 1 of this Act,[3] for any such damage;

then, notwithstanding that subsection (1) (*b*) of that section does not apply, he shall be liable for the cost of the measures, whether or not the person taking them does so for the protection of his interests or in the performance of a duty.[4]

(2) For the purposes of section 503 of the Merchant Shipping Act 1894 (limitation of liability) any liability incurred under this section shall be deemed to be a liability to damages in respect of such loss, damage or infringement as is mentioned in subsection (1) (*d*) of that section.

1522 [1] See note (2) to s. 1.
[2] As for hovercraft, see s. 17.
[3] *i.e.* a person other than the owner.
[4] This subsection appears to have been wholly prompted by the *Torrey Canyon* case. The vessel stranded on the Seven Stones in March 1967, and a large proportion of her 100,000 ton cargo of crude oil escaped. Thereafter, at the request of various local authorities the British Government expended substantial sums in an effort to prevent or minimise the effects of pollution on the coasts of Cornwall. Doubts were expressed at the time as to whether the Government had any cause of action against the owners for the recovery of the costs of these measures. In particular, it was maintained that the Government had neither a sufficient proprietorial interest in the shore that was threatened nor any duty to perform activities in the nature of a rescue.

Saving for recourse actions

1523 **16.** Nothing in this Act shall prejudice any claim, or the enforcement of any claim, a person incurring any liability under this Act may have against another person in respect of that liability.

Application to hovercraft

1524 **17.** The enactments and instruments with respect to which provision may be made by an Order in Council [1] under section 1 (1) (*h*) of the

Hovercraft Act 1968 shall include this Act and any instrument made under it.

[1] No order has yet been made under this section.

Extensions to British possessions, etc.

1525 **18.**—(1) Her Majesty may by Order in Council [1] direct that this Act shall extend, subject to such exemptions, modifications or adaptations as may be specified in the Order, to any of the following countries, that is to say—

(*a*) the Isle of Man [2];
(*b*) any of the Channel Islands;
(*c*) any colony other than one for whose external relations a country other than the United Kingdom is responsible;
(*d*) any country outside Her Majesty's dominions in which Her Majesty has jurisdiction in right of Her Majesty's Government of the United Kingdom.

(2) Her Majesty may by Order in Council [1] provide that this Act shall have effect as if any reference therein to the United Kingdom included a reference to any of the countries mentioned in the preceding subsection.

(3) Any statutory instrument made by virtue of subsection (2) of this section shall be subject to annulment in pursuance of a resolution of either House of Parliament.

1526 [1] No order has yet been made under this section.
[2] *i.e.* Guernsey, Jersey, Alderney and Sark and their respective dependencies: see the Customs and Excise Act 1952, s. 37 (3).

Meaning of " the Convention," " Convention country " and " Convention State "

1527 **19.**—(1) *In this Act—*

" the Convention " means the International Convention on Civil Liability for Oil Pollution Damage signed in Brussels in 1969 [1];
" Convention country " means a country in respect of which the Convention is in force; and
" Convention State " means a State which is a party to the Convention.

(2) *If Her Majesty by Order in Council declares that any State specified in the Order is a party to the Convention in respect of any country so specified the Order shall, while in force, be conclusive evidence that that State is a party to the Convention in respect of that country.*

[1] See Cmnd. 4403.

Interpretation of other expressions

1528 **20.**—(1) In this Act—

"damage" includes loss;

"owner", in relation to a registered ship,[1] means the person registered as its owner, except that in relation to a ship owned by a State which is operated by a person registered as the ship's operator, it means the person registered as its operator;

"the court" means the High Court in England and Wales, the Court of Session or the High Court in Northern Ireland or a judge thereof.

(2) In relation to any damage or cost resulting from the discharge or escape of any oil carried in a ship references in this Act to the owner of the ship are references to the owner at the time of the occurrence or first of the occurrences resulting in the discharge or escape.

(3) References in this Act to the area of any country include the territorial sea[2] of that country.

[1] As for hovercraft, see s. 17.
[2] See note (2) to s. 10.

Citation, construction, commencement and extent

1529 **21.**—(1) This Act may be cited as the Merchant Shipping (Oil Pollution) Act 1971, and this Act and the Merchant Shipping Acts 1894 to 1970 may be cited together as the Merchant Shipping Acts 1894 to 1971.[1]

(2) This Act shall be construed as one[2] with the Merchant Shipping Acts 1894 to 1970.

(3) This Act shall come into force on such day as the Secretary of State may by order made by statutory instrument appoint,[3] and different days may be so appointed for different provisions of this Act.

(4) This Act extends to Northern Ireland.

1530 [1] The following unrepealed Acts are included in this collective title:

(i) The Merchant Shipping Act 1894, c. 60.
(ii) The Merchant Shipping Act 1897, c. 59.
(iii) The M.S. (Mercantile Marine Fund) Act 1898, c. 44.
(iv) The M.S. (Liability of Shipowners and Others) Act 1900, c. 32.
(v) The Merchant Shipping Act 1906, c. 48.
(vi) The Merchant Shipping Act 1911, c. 42.
(vii) The Pilotage Act 1913, c. 31.
(viii) The M.S. (Certificates) Act 1914, c. 42.
(ix) The M.S. (Amendment) Act 1920, c. 2.
(x) The M.S. (Scottish Fishing Boats) Act 1920, s. 39.
(xi) The Merchant Shipping Act 1921, c. 28.
(xii) The Fees Increase Act 1923, c. 4 (so far as it amends the Merchant Shipping Acts 1894 to 1921).
(xiii) The M.S. (Equivalent Provisions) Act 1925, c. 37.
(xiv) The M.S. (International Labour Conventions) Act 1925, c. 42.
(xv) The M.S. (Safety and Load Line Conventions) Act 1932, c. 9.
(xvi) The Merchant Shipping Act 1948, c. 44.
(xvii) The M.S. (Safety Convention) Act 1949, c. 43.
(xviii) The Merchant Shipping Act 1950, c. 9.

(xix) The Merchant Shipping Act 1952, c. 14.
(xx) The M.S. (Liability of Shipowners and Others) Act 1958, c. 62.
(xxi) The M.S. (Minicoy Lighthouse) Act 1960, c. 42.
(xxii) The Merchant Shipping Act 1964, c. 47.
(xxiii) The Merchant Shipping Act 1965, c. 47.
(xxiv) The Merchant Shipping Act 1967, c. 26.
(xxv) The M.S. (Load Lines) Act 1967, c. 27.
(xxvi) The Fishing Vessels (Safety Provisions) Act 1970, c. 27.
(xxvii) The Merchant Shipping Act 1970, c. 36.
(xxviii) The M.S. (Oil Pollution) Act 1971, c. 59.
(xxix) The Merchant Shipping Act 1974, c. 43.

[2] This means that every part of each of the Acts has to be construed as if it had been contained in one Act. Unless there is some manifest discrepancy, making it necessary to hold that the later Act has to some extent modified something found in the earlier Act: *per* Earl of Selborne L.C. in *Canada Southern Ry. Co.* v. *International Bridge Co.* (1883) 8 App.Cas. 723 at p. 727; principle applied in *Hart* v. *Hudson Bros. Ltd.* [1928] 2 K.B. 629 and in *Phillips* v. *Parnaby* [1934] 2 K.B. 299. Accordingly definition in an earlier Act may be relevant: *cf. Kirkness* v. *John Hudson & Co. Ltd.* [1955] A.C. 696; *Solomons* v. *R. Gertzenstein Ltd.* [1954] 2 Q.B. 243; *Crowe* (*Valuation Officer*) v. *Lloyd's British Testing Co. Ltd.* [1960] 1 Q.B. 592.

In addition to the statutes set out in (i), (iii), (iv), (v), (vi), (vii), (xi), (xii), (xiii), (xiv), (xv), (xvi), (xvii), (xviii), (xx), (xxii), (xxiii), (xxv), (xxvi), (xxvii), (xxviii), (xxix), the Maritime Conventions Act 1911, is also construed as one with this Act.

[3] See the M.S. (Oil Pollution) Act 1971 (Commencement) Order 1971, (S.I. No. 1423) bringing into force: ss. 1 (excluding subs. (2)), 2, 3, 9, 13, (1), 14 (1), 15–18, 20 and 21. See also the M.S. (Oil Pollution) Act 1971 (Commencement No. 2) Order 1975 (S.I. No. 867) bringing into force ss. 1 (2), 4–8, 10–12, 13 (2) and (3), 14 (2) and (3) and 19.

PREVENTION OF OIL POLLUTION ACT 1971

[1971 c. 60]

An Act to consolidate the Oil in Navigable Waters Acts 1955 to 1971 and section 5 of the Continental Shelf Act 1964. [27th July 1971]

Be it enacted etc.:

1531 INTRODUCTORY NOTE. By consolidating the provisions of the Oil in Navigable Waters Acts 1955, 1963 and 1971, together with section 5 of the Continental Shelf Act 1964, this Act gave effect to two Conventions and part of a third:

(*a*) The International Convention for the Prevention of Pollution of the Sea by Oil 1954 (Cmnd. 9197) as amended in 1962 (Cmnd. 1801) and in 1970 (Cmnd. 4347);

(*b*) The International Convention relating to the Intervention on the High Seas in cases of Oil Pollution, Accidents and Collisions, 1969;

(*c*) Part of the Convention on the High Seas 1958 (Art. 24).

The Act came into force on March 1, 1973; see the Prevention of Oil Pollution Act 1971 (Commencement) Order 1973 (S.I. No. 203).

General provisions for preventing oil pollution

Discharge of certain oils into sea outside territorial waters

1532 **1.**—(1) If any oil to which this section applies or any mixture containing such oil is discharged [1] from a ship [2] registered in the United Kingdom into any part of the sea [3] outside the territorial waters [4] of the United Kingdom, the owner or master [5] of the ship shall, subject to the provisions of this Act, be guilty of an offence.[6]

(2) This section applies—

(*a*) to crude oil, fuel oil and lubricating oil; and

(*b*) to heavy diesel oil, as defined by regulations [7] made under this section by the Secretary of State;

and shall also apply to any other description of oil [8] which may be specified by regulations made by the Secretary of State, having regard to the provisions of any Convention accepted by Her Majesty's Government in the United Kingdom in so far as it relates to the prevention of pollution of the sea by oil,[9] or having regard to the persistent character of oil of that description and the likelihood that it would cause pollution if discharged from a ship into any part of the sea outside the territorial waters of the United Kingdom.

(3) Regulations [10] made by the Secretary of State may make exceptions from the operation of subsection (1) of this section, either generally or with respect to particular classes of ships, particular descriptions of oil or mixtures [11] containing oil or the discharge of oil or mixtures in particular circumstances or into particular areas of the sea, and may do so either absolutely or subject to any specified conditions.

(4) A person guilty of an offence under this section shall be liable on summary conviction to a fine not exceeding £50,000 or on conviction on indictment to a fine.

1533 [1] See s. 29 (3).
[2] See s. 29 (4). As for hovercraft, see s. 31.
[3] See s. 29 (1).
[4] See note (2) to the M.S. (Oil Pollution) Act 1971, s. 10.
[5] *Both* the owners and master may be prosecuted and convicted of an offence under the section arising out of the same facts: *cf. R.* v. *Federal Steam Navigation Co*; *R.* v. *Moran* [1973] 1 W.L.R. 1373.
[6] Accordingly, it is an absolute offence, not requiring *mens rea*: see ***Brentnall and Cleland Ltd.*** v. *L.C.C.* [1945] K.B. 115.
[7] See the Oil in Navigable Waters (Heavy Diesel Oil) Regs. 1967 (S.I. No. 710), saved by virtue of s. 33 (2).
[8] See s. 29 (1).
[9] See the Introductory Note. This expression would also include the International Convention on Civil Liability for Oil Pollution Damage 1969, which forms the basis of the M.S. (Oil Pollution) Act 1971.
[10] See the Oil in Navigable Waters (Exceptions) Regulations 1972 (S.I. No. 1928).
[11] See s. 29 (2).

Discharge of oil into United Kingdom waters

1534 **2.**—(1) If any oil [1] or mixture [2] containing oil is discharged as mentioned in the following paragraphs into waters to which this section applies, then, subject to the provisions of this Act, the following shall be guilty of an offence, that is to say—

(*a*) if the discharge is from a vessel,[3] the owner or master of the vessel, unless he proves that the discharge took place and was caused as mentioned in paragraph (*b*) of this subsection;

(*b*) if the discharge is from a vessel but takes place in the course of a transfer [1] of oil to or from another vessel or a place on land and is caused by the act or omission of any person in charge [4] of any apparatus in that other vessel or that place, the owner or master of that other vessel or, as the case may be, the occupier of that place;

(*c*) if the discharge is from a place on land, the occupier of that place, unless he proves that the discharge was caused as mentioned in paragraph (*d*) of this subsection;

(*d*) if the discharge is from a place on land and is caused by the act of a person who is in that place without the permission (express or implied) of the occupier, that person;

(*e*) if the discharge takes place otherwise than as mentioned in the preceding paragraphs and is the result of any operations for the exploration of the sea-bed and sub-soil or the exploitation of their natural resources, the person carrying on the operations.

(2) This section applies to the following waters, that is to say,—

(*a*) the whole of the sea within the seaward limits of the territorial waters [5] of the United Kingdom; and

(*b*) all other waters (including inland waters [6]) which are within those limits and are navigable by sea-going ships.[7]

(3) In this Act " place on land " includes anything resting on the bed or shore of the sea, or of any other waters to which this section applies, and also includes anything afloat (other than a vessel) if it is anchored or attached to the bed or shore of the sea or of any such waters; and " occupier ", in relation to any such thing as is mentioned in the preceding provisions of this subsection, if it has no occupier, means the owner thereof, and, in relation to a railway wagon or road vehicle, means the person in charge of the wagon or vehicle and not the occupier of the land on which the wagon or vehicle stands.

(4) A person guilty of an offence under this section shall be liable on summary conviction to a fine not exceeding £50,000 or on conviction on indictment to a fine.

1535 [1] See s. 29 (1). [2] See s. 29 (2). [3] See s. 29 (4). As for hovercraft, see s. 31.

[4] For the meaning of " in charge " *cf. Leach* v. *Evans* [1952] 2 All E.R. 264; *Haines* v. *Roberts* [1953] 1 All E.R. 344; and *Ellis* v. *Smith* [1962] 1 W.L.R. 1486.

[5] See note 2 to s. 10 of the M.S. (Oil Pollution) Act 1971.

[6] *Cf.* the definition in the Mineral Workings (Offshore Installations) Act 1971, s. 1 (2) (*b*).

[7] A dry dock forming part of the Port of London may be " navigable by sea-going ships " even when the water has been so far pumped out that the vessel is resting on blocks: *cf. Rankin* v. *De Coster* [1975] 1 W.L.R. 606.

Discharge of certain oils from pipe-lines or as the result of exploration etc. in designated areas

1536 3.—(1) If any oil to which section 1 of this Act applies, or any mixture [1] containing such oil, is discharged [2] into any part of the sea [3]—

(*a*) from a pipe-line; or

(*b*) (otherwise than from a ship) as the result of any operation for the exploration of the sea-bed and subsoil or the exploitation of their natural resources in a designated area,

then, subject to the following provisions of this Act,[4] the owner of the pipe-line or, as the case may be, the person carrying on the operations shall be guilty of an offence unless the discharge was from a place in his occupation and he proves [5] that it was due to the act of a person who was there without his permission (express or implied).

(2) In this section " designated area " means an area for the time being designated by an Order [6] made under section 1 of the Continental Shelf Act 1964.

(3) A person guilty of an offence under this section shall be liable on summary conviction to a fine not exceeding £50,000 or on conviction on indictment to a fine.

1537 [1] See s. 29 (2).
[2] See s. 29 (3).
[3] See s. 29 (1).
[4] By virtue of s. 25, this section cannot be applied by Order in Council to the Isle of Man, the Channel Islands or any colony or extended by Order in Council under the Foreign Jurisdiction Act 1890, to foreign countries in which Her Majesty has jurisdiction.
[5] *i.e.* on the balance of probabilities, *cf. R.* v. *Carr-Briant* [1943] K.B. 607.
[6] See the Continental Shelf (Designation of Areas) Order 1964 (S.I. No. 697) and the Continental Shelf (Designation of Additional Areas) Orders 1965 (S.I. No. 1531), 1968 (S.I. No. 891) and 1971 (S.I. No. 594).

Equipment in ships to prevent oil pollution

1538 4.—(1) For the purpose of preventing or reducing discharges of oil [1] and mixtures [2] containing oil into the sea, the Secretary of State may make regulations [3] requiring ships [4] registered [5] in the United Kingdom to be fitted with such equipment and to comply with such other requirements as may be specified in the regulations.

(2) Without prejudice to the generality of subsection (1) of this section, where any regulations made thereunder require ships to be fitted with equipment of a specified description, the regulations may provide that equipment of that description—

(*a*) shall not be installed in a ship to which the regulations apply unless it is of a type tested and approved by a person appointed by the Secretary of State;

(*b*) while installed in such a ship, shall not be treated as satisfying the requirements of the regulations unless, at such times as may be specified in the regulations, it is submitted for testing and approval by a person so appointed.

(3) The Secretary of State may appoint persons to carry out tests for the purposes of any regulations made under this section, and, in respect of the carrying out of such tests, may charge such fees as, with the approval of the Treasury, may be prescribed by the regulations.

(4) Every surveyor [6] of ships shall be taken to be a person appointed by the Secretary of State to carry out tests for the purposes of any regulations made under this section, in so far as they relate to tests required in accordance with paragraph (*b*) of subsection (2) of this section.

(5) If, in the case of any ship, the provisions of any regulations made under this section which apply to that ship are contravened, the owner or master of the ship shall be guilty of an offence.

(6) A person guilty of an offence under this section shall be liable on summary conviction to a fine not exceeding £1,000 or on conviction on indictment to a fine.

539 [1] See s. 29 (1).
[2] See s. 29 (2).
[3] See the Oil in Navigable Waters (Ship's Equipment) (No. 1) Regulations 1956 (S.I. No. 1423) and the Oil in Navigable Waters (Ship's Equipment) Regulations 1957 (S.I. No. 1424), saved by virtue of s. 33 (2).
[4] See s. 29 (4). As for hovercraft, see s. 31.
[5] For provisions as to registration, see the M.S.A. 1894, s. 2. Regulations made under this section can be extended to vessels registered outside the U.K. See s. 22 (1).
[6] For provisions as to surveyors, see the M.S.A. 1894, ss. 724 *et seq.* Such surveyors are deemed inspectors pursuant to s. 18 (1); see s. 18 (2). As for powers of inspector, see s. 18 (3) and the M.S.A. 1894, s. 729 and notes thereon.

Defences of owner or master charged with offence under s. 1 or s. 2

540 **5.**—(1) Where a person is charged with an offence under section 1 of this Act, or is charged with an offence under section 2 of this Act as the owner or master of a vessel,[1] it shall be a defence to prove that the oil [2] or mixture [3] was discharged [4] for the purpose of securing the safety of any vessel, or of preventing damage to any vessel or cargo, or of saving life, unless the court is satisfied that the discharge of the oil or mixture was not necessary for that purpose or was not a reasonable step to take in the circumstances.

(2) Where a person is charged as mentioned in subsection (1) of this section, it shall also be a defence to prove—

(*a*) that the oil or mixture escaped in consequence of damage to the vessel, and that as soon as practicable after the damage occurred all reasonable steps were taken for preventing, or (if it could not be prevented) for stopping or reducing, the escape of the oil or mixture, or

(*b*) that the oil or mixture escaped by reason of leakage,[5] that neither the leakage nor any delay in discovering it was due to any want of reasonable care, and that as soon as practicable [6] after the escape was discovered all reasonable steps were taken for stopping or reducing it.

1541 [1] See s. 29 (1).
[2] See s. 29 (1).
[3] See s. 29 (2).
[4] See s. 29 (3).
[5] " Leakage " is not intended to apply to an escape of oil brought about by some physical force such as air pressure built up by hydrodynamic power; see *Nicholson* v. *Fremantle Port Authority* [1970] 1 Lloyd's Rep. 391 (Aust.).
[6] For meaning of " practicable " see *Marshall* v. *Gotham Ltd.* [1954] A.C. 360; *Moorcraft* v. *Th. Powles & Sons Ltd.* [1962] 1 W.L.R. 1447; *Jayne* v. *N.C.B.* [1963] 2 All E.R. 220.

Defences of other persons charged with offences under s. 2 or s. 3

1542 **6.**—(1) Where a person is charged, in respect of the escape of any oil [1] or mixture [2] containing oil, with an offence under section 2 or 3 of this Act—

(*a*) as the occupier [3] or a place on land [3]; or

(*b*) as a person carrying on operations for the exploration of the sea-bed and subsoil or the exploitation of their natural resources; or

(*c*) as the owner of a pipe-line,

it shall be a defence to prove that neither the escape nor any delay in discovering it was due to any want of reasonable care and that as soon as practicable [4] after it was discovered all reasonable steps were taken for stopping or reducing it.

(2) Where a person is charged with an offence under section 2 of this Act in respect of the discharge [5] of a mixture containing oil from a place on land, it shall also, subject to subsection (3) of this section, be a defence to prove—

(*a*) that the oil was contained in an effluent produced by operations for the refining of oil;

(*b*) that it was not reasonably practicable [6] to dispose of the effluent otherwise than by discharging it into waters to which that section applies; and

(*c*) that all reasonably practicable steps had been taken for eliminating oil from the effluent.

(3) If it is proved that, at a time to which the charge relates, the surface of the waters into which the mixture was discharged from the place on land, or land adjacent to those waters, was fouled by oil, subsection (2) of this section shall not apply unless the court is satisfied that the fouling was not caused, or contributed to, by oil contained in any effluent discharged at or before that time from that place.

1543 [1] See s. 29 (1).
[2] See s. 29 (2).
[3] See s. 2 (3).

4 See note 6 to s. 5.
5 See s. 29 (3).
6 See note 6 to s. 5. Also see *Braham* v. *J. Lyons & Co. Ltd.* [1962] 1 W.L.R. 1048 and *Dorman Long (Steel) Ltd.* v. *Bell* [1964] 1 W.L.R. 333.

Protection of acts done in exercise of certain powers of harbour authorities etc.

544 **7.**—(1) Where any oil,[1] or mixture [2] containing oil, is discharged [3] in consequence of—

(*a*) the exercise of any power conferred by sections 530 to 532 of the Merchant Shipping Act 1894 (which relate to the removal of wrecks by harbour, conservancy and lighthouse authorities); or

(*b*) the exercise, for the purpose of preventing an obstruction or danger to navigation, of any power to dispose of sunk, stranded or abandoned vessels [4] which is exercisable by a harbour authority [5] under any local enactment [1];

and apart from this subsection the authority exercising the power, or a person employed by or acting on behalf of the authority, would be guilty of an offence under section 1 or section 2 of this Act in respect of that discharge, the authority or person shall not be convicted of that offence unless it is shown that they or he failed to take such steps (if any) as were reasonable in the circumstances for preventing, stopping or reducing the discharge.

(2) Subsection (1) of this section shall apply to the exercise of any power conferred by section 13 of the Dockyard Ports Regulation Act 1865 (which relates to the removal of obstructions to dockyard ports) as it applies to the exercise of any such power as is mentioned in paragraph (*a*) of that subsection, and shall, as so applying, have effect as if references to the authority exercising the power were references to the Queen's harbour master for the port in question.

545 1 See s. 29 (1).
2 See s. 29 (2).
3 See s. 29 (3).
4 See s. 29 (4).
5 See s. 8 (2).

Discharge of certain ballast water into harbours

546 **8.**—(1) A harbour authority may appoint a place within their jurisdiction where the ballast water of vessels [1] in which a cargo of petroleum-spirit [2] has been carried may be discharged into the waters of the harbour, at such times, and subject to such conditions, as the authority may determine; and, where a place is so appointed, the discharge of ballast water from such a vessel shall not constitute an offence under section 2 of this Act, if the ballast water is discharged at that place, and at a time and in accordance with the conditions so determined, and the ballast water contains no oil [2] other than petroleum-spirit.

(2) In this Act—

" harbour authority " means a person or body of persons empowered by an enactment [3] to make charges in respect of vessels entering a harbour in the United Kingdom or using facilities therein;

" harbour in the United Kingdom " means a port, estuary, haven, dock, or other place which fulfils the following conditions, that is to say,—

(*a*) that it contains waters to which section 2 of this Act applies, and

(*b*) that a person or body of persons is empowered by an enactment to make charges in respect of vessels entering that place or using facilities therein.

In this subsection " enactment " includes a local enactment,[2] and " charges " means any charges with the exception of light dues, local light dues and any other charges payable in respect of lighthouses, buoys or beacons, and of charges in respect of pilotage.

1547 [1] See s. 29 (4). As for hovercraft, see s. 31.
[2] See s. 29 (1).
[3] See s. 29 (7).

Cases excluded from sections 4 to 8

1547a See new section 8A, *post* § 1619, added by M.S.A. 1974, s. 9.

Facilities in harbour for disposal of oil residues

1548 **9.**—(1) The powers exercisable by a harbour authority [1] in respect of any harbour [1] in the United Kingdom shall include power to provide facilities for enabling vessels [2] using the harbour to discharge [3] or deposit oil residues [4] (in this Act referred to as " oil reception facilities ").

(2) Any power of a harbour authority to provide oil reception facilities shall include power to join with any other person in providing them, and references in this section to the provision of oil reception facilities by a harbour authority shall be construed accordingly; and any such power shall also include power to arrange for the provision of such facilities by any other person.

(3) A harbour authority providing oil reception facilities, or a person providing such facilities by arrangement with a harbour authority, may make reasonable charges for the use of the facilities, and may impose reasonable conditions in respect of the use thereof.

(4) Subject to the following provisions of this section, any oil reception facilities provided by, or by arrangement with, a harbour authority shall be open to all vessels using the harbour on payment of any charges, and subject to compliance with any conditions, imposed in accordance with subsection (3) of this section.

(5) Where in the case of any harbour in the United Kingdom it appears to the Secretary of State, after consultation with the harbour authority and with any organisation appearing to the Secretary of State to be representative of owners of ships registered [5] in the United Kingdom,—

(*a*) if the harbour has oil reception facilities, that those facilities are inadequate, or

(*b*) if the harbour has no such facilities, that the harbour has need of such facilities,

the Secretary of State may direct the harbour authority to provide, or arrange for the provision of, such oil reception facilities as may be specified in the direction.

549 (6) Notwithstanding the provisions of subsection (4) of this section, a harbour authority providing oil reception facilities, or a person providing such facilities by arrangement with a harbour authority, shall not be obliged to make those facilities available for use by tankers, or for the reception of oil residues discharged for the purpose of enabling a vessel to undergo repairs; and the requirements of tankers, and the reception of oil residues so discharged, shall be disregarded by the Secretary of State in exercising his powers under subsection (5) of this section.

(7) Nothing in this section shall be construed as requiring a harbour authority to allow untreated ballast water (that is to say, ballast water which contains oil and has not been subjected to an effective process for separating the oil from the water) to be discharged into any oil reception facilities provided by, or by arrangement with, the authority; and the Secretary of State shall exercise his powers under subsection (5) of this section accordingly.

(8) Any harbour authority failing to comply with any direction given under subsection (5) of this section within the period specified in the direction, or within any extended period allowed by the Secretary of State (whether before or after the end of the period so specified), shall be guilty of an offence, and liable on summary conviction to a fine not exceeding £10 for each day during which the default continues, from the day after the end of the period specified in the direction, or any extended period allowed by the Secretary of State, as the case may be, until the last day before that on which the facilities are provided in accordance with the direction.

(9) Subsections (1), (2), (5) and (8) of this section shall have effect in relation to arrangements for disposing of oil residues discharged or deposited by vessels using a harbour's oil reception facilities, and to the making of such arrangements, as those subsections have effect in relation to oil reception facilities and the provision of such facilities.

550 [1] See s. 8 (2).
[2] See s. 29 (4). As for hovercraft, see s. 31.

[3] See s. 29 (3).
[4] See s. 29 (1).
[5] For registration, see the M.S.A. 1894, s. 2.

Restrictions on transfer of oil at night

1551 **10.**—(1) No oil [1] shall be transferred [1] between sunset and sunrise to or from a vessel [2] in any harbour [3] in the United Kingdom unless the requisite notice has been given in accordance with this section or the transfer is for the purposes of a fire brigade.

(2) A general notice may be given to the harbour master [1] of a harbour that transfers of oil between sunset and sunrise will be frequently carried out at a place in the harbour within such period, not ending later than twelve months after the date on which the notice is given, as is specified in the notice; and if such a notice is given it shall be the requisite notice for the purposes of this section as regards transfers of oil at that place within the period specified in the notice.

(3) Subject to subsection (2) of this section, the requisite notice for the purposes of this section shall be a notice given to the harbour master not less than three hours nor more than ninety-six hours before the transfer of oil begins.

(4) In the case of a harbour which has no harbour master, references in this section to the harbour master shall be construed as references to the harbour authority.[3]

(5) If any oil is transferred to or from a vessel in contravention of this section, the master of the vessel, and, if the oil is transferred from or to a place on land,[4] the occupier [4] of that place, shall be liable on summary conviction to a fine not exceeding £100.

1552 [1] See s. 29 (1).
[2] See s. 29 (4). As for hovercraft, see s. 31.
[3] See s. 8 (2).
[4] See s. 2 (5).

Duty to report discharge of oil into waters of harbours

1553 **11.**—(1) If any oil [1] or mixture [2] containing oil—

(*a*) is discharged from a vessel [3] into the waters of a harbour [4] in the United Kingdom; or

(*b*) is found to be escaping or to have escaped from a vessel into any such waters; or

(*c*) is found to be escaping or to have escaped into any such waters from a place on land [5];

the owner or master of the vessel, or the occupier [5] of the place on land, as the case may be, shall forthwith [6] report the occurrence to the harbour master,[1] or, if the harbour has no harbour master, to the harbour authority.[4]

(2) A report made under subsection (1) of this section by the owner or master of a vessel shall state whether the occurrence falls within paragraph (*a*) or paragraph (*b*) of that subsection.

(3) If a person fails to make a report as required by this section he shall be liable on summary conviction to a fine not exceeding £200.

54 [1] See s. 29 (1).
[2] See s. 29 (2).
[3] See s. 29 (4). As for hovercraft, see s. 31.
[4] See s. 8 (2).
[5] See s. 2 (3).
[6] For meaning of " forthwith " in other contexts, see *Re Southam, ex p. Lamb* (1881) 19 Ch.D. 169; *Re Muscovitch, ex p. Muscovitch* [1939] Ch. 694.

Shipping casualties

Shipping casualties

55 **12.**—(1) The powers conferred by this section shall be exercisable where—

(*a*) an accident [1] has occurred to or in a ship [2]; and

(*b*) in the opinion of the Secretary of State oil [3] from the ship will or may cause pollution on a large scale in the United Kingdom or in the waters in or adjacent to the United Kingdom up to the seaward limits of territorial waters [4]; and

(*c*) in the opinion of the Secretary of State the use of the powers conferred by this section is urgently needed.

(2) For the purpose of preventing or reducing oil pollution, or the risk of oil pollution, the Secretary of State may give directions as respects the ship or its cargo—

(*a*) to the owner of the ship, or to any person in possession of the ship; or

(*b*) to the master of the ship; or

(*c*) to any salvor in possession of the ship, or to any person who is the servant or agent of any salvor in possession of the ship, and who is in charge [5] of the salvage operation.

(3) Directions under subsection (2) of this section may require the person to whom they are given to take, or refrain from taking, any action of any kind whatsoever, and without prejudice to the generality of the preceding provisions of this subsection the directions may require—

(*a*) that the ship is to be, or is not to be, moved, or is to be moved to a specified [1] place, or is to be removed from a specified area or locality; or

(*b*) that the ship is not to be moved to a specified place or area, or over a specified route; or

(*c*) that any oil or other cargo is to be, or is not to be, unloaded or discharged [3]; or

(*d*) that specified salvage measures are to be, or are not to be, taken.

(4) If in the opinion of the Secretary of State the powers conferred by subsection (2) of this section are, or have proved to be, inadequate for the purpose, the Secretary of State may, for the purpose of preventing or reducing oil pollution, or the risk of oil pollution, take, as respects the ship or its cargo, any action of any kind whatsoever, and without prejudice to the generality of the preceding provisions of this subsection the Secretary of State may—

(*a*) take any such action as he has power to require to be taken by a direction under this section;

(*b*) undertake operations for the sinking or destruction of the ship, or any part of it, of a kind which is not within the means of any person to whom he can give directions;

(*c*) undertake operations which involve the taking over of control of the ship.

(5) The powers of the Secretary of State under subsection (4) of this section shall also be exercisable by such persons as may be authorised in that behalf by the Secretary of State.

(6) Every person concerned with compliance with directions given, or with action taken, under this section shall use his best endeavours to avoid any risk to human life.

(7) The provisions of this section and of section 16 of this Act are without prejudice to any rights or powers of Her Majesty's Government in the United Kingdom exercisable apart from those sections whether under international law or otherwise.

(8) It is hereby declared that any action taken as respects a ship which is under arrest or as respects the cargo of such a ship, being action duly taken in pursuance of a direction given under this section, or being any action taken under subsection (4) or (5) of this section—

(*a*) does not constitute contempt of court; and

(*b*) does not in any circumstances make the Admiralty Marshal liable in any civil proceedings.

(9) In this section, unless the context otherwise requires—

"accident" includes the loss, stranding, abandonment of or damage to a ship; and

"specified", in relation to a direction under this section, means specified by the direction;

and the reference in subsection (8) of this section to the Admiralty Marshal includes a reference to the Admiralty Marshal of the Supreme Court of Northern Ireland.

1556 [1] See subs. (9).
[2] See s. 29 (4). As for hovercraft, see s. 31.
[3] See s. 39 (1).
[4] See note (2) to the M.S. (Oil Pollution) Act 1971, s. 10.
[5] See note (4) to s. 2.

Right to recover in respect of unreasonable loss or damage

557 **13.**[1]—(1) If any action duly taken by a person in pursuance of a direction given to him under section 12 of this Act, or any action taken under subsection (4) or (5) of that section—

(*a*) was not reasonably necessary to prevent or reduce oil pollution, or risk of oil pollution; or

(*b*) was such that the good it did or was likely to do was disproportionately less than the expense incurred, or damage suffered, as a result of the action,

a person incurring expense or suffering damage as a result of, or by himself taking, the action shall be entitled to recover compensation from the Secretary of State.

(2) In considering whether subsection (1) of this section applies, account shall be taken of—

(*a*) the extent and risk of oil pollution if the action had not been taken;

(*b*) the likelihood of the action being effective; and

(*c*) the extent of the damage which has been caused by the action.

(3) Any reference in this section to the taking of any action includes a reference to a compliance with a direction not to take some specified action.

(4) The Admiralty jurisdiction of the High Court,[2] of the Court of Session and of the Supreme Court of Northern Ireland shall include jurisdiction to hear and determine any claim arising under this section.

558 [1] This section may be applied to certain foreign and other ships; see s. 16.

[2] This jurisdiction is assigned to the Queen's Bench Division (Admiralty Court); see the Administration of Justice Act 1956, ss. 1, 2.

Offences in relation to s. 12

559 **14.**[1]—(1) If the person to whom a direction is duly given under section 12 of this Act contravenes, or fails to comply with, any requirement of the direction, he shall be guilty of an offence.

(2) If a person wilfully obstructs any person who is—

(*a*) acting on behalf of the Secretary of State in connection with the giving or service of a direction under section 12 of this Act;

(*b*) acting in compliance with a direction under that section; or

(*c*) acting under subsection (4) or (5) of that section;

he shall be guilty of an offence.

(3) In proceedings for an offence under subsection (1) of this section, it shall be a defence for the accused to prove that he has used all due diligence to ensure compliance with the direction, or that he had reason-

able cause for believing that compliance with the direction would have involved a serious risk to human life.

(4) A person guilty of an offence under this section shall be liable on summary conviction to a fine not exceeding £50,000, or on conviction on indictment to a fine.

[1] This section may be applied to certain foreign and other ships; see s. 16.

Service of directions under s. 12

1560 **15.**—(1) If the Secretary of State is satisfied that a company or other body is not one to whom section 412 or section 437 of the Companies Act 1948 (service of notices) applies so as to authorise the service of a direction on that body under either of those sections, he may give a direction under section 12 of this Act—

(*a*) to that body, as the owner of, or the person in possession of, a ship,[1] by serving the direction on the master of the ship; or

(*b*) to that body, as a salvor, by serving the direction on the person in charge of the salvage operations.

(2) For the purpose of giving or serving a direction under section 12 of this Act to or on any person on a ship, a person acting on behalf of the Secretary of State shall have the right to go on board the ship.

(3) In the application of subsection (1) of this section to Northern Ireland, for references to sections 412 and 437 of the Companies Act 1948 there shall be substituted references to sections 361 and 385 of the Companies Act (Northern Ireland) 1960.

[1] See s. 29 (4). As for hovercraft, see s. 31.

Application of ss. 12 to 15 to certain foreign and other ships

1561 **16.**—(1) Her Majesty may by Order in Council [1] provide that sections 12 to 15 of this Act, together with any other provisions of this Act, shall apply to a ship [2]—

(*a*) which is not a ship registered [3] in the United Kingdom; and

(*b*) which is for the time being outside the territorial waters [4] of the United Kingdom;

in such cases and circumstances as may be specified in the Order, and subject to such exceptions, adaptations and modifications, if any, as may be so specified.

(2) An Order in Council under subsection (1) of this section may contain such transitional and other consequential provisions as appear to Her Majesty to be expedient.

(3) Except as provided by an Order in Council under subsection (1) of this section, no direction under section 12 of this Act shall apply to a ship which is not registered in the United Kingdom and which is for the time

being outside the territorial waters of the United Kingdom, and no action shall be taken under subsection (4) or (5) of section 12 of this Act as respects any such ship.

(4) No direction under section 12 of this Act shall apply to any vessel of Her Majesty's navy or to any Government ship (within the meaning of section 80 of the Merchant Shipping Act 1906) and no action shall be taken under subsection (4) or (5) of that section as respects any such vessel or ship.

62 [1] See the Oil in Navigable Waters (Shipping Casualties) Order 1971 (S.I. No. 1736), saved by s. 33 (2).
[2] See s. 29 (4). As for hovercraft, see s. 31.
[3] See the M.S.A. 1894, s. 2.
[4] See note (2) to the M.S. (Oil Pollution) Act 1971, s. 10.

Enforcement

Oil records

63 **17.**—(1) The Secretary of State may make regulations [1] requiring oil record books to be carried in ships [2] registered [3] in the United Kingdom and requiring the master of any such ship to record in the oil record book carried by it—

(*a*) the carrying out, on board or in connection with the ship, of such of the following operations as may be prescribed, that is to say, operations relating to—

(i) the loading of oil [4] cargo, or

(ii) the transfer [4] of oil cargo during a voyage, or

(iii) the discharge [5] or oil cargo, or

(iv) the ballasting or oil tanks (whether cargo or bunker fuel tanks) and the discharge of ballast from, and cleaning of, such tanks, or

(v) the separation of oil from water, or from other substances, in any mixture [6] containing oil, or

(vi) the disposal of any oil or water, or any other substance, arising from operations relating to any of the matters specified in the preceding sub-paragraphs, or

(vii) the disposal of any other oil residues [4];

(*b*) any occasion on which oil or a mixture containing oil is discharged from the ship for the purpose of securing the safety of any vessel, or of preventing damage to any vessel or cargo, or of saving life;

(*c*) any occasion on which oil or a mixture containing oil is found to be escaping, or to have escaped, from the ship in consequence of damage to the ship, or by reason of leakage.

(2) The Secretary of State may make regulations [7] requiring the keeping of records relating to the transfer of oil to and from vessels while

they are within the seaward limits of the territorial waters of the United Kingdom; and the requirements of any regulations made under this subsection shall be in addition to the requirements of any regulations made under subsection (1) of this section.

(3) Any records required to be kept by regulations made under subsection (2) of this section shall, unless the vessel is a barge,[4] be kept by the master of the vessel, and shall, if the vessel is a barge, be kept, in so far as they relate to the transfer of oil to the barge, by the person supplying the oil and, in so far as they relate to the transfer of oil from the barge, by the person to whom the oil is delivered.

1564 (4) Regulations under this section requiring the carrying of oil record books or the keeping of records may—

(*a*) prescribe the form of the oil record books or records and the nature of the entries to be made in them;

(*b*) require the person providing or keeping the books or records to retain them for a prescribed period;

(*c*) require that person, at the end of the prescribed period, to transmit the books or records to a place or person determined by or under the regulations;

(*d*) provide for the custody or disposal of the books or records after their transmission to such a place or person.

(5) If any ship fails to carry such an oil record book as it is required to carry under this section the owner or master shall be liable on summary conviction to a fine not exceeding £500; if any person fails to comply with any requirements imposed on him by or under this section, he shall be liable on summary conviction to a fine not exceeding £500; and if any person makes an entry in any oil record book carried or record kept under this section which is to his knowledge false or misleading in any material particular, he shall be liable on summary conviction to a fine not exceeding £500, or imprisonment for a term not exceeding six months, or both, or on conviction on indictment to a fine or to imprisonment for a term not exceeding two years or both.

(6) In any proceedings under this Act—

(*a*) any oil record book carried or record kept in pursuance of regulations made under this section shall be admissible as evidence, and in Scotland shall be sufficient evidence, of the facts stated in it;

(*b*) any copy of an entry in such an oil record book or record which is certified by the master of the ship in which the book is carried or by the person by whom the record is required to be kept to be a true copy of the entry shall be admissible as evidence, and in Scotland shall be sufficient evidence, of the facts stated in the entry;

(*c*) any document purporting to be an oil record book carried or record kept in pursuance of regulations made under this section, or purporting to be such a certified copy as is mentioned in the preceding paragraph, shall, unless the contrary is proved, be presumed to be such a book, record or copy, as the case may be.

65 [1] See the Oil in Navigable Waters (Transfer Records) Regulations 1957 (S.I. No. 358) saved by s. 33 (2).
[2] See s. 29 (4). As for hovercraft, see s. 31.
[3] See the M.S.A. 1894, s. 2.
[4] See s. 29 (1).
[5] See s. 29 (3).
[6] See s. 29 (2).
[7] See the Oil in Navigable Waters (Records) Regulations 1972 (S.I. 1929).

Powers of inspection

66 **18.**—(1) The Secretary of State may appoint any person as an inspector to report to him—

(*a*) whether the prohibitions, restrictions and obligations imposed by virtue of this Act (including prohibitions so imposed by the creation of offences under any provision of this Act other than section 3) have been complied with;

(*b*) what measures (other than measures made obligatory by regulations made under section 4 of this Act) have been taken to prevent the escape of oil [1] and mixtures [2] containing oil;

(*c*) whether the oil reception facilities [3] provided in harbours are adequate;

and any such inspector may be so appointed to report either in a particular case or in a class of cases specified in his appointment.

(2) Every surveyor of ships shall be taken to be a person appointed generally under the preceding subsection to report to the Secretary of State in every kind of case falling within that subsection.

(3) Section 729 of the Merchant Shipping Act 1894 (powers of inspectors) shall apply to persons appointed or taken to be appointed under subsection (1) of this section as it applies to the inspectors referred to in that section and shall, as so applying, have effect as if—

(*a*) in paragraph (*a*) of subsection (1) of that section, the reference to a ship included any vessel, and the reference to that Act were a reference to this Act and any regulations made under this Act; and

(*b*) any power under that section to inspect premises included power to inspect any apparatus used for transferring [1] oil.

(4) Any power of an inspector, under section 729 as applied by the preceding subsection, to inspect a vessel shall include power to test [4] any

equipment with which the vessel is required to be fitted in pursuance of regulations made under section 4 of this Act.

1567 (5) Any power of an inspector, under section 729 as so applied, to require the production of any oil record book [5] required to be carried or records required to be kept in pursuance of regulations made under section 17 of this Act shall include power to copy any entry therein and require the master to certify the copy as a true copy of the entry; and in subsection (3) of section 729, as so applied, the reference to making a declaration shall be construed as a reference to the certification of such a copy.

(6) Without prejudice to any powers exercisable by virtue of the preceding provisions of this section, in the case of a vessel which is for the time being in a harbour [6] in the United Kingdom the harbour master,[1] and any other person appointed by the Secretary of State under this subsection (either generally or in relation to a particular vessel), shall have power—

(*a*) to go on board and inspect the vessel or any part thereof, or any of the machinery, boats, equipment or articles on board the vessel, for the purpose of ascertaining the circumstances relating to an alleged discharge [7] of oil or a mixture containing oil from the vessel into the waters of the harbour;

(*b*) to require the production of any oil record book required to be carried or records required to be kept in pursuance of regulations made under section 17 of this Act; and

(*c*) to copy any entry in any such book or record and require the master to certify the copy as a true copy of the entry.

(7) A person exercising any powers conferred by subsection (6) of this section shall not unnecessarily detain or delay the vessel from proceeding on any voyage.

(8) If any person fails to comply with any requirement duly made in pursuance of paragraph (*b*) or paragraph (*c*) of subsection (6) of this section, he shall be liable on summary conviction to a fine not exceeding £10; and if any person wilfully obstructs a person acting in the exercise of any power conferred by virtue of this section, he shall be liable on summary conviction to a fine not exceeding £100.

1568 [1] See s. 29 (1).
[2] See s. 29 (2).
[3] See s. 9 (1).
[4] See s. 29 (5).
[5] See s 17.
[6] See s. 8 (2).
[7] See s. 29 (3).

Prosecutions

569 **19.**—(1) Proceedings for an offence under this Act may, in England or Wales, be brought only—

(*a*) by or with the consent of the Attorney General, or

(*b*) if the offence is one to which subsection (2) of this section applies, by the harbour authority,[1] or

(*c*) unless the offence is one mentioned in paragraph (*b*), (*c*) or (*d*) of subsection (2) of this section, by the Secretary of State or a person authorised by any general or special direction of the Secretary of State.

(2) This subsection applies to the following offences—

(*a*) any offence under section 2 of this Act which is alleged to have been committed by the discharge[2] of oil,[3] or a mixture[4] containing oil, into the waters of a harbour[1] in the United Kingdom;

(*b*) any offence in relation to such a harbour under section 10 or section 11 of this Act;

(*c*) any offence under section 17 of this Act relating to the keeping of records of the transfer[3] of oil within such a harbour; and

(*d*) any offence under section 18 of this Act in respect of a failure to comply with a requirement of a harbour master,[3] or in respect of obstruction of a harbour master acting in the exercise of any power conferred by virtue of that section.

(3) The preceding provisions of this section shall apply in relation to any part of a dockyard port within the meaning of the Dockyard Ports Regulation Act 1865 as follows, that is to say—

(*a*) if that part is comprised in a harbour in the United Kingdom, the reference to the harbour authority shall be construed as including a reference to the Queen's harbour master for the port;

(*b*) if that part is not comprised in a harbour in the United Kingdom, the references to such a harbour shall be construed as references to such a dockyard port and the reference to the harbour authority as a reference to the Queen's harbour master for the port.

(4) Where, immediately before the date on which (apart from this subsection) the time for bringing summary proceedings for an offence under this Act would expire, the person to be charged is outside the United Kingdom, the time for bringing the proceedings shall be extended until the end of the period of two months beginning with the date on which he next enters the United Kingdom.

570 (5) Proceedings for any offence under this Act may (without prejudice to any jurisdiction exercisable apart from this subsection) be taken against a person at any place at which he is for the time being.

(6) If a local fisheries committee constituted by an order made, or having effect as if made, under section 1 of the Sea Fisheries Regulation Act 1966 or any of its officers is authorised in that behalf under subsection (1) of this section, the committee may institute proceedings for any offence under this Act committed within the district of the committee.

(7) The preceding provisions of this section do not apply in relation to an offence under section 3 of this Act, but proceedings for such an offence may—

(*a*) in England and Wales, be brought only by or with the consent of the Director of Public Prosecutions; and

(*b*) in Northern Ireland, be brought only by or with the consent of the Attorney General for Northern Ireland;

and any such proceedings may be taken, and the offence may for all incidental purposes be treated as having been committed, in any place in the United Kingdom.

(8) Where a body corporate is guilty of an offence under section 3 of this Act and the offence is proved to have been committed with the consent or connivance of, or to be attributable to any neglect on the part of, any director, manager, secretary or other similar officer of the body corporate or any person who was purporting to act in any such capacity he, as well as the body corporate, shall be guilty of the offence and shall be liable to be proceeded against and punished accordingly.

In this subsection, " director " in relation to a body corporate established for the purpose of carrying on under national ownership any industry or part of an industry or undertaking, being a body corporate whose affairs are managed by its members, means a member of that body corporate.

1571 [1] See s. 8 (2).
[2] See s. 29 (3).
[3] See s. 29 (1).
[4] See s. 29 (2).

Enforcement and application of fines

1572 **20.**—(1) Where a fine imposed by a court in proceedings against the owner or master of a vessel [1] for an offence under this Act is not paid at the time ordered by the court, the court shall, in addition to any other powers for enforcing payment, have power to direct the amount remaining unpaid to be levied by distress or poinding and sale of the vessel, her tackle, furniture and apparel.

(2) Where a person is convicted of an offence under section 1 or section 2 of this Act, and the court imposes a fine in respect of the offence, then if it appears to the court that any person has incurred, or will incur, expenses in removing any pollution, or making good any damage, which is

attributable to the offence, the court may order the whole or part of the fine to be paid to that person for or towards defraying those expenses.

[1] See s. 29 (4). As for hovercraft, see s. 31.

Enforcement of Conventions relating to oil pollution

73 **21.**—(1) Her Majesty may by Order in Council [1] empower such persons as may be designated by or under the Order to go on board any Convention ship [2] while the ship is within a harbour [3] in the United Kingdom, and to require production of any oil record book [4] required to be carried in accordance with the Convention.

(2) An Order in Council [1] under this section may, for the purposes of the Order, and with any necessary modifications, apply any of the provisions of this Act relating to the production and inspection of oil record books and the taking of copies of entries therein, and to the admissibility in evidence of such oil record books and copies, including any provisions of the Merchant Shipping Act 1894 applied by those provisions, and including any penal provisions of this Act in so far as they relate to those matters.

(3) Her Majesty, if satisfied that the government of any country has accepted, or denounced, the Convention, or that the Convention extends, or has ceased to extend, to any territory, may by Order in Council [5] make a declaration to that effect.

(4) In this section " the Convention " means any Convention accepted by Her Majesty's Government in the United Kingdom in so far as it relates to the prevention of pollution of the sea by oil; and " Convention ship " means a ship registered in—

(*a*) a country the government of which has been declared by an Order in Council under the preceding subsection to have accepted the Convention, and has not been so declared to have denounced it; or

(*b*) a territory to which it has been so declared that the Convention extends, not being a territory to which it has been so declared that the Convention has ceased to extend.

574 [1] See the Oil in Navigable Waters (Enforcement of Convention) Order 1958 (S.I. No. 1526), saved by s. 33 (2).

[2] See s. 29 (4). As for hovercraft, see s. 31.

[3] See s. 8 (2).

[4] See s. 17.

[5] See the Prevention of Oil Pollution (Convention Countries) (Fiji) Order1973 (S.I. No. 613). Also see the following Orders, saved by s. 33 (2):

(i) 1958 S.I. No. 1527 (Belgium, Canada, Denmark, Germany, France, Ireland, Mexico, Netherlands, Norway, Sweden, and the U.K.);
(ii) 1962 S.I. No. 2189 (Netherlands Antilles);
(iii) 1964 S.I. No. 280 (Algeria);
(iv) 1962 S.I. No. 2354 (Australia);
(v) 1963 S.I. No. 1317 (Dominican Republic);
(vi) 1962 S.I. No. 1657 (Ghana);
(vii) 1959 S.I. No. 869 (Finland);
(viii) 1967 S.I. No. 814 (Greece);

(ix) 1962 S.I. No. 1092 (Iceland);
(x) 1966 S.I. No. 189 (Israel);
(xi) 1964 S.I. No. 931 (Italy);
(xii) 1967 S.I. No. 814 (Ivory Coast);
(xiii) 1967 S.I. No. 1680 (Japan);
(xiv) 1963 S.I. No. 1149 (Jordan);
(xv) 1962 S.I. No. 174 (Kuwait);
(xvi) 1967 S.I. No. 1153 (Lebanon);
(xvii) 1962 S.I. No. 1345 (Liberia);
(xviii) 1972 S.I. No. 1591 (Libya);
(xix) 1965 S.I. No. 976 (Malagasy);
(xx) 1970 S.I. No. 824 (Monaco);
(xxi) 1968 S.I. No. 730 (Morocco);
(xxii) 1971 S.I. No. 1735 (New Zealand);
(xxiii) 1968 S.I. No. 468 (Nigeria);
(xxiv) 1963 S.I. No. 1931 (Panama);
(xxv) 1964 S.I. No. 60 (Philippines);
(xxvi) 1961 S.I. No. 1008 (Poland);
(xxvii) 1967 S.I. No. 1680 (Portugal);
(xxviii) 1972 S.I. No. 1591 (Senegal);
(xxix) 1964 S.I. No. 281 (Spain);
(xxx) 1969 S.I. No. 1085 (South Yemen);
(xxxi) 1966 S.I. No. 392 (Switzerland);
(xxxii) 1969 S.I. No. 387 (Syria);
(xxxiii) 1973 S.I. No. 1752 (Tunisia);
(xxxiv) 1963 S.I. No. 1150 (U.A.R.);
(xxxv) 1961 S.I. No. 2277 (U.S.A.);
(xxxvi) 1970 S.I. No. 638 (U.S.S.R.);
(xxxvii) 1964 S.I. No. 64 (Venezuela).

Miscellaneous and supplementary

Power to apply certain provisions to ships registered outside United Kingdom

1575 **22.**—(1) Her Majesty may by Order in Council [1] direct that, subject to such exceptions and modifications as may be specified in the Order, any regulations made under section 4 or section 17 (1) of this Act shall apply to ships [2] registered in countries and territories other than the United Kingdom at any time when they are in a harbour [3] in the United Kingdom, or are within the seaward limits of the territorial waters of the United Kingdom while on their way to or from a harbour in the United Kingdom.

(2) An Order in Council under subsection (1) of this section shall not be made so as to impose different requirements in respect of ships of different countries or territories; but if Her Majesty is satisfied, as respects any country or territory, that ships registered there are required, by the law of that country or territory, to comply with provisions which are substantially the same as, or equally effective with, the requirements imposed by virtue of the Order, Her Majesty may by Order in Council direct that those requirements shall not apply to any ship registered in that country or territory if the ship complies with such of those provisions as are applicable thereto under the law of that country or territory.

(3) No regulation shall by virtue of an Order in Council under this section apply to any ship as being within a harbour in the United Kingdom, or on her way to or from such a harbour, if the ship would not have been within the harbour, or, as the case may be, on her way to or from the

harbour, but for stress of weather or any other circumstances which neither the master nor the owner nor the charterer (if any) of the ship could have prevented or forestalled.

76 [1] No Order in Council has yet been made.
[2] See s. 29 (4). As for hovercraft, see s. 31.
[3] See s. 8 (2).

Power of Secretary of State to grant exemptions

77 **23.** The Secretary of State may exempt any vessels or classes of vessels from any of the provisions of this Act or of any regulations made thereunder, either absolutely or subject to such conditions as he thinks fit.

Application of Act to Government ships

78 **24.**—(1) The provisions of this Act do not apply to vessels of Her Majesty's navy, nor to Government ships in the service of the Secretary of State while employed for the purposes of Her Majesty's navy.

(2) Subject to subsection (1) of this section and subsection (4) of section 16 of this Act—

(*a*) provisions of this Act which are expressed to apply only to ships registered in the United Kingdom apply to Government ships so registered and also to Government ships not so registered but held for the purposes of Her Majesty's Government in the United Kingdom;

(*b*) provisions of this Act which are expressed to apply to vessels generally apply to Government ships.

(3) In this section " Government ships " has the same meaning as in section 80 of the Merchant Shipping Act 1906.

Provisions as to Isle of Man, Channel Islands, colonies and dependencies

79 **25.**—(1) Her Majesty may by Order in Council [1] direct that such of the provisions of this Act, other than section 3, or of any enactment for the time being in force amending or replacing them, as may be specified in the Order shall extend, with such exceptions and modifications, if any, as may be specified in the Order, to the Isle of Man, any of the Channel Islands, or any colony.

(2) The Foreign Jurisdiction Act 1890 shall have effect as if the provisions of this Act, other than section 3, were included among the enactments which, by virtue of section 5 of that Act, may be extended by Order in Council to foreign countries in which for the time being Her Majesty has jurisdiction.

(3) Her Majesty may by Order in Council direct that, subject to such exceptions and modifications as may be specified in the Order, the provisions of this Act which (apart from sections 22 and 24 of this Act) apply

only to ships registered in the United Kingdom shall apply also to ships registered in any country or territory specified in the Order, being a country or territory to which the provisions of this Act can be extended by virtue of either of the preceding subsections.

1580 [1] (i) As for the Isle of Man, see the Oil in Navigable Waters (Isle of Man) Order 1966 (S.I. No. 394) and Regulations 1966 (S.I. No. 426).
(ii) As for Hong Kong, see the Oil in Navigable Waters (Hong Kong) Order 1963 (S.I. No. 788) and Regulations 1963 (S.I. No. 848).
(iii) As for Guernsey, see the Oil in Navigable Waters (Guernsey) Order 1966 (S.I. No. 393) and Regulation 1966 (S.I. No. 425).
(iv) As for Jersey, see the Oil in Navigable Waters (Jersey) Order 1966 (S.I. No. 395) and Regulations 1966 (S.I. No. 427).

Annual report

1581 **26.** The Secretary of State shall, as soon as possible after the end of each calendar year, make a report on the exercise and performance of his functions under this Act during that year, which shall include such observations as he may think fit to make on the operation during that year of this Act and of any Convention accepted by Her Majesty's Government in the United Kingdom in so far as it relates to the prevention of pollution of the sea by oil, and the Secretary of State shall lay a copy of every such report before each House of Parliament.

General provisions as to Orders in Council, regulations and orders

1582 **27.**—(1) Any power to make regulations or an order under this Act shall be exercisable by statutory instrument.

(2) Any statutory instrument made by virtue of this Act, other than an Order in Council under section 25 or an order under section 34 of this Act, shall be subject to annulment in pursuance of a resolution of either House of Parliament.

(3) Any Order in Council, or other order, made under any provision of this Act may be varied or revoked by a subsequent Order in Council or order made thereunder.

(4) Where a power to make regulations is conferred by any provision of this Act, regulations made under that power may be made with respect to all or with respect to any one or more of the classes of vessel or other matters to which the provision relates, and different provision may be made by any such regulations for different classes of vessel or otherwise for different classes of case or different circumstances.

Financial provisions

1583 **28.**—(1) There shall be defrayed out of moneys provided by Parliament any administrative expenses of the Secretary of State under this Act.

(2) Any fees received by the Secretary of State under this Act shall be paid into the Consolidated Fund.

Interpretation

584 **29.**—(1) In this Act—

"barge" includes a lighter and any similar vessel;

"harbour authority" and "harbour in the United Kingdom" have the meanings assigned to them by section 8 (2) of this Act;

"harbour master" includes a dock master or pier master, and any person specially appointed by a harbour authority for the purpose of enforcing the provisions of this Act in relation to the harbour;

"local enactment" means a local or private Act, or an order confirmed by Parliament or brought into operation in accordance with special parliamentary procedure;

"oil" means oil of any description [1] and includes spirit produced from oil of any description, and also includes coal tar;

"oil reception facilities" has the meaning assigned to it by section 9 (1) of this Act;

"oil residues" means any waste consisting of, or arising from, oil or a mixture containing oil;

"outside the territorial waters [2] of the United Kingdom" means outside the seaward limits of those waters;

"petroleum-spirit" has the same meaning as in the Petroleum (Consolidation) Act 1928[3];

"place on land" has the meaning assigned to it by section 2 (3) of this Act;

"sea" includes any estuary or arm of the sea;

"transfer", in relation to oil, means transfer in bulk.

585 (2) Any reference in any provision of this Act to a mixture containing oil shall be construed as a reference to any mixture of oil (or, as the case may be, of oil of a description referred to in that provision) with water or with any other substance.

(3) Any reference in the provisions of this Act other than section 11 to the discharge of oil or a mixture containing oil, or to its being discharged, from a vessel, place or thing, except where the reference is to its being discharged for a specified purpose, includes a reference to the escape of the oil or mixture, or (as the case may be) to its escaping, from that vessel, place or thing.

(4) For the purposes of any provision of this Act relating to the discharge of oil or a mixture containing oil from a vessel, any floating craft (other than a vessel) which is attached to a vessel shall be treated as part of the vessel.[4]

(5) Any power conferred by this Act to test any equipment on board a vessel shall be construed as including a power to require persons on board

the vessel to carry out such work as may be requisite for the purpose of testing the equipment; and any provision of this Act as to submitting equipment for testing shall be construed accordingly.

(6) Subject to the preceding subsections, expressions used in this Act and in the Merchant Shipping Act 1894,[5] have the same meanings in this Act as in that Act.

(7) Except in so far as the context otherwise requires, any reference in this Act to an enactment shall be construed as a reference to that enactment as amended by or under any other enactment.

1586 [1] This includes vegetable oils as well as mineral oils (*e.g.* sunflower seed oil); see *Cosh* v. *Larsen* [1971] 1 Lloyd's Rep. 557.

[2] See note (2) to the M.S. (Oil Pollution) Act 1971 s. 10.

[3] See *ibid.* s. 23.

[4] As for hovercraft, see s. 31.

[5] See, particularly, the definitions in the M.S.A. 1894, s. 742, where " vessel," " ship," " master," and " harbour," are each referred to.

Provisions as to Northern Ireland

1587 **30.**—(1) This Act extends to Northern Ireland and the following provisions of this section shall have effect with respect to the application of this Act to Northern Ireland.

(2) References in section 9 of this Act to the Secretary of State shall be construed as references to the Ministry of Commerce for Northern Ireland (in this section referred to as " the Ministry of Commerce ").

(3) In relation to places on land [1] in Northern Ireland, and to apparatus located in Northern Ireland otherwise than on board a vessel,[2]—

(*a*) persons appointed by the Secretary of State as inspectors under section 18 of this Act, and surveyors of ships in their capacity as persons so appointed, shall have no powers of entry or inspection; but

(*b*) persons appointed by the Ministry of Commerce shall have the like powers as (but for the preceding paragraph) persons appointed by the Secretary of State would have by virtue of that section, and the provisions of that section shall have effect in relation to persons appointed by the Ministry of Commerce as, in England and Wales, they have effect in relation to persons appointed by the Secretary of State.

(4) Subsection (1) of section 19 of this Act shall apply to proceedings in Northern Ireland as it applies to proceedings in England and Wales, but with the substitution, for references to the Attorney General, of references to the Attorney General for Northern Ireland; except that, in relation to proceedings for an offence under section 2 of this Act—

(*a*) if the alleged offence relates to the discharge [3] of oil [4] of a mixture [5] containing oil from a vessel in a harbour or inland waterway in Northern Ireland, the references in that subsection to the

Secretary of State shall be construed as references to the Secretary of State or the Ministry of Commerce;

(*b*) if the alleged offence relates to the discharge of oil or a mixture containing oil from a place on land in Northern Ireland, or from apparatus located in Northern Ireland otherwise than on board a vessel, the references in that subsection to the Secretary of State shall be construed as references to the Ministry of Commerce.

(5) In the definition of " local enactment " in subsection (1) of section 29 of this Act the reference to a local or private Act includes a reference to a local or private Act of the Parliament of Northern Ireland, and the reference to an order confirmed by Parliament includes a reference to an order confirmed by that Parliament; and the reference in that subsection to the Petroleum (Consolidation) Act 1928 shall be construed as a reference to the Petroleum (Consolidation) Act (Northern Ireland) 1929.

(6) The provisions of this Act, so far as they relate to matters with respect to which the Parliament of Northern Ireland has power to make laws, shall not be taken to restrict that power, and any laws made by that Parliament in the exercise of that power shall have effect notwithstanding anything in those provisions.

588 [1] See s. 2 (3).
[2] See s. 29 (4). As for hovercraft, see s. 31.
[3] See s. 29 (3).
[4] See s. 29 (1).
[5] See s. 29 (2).

Application to hovercraft

589 **31.** The enactments and instruments with respect to which provision may be made by an Order in Council [1] under section 1 (1) (*h*) of the Hovercraft Act 1968 shall include this Act and any instrument made under it.

[1] No such provision has yet been made.

Saving for other restrictions, rights of action etc.

590 **32.** Subject to section 33 of the Interpretation Act 1889 (offence under two or more laws) nothing in this Act shall affect any restriction imposed by or under any other enactment, whether contained in a public general Act or in a local or private Act, or shall derogate from any right of action or other remedy (whether civil or criminal) in proceedings instituted otherwise than under this Act.

Repeals and savings

591 **33.**—(1) The enactments specified in the Schedule to this Act are hereby repealed to the extent specified in the third column of that Schedule.

(2) In so far as any instrument made or other thing done under any

enactment repealed by this Act could have been made or done under any provision of this Act it shall have effect as if made or done under that provision; and references in any such instrument to any such enactment shall be construed as referring to the corresponding provision of this Act or, as the case may be, to this Act.

(3) Nothing in the foregoing provisions of this section shall be taken as prejudicing the operation of section 38 of the Interpretation Act 1889 (which relates to the effect of repeals).

Short title and commencement

1592 **34.**—(1) This Act may be cited as the Prevention of Oil Pollution Act 1971.

(2) This Act shall come into force on such day as the Secretary of State may by order [1] appoint; but the day so appointed shall not be earlier than the day or, if more than one, the latest day, appointed under section 12 (3) of the Oil in Navigable Waters Act 1971 for the coming into force of the provisions of that Act.

[1] *viz.* March 1, 1973; see the Prevention of Oil Pollution Act 1971 (Commencement) Order 1973 (S.I. No. 203).

SCHEDULE

1593 ENACTMENTS REPEALED

Chapter	Short Title	Extent of Repeal
3 & 4 Eliz. 2. c. 25.	The Oil in Navigable Waters Act 1955.	The whole Act.
1963 c. 28.	The Oil in Navigable Waters Act 1963.	The whole Act.
1964 c. 29.	The Continental Shelf Act 1964.	Section 5.
1966 c. 38.	The Sea Fisheries Regulation Act 1966.	Section 21 (7).
1971 c. 21.	The Oil in Navigable Waters Act 1971.	The whole Act.
1971 c. 61.	The Mineral Workings (Offshore Installations) Act 1971.	Section 10 (1) (*c*).

PROTECTION OF WRECKS ACT 1973

[1973 c. 33]

An Act to secure the protection of wrecks in territorial waters and the sites of such wrecks, from interference by unauthorised persons; and for connected purposes. [18th July 1973]

Be it enacted, etc.:

Protection of sites of historic wrecks

1594 **1.**—(1) If the Secretary of State is satisfied with respect to any site in United Kingdom waters [1] that—

(*a*) it is, or may prove to be, the site of a vessel lying wrecked on or in the sea bed; and

(*b*) on account of the historical, archaeological or artistic importance of the vessel, or of any objects contained or formerly contained in it which may be lying on the sea [1] bed in or near the wreck, the site ought to be protected from unauthorised interference,

he may by order [2] designate an area round the site as a restricted area.

(2) An order under this section shall identify the site where the vessel lies or formerly lay, or is supposed to lie or have lain, and—

(*a*) the restricted area shall be all within such distance of the site (so identified) as is specified in the order, but excluding any area above high water mark of ordinary spring tides; and

(*b*) the distance specified for the purposes of paragraph (*a*) above shall be whatever the Secretary of State thinks appropriate to ensure protection for the wreck.

(3) Subject to section 3 (3) below, a person commits an offence if, in a restricted area, he does any of the following things otherwise than under the authority of a licence granted by the Secretary of State—

(*a*) he tampers with, damages or removes any part of a vessel lying wrecked on or in the sea bed, or any object formerly contained in such a vessel; or

(*b*) he carries out diving or salvage operations directed to the exploration of any wreck or to removing objects from it or from the sea bed, or uses equipment constructed or adapted for any purpose of diving or salvage operations; or

(*c*) he deposits, so as to fall and lie abandoned on the sea bed, anything which, if it were to fall on the site of a wreck (whether it so falls or not), would wholly or partly obliterate the site or obstruct access to it, or damage any part of the wreck;

and also commits an offence if he causes or permits any of those things to be done by others in a restricted area, otherwise than under the authority of such a licence.

1595 (4) Before making an order under this section, the Secretary of State shall consult with such persons as he considers appropriate having regard to the purposes of the order; but this consultation may be dispensed with if he is satisfied that the case is one in which an order should be made as a matter of immediate urgency.

(5) A licence granted by the Secretary of State for the purposes of subsection (3) above shall be in writing and—

(*a*) the Secretary of State shall in respect of a restricted area grant licences only to persons who appear to him either—

(i) to be competent, and properly equipped, to carry out salvage operations in a manner appropriate to the historical, archaeological or artistic importance of any wreck which may be lying in the area and of any objects contained or formerly contained in a wreck, or

(ii) to have any other legitimate reason for doing in the area that which can only be done under the authority of a licence;

(*b*) a licence may be granted subject to conditions or restrictions, and may be varied or revoked by the Secretary of State at any time after giving not less than one week's notice to the licensee; and

(*c*) anything done contrary to any condition or restriction of a licence shall be treated for purposes of subsection (3) above as done otherwise than under the authority of the licence.

(6) Where a person is authorised, by a licence of the Secretary of State granted under this section, to carry out diving or salvage operations, it is an offence for any other person to obstruct him, or cause or permit him to be obstructed, in doing anything which is authorised by the licence, subject however to section 3 (3) below.

1596 [1] See s. 3 (1).

[2] (i) Protection of Wrecks (Designation) Order 1973 (S.I. No. 1531 as amended by S.I. 1975 No 262).
(ii) Protection of Wrecks (Designation No. 2) Order 1973 (S.I. No. 1690).
(iii) Protection of Wrecks (Designation No. 1) Order 1974 (S.I. No. 55).
(iv) Protection of Wrecks (Designation No. 2) Order 1974 (S.I. No. 56).
(v) Protection of Wrecks (Designation No. 3) Order 1974 (S.I. No. 57).
(vi) Protection of Wrecks (Designation No. 4) Order 1974 (S.I. No. 58).
(vii) Protection of Wrecks (Designation No. 5) Order 1974 (S.I. No. 457).
(viii) Protection of Wrecks (Designation No. 6) Order 1974 (S.I. No. 458).
(ix) Protection of Wrecks (Designation No. 7) Order 1974 (S.I. No. 910).
(x) Protection of Wrecks (Designation No. 1) Order 1975 (S.I. No. 174).
(xi) Protection of Wrecks (Designation No. 2) Order 1975 (S.I. No. 726).

Prohibition on approaching dangerous wrecks

1597 **2.**—(1) If the Secretary of State is satisfied with respect to a vessel lying wrecked in United Kingdom waters [1] that—

(*a*) because of anything contained in it, the vessel is in a condition which makes it a potential danger to life or property; and

(*b*) on that account it ought to be protected from unauthorised interference,

he may by order [2] designate an area round the vessel as a prohibited area.

(2) An order under this section shall identify the vessel and the place where it is lying and—

(*a*) the prohibited area shall be all within such distance of the vessel as is specified by the order, excluding any area above high water mark of ordinary spring tides; and

(*b*) the distance specified for the purposes of paragraph (*a*) above shall be whatever the Secretary of State thinks appropriate to ensure that unauthorised persons are kept away from the vessel.

(3) Subject to section 3 (3) below, a person commits an offence if, without authority in writing granted by the Secretary of State, he enters a prohibited area, whether on the surface or under water.

[1] See s. 3 (1).
[2] No order has yet been made under this section.

Supplementary provisions

1598 3.—(1) In this Act—

" United Kingdom waters " means any part of the sea within the seaward limits of United Kingdom territorial waters and includes any part of a river within the ebb and flow of ordinary spring tides;

" the sea " includes any estuary or arm of the sea; and

references to the sea bed include any area submerged at high water of ordinary spring tides.

(2) An order under section 1 or section 2 above shall be made by statutory instrument subject to annulment in pursuance of a resolution of either House of Parliament and may be varied or revoked by a subsequent order under the section; and the Secretary of State shall revoke any such order if—

(*a*) in the case of an order under section 1 designating a restricted area, he is of opinion that there is not, or is no longer, any wreck in the area which requires protection under this Act;

(*b*) in the case of an order under section 2 designating a prohibited area, he is satisfied that the vessel is no longer in a condition which makes it a potential danger to life or property.

(3) Nothing is to be regarded as constituting an offence under this Act where it is done by a person—

(*a*) in the course of any action taken by him for the sole purpose of dealing with an emergency of any description; or (*b*) in exercising, or seeing to the exercise of, functions conferred by or under an enactment (local or other) on him or a body for which he acts; or

(*c*) out of necessity due to stress of weather or navigational hazards.

(4) A person guilty of an offence under section 1 or section 2 above shall be liable on summary conviction to a fine of not more than £400, or on conviction on indictment to a fine; and proceedings for such an offence may be taken, and the offence may for all incidental purposes be treated as having been committed, at any place in the United Kingdom where he is for the time being.

Citation

1599 **4.** This Act may be cited as the Protection of Wrecks Act 1973.

MERCHANT SHIPPING ACT 1974

[1974 c. 43]

An Act to make further provision concerning oil pollution by ships and related matters; to give power to protect shipping and trading interests against foreign action concerning or affecting carriage of goods by sea; to make provision relating to the operation of submersible apparatus; to alter the constitution of the Commissioners of Northern Lighthouses; and to amend certain provisions of the Merchant Shipping Act 1970 relating to offences committed by seamen. [31st July 1974]

1600 INTRODUCTORY NOTE: Part I of the Act gives effect to the provisions of the International Convention on the Establishment of an International Fund for Compensation for Oil Pollution Damage, dated Brussels December 18, 1971. The 1971 Convention is linked to the International Convention on Civil Liability for Oil Pollution Damage dated Brussels, November 29, 1969, to which effect was given by the Merchant Shipping (Oil Pollution) Act 1971, § 1497, *ante*. The object of the Fund to be established under this Act is to provide compensation for victims of oil pollution damage who have been unable to obtain full recompense under the 1971 Act. Part II of the Act implements the 1971 amendments to the Prevention of the Pollution of the Sea by Oil Convention 1954, concerning the design and construction of oil tankers. The principal purpose is to limit the size of individual cargo tanks. Part III of the Act confers powers on the Secretary of State to meet flag discrimination and other action by foreign governments whereby U.K. shipping or trading interests are adversely affected or where such powers are needed to effect compliance with the international obligation of the U.K. Part IV of the Act contains provisions relating to the safety of any submersible apparatus and the welfare of those using it. Regulations made thereunder apply in a modified form the provisions of Part VI of the 1894 Act and s. 66 of the 1906 Act to diving operations: see the M.S. (Diving Operations) Regulations 1975 (S.I. No. 116). Part V contains miscellaneous provisions.

PART I

THE INTERNATIONAL OIL POLLUTION COMPENSATION FUND

Interpretation of Part I (not in force at June 1975)

1601 **1.**—(1) In this Part of this Act—

(*a*) the " Liability Convention " means the International Convention on Civil Liability for Oil Pollution Damage opened for signature in Brussels on 29th November 1969;

(*b*) the " Fund Convention " means the International Convention on the Establishment of an International Fund for Compensation for Oil Pollution Damage opened for signature in Brussels on 18th December 1971;

(*c*) " the Fund " means the International Fund established by the Fund Convention; and

(*d*) " Fund Convention country " means a country in respect of which the Fund Convention is in force.

(2) If Her Majesty by Order in Council declares that any State specified in the Order is a party to the Fund Convention in respect of any country so specified the Order shall, while in force, be conclusive evidence that that State is a party to the Convention in respect of that country.

1602 (3) In this Part of this Act, unless the context otherwise requires—

the " Act of 1971 " means the Merchant Shipping (Oil Pollution) Act 1971,

" damage " includes loss,

" discharge or escape ", in relation to pollution damage, means the discharge or escape of oil carried by the ship,

" guarantor " means any person providing insurance or other financial security to cover the owner's liability of the kind described in section 10 of the Act of 1971,

" oil ", except in sections 2 and 3, means persistent hydrocarbon mineral oil,

" owner " means the person or persons registered as the owner of the ship or, in the absence of registration, the person or persons owning the ship, except that in relation to a ship owned by a State which is operated by a person registered as the ship's operator, it means the person registered as its operator,

"pollution damage" means damage caused outside the ship carrying oil by contamination resulting from the escape or discharge of oil from the ship, wherever the escape or discharge may occur, and includes the cost of preventive measures and further damage caused by preventive measures,

"preventive measures" means any reasonable measures taken by any person after the occurrence to prevent or minimise pollution damage,

"ship" means any sea-going vessel and any seaborne craft of any type whatsoever carrying oil in bulk as cargo.

(4) For the purposes of this Part of this Act a ship's tonnage shall be the net tonnage of the ship with the addition of the amount deducted from the gross tonnage on account of engine room space for the purpose of ascertaining the net tonnage.

If the ship cannot be measured in accordance with the normal rules, its tonnage shall be deemed to be 40 per cent. of the weight in tons (of 2240 lbs.) of oil which the ship is capable of carrying.

(5) For the purposes of this Part of this Act, where more than one discharge or escape results from the same occurrence or from a series of occurrences having the same origin, they shall be treated as one.

(6) In this Part of this Act a franc shall be taken to be a unit of $65\frac{1}{2}$ milligrammes of gold of millesimal fineness 900.

(7) The Secretary of State may from time to time by order made by statutory instrument specify the amounts which for the purposes of this Part of this Act are to be taken as equivalent to any specified number of francs.

Contributions to Fund

Contributions by importers of oil and others (not in force at June 1975)

1603 **2.**—(1) Contributions shall be payable to the Fund[1] in respect of oil[2] carried by sea[3] to ports or terminal installations[2] in the United Kingdom.

(2) Subsection (1) above applies whether or not the oil is being imported, and applies even if contributions are payable in respect of carriage of the same oil on a previous voyage.

(3) Contributions shall also be payable to the Fund[1] in respect of oil when first received in any installation in the United Kingdom after having been carried by sea and discharged in a port or terminal installation in a country which is not a Fund Convention country.[4]

(4) The person liable to pay contributions is—

(*a*) in the case of oil which is being imported into the United Kingdom, the importer, and

(*b*) otherwise, the person by whom the oil is received.

(5) A person shall not be liable to make contributions in respect of the oil imported or received by him in any year if the oil so imported or received in the year does not exceed 150,000 tonnes.

(6) For the purpose of subsection (5) above—

(*a*) all the members of a group of companies shall be treated as a single person, and

(*b*) any two or more companies which have been amalgamated into a single company shall be treated as the same person as that single company.

(7) The contributions payable by a person for any year shall—

(*a*) be of such amount as may be determined by the Assembly of the Fund[1] under Articles 11 and 12 of the Fund Convention and notified to him by the Fund[1];

(*b*) be payable in such instalments, becoming due at such times, as may be so notified to him;

and if any amount due from him remains unpaid after the date on which it became due, it shall from then on bear interest, at a rate determined from time to time by the said Assembly, until it is paid.

604 (8) The Secretary of State may by regulations contained in a statutory instrument impose on persons who are or may be liable to pay contributions under this section obligations to give security for payment to the Secretary of State, or to the Fund.[1]

Regulations under this subsection—

(*a*) may contain such supplemental or incidental provisions as appear to the Secretary of State expedient,

(*b*) may impose penalties for contravention of the regulations punishable on summary conviction by a fine not exceeding £400, or such lower limit as may be specified in the regulations, and

(*c*) shall be subject to annulment in pursuance of a resolution of either House of Parliament.

(9) In this and the next following section, unless the context otherwise requires—

" company " means a body incorporated under the law of the United Kingdom, or of any other country;

" group " in relation to companies, means a holding company and its subsidiaries as defined by section 154 of the Companies Act 1948 (or for companies in Northern Ireland section 148 of the Companies Act (Northern Ireland) 1960), subject, in the case of a company incorporated outside the United Kingdom, to any necessary modifications of those definitions;

"importer" means the person by whom or on whose behalf the oil in question is entered for customs purposes on importation, and "import" shall be construed accordingly;

"oil" means crude oil and fuel oil, and

(*a*) "crude oil" means any liquid hydrocarbon mixture occurring naturally in the earth whether or not treated to render it suitable for transportation, and includes—

(i) crude oils from which distillate fractions have been removed, and

(ii) crude oils to which distillate fractions have been added,

(*b*) "fuel oil" means heavy distillates or residues from crude oil or blends of such materials intended for use as a fuel for the production of heat or power of a quality equivalent to the "American Society for Testing and Materials' Specification for Number Four Fuel Oil (Designation D 396-69)", or heavier.

"terminal installation" means any site for the storage of oil in bulk which is capable of receiving oil from waterborne transportation, including any facility situated offshore and linked to any such site.

(10) In this section "sea" does not include any waters on the landward side of the baselines from which the territorial sea of the United Kingdom is measured.

1605 [1] See s. 1 (1) (*c*).
[2] See subs. (9).
[3] See subs. (10).
[4] See s. 1 (1) (*d*).

Power to obtain information (now in force [1a])

1606 **3.**—(1) For the purpose of transmitting to the Fund [1] the names and addresses of the persons who under the last preceding section are liable to make contributions to the Fund [1] for any year, and the quantity of oil [2] in respect of which they are so liable, the Secretary of State may by notice require any person engaged in producing, treating, distributing or transporting oil [2] to furnish such information as may be specified in the notice.

(2) A notice under this section may require a company to give such information as may be required to ascertain whether its liability is affected by subsection (6) of the last preceding section.

(3) A notice under this section may specify the way in which, and the time within which, it is to be complied with.

(4) In proceedings by the Fund [1] against any person to recover any amount due under the last preceding section, particulars contained in

any list transmitted by the Secretary of State to the Fund [1] shall, so far as those particulars are based on information obtained under this section, be admissible as evidence of the facts stated in the list; and so far as particulars which are so admissible are based on information given by the person against whom the proceedings are brought, those particulars shall be presumed to be accurate until the contrary is proved.

(5) If a person discloses any information which has been furnished to or obtained by him under this section, or in connection with the execution of this section, he shall, unless the disclosure is made—

(*a*) with the consent of the person from whom the information was obtained, or

(*b*) in connection with the execution of this section, or

(*c*) for the purposes of any legal proceedings arising out of this section or of any report of such proceedings,

be liable on summary conviction to a fine not exceeding £400.

(6) A person who—

(*a*) refuses or wilfully neglects to comply with a notice under this section, or

(*b*) in furnishing any information in compliance with a notice under this section makes any statement which he knows to be false in a material particular, or recklessly makes any statement which is false in a material particular,

shall be liable—

(i) on summary conviction to a fine not exceeding £400, and

(ii) on conviction on indictment to a fine, or to imprisonment for a term not exceeding twelve months, or to both.

1607 [1] See s. 1 (1) (*c*).
[1a] Brought into force by S.I. 1974 No. 1792 (C.31) as from November 1, 1974.
[2] See s. 2 (9).

Compensation for persons suffering pollution damage

Liability of the Fund (not in force at June 1975)

1608 **4.**—(1) The Fund [1] shall be liable for pollution damage [2] in the United Kingdom if the person suffering the damage [2] has been unable to obtain full compensation under section 1 of the Act of 1971 [3] (which gives effect to the Liability Convention [2])—

(*a*) because the discharge or escape [2] causing the damage—

(i) resulted from an exceptional, inevitable and irresistible phenomenon, or

(ii) was due wholly to anything done or left undone by another person (not being a servant or agent of the owner) with intent to do damage, or

(iii) was due wholly to the negligence or wrongful act of a government or other authority in exercising its function of maintaining lights or other navigational aids for the maintenance of which it was responsible,

(and because liability is accordingly wholly displaced by section 2 [4] of the Act of 1971), or

(*b*) because the owner [2] or guarantor [2] liable for the damage cannot meet his obligations in full, or

(*c*) because the damage exceeds the liability under section 1 of the Act of 1971 as limited—

(i) by section 4 of the Act of 1971, or

(ii) (where the said section 4 is displaced by section 9 of this Act) by section 503 of the Merchant Shipping Act 1894.

(2) Subsection (1) above shall apply with the substitution for the words " the United Kingdom " of the words " a Fund Convention country " [5] where—

(*a*) the headquarters of the Fund is for the time being in the United Kingdom, and proceedings under the Liability Convention for compensation for the pollution damage have been brought in a country which is not a Fund Convention country, or

(*b*) the incident has caused pollution damage both in the United Kingdom and in another Fund Convention country, and proceedings under the Liability Convention for compensation for the pollution damage have been brought in a country which is not a Fund Convention country or in the United Kingdom.

(3) Where the incident has caused pollution damage both in the United Kingdom and in another country in respect of which the Liability Convention is in force, references in this section to the provisions of the Act of 1971 shall include references to the corresponding provisions of the law of any country giving effect to the Liability Convention.

(4) Where proceedings under the Liability Convention for compensation for pollution damage have been brought in a country which is not a Fund Convention country and the Fund is liable for that pollution damage by virtue of subsection (2) (*a*) above, references in this section to the provisions of the Act of 1971 shall be treated as references to the corresponding provisions of the law of the country in which those proceedings were brought.

(5) For the purposes of this section an owner or guarantor is to be treated as incapable of meeting his obligations if the obligations have not been met after all reasonable steps to pursue the legal remedies available have been taken.

1609 (6) Expenses reasonably incurred, and sacrifices reasonably made, by the owner voluntarily to prevent or minimise pollution damage shall be treated as pollution damage for the purposes of this section, and accordingly he shall be in the same position with respect to claims against the Fund under this section as if he had a claim in respect of liability under section 1 of the Act of 1971.

(7) The Fund shall incur no obligation under this section if—

(*a*) it proves that the pollution damage—

(i) resulted from an act of war, hostilities, civil war or insurrection, or

(ii) was caused by oil which has escaped or been discharged from a warship or other ship owned or operated by a State and used, at the time of the occurrence, only on Government non-commercial service, or

(*b*) the claimant cannot prove that the damage resulted from an occurrence involving a ship identified by him, or involving two or more ships one of which is identified by him.

(8) If the Fund proves that the pollution damage resulted wholly or partly—

(*a*) from an act or omission done with intent to cause damage by the person who suffered the damage, or

(*b*) from the negligence of that person,

the Fund may be exonerated wholly or partly from its obligation to pay compensation to that person:

Provided that this subsection shall not apply to a claim in respect of expenses or sacrifices made voluntarily to prevent or minimise pollution damage.

(9) Where the liability under section 1 of the Act of 1971 is limited to any extent by subsection (5) of that section (contributory negligence), the Fund shall be exonerated to the same extent.

(10) The Fund's liability under this section shall be subject to the limits imposed by paragraphs 4, 5 and 6 of Article 4 of the Fund Convention which impose an overall liability on the liabilities of the owner and of the Fund, and the text of which is set out in Schedule 1 to this Act.

(11) Evidence of any instrument issued by any organ of the Fund or of any document in the custody of the Fund, or any entry in or extract from such a document, may be given in any legal proceedings by production of a copy certified as a true copy by an official of the Fund; and any document purporting to be such a copy shall be received in evidence without proof of the official position or handwriting of the person signing the certificate.

(12) For the purpose of giving effect to the said provisions of Article 4 of the Fund Convention a court giving judgment against the Fund in proceedings under this section shall notify the Fund, and—

(*a*) no steps shall be taken to enforce the judgment unless and until the court gives leave to enforce it, (*b*) that leave shall not be given unless and until the Fund notifies the court either that the amount of the claim is not to be reduced under the said provisions of Article 4 of the Fund Convention, or that it is to be reduced to a specified amount, and

(*c*) in the latter case the judgment shall be enforceable only for the reduced amount.

1610 [1] See s. 1 (1) (*c*).
[2] See s. 1 (3).
[3] See § 1497, *ante*.
[4] A discharge or escape resulting from an act of war, hostilities, civil war or insurrection is excluded from both the 1971 and the 1974 Acts: see s. 7 (*a*) (i), *post*.
[5] See s. 1 (1) (*d*).

Indemnification of shipowners

Indemnification where damage is caused by ship registered in Fund Convention country (not in force at June 1975)

1611 **5.**—(1) Where a liability is incurred under section 1 of the Act of 1971 [1] in respect of a ship [1] registered in a Fund Convention country [2] the Fund [3] shall indemnify the owner [1] and his guarantor [1] for that portion of the aggregate amount of the liability which—

(*a*) is in excess of an amount equivalent to 1500 francs [4] for each ton of the ship's tonnage [5] or of an amount of 125 million francs, whichever is the less, and

(*b*) is not in excess of an amount equivalent to 2000 francs for each ton of the said tonnage or an amount of 210 million francs, whichever is the less.

(2) Where proceedings under the Liability Convention [6] for compensation for pollution damage [1] have been brought in a country which is not a Fund Convention country (but is a country in respect of which the Liability Convention is in force), and either—

(*a*) the incident [7] has caused pollution damage in the United Kingdom (as well as in that other country); or

(*b*) the headquarters of the Fund is for the time being in the United Kingdom,

subsection (1) above shall apply with the omission of the words " under section 1 of the Act of 1971 ".

(3) The Fund shall not incur an obligation under this section where the pollution damage resulted from the wilful misconduct [8] of the owner.

(4) In proceedings to enforce the Fund's obligation under this section the court may exonerate the Fund wholly or partly if it is proved that, as a result of the actual fault or privity [9] of the owner—

(*a*) the ship did not comply with such requirements as the Secretary of State may by order prescribe for the purposes of this section, and (*b*) the occurrence or damage was caused wholly or partly by that non-compliance.

(5) The requirements referred to in subsection (4) above are such requirements as appear to the Secretary of State appropriate to implement the provisions of—

(*a*) article 5 (3) of the Fund Convention (marine safety conventions), and

(*b*) article 5 (4) of the Fund Convention (which enables the Assembly of the Fund to substitute new conventions).

(6) An order made under subsection (4) above—

(*a*) may be varied or revoked by a subsequent order so made,

(*b*) may contain such transitional or other supplemental provisions as appear to the Secretary of State to be expedient, and

(*c*) shall be contained in a statutory instrument subject to annulment in pursuance of a resolution of either House of Parliament.

(7) Expenses reasonably incurred, and sacrifices reasonably made, by the owner voluntarily to prevent or minimise the pollution damage shall be treated as included in the owner's liability for the purposes of this section.

1612 [1] See s. 1 (3).
[2] See s. 1 (1) (*d*).
[3] See s. 1 (1) (*c*).
[4] See s. 1 (6).
[5] See s. 1 (4).
[6] See s. 1 (1) (*a*).
[7] This expression is not defined in the Act, but see the Convention: " any occurrence or series of occurrences, having the same origin which causes pollution damage."
[8] This expression is more commonly found in legislation relating to liability arising out of the operation of aircraft. See generally McNair, *The Law of the Air*, 4th ed.
[9] See note (4) to s. 503 of the 1894 Act, § 427, *ante*.

Supplemental

Jurisdiction and effect of judgments (not in force at June 1975)

1613 **6.**—(1) Paragraph (*d*) of section 1 (1) of the Administration of Justice Act 1956 [1] and paragraph 1 (1) (*d*) of Schedule 1 to that Act (Admiralty jurisdiction in claims for damage done by ships) shall be construed as extending to any claim in respect of a liability falling on the Fund [2] under this Part of this Act; and the Admiralty jurisdiction of the Court of Session shall extend to any case arising out of any such claim.

(2) Where in accordance with rules of court made for the purposes of this subsection the Fund has been given notice of proceedings brought against an owner [3] or guarantor [3] in respect of liability under section 1 of the Act of 1971,[3] any judgment given in the proceedings shall, after it has become final and enforceable, become binding upon the Fund in the sense

that the facts and evidence in the judgment may not be disputed by the Fund even if the Fund has not intervened in the proceedings.

(3) Where a person incurs a liability under the law of a Fund Convention country [4] corresponding to the Act of 1971 for damage which is partly in the area of the United Kingdom, subsection (2) above shall, for the purpose of proceedings under this Part of this Act, apply with any necessary modifications to a judgment in proceedings under that law of the said country.

(4) Subject to subsection (5) below, Part I of the Foreign Judgments (Reciprocal Enforcement) Act 1933 shall apply, whether or not it would so apply apart from this subsection, to any judgment given by a court in a Fund Convention country to enforce a claim in respect of liability incurred under any provision corresponding to section 4 or 5 of this Act; and in its application to such a judgment the said Part I shall have effect with the omission of subsections (2) and (3) of section 4 of the Act of 1933.

(5) No steps shall be taken to enforce such a judgment unless and until the court in which it is registered under Part I of the Act of 1933 gives leave to enforce it; and—

(*a*) that leave shall not be given unless and until the Fund notifies the court either that the amount of the claim is not to be reduced under paragraph 4 of Article 4 of the Fund Convention (as set out in Schedule 1 to this Act) or that it is to be reduced to a specified amount; and

(*b*) in the latter case, the judgment shall be enforceable only for the reduced amount.

1614 [1] See App. 8, § 3167, *post*.
[2] See s. 1 (1) (*c*).
[3] See s. 1 (3).
[4] See s. 1 (1) (*d*).

Extinguishment of claims (not in force at June 1975)

1615 **7.**—(1) No action to enforce a claim against the Fund [1] under this Part of this Act shall be entertained by a court in the United Kingdom unless—

(*a*) the action is commenced, or

(*b*) a third-party notice of an action to enforce a claim against the owner [2] or his guarantor [2] in respect of the same damage is given to the Fund,

not later than three years after the claim against the Fund arose.[3]

In this subsection "third party notice" means a notice of the kind described in subsections (2) and (3) of the last preceding section.

(2) No action to enforce a claim against the Fund under this Part of this Act shall be entertained by a court in the United Kingdom unless the action is commenced not later than six years after the occurrence, or

first of the occurrences, resulting in the discharge or escape [2] by reason of which the claim against the Fund arose.

(3) Notwithstanding the preceding provisions of this section, a person's right to bring an action under section 5 of this Act shall not be extinguished before six months from the date when that person first acquired knowledge of the bringing of an action against him under the Act of 1971 [2] (that is to say an action to enforce a liability against which he seeks indemnity), or under the corresponding provisions of the law of any country outside the United Kingdom giving effect to the Liability Convention.

1616 [1] See s. 1 (1) (*c*).
[2] See s. 1 (3).
[3] Presumably the claim arises when the pollution damage is sustained.

Subrogation and rights of recourse (not in force at June 1975)

1617 **8.**—(1) In respect of any sum paid under section 4 (1) (*b*) of this Act (default by owner or guarantor on liability for pollution damage) the Fund [1] shall acquire by subrogation the rights of the recipient against the owner [2] or guarantor.[2]

(2) The right of the Fund under subsection (1) above is subject to any obligation of the Fund under section 5 of this Act to indemnify the owner or guarantor for any part of the liability on which he has defaulted.

(3) In respect of any sum paid—

(*a*) under paragraph (*a*) or paragraph (*c*) of section 4 (1); or

(*b*) under section 5,

the Fund shall acquire by subrogation any rights of recourse or subrogation which the owner or guarantor or any other person has in respect of his liability for the damage in question.

(4) In respect of any sum paid by a public authority in the United Kingdom as compensation for pollution damage,[2] that authority shall acquire by subrogation any rights which the recipient has against the Fund under this Part of this Act.

1618 [1] See s. 1 (1) (*c*).
[2] See s. 1 (3).

Modification of limitation of liability under Act of 1971 (now in force [1a])

1619 **9.** In the Act of 1971 [1] after section 8 there shall be inserted the following section—

Cases excluded from sections 4 to 8

" **8A.**—(1) Sections 4 to 8 of this Act shall not apply to a ship which at the time of the discharge or escape was registered in a country—

(*a*) which was not a Convention country, and

(*b*) which was a country in respect of which the 1957 Convention was in force.

(2) In this section ' the 1957 Convention ' means the International Convention relating to the Limitation of the Liability of Owners of Seagoing Ships signed in Brussels on 10th October 1957.

(3) If Her Majesty by Order in Council declares that any country—

(*a*) is not a Convention country within the meaning of this Act, and

(*b*) is a country in respect of which the 1957 Convention is in force,

or that it was such a country at a time specified in the Order, the Order shall, while in force, be conclusive evidence of the facts stated in the Order."

1620 NOTE. The effect of this section is to apply the lower limits provided by s. 503 of the 1894 Act to ships which are registered in States who are parties to the 1957 Convention but not the 1969 Convention.

[1a] Brought into force by S.I. 1975 No. 866 as from June 19, 1975.

[1] " Act of 1971 ": M.S.A. 1971, see § 1497, *ante*.

PART II

OIL TANKERS

Interpretation of Part II (now in force [1])

1621 **10.**—(1) In this Part of this Act " the Conventions " means—

(*a*) Article VI bis and Annex C of the International Convention, signed in London on 12th May 1954, for the Prevention of Pollution of the Sea by Oil, which Article and Annex were added on 15th October 1971 by resolution of the Assembly of the Inter-governmental Maritime Consultative Organisation; and

(*b*) any other international convention, or amendment of an international convention, which relates in whole or in part to prevention of pollution of the sea by oil, and which has been signed for the United Kingdom before the passing of this Act, or later.

(2) In this Part of this Act " Convention country " means a country in respect of which a State is a party to any of the Conventions.

(3) If Her Majesty by Order in Council declares that any State specified in the Order is a party to any of the Conventions in respect of any country so specified, the Order shall, while in force, be conclusive evidence that that State is a party to the Convention in respect of that country.

(4) In this Part of this Act—

" oil tanker " means a ship which is constructed or adapted primarily to carry oil in bulk in its cargo spaces (whether or not it is also so constructed or adapted as to be capable of carrying other cargoes in those spaces),

" United Kingdom oil tanker " means an oil tanker registered in the United Kingdom,

" oil " means crude oil, fuel oil (including diesel oil) and lubricating oil,

" port " includes an off-shore terminal, and references to entering or leaving a port shall include references to using or ceasing to use an off-shore terminal.

[1] See note ([1a]) to s. 3, *ante*, § 1606.

Design and construction of oil tankers (now in force [1a])

1622 **11.**—(1) For the purpose of preventing pollution of the sea by oil,[1] the Secretary of State may make rules (called " oil tanker [1] construction rules ") prescribing requirements to be complied with by United Kingdom, oil tankers [1] in respect of their design and construction.

(2) The said rules may include such requirements as appear to the Secretary of State to implement any of the provisions of the Conventions, so far as they relate to prevention of pollution of the sea by oil.

This subsection applies whether or not the said provisions are for the time being binding on Her Majesty's Government in the United Kingdom.

(3) Oil tanker construction rules may provide—

(*a*) for oil tankers to be surveyed and inspected with a view to determining whether they comply with the rules,

(*b*) for a tanker which on a survey is found to comply to be issued with a certificate called a " tanker construction certificate ", and

(*c*) for a tanker which is not required to comply with the rules to be issued with a certificate called a " tanker exemption certificate ".

(4) Schedule 2 to this Act shall have effect for supplementing this Part of this Act.

(5) It is hereby declared that the oil tankers to which rules under this section may be applied include those designed or constructed before the rules come into force, and that the following provisions of this Part of this Act apply whether the oil tanker in question was designed or constructed before or after the relevant requirements as to design or construction came into force.

(6) Oil tanker construction rules shall be contained in a statutory instrument subject to annulment in pursuance of a resolution of either House of Parliament.

[1a] See note ([1a]) to s. 3, *ante*, § 1606.
[1] See s. 10 (4).

Restrictions on tankers sailing from U.K. ports (not in force at June 1975)

1623 **12.**—(1) No oil tanker shall proceed, or attempt to proceed, to sea unless—

(*a*) it is a certificated oil tanker [1] (within the meaning of Schedule 3 to this Act), or

(*b*) it is not registered in the United Kingdom, and—

(i) if it were a United Kingdom oil tanker,[1] it would qualify for the issue of a tanker exemption certificate,[2] or

(ii) its gross tonnage is less than 150 tons, or

(*c*) the Secretary of State has issued it with leave to sail.

(2) Where an application is made for leave to sail to be issued to an oil tanker, then—

(*a*) if the tanker is registered in the United Kingdom, the Secretary of State may issue it with leave to sail where he considers it appropriate to do so;

(*b*) if the tanker is not registered in the United Kingdom, the Secretary of State—

(i) shall issue it with leave to sail if he is satisfied that it would qualify for the issue of a tanker construction certificate [3] if it were a United Kingdom oil tanker; and

(ii) may, if he is not so satisfied, issue it with leave to sail where he considers it appropriate to do so.

(3) Leave to sail issued under paragraph (*a*) or (*b*) (ii) of subsection (2) above may be issued subject to conditions imposed with a view to preventing or limiting the danger of oil [1] pollution, including—

(*a*) conditions as to the cargo with which the tanker may sail;

(*b*) a condition that the tanker sails only to a specified port [1] in the United Kingdom or elsewhere.

(4) Subject to subsection (5) below, if—

(*a*) an oil tanker proceeds, or attempts to proceed, to sea in contravention of subsection (1) above; or

(*b*) leave to sail having been issued to an oil tanker under this section subject to conditions, it proceeds to sea but the conditions are not complied with,

the owner and master of the tanker shall each be liable on summary conviction to a fine of not more than £10,000, or on conviction on indictment to a fine.

(5) In proceedings under subsection (4) above, it shall be a defence to prove that in order—

(*a*) to ensure the safety of the oil tanker, or

(*b*) to reduce the risk of damage to any other vessel or property, it was necessary for the tanker to proceed to sea in contravention of subsection (1) above or, as the case may be, without complying with the conditions mentioned in paragraph (*b*) of subsection (4).

In this section " damage " does not include damage caused by contamination resulting from the escape or discharge of oil from a tanker.

624 [1] See s. 10 (4).
[2] See s. 11 (3) (*c*).
[3] See s. 11 (3) (*b*).

Restrictions on uncertificated tankers (not in force at June 1975)

625 **13.**—(1) If it appears to the Secretary of State that an oil tanker [1] is not certificated (within the meaning of Schedule 3 to this Act) [2] he may direct the oil tanker—

(*a*) not to enter any port [1] in the United Kingdom (or not to enter one or more specified ports in the United Kingdom); or

(*b*) not to enter all or any ports in the United Kingdom except subject to specified conditions.

(2) A direction may be given under this section in respect of an oil tanker which is for the time being in a port in the United Kingdom, so as to apply after it leaves that port.

(3) Directions under this section shall be addressed to the master or owner of the tanker, or to both, and may be communicated by any means which appear to the Secretary of State suitable for the purpose.

(4) Subject to subsection (5) below, if an oil tanker enters a port in the United Kingdom in contravention of a direction under this section, or without complying with any conditions imposed under this section, the owner and the master of the tanker shall each be liable on summary conviction to a fine not exceeding £15,000, or on conviction on indictment to a fine.

(5) In proceedings under subsection (4) above, it shall be a defence to prove that the tanker entered the port out of necessity due—

(*a*) to an emergency involving a threat to any person's life or the safety of the tanker, or

(*b*) to circumstances outside the control of the tanker's master.

626 [1] See s. 10 (4).
[2] See § 1643, *post*.

PART III

PROTECTION OF SHIPPING AND TRADING INTERESTS

Foreign action affecting shipping (not in force at June 1975)

627 **14.**—(1) The Secretary of State may exercise the powers conferred by this section if he is satisfied that a foreign government, or any agency or

authority of a foreign government, have adopted, or propose to adopt, measures or practices concerning or affecting the carriage of goods by sea which—

(*a*) are damaging or threaten to damage the shipping or trading interests of the United Kingdom, or

(*b*) are damaging or threaten to damage the shipping or trading interests of another country, and the Secretary of State is satisfied that action under this section would be in fulfilment of the international obligations of Her Majesty's Government to that other country.

(2) The Secretary of State may by order make provision for requiring persons in the United Kingdom carrying on any trade or business to provide the Secretary of State with all such information as he may require for the purpose of enabling him—

(*a*) to determine what further action to take under this section, and

(*b*) to ensure compliance with any orders or directions made or given under this section.

(3) The Secretary of State may by order provide for—

(*a*) regulating the carriage of goods in ships and the rates which may or must be charged for carrying them;

(*b*) regulating the admission and departure of ships to and from United Kingdom ports,[1] the cargoes they may carry, and the loading or unloading of cargoes;

(*c*) regulating the making and implementation of agreements (including charter-parties) whose subject matter relates directly or indirectly to the carriage of goods by sea, and requiring such agreements to be subject to the Secretary of State's approval in such cases as he may specify;

(*d*) imposing charges in respect of ships which enter United Kingdom ports to load or unload cargo.

(4) In a case falling within subsection (1) (*a*) above, an order under subsection (3) above shall specify the measures or practices which in the opinion of the Secretary of State are damaging or threaten to damage shipping or trading interests of the United Kingdom.

(5) An order under this section may authorise the Secretary of State to give directions to any person for the purposes of the order:

Provided that this subsection shall not apply for the purpose of recovering charges imposed under subsection (3) (*d*) above.

(6) Any order or direction made or given under this section—

(*a*) may be either general or special, and may be subject to such conditions or exceptions as the Secretary of State specifies (including conditions and exceptions operating by reference to the giving or withholding of his approval for any course of action);

(*b*) may be in terms that require compliance either generally or only in specified cases;

(*c*) may be varied or revoked by a subsequent order, or as the case may be, a subsequent direction, so made or given,

and an order made pursuant to this section shall be contained in a statutory instrument.

628 (7) Before the Secretary of State makes an order under this section he shall consult such representatives of the shipping or trading interests of the United Kingdom, and such other persons, as appear to him appropriate.

(8) If a person discloses any information which has been furnished to or obtained by him under this section, or in connection with the execution of this section, he shall, unless the disclosure is made—

(*a*) with the consent of the person from whom the information was obtained, or

(*b*) in connection with the execution of this section, or

(*c*) for the purposes of any legal proceedings arising out of this section or of any report of such proceedings,

be liable on summary conviction to a fine not exceeding £400.

(9) A person who—

(*a*) refuses or wilfully neglects to furnish any information which he is required to furnish under this section, or

(*b*) in furnishing any such information makes any statement which he knows to be false in a material particular, or recklessly makes any statement which is false in a material particular,

shall be liable on summary conviction to a fine not exceeding £400.

(10) A person who wilfully contravenes or fails to comply with any provision of an order or direction made or given pursuant to this section, other than a provision requiring him to give any information, shall be liable—

(*a*) on summary conviction to a fine of not more than £5,000;

(*b*) on conviction on indictment to a fine;

and where the order or direction requires anything to be done, or not to be done, by, to or on a ship, and the requirement is not complied with, the owner and master of the ship are each to be regarded as wilfully failing to comply, without prejudice to the liability of anyone else.

(11) In this section " foreign government " means the government of any country outside the United Kingdom; and references to ships are to ships of any registration.

(12) Schedule 4 to this Act shall have effect for supplementing this section, which in that Schedule is called " the principal section ".

1629 [1] See Sched. 4, para. 4, § 1644, *post*.

Parliamentary control of orders under Part III (not in force at June 1975)

1630 **15.**—(1) No order shall be made in exercise of the powers conferred by subsection (3) of the last preceding section unless—

(*a*) a draft has been approved by resolution of each House of Parliament, or

(*b*) it is declared in the order that it appears to the Secretary of State that by reason of urgency it is necessary to make the order without a draft having been so approved.

(2) An order made in exercise of the powers conferred by the said subsection (3) without a draft having been approved by resolution of each House of Parliament shall cease to have effect at the expiration of a period of 28 days beginning with the date on which it was made unless before the expiration of that period it has been approved by resolution of each House of Parliament, but without prejudice to anything previously done, or to the making of a new order.

In reckoning for the purposes of this subsection any period of 28 days, no account shall be taken of any period during which Parliament is dissolved or prorogued or during which both Houses are adjourned for more than four days.

(3) An order under the last preceding section which is not made in exercise of the powers conferred by subsection (3) of that section shall be subject to annulment in pursuance of a resolution of either House of Parliament.

(4) If an order under that section recites that it is not made in exercise of the powers conferred by the said subsection (3), the recital shall be conclusive.

PART IV

SUBMERSIBLE APPARATUS

Apparatus to which Part IV applies (now in force)

1631 **16.**—(1) This Part of this Act applies to any submersible or supporting apparatus—

(*a*) operated within waters which are in the United Kingdom or which are adjacent thereto and within the seaward limits of territorial waters, or

(*b*) launched or operated from, or comprising, a ship registered in the United Kingdom or a British ship of a specified description (being a British ship which is not registered in the United Kingdom).

(2) In this section—

" apparatus " includes any vessel, vehicle or hovercraft, any structure, any diving plant or equipment and any other form of equipment,

" specified " means specified in regulations made by the Secretary of State for the purposes of this section,

" submersible apparatus " means any apparatus used, or designed for use, in supporting human life on or under the bed of any waters or elsewhere under the surface of any waters, and

" supporting apparatus " means any apparatus used, or designed for use, in connection with the operation of any submersible apparatus.

Safety of submersible and supporting apparatus (now in force)

32 **17.**—(1) The Secretary of State may make regulations [1]—

(*a*) for the safety of submersible and supporting apparatus;

(*b*) for the prevention of accidents in or near submersible or supporting apparatus;

(*c*) for the safety, health and welfare of persons on or in submersible and supporting apparatus;

(*d*) for prohibiting or otherwise restricting the operation of any submersible apparatus except in accordance with the conditions of a licence granted under the regulations; and

(*e*) for the registration of submersible apparatus.

(2) Regulations made under this section shall be contained in a statutory instrument subject to annulment in pursuance of a resolution of either House of Parliament.

(3) Schedule 5 to this Act shall have effect for supplementing the provisions of this section.

[1] See the M.S. (Diving Operations) Regulations 1975 (S.I. No. 116).

Part V

Miscellaneous and Supplemental

Miscellaneous

Commissioners of Northern Lighthouses (now in force)

33 **18.**—(1) Section 668 of the Merchant Shipping Act 1894 [1] (constitution of Commissioners of Northern Lighthouses) shall be amended as follows.

(2) After paragraph (*d*) of subsection (1) there shall be inserted—

" (*dd*) a person nominated by the Lieutenant-Governor of the Isle of Man and appointed by the Secretary of State ".

(3) At the end of the said section 668 there shall be added—

" (4) The Commissioners may elect, as members of their body, not more than four other persons.

(5) A person appointed by the Secretary of State under subsection (1) (*dd*) above, or a person appointed by the Commissioners under subsection (4) above, shall hold office for three years, but shall be eligible for re-appointment."

[1] See § 581, *ante*.

Offences by seamen (now in force)

1634 **19.**—(1) The Merchant Shipping Act 1970 shall be amended in accordance with the following provisions of this section.

(2) In section 27 (which creates an offence in relation to misconduct endangering a ship or persons on board, punishable on summary conviction with a fine not exceeding £200) for the words " £200 " there shall be substituted the words " £400 ".

(3) Section 29 (which makes it an offence wilfully to disobey a lawful command relating to, or likely to affect, the operation of a ship or of its equipment) and section 31 (which makes it an offence in certain circumstances for a seaman to be absent without leave at the time of sailing) are hereby repealed.

(4) In section 30 (continued or concerted disobedience, neglect of duty, etc.) for the words from the beginning of paragraph (*c*) to the end there shall be substituted:—

" (*c*) combines with other seamen employed in that ship—

(i) to disobey lawful commands which are required to be obeyed at a time while the ship is at sea;

(ii) to neglect any duty which is required to be discharged at such a time; or

(iii) to impede, at such a time, the progress of a voyage or the navigation of the ship,

he shall be liable on summary conviction to a fine not exceeding £100.

For the purposes of this section a ship shall be treated as being at sea at any time when it is not securely moored in a safe berth."

(5) In section 34 (2) (which imposes a limit of £10 on the amount of any fine which may be imposed on a seaman for a " disciplinary offence ") for the words " £10 " there shall be substituted the words " £20 ".

(6) The following provisions referring to sections repealed by subsection (3) above shall be amended, that is to say—

(*a*) in section 32 the words " 29 " shall be omitted;

(*b*) in paragraph 2 of Schedule 2 the words " 29 ", in both places, and the words " or 31 " shall be omitted;

(*c*) in section 95 (1) (*a*) for the words " 29 to " there shall be substituted the words " 30 and ".

Supplemental

Extensions to British possessions etc. (now in force)

635 **20.**—(1) Her Majesty may by Order in Council direct that specified provisions of this Act shall extend, subject to specified exceptions, modifications or adaptations, to any of the following countries, that is to say—

(*a*) the Isle of Man;

(*b*) any of the Channel Islands;

(*c*) any colony other than one for whose external relations a country other than the United Kingdom is responsible;

(*d*) any country outside Her Majesty's dominions in which Her Majesty has jurisdiction in right of Her Majesty's Government in the United Kingdom.

(2) In respect of any country falling within any of paragraphs (*a*) to (*d*) of subsection (1) above, Her Majesty may by Order in Council, specifying that country, direct that, with specified exceptions, adaptations or modifications, specified provisions of this Act shall have effect as if references therein to the United Kingdom included references to that country.

(3) In subsections (1) and (2) above " specified " means specified by an Order under this section.

(4) Any Order made under subsection (2) above shall be subject to annulment in pursuance of a resolution of either House of Parliament.

Financial provisions (now in force)

636 **21.** Any sum received by a Minister under this Act shall be paid into the Consolidated Fund.

Offences by bodies corporate (now in force)

637 **22.** Where an offence under this Act, or under regulations made under any of its provisions, which has been committed by a body corporate is proved to have been committed with the consent or connivance of, or to be attributable to any neglect on the part of, a director, manager, secretary or other similar officer of the body corporate, or any person who was purporting to act in any such capacity, he, as well as the body cor-

porate, shall be guilty of that offence and shall be liable to be proceeded against and punished accordingly.

In this section " director ", in relation to a body corporate established by or under any enactment for the purpose of carrying on under public ownership any industry or part of an industry or undertaking, being a body corporate whose affairs are managed by its members, means a member of that body corporate.

Construction and interpretation (now in force)

1638 **23.**—(1) This Act shall be construed as one with the Merchant Shipping Acts 1894 to 1971, and without prejudice to the generality of this provision, references in those Acts to the Merchant Shipping Acts shall be construed as including references to this Act.

(2) References in this Act to the area of any country include the territorial sea of that country, and references to pollution damage in the United Kingdom shall be construed accordingly.

(3) It is hereby declared that any power to give directions conferred by this Act includes a power to vary or revoke directions so given.

(4) Except so far as the context otherwise requires, any reference in this Act to an enactment shall be construed as a reference to that enactment as amended or extended by or under any other enactment.

Citation, commencement, repeals and extent (now in force)

1639 **24.**—(1) This Act may be cited as the Merchant Shipping Act 1974; and this Act and the Merchant Shipping Acts 1894 to 1971 may be cited together as the Merchant Shipping Acts 1894 to 1974.[1]

(2) This Act shall come into force on such day as the Secretary of State may appoint by order made by statutory instrument; and different days may be appointed for different provisions, or for different purposes.[2]

(3) An order under subsection (2) above may make such transitional provision as appears to the Secretary of State to be necessary or expedient in connection with the provisions thereby brought into force, including such adaptations of those provisions, or any provisions of this Act then in force, as appear to him to be necessary or expedient in consequence of the partial operation of this Act (whether before or after the day appointed by the order).

(4) Sections 324 to 326 and sections 330 and 331 of the Customs Consolidation Act 1853 (which relate to reciprocity in international commerce) are hereby repealed.

(5) This Act extends to Northern Ireland.

[1] See § 1530, *ante*.

[2] See the M.S.A. 1974 (Commencement No. 1) Order 1974 (S.I. No. 1792) and the M.S.A. 1974 (Commencement No. 2) Order 1975 (S.I. No. 866).

SCHEDULES

SCHEDULE 1 [1] **Sections 4 (10), 6 (5)**

Overall Limit on Liability of Fund

Article 4—paragraphs 4, 5 *and* 6

640 4. (*a*) Except as otherwise provided in sub-paragraph (*b*) of this paragraph, the aggregate amount of compensation payable by the Fund under this Article shall in respect of any one incident be limited, so that the total sum of that amount and the amount of compensation actually paid under the Liability Convention for pollution damage caused in the territory of the Contracting States, including any sums in respect of which the Fund is under an obligation to indemnify the owner pursuant to Article 5, paragraph 1, of this Convention, shall not exceed 450 million francs.

(*b*) The aggregate amount of compensation payable by the Fund under this Article for pollution damage resulting from a natural phenomenon of an exceptional, inevitable and irresistible character shall not exceed 450 million francs.

5. Where the amount of established claims against the Fund exceeds the aggregate amount of compensation payable under paragraph 4, the amount available shall be distributed in such a manner that the proportion between any established claim and the amount of compensation actually recovered by the claimant under the Liability Convention and this Convention shall be the same for all claimants.

6. The Assembly of the Fund (hereinafter referred to as " the Assembly ") may, having regard to the experience of incidents which have occurred and in particular the amount of damage resulting therefrom and to changes in the monetary values, decide that the amount of 450 million francs referred to in paragraph 4, sub-paragraph (*a*) and (*b*), shall be changed; provided, however, that this amount shall in no case exceed 900 million francs or be lower than 450 million francs. The changed amount shall apply to incidents which occur after the date of the decision effecting the change.

[1] This Schedule is not in force at June 1975.

SCHEDULE 2 [1] **Section 11 (4)**

Oil Tankers

Surveys, inspections and certificates

641 1.—(1) Oil tanker construction rules may provide for any surveys of inspections under the rules to be undertaken, and certificates to be issued,

in such circumstances as may be specified in the rules, by persons appointed by such organisations as may be authorised for the purpose by the Secretary of State.

(2) Sub-paragraph (1) above shall have effect notwithstanding section 86 of the Merchant Shipping Act 1894 (which requires certain surveys and measurements to be carried out by officers of the Secretary of State).

(3) The rules may apply any of the following provisions of the Merchant Shipping Act 1894 with such exceptions or modifications as may be prescribed by the rules, that is—

(*a*) section 272 (2) (surveyor to deliver declaration of survey to owner),

(*b*) section 273 (owner to deliver declaration to Secretary of State),

(*c*) section 275 (appeal to court of survey),

(*d*) section 276 and sections 278 to 281 (provisions about certificates),

(*e*) section 282 (forgery of certificate or declaration of survey).

Duty to notify alterations

2.—(1) The rules may require the owner of a United Kingdom oil tanker to notify the Secretary of State of any alteration to the tanker which may affect the question of its qualification or continued qualification for a tanker construction certificate or a tanker exemption certificate.

(2) If any person contravenes the rules by failing to notify such an alteration, he shall be guilty of an offence and liable on summary conviction to a fine not exceeding £1,000.

Clearance of outgoing tanker

3.—(1) Before a certificated oil tanker proceeds to sea, the master of the tanker shall produce the certificate to the officer of customs from whom a clearance for the ship is demanded.

(2) Before any oil tanker which is not certificated proceeds to sea, the master of the tanker shall produce to the officer of customs from whom a clearance for the ship is demanded evidence to the satisfaction of the officer that the departure will not be in contravention of section 12 of this Act.

(3) A clearance shall not be granted, and the tanker may be detained, until the certificate or other evidence is so produced.

Inspection of foreign tanker

1642 4.—(1) For the purpose of determining whether an oil tanker not registered in the United Kingdom is certificated, or whether, if it were a United Kingdom oil tanker, it would qualify for the issue of a tanker construction certificate or a tanker exemption certificate, a competent officer may at all reasonable times go on board the tanker and inspect any part of it, and call for the production of any document carried in the tanker.

(2) An officer exercising powers under this paragraph shall not unnecessarily detain or delay a tanker but may, if he considers it necessary in order to determine—

(*a*) whether the tanker should be issued with leave to sail under section 12 of this Act, or whether leave to sail should be issued subject to any conditions under subsection (3) of that section, or

(*b*) whether an order should be issued in respect of the tanker under section 13 of this Act,

require the tanker to be taken into dock for a survey of its hull, cargo-spaces or fuel-tanks.

(3) If any person obstructs an officer acting under this paragraph, or fails to comply with a requirement made under sub-paragraph (2) above, or fails to produce a document carried in the tanker when called on by the officer to produce it, he shall be guilty of an offence and liable on summary conviction to a fine of not more than £100.

(4) In this paragraph " competent officer " means an officer of the Secretary of State authorised by him to act thereunder.

(5) Nothing in this paragraph prejudices section 76 of the Merchant Shipping Act 1970 (general powers of inspection).

Offences

5.—(1) Oil tanker construction rules may provide for the punishment of any contravention of or failure to comply with the rules by making a person liable on summary conviction to a fine not exceeding £100, or such lower limit as may be specified in the rules.

(2) This paragraph is without prejudice to liability for any offence against the rules for which a punishment is provided by some other provision of this Act.

Fees

6. Oil tanker construction rules—

(*a*) may, with the approval of the Treasury, prescribe the fees payable in respect of surveys and inspections carried out, and certificates issued, under the rules;

(*b*) shall, subject to sub-paragraph (*c*) below, provide for all fees payable under the rules to be paid to the Secretary of State; and

(*c*) may, in the case of surveys and inspections carried out, and certificates issued, by persons appointed by organisations authorised under paragraph 1 above, provide for fees to be payable to those persons or organisations.

[1] Paragraphs 3 and 4 of this Schedule are not in force at June 1975, the rest was brought into effect by S.I. 1974 No. 1792 (C. 31) as from November 1, 1974.

SCHEDULE 3 [1] Section 12 (1)

Certificated Oil Tankers

1643 1. In Part II of this Act a " certificated oil tanker " means one falling within paragraphs 2, 3 or 4 below.

2. An oil tanker is certificated if it is a United Kingdom oil tanker in respect of which a tanker construction certificate or a tanker exemption certificate is in force.

3.—(1) An oil tanker registered in a Convention country (other than the United Kingdom) is certificated if a certificate corresponding to a tanker construction certificate or tanker exemption certificate duly issued under the law of that country is in force in respect of the tanker.

(2) The Secretary of State may by order in a statutory instrument declare that for the purposes of this paragraph a certificate of a kind specified in the order is one which corresponds to a tanker construction certificate or tanker exemption certificate, and is of a kind which is issued under the law of a Convention country so specified.

(3) An order under this paragraph shall, while the order is in force, be conclusive evidence of the facts stated in the order.

4.—(1) An oil tanker is certificated if a certificate of a prescribed kind issued under the law of a country which is not a Convention country is in force as respects the oil tanker.

(2) In this paragraph " prescribed " means prescribed by order of the Secretary of State contained in a statutory instrument.

5. An order made under this Schedule may be varied or revoked by a subsequent order so made.

[1] Not in force at June 1975.

SCHEDULE 4 [1] Section 14 (12)

Protection of Shipping and Trading Interests

Customs powers

1644 1.—(1) An order made under the principal section with the consent of the Commissioners of Customs and Excise may provide for the enforcement and execution of any order or direction under the principal section by officers of customs and excise.

(2) Officers of customs and excise acting under any provision made under sub-paragraph (1) above shall have power to enter any premises or vessel.

(3) Section 53 of the Customs and Excise Act 1952 (power to refuse or cancel clearance of ship or aircraft) shall apply as if the principal section and this Schedule were contained in that Act.

Orders imposing charges

2.—(1) An order under subsection (3) (*d*) of the principal section—

(*a*) may apply to ships of any description specified in the order, and may apply in particular to ships registered in a specified country, or ships carrying specified goods or cargoes, and

(*b*) may contain such provisions as appear to the Secretary of State expedient to enable the Commissioners of Customs and Excise to collect any charge imposed by the order, and

(*c*) may apply any of the provisions of the customs Acts which relate to duties of customs, subject to any modifications or exceptions specified in the order.

(2) The charge so imposed may be a fixed amount, or may be an amount depending on the tonnage of the ship.

(3) Any such charge shall be payable to the Secretary of State.

Criminal proceedings

3. A person shall not be guilty of an offence against any provision contained in or having effect under the principal section or this Schedule by reason only of something done by that person wholly outside the area of the United Kingdom unless that person is a British subject or a company incorporated under the law of any part of the United Kingdom.

Interpretation

4. In the principal section " port " includes an off-shore terminal, and references to entering or leaving a port shall include references to using or ceasing to use an off-shore terminal.

[1] Not in force at June 1975.

SCHEDULE 5

Section 17 (3)

Regulations Relating to Submersible and Supporting Apparatus

1645 1.—(1) In this Schedule [1] " regulations " means regulations made under section 17 of this Act, and " prescribed " means prescribed by regulations.

(2) Nothing in this Schedule shall be taken to prejudice the generality of section 17 of this Act.

Registration of submersible apparatus

2. Regulations made by virtue of section 17 (1) (*e*) of this Act may make provision—

(*a*) for all matters relevant to the maintenance of a register of submersible apparatus,

(b) without prejudice to sub-paragraph (a) above, for the period for which any registration or exemption is to remain effective without renewal, the alteration or cancellation in any prescribed circumstances of registration or exemption or of any conditions attached thereto, the person by whom and manner in which applications in connection with any registration or exemption are to be made, and information and evidence to be furnished in connection with any such application,

(c) for the marking or other means of identification of any submersible apparatus,

(d) for the issue of certificates of registration or exemption, and the custody, surrender, production or display of the certificates or copies of them,

(e) for matters arising out of the termination of any registration or exemption, or any conditions attached thereto.

Offences

3.—(1) Subject to sub-paragraph (2) below, regulations—

(a) may provide for the creation of offences and for their punishment on summary conviction or on conviction on indictment, and

(b) may afford, in respect of any description of offence created by the regulations, such defence (if any) as may be prescribed.

(2) The punishment for an offence created by regulations shall be—

(a) on summary conviction a fine not exceeding £400,

(b) on conviction on indictment imprisonment for a term not exceeding 2 years, or a fine, or both,

but without prejudice to any further restriction contained in the regulations on the punishments which can be awarded and without prejudice to the exclusion by the regulations of proceedings on indictment.

Exemptions from regulations

4.—(1) The operation of any regulations may be excluded in whole or in part in relation to any class or description of submersible or supporting apparatus by regulations, or in relation to any particular apparatus by the direction of the Secretary of State given in such manner as he thinks appropriate.

(2) Any exemption or exclusion by regulations or by directions of the Secretary of State under this paragraph may be made subject to the imposition of conditions specified by the regulations or directions.

(3) Where, in pursuance of this paragraph, a person is exempted or excluded from the requirements of the provisions of regulations but,

subject to a condition, and the condition is not observed, the exemption or exclusion shall not have effect, and accordingly proceedings may be brought in respect of any offence created by the regulations.

General

646 5. Regulations—

(*a*) may provide for their operation anywhere outside the United Kingdom and for their application to persons, whether or not British subjects, and to companies, whether or not incorporated under the law of any part of the United Kingdom,

(*b*) may provide that in any proceedings for an offence under the regulations an averment in any process of the fact that anything was done or situated within waters to which this Act applies shall, until the contrary is proved, be sufficient evidence of that fact as stated in the averment,

(*c*) may provide that proceedings for any offence under the regulations may be taken, and the offence be treated for all incidental purposes as having been committed, in any place in the United Kingdom,

(*d*) may provide for any provisions of the Merchant Shipping Acts 1894 to 1970 relating to inquiries and investigations into shipping casualties to apply (with such modifications as may be specified) in relation to casualties involving any submersible apparatus which is not a ship as they apply to ships,

(*e*) may provide that specified provisions of any enactment (other than this Act) shall, in such circumstances as may be prescribed, not have effect in relation to such class or description of, or to such particular, submersible or supporting apparatus as may be prescribed;

(*f*) may make different provision for different classes or descriptions of submersible or supporting apparatus and for different circumstances,

(*g*) may contain such supplemental and incidental provisions as appear to the Secretary of State to be expedient, including provision for requiring the payment of fees in connection with the making of applications and the granting of licences or issue of certificates, or other matters.

[1] See the M.S. (Diving Operations) Regulations 1975 (S.I. No. 116).

APPENDICES

APPENDIX 1

NOTES ON THE ENGAGEMENT AND DISCHARGE OF SEAMEN UNDER THE MERCHANT SHIPPING ACT 1970: MERCHANT SHIPPING (CREW AGREEMENTS, LISTS OF CREW AND DISCHARGE OF SEAMEN) REGULATIONS

[Department of Trade]
Notes for Owners of Merchant Ships, Masters, Officers and Seamen on the Implementation of the Merchant Shipping Act 1970

01 **1.** Merchant Shipping Notice M 649 listed the sections of the Merchant Shipping Act 1970 and the regulations made under the Act which will come into force on 1 January 1973. The Department wishes to draw attention to certain consequential changes in the functions of superintendents and proper officers which will bring about some changes in current practices, particularly in relation to the engagement and discharge of seamen. They are as follows:—

Engagement

02 **2.** Mercantile marine superintendents and proper officers will no longer attend as a matter of course at and witness the engagement and discharge of seamen on United Kingdom registered ships. When attending at engagements it has been the practice for superintendents to take with them the necessary official documents and forms, eg, crew agreements, log books, and forms for notifying crew changes. From 1 January 1973 it will be necessary for employers to make arrangements for these forms and documents to be obtained from mercantile marine offices or from the Department's forms store at Eileen House, Newington Causeway, London SE1.

3. It has been the practice too for superintendents to enter seamen's particulars on the list of crew and to see that the crew agreement is properly signed and completed. In the absence of the superintendents employers will need to make other arrangements for the completion of these documents.

4. Although superintendents and proper officers will not be required to attend at the engagement of seamen, notification of the intention to employ a seaman must be given to the appropriate superintendent or proper officer in accordance with regulation 4 of the Merchant Shipping (Crew Agreements. Lists of Crew and Discharge of Seamen) Regulations 1972. And copies of the crew agreement must be delivered in accordance with regulation 6 of those regulations; and copies of crew lists (where they are separate from crew agreements) in accordance with regulation 15.

Clearance Certificates

03 **5.** Masters of United Kingdom registered ships will not be required to obtain a clearance certificate from a superintendent before sailing. They will, however, still be required to obtain clearance by an officer of Customs and Excise.

3004 *Discharge*

6. Although superintendents and proper officers will not attend as a matter of course at the discharge of seamen, notice of the intention to discharge a seaman must be given to the appropriate superintendent or proper officer in accordance with regulations 23, 24 and 25 of the Discharge Regulations, and the seaman must be discharged in accordance with the procedure prescribed in regulation 26.

3005 *Seamen left behind abroad*

7. Employers will be responsible for returning seamen left behind abroad and to provide for their relief and maintenance until they are returned in accordance with the Merchant Shipping (Repatriation) Regulations 1972. And they will be responsible under these regulations for dealing with the property and wages of these seamen. Facilities for depositing the wages and effects of seamen left behind will no longer be available at mercantile marine offices.

3006 *Seamen's savings bank*

8. No further sums for deposit in the Seamen's Savings Bank will be accepted by mercantile marine offices after 31 December 1972. Up to the 20th May 1973 depositors may obtain repayment of deposits or apply for them to be transferred to the National Savings Bank. On 31 May 1973 all remaining deposits will be transferred to the National Savings Bank.

3007 *Issue of money orders and transmission of wages*

9. Facilities provided by the mercantile marine offices for the safe custody and transmission of seamen's wages and for the issue of money orders to seamen will cease to be available after 31 December 1972.

3008 *Inspection*

10. Although mercantile marine superintendents and proper officers will not be required to attend at the engagement and discharge of seamen, they are empowered under section 76 of the 1970 Act to go on board a ship and inspect any document carried in the ship in pursuance of the Merchant Shipping Acts or the regulations and rules made under the Acts. On receipt of a notification of the engagement or discharge of a crew, superintendents may from time to time go on board a ship to inspect such documents as crew agreements, crew lists and log books and to carry out checks on the safe manning of the ship. They may undertake inspections of this kind also when they go on board a ship to deal, for example, with an appeal under section 35 of the 1970 Act against a fine, or to deal with a wages dispute under section 10, to hold a death inquiry under section 61 or to deal with complaints about provisions and water under section 21.

3009 **Merchant Shipping (Crew Agreements, Lists of Crew and Discharge of Seamen) Regulations 1972**

(S.I. 1972 No. 918)

Regulations made under sections 1(5)(7), 2, 3, 68(2)(5) *and* 69 *of the Merchant Shipping Act* 1970 *dated June* 20, 1972.

EXPLANATORY NOTE [1]

These Regulations, which are made under the Merchant Shipping Act 1970 apply to ships registered in the United Kingdom other than fishing vessels.

Part I provides for exemption from the requirements of section 1 of that Act (which relates to crew agreements) in relation to the ships, voyages and seamen described in regulation 3, for the giving of notice before crew agreements are made and for other matters relating to crew agreements.

Part II provides for the exemption from the requirements of section 69 of that Act (which relates to lists of crew) of the ships described in regulation 12, for the particulars to be specified in lists of crew and for other matters relating to such lists.

Part III provides for the procedure to be followed in connection with the discharge of seamen from ships, for the giving of notice and for the recording of such discharge.

Citation, commencement and interpretation

3010 **1.**—(1) These Regulations may be cited as the Merchant Shipping (Crew Agreements, Lists of Crew and Discharge of Seamen) Regulations 1972 and shall come into operation on 1st January 1973.

(2) In these Regulations—

"the Act" means the Merchant Shipping Act 1970;

"coastal voyage" means a voyage between places in the British Islands (including the Republic of Ireland) or from and returning to such a place during which, in either case, no call is made at any place outside those islands;

"ship" means a ship registered in the United Kingdom but does not include a fishing vessel; and

references to the gross or to the register tonnage of a ship are, in the case of a ship having alternative gross or alternative register tonnages, references to the larger of its gross tonnages or to the larger of its register tonnages, as the case may be.

(3) The Interpretation Act 1889 shall apply to the interpretation of these Regulations as it applies to the interpretation of an Act of Parliament.

1 This Note is not part of the Regulations.

PART I

ENGAGEMENT OF SEAMEN

Interpretation of Part I

3011 **2.** In this Part of these Regulations "the appropriate superintendent or proper officer" means a superintendent or proper officer for the place at which a crew agreement, or an agreement with any person added to those contained in a crew agreement, is or is to be made.

Exemptions from requirements of section 1 (*crew agreements*)

3012 **3.** The requirements of section 1 of the Act relating to crew agreements shall not apply to—

(*a*) the following descriptions of ships and voyages:—

(i) a ship belonging to a general lighthouse authority;

(ii) a ship of less than 80 register tons engaged solely on coastal voyages;

(iii) a pleasure yacht which is—

(*a*) engaged on a coastal voyage; or

(*b*) engaged on any other voyage, provided that not more than 4 members of the crew receive wages for their employment;

(iv) a coastal voyage by any ship solely for the purpose of trials of the ship, its machinery or equipment;

(*b*) the following descriptions of seamen:—

(i) a person employed in a ship solely in connection with the construction, alteration, repair or testing of the ship, its machinery or equipment, and not engaged in the navigation of the ship;

(ii) a person employed in a ship solely to provide goods, personal services or entertainment on board, who is employed by a person other than the owner or the persons employing the master and who is not a member of the medical or catering staff in the ship;

(iii) a member of the naval, military or air forces of the Crown or of any service administered by the Defence Council, when acting as such a member.

Notice of intention to employ a seaman under a crew agreement

3013 **4.**—(1) Except in the circumstances specified in paragraph (4) of this regulation, any person, before employing a seaman under a crew agreement, shall give prior notice to the appropriate superintendent or proper officer.

(2) A notice under this regulation shall be given before the period of 24 hours ending with the time when the crew agreement is made or the agreement is added, as the case may be; provided that, if it is not possible to give the notice before the beginning of that period, it shall be given as early as practicable within that period.

(3) A notice under this regulation shall contain the following particulars:—

(*a*) the name of the ship (or, if the crew agreement relates to more than one ship, of each ship to which the agreement relates), its port of registry and official number;

(*b*) whether a new crew agreement is to be made or whether an agreement with any person is to be added to those contained in a crew agreement;

(*c*) the date on which, and the place and time at which, the crew agreement is to be made or an agreement with any person is to be added to those contained in the crew agreement;

(*d*) the capacity in which each person to whom the notice relates is to be employed.

(4) The circumstances in which no notice need be given under paragraph (1) of this regulation are—

(*a*) where it is not practicable without unreasonably delaying the ship to give notice before employing the seaman; or

(*b*) where the person who would, but for this paragraph, be required to give such notice has reasonable grounds for believing that the total number of seamen agreements with whom will be added to a crew agreement relating to a single ship, while that ship remains at one place in the United Kingdom, will not exceed two.

Carrying of copy of crew agreement in ships

014 5.—(1) A ship required under section 1 of the Act to carry a crew agreement may, in the case of an agreement which relates both to that and to other ships and which is kept at an address ashore in the United Kingdom, comply with that requirement by carrying a copy of the agreement certified in the manner provided by paragraph (2) of this regulation.

(2) A copy of a crew agreement carried in a ship in accordance with paragraph (1) of this regulation shall bear a certificate signed by the master certifying that it is a true copy of the crew agreement and specifying the address in the United Kingdom at which the crew agreement is kept and the name of the person by whom it is so kept.

Delivery of crew agreement and copies

15 6.—(1) The employer shall, within 2 days of the date on which a crew agreement is made or any agreement is added to those contained in a crew agreement or, if it is not practicable within that period, as soon as practicable thereafter, deliver to the appropriate superintendent or proper officer a copy of the crew agreement and of any agreement so added.

(2) The employer shall, within 7 days of the date when the last person remaining employed under the crew agreement ceases to be employed under that agreement, deliver the crew agreement to a superintendent or proper officer for the place where the ship was when that person ceased to be so employed.

Display of crew agreement

016 7. The master of a ship shall cause—

(*a*) a copy of any crew agreement relating to the ship; or

(*b*) an extract containing the terms of that agreement applicable—

(i) to all seamen employed under it, and

(ii) to each description of seamen so employed;

to be posted in some conspicuous place on board the ship where it can be read by the persons employed under the crew agreement and he shall cause it to be kept so posted and legible so long as any seaman is employed in the ship under the crew agreement.

Supply and production of copy documents

3017 **8.** Upon a seaman making a demand of his employer or of the master, the employer or the master, as the case may be, shall within a reasonable time—

(*a*) cause to be supplied to him a copy of the crew agreement under which he is employed or such extracts therefrom as are necessary to show the terms on which he is employed; and

(*b*) cause to be made available to him a copy of any document referred to in the agreement.

Production of documents to officer of customs and excise

3018 **9.** The master shall, on demand by an officer of customs and excise, produce to him—

(*a*) any crew agreement, or the copy of any crew agreement carried in the ship in pursuance of regulation 5; and

(*b*) any certificate evidencing an exemption granted by the Secretary of State from the requirements of section 1 of the Act with respect to the ship or to any person in it.

Offences under Part I

3019 **10.**—(1) A person who fails to comply with an obligation imposed on him by or under regulation 4, 6 or 8 shall be guilty of an offence.

(2) A master who fails to comply with an obligation imposed on him by or under regulation 7, 8 or 9 shall be guilty of an offence.

(3) Any offence under this regulation shall be punishable on summary conviction with a fine not exceeding £50.

PART II

LISTS OF CREW

Interpretation of Part II

3020 **11.** In this Part of these Regulations—

"seaman" includes the master of a ship;

except where the context otherwise requires, references to the employment of a seaman in a ship include references to engagement; and references to discharge include references to termination of engagement.

Exemptions from the requirements of section 69 of the Act (*lists of crew*)

3021 **12.** The duty imposed by section 69 of the Act to make and maintain a list of the crew shall not apply in relation to a pleasure yacht which is—

(*a*) engaged on a coastal voyage; or

(*b*) engaged on any other voyage, provided that not more than 4 members of the crew receive wages for their employment.

Lists of crew contained in crew agreement

3022 **13.** A list of crew may be contained in the same document as a crew agreement relating to one ship only and any particulars entered in the crew agreement shall be treated as forming part of the particulars entered in the list.

Particulars to be specified in lists of crew

3 **14.**—(1) Subject to paragraphs (2) and (3) of this regulation, a list of crew shall contain the following particulars—

(*a*) (i) the name of the ship, its port of registry and official number;

(ii) the name of the owner of the ship and his address; and

(iii) the number of the certificate evidencing an exemption granted by the Secretary of State from the requirements of section 1 of the Act (which relates to crew agreements) with respect to the ship or any person in it; and

(*b*) subject to paragraph (4) of this regulation, in respect of every seaman from time to time on board the ship, whether or not he is employed under a crew agreement—

(i) his name;

(ii) his address;

(iii) the number of his current discharge book (if any) or the date and place of his birth;

(iv) the name of the ship in which he was last employed, and, if he was discharged from that ship more than 12 months before he became employed in the ship to which the list of crew relates, the year in which he was so discharged;

(v) the capacity in which he is employed in the ship;

(vi) the grade and number of any certificate of competency held by him;

(vii) the date on which he went on board the ship to commence his employment in it;

(viii) the date on and place at which he left the ship and, if he left on discharge, the reason for his discharge;

(ix) if he is left behind otherwise than on discharge, the date and place of and the reason (if known to the master) for this being done; and

(x) the name and relationship of his next of kin and the address of his next of kin, if different from that of the seaman.

4 (2) A list of crew which relates to a ship belonging to a general lighthouse authority need contain only the particulars referred to in paragraph (1)(*a*)(i) and in (i), (ii), (vii) and (viii) of paragraph (1)(*b*) of this regulation.

(3) A list of crew which relates to seamen employed under a crew agreement need contain only the particulars referred to in paragraph (1)(*a*)(i) of this regulation and, in respect of each seaman, the particulars referred to in (i), (ii), (iii), (v), (vii) and (viii) of paragraph (1)(*b*) if the remaining particulars referred to in paragraph (1) are contained in the crew agreement.

(4) In respect of a member of the naval, military or air forces of the Crown or of any service administered by the Defence Council when acting as such a member, a list of crew need contain only the particulars referred to in (i), (ii), (vii) and (viii) of paragraph (1)(*b*) of this regulation.

Delivery of copies of lists of crew and notification of changes

3025 **15.**—(1) When—

(*a*) a new list of crew is made relating to a ship of 25 gross tons or more, other than one belonging to a general lighthouse authority; or

(*b*) any change (including the addition of any particulars) is made in a list of crew relating to a ship of 200 gross tons or more, other than one belonging to a general lighthouse authority;

the master shall, within 2 days thereafter or, if it is not practicable within that period, as soon as practicable thereafter, deliver to a superintendent or proper officer a copy of the list of crew or notification of the change, as the case may be.

(2) The master shall endorse the copy of a list of crew or the notification of any change with a certificate that it is a true copy.

Copies of list of crew

3026 **16.**—(1) A copy of every list of crew (including all changes in it notified to the owner) shall be maintained by the owner of the ship at an address in the United Kingdom.

(2) The master shall, as soon as practicable and in any event within 3 days of any change being made in the list of crew, notify the change to the owner of the ship.

(3) In this regulation, "owner of the ship" means—

(*a*) the person registered as managing owner, ship's husband or manager; or

(*b*) if there is no such person, the owner of the ship.

3027 **17.** When any person having in his possession the copy of a list of crew required to be maintained under regulation 16 has reason to believe that the ship to which it relates has been lost or abandoned, he shall immediately deliver the copy of the list to a superintendent.

3028 **18.** A person having in his possession a copy of a list of crew relating to a ship of less than 25 gross tons or to a ship belonging to a general lighthouse authority shall deliver it on demand to a superintendent.

Duration of lists of crew

3029 **19.** A list of crew shall remain in force—

(*a*) if any person is employed in the ship under a crew agreement, until all the persons employed under that agreement in that ship have been discharged; and

(*b*) in any other case, until the ship first calls at a port more than 6 months after the first entry relating to a seaman is made in the list.

Delivery of lists of crew

30 **20.** The master shall, within 2 days after a list of crew (other than one relating to a ship of less than 25 gross tons or to a ship belonging to a general lighthouse authority) has ceased to be in force or, if it is not practicable within that period, as soon as practicable thereafter, deliver the list to a superintendent or proper officer for the place where the ship is when the list of crew ceases to be in force.

Production of lists of crew

31 **21.** A master shall, on demand, produce to the Registrar General of Shipping and Seamen, a superintendent or proper officer or an officer of customs and excise the list of crew required to be maintained in the ship.

Offences under Part II

32 **22.**—(1) A master who fails to comply with an obligation imposed on him by or under regulation 15(1), 15(2), 16(2), 20 or 21 shall be guilty of an offence.

(2) A person who fails to comply with an obligation imposed on him by regulation 16(1), 17 or 18 shall be guilty of an offence.

(3) Any offence under this regulation shall be punishable on summary conviction with a fine not exceeding £20.

PART III

DISCHARGE OF SEAMEN

Notice of discharge

33 **23.**—(1) Subject to regulation 24, the master of a ship shall, not less than 48 hours before a seaman is discharged from the ship or, if it is not practicable within that period, as soon as practicable thereafter, give a notice of discharge in writing to a superintendent or proper officer for the place where the seaman is to be discharged.

(2) A notice of discharge shall contain the following particulars—

(*a*) the name of the ship, its port of registry and official number;

(*b*) the place, date and time of the seaman's discharge;

(*c*) the capacity in which the seaman is employed in the ship;

(*d*) if the seaman is to be discharged outside the United Kingdom, whether or not the consent of a proper officer to the seaman's discharge is required;

(*e*) if the seaman is to be discharged outside the United Kingdom and the consent of a proper officer is not required, which of the reasons specified in regulation 25(1) is the reason for that consent not being required; and

(*f*) the seaman's name if, at the time of discharge, a dispute about his wages is to be submitted to a superintendent or proper officer under section 10 of the Act (which relates to disputes about seamen's wages) or an appeal is to be made by the seaman to a superintendent or proper officer under section 35 of the Act (which relates to appeals against fines for disciplinary offences).

(3) If a notice of discharge relates to more than one seaman, it shall state, in addition to the particulars specified in paragraph (2) of this regulation, the number of seamen being discharged.

Discharge in the United Kingdom

3034 **24.** A notice of discharge is not required in respect of a seaman discharged in the United Kingdom—

(*a*) if—

(i) at the time of discharge, no such dispute or appeal as is referred to in regulation 23(2)(*f*) is to be submitted or made to a superintendent; and

(ii) the master has reasonable grounds for believing that the total number of seamen, (other than seamen exempted by regulation 3(*b*) from the requirements of section 1 of the Act, which relates to crew agreements) who will be discharged from the ship, while it remains in the place where the seaman is being discharged, will not exceed two; or

(*b*) if the seaman is to be discharged from a ship exempted from the requirements of section 1 of the Act by regulation 3(*a*); or

(*c*) if the seaman is exempted from the requirements of section 1 of the Act by regulation 3(*b*).

Discharge outside the United Kingdom

3035 **25.**—(1) A seaman employed in a ship (other than a ship belonging to a general lighthouse authority) shall not be discharged from the ship outside the United Kingdom without the consent of a proper officer, except where—

(*a*) the seaman is employed under an agreement for one or more voyages and he is to be discharged either at the end of that voyage or of the last of such voyages; or

(*b*) the seaman is employed under an agreement for a specified period and he is to be discharged at the end of that period; or

(*c*) the seaman and the master agree (notwithstanding anything in the agreement under which the seaman is employed) that he should be discharged at the place and at the time when he is discharged; or

(*d*) it appears to the master that it is not practicable without unreasonably delaying the ship to obtain the consent of a proper officer to a seaman's discharge and that either—

(i) in the interests of safety or for the preservation of good order and discipline on board the ship, it is necessary that the seaman should be discharged; or

(ii) the seaman is incapable of performing his duties by reason of illness or injury and is in urgent need of medical or surgical attention which cannot be provided on board the ship.

(2) Where a proper officer consents to the discharge of a seaman outside the United Kingdom, he shall, if it is practicable for him to do so, make and sign an entry in the ship's official log book recording his consent; but if he does not make and sign an entry, the master shall make and sign an entry recording that such consent has been given.

Procedure on discharge

36 **26.**—(1) Where a seaman is present when he is discharged—

(*a*) the master, or one of the ship's officers authorised by him in that behalf, shall, before the seaman is discharged—

(i) if the seaman produces his discharge book to him, record in it the name of the ship, its port of registry, gross or register tonnage and official number, the description of the voyage, the capacity in which the seaman has been employed in the ship, the date on which he began to be so employed and the date and place of his discharge; or

(ii) if the seaman does not produce his discharge book to him, give to the seaman a certificate of discharge containing the like particulars;

(*b*) the master shall ensure that the seaman is discharged in the presence of—

(i) the master himself, or

(ii) the seaman's employer, or

(iii) a person authorised in that behalf by the master or employer;

(*c*) the person mentioned in paragraph (1)(*b*) of this regulation in whose presence the seaman is being discharged shall—

(i) make and sign an entry in the official log book recording the place, date and time of the seaman's discharge; and

(ii) make and sign an entry in the crew agreement or, if there is a list of crew separate from a crew agreement, in the list of crew, recording the place and date of, and the reason for, the seaman's discharge;

(*d*) the seaman shall sign the entry in the crew agreement and list of crew referred to in paragraph (1)(*c*)(ii) of this regulation.

(2) Where a seaman is not present when he is discharged, the master, or a person authorised in that behalf by the master, shall make the entries referred to in paragraph (1)(*c*) of this regulation.

(3) All entries in the official log book required under the preceding paragraphs of this regulation shall, in addition to being signed by the person making the entry, be signed also by a member of the crew.

(4) If a seaman so requests, the master, or one of the ship's officers authorised by him in that behalf, shall give to the seaman a certificate (which shall be separate from any other document) either as to the quality of his work or indicating whether he has fully discharged his obligations under his contract of employment.

Offences under Part III

037 **27.**—(1) Any person (including a master)—

(*a*) who discharges a seaman in contravention of any of the provisions of regulation 25(1); or

(*b*) who fails to comply with an obligation imposed on him by or under paragraph (1)(*a*), (1)(*c*)(ii) or (4) of regulation 26; or

(*c*) who fails to comply with an obligation imposed on him by regulation 26(2) in relation to an entry in a crew agreement or in a list of crew; or

(*d*) who fails to make an entry in an official log book required by regulation 26(1)(*c*)(i); or (*e*) who fails to comply with an obligation imposed on him by regulation 26(2) in relation to an entry in an official log book;

shall be guilty of an offence.

(2) A master—

(*a*) who fails to comply with an obligation imposed on him under regulation 23(1), or 26(1)(*b*); or

(*b*) who fails to make an entry in an official log book required by regulation 25(2);

shall be guilty of an offence.

(3) A seaman who fails to comply with an obligation imposed on him by regulation 26(1)(*d*) shall be guilty of an offence.

(4) Any offence under this regulation shall be punishable on summary conviction—

(*a*) in the case of an offence referred to in paragraph (1)(*a*), (1)(*b*), (1)(*c*) or (2)(*a*) of this regulation, with a fine not exceeding £100;

(*b*) in the case of an offence referred to in paragraph (1)(*d*), (1)(*e*) or (2)(*b*) of this regulation, with a fine not exceeding £20; and

(*c*) in the case of an offence referred to in paragraph (3) of this regulation, with a fine not exceeding £10.

Appendix 2

NOTES ON AGREEMENTS WITH CREW

Notes for all Owners of Merchant Ships and Fishing Vessels, and Masters and Seamen on the Approval of Crew Agreements

038 **1.** Section 1(3) of the Merchant Shipping Act 1970 provides that the provisions and form of a crew agreement must be of a kind approved by the Department and different provisions and forms may be so approved for different circumstances.

2. The [Department of Trade] in consultation with the shipping and fishing industries have produced standard agreements which will be available from Mercantile Marine Offices and proper officers abroad. There are 3 standard agreements:—

(1) An agreement appropriate for use on ships operating under National Maritime Board conditions. (Form ALC/NMB 1)

(2) An agreement for ships not operating under National Maritime Board conditions. (Form ALC/NFD 1) and

(3) An agreement suitable for use on fishing vessels. (Form ALC/FSG 1)

These standard agreements will be regarded as approved agreements and subject to the comments in paragraphs 9 and 10 below may be used without individual submission to the Department for approval provided that they are not modified in any way by those who use them.

3. Employers who wish to use agreements other than the standard forms or who wish to use modified versions of the standard forms will be required to submit them to the Department for approval not less than 14 days before the agreement is to be used. Approval will not be given to such agreements unless they comply with ILO Convention 22 (Seamen's articles of agreement) or ILO Convention 114 (Fishermen's articles of agreement) as may be appropriate; are in the form prescribed for standard agreements (see paragraph 6 below) and contain contractual provisions dealing with the matters set out in paragraph 7 of this notice. In considering requests for approval of non-standard agreements the Department will have regard to the need to ensure that the seamen are as adequately protected under these agreements as they would be under the provisions set out in the standard form of agreement. Before approving a non-standard agreement or a modified version of a standard agreement the Department will wish to know the views of the seafarers' organisations on the proposed agreement or modification.

4. Non-standard agreements or modifications to standard agreements may be submitted for approval either direct to Marine Division (Branch 6), Department of Trade and Industry, Sunley House, 90–93 High Holborn, London WC1, to superintendents or proper officers abroad.

Multiple agreements

3039 **5.** Section 1(2)(*b*) provides that agreements with the several persons employed in a ship shall be contained in one document except that in such cases as the Department may approve one crew agreement may relate to more than one ship. The Department propose to approve crew agreements (to be known as multiple ship agreements) in circumstances where several ships regularly making journeys between the same ports need to be able to employ individual crew members on any of these ships during the currency of an agreement. These standard multiple ship agreements will be in the same form and contain the same provisions as those for the standard agreements except that the name of each of the ships to which they relate will be entered on the outer cover.

APPENDIX 3

DISCIPLINARY OFFENCES REGULATIONS

Merchant Shipping (Disciplinary Offences) Regulations 1972

(S.I. 1972 No. 1294)

Regulations made under sections 34, 35, 38(3) *and* 68(2) *of the Merchant Shipping Act* 1970, *dated August* 17, 1972.

40 EXPLANATORY NOTE [1]

These Regulations, made under the Merchant Shipping Act 1970, make provision for the maintenance of discipline on board ships (other than fishing vessels) registered in the United Kingdom. They apply to all seamen, except certificated officers, employed in such ships otherwise than as specified in regulation 2. The Regulations—

(*a*) specify the types of misconduct which constitute disciplinary offences on board all such ships (regulation 3);

(*b*) specify the types of misconduct which constitute disciplinary offences on board the ships described in regulation 4(3) in which there is a special risk of fire or explosion (regulation 4);

(*c*) prescribe the procedure to be followed in dealing with disciplinary offences (regulations 5-7), the fines which may be imposed (regulation 8) and make provision for matters relating to such fines (regulations 9 and 10);

(*d*) provide for appeals against fines for disciplinary offences, including the procedure to be followed on any such appeal (regulations 11-20).

Citation, commencement and interpretation

041 **1.**—(1) These Regulations may be cited as the Merchant Shipping (Disciplinary Offences) Regulations 1972 and shall come into operation on 1st January 1973.

(2) In these Regulations—

"the Act" means the Merchant Shipping Act 1970;

"the 1894 Act" means the Merchant Shipping Act 1894(c);

"intermediate port", in relation to an appeal by a seaman to a superintendent or proper officer, means a port at which a ship calls before arriving at the port at which, or nearest to the place at which, the seaman is to be discharged;

"master" includes (except in regulation 5) any officer authorised under regulation 5(2) to exercise the powers of the master and to perform his duties in relation to a disciplinary offence;

"officer" means an officer qualified for the purposes of section 43 of the Act or duly certificated under the 1894 Act;

"seaman" does not include an officer;

"ship" means a ship registered in the United Kingdom.

(3) The Interpretation Act 1889 shall apply to the interpretation of these Regulations as it applies to the interpretation of an Act of Parliament.

[1] This Note is not part of the Regulations.

Application

3042 **2.**—(1) These Regulations apply to any seaman employed in a ship otherwise than—

(*a*) in a pleasure yacht;

(*b*) in a ship belonging to a general lighthouse authority;

(*c*) in a ship of less than 200 tons engaged solely on coastal voyages;

(*d*) solely in connection with the construction, alteration, repair or testing of the ship, its machinery or equipment, and not engaged in the navigation of the ship;

(*e*) in a ship engaged solely on a coastal voyage for the purpose of trials of the ship, its machinery or equipment.

(2) For the purposes of paragraph (1)(*c*) and (*e*) of this regulation—

"coastal voyage" means a voyage between places in the British Islands (including the Republic of Ireland) or from and returning to such a place during which, in either case, no call is made at any place outside those islands;

"tons" means tons gross tonnage and the gross tonnage of a ship having alternative tonnages shall be the larger of those tonnages.

Part I

Disciplinary Offences

3043 **3.** It is a disciplinary offence on board a ship for a seaman to whom these Regulations apply—

(*a*) wilfully to strike any person;

(*b*) wilfully to disobey a lawful command;

(*c*) without reasonable cause—

(i) to fail to be available for duty at a time when he is required by the master or by a person authorised by the master to be so available; or

(ii) to fail to report or to remain at his place of duty at a time when he is so required to be at that place; or

(iii) while on duty, to be asleep at his place of duty;

(*d*) to be under the influence of drink or a drug (whether alone or in combination) to such an extent that he behaves in a disorderly manner or is unfit to be entrusted with his duty or with any duty which he might be called upon to perform, unless the drug was taken by him for medical purposes and either—

(i) he took it on medical advice and complied with any directions given as part of that advice; or

(ii) he had no reason to believe that the drug might have the influence it had;

(*e*) without the consent of the master or of any other person authorised to give it, to bring on board the ship or to have in his possession on board any offensive weapon;

(*f*) wilfully and without reasonable cause—

(i) to damage the ship; or

(ii) to damage any property on board the ship; or

(iii) to throw any such property overboard;

(*g*) without reasonable cause, to take or to be in possession of any property belonging to or in the custody of any person on board the ship;

(*h*) to cause or knowingly to permit to be on board the ship any person who, being neither in Her Majesty's service nor authorised by law to be on board the ship, is on board without the consent of the master or of any other person authorised to give it.

Disciplinary offences on board certain ships

3044 **4.**—(1) It is a disciplinary offence on board a ship described in paragraph (3) of this regulation for a seaman to whom these Regulations apply—

(*a*) to smoke; or

(*b*) to use a naked light or mechanical lighter; or

(*c*) to use an electric torch which is not of a type approved by the master;

in any part of the ship in which smoking or the use of such a light, mechanical lighter or torch is prohibited by the master or the employer.

(2) It is a disciplinary offence on board a ship described in paragraph (3) of this regulation for a seaman to whom these Regulations apply, without the consent of the master or of any other person authorised to give it, to bring on board the ship or to have in his possession on board any matches or a mechanical lighter.

(3) The description of ship referred to in paragraphs (1) and (2) of this regulation is any ship in which—

(i) by reason of the cargo or stores which are or have been carried in the ship, there is a special risk of fire or explosion; and

(ii) the master or the employer has given notice to seamen in the ship (whether by means of notices displayed in the ship or otherwise) that the acts mentioned in sub-paragraphs (*a*), (*b*) and (*c*) of paragraph (1) of this regulation are prohibited, either in all or specified parts of the ship.

(4) In this regulation—

"mechanical lighter" includes any mechanical, chemical or electrical contrivance designed or adapted for or capable of causing fire or explosion.

Procedure relating to disciplinary offences

3045 **5.**—(1) Subject to paragraph (2) of this regulation, a disciplinary offence may be dealt with only by the master of the ship on board which the offence is alleged to have occurred and the master may impose a fine (not exceeding such an amount as is specified in regulation 8) on the seaman whom he finds has committed the offence.

(2) The powers of the master in relation to a disciplinary offence may be exercised and his duties may be performed by any officer authorised for the purpose by the master; and the name of any officer so authorised shall be entered by the master in the official log book.

6. A disciplinary offence shall be dealt with within 24 hours of the time it comes to the notice of the master, unless it is not practicable to deal with it within that time, in which case it shall be dealt with as soon as practicable thereafter.

3046 **7.** In dealing with a disciplinary offence, the following procedure shall be followed—

(*a*) A seaman charged with a disciplinary offence shall, if he so requests, be permitted at the hearing before the master to be accompanied by a friend for the purpose of advising him and the friend may speak on behalf of the seaman.

(*b*) The charge shall be entered by the master in the official log book and shall be read to the seaman by the master, who shall record therein that it has been so read.

(*c*) The seaman shall then be asked whether or not he admits the charge. If he does admit it, the admission shall be recorded by the master in the official log book. In all other cases an entry to the effect that the seaman does not admit the charge shall be recorded therein.

(*d*) The evidence of any witness called by the master shall be heard in the presence of the seaman, who shall be afforded reasonable opportunity to question the witness on his evidence.

(*e*) The seaman shall be given an opportunity to make a statement in answer to the charge, including any comments on the evidence produced against him. Particulars of the statement (or a record that the seaman declined to make one, if such should be the case) shall be entered by the master in the official log book or contained in a separate document annexed to, and referred to in an entry made by the master in, the official log book.

(*f*) The seaman shall be permitted to call witnesses to give evidence on his behalf, and any such witness may be questioned by the master on his evidence.

(*g*) The master shall, after consideration of all the evidence given before him, give his decision in the presence of the seaman as to whether he finds the seaman has committed the offence charged and—

(i) if he does not find that the seaman has committed the offence, he shall dismiss the charge;

(ii) if he finds that the seaman has committed the offence, he shall, after having regard to any mitigating circumstances brought to his notice, give his decision either as to the amount of the fine he is imposing or that he is imposing no fine;

and the master shall record his decisions in the official log book.

(*h*) The master shall—

(i) inform a seaman on whom a fine has been imposed, of his right of appeal under section 35 of the Act and of the time within which notice of intended appeal must be given in accordance with these Regulations;

(ii) if the seaman so requests, supply to him copies of all entries in the official log book (including any annexes thereto) referring to the disciplinary offence to which the fine relates.

Fines

47 **8.**—(1) The fine that may be imposed on a seaman for a disciplinary offence under regulation 3 shall be an amount not exceeding £2 or, in the case of a second or subsequent commission of that offence before the seaman is discharged from the ship, an amount not exceeding £5.

(2) The fine that may be imposed on a seaman for a disciplinary offence under regulation 4 shall be an amount not exceeding £10.

9. A fine imposed on a seaman for a disciplinary offence may be remitted in whole or in part by the master—

(*a*) if the master is of the opinion that the seaman's conduct since the fine was imposed has been such as to justify the remission; or

(*b*) if new evidence has been discovered which was not known to the master at the time he dealt with the offence and which, in his opinion, justifies the remission;

and a record of every such remission shall be entered in the official log book by the master.

10. A fine imposed on a seaman for a disciplinary offence and against which an appeal is pending at the time mentioned in section 38(2) of the Act may be provisionally deducted from the seaman's wages pending the appeal.

PART II

Appeals against a fine for a disciplinary offence

48 **11.** Subject to regulations 14 and 15, an appeal by a seaman against a fine for a disciplinary offence shall be heard by a superintendent or proper officer at the place at which the seaman is discharged.

12. Subject to regulation 14, if a seaman on whom a fine has been imposed for a disciplinary offence wishes to appeal against the decision to a superintendent or proper officer, he shall give notice of intended appeal to the master within 2 days of the decision; provided that if the decision is given within 2 days of the ship's expected time of arrival at the port at which, or nearest to the place at which, the seaman is to be discharged, the notice shall be given before the seaman is discharged.

13. Upon receipt of a notice of intended appeal from the seaman, the master shall—

(*a*) make an entry in the official log book recording the date of receipt of the notice; and

(*b*) subject to regulation 14, give notice of the appeal, not later than 36 hours before the ship's expected time of arrival at the port at which, or nearest to the place at which, the seaman is to be discharged, to the superintendent or proper officer for that port; provided that if it is not practicable for the notice to be given within that period, it shall be given as soon as practicable thereafter.

49 **14.**—(1) Notwithstanding anything contained in regulations 11, 12 or 13(b), an appeal by a seaman against a fine for a disciplinary offence may be heard at an intermediate port by the superintendent or proper officer for that port if—

(*a*) either the master or the seaman requests that superintendent or proper officer to hear the appeal; and

(*b*) notice of intended appeal is given by the seaman to the master and by the master to the superintendent or proper officer within a reasonable time of the ship's expected time of arrival at the intermediate port; and

(*c*) the superintendent or proper officer is of the opinion that it is desirable that the appeal should be heard by him.

(2) If an appeal is to be heard at an intermediate port, the master shall make an entry to that effect in the official log book.

15. Notwithstanding anything contained in regulation 11, if an appeal has not been determined at an intermediate port and either—

(*a*) there is no superintendent or proper officer available to hear the appeal at the place, date and time at which the seaman is discharged; or

(*b*) the Secretary of State is of the opinion, that, having regard to all the circumstances of the case, it is expedient that the appeal should be heard at a place other than that at which the seaman is discharged;

the appeal shall be heard at such other place as the Secretary of State may direct.

3050 **16.**—(1) The superintendent or proper officer to whom a notice of intended appeal has been given shall make arrangements as to the place, date and time at which the appeal is to be heard and shall inform the master of those arrangements.

(2) The master shall, upon being informed by the superintendent or proper officer of the arrangements which have been made for hearing the appeal, inform the seaman of those arrangements.

(3) The master shall supply to the seaman copies of all entries in the official log book (including any annexes thereto) referring to the disciplinary offence to which the appeal relates, unless he has already supplied those copies in accordance with regulation 7(*h*)(ii).

17. The master shall, upon request, supply the superintendent or proper officer with copies of all entries in the official log book (including any annexes thereto) referring to the disciplinary offence to which the appeal relates and, if so required, produce to him the official log book.

3051 **18.**—(1) In hearing an appeal, the following procedure shall be followed—

(*a*) The seaman shall, if he so requests, be permitted at the hearing to be accompanied by a friend for the purpose of advising him and the friend may speak on behalf of the seaman.

(*b*) The seaman shall be given an opportunity to state the grounds of his appeal, to produce supporting evidence and to call witnesses to give evidence on his behalf.

(*c*) Subject to paragraph (2) of this regulation, the master shall be given an opportunity to call witnesses and to give evidence himself.

(*d*) The evidence of any witness (whether called by the superintendent or proper officer or otherwise) shall be heard in the presence of the seaman.

(*e*) Subject to paragraph (2) of this regulation, both the seaman and the master shall be afforded reasonable opportunity to question any witness on his evidence and to comment upon it.

(*f*) The superintendent or proper officer shall notify the seaman and the employer of his decision regarding the appeal and shall record that decision in the official log book.

(2) If the master is absent from the hearing of the appeal and the superintendent or proper officer is satisfied that no injustice will result, the appeal may (notwithstanding sub-paragraphs (*c*) and (*e*) of paragraph (1) of this regulation) be heard and determined by the superintendent or proper officer in the absence of the master.

3052 **19.**—(1) Where a seaman is not present at the place, date and time arranged for the hearing of his appeal—

(*a*) if the seaman so requests within 6 months from the date on which he was discharged from the ship; and

(*b*) if the seaman had not been informed of those arrangements or had other reasonable excuse for not being present;

the superintendent or proper officer shall make further arrangements for the appeal to be heard.

(2) If the superintendent or proper officer makes further arrangements for the appeal to be heard, he shall notify them to the seaman and to the employer.

(3) If the superintendent or proper officer does not make further arrangements for the appeal to be heard, he shall notify his reasons to the seaman and to the employer.

(4) It shall be sufficient compliance with the requirements of paragraphs (2) or (3) of this regulation for the notification to be sent by registered post to the last known address of the seaman and to the last known address of the employer.

20.—(1) All entries in the official log book (including annexes thereto) required to be made by the master under these Regulations shall be signed by the master and by a member of the crew.

(2) A master or the officer authorised by him under regulation 5(2) to exercise the powers of the master and to perform his duties in relation to a disciplinary offence, who fails to make an entry in an official log book required to be made by the master under these Regulations (except regulation 14(2)), shall be guilty of an offence and shall be punishable on summary conviction with a fine not exceeding £20.

Appendix 4

TONNAGE REGULATIONS

Merchant Shipping (Tonnage) Regulations 1967

(S.I. 1967 No. 172)

Regulations made under section 1 *of the Merchant Shipping Act* 1965, *dated February* 10, 1965.

3053 Explanatory Note [1]

These Regulations are made under the Merchant Shipping Act 1965 which came into operation on March 1, 1967. They replaced with minor amendments the provisions of the Merchant Shipping Acts relating to tonnage measurement which were repealed by that Act, and gave effect to a recommendation of the Inter-Governmental Maritime Consultative Organisation regarding the treatment for tonnage measurement purposes of the shelter deck and certain other spaces on board ship.

The principal changes were:

(1) Shelter deck ships had hitherto been allocated reduced tonnages by virtue of openings in the shelter deck known as tonnage openings. Provision is made for the allocation of alternative tonnages or in certain circumstances, if the owners so desire, permanently reduced tonnages. When alternative tonnages are allocated the submersion or non-submersion of a tonnage mark on the side of the ship will indicate which tonnage is to be applied. The effect of these provisions will be to enable tonnage openings to be permanently closed for reasons of safety without prejudicing the reduced tonnage of the ship.

(2) Certain spaces occupied by goods are exempted from measurement under Section 85 of the Merchant Shipping Act 1894 notwithstanding that they are not included in the register tonnage of the ship.

[1] This Note is not part of the Regulations.

PART I

Ascertainment of Tonnage

054 **1.** The tonnage of any ship to be registered in the United Kingdom under the principal Act, whether under Part I or Part IV thereof, shall be ascertained in accordance with these Regulations.

Method of Measurement

2.—(1) The owner and the master of a ship to be measured shall make it available for measurement by a surveyor of ships pursuant to section 6 of the principal Act and afford all necessary facilities for its inspection and measurement and shall produce for the surveyor's use and retention if required such plans, drawings, specifications and other documents relating to the ship as he may require.

(2) Subject to paragraph (3) of this Regulation, the tonnage of a ship shall be measured in the manner specified in Rule I of Schedule 1 and in Schedule 2 to these Regulations.

(3) In any case in which the surveyor is satisfied that by reason of the ship's being laden or otherwise measurement of the tonnage of the ship below the upper deck in accordance with paragraph (2) of this Regulation is not reasonably practicable, such tonnage shall be measured in the manner specified in Rule II of Schedule 1 and in the case of a ship so measured the provisions of Regulations 11 and 12 shall not apply.

(4) The [Department] may on the application of the owner of any ship the tonnage of which below the upper deck has been measured in accordance with paragraph (3) direct such tonnage to be measured in accordance with paragraph (2) and [See App. 4a, *post*, § 3071a].

(5) All measurements required by these Regulations shall be taken and expressed in feet and fractions of a foot, and such fractions shall be expressed in decimals.

(6) Tonnage in relation to any ship or space in a ship shall be measured in terms of cubic capacity, 100 cubic feet representing one ton.

Certificates of British Tonnage

55 **3.**—(1) The [Department] shall issue to the owner of every ship registered in the United Kingdom under the principal Act, the tonnage of which has been ascertained in accordance with these Regulations, a certificate of British tonnage certifying the registered tonnage of the ship and containing the following particulars:—

(*a*) the name, port of registry and official number of the ship;

(*b*) its registered dimensions;

(*c*) its gross tonnage and the tonnage of each of the components thereof specified in Regulation 4(1);

(*d*) its register tonnage and the deductions and allowances made pursuant to Regulations 9 and 10 respectively in ascertaining that tonnage;

(*e*) in the case of a ship to which gross and register tonnages have been assigned in accordance with Regulation 11, or to which alternative tonnages have been assigned in accordance with Regulation 12, particulars of the spaces the tonnage of which has been excluded by virtue of the provisions of Regulation 11 or Regulation 12, as the case may be, in ascertaining such tonnages;

(*f*) the position in which any tonnage mark assigned to the ship is to be placed.

(2) For the purpose of ascertaining in relation to ships not registered in the United Kingdom the amount of rates and charges based upon tonnage, the Board may issue to the owner of any such ship the tonnage of which has been ascertained in accordance with these Regulations a certificate of British tonnage as aforesaid, and the gross and register tonnages as stated in that certificate shall, unless any alteration is made in the form or capacity of the ship or it is discovered that the tonnage of the ship has been erroneously computed, be taken for that purpose to be the gross and register tonnages of the ship.

(3) On remeasurement of a ship any certificate of British tonnage in force in relation to that ship shall be delivered up to the [Department] and the [Department] shall issue a new certificate in place thereof.

Part II

A. Gross Tonnage

Components of Gross Tonnage

3056 **4.**—(1) Subject to the provisions of Part III of these Regulations, the gross tonnage of a ship shall be the sum of—

(*a*) the underdeck tonnage of the ship ascertained in accordance with the provisions of Regulation 5 and paragraph 1 of Rule I of Schedule 1 to these Regulations;

(*b*) the tonnage of betweendeck space between the second deck and the upper deck ascertained in accordance with the provisions of paragraph 2 of the said Rule I;

(*c*) the tonnage of permanently closed-in spaces on or above the upper deck including that of breaks situated above the line of the deck but excluding—

(i) the tonnage of hatchways described in Regulation 6;

(ii) the tonnage of framed-in spaces on or above the upper deck which contain any part of the propelling machinery or which light or ventilate space appropriated for such machinery;

(iii) any space excluded by virtue of the provisions of Regulation 7,

ascertained in accordance with the provisions of paragraphs 3, 4 and 5 of the said Rule I;

(*d*) the tonnage of hatchways described in Regulation 6, ascertained in accordance with the provisions of that Regulation and paragraph 5 of the said Rule I;

(*e*) the tonnage of framed-in spaces on or above the upper deck which contain any part of the propelling machinery or which light or ventilate space appropriated for such machinery, ascertained in accordance with the provisions of paragraph 5 of the said Rule I, subject to the conditions that—

(i) the owner of the ship has made written application to the Board for the inclusion of such spaces in the propelling machinery space of the ship;

(ii) they are permanently marked by a notice stating their purpose; and

(iii) they are certified by a surveyor of ships as safe and seaworthy and properly constructed for their purpose, as reasonable in extent for that purpose, and as being such that they cannot be used for any other purpose.

(2) In the case of a ship the tonnage of which below the upper deck has been measured in accordance with Rule II of Schedule 1, that tonnage shall be included instead of the tonnages specified at (*a*) and (*b*) in paragraph (1).

(3) For the purpose of these Regulations the expression " permanently closed-in spaces on or above the upper deck " shall include:—

(*a*) a poop, bridge or forecastle notwithstanding the presence of an opening in the end transverse bulkhead thereof, unless the opening extends from deck to deck for one half or more of the breadth of the deck in way of the bulkhead;

(*b*) a deck house notwithstanding the presence of an opening in one of the boundary bulkheads thereof exposed to the weather, unless the opening extends from deck to deck for one half or more of the length of the bulkhead in which it is situated and is 4 feet wide or more;

(*c*) a structure extending from side to side of the ship notwithstanding the presence in it of an opening in the ship's side, unless the opening extends for one half or more of the length of the space which it serves and exceeds in height one third of the distance from deck to deck in way of the opening or 2 feet 6 inches, whichever is the greater;

(*d*) a passage way at the ship's side, unless it is 4 feet wide or more and is completely open to the weather at one end, or both ends, of its length;

(*e*) a recess, unless it extends from deck to deck for 3 feet or more of its width and is exposed to the weather; and

(*f*) any space having an opening in the deck over being a deck exposed to the weather, unless the area of the opening is one quarter or more of the deck area over the space.

Underdeck Tonnage

57 **5.** The underdeck tonnage of a ship shall be the sum of—

(*a*) the tonnage of the space below the tonnage deck bounded by—

(i) the tonnage deck,

(ii) the upper surface of the double bottom tanks, open floors or ceiling as the case may be, and

(iii) the inner face of the timbers, frames or sparring as the case may be,

measured in accordance with the provisions of paragraph 1 of Rule I of Schedule 1 to these Regulations, but subject to such limitations specified in Schedule 2 as may be applicable in the circumstances of the case, and excluding the tonnage of breaks above the line of the tonnage deck; and

(*b*) the tonnage of shaft bossings and any other appendages forming part of the hull of the ship below the tonnage deck whether or not they project beyond the extreme points of measurement of that deck.

Tonnage of Hatchways

6. The tonnage of all hatchways leading to space included in the gross tonnage of the ship other than internal hatchways totally enclosed within such space shall be measured in accordance with paragraph 5 of Rule I of Schedule 1 to these Regulations and from the aggregate thereof there shall be deducted ½ of 1 per cent. of the ship's gross tonnage excluding such aggregate. The remainder (if any) shall be the tonnage of hatchways, customarily referred to as " excess of hatchways ", to be included in the gross tonnage of the ship.

Closed-in spaces on or above the upper deck not to be included in Gross Tonnage

7. Permanently closed-in spaces of the following kinds situated on or above the upper deck shall not be included in the gross tonnage of the ship:—

(*a*) dry cargo space, unless situated in a break above the line of the upper deck;

(*b*) space fitted with and appropriated for the use of machinery or condensers;

(*c*) the wheelhouse and chartroom, and space fitted with and appropriated for the use of radio and navigational aids;

(*d*) skylights, domes and trunks which light or ventilate the space they serve;

(*e*) chain lockers, and space appropriated for working the anchor gear and capstan;

(*f*) space appropriated for the storage of safety equipment or batteries;

(*g*) companions and access hatches serving as protection for stairways or ladderways leading to space below, and openings over such stairways and ladderways;

(*h*) the galley, and any separate bakery fitted with ovens, provided in either case that no part thereof is appropriated for use for any other purpose;

(*i*) washing and sanitary accommodation forming part of the crew accommodation or appropriated for the use of the master;

(*j*) workshops and storerooms appropriated for the use of pumpmen, engineers, electricians, carpenters and boatswains, and the lamp-room;

(*k*) water ballast tanks not appropriated for use for any other purpose;

(*l*) shelter space providing weather protection only for use, free of charge, by deck passengers in ships intended for use only on voyages not exceeding 10 hours duration;

(*m*) sheltered promenade space, glassed in and unfurnished except for deckchairs or similar light portable seating, in ships intended for use on international voyages:

Provided that this Regulation shall not apply in any case other than that specified at sub-paragraph (*a*) unless the space is certified by a surveyor of ships as being reasonable in extent, and properly constructed, for its purpose and is permanently marked by a notice stating that purpose.

[New Reg. 7A. See App. 4a, § 3071b, *post*.]

B. Register Tonnage

Ascertainment of Register Tonnage

3058 **8.** Subject to the provisions of Part III of these Regulations, the register tonnage of a ship shall be the tonnage obtained by deducting from its gross tonnage—

(*a*) the tonnage of spaces specified in Regulation 9, and

(*b*) the tonnage allowance for propelling machinery space described in Regulation 10:

Provided that—

(i) the deduction shall in each case be subject to any condition, limit or restriction expressed to be applicable in that case; and

(ii) no deduction shall be made of or in respect of the tonnage of any space which has not first been included in the ship's gross tonnage.

Space to be Deducted

9. The spaces referred to in Regulation 8(*a*) are—

(*a*) space appropriated for the accommodation of the master;

(*b*) crew accommodation, except space appropriated for the storage of fresh water and space appropriated for the storage of provisions (other than fresh water), being in the latter case space in excess of 15 per cent. of the aggregate of—

(i) space appropriated for the accommodation of the master; and

(ii) crew accommodation other than space appropriated for the storage of provisions and fresh water;

(*c*) the wheelhouse and chartroom, and space fitted with and appropriated for the use of radio and navigational aids;

(*d*) chain lockers and space appropriated for, or for the working of, the steering gear, anchor gear and capstan;

(*e*) space appropriated for the storage of safety equipment or batteries;

(*f*) workshops and storerooms appropriated for the use of pumpmen, electricians, carpenters and boatswains, and the lamp-room;

(*g*) space occupied by the donkey engine and boiler if they are outside the propelling machinery space and connected to the main pumps of the ship;

(*h*) space occupied by the main pumps of the ship if they are outside the propelling machinery space;

(*i*) in the case of ships wholly propelled by sails, space appropriated for the storage of sails, so however that the total tonnage of such space does not exceed 2½ per cent. of the ship's gross tonnage; and

(*j*) water ballast tanks not appropriated for use for any other purpose, so however that the total tonnage so to be deducted, when added to the tonnage of spaces appropriated for water ballast not included in the gross tonnage of the ship consisting of double bottom space, space below bottom floor level or space above the upper deck, does not exceed 19 per cent. of the ship's gross tonnage:

Provided that no deduction shall be made—

(i) in respect of any space specified in sub-paragraph (*b*) unless it is certified by a surveyor of ships as complying with all applicable provisions as to crew accommodation contained in the Merchant Shipping Acts 1894 to 1965 and regulations made thereunder; and

(ii) in respect of any space specified in sub-paragraphs (*a*) or (*c*) to (*j*) unless it is certified by a surveyor of ships to be reasonable in extent, and properly constructed, for its purpose and is permanently marked by a notice stating that purpose.

Allowance for Propelling Machinery Space

3060 **10.** The tonnage allowance for propelling machinery space to be deducted pursuant to Regulation 8(*b*) shall be determined as follows:—

(*a*) in the case of ships propelled by screws—

(i) if the tonnage of the propelling machinery space is 13 per cent. or over but less than 20 per cent. of the gross tonnage the allowance shall be 32 per cent. of the gross tonnage;

(ii) if the tonnage of the propelling machinery space is less than 13 per cent. of the gross tonnage the allowance shall be that lesser percentage of the gross tonnage multiplied by $\frac{32}{13}$;

(*b*) in the case of ships propelled by paddle wheels—

(i) if the tonnage of the propelling machinery space is 20 per cent. or over but less than 30 per cent. of the gross tonnage the allowance shall be 37 per cent. of the gross tonnage;

(ii) if the tonnage of the propelling machinery space is less than 20 per cent. of the gross tonnage the allowance shall be that lesser percentage of the gross tonnage multiplied by $\frac{37}{20}$;

(*c*) in the case of ships to which sub-paragraphs (*a*) and (*b*) do not apply, the allowance shall be—

(i) in the case of ships propelled by screws, $1\frac{3}{4}$ times the tonnage of the propelling machinery space;

(ii) in the case of ships propelled by paddle wheels, $1\frac{1}{2}$ times the tonnage of the propelling machinery space:

Provided that—

(i) in no case save that of tugs intended to be used exclusively as such shall the allowance exceed 55 per cent. of that portion of the tonnage of the ship which remains after deducting from its gross tonnage the deductions authorised by Regulation 8(*a*); and

(ii) such deductions shall be subject to the propelling machinery space and space appropriated for its lighting and ventilation being certified as adequate by a surveyor of ships and being permanently marked by notices stating their purpose.

Part III

Modified and Alternative Tonnages and Tonnage Marks

Modified gross and register tonnage of ships with certain freeboards

3061 **11.**—(1) This Regulation shall apply to a ship in respect of which—

(*a*) greater than minimum freeboards have been assigned under the Load Line Rules;

(*b*) the positions of the load lines are not higher than would have been the case if the freeboards assigned to the ship and the position of the load lines appropriate thereto had been calculated treating the second deck as the freeboard deck.

(2) The Board may, on the application of the owner of a ship to which this Regulation applies, assign to the ship as its gross tonnage and register tonnage a modified gross tonnage and modified register tonnage ascertained in accordance with paragraph (3) of this Regulation instead of the gross tonnage and register tonnage ascertained in accordance with Part II of these Regulations.

(3) The modified gross tonnage and modified register tonnage so to be assigned shall be ascertained in accordance with Part II of these Regulations subject to the following modifications:—

(*a*) for references to the upper deck in—
Regulation 4(1)(*c*) and (*e*), and (3);
Regulation 7; [Regulation 7A, *q.v.* App. 4, § 3071b, *post.*];
Regulation 9(*j*),
the definition of " propelling machinery space " in Regulation 16;
and Schedule 1, paragraphs 3, 5 and 6,
there shall be substituted references to the second deck; and

(*b*) Regulation 4(1)(*b*) and paragraph 2 of Rule I of Schedule 1 shall be omitted.

(4) Where such tonnages have been assigned to a ship there shall be placed on each side of the ship a tonnage mark in the form described in Schedule 3 to these Regulations, in a position in line with the deepest load line to which the ship may be loaded, no account being taken for this purpose of timber load lines, but subject to the foregoing in a position determined in accordance with Schedule 4.

Alternative Tonnages

12.—(1) The Board may, on the application of the owner of a ship, assign to the ship, as an alternative to its gross tonnage and register tonnage ascertained in accordance with Part II of these Regulations, the modified gross tonnage and modified register tonnage ascertained in accordance with the provisions of paragraph (3) of Regulation 11.

(2) Where alternative tonnages have been assigned to a ship there shall be placed on each side of that ship a tonnage mark in the form described in Schedule 3 to these Regulations in a position determined in accordance with the provisions of Schedule 4.

(3) The gross tonnage and register tonnage of the ship shall be taken to be respectively the modified gross tonnage and modified register tonnage when the ship is so loaded that the tonnage mark is not submerged. At all other times the gross and register tonnages of the ship shall be those ascertained in accordance with Part II of these Regulations.

Part IV

General

Fishing boats

2 **13.**—(1) Except as provided in paragraph (2) of this Regulation these Regulations shall not apply in relation to a British fishing boat to be registered under Part IV only of the principal Act.

(2) The tonnage of a British fishing boat to be registered under Part IV only of the principal Act shall be ascertained in accordance with the provisions made with respect to the ascertainment of tonnage by the Merchant Shipping (Fishing Boats Registry) Order 1927 [2] (which by virtue of section 3 of the 1965 Act have effect as if contained in these Regulations) and the tonnage so ascertained shall be taken to be the gross and register tonnage of the ship.

Remeasurement of tonnage of ships already registered

14.—(1) The Board may on the application of the owner of a ship registered under Part I of the principal Act before the coming into operation of these

[2] S.R. & O. 1927 No. 642.

Regulations direct that the tonnage of the ship be remeasured in accordance with the provisions of these Regulations.

(2) In such a case, after remeasurement of the ship the ship's existing certificate of registry shall be delivered up to the registrar of the ship's port of registry or of any other port of registry.

(3) Such registrar shall on receipt of the surveyor's certificate giving particulars of the ship as remeasured grant a new certificate of registry in place of the existing certificate and, unless he is the registrar of the ship's port of registry, shall forward the surveyor's certificate to that registrar and notify him of the issue of the new certificate.

(4) The registrar of the ship's port of registry shall alter the particulars respecting the ship in his register book accordingly and record therein the grant of the new certificate.

Space for the purposes of section 85 *of the principal Act*

[**15.**—(1) Space to be taken into account for the purposes of section 85 of the principal Act (payment of dues where goods carried in spaces not forming part of registered tonnage) shall be ascertained in accordance with the provisions of paragraph 5 of Rule I of Schedule 1 to these Regulations.

(2) Permanently closed-in space not included in the registered tonnage of a ship consisting of—

(*a*) dry cargo spaces, or

(*b*) workshops and store rooms appropriated for the use of pumpmen, engineers, electricians, carpenters and boatswains, or

(*c*) the lamp-room,

shall be exempt from being taken into account for the purposes of the said section 85.

(3) Goods or stores shall not be carried in any permanently closed-in space on board ship which has not been included in the registered tonnage of the ship, other than a double bottom tank or space described in paragraph (2).

(4) If goods or stores are carried in a permanently closed-in space on board ship in contravention of paragraph (3), the master and the owner of the ship shall each be liable to a fine not exceeding £100.] See App. 4A, § 3071c, *post*.

Interpretation

3063 **16.**—(1) In these Regulations, unless the context otherwise requires—

" the [Department] " means the [Department of Trade];

" the principal Act " means the Merchant Shipping Act 1894;

" the 1965 Act " means the Merchant Shipping Act 1965;

" crew accommodation " has the same meaning as in the Merchant Shipping Act 1948;

" dry cargo space " means space appropriated for the carriage of cargo other than liquid or gaseous matter in bulk;

["Load Line Rules " means the Merchant Shipping (Load Line) Rules 1968 as amended and includes in relation to any ship not registered in the United Kingdom any corresponding rules of the country in which the ship is registered."]

" passenger " has the same meaning as in the Merchant Shipping (Safety Convention Act 1949;

" propelling machinery space " means space below the upper deck appropriated for the main or auxiliary propelling machinery of a ship, and includes—

(*a*) ventilation, light or escape trunks serving any such space;

(*b*) space appropriated for boilers serving such machinery;

(*c*) shaft tunnels;

(*d*) engineers' storerooms and workshops not exceeding in total tonnage ¾ of 1 per cent. of the gross tonnage of the ship;

(*e*) oil fuel settling tanks serving the main or auxiliary propelling machinery, having a total capacity sufficient to provide not less than 24 or more than 96 hours steaming for the ship at maximum speed;

and shall also include framed-in spaces on or above the upper deck described in Regulation 4(1)(*e*) and included in the gross tonnage of the ship in accordance with that provision;

" second deck " means the deck next below the upper deck, being a deck—

(*a*) which is fitted as an integral part of the ship's structure;

(*b*) which is continuous at least between peak bulkheads both fore and aft and transversely, and

(*c*) in which all hatchways are fitted with substantial and durable covers,

a deck being taken to be continuous for this purpose notwithstanding the presence in it of—

(i) openings serving propelling machinery space or leading to ladderways or stairways;

(ii) hatch or ventilation trunks, provided that they do not extend fore and aft from one main transverse bulkhead to another;

(iii) chain lockers or cofferdams; or

(iv) a break or breaks the aggregate height of which above the line of continuation of the deck does not exceed 4 feet;

" tonnage deck " means the second deck except in the case of single deck ships, in which case it means the upper deck;

" upper deck " means the uppermost complete deck exposed to sea and weather fitted as an integral part of the ship's structure, being a deck all openings in the weather portions of which are fitted with permanent means of closing and below which all openings in the sides of the ship are fitted with permanent means of watertight closing, but shall in the case of an open ship be taken to be the upper edge of the upper strake of the gunwale.

(2) The Interpretation Act 1889 shall apply to the interpretation of these Regulations as it applies to the interpretation of an Act of Parliament.

Citation and Commencement

17. These Regulations may be cited as the Merchant Shipping (Tonnage) Regulations 1967 and shall come into operation on 1st March 1967.

SCHEDULE 1

MEASUREMENT OF TONNAGE

RULE I

Regulation 2

3064 1. *Underdeck tonnage*

(1) The length of the tonnage deck shall be measured in a straight line in the middle plane of the ship between the points at the forward and after ends of the deck where the underside of the deck, or the line of continuation thereof in way of breaks or discontinuations of the deck, meets the inner face of the frames, timbers, ceiling or sparring as the case may be. Such length so measured is hereafter referred to in this Schedule and in Schedule 2 to these Regulations as the " tonnage length ".

(2) In ships which have a break, or breaks, in a double bottom the tonnage length shall be measured in parts corresponding to the number and position of such break or breaks.

(3) The tonnage length, or the length of each of the several parts thereof obtained in accordance with sub-paragraph (2), shall be divided into equal parts as shown in the following table:—

length 50 feet or under, into 4 equal parts;

length above 50 feet but not exceeding 120 feet, into 6 equal parts;

length above 120 feet but not exceeding 180 feet, into 8 equal parts;

length above 180 feet but not exceeding 225 feet, into 10 equal parts;

length above 225 feet, into 12 equal parts:

Provided that the length of any of the several parts obtained in accordance with sub-paragraph (2) may be divided into 2 equal parts if such length is 30 feet or under.

(4) The transverse area of the ship at each point of division of the tonnage length, or of parts of that length as aforesaid, shall be calculated as follows:—

(*a*) The depth in the middle plane of the ship from the underside of the tonnage deck to the top of the open floor or double bottom as the case may be shall be measured, deducting therefrom the average thickness of ceiling, if fitted, and one-third the round of beam. If the top of the double bottom falls from the middle plane of the ship, there shall be added to the depth the mean of the fall; if the top of the double bottom rises from the middle plane, a corresponding correction shall be deducted from the depth.

In ships of wooden construction the lower terminal point of the depth shall be the upper side of the floor timber at the inside of the limber strake, after deducting therefrom the average thickness of ceiling between the bilge planks and the limber strake.

(*b*) If the depth so obtained does not exceed 16 feet at the amidship division of the total tonnage length, the depth at each point of division of the tonnage length, or of parts of that length as aforesaid, shall be divided into 4 equal parts; depths in excess of 16 feet shall be divided into 6 equal parts.

(*c*) At the point of division between each of the parts obtained in accordance with sub-paragraph (*b*) the horizontal breadths to the inner face of the timber, frame or sparring as the case may be shall be measured. Numbering these breadths from the tonnage deck, the even numbered breadths shall be multiplied by 4 and the others, with the exception of the first and last, by 2; these products shall be added together, and to the sum there shall be added the first and last breadths; the quantity thus obtained shall be multiplied by one-third of the common interval between the breadths and the product shall be the transverse area in square feet.

(5) The transverse areas so obtained shall be numbered from the extreme forward point of measurement of the tonnage length, or of the parts thereof as the case may be; the even numbered areas shall be multiplied by 4 and the odd numbered areas, other than the first and last, by 2; these products shall be added together and to the sum there shall be added the area (if any) of the first and last; the quantity thus obtained shall be multiplied by one-third of the common interval between the areas; the product so obtained divided by 100 shall be the underdeck tonnage of the ship exclusive of the tonnage of spaces to be included therein pursuant to Regulation 5(*b*) (appendages).

2. *Betweendeck space between the second deck and the upper deck*

(1) (*a*) Betweendeck space between the second deck and the upper deck shall be measured for length in a straight line in the middle plane of the ship between the points at the forward and after ends of the space where the inner surface of the frames, timbers, ceiling or sparring as the case may be meets the middle plane of the ship at half the height between the upper surface of the deck and the underside of the deck over.

(*b*) Where a break exists in the second deck or the upper deck the line of the deck shall be extended through the break parallel to the raised part of the break; and the tonnage of the betweendeck space shall be measured in such a case by reference to the line of the deck so extended.

(2) The length shall be divided into equal parts as provided in paragraph 1(3) of this Rule. At each of these points of division the horizontal breadth from the inner face of the frames, timbers or sparring as the case may be, shall be measured at half the height of the betweendeck space.

(3) These breadths shall be numbered from the stem, the stem being number 1. The even numbered breadths shall be multiplied by 4 and the odd numbered, other than the first and last, by 2. The products shall be added together and the first and the last breadths shall be added to the sum. The quantity thus obtained shall be multiplied by one-third of the common interval between the breadths, and the area thus obtained shall be multiplied by the mean height between the upper surface of the deck and the underside of the deck over. The product so obtained divided by 100 shall be the tonnage of the betweendeck space.

3. *Breaks in the upper deck*

Breaks in the upper deck shall be measured for length in a straight line in the middle plane of the ship between the extremities of the break at half the height of the break, terminal points at the stem or stern being taken as described in paragraph 2(1) of this Rule. The length so obtained shall be divided into 2 equal parts for lengths of 50 feet or less, 4 equal parts for lengths above 50 feet but not more than 225 feet and 6 equal parts for lengths over 225 feet. At each of the points of division the horizontal breadth at half the height of the break at the ship's side to the inner face of the frames, timbers or sparring as the case may be shall be measured. Numbering these breadths from the foremost terminal point, the even numbered breadths shall be multiplied by 4 and the odd numbered, other than the first and last, by 2. The products shall be added together and to the sum there shall be added the first and last breadths. The quantity thus obtained shall be multiplied by one-third of the common interval between the breadths. The area thus obtained shall be multiplied by the height of the break. The product divided by 100 shall be the tonnage of the break.

4. *Poop, bridge and forecastle*

A poop, bridge or forecastle shall be measured as follows:—

The mean length thereof shall be measured at half the height between the upper surface of the deck and the underside of the deck over, terminal points at the stem and stern being taken as described in paragraph 2(1) of this Rule. The length so obtained shall be divided into 2 equal parts for lengths of 50 feet or under, 4 equal parts for lengths over 50 feet but not exceeding 225 feet, and 6 equal parts for lengths exceeding 225 feet. At each of the points of division the horizontal breadth shall be measured from the inner face of the frames, timbers or sparring as the case may be at half the height between the upper surface of the deck and the underside of the deck over. Numbering these breadths from the foremost terminal point, the even numbered breadths shall be multiplied by 4 and the odd numbered, other than the first and last, by 2. The products shall be added together and to the sum there shall be added the first and last breadths. The quantity thus obtained shall be multiplied by one-third of the common interval between the breadths, and the area thus obtained shall be multiplied by the mean height of the poop, bridge or forecastle. The product divided by 100 shall be the tonnage of the poop, bridge or forecastle.

5. *Other permanently closed-in spaces on or above the upper deck*

Permanently closed-in spaces on or above the upper deck other than those dealt with in paragraph 4 shall be measured by ascertaining their mean length, breadth and height and the product of multiplying these dimensions together shall, when divided by 100, be the tonnage of the space.

6. *Propelling machinery space*

(1) Propelling machinery space which extends to the ship's side and is situated below the upper deck shall be measured as follows:—

The mean length shall be measured in each space at half the mean depth, which shall be measured in the middle plane of the ship from the underside of the deck forming the crown of the space to the top of the double bottom or open floors, allowance being made for ceiling if fitted; for amidship spaces 3 equally spaced breadths shall be used and for spaces abaft amidships 3 equally spaced breadths shall be used for lengths up to 30 feet, 5 equally spaced breadths for lengths over 30 feet to 50 feet and 7 equally spaced breadths for lengths over 50 feet, the breadths being measured from the inner face of the frames, timbers or sparring as the case may be at half the depth of the space at that point. The mean length, mean breadth and mean depth so ascertained shall be multiplied together and the product divided by 100 shall be the tonnage of the space.

(2) Propelling machinery space which does not extend to the ship's side and is situated below the upper deck shall be measured by ascertaining its mean length, mean breadth and mean depth, and the product of multiplying these dimensions together shall, when divided by 100, be the tonnage of the space.

7. *Shaft bossings and appendages*

The tonnage of shaft bossings and other appendages referred to in Regulation 5(*b*) shall be ascertained by measuring the internal cubic capacity of the space as accurately as practicable and dividing the result by 100.

6 RULE II

Measurement of tonnage below the upper deck where measurement in accordance with Rule I is impracticable

1. The length of the ship shall be measured on the upper side of the upper deck from the inside of the outer plate or plank at the stem to the aft side of the stern-post, or to the fore side of the rudder stock where no stern-post is fitted. The extreme breadth of the ship shall be measured, excluding rubbers or fenders. The girth, from the upper edge of the upper deck at side on one side of the ship to the same point at the other side, shall be measured on the outside of the ship at the greatest breadth. To half the girth thus measured there shall be added half the aforesaid breadth. The square of the sum shall be multiplied by the aforesaid length. This product multiplied by ·0017 in the case of ships built of wood and by ·0018 in the case of other ships shall be the tonnage of the ship below the upper deck.

2. In any case in which the surveyor is satisfied that by reason of the size of the ship it is not reasonably practicable to measure its girth as provided in paragraph 1, such girth shall be ascertained by adding the aforesaid breadth of the ship to twice the depth of the ship from the top of the upper deck at the side of the ship to the bottom of the keel and multiplying this sum by 0·98.

67 **SCHEDULE 2**

LIMITATION OF HEIGHT OF OPEN FLOORS AND DOUBLE BOTTOMS, AND OF DEPTHS OF FRAMES AND SIDE BRACKETS, FOR PURPOSES OF MEASUREMENT OF UNDERDECK TONNAGE

Regulation 5

The provisions of this Schedule shall have effect for the purposes of the measurement of underdeck tonnage.

1. *Open floors*

(1) Any part of an open floor, other than a floor in the main space for the propelling machinery of a ship, which is situated above the horizontal line hereinafter described shall be disregarded for the purposes of measurement of underdeck tonnage, which shall be measured accordingly by reference to the said line.

(2) The line above referred to shall be a line passing through a point in the middle plane of the ship at a height consisting of the maximum height of open floors applicable to a ship of the tonnage length of the ship undergoing measurement, ascertained by reference to columns A and B of Table I and corrected by the addition of a distance equal to the rise of the moulded frame line at one quarter of the breadth of the ship between moulded frame lines at the said maximum height.

(3) The provisions of this paragraph shall also apply in the case of ships fitted with longitudinal floors and/or frames.

2. *Double Bottoms*

A double bottom, situated in any part of a ship other than the main space for the propelling machinery, which is of greater height than a height consisting of the maximum height of double bottom applicable to a ship of the tonnage length of the ship undergoing measurement, ascertained by reference to columns A and C of Table I and corrected by the addition of a distance equal to the rise of the moulded frame line at one quarter of the breadth of the ship between moulded frame lines at the said maximum height, shall be treated not as a double bottom but as an open floor of such height ascertained in accordance with the provisions of paragraph 1(2) of this Schedule as would be applicable in the case of a ship of the tonnage length of the ship undergoing measurement.

3. *Bilge brackets*

(1) The horizontal width of bilge brackets measured from the shell of the ship to the inboard toe of the bracket shall not—

(*a*) if taken at the level of the top of an open floor, exceed the maximum height of open floor applicable to the ship obtained by reference to columns A and B of Table I;

(*b*) if taken at the level of the top of a double bottom, exceed the maximum height of double bottom applicable to the ship obtained by reference to columns A and C of that Table.

(2) In any case in which underdeck tonnage is measured by reference to a height ascertained and applied in accordance with the provisions of paragraphs 1 and 2 of this Schedule, the lowest breadth used in the measurement of underdeck tonnage area shall be the breadth between the inner sides of the shell of the ship taken at that height, less twice the maximum height of open floor applicable to the ship obtained by reference to columns A and B of Table I or twice the width of the bilge bracket whichever is the less.

4. *Allowance for ceiling*

The limitations imposed by the preceding three paragraphs are exclusive of an allowance for ceiling, if fitted.

5. *Depth of frames*

(1) Subject to sub-paragraph (2), the extent to which the depth of transverse or longitudinal ship side framing in the case of any ship, measured from its shell, exceeds the maximum depth of frame applicable to a ship of the registered breadth of the ship undergoing measurement ascertained by reference to Table II shall be disregarded and underdeck tonnage shall be measured accordingly by reference to the maximum depth of frame so ascertained.

(2) In the case of a ship in which alternate deep and shallow frames are fitted, the depth of frame used for purposes of measurement, measured from the shell of the ship, shall not exceed whichever is the lesser of the following dimensions:—

(*a*) twice the depth of the shallow frame, or

(*b*) the maximum depth of frame applicable to the ship ascertained as aforesaid.

(3) The limitations imposed by sub-paragraphs (1) and (2) are exclusive of an allowance for sparring fitted on the toe of the frames.

TABLE I

A	B	C
TONNAGE LENGTH OF SHIP	MAXIMUM HEIGHT OF OPEN FLOORS	MAXIMUM HEIGHT OF DOUBLE BOTTOM
	The dimensions shown are to be increased by 50 per cent. for the foremost 25 per cent. and aftermost 15 per cent. of the tonnage length of the ship.	
in feet	*in inches*	*in inches*
Not exceeding 60	23	34·5
80	24	36
100	25	37·5
120	26	39
140	27	40·5
160	28	42
180	29	43·5
200	30	45
220	31	46·5
240	32	48
260	33	49·5
280	34	51
300	35	52·5
320	36	54
340	37	55·5
360	38	57
380	39	58·5
400	40	60
420	41	61·5
440	42	63
460	43	64·5
480	44	66
500	45	67·5
520	46	69
540	47	70·5
560	48	72
580	49	73·5
600	50	75
620	51	76·5
640	52	78
660	53	79·5
680	54	81
700	55	82·5

In the case of ships of intermediate length, the maximum height of floors or double bottoms shall be obtained by interpolation, and in the case of ships exceeding 700 feet, by linear extrapolation.

TABLE II

REGISTERED BREADTH *in feet*	MAXIMUM DEPTH OF FRAME *in inches*
Not exceeding 20	14
30	16
40	18
50	20
60	22
70	25
80	28
90	31
100 and above	34

In the case of ships of intermediate breadths, the maximum depth of frame shall be obtained by interpolation.

3069

SCHEDULE 3
TONNAGE MARK

Regulations 11 and 12

1. Save as otherwise provided in paragraph 2, the tonnage mark shall consist as shown in Figure I of a horizontal line 15 inches long and 1 inch wide upon which shall be placed for identification purposes an inverted equilateral triangle, each side of which is 12 inches long and 1 inch wide, having its apex on the mid-point of the horizontal line.

2. In the case of a ship intended to operate in fresh or tropical waters as defined in the Load Line Rules (not being a ship on which tonnage marks have been placed in accordance with Regulation 11), an additional horizontal line may on the application of the owner of the ship be placed above the tonnage mark described in paragraph 1 at a distance of one forty-eighth (1/48th) of the moulded draught to that tonnage mark. This additional line shall be 9 inches long and 1 inch wide measured from a 1 inch wide vertical line (shown marked " W " in Figure 1) at the after end of, and perpendicular to, that tonnage mark. In such a case, at all such times as the ship so marked is operating in fresh or tropical waters as aforesaid, this additional line shall be taken to be the tonnage mark in lieu of that described in paragraph 1.

3. The lines and triangle above mentioned shall be painted in white or yellow on a dark ground or in black on a light ground, and carefully cut in, centre punched or welded on the sides of the ship. They shall be so kept and maintained as to be plainly visible at all times save when submerged.

3070

SCHEDULE 4
POSITION OF TONNAGE MARKS

Regulations 11 and 12

1. The tonnage mark shall be placed on each side of the ship at a distance below the line where the underside of the second deck stringer plate meets the ship's side plating amidships, or below the line equivalent to that line as shown in Figure 2 in cases where the deck is stepped, to be ascertained by reference to the Tonnage Mark Table at the end of this Schedule.

2. In that Table—

(1) the length Lt in column A is the distance in feet on the second deck between the points at the forward and after ends of the deck where the underside of the deck or line of continuation thereof meets the inner surface of the frames, ceiling or sparring as the case may be in the middle plane of the ship, using an equivalent length in cases where the deck is stepped as shown in Figure 2;

(2) the depth Ds is the depth in feet amidships from the top of the keel

FORWARD
TONNAGE MARK
1 INCH
12 INCHES
12 INCHES
1 INCH
7½ INCHES
7½ INCHES
W
1 INCH
9 INCHES
OPTIONAL TONNAGE MARK FOR FRESH OR TROPICAL WATERS
1 INCH

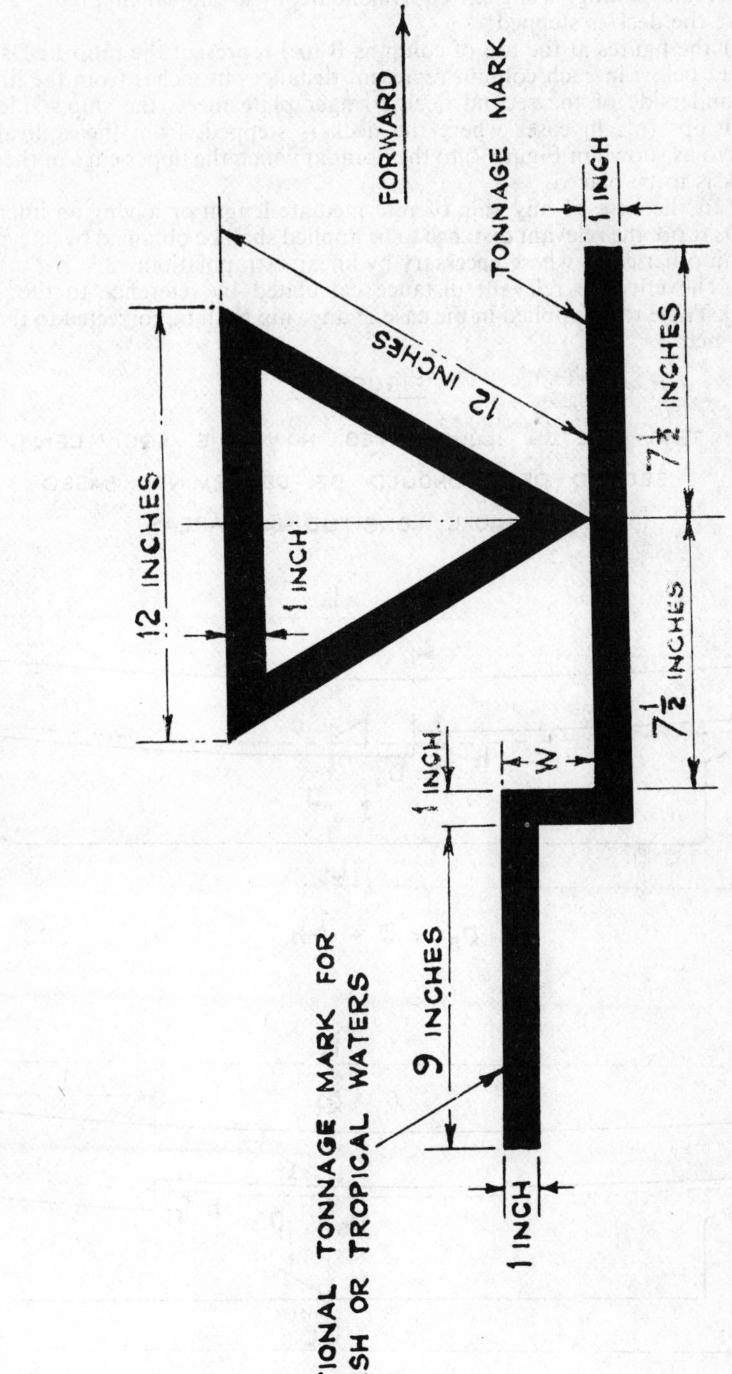

FIGURE 1

to the point at which the underside of the second deck stringer plate meets the ship's side plating, using an equivalent depth as shown in Figure 2 in cases where the deck is stepped;

(3) the figures at the top of columns B to J represent the ratio Lt/Ds and the figures below in each column represent distances in inches from the line where the underside of the second deck stringer plate meets the ship's side plating amidships (or, in cases where the deck is stepped, from the equivalent line thereto as shown in Figure 2) to the point at which the upper edge of the tonnage mark is to be placed.

3. In the case of any ship of intermediate length or having an intermediate Lt/Ds ratio, the relevant distance to be applied shall be obtained by interpolation, and in other cases where necessary by linear extrapolation.

4. The effective relevant distance calculated by reference to the Tonnage Mark Table to be applied in the case of any ship shall be corrected to the nearest half-inch.

FIGURE 2

THIS SKETCH ILLUSTRATES HOW THE EQUIVALENT SECOND DECK SHOULD BE DETERMINED, BASED ON EQUAL LONGITUDINAL AREAS

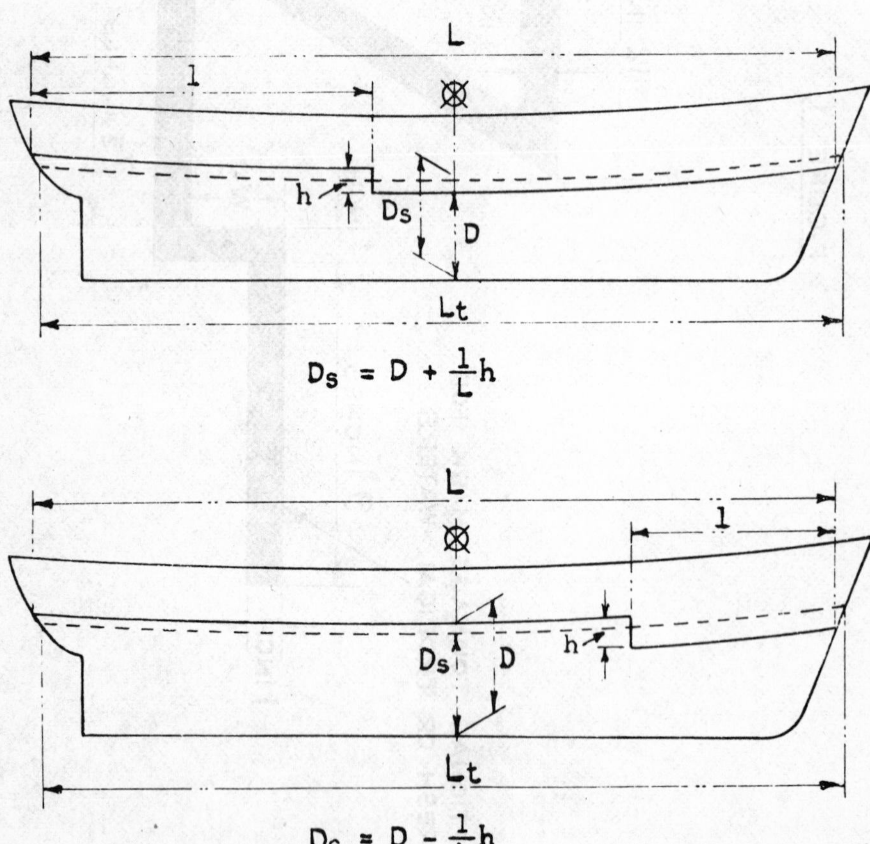

5. In the case of a ship to which load lines have been assigned the tonnage marks shall, subject to the provisions of Regulation 11, be placed in a position ascertained in accordance with the foregoing provisions of this Schedule with the apex of the identification triangle at a distance of 21 inches horizontally aft of the centre line of the load line disc:

Provided—

(i) that in cases in which a timber load line has been assigned to the ship such distance shall be 42 inches;

(ii) that in no case shall the tonnage marks be placed above the deepest load line to which the ship may be loaded, no account being taken for this purpose of timber load lines.

6. In the case of a ship to which load lines have not been assigned the tonnage marks shall be placed in a position ascertained in accordance with the foregoing provisions of this Schedule with the apex of the identification triangle at the middle of the length Lt. In every such case the line of the upper deck shall be shown by a deck line corresponding in form to that required by the Load Line Rules and placed centrally to a vertical line bisecting the identification triangle of the tonnage mark.

1 TONNAGE MARK TABLE

A	B	C	D	E	F	G	H	I	J
Lt/Ds	12	13	14	15	16	17	18	19	20
Length *Lt in feet*	*Distances in inches*								
220 and under	2.0	2.0	2.0	2.0	2.0	2.0	2.0	2.0	2.0
230	3.2	2.0	2.0	2.0	2.0	2.0	2.0	2.0	2.0
240	4.7	2.0	2.0	2.0	2.0	2.0	2.0	2.0	2.0
250	6.3	3.3	2.0	2.0	2.0	2.0	2.0	2.0	2.0
260	8.0	4.8	2.1	2.0	2.0	2.0	2.0	2.0	2.0
270	9.9	6.4	3.5	2.0	2.0	2.0	2.0	2.0	2.0
280	11.8	8.1	4.9	2.1	2.0	2.0	2.0	2.0	2.0
290	13.9	9.9	6.5	3.5	2.0	2.0	2.0	2.0	2.0
300	16.0	11.7	8.1	4.9	2.1	2.0	2.0	2.0	2.0
310	18.3	13.7	9.8	6.4	3.5	2.0	2.0	2.0	2.0
320	20.7	15.8	11.7	8.1	4.9	2.1	2.0	2.0	2.0
330	23.2	18.0	13.6	9.8	6.4	3.5	2.0	2.0	2.0
340	25.9	20.4	15.7	11.6	8.1	4.9	2.1	2.0	2.0
350	28.7	22.9	17.9	13.6	9.8	6.5	3.6	2.0	2.0
360	31.7	25.5	20.2	15.7	11.7	8.2	5.0	2.2	2.0

A	B	C	D	E	F	G	H	I	J
Lt/Ds	12	13	14	15	16	17	18	19	20
Length *Lt in feet*				*Distances in inches*					
370	34.7	28.3	22.7	17.9	13.6	9.9	6.6	3.7	2.0
380	38.0	31.1	25.3	20.2	15.7	11.8	8.3	5.2	2.4
390	41.3	34.1	27.9	22.6	17.9	13.8	10.1	6.8	3.8
400	44.8	37.2	30.7	25.0	20.1	15.8	11.9	8.4	5.3
410	48.2	40.3	33.5	27.7	22.6	18.1	14.0	10.4	7.2
420	51.5	43.4	36.4	30.4	25.2	20.6	16.4	12.7	9.4
430	54.8	46.5	39.4	33.3	27.9	23.2	19.0	15.2	11.8
440	58.4	49.9	42.6	36.4	30.9	26.0	21.7	17.8	14.4
450	62.1	53.4	46.0	39.6	33.9	29.0	24.6	20.6	17.1
460	65.9	57.0	49.5	42.9	37.1	32.1	27.6	23.5	19.9
470	69.8	60.7	53.0	46.3	40.4	35.2	30.6	26.5	22.8
480	73.7	64.4	56.5	49.7	43.7	38.4	33.7	29.5	25.7
490	77.5	68.1	60.0	53.0	46.9	41.5	36.7	32.4	28.5
500	81.2	71.6	63.4	56.2	50.0	44.5	39.6	35.2	31.2
510	84.9	75.1	66.7	59.4	53.0	47.4	42.4	37.9	33.9
520	88.4	78.4	69.9	62.4	55.9	50.2	45.1	40.5	36.4
530	91.8	81.6	72.9	65.3	58.7	52.9	47.7	43.0	38.8
540	95.2	84.8	75.9	68.1	61.4	55.5	50.2	45.4	41.2
550	98.4	87.8	78.8	70.9	64.0	58.0	52.6	47.8	43.4
560	101.6	90.8	81.6	73.6	66.6	60.5	55.0	50.1	45.6
570	104.8	93.8	84.4	76.3	69.2	62.9	57.3	52.3	47.8
580	107.9	96.8	87.2	78.9	71.7	65.3	59.6	54.5	49.9
590	111.0	99.7	90.0	81.5	74.2	67.7	61.9	56.7	52.0
600	114.0	102.5	92.6	84.0	76.5	69.9	64.0	58.8	54.0
610	117.0	105.3	95.2	86.5	78.9	72.1	66.2	60.8	56.0
620	120.0	108.0	97.8	88.9	81.2	74.4	68.3	62.8	58.0
630	122.9	110.7	100.4	91.3	83.5	76.6	70.4	64.8	59.9

A	B	C	D	E	F	G	H	I	J
Lt/Ds	12	13	14	15	16	17	18	19	20
Length *Lt in feet*				*Distances in inches*					
640	125.7	113.4	102.9	93.7	85.8	78.7	72.4	66.8	61.7
650	128.6	116.1	105.4	96.1	88.0	80.8	74.4	68.7	63.6
660	131.4	118.7	107.8	98.3	90.1	82.8	76.3	70.6	65.3
670	134.2	121.2	110.2	100.6	92.2	84.8	78.3	72.4	67.1
680	136.9	123.8	112.6	102.9	94.3	86.8	80.2	74.2	68.9
690	139.6	126.3	115.0	105.1	96.4	88.8	82.1	76.0	70.6
700	142.3	128.8	117.3	107.3	98.5	90.8	83.9	77.8	72.3
710	144.9	131.3	119.6	109.4	100.5	92.7	85.7	79.5	73.9
720	147.5	133.7	121.8	111.5	102.5	94.6	87.5	81.2	75.5
730	150.1	136.1	124.0	113.6	104.5	96.5	89.3	82.9	77.1
740	152.7	138.5	126.2	115.7	106.5	98.3	91.1	84.5	78.7
750	155.3	140.8	128.5	117.8	108.4	100.1	92.8	86.1	80.3
760	157.8	143.1	130.6	119.7	110.3	101.9	94.4	87.8	81.7
770	160.2	145.4	132.7	121.7	112.1	103.6	96.0	89.3	83.2
780	162.6	147.6	134.8	123.7	113.9	105.3	97.6	90.8	84.7
790	165.1	149.9	136.9	125.6	115.7	107.0	99.2	92.3	86.1
800	167.5	152.1	138.9	127.4	117.4	108.6	100.8	93.8	87.4

[The next page is 789/1.]
[The next paragraph number is 3071a.]

APPENDIX 4A

TONNAGE AMENDMENT REGULATIONS

3071a Regulation 2 (4) (*ante*, § 3054) of the main Regulations should read as follows:

" The [Department] may on the application of the owner of any ship, the tonnage of which below the upper deck has been measured in accordance with paragraph (3), direct such tonnage to be measured in accordance with paragraph (2) and *furnish the particulars of such measurements to the Registrar of British ships at the port at which the ship is registered, and that Registrar shall alter the particulars relating to the registered tonnage accordingly.*" [1]

3071b The following *new* regulation 7A was added to the main Regulations by M.S. (Tonnage) (Amendment) Regulations 1972 (S.I. 1972 No. 656):

"7A—(1) Paragraph (2) of this Regulation applies—

(*a*) to ships registered in the United Kingdom under Part 1 of the principal Act before 1st March 1967 the tonnage of which is to be measured under these Regulations; and

(*b*) to ships previously registered elsewhere than in the United Kingdom which are to be so registered; and

(*c*) to ships registered elsewhere than in the United Kingdom in respect of which application is made for a certificate of British tonnage pursuant to Regulation 3(2).

(2) Without prejudice to the provisions of Regulation 7, space situated on or above the upper deck of a ship to which this paragraph applies, being space—

(*a*) which, in the case of a ship described in sub-paragraph (1)(*a*), was by virtue of openings in it not included in the gross tonnage of the ship under the law in force immediately prior to 1st March 1967(e), or

(*b*) which, in the case of a ship described in sub-paragraph 1(*b*) or (*c*), was by virtue of there being or having been openings in it not included in the gross tonnage of the ship specified in the national certificate of registry in force in respect of the ship immediately prior to her registry in the United Kingdom or the said application as the case may be,

shall not be included in the gross tonnage of the ship irrespective of whether such openings have been closed or not, if—

(i) there has been no change since the date on which the tonnage of the ship was last measured in the purpose for which the space is used; and

[1] Words in italics substituted by M.S. (Tonnage) (Amendment) Regulations 1975 (S.I. 1975 No. 594) coming into effect June 1, 1975.

(ii) in the case of a ship described in sub-paragraph (1)(*b*) or (*c*), the space is such that it would not, had the ship been registered in the United Kingdom prior to 1st March 1967 with the openings unclosed, have been included in her gross tonnage."

The following *new* regulation was *substituted* for the previous regulation 15 by M.S. (Tonnage) (Amendment) Regulations 1967 (S.I. 1967 No. 1093):

"15(1) Space to be taken into account for the purposes of section 85 of the principal Act (payment of dues where goods carried in spaces not forming part of registered tonnage) shall, subject to paragraph (2) of this Regulation, be ascertained in accordance with the provisions of paragraph 5 of Rule 1 of Schedule 1 to these Regulations.

(2) Where—

(*a*) a ship has been assigned alternative tonnages in pursuance of Regulation 12, and

(*b*) the tonnages applicable to the ship are the modified tonnages ascertained in accordance with Regulation 11(3),

no account shall be taken for the purpose of the said section 85 of any space, which is included in the register tonnage ascertained in accordance with Part II of these Regulations but which is not included in the modified register tonnage, to the extent that the tonnage of such space exceeds the difference between those register tonnages.

(3) Goods or stores shall not be carried in any permanently closed in space on board the ship which has not been included in the registered tonnage of the ship other than

(*a*) dry cargo spaces;

(*b*) workshops or storerooms appropriated for the use of pump men, engineers, electricians, carpenters and boatswains;

(*c*) the lamp room; or

(*d*) double bottom tanks.

(4) If goods or stores are carried in a permanently closed in space on board ship in contravention of paragraph (3) of this Regulation, the master and the owner of the ship shall each be liable to a fine not exceeding £100."

The regulations of 1975 (see n. (1) to § 3071a, *ante*) contained further additional regulations as follows:

Part 3: Delegation of tonnage measurement surveys

4. The measurement and survey of a ship for the purpose of ascertaining its tonnage may, if the ship is classed with Lloyd's Register of Shipping, be undertaken by a surveyor appointed by Lloyd's Register of Shipping (being an organisation authorised in that behalf by the Secretary of State), instead of by a surveyor of ships.

5. In any case in which a ship is, pursuant to Regulation 4 of these Regulations, to be measured by a surveyor so appointed—

(*a*) the owner and the master of the ship shall make it available for measurement to the surveyor and shall afford him all such facilities and produce for him all such documents as are required by Regulation 2 (1) of the principal Regulations to be afforded to or produced for a surveyor of ships;

(*b*) any function to be performed by the Board in accordance with the principal Regulations shall in relation to that ship be performed by Lloyd's Register of Shipping;

(*c*) any application required by the principal Regulations to be made to the Board shall in relation to that ship be made to Lloyd's Register of Shipping;

(*d*) any function required by the principal Regulations to be performed by a surveyor of ships (except the function of certification referred to in paragraph (i) of the proviso to Regulation 9 of the principal Regulations which shall in every case be performed by a surveyor of ships) shall be performed by the surveyor so appointed;

and the principal Regulations shall be construed accordingly.

3071e *Part 4: Tonnage Measurement for pleasure yachts*

6.—(1) This Part of these Regulations applies only in relation to pleasure yachts under 45 feet (13·7 metres) in overall length which either—

(*a*) are to be registered in the United Kingdom under Part I of the principal Act on or after the coming into operation of these Regulations; or

(*b*) being so registered before the coming into operation of these Regulations, fall to be re-measured thereafter pursuant to the provisions of section 82 of the principal Act.

(2) The principal Regulations shall not apply in relation to pleasure yachts to which this Part of these Regulations applies.

7. The tonnage of a pleasure yacht to which this Part of these Regulations applies shall be ascertained in accordance with these Regulations and the tonnage so ascertained shall be taken to be its gross and register tonnage.

8.—(1) The owner of such a pleasure yacht to be measured shall make it available for measurement pursuant to section 6 of the principal Act by either—

(*a*) a surveyor appointed by Lloyd's Register of Shipping or a measurer appointed by the Royal Yachting Association or the Yacht Brokers Designers and Surveyors Association being organisations authorised by the Secretary of State under section 1 (4) of the Merchant Shipping Act 1965 (*ante*) to appoint persons to undertake the measurement of pleasure yachts to which this Part of these Regulations applies; or

(*b*) a surveyor of ships;

and shall afford all necessary facilities for its inspection and measurement and shall produce for the surveyor's or measurer's use and retention if required such plans, drawings, specifications and other documents relating to the pleasure yacht as he may require.

(2) The tonnage of a pleasure yacht to which this Part of these Regulations applies shall be measured in the manner specified in the Schedule to these Regulations.

3071f SCHEDULE

1. Tonnage in relation to any pleasure yacht to which Part 4 of these Regulations applies shall be measured in terms of cubic capacity.

2.—(1) The tonnage of the yacht shall be the sum of—

(*a*) the product of multiplying together its overall length, breadth and depth, and multiplying the resultant figure by 0·0045; and

(*b*) the tonnage of any break or breaks defined in paragraph 3 and calculated in accordance with the provisions of that paragraph.

(2) The breadth of a yacht for this purpose shall be its extreme breadth over the outside plating, planking or hull, no account being taken of rubbers or fenders even if they are moulded so as to be integral with the hull.

(3) (*a*) The depth of a yacht for this purpose shall be measured vertically midway between the foremost and aftermost points of measurement of its length.

(*b*) The upper terminal point for depth shall be —

(i) in the case of a decked yacht, the underside of deck on the middle line or, if there is no deck at the middle line at the point of measurement, the underside of the deck at side of the yacht plus the full deck camber;

(ii) in the case of an open yacht, the top of the upper strake or gunwale.

(*c*) The lower terminal point for depth shall be—

(i) in the case of a wooden yacht, the upper side of planking at side of keel or hog;

(ii) in the case of a metal yacht, the top of plating at side of keel;

(iii) in the case of a glass reinforced plastic yacht, the inside of hull. Where no keel member is fitted and the keel is of open trough construction, the lower terminal point for depth shall be the top of the keel filling, if fitted, or the level at which the inside breadth of the trough is 4 inches, whichever gives the lesser depth.

(*d*) Where a break exists in way of the point of measurement for depth, the height of the break shall not be included in the measurement of depth.

3. A break for the purpose of paragraph 2(1)(*b*) shall be a side to side break existing in the line of the deck, and its tonnage shall be the figure obtained by multiplying together the mean length, mean breadth and mean height of the break and dividing the product by 100.

4. In the case of a catamaran or trimaran the tonnage of each hull shall be measured separately, using the breadth of each hull for the purposes of its measurement, and the sum of such tonnages shall be the tonnage of the yacht.

5. All measurements shall be taken and expressed in feet and decimals of 1 foot to the nearest one-tenth of 1 foot.

6. Tonnage shall be expressed to two decimal places, the second decimal place being increased by 1 if the third decimal place is 5 or more.

[The next page is 790.]
[The next paragraph number is 3072.]

APPENDIX 5

LOAD LINE RULES

Merchant Shipping (Load Line) Rules 1968

(S.I. 1968 No. 1053)

Rules made under sections 2, 5, 6, 8, 12, 20, 21, 22 *and* 30 *of the Merchant Shipping (Load Lines) Act 1967, dated* July 4, 1968.

3072 EXPLANATORY NOTE [1]

These Rules, made by the then Board of Trade under the Merchant Shipping (Load Lines) Act 1967, came into force on July 21, 1968. They contain revised requirements relating to the surveying of and assignment of freeboards to ships, the marking of load lines and the issue of load line certificates, in order to enable the United Kingdom to give effect to the International Convention on Load Lines 1966 (Cmnd. 3070). The Rules replaced the Load Line Rules 1959 (S.I. 1959 No. 2238) made under provisions of the Merchant Shipping (Safety and Load Line Conventions) Act 1932 which were repealed by the 1967 Act with effect from that date.

The principal change is that new ships as defined in section 32(4) of the 1967 Act are required to comply with more stringent constructional requirements (conditions of assignment) specified in Schedule 4. This qualifies them for reduced freeboards under Schedule 5, thus enabling them to be more deeply loaded than heretofore. Existing ships as so defined are not required to meet the new conditions of assignment and will continue to be assigned freeboards calculated in accordance with the 1959 Rules for which purpose they must comply with the conditions of assignment applicable to them under those Rules.

The Zones and Seasonal Areas specified in the 1959 Rules have been revised by the Convention, and the new Zones, Areas and Seasonal Periods set out in Schedule 2 to these Rules are applicable to all ships to which the Rules apply.

The Rules also prescribe particulars as to the information relating to stability, loading and ballasting to be supplied to the masters of ships. These replace the more general requirements of section 18 of the Merchant Shipping (Safety Convention) Act 1949 and section 14 of the Merchant Shipping Act 1964, which sections are repealed by the 1967 Act.

[1] This Note is not part of the Rules.

ARRANGEMENT OF RULES

PART IV
FREEBOARDS

PART V
GENERAL

PART VI
INTERPRETATION, CITATION, AND COMMENCEMENT

SCHEDULES

Ships to which the Rules apply

74 **1.** These Rules apply to all ships except—

(*a*) ships of war;

(*b*) ships solely engaged in fishing; and

(*c*) pleasure yachts.

PART I

SURVEYS AND CERTIFICATES

Application to Assigning Authority for the assignment of freeboards and issue of load line certificates

75 **2.**—(1) The Assigning Authorities for the purposes of these Rules shall be the [Department], Lloyd's Register of Shipping, the British Committee of Bureau Veritas, the British Technical Committee of the American Bureau of Shipping, the British Committee of Det norske Veritas and the British Committee of Germanischer Lloyd.

(2) Application for the assignment of freeboards to a ship and for the issue of a load line certificate in respect of the ship shall be made to an Assigning Authority by or on behalf of the owner of the ship, who shall furnish to the Authority such plans, drawings, specifications and other documents and information relating to the design and construction of the ship as the Authority may require.

Load Line Survey

3.—(1) After receipt of the application and the documents and information required by the preceding Rule the Assigning Authority shall cause the ship to be surveyed by a Surveyor in order to ascertain—

(*a*) whether the ship complies with such of the requirements of Rule 23 and Schedule 4 to these Rules as are applicable to the ship; and

(*b*) such other data as may be necessary—

(i) for the assignment of freeboards to the ship in accordance with Part IV and Schedule 5 to these Rules and

(ii) to enable information to be supplied to the master of the ship pursuant to Rules 30 and 31.

(2) In the course of the survey to be carried out pursuant to the preceding paragraph of this Rule the ship and any of her fittings or equipment shall be submitted to such tests as may in the opinion of the Assigning Authority be necessary to ascertain the matters referred to in that paragraph. Tests carried out as to stability shall be subject to the requirements of Rule 30 and of paragraph 2(3) of Schedule 4.

(3) The owner of the ship shall afford all necessary facilities for such survey and shall at the request of the Assigning Authority furnish for the Authority's use and retention if required such further documents or information relating to the ship as the Authority may require.

Surveyor's Report

3076 **4.**—(1) On completion of the survey the Surveyor shall furnish to the Assigning Authority a report giving the results of the survey and his findings in relation to the matters specified in Rule 3.

(2) There shall be appended to the report the record of particulars required for the purposes of section 2(3)(*b*) of the Act and the requirements of Rule 25 shall apply in respect of that record.

(3) In the case of a ship which is required to comply with the requirements of Schedule 4 to these Rules relating to stability the Surveyor shall furnish to the [Department] information necessary to enable the [Department] to determine whether the ship complies with those requirements.

Assignment of Freeboards

5.—(1) The Assigning Authority shall—

(*a*) if satisfied on receipt of the Surveyor's report that the ship complies with the requirements of Rule 23 and Schedule 4 (other than those relating to stability) applicable to her, and

(*b*) on receipt from the [Department] of notification that the [Department] are satisfied that the ship complies with those requirements insofar as they relate to stability—

assign freeboards to the ship in accordance with Part IV and Schedule 5.

(2) On assigning freeboards the Assigning Authority shall furnish to the owner of the ship—

(*a*) particulars of the freeboards so assigned ;

(*b*) directions specifying—

(i) which of the load lines described in Part II of these Rules are to be marked on the sides of the ship in accordance with the requirements of that Part, and

(ii) the position in which those load lines, the deck-line and the load line mark are to be so marked ; and

(*c*) two copies of the Surveyor's report.

Issue and form of Load Line Certificates

3077 **6.** Subject to the provisions of Rule 11 (Exemption and Exemption Certificates) the Assigning Authority shall, on being satisfied that the ship has been duly marked in accordance with the directions referred to in the preceding Rule, issue to the owner of the ship either an International Load Line Certificate (1966) or a United Kingdom load line certificate, as may be required by the Act, in the form set out for such certificates respectively in Schedule 1 to these Rules ; and for that purpose each of the Assigning Authorities other than the [Department] is hereby authorised by the [Department] to issue load line certificates in pursuance of section 6(3)(*a*) of the Act.

Duration

7. Subject to the provisions of section 15(3) of the Act (Cancellation of United Kingdom load line certificates of ships plying on international voyages) and except as otherwise provided in the following Rules of this Part, a load line certificate shall be valid until a date to be determined by the Assigning Authority, not being a date more than five years after the date of completion of the survey referred to in Rule 3.

Extension

078 **8.**—(1) Subject to paragraph (2) of this Rule, where—

(*a*) application has been made to an Assigning Authority by the owner of a ship in respect of which a load line certificate is in force for the issue of a load line certificate in respect of the ship to take effect on the expiry of the current certificate, and

(*b*) following such application the ship has been duly surveyed in accordance with Rule 3.

the Assigning Authority may, if it is satisfied on receipt of the Surveyor's report that the ship complies with the requirements of Rule 23 and Schedule 4 (other than those relating to stability) applicable to her and has received notification from the [Department] that the ship complies with those requirements insofar as they relate to stability, but considers that it will not be reasonably practicable under the circumstances to issue the load line certificate applied for before the date of expiry of the current certificate, extend the period of validity specified in the current certificate for a period not exceeding 5 months.

(2) No such extension shall have effect unless particulars of the date to which the period of validity is extended, together with particulars of the place at and date on which such extension was given, are endorsed by the Assigning Authority on the current certificate.

(3) The period of validity of any load line certificate coming into effect immediately on the expiry of a certificate extended pursuant to this Rule shall not exceed a period of 5 years commencing on the date of completion of the survey referred to in paragraph (1) of this Rule.

Cancellation

9.—(1) The [Department] may cancel a load line certificate—

(*a*) if satisfied (whether by a report from an Assigning Authority or otherwise) that—

(i) the ship to which the certificate relates does not comply with the conditions of assignment ; or

(ii) the structural strength of the ship is lowered to such an extent that the ship is unsafe ; or

(iii) information on the basis of which freeboards were assigned to the ship was incorrect in a material particular ;

(*b*) if the certificate is not endorsed in accordance with the requirements of Rule 10 to show that the ship has been inspected in accordance with the requirements of that Rule ;

(*c*) if a new certificate is issued in respect of the ship ;

(*d*) if the ship was registered in the United Kingdom when the certificate was issued and has ceased to be so registered.

(2) In every such case the [Department] shall notify the owner of the ship in writing of the cancellation specifying the grounds therefor and the date on which it is to take effect.

(3) The provisions of this Rule other than those of paragraph (1)(*b*) shall apply to load line certificates issued under the provisions of the law in force immediately prior to the coming into operation of these Rules and continued in force by the Merchant Shipping (Load Lines) (Transitional Provisions) Regulations 1968 (S.I. 1968 No. 1052).

Periodical Inspection of Ships

3079 **10.**—(1) Every ship in respect of which a load line certificate is in force shall be periodically inspected by a Surveyor in accordance with the provisions of this Rule in order to ensure that—

(*a*) the fittings and appliances for the protection of openings, the guard rails, the freeing ports and the means of access to the crew's quarters in the ship are in an effective condition ; and

(*b*) no changes have been made or taken place in the hull or superstructures of the ship such as to render no longer accurate data on the basis of which freeboards were assigned to the ship.

(2) Application for the inspection shall be made by or on behalf of the owner of the ship to an Assigning Authority, who shall appoint a Surveyor to carry out the inspection.

(3) The Surveyor may in the course of any such inspection require the carrying out of tests considered by him to be necessary to establish that the ship complies with the requirements of paragraph (1) of this Rule.

(4) Inspection of a ship pursuant to this Rule shall be carried out on or within 3 months before or after each anniversary of the date of completion of the survey leading to the issue of the certificate :

Provided that unless the Assigning Authority otherwise consents the intervals between inspections shall not be less than 9 or more than 15 months.

(5) The Surveyor, if satisfied after inspection that the ship complies with the requirements of paragraph (1) of this Rule, shall endorse a record of the inspection and of the fact—

(*a*) in the case of an International Load Line Certificate (1966), that the ship was found to comply with the relevant provisions of the Convention, and

(*b*) in the case of a United Kingdom load line certificate, that the ship was found to comply with the relevant provisions of these Rules,

on the load line certificate in the space provided, specifying the Assigning Authority by which he was appointed to carry out the inspection.

Exemption and Exemption Certificates

3080 **11.**—(1) Where the [Department] exempt a ship pursuant to section 19 of the Act, the International Load Line Exemption Certificate or United Kingdom load line exemption certificate to be issued to the owner of the ship by the Board as required by section 20 of the Act shall be in the form set out for such certificates respectively in Schedule 1 to these Rules.

(2) Except in so far as the nature or terms of any such exemption require the contrary the provisions of Rules 2 to 5 and 7 to 10 shall have effect in the case of any ship so exempted and of any exemption certificate issued in respect of

such a ship as they have effect in the case of a ship in respect of which a load line certificate has been issued and of such a certificate, subject to the substitution—

(*a*) for references in the said Rules to an Assigning Authority, of references to the [Department];

(*b*) for paragraph (5) of Rule 10, of the following:—
"(5) The Surveyor, if satisfied after inspection that the ship continues to comply with the conditions subject to which the exemption was granted, shall endorse a record of the inspection and of that fact on the exemption certificate in the space provided."

PART II

LOAD LINES AND MARKS

"Appropriate Marks"

81 **12.** In this Part of the Rules the expression "the appropriate marks" in relation to a ship means the load lines directed to be marked on the ship pursuant to Rule 5(2)(*b*) and the deck-line and load line mark.

Marking

13. On receipt from the Assigning Authority of the particulars and directions referred to in Rule 5 the owner of the ship shall cause the appropriate marks to be marked on each side of the ship in accordance with the said directions and the requirements of this Part of the Rules.

Deck-line

14.—(1) The deck-line shall consist of a horizontal line 300 millimetres in length and 25 millimetres in width and shall be marked amidships on each side of the ship in accordance with the following provisions of this Rule so as to indicate the position of the freeboard deck.

(2) Subject to paragraph (3) of this Rule, the deck-line shall be marked in such a position on the side of the ship that its upper edge passes through the point amidships where the continuation outwards of the upper surface of the freeboard deck, or of any sheathing of that deck, intersects the outer surface of the shell of the ship as shown in Figure 1.

(3) Where the design of the ship or other circumstances render it in the opinion of the Assigning Authority impracticable to mark the deck-line in accordance with paragraph (2), the Authority may include in the directions given pursuant to Rule 5 a direction that it may be marked by reference to another fixed point in the ship as near as practicable to the position described in paragraph (2).

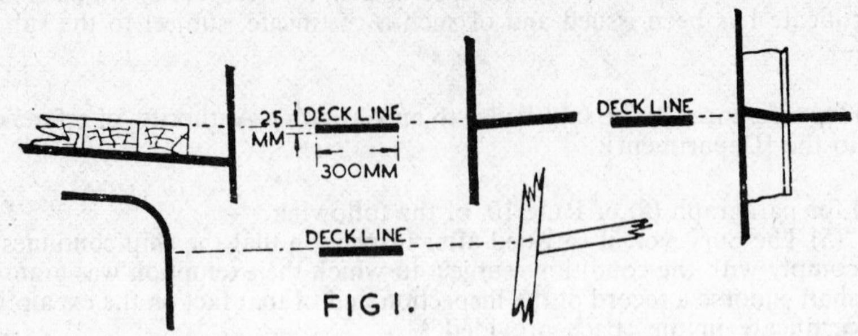

FIG1.

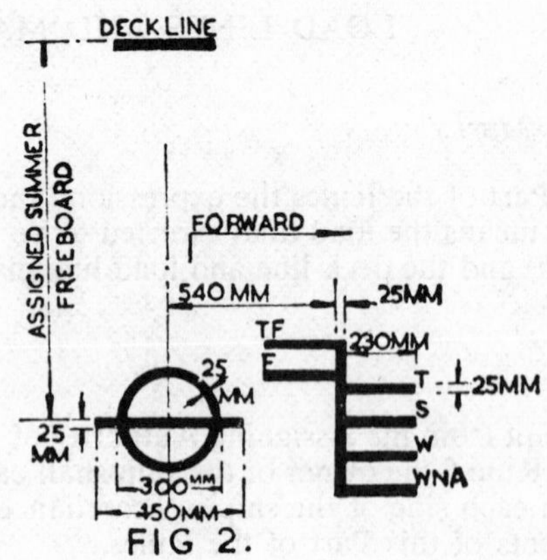

FIG 2.

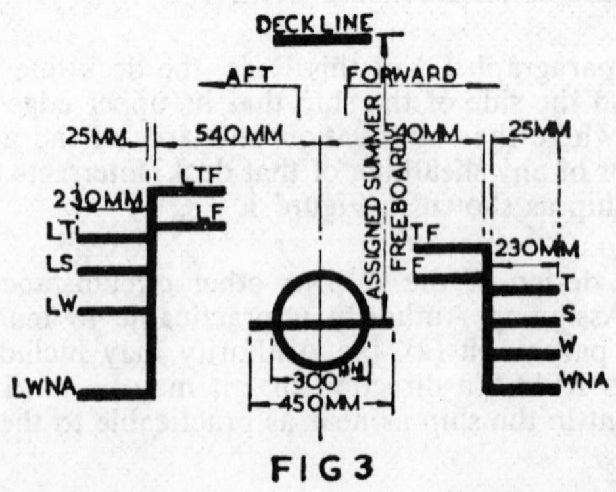

FIG3

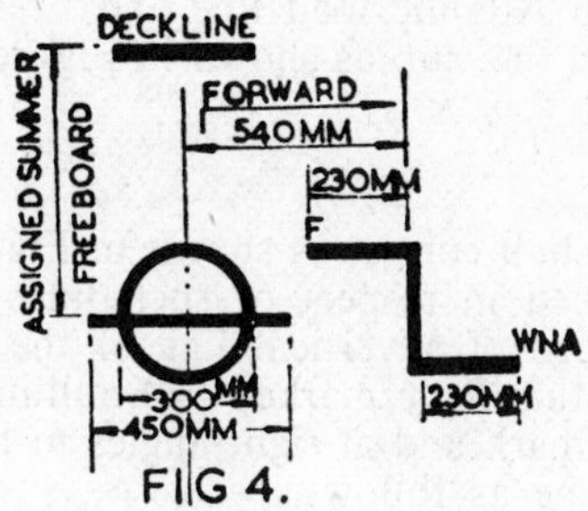

FIG 4.

Load Line Mark

82 **15.** The load line mark shall consist, as shown by Figure 2, of a ring 300 millimetres in outside diameter and 25 millimetres wide, intersected by a horizontal line 450 millimetres long and 25 millimetres wide the upper edge of which passes through the centre of the ring. The centre of the ring shall be marked amidships vertically below the deck-line, so that, except as otherwise provided in Rule 28 (Greater than minimum freeboards), the distance from the centre of the ring to the upper edge of the deck-line is equal to the Summer freeboard assigned to the ship.

Load Lines

16.—(1) Load lines as described in this and the following Rule indicate the maximum depth to which a ship marked therewith may be loaded in the circumstances described in Schedule 2 (Appropriate Load Lines—Zones, Areas and Seasonal Periods).

(2) Except as otherwise provided in paragraph (3) of this Rule, the following Rule and Rule 28 (Greater than minimum freeboards), load lines shall consist as shown in Figure 2 of horizontal lines each 230 millimetres in length and 25 millimetres in width extending forward or abaft of a vertical line 25 millimetres in width marked 540 millimetres forward of the centre of the ring of the load line mark and at right angles to that line, and individual load lines shall be as follows :—

the *Summer load line,* which shall extend forward of the said vertical line and be marked S, and shall correspond horizontally with the line passing through the centre of the ring of the load line mark ;

the *Winter load line,* which shall extend forward of the said vertical line and be marked W ;

the *Winter North Atlantic load line,* which shall extend forward of the said vertical line and be marked WNA ;

the *Tropical load line,* which shall extend forward of the said vertical line and be marked T ;

the *Fresh Water load line,* which shall extend abaft the said vertical line and be marked F ;

the *Tropical Fresh Water load line,* which shall extend abaft the said vertical line and be marked TF.

The maximum depth of loading referred to in paragraph (1) shall be the depth indicated by the upper edge of the appropriate load line.

(3) In the case of a sailing ship—

(*a*) the Summer load line shall consist of the line passing through the centre of the ring of the load line mark ; and (*b*) the Winter North Atlantic load line and Fresh Water load line only shall be marked on the ship as shown in Figure 4.

Timber Load Lines

3083 **17.** Timber load lines shall consist as shown in Figure 3 of horizontal lines of the dimensions specified in respect of such lines in the preceding Rule, extending abaft or forward of a vertical line of the dimensions specified in respect of such a line in that Rule marked 540 millimetres abaft the centre of the ring of the load line mark and at right angles to that line; and individual Timber load lines shall be as follows:—

the *Summer Timber load line*, which shall extend abaft the said vertical line and be marked LS;

the *Winter Timber load line*, which shall extend abaft the said vertical line and be marked LW;

the *Winter North Atlantic Timber load line*, which shall extend abaft the said vertical line and be marked LWNA;

the *Tropical Timber load line*, which shall extend abaft the said vertical line and be marked LT;

the *Fresh Water Timber load line*, which shall extend forward of the said vertical line and be marked LF;

the *Tropical Fresh Water Timber load line*, which shall extend forward of the said vertical line and be marked LTF.

The maximum depth of loading referred to in Rule 16(1) shall be the depth indicated by the upper edge of the appropriate Timber load line.

Appropriate Load Line

18. The appropriate load line in respect of a ship at any particular place and time shall be ascertained in accordance with the provisions of Schedule 2.

Position of Load Lines

19. Each load line required to be marked on a ship shall be marked in such a position on each side of the ship that the distance measured vertically downwards from the upper edge of the deck-line to the upper edge of the load line is equal to the freeboard assigned to the ship which is appropriate to that load line.

Method of marking

3084 **20.**—(1) The appropriate marks shall be marked on each side of a ship in accordance with the requirements of this Rule in such a manner as to be plainly visible.

(2) If the sides of the ship are of metal, the appropriate marks shall be cut in, centre punched or welded; if the sides of the ship are of wood, the marks shall be cut into the planking to a depth of not less than 3 millimetres; if the sides are of other materials to which the foregoing methods of marking cannot effectively be applied, the marks shall be permanently affixed to the sides of the ship by bonding or some other effective method.

(3) The appropriate marks shall be painted in white or yellow if the background is dark, and in black if the background is light.

Authorisation of removal, etc., of appropriate marks

21. After the appropriate marks have been marked on a ship, such marks may not be concealed, removed, altered, defaced or obliterated except under the authority of an Assigning Authority.

Mark of Assigning Authority

22.—(1) The mark of the Assigning Authority as described in the following paragraph of this Rule may be marked on each side of the ship in a position alongside the load line mark either above the horizontal line forming part of that mark, or above and below it.

(2) An Assigning Authority's mark for this purpose shall consist of not more than four initials to identify the Authority's name, each measuring approximately 115 millimetres in height and 75 millimetres in width.

PART III

RULES AS TO CONDITIONS OF ASSIGNMENT

Requirements relevant to the assignment of freeboards

85 **23.**—(1) The requirements specified in this Rule and in Schedule 4 in respect of the hulls, superstructures, fittings and appliances of ships are requirements considered by the Board to be relevant to the assignment of freeboards to ships and are prescribed as such for the purposes of section 2(3)(*a*) of the Act.

(2) Except as otherwise provided in paragraphs (3) and (4) of this Rule, every ship to which freeboards are to be assigned under these Rules shall comply with the requirements applicable to her under Part I of Schedule 4.

(3) Every ship to which Part II (Special Requirements applicable to Type "A" ships), Part III (Special Requirements applicable to certain Type "B" ships) or Part IV (Special Requirements applicable to ships to be assigned Timber Freeboards) of Schedule 4 applies shall comply with the requirements of such Part applicable to her and with the requirements of Part I of that Schedule except in so far as compliance with those of the said Part II, III or IV as the case may be otherwise requires.

(4) Every existing ship, not being a ship to which freeboards are to be assigned in accordance with Rule 27(1) by virtue of the proviso to Rule 27(2), shall comply with such of the requirements relevant to the assignment of freeboards to ships as were applicable to her under the law in force immediately prior to the coming into operation of these Rules.[2]

Compliance with conditions of assignment

24.—(1) Except as otherwise provided in paragraph (2) of this Rule, a ship shall for the purposes of the Act be taken not to comply with the conditions of assignment—

(*a*) if at any time after the assignment of freeboards to the ship there has been any alteration of the hull, superstructures, fittings or appliances of the ship such that either—

(i) any requirement applicable to the ship under the preceding Rule is not complied with in respect of the ship ; or

(ii) the record of particulars made in relation to the ship pursuant to the following Rule is rendered inaccurate in a material respect ;

[2] See Load Line Rules 1959 (S.I. 1959 No. 2238) as amended by Load Line (Amendment) (No. 3) Rules 1961 (S.I. 1961 No. 1920).

or (*b*) if that record of particulars is not kept on board the ship in accordance with paragraph (2) of that Rule.

(2) A ship shall be taken to comply with the conditions of assignment notwithstanding an alteration described in paragraph (1)(*a*) of this Rule if either—

(*a*) fresh freeboards appropriate to the condition of the ship after the alteration have been assigned to the ship and the ship has been marked with load lines and a fresh certificate issued to the owner of the ship accordingly ; or

(*b*) the alteration has been inspected by a Surveyor on behalf of the Assigning Authority, that Authority is satisfied that the alteration is not such as to require any change in the freeboards assigned to the ship, and full particulars of the alteration together with the date and place of his inspection have been endorsed by the Surveyor on the record above referred to.

Record of Particulars

3086 **25.**—(1) The record required by section 2(3)(*b*) of the Act of particulars of requirements in respect of the hull, superstructures, fittings and appliances of a ship to which freeboards are assigned shall be in the form set out in Schedule 3 to these Rules or a form as near thereto as circumstances permit and shall contain the particulars required by that form. Such particulars may be given by attaching to the record a copy of the Surveyor's report and specifying in the record passages in that report in which those particulars are given.

(2) The record shall be completed by the Surveyor carrying out the survey of the ship pursuant to Rule 3 and shall be furnished by him to the Assigning Authority in accordance with Rule 4. Two copies of the record shall be sent by the Assigning Authority to the owner of the ship together with the particulars, directions and copies of the Surveyor's report required to be so furnished under Rule 5, and one copy (including a copy of the Surveyor's report if it is attached to the record) shall be kept on the ship at all times in the custody of the master.

Part IV

FREEBOARDS

Types of freeboard

3087 **26.** The freeboards assignable to a ship under these Rules are the Summer freeboard, Tropical freeboard, Winter freeboard, Winter North Atlantic freeboard, Fresh Water freeboard, and Tropical Fresh Water freeboard, and in the case of ships to which Timber freeboards are to be assigned the Summer Timber freeboard, Winter Timber freeboard, Winter North Atlantic Timber freeboard, Tropical Timber freeboard, Fresh Water Timber freeboard and Tropical Fresh Water Timber freeboard.

Determination of freeboards

27. Except as otherwise provided in the following Rule—

(1) the freeboards to be assigned to a new ship shall be determined in accordance with the provisions of Schedule 5 to these Rules ; and

(2) the freeboards to be assigned to an existing ship shall be determined in accordance with the provisions applicable in that behalf to the ship under the law in force immediately prior to the coming into operation of these Rules[3]:

[3] See Load Line Rules 1959 (S.I. 1959 No. 2238) as amended by Load Line (Amendment) Rules 1967 (S.I. 1967 No. 173).

Provided that if an existing ship has been so constructed or modified as to comply with all the requirements of Schedule 4 applicable to a new ship of her type and application is made for the assignment to her of freeboards determined in accordance with the provisions of Schedule 5, such freeboards shall be assigned to her.

Greater than minimum freeboards

088 **28.**—(1) A freeboard determined in accordance with the preceding Rules of this Part is hereafter referred to in this Rule as a minimum freeboard.

(2) The owner of a ship may, when making application under Rule 2 for the assignment of freeboards in respect of the ship, request the assignment of freeboards greater than minimum freeboards.

(3)(*a*) In any such case the Assigning Authority may, if satisfied after survey of the ship pursuant to Rule 3 that the ship complies with the requirements of Rule 23 and Schedule 4 (other than those relating to stability) and if the Authority has received notification from the [Department] that the ship complies with those requirements in so far as they relate to stability, assign to the ship freeboards (other than timber freeboards) exceeding the minimum freeboards appropriate to the ship by such amount as they may determine, and furnish to the owner of the ship particulars thereof in accordance with Rule 5. Such freeboards are hereafter referred to in this Rule as greater than minimum freeboards.

(*b*) Timber freeboards shall not be assigned to a ship to which greater than minimum freeboards have been assigned.

(4) In any case in which the greater than minimum Summer freeboard assigned to a ship in accordance with the provisions of the preceding paragraph is such that the position on the sides of the ship of the load line appropriate to that freeboard would correspond to, or be lower than, the position at which the lowest of the load lines appropriate to minimum freeboards for the ship would be marked—

(*a*) the following load lines only shall be marked on the sides of the ship, that is to say, those appropriate to the greater than minimum Summer freeboard and Fresh Water freeboard;

(*b*) the load line appropriate to the greater than minimum Summer freeboard shall be known as the "All Seasons load line" and shall consist of the horizontal line intersecting the load line mark and such mark shall be placed accordingly;

(*c*) the vertical line described in Rule 16 shall be omitted;

(*d*) subject to the provisions of sub-paragraph (*c*), the Fresh Water load line shall be as described in Rule 16(2) and be marked accordingly.

Special position of deck-line: correction of freeboards

29. In any case in which the deck-line is to be marked on the sides of a ship as provided in Rule 14(3), the freeboards to be assigned to the ship shall be corrected to allow for the vertical distance by which the position of the deck-line is altered by virtue of that paragraph. The location of the point by reference to which the deck-line has been so marked and the identity of the deck which has been taken as the freeboard deck shall be specified in the load line certificate issued in respect of the ship.

[4] See the Merchant Shipping (Safety Convention) Act 1949, s. 18, and the Merchant Shipping Act 1964.

PART V

GENERAL

Information as to stability of ships

3089 **30.**—(1) The owner of any ship to which freeboards are assigned under these Rules shall provide for the guidance of the master of the ship information relating to the stability of the ship in accordance with the following provisions of this Rule.

(2) Except as otherwise provided in paragraph (6) of this Rule, such information shall include particulars appropriate to the ship in respect of all matters specified in Schedule 7 to these Rules and shall be in the form required by that Schedule.

(3) Subject to the following paragraph, the information shall, when first supplied, be based on the determination of stability by means of an inclining test which shall unless the [Department] otherwise permits be carried out in the presence of a surveyor appointed by the [Department]. The information first supplied shall be replaced by fresh information whenever its accuracy is materially affected by alteration of the ship. Such fresh information shall if the [Department] so require be based on a further inclining test.

(4) The [Department] may—

(*a*) in the case of any ship allow the information to be based on the determination, by means of an inclining test, of the stability of a sister ship;

(*b*) in the case of a ship specially designed for the carriage of liquids or ore in bulk, or of any class of such ships, dispense with an inclining test if satisfied from the information available in respect of similar ships that the ship's proportions and arrangements are such as to ensure more than sufficient stability in all probable loading conditions.

[(5) The information, and any fresh information to replace the same pursuant to paragraph (3) of this Rule, shall before issue to the master be submitted by or on behalf of the owner of the ship to the [Department] for their approval, together with a copy thereof for retention by the [Department], and shall incorporate such additions and amendments as the [Department] may in any particular case require.] See App. 5A, § 3139a, *post*.

(6)(*a*) *This paragraph shall apply to any ship in respect of which a load line certificate issued under the Merchant Shipping (Safety and Load Line Conventions) Act* 1932 *was in force on* 21*st July* 1968 (*the date on which these Rules came into operation) not being a ship in respect of which information as to stability including particulars appropriate to the ship in respect of the matters specified in Schedule* 7 *has been approved by the* [*Department*] *under paragraph* (5) *of this Rule.*

(*b*) *The owner of a ship to which this paragraph applies shall provide for the information of the master such information relating to the stability of the ship as was required to be provided under the law in force immediately prior to* 21*st July* 1968.[4]

(*c*) *The preceding sub-paragraph shall have effect in relation to any ship until either—*

(i) *the expiration of the period of* 12 *months next following the date of issue of the first load line certificate to be issued in respect of the ship after* 20*th July* 1970; *or*

(ii) 20*th July* 1975

whichever shall first occur.[5]

(7) Information provided pursuant to the foregoing provisions of this Rule shall be furnished by the owner of the ship to the master in the form of a book which shall be kept on the ship at all times in the custody of the master.

[5] This paragraph was substituted by the Merchant Shipping (Load Line) (Amendment) Rules 1970 (S.I. 1970 No. 1003.

Information as to loading and ballasting of ships

3090 **31.**—(1) The owner of any ship to which freeboards are assigned under these Rules, being a ship of more than 150 metres in length specially designed for the carriage of liquids or ore in bulk, shall provide for the information of the master information relating to the loading and ballasting of the ship in accordance with the following provisions of this Rule.

(2) Such information shall consist of working instructions specifying in detail the manner in which the ship is to be loaded and ballasted so as to avoid the creation of unacceptable stresses in her structure and shall indicate the maximum stresses permissible for the ship.

(3) The provisions of paragraph (5) of the preceding Rule shall have effect in respect of information required under this Rule, and the information duly approved in accordance with that paragraph shall be contained in the book to be furnished to the master of the ship pursuant to paragraph (7) of that Rule, so however that the information to be provided pursuant to each Rule is separately shown in the book under separate headings specifying the number and heading of each Rule.

Recognition of certificates issued by other Governments

3091 **32.**—(1) In this Rule, "Convention ship" means a ship to which section 12 of the Act applies.

(2) The circumstances in which certificates which are issued as International Load Line Certificates (1966) in respect of Convention ships by Governments other than Her Majesty's Government in the United Kingdom shall be recognised for the purposes of the Act are as follows :—

(*a*) the certificate shows by its terms that it was issued in respect of the ship by a Government, being either—

- (i) the Government of the Convention country in which the ship is registered or, if the ship is not registered in any such country or elsewhere, the Government of the Convention country whose flag she flies ; or
- (ii) the Government of any other Convention country stated in the certificate to have issued the certificate at the request of a country specified in sub-paragraph (i),

or by a person or organisation under the authority of such a Government ;

(*b*) the certificate is in the official language or languages of the issuing country and, if the language used is neither English nor French, includes in its text a translation into one of those languages ;

(*c*) the certificate is in the form set out in Annex III to the Convention of 1966 for an International Load Line Certificate (1966) and contains all the particulars required by such form ;

(*d*) the certificate shows that it is currently in force and applicable to the voyage in respect of which clearance or transire is required ;

(*e*) the period for which the certificate is expressed to be valid does not exceed 5 years from the date of issue ;

(*f*) any extension of the period for which the certificate is expressed to be valid is duly endorsed on the certificate by the issuing authority and does not exceed 5 months ;

(*g*) periodical inspections of the ship to which the certificate relates, being inspections required by Article 14(1)(*c*) of the Convention of 1966, are shown duly endorsed on the certificate by the issuing authority ;

(*h*) the ship to which the certificate relates—

(i) if registered in a Convention country when the certificate was issued, remains registered in that country, or

(ii) if not so registered when the certificate was issued, either has since been registered in the Convention country by or on behalf of the Government of which the certificate was issued and remains so registered, or flies the flag of that Convention country.

(3) The circumstances in which exemption certificates which, in accordance with the Convention of 1966, are issued in respect of Convention ships by Governments other than Her Majesty's Government in the United Kingdom shall have the like effect for the purposes of the Act as if they were valid Convention certificates are those specified in sub-paragraphs (*a*) to (*h*) of paragraph (2) of this Rule subject to the substitution for the reference in sub-paragraph (*c*) to an International Load Line Certificate (1966) of reference to an International Load Line Exemption Certificate.

PART VI

INTERPRETATION, CITATION AND COMMENCEMENT

Interpretation

3092 **33.**—(1) In these Rules, except where the context otherwise requires—

"the Act" means the Merchant Shipping (Load Lines) Act 1967 ;

"amidships" means the middle of the ship's length (L) ;

"the [Department]" means the [Department of Trade];

"deck cargo regulations" means the deck cargo regulations for the time being in force under section 24 of the Act ;

"freeboard" means the distance measured vertically downwards amidships from the upper edge of the deck-line described in Rule 14 of these Rules to the position at which the upper edge of the load line appropriate to the freeboard is to be marked ;

"freeboard deck" in relation to a ship means the deck from which the freeboards assigned to the ship are calculated, being either—

(*a*) the uppermost complete deck exposed to weather and sea, which has permanent means of closing all openings in its weather portions, and below which all openings in the sides of the ship are fitted with permanent means of watertight closing ; or

(*b*) at the request of the owner and subject to the approval of the [Department] a deck lower than that described in paragraph (*a*), subject to its being a complete and permanent deck which is continuous both (i) in a fore and aft direction at least between the machinery space and peak bulkheads of the ship and (ii) athwartships,

a deck which is stepped being taken to consist for this purpose of the lowest line of the deck and the continuation of that line parallel to the upper part of the deck ;

"length" and the symbol "(L)" in relation to a ship mean the length of the ship ascertained in accordance with the regulations made under section 32(6) of the Act ;

"load line certificate" means a load line certificate issued pursuant to these Rules ;

"sailing ship" means a ship designed to carry sail, whether as the sole means of propulsion or as a supplementary means ;

"Surveyor" means a surveyor of ships appointed either by the [Department] under the Merchant Shipping Acts or by any other Assigning Authority;

"watertight" means capable of preventing the passage of water in any direction.

(2) References in these Rules to ships registered in the United Kingdom include references to ships which not being so registered are to be treated as so registered for the purposes of the Act by virtue of an order for the time being in force under section 29 of the Act.

(3) The Interpretation Act 1889 shall apply to the interpretation of these Rules as it applies to the interpretation of an Act of Parliament ; and without prejudice to the generality of the foregoing the expressions "alteration", "Convention of 1966", "Convention country", "existing ship" and "new ship" have in these Rules the meanings given to them respectively by the Act.

Citation and Commencement

34. These Rules may be cited as the Merchant Shipping (Load Line) Rules 1968 and shall come into operation on 21st July 1968.

SCHEDULE 1

FORMS OF CERTIFICATES

(Rules 6 and 11)

3093 **1.** *Form of International Load Line Certificate* (1966):—

INTERNATIONAL LOAD LINE CERTIFICATE (1966)

(Official Seal)

Issued under the provisions of the International Convention on Load Lines, 1966, under the authority of the Government of the United Kingdom of Great Britain and Northern Ireland by (full official designation of the Assigning Authority).

Name of Ship	Distinctive Number or Letters	Port of Registry	Length (L) as defined in Article 2(8)	Gross Tonnage

*Freeboard assigned as: A new ship, An existing ship.

*Type of Ship: Type A, Type B, Type B with reduced/increased freeboard/timber freeboard.

	Freeboard from Deck Line	*Load Line*
Tropical	..........mm. (T)	..........mm. above (S)
Summer	..........mm. (S)	Upper edge of line through centre of ring
Winter	..........mm. (W)	..........mm. below (S)
Winter North Atlantic	..........mm. (WNA)	..........mm. below (S)
Timber tropical	..........mm. (LT)	..........mm. above (LS)
Timber summer	..........mm. (LS)	..........mm. above (S)
Timber winter	..........mm. (LW)	..........mm. below (LS)
Timber winter North Atlantic	..........mm. (LWNA)	..........mm. below (LS)

Note: Freeboards and Load Lines which are not applicable need not be entered on the certificate.

3094 Allowance for Fresh Water for all freeboards other than timber..........mm.

Allowance for Fresh Water for Timber freeboards..........mm.

The upper edge of the deck line from which these freeboards are measured is....................

....mm. ....

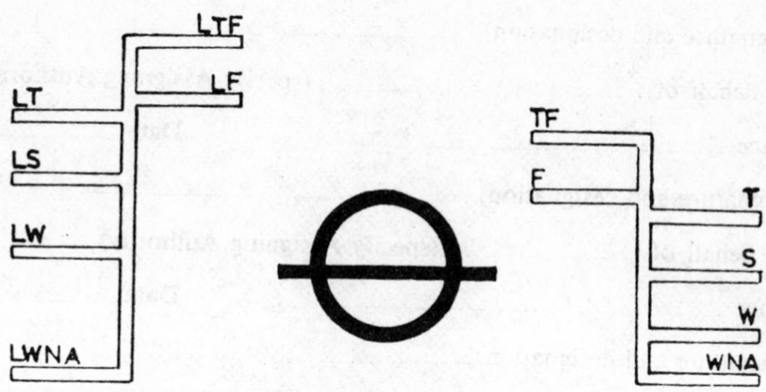

Note: Applicable load lines to be indicated.

3095 Date of initial or periodical survey..

This is to certify that this ship has been surveyed and that the freeboards have been assigned and load lines shown above have been marked in accordance with the International Convention on Load Lines 1966.

This certificate is valid until..................................subject to periodical inspections in accordance with Article 14(1)(*c*) of the Convention.

Issued at..on....... ....19..........

The undersigned declares that

†he is duly authorised

†......................(specify Assigning Authority) are duly authorised by the said Government to issue this Certificate.

....
(Signature and designation)

NOTE

1. When a ship departs from a port situated on a river or inland water, deeper loading shall be permitted corresponding to the weight of fuel and all other materials required for consumption between the point of departure and the sea.

2. When a ship is in fresh water of unit density the appropriate load line may be submerged by the amount of the fresh water allowance shown above. Where the density is other than unity an allowance shall be made proportional to the difference between 1.025 and the actual density.

* Delete whichever is inapplicable.

† The first alternative is to be used if the Certificate is issued by the [Department of Trade] and the second where it is issued by an Assigning Authority other than the [Department]. Delete whichever is inapplicable.

3096 This is to certify that at a periodical inspection required by Article 14(1)(*c*) of the Convention, this ship was found to comply with the relevant provisions of the Convention.

Place.. Date..........................

(Signature and designation)..

on behalf of.......................................(specify Assigning Authority)

Place.. Date..........................

(Signature and designation)..

on behalf of.......................................(specify Assigning Authority)

Place.. Date..........................

(Signature and designation)..

on behalf of.......................................(specify Assigning Authority)

Place.. Date..........................

(Signature and designation)..

on behalf of.......................................(specify Assigning Authority)

The provisions of the Convention being fully complied with by this ship, the validity of this certificate is, in accordance with Article 19(2) of the Convention, extended

until..

Place.. Date..........................

(Signature and designation)..

on behalf of ....(specify Assigning Authority)

NOTE

This Certificate must be kept framed and posted up in some conspicuous place on board the ship, so long as it remains in force and the ship is in use.

3097 2. *Form of International Load Line Exemption Certificate*:—

INTERNATIONAL LOAD LINE EXEMPTION CERTIFICATE

(Official seal)

Issued under the provisions of the International Convention on Load Lines, 1966, under the authority of the Government of the United Kingdom of Great Britain and Northern Ireland by the [Department of Trade].

Name of Ship	Distinctive Number or Letters	Port of Registry

This is to certify that the above-mentioned ship is exempted from the provisions of the 1966 Convention, under the authority conferred by Article 6(2)/Article 6(4)* of the Convention referred to above.

The provisions of the Convention from which the ship is exempted under Article 6(2) are:

....

....

....

The voyage for which exemption is granted under Article 6(4) is:

From:..

To:..

Conditions, if any, on which the exemption is granted under either Article 6(2) or Article 6(4):

....

....

....

....

....

....

This certificate is valid until..**subject, where appropriate, to periodical inspections in accordance with Article 14(1)(*c*) of the Convention.**

Issued at..**on**..**19**..........

The undersigned declares that he is duly authorised by the said Government to issue this certificate.

....

An authorised officer of the [Department of Trade].

*** Delete whichever is inapplicable.**

This is to certify that this ship continues to comply with the conditions under which this exemption was granted.

Place.. Date..................................

.... Surveyor [Department of Trade].

Place.. Date..................................

.... Surveyor [Department of Trade].

Place.. Date..................................

.... Surveyor [Department of Trade].

Place.. Date..................................

.... Surveyor [Department of Trade].

This ship continues to comply with the conditions under which this exemption was granted, and the validity of this certificate is, in accordance with Article 19(4)(*a*) of the Convention, extended until..

Place.. Date..................................

....

authorised by the [Department of Trade]

3099 3. *Form of United Kingdom load line certificate*:

UNITED KINGDOM LOAD LINE CERTIFICATE

(Official Seal)

Issued *by the [Department of Trade]/*under the authority of the [Department of Trade] by (full official designation of the Assigning Authority).

Name of Ship	Distinctive Number or Letters	Port of Registry	Length (L) as defined by regulations under section 32(6) of the Merchant Shipping (Load Lines) Act 1967	Gross Tonnage

*Freeboard assigned as: A new ship, An existing ship.

*Type of Ship: Type A, Type B, Type B with reduced/increased freeboard.

Freeboard from Deck Line *Load Line*

Tropical................................mm. (T)....................mm. above (S).

Summer................................mm. (S) Upper edge of line through centre of ring.

Winter................................mm. (W)....................mm. below (S).

Winter North Atlantic....................mm. (WNA)....................mm. below (S).

Allowance for fresh water for all freeboards....................................mm.

The upper edge of the deck line from which these freeboards are measured is..................

....

This is to certify that this ship has been surveyed and the freeboards and load lines shown above have been assigned in accordance with the Merchant Shipping (Load Line) Rules 1968.

This Certificate is valid until....................................subject to periodical inspections in accordance with those Rules.

Issued at....................................on....................................19..........

Signature and designation....................................

on behalf of....................................

(specify Assigning Authority)

NOTE:

1. When a ship departs from a port situated on a river or inland water, deeper loading shall be permitted corresponding to the weight of fuel and all other materials required for consumption between the point of departure and the sea.

2. When a ship is in fresh water of unit density the appropriate load line may be submerged by the amount of the fresh water allowance shown above. Where the density is other than unity, an allowance shall be made proportional to the difference between 1.025 and the actual density.

* Delete whichever is inapplicable.

---

00 This is to certify that at a periodical inspection required by the Merchant Shipping (Load Line) Rules 1968 this ship was found to comply with the relevant provisions of the Rules.

Place.. Date....................

(Signature and designation)....................................

On behalf of....................................(specify Assigning Authority)

Place.. Date....................

(Signature and designation)....................................

On behalf of....................................(specify Assigning Authority)

Place.. Date....................

(Signature and designation)....................................

On behalf of....................................(specify Assigning Authority)

Place.. Date....................

(Signature and designation)....................................

On behalf of....................................(specify Assigning Authority)

Survey of this ship having been satisfactorily completed in accordance with the requirements of the Merchant Shipping (Load Line) Rules 1968, this Certificate is extended until..

Place.. Date..........................

(Signature and designation)..

On behalf of..........................(specify Assigning Authority)

NOTE

This Certificate must be kept framed and posted up in some conspicuous place on board the ship, so long as it remains in force and the ship is in use.

3101 4. *Form of United Kingdom load line exemption certificate:—*

UNITED KINGDOM LOAD LINE EXEMPTION CERTIFICATE

(Official Seal)

Issued by the [Department of Trade]

Name of Ship	Distinctive Number or Letters	Port of Registry

This is to certify that the above-mentioned ship is exempted pursuant to Section 19(3) of the Merchant Shipping (Load Lines) Act 1967 from—

*All the provisions of that Act and of the Merchant Shipping (Load Line) Rules 1968

*The following provisions of that Act and of the Merchant Shipping (Load Line) Rules 1968:—

....

....

....

Subject to the following conditions†:—

....

....

....

* Delete whichever is inapplicable.

† Delete if inapplicable.

This Certificate is valid until.................................subject, where appropriate, to periodical inspections in accordance with the Merchant Shipping (Load Line) Rules 1968.

Issued at..on...19.........

....

An authorised officer of the [Department of Trade]

This is to certify that this ship continues to comply with the conditions under which this exemption was granted—

Signed.................................... **Place**.................................... **Date**....................
Surveyor [Department of Trade]

Signed.................................... **Place**.................................... **Date**....................
Surveyor [Department of Trade]

Signed.................................... **Place**.................................... **Date**....................
Surveyor [Department of Trade]

Signed.................................... **Place**.................................... **Date**....................
Surveyor [Department of Trade]

3102 **SCHEDULE 2**

APPROPRIATE LOAD LINES—ZONES, AREAS AND SEASONAL PERIODS [6]

PART I

Appropriate Load Lines (Rules 16 to 18)

1. Subject to paragraphs 3-6 of this Part, the load line appropriate to a ship shall be—

(1) the Summer load line when the ship is in a summer zone (excluding any part of such a zone which is to be regarded as a seasonal area in relation to the ship);

(2) the Tropical load line when the ship is in the tropical zone;

(3) when the ship is in a seasonal zone or area (including any part of a summer zone which is to be regarded as a seasonal area in relation to the ship) the Summer load line, the Winter load line or the Tropical load line according to whether the seasonal period applicable in that zone or area to that ship is respectively summer, winter or tropical.

2.—(1) The zones,

(2) the seasonal zones, seasonal areas and seasonal periods applicable to a ship, shall be those set out in Part II of this Schedule and shown by way of illustration on the Chart annexed to these Rules.

3. In the case of a ship of 100 metres or less in length, the appropriate load line shall be the Winter North Atlantic load line in—

(1) the North Atlantic Winter Seasonal Zone I as described in paragraph 1(1) of Part II of this Schedule;

(2) so much of North Atlantic Winter Seasonal Zone II, as so described, as lies between the meridians of longitude of 15°W and 50°W

during the winter seasonal periods respectively applicable in those zones.

4. In the case of a sailing ship the appropriate load line shall except in circumstances in which paragraph 3 applies, be the Summer load line.

5. In the case of a ship marked with an All Seasons load line in accordance with Rule 28 that load line shall be the appropriate load line in all circumstances.

6. In the case of a ship marked with Timber load lines and carrying timber deck cargo in accordance with the requirements of the deck cargo regulations, the load line to be observed in any particular circumstances shall be the Timber load line corresponding to the load line which would be applicable in those circumstances under paragraphs 1 to 5 of this Schedule if the ship were not so marked.

PART II

Zones, Areas and Seasonal Periods

3103 1. NORTHERN WINTER SEASONAL ZONES AND AREA

(1) *North Atlantic Winter Seasonal Zones I and II*

(*a*) The North Atlantic Winter Seasonal Zone I lies within the meridian of longitude 50°W from the coast of Greenland to latitude 45°N, thence the parallel of latitude 45°N to longitude 15°W, thence the meridian of longitude 15°W to latitude 60°N, thence the parallel of latitude 60°N to the Greenwich Meridian, thence this meridian northwards.

Seasonal periods:

Winter: 16 October to 15 April.

Summer: 16 April to 15 October.

[6] The H.M.S.O. version of this Statutory Instrument contains a map of the world showing relevant zones, areas and seasonal periods.

(*b*) The North Atlantic Winter Seasonal Zone II lies within the meridian of longitude 68°30 W from the coast of the United States to latitude 40°N thence the rhumb line to the point latitude 36°N longitude 73°W thence the parallel of latitude 36°N to longitude 25°W and thence the rhumb line to Cape Toriñana.

Excluded from this zone are the North Atlantic Winter Seasonal Zone I, the North Atlantic Winter Seasonal Area and the Baltic Sea bounded by the parallel of latitude of The Skaw in the Skagerrak.

Seasonal periods:

Winter: 1 November to 31 March.

Summer: 1 April to 31 October.

The Shetland Islands are to be considered as being on the boundary line between the North Atlantic Winter Seasonal Zones I and II.

(2) *North Atlantic Winter Seasonal Area*

The boundary of the North Atlantic Winter Seasonal Area is—
the meridian of longitude 68°30′ W from the coast of the United States to latitude 40°N, thence the rhumb line to the southernmost intersection of the meridian of longitude 61°W with the coast of Canada and thence the east coasts of Canada and the United States.

Seasonal periods:

For ships over 100 metres in length:

Winter: 16 December to 15 February.

Summer: 16 February to 15 December.

For ships of 100 metres or less in length:

Winter: 1 November to 31 March.

Summer: 1 April to 31 October.

(3) *North Pacific Winter Seasonal Zone*

The southern boundary of the North Pacific Winter Seasonal Zone is—
the parallel of latitude 50°N from the east coast of the USSR to the west coast of Sakhalin, thence the west coast of Sakhalin to the southern extremity of Cape Kril'on, thence the rhumb line to Wakkanai, Hokkaido, Japan, thence the east and south coasts of Hokkaido to longitude 145°E, thence the meridian of longitude 145°E to latitude 35°N, thence the parallel of latitude 35°N to longitude 150°W and thence the rhumb line to the southern extremity of Dall Island, Alaska.

Seasonal periods:

Winter: 16 October to 15 April.

Summer: 16 April to 15 October.

04 2. SOUTHERN WINTER SEASONAL ZONE

The northern boundary of the Southern Winter Seasonal Zone is—

the rhumb line from the east coast of the American continent at Cape Tres Puntas to the point latitude 34°S, longitude 50°W, thence the parallel of latitude 34°S to longitude 17°E, thence the rhumb line to the point latitude 35°10′S, longitude 20°E, thence the rhumb line to the point latitude 34°S, longitude 28°E, thence the rhumb line to the point latitude 35°30′S, longitude 118°E, and thence the rhumb line to Cape Grim on the northwest coast of Tasmania; thence along the north and east coasts of Tasmania to the southernmost point of Bruny Island, thence the rhumb line to Black Rock Point on Stewart Island, thence the rhumb line to the point latitude 47°S, longitude 170°E, thence the rhumb line to the point latitude 33°S, longitude 170°W, and thence the parallel of latitude 33°S to the west coast of the American continent.

Seasonal periods:

Winter: 16 April to 15 October.

Summer: 16 October to 15 April.

Valparaiso is to be considered as being on the boundary line of the Summer and Winter Seasonal Zones.

3105 3. TROPICAL ZONE

(1) *Northern Boundary of the Tropical Zone*

The northern boundary of the Tropical Zone is—

the parallel of latitude 13°N from the east coast of the American continent to longitude 60°W, thence the rhumb line to the point latitude 10°N, longitude 58°W, thence the parallel of latitude 10°N to longitude 20°W, thence the meridian of longitude 20°W to latitude 30°N and thence the parallel of latitude 30°N to the west coast of Africa; from the east coast of Africa the parallel of latitude 8°N to longitude 70°E, thence the meridian of longitude 70°E to latitude 13°N, thence the parallel of latitude 13°N to the west coast of India; thence the south coast of India to latitude 10°30′N on the east coast of India, thence the rhumb line to the point latitude 9°N, longitude 82°E, thence the meridian of longitude 82°E to latitude 8°N, thence the parallel of latitude 8°N to the west coast of Malaysia, thence the coast of South-East Asia to the east coast of Vietnam at latitude 10°N, thence the parallel of latitude 10°N to longitude 145°E, thence the meridian of longitude 145°E to latitude 13°N and thence the parallel of latitude 13°N to the west coast of the American continent.

Saigon is to be considered as being on the boundary line of the Tropical Zone and the Seasonal Tropical Area.

(2) *Southern Boundary of the Tropical Zone*

The southern boundary of the Tropical Zone is—

the rhumb line from the Port of Santos, Brazil, to the point where the meridian of longitude 40°W intersects the Tropic of Capricorn; thence the Tropic of Capricorn to the west coast of Africa; from the east coast of Africa the parallel of latitude 20°S to the west coast of Madagascar, thence the west and north coasts of Madagascar to longitude 50°E, thence the meridian of longtitude 50°E to latitude 10°S, thence the parallel of latitude 10°S to longitude 98°E, thence the rhumb line to Port Darwin, Australia, thence the coasts of Australia and Wessel Island eastwards to Cape Wessel, thence the parallel of latitude 11°S to the west side of Cape York; from the east side of Cape York the parallel of latitude 11°S to longitude 150°W, thence the rhumb line to the point latitude 26°S, longitude 75°W, and thence the rhumb line to the west coast of the American continent at latitude 30°S.

Coquimbo and Santos are to be considered as being on the boundary line of the Tropical and Summer Zones.

(3) *Areas to be included in the Tropical Zone*

The following areas are to be treated as included in the Tropical Zone—

(*a*) The Suez Canal, The Red Sea and the Gulf of Aden, from Port Said to the meridian of longitude 45°E.

Aden and Berbera are to be considered as being on the boundary line of the Tropical Zone and the Seasonal Tropical Area.

(*b*) The Persian Gulf to the meridian of longitude 59°E.

(*c*) The area bounded by the parallel of latitude 22°S from the east coast of Australia to the Great Barrier Reef, thence the Great Barrier Reef to latitude 11°S. The northern boundary of the area is the southern boundary of the Tropical Zone.

106 4. Seasonal Tropical Areas

The following are Seasonal Tropical Areas:—

(1) *In the North Atlantic*

An area bounded—

on the north by the rhumb line from Cape Catoche, Yucatan, to Cape San Antonio, Cuba, the north coast of Cuba to latitude 20°N and thence the parallel of latitude 20°N to longitude 20°W;

on the west by the coast of the American continent;

on the south and east by the northern boundary of the Tropical Zone.

Seasonal periods:

Tropical: 1 November to 15 July.

Summer: 16 July to 31 October.

(2) *In the Arabian Sea*

An area bounded—

on the west by the coast of Africa, the meridian of longitude 45°E in the Gulf of Aden, the coast of South Arabia and the meridian of longitude 59°E in the Gulf of Oman;

on the north and east by the coasts of Pakistan and India;

on the south by the northern boundary of the Tropical Zone.

Seasonal periods:

Tropical: 1 September to 31 May.

Summer: 1 June to 31 August.

(3) *In the Bay of Bengal*

The Bay of Bengal north of the northern boundary of the Tropical Zone.

Seasonal Periods:

Tropical: 1 December to 30 April.

Summer: 1 May to 30 November.

(4) *In the South Indian Ocean*

(*a*) An area bounded—

on the north and west by the southern boundary of the Tropical Zone and the east coast of Madagascar;

on the south by the parallel of latitude 20°S;

on the east by the rhumb line from the point latitude 20°S, longitude 50°E, to the point latitude 15°S, longitude 51°30′E, and thence by the meridian of longitude 51°30′E to latitude 10°S.

Seasonal periods:

Tropical: 1 April to 30 November.

Summer: 1 December to 31 March.

(*b*) An area bounded—

on the north by the southern boundary of the Tropical Zone;

on the east by the coast of Australia;

on the south by the parallel of latitude 15°S from longitude 51°30′E, to longitude 120°E and thence the meridian of longitude 120°E to the coast of Australia;

on the west by the meridian of longitude 51°30′E.

Seasonal periods:

Tropical: 1 May to 30 November.

Summer: 1 December to 30 April.

3107 (5) *In the China Sea*

An area bounded—

on the west and north by the coasts of Vietnam and China from latitude 10°N to Hong Kong;

on the east by the rhumb line from Hong Kong to the Port of Sual (Luzon Island) and the west coasts of the Islands of Luzon, Samar and Leyte to latitude 10°N;

on the south by the parallel of latitude 10°N.

Hong Kong and Sual are to be considered as being on the boundary of the Seasonal Tropical Area and Summer Zone.

Seasonal periods:

Tropical: 21 January to 20 April.

Summer: 1 May to 20 January.

(6) *In the North Pacific*

(*a*) An area bounded—

on the north by the parallel of latitude 25°N;

on the west by the meridian of longitude 160°E;

on the south by the parallel of latitude 13°N;

on the east by the meridian of longitude 130°W.

Seasonal periods:

Tropical: 1 April to 31 October.

Summer: 1 November to 31 March.

(*b*) An area bounded—

on the north and east by the west coast of the American continent;

on the west by the meridian of longitude 123°W from the coast of the American continent to latitude 33°N and by the rhumb line from the point latitude 33°N, longitude 123°W to the point latitude 13°N, longitude 105°W;

on the south by the parallel of latitude 13°N.

Seasonal periods:

Tropical: 1 March to 30 June and 1 November to 30 November.

Summer: 1 July to 31 October and 1 December to 28/29 February.

(7) *In the South Pacific*

(*a*) The Gulf of Carpentaria south of latitude 11°S.

Seasonal periods:

Tropical: 1 April to 30 November.

Summer: 1 December to 31 March.

(*b*) An area bounded—

on the north and east by the southern boundary of the Tropical Zone;

on the south by the Tropic of Capricorn from the east coast of Australia to longitude 150°W, thence by the meridian of longitude 150°W to latitude 20°S and thence by the parallel of latitude 20°S to the point where it intersects the southern boundary of the Tropical Zone;

on the west by the boundaries of the area within the Great Barrier Reef included in the Tropical Zone and by the east coast of Australia.

Seasonal periods:

Tropical: 1 April to 30 November.

Summer: 1 December to 31 March.

108 5. SUMMER ZONES

The remaining sea areas constitute the summer Zones.

However, for ships of 100 metres or less in length, the area bounded—

on the north and west by the east coast of the United States;

on the east by the meridian of longitude 68°30′W from the coast of the United States to latitude 40°N and thence by the rhumb line to the point latitude 36°N longitude 73°W;

on the south by the parallel of latitude 36°N;

is a Winter Seasonal Area.

Seasonal periods:

Winter: 1 November to 31 March.

Summer: 1 April to 31 October.

109 6. ENCLOSED SEAS

(1) *Baltic Sea*

This sea bounded by the parallel of latitude of The Skaw in the Skagerrak is included in the Summer Zones.

However, for ships of 100 metres or less in length, it is a Winter Seasonal Area.

Seasonal periods:

Winter: 1 November to 31 March.

Summer: 1 April to 31 October.

(2) *Black Sea*

This sea is included in the Summer Zones.

However, for ships of 100 metres or less in length, the area north of latitude 44°N is a Winter Seasonal Area.

Seasonal periods:

Winter: 1 December to 28/29 February.

Summer: 1 March to 30 November.

(3) *Mediterranean*

This sea is included in the Summer Zones.

However, for ships of 100 metres or less in length, the area bounded—

on the north and west by the coasts of France and Spain and the meridian of longitude 3°E from the coast of Spain to latitude 40°N;

on the south by the parallel of latitude 40°N from longitude 3°E to the west coast of Sardinia;

on the east by the west and north coasts of Sardinia from latitude 40°N to longitude 9°E, thence by the meridian of longitude 9°E to the south coast of Corsica, thence by the west and north coasts of Corsica to longitude 9°E and thence by the rhumb line to Cape Sicié,

is a Winter Seasonal Area.

Seasonal periods:

Winter: 16 December to 15 March.

Summer: 16 March to 15 December.

(4) *Sea of Japan*

This sea south of latitude 50°N is included in the Summer Zones.

However, for ships of 100 metres or less in length, the area between the parallel of latitude 50°N and the rhumb line from the east coast of Korea at latitude 38°N to the west coast of Hokkaido, Japan, at latitude 43°12′N is a Winter Seasonal Area.

Seasonal periods:

Winter: 1 December to 28/29 February.

Summer: 1 March to 30 November.

(7) *Ports on Boundary Lines*

For the purposes of the application of the provisions of this Schedule to a ship at a port which stands on the boundary line between two zones or areas or between a zone and an area, or which is required under the foregoing provisions of this Schedule to be considered as being on such a boundary line, the port shall be deemed to be within the zone or area into which the ship is about to proceed or from which she has arrived as the case may be.

SCHEDULE 3

Record of Particulars

(Rule 25)

The following is the form of record of particulars referred to in Rule 25:—

MERCHANT SHIPPING (LOAD LINE) RULES 1968

RECORD OF PARTICULARS RELATING TO CONDITIONS OF ASSIGNMENT

1. Reference to paragraphs in this record are references to paragraphs of Schedule 4 (Conditions of Assignment) to the above mentioned Rules.

2. Particulars required by this record may be given by attaching to the record a copy of the Surveyor's report made pursuant to Rule 4 of the above mentioned Rules and specifying in the record the passages in that report in which those particulars are given.

NAME OF SHIP **PORT OF REGISTRY**

DISTINCTIVE NUMBER OR LETTERS

DIMENSIONS OF SHIP: LENGTH (L) BREADTH (B) DEPTH (D)

PORT OF SURVEY DATE OF SURVEY YEAR OF BUILD

ASSIGNING AUTHORITY

CLASSIFICATION NOTATION

SURVEYOR'S SIGNATURE

Superstructure End Bulkheads (Paragraph 3)

1.(*a*) Give particulars of the construction of bulkheads at exposed ends of enclosed superstructures.

(*b*) Is such construction efficient?

Hatchways on Freeboard and Superstructure Decks Closed by Portable Covers and Secured Weathertight by Tarpaulins and Battening Devices (Paragraph 5)

2. If the material used for coamings is not mild steel, specify it. Is the strength and stiffness of the coaming equivalent to that of a coaming constructed of mild steel?

3.(*a*) Specify the material used for hatch covers.

(*b*) If not of mild steel or wood, is the strength and stiffness of the cover equivalent to that of a cover constructed of mild steel?

4. Are the galvanised steel bands protecting the ends of wooden hatch covers efficiently secured?

5.(*a*) Specify the material used for portable beams.

(*b*) If not of mild steel, are the strength and stiffness of the beams equivalent to those of beams of mild steel?

6.(*a*) Give particulars of the construction of carriers or sockets for portable beams.

(*b*) Are such carriers or sockets of substantial construction and efficient for their purpose?

(*c*) Are rolling types of beams used? If so, give particulars of securing arrangements.

7.(*a*) Are battens and wedges efficient and in good condition?

(*b*) Specify the material used for wedges. If not of tough wood, is the material used equivalent to tough wood?

8. Are tarpaulins waterproof, in good condition and of material of suitable strength and quality?

9.(*a*) State material of bars used for securing of hatchway covers.

(*b*) If not of steel, state whether the strength and stiffness of the bars is equivalent to that of steel bars.

(*c*) Are the numbers of bars supplied for each hatchway sufficient to ensure compliance with paragraph 5(9)?

(*d*) If covers are secured otherwise than by bars, give particulars. Are means used acceptable under the provisions of paragraph 5(9)(*b*)?

3111 HATCHWAYS ON FREEBOARD AND SUPERSTRUCTURE DECKS CLOSED BY WEATHERTIGHT COVERS OF STEEL OR EQUIVALENT MATERIAL FITTED WITH GASKETS AND CLAMPING DEVICES (Paragraph 6)

10.(*a*) If coamings are less than the height required by paragraph 6(1) or are omitted specify the arrangements relied on to ensure that the safety of the ship will not in consequence by impaired in the worst sea and weather conditions likely to be encountered by the ship in service.

(*b*) Are such arrangements sufficient for that purpose?

11.(*a*) Specify the means for securing covers and making them weathertight.

(*b*) Are such means, including gaskets and clamping devices, efficient and in good condition?

12.(*a*) Specify the material used for hatch covers.

(*b*) If not of mild steel, is the strength and stiffness of the cover equivalent to that of a cover constructed of mild steel?

MACHINERY SPACE OPENINGS (Paragraph 7)

13.(*a*) Give particulars of the framing and of the steel casings enclosing all machinery space openings in Positions 1 and 2.

(*b*) Is such framing efficient?

(*c*) Are such casings of substantial strength?

14.(*a*) Give particulars of the heights above deck of coamings of fiddleys, funnels and machinery space ventilators situated in exposed positions on freeboard and superstructure decks.

(*b*) Do such heights provide adequate protection in the circumstances?

MISCELLANEOUS OPENINGS IN FREEBOARD AND SUPERSTRUCTURE DECKS (Paragraph 8)

15.(*a*) Give particulars of the construction and material of covers fitted to manholes and flush scuttles.

(*b*) Is such construction and material acceptable under paragraph 8(1)?

16. Specify the means by which such covers can be secured and maintained watertight, and state whether they are efficient.

17. If such covers are not secured by closely spaced bolts, give particulars of means of permanent attachment.

112 VENTILATORS IN EXPOSED POSITIONS ON FREEBOARD AND SUPERSTRUCTURE DECKS (Paragraph 9)

18.(*a*) Specify the material used for coamings.

(*b*) If the coamings are not of steel, is the material used equivalent to steel?

19. Are all coamings of ventilators in Positions 1 and 2 of substantial construction and efficiently connected to the deck?

20.(*a*) Specify the ventilators (if any) situated in positions particularly subjected to weather and sea.

(*b*) Have the heights of the coamings of such ventilators been increased in accordance with paragraph 9(1)(*b*) above the height required by paragraph 9(1)(*a*)? If so, specify such increase for each ventilator.

(*c*) Is the increased height acceptable under paragraph 9(1)(*b*)?

21. Is the coaming of every ventilator exceeding 900 millimetres in height efficiently supported? By what means?

22. State whether any ventilator in Position 1 or 2 which exceeds the height specified in paragraph 9(5) and is not fitted with a closing appliance should be so fitted, giving reasons.

AIR PIPES IN EXPOSED POSITIONS ON FREEBOARD AND SUPERSTRUCTURE DECKS (Paragraph 10)

23 (*a*) Give particulars of the construction of exposed parts of air pipes.

(*b*) Is such construction acceptable under paragraph 10(1)?

24.(*a*) Give particulars of any exposed air pipe openings on a superstructure deck where the superstructure is less than standard height, specifying the height above deck of the pipe opening.

(*b*) Is such height acceptable under the provisions of paragraph 10(3)(*b*)?

25.(*a*) Give particulars of any exposed air pipe openings which are less than (i) 760 mm. if on the freeboard deck (ii) 450 mm. if on a superstructure deck, specifying the height above deck of the pipe opening.

(*b*) Is such height acceptable under the provisions of paragraph 10(4)(*a*) and (*b*)?

CARGO PORTS AND SIMILAR OPENINGS (Paragraph 11)

26(*a*) Give particulars and specify the number of cargo ports and similar openings in the ship's side below the freeboard deck and in the sides and ends of superstructures which form part of the shell of the ship.

(*b*) Are such ports and openings compatible with the design of the ship?

(*c*) Is their number necessary for the proper working of the ship?

(*d*) Will the lower edge of any such cargo port or similar opening be below a line parallel to the freeboard deck at side and having as its lowest point the upper edge of the uppermost load line, and if so by what distance?

(*e*) Give particulars of closing appliances of the cargo ports and openings referred to in (*a*) above.

(*f*) Are such closing appliances such as to ensure watertightness, and structural integrity commensurate with the surrounding shell plating?

3113 **Scuppers, Inlets and Discharges (Paragraph 12)**

27.(*a*) Give particulars of the positions from where single automatic non-return valves fitted pursuant to paragraph 12(2) can be closed.

(*b*) Are these positions readily accessible at all times under service conditions?

28.(*a*) Where two automatic non-return valves are fitted give particulars of the position of the inboard valve.

(*b*) Is this position readily accessible at all times for examination under service conditions?

29.(*a*) Give particulars of the location of the controls of valves in (*i*) manned machinery spaces and (*ii*) unattended machinery spaces.

(*b*) Are the controls of the valves referred to in (*a*) readily accessible at all times under service conditions?

30.(*a*) Give particulars of the devices giving warning of entry of water into unattended machinery spaces.

(*b*) Are such devices acceptable under paragraph 12(4)(*b*)?

31.(*a*) Give particulars of the locations in the ship of the control positions at which warning is given by the devices referred to in 30(*a*).

(*b*) Are such positions acceptable under paragraph 12(4)(*b*)?

Side Scuttles (Paragraph 13)

32. Are the sills of all side scuttles at or above a line drawn parallel to the freeboard deck at side having as its lowest point:

(*a*) 2·5 per cent of (B) above the Summer load line or

(*b*) 500 millimetres above the Summer load line,

whichever is the greater?

33.(*a*) Give particulars of the construction of side scuttles, deadlights and glasses (if fitted).

(*b*) Are they efficiently fitted?

Freeing Ports and Arrangements (Paragraph 14)

34.(*a*) Give particulars of the distance above deck of the lower edges of freeing ports.

(*b*) Are such lower edges as near to the deck as practicable?

35.(*a*) Give particulars of the provision made for freeing from water superstructures other than enclosed superstructures.

(*b*) Is such provision efficient?

Protection of the Crew (Paragraph 15)

36.(*a*) Give particulars of the construction of deckhouses used for the accommodation of crew.

(*b*) Is such construction efficient?

37.(*a*) Give particulars, including spacing and height, of guard rails, guard wires and stanchions fitted at the perimeter of exposed parts of the freeboard and superstructure decks.

(*b*) Are such guard rails, guard wires and stanchions acceptable under paragraph 15(2)?

38.(*a*) Are guard rails, guard wires or bulwarks less at any point than 1 metre in height?

(*b*) If so, specify their height. Would they, if they were 1 metre in height or more, interfere with the normal operation of the ship?

(*c*) Give particulars of the protection provided at that point. Is it adequate?

39.(*a*) Give particulars of the gangways, underdeck passages and other means of access enabling the crew to pass between their quarters, the machinery space and other spaces used in the ordinary course of their work.

(*b*) Give particulars of life lines, access ladders, guard rails, guard wires, hand rails and other safety fittings provided.

(*c*) Are these arrangements acceptable under the provisions of paragraph 15(5)?

114 SPECIAL REQUIREMENTS APPLICABLE TO TYPE "A" SHIPS

MACHINERY CASINGS (Paragraph 17)

40.(*a*) Are all casings enclosing machinery space openings in Position 1 or Position 2 protected by a poop, bridge or deckhouse in accordance with paragraph 17?

(*b*) If not—

(i) specify any casings not so protected;

(ii) state in the case of each whether or not there is an opening in the casing giving direct access from the freeboard deck to the machinery space;

(iii) if there is an opening described in (ii)—

does the only opening in the casing have a steel weathertight door?

does that door lead to a space or passageway which is as strongly constructed as the casing, and is it separated from the stairway to the machinery space by a second steel weathertight door?

GANGWAY AND ACCESS (Paragraph 18)

41.(*a*) Where access betweeen the poop and the détached bridge is obtained other than by a permanent gangway or an underdeck passage, give particulars of the arrangements provided for such access.

(*b*) Are such arrangements equivalent to the provision of access by means of a permanent gangway or underdeck passage?

42.(*a*) If a walkway is fitted pursuant to paragraph 18(4)(*c*), is it obstructed by pipes or other fittings of a permanent nature?

(*b*) If so—

(i) give particulars of the means of passage over the obstruction;

(ii) are such means acceptable under the provisions of paragraph 18(5)(*e*)?

FREEING ARRANGEMENTS (Paragraph 20)

43.(*a*) Where guard rails, guard wires and stanchions are not provided for at least a half of the length of the freeboard and superstructure decks, give particulars of the freeing arrangements in lieu.

(*b*) Are such freeing arrangements equally effective?

44. (*a*) Give the height above deck of the upper edge of the sheer strake.

(*b*) Is this height as low as practicable?

45.(*a*) Give particulars of the numbers, type and positions of breakwaters fitted.

(*b*) Are such breakwaters efficient and acceptable for the conditions likely to be encountered by the ship in service?

3115 **SPECIAL REQUIREMENTS APPLICABLE TO CERTAIN TYPE "B" SHIPS (Paragraph 21)**

MACHINERY CASINGS (Applicable only to Type "B" ships to be assigned Type "A" freeboards under paragraph 5(5) of Schedule 5)

46.(*a*) Are all casings enclosing machinery space openings in Position 1 or Position 2 protected by a poop, bridge or deckhouse in accordance with paragraph 17?

(*b*) If not—

(i) specify any casings not so protected;

(ii) state in the case of each whether or not there is an opening in the casing giving direct access from the freeboard deck to the machinery space;

(iii) if there is an opening described in (ii)—

does the only opening in the casing have a steel weathertight door?

does that door lead to a space or passageway which is as strongly constructed as the casing, and is it separated from the stairway to the machinery space by a second steel weathertight door?

GANGWAY AND ACCESS (Paragraph 22)

47.(*a*) Where access between the poop and the detached bridge is obtained otherwise than by a permanent gangway or an underdeck passage or gangway constructed according to paragraph 23(2), give particulars of the arrangements provided for such access.

(*b*) Are such arrangements equivalent to the provision of access by means of a permanent gangway or underdeck passage or gangway constructed according to paragraph 23(2)?

FREEING ARRANGEMENTS (Applicable only to Type "B" ships to be assigned Type "A" freeboards under paragraph 5(5) of Schedule 5)

48.(*a*) Where guard rails, guard wires and stanchions are not provided for at least a half of the length of the freeboard and superstructure decks give details of freeing arrangements.

(*b*) Are such freeing arrangements equally effective?

49.(*a*) Give the height above deck of the upper edge of the sheer strake.

(*b*) Is this height as low as practicable?

50.(*a*) Give particulars of the numbers, type and positions of breakwaters fitted.

(*b*) Are such breakwaters efficient and acceptable for the conditions likely to be encountered by the ship in service?

SPECIAL REQUIREMENTS APPLICABLE TO SHIPS TO BE ASSIGNED TIMBER FREEBOARDS (Paragraph 26)

BULWARKS, GUARD RAILS AND STANCHIONS (Paragraph 29)

51.(*a*) Give particulars of the stiffening of bulwarks and of supports.

(*b*) Are such stiffening and supports acceptable under paragraph 29(1)?

52.(*a*) Where bulwarks are not fitted, give particulars of guard rails and stanchions provided as an alternative.

(*b*) Are such guard rails and stanchions efficient and acceptable under paragraph 29(2)?

16 ## SCHEDULE 4

Conditions of Assignment

(Rule 23)

Interpretation

1. In this Schedule, except where the context otherwise requires—

"breadth" and the symbol "(B)" in relation to a ship mean the maximum breadth of the ship measured amidships to the moulded line of the frame in the case of a ship having a metal shell, or to the outer surface of the hull in the case of a ship having a shell of any other material;

"enclosed superstructure" means a superstructure—

(*a*) which has enclosing bulkheads of efficient construction in which all access openings are fitted with sills and weathertight doors, and

(*b*) in which all other openings in sides or ends thereof are fitted with efficient weathertight means of closing,

but shall not include a bridge or poop fulfilling these requirements unless access is provided by which the crew can reach machinery and other working spaces within the bridge or poop by alternative means which are available for the purpose at all times when access openings in the bulkheads of the bridge or poop are closed;

"exposed position" means a position which is either—

(*a*) exposed to weather and sea, or

(*b*) within a structure so exposed other than an enclosed superstructure;

"forward perpendicular" means the perpendicular taken at the forward end of the ship's length (L), coinciding with the foreside of the stem on the waterline on which such length is measured; and "after perpendicular" means the perpendicular taken at the after end of such length;

"height" in relation to a superstructure means the least vertical height measured at side from the top of the superstructure deck beams to the top of the freeboard deck beams; and the "standard height" of a superstructure means the height ascertained in accordance with the provisions of paragraph 9 of Schedule 5;

"Summer load waterline" in relation to a ship means the waterline which corresponds, or will when load lines have been marked on the sides of the ship correspond, to the Summer load line of the ship;

"superstructure" means a decked structure (including a raised quarter deck) situated on the freeboard deck which either extends from side to side of the ship or is such that its side plating is not inboard of the shell plating of the ship by more than 4 per cent of the breadth (B) of the ship; and, where the freeboard deck of the ship consists of a lower deck as described in sub-paragraph (*b*) of the definition of "freeboard deck" in Rule 33, includes that part of the hull of the ship which extends above the freeboard deck;

"superstructure deck" means a deck forming the top of a superstructure;

"Type "A" ship" means a ship which is designed to carry only liquid cargoes in bulk and has the characteristics set out below:—

(*a*) The cargo tanks of the ship have only small access openings closed by watertight gasketed covers of steel.

(*b*) The ship in consequence of its design has high integrity of the exposed deck and has a high degree of safety against flooding in consequence of the low permeability of loaded cargo spaces and the degree of subdivision therein.

(*c*) If over 150 metres in length and designed to have empty compartments when loaded to the Summer load waterline, the ship shall be capable of remaining afloat after the flooding of any one of such empty compartments, at an assumed permeability of 0·95 in the condition of equilibrium described in the following sub-paragraph;

Provided that if the ship exceeds 225 metres in length its machinery space shall also be treated as one of the floodable compartments above mentioned but with an assumed permeability of 0·85.

(*d*) The condition of equilibrium referred to in sub-paragraph (*c*) is as follows:—

(i) the final water line after the flooding specified in that sub-paragraph is below the top of any ventilator coaming, the lower edge of any air pipe opening, the upper edge of the sill of any access opening fitted with a weathertight door, and the lower edge of any other opening through which progressive flooding may take place;

(ii) the angle of heel due to unsymmetrical flooding does not exceed 15 degrees;

(iii) the metacentric height calculated using the constant displacement method has a positive value of at least 50 millimetres in the upright condition after the flooding specified in that sub-paragraph; and

(iv) the ship has adequate residual stability.

"Type "B" ship" means either—

(*a*) a new ship other than a Type "A" ship, or

(*b*) an existing ship which, being so constructed or modified as to comply with all the requirements of this Schedule applicable to a new ship of her type, is to be assigned freeboards determined in accordance with Schedule 5;

"weathertight" in relation to any part of a ship other than a door in a bulkhead means that the part is such that water will not penetrate it and so enter the hull of the ship in the worst sea and weather conditions likely to be encountered by the ship in service; and in relation to a door in a bulkhead means a door which—

(*a*) is constructed of steel or other equivalent material, is permanently and strongly attached to the bulkhead, and is framed, stiffened and fitted so that the whole structure in which it is set is of equivalent strength to the unpierced bulkhead;

(*b*) is closed by means of gaskets, clamping devices or other equivalent means permanently attached to the bulkhead or to the door itself;

(*c*) when closed, is weathertight as above defined; and

(*d*) is so arranged that it can be operated from either side of the bulkhead.

References to any structure, opening or fitting as being in Position 1 or Position 2 shall be construed as references to its being in the following positions respectively:—

Position 1: in an exposed position on either (*a*) the freeboard deck or a raised quarter deck or (*b*) a superstructure deck and forward of a point one quarter of the ship's length (L) from the forward perpendicular;

Position 2: in an exposed position on a superstructure deck and abaft the said point.

PART I

3117

SHIPS IN GENERAL

Structural Strength and Stability

2.—(1) The construction of the ship shall be such that her general structural strength will be sufficient for the freeboards to be assigned to her.

(2) The design and construction of the ship shall be such as to ensure that her stability in all probable loading conditions will be sufficient for the freeboards to be assigned to her, and for this purpose regard shall be had, in addition to the intended service of the ship and to any relevant requirements of Rules made under the Merchant Shipping (Safety Convention) Act 1949 and the Merchant Shipping Act 1964, to the following criteria:—

(*a*) The area under the curve of Righting Levers (GZ curve) shall not be less than—

(i) 0·055 metre-radians up to an angle of 30 degrees;

(ii) 0·09 metre-radians up to an angle of either 40 degrees or the angle at which the lower edges of any openings in the hull, superstructures or deckhouses, being openings which cannot be closed weathertight, are immersed if that angle be less;

(iii) 0·03 metre-radians between the angles of heel of 30 degrees and 40 degrees or such lesser angle as is referred to in (ii).

(*b*) The Righting Lever (GZ) shall be at least 0·20 metres at an angle of heel equal to or greater than 30 degrees.

(*c*) The maximum Righting Lever (GZ) shall occur at an angle of heel not less than 30 degrees.

(*d*) The initial transverse metacentric height shall not be less than 0·15 metres. In the case of a ship carrying a timber deck cargo which complies with sub-paragraph (*a*) by taking into account the volume of timber deck cargo the initial transverse metacentric height shall not be less than 0·05 metres.

(3) To determine whether the ship complies with the requirements of sub-paragraph (2) the ship shall, unless the Board otherwise permit, be subjected to an inclining test carried out in the presence of a surveyor appointed by the Board, and the Board shall notify the Assigning Authority whether or not they are satisfied that the ship complies with those requirements.

Superstructure End Bulkheads

3. Bulkheads at exposed ends of enclosed superstructures shall be of efficient construction. The height of any sill in an access opening in such a bulkhead shall except where otherwise stated be at least 380 millimetres above the deck.

Hatchways: General

4.—(1) The provisions of this paragraph and of paragraphs 5 and 6 apply to all hatchways in Position 1 or in Position 2 except where otherwise stated.

(2) Subject to sub-paragraph (3), the construction and the means for securing the weathertightness of a hatchway shall—

(*a*) in the case of a hatchway closed by a portable cover and secured weathertight by tarpaulins and battening devices, comply with the requirements of paragraph 5; and.

(*b*) in the case of a hatchway closed by a weathertight cover of steel or other equivalent material fitted with gaskets and clamping devices, comply with the requirements of paragraph 6.

(3) Every hatchway in an exposed position on a deck above a superstructure deck and leading to space below that superstructure deck shall be of such construction and be fitted with such means for securing the weathertightness of the hatchway as are adequate having regard to its position.

Hatchways Closed by Portable Covers and Secured Weathertight by Tarpaulins and Battening Devices.

5.—(1) *Coamings:* Every hatchway shall have a coaming of substantial construction. The coaming shall be constructed of mild steel but may be constructed of other material provided that the strength and stiffness of the coaming are equivalent to those of a coaming of mild steel. The height of the coaming above the deck shall be at least—

600 millimetres if the hatchway is in Position 1;

450 millimetres if the hatchway is in Position 2.

(2) *Covers:* (*a*) The width of every bearing surface for a hatchway cover shall be at least 65 millimetres.

(*b*) In the case of a cover made of wood—

(i) the finished thickness of the cover shall be at least 60 millimetres in association with a span of not more than 1·5 metres, and the thickness of covers for larger spans shall be increased in the ratio of 60 millimetres to a span of 1·5 metres;

(ii) the ends of the cover shall be protected by galvanised steel bands efficiently secured.

(*c*) In the case of a cover made of mild steel—

(i) the strength of the cover shall be calculated with an assumed load ascertained in accordance with the following Table, and the product of the maximum stress thus calculated and the factor 4·25 shall not exceed the minimum ultimate strength of the material:—

3119 TABLE

	Assumed Load, per square metre	
Ship's Length (L)	Hatchway in Position 1	Hatchway in Position 2
24 metres	1 metric ton	·75 metric ton
100 metres or over	1·75 metric tons	1·30 metric tons
Over 24 metres but less than 100 metres	to be ascertained by linear interpolation	

(ii) the cover shall be so designed as to limit the deflection to not more than 0·0028 times the span under the load appropriate to the hatchway cover under sub-paragraph (i).

(*d*) In the case of a cover made neither of mild steel nor wood the strength and stiffness of the cover shall be equivalent to those of a cover of mild steel.

(3) *Portable beams:* (*a*) Where portable beams for supporting hatchway covers are made of mild steel, the strength of such beams shall be calculated with the appropriate assumed load ascertained in accordance with the Table in sub-paragraph (2) and the product of the maximum stress thus calculated and the factor 5 shall not exceed the minimum ultimate strength of the material.

(b) Such beams shall be so designed as to limit the deflection to not more than 0·0022 times the span under the load appropriate to the beam under sub-paragraph (*a*).

(*c*) In the case of portable beams not made of mild steel, the strength and stiffness of the beams shall be equivalent to those of beams of mild steel.

(4) *Pontoon covers:* (*a*) Where pontoon covers of mild steel are used in place of portable beams and covers their strength shall be calculated with the appropriate assumed load ascertained in accordance with the Table in sub-paragraph (2) and the product of the maximum stress thus calculated and the factor 5 shall not exceed the minimum ultimate strength of the material.

(*b*) Such pontoon covers shall be so designed as to limit the deflection to not more than 0·0022 times the span under the load appropriate to a pontoon cover under sub-paragraph (*a*).

(*c*) Mild steel plating forming the tops of such covers shall be not less in thickness than 1 per cent of the spacing of the stiffeners or 6 millimetres, whichever is the greater.

(*d*) In the case of pontoon covers not made of mild steel, the strength and stiffness of the cover shall be equivalent to those of a cover of mild steel.

(5) *Carriers or sockets:* Carriers or sockets for portable beams shall be of substantial construction, and shall provide efficient means for the fitting and securing of the beams. Where rolling types of beams are used the arrangements shall ensure that the beams remain properly in position when the hatchway is closed.

(6) *Cleats:* Cleats shall be set to fit the taper of the wedges. They shall be at least 65 millimetres wide and spaced not more than 600 millimetres centre to centre. The end cleats along each side or end of the hatchway shall be not more than 150 millimetres from the hatch corners.

(7) *Battens and wedges:* Battens and wedges shall be efficient for their purpose and in good condition. Wedges shall be of tough wood or equivalent material cut to a taper of not more than 1 in 6 and shall be not less than 13 millimetres thick at the toes.

(8) *Tarpaulins:* At least two layers of tarpaulins shall be provided for every hatchway. Such tarpaulins shall be waterproof, in good condition, and of material of satisfactory strength and quality.

(9) *Security of hatchway covers:* (*a*) Except as otherwise provided in sub-paragraph (*b*), steel bars shall be provided for every hatchway sufficient to ensure that each section of hatchway covers can be efficiently and independently secured after the tarpaulins have been battened down and that hatchway covers more than 1·5 metres in length are so secured by at least two such bars.

(*b*) Bars of material other than steel, or means of securing hatchway covers otherwise than by bars, may be so used, provided:

(i) that in the case of the former, the strength and stiffness of the bars used are equivalent to those of steel bars;

(ii) that in either case the degree of security so achieved is not less than that which would be achieved by the use of steel bars.

Hatchways closed by Weathertight Covers of Steel or equivalent material fitted with Gaskets and Clamping Devices

6.—(1) *Coamings:* (*a*) Except as otherwise provided in sub-paragraph (*b*), every hatchway shall have a coaming of substantial construction the height of which above the deck shall be at least—

600 millimetres if the hatchway is in Position 1;

450 millimetres if the hatchway is in Position 2.

(*b*) A hatchway may have a coaming of less than the height applicable under the provisions of sub-paragraph (*a*), or in exceptional circumstances a coaming may be dispensed with, provided:

(i) that the safety of the ship will not be impaired in consequence in the worst sea and weather conditions likely to be encountered by the ship in service, and

(ii) that any coaming fitted pursuant to this sub-paragraph is of substantial construction.

(2) *Weathertight Covers:* (*a*) The strength of every cover of mild steel shall be calculated with an assumed load ascertained in accordance with the Table set out in paragraph 5(2) and the product of the maximum stress thus calculated and the factor 4·25 shall not exceed the minimum ultimate strength of the material. Every such cover shall be so designed as to limit the deflection under such a load to not more than 0·0028 times the span.

(*b*) Every cover constructed of material other than mild steel shall have strength and stiffness equivalent to those required in the case of a cover of mild steel.

(*c*) Every cover shall be fitted with efficient means by which it can be secured and made weathertight.

(*d*) Mild steel plating forming the top of any cover shall be not less in thickness than one per cent. of the spacing of the stiffeners or 6 millimetres whichever is the greater.

Machinery Space Openings

3120 7.—(1) Every machinery space opening situated in Position 1 or Position 2 shall be efficiently framed and enclosed by a steel casing of substantial strength, account being taken of the extent, if any, to which the casing is protected by other structures.

(2) Every doorway in a casing referred to in the preceding sub-paragraph shall be fitted with a steel weathertight door having a sill the height of which shall be at least—

(*a*) 600 millimetres above the deck if the opening is in Position 1;

(*b*) 380 millimetres above the deck if the opening is in Position 2.

(3) Every opening in such a casing other than a doorway shall be fitted with a permanently attached cover of steel, which is fitted with efficient means by which it can be secured and maintained weathertight and, except in the case of a cover consisting of a plate secured by bolts, is capable of being operated from either side of the opening.

(4) Every fiddley, funnel or machinery space ventilator situated in an exposed position on the freeboard deck or on a superstructure deck shall have a coaming of such height above the deck as will provide adequate protection having regard to its position.

Miscellaneous Openings in Freeboard and Superstructure Decks

8.—(1) Every manhole and flush scuttle in Position 1 or Position 2 shall be provided with a substantial cover fitted with efficient means by which it can be secured and maintained watertight. Unless secured by closely spaced bolts, every such cover shall be permanently attached by a chain or equivalent means so as to be available for immediate use at all times.

(2) Every opening in a deck other than a hatchway, machinery space opening, manhole or flush scuttle shall—

(*a*) if situated in the freeboard deck be protected either by an enclosed superstructure or by a deckhouse or companionway equivalent in strength and weathertightness to an enclosed superstructure;

(*b*) if situated in an exposed position either—

(i) in a deck over an enclosed superstructure and giving access to space within that superstructure, or

(ii) on top of a deckhouse on the freeboard deck and giving access to space below that deck,

be protected by an efficient deckhouse or companionway fitted with weathertight doors;

(*c*) if situated in an exposed position in a deck above the deck over an enclosed superstructure and giving access to space within that superstructure, be protected either in accordance with the requirements of sub-paragraph (*b*) or to such lesser extent as may be adequate having regard to its position.

(3) Every door in a companionway, deckhouse or enclosed superstructure referred to in sub-paragraph 2(*a*) or (*b*) shall have a sill the height of which shall be at least—

(*a*) 600 millimetres if the structure is in Position 1;

(*b*) 380 millimetres if the structure is in Position 2.

Ventilators

9.—(1)(*a*) Except as otherwise provided in sub-paragraph (*b*), every ventilator in Position 1 or Position 2 leading to space below the freeboard deck or below the deck of an enclosed superstructure shall have a coaming of steel or equivalent material, substantially constructed and efficiently connected to the deck. The height of such coamings shall be at least—

(i) 900 millimetres above the deck if the ventilator is in Position 1;

(ii) 760 millimetres above the deck if the ventilator is in Position 2.

(*b*) Where the coaming for any ventilator referred to in sub-paragraph (*a*) is situated in a position in which it will be particularly subjected to weather and sea the height of the coaming shall exceed the relevant minimum height above specified by such amount as is necessary to provide adequate protection having regard to its position.

(2) If the coaming of any ventilator referred to in the preceding sub-paragraph exceeds 900 millimetres in height above the deck it shall be efficiently supported by stays, brackets or other means.

(3) Every ventilator in Position 1 or Position 2 which passes through a superstructure other than an enclosed superstructure shall have a coaming of steel or equivalent material at the freeboard deck, substantially constructed and efficiently connected to that deck and at least 900 millimetres in height above that deck.

(4) Subject to the following sub-paragraph, every ventilator opening in Position 1 or Position 2 shall be provided with an efficient appliance by which it can be closed and secured weathertight. Every such closing appliance so provided on board a ship of not more than 100 metres in length shall be permanently attached to, and in the case of any other ship shall either be so attached or be conveniently stowed near to, the ventilator for which it is provided.

(5)(*a*) A ventilator in Position 1 the coaming of which exceeds 4·5 metres in height above the deck, and a ventilator in Position 2 the coaming of which exceeds 2·3 metres in height above the deck, need not be fitted with a closing appliance unless either—

(i) it serves the machinery spaces or a cargo compartment, or

(ii) the fitting of such an appliance is necessary in the circumstances in order to provide adequate protection.

(*b*) A ventilator in Position 1 or Position 2 leading to space in a battery room shall not be fitted with a closing appliance.

Air pipes

10.—(1) The exposed parts of any air pipe leading to a ballast or other tank and extending above the freeboard deck or a superstructure deck shall be of substantial construction.

(2) The exposed opening of any such air pipe shall be fitted with efficient means of closing the opening weathertight, which shall be permanently attached in a position ready for immediate use.

(3) Subject to sub-paragraph (4), the height above deck of the exposed opening of any such airpipe shall be—

(*a*) at least 760 millimetres if that deck is the freeboard deck;

(*b*) if that deck is a superstructure deck, at least 450 millimetres or, if the superstructure is of less than standard height, such greater height as is necessary to provide adequate protection having regard to the lower height of the superstructure.

(4) The height described in the preceding sub-paragraph may in any particular case be lower than the minimum specified in relation thereto in that sub-paragraph if—

(*a*) the working of the ship would be unreasonably interfered with if such minimum heights were adhered to, and

(*b*) the closing arrangements are such as to ensure that such lower height is adequate in the circumstances.

Cargo ports and similar openings

11.—(1) Cargo ports and similar openings in the ship's side below the freeboard deck or in the sides or ends of superstructures which form part of the shell of the ship shall be compatible with the design of the ship and shall not exceed in number those necessary for the proper working of the ship.

(2) Every such cargo port and opening shall be provided with a door or doors so fitted and designed as to ensure watertightness and structural integrity commensurate with the surrounding shell plating.

(3) No such cargo port or opening below the freeboard deck shall, unless the Board otherwise consents, be so situated that when load lines have been marked on the ship's side the lower edge of the port or opening will be below a line drawn parallel to the freeboard deck at side having as its lowest point the upper edge of the uppermost load line.

Scuppers, inlets and discharges

3121 12.—(1) Every discharge led through the shell of a ship either—

(*a*) from spaces below the freeboard deck, or

(*b*) from within any enclosed superstructure, or from within any deckhouse on the freeboard deck which is fitted with weathertight doors,

shall be fitted in accordance with sub-paragraphs (2) and (3) with efficient means for preventing water from passing inboard.

(2) Subject to sub-paragraph (3), such means shall consist of a single automatic non-return valve fitted at the shell of the ship and having positive means of closure from a position or positions above the freeboard deck. Such positions shall be readily accessible at all times under service conditions and shall be provided with an indicator showing whether the valve is open or closed.

(3)(*a*) If when load lines are marked on the ship's side the vertical distance from the Summer load waterline to the inboard end of a discharge pipe will exceed 0·01(L), such means may consist of two automatic non-return valves having no positive means of closure, one of which shall be situated as close to the ship's shell as practicable and be substantially connected thereto and the inboard one of which is so situated that it will at all times under service conditions be readily accessible for examination.

(*b*) Where the vertical distance referred to in sub-paragraph (*a*) will exceed 0·02(L) such means may consist, if in the circumstances the following would be equally effective, of a single automatic non-return valve having no positive means of closure, situated as close to the ship's shell as practicable and substantially connected thereto.

(4)(*a*) The controls of any valve situated in a manned machinery space, and serving a main or auxiliary sea inlet or discharge or bilge injection system shall be so sited as to be readily accessible at all times under service conditions. Valves referred to in this and the following sub-paragraph shall be equipped with an indicator showing whether the valve is open or closed.

(*b*) The controls of any valve situated in an unattended machinery space and serving a sea inlet or discharge or bilge injection system shall be so sited as to be readily accessible at all times under service conditions, particular attention being paid in this regard to possible delay in reaching or operating the controls. In addition, the machinery space in which the valve is situated shall be equipped with an efficient warning device to give warning at suitable control positions of any entry of water into the machinery space other than water resulting from the normal operation of the machinery.

(*c*) In this sub-paragraph "unattended machinery space" means a machinery space which during the normal operation of the ship at sea is unmanned for any period, and "manned machinery space" means a machinery space other than an unattended machinery space.

(5) Every scupper and discharge pipe originating at any level and penetrating the shell of the ship either—

(*a*) more than 450 millimetres below the freeboard deck, or

(*b*) less than 600 millimetres above the Summer load waterline

shall be equipped with an automatic non-return valve situated as close to the ship's shell as practicable and substantially connected thereto:

Provided that this paragraph shall not apply—

(i) where the scupper or discharge pipe is fitted with means for preventing water from passing inboard in accordance with the provisions of sub-paragraphs (1) to (3); or

(ii) in any case in which the piping of the scupper or discharge pipe is of substantial thickness.

(6) Every scupper leading from a superstructure other than an enclosed superstructure or from a deckhouse not fitted with weathertight doors shall be led overboard.

(7) All valves and shell fittings required by the provisions of this paragraph shall be of steel, bronze or other suitable ductile material, and all pipes referred to in this paragraph shall be of steel or equivalent material.

Side Scuttles

13.—(1) Every side scuttle to space below the freeboard deck or to space within an enclosed superstructure shall be fitted with a hinged inside deadlight by which it can be effectively closed and secured watertight.

(2) No side scuttle shall be fitted in a position such that its sill, when load lines have been marked on the ship's side, will be below a line drawn parallel to the freeboard deck at side having as its lowest point—

(*a*) 2·5 per cent. of the breadth of the ship (B) above the Summer load line, or

(*b*) 500 millimetres above the Summer load line,

whichever is the greater.

(3) Every side scuttle, deadlight and glass (if fitted) shall be of substantial construction and be efficiently fitted.

Freeing ports and arrangements

14.—(1) Where bulwarks on the weather portions of the freeboard deck, a raised quarter deck or a superstructure deck form wells, efficient provision shall be made for rapidly freeing the decks of water in bulk and for draining them, and in particular the requirements set out in sub-paragraphs (2) to (7) below shall be complied with.

(2) Except as otherwise provided in sub-paragraphs (3) and (4), the sum of the areas of the openings of freeing ports on each side of the ship for each such well (hereafter referred to in this paragraph as "the freeing port area" and by the symbol "(A)") shall—

(*a*) if the well is on the freeboard deck or on a raised quarter deck be not less than the area ascertained in accordance with the following formula, and

(*b*) if the well is on a superstructure deck other than a raised quarter deck be not less than one half of that area:—

Formula

(i) Where the length of a bulwark (*l*) in the well is 20 metres or less

(A)=0·7+0·035 (*l*) (square metres); and where (*l*) exceeds 20 metres, (A)=0·07 (*l*) (square metres).

(*l*) need in no case be taken as greater than 0·7(L).

(ii) If the bulwark is more than 1·2 metres in average height the required area shall be increased by 0·004 square metres per metre of length of well for each 0·1 metre difference in height. If the bulwark is less than 0·9 metre in average height, the required area may be decreased by 0·004 square metre per metre of length of well for each 0·1 metre difference in height.

(3)(*a*) If the deck on which the well is situated has no sheer, the area (A) shall be the area ascertained in accordance with sub-paragraph (2) increased by 50 per cent.

(*b*) If the deck on which the well is situated has sheer less than standard sheer, the area (A) shall be the area ascertained in accordance with subparagraph (2) increased by a percentage to be obtained by linear interpolation.

(*c*) If the deck on which the well is situated has sheer, two thirds of the freeing port area (A) shall be situated in the half of the well which is nearest to the lowest point of the sheer.

(4) The lower edge of every freeing port shall be as near to the deck as practicable.

(5) Every freeing port more than 230 millimetres in depth shall be protected by rails or bars so fixed that the distance between the lowest rail or bar and the lower edge of the freeing port does not exceed 230 millimetres.

(6) Every freeing port which is fitted with a shutter shall have sufficient clearance to prevent jamming of the shutter, and the shutter hinges shall have pins or bearings of efficient non-corrodible material.

(7) Efficient provision shall be made for freeing from water any superstructure other than an enclosed superstructure.

Protection of the Crew

3122 15.—(1) Every deckhouse used for the accommodation of members of the crew shall be of efficient construction.

(2) Except as otherwise provided in sub-paragraph (3), all exposed parts of the freeboard deck and of every superstructure deck shall be fitted at their perimeter either with efficient guard rails or guard wires and stanchions complying with the requirements of sub-paragraph (4) or with bulwarks, being in either case at least 1 metre in height from the deck at side.

(3) The height specified in relation to guard rails or guard wires and bulwarks in sub-paragraph (2) may be reduced at any particular point if—

(*a*) the working of the ship would be unreasonably interfered with if such minimum height were adhered to at that point, and

(*b*) adequate protection is provided at that point.

(4) Guard rails or guard wires fitted pursuant to sub-paragraph (2) shall consist of courses of rails or wires supported by stanchions efficiently secured to the deck. The opening between the lowest course of the rails or wires and the deck shall not exceed 230 millimetres in height, and no opening above that course of rails or wires shall exceed 380 millimetres in height. Where the ship has rounded gunwales the stanchions shall be secured at the perimeter of the flat of the deck.

(5) Gangways, underdeck passages and all other means of access by which members of the crew pass between their quarters, the machinery space and any other space in the ship used by them in the course of their necessary work about the ship shall be so designed and constructed, and be fitted where necessary with such life lines, access ladders, guard rails or guard wires, hand rails or other safety fittings, as to afford effective protection for the crew.

(6) The requirements of this paragraph shall not apply in the case of unmanned barges.

Part II

Special Requirements Applicable to Type "A" Ships

Application

3123 16. The requirements of paragraphs 17 to 20 of this Part apply in the case of Type "A" ships only.

Machinery casings

17. Every casing enclosing a machinery space opening in Position 1 or Position 2 shall be protected by either—

(1) an enclosed poop or bridge of at least standard height, or

(2) a deckhouse of equal height and equivalent strength and weathertightness:

Provided that this requirement shall not apply and the casing may accordingly be exposed—

(*a*) if there is no opening in the casing which gives direct access from the freeboard deck to the machinery space; or

(*b*) if the only opening in the casing has a steel weathertight door and leads to a space or passageway which is as strongly constructed as the casing and is separated from the stairway to the machinery space by a second steel weathertight door.

Gangway and access

18.—(1) References in this paragraph to a poop or detached bridge include references to a deckhouse fitted in lieu of and serving the purpose of a poop or detached bridge.

(2) Access between the poop and the detached bridge shall be by means of either—

(*a*) a permanent and efficiently constructed gangway of substantial strength connecting those structures. The gangway shall be at the level of the superstructure deck and have a platform at least 1 metre in width and of non-slip material. Efficient means of access from gangway level to the deck shall be provided at each terminal point. The platform shall be fitted at each side throughout its length with guard rails or guard wires supported by stanchions. Such rails or wires shall consist of not less than 3 courses, the lowest being not more than 230 millimetres, and the uppermost being at least 1 metre, above the platform, and no intermediate opening being more than 380 millimetres in height. Stanchions shall be at intervals of not more than 1·5 metres;

or (*b*) an underdeck passage connecting and providing unobstructed access between those structures and complying with the requirements of sub-paragraph (3);

or (*c*) equivalent means of access.

(3) An underdeck passage provided pursuant to sub-paragraph (2)(*b*) shall comply with the following requirements:—

(*a*) the passage and all fittings therein shall be oil and gas tight;

(*b*) the passage shall be well lighted, and be fitted with efficient gas detection and ventilation systems;

(*c*) it shall be situated immediately below the freeboard deck;

(*d*) its distance from the shell plating shall at no point throughout its length be less than one fifth of the breadth (B) of the ship:

Provided that in the case of a ship so designed as to render compliance with this requirement not reasonably practicable, two underdeck passages may be provided one to port and one to starboard each of which shall comply with all requirements of this paragraph except this requirement;

(*e*) means of exit from the passage to the freeboard deck shall be—

(i) so arranged as to be as near as practicable to the working areas to be used by the crew,

(ii) in no case be more than 90 metres apart, and

(iii) fitted with efficient means of closing which are capable of quick release and operable from either side;

(*f*) openings in the freeboard deck corresponding to the means of exit referred to in sub-paragraph (*e*) shall be protected in accordance with the requirements of paragraph 8(2)(*a*).

(4) In the case of a ship the crew of which may in the course of their duties be required to go in adverse weather conditions to a position or positions forward of the detached bridge, or forward of the poop in cases where there is no detached bridge and all crew accommodation and machinery spaces are situated at the after end of the ship, access to such positions shall be by means of either—

(*a*) a gangway complying with the requirements of sub-paragraph (2)(*a*), or

(*b*) an underdeck passage complying with the requirements of sub-paragraph (3), or

(*c*) a walkway complying with the requirements of sub-paragraph (5).

(5) A walkway provided pursuant to sub-paragraph (4)(*c*) shall—

(*a*) be not less than 1 metre in width and be situated on or as near as practicable to the centre line of the ship;

(*b*) be fitted at each side throughout its length with guard rails or guard wires complying with the requirements set out in relation to such rails or wires in sub-paragraph (2)(*a*);

(*c*) have openings giving free access to and from the freeboard deck, set in such guard rails or guard wires as near as practicable to the working areas to be used by the crew, so however that such openings shall be on alternate sides of the walkway and be situated not more than 90 metres apart on either side;

(*d*) if the length of exposed deck to be traversed exceeds 70 metres, have shelters of substantial construction set in way of the walkway at intervals not exceeding 45 metres, every such shelter being capable of accommodating at least one person and so constructed as to afford weather protection on the forward, port and starboard sides;

(*e*) if obstructed by pipes or other fittings of a permanent nature, be provided with efficient means of passage over such obstruction.

(6) The requirements of this paragraph shall not apply in the case of unmanned barges.

Hatchway covers

3124 19. The covers of hatchways in an exposed position on the freeboard deck, on a forecastle deck or on the top of an expansion trunk shall be of steel, of efficient construction, and watertight when secured.

Freeing arrangements

20.—(1) All exposed parts of the freeboard deck and superstructure decks shall be fitted at their perimeter for at least half their length with guard rails or guard wires in lieu of bulwarks or with other equally effective freeing arrangements. Such guard rails or guard wires shall comply with the requirements set out in relation to such rails or wires in paragraph 18(2)(*a*).

(2) The upper edge of the sheer strake shall be as low as practicable.

(3) If superstructures of the ship are connected by a trunk, the exposed parts of the freeboard deck in way of the trunk shall be fitted at their perimeter throughout their length with guard rails or guard wires complying with the requirements set out in relation to such rails or wires in paragraph 18(2)(*a*).

(4) If the ship is so constructed that notwithstanding the provision of freeing ports and arrangements it will be particularly subjected under service conditions to the building up of quantities of water on the freeboard deck, efficient breakwaters shall be fitted in suitable positions on that deck.

PART III

SPECIAL REQUIREMENTS APPLICABLE TO CERTAIN TYPE "B" SHIPS

Application

21. The requirements of paragraphs 22 to 25 apply only in the case of Type "B" ships to be assigned a reduced freeboard under the provisions of paragraph 5(3) of Schedule 5.

Gangway and access

22. The ship shall comply with the requirements of either—

(1) paragraph 18 as if it were a Type "A" ship, or

(2) paragraphs 23 and 24.

23.—(1) References in this paragraph to a poop or detached bridge include references to a deckhouse fitted in lieu of and serving the purpose of a poop or detached bridge.

(2) Access between the poop and the detached bridge shall be by means of an efficiently constructed gangway of substantial strength connecting those structures, fitted on or near the centre line of the ship. The gangway shall be at least 1 metre in width and shall be fitted at each side throughout its length with guard rails or guard wires complying with the requirements set out in relation to such rails or wires in paragraph 18(2)(*a*). If the length of the gangway exceeds 70 metres, shelters complying with the requirements set out in relation to shelters in paragraph 18(5)(*d*) shall be provided in way of the gangway.

24. In the case of a ship the crew of which may in the course of their duties be required to go in adverse weather conditions to a position or positions forward of the detached bridge, or forward of the poop in cases where there is no detached bridge and all crew accommodation and machinery spaces are situated at the after end of the ship, access to such positions shall be—

(1) by the means described in paragraph 18(4), or

(2) by the means described in paragraph 23(2), or

(3) equivalent means of access:

Provided that in the case of a ship the hatchway coamings of which are 600 millimetres or more in height from the deck, two walkways giving access to the said positions and complying with the following requirements may be provided:—

(i) the walkways shall be efficiently constructed and of satisfactory strength;

(ii) the walkways shall each be at least 1 metre in width and shall be fitted on the freeboard deck alongside the outboard structure of the hatchway coamings, one to port and the other to starboard of the hatchways;

(iii) each walkway shall be fitted on the side outboard of the hatchways with guard rails or guard wires complying with the requirements set out in relation to such rails or wires in paragraph 18(2)(*a*).

Freeing arrangements

25. The ship shall comply with the requirements of paragraph 20(4).

3126 **PART IV**

SPECIAL REQUIREMENTS APPLICABLE TO SHIPS TO BE ASSIGNED TIMBER FREEBOARDS

Application

26. The requirements of paragraphs 27 to 29 of this Part apply only in the case of ships to be assigned Timber freeboards.

Superstructures

27.—(1) The ship shall have a forecastle of not less than the standard height of an enclosed superstructure and not less in length than 0·07(L).

(2) If the ship is less than 100 metres in length it shall be fitted aft with either—

(i) a poop of not less than standard height, or

(ii) a raised quarter deck having either a deck house or a strong steel hood, so that the total height thereof is not less than the standard height of an enclosed superstructure.

Double Bottom Tanks

28. Double bottom tanks where fitted within the midship half length of the ship shall have satisfactory watertight longitudinal subdivision.

Bulwarks, guard rails and stanchions

29. The ship shall be fitted with either—

(1) permanent bulwarks at least 1 metre in height which are specially stiffened on the upper edge and supported by strong bulwark stays attached to the deck, and are provided with freeing ports complying with the requirements of paragraph 14(1) to (6), or

(2) efficient guard rails and stanchions at least 1 metre in height, of specially strong construction, and complying with the requirements of paragraph 15(4).

PART V

GENERAL

Equivalent or exceptional provision

30. The Assigning Authority may with the approval of the [Department]—

(1) allow any fitting, material, appliance or apparatus to be fitted in a ship, or allow other provision to be made in a ship, in the place of any fitting, material, appliance, apparatus or provision respectively which is required under any of the provisions of this Schedule, if satisfied by trial thereof or otherwise that it is at least as effective as that so required; or

(2) allow in any exceptional case departures from the requirements of any of the said provisions on condition that the freeboards to be assigned to the ship are increased to such an extent as to satisfy the [Department] that the safety of the ship and protection afforded to the crew will be no less effective than would be the case if the ship fully complied with those requirements and there were no such increase of freeboards.

SCHEDULE 5

FREEBOARDS

(Rule 27)

Interpretation

1. In this Schedule expressions defined in Schedule 4 have the meanings thereby assigned to them respectively, and—

"block coefficient" or the symbol "(C_b)" in relation to a ship means the product of—

$$\frac{\nabla}{L.Bd_1}$$

where—

∇ is the volume of the moulded displacement of the ship (excluding bossing) if the ship has a metal shell, and of displacement to the outer surface of the hull if the ship has a shell of any other material, displacement being taken in each case at a moulded draught of d_1, and

d_1 is 85 per cent of the least moulded depth;

provided that in no case shall the block coefficient (C_b) be taken to be less than 0·68;

"depth for freeboard" and the symbol "(D)" in relation to a ship—

(*a*) means, except as otherwise stated in sub-paragraph (*b*), the moulded depth of the ship amidships plus the thickness of the freeboard deck stringer plate where fitted, plus, if the exposed freeboard deck is sheathed, the product of $\frac{T((L)—(S))}{(L)}$ where T is the mean thickness of the exposed sheathing clear of deck openings;

(*b*) in the case of a ship having a rounded gunwale with a radius greater than 4 per cent of the breadth of the ship (B) or having topsides of unusual form, means the depth, calculated in accordance with sub-paragraph (*a*), which would be the depth for freeboard purposes of a ship having a midship section with vertical topsides and with the same round of beam and the same area of topside section as that of the midship section of the first mentioned ship;

"effective length "and the symbol "(E)" in relation to a superstructure means the effective length of the superstructure ascertained in accordance with the provisions of paragraph 9 of this Schedule;

"flush deck ship" means a ship which has no superstructure on the freeboard deck;

"length" and the symbol "(S)" in relation to a superstructure means the length of the superstructure ascertained in accordance with the provisions of paragraph 9 of this Schedule;

"moulded depth" in relation to a ship means the vertical distance measured from the top of the keel to the top of the freeboard deck beam at side;

Provided that—

(*a*) in the case of a wood or composite ship, it shall be measured from the lower edge of the keel rabbet;

(*b*) if the form at the lower part of the midship section of the ship is of a hollow character, or if thick garboards are fitted, it shall be measured from the point where the line of the flat of the bottom continued inwards cuts the side of the keel;

(*c*) in the case of a ship having rounded gunwales, it shall be measured to the point of intersection of the moulded lines of the deck and side shell plating, the lines extending as though the gunwale were of angular design;

(*d*) if the freeboard deck is stepped and the raised part of the deck extends over the point at which the moulded depth is to be determined, it shall be measured to a line of reference extending from the lower part of the deck along a line parallel to the raised part of the deck.

"summer draught" in relation to a ship means the draught measured from—

(*a*) in the case of a wood or composite ship, the lower edge of the keel rabbet;

(*b*) if the form at the lower part of the midship section is of a hollow character, or if thick garboards are fitted, the point where the line of the flat of the bottom continued inwards cuts the side of the keel, and

(*c*) in any other case from the top of the keel,

to the point which when load lines and marks have been marked on the ship's side will correspond to the centre of the ring of the load line mark;

"summer timber draught" in relation to a ship means the draught measured from point (*a*), (*b*) or (*c*) described in the preceding definition to the point which when timber load lines have been marked on the ship's side will correspond to the upper edge of the Summer Timber load line;

"tabular freeboard" means in the case of a Type "A" ship the freeboard appropriate to the ship's length under Freeboard Table A set out in Schedule 6 to these Rules and in the case of a Type "B" ship the freeboard appropriate to the ship's length under Freeboard Table B in that Schedule.

Freeboards: general

2.—(1) Except as otherwise provided in sub-paragraphs (2) and (3), the freeboards to be assigned to a ship other than Timber freeboards shall be determined in accordance with the provisions of Part I of this Schedule, and Timber freeboards to be assigned to a ship shall be determined in accordance with Part II.

(2) Freeboards determined as described in sub-paragraph (1) are the freeboards appropriate to ships the structural strength of which complies with the highest standard required by an Assigning Authority; and the freeboards to be assigned to ships the structural strength of which does not comply with that standard shall be freeboards so determined but increased in each case by such amount as the Assigning Authority with the approval of the Board may determine as appropriate to the ship's structural strength.

(3) The freeboards to be assigned to—

sailing ships;
tugs;
ships of wood or of composite construction or of other materials;
ships with constructional features such as to render freeboards determined as described in sub-paragraph (1) unreasonable or impracticable; and
unmanned barges having on the freeboard deck only small access openings closed by watertight gasketed covers of steel,

shall be determined in accordance with the provisions of Part III of this Schedule.

3128

PART I

FREEBOARDS OTHER THAN TIMBER FREEBOARDS

Determination of freeboards

3.—(1) The Summer freeboard shall be determined in accordance with the provisions of paragraphs 4 to 16 of this Schedule:

Provided that the freeboard so obtained but omitting any correction made for deck-line as provided in paragraph 8 shall be not less than 50 millimetres except in the case of a ship with hatchways in Position 1 to which paragraph 5 of Schedule 4 applies but which do not have pontoon covers, in which case it shall be not less than 150 millimetres.

(2) The Tropical freeboard shall be obtained by deducting from the Summer freeboard applicable to the ship one forty-eighth (1/48th) of the summer draught of the ship:

Provided that the freeboard so obtained but omitting any correction made for deck-line as provided in paragraph 8 shall be not less than 50 millimetres except in the case of a ship with hatchways in Position 1 to which paragraph 5 of Schedule 4 applies but which do not have pontoon covers, in which case it shall be not less than 150 millimetres.

(3) The Winter freeboard shall be obtained by adding to the Summer freeboard applicable to the ship one forty-eighth (1/48th) of the summer draught of the ship.

(4) The Winter North Atlantic freeboard shall be obtained by adding to the Winter freeboard applicable to the ship a distance of 50 millimetres.

(5)(*a*) The Fresh Water freeboard shall, subject to sub-paragraph (*b*), be obtained by deducting from the Summer freeboard the quantity—

$$\frac{\Delta}{4T} \text{ millimetres}$$

where Δ is the displacement in salt water in metric tons at the Summer load waterline, and T represents metric tons per centimetre immersion in salt water at that waterline.

(*b*) In any case in which the displacement at that waterline cannot be ascertained the deduction shall be one forty-eighth (1/48th) of the summer draught of the ship.

Summer freeboard: Type "A" ships

29 4. The Summer freeboard to be assigned to a Type "A" ship shall be determined as follows:—

(1) There shall first be ascertained the ship's tabular freeboard.

(2) If the block coefficient (C_b) of the ship exceeds 0·68 the tabular freeboard shall be multiplied by the factor $\frac{(C_b)+0{\cdot}68}{1{\cdot}36}$.

(3) Corrections in accordance with paragraphs 6 to 16 of this Schedule shall be applied to the freeboard ascertained in accordance with sub-paragraphs (1) and (2).

(4) Subject to the proviso to paragraph 3(1), the freeboard so corrected shall be the Summer freeboard to be assigned to the ship.

Summer freeboard: Type "B" ships

5. The Summer freeboard to be assigned to a Type "B" ship shall be determined as follows:—

(1) There shall first be ascertained the ship's tabular freeboard.

(2)(*a*) If the ship has hatchways in Position 1 the covers of which are either (i) pontoon covers complying with the requirements of paragraph 5 (4)of Schedule 4 or (ii) covers which comply with those of paragraph 6 of that Schedule, the tabular freeboard may be corrected in accordance with such of the provisions of sub-paragraphs (3) to (7) of this paragraph as are applicable to the ship.

(*b*) If the ship has hatchways in Position 1 the covers of which comply with the requirements of paragraph 5 of Schedule 4 except those of sub-paragraph(4) of that paragraph, the tabular freeboard shall be corrected in accordance with the provisions of sub-paragraph (8) of this paragraph.

(3) The tabular freeboard of a ship to which sub-paragraph (2)(*a*) applies and which exceeds 100 metres in length may be reduced by an amount not exceeding the maximum applicable under sub-paragraphs (4) and (5) if the Assigning Authority is satisfied that—

(*a*) the measures for the protection of the crew comply with the requirements of paragraph 15 of Schedule 4;

(*b*) the freeing arrangements comply with the requirements of paragraph 14 of Schedule 4;

(*c*) all covers of hatchways in Positions 1 and 2 comply with the requirements of paragraph 6 of Schedule 4;

(*d*) the ship when loaded to the Summer load waterline will remain afloat, after the flooding of any single damaged compartment other than the machinery space at an assumed permeability of 0·95, in the condition of equilibrium described in sub-paragraph (6):

Provided that if the length of the ship exceeds 225 metres the machinery space shall rank as a floodable compartment for the purposes of this requirement having for the purpose an assumed permeability of 0·85.

(4) Subject to sub-paragraph (5) no reduction of freeboard pursuant to sub-paragraph (3) shall exceed 60 per cent of the difference between the tabular freeboards appropriate to the ship's length under Freeboard Table A and Freeboard Table B.

(5) The reduction of 60 per cent referred to in the preceding paragraph may be increased to 100 per cent if the Assigning Authority is satisfied that—

(*a*) the ship complies with the requirements of paragraphs 17 and 20 of Schedule 4 as if it were a Type "A" ship and with those of paragraph 22 of that Schedule;

(*b*) the ship complies with the requirements of sub-paragraph (3)(*a*) to (*c*); and

(*c*) the ship when loaded to the Summer load waterline will remain afloat in the condition of equilibrium described in sub-paragraph (6) after the flooding—

(i) of any two compartments adjacent fore and aft, neither of which is the machinery space, at an assumed permeability of 0·95, and

(ii) in the case of a ship exceeding 225 metres in length, of the machinery space alone, at an assumed permeability of 0·85.

(6) The condition of equilibrium referred to in sub-paragraphs (3) and (5) above is as follows:—

(*a*) the final waterline after flooding is below the top of any ventilator coaming, the lower edge of any air pipe opening, the upper edge of the sill of any access opening fitted with a weathertight door, and the lower edge of any other opening through which progressive flooding may take place;

(*b*) the angle of heel due to unsymmetrical flooding does not exceed 15 degrees;

(*c*) the metacentric height calculated using the constant displacement method has a positive value of at least 50 millimetres in the upright condition after flooding; and

(*d*) the ship has adequate residual stability.

(7) The following assumptions shall be made for the purposes of calculations pursuant to sub-paragraphs (3)(*d*) and (5)(*c*):—

(*a*) that the vertical extent of damage is equal to the depth of the ship at the point of damage, measured from and including the freeboard deck at side to the underside of the keel;

(*b*) that the transverse penetration of damage is not more than one fifth of the breadth of the ship (B), this distance being measured inboard from the ship's side at right angles to the centre line of the ship at the level of the Summer load waterline:

Provided that if damage of a lesser extent results in a more severe condition, such lesser extent shall be assumed;

(*c*) that, except in the case of compartments referred to in sub-paragraph (5)(*c*)(i), no main transverse bulkhead is damaged;

(*d*) that the height of the centre of gravity above the base-line is assessed allowing for homogeneous loading of cargo holds and for 50 per cent. of the designed capacity of consumable fluids and stores.

(8) The tabular freeboard of a ship to which sub-paragraph (2)(*b*) of this paragraph applies shall be increased by the amount shown by the following Table to be approriate to the ship's length:—

TABLE

Length of ship (metres)	Freeboard increase (millimetres)	Length of ship (metres)	Freeboard increase (millimetres)	Length of ship (metres)	Freeboard increase (millimetres)
108 and below	50	139	175	170	290
109	52	140	181	171	292
110	55	141	186	172	294
111	57	142	191	173	297
112	59	143	196	174	299
113	62	144	201	175	301
114	64	145	206	176	304
115	68	146	210	177	306
116	70	147	215	178	308
117	73	148	219	179	311
118	76	149	224	180	313
119	80	150	228	181	315
120	84	151	232	182	318
121	87	152	236	183	320
122	91	153	240	184	322
123	95	154	244	185	325
124	99	155	247	186	327
125	103	156	251	187	329
126	108	157	254	188	332
127	112	158	258	189	334
128	116	159	261	190	336
129	121	160	264	191	339
130	126	161	267	192	341
131	131	162	270	193	343
132	136	163	273	194	346
133	142	164	275	195	348
134	147	165	278	196	350
135	153	166	280	197	353
136	159	167	283	198	355
137	164	168	285	199	357
138	170	169	287	200	358

Freeboards at intermediate lengths of ship shall be obtained by linear interpolation. The increase in the case of ships of more than 200 metres in length shall be such amount as the [Department] may determine in each particular case.

(9)(*a*) This sub-paragraph applies to every Type "B" ship of not more than 100 metres in length having enclosed superstructures the total effective length of which does not exceed 35 per cent. of the ship's length (L).

(*b*) the freeboard calculated in respect of such a ship in accordance with sub-paragraphs (1), (2) and (8) above shall be increased by an amount ascertained in accordance with the formula $7{\cdot}5\left(100-(L)\right)\left(0{\cdot}35-\frac{(E)}{(L)}\right)$ millimetres.

(10) In the case of a ship the block coefficient (C_b) of which exceeds 0·68 the freeboard calculated in respect of the ship in accordance with sub-paragraphs (1) to (9) above shall be multiplied by the factor $\frac{(C_b)+0{\cdot}68}{1{\cdot}36}$

(11) Corrections in accordance with paragraphs 6 to 16 of this Schedule shall be applied to the freeboard ascertained in accordance with sub-paragraphs (1) to (10) above and subject to the proviso to paragraph 3(1) the freeboard so corrected shall be the Summer freeboard to be assigned to the ship.

Basic freeboard

6. In the following paragraphs of this Schedule "basic freeboard" in relation to a ship means the Summer freeboard calculated for the ship in accordance with paragraph 4 or 5 whichever is applicable, but omitting in the case of a Type "A" ship the corrections referred to in paragraph 4(3) and in the case of a Type "B" ship the corrections referred to in paragraph 5(11).

Correction for Depth

3130 7.—(1) If the depth for freeboard (D) of a ship exceeds $\frac{(L)}{15}$, the basic freeboard of the ship shall be increased by $\left((D)-\frac{(L)}{15}\right)$ R millimetres, R for this purpose being taken to be $\frac{(L)}{0\cdot48}$ in the case of a ship less than 120 metres in length, and 250 in the case of a ship of 120 metres or more in length.

(2) If the depth for freeboard (D) of a ship is less than $\frac{(L)}{15}$, the basic freeboard of the ship shall be reduced by $\left((D)-\frac{(L)}{15}\right)$ R millimetres if, but only if, the ship has either (*a*) an enclosed superstructure covering at least 0·6 (L) amidships, or (*b*) an efficient trunk extending for the ship's length (L), or (*c*) a combination of enclosed superstructures connected by efficient trunks, being a combination extending for the ship's length (L):

Provided that if the height of any such superstructure or trunk is less than standard height the amount of such reduction shall be reduced in the ratio of the actual to the standard height of the superstructure or trunk.

Correction for position of deck-line

8. If the actual depth to the upper edge of the deck-line is greater or less than the depth for freeboard (D), the difference if greater shall be added to, or if less shall be deducted from, the basic freeboard of the ship:

Provided that in a case in which the position of the deck-line has been fixed in accordance with the provisions of Rule 14(3), the actual depth of the ship shall be taken for the purposes of the foregoing requirement to the point amidships where the continuation outwards of the upper surface of the freeboard deck or of any sheathing of that deck intersects the outer surface of the shell of the ship.

Standard height, length and effective length of superstructures

9.—(1) The standard height of a superstructure shall be the height appropriate to the ship's length (L) determined in accordance with the following Table:—

Length of ship (L) (metres)	Standard Height (metres)	
	of a raised quarter deck	of a superstructure other than a raised quarter deck
30 or less	0·90	1·80
75	1·20	1·80
125 or more	1·80	2·30

Standard heights for intermediate lengths of ship shall be obtained by linear interpolation.

(2)(*a*) Subject to sub-paragraph (*b*), the length of a superstructure (S) shall be the mean length of the parts of the superstructure which lie within the length of the ship (L).

(*b*) In the case of an enclosed superstructure having an end bulkhead which extends in a fair convex curve beyond its intersection with the superstructure sides, the length of the superstructure (S) may be taken as its length ascertained in accordance with sub-paragraph (*a*) increased on the basis of an equivalent plane bulkhead by the amount of two-thirds of the fore and aft extent of the curvature:

Provided that the amount of the curvature to be taken into account shall not exceed one half the breadth of the superstructure at the point of intersection of the curved end of the superstructure with its side.

(3) The effective length of a superstructure (E) shall be as follows:—

(*a*) Subject to sub-paragraph (*c*), (E) in the case of an enclosed superstructure of standard height shall be either—

(i) its length (S), or

(ii) if the superstructure is set in from the sides of the ship, its length (S) modified in the ratio b/Bs, where—

"b" is the breadth of the superstructure at the middle of its length (S) and

"Bs" is the breadth of the ship at the middle of the length of the superstructure (S):

Provided that if the superstructure is so set in for part only of its length, such modification shall be applied only to that part.

(*b*) Subject to sub-paragraph (*c*), (E) in the case of an enclosed superstructure of less than standard height shall be its length (S) reduced in the ratio of the actual height of the superstructure to its standard height.

(*c*) (E) in the case of an enclosed superstructure consisting of a raised quarter deck shall, if the deck is fitted with an intact front bulkhead, be its length (S) subject to a maximum of 0·6 of the ship's length (L); and if not so fitted, be ascertained by treating the raised quarter deck as a poop of less than standard height.

(*d*) A superstructure which is not an enclosed superstructure shall have no effective length.

Standard height and effective length of trunks

131 10.—(1) The standard height of a trunk shall be determined in the same manner as that applicable to a superstructure other than a raised quarter deck under paragraph 9(1).

(2) The effective length of a trunk shall be determined as follows:—

(*a*) A trunk which is not an efficient trunk as described in sub-paragraph (*b*) shall have no effective length.

(*b*) A trunk shall be treated as an efficient trunk subject to the following conditions:—

(i) that it shall be at least as strong as a superstructure;

(ii) that the hatchways in way of the trunk are in the trunk deck, and the hatchway coamings and covers comply with the requirements of paragraphs 4 to 6 of Schedule 4:

Provided that small access openings with watertight covers may be permitted in the freeboard deck;

(iii) that the width of the trunk deck stringer provides a satisfactory gangway and sufficient lateral stiffness;

(iv) that a permanent working platform fore and aft fitted with guard rails or guard wires complying with the requirements applicable thereto under paragraph 18(2)(*a*) of Schedule 4 is provided by the trunk deck, or by detached trunks connected to superstructures by efficient permanent gangways;

(v) that ventilators are protected by the trunk, by watertight covers or by equivalent means;

(vi) that open rails or wires are fitted on the weather parts of the freeboard deck in way of the trunk for at least half their length;

(vii) that the machinery casings are protected by the trunk, or by an enclosed superstructure of at least standard height, or by a deckhouse of the same height and of strength and weathertightness equivalent to those of such a superstructure;

(viii) that the breadth of the trunk is at least 60 per cent of the breadth of the ship (B);

(ix) that where there is no superstructure the length of the trunk is at least 0·6(L).

(*c*) Except as otherwise provided in sub-paragraph (*d*), the effective length of an efficient trunk shall be its full length reduced in the ratio of its mean breadth to the breadth of the ship (B).

(*d*) If the actual height of an efficient trunk is less than the standard height, its effective length shall be the length calculated in accordance with sub-paragraph (*c*) reduced in the ratio of the actual to the standard height of the trunk. In addition, if the ship is a Type "B" ship and the height of hatchway coamings on the trunk deck is less than that required by paragraph 5(1) or 6(1) of Schedule 4 a reduction from the actual height of the trunk shall be made of an amount corresponding to the difference between the actual height of such coamings and the height so required for them.

Deduction for effective length of Superstructures and Trunks

3132 11.—(1) Where the sum of the effective lengths of superstructures of a ship is 1·0(L), the basic freeboard of the ship shall be reduced:—

by 350 millimetres if the ship is 24 metres in length (L);
„ 860 „ „ „ „ „ 85„ „ „ „ „
„ 1070 „ „ „ „ „ 122 „ „ „ „ „ or more;

and by amounts obtained by linear interpolation in the case of ships of intermediate length.

(2) The basic freeboard of a ship shall be reduced according to the total effective length of her superstructures and trunks as follows:—

(*a*) in the case of a Type "A" ship, by a percentage ascertained by reference to the following Table, the percentage in the case of a ship having superstructures and trunks of an effective length intermediate to those specified in the Table being obtained by linear interpolation:—

TABLE

PERCENTAGE OF DEDUCTION FOR TYPE 'A' SHIPS

	Total effective length of superstructures and trunks										
	0	0·1 (L)	0·2 (L)	0·3 (L)	0·4 (L)	0·5 (L)	0·6 (L)	0·7 (L)	0·8 (L)	0·9 (L)	1·0 (L)
Percentage of deduction for all types of superstructures	0	7	14	21	31	41	52	63	75·3	87·7	100

(*b*) in the case of a Type "B" ship, by a percentage ascertained by reference to the following Table and to such of directions (i) to (iii) appended thereto as apply in the circumstances, the percentage in the caseo f a ship having superstructures and trunks of an effective length intermediate to those specified in the Table being obtained by linear interpolation:—

TABLE

PERCENTAGE OF DEDUCTION FOR TYPE 'B' SHIPS

		Total effective length of superstructures and trunks										
	Line	0	0·1 (L)	0·2 (L)	0·3 (L)	0·4 (L)	0·5 (L)	0·6 (L)	0·7 (L)	0·8 (L)	0·9 (L)	1·0 (L)
Ships with forecastle and without detached bridge	I	0	5	10	15	23·5	32	46	63	75·3	87·7	100
Ships with forecastle and detached bridge	II	0	6·3	12·7	19	27·5	36	46	63	75·3	87·7	100

(i) Where the effective length of a bridge covers less than 0·1 (L) before amidships and 0·1 (L) abaft amidships the percentages shall be obtained by linear interpolation between the lines I and II.

(ii) Where the effective length of a forecastle is more than 0·4 (L), the percentages shall be obtained from line II.

(iii) Where the effective length of a forecastle is less than 0·07 (L), the above percentages shall be reduced by:

$$5 \times \frac{(0{\cdot}07(L) - f)}{0{\cdot}07(L)}$$

where "f" is the effective length of the forecastle.

Measurement of Sheer

33 12.—(1) The sheer shall be measured from the deck at side to a line of reference drawn parallel to the keel through the sheer line at amidships.

(2) In ships designed with a rake of keel, the sheer shall be measured in relation to a line of reference drawn parallel to the Summer load waterline.

(3) In flush deck ships and in ships with detached superstructures the sheer shall be measured at the freeboard deck.

(4) In ships with topsides of unusual form in which there is a step or break in the topsides, the sheer shall be considered in relation to the equivalent depth amidships.

(5) In ships with a superstructure of standard height which extends over the whole length of the freeboard deck, the sheer shall be measured at the superstructure deck. Where the height of the superstructure exceeds the standard height the least difference (Z) between the actual and standard heights shall be added to each end ordinate. Similarly, the intermediate ordinates at distances of 1/6 (L) and 1/3 (L) from each perpendicular shall be increased by 0·444 (Z) and 0·111 (Z) respectively.

(6) Where the deck of an enclosed superstructure has at least the same sheer as the exposed freeboard deck, the sheer of the enclosed portion of the freeboard deck shall not be taken into account.

(7) Where an enclosed poop or forecastle is either (*a*) of standard height with greater sheer than that of the freeboard deck, or (*b*) is of more than standard height, an addition to the sheer of the freeboard deck shall be made calculated in accordance with paragraph 14(4).

Standard Sheer Profile

13. The ordinates of the standard sheer profile are given in the following Table:

	Station	Ordinate (in millimetres)	Factor
After half	After perpendicular....................	$25 \left(\frac{(L)}{3} + 10\right)$	1
	1/6 (L) from A.P........................	$11{\cdot}1 \left(\frac{(L)}{3} + 10\right)$	3
	1/3 (L) from A.P........................	$2{\cdot}8 \left(\frac{(L)}{3} + 10\right)$	3
	Amidships................................	0	1
Forward half	Amidships................................	0	1
	1/3 (L) from F.P........................	$5{\cdot}6 \left(\frac{(L)}{3} + 10\right)$	3
	1/6 (L) from F.P........................	$22{\cdot}2 \left(\frac{(L)}{3} + 10\right)$	3
	Forward perpendicular..............	$50 \left(\frac{(L)}{3} + 10\right)$	1

Measurement of Variation from Standard Sheer Profile

14.—(1) Where the sheer profile of a ship differs from the standard sheer profile, the four ordinates of each profile in the forward and after halves of the ship shall be multiplied by the appropriate factors given in the Table of ordinates in the preceding paragraph. The difference between the sums of the respective products and those of the standard divided by 8 shall be the deficiency or excess of sheer in the forward or after half. The arithmetical mean of the excess or deficiency in the forward and after halves shall be the excess or deficiency of sheer.

(2) Where the after half of the sheer profile is greater than the standard sheer profile and the forward half is less than the standard sheer profile, no credit shall be allowed for the part in excess, and deficiency only shall be measured.

(3) Where the forward half of the sheer profile exceeds the standard sheer profile, and the after half of the sheer profile is not less than 75 per cent. of the standard sheer profile, credit shall be allowed for the part in excess.

Where the after half of the sheer profile is less than 50 per cent. of the standard sheer profile, no credit shall be given for the excess of sheer forward.

Where the sheer in the after half is between 50 per cent. and 75 per cent. of the standard sheer profile, intermediate allowances may be granted for excess sheer forward.

(4) Where sheer credit is given for a poop or forecastle the following formula shall be used:

$$s = \frac{y}{3} \times \frac{L'}{(L)}$$

Where s = sheer credit, to be deducted from the deficiency or added to the excess of sheer;

y = difference between actual and standard height of superstructure at the end ordinate of sheer; and

L′ = mean enclosed length of poop or forecastle up to a maximum length of 0·5 (L).

The above formula provides a curve in the form of a parabola tangential to the actual sheer curve at the freeboard deck and intersecting the end ordinate at a point below the superstructure deck at a distance equal to the standard height of the poop or forecastle. The superstructure deck shall not be less than standard height above this curve at any point. This curve shall be used in determining the sheer profile for forward and after halves of the ship.

Correction for Variations from Standard Sheer Profile

15.—(1) The correction for sheer shall be the deficiency or excess of sheer determined in accordance with paragraph 14 multiplied by

$$0 \cdot 75 - \frac{S}{2\,(L)}$$

(2) In the case of a ship with sheer less than the standard sheer profile, the correction for deficiency of sheer determined in accordance with sub-paragraph (1) shall be added to the basic freeboard of the ship.

(3) Subject to sub-paragraph (4), in the case of a ship having an excess of sheer—

(*a*) if an enclosed superstructure covers 0·1 (L) before and 0·1 (L) abaft amidships, the correction for excess of sheer determined in accordance with sub-paragraph (1) shall be deducted from the basic freeboard of the ship;

(*b*) if no enclosed superstructure covers amidships, no deductions shall be made from the basic freeboard of the ship;

(*c*) if an enclosed superstructure covers less than 0·1 (L) before and 0·1 (L) abaft amidships, the correction for excess of sheer determined in accordance with sub-paragraph (1) shall be modified in the ratio of the amount of 0·2 (L) amidships which is covered by the superstructure, to 0·2 (L).

(4) The maximum deduction for excess sheer shall be at the rate of 125 millimetres per 100 metres of length (L).

Correction for Minimum Bow Height

34 16.—(1) Except as otherwise provided in sub-paragraphs (2) and (3), where the bow height of a ship determined in accordance with sub-paragraph (4) is less than the minimum bow height appropriate to the ship determined in accordance with sub-paragraph (5), the freeboard determined for the ship in accordance with the foregoing paragraphs shall be increased by an amount equal to the difference between the bow height and the minimum bow height.

(2) Where an existing ship to which sub-paragraph (1) applies has been so constructed or modified as to comply with all the requirements of Schedule 4 applicable to a new ship of her type and is to be assigned freeboards determined in accordance with this Schedule, and/or—

(*a*) the forecastle is less than 0·07 (L);

(*b*) the sheer extends for less than 15 per cent. of the ship's length (L) measured from the forward perpendicular,

the freeboard determined for the ship in accordance with the foregoing paragraphs shall be increased by such amount as the [Department] may determine in each particular case.

(3) In the case of a ship to which sub-paragraph (1) applies, being a ship which is constructed to meet exceptional operational requirements, the correction to be made pursuant to the preceding sub-paragraphs may be reduced or waived if the Board are satisfied that the safety of the ship will not be impaired in consequence in the worst sea and weather conditions likely to be encountered by the ship in service.

(4) The bow height of a ship is the vertical distance at the forward perpendicular between the Summer load waterline of the ship at the designed trim and the top of the exposed deck at side ascertained as follows:—

(*a*) Where the bow height is obtained by including sheer, the sheer shall extend for not less than 15 per cent. of the ship's length (L) measured from the forward perpendicular.

(*b*) Where the bow height is obtained by including the height of a superstructure, such superstructure shall:—

(i) extend from the stem to a point not less than 0·07 of the ship's length (L) measured from the forward perpendicular;

(ii) if the ship's length (L) is 100 metres or less, be an enclosed superstructure; and

(iii) if the ship's length (L) exceeds 100 metres in length, be fitted with satisfactory closing appliances.

(5) The minimum bow height for a ship shall be derived from formula 1 in the case of a ship of less than 250 metres in length (L) and from formula 2 in the case of a ship of 250 metres or more in length (L):—

Formula 1

$$56(L)\left(1-\frac{(L)}{500}\right)\left(\frac{1\cdot 36}{C_b+0\cdot 68}\right) \text{ millimetres}$$

Formula 2

$$7000\left(\frac{1\cdot 36}{C_b+0\cdot 68}\right) \text{ millimetres}$$

C_b being taken as not less than 0·68 in the case of each formula.

PART II

TIMBER FREEBOARDS

Summer Timber freeboard

17. The Summer Timber freeboard shall be determined as follows:—

(1) There shall first be ascertained the freeboard appropriate to the ship under the provisions of sub-paragraphs (1), (2)(*a*), (9) and (10) of paragraph 5 of this Schedule.

(2) Corrections shall be applied to the freeboard so obtained in accordance with the provisions of paragraphs 6 to 10 of this Schedule.

(3) Deductions for the effective length of superstructures only shall be made from the freeboard obtained pursuant to the preceding sub-paragraphs, in accordance with the provisions of paragraph 11(1) and (2)(*b*) of this Schedule but substituting for the Table "Percentage of Deduction for Type "B" ships" therein the following Table:-

TABLE

	Total effective length of superstructures										
	0	0·1 (L)	0·2 (L)	0·3 (L)	0·4 (L)	0·5 (L)	0·6 (L)	0·7 (L)	0·8 (L)	0·9 (L)	1·0 (L)
Percentage of deduction for all types of superstructures	20	31	42	53	64	70	76	82	88	94	100

Percentages at intermediate lengths of superstructures shall be obtained by linear interpolation.

(4) Corrections shall be applied to the freeboard obtained pursuant to the preceding sub-paragraphs in accordance with the provisions of paragraphs 12 to 15 of this Schedule, and the freeboard so corrected shall be the Summer Timber freeboard to be assigned to the ship.

Other Timber freeboards

18.—(1) The Winter Timber freeboard shall be obtained by adding to the Summer Timber freeboard one thirty-sixth (1/36th) of the summer timber draught of the ship.

(2) The Winter North Atlantic Timber freeboard shall be the same as the Winter North Atlantic freeboard assigned to the ship.

(3) The Tropical Timber freeboard shall be obtained by deducting from the Summer Timber freeboard one forty-eighth (1/48th)of the summer timber draught of the ship.

(4)(*a*) The Fresh Water Timber freeboard shall, subject to sub-paragraph (*b*), be obtained by deducting from the Summer Timber freeboard the quantity—

$$\frac{\Delta}{4\,T} \text{ millimetres}$$

where Δ is the displacement in salt water in metric tons at the waterline which will when load lines have been marked on the ship's side correspond to the Summer Timber load line, and T represents metric tons per centimetre immersion in salt water at that waterline.

(*b*) In any case in which the displacement at that waterline cannot be ascertained the deduction shall be one forty-eighth (1/48th) of the summer timber draught of the ship.

Part III

Sailing Ships And Other Ships

Sailing ships and tugs

19. The freeboards to be assigned to sailing ships and tugs shall be freeboards determined in accordance with the provisions of Part I of this Schedule increased by such amounts as the [Department] may direct in each particular case.

Ships of wood and other ships

20. The freeboards to be assigned to ships of wood or of composite construction or of other materials, or to ships with constructional features such as to render freeboards calculated in accordance with **Part I** of this Schedule unreasonable or impracticable shall be determined by the [Department] in each particular case.

Unmanned barges

21. The freeboards to be assigned to unmanned barges having on the freeboard deck only small access openings closed by watertight gasketed covers of steel shall be freeboards determined in accordance with the provisions of Part I of this Schedule omitting paragraphs 5 and 16. Such freeboards may be reduced by such amounts not exceeding 25 per cent. as the [Department] may direct in each particular case.

3136 ## SCHEDULE 6

FREEBOARD TABLES

(Schedule 5)

1. The following is Freeboard Table A referred to in the definition of "tabular freeboard" in paragraph 1 of Schedule 5:—

TABLE A

FREEBOARD TABLE FOR TYPE "A" SHIPS

Length of ship (metres)	Freeboard (millimetres)	Length of ship (metres)	Freeboard (millimetres)	Length of ship (metres)	Freeboard (millimetres)
24	200	64	626	104	1196
25	208	65	639	105	1212
26	217	66	653	106	1228
27	225	67	666	107	1244
28	233	68	680	108	1260
29	242	69	693	109	1276
30	250	70	706	110	1293
31	258	71	720	111	1309
32	267	72	733	112	1326
33	275	73	746	113	1342
34	283	74	760	114	1359
35	292	75	773	115	1376
36	300	76	786	116	1392
37	308	77	800	117	1409
38	316	78	814	118	1426
39	325	79	828	119	1442
40	334	80	841	120	1459
41	344	81	855	121	1476
42	354	82	869	122	1494
43	364	83	883	123	1511
44	374	84	897	124	1528
45	385	85	911	125	1546
46	396	86	926	126	1563
47	408	87	940	127	1580
48	420	88	955	128	1598
49	432	89	969	129	1615
50	443	90	984	130	1632
51	455	91	999	131	1650
52	467	92	1014	132	1667
53	478	93	1029	133	1684
54	490	94	1044	134	1702
55	503	95	1059	135	1719
56	516	96	1074	136	1736
57	530	97	1089	137	1753
58	544	98	1105	138	1770
59	559	99	1120	139	1787
60	573	100	1135	140	1803
61	587	101	1151	141	1820
62	600	102	1166	142	1837
63	613	103	1181	143	1853

TABLE A (*continued*)

Length of ship (metres)	Freeboard (millimetres)	Length of ship (metres)	Freeboard (millemitres)	Length of ship (metres)	Freeboard (millimetres)
144	1870	197	2582	250	3012
145	1886	198	2592	251	3018
146	1903	199	2602	252	3024
147	1919	200	2612	253	3030
148	1935	201	2622	254	3036
149	1952	202	2632	255	3042
150	1968	203	2641	256	3048
151	1984	204	2650	257	3054
152	2000	205	2659	258	3060
153	2016	206	2669	259	3066
154	2032	207	2678	260	3072
155	2048	208	2687	261	3078
156	2064	209	2696	262	3084
157	2080	210	2705	263	3089
158	2096	211	2714	264	3095
159	2111	212	2723	265	3101
160	2126	213	2732	266	3106
161	2141	214	2741	267	3112
162	2155	215	2749	268	3117
163	2169	216	2758	269	3123
164	2184	217	2767	270	3128
165	2198	218	2775	271	3133
166	2212	219	2784	272	3138
167	2226	220	2792	273	3143
168	2240	221	2801	274	3148
169	2254	222	2809	275	3153
170	2268	223	2817	276	3158
171	2281	224	2825	277	3163
172	2294	225	2833	278	3167
173	2307	226	2841	279	3172
174	2320	227	2849	280	3176
175	2332	228	2857	281	3181
176	2345	229	2865	282	3185
177	2357	230	2872	283	3189
178	2369	231	2880	284	3194
179	2381	232	2888	285	3198
180	2393	233	2895	286	3202
181	2405	234	2903	287	3207
182	2416	235	2910	288	3211
183	2428	236	2918	289	3215
184	2440	237	2925	290	3220
185	2451	238	2932	291	3224
186	2463	239	2939	292	3228
187	2474	240	2946	293	3233
188	2486	241	2953	294	3237
189	2497	242	2959	296	3241
190	2508	243	2966	296	3246
191	2519	244	2973	297	3250
192	2530	245	2979	298	3254
193	2541	246	2986	299	3258
194	2552	247	2993	300	3262
195	2562	248	3000	301	3266
196	2572	249	3006	302	3270

TABLE A (*continued*)

Length of ship (metres)	Freeboard (millimetres)	Length of ship (metres)	Freeboard (millimetres)	Length of ship (metres)	Freeboard (millimetres)
303	3274	324	3342	345	3394
304	3278	325	3345	346	3396
305	3281	326	3347	347	3399
306	3285	327	3350	348	3401
307	3288	328	3353	349	3403
308	3292	329	3355	350	3406
309	3295	330	3358	351	3408
310	3298	331	3361	352	3410
311	3302	332	3363	353	3412
312	3305	333	3366	354	3414
313	3308	334	3368	355	3416
314	3312	335	3371	356	3418
315	3315	336	3373	357	3420
316	3318	337	3375	358	3422
317	3322	338	3378	359	3423
318	3325	339	3380	360	3425
319	3328	340	3382	361	3427
320	3331	341	3385	362	3428
321	3334	342	3387	363	3430
322	3337	343	3389	364	3432
323	3339	344	3392	365	3433

Freeboards at intermediate lengths of ship shall be obtained by linear interpolation.

137 2. The following is Freeboard Table B referred to in the definition of "tabular freeboard" in paragraph 1 of Schedule 5:—

TABLE B

FREEBOARD TABLE FOR TYPE "B" SHIPS

Length of ship (metres)	Freeboard (millimetres)	Length of ship (metres)	Freeboard (millimetres)	Length of ship (metres)	Freeboard (millimetres)
24	200	72	754	120	1690
25	208	73	769	121	1709
26	217	74	784	122	1729
27	225	75	800	123	1750
28	233	76	816	124	1771
29	242	77	833	125	1793
30	250	78	850	126	1815
31	258	79	868	127	1837
32	267	80	887	128	1859
33	275	81	905	129	1880
34	283	82	923	130	1901
35	292	83	942	131	1921
36	300	84	960	132	1940
37	308	85	978	133	1959
38	316	86	996	134	1979
39	325	87	1015	135	2000
40	334	88	1034	136	2021
41	344	89	1054	137	2043
42	354	90	1075	138	2065
43	364	91	1096	139	2087
44	374	92	1116	140	2109
45	385	93	1135	141	2130
46	396	94	1154	142	2151
47	408	95	1172	143	2171
48	420	96	1190	144	2190
49	432	97	1209	145	2209
50	443	98	1229	146	2229
51	455	99	1250	147	2250
52	467	100	1271	148	2271
53	478	101	1293	149	2293
54	490	102	1315	150	2315
55	503	103	1337	151	2334
56	516	104	1359	152	2354
57	530	105	1380	153	2375
58	544	106	1401	154	2396
59	559	107	1421	155	2418
60	573	108	1440	156	2440
61	587	109	1459	157	2460
62	601	110	1479	158	2480
63	615	111	1500	159	2500
64	629	112	1521	160	2520
65	644	113	1543	161	2540
66	659	114	1565	162	2560
67	674	115	1587	163	2580
68	689	116	1609	164	2600
69	705	117	1630	165	2620
70	721	118	1651	166	2640
71	738	119	1671	167	2660

TABLE B (*continued*)

Length of ship (metres)	Freeboard (millimetres)	Length of ship (metres)	Freeboard (millimetres)	Length of ship (metres)	Freeboard (millimetres)
168	2680	221	3601	274	4327
169	2698	222	3615	275	4339
170	2716	223	3630	276	4350
171	2735	224	3645	277	4362
172	2754	225	3660	278	4373
173	2774	226	3675	279	4385
174	2795	227	3690	280	4397
175	2815	228	3705	281	4408
176	2835	229	3720	282	4420
177	2855	230	3735	283	4432
178	2875	231	3750	284	4443
179	2895	232	3765	285	4455
180	2915	233	3780	286	4467
181	2933	234	3795	287	4478
182	2952	235	3808	288	4490
183	2970	236	3821	289	4502
184	2988	237	3835	290	4513
185	3007	238	3849	291	4525
186	3025	239	3864	292	4537
187	3044	240	3880	293	4548
188	3062	241	3893	294	4560
189	3080	242	3906	295	4572
190	3098	243	3920	296	4583
191	3116	244	3934	297	4595
192	3134	245	3949	298	4607
193	3151	246	3965	299	4618
194	3167	247	3978	300	4630
195	3185	248	3992	301	4642
196	3202	249	4005	302	4654
197	3219	250	4018	303	4665
198	3235	251	4032	304	4676
199	3249	252	4045	305	4686
200	3264	253	4058	306	4695
201	3280	254	4072	307	4704
202	3296	255	4085	308	4714
203	3313	256	4098	309	4725
204	3330	257	4112	310	4736
205	3347	258	4125	311	4748
206	3363	259	4139	312	4757
207	3380	260	4152	313	4768
208	3397	261	4165	314	4779
209	3413	262	4177	315	4790
210	3430	263	4189	316	4801
211	3445	264	4201	317	4812
212	3460	265	4214	318	4823
213	3475	266	4227	319	4834
214	3490	267	4240	320	4844
215	3505	268	4252	321	4855
216	3520	269	4264	322	4866
217	3537	270	4276	323	4878
218	3554	271	4289	324	4890
219	3570	272	4302	325	4899
220	3586	273	4315	326	4909

TABLE B *(continued)*

Length of ship (metres)	Freeboard (millimetres)	Length of ship (metres)	Freeboard (millimetres)	Length of ship (metres)	Freeboard (millimetres)
327	4920	340	5055	353	5190
328	4931	341	5065	354	5200
329	4943	342	5075	355	5210
330	4955	343	5086	356	5220
331	4965	344	5097	357	5230
332	4975	345	5108	358	5240
333	4985	346	5119	359	5250
334	4995	347	5130	360	5260
335	5005	348	5140	361	5268
336	5015	349	5150	362	5276
337	5025	350	5160	363	5285
338	5035	351	5170	364	5294
339	5045	352	5180	365	5303

Freeboards at intermediate lengths of ship shall be obtained by linear interpolation.

3138 **SCHEDULE 7**

INFORMATION AS TO STABILITY OF SHIPS

(Rule 30)

The information relating to the stability of a ship to be provided for the master pursuant to Rule 30 of these Rules shall include particulars appropriate to the ship of the matters specified below. Such particulars shall be in the form of a statement unless the contrary is indicated.

1. The ship's name, official number, port of registry, gross and register tonnages, principal dimensions, displacement, deadweight and draught to the Summer load line.

2. A profile view and, if the [Department] so require in a particular case, plan views of the ship drawn to scale showing with their names all compartments, tanks, storerooms and crew and passenger accommodation spaces, and also showing the mid-length position.

3. The capacity and the centre of gravity (longitudinally and vertically) of every compartment available for the carriage of cargo, fuel, stores, feed water, domestic water or water ballast.

In the case of a vehicle ferry, the vertical centre of gravity of compartments for the carriage of vehicles shall be based on the estimated centres of gravity of the vehicles and not on the volumetric centres of the compartments.

4. The estimated total weight of (*a*) passengers and their effects and (*b*) crew and their effects, and the centre of gravity (longitudinally and vertically) of each such total weight. In assessing such centres of gravity passengers and crew shall be assumed to be distributed about the ship in the spaces they will normally occupy, including the highest decks to which either or both have access.

5. The estimated weight and the disposition and centre of gravity of the maximum amount of deck cargo which the ship may reasonably be expected to carry on an exposed deck. The estimated weight shall include in the case of deck cargo likely to absorb water the estimated weight of water likely to be so absorbed and allowed for in arrival conditions, such weight in the case of timber deck cargo being taken to be 15 per cent by weight.

6. A diagram or scale showing the load line mark and load lines with particulars of the corresponding freeboards, and also showing the displacement, metric tons per centimetre immersion, and deadweight corresponding in each case to a range of mean draughts extending between the waterline representing the deepest load line and the waterline of the ship in light condition.

7. A diagram or tabular statement showing the hydrostatic particulars of the ship, including—

(1) the heights of the transverse metacentre and

(2) the values of the moment to change trim one centimetre,

for a range of mean draughts extending at least between the waterline representing the deepest load line and the waterline of the ship in light condition. Where a tabular statement is used, the intervals between such draughts shall be sufficiently close to permit accurate interpolation. In the case of ships having raked keels, the same datum for the heights of centres of bouyancy and metacentres shall be used as for the centres of gravity referred to in paragraphs 3, 4 and 5.

8. The effect on stability of free surface in each tank in the ship in which liquids may be carried, including an example to show how the metacentric height is to be corrected.

9.—(1) A diagram showing cross curves of stability indicating the height of the assumed axis from which the Righting Levers are measured and the trim which has been assumed. In the case of ships having raked keels, where a datum other than the top of keel has been used the position of the assumed axis shall be clearly defined.

(2) Subject to the following sub-paragraph, only (*a*) enclosed superstructures and (*b*) efficient trunks as defined in paragraph 10 of Schedule 5 shall be taken into account in deriving such curves.

(3) The following structures may be taken into account in deriving such curves if the Board are satisfied that their location, integrity and means of closure will contribute to the ship's stability:—

(*a*) superstructures located above the superstructure deck;

(*b*) deckhouses on or above the freeboard deck, whether wholly or in part only;

(*c*) hatchway structures on or above the freeboard deck.

Additionally, in the case of a ship carrying timber deck cargo, the volume of the timber deck cargo, or a part thereof, may with the Board's approval be taken into account in deriving a supplementary curve of stability appropriate to the ship when carrying such cargo.

(4) An example shall be given showing how to obtain a curve of Righting Levers (GZ) from the cross curves of stability.

(5) Where the buoyancy of a superstructure is to be taken into account in the calculation of stability information to be supplied in the case of a vehicle ferry or similar ship having bow doors, ship's side doors or stern doors, there shall be included in the stability information a specific statement that such doors must be secured weathertight before the ship proceeds to sea and that the cross curves of stability are based upon the assumption that such doors have been so secured.

139 10—(1) The diagram and statements referred to in sub-paragraph (2) of this paragraph shall be provided separately for each of the following conditions of the ship:—

(*a*) *Light condition*. If the ship has permanent ballast, such diagram and statements shall be provided for the ship in light condition both (i) with such ballast, and (ii) without such ballast.

(*b*) *Ballast condition*, both (i) on departure, and (ii) on arrival, it being assumed for the purpose of the latter in this and the following sub-paragraphs that oil fuel, fresh water, consumable stores and the like are reduced to 10 per cent of their capacity.

(*c*) Condition both (i) on departure, and (ii) on arrival, when loaded to the Summer load line with cargo filling all spaces available for cargo, cargo for this purpose being taken to be homogeneous cargo except where this is clearly inappropriate, for example in the case of cargo spaces in a ship which are intended to be used exclusively for the carriage of vehicles or of containers.

(*d*) Service loaded conditions, both (i) on departure and (ii) on arrival.

(2)(*a*) A profile diagram of the ship drawn to a suitable small scale showing the disposition of all components of the deadweight.

(*b*) A statement showing the lightweight, the disposition and the total weights of all components of the deadweight, the displacement, the corresponding positions of the centre of gravity, the metacentre and also the metacentric height (GM).

(*c*) A diagram showing a curve of Righting Levers (GZ) derived from the cross curves of stability referred to in paragraph 9. Where credit is shown for the buoyancy of a timber deck cargo the curve of Righting Levers (GZ) must be drawn both with and without this credit.

(3) The metacentric height and the curve of Righting Levers (GZ) shall be corrected for liquid free surface.

(4) Where there is a significant amount of trim in any of the conditions referred to in sub-paragraph (1) the metacentric height and the curve of Righting Levers (GZ) may be required to be determined from the trimmed waterline.

(5) If in the opinion of the [Department] the stability characteristics in either or both of the conditions referred to in sub-paragraph (1)(*c*) are not satisfactory, such conditions shall be marked accordingly and on appropriate warning to the master shall be inserted.

11. Where special procedures such as partly filling or completely filling particular spaces designated for cargo, fuel, fresh water or other purposes are necessary to maintain adequate stability, a statement of instructions as to the appropriate procedure in each case.

12. A copy of the report on the inclining test and of the calculation therefrom of the light condition particulars.

[The next page is 864/1.]
[The next paragraph is 3139a.]

APPENDIX 5A

LOAD LINE AMENDMENT RULES

39a Rule 30 (5) (*ante*, § 3089) of the main Rules has been substituted as follows:

"(5) The information, and any fresh information to replace the same pursuant to paragraph (3) of this Rule, shall before issue to the master:—

(*a*) if it relates to a ship which is classed with Lloyd's Register of Shipping and is—

(i) an oil tanker over 100 metres in length;

(ii) a bulk carrier, or an ore carrier, over 150 metres in length;

(iii) a single deck bulk carrier over 100 metres but not exceeding 150 metres in length;

(iv) a single deck dry cargo ship over 100 metres in length; or

(v) a purpose built container ship over 125 metres in length;

be submitted in duplicate by or on behalf of the owner of the ship either to the Secretary of State or to Lloyd's Register of Shipping for approval; or

(*b*) if it relates to any other ship, be submitted in duplicate by or on behalf of the owner of the ship to the Secretary of State for approval.

The information shall incorporate such additions and amendments as the Secretary of State or Lloyd's Register of Shipping, as the case may be, may in any particular case specify for the purpose of ensuring that the information complies with the provisions of this Rule."

[1] Substitution made by M.S. (Load Line) (Amendment) Rules 1975 (S.I. 1975 No. 595), coming into effect June 1, 1975.

[The next page is 865.]
[The next paragraph number is 3140.]

Appendix 6

HOVERCRAFT (APPLICATION OF ENACTMENTS) ORDER

Hovercraft (Application of Enactments) Order 1972

(S.I. 1972 No. 971)

Order made under sections 1(1)(*h*)(*j*),(3) *of the Hovercraft Act* 1968, *dated June* 28, 1972.

3140 Explanatory Note [1]

This Order applies to hovercraft, with modifications, a number of enactments and instruments relating to ships, aircraft and motor vehicles. Amongst those relating to ships which are applied to hovercraft are Part VI of the Merchant Shipping Act 1894, which provides for the investigation of casualties, and the various enactments and instruments dealing with wreck, salvage and distress.

The Order also substitutes references to hovercraft in some enactments for references to hover vehicles.

3141 ARRANGEMENT OF ORDER

Article

1. Citation and Commencement
2. Application
3. Interpretation
4. Application to hovercraft of enactments and instruments relating to vessels
5. Application to hovercraft of enactments and instruments relating to aircraft
6. Application to hovercraft of enactments and instruments relating to motor vehicles
7. Insurance
8. Wreck, salvage and distress
9. Investigation of casualties
10. Nomenclature

SCHEDULES

Schedule

1. Part A: Enactments relating to vessels applied to hovercraft
   Part B: Instruments relating to vessels applied to hovercraft
2. Part A: Enactments relating to aircraft applied to hovercraft
   Part B: Instruments relating to aircraft applied to hovercraft

[1] This Note is not part of the Order.

3. Part A: Enactments relating to motor vehicles applied to hovercraft
   Part B: Instruments relating to motor vehicles applied to hovercraft
4. Investigation of casualties

Citation and Commencement

3142 **1.** This Order may be cited as the Hovercraft (Application of Enactments) Order 1972 and shall come into operation 14 days after the date of making.

Application

2. This Order applies to hovercraft which are used—

(i) wholly or partly on or over the sea or navigable waters; or

(ii) on or over land to which the public have access or non-navigable waters to which the public have access; or

(iii) elsewhere for the carriage of passengers for reward:

Provided that this Order shall not:

(*a*) apply to hovertrains; nor
(*b*) prejudice the operation of section 19 of the Road Traffic Act 1962.[2]

Interpretation

3.—(1) In this Order, unless the context otherwise requires—

"Captain" means the person who is designated by the operator to be in charge of a hovercraft during any journey, or, failing such designation, the person who is for the time being lawfully in charge of the hovercraft;

"Hovertrains" means hovercraft which are at all times guided by tracks, rails or guides fixed to the ground;

"Navigable water" means any water which is in fact navigable by ships or vessels, whether or not the tide ebbs and flows there, and whether or not there is a public right of navigation in that water;

(2) The Interpretation Act 1889 shall apply to the interpretation of this Order as it applies to the interpretation of an Act of Parliament.

[2] Now s. 192 of the Road Traffic Act 1972.

Application to hovercraft of enactments and instruments relating to vessels

143 **4.** The enactments mentioned in column 1 of Part A of Schedule 1 to this Order, and the statutory instruments mentioned in column 1 of Part B of Schedule 1 to this Order, shall have effect as if any reference therein in whatever terms to ships, vessels or boats or activities or places connected therewith included a reference to hovercraft or activities or places connected with hovercraft, subject to the modifications (if any) contained in column 3 or Parts A and B respectively.

Application to hovercraft of enactments and instruments relating to aircraft

5. The enactments mentioned in column 1 of Part A of Schedule 2 to this Order and the statutory instruments mentioned in column 1 of Part B of Schedule 2 to this Order shall have effect as if any reference therein in whatever terms to aircraft or activities or places connected therewith included a reference to hovercraft or activities or places connected with hovercraft, subject to the modifications (if any) contained in column 3 of Parts A and B respectively.

Application to hovercraft of enactments and instruments relating to motor vehicles

6. The enactments mentioned in column 1 of Part A of Schedule 3 to this Order, and the statutory instruments mentioned in column 1 of Part B of Schedule 3 to this Order, shall have effect as if any reference therein in whatever terms to motor vehicles or activities or places connected therewith included a reference to hovercraft or activities or places connected with hovercraft, subject to the modifications (if any) contained in column 3 of Parts A and B respectively.

Insurance

7.—(1) The Insurance Companies Acts 1958 to 1967 shall have effect as if any reference therein to "vessels or aircraft" included a reference to hovercraft.

(2) Section 94 of the Companies Act 1967 shall have effect as if there were added to section 94 the following sub-section—

"(7) For the purposes of this Part of this Act, the business of effecting and carrying out contracts of insurance against loss of, or damage to, or arising out of or in connection with the use of, hovercraft, inclusive of third-party risks but exclusive of transit risks, if carried on by a person who at the same time carries on motor vehicle insurance business but does not otherwise carry on marine, aviation and transport business, shall be taken to be motor vehicle insurance business".

Wreck, salvage and distress

144 **8.**—(1) The following enactments and instruments shall have effect as if any reference therein, in whatever terms, to ships, vessels or boats, or activities or places connected therewith, included a reference to hovercraft, or activities or places connected with hovercraft, namely—

(*a*) Sections 510 to 516, 518 to 537 and 544 to 571 of the Merchant Shipping Act 1894;

(*b*) Section 72 of the Merchant Shipping Act 1906;

(*c*) Sections 6 and 7 of the Maritime Conventions Act 1911;

(*d*) Section 24 of the Merchant Shipping (Safety and Load Line Conventions) Act 1932;

(*e*) Section 8 of the Crown Proceedings Act 1947;

(*f*) The Merchant Shipping (Navigational Warnings) Rules 1965 [3];

(*g*) The Merchant Shipping (Signals of Distress) Rules 1965 (s. 1965 No. 1550).

In relation to the above enactments, as so applied, the expression "wreck" (save and except in so far as relates to the claims of any Admiral, Vice-Admiral, Lord of the Manor, heritable proprietor duly infeft, or any person other than Her Majesty and Her Royal Successors to unclaimed wreck for his own use) shall include any hovercraft or any part thereof or cargo thereof found sunk, stranded or abandoned in or on any navigable water, or on or over the foreshore, or place where the tide normally ebbs or flows.

(2) (*a*) Sections 56 and 57 of the Harbours, Docks and Piers Clauses Act, 1847 as incorporated with any local or special Act, whenever passed, and the provisions relating to the same subject matters as those sections of any local or special Act for the time being in force, shall apply in relation to hovercraft as those provisions apply to vessels, and the expressions "wreck" and "vessel" in those sections shall be deemed to include wreckage of or from hovercraft, and hovercraft, respectively;

(*b*) In the application in relation to hovercraft of the provisions of the said sections, the expressions "owner" shall mean the owner of the hovercraft at the time it was wrecked or laid by or neglected.

(3) Any services rendered in assisting, or in saving life from, or in saving the cargo or apparel of, hovercraft in, on or over navigable water or on or over the foreshore or place where the tide normally ebbs and flows shall be deemed to be salvage services in all cases in which they would have been salvage services if they had been rendered in relation to a vessel; and where salvage services are rendered by hovercraft to any property or person, the owner and crew of the hovercraft shall be entitled to the same reward for those services as they would have been entitled to if the hovercraft had been a vessel.

The foregoing provisions of this sub-section shall have effect notwithstanding that the hovercraft concerned is not registered in the United Kingdom and notwithstanding that the services in question are rendered elsewhere than within the limits of the territorial waters adjacent to any part of Her Majesty's dominions.

Investigation of casualties

9. Part VI of the Merchant Shipping Act 1894 (Special Shipping Inquiries and Courts), s. 66 of the Merchant Shipping Act 1906 and the Shipping Casualties and Appeals and Re-hearings Rules 1923 [4] shall have effect as if references therein, in whatever terms, to ships or activities connected therewith included references to hovercraft or activities connected with hovercraft, subject to the modifications set out in Schedule 4 to this Order.

[3] S.I. 1965 No. 105.
[4] S.R. & O. 1923 No. 752.

Nomenclature

145 **10.**—(1) There shall be substituted a reference to "hovercraft" for the reference to "hover vehicles" in the British Railways Acts 1966 and 1967.

(2) The reference to machines designed or adapted for use in agriculture in the definition of "field machine" in the Agriculture (Field Machinery) Regulations 1962 [5] shall be deemed to include a reference to hovercraft used for agricultural purposes.

(3) For the reference in s. 13(4) of the Sea Fisheries (Shellfish) Act 1967 to "hover vehicle", there shall be substituted a reference to "hovercraft".

W. G. Agnew.

[5] S.I. 1962 No. 1472.

Article 4

3146 SCHEDULE 1

APPLICATION TO HOVERCRAFT OF CERTAIN ENACTMENTS AND INSTRUMENTS RELATING TO VESSELS

PART A:—Enactments applied, and modifications

Column 1 Enactments applied	Column 2 References	Column 3 Modifications in relation to hovercraft or activities or places connected therewith (if any)
The Harbours, Docks and Piers Clauses Act 1847, sections 28, 52 and 53, and as incorporated in any local or special Act whenever passed	1847 c. 27.	
The General Pier and Harbour Act 1861	1861 c. 45.	
The General Pier and Harbour Act 1861 Amendment Act 1862	1862 c. 19.	
The Naval Agency and Distribution Act 1864, section 3	1864 c. 24.	
The Naval Prize Act 1864	1864 c. 25.	
The Public Stores Act 1875	1875 c. 25.	
The Territorial Waters Jurisdiction Act 1878	1878 c. 73.	
The Merchant Shipping Act 1894, sections 418, 419, 421, 422 and 446 to 450	1894 c. 60.	
The Congested Districts (Scotland) Act 1897	1897 c. 53.	
The Marine Insurance Act 1906	1906 c. 41.	
The Official Secrets Acts 1911 and 1920	1911 c. 28. 1920 c. 75.	
The Salmon and Freshwater Fisheries Acts 1923 to 1965	1923 c. 16. 1935 c. 43. 1965 c. 68.	
The Land Drainage Act 1930	1930 c. 44.	
The Improvement of Livestock (Licensing of Bulls) Act 1931, (as amended and extended)	1931 c. 43.	
The Manchester Ship Canal Act 1936	1936 c. cxxiv.	
The Harbours, Piers and Ferries (Scotland) Act 1937	1937 c. 28.	

Column 1 Enactments applied	Column 2 References	Column 3 Modifications in relation to hovercraft or activities or places connected therewith (if any)
The Crown Proceedings Act 1947, sections 10 and 29	1947 c. 44.	
The Merchant Shipping (Safety Convention) Act 1949, sections 21 to 23	1949 c. 43.	In section 23(3), the words "and the ship shall be deemed for the purposes of Part V of the principal Act to be unsafe by reason of improper loading" shall not apply.
The Wireless Telegraphy Act 1949 (as modified by the Wireless Telegraphy Act 1967)	1949 c. 54. 1967 c. 72.	
The Prevention of Damage by Pests Act 1949	1949 c. 55.	
The Diseases of Animals Act 1950	1950 c. 36.	
The Visiting Forces Act 1952	1952 c. 67.	
The Pests Act 1954	1954 c. 68.	
The Army Act 1955, sections 25(3)(*a*) and (*b*), 60(2)(*a*) and (*b*), 148(2) and (198(8)(*c*)	1955 c. 18.	
The Air Force Act 1955, sections 25(3)(*a*) and (*b*), 60(2)(*a*) and (*b*) and 148(2)	1955 c. 19.	
The Naval Discipline Act 1957	1957 c. 53.	
The Registration of Births, Deaths and Marriages (Special Provisions) Act 1957	1957 c. 58.	
The Horse Breeding Act 1958, as extended by section 16(4) of the Agriculture (Miscellaneous Provisions) Act 1963	1958 c. 43. 1963 c. 11.	
The Highlands and Islands Shipping Services Act 1960	1960 c. 31.	
The Public Health Act 1961, section 76	1961 c. 64.	
The Water Resources Act 1963	1963 c. 38.	
The Wills Act 1963	1963 c. 44.	
The Fishery Limits Act 1964	1964 c. 72.	
The National Insurance Act 1965, section 100	1965 c. 51.	

Column 1 Enactments applied	Column 2 References	Column 3 Modifications in relation to hovercraft or activities or places connected therewith (if any)
The National Insurance (Industrial Injuries) Act 1965, section 75; Schedule 1, Part I, paragraphs 2 to 5; and Schedule 1, Part II, paragraphs 2 and 3	1965 c. 52.	(1) For paragraph 2(2)(*b*) and (*c*) of Schedule 1, Part I there shall be substituted:— "(*b*) to all hovercraft registered in the United Kingdom, not being hovercraft whose owner (or managing owner if there is more than one owner) or manager resides or has his principal place of business in Northern Ireland; or whose owner (or managing owner if there is more than one owner) has no place of business in the United Kingdom." (2) In paragraph 2(3) of the said Schedule 1, Part I, the words "ship's husband or other" shall be omitted.
The Sea Fisheries Regulation Act 1966	1966 c. 38.	
The Marine, &c., Broadcasting (Offences) Act 1967	1967 c. 41.	
The Sea Fish (Conservation) Act 1967	1967 c. 84.	
The Firearms Act 1968	1968 c. 27.	
The Sea Fish Industry Act 1970	1970 c. 11.	
The Destructive Imported Animals Act (N.I.) 1933	23 Geo 5 c. 5. (N.I.)	
The Foyle Fisheries Acts (N.I.) 1952 and 1962	1952 c. 5 (N.I.) 1962 c. 5 (N.I.)	
The Exported Animals (Compensation) Act (N.I.) 1952	1952 c. 24 (N.I.)	
The Diseases of Animals Act (N.I.) 1958	1958 c. 13 (N.I.)	
The Marketing of Potatoes Act (N.I.) 1964	1964 c. 8 (N.I.)	
The Agriculture (Miscellaneous Provisions) Act (N.I.) 1965	1965 c. 3 (N.I.)	
The Seeds Act (N.I.) 1965	1965 c. 22 (N.I.)	
The National Insurance Act (Northern Ireland) 1966, section 95	1966 c. 6 (N.I.)	

Column 1 Enactments applied	Column 2 References	Column 3 Modifications in relation to hovercraft or activities or places connected therewith (if any)
The National Insurance (Industrial Injuries) Act (Northern Ireland) 1966, section 71, Schedule 1, Part I, paragraphs 2, 3 and 4; and Schedule 1, Part II, paragraphs 2 and 3	1966 c. 9 (N.I.)	(1) For paragraph 2(2) of Part I of Schedule 1, there shall be substituted:— "This paragraph applies, with such exceptions as may be prescribed, to all hovercraft registered in the United Kingdom, not being hovercraft whose owner (or managing owner if there is more than one owner), or manager resides or has his principal place of business in Great Britain, or whose owner (or managing owner if there is more than one owner) has no place of business in the United Kingdom". (2) In paragraph 2(3) of the said Schedule 1, Part I, the words "ship's husband or other" shall be omitted.
The Horticulture Act (N.I.) 1966	1966 c. 15 (N.I.)	
The Fisheries Acts (N.I.) 1966 & 1968	1966 c. 17 (N.I.) 1968 c. 31 (N.I.)	
The Diseases of Animals (Amendment) Act (N.I.) 1966	1966 c. 23 (N.I.)	

3147 PART B:—Instruments applied, and modifications

Column 1 Instruments applied	Column 2 References	Column 3 Modifications in relation to hovercraft or activities or places connected therewith (if any)
The Conveyance of Live Poultry Order of 1919 as amended	S.R. & O. 1919/933 (Rev. XVIII, p. 434: Noted 1919, p. 966).	
The Transit of Animals Order of 1927 as amended	S.R. & O. 1927/289 (Rev. II, p. 259: 1927, p. 57)	
The Foot-and-Mouth Disease Order of 1928 as amended	S.R. & O. 1928/133 (Rev. II, p. 499: 1928, p. 94).	
The Pleuro-Pneumonia Order of 1928	S.R. & O. 1928/205 (Rev. II, p. 567; 1928, p. 118).	
The Cattle Plague Order of 1928	S.R. & O. 1928/206 (Rev. II, p. 472; 1928, p. 78).	
The Importation of Dogs and Cats Order of 1928 as amended	S.R. & O. 1928/922 (Rev. II, p. 399; 1928, p. 177).	
The Animals (Importation) Order of 1930 as amended	S.R. & O. 1930/922 (Rev. II, p. 331; 1930, p. 52).	
The Animals (Sea Transport) Order of 1930 as amended	S.R. & O. 1930/923 (Rev. II, p. 284; 1930, p. 78).	
The Importation of Meat, &c. (Wrapping Materials) Order of 1932 as amended	S.R. & O. 1932/317 (Rev. II, p. 409; 1932, p. 107).	
The Fowl Pest Order of 1936 as amended	S.R. & O. 1936/1297 (Rev. XVIII, p. 442; 1936 II, p. 2086).	
The Epizootic Lymphangitis Order of 1938	S.R. & O. 1938/193 (Rev. II, p. 490; 1938 I, p. 141).	
The Sheep Scab Order of 1938 as amended	S.R. & O. 1938/196 (Rev. II, p. 602; 1938 I, p. 234).	
The Anthrax Order of 1938	S.R. & O. 1938/204 (Rev. II, p. 457; 1938 I, p. 124).	

Column 1 Instruments applied	Column 2 References	Column 3 Modifications in relation to hovercraft or activities or places connected therewith (if any)
The Parasitic Mange Order of 1938	S.R. & O. 1938/227 (Rev. II, p. 556; 1938 I, p. 191).	
The Glanders or Farcy Order of 1938	S.R. & O. 1938/228 (Rev. II, p. 545; 1938 I, p. 178).	
The Sheep-Pox Order of 1938	S.R. & O. 1938/229 (Rev. II, p. 588; 1938 I, p 216).	
The Foot-and-Mouth Disease (Infected Areas Restrictions) Order of 1938 as amended	S.R. & O. 1938/1434 (Rev. II, p. 528; 1938 I, p. 155).	
The Foot-and-Mouth Disease (Controlled Areas Restrictions) Order of 1938 as amended	S.R. & O. 1938/1435 (Rev. II, p. 520; 1938 I, p. 169).	
The Poultry and Hatching Eggs (Importation) Order of 1947 as amended	S.R. & O. 1947/1426 (Rev. XVIII, p. 450; 1947 I, p. 1841).	
The National Insurance (Industrial Injuries) Mariners Regulations 1948, as amended, regulations 1, 3, 7(1), 8, 10, 12, 13 and 14	S.R. & O. 1948/1471 (Rev. XVI, p. 432; 1948 I, p. 2990).	(1) In regulation 1(2) the definition of "home-trade ship" and the words "and, subject as aforesaid, expressions to which meanings are assigned in the Merchant Shipping Acts 1894 to 1938 have the same meanings as in those Acts" shall not apply; and in the definition of "mariner" for the words from "under the Act" to "thereto", there shall be substituted the words "under the National Insurance (Industrial Injuries) Act 1965 by virtue of the provisions of paragraphs 2 (as modified by Schedule 1 to the Hovercraft (Application of Enactments) Order 1972) and 3-5 of Part 1 of Schedule 1 to that Act". (2) In regulation 3, the words "Subject to the provisions of the two next following regulations" shall be omitted; for the words "or of any regulations for the time being in force as to the payment of contributions under the National Insurance

Column 1 Instruments applied	Column 2 References	Column 3 Modifications in relation to hovercraft or activities or places connected therewith (if any)
		Act in respect of share fishermen" there shall be substituted the words "as applied by Schedule 1 to the Hovercraft (Application of Enactments) Order 1972" and after the words "by virtue of these regulations", there shall be inserted the words "as applied by Schedule 1 to the Hovercraft (Application of Enactments) Order 1972". (3) In regulation 8, for the words "to which paragraph 2 of Part 1 of the First Schedule to the Act applies, or by virtue of employment as a pilot within paragraph 3 thereof", there shall be substituted the words "to which paragraph 2 of Part 1 of Schedule 1 to the National Insurance (Industrial Injuries) Act 1965 as modified by Schedule 1 to the Hovercraft (Application of Enactments) Order 1972 applies"; for the words "at a port other than a proper return port", there shall be substituted the words "outside Great Britain"; for the words "to such a port", there shall be substituted the words "to Great Britain"; and paragraph (*d*) shall not apply. (4) In regulation 10, for the words "to which paragraph 2 of Part I of the First Schedule to the Act applies or as a pilot within paragraph 3 thereof", there shall be substituted the words "to which paragraph 2 of Part I of Schedule 1 to the National Insurance (Industrial Injuries) Act 1965 as modified by Schedule 1 to the Hovercraft (Application of Enactments) Order 1972 applies". (5) In regulation 13, the words "or by a superintendent" shall be omitted.
The Prevention of Damage by Pests (Application to Shipping) Order 1951 as amended	S.I. 1951/967 (1951 II, p. 197).	
The Poultry Pens, Fittings and Receptacles (Disinfection) Order 1952 as amended	S.I. 1952/437 (1952 III, p. 2628).	
The Horses (Sea Transport) Order 1952 as amended	S.I. 1952/1291 (1952 I, p. 146).	

Column 1 Instruments applied	Column 2 References	Column 3 Modifications in relation to hovercraft or activities or places connected therewith (if any)
The Horses (Landing from Northern Ireland and the Republic of Ireland) Order 1954	S.I. 1954/698 (1954 I, p. 133).	
The Importation of Carcases and Animal Products Order 1954, as amended	S.I. 1954/853 (1954 I, p. 136).	
The Poultry Carcases (Landing) Order 1955 as amended	S.I. 1955/147 (1955 II, p. 2052).	
The Animals (Landing from Channel Islands, Isle of Man, Northern Ireland and Republic of Ireland) Order 1955 as amended	S.I. 1955/1310 (1955 I, p. 190).	
The Importation of Animal Semen Order 1955 as amended	S.I. 1955/1390 (1955 I, p. 207).	
The Poultry Premises and Vehicles (Disinfection) Order 1956	S.I. 1956/11 (1956 II, p. 1895).	
The Prevention of Damage by Pests (Application to Shipping) (Amendment No. 2) Order 1956	S.I. 1956/420 (1956 II, p. 1754).	
The Fowl Pest (Infected Areas Restrictions) Order 1956 as amended	S.I. 1956/1611 (1956 II, p. 1883).	
The Swine Fever (Infected Areas Restrictions) Order 1956 as amended	S.I. 1956/1750 (1956 I, p. 180).	
The Diseases of Animals (Waste Foods) Order 1957	S.I. 1957/628 (1957 I, p. 148).	
The Service Departments Registers Order 1959 as amended	S.I. 1959/406 (1959 II, p. 2303).	
The Movement of Animals (Records) Order 1960 as amended	S.I. 1960/105 (1960 I, p. 302).	
The Landing of Unbarked Coniferous Timber Order 1961	S.I. 1961/656 (1961 I, p. 1395).	
The Importation of Hay, Straw and Dried Grass Order 1961	S.I. 1961/946 (1961 II, p. 1841).	

Column 1 Instruments applied	Column 2 References	Column 3 Modifications in relation to hovercraft or activities or places connected therewith (if any)
The Swine Fever Order 1963	S.I. 1963/286 (1963 I, p. 239).	
The Exported Animals Protection Order 1964	S.I. 1964/704 (1964 II, p. 1352).	
The Collision Regulations (Ships and Seaplanes on the Water) and Signals of Distress (Ships) Order 1965	S.I. 1965/1525 (1965 II, p. 4411).	(1) For Article 3 there shall be substituted "the Collision Regulations shall apply to all United Kingdom registered hovercraft and to all other hovercraft within United Kingdom territorial waters". (2) For Article 4(2) there shall be substituted "The provisions of the said section 21 shall apply to all United Kingdom hovercraft, and to all other hovercraft within United Kingdom territorial waters". (3) In Rule 1(*a*) the words "or hovercraft" shall be added after "seaplanes" in the second sentence. (4) There shall be added to Schedule 1, Part B as Rule 7A the following Rule— (*a*) "In addition to the lights prescribed in Rule 2 and Rule 7 for a power driven vessel under way a hovercraft when under way and supported (wholly or partly) on its cushion of air shall carry where it can best be seen an amber flashing light flashing 60 times per minute and of such a character as to be visible all round the horizon at a distance of at least 5 miles. (*b*) A hovercraft when complying with the carriage of lights prescribed in Rule 4(*a*), Rule 4(*c*) and Rule 5(*a*) and (*c*) shall not carry an amber flashing light prescribed above." (5) There shall be added as paragraph (3) to the Preliminary to Part C—Sound Signals and Conduct in Restricted Visibility the following:—

Column 1 Instruments applied	Column 2 References	Column 3 Modifications in relation to hovercraft or activities or places connected therewith (if any)
		"(3) It should be noted that because of the noise of operation of some types of hovercraft, sound signals may not be heard from them and they may not be able to hear sound signals made by other vessels". (6) There shall be added as paragraph (5) of the Preliminary to Part D—Steering and Sailing Rules, the following:— "(5) In complying with the Steering and Sailing Rules it should be borne in mind that hovercraft operate at high speed and that under certain circumstances the aspect presented by the hovercraft to other vessels is not always a true indication of its direction of travel."
The Merchant Shipping (Dangerous Goods) Rules 1965 as amended	S.I. 1965/1067 (1965 II, p. 2681).	(1) For "passenger steamer" wherever it appears, there shall be substituted "hovercraft carrying more than 12 passengers", and (2) The definition of "passenger steamer" and "steamer" shall not apply.
The Hares (Control of Importation) Order 1965	S.I. 1965/2040 (1965 III, p. 6030).	
The Export of Horses (Veterinary Examination) Order 1966	S.I. 1966/507 (1966, I p. 1071).	
The National Insurance (Mariners) Regulations 1967 as amended Regulations 1, 2, 10, 14 and 24	S.I. 1967/386 (1967 I, p. 1294).	(1) In regulation 1(2), the definitions of "share fisherman", "home-trade ship", "home-trade port", "foreign-going ship", "passenger" and "passenger ship" and the words "and, subject as aforesaid, expressions to which meanings are assigned in the Merchant Shipping Acts 1894 to 1965 have the same meanings as in those Acts" shall not apply: in the definition of "mariner" the words "and includes a share fisherman" shall be omitted; in the definition of "manager" the words "ship's husband or other" shall be omitted; and

Column 1 Instruments applied	Column 2 References	Column 3 Modifications in relation to hovercraft or activities or places connected therewith (if any)
		the definition of "British ship" shall have effect subject to the modifications of paragraph 2 of Part I of Schedule 1 to the National Insurance (Industrial Injuries) Act 1965, effected by this Schedule. (2) In regulation 2, the proviso to paragraph (1) thereof, and paragraphs (2), (5) and (6) thereof, shall not apply. (3) In regulation 10, in paragraph (*b*), the words "superintendent or" shall be omitted; and in provisos (*b*) and (*c*) for the words "a proper return port" wherever they appear, there shall be substituted the words "Great Britain". (4) In regulation 14, paragraph (3) shall not apply.
The Equine Animals (Importation) Order 1969 as amended	S.I. 1969/915 (1969 II, p. 2791).	
The Exotic Animals (Importation) Order 1969	S.I. 1969/1737 (1969 III, p. 5450).	
The Export of Horses (Excepted Cases) Order 1969	S.I. 1969/1742 (1969 III, p. 5470).	
The Export of Horses (Protection) Order 1969	S.I. 1969/1784 (1969 III, p. 5582).	
The Cattle Plague (Ireland) Order of 1900	S.R. & O. 1901/7	
The Pleuro-Pneumonia (Ireland) Order of 1900	S.R. & O. 1901/8	
The Sheep Pox (Ireland) Order of 1900	S.R. & O. 1901/10	
The Glanders or Farcy (Ireland) Order of 1900 as amended	S.R. & O. 1901/15	
The Importation of Animals (Ireland) Order 1900	S.R. & O. 1901/17	
The Foreign Animals (Ireland) Order of 1901	S.R. & O. 1901/959	
The Importation of Horses, Asses and Mules (Ireland) Order 1907 as amended	S.R. & O. 1907/59	

Column 1 Instruments applied	Column 2 References	Column 3 Modifications in relation to hovercraft or activities or places connected therewith (if any)
The Animals (Transit & General) (Ireland) Order of 1913 as amended	S.R. & O. 1913/604	
The Portal Inspection (Ireland) Order of 1914 as amended	S.R. & O. 1914/1564	
The Parasitic Mange (Ireland) Order of 1919 as amended	S.R. & O. 1919/737	
The Conveyance of Live Poultry (Ireland) Order of 1919 as amended	S.R. & O. 1919/1066	
The Animals Quarantine Order (N.I.) 1923	S.R. & O. 1923/501	
The Exportation of Animals (N.I.) Order 1923 as amended	S.R. & O. 1923/1076	
The Swine Fever Order (N.I.) 1926	S.R. & O. 1926/95	
The Animals Disinfection (N.I.) Order 1927 as amended	S.R. & O. 1927/52	
The Transit of Animals (N.I.) Order 1927 as amended	S.R. & O. 1927/38	
The Foreign Animals (N.I.) Order 1928	S.R. & O. 1928/88	
The Musk Rats (N.I.) Order 1933	S.R. & O. 1933/46	
The Bovine Tuberculosis (N.I.) Order 1935 as amended	S.R. & O. 1935/39	
The Grey Squirrels (N.I.) Order 1936	S.R. & O. 1936/65	
The Diseases of Animals (Poultry) Order (N.I.) 1949 as amended	S.R. & O. 1949/192	
The Horses (Sea Transport) Order (N.I.) 1953	S.R. & O. 1953/87	
The Diseases of Animals (Therapeutic Substances) (N.I.) Order 1953 as amended	S.R. & O. 1953/169	
The Non-Indigenous Rabbits (Prohibiting of Importation and Keeping) Order (N.I.) 1954	S.R. & O. 1954/161	
The Animals (Sea Transport) Order (N.I.) 1958	S.R. & O. 1958/5	

Column 1 Instruments applied	Column 2 References	Column 3 Modifications in relation to hovercraft or activities or places connected therewith (if any)
The Importation of Foreign Vegetables Order (N.I.) 1961	S.R. & O. 1961/28	
The Importation of Dogs and Cats Order (N.I.) 1961 as amended	S.R. & O. 1961/29	
The Hay, Straw & Grass Meal Order (N.I.) 1962 as amended	S.R. & O. 1962/62	
The Diseases of Animals (Boiling of Animal Food) Order (N.I.) 1962	S.R. & O. 1962/72	
The Foot and Mouth Disease Order (N.I.) 1962	S.R. & O. 1962/209	
The Unlawful Importations Order (N.I.) 1963	S.R. & O. 1963/178	
The Coypus Order (N.I.) 1963	S.R. & O. 1963/234	
The Foreign Animals Order (N.I.) 1964	S.R. & O. 1964/81	
The Diseases of Animals (Importation of Poultry) Order (N.I.) 1965 as amended	S.R. & O. 1965/175	
The Foyle Area (Control of Netting) Regulations (N.I.) 1966	S.R. & O. 1966/72	
The Destructive Pests and Diseases of Plants Order (N.I.) 1966	S.R. & O. 1966/313	
The Importation of Dung Order (N.I.) 1967	S.R. & O. 1967/179	
The Rabbits and Hares (Control of Importation) Order (N.I.) 1967	S.R. & O. 1967/294	
The Mink Order (N.I.) 1967	S.R. & O. 1967/346	
The Mink (Importation and Keeping) Regulations (N.I.) 1968	S.R. & O. 1968/8	
The Fisheries Consolidated, Amendment and Licence Duties Bye-Laws (N.I.) 1969	S.R. & O. 1969/91	
The Exotic Animals Importation Order (N.I.) 1969 as amended	S.R. & O. 1969/334	
The Landing of Carcases and Animal Products Order (N.I.) 1970	S.R. & O. 1970/145	

Column 1 Instruments applied	Column 2 References	Column 3 Modifications in relation to hovercraft or activities or places connected therewith (if any)
The Foyle Area (Control of Netting) (Amendment) Regulations (N.I.) 1970	S.R. & O. 1970/200	
The Sheep Scab Order (N.I.) 1970	S.R. & O. 1970/240	
The Exported Animals (Amendment of Charges) Order (N.I.) 1971	S.R. & O. 1971/56	
The Importation of Peat Moss Litter Order (N.I.) 1971	S.R. & O. 1971/186	

3148

SCHEDULE 2

Article 5

Application to Hovercraft of Certain Enactments and Instruments Relating to Aircraft

Part A:—Enactments applied and modifications

Column 1 Enactments applied	Column 2 References	Column 3 Modifications in relation to hovercraft or activities or places connected with hovercraft (if any)
The Civil Aviation Act 1949 sections 52 and 55 as amended by the Civil Aviation Act 1971.	1949 c. 67. 1971 c. 75.	(1) In section 52, subsections (1), (2) and (4) shall not apply. (2) In section 52, subsection (3) the words "when on the surface of the water" shall be omitted. (3) In section 52, subsection (5), paragraphs (*c*) and (*d*) shall not apply. (4) In section 55— (i) references to the "Air Register Book of Births and Deaths" shall be deemed to be references to "the Hovercraft Register Book of Births and Deaths", and (ii) references to 'aircraft registered in Great Britain and Northern Ireland' shall be deemed to include references (as well as to hovercraft registered in Great Britain and Northern Ireland) to hovercraft not so registered which carry passengers to or from any port in the United Kingdom. (iii) References to the Civil Aviation Authority substituted for "the Minister" by the Civil Aviation Act 1971 shall in relation to hovercraft be deemed to be references to the Secretary of State, and references to the Authority substituted as aforesaid for references to his Department shall be deemed to be references to the Department of Trade and Industry.

Column 1 Enactments applied	Column 2 References	Column 3 Modifications in relation to hovercraft or activities or places connected with hovercraft (if any)
The Army Act 1955 sections 24(1)(*h*), 24(3), 36(2), 44(2) and (3), 46(*aa*) and (*ab*), 48(2), 49, 50, 177(2) and 198	1955 c. 18.	
The Air Force Act 1955 sections 24(1)(*h*), 24(3), 36(2), 44(2) and (3), 46(*b*) and (*c*), 48(2), 49, 50, 172, 177(2) and 198	1955 c. 19.	
The Licensing Act 1964 section 87	1964 c. 26.	In section 87— (i) In sub-section (1), for "the examination station approved for the airport under section 16 of the Customs and Excise Act 1952" there shall be substituted "the approved wharf approved for the hoverport under section 14 of the Customs and Excise Act 1952 as applied by section 10 of the Finance Act 1966". (ii) In sub-section (2) "The Secretary of State" shall be substituted for the words from "This section" (where they first appear) to "Aviation"; and the words "and any order under the said Act of 1956", shall be omitted. (iii) In sub-section (3), for "Minister" there shall be substituted "Secretary of State". (iv) In sub-section (3), for "examination station" there shall be substituted "approved wharf".
The Registration of Births, Deaths and Marriages (Scotland) Act 1965	1965 c. 49.	
The Tokyo Convention Act 1967	1967 c. 52.	(1) For references to "flight" where they occur shall be substituted references to "journey"; and for references to "commander" wherever they occur there shall be substituted references to "captain".

Column 1 Enactments applied	Column 2 References	Column 3 Modifications in relation to hovercraft or activities or places connected with hovercraft (if any)
		(2) In section 1(2) the words in brackets shall be omitted;
		(3) In section 1(3) from "and section 62(1)" to the end shall be omitted;
		(4) In section 2 for "registered in a Convention country" there shall be substituted "registered in any country other than the United Kingdom";
		(5) In section 3(5)(*b*)(ii) and 3(6)(*b*) "which is a Convention country" shall be omitted;
		(6) Section 4 shall not apply;
		(7) Section 5 shall not apply;
		(8) In section 6(1)(*a*) for sub-paragraphs (i) and (ii) there shall be substituted "an Order in Council made under the Hovercraft Act 1968".
		(9) In section 6(1)(*a*) "or the Air Transport Licensing Board" shall be omitted.
		(10) Section 6(1)(*b*) and 6(2) shall not apply.
		(11) In section 7(1) the definitions of "commander" "Convention country", "pilot in command" and "Tokyo Convention" shall not apply.
		(12) In section 7(2)(*a*), for from "taking off" to the end there shall be substituted "moving off on a journey until the moment when the hovercraft comes to a halt at the end of that journey; and"
		(13) Section 7(4) and (5)(*b*) shall not apply;
		(14) Sections 8 and 9 and the Schedule shall not apply.

Column 1 Enactments applied	Column 2 References	Column 3 Modifications in relation to hovercraft or activities or places connected with hovercraft (if any)
The Civil Aviation Act 1968 section 16	1968 c. 61.	In section 16(2)(*b*) the words "and rights under section 14 of this Act or under regulations made by virtue of section 7(2) of the Civil Aviation (Eurocontrol) Act 1962" shall not apply.
The Civil Aviation Act 1971 section 27	1971 c. 75.	In sub-section (2) references to "certificates of airworthiness to be granted or renewed in pursuance of the Air Navigation Orders" shall include references to any certificates to be granted or renewed in pursuance of Part II of the Hovercraft (General) Order 1972.

PART B:—Instruments applied

Column 1 Instruments applied	Column 2 References	Column 3 Modifications in relation to hovercraft or activities or places connected with hovercraft (if any)
The Destructive Pests and Diseases of Plants Order 1965	S.I. 1965/216 (1965 I, p. 510).	
The Importation of Forest Trees (Prohibition) (Great Britain) Order 1965	S.I. 1965/2121 (1965 III, p. 6236)	
The Destructive Pests and Diseases of Plants (Scotland) Order 1966	S.I. 1966/1533 (1966 III, p. 4353)	
The Examination of Seed Potatoes (Scotland) Order 1970	S.I. 1970/1287 (1970 III, p. 4264)	

SCHEDULE 3

Article 6

Application to Hovercraft of Certain Enactments and Instruments Relating to Motor Vehicles

Part A: Enactments applied

Column 1 Enactments applied	Column 2 References	Column 3 Modifications in relation to hovercraft or activities or places connected therewith (if any)
The Army Act 1955 sections 47(*b*), 172, 173, 184(1)(*b*) and (*c*)	1955 c. 18.	
The Air Force Act 1955 sections 47(*b*), 48(1), 173, 184(*a*), (*b*) and (*c*)	1955 c. 19.	

Part B: Instruments applied

Column 1 Instruments applied	Column 2 References	Column 3 Modifications in relation to hovercraft or activities or places connected therewith (if any)
The Royal Botanic Gardens Kew Regulations 1957	S.I. 1957/710	
The Wakehurst Place Regulations 1969	S.I. 1969/1000	
The Agricultural Statistics (England and Wales) Regulations of 1948 as amended	S.R. & O. 1948/2294 (Rev. I, p. 583; 1948 I, p. 30).	

3149

SCHEDULE 4

Article 9

INVESTIGATION OF CASUALTIES

PART A

MODIFICATIONS OF PART VI OF THE MERCHANT SHIPPING ACT 1894

The following are modifications of Part VI of the Merchant Shipping Act 1894 referred to in Article 9 of this Order:—

(1) For section 464 there shall be substituted—

"For the purposes of inquiries and investigations under this Part of this Act, a hovercraft casualty shall be deemed to occur when a hovercraft—

(*a*) has sustained, caused or been involved in any accident occasioning loss of life or any serious injury to any person;

(*b*) becomes lost, abandoned, missing or stranded;

(*c*) suffers such damage as the result of any accident that its safety is impaired; or

(*d*) becomes involved in a collision with another hovercraft or ship;

but only when the occurrence takes place—

(i) on or over the sea or other navigable water; or

(ii) between the time when any person goes on board the hovercraft for the purpose of making a journey which would involve crossing the sea or other navigable water and the time when it comes to rest at the end of such a journey; or

(iii) during the testing or maintenance of a hovercraft which normally makes journeys on or over the sea or other navigable water

and also only if at the time the occurrence takes place, the hovercraft was registered in the United Kingdom or was operating unregistered in accordance with any provisions of any Order made under section 1(1)(a) of the Hovercraft Act 1968 or was within the United Kingdom or United Kingdom territorial waters.

(2) For section 465 there shall be substituted—

"(1) Where a hovercraft casualty has occurred a preliminary inquiry may be held respecting the casualty by a person appointed for the purpose by the Secretary of State.

(2) A person appointed under this section to hold a preliminary inquiry into a hovercraft casualty shall for the purpose of the inquiry have the powers conferred on an inspector by section 729 of this Act as if the reference therein to a ship were a reference to a hovercraft".

(3) For section 466(1) there shall be substituted—

"The Secretary of State may cause a formal investigation to be held, if in England, Wales, or Northern Ireland, by a wreck commissioner, and in Scotland, by a sheriff, and any reference to the court holding an investigation under this section means a wreck commissioner or sheriff, as the case may be, holding such an investigation".

(4) Section 466(2) shall not apply.

(5) For section 466(3) there shall be substituted—

"The court holding any such formal investigation shall hold the same with the assistance of one or more assessors of nautical, engineering, hovercraft or other special skill or knowledge to be appointed by the Lord Chancellor".

(6) Section 466(4) and (5) shall not apply.

(7) Section 467 to 474 shall not apply.

(8) In section 475(1) the words "or an inquiry into the conduct of a master, mate or engineer" shall be omitted.

(9) Section 475(3) shall not apply.

(10) Section 476 shall not apply.

(11) For section 477 there shall be substituted—

"(1) The Lord Chancellor may appoint such number of persons as he thinks fit to be wreck commissioners and may remove any wreck commissioners appointed by him.

(2) Before appointing a person as wreck commissioner in Northern Ireland, the Lord Chancellor shall consult the Lord Chief Justice of Northern Ireland".

(12) Section 478 shall not apply.

(13) Sections 480-490 shall not apply.

(14) For section 491 there shall be substituted—

"There may be paid out of the money provided by Parliament to any wreck commissioner, sheriff, assessor in any court of investigation under this part of this Act, registrar of a court, or any other officer, or person appointed for the purpose of any court of investigation under this part of this Act, such salary or remuneration (if any) as the Treasury may direct."

PART B

MODIFICATIONS OF THE SHIPPING CASUALTIES AND APPEALS AND RE-HEARINGS RULES 1923

The following are modifications of the Shipping Casualties and Appeals and Re-hearings Rules 1923 referred to in Article 9 of this Order:—

(1) After the word "owner", wherever it appears, there shall be added "or operator".

(2) Rule 1 shall not apply.

(3) In Rule 2 the definition of "List of Assessors" shall be deleted and in the definition of judge the words "sheriff substitute, stipendiary magistrate, justices" shall be omitted.

(4) In Rule 15 the words "Except where the certificate of an officer is cancelled or suspended in which case the decision shall always be given in open Court" shall be omitted.

(5) In Rule 19 the words "other than an appeal under section 68 of the Merchant Shipping Act 1906" shall be omitted.

(6) For Rule 20(*e*) there shall be substituted the following—

"The Court of Appeal shall be assisted by not less than two suitably qualified or experienced persons to be selected by the Court who shall have regard to the nature of the case."

(7) In Rule 21(*a*) the words "or 478" shall be omitted and after "1894" there shall be inserted the words "as applied by the Hovercraft (Application of Enactments) Order 1972".

(8) Rules 22 to 26 shall not apply.

(9) Rules 30 and 31 shall not apply.

(10) Part II of the Appendix shall not apply.

APPENDIX 7

HOVERCRAFT: REGISTRATION AND SAFETY ORDER

Hovercraft (General) Order 1972

(S.I. 1972 No. 674)

Order made under section 1(1)(*a*)-(*c*),(*e*),(*l*),(*n*)-(*p*),(3) *of the Hovercraft Act* 1968, *dated April* 28, 1972.

8150 EXPLANATORY NOTE [1]

This Order makes provision for the registration, safety certification, maintenance and operational safety of hovercraft. It also includes provision as to ancillary matters affecting the safety of hovercraft and persons and property thereon.

Under the Order the Secretary of State will be the authority for the registration of hovercraft and for issuing Operating Permits, while the Civil Aviation Authority will be the authority for certifying the safe construction of hovercraft.

The Order empowers the Secretary of State to make regulations by Statutory Instrument prescribing fees, with the approval of the Treasury, in respect of matters relating to hovercraft.

8151 ARRANGEMENT OF ORDER

Article

[1] This Note is not part of the Order.

PART III

DUTIES OF OPERATOR AND CAPTAIN

18. Operating Permits
19. Duties of operator
20. Duties of captain
21. Operational records
22. Medical equipment
23. Documents to be carried
24. Notification of casualties

PART IV

SUPPLEMENTARY PROVISIONS

25. Right of access to hoverports
26. Safety of persons and property
27. Duty to obey captain
28. Power to prevent hovercraft operating
29. Revocation etc. of Certificates etc.
30. Obstruction of persons
31. Enforcement of directions
32. Exemption from Order
33. Penalties
34. Crown application
35. Fees
36. Extra-territorial effect of the Order

SCHEDULE

Schedule: Penalties

Citation and Commencement

3152 **1.**—(1) This Order may be cited as the Hovercraft (General) Order 1972.

(2)(*a*) Article 35 of this Order shall come into operation on 31st May 1972;

(*b*) The remainder of the Order shall come into operation on 26th June 1972.

(a) 1968 c. 59.

Application

2. This Order applies to hovercraft which are used—

(i) wholly or partly on or over the sea or navigable waters; or

(ii) on or over land to which the public have access or non-navigable waters to which the public have access; or

(iii) elsewhere for the carriage of passengers for reward:

Provided that this Order shall not:

(*a*) apply to hovertrains; nor

(*b*) prejudice the operation of section 19 of the Road Traffic Act 1962.[2]

Interpretation

3.—(1) In this Order, unless the context otherwise requires—

"Authorised person" for the purposes of any provision of this Order means—

(*a*) any constable; and

(*b*) any person authorised in writing by the Secretary of State either generally or in relation to a particular case or class of cases;

"Beneficial interest" includes interests arising under contract and other equitable interests;

"The CAA" means the Civil Aviation Authority;

"Captain" means the person who is designated by the operator to be in charge of a hovercraft during any journey, or, failing such designation, the person who is for the time being lawfully in charge of the hovercraft;

"Hovertrains" means hovercraft which are at all times guided by tracks, rails or guides fixed to the ground;

"Military hovercraft" means the naval, military or air force hovercraft of any country and includes—

(*a*) any hovercraft being constructed for the naval, military or air force of any country under a contract entered into by the Secretary of State; and

(*b*) any hovercraft in respect of which there is in force a certificate issued by the Secretary of State that the hovercraft is to be treated for the purposes of this Order as a military hovercraft;

"Navigable water" means any water which is in fact navigable by ships or vessels, whether or not the tide ebbs and flows there, and whether or not there is a public right of navigation in that water;

"Operator" in relation to a hovercraft means the person for the time being having the management of the hovercraft;

"Passenger" means any person carried in a hovercraft, except a person employed or engaged in any capacity on board the hovercraft on the business of the hovercraft;

"Unladen weight" in relation to a hovercraft means the weight of a hovercraft ready for use, excluding the weight of usable fuel, occupants, baggage, cargo, stores, buoyant life-saving equipment, portable fire-fighting equipment, portable emergency equipment and non-permanent ballast;

[2] See Note (2) § 3142, *supra*.

"United Kingdom" includes the territorial waters adjacent to the United Kingdom;

"Unqualified person" means a person not qualified in accordance with Article 5(3) to be the holder of a legal or beneficial interest by way of ownership in the hovercraft.

(2) The Interpretation Act 1889 shall apply to the interpretation of this Order as it applies to the interpretation of an Act of Parliament.

PART I
REGISTRATION

Hovercraft to be registered

3153 **4.** Subject to Article 7, a hovercraft shall, if used in the United Kingdom, be registered in the United Kingdom unless—

(*a*) it is registered in some other country; or

(*b*) an unqualified person holds a legal or beneficial interest in the hovercraft by way of ownership or share therein, and the Secretary of State consents to its use unregistered in the United Kingdom, subject to such conditions as he thinks fit:

Provided that a hovercraft may also be used unregistered in the United Kingdom if:

(i) (*a*) it has been issued with an Experimental Certificate in accordance with Article 9, and

(*b*) it is marked in a manner approved by the Secretary of State; or

(ii) it has an unladen weight of less than 1,000 kg. and is not used for reward.

Registration of hovercraft in the United Kingdom

3154 **5.**—(1) The Secretary of State shall be the authority for registration of hovercraft in the United Kingdom.

(2) Subject to the provisions of this Article a hovercraft shall not be registered or continue to be registered in the United Kingdom if it appears to the Secretary of State that—

(*a*) the hovercraft is registered outside the United Kingdom and that such registration does not cease by operation of law upon the hovercraft being registered in the United Kingdom; or

(*b*) an unqualified person holds any legal or beneficial interest in the hovercraft by way of ownership or any share therein.

(3) Subject to paragraph (4) of this Article the following persons and no others shall be qualified to be the holder of a legal or beneficial interest by way of ownership in a hovercraft registered in the United Kingdom or a share therein—

(*a*) the Crown in right of Her Majesty's Government in the United Kingdom;

(*b*) persons ordinarily resident in the United Kingdom;

(*c*) bodies incorporated in the United Kingdom and having their principal place of business in the United Kingdom;

(*d*) firms carrying on business in Scotland;

In this sub-paragraph "firm" has the same meaning as in the Partnership Act 1890.

(4) If an unqualified person holds a legal or beneficial interest by way of ownership in a hovercraft or a share therein, or is charterer by demise thereof, the Secretary of State may register the hovercraft in the United Kingdom subject to such conditions as he thinks fit. The Secretary of State may at any time cancel the registration of a hovercraft registered under this paragraph.

(5) Application for the registration of a hovercraft in the United Kingdom shall be made in writing to the Secretary of State and shall include or be accompanied by such particulars and evidence relating to the hovercraft and the ownership and chartering thereof as he may require to enable him to determine whether the hovercraft may properly be registered in the United Kingdom and to issue the certificate referred to in paragraph (7) of this Article.

(6) Upon receiving an application for the registration of a hovercraft in the United Kingdom and being satisfied that the hovercraft may properly be so registered, the Secretary of State shall (or, in the case of an application under paragraph (4) of this Article, may) register the hovercraft, wherever it may be, and shall include in the register the following particulars—

(*a*) the number of the certificate;

(*b*) the registration mark assigned to the hovercraft by the Secretary of State;

(*c*) the name of the constructor of the hovercraft, its type and constructor's number;

(*d*) (i) the name and address of every person who holds a legal interest in the hovercraft by way of ownership or a share therein, or, in the case of a hovercraft which is the subject of a hire-purchase agreement, the name and address of the hirer; and

(ii) in the case of a hovercraft registered in pursuance of paragraph (4) of this Article, an indication that it is so registered, and an indication as to whether the person in whose name it is registered is the owner or charterer by demise.

(7) The Secretary of State shall furnish to the person in whose name the hovercraft is registered (hereinafter in this Article referred to as "the registered owner") a certificate of registration, which shall include the foregoing particulars and the date on which the certificate was issued.

(8) Subject to paragraph (4) of this Article, if at any time after a hovercraft has been registered in the United Kingdom an unqualified person becomes the holder of a legal or beneficial interest in the hovercraft by way of ownership or a share therein, the registration of the hovercraft shall thereupon become void and the certificate of registration shall forthwith be returned by the registered owner to the Secretary of State for cancellation.

(9) Any person who is registered as the owner of a hovercraft registered in the United Kingdom shall forthwith inform the Secretary of State in writing of—

(*a*) any change in the particulars which were furnished to the Secretary of State upon application being made for the registration of the hovercraft;

(a) 1890 c. 39.

(*b*) the destruction of the hovercraft, or its permanent withdrawal from use;

(*c*) in the case of a demise chartered hovercraft registered in pursuance of paragraph (4) of this Article, the termination of the demise charter.

(10) Any person who becomes the owner of a hovercraft registered in the United Kingdom shall forthwith inform the Secretary of State in writing to that effect.

(11) The Secretary of State may, whenever it appears to him necessary or appropriate to do so for giving effect to this Order or for bringing up to date or otherwise correcting the particulars entered on the register, amend the register or, if he thinks fit, may cancel the registration of the hovercraft, and shall cancel that registration if he is satisfied that there has been a change in the ownership of the hovercraft.

(12) In this Article references to an interest in a hovercraft do not include references to an interest in a hovercraft to which a person is entitled only by virtue of his membership of a hovercraft club and the reference in paragraph (9) of this Article to the registered owner of a hovercraft includes in the case of a deceased person, his legal personal representative, and in the case of a body corporate which has been dissolved, its successor.

Nationality and registration marks

3155 **6.**—(1) A hovercraft registered in the United Kingdom shall not be used unless—

(i) it bears prominently and clearly painted or affixed to the craft its nationality and registration marks; and

(ii) the nationality and registration marks together with the name and address of the registered owner are engraved on a fire proof metal plate affixed in a prominent position inside the hovercraft near an entrance.

(2) The nationality mark of a hovercraft registered in the United Kingdom shall be the capital letters "GH" in Roman characters and the registration mark shall be a group of four digits assigned by the Secretary of State on the registration of the hovercraft. The letters and digits shall be without ornamentation and a hyphen shall be placed between the nationality mark and the registration mark.

(3) The nationality and registration marks of a hovercraft shall be used as the sole means of identification of the craft by radio.

Hovercraft registered outside the United Kingdom

7.—(1) A hovercraft registered in a country other than the United Kingdom shall not be used for reward or in connection with a trade or business in or over the United Kingdom, except with the permission of the Secretary of State granted under this Article to the operator or charterer of the hovercraft and in accordance with any conditions to which such permission may be subject.

(2) Nothing in this Article shall apply to the use of a hovercraft for passage through the territorial waters of the United Kingdom.

Part II

Certification and Maintenance

Safety Certificate to be in force

156 **8.** A hovercraft registered in the United Kingdom shall not be used unless there is in force in respect thereof a current Safety Certificate issued in accordance with this Order and any conditions subject to which the Certificate was issued are complied with:

Provided that the foregoing prohibition shall not apply to—

(*a*) a hovercraft used in accordance with the conditions of an Experimental Certificate issued by the CAA in respect of that hovercraft; or

(*b*) subject to the prior consent of the CAA and to any conditions subject to which that consent was given, a hovercraft in respect of which a Safety Certificate has previously been in force, which is used solely for the purpose of enabling it to—

(i) qualify for a renewal of a Safety Certificate or a variation of a certificate after an application has been made for such renewal or variation;

(ii) proceed to or from a place at which any inspection or test of the hovercraft is to take place for the purpose referred to in sub-paragraph (i) above; or

(iii) proceed to a place at which repairs can be effected.

Issue and renewal of Experimental Certificates

9.—(1) The CAA may, if satisfied by such investigations relating to the safe use of the hovercraft as it may require, issue in respect of any hovercraft an Experimental Certificate, which shall be subject to the condition that the hovercraft is not to carry any persons other than those engaged on the business of the hovercraft, unless the CAA specifically permits such other persons to be carried in a particular case. The Experimental Certificate shall be issued subject to such further conditions relating to safety as the CAA thinks fit.

(2) The CAA may, if satisfied by such investigations relating to the safe use of the hovercraft as it may require, vary an Experimental Certificate at the request of an applicant. Such variation may be subject to such further conditions relating to safety as the CAA thinks fit.

(3) An Experimental Certificate shall, unless cancelled or suspended, remain in force for such period not exceeding one year as may be specified therein, and may be renewed from time to time by the CAA for such further period not exceeding one year as it thinks fit.

Issue of Type Certificates

10.—(1) The CAA may, if satisfied by such investigations of one or more hovercraft as it may require, or by a study of relevant specifications, or by a combination of investigations and a study of relevant specifications, that individual examples of a particular type of hovercraft would if suitably constructed be capable of safe use, issue a Type Certificate in respect of the type of hovercraft specified in the Certificate.

(2) The CAA may, if satisfied by such investigations as it may require or by a study of relevant specifications, or by a combination of investigations and a study of relevant specifications, that individual examples of an engine, component, instrument, or equipment intended for use in a hovercraft would if suitably constructed safely fulfil the function for which they are intended, issue a Type Certificate in respect of that type of engine, component, instrument, or equipment.

(3) The CAA may, if satisfied by such investigations as it may require, vary a Type Certificate issued under paragraph (1) and (2) of this Article, at the request of an applicant.

(4) A Type Certificate shall remain in force until cancelled or suspended.

Issue of Safety Certificates

3157 **11.**—(1) The CAA may issue a Safety Certificate in respect of a hovercraft registered in the United Kingdom upon being satisfied that it is fit to be used, having regard, in particular, to—

(*a*) the conformity of the hovercraft, its engines, components, instruments, and equipment to a relevant Type Certificate, and compliance with any conditions subject to which that certificate may have been issued;

(*b*) the results of such investigations of the hovercraft as the CAA may require; and

(*c*) the quality of the hovercraft's construction.

(2) (*a*) Every Safety Certificate may specify such categories as have been applied for and are, in the opinion of the CAA, appropriate to the hovercraft, and the Safety Certificate shall be issued subject to the condition that the hovercraft shall be used only for the purposes indicated in sub-paragraph (*c*) of this paragraph in relation to such categories;

(*b*) The categories referred to in sub-paragraph (*a*) of this paragraph are—

Passenger
Cargo
Special

(*c*) The purposes for which hovercraft may be used are as follows—

Passenger Category:	Carriage of passengers and their baggage, and any other purpose specified in the Certificate.
Cargo Category:	The carriage of cargo generally, or of such cargo as may be specified in the Certificate.
Special Category:	Any purpose specified in the Certificate, but not including the carriage of passengers except as expressly permitted.

(3) The CAA may issue the Safety Certificate subject to such other conditions relating to the safety of the hovercraft as it thinks fit.

(4) The CAA may, having regard to such investigations as it may require, vary a Safety Certificate at the request of an applicant. Such variation may be subject to such other conditions relating to the safety of hovercraft as it thinks fit.

Period of validity of Certificates

12. Subject to the provisions of Articles 11 and 15, a Safety Certificate shall remain in force for such period not exceeding one year as may be specified therein, and may be renewed from time to time by the CAA for such further period not exceeding one year as it thinks fit. A Safety Certificate shall cease to be valid in the event of a hovercraft ceasing to be registered in the United Kingdom.

Maintenance

158 **13.** A hovercraft in respect of which a Safety Certificate is in force under this Order shall not be used unless it is maintained in a condition satisfactory to the CAA, and in accordance with arrangements approved by the CAA.

Approvals

14. For the purposes of this Part of this Order the CAA may accept reports furnished to it by a person whom it may for the time being approve either absolutely or subject to such conditions as it thinks fit as qualified to furnish such reports.

Revocation etc., of Certificates etc., and power to prevent hovercraft being used

15.—(1) The CAA may, if it thinks fit, provisionally suspend or vary any Certificate, approval or other document issued, granted or having effect under this part of this Order, pending inquiry into or consideration of the case. Without prejudice to Article 10(3) or 11(4); the CAA may, on sufficient ground being shown to its satisfaction after due inquiry, revoke, suspend or vary any such Certificate, approval or other document.

(2) The holder or any person having the possession or custody of any Certificate, approval or other document which has been revoked, suspended or varied under this Part of this Order shall surrender it to the CAA within a reasonable time after being required to do so by it.

(3) The breach of any condition subject to which any Certificate, approval or other document, has been granted or issued, or which has effect under this Order shall render the document invalid during the continuance of the breach.

(4) If it appears likely to the CAA that a hovercraft is intended or likely to be used—

(*a*) in such circumstances that any conditions on which the Safety Certificate has been granted are breached;

(*b*) whilst the approved maintenance arrangements are not adhered to;

(*c*) whilst materially damaged; or

(*d*) in such circumstances that the CAA has reason to believe that the hovercraft is or may be unsafe;

the CAA may direct the operator or the captain of the hovercraft that he is not to permit the hovercraft to make the particular journey or any other journey of such description as may be specified in the direction, until the direction has been revoked by the CAA, and the CAA may take such steps as are necessary to detain the hovercraft for a period not exceeding seven days.

(5) In the event of the CAA provisionally suspending any Certificate, approval or other document under paragraph (1), or detaining a hovercraft under paragraph (4) above, the CAA shall, within 48 hours, send to the holder of such Certificate, approval or other document a statement in writing of its reasons.

(6) Notwithstanding paragraph (1) of this Article any document incorporated by reference in any Certificate may be varied on sufficient ground being shown to the satisfaction of the CAA, whether or not after due inquiry.

Inspection of hovercraft

3159 **16.** The CAA may at any reasonable time inspect a hovercraft or part or equipment thereof in respect of which an Experimental or Safety Certificate—

(*a*) has been applied for, or

(*b*) has been issued and is still in force, or

(*c*) has been issued and has ceased within the preceding period of 3 months to be in force,

and may for that purpose enter any premises where persons are employed in the design, construction, maintenance or storage of the hovercraft, or any hoverport.

International Certificates

17.—(1) The Secretary of State may issue in respect of a hovercraft registered in the United Kingdom such certificates as he deems appropriate, as a result of inspection and survey of the hovercraft by the CAA, under the International Convention for the Safety of Life at Sea [3] and the Internationl Convention on Load Lines 1966 [4] for the purpose of complying with the law of a country other than the United Kingdom.

(2) The Secretary of State may cancel or suspend any certificate issued under this Article where he has reason to believe—

(*a*) that the certificate has been issued on the basis of inaccurate information; or

(*b*) that since the issue of the certificate the hovercraft has sustained any material damage or that the condition of the hovercraft or of its equipment does not correspond substantially with the particulars of that certificate.

(3) The Secretary of State may require any certificate, issued under this Article which has expired or been suspended or cancelled to be delivered up as he directs.

PART III

DUTIES OF OPERATOR AND CAPTAIN

Operating Permits

3160 **18.**—(1) Hovercraft registered in the United Kingdom shall not be used for reward or in connection with a trade or business, otherwise than under and in accordance with a Permit (hereinafter called an "Operating Permit") granted to the operator of the hovercraft under paragraph (2) of this Article. Operating

[3] Cmnd. 2812. 2812. [4] Cmnd. 3070.

Permits shall be granted with a view to securing the safe operation of the hovercraft. However this Article shall not apply to a hovercraft operating in accordance with an Experimental Certificate issued pursuant to Article 9.

(2) The Secretary of State may grant or renew to any person applying therefor an Operating Permit for the operation of hovercraft of the types and in relation to the areas of operation specified in the Operating Permit for the purposes so specified. The Operating Permit may be granted subject to such conditions as the Secretary of State thinks fit to impose with a view to securing the safe operation of hovercraft and shall remain in force for such time as may be specified in the Operating Permit or until suspended or revoked by the Secretary of State and may be renewed from time to time by the Secretary of State for such further period as he thinks fit. The Secretary of State may vary an Operating Permit on application by the holder.

(3) The conditions to which the Operating Permit may be subject may include, without prejudice to the generality of the foregoing paragraph, conditions in respect of the following matters—

(*a*) crew complement and qualifications;

(*b*) type of hovercraft;

(*c*) area of operation;

(*d*) restrictions with regard to working hours and rest periods of crew;

(*e*) safety arrangements at hoverports or terminal areas;

(*f*) the weather conditions in which the hovercraft may operate;

(*g*) day or night operation;

(*h*) life-saving equipment and procedures;

(*i*) other equipment and procedures necessary for safety of operation;

(*j*) radio and radar;

(*k*) the keeping of records.

Duties of operator

19.—(1) The operator of a hovercraft registered in the United Kingdom or operating unregistered in the United Kingdom in accordance with proviso(i) in Article 4 of this Order shall not permit the hovercraft to be used without first—

(*a*) designating a member of the crew to be captain on that journey;

(*b*) ensuring that a minimum number of the crew corresponding to the complement necessary for the journey are adequately trained for their duties for that journey;

(*c*) ensuring that the safety equipment required to be carried is in working order.

(2) Without prejudice to his other duties under this Order an operator shall at all times take all reasonable precautions at hoverports and terminal areas so as to ensure the safety of persons and property in the hovercraft and on the ground.

(3) An operator shall not permit any hovercraft to be used if he has reason to believe or suspect it is in an unsafe condition.

Duties of captain

3161 **20.** The captain, before the departure of the hovercraft—

(*a*) shall take reasonable steps to ensure

(i) that the craft is properly loaded and any cargo adequately secured in the craft;

(ii) that there is adequate supply of fuel; and

(iii) that the craft is in a fit state and that the safety equipment required to be carried is in a fit condition and ready to be used; and

(*b*) shall satisfy himself that the journey can safely be made, taking into account the latest information available to him as to the route and weather.

Operational records

21.—(1) The captain of every hovercraft registered in the United Kingdom shall ensure that records are kept of the following matters relating to any journey of the hovercraft—

(*a*) Names of terminal and any intermediate points, and the times of departure from and arrival at such points;

(*b*) Weather conditions, such as wind, sea condition and visibility experienced;

(*c*) Any accidents or unusual occurrences on the journey;

(*d*) Any births or deaths which occur on the journey;

(*e*) A summary of all communications relating to distress, urgency and safety traffic.

(2) The operator of every hovercraft registered in the United Kingdom shall keep records of—

(*a*) crew emergency and distress drills (including names of persons present);

(*b*) the names of all crew aboard a hovercraft on any journey.

(3) The captain or operator, as the case may be, shall within a reasonable time after being requested to do so by an authorised person, cause to be produced to that person the records referred to in paragraphs (1) and (2) above respectively.

(4) (*a*) The records mentioned above shall be preserved by the operator for at least 12 months after any journey or drill to which they refer;

(*b*) The records referred to in paragraph (1) of this Article shall be delivered to the operator of the hovercraft to which the records relate by the captain at the time he ceases to be the captain, or when the operator requires their delivery;

(*c*) A person required to preserve any record by reason of his being the operator of a hovercraft shall, if he ceases to be the operator of the hovercraft continue to preserve the record as if he had not ceased to be the operator, and in the event of his death the duty to preserve the record shall fall upon his personal representative.

Medical equipment

22. A hovercraft registered in the United Kingdom or used unregistered in accordance with proviso (i) in Article 4, shall carry when in use first-aid equipment of good quality, sufficient in quantity having regard to the number of persons on board and the circumstances of the use of the hovercraft, and including the following—

Roller bandages, triangular bandages, absorbent gauze, adhesive plaster, white absorbent lint, cotton wool (or wound dressings in place of the lint and cotton wool), burn dressings, safety pins; haemostatic bandages or tourniquets, scissors; antiseptic, analgesic and stimulant drugs; a handbook on First Aid.

Documents to be carried

62 **23.**—(1) A hovercraft registered in the United Kingdom, or operating unregistered in the United Kingdom in accordance with proviso (i) in Article 4 shall, when in operation, carry the following documents or true copies thereof—

(*a*) its Safety Certificate, or Experimental Certificate if any;

(*b*) its certificate of registration if any;

(*c*) any certificate issued to the hovercraft under Article 17.

(2) The Safety Certificate and any certificate issued to the hovercraft under Article 17 or true copies thereof shall be posted in some conspicuous place in the hovercraft.

Notification of casualties

24.—(1) When a hovercraft casualty has occurred, the captain or if the captain is incapacitated, the operator of the hovercraft shall—

(*a*) by the quickest available means, inform the Secretary of State of the happening of the casualty, stating the registration number or identity of the hovercraft and the place where the casualty occurred or is believed to have occurred and, in the case of a hovercraft which is missing, the route it was on; and

(*b*) within 48 hours, or as soon thereafter as possible, transmit to the Secretary of State a report, signed by the captain or operator, of the casualty and of the probable occasion thereof, stating the registration number or identity of the hovercraft and the place where the casualty occurred or is believed to have occurred:

Provided that this Article shall not apply to hovercraft which are less than 1,000 kg. unladen weight and are not used for reward.

(2) For the purpose of this Article a hovercraft casualty shall be deemed to occur when a hovercraft—

(*a*) has sustained, caused or been involved in any accident occasioning loss of life or any serious injury to any person;

(*b*) becomes lost, abandoned, missing or stranded;

(*c*) suffers such damage as the result of any accident that its safety is impaired; or

(*d*) becomes involved in a collision with another hovercraft or ship;

but only when the occurence takes place—

(i) on or over the sea or other navigable water; or

(ii) between the time when any person goes on board the hovercraft for the purpose of making a journey which would involve crossing the sea or other navigable water and the time when it comes to rest at the end of such a journey; or

(iii) during the testing or maintenance of a hovercraft which normally makes journeys on or over the sea or other navigable water

and also only if at the time the occurrence takes place, the hovercraft was registered in the United Kingdom or was operating unregistered in accordance with proviso(i) in Article 4 of this Order or was within the United Kingdom.

PART IV

SUPPLEMENTARY PROVISIONS

Right of access to hoverports

3163 **25.** The Secretary of State and any authorised person shall have the right of access at all reasonable times to any hoverport and any place where a hovercraft is for the purpose of inspecting any hovercraft or any document which they have power to demand under this Order, and for the purpose of detaining any hovercraft under the provisions of this Order.

Safety of persons and property

26.—(1) A person shall not wilfully or negligently—

(*a*) act in a manner likely to endanger a hovercraft, or any person therein; or

(*b*) go or attempt to go on a journey on a hovercraft without the consent of the captain or other person authorised to give it.

(2) A person shall not—

(*a*) enter a hovercraft when drunk, or be drunk in a hovercraft; or

(*b*) smoke in a place in a hovercraft or at a hoverport where and when smoking is prohibited by notice.

Duty to obey captain

27. Every person in a hovercraft shall obey all lawful commands which the captain may give for the purpose of securing the safety of the hovercraft and of persons or property carried therein, or the safety, efficiency or regularity of navigation.

Power to prevent hovercraft operating

28.—(1) If it appears to the Secretary of State or an authorised person that any hovercraft is intended or likely to be operated—

(*a*) in such circumstances that any provision of Articles 4, 6, 7, 8, 13 or 18 of this Order would be contravened in relation to the journey; or

(*b*) in such circumstances that the journey would be in contravention of any other provision of this Order and be a cause of danger to any person or property whether or not in the hovercraft; or

(*c*) while in a condition unfit for operation whether or not the journey would otherwise be in contravention of any provision of this Order,

the Secretary of State or that authorised person may direct the operator or the captain of the hovercraft that he is not to permit the hovercraft to make the particular journey or any other journey of such description as may be specified in the direction, until the direction has been revoked by the Secretary of State or by an authorised person, and the Secretary of State, or that person may take such steps as are necessary to detain the hovercraft.

(2) For the purposes of paragraph (1) of this Article the Secretary of State or any authorised person may enter upon and inspect any hovercraft.

Revocation etc. of Certificates etc.

3164 **29.**—(1) The Secretary of State may, if he thinks fit, provisionally suspend any certificate, licence, approval, permission, exemption or other document issued, granted or having effect under this Order other than under Part II, pending inquiry into or investigation of the case. Without prejudice to Article 18(2) of this Order the Secretary of State may on sufficient ground being shown to his satisfaction after due inquiry, revoke, suspend or vary any such certificate, licence, approval, permission, exemption or other document.

(2) The holder or any person having the possession or custody of any certificate, licence, approval, permission, exemption or other document which has been revoked, suspended or varied under this Article shall surrender it to the Secretary of State within a reasonable time after being required to do so by him.

(3) The breach of any condition subject to which any certificate, licence, approval, permission, exemption or other document has been granted or issued, or which has effect under this Order, shall render the document invalid during the continuance of the breach.

Obstruction of persons

30. A person shall not wilfully obstruct or impede any person acting in the exercise of his powers or the performance of his duties under this Order.

Enforcement of directions

31. Any person who fails to comply with any direction given to him by the Secretary of State or by any authorised person under any provision of this Order shall be deemed for the purpose of this Order to have contravened that provision.

Exemption from Order

32. The Secretary of State may exempt from any of the provisions of this Order or any regulations made thereunder any hovercraft or persons or classes of hovercraft or persons, either absolutely or subject to such conditions as he thinks fit.

Penalties

65 **33.**—(1) If any provision of this Order is contravened in relation to a hovercraft, the operator of that hovercraft and the captain thereof, shall (without prejudice to the liability of any other person under this Order for that contravention) be deemed for the purposes of sub-paragraphs (3) to (5) of this Article to have contravened that provision unless he proves that the contravention occurred without his consent or connivance and that he exercised all due diligence to prevent the contravention.

(2) If it is proved that an act or omission of any person which would otherwise have been a contravention by that person of a provision of this Order was due to any cause not avoidable by the exercise of reasonable care by that person the act or omission shall be deemed not to be a contravention by that person of that provision.

(3) If any person contravenes any provision of this Order, not being a provision referred to in paragraph (4) or paragraph (5) of this Article, he shall be liable on summary conviction to a fine not exceeding ten pounds; or in the case of a second or subsequent conviction for the like offence to a fine not exceeding twenty pounds.

(4) If any person contravenes any provision specified in Part A of the Schedule to this Order he shall be liable on summary conviction to a fine not exceeding fifty pounds; or in the case of a second or subsequent conviction for the like offence to a fine not exceeding one hundred pounds, or on indictment both to such fine and to imprisonment for a term not exceeding three months.

(5) If any person contravenes any provision specified in Part B of the said Schedule he shall be liable on summary conviction to a fine not exceeding two hundred pounds or, on indictment both to such fine and to imprisonment for a term not exceeding six months.

Crown application

34.—(1) Subject to the following provisions of this Article, the provisions of this Order shall apply to or in relation to hovercraft belonging to or exclusively employed in the service of Her Majesty, as they apply to or in relation to other hovercraft and for the purposes of such application the Government Department or other authority for the time being responsible on behalf of Her Majesty for the operational management of the hovercraft shall be deemed to be the operator of the hovercraft and in the case of a hovercraft belonging to Her Majesty to be the owner of the interest of Her Majesty in the hovercraft:

Provided that nothing in this Article shall render liable to any penalty any Department or other authority responsible on behalf of Her Majesty for the management of the hovercraft.

(2) Save as provided in paragraph (3) of this Article nothing in this Order shall apply to or in relation to any military hovercraft.

(3) Where a military hovercraft is operated by a civilian and is not commanded by a person who is acting in the course of his duty as a member of any of Her Majesty's naval or military or air forces or as a member of a visiting force or international headquarters, Article 20 shall apply on the occasion of that journey.

Fees

35. The Secretary of State may, by regulations made by statutory instrument, require the payment of fees in respect of any matter relating to hovercraft which is specified in this Order, and may prescribe with the approval of the Treasury the amount of any such fee or the manner in which that amount is to be determined, and sections 1, 2 and 3 of the Statutory Instruments Act 1946 shall apply to the regulations.

Extra-territorial effect of the Order

36.—(1) Except where the context otherwise requires, the provisions of this Order—

(*a*) in so far as they apply (whether by express reference or otherwise) to hovercraft registered in the United Kingdom, shall apply to such hovercraft wherever they may be;

(*b*) in so far as they apply as aforesaid to other hovercraft shall apply to such hovercraft when they are within the United Kingdom;

(*c*) in so far as they prohibit, require or regulate (whether by express reference or otherwise) the doing of anything by persons in, or by any of the crew of, any hovercraft registered in the United Kingdom, shall apply to such persons and crew, wherever they may be; and

(*d*) in so far as they prohibit, require or regulate as aforesaid the doing of anything in relation to any hovercraft registered in the United Kingdom by other persons shall, where such persons are British subjects, apply to them wherever they may be.

(2) Nothing in this Article shall be construed as extending to make any person guilty of an offence in any case in which it is provided by section 3(1) of the British Nationality Act 1948(**a**) (which limits the criminal liability of certain persons who are not citizens of the United Kingdom and colonies) that that person shall not be guilty of an offence.

W. G. Agnew.

SCHEDULE

Article 33

PENALTIES

PART A: Provisions referred to in Article 33(4); Articles 4, 6, 21, 23, 24 and 30

PART B: Provisions referred to in Article 33(5); Articles 7, 8, 13, 15, 18, 19, 20, 22, 26, 27 and 28

APPENDIX 8

ADMIRALTY JURISDICTION OF THE HIGH COURT

Administration of Justice Act 1956

(4 & 5 Eliz. 2, c. 46)

An Act to amend the law relating to Admiralty jurisdiction, legal proceedings in connection with ships and aircraft and the arrest of ships and other property . . . [5th July, 1956]

PART I
ADMIRALTY JURISDICTION AND OTHER PROVISIONS AS TO SHIPS

Admiralty jurisdiction of the High Court

3167 **1.**—(1) The Admiralty jurisdiction of the High Court shall be as follows, that is to say, jurisdiction to hear and determine any of the following questions or claims—

(*a*) any claim to the possession or ownership of a ship or to the ownership of any share therein;

(*b*) any question arising between the co-owners of a ship as to possession, employment or earnings of that ship;

(*c*) any claim in respect of a mortgage of or charge on a ship or any share therein;

(*d*) any claim for damage done by a ship;

(*e*) any claim for damage received by a ship;

(*f*) any claim for loss of life or personal injury sustained in consequence of any defect in a ship or in her apparel or equipment, or of the wrongful act, neglect or default of the owners, charterers or persons in possession or control of a ship or of the master or crew thereof or of any other person for whose wrongful acts, neglects or defaults the owners, charterers or persons in possession or control of a ship are responsible, being an act, neglect or default in the navigation or management of the ship, in the loading, carriage or discharge of goods on, in or from the ship or in the embarkation, carriage or disembarkation of persons on, in or from the ship;

(*g*) any claim for loss of or damage to goods carried in a ship;

(*h*) any claim arising out of any agreement relating to the carriage of goods in a ship or to the use or hire of a ship;

(*j*) any claim in the nature of salvage (including any claim arising by virtue of the application, by or under section fifty-one of the Civil Aviation Act, 1949, of the law relating to salvage to aircraft and their apparel and cargo);

(*k*) any claim in the nature of towage in respect of a ship or an aircraft;

(*l*) any claim in the nature of pilotage in respect of a ship or an aircraft;

(*m*) any claim in respect of goods or materials supplied to a ship for her operation or maintenance;

(*n*) any claim in respect of the construction, repair or equipment of a ship or dock charges or dues;

(*o*) any claim by a master or members of the crew of a ship for wages and any claim by or in respect of a master or member of the crew of a ship for any money or property which, under any of the provisions of the Merchant Shipping Acts, 1894 to 1954, is recoverable as wages or in the court and in the manner in which wages may be recovered;

(*p*) any claim by a master, shipper, charterer or agent in respect of disbursements made on account of a ship;

(*q*) any claim arising out of an act which is or is claimed to be a general average act;

(*r*) any claim arising out of bottomry;

(*s*) any claim for the forfeiture or condemnation of a ship or of goods which are being or have been carried, or have been attempted to be carried, in a ship, or for the restoration of a ship or any such goods after seizure, or for droits of Admiralty,

together with any other jurisdiction which either was vested in the High Court of Admiralty immediately before the date of the commencement of the Supreme Court of Judicature Act, 1873 (that is to say, the first day of November, eighteen hundred and seventy-five) or is conferred by or under an Act which came into operation on or after that date on the High Court as being a court with Admiralty jurisdiction and any other jurisdiction connected with ships or aircraft vested in the High Court apart from this section which is for the time being assigned by rules of court to the *Queen's Bench Division and directed by the rules to be exercised by the Admiralty Court.*[1]

3168 (2) The jurisdiction of the High Court under paragraph (*b*) of subsection (1) of this section includes power to settle any account outstanding and unsettled between the parties in relation to the ship, and to direct that the ship, or any share thereof, shall be sold, and to make such other order as the court thinks fit.

(3) The reference in paragraph (*j*) of subsection (1) of this section to claims in the nature of salvage includes reference to such claims for services rendered in saving life from a ship or an aircraft or in preserving cargo, apparel or wreck as, under sections five hundred and forty-four to five hundred and forty-six of the Merchant Shipping Act, 1894, or any Order in Council made under section fifty-one of the Civil Aviation Act, 1949, are authorised to be made in connection with a ship or an aircraft.

(4) The preceding provisions of this section apply—

(*a*) in relation to all ships or aircraft, whether British or not and whether registered or not and wherever the residence or domicile of their owners may be;

(*b*) in relation to all claims, wheresoever arising (including, in the case of cargo or wreck salvage, claims in respect of cargo or wreck found on land); and

(*c*) so far as they relate to mortgages and charges, to all mortgages or charges, whether registered or not and whether legal or equitable, including mortgages and charges created under foreign law:

Provided that nothing in this subsection shall be construed as extending the cases in which money or property is recoverable under any of the provisions of the Merchant Shipping Acts, 1894 to 1954.

169 [1] The words in italics were substituted by the Administration of Justice Act 1970, s. 2 (4). Jurisdiction was formerly exercised by the Probate, Divorce and Admiralty Division.

Mode of exercise of Admiralty jurisdiction

3170 **3.**—(1) Subject to the provisions of the next following section, the Admiralty jurisdiction of the High Court, *the Liverpool Court of Passage* [1] [and any county court] [2] may in all cases be invoked by an action in personam.

(2) The Admiralty jurisdiction of the High Court may in the cases mentioned in paragraphs (*a*) to (*c*) and (*s*) of subsection (1) of section one of this Act be invoked by an action in rem against the ship or property in question.

(3) In any case in which there is a maritime lien or other charge on any ship, aircraft or other property for the amount claimed, the Admiralty jurisdiction of the High Court, *the Liverpool Court of Passage* [1] [and any county court] [2] may be invoked by an action in rem against that ship, aircraft or property.

(4) In the case of any such claim as is mentioned in paragraphs (*d*) to (*r*) of subsection (1) of section one of this Act, being a claim arising in connection with a ship, where the person who would be liable on the claim in an action in personam was, when the cause of action arose, the owner or charterer of, or in possession or in control of, the ship, the Admiralty jurisdiction of the High Court and (*where there is such jurisdiction*) *the Admiralty jurisdiction of the Liverpool Court of Passage* [1] [or any county court] [2] may (whether the claim gives rise to a maritime lien on the ship or not) be invoked by an action in rem against—

(*a*) that ship, if at the time when the action is brought it is beneficially owned as respects all the shares therein by that person; or

(*b*) any other ship which, at the time when the action is brought, is beneficially owned as aforesaid.

3171 (5) In the case of a claim in the nature of towage or pilotage in respect of an aircraft, the Admiralty jurisdiction of the High Court, *the Liverpool Court of Passage* [1] [and any county court] [2] may be invoked by an action in rem against that aircraft if at the time when the action is brought it is beneficially owned by the person who would be liable on the claim in an action in personam.

(6) Notwithstanding anything in the preceding provisions of this section, the Admiralty jurisdiction of the High Court, *the Liverpool Court of Passage* [1] [or any county court] [2] shall not be invoked by an action in rem in the case of any such claim as is mentioned in paragraph (*o*) of subsection (1) of section one of this Act unless the claim relates wholly or partly to wages (including any sum allotted out of wages or adjudged by a superintendent to be due by way of wages).

(7) Where, in the exercise of its Admiralty jurisdiction, the High Court, *the Liverpool Court of Passage* [1] [or any county court] [2] orders any ship, aircraft or other property to be sold, the court shall have jurisdiction to hear and determine any question arising as to the title to the proceeds of sale.

(8) In determining for the purposes of subsections (4) and (5) of this section whether a person would be liable on a claim in an action in personam it shall be assumed that he has his habitual residence or a place of business within England and Wales.

3172 [1] The words in italics were repealed by the Courts Act 1971, s. 56, Sched. II, Pt. II.
[2] The words in square brackets were repealed by the County Courts Act 1959, s. 202, Sched. III. See now ss. 55–61 of that Act, *infra*, Appendix 9.

Jurisdiction in personam of courts in collision and other similar cases

73 **4.**—(1) No court in England and Wales shall entertain an action in personam to enforce a claim to which this section applies unless—

(*a*) the defendant has his habitual residence or a place of business within England and Wales; or

(*b*) the cause of action arose within inland waters of England and Wales or within the limits of a port of England and Wales; or

(*c*) an action arising out of the same incident or series of incidents is proceeding in the court or has been heard and determined in the court.

In this subsection—

"inland waters" includes any part of the sea adjacent to the coast of the United Kingdom certified by the Secretary of State to be waters falling by international law to be treated as within the territorial sovereignty of Her Majesty apart from the operation of that law in relation to territorial waters;

"port" means any port, harbour, river, estuary, haven, dock, canal or other place so long as a person or body of persons is empowered by or under an Act to make charges in respect of ships entering it or using the facilities therein, and "limits of a port" means the limits thereof as fixed by or under the Act in question or, as the case may be, by the relevant charter or custom;

"charges" means any charges with the exception of light dues, local light dues and any other charges in respect of lighthouses, buoys or beacons and of charges in respect of pilotage.

(2) No court in England and Wales shall entertain an action in personam to enforce a claim to which this section applies until any proceedings previously brought by the plaintiff in any court outside England and Wales against the same defendant in respect of the same incident or series of incidents have been discontinued or otherwise come to an end.

(3) The preceding provisions of this section shall apply to counter-claims (not being counter-claims in proceedings arising out of the same incident or series of incidents) as they apply to actions in personam, but as if the references to the plaintiff and the defendant were respectively references to the plaintiff on the counter-claim and the defendant to the counter-claim.

(4) The preceding provisions of this section shall not apply to any action or counter-claim if the defendant thereto submits or has agreed to submit to the jurisdiction of the court.

4 (5) Subject to the provisions of subsection (2) of this section, the High Court shall have jurisdiction to entertain an action in personam to enforce a claim to which this section applies whenever any of the conditions specified in paragraphs (*a*) to (*c*) of subsection (1) of this section are satisfied, and the rules of court relating to the service of process outside the jurisdiction shall make such provision as may appear to the rule-making authority to be appropriate having regard to the provisions of this subsection.

(6) Nothing in this section shall prevent an action or counter-claim which is brought in accordance with the provisions of this section in the High Court, *the Liverpool Court of Passage* [1] [or a county court] [2] being transferred, in accordance with the enactments in that behalf, to some other court.

5 [1] The words in italics were repealed by the Courts Act 1971, s. 56, Sched. 111, Part II. See note (1) to section 2, *supra*.

[2] The words in square brackets were repealed by the County Courts Act 1959, s. 202, Sched. III. See now ss. 55–61 of that Act, *infra*, Appendix 9.

(7) The claims to which this section applies are claims for damage, loss of life or personal injury arising out of a collision between ships or out of the carrying out of or omission to carry out a manoeuvre in the case of one or more of two or more ships or out of non-compliance, on the part of one or more of two or more ships, with the collision regulations.

(8) For the avoidance of doubt it is hereby declared that this section applies in relation to the jurisdiction of any court not being Admiralty jurisdiction, as well as in relation to its Admiralty jurisdiction, if any.

Wages

3176 **5.**—(1) Section one hundred and sixty-five of the Merchant Shipping Act, 1894 (which imposes restrictions on suits for wages), is hereby repealed.

(2) Nothing in this Part of this Act shall be construed as limiting the jurisdiction of the court to refuse to entertain an action for wages by the master or a member of the crew of a ship, not being a British ship.

Courts in England and Wales not to have jurisdiction in cases falling within Rhine Convention

3177 **6.** No court in England and Wales shall have jurisdiction to determine any claim or question certified by the Secretary of State to be a claim or question which, under the Rhine Navigation Convention, falls to be determined in accordance with the provisions thereof and any proceedings to enforce such a claim which are commenced in any such court shall be set aside.

Repeals and savings

3178 **7.**—(1) Section six hundred and eighty-eight of the Merchant Shipping Act, 1894, the Shipowners' Negligence (Remedies) Act, 1905 and the Merchant Shipping (Stevedores and Trimmers) Act, 1911 (which relate to the detention of ships by customs officers in certain cases), and so much of subsection (2) of section seventy-five of the Diseases of Animals Act, 1950, as enables a local authority to recover expenses in burying or destroying carcases in the same manner as salvage is recoverable, shall cease to have effect, but nothing in this Part of this Act, affects the provisions of section five hundred and fifty-two of the Merchant Shipping Act, 1894 (which relates to the power of a receiver of wreck to detain a ship in respect of a salvage claim).

(2) The provisions of sections one to three of this Act shall, as respects the High Court, have effect in lieu of sections twenty-two and thirty-three of the Supreme Court of Judicature (Consolidation) Act, 1925 [and, as respects the Liverpool Court of Passage and the county court, in lieu of subsections (1) to (7) of section fifty-six of the County Courts Act, 1934] [1] and those Acts, and in particular any provision of the first-mentioned Act referring to the Admiralty jurisdiction of the High Court, shall be construed accordingly.

(3) Nothing in this Part of this Act shall authorise proceedings in rem in respect of any claim against the Crown, or the arrest, detention or sale of any of Her Majesty's ships or Her Majesty's aircraft, or of any cargo or other property belonging to the Crown.

In this subsection "Her Majesty's ships" and "Her Majesty's aircraft" have the meanings assigned to them by subsection (2) of section thirty-eight of the Crown Proceedings Act, 1947.

(4) *Nothing in this Part of this Act shall affect section five of the Mail Ships Act,* 1891 (*which protects certain mail ships from arrest in certain circumstances*).[2]

3179 [1] The words in square brackets were repealed by the County Courts Act 1959, s. 202, Sched. III. See now ss. 55–61 of that Act, *infra*, Appendix 9.

[2] The words in italics were repealed by the Statute Law Revision Act 1963, s. 1, Sched.

Supplemental and Transitional provisions

80 **8.**—(1) In this Part of this Act, unless the context otherwise requires,—

"ship" includes any description of vessel used in navigation;

"goods" includes baggage;

"collision regulations" means regulations under section four hundred and eighteen of the Merchant Shipping Act, 1894, or any such rules as are mentioned in subsection (1) of section four hundred and twenty-one of that Act or any rules made under subsection (2) of the said section four hundred and twenty-one;

"master" has the same meaning as in the Merchant Shipping Act, 1894, and accordingly includes every person (except a pilot) having command or charge of a ship;

"towage" and "pilotage", in relation to an aircraft, means towage and pilotage while the aircraft is waterborne;

"the Rhine Navigation Convention" means the Convention of the seventh of October, eighteen hundred and sixty-eight, as revised by any subsequent Convention.

(2) Nothing in any provision in this Part of this Act or in any repeal consequential thereon shall affect proceedings in respect of any cause of action arising before the coming into operation thereof.

APPENDIX 9

ADMIRALTY JURISDICTION OF THE COUNTY COURT

County Courts Act 1959

(7 & 8 Eliz. 2, c. 22)

Admiralty Proceedings

Districts for Admiralty purposes

3181 **55.**—(1) If at any time it appears expedient to the Lord Chancellor that any county court should have Admiralty jurisdiction, it shall be lawful for him by order—

(*a*) to appoint that court to have, as from such date as may be specified in the order, such Admiralty jurisdiction as is hereafter provided in this Act; and

(*b*) to assign to that court as its district for Admiralty purposes any part or parts of any county court district or of two or more county court districts:

Provided that no court except the Mayor's and City of London Court shall have Admiralty jurisdiction in the City of London.[1]

(2) Where a district has been assigned to a court as its district for Admiralty purposes, the parts of the sea (if any) adjacent to that district to a distance of three miles from the shore thereof shall be deemed to be included in that district, and the judge and all officers of the court shall have jurisdiction and authority for those purposes throughout that district as if it were the district for the court for all purposes.

(3) Any order made under this section may be varied from time to time or revoked, as appears expedient, by a subsequent order made thereunder.

(4) Where an order is made under this section for the discontinuance of the Admiralty jurisdiction of any county court, whether wholly or within a part of the district assigned to it for Admiralty purposes, provision may be made in the order with respect to any Admiralty proceedings commenced in that court before the order comes into operation.

(5) The power to make orders under this section shall be exercisable by statutory instrument.

3182 [1] The words in italics were repealed by the Courts Act 1967, s. 56, Sched. 11, Part III.

3183 **Admiralty jurisdiction**

56.—(1) Subject to the limitations of amount specified in subsection (2) of this section, an Admiralty county court shall have the following Admiralty jurisdiction, that is to say, jurisdiction to hear and determine any of the following claims:—

(*a*) any claim for damage done by a ship;

(*b*) any claim for damage received by a ship;

(*c*) any claim for loss of life or personal injury sustained in consequence of any defect in a ship or in her apparel or equipment, or of the wrongful act, neglect or default of the owners, charterers or persons in possession or control of a ship or of the master or crew thereof or of any other person for whose wrongful acts, neglects or defaults the owners, charterers or persons in possession or control of a ship are responsible, being an act, neglect or default in the navigation or management of the ship, in the loading, carriage or discharge of goods on, in or from the ship or in the embarkation, carriage or disembarkation of persons on, in or from the ship;

(*d*) any claim for loss of or damage to goods carried in a ship;

(*e*) any claim arising out of any agreement relating to the carriage of goods in a ship or to the use or hire of a ship;

(*f*) any claim in the nature of salvage (including any claim arising by virtue of the application, by or under section fifty-one of the Civil Aviation Act, 1949, of the law relating to salvage to aircraft and their apparel and cargo);

(*g*) any claim in the nature of towage in respect of a ship or an aircraft;

(*h*) any claim in the nature of pilotage in respect of a ship or an aircraft;

(*j*) any claim in respect of goods or materials supplied to a ship for her operation or maintenance;

(*k*) any claim in respect of the construction, repair or equipment of a ship or dock charges or dues;

(*l*) any claim by a master or member of the crew of a ship for wages and any claim by or in respect of a master or member of the crew of a ship for any money or property which, under any of the provisions of the Merchant Shipping Acts, 1894 to 1954, is recoverable as wages or in the court and in the manner in which wages may be recovered;

(*m*) any claim by a master, shipper, charterer or agent in respect of disbursements made on account of a ship.

(2) The limitations of amount referred to in subsection (1) of this section are as follows, that is to say, that the court shall not have jurisdiction to hear and determine any claim mentioned in that subsection for an amount exceeding one thousand pounds, except in the case of a claim in the nature of salvage where the value of the property saved does not exceed three thousand five hundred pounds.

84 (3) References in the foregoing provisions of this section to claims in the nature of salvage include references to such claims for services rendered in saving life from a ship or an aircraft or in preserving cargo, apparel or wreck as, under sections five hundred and forty-four to five hundred and forty-six of the Merchant Shipping Act, 1894, or any Order in Council made under section fifty-one of the Civil Aviation Act, 1949, are authorised to be made in connection with a ship or an aircraft.

(4) The preceding provisions of this section apply—

(*a*) in relation to all ships or aircraft whether British or not and whether registered or not and wherever the residence or domicile of their owners may be; and

(*b*) in relation to all claims, wheresoever arising (including, in the case of cargo or wreck salvage, claims in respect of cargo or wreck found on land):

Provided that nothing in this subsection shall be construed as extending the cases in which money or property is recoverable under any of the provisions of the Merchant Shipping Acts, 1894 to 1954.

(5) If, as respects any proceedings as to any such claim as is mentioned in subsection (1) of this section, the parties agree, by a memorandum signed by them or by their respective solicitors or agents, that a particular county court specified in the memorandum shall have jurisdiction in the proceedings, that court shall, notwithstanding anything in subsection (2) of this section or in any rules made under subsection (3) of section one hundred and two of this Act for prescribing the courts in which proceedings shall be brought, have jurisdiction to hear and determine the proceedings accordingly.

(6) Nothing in this section shall be taken to affect the jurisdiction of any county court to hear and determine any proceedings in which it has jurisdiction by virtue of section thirty-nine or forty-one of this Act.

(7) Nothing in this section, or in the last foregoing section or any order made thereunder, shall be taken to confer on a county court the jurisdiction of a prize court within the meaning of the Naval Prize Acts, 1864 to 1916.

(8) Section five hundred and fifty-five of the Merchant Shipping Act, 1894, shall have effect as if there were inserted after the word "agreement" the words "or by a county court in England or Wales".

Mode of exercise of Admiralty jurisdiction.

3185 **57.**—(1) Subject to the following provisions of this Part of this Act, the Admiralty jurisdiction of a county court may in all cases be invoked by an action in personam.

(2) In any case in which there is a maritime lien or other charge on any ship, aircraft or other property for the amount claimed, the Admiralty jurisdiction of a county court may be invoked by an action in rem against that ship, aircraft or property.

(3) In the case of any such claim as is mentioned in subsection (1) of the last foregoing section, being a claim arising in connection with a ship, where the person who would be liable on the claim in an action in personam was, when the cause of action arose, the owner or charterer of, or in possession or in control of, the ship, the Admiralty jurisdiction of a county court may (whether the claim gives rise to a maritime lien on the ship or not) be invoked by an action in rem against—

(*a*) that ship, if at the time when the action is brought it is beneficially owned as respects all the shares therein by that person; or

(*b*) any other ship which, at the time when the action is brought, is beneficially owned as aforesaid.

(4) In the case of a claim in the nature of towage or pilotage in respect of an aircraft, the Admiralty jurisdiction of a county court may be invoked by an action in rem against that aircraft if at the time when the action is brought it is beneficially owned by the person who would be liable on the claim in an action in personam.

(5) Notwithstanding anything in the preceding provisions of this section, the Admiralty jurisdiction of a county court shall not be invoked by an action

in rem in the case of any such claim as is mentioned in paragraph (*l*) of subsection (1) of the last foregoing section unless the claim relates wholly or partly to wages (including any sum allotted out of wages or adjusted by a superintendent to be due by way of wages).

(6) Where, in the exercise of its Admiralty jurisdiction, a county court orders any ship, aircraft or other property to be sold, the court shall have jurisdiction to hear and determine any question arising as to the title to the proceeds of sale.

(7) In determining for the purposes of subsections (3) and (4) of this section whether a person would be liable on a claim in an action in personam it shall be assumed that he has his habitual residence or a place of business within England or Wales.

Transfer of Admiralty proceedings from county court to High Court

86 **58.**—(1) The High Court, on the application of any party to Admiralty proceedings pending in a county court, may, if it thinks fit, after notice has been given to the other party, order that the proceedings be transferred to the High Court and order security for costs or impose such other terms as the court thinks fit.

(2) If, during the progress of any Admiralty proceedings in a county court, it appears to the county court that the proceedings could be more conveniently prosecuted in the High Court, the county court may order that the proceedings be transferred to the High Court.

Transfer of Admiralty proceedings from High Court to county court

87 **59.**—(1) In any action commenced in the High Court to which this section applies —

(*a*) any party may at any time apply to the High Court or a judge thereof for an order that the claim and counter-claim (if any) or, if the only matter remaining to be tried is a counterclaim, the counterclaim, shall be transferred to an Admiralty county court; and

(*b*) the High Court or judge may thereupon if it or he thinks fit, order that the claim and counterclaim (if any) or, if the only matter remaining to be tried is a counterclaim, the counterclaim, be transferred to any Admiralty county court which the court or judge may deem the most convenient to the parties.

(2) This section applies to any action where the plaintiff's claim is any such claim as is mentioned in subsection (1) of section fifty-six of this Act and the amount claimed or remaining in dispute does not exceed the amount specified in subsection (2) of that section—

(*a*) whether the action could or could not have been commenced in a county court; and

(*b*) whether the defendant does or does not set up or intend to rely on a counterclaim; and

(*c*) whether the counterclaim (if any), if it had been a claim in an action, would or would not have been within the jurisdiction of a county court.

(3) Where an action is transferred to a county court under this section, any vessel or other property which has been arrested in the action before the transfer shall, notwithstanding the transfer, remain in the custody of the

Admiralty Marshal who shall, subject to any directions of the High Court, comply with any orders made by the county court with respect to that vessel or property.

Costs of certain Admiralty proceedings commenced in High Court which could have been commenced in county court

3188 **60.**—(1) The following provisions of this section shall have effect in relation to the exercise by the High Court of the Admiralty jurisdiction of that Court.

(2) Subject to the provisions of subsection (5) of this section, if in any claim for salvage services the plaintiff does not recover more than one thousand pounds, he shall not be entitled to recover any costs of the proceedings unless it is certified by the court or a judge that the case was a fit one to be tried otherwise than in a county court.

(3) Subject to the provisions of subsection (5) of this section, if in any claim arising out of an agreement relating to the use or hire of a ship, or any claim relating to the carriage of goods in a ship, or any claim in tort in respect of goods carried in a ship, the plaintiff recovers a less amount than *one hundred pounds*,[1] he shall not be entitled to any costs of the proceedings unless it is certified by the court or a judge that there was sufficient reason for bringing the proceedings in the High Court.

(4) Subject to the provisions of the next following subsection, if in any such claim as is mentioned in subsection (3) of this section the plaintiff recovers a less amount than one thousand pounds, he shall not be entitled to any more costs than those to which he would have been entitled if the proceedings had been brought in a county court, unless it is certified by the court or a judge that there was sufficient reason for bringing the proceedings in the High Court.

(5) Subsections (2) to (4) of this section shall not affect any question as to costs in any case where it appears to the High Court or a judge thereof that there was reasonable ground for supposing the amount recoverable in respect of the plaintiff's claim to be in excess of the amount recoverable in proceedings commenced in a county court; and for the purposes of the said subsections, a plaintiff shall be treated as recovering the full amount recoverable in respect of his claim without regard to any deduction made in respect of contributory negligence on his part or otherwise in respect of matters not falling to be taken into account in determining whether the action could have been commenced in the county court.

Supplementary provisions as to Admiralty proceedings

3189 **61.**—(1) In the foregoing provisions of this Part of this Act relating to Admiralty proceedings, unless the context otherwise requires,—

"goods" includes baggage;

"master" has the same meaning as in the Merchant Shipping Act, 1894, and accordingly includes every person (except a pilot) having command or charge of a ship;

"towage" and "pilotage", in relation to an aircraft, mean towage and pilotage while the aircraft is waterborne.

(2) Nothing in the said provisions shall—

(*a*) be construed as limiting the jurisdiction of a county court to refuse

[1] Words in italics substituted by the Administration of Justice Act 1969, s. 4 (3).

to entertain an action for wages by the master or a member of the crew of a ship, not being a British ship;

(*b*) affect the provisions of section five hundred and fifty-two of the Merchant Shipping Act, 1894 (which relates to the power of a receiver of wreck to detain a ship in respect of a salvage claim);

(*c*) authorise proceedings in rem in respect of any claim against the Crown, or the arrest, detention or sale of any of Her Majesty's ships or Her Majesty's aircraft, or of any cargo or other property belonging to the Crown;

(*d*) *affect section five of the Mail Ships Act, 1891 (which protects certain mail ships from arrest in certain circumstances).*[1]

In this subsection "Her Majesty's ships" and "Her Majesty's aircraft" have the meanings assigned to them by subsection (2) of section thirty-eight of the Crown Proceedings Act, 1947.

[1] The words in italics were repealed by the Statute Law Revision Act 1963, s. 1, Sched.

Appendix 10

RULES OF THE SUPREME COURT

Applications and Appeals under the Merchant Shipping Acts 1894 to 1970

(R.S.C., Order 74)

3190 **Assignment of proceedings**

1.—(1) Subject to paragraph (2), proceedings by which any application is made to the High Court under the Merchant Shipping Acts 1894 to 1970 *shall be assigned to the Queen's Bench Division and taken by the Admiralty Court.*[1]

(2) Proceedings by which an application under section 55 of the Merchant Shipping Act 1894 is made shall be assigned to the Chancery Division . . .[2]

Appeals

2.—(1) An appeal to the High Court under section 68 of the Merchant Shipping Act 1906 against an order or decision of a naval court and an appeal to that Court under section 28 of the Pilotage Act 1913 against a decision of a county court judge or a magistrate, shall be heard and determined by a Divisional Court of the *Queen's Bench Division constituted so far as practicable of Admiralty Judges.*[1]

(2) Order 55, rule 4 (1) (*a*), shall apply in relation to an appeal under the said section 68 as if the words " the registrar or clerk of the court and " were omitted.

(3) Order 55, rule 4 (2), shall apply in relation to an appeal under the said section 68 as if for the period of 28 days therein specified there were substituted a period of 3 months.

(4) A copy of the report of the proceedings before the naval court against whose order or decision an appeal is brought, being the report made to the [Department] of Trade under section 484 of the Merchant Shipping Act 1894, must be left at the Admiralty Registry when the appeal is set down for hearing.

(5) The proper officer shall notify the [Department] of Trade of the decision of the Court on an appeal under the said section 68.

Appeals to which other rules apply

3. Orders 55 and 57 shall not apply in relation to an appeal to the High Court which is to be subject to and conducted in accordance with conditions and regulations prescribed by rules made in relation thereto under the powers contained in Part VI of the Merchant Shipping Act 1894.

3191 [1] The words in italics were substituted by R.S.C. (Amendment No. 4) 1971 (S.I. 1971 No. 1269).
[2] Words deleted by R.S.C. (Amendment No. 4) 1971 (S.I. 1971 No. 1269).

Appendix 11

SHIPPING CASUALTIES ETC. RULES

Shipping Casualties and Appeals and Re-hearings Rules 1923 Codifying Act of Sederunt 1913

(S.R. & O. 1923 No. 752)

Rules made under section 479 *of the Merchant Shipping Act* 1894, *dated May* 4, 1923

Short Title and Commencement

92 **1.** These Rules may be cited as the Shipping Casualties and Appeals and Re-hearings Rules, 1923. They shall come into operation on the 1st August, 1923, and shall, so far as practicable, and unless otherwise expressly provided, apply to all matters arising in any pending investigation or proceeding, and also to all investigations or proceedings instituted on or after the said day.

Interpretation

2. In these Rules, unless the context or subject-matter otherwise requires—

"Investigation" means a formal investigation into a shipping casualty:

"Judge" means the Wreck Commissioner, sheriff, sheriff-substitute, stipendiary magistrate, justices, or other authority empowered to hold an investigation:

"List of assessors" means the existing list and classification of assessors for shipping casualties approved by the Secretary of State set out in Part II of the Appendix to these Rules, or the list and classification of assessors for the time being approved by the Secretary of State:

"Court of Appeal" means the court by which appeals from decisions given in investigations or inquiries are for the time being heard, under the Merchant Shipping Acts, 1894 to 1921, or any Act amending the same.

Notice of Investigation

3. When an investigation has been ordered, the [Secretary of State for Trade] may cause a notice, to be called a notice of investigation, to be served [1] upon the owner, master, and officers of the ship, as well as upon any person who in [his] opinion ought to be served with such notice. The notice shall contain a statement of the questions which, on the information then in possession of the [Secretary of State for Trade], [he intends] to raise on the hearing of the investigation, and shall be in the form No. 1 in Part I of the Appendix,[2] with such variations as circumstances may require. The[Secretary of State for Trade] may, at any time before the hearing [3] of the investigation, by a subsequent notice amend, add to, or omit any of the questions specified in the notice of investigation.

[1] As to service, see Rule 28, *post*. As to proof of service, see Rule 29, *post*.

[2] The form also provides that a copy of a report, or statement of the case, upon which the investigation has been ordered shall be subjoined to the notice. A copy of the report of a Receiver of Wreck (*The Dinorah and the Dorunda*) (1876) 21 S.J. 31) and a copy of notes taken at a coroner's inquest (*Ex p. Ferguson* (1871) 6 Q.B. 280) have each been held to be a sufficient statement of the case.

[3] The questions may be further amended when the examination of witnesses called by the Secretary of State has been concluded; see Rule 11, *post*.

4. The [Secretary of State for Trade], the owner, the master, and any certificated officer or other person upon whom a notice of investigation has been served, shall be deemed to be parties to the proceedings.

5. Any other person may, by leave of the Judge, appear, and any person who appears under this Rule shall thereupon become a party to the proceedings.

Notice to Produce

6. A party may give to any other party notice in writing to produce any documents (saving all just exceptions) relating to the matters in question, and which are in the possession or under the control of such other party; and, if the notice is not complied with, secondary evidence of the contents of the documents may be given by the party who gave the notice.[1]

[1] The notice of investigation itself contains a general notice to produce all relevant documents; see Form No. 1 in Part I of the Appendix, *post*.

Notice to Admit

7. A party may give to any other party notice in writing to admit any documents (saving all just exceptions), and in case of neglect or refusal to admit after such notice, the party so neglecting or refusing shall be liable for all the costs of proving the documents, whatever may be the result, unless the Judge is of opinion that the refusal to admit was reasonable; and no costs of proving any document shall be allowed unless such notice has been given, except where the omission to give the notice has, in the opinion of the officer by whom the costs are taxed, caused a saving of expense.

Evidence

3193 **8.** Affidavits and statutory declarations may, by permission of the Judge, and saving all just exceptions, be used as evidence at the hearing.[1]

[1] For documents expressly declared to be admissible in evidence upon certain conditions, see M. S. A., 1894, ss. 64, 239 (6), 256, 691, 695, 719.

Proceedings in Court

9. At the time and place appointed for holding the investigation the Court may proceed with the investigation, whether the parties, upon whom a notice of investigation has been served, or any of them, are present or not.

10. The proceedings on the investigation shall commence with the production and examination of witnesses by the [Secretary of State for Trade].[1] These witnesses, after being examined on behalf of the [Secretary of State for Trade,] may be cross-examined by the parties in such order as the Judge may direct, and may then be re-examined by the [Secretary of State for Trade]. Questions asked, and documents tendered as evidence in the course of the examination of these witnesses, shall not be open to objection merely on the ground that they do or may raise questions which are not contained in, or which vary from, the statement of the case, or questions specified in the notice of investigation or subsequent notices referred to in Rule 3.

[1] The purpose of the legislation governing these Inquiries was summarised by Lord MacDermott C.J. in *The Princess Victoria* (1953) 2 Lloyd's Rep. 619 at p. 628:—"It is to ensure, in the public interest, that shipping casualties will be adequately investigated and the material facts and causes ascertained and brought to light if possible." With these objects in view, it is the practice of the Minister to adduce all the evidence which he considers might assist the court, including that of persons whose conduct he may ask the court to criticise. It is the duty of the Secretary of State's representative, before concluding his examination, to put to a witness any criticism of his conduct which he intends to suggest to the court.

11. When the examination of the witnesses produced by the [Secretary of State for Trade] has been concluded, the [Secretary of State for Trade] shall state in open Court[1] the questions in reference to the casualty, and the conduct of the certified officers, or other persons connected therewith, upon which the opinion of the Court is desired. In framing the questions for the opinion of the Court the [Secretary of State for Trade] may make such modifications in, additions to, or omissions from the questions in the notice of investigation or subsequent notices referred to in Rule 3, as, having regard to the evidence which has been given, the [Secretary of State for Trade] may think fit.

[1] In the public interest, a part of the evidence in the Inquiry into the loss of the "Lusitania" was heard *in camera*.

12. After the questions for the opinion of the Court have been stated, the Court shall proceed to hear the parties to the investigation upon, and determine the questions so stated. Each party to the investigation shall be entitled to address the Court and produce witnesses, or recall any of the witnesses who have already been examined for further examination, and generally adduce evidence. The parties shall be heard and their witnesses examined, cross-examined, and re-examined in such order as the Judge shall direct. The [Secretary of State for Trade] may also produce and examine further witnesses, who may be cross-examined by the parties, and re-examined by the [Secretary of State for Trade].

13. When the whole of the evidence in relation to the questions for the opinion of the Court has been concluded, any of the parties who desire so to do may address the Court upon the evidence, and the [Secretary of State for Trade] may address the Court in reply upon the whole case.[1]

[1] The Secretary of State for Trade must advise the court whether he considers that an officer's certificate ought to be cancelled or suspended by the court under M. S. A., 1894, s. 470 (1)(*a*); *The Carlisle* [1906] P. 301 at pp. 313 *et seq.* It is also the practice of the Secretary of State to indicate to the court whether he considers that the conduct of any party should be criticised, and also to suggest to the court any recommendations arising out of the evidence which it might usefully make for the benefit of shipping in general.

14. The Judge may adjourn the investigation from time to time and from place to place, and where an adjournment is asked for by a party to the investigation or by the [Secretary of State for Trade], the Judge may impose such terms as to payment of costs or otherwise as he may think just as a condition of granting the adjournment.

194 **15.** Except when the certificate of an officer is cancelled, or suspended in which case the decision shall always be given in open Court, the Judge may deliver the decision of the Court either *viva voce* or in writing, and if in writing it may be sent or delivered to the parties. In the latter case it shall not be necessary to hold a Court merely for the purpose of delivering the decision of the Court.

16. The Judge may order the costs and expenses of the investigation, or any part thereof, to be paid by the [Secretary of State for Trade] or by any other party.[1] An order for payment of costs shall be in the Form No. 2 in Part I of the Appendix, with such variations as circumstances may require.

[1] See note (6) to M. S. A., 1894, s. 466.

17. At the conclusion of the investigation the Judge shall report to the [Secretary of State for Trade]. The report shall be in the Form No. 3 in Part I of the Appendix, with such modifications as circumstances may require.

Copy of Report

18. The [Secretary of State for Trade] shall, on application by any party to the proceedings, give him a copy of the report made to the [Secretary of State].

Appeals

3195 **19.** Where an appeal is given from the decision of any Court or authority other than an appeal under section 68 of the Merchant Shipping Act, 1906, to the High Court in England, it shall be to a Divisional Court of the Probate, Divorce and Admiralty Division of the High Court.[1]

[1] Now the Admiralty Law of the Queen's Bench Division.

20. Every such appeal shall be conducted in accordance with the conditions and regulations following (namely):—

(*a*) The appellant shall, within the time hereinafter mentioned, serve on such of the other parties to the proceeding as he may consider to be directly affected by the appeal, notice of his intention to appeal, and shall also, within two days after setting down the appeal, give to the said parties notice of the general grounds of the appeal.

(*b*) Notice of appeal shall be served within twenty-eight days from the date on which the decision is pronounced or, within twenty-one days from the date on which the report is issued in print in London by the [Secretary of State for Trade]: or if the report is not issued in print, as aforesaid, then within 21 days from the date of the London Gazette in which a notice is published of the receipt by the [Secretary of State for Trade] of the report of the Court.

(*c*) If the appeal is brought by any party other than the [Secretary of State for Trade], the appellant shall before the appeal is heard give such security, if any, by deposit of money or otherwise, for the costs to be occasioned by the appeal as the Judge from whose decision the appeal is brought on application made to him for that purpose may direct; or in the case of an appeal from the decision of a Court outside the United Kingdom as may be directed by the Court of Appeal.

(*d*) The appellant shall, before the expiration of the time within which notice of appeal may be given, leave with the officer for the time being appointed for that purpose by the Court of Appeal, a copy of the notice of appeal, and the officer shall thereupon set down the appeal by entering it in the proper list.

(*e*) The Court of Appeal shall be assisted by not less than two assessors to be selected, in the discretion of that Court, having regard to the nature of each case, from either or both of the following classes:—

1. Elder Brethren of Trinity House.
2. Persons approved from time to time by the Secretary of State as assessors for the purpose of formal investigations into shipping casualties, under sections 466 and 467 of the Merchant Shipping Act, 1894.

(*f*) The Court of Appeal may, if it thinks fit, order any other person, other than the parties served with the notice of appeal, to be added as a party or parties to the proceedings for the purposes of the appeal, on such terms with respect to costs and otherwise as the Court of Appeal may think fit. Any party to the proceedings may object to the appearance on the appeal of any other party to the proceedings as unnecessary.

(*g*) The evidence taken before the Judge from whose decision the appeal is brought shall be proved before the Court of Appeal by a copy of the notes of the Judge, or of the shorthand writer, clerk, secretary, or other person authorised by him to take down the evidence, or by such other materials as the Court of Appeal thinks expedient; and a copy of the evidence, and of the report to the [Secretary of State for Trade] containing the decision from which the appeal is brought, and of the notice of the general grounds of the appeal, shall be left with the officer for the time being appointed for that purpose by the Court of Appeal before the appeal comes on for hearing. For the purpose of this Rule, copies of the notes of the evidence, and of the report, shall be supplied to the appellant, on request, by the Judge or other person having charge thereof, on payment of the usual charge for copying.

(*h*) The Court of Appeal shall have full power to receive further evidence on questions of fact, such evidence to be either by oral examination in court, by affidavit, or by deposition taken before an examiner or commissioner. Evidence may also be given with special leave of the Court of Appeal as to matters which have occurred since the date of the decision from which the appeal is brought.

(*i*) The Court of Appeal shall have power to make such order as to the whole or any part of the costs of and occasioned by the appeal as the Court may think just.

(*j*) Subject to the foregoing provisions of this Rule, every appeal shall be conducted under and in accordance with the general rules and regulations applicable to ordinary proceedings before the Court of Appeal, but there shall not be anything in the nature of pleadings other than the notice of the general grounds of the appeal, except by special permission of the Court of Appeal.

(*k*) On the conclusion of an appeal the Court of Appeal shall send to the [Secretary of State for Trade] a report of the case in such form as the Court of Appeal may think fit.

Re-hearings by Order of [the Minister of Transport]

3196 **21.**—(*a*) Where the [Secretary of State for Trade directs] a re-hearing, under section 475 or 478 of the Merchant Shipping Act, 1894, [he] shall cause such reasonable notice to be given to the parties whom [he considers] to be affected by the re-hearing as the circumstances of the case may, in the opinion of the [Secretary of State for Trade], permit.

(*b*) The provisions distinguished as (*e*), (*f*), (*g*), (*h*), (*i*), (*j*), and (*k*), of the last foregoing rule shall apply to a re-hearing as if it were an appeal, and as if the Court or authority before whom the re-hearing takes place were the Court of Appeal.

Appointment of Assessors

22. Subject to these Rules assessors for investigations into shipping casualties shall be appointed from the list of assessors by the Secretary of State.

23. If any investigation involves or appears likely to involve the cancelling or suspension of the certificate of a master, mate, or engineer, there shall be appointed from the list of assessors not less than two assessors from Class I and Class II or from either of those classes.

24. Subject to any special appointment or appointments which the Secretary of State may think it expedient to make in any case where special circumstances appear to him to require a departure from these rules (the requirements of the last preceding Rule being always complied with) assessors shall be appointed as follows:—

(1) Where the investigation involves or appears likely to involve the cancelling or suspension of the certificate of a master or mate, but not of an engineer, at least two assessors shall be appointed from Class I.

(2) Where the investigation involves or appears likely to involve the cancelling or suspension of the certificate of a master or mate of a sailing ship, one at least of the assessors shall be appointed from subsection (*a*) of Class I, and where the investigation involves or appears likely to involve the cancelling or suspension of the certificate of a master or mate of a steamship, one at least of the assessors shall be appointed from sub-section (*b*) of Class I.

(3) Where the investigation involves or appears likely to involve the cancelling or suspension of the certificate of an engineer, one at least of the assessors shall be appointed from Class II.

25. The [Secretary of State for Trade] shall inform the Secretary of State when assessors are required, and shall state from which of the aforesaid classes assessors ought in [his] opinion to be appointed but the [Secretary of State for Trade] shall not request the appointment of any individual assessor.

26. An appointment made by the Secretary of State of any assessor or assessors for an investigation shall not be open to question on the ground that it was not in accordance with these Rules, or does not give full effect to the requirements of these Rules.

Computation of Time

3197 **27.** In computing the number of days within which any act is to be done they shall be reckoned exclusive of the first and inclusive of the last day, unless the last day shall happen to fall on a Sunday, Christmas Day, or Good Friday, or on a day appointed for a public fast or thanksgiving or holiday, in which case the time shall be reckoned exclusive of that day also.

Service of Notices

28. Any notice, summons, or other document issued under these Rules may be served by sending the same by registered letter to the address of the person to be served.

29. The service of any notice, summons, or other document may be proved by the oath or affidavit of the person by whom it was served.

Repealing Clause

30. The under-mentioned Rules are hereby annulled, but nothing in these Rules shall affect the previous operation of, or anything done or suffered under, any of the said Rules—

The Shipping Casualties and Appeals and Re-hearings Rules, 1907.

Publication of Rules

31. A copy of these Rules shall be kept at every Custom House and Mercantile Marine Office in the United Kingdom, and any person desiring to peruse them shall be entitled to do so.

APPENDIX

3198 PART I

FORMS

The following forms shall be used, as far as possible, with such alterations as circumstances may require, but no deviation from the prescribed forms shall invalidate the proceedings, unless the Judge shall be of opinion that the deviation was material: —

No. 1.—Notice of Investigation

To master, mate, engineer, owner, etc., of
of or belonging to the ship

I hereby give you notice that the [Secretary of State for Trade has] ordered a formal investigation into the circumstances attending the

and that subjoined hereto is a copy of a report [or statement of the case] upon which the said investigation has been ordered. I further give you notice to produce to the Court [your [Secretary of State for Trade] certificate, the log books of the vessel, and] any [other] documents relevant to this case which may be in your possession.

I have further to give you notice that on the information at present obtained by the [Secretary of State for Trade] the questions annexed hereto are those upon which it appears desirable, and upon which they propose, to take the opinion of the Court; but these questions will be subject to alteration, addition, omission, or amendment by the representative of the [Secretary of State for Trade] at the investigation, after the witnesses called by the [Secretary of State for Trade] have been examined.

Dated this day of 19 .

Solicitor, [Department of Trade].

I. *Report* [*or statement of case.*]

II. *Questions*

1. Whether the

[*Here insert the proposed questions*]

No. 2.—Order on a Party for Payment of Costs of Investigation

In the matter of a formal investigation held at on the (*here state all the days on which the Court sat*) days of before assisted by into the circumstances attending the

The Court orders—

(1) That *A.B.*, of , do pay to the Solicitor to the [Department of Trade] [the sum of pounds on account of] the expenses of this investigation.

Or (2) That the [Department of Trade] do pay to *A.B.*, of [the sum of pounds on account of] the expenses of this investigation.

Given under my hand this day of 19 .

Judge.

3199 **No. 3.—Report of Court**

In the matter of a formal investigation held at on the (*here state all the days on which the Court sat*) days of before assisted by into the circumstances attending the

The Court, having carefully inquired into the circumstances attending the above-mentioned shipping casualty, finds for the reasons stated in the Annex

hereto, that the (*here state findings of Court*).
Dated this day of 19 .

Judge.

We [or I] concur in the above report.

Assessor.
Assessor.

Annex to the Report

(*Here state fully the circumstances of the case, the opinion of the Court touching the causes of the casualty, and the conduct of any persons implicated therein, and whether the certificate of any officer is either suspended or cancelled, and if so for what reasons.*)

Editor's Note:

If an officer's certificate is cancelled or suspended, it is usual (*semble* obligatory; see *The Corchester* [1957] P. 84 at 96) to state this also in the Report itself, and further to state in the Report that the fault of the officer concerned caused or contributed to the casualty.

PART II

3200 **CLASSIFICATION OF LIST OF ASSESSORS, AND QUALIFICATIONS PRESCRIBED FOR EACH CLASS**

The Merchant Shipping Act, 1894

57 & 58 Vict. c. 60

Whereas by section 466 of the Merchant Shipping Act, 1894, it is provided that—

The Court holding a formal investigation into a shipping casualty shall hold the same with the assistance of one or more assessors of nautical, engineering or other special skill or knowledge, to be appointed out of a list of persons for the time being approved for the purpose by a Secretary of State in such manner and according to such regulations as may be prescribed by Rules made under this Act with regard thereto.

And whereas by section 467 of the Merchant Shipping Act, 1894, it is enacted as follows:—

(1) The list of persons approved as assessors for the purpose of formal investigations into shipping casualties shall be in force for three years only, but persons whose names are on any such list may be approved for any subsequent list.

(2) The Secretary of State may at any time add or withdraw the name of any person to or from the list.

(3) The list of assessors in force at the passing of this Act shall subject as aforesaid continue in force till the end of the year one thousand eight hundred and ninety-five.

The Secretary of State has directed that the assessors shall, so far as in his opinion circumstances permit, be taken in order of rotation within each class or sub-class, and has further directed that the assessors placed by him on the list of assessors shall be classified according to their qualifications, as follows:—

Class I—Mercantile Marine Masters

3201 (*a*) Five years' service in any certificated capacity on a British sailing ship of not less than 1,000 tons gross and two years' service as a certificated Master in command of a British sailing or steamship.

(*b*) Five years' service as a certificated Master in command of British Merchant vessels of which two years must have been service in command of a steamship.

Class II—Mercantile Marine Engineers

Five years' service as an Engineer in a Merchant vessel. A candidate for appointment must hold a first-class certificate of competency as Engineer in the

Mercantile Marine, and have had two years' experience as a Chief Engineer in vessels of not less than 1,000 tons gross.

Class III—Royal Navy

(*a*) Rank of Admiral or Captain and three years' service in command of one of His Majesty's ships at sea.

(*b*) Rank of Staff Commander and three years' service in that rank of one of His Majesty's ships at sea.

(*c*) Rank of Commander (N.) or Lieutenant (N.) and three years' service as Navigator since passing Navigation for 1st Class ships.

Class IV—Persons of Fishery, Naval Architectural or other Special Skill or Knowledge

(*a*) Special knowledge and experience of Fishing Vessels; or

(*b*) Special knowledge and experience of Naval Architecture; or

(*c*) Such qualification as is in the opinion of the Secretary of State requisite.

Appendix 12

PILOTAGE APPEALS TO STIPENDIARY MAGISTRATES IN ENGLAND: PROCEDURE: PILOTAGE ACT 1913, S. 28

Appeals to Stipendiary and Magistrates' Courts—Rules

(S.R. & O. 1916 No. 62)

Rules, dated January 27, 1916, *made under section* 28 *of the Pilotage Act* 1913.

3202 **1.** Every complaint [1] for the purpose of an appeal under section 28 of the Pilotage Act, 1913, shall be in writing and shall state the specific ground on which the appeal is based and shall be made within one month from the time when the matter of such complaint arose.

Where the complaint is in respect of the suspension or revocation of a licence, or the refusal to renew a licence or the refusal to return a licence of which the pilotage authority have obtained possession or the imposition by the pilotage authority of a fine exceeding £2, the matter of the complaint shall be deemed to have arisen on the day on which the appellant shall have been informed by the pilotage authority of such suspension, revocation or refusal or the imposition of such fine.

Where the complaint is in respect of the failure of the pilotage authority to renew a licence, the matter of the complaint shall be deemed to have arisen on the day on which such licence expired.

Where the complaint is in respect of the failure of the pilotage authority to return a licence of which they have obtained possession, the matter of such complaint shall be deemed to have arisen three days after the appellant has addressed a written application to such authority for the return of his licence.

2. The appellant shall within four days after the time of making his complaint deposit with the clerk of the magistrate the sum of £5 and enter into a recognisance in the further sum of £10, with or without sureties as the magistrate may direct, conditioned to appear before the said magistrate and abide his judgment on such appeal, and to pay such further costs, if any, as may be awarded by such magistrate; and the sum so deposited shall be applicable to the payment of the costs of the appeal and the costs occasioned by the appellant by way of objection, if any, to an assessor, or shall, in whole or in part, be returned to the appellant, as the magistrate on the termination of the case may direct.

3. When the magistrate issues his summons to the pilotage authority he shall at the same time in writing require from such authority a statement showing the exact particulars of the proceeding of the authority in respect of which the complaint is made and the grounds of such proceeding, and such statement shall be forwarded by the pilotage authority to the magistrate's clerk and the appellant within seven days from the requirement, or within such extended time as may be allowed by the magistrate.

3203 **4.** If in the statement of the pilotage authority the grounds of the proceeding of that authority are stated to be that the appellant had been convicted of or charged with an offence in a Court of criminal jurisdiction, the pilotage authority shall add to the statement required by the magistrate full particulars of the hearing of such charge, or (if not already disposed of) of the proceedings taken thereon.

5. The magistrates shall with as little delay as possible notify in writing to each party to the appeal the name of the assessor proposed to be selected.

6. If either party objects to the assessor proposed to be selected, notice in writing of the objection shall be given to the magistrate and to the other party within five days after the receipt of the notification mentioned in Rule 5, and the notice shall state briefly the ground of the objection. The magistrate shall thereupon fix a day for the hearing of the objection. Any costs occasioned by objection to the assessor proposed to be selected may, if the magistrate thinks fit, be ordered to be paid by the objecting party.

7. For the better selection of assessors, magistrates shall, if the Secretary of State so require, cause to be hung up within their courts lists of such persons (including Brethren of the Trinity House) as are known to them to be of nautical and pilotage experience willing to act as assessors, and such lists may be amended from time to time as may be found necessary.

8. The remuneration of assessors shall be at the rate of two guineas for each day's attendance, together with any allowance for expenses that the magistrate may expressly order; and such remuneration and allowance shall be considered as costs.

9. The fees to be taken by the magistrate's clerk shall be as follows: —

	s.	d.
For all services rendered in connection with the hearing of an appeal	15	0
For all services rendered in connection with the hearing of an objection raised against an assessor proposed to be appointed	6	0

such fees to be paid by the magistrate's clerk to the fund to which other fees taken for services rendered by him are at present or shall be from time to time payable.

10. An appeal under section 28 (4) from the decision of a magistrate to the High Court, shall take place in the same manner as an appeal from a Court of Summary Jurisdiction by special case, and section 33 of the Summary Jurisdiction Act, 1879, and the Rules for the time being in force shall apply to such appeal as if it were an appeal from a Court of Summary Jurisdiction under that section.

Editors' Note:

3204 An appeal to a magistrates' court must be by way of complaint for an order: Magistrates' Courts Rules 1968 (S.I. 1968 No. 1920), r. 30.

Appendix 13

PILOTAGE APPEALS TO SHERIFFS IN SCOTLAND: PROCEDURE

Codifying Act of Sederunt 1913

(S.R. & O. 1913 No. 638)

Book L. Sheriff Courts

3205 Chapter XI.—Appeals to the Sheriff under the Pilotage Act, 1913 (2 & 3 Geo. 5, c. 31, s. 28)[1]

1. *Procedure by Initial Writ*

Appeals to the sheriff under section 28 of the Pilotage Act, 1913, shall be by initial writ under the Sheriff Courts (Scotland) Acts, 1907 and 1913 (7 Edw. 7, c. 51 and 2 & 3 Geo. 5, c. 28), and the proceedings thereon shall be as laid down in those statutes.

2. *Time for Appeal*

Such initial writ shall be presented to the sheriff within twenty-one days from the date of the decision appealed from, and there shall be produced along with it two copies of the decision, one of which shall be certified to be a true copy by the clerk or secretary of the Pilotage Authority.

3. *Citation of Pilotage Authority*

On the initial writ being presented the sheriff-clerk shall grant warrant to cite the Pilotage Authority, which citation shall be made by serving a copy of the writ and of the warrant of citation upon the clerk or secretary of the Pilotage Authority.

4. *Expenses and Fees*

The expenses and Court fees connected with the appeal shall be the same as prescribed for civil causes in the Sheriff Courts.

5. *Nautical Assessor*

The provisions of the Nautical Assessors (Scotland) Act, 1894, and relative provisions in Book L, Chapter 1 hereof, shall apply to the assessor of nautical and pilotage experience provided for by the said section of the Merchant Shipping Act.

Editors' Note:

[1] The heading and Rule 1 as printed in the text reproduce the amendments to the Rules of 1913 effected by S.R. & O. 1919, No. 1615/S.47.

Appendix 14

3206 **NOTICE OF LIEN FOR FREIGHT**

[N.B.—*Editors' Note*: This is not an official form of notice, but it is thought that it satisfies the requirements of the statute; see notes to M.S.A., 1894, s. 494.]

To Wharfinger
[Warehouseman].

Address.

TAKE NOTICE that the goods mentioned in the Schedule hereto which are being and/or have been landed from the [steamship] " " and placed in your custody as wharfinger and/or warehouseman are to remain subject to a lien for freight and/or other charges payable to (shipowner) to the amount mentioned in the said Schedule.

This Notice is given pursuant to section 494 of the Merchant Shipping Act, 1894, under which you are to retain the said goods until the said lien is discharged in accordance with provisions of the Act and, on failure to do so, will be liable to make good to (shipowner) any loss thereby occasioned to him.

(Signature.)

Date.

SCHEDULE

Quantity	Marks	Description of Goods	Freight	Other Charges	Total
100	A △ B	Barrels Tallow, ex S.S.	£25......	Landing* charges, £5............	£30

Total payable......£30

* Insert particulars and amounts of charges on each item of cargo, *e.g.*, landing charges, demurrage, dead-freight, etc., as the case may require.

INDEX

INDEX

[*All references are to paragraph numbers*]

[*All references are to paragraph numbers*]

[*All references are to paragraph numbers*]

[*All references are to paragraph numbers*]

[*All references are to paragraph numbers*]

[*All references are to paragraph numbers*]

[*All references are to paragraph numbers*]

[*All references are to paragraph numbers*]

[*All references are to paragraph numbers*]

[*All references are to paragraph numbers*]

[*All references are to paragraph numbers*]

[*All references are to paragraph numbers*]

[*All references are to paragraph numbers*]

[*All references are to paragraph numbers*]